CW00591416

Harden's

Best UK Restaurants 2024

ESTABLISHED 1991

INDEPENDENT AND UNBIASED REVIEWS OF 3,000 RESTAURANTS

'It will tell you what Diners actually like as opposed to mere Restaurant Critics'

Richard Vines, Restaurant Critic, Koffmann & Vines

ISBN 978-1-9160761-7-4

British Library Cataloguing-in-Publication data: a catalogue record for this book is available from the British Library.

Printed in Britain by Short Run Press, Exeter

Assistant editors: Clodagh Kinsella, Bruce Millar, Antonia Russell
Design: paulsmithdesign.com

Harden's Limited
MissionWorks, 41 Iffley Road, London W6 0PB

Would restaurateurs (and PRs) please address communications to 'Editorial' at the above address, or ideally by email to: editorial@hardens.com The contents of this book are believed correct at the time of printing. Nevertheless, the publisher can accept no responsibility for errors or changes in or omissions from the details given.

Harden's 100

The UK's 100 Best Restaurants for 2024, as dictated by Harden's annual survey of diners

1 L'Enclume, Cartmel (8)

2 Outlaw's New Road, Port Isaac (44)

3 Andrew Fairlie, Gleneagles Hotel, Auchterarder (1)

4 Paul Ainsworth at No 6, Padstow (29)

5 Endo at The Rotunda, TV Centre, London W12 (4)

6 Moor Hall, Aughton (77)

7 Core by Clare Smyth, London W11 (6)

8 Restaurant Martin Wishart, Edinburgh (14)

9 Midsummer House, Cambridge (75)

10 Da Terra, Town Hall Hotel, London E2 (11)

11 Lympstone Manor, Exmouth (24)

12 A Wong, London SW1 (36)

13 The Kitchin, Edinburgh (5)

14 Hjem, Wall (15)

15 Solstice, Newcastle upon Tyne

16 Cail Bruich, Glasgow (50)

17 Ynyshir Restaurant and Rooms, Ynyshir Hall, Eglwys Fach (37)

18 Sorrel, Dorking (13)

19 Sketch, The Lecture Room and Library, London W1 (93)

20 Meadowsweet, Holt (38)

21 The Ledbury, London W11 (39)

22 Alex Dilling Café Royal, London W1

23 Restaurant Twenty Two, Cambridge (62)

24 Outlaw's Fish Kitchen, Port Isaac (63)

25 PLU, London NW8 (18)

26 Maru, London W1 (9)

27 Gravetye Manor, East Grinstead

28 Roots, York (41)

29 The Five Fields, London SW3 (12)

30 Latymer, Pennyhill Park Hotel, Bagshot (46)

31 Ugly Butterfly, St Ives

32 The Forest Side, Grasmere (27)

33 Anglo, London EC1 (34)

34 The Black Swan, Oldstead (65)

35 Etch, Brighton

36 La Dame de Pic London, Four Seasons Hotel, London EC3

37 Frog by Adam Handling, London WC2 (66)

38 Sushi Tetsu, London EC1

39 Restaurant Sat Bains, Nottingham

40 Muse, London SW1 (20)

41 Waterside Inn, Bray (3)

42 Adam's, New Oxford House, Birmingham (17)

43 Hambleton Hall, Hambleton (26)

44 Behind, London E8 (85)

45 SOLA, London W1 (32)

46 Lumière, Cheltenham (21)

47 Pine, East Wallhouses (10)

48 Where The Light Gets In, Stockport

49 Morston Hall, Morston (35)

50 Club Gascon, London EC1 (47)

GUSBOURNE
TWENTY FOURTEEN
GUSBOURNE
BLANC DE BLANCS

Harden's 100

The UK's 100 Best Restaurants for 2024, as dictated by Harden's annual survey of diners

51 The Sportsman, Seasalter (70)

52 Bohemia, The Club Hotel & Spa, Jersey (61)

53 Restaurant Roots, Southbourne

54 Chez Bruce, London SW17 (53)

55 The Ritz, London W1 (91)

56 Le Manoir aux Quat' Saisons, Belmond, Great Milton (16)

57 The Fat Duck, Bray (96)

58 Pied à Terre, London W1 (71)

59 Hakkasan Mayfair, London W1

60 Paris House, Woburn

61 Barrafina, London W1

62 The Wilderness, Birmingham (92)

63 The Ninth, London W1

64 Fhior, Edinburgh

65 Restaurant St. Barts, London EC1

66 Otto's, London WC1

67 BiBi, London W1 (88)

68 Evelyn's Table at The Blue Posts, The Blue Posts, London W1 (2)

69 The Small Holding, Goudhurst (98)

70 Northcote, Langho

71 Bulrush, Bristol

72 Riva, London SW13

73 Vanderlyle, Cambridge

74 White Swan at Fence, Fence

75 Shaun Rankin at Grantley Hall, Grantley

76 The Dining Room, Beaverbrook, Leatherhead

77 Woven by Adam Smith, Coworth Park, Ascot

78 John's House, Mountsorrel

79 Salt, Stratford upon Avon

80 The Three Chimneys, Dunvegan

81 The Neptune, Old Hunstanton

82 Stark, Broadstairs

83 SY23, Aberystwyth (54)

84 The Fordwich Arms, Fordwich

85 Wheelers Oyster Bar, Whitstable

86 Allium at Askham Hall, Penrith

87 Sollip, London SE1 (82)

88 The Whitebrook, Whitebrook (78)

89 Wilson's, Bristol (87)

90 The Nut Tree Inn, Murcott

91 Bouchon Racine, London EC1

92 The Fernery, Grove of Narberth, Dyfed

93 Pollen Street Social, London W1

94 JKS Restaurants, Kitchen Table, London W1 (25)

95 Hide & Fox, Saltwood

96 Sabor, London W1

97 Mana, Manchester (73)

98 Nobu, Metropolitan Hotel, London W1 (40)

99 Clarke's, London W8

100 Grace & Savour, Hampton-in-Arden

CONTENTS

The Lanesborough Grill SW1

Circolo Popolare W1

Etch, Brighton

RATINGS & PRICES

Ratings

Our rating system does not tell you as most guides do that expensive restaurants are often better than cheap ones! What we do is compare each restaurant's performance as judged by the average ratings awarded by reporters in the survey with other similarly-priced restaurants. This approach has the advantage that it helps you find whatever your budget for any particular meal where you will get the best 'bang for your buck'.

The following qualities are assessed:

F — Food
S — Service
A — Ambience

The rating indicates that, **in comparison with other restaurants in the same price-bracket**, performance is…

5 — Exceptional
4 — Very good
3 — Good
2 — Acceptable
1 — Poor

Prices

The price shown for each restaurant is the cost for one (1) person of an average three-course dinner with half a bottle of house wine and coffee, any cover charge, service and VAT. Lunch is often cheaper. With BYO restaurants, we have assumed that two people share a £7 bottle of off-licence wine.

Small print

Telephone number – including area code.

Map reference – shown immediately after the telephone number.

Full postcodes – for non-group restaurants, the first entry in the 'small print' at the end of each listing, so you can set your sat-nav.

Website and Instagram – shown in the small print, where applicable.

Last orders time – listed after the website (if applicable); Sunday may be up to 90 minutes earlier.

Sustainability – if a restaurant or group has a star rating from the Sustainable Restaurants Association, this is shown.

YOUR CONTRIBUTION

Celebrating our 33rd year!

This guide is based on our annual poll of what 'ordinary' diners-out think of London's restaurants. The first such survey was in 1991 with a few over 100 people taking part. This year, the total number of reporters in our combined London/UK survey, conducted mainly online, numbered 2,500, and, between them, they contributed 30,000 individual reports.

How intelligent is AI?

At a time when the credibility of online reviews and influencer posts are under ongoing scrutiny, there is an ever-greater need for trusted sources such as the Harden's annual national diners' poll. In particular, the active curation by humans that we provide. For – while obviously folks can attempt to stuff the Harden's ballot too – our high degree of editorial oversight, plus our historical data about both the restaurants and those commenting, makes it much harder to cheat. In this way Harden's can socially source restaurant feedback, but – vitally – curate it carefully. It is this careful curation that provides extra 'value-added' for diners.

How we determine the ratings

In general, ratings are arrived at statistically. We create a ranking akin to football leagues, with the most expensive restaurants in the top league and the cheaper ones in lower ones. Any restaurant's ranking within its own particular league determines its ratings. In cases of limited feedback, editorial judgement may be used to smooth variations in ratings and reports from year to year. The guiding principle is not to assert the editor's opinions, but to try and reflect back to readers as faithful a picture as possible from the feedback of fellow diners.

How we write the reviews

The tone of each review and the ratings are guided by the ranking of the restaurant concerned, derived as described above. At the margin, we may also pay regard to the balance of positive votes (such as for 'favourite restaurant') against negative ones (such as for 'most overpriced'). To explain why an entry has been rated as it has, we extract snippets from user comments ("enclosed in double quotes"). On well-known restaurants, we may receive over a hundred reports, and a short summary cannot do individual justice to all of them. What we seek to do – without any regard to our own *personal opinions* – is to illustrate key themes in the collective feedback.

How do we find our reporters?

Anyone can take part. Register now at www.hardens.com if you have not already done so! In fact, we find that once people have taken part, they often continue to do so.

Consequently, many people who complete the survey have done so before. With high repeat-participation, the endresult is really more the product of a very large and everevolving panel, or jury, than a random 'poll'.

This is a tough time to be running a restaurant. Operators are dealing with the cost-of-living crisis, skyrocketing energy bills, supply chain disruptions and ongoing staffing issues – all while the impacts of Brexit and the pandemic still linger. At the same time, the climate crisis is at a breaking point. Talk of sustainability is everywhere, and restaurants are under increasing pressure from every direction to implement transparent and measurable sustainability practices.

As customers, we're feeling the pinch, too, and money is tighter in many of our households these days. When we do get out for a bite to eat, most of us want to know that we're supporting the right sort of business: one that makes a positive contribution to our world.

The number of environmental marks and green awards seems to grow by the moment, and it can be impossible to know which is the most meaningful. At The Sustainable Restaurant Association, we've been working directly with the hospitality industry since 2010, and we've poured all of this knowledge into creating a new edition of the Food Made Good Standard. Relaunched earlier this year, this is the only global sustainability accreditation built especially for restaurants and other hospitality businesses.

When you see a restaurant sporting the Food Made Good logo, you know they're committed to sustainability in a tangible, measurable and transparent way – we make a point of rewarding action over intention. Completing the Food Made Good Standard is rigorous and requires an ongoing commitment; the accreditation must be renewed every two years, and each time, the restaurant receives a tailored report outlining practical steps they can take to improve further. The FMG Standard is a significant step forward for any restaurant, one that better informs their practices and guides them in a process of continuous improvement.

Food Made Good also takes a holistic, big-picture view of sustainability efforts. While carbon is of critical importance, it's far from the only metric that needs to be measured. Sustainability is a much bigger story, and taking a 360-degree approach is a more meaningful way to have an impact. We focus on 10 key focus areas across three pillars (Sourcing, Society and Environment) to ensure that every part of a restaurant's operation is actively contributing towards a better future for both people and planet.

The people element of this is important. Society – the 'S' in ESG – is too often forgotten when it comes to sustainability; however, in an industry built on people and personality, it needs to be a key concern. Things like diversity and equity, work-life balance, career development, zero tolerance for bullying and harassment and reasonable compensation have not always been a given in this industry, but we believe they must play a role in any restaurant's sustainability ambitions. Because restaurants also provide spaces for people to come together and help to define culture on a local level, community engagement is central to what it means to be a sustainable restaurant.

There are lots of accreditations out there, but the Food Made Good Standard is the only one specifically tailored to fit the needs of the hospitality industry. We see where restaurants are now, we know where they need to go, and we provide clear, measurable and practical directions for how they can get there. Whether you're considering a fine dining restaurant or a cosy neighbourhood hangout for your next meal, ask if they've done the Food Made Good Standard. It's how you can rest assured that they're playing their part in building a more sustainable future for all of us.

Stay up to date with The Sustainable Restaurant Association and our latest Food Made Good accredited businesses.

Website: www.thesra.org Instagram: @foodmadegood

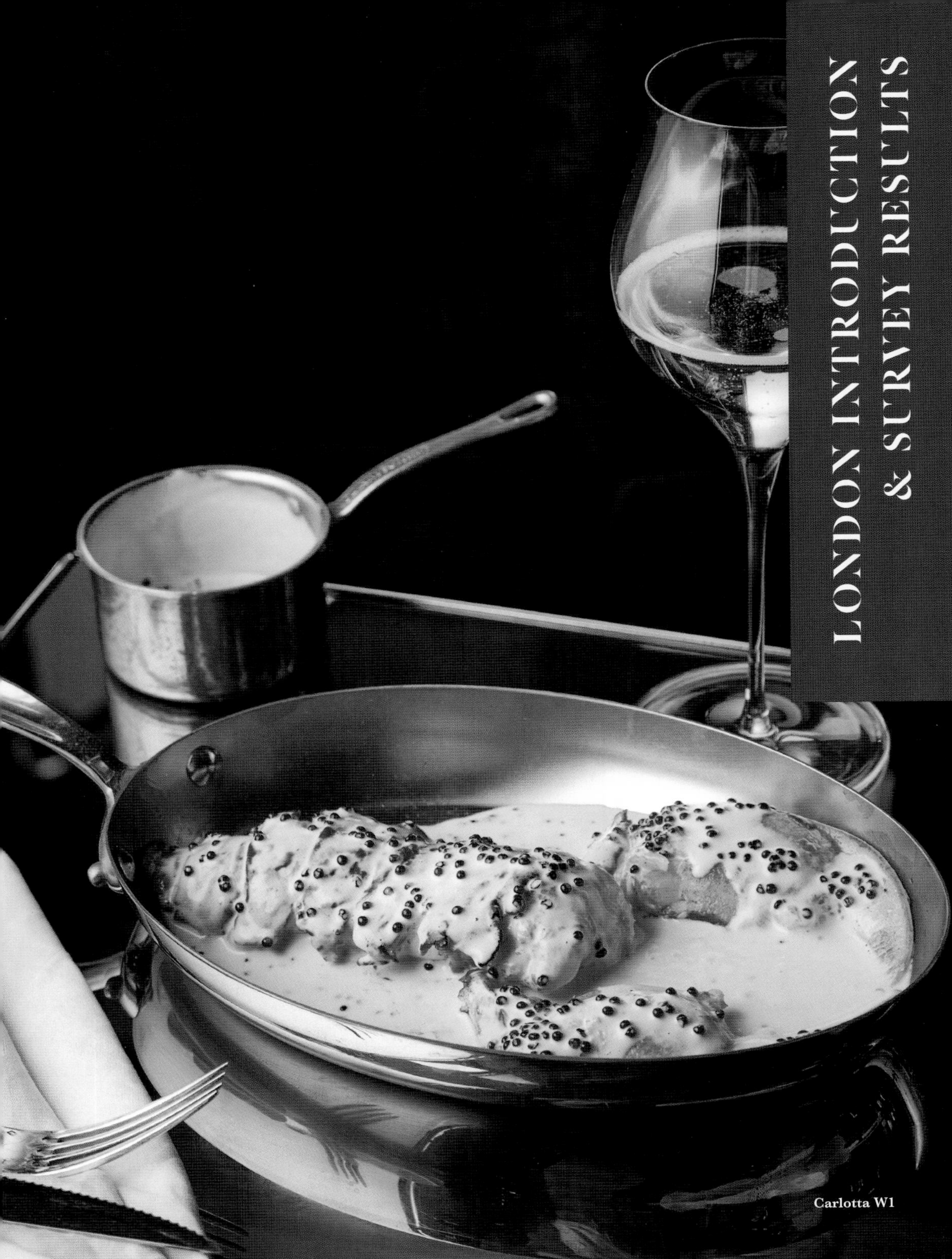

LONDON INTRODUCTION & SURVEY RESULTS

Carlotta W1

SURVEY MOST MENTIONED

RANKED BY THE NUMBER OF REPORTERS' VOTES

These are the restaurants which were most frequently mentioned by reporters. (Last year's position is given in brackets.)

1 J Sheekey (1)
2 Scott's (2)
3 Chez Bruce (3)
4 Noble Rot (11)
5 The Wolseley (4)
6 Clos Maggiore (6)
7 The River Café (7)
8 Core by Clare Smyth (5)
9 Brasserie Zédel (8)
10 Medlar (24)
11 Bocca di Lupo (15)
12 The Delaunay (8)
13 Andrew Edmunds (13)
14 The Cinnamon Club (22)
15 Noble Rot Soho (20)
16 La Trompette (16)
17 The Ritz (21)
18 Sam's Riverside (30)
19 La Poule au Pot (23)
20 A Wong (12)
21 Gymkhana (14)
22 Bentley's (19)
23 Trinity (25)
24 The Five Fields (17)
25 The Anchor & Hope (-)
26 Rules (-)
27 Galvin La Chapelle (38)
28 Benares (-)
29 Wiltons (32)
30 Gordon Ramsay (26)
31 Pied à Terre (28)
32 Moro (-)
33 Sessions Arts Club (-)
34 The Ledbury (-)
35 Lorne (34)
36 Oxo Tower (Restaurant) (-)
37 Harwood Arms (-)
38 Caraffini (-)
39 The Ivy (18)
40 St John Smithfield (39)

J Sheekey

SURVEY NOMINATIONS

Top gastronomic experience
1 Core by Clare Smyth (1)
2 Chez Bruce (2)
3 Bouchon Racine*
4 Pied à Terre (-)
5 The Ledbury (8)
6 The Five Fields (3)
7 Frog by Adam Handling (5)
8 The Ritz (7)
9 The River Café (-)
10 Medlar (10)

Favourite
1 Chez Bruce (1)
2 Sam's Riverside (10)
3 Bouchon Racine*
4 The Wolseley (2)
5 The River Café (3)
6 La Trompette (8)
7 Bocca di Lupo (-)
8 Medlar (-)
9 Hawksmoor (Group) (-)
10 J Sheekey (-)

Best for romance
1 Clos Maggiore (1)
2 La Poule au Pot (2)
3 Andrew Edmunds (3)
4 Core by Clare Smyth (7)
5 Sessions Arts Club (5)
6 Galvin La Chapelle (-)
7 Medlar (-)
8 Chez Bruce (6)
9 Scott's (8)
10 Pied à Terre (-)

Best bar/pub food
1 Harwood Arms (1)
2 The Anchor & Hope (3)
3 The Anglesea Arms (4)
4 The Eagle (8)
5 Bull & Last (7)
6 The Wigmore, The Langham (
7 The Drapers Arms (-)
8 The Ladbroke Arms (-)
9 The Pelican (-)
10 The Red Lion & Sun (6)

Best for business
1 The Wolseley (1)
2 The Delaunay (3)
3 Hawksmoor (Group) (3)
4 Scott's (6)
5 Rules (-)
6 Coq d'Argent (4)
7 Galvin La Chapelle (8)
8 Cabotte (8)
8= The Dining Room, The Goring Hotel (10)
10 Bleeding Heart Bistro (-)

Best breakfast/ brunch
1 The Wolseley (1)
2 Dishoom (2)
3 The Delaunay (4)
4 Granger & Co (5)
5 Breakfast Club (10)
6 Côte (3)
7 Caravan (7)
8 Megan's (8)
9 The Ivy Grills & Brasseries (6)
10 Claridges Foyer & Reading Room (-)

Most disappointing cooking
1 Oxo Tower (Restaurant) (1)
2 The Ivy (2)
3 The Wolseley (-)
4 Dinner Mandarin Oriental (-)
5 Gordon Ramsay (3)
6 Mere (-)
7 Hot Stone (-)
8 Jacuzzi (-)
9 Rick Stein (5)
10 Skylon (-)

Most overpriced restaurant
1 The River Café (1)
2 Gordon Ramsay (5)
3 Oxo Tower (Restaurant) (4)
4 Sexy Fish (2)
5 Hélène Darroze, Connaught (3
6 Dinner Mandarin Oriental (-)
7 J Sheekey (-)
8 Scott's (10)
9 Langan's Brasserie (-)
10 Estiatorio Milos (-)

SURVEY HIGHEST RATINGS

	FOOD	SERVICE	AMBIENCE	OVERALL
£130+				
1	Endo at The Rotunda	Core by Clare Smyth	Sketch (Lecture Room)	Sketch (Lecture Room)
2	Core by Clare Smyth	Da Terra	Endo at The Rotunda	Endo at The Rotunda
3	Da Terra	Endo at The Rotunda	Core by Clare Smyth	Core by Clare Smyth
4	A Wong	The Five Fields	The Ledbury	Da Terra
5	Sketch (Lecture Room)	Muse	Da Terra	The Ledbury
£100–£129				
1	Chez Bruce	Charlie's at Brown's	Charlie's at Brown's	Charlie's at Brown's
2	SOLA	The Ritz	The Ritz	The Ritz
3	Otto's	Clarke's	Min Jiang	Hutong, The Shard
4	Hutong, The Shard	Otto's	Galvin at Windows	Min Jiang
5	The Ninth London	Chez Bruce	Hutong, The Shard	Otto's
£75–£99				
1	BiBi	The Dysart Petersham	Clos Maggiore	The Dysart Petersham
2	The Barbary	Theo Randall	The Dysart Petersham	BiBi
3	Myrtle	Cornerstone	The Barbary	The Barbary
4	The Dysart Petersham	Myrtle	Sam's Riverside	Cornerstone
5	Brat	BiBi	The Cinnamon Club	Norma
£55–£74				
1	Sabor	Oslo Court	Sessions Arts Club	Sabor
2	Jin Kichi	Café Spice Namaste	Andrew Edmunds	The French House
3	Bombay Bustle	Hereford Road	Cafe Cecilia	Cafe Cecilia
4	The French House	The French House	Sabor	Café Spice Namaste
5	Berber & Q	Mazi	The French House	Sessions Arts Club
£54 or less				
1	Dastaan	Cinquecento	Bar Italia	Cinquecento
2	Roti King	Dastaan	Trattoria Brutto	Trattoria Brutto
3	Supawan	Monmouth Coffee Co	Maison Bertaux	Dastaan
4	Manteca	Lupins	Granary Square Brasserie	Supawan
5	Kiln	Kiln	Cinquecento	Bar Italia

SURVEY BEST BY CUISINE

These are the restaurants which received the best average food ratings (excluding establishments with a small or notably local following).

Where the most common types of cuisine are concerned, we present the results in two price-brackets. For less common cuisines, we list the top three, regardless of price.

British, Modern

£75 and over

1 Core by Clare Smyth
2 The Ledbury
3 Chez Bruce
4 Muse
5 The Five Fields

Under £75

1 The French House
2 Cafe Cecilia
3 The Plimsoll
4 12:51
5 Lupins

French

£75 and over

1 Sketch (Lecture Room)
2 La Dame de Pic London
3 Otto's
4 The Ninth London
5 Galvin La Chapelle

Under £75

1 Casse-Croute
2 Café du Marché
3 Galvin Bistrot & Bar
4 The Wells Tavern
5 Petit Ma Cuisine

Italian/Mediterranean

£75 and over

1 Norma
2 Theo Randall
3 Murano
4 Luca
5 Enoteca Turi

Under £75

1 Pentolina
2 Manteca
3 Padella
4 Bocca di Lupo
5 Flour & Grape

Indian & Pakistani

£75 and over

1 BiBi
2 Bombay Bustle
3 Gymkhana
4 Trishna
5 Tamarind

Under £75

1 Dastaan
2 Café Spice Namaste
3 Kricket
4 Pure Indian Cooking
5 Lahore Kebab House

Chinese

£75 and over

1 A Wong
2 Hutong, The Shard
3 Min Jiang
4 China Tang
5 Hunan

Under £75

1 Three Uncles
2 Barshu
3 Master Wei
4 Mandarin Kitchen
5 Four Seasons

Japanese

£75 and over

1 Endo at Rotunda
2 Dinings
3 Nobu Portman Square
4 Zuma
5 Nobu

Under £75

1 Jin Kichi
2 Oka
3 Akira at Japan House
4 Eat Tokyo
5 Sticks'n'Sushi

British, Traditional

1 The Ritz
2 St John Smithfield
3 Scott's

Vegetarian

1 Bubala
2 Apricity
3 Ragam

Burgers, etc

1 Burger & Lobster
2 MEATLiquor
3 Patty and Bun

Pizza

1 Santa Maria
2 Cinquecento
3 50 Kalò di Ciro Salvo

Fish & Chips

1 Nautilus
2 Toff's
3 fish!

Thai

1 Supawan
2 Kiln
3 Smoking Goat

Steaks & Grills

1 Lurra
2 Goodman
3 Hawksmoor

Fish & Seafood

1 Cornerstone
2 The Oystermen
3 Bentley's

Fusion

1 Da Terra
2 Paladar
3 Scully

Spanish

1 Sabor
2 Brat
3 José

Los Mochis

Blacklock

dland Grand Dining Room NW1

THE RESTAURANT SCENE

Headwinds continue to constrain growth

We recorded 123 new openings in the last 12 months. Like last year, this is the lowest level of openings since the 2012 edition. Yet again, the rate falls near the bottom of the range of 107-200 openings per annum since the year 2000.

By contrast, the rate of closures stands at 77, which – while not high – isn't a low rate either. Subtracting this figure from the openings gives net growth of 46, continuing the tame run of growth seen since 2018. London's quality restaurant scene nowadays is expanding at a rate more in keeping with the 1990s than the previous millennial trend. When you consider that the population today is over 30% higher than it was in 2000, it underlines the tepid nature of current activity.

Hold onto your hats!

One area of undoubted growth is restaurant bills! The average price of dinner for one at establishments listed in this guide is £75.65 (c.f. £69.28 last year). This represents an annualised increase of 9.2% in the past year: well above CPI growth of 6.4% for the 12 months to July 2022 (although food inflation in this period was higher).

Continuing a trend seen last year, the rise is most marked amongst the most pricey restaurants (those charging over £100 per head). In this group, the annualised growth rate is again higher than for restaurants generally, at 10.7% (down a fraction from 11.7% last year).

This last factor continues to produce ever-new, vertigo-inducing price points that would have seemed far-fetched in the capital barely five years ago. Last year, we noted that £100 per head is no longer enough for our highest price category (now redefined to £130+). Next year, we will have to redefine our top category at £150+.

Growth at the loftiest price-levels is particularly eyecatching: becoming more so the higher you move up the price scale. There are now 191 restaurants in the guide charging over £100 per head (up 24% from last year's 154); there are 54 restaurants charging over £150 per head (up 46% from last year's 37); above £200 per head, there are 27 establishments (up 59%) and above £250 per head now 11 (up 83% from 6 last year). And these figures do not include establishments such as those in Whitehall's new OWO hotel, flagged in the guide but not yet part of our stats.

Rich person's playground?

Beyond the global pressure on prices, it is tempting to look for other long-term trends that may account for shifting the price-landscape at the top of the London restaurant scene. In September 2023, London's Evening Standard ran a front page with the headline "London's 7-star gold rush" in which it charted the large number of über-luxe new hotel projects approaching completion. Pricewise, these establishments are seeking a room rate of £1000+ per night – breaking new ground for the capital. Many of London's splashiest new eateries operate from within such ventures.

Another factor adding to the top-end price category is the rise of luxury Japanese dining in London. Nearly half of the £250+ establishments are Japanese, yet this is a category of restaurant that didn't exist in London 10 years ago. And many of the more expensive Modern European and fusion restaurants in the upper price categories ape this counterbased style of dining. It's a form of top-end meal that would not be recognisable to previous generations of Londoners: often based around a chef's table with the focus on foodie reverie rather than the traditional image of gilded chambers, candle-light, flunkies, gueridons, and napery.

It is tempting to conclude that the capital is becoming a playground for what used to be called "the jet set", with most of its own residents consigned to looking on enviously on Insta and in colour supplements. But historically one of the striking features of the London restaurant scene has been its lack of a top tier of splurgy, expensive destinations such as those that have long characterised top-end dining in Paris and Tokyo. Perhaps it is perverse to complain if London can now hold its own internationally.

Changing of the guard

Although this year has not been exceptional for closures, what has caught attention is the number of famous names and stalwart institutions that have given up the ghost.

Le Gavroche (open till January, but now booked solid on the news of its demise) is the most notable, with Michel Roux Jr now seemingly focusing purely on his media and consultancy commitments. In a similar vein, Marcus Wareing has also announced that he is stepping back this year.

The very venerable Simpsons Tavern (which dated from 1757), Julies, The India Club and Banners all chose to go this year, while Simpsons in the Strand (est. 1828) sold off its famous carving trollies and is to be relaunched with an as-yet-to-be-revealed new look.

Japanese most popular non-European cuisine

In terms of cuisines, this year's openings mirrored last year's. After Modern British (30) openings, Italian cuisine was next favourite (with 18 debuts), followed by Japanese cuisine (with 10 openings).

In terms of location, Central London remained dominant, with 50 arrivals. In the 'burbs, South London led the way for once (with 21 openings) boosted by the Battersea Power Station development. East London followed (with 19 openings); while West London equalled North London's rate of opening (with 16 apiece).

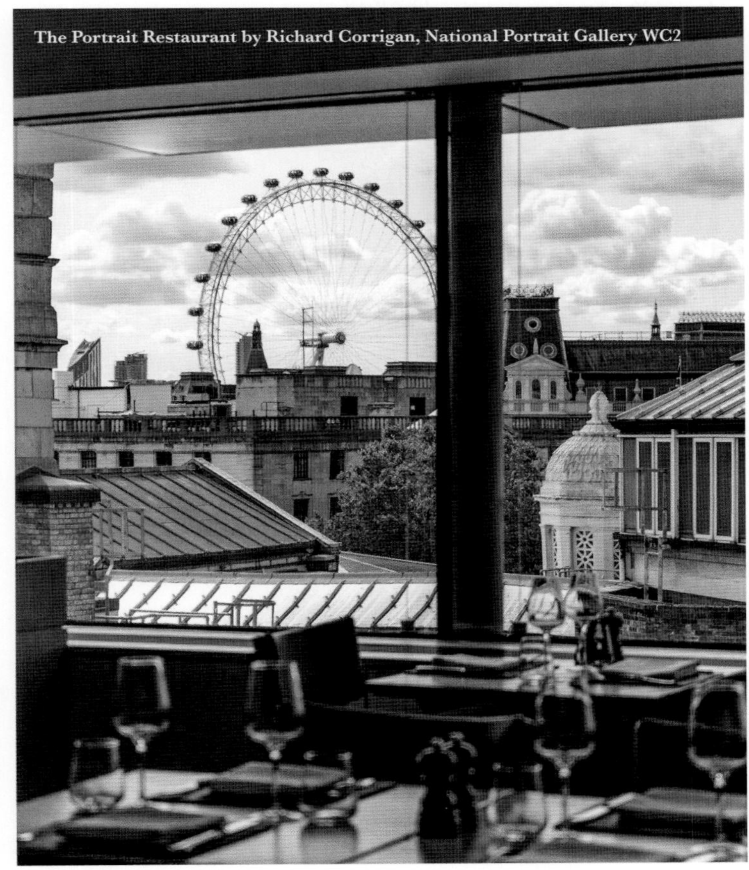
The Portrait Restaurant by Richard Corrigan, National Portrait Gallery WC2

OPENINGS AND CLOSURES

The listings below relate to the period from Autumn 2022 to Autumn 2023. In one or two cases (Le Gavroche, Marcus) we have anticipated a closure due shortly post-publication.

Only branches of small groups in the listings below contribute to the grand total figures. (It is beyond the scope of this book to track comings and goings at the large multiples.)

* temporarily closed as we to go to press.

Openings (123)

The Apollo Arms
Archway
ArtSpace Café, Claridge's
Attica
Audrey Green, NPG
Bancone *(SE1)*
Bao Battersea *(SW11, W1)*
Bar Kroketa
The Barley Mow
The Beefsteaks @ M. Manze
Berbere Pizza
Berenjak Borough *(SE1)*
Blacklock *(E14)*
Block Soho
Bone Daddies *(W8)*
Bouchon Racine
Boudica
Brooklands
Café Lapérouse, The OWO
Capri
Caravan *(WC2)*
Carlotta
Casa do Frango *(SW1, W1)*
Chet's, Hoxton Hotel
Chungdam
Cilantro Putney
Cinder *(NW8)*
Cinquecento *(W1, NW3)*
Claridges Restaurant
Contigo
Crisp Pizza, The Chancellors
The Devonshire
Diba *(SW3)*
Doppo
Dorian
Dorothy & Marshall
Dovetale by Tom Sellers
EDIT
081 Pizzeria, Peckham Levels
Eline
Emmanuelle
Empire Empire
Endo Kazutoshi, The OWO
Epicurus
Evernight
Fatto A Mano *(N1)*
Flat Iron *(W8)*
Freak Scene
La Gamba
Giacco's
Gouqi
The Gurkhas
Harvest
Hawthorn
Hicce Hart
Homies on Donkeys
Humo
Izakaya Nights
Kanada-Ya *(W5)*
Kapara by Bala Baya
Kettners
Kibako
Kima
Kuro Eatery
The Lanesborough Grill
Langosteria, The OWO
Lasdun, National Theatre
Lavo, The BoTree
Leo's
Lilienblum
Lina Stores *(SW4)*
Little Kudu
Little Pizza Hicce
Llama Inn, The Hoxton
Lusin
Maene
Maresco
Maria G's *(SW6)*
Masala Zone *(W1)*
Mauro Colagreco, The OWO
Mayha
Meet Bros
Midland Grand Dining Room
Miznon *(W11)*
Los Mochis *(EC2)*
Mount Street Restaurant, The Audley
Mountain
Mr Ji *(NW1)*
Nammos
1905
Noble Rot Mayfair
Noci *(SW11, EC1)*
Notto
Oak & Poppy
Ochre
The Orangery
Paper Moon, The OWO
Papi
The Parakeet
The Park
Pavyllon
Ploussard
The Portrait Restaurant by Richard Corrigan, NPG
Rasa Street
Sam's Kitchen
Sheesh
Shiro
64 Goodge Street
Souvlaki Street
Sticks n Sushi *(W12, E1)*
Sticky Mango Butler's Wharf *(SE1)*
Story Cellar
Studio Gauthier
Supa Ya Ramen *(SE15)*
Sushi Kanesaka
TAKU
Terra Moderna
Terra Rossa *(EC4)*
The eight Restaurant
Toba
Tofu Vegan *(E1)*
Tozi Grand Cafe *(SW11)*
Trinco
20 Berkeley
Uli Marylebone *(W1)*
Via Emilia *(W1T)*
Vori
The Waterman's Arms
The Wolseley City
Yaatra
Zapote
Zia Lucia *(NW6, E14)*

Closures (77)

Amethyst
Antillean
Aquavit
Attawa
Attimi
The Avenue
Banners
Bao Bar* *(E8)*
Bao Fitzrovia *(W1)*
Bermondsey Larder*
Black Radish
BOB's Lobster
Boiler & Co
Boudin Blanc
Bright
Celeste at The Lanesborough
Chameleon
Cincinnati Chilibomb
Dai Chi
Dumpling Shack x Fen Noodles
FENN
Fiend
Folie*
Le Gavroche
Giannino Mayfair*
Goddard & Gibbs
Grand Trunk Road
Ham
Hankies Marble Arch *(W1)*
Haugen
The Hero of Maida
Hood
India Club, Strand Continental Hotel
Isibani
Itaku
Joanna's
The Jones Family Affair
Julie's
Lino's
The Tent (at the End of the Universe)
M Restaurant Victoria Street *(SW1)*
Ma Goa
Made in Italy *(SW19)*
Marcus, The Berkeley
Mathura
Maya
Mike's Peckham
Miscusi *(N1)*
Mr Ji *(W1)*
Mr Todiwala's Petiscos
The Narrow
Native at Browns
Ngon
Nutshell
Off the Hook
Oklava *(EC2)*
Olivocarne
Oxeye
P Franco
Pizza East Portobello *(W10)*
Plateau
Rabot 1745
Radici
The Red Duck
The Residency
Sarap Filipino Bistro
SeaSons
7 Saints
Simpson's Tavern
Sparrow
St Martin's House
Stem & Glory *(EC1, EC2)*
Tatale
Tokyo Sukiyaki-Tei & Bar Walter's
West 4th
Wun's *(W1)*

Midland Grand Dining Room NW1

LONDON DIRECTORY

Claridge's Restaurant W1

LONDON DIRECTORY

A CENA TW1 £79 4|4|3

418 RICHMOND ROAD
020 8288 0108 1–*4A*

With its "traditional tablecloths and a sense of comfort", this "really strong and inventive neighbourhood Italian" close to Richmond Bridge in St Margaret's appeals to a broad local constituency – "you can tell because it can be hard to get a table!". The food is "always a treat" – and "the menu changes regularly, which makes eating here frequently even more of a pleasure". / TW1 2EB; www.acena.co.uk; acenarestaurant; Tue-Sat 10 pm.

A WONG SW1 £252 5|2|2

70 WILTON RD 020 7828 8931 2–*4B*

"Without a shadow of a doubt the very best Chinese restaurant in town" – Andrew Wong is "such a talent" and his "genius" cuisine inspires unending superlatives regarding his Pimlico HQ (previously run for decades by his parents as Kym's). "Exceptional craft is on display" in the preparation of the "exquisite dim sum" and other "clearly Chinese dishes" ("none of your fusion nonsense here!") and for some reporters it is "one of the most extraordinary culinary experiences ever". But since the award of a second Michelin star (the first ever for a Chinese establishment) a meal here risks becoming "prohibitively expensive", with minimum spends for lunch and tasting menus only in the evening. On most accounts it's "worth it despite the high cost", but the equation is more evenly balanced now, and the levels of service and ambience have struggled to keep up with the "hellish" bill. Even so, "there's scarce table availability even with the extension into the outer terrace". / SW1V 1DE; www.awong.co.uk; awongsw1; Wed-Sat, Tue 8.30 pm.

THE ABINGDON W8 £67 3|3|3

54 ABINGDON RD 020 7937 3339 6–*2A*

"A very special gastropub tucked away in a quiet street off Kensington High Street", which has been run for 25 years by the Staples family, who have remodelled what was built as a classic Victorian corner tavern into an "all-round reliable local restaurant" and bar fit for its chichi environs. / W8 6AP; www.theabingdon.co.uk; theabingdon; Mon-Sat 10 pm, Sun 9 pm.

ACME FIRE CULT E8 £55 2|1|3

THE BOOTYARD, ABBOT STREET NO TEL
14–*1A*

"Don't be put off by what looks like a dodgy side street to get there", say fans of Andrew Clarke and Daniel Watkins's Dalston BBQ, who say that the "great food cooked with fire and flames" (and served "in the classic small plates style") justifies eating "in a tent! in January!" ("you get blankets… it's worth it and fun"). And there's "amazing vegetarian options as well as the fish and meat". But other diners in our annual poll are less sure. "Haphazard" or "too-cool-for-school" service is a recurrent theme. And overall ratings were dragged down by the minority who found the food itself to be "a real let down" ("considering everything is prepared over coals, it was not the charry interesting place we'd heard of, in fact somewhat bland"). / E8 3DP; www.acmefirecult.com; acmefirecult; Tue-Sat 10 pm, Sun 4 pm.

AFGHAN KITCHEN N1 £37 3|2|2

35 ISLINGTON GREEN
020 7359 8019 9–*3D*

This "tiny hole in the wall with an even tinier kitchen" on Islington Green "delivers time and time again" with its tasty and good-value Afghan cooking. Top Menu Tip – "get the pumpkin curry". / N1 8DU; kubiti.blog/afghan-kitchen; afghankitchenldn; Wed & Thu, Sun 9.30 pm, Fri & Sat 10 pm.

AGLIO E OLIO SW10 £52 3|3|2

194 FULHAM RD 020 7351 0070 6–*3B*

"Spot-on pasta" is a key draw at this "excellent local Italian" near Chelsea & Westminster Hospital "that welcomes kids" and "always delivers with charming service". It's the sort of place regulars "go to at least once a month, love it!" – which means it's typically rammed. / SW10 9PN; www.aglioeolio.co.uk; Mon-Sun 11 pm.

AKARI N1 £45 4|3|3

196 ESSEX RD 020 7226 9943 9–*3D*

"Still a bit of a hidden gem, which is a real shame as this place should be packed" – this converted pub by Essex Road station is a longstanding fixture of the area. With its mix of sushi and other "enjoyable and very tasty" fare, fans say it serves "really wonderful izakaya dishes in a pretty chilled-out environment"; and that even if "it's not as cheap as it once was, it's still good value". / N1 8LZ; www.akarilondon.co.uk; akari_islington; Tue-Thu, Sun 10.30 pm, Fri 10 pm, Sat 11 pm.

AKIRA AT JAPAN HOUSE W8 £74 3|3|2

101-111 KENSINGTON HIGH STREET
020 3971 4646 6–*1A*

"Exquisite" (or "expensive"?) is the apposite word to describe a meal at the first-floor restaurant of the Japan House cultural centre on Kensington High Street, where tableware and presentation are given equal billing with the food. "The bento boxes are beautiful", too. / W8 5SA; www.japanhouselondon.uk; japanhouseldn; Tue-Sat 11 pm, Sun.

AKOKO W1 £164 4|4|3

21 BERNERS STREET
020 7323 0593 5–*1A*

Ayo Adeyemi is now at the stoves of Aji Akokomi's groundbreaking Fitzrovia West African, after the departure of Theo Clench in March 2022. Clench held a Michelin star at his previous gig (Bonham's) and was instantly awarded one at his new home (Cycene) so it's slightly puzzling why one was withheld from him here? Perhaps Ayo will eventually succeed where Theo did not? The intriguing cooking uses West African ingredients and spicing as inspiration for an 'haute' take on these cuisines, and though feedback was limited this year it seems to continue at the same "brilliant, creative and delicious" level set by his predecessor. Add in the vibey interior using a palette inspired by African village culture, and the establishment has helped move the goalposts of what can be expected in terms of sophistication for an African-inspired venture in London. BREAKING NEWS. In September 2023, Aji announced a spin-off venture in Borough Yards called Akara – also West African but in a cheaper, more accessible format. / W1T 3LJ; akoko.co.uk; akokorestaurant; Tue-Sat 9 pm.

AKUB W8 £70 2|3|4

27 UXBRIDGE STREET
07729 039206 7–*2B*

Fadi Kattan's three-floor Palestinian newcomer in Notting Hill inspires mixed reviews. Everyone agrees it's a "beautiful room" with a "bubbling" atmosphere; and welcomes the fact that its Middle Eastern menu is "just a bit different, with a nice twist on more familiar fare". But while some reporters (especially veggie ones) feel the cuisine is outstanding, too many feel it is "heavy handed" – "a baffling series of dishes, some of them good, some of them unappetising, with no coherent pattern of size or flavour". "I was so looking forward to this one – the service was great and so was the ambience but the food was disappointing". / W8 7TQ; www.akub-restaurant.com; akub.london; Tue-Thu 11 pm, Fri & Sat 11.30 pm, Sun 4 pm.

AL DUCA SW1 £90 3 2 3

4-5 DUKE OF YORK ST
020 7839 3090 3–*3D*

"Very well-presented Italian food" and "an atmosphere quiet enough for conversation" make this straightforward trattoria on a corner site in St James's a useful and reasonably priced option in an expensive part of town. / SW1Y 6LA; www.alduca-restaurant.co.uk; al_duca; Mon-Sat 11 pm.

ALAIN DUCASSE AT THE DORCHESTER W1 £278 3 3 2

53 PARK LANE 020 7629 8866 3–*3A*

"A perfect menu that will forever stay in the mind" is how some reporters remember this luxurious Mayfair outpost of France's most celebrated restaurateur, whose kitchen is run by chef-patron Jean-Philippe Blondet. Often indifferently rated in our survey over the years, it was more regularly acclaimed this year as offering "the very best of French cuisine" to match its Michelin three-star renown, although even those acknowledging the "impeccable food and service" sometimes note that "the room itself is a bit soulless and rather boring". And there remains an undercurrent in sentiment of the view that the performance is "uninspiring and poor value". Top Menu Tip – save yourself for the signature dish, which is rum baba, with Chantilly cream and rum. / W1K 1QA; www.alainducasse-dorchester.com; alainducasseatthedorchester.

ALEX DILLING CAFÉ ROYAL W1 £212 5 4 3

68 REGENT STREET 020 7406 3333 4–*4C*

Ex-Greenhouse chef, Alex Dilling, "has hit the ground running" at this West End yearling, overlooking Regent Street: one of the highest quality arrivals of the last twelve months (for which he was awarded two Michelin stars in no seconds flat). Feedback is full of superlatives for his "exceptional cuisine" which is in a "classic" style rooted in tradition ("it was some of the most technically accomplished food I have ever been served…"). Overall it's an "elegant" experience, but the "dining room could do with a little refresh (staff indicated plans are in the pipeline for this)". / W1B 4DY; www.hotelcaferoyal.com; alexdillingcaferoyal; Tue-Sun 8.30 pm.

ALEXANDRIE W8 £74 3 3 3

38C KENSINGTON CHURCH STREET
020 7937 2244 6–*1A*

This relatively unsung Kensington outfit is worth knowing about, if on limited feedback, for its refined French-influenced Egyptian cooking – of the style enjoyed in sophisticated homes rather than in tourist traps. / W8 4BX; alexandrie_kensington; Wed-Sat 10 pm, Sun 9.30 pm.

ALLEGRA E20 £95 3 2 2

THE STRATFORD, 20-22 INTERNATIONAL WAY 020 3973 0545 14–*1D*

Patrick Powell's "adventurous and well-crafted" cuisine on the 7th floor of this glossy design hotel (part of the Manhattan Loft Gardens apartment block) "is something far beyond other restaurants in the area, with real delicacy and touch, particularly in the fish cookery… if it were more central it would be constantly packed to bursting". On the downside, "despite the pleasant decor and the great view you can't quite shake the feeling that it's part of a hotel… which of course it is…" / E20 1GQ; www.allegra-restaurant.com; allegrarestaurant; Wed-Sat 10 pm, Sun 3 pm.

THE ALMA SE19 £69 3 3 4

95 CHURCH ROAD 020 8768 1885 1–*4D*

This "lovely food-led pub" – a carefully modernised beauty from 1854 on Crystal Palace's thriving 'Triangle' – showcases chef David Yorkiston's "really great cooking – way, way above typical gastroboozer fare". "Controversially, it has banned kids under 10" but not everyone objects ("we think the atmosphere is all the better for it, even if it means we can't go there as often as we'd like)". / SE19 2TA; thealmapub.com; thealmacp; Mon-Sat 10 pm, Sun 9 pm.

ALOO TAMA SW1 £47 4 3 2

18 GREENCOAT PLACE
020 7834 9873 2–*4C*

"Terrific Nepalese dishes in a basic setting" behind Victoria station. "The manager is exceptionally friendly and skillful – they were happy to make black lentils for us despite not being on the menu". They also have a lunchtime food truck at Merchant Square in Paddington. Top Tip – "BYO, so don't turn up empty-handed expecting a beer or glass of wine". / SW1P 1PG; www.alootama.com; alootamaofficial; Tue-Sat 10 pm, Sun 9 pm.

ALTER E1 £34 4 3 2

15 LEMAN STREET NO TEL 10–*2D*

Within Leman Locke Hotel in Aldgate East, Andy Goodwin's modern dining room (with floor-to-ceiling windows looking out onto the nearby offices) aims to 'challenge the common perceptions of vegan cooking by drawing inspiration from global street food cultures'. Feedback on his interesting meat-free creations remains limited, but very enthusiastic. Top Tip – dip your toe in the water with the £28 early evening menu. / E1 8EN; www.alterldn.com; alter_ldn; Mon-Sat 10 pm.

AMAYA SW1 £96 4 4 4

HALKIN ARCADE, 19 MOTCOMB ST
020 7823 1166 6–*1D*

"Sophisticated flavours run through outstanding quality grill and tandoori dishes" – "beautiful" food from a "cleverly designed menu" using a wide variety of cooking techniques – at this Belgravia pioneer of Indian tapas (part of MW Eats, which owns Masala Zone, Chutney Mary, et al). With its stylish design, built around an open kitchen, it falls under the heading: "pricey but worth it". / SW1X 8JT; www.amaya.biz; amaya.ldn; Tue-Sat 10.30 pm, Sun 10 pm.

AMAZONICO W1 £144 2 3 4

10 BERKELEY SQUARE
020 7404 5000 3–*3B*

"If you feel like a party this is a good place to come" – this lavish, foliage-filled Mayfair haunt 'goes for it' with its "live music, nice cocktails and lively ambience" and provides a "great setting" (including for romance). Fans say "the food is as good as the music" and applaud a "superb overall experience". But there are also those – particularly who focus on the sushi and luxurious grills rather than the complete package – for whom it's just far too overpriced. / W1J 6EF; www.amazonicorestaurant.com; amazonicolondon; Mon-Sat 1 am, Sun midnight.

THE AMERICAN BAR, THE STAFFORD SW1 £82 3 3 4

16-18 SAINT JAMES'S PLACE
020 7493 0111 3–*4C*

The "great vibe" created by its tranquil St James's location and retro Americana helps create a feeling of luxurious nostalgia at this long-standing fixture. With the hotel catering now overseen by Northcote's Lisa Goodwin-Allen, the menu has been usefully re-imagined in recent times and has a heartier, more distinctive US spin (steaks, dogs, pastrami rolls) than it did of old. / SW1A 1NJ; thestaffordlondon.com; Sun-Wed midnight, Thu-Sat 1 am.

L'AMOROSA W6 £67 4 4 3

278 KING ST 020 8563 0300 8–*2B*

This "lovely local Italian" near Ravenscourt Park tube is getting back into its stride after "a dreadful time with lockdown followed by a flood at the premises". Ex-Zafferano chef Andy Needham and his team offer a "really warm welcome and a beautifully executed short menu". Top Menu Tip – "excellent pasta and specials". / W6 0SP; www.lamorosa.co.uk; lamorosa_london; Thu, Sat 9 pm.

AMPÉLI W1 £93 3 3 2

18 CHARLOTTE STREET
020 3355 5370 2–*1C*

Opened a matter of weeks before Covid struck in 2020, photographer Jenny Pagoni's debut restaurant on Fitzrovia's foodie Charlotte Street was inspired by contemporary Athenian wine bars, and has a "very interesting all-Greek list" emphasising indigenous grape varieties, accompanied by a menu of eastern Mediterranean dishes. / W1T 2LZ; www.ampeli.london; ampeli.london; Tue-Sat 9.30 pm.

AMRUTHA SW18 £37 342

326 GARRATT LANE 020 8001 4628 11–2B

"Vegan food that's as good as can be" – from a selection of broadly Asian choices – inspires devotees of this 'vegan soul food' venture in Earlsfield (now with a spin-off in Honor Oak Park) from school friends Arvin Suntaramoorphy and Shyam Kotecha. "Being able to ask for additional dishes until satisfied means you never leave disappointed". Guests are invited to BYO without charge, and to reduce the bill if they believe it is too high – while the truly hard-up can eat for free in return for a couple of hours' work. / SW18 4EJ; www.amrutha.co.uk; amruthauk; Tue-Sat 10 pm, Sun 9 pm.

THE ANCHOR & HOPE SE1 £69 433

36 THE CUT 020 7928 9898 10–4A

"Still fantastic after all these years" – this celebrated foodie favourite near the Old Vic returned to being London's No.1 gastropub this year, in a dead heat with Fulham's Harwood Arms. "It's a bit insulting to call it bar/ pub food as it's a level up from that" – "very strong, British traditional fare is made with added flair and style" from a "daily changing menu with lots of options" ("the shared roast and other meat dishes are quite unique and the eclectic wine list a joy"). And "nowadays they serve a well-priced lunch as well as its always-magnificent evening menu". / SE1 8LP; www.anchorandhopepub.co.uk; anchorhopecut; Mon & Tue 10 pm, Wed-Sat 10.30 pm, Sun 3.15 pm.

ANDANZA SE1 £54 433

66 WESTON STREET 020 7967 1972 10–4C

This "buzzing tapas bar, hidden away from the tourist traps of Borough Market", occupies a former bookies' in the shadow of the Shard, and offers some "great, non-standard" pintxo, pequeno and other options. If "the set-up's a little bit cramped, that does give it the feel of the tightest of tapas bars in Catalonia". / SE1 3QJ; www.andanza.co.uk; andanza.se1; Mon-Sun 11 pm.

THE ANDOVER ARMS W6 £53 344

57 ALDENSLEY RD 020 8748 2155 8–1C

"Now under new management", this "small and friendly" pub – in the picturesque Hammersmith backstreets known as 'Brackenbury Village' – has gone from good to better. It has always been a "solid, welcoming local, with good food and well-kept beer" and its new incarnation is just that bit 'next-level': with its "well judged and executed seasonal menus and quality wines by the glass" it's "buzzing". / W6 0DL; www.theandoverarmsw6.com; theandoverarms; Mon-Sat 10 pm, Sun 9 pm.

ANDREW EDMUNDS W1 £71 345

46 LEXINGTON STREET 020 7437 5708 4–2C

"If your date is going badly here, it's not destined to be" at this "gorgeous", candle-lit Soho townhouse – one of the capital's prime destinations "for a tête-a-tête lunch or smoochy dinner". "All bare wood, nooks, and snugs", it is "very tightly packed" and down-to-earth and for its legions of fans captures "just what I want from a restaurant. OK, the setting could be more comfy, but it has a superb vibe", "amenable" and "charming" service, and "British seasonal food with a twist" that's not aiming for fireworks but which is "always reliable". Crucially, all this is backed up by "a short wine selection that's second to none and at absolutely outstanding prices". Andrew Edmunds himself unexpectedly passed away in September 2022, but the business (now run by his family) "continues to honour his legacy": "I've been coming here since the 90's and I'm so glad the team have carried on without Andrew – the place goes from strength to strength". / W1F 0LP; www.andrewedmunds.com; andrew.edmunds; Mon-Sun 10.30 pm.

The Apollo Arms SW4

ANGELINA E8 £72 534

56 DALSTON LANE 020 7241 1851 14–1A

"Every time is a different experience thanks to the ever changing menu" at this "imaginative and wonderful" Dalston venture. "The food really is a mix of European and Japanese influences" and served in a tasting menu format (either the 10-course 'kaiseki' or 4-course 'omakase') that's "excellent, without feeling too fussy, and great value for money". The "dark and moody interior" creates a "pared-back but buzzy atmosphere, which makes this a perfect pick for a special dinner". / E8 3AH; angelina.london; angelina.dalston; Mon-Fri 10 pm, Sat 10.30 pm.

ANGLER, SOUTH PLACE HOTEL EC2 £118 342

3 SOUTH PL 020 3215 1260 13–2A

"Fine fish, delicately cooked and served" is the speciality at this "smart modern restaurant on the top floor of a hotel" near Broadgate, from D&D London. Food of this standard is rare in the City, and "not even the dullest business chat can take the edge off the outstanding cooking and wines". It's a discreet place, too, "and the team knows when to shoot the breeze with diners and when to withdraw to let the serious negotiations take place". / EC2M 2AF; www.anglerrestaurant.com; angler_restaurant; Tue-Sat 9.15 pm. SRA – accredited

THE ANGLESEA ARMS W6 £67 435

35 WINGATE RD 020 8749 1291 8–1B

A "favourite in West London" – this very popular hostelry sits on "a quiet tree-lined street" near Ravenscourt Park, and has a small, sunny outside terrace. Its legions of fans say it's "the perfect gastropub" thanks to its "continually brilliant food" over many years, its "perfectly informal service" and its "cosy and intimate" style. "It still feels like a pub and not a restaurant, but the cooking is better than practically any other pub and most restaurants". / W6 0UR; www.angleseaarmspub.co.uk; theangleseaarmsw6; Mon-Wed, Fri & Sat 11 pm, Sun 10.30 pm.

ANGLO EC1 £111 543

30 ST CROSS STREET 020 7430 1503 10–1A

"Surely the best restaurant in London without a Michelin star!" Chef Anthony Raffo provides "modern British cooking at its finest" at this "tiny" Farringdon venture, with "novel flavours and combinations, cleverly incorporating a perfect balance of umami and other tastes; all whilst using seasonal ingredients and looking incredible". Meanwhile, manager, Marie Danzanvilliers, presides "with great charm and hospitality". "The venue itself is quite hipster-cool but pretty low key. At the end of the day, it is all about the food offer and they absolutely nail that!". "It really is a hidden gem"… "No idea why the Tyre Man hasn't come calling." / EC1N 8UH; www.anglorestaurant.com; anglorestaurant; Tue-Sat 11 pm.

ANIMA E CUORE NW1 £59 432

129 KENTISH TOWN RD 07590 427171 9–2B

"Tucked away behind an ice-cream parlour" in Kentish Town, "this lovely local restaurant produces dishes that would shame a far more expensive West End place". Calabrian-born with Moroccan heritage, chef Mustapha Mouflih conjures up "exceptional real Italian cuisine" in a "no-frills" setting which is "reflected in the prices" – and "a bargain deal on corkage". / NW1 8PB; www.animaecuore.co.uk; animaecuoreuk; Tue-Sat 10.30 pm.

ANJANAAS NW6 £39 342

57-59 WILLESDEN LANE 020 7624 1713 1–1B

"Super southern Indian dishes at reasonable prices too" win a following for this family run Keralan in Kilburn. It's either "brilliant and low key" or "very good but with slightly disappointing surroundings" depending on your tastes. / NW6 7RL; www.anjanaas.com; anjanaaslondon; Mon, Wed & Thu 10.30 pm, Fri & Sat 11 pm, Sun 10 pm.

ANNIE'S W4 £65 234

162 THAMES RD 020 8994 9080 1–3A

"A favourite local, always to be relied on" – this cosy, all-day fixture in Strand on the Green, from Lorraine Angliss, is still popular after 24 years. A branch in Barnes hit the buffers a while ago, but three other sister venues are still thriving – Little Bird in Battersea and Rock & Rose in Richmond and most recently Chiswick High Road. / W4 3QS; www.anniesrestaurant.co.uk; anniesrestaurant; Tue-Thu 9 pm, Fri & Sat 10 pm, Sun 5 pm.

THE APOLLO ARMS SW4

13-19 OLD TOWN 020 3827 1213 11–1D

Clapham pub, taken over by the operator behind Ganymede in Belgravia and The Hunter's Moon in South Kensington. It re-opened in May 2023, too late for survey feedback, but it looks worth knowing about, if for no other reason than its spacious terrace. / SW4 0JT; apolloarms.co.uk; theapolloarms; Mon-Sat 10 pm, Sun 9 pm.

APPLEBEE'S FISH SE1 £75 332

5 STONEY ST 020 7407 5777 10–4C

This "reliable" fish specialist on the edge of Borough Market has raised its game in line with the location's emergence as a culinary mecca, and can accommodate guests year-round, either indoors or on its street terrace. The team has recently opened La Gamba tapas bar at the Southbank Centre. / SE1 9AA; www.applebeesfish.com; applebeesfishlondon; Mon-Thu 10 pm, Fri & Sat 11 pm, Sun 6 pm.

APRICITY W1 £105 332

68 DUKE STREET 020 8017 2780 3–2A

Chantelle Nicholson's Mayfair yearling has "a menu balance that's the opposite way around to most restaurants, with an emphasis on vegetarian/vegan cooking, but also with a few meat/fish options". Although some more critical reviewers "were expecting more after reading the glowing reviews", even they said it was "perfectly good". And most feedback this year was uniformly positive, hailing it as an unqualified "winner": "there was no need to order any meat or fish: the vegetarian and vegan dishes we had were spectacular!". / W1K 6JU; www.apricityrestaurant.com; apricityrestaurant; Tue-Sat 9 pm.

APULIA EC1 £71 223

50 LONG LANE 020 7600 8107 10–2B

"In a great location opposite Smithfield Market", and "an excellent pre-theatre option near the Barbican" – this "cheap 'n' cheerful" Italian is "very popular" for its "decent, solid staples" (in particular "good – and huge – pizzas"). "Go hungry." / EC1A 9EJ; apuliarestaurant.co.uk; apuliarestaurant; Mon-Fri 10.30 pm, Sat 10.45 pm, Sun 10.15 pm.

AQUA SHARD SE1 £115 224

31 ST THOMAS ST 020 3011 1256 10–4C

"Everyone is here for the view" on the 31st floor of the Shard, with "all diners glammed up to celebrate something special": "it's what you are paying for". "And boy are you paying!" – "when you consider the sky-high bills", the cuisine is somewhere between "decent enough" and "bog standard". In a similar vein, "service is fine, but could use some improvements… with views to attract the crowds anyway, perhaps management aren't super-worried about the service levels". Overall, though, it's a Faustian bargain many reporters are prepared to make, especially for afternoon tea or a date… or both! / SE1 9RY; www.aquashard.co.uk; aquashard; Sun-Thu 10 pm, Fri & Sat 10.30 pm.

AQUAVIT SW1 £114

ST JAMES'S MARKET, 1 CARLTON ST 020 7024 9848 4–4D

A sense of nearly-but-not-quite hovers over this Scandi NYC-import, whose 1980s namesake is a legend of the Manhattan restaurant scene, but whose London branch (opened in 2016) has never really made waves. A location in the un-loved St James's Market development doesn't help, nor does the atmosphere which can appear gorgeous and glam but can also feel "sterile, despite the best attempts of expensive interior decor". Ultimately, the impression of there being more this place could give "probably comes down to the pricey, decent-but-not-brilliant food". BREAKING NEWS: in September 2023, the restaurant closed unexpectedly, although the owners of NYC Aquavit (who had no stake in the London spin-off) announced a desire to re-establish the brand in London. / SW1Y 4QQ; www.aquavitrestaurants.com; aquavitlondon; Tue-Thu 9 pm, Fri & Sat 10 pm.

ARABICA £60 333

7 LEWIS CUBITT WALK, N1 020 3747 4422 9–3C
3 ROCHESTER WALK, SE1 020 3011 5151 10–4C

"The food is always a delight" at this "consistently high-quality" Levantine specialist "with an emphasis on inventive veg". Originally a market stall, it graduated to a restaurant inside a Borough railway arch, with a second branch in King's Cross. Top Menu Tips – "the stand-out cod dish with chunky flakes cooked just perfectly" and "the toasted flatbread that comes hot in rustling bags". / www.arabicalondon.com; arabicalondon.

THE ARAKI W1 £398 453

UNIT 4 12 NEW BURLINGTON ST 020 7287 2481 4–3A

When it first touched down in 2014 under founder Matsuhiro Araki, this nine-seat Mayfair venue broke the mould for London in the level of ambition for its top-end sushi omakase (gaining three Michelin stars in the bargain). When Master Araki returned to the Far East in 2019, his protégé, UK-born Marty Lau, took over and Michelin removed all three stars never to return any. Why always puzzled us, as little other than very good or outstanding meals are reported here. "You sit at the sushi bar, watching the chef produce the most incredible sushi ever, with the theatre of exceptional fish being filleted", and if there's a quibble it's that "even though the sushi is superb, it's hard not to wonder what it was like when Master Araki himself was still here". There is also the issue that this genre of high-end sushi experiences have multiplied in the capital in recent years and so it is no longer unique in the way it was in the early days. / W1S 3BH; the-araki.co.uk; the_araki_london; Tue-Sat 9 pm.

ARCADE FOOD HALL WC1 £35 222

103-105 NEW OXFORD STREET 020 7519 1202 5–1A

As a "buzzy venue for the young, after-work crowd", this JKS Restaurants food court at the foot of Centre Point does have its fans, who feel that as a "cheap 'n' cheerful" option it's "phenomenal, with such a great variety of street food to try all under one roof – ideal for big groups". Ratings are undercut, though, by those who just find it "very noisy", "pricey" and "average". (In July 2023, JKS launched a second Arcade in the new Battersea Power Station complex, mixing brands from the original together with a new selection of offerings.) / WC1A 1DB; www.arcade-london.com; arcadefoodhall; Tue-Sat 11.30pm, Sun 9.30 pm.

ARCHWAY SW8 £70 444

ARCH 65, QUEEN'S CIRCUS 020 3781 1102 11–1C

"This new spot under the railway arches by Battersea Power Station has some really good cooking" from ex-River Café chef, Alex Owens, to the extent that one early reporter thought it this year's "top opening". It helps too that it has a very attractive interior and "amazing service", led by the other woman behind the new place: owner and CEO Emily Few Brown, who launched the catering company Spook almost ten years ago. / SW8 4NE; www.archwaybattersea.co.uk; archwaybattersea; Wed-Sat midnight.

ARK FISH E18 £55 332

142 HERMON HILL 020 8989 5345 1–1D

"With a varied fish menu", "nice interior" and "very friendly staff", this spacious South Woodford chippy is "great for a family lunch". / E18 1QH; www.arkfishrestaurant.co.uk; ark_fish_restaurant; Tue-Thu 9.45 pm, Fri & Sat 10.15 pm, Sun 8.45 pm.

AROMA BUFFET W12

FIRST FLOOR, WEST 12 SHOPPING CENTRE 020 8746 7625 8–1C

All spent out at Westfield? Head for this large first-floor eatery within the much-less-glam'-looking West 12 Shopping Centre on the other side of Shepherd's Bush Green. Reports on the all-you-can-eat £15 pan-Asian buffet are few, but The Guardian's Grace Dent in late 2022 was a fan, describing a "vast" array of "feisty flavours" (with diverse dishes from as far afield as Canton and West Sumatra) whose "pleasing" prices spark "joy through dark times and ransacked wallets". / W12 8PP; www.aromabuffet.co.uk; aromabuffetw12; Mon, Fri-Sun 10.30 pm.

ARROS QD W1 £100 232

64 EASTCASTLE STREET 020 3883 3525 3–1D

No-one, it seems, told star Spanish chef Quique Dacosta (whose Alicante restaurants hold three Michelin stars) that you don't launch an ambitious foodie venue just off the shopping hell of Oxford Street. This impressive-looking four-year-old – complete with a large open kitchen – offers high quality grills, with the speciality being a selection of paella dishes. Feedback remains quite limited (not helped by its location) – neither huge criticism, nor huge praise is present. / W1W 8NQ; www.arrosqd.com; arrosqd; Mon-Sat 11 pm, Sun 3 pm.

L'ARTISTA NW11 £52 233

917 FINCHLEY RD 020 8731 7501 1–1B

Celebrating its 40th anniversary next year, this "big, bustling old favourite in the heart of Golders Green" (occupying a railway arch by the tube) has itself hosted more than its fair share of birthdays over the years thanks to a crowd-pleasing combination of "generous portions of pasta and pizza" at "very reasonable prices". / NW11 7PE; www.lartistapizzeria.com; lartistalondon; Mon-Sun midnight.

ARTSPACE CAFÉ, CLARIDGE'S W1

BROOK'S MEWS 020 7409 6424 3–2B

Jet-set living for the price of a (admittedly relatively expensive) croissant and a coffee? That's the promise of this new café within Claridge's, serving up toasties, crepes and cakes in a new space with a small art gallery attached designed by John Pawson. / W1K 4HR; www.claridges.co.uk; claridgeshotel; Mon-Fri 6 pm, Sat & Sun 4 pm.

ARTUSI SE15 £61 332

161 BELLENDEN RD 020 3302 8200 1–4D

As it celebrates its tenth anniversary, this small Peckham Italian – named after Pellegrino Artusi, author of nineteenth-century classic 'La Scienza in Cucina' – is "still a destination" for its dedicated southeast London fans. / SE15 4DH; www.artusi.co.uk; artusipeckham; Tue-Thu 9.30 pm, Fri & Sat 10 pm, Sun 4 pm.

ASSAGGI W2 £90 453

39 CHEPSTOW PL 020 7792 5501 7–1B

"A classic that's every bit as good as when it first started", claim fans of Nino Sassu's quirky Italian, which has occupied this room above a Bayswater pub for over 25 years. Compared to its glory days – when it was the talk of the town – feedback is nowadays very limited. But its diehard fan club are unanimous regarding this "perennial favourite" and its "incredible, genuine dishes": "it feels very special to take the family there and everyone is always greeted with such warmth". / W2 4TS; www.assaggi.co.uk; assagginottinghill; Tue-Sat 10 pm.

L'ATELIER ROBUCHON W1 £140

6 CLARGES STREET 020 8076 0570 3–4C

As Le Comptoir Robuchon (RIP), this Mayfair outpost of the famous French chef's global empire (which opened after his death) has never been a huge talking point for the fooderati. This was despite it providing a "top gastronomic experience" combining a very elegant interior with traditional Gallic fare that's "worth the price". Now, from September 2023, it's being re-jigged to sit under the group's international, flagship 'Atelier' brand – so creating a successor to the erstwhile Covent Garden site of that name that closed in 2018. Chef Andrea Cofini will be at the stoves, and doubtless aiming to put it on a par with its siblings in Hong Kong, Miami, Taipei, Vegas and Geneva, each of which holds at least one Michelin star (and most two or three). / W1J 8AE; www.robuchonlondon.co.uk; lecomptoirrobuchon; Mon-Sat 11 pm.

THE ATLAS SW6 £54 344

16 SEAGRAVE RD 020 7385 9129 6–3A

This "traditional backstreet pub – wood-panelled and with a walled garden" – is a good find in the thin area surrounding West Brompton tube and makes a cosy winter destination or – in summer – "the terrace is a great sun trap in the afternoon". Its Med-inspired cuisine is a cut-above typical gastropub standards. / SW6 1RX; www.theatlaspub.co.uk; theatlaspub; Mon-Sat 9.30 pm, Sun 8.30 pm.

ATTICA EC1 £58 233

56-60 ROSEBERY AVE 020 7837 8367 10–1A

Like Jay Rayner of The Observer, reporters in our annual diners' poll remember this Clerkenwell site from its days as The Kolossi Grill (RIP), which for decades provided a good, post-work piss-up, but which has faded from view in recent years. In early 2023 it was relaunched (first under the old Kolossi flag, then changing its name to Attica). But our diners disagreed with Jay's upbeat April 2023 assessment. He found Greek cuisine that's "so much better than [revelatory]… the essentials done with due care and attention" making it "a venerable restaurant that has found a way to avoid decline and start afresh". Our early reporters feel that "despite glowing press reviews we found the food between average to disappointing"… "a shadow of the former taverna experience"… "nice people, but not a great meal". / EC1R 4RR; Tue-Sat 9.15 pm.

THE AUDLEY W1 £57 324

43 MOUNT STREET 020 3840 9862 3–3A

"Fantastic looking, cleaned up and with an amazing ceiling by the late Phyllida Barlow" (who completed the work shortly before she died in March 2023) – ArtFarm's newly relaunched "posh boozer" in Mayfair has five storeys (with the Mount Street Restaurant on the first – see also – and with the upper floors dedicated to art events supporting Hauser & Wirth's roster of artists). Aside from "loads of interesting art and a good backstory", the traditional British grub (pint of prawns, oysters, shepherd's pie, fish finger sarnie, Chelsea bun…) is pricey but "decent". / W1K 3AH; theaudleypublichouse.com; audleypublichouse; Mon-Fri 11.30 pm, Sat midnight, Sun 10.30 pm.

AUDREY GREEN, NATIONAL PORTRAIT GALLERY WC2

ST MARTIN'S PLACE 020 3822 0246 2–2C

After being closed for several years for a major refurbishment, the NPG re-opened in June 2023 (too late for our survey), with a new all-day café on the ground floor and in the intriguing vaulted basement. The latter was always a surprisingly attractive, but completely undiscovered feature of the West End – now it's to be better publicised as 'Larry's Bar', with a late-night bar and small-plates menu. / WC2H 0HE; www.npg.org.uk; Mon & Tue, Sun 5.30 pm, Wed-Sat 10.30 pm.

AUGUSTINE KITCHEN SW11 £68 3 2 3

63 BATTERSEA BRIDGE RD
020 7978 7085 6–*4C*

"Just the job for a simple, casual supper" – this bistro in an "unlikely spot" just south of Battersea Bridge is inspired by the cuisine of Evian in the French Alps, hometown of patron Franck Raymond, who is "completely invested in making sure you have a great experience". / SW11 3AU; www.augustine-kitchen.co.uk; augustinesw11; Tue-Sat 9 pm.

AULIS LONDON W1 £236 5 4 3

16A ST ANNE'S COURT
020 3948 9665 4–*1D*

"If you can't make it to Cartmel to visit L'Enclume, enjoy Simon Rogan's innovative cuisine here in London in a strange combination of chef's table and culinary laboratory: a unique gastronomic and social experience in all respects!". From May 2023, the star chef's Soho outpost grew (a little) in size to seat 12 guests (up from the original 8) together with a complete refurb. But fans say "they didn't need to bother with the decor when the food (from executive head chef Oli Marlow and head chef Charlie Tayler) is this spectacular"; and they hail it as "the top spot in the capital for those who want to focus on what's on the plate" (for which the ingredients are primarily sourced from 'Our Farm' – Simon's Lake District property). Compared with the culinary pyrotechnics and inventiveness, the "wine list is quite simple by comparison". / W1F 0BF; aulis.london; aulissimonrogan; Tue-Sat 11.30 pm.

AUTHENTIQUE EPICERIE & BAR NW5 £54 3 3 3

114-116 FORTESS ROAD
020 3609 6602 9–*2C*

800+ wines by the bottle and a selection of 75 craft beers are the USP of this intriguing Tufnell Park showcase for regional French drinks and produce. The menu changes every six weeks with a different region moving into focus – it's short and in a supporting role to all the delicious grog, but good value. / NW5 5HL; authentique-epicerie.com; authentiquelondon; Tue-Sat 11 pm, Sun 8 pm.

AVANTI W4 £53 2 2 3

SOUTH PARADE 020 8994 9444 8–*1A*

"The mixture of tapas and pizzas works well for a family meal" at this handy local on the edge of Bedford Park in Chiswick, where "the ambience is nice, particularly out on the terrace on a warm evening". If there's a complaint, it's that standards can be "a bit hit 'n' miss". / W4 1LD; avantichiswick.com; avantichiswick; Mon-Sun 10 pm.

AVE MARIO WC2 £67 3 3 4

15 HENRIETTA STREET NO TEL 5–*3C*

"We all loved it – especially the kids", is the most popular view of this vast and OTT mock-Italian operation in Covent Garden from French group Big Mamma, whose "funky interior, fun staff and really positive vibe" create a jolly backdrop to some "surprisingly good and cheaply priced food" – mainly pizza and pasta. Moaning "shame about the Instagramming teenagers" rather misses the point of the whole enterprise, although the odd 'off' report suggests that the joke can fall flat on a bad day – "indifferent service, a quiet atmosphere and disappointing grub: what went wrong? They had something but blew it!". / WC2E 8QG; www.bigmammagroup.com; bigmamma.uk; Sun-Wed 10.30 pm, Thu-Sat 10.45 pm.

L'AVENTURE NW8 £80 4 5 4

3 BLENHEIM TERRACE
020 7624 6232 9–*3A*

This "consistently fabulous restaurant" in St John's Wood has a "special and romantic atmosphere" thanks to its "charming" French owner Catherine Parisot, who has run it for 42 years and ensures the "service is so good and personal" that "you can't fail to feel boosted by a visit". The classic 'cuisine bourgeoise' hits the spot every time, too. / NW8 0EH; www.laventure.co.uk; Mon-Sat 11 pm.

AWESOME THAI SW13 £39 3 3 2

68 CHURCH RD 020 8563 7027 11–*1A*

With its "above-average food and friendly staff" this "fine, family-run Thai" is a "popular Barnes local that also delivers" – and that takes full advantage of its prime position directly opposite the Olympic Studios indie cinema. ("The menu has remained the same for a long while – some new dishes wouldn't harm!") / SW13 0DQ; www.awesomethai.co.uk; Mon-Sat 10.45 pm, Sun 10 pm.

LE BAB £61 4 3 2

TOP FLOOR, KINGLY COURT, W1
020 7439 9222 4–*2B*
4 MERCER WALK, WC2
020 7240 9781 5–*2C*
CIRCUS WEST VILLAGE, BATTERSEA POWER STATION, SW11
020 7864 354 11–*1C*
408 COLDHARBOUR LANE, SW9
020 7864 354 11–*2D*
KINGSLAND LOCKE, 130 KINGSLAND HIGH STREET, E8 020 3877 0865 14–*1A*
231 OLD STREET, EC1
020 3456 7890 13–*1A*

"Tasty kebabs and sides" that "offer a modern twist on traditional Middle Eastern cuisine" make this "brilliant" Carnaby Street outfit "a must-visit", "in the lovely setting of Kingly Court". The Battersea branch is "an absolute gem", and there are now half a dozen outlets around town, including at the Market Halls in Oxford Street and Canary Wharf. See also Kebab Queen. / www.eatlebab.com; eatlebab.

BABUR SE23 £58 4 4 3

119 BROCKLEY RISE 020 8291 2400 1–*4D*

To its many fans, this "small place" off the gastronomic track in Honor Oak Park "remains the best Indian in South London", and its "engaging staff" delivering "very different food with panache and skill", "after almost 40 years". "Unless you're local, it's not entirely easy to get to, but it's well worthy of a journey." / SE23 1JP; www.babur.info; baburrestaurant; Mon-Sat 11 pm, Sun 10.30 pm.

BACCHANALIA W1 £189 2 2 4

1 MOUNT STREET 020 3161 9720 3–*3B*

"A complete circus!" – Richard Caring jovially sticks two fingers up to good taste at his willfully opulent and theatrical riff on Mayfair-meets-Roman-orgy, where staff are clad in togas, and winged statues and nymphs flying around in the ceiling murals look down on you as you eat. Compared to the "OTT" riot of the decor, it's easy to overlook the luxurious menu, which is Italian- and Greek-accented, with a bit of caviar thrown in for good measure. There's the odd report of "appalling service" ("trying to hurry us to meet their deadline") or dishes that misfire badly, but savage put-downs are absent from reports; even while acknowledging that it is "crazily expensive" and "full of selfie takers" (obvs!). / W1K 3NA; bacchanalia.co.uk; bacchanalialdn; Mon-Sat 12.30 am, Sun midnight.

BACCO TW9 £74 3 3 2

39-41 KEW RD 020 8332 0348 1–*4A*

"An excellent venue for a meal before a performance at Richmond Theatre" – this "good value" Italian restaurant near the station has long been a mainstay of the area. Top Tips – set menus are a feature for lunch and pre-theatre, and the wine list is extensive. / TW9 2NQ; www.bacco-restaurant.co.uk; Mon-Sat 9.30 pm.

BAGERIET WC2 £21 4 2 2

24 ROSE ST 020 7240 0000 5–*3C*

"Cakes to die for!" say fans of this tiny Scandi café in a cute Covent Garden cut-through, with a handful of seats outside in summer. Top Menu Tip – Prinsesstårta (a Swedish cake, layering sponge, cream and marzipan). / WC2E 9EA; www.bageriet.co.uk; bageriet_london; Mon-Fri 6.30 pm, Sat 6 pm.

BALA BAYA SE1 £74 4 3 3

ARCH 25, OLD UNION YARD ARCHES, 229 UNION STREET 020 8001 7015 10–*4B*

Former Ottolenghi chef Eran Tibi showcases his accomplished take on modern Israeli cuisine at this fun Tel Aviv-style venue in a Southwark railway arch, on which all reports were upbeat this year. / SE1 0LR; balabaya.co.uk; bala_baya; Mon-Sat 11 pm, Sun 10 pm.

BALHAM SOCIAL SW12 £38 342

2 STATION PARADE ROAD, BALHAM HIGH ROAD 020 4529 8222 11–*2C*

The latest opening from the team behind Putney's popular Chook Chook 'Indian Railway Kitchen' is a flamboyant Balham hangout in the former premises of long-serving Lamberts (RIP). A café by day, it switches in the evening to 'high-end' modern cuisine with an "interesting South Indian influence", under head chef Imran Mansuri, whose Mayfair-heavy CV takes in Jamavar, Tamarind and Annabel's. / SW12 9AZ; balhamsocial.com; balham.social; Mon-Sun 10.30 pm.

BALTHAZAR WC2 £85 123

4-6 RUSSELL STREET 020 3301 1155 5–*3D*

"Like being in an old fashioned Parisian brasserie", this big venue, "centrally located by Covent Garden Piazza", provides a "hectic but impressive" backdrop to a meal. Many reporters feel "it has a whole lot going for it", but even they often acknowledge either "seriously poor" cooking, or the trade-offs that a visit entails: "Yes it's on the pricey side and the food is average really, but it's still a tradition that we enjoy." / WC2B 5HZ; www.balthazarlondon.com; balthazarldn; Mon-Sat 10.45 pm, Sun 9.45 pm.

BALUCHI, LALIT HOTEL LONDON SE1 £79 334

181 TOOLEY ST 020 3765 0000 10–*4D*

"Hints of the Raj" at the Lalit Hotel Group's flagship property in the UK (the group has sites across India), occupying "the old hall of a former grammar school" near City Hall (a big property, designed by the architect of the Old Bailey). Reports are not huge in number, but cite "attentive service" and "refined dishes from across the subcontinent". / SE1 2JR; www.thelalit.com; thelalitlondon; Mon-Sun 10 pm.

BANCONE £59 233

10 LOWER JAMES STREET, W1 020 3034 0820 4–*3C*
39 WILLIAM IV STREET, WC2 020 7240 8786 5–*4C*
BOROUGH YARDS, STONEY STREET, SE1 NO TEL 10–*4C*

"Elevating accessible pasta to another level" and "at fair prices" has won a huge fan club for these pasta pit-stops, which – in July 2023 – added a Borough Yards location to their outlets in Soho and off Trafalgar Square. It's the "narrow" WC2 branch that's best known, and, despite the weight of custom, "helpful staff do their best" and it delivers "lots of atmosphere". The food rating dipped this year, though, due to a few refuseniks who say "it used to be good, but is becoming a victim of its own success". / www.bancone.co.uk; bancone.pasta.

BANG BANG ORIENTAL NW9 £44 322

399 EDGWARE ROAD NO TEL 1–*1A*

"The Oriental food hall of your dreams" – this gastro-warehouse in Colindale offers a vast choice. "The quality ranges extremely widely between the various stalls", but choose carefully and you'll be well fed. / NW9 0AS; www.bangbangoriental.com; bangbangoriental; Sun-Thu 9.30 pm, Fri & Sat 10 pm.

BAO £40 344

53 LEXINGTON ST, W1 07769 627811 4–*2C*
56 JAMES ST, W1 NO TEL 3–*1A*
4 PANCRAS SQUARE, N1 NO TEL 9–*3C*
13 STONEY STREET, SE1 020 3967 5407 10–*4C*
BATTERSEA POWER STATION, SW11 NO TEL 11–*1C*
1 REDCHURCH STREET, E2 NO TEL 13–*1B*

"A first-choice Asian restaurant" – say fans of this "friendly, buzzy" chain serving "delicious" Taiwanese filled buns that can constitute "a quick bite for lunch, or a longer meal with friends". Launched as a street-food stand in 2012 by Erchen Chang, her husband Shing Tat and his sister Wai Ting Chung, the group is now backed by the all-conquering JKS Restaurants and opened its sixth venue in Battersea Power Station in 2023. Top Tip – "beef with black pepper sauce and rice is a must-order at King's Cross". / baolondon.com; bao_london.

BAOZI INN £37 322

24 ROMILLY STREET, W1 020 7287 3266 5–*3A*
34-36 SOUTHWARK STREET, SE1 020 8037 5875 10–*4C*

Northern Chinese fare including "authentic and tasty dumplings and noodles" make either of Wei Shao's duo (Borough Market and Soho) "a great standby for a quick and fun meal". "A Chinese that's worth a visit for an evening bite and not just for dim sum – and which doesn't break the bank – is a rare find in London." / baoziinn.com.

BAR DES PRÉS W1 £129 243

16 ALBEMARLE STREET 020 3908 2000 3–*3C*

This 'Franco-Japanese fusion' – a two-year-old Mayfair spin-off from TV chef Cyril Lignac's Paris restaurant St Germain des Prés – excites contradictory responses (and relatively little feedback overall). For fans, "the fusion of Japanese food with French expertise has resulted in an excellent dining experience". For the odd critic, though, it's nothing more than a "flash, cramped and noisy Euro place with prices that reflect the name of the celebrity French chef and the fancy crowd". / W1S 4HW; bardespres.com; bardespres; Mon-Sat 11 pm, Sun 10 pm.

BAR DOURO SE1 £55 334

ARCH 35B, 85B SOUTHWARK BRIDGE RD 020 7378 0524 10–*4B*

"Fresh, pungent sharing plates", "cooked in front of you", backed up by "good wine options" – win praise for this tiled bar in a railway arch near Borough Market (founded by Max Graham, from the Churchill's port family), which does "just what Portuguese tapas should do". "Characterful service" contributes to a "wonderfully relaxed" atmosphere. / SE1 0NQ; www.bardouro.co.uk; bardouro; Tue-Sat 10 pm, Sun 9 pm.

BAR ESTEBAN N8 £61 344

29 PARK RD 020 8340 3090 1–*1C*

This Crouch End spot has built a strong local name over more than a decade, and is known for its superior tapas and a "really good selection of Spanish wine, by the glass or bottle". Founder Stephen ('Esteban') Lironi is a Glasgow-born music producer and sherry aficionado, while Barcelona-born chef Pablo Rodriguez arrived via Barrafina. / N8 8TE; www.baresteban.com; bar__esteban; Fri & Sat 11 pm, Tue-Thu 10 pm.

BAR ITALIA W1 £42 245

22 FRITH ST 020 7437 4520 5–*2A*

This "Soho institution" stands for "tradition and location", offering "the best coffee 24/7" along with "the most atmospheric counter seating in London". Founded in 1949 by the Polledri family, who still own it, it is a rare survivor of Soho's once-thriving Italian community. / W1D 4RF; www.baritaliasoho.co.uk; Mon-Sun 5 am.

BAR KROKETA W1

21 BEAK STREET 0203 954 8888 4–*2B*

With 'croquetas at its core', this small, December 2022 newcomer, south of Carnaby Street, promises to bring 'Spanish bar culture with regional sensibilities to Soho'. Run by Brindisa, it's a non-branded attempt at a funkier outlet for their Hispanic produce and wines. No survey feedback as yet, but in a March 2023 review, The Independent's Lucy Thackray hailed a "cosy, convivial Spanish hangout" that's "a potentially chemistry-crackling date place" – "the spelling may be gimmicky but the food is not". / W1F 9RR; www.kroketa.co.uk; bar.kroketa; Mon-Sun 11 pm.

THE BARBARY WC2 £83 544

16 NEAL'S YARD NO TEL 5–*2C*

"Stunning in every respect" – this "tiny, dark, smoky, and cool" North African-inspired venue in Neal's Yard is "a superb place where they really make use of the counter service to engage you in the cooking". "No matter how many times I go I always need the menu explained" – "beautifully spiced" small plates ("a bit salty at times") plus "great, unusual wines" all

Archway SW8

served by "enthusiastic staff". / WC2H 9DP; www.thebarbary.co.uk; the barbary; Mon-Sat 10 pm, Sun 9 pm.

THE BARBARY NEXT DOOR WC2 £49 432

16A NEAL'S YARD NO TEL 5–*2C*

This "fab, tiny little counter bar" next door to its grown-up sibling in Neal's Yard, Covent Garden, offers "superb" Middle Eastern/ Moroccan food accompanied by biodynamic wines. "Sooo sad they stopped doing breakfast!". The site's previous occupant was the much-loved Jacob the Angel (RIP). / WC2H 9DP; thebarbarynextdoor.co.uk; thebarbarynextdoor; Mon-Sat 11 pm.

BARBICAN BRASSERIE, BARBICAN CENTRE (FKA OSTERIA) EC2 £53 333

LEVEL 2 SILK STREET
020 7588 3008 10–*1B*

"The restaurant formerly known as Osteria has recently re-emerged from a makeover as the Barbican Brasserie, but still operated by catering company Searcy's"; and still with a vaguely Italian spin on its selection of modern European dishes. It's "a smart venue overlooking the lake", which this year was more often "recommended for reasonably priced dinner" – especially prior to a show within the centre. / EC2Y 8DS; osterialondon.co.uk; searcyslondon; Mon-Wed, Sat 7 pm, Thu & Fri 9 pm.

LA BARCA SE1 £90 333

80-81 LOWER MARSH
020 7928 2226 10–*4A*

"From a bygone era, and all the better for it!" – this family-run Italian restaurant behind Waterloo station set sail almost 50 years ago, offering "a combination of excellent traditional dishes, lively atmosphere and attentive service from staff, many of whom have worked there for years". / SE1 7AB; www.labarca-ristorante.com; labarca1976; Mon-Sat 10.30 pm.

BARGE EAST E9 £68 435

RIVER LEE, SWEETWATER MOORING, WHITE POST LANE 020 3026 2807 14–*2C*

"It's so fun being on board a boat!" – this 120-year-old barge is moored in Hackney Wick, near the Olympic stadium, and is also surrounded by gardens providing an alternative backdrop to a meal. All reports agree on its "fantastic food and atmosphere": there are a variety of menus, including tasting and group options, all featuring imaginative modern British dishes. / E9 5EN; www.bargeeast.com; bargeeast; Wed-Sun midnight.

THE BARING N1 £85 433

55 BARING STREET 020 7359 5785 14–*2A*

"It's probably unfair to call it pub food though it is food in a pub!" – Re-opened in 2022, this revamped Islington boozer has built a major following thanks to offering "an all-round five-star experience" that's very superior for the gastropub genre. Staff who are "charming, friendly and fast" provide "simple"-sounding yet "fabulous" and "sustainably sourced" dishes ("the almond financier made me smile so much the chef came over to see what was entertaining me"). "The only downside is the slightly out-of-the-way location" that's "hard to get to on public transport". / N1 3DS; www.thebaring.co.uk; thebaring; Tue-Sat 9.30 pm, Sun 4 pm.

THE BARLEY MOW W1 £98 333

82 DUKE STREET 020 7730 0070 3–*2A*

"All of the Cubitt's pubs are class acts", and this recent (2022) addition to their glossy tribe is a gentrified Mayfair boozer with fine period features. In culinary terms, it fits the "pricey but good quality" DNA of the group – in fact, it's at the upper level of achievement in that respect. There's a bar downstairs and a more formal restaurant on the first floor. / W1K 6JG; www.cubitthouse.co.uk; cubitthouse; Mon-Sat 10 pm, Sun 5 pm.

BARRAFINA £70 544

26-27 DEAN STREET, W1
020 7813 8016 4–*1D*
10 ADELAIDE ST, WC2
020 7440 1456 5–*4C*
43 DRURY LANE, WC2
020 7440 1456 5–*2D*
COAL DROPS YARD, N1
0207 440 1486 9–*3C*
2 DIRTY LANE, SE1 0207 440 1486 10–*4C*

"It's a great show to watch the chefs at work", perched on a stool at the counter of the Hart Bros' "incredibly busy and buzzy" bars – their hyper-successful homage to Barcelona's Cal Pep. "The tapas is always first rate" with "succulent grilled seafood all prepared in front of your very eyes" a highlight. "Staff are friendly and efficient and take such pride in the dishes and their presentation". (In April 2023, executive chef Angel Zapata Martin left the group after six years, leaving Antonio Gonzales Milla minding the central Barrafina locations, and Francisco Jose Torrico in charge of Coal Drops Yard and Borough). / www.barrafina.co.uk.

BARSHU W1 £71 532

28 FRITH ST 020 7287 6688 5–*3A*

"Spicy, authentic Sichuan cuisine" makes this Chinatown destination "worth hunting out" – it's "way above the bog-standard fare nearby", with "amazing taste sensations including a lot more besides the fragrant heat of the eponymous Sichuan pepper". And "friendly staff made choosing from the huge menu easier". Top Tip – find a table downstairs if you can, to avoid the "weak ambience on the first floor". / W1D 5LF; www.barshurestaurant.co.uk; barshurestaurant; Sun-Thu 10 pm, Fri & Sat 10.30 pm.

BASE FACE PIZZA W6 £38 443

300 KING STREET 020 8617 1092 8–*2B*

"A true find" – jazz bassist Tim Thornton's lockdown pizza project-gone-permanent goes from strength to strength, serving "top sourdough pizzas" at his original pizzeria on King Street in Hammersmith and a more recent addition across the river in Barnes. "Lovely staff and a great atmosphere" add to the package. / W6 0RR; www.basefacepizza.com; base.face.pizza; Tue-Sat 10 pm, Sun 9 pm.

BAYLEAF N20 £25 433

1282 HIGH ROAD 020 8446 8671 1–*1B*

Established on the foundation of a long-running takeaway business, this highly rated Whetstone curry house serves "high-quality" food with a focus on "super-dramatic presentation" of dishes, with "steam rising from the table". / N20 9HH; www.bayleaf.co.uk; bayleafofficial; Mon-Sun 10 pm.

THE BEEFSTEAKS @ M. MANZE N1

74 CHAPEL MARKET NO TEL 9–*3D*

Due to open in the second half of 2023 – this historic Islington pie 'n' mash shop in Chapel Market closed in 2018 but has been rescued by Alex Pashby of street-food trader The Beefsteaks ('An exclusive 18th Century London steak club reimagined as inclusive 21st Century street food'). At first it will operate as a low-intervention wine bar serving British small plates – as it takes off, the hope is for the food offering to expand. / N1 9ER; thebeefsteaks.

BEHIND E8 £140 543

20 SIDWORTH STREET NO TEL 14–*2B*

"Wow!" "Andy Beynon continues to produce superb, good-value cuisine in a relaxed and intimate setting" at his small venue, near London Fields: "an immersive experience, where the chefs prepare the food around you as you sit at the bar". "There are no waiters: the chefs cover service, chat about the food and ferry each new course from the nearby open preparation areas"; and the team gives the impression of being "super keen and far from weary, jaded or sitting on their laurels". "Sustainable fish is the clear focus here, and everything is on point in each exceptional dish". / E8 3SD; www.behindrestaurant.co.uk; behindrestaurant; Wed-Sat 11 pm.

BELLAMY'S W1 £80 344

18-18A BRUTON PLACE
020 7491 2727 3–*2B*

"A haven of calm in an ever-changing world": "they cater for the most conservative of palates (and the deepest pockets)" at Gavin Rankin's "old-school, brasserie-style restaurant in Mayfair" (which had the rare privilege of hosting the late Queen Elizabeth on a couple of occasions). Its Anglo-French fare is "super reliable, if not exciting" and service "immaculate". "If you like the kind of place where you still need to dress up a bit, this is it", but "the ambience is set by its older, quietly-spoken crowd: don't visit if you are planning a loud-laughing night!". Top Menu Tip – "good value lunch menu; and staples such as iced lobster soufflé, smoked eel mousse and steak tartare". / W1J 6LY; www.bellamysrestaurant.co.uk; bellamysmayfair; Mon-Fri 10.30 pm, Sat.

BELLANGER N1 £58

9 ISLINGTON GREEN 020 7226 2555 9–*3D*

"Evoking a big Parisian brasserie", this Wolseley Group venture on Islington Green has had a chequered history. Opened in 2015, when Corbin & King owned the business, they closed it again in 2019 saying "we just couldn't make it the success we aspired to". But then, in 2020 – having failed to sell the property – they re-opened and had a second run at making a go of it. With Corbin & King then forced to exit the business in 2022, we are now going around again under the new owners. In June 2023, after our survey had completed, the restaurant re-opened yet again after a complete refit of the vast space and a new menu. Though brighter, the decor is still in the traditional brasserie mould. When it comes to food: out go the retro 'tarte flambées' and the chicken schnitzel – in comes the focaccia and – according to the PR – an 'evolving seasonal menu… taking inspiration from the southern Mediterranean coastal regions'. Er, except it also includes very un-Mediterranean dishes like Dressed Dorset Crab, Loch Duart Salmon with jersey royals and a watercress velouté and Flat Iron Steak Frites. The weekend brunch – with its pancakes and Eggs Benedict – also owes little to Spain, Italy and Greece. Other novelties are a new cocktail bar, and a DJ booth (the latter of which really risks 'Dad dancing' for this kind of venue). Our pre-revamp feedback suggested the same rather 'OK but not particularly distinguished' performance of old. But we've left it unrated on the basis of the latest changes, as this sounds like a case of 'outlook negative'. / N1 2XH; www.bellanger.co.uk; bellanger_n1; Mon-Sat 10 pm, Sun 9 pm.

BELVEDERE W8 £72 334

OFF ABBOTSBURY RD IN HOLLAND PARK
020 7602 1238 8–*1D*

Is it London? It doesn't feel like it at this enchanting, 17th-century ballroom adjoining Holland House, and surrounded by the tranquility of Holland Park. As a restaurant, it's had many ups and downs over the years (there's always a temptation here to coast on the location), and its latest incarnation was launched without fanfare in December 2022 by George Bukhov-Weinstein and Ilya Demichev, of Goodman, Burger & Lobster and Wild Tavern. True to the DNA of these other offerings, it's been handsomely revamped and now serves an Italian-influenced menu centred on luxe casual dining – raw seafood, USDA steak, plus fancy pizza and pasta. In a February 2023 review, Giles Coren of The Times decried it as akin to "the second-best Italian restaurant in Dubai" whose unifying principle is "expensive" not Italian. Our initial reports are less sniffy: "an amazing meal with attentive service, and good ambience even if the decor is a bit overdone for my taste and the food is on the pricey side for what it is". / W8 6LU; www.belvedererestaurant.co.uk; belvedere_holland_park; Mon-Sat 10.30 pm, Sun 9.30 pm.

BENARES W1 £94 432

12A BERKELEY SQUARE HOUSE,
020 7629 8886 3–*3B*

"Outstandingly good Indian fine dining, curated by head chef Sameer Taneja, whose forte is a tasting menu with a strong seafood offering" wins strong approval for this "sophisticated" nouvelle Indian, located in a large first-floor space above Berkeley Square, whose "helpful service" offsets the "rather soulless" decor. Top Tip – "their bottomless thali lunchtime meal deal is amazing value for a Michelin-starred restaurant. Not to be missed!!" / W1J 6BS; www.benaresrestaurant.co.uk; benaresofficial; Mon-Sat 10.30 pm, Sun 9.30 pm.

BENTLEY'S W1 £106 344

11-15 SWALLOW ST 020 7734 4756 4–*4B*

"Owner Richard Corrigan is often around and the food is always good" at this "iconic" fish and seafood "classic" – 107 years old (est. 1916) – which is to be found in a side street, near Piccadilly Circus. It offers two distinct experiences: "upstairs for very elegant fine dining, or in the bar downstairs for top-notch seafood with less formality – both excellent" (although the latter gets many people's vote, as "there is always a good buzz in the bar area with a few famous faces sometimes"). "Possibly the best oysters in town (and the best shuckers too)" number alongside "top crab" and "the notably good fish pie" as its best menu options, all in a "reassuringly good-but-expensive" mould ("comfort seafood at West End prices"). Service that's "very attentive and kind" from long-serving staff is intrinsic to the performance. / W1B 4DG; www.bentleys.org; bentleysoysterbar; Mon-Sat 9.30 pm, Sun 9 pm.

BERBER & Q £61 543

ARCH 338 ACTON MEWS, E8
020 7923 0829 14–*2A*
EXMOUTH MARKET, EC1
020 7837 1726 10–*1A*

"Never had a bad trip here!" – a common experience at these impressively consistent hipster grills where the "great and tasty mezze and flatbreads" are inspired by North Africa and the eastern Med: "delicious dishes with explosive flavours" that are "well-priced and extremely fresh tasting". They "can get very noisy" ("it was as easy to talk as sitting in a rock concert!") "but an excellent meal is your reward!" / www.berberandq.com; berberandq.

BERBERE PIZZA NW5 £42 433

300 KENTISH TOWN ROAD
020 3417 7130 9–*2C*

"Really good Calabrian pizza made with sourdough" is winning attention for this Kentish Town newcomer, which opened in November 2022, with a mix of standard and unusual toppings, such as 'Orange Crush' (creamed butternut squash, leeks, olives, chilli and peanut butter). It also has an often overlooked Clapham sibling (not listed), that's been open for three years; and is part of a wider genuinely Italian chain with branches in numerous cities, founded in Bologna in 2010. / NW5 2TG; www.berberepizzeria.co.uk; berberepizzeria_ldn; Sun-Thu 10 pm, Fri & Sat 10.30 pm.

BERENJAK £64 544

27 ROMILLY STREET, W1
020 3319 8120 5–*2A*
1 BEDALE STREET, SE1
020 3011 1021 10–*4C*

"Sit at the counter and watch the magic", say fans of Kian Samyani's "rammed-to-the-rafters" charcoal grill in Soho, which aims (with the help of JKS Restaurants) to bring to London the childhood tastes of his Iranian upbringing. The result: "delicious food, super

BAO

friendly front-of-house staff, and a great atmosphere, especially at the counter" (although there is also a more conventional seating area). It now has a similar Borough Market spin-off too, on the two-storey site of the short-lived Flor (RIP), which scores highly, but is slightly less venerated than its more established sibling: "there is no doubting that the food is excellent here too. But the price for a lamb or chicken kebab is more Salt Bae than Efes!" / berenjaklondon.com; berenjaklondon.

THE BERNERS TAVERN W1 £107 345

10 BERNERS STREET
020 7908 7979 3–*1D*

"The impressive room is good as it looks in the photos" and "the bar is one of the most beautiful in central London" at Jason Atherton's sparkling venue: a converted banking hall that's part of a glam (Ian Shrager-designed) hotel, north of Oxford Street. With its "big and well-spaced tables" it's "sure to wow your customers", catch the attention of your date or set the scene for a "lovely special occasion". Historically, other aspects of the performance have played second fiddle to the surroundings here, but this year it won all-round praise for its "excellent" luxury brasserie cuisine and "knowledgeable" service too. / W1T 3NP; www.editionhotels.com; bernerstavern; Mon-Sat 9.45 pm.

BEST MANGAL £52 442

619 FULHAM RD, SW6
020 7610 0009 6–*4A*
104 NORTH END RD, W14
020 7610 1050 8–*2D*

A handy "cheap 'n' cheerful" option – these traditional Turkish venues, near West Kensington tube and on Fulham Broadway are a favourite stop-off for a freshly BBQ'd kebab. (The West Ken branch is not to be confused with 'Best Mangal 1996' – a similar venture at 66 North End Road). / www.bestmangal.com.

BIBENDUM SW3 £225 333

81 FULHAM RD 020 7589 1480 6–*2C*

"The lovely Michelin building is so cool", and its "well-spaced, light and airy dining room" is perhaps the late Sir Terence Conran's most enduring contribution to London's restaurant scene (best visited at lunch, when all the natural daylight makes it serene and "romantic"). Under Claude Bosi, its foodie renown has grown, and fans say he is "still setting the bar for outstanding contemporary French cooking in the capital" (for which he's held two Michelin stars since 2017). Its ratings blipped rather this year, however – as at a number of other top restaurants coping with the cost of living crisis, it can now just seem "too expensive" ("used to be great – recently disappointing"). / SW3 6RD; www.claudebosi.com; claudebosiatbibendum; Tue-Sat 9.30 pm.

BIBENDUM OYSTER BAR SW3 £87 334

MICHELIN HOUSE, 81 FULHAM ROAD
020 7581 5817 6–*2C*

The "plateau de fruits de mer takes some beating" at Claude Bosi's oyster bar, downstairs from his grand – and rather more expensive – flagship restaurant, in the foyer of Chelsea's iconic Michelin building. (Some hot alternatives to the cold luxurious seafood bites were introduced a couple of years ago.) / SW3 6RD; www.claudebosi.com; claudebosiatbibendum; Mon-Sun 9.30 pm.

BIBI W1 £87 554

42 NORTH AUDLEY STREET
020 3780 7310 3–*2A*

"Creative and fascinating riffs on classic Indian cooking" by chef Chet Sharma inspire another year of rapturous reviews ("quite simply the best Indian food I have ever eaten") for this JKS Restaurants property in Mayfair; on the (somewhat "narrow") site that was Truc Vert (RIP). "The friendly, charming team makes the experience a true delight, and there's a cracking playlist as well!" Caveats? "It's another case of a restaurant going set menu only in the evenings", which limits a less expensive à la carte option to lunch. / W1K 6ZR; www.bibirestaurants.com; bibi_ldn; Wed-Sat 9.30 pm.

BIBIDA W8 £45 342

1 HILLGATE STREET 020 7221 0151 7–*2B*

This "great local Korean" close to Notting Hill Gate tube station offers a "good variety of dishes" – including Japanese sushi and "super lunchtime bento boxes". "It can get very busy, so booking is advised". / W8 7SP; www.bibida.co.uk; Mon-Sat 10.30 pm, Sun 10 pm.

BIBO BY DANI GARCÍA, MONDRIAN HOTEL EC2 £86 223

45 CURTAIN ROAD 020 3146 4545 13–*1B*

Star chef Dani Garcia opened his first UK venture in Shoreditch's Mondrian Hotel a couple of years ago, to mixed reviews. This up-and-down sentiment continues in feedback to date – some reporters think the Spanish cuisine – paellas, roast and grilled fish and meat, tapas – is "very good" (but encountered "an empty room on a Sunday lunch"); other well-travelled types thought it "underwhelming compared to the wonders of his native Andalusian restaurants". / EC2A 4PJ; www.sbe.com; bibo_shoreditch; Sun-Wed 9 pm, Thu-Sat 10 pm.

BIG EASY £72 223

12 MAIDEN LN, WC2 020 3728 4888 5–*3D*
332-334 KING'S RD, SW3
020 7352 4071 6–*3C*
CROSSRAIL PL, E14 020 3841 8844 12–*1C*

"BBQ, live music, decent cocktails and craft beer" channel the spirit of the American South at this "buzzy", long-running spot in Chelsea and its more recent spin-offs in Covent Garden and Canary Wharf. The food is "more about quantity than quality", although the "great-value lunch deals" are popular: "£10 meat taster is unbeatable". / www.bigeasy.co.uk; bigeasylondon.

BIG FERNAND SW7 £43 332

39 THURLOE PLACE 020 3031 8330 6–*2C*

"French… and have to admit pretty good" – London's outpost of this Gallic 'Maison du Hamburgé' chain (that's 50-strong over the Channel) is to be found in South Kensington's 'Little France' and gets a consistent thumbs up. The addition of lashings of different French regional cheeses is key to distinguishing its menu options. / SW7 2HP; www.bigfernanduk.com; bigfernand_uk; Mon-Sun 10 pm.

THE BIRD IN HAND W14 £56 333

88 MASBRO ROAD 020 7371 2721 8–*1C*

"Great food and drink, especially pizza" makes it worth remembering this stylish (if sometimes noisy) Olympia pub-conversion, a few minutes' walk from Brook Green (part of the Oak group). / W14 0LR; www.thebirdinhandlondon.com; thebirdw14; Tue-Fri 11 pm, Sat & Sun 10 pm.

BISTRO UNION SW4 £64 332

40 ABBEVILLE RD 020 7042 6400 11–*2D*

"Good food, leaning towards the hearty end of the spectrum rather than the refined", is enjoyed by most reporters at this 'Abbeville village' bistro from star Clapham chef Adam Byatt. If there's a grumble, it is that it can seem "disappointing given its link to Trinity", his flagship across the Common. / SW4 9NG; www.bistrounion.co.uk; bistrounionclapham.

BLACK BEAR BURGER £48 432

11-13 MARKET ROW, SW9
020 7737 3444 11–*2D*
CANADA SQUARE, E14
020 7737 3444 12–*1C*
2-10 BETHNAL GREEN ROAD, E1 NO TEL 13–*2B*
17 EXMOUTH MARKET, EC1
020 7837 1039 10–*1A*

"Smoky, flavourful, moist, DEELICIOUS – the burger is so well done, I go back again and again", chorus fans of this five-year-old independent with five outlets around London. Some hail the burgers – made from high-welfare native breed grass-fed West Country beef, dry-aged on the bone – as "the best in town". Founders Liz & Stew dreamt up the project while working ski seasons in Canada – hence the name. / blackbearburger.com; black_bear_burger.

THE BLACK BOOK W1 £54 344

23 FRITH STREET 020 7434 1724 5–*2A*

Snug Soho bar, whose superior wine list belies its founding by two Master Sommeliers: Gearoid Devaney and Xavier Rousset. To help soak up the vino: well-rated small plates, cheese and charcuterie. Top Tip – head here in the wee hours: it's open till 3am later in the week. / W1D 4RR; blackbooksoho.co.uk; theblackbooksoho; Tue, Wed 1 am, Thu-Sat 3 am.

BLACK DOG BEER HOUSE TW8 £57 333

17 ALBANY ROAD 020 8568 5688 1–*3A*

"Great, hearty gastro-food" with "no pretensions" along with an "excellent array of beers" (14 from the keg, five real ales, 50 bottled or canned) leave guests spoilt for choice at this "very welcoming" backstreet free house in Brentford. Landlord Pete Brew (sic) even has his own in-house nano-brewery, Fearless Nomad. Top Menu Tip – "the fantastic salt-beef sandwich". / TW8 0NF; www.blackdogbeerhouse.co.uk; blackdogbeerhouse; Mon, Wed-Sat 11 pm, Sun 10.30 pm.

THE BLACK LAMB SW19 £60 322

67 HIGH STREET 020 8947 8278 11–*2B*

"The cooking is interesting, vegetable heavy, but accessible to all", say fans of the Gladwin family's field-to-fork yearling (supplied by their Sussex farm), which has proved to be one of their more commented-on recent openings. But even those who feel it's "a great addition to the dining choices in Wimbledon Village" say "the food is perhaps not always as good as they think it is (some portions are tiny)". And it does also attract one or two really harsh critiques: "as a replacement for The White Onion (RIP) – an outstanding local – The Black Lamb is a disappointment and can be totally lacking in atmosphere". / SW19 5EE; www.theblacksheep-restaurant.com; theblacklamb_resto; Wed-Fri 10.30 pm, Tue 10 pm, Sat 11.30 pm, Sun 8.30 pm.

BLACK SALT SW14 £49 443

505-507 UPPER RICHMOND ROAD WEST
020 4548 3327 11–*2A*

"Oh, you lucky punters of East Sheen… rejoice!" – this "unexpected" two-year-old is a spin-off from Ewell's legendary Dastaan, and is praised in numerous reports for chef Manish Sharma's "extraordinary Indian cuisine at fair prices": "big, complex punches of flavour but all nicely balanced". On the downside, ratings are capped by the odd reporter who feels it's "OK, but not quite as good as its reviews and reputation would suggest". / SW14 7DE; blacksaltsheen.com; blacksaltsheen; Tue-Thu 10 pm, Fri & Sat 10.30 pm, Sun 9 pm.

BLACKLOCK £54 344

24 GREAT WINDMILL ST, W1
020 3441 6996 4–*3D*
16A BEDFORD STREET, WC2
020 303 4139 5–*3C*
5 FROBISHER PASSAGE, E14
020 3034 0230 12–*1C*
28 RIVINGTON STREET, EC2
AWAITING TEL 13–*1B*
13 PHILPOT LANE, EC3
020 7998 7676 10–*3D*

"Absolutely delicious grilled meats with equally tasty accompaniments, all in a buzzy and fun setting" inspire many loyalists for Gordon Ker's "go-to" chain, which in May 2023 added a fifth branch in Canary Wharf's North Dock. "Hawksmoor every week could be financially ruinous, but this never disappoints, be it lunch or dinner, for half the money". Top Tips – "Butchers Block Monday prices, and regular £10 corkage. Get in!" Also the "all-in" meat-fest of lamb and pork chops, steak and bacon: "it uses cheaper cuts and preparation is basic, but juices drip over the plate, and the peppercorn sauce is delicious!" / theblacklock.com; blacklockchops.

BLANCHETTE W1 £82 332

9 D'ARBLAY ST 020 7439 8100 4–*1C*

"Excellent, stylish Gallic fare" sets the tone at this "friendly" bistro, run by a trio of French brothers who named it after their mother, that has notched up a decade in Soho. "I'm already planning my next visit!". The only real complaint is that "in true Gallic style, the settings can be a bit cramped". / W1F 8DS; www.blanchettesoho.co.uk; blanchettelondon; Mon-Sat 11 pm.

BLANDFORD COMPTOIR W1 £75 343

1 BLANDFORD STREET
020 7935 4626 2–*1A*

Sommelier Xavier Rousset is behind this "wonderful and quiet little restaurant" and wine bar in Marylebone, "serving delicious, serious food" – mostly inspired by Italy – and "an outstanding Rhône-specialist wine list". Service is notably "friendly, with a relaxed vibe". / W1U 3DA; blandford-comptoir.co.uk; blandfordcomptoir; Tue-Sat 11 pm.

BLEECKER BURGER £29 422

205 VICTORIA ST, SW1 NO TEL 2–*4B*
THE BALCONY, WESTFIELD WHITE CITY, W12 020 3582 2930 1–*3B*
UNIT B PAVILION BUILDING, SPITALFIELDS MKT, E1 07712 540501 13–*2B*
QUEEN VICTORIA STREET, EC4
AWAITING TEL 10–*3C*

"Still the best burger in town in my opinion" is a widely shared view of this independent chain with four sit-down and three delivery-only kitchens. "No matter how many burgers I try in London, I can't beat Bleecker" – "they get the simple stuff right: quality of meat, how the patty is made, doneness, ratio of meat to bread, and it adds up to a serious burger". Zan Kaufman, a former New York corporate lawyer, launched her brand from the back of a truck 12 years ago, naming it after a Greenwich Village street. / www.bleecker.co.uk; bleeckerburger.

BLEEDING HEART BISTRO EC1 £64 334

BLEEDING HEART YARD
0207 2428238 10–*2A*

This "impressive French-inspired bistro" is cutely tucked away in a historic yard on the fringe of the City, and thrives on its "simple typically Gallic cooking with good ingredients", its high-quality wine list, and its "attentive and friendly service". "It's not quite what it was" when the adjoining buildings held a posher sister restaurant, but "a reliable mainstay that's still well worth a visit", and which is still a go-to business entertaining venue. Top Tip – large and very attractive terrace for the summer months; and "the set menu isn't bad value either". / EC1N 8SJ; www.bleedingheart.co.uk; bleeding_heart_restaurants; Mon-Sat 9 pm.

BLOCK SOHO W1 £53 222

CLARION HOUSE, 2 SAINT ANNE'S COURT
020 3376 9999 4–*1D*

On a cute, pedestrianised Soho cut-through, this year-old chop-house has seen lots of restaurants come and go over the years (most recently, Zelman Meats, RIP). Many reporters went in days of the 50%-off soft launch offer, and said they "would not pay the full price" due to inept service and either "too much char, char, char" or – conversely – "a lack of the flavour you'd expect from somewhere promoting itself by reference to its flame-grilled dishes". Post-launch comments veer in the other direction: "excellent meat… but wow the prices!" / W1F 0AZ; www.blocksoho.com; blocksoho; Sun-Thu midnight, Fri & Sat 12.30 am.

BLUE BOAR PUB, CONRAN LONDON ST JAMES SW1 £80 222

22-28 BROADWAY 020 3301 1400 2–*3C*

This stab at a 'modern British pub' from a posh Westminster hotel has not really convinced reporters, despite the appointment of high-profile chef, Sally Abé, from Fulham's brilliant Harwood Arms (she also runs the hotel's flagship restaurant, The Pem). "There isn't a lot of choice round this way" but BB is "expensive for what it is and full of a combination of mid-ranking politicians and journalists" – ouch! / SW1H 0BH; blueboarlondon.com; blueboarpub; Mon-Sun 11 pm.

BLUEBIRD SW3 £93 213

350 KING'S ROAD 020 7559 1000 6–*3C*

It has a "very attractive site" – a landmark 1920s car showroom on King's Road Chelsea, with a "trendy vibe" – but is perennially "let down by a tired menu which is not well executed" and mediocre service. Why D&D London have never sorted this place out is a bit of a mystery – it could be so good. / SW3 5UU;

www.bluebird-restaurant.co.uk; bluebirdchelsea; Mon-Wed, Fri, Thu, Sat 10.30 pm, Sun 9.30 pm. SRA – accredited

BOB BOB RICARD £91 244

1 UPPER JAMES STREET, W1
020 3145 1000 4–*2C*
LEVEL 8, 122 LEADENHALL STREET, EC3
020 3145 1000 10–*2D*

The 'Press for Champagne' button has become an Instagram classic – made famous by the original Soho branch of Leonid Shutov's decadent diners, which provide luxurious treats like caviar and beef Wellington all served in a sumptuous environment, whose dark wood and polished surfaces evoke the deco glam of a trip on the Orient Express. "A fun place for a celebration" or romance, they are also notably "overpriced" – a factor harder to overlook in the era of straitened post-Covid expense accounts, when splashy business dining (for which they are a favourite) has been reined in. Perhaps that's why the renamed 'Bob Bob Cité' – a "nightclub-like space" occupying a floor of the City's Cheesegrater – has failed to make waves, and generates very few (albeit positive) reports. In August 2023, the group (celebrating its fifteenth year) started a new, 56-seat spin-off, a few doors down from the original, called 'Bébé Bob': the offering here will shoehorn champagne and caviar into a more dressed-down offering, alongside rotisserie chicken as the main event.

BOCCA DI LUPO W1 £67 443

12 ARCHER ST 020 7734 2223 4–*3D*

"Jacob Kenedy's terrific Italian restaurant in the heart of the West End hasn't lost its edge in 15-plus years" (est. 2008) and is one of the most popular London destinations in our annual diners' poll. It serves "inspired, regional-Italian dishes" – "lots of interesting choices from an original, constantly-changing, seasonal menu" – all at notably "sensible prices". "The sommelier will assist you to navigate a marvellous Italian list and introduce you to some new wines; and service generally is both professional yet very friendly". Many diners "prefer sitting at the counter" watching the chefs to the "more formal" tables at the back, "but you always get a good meal either way". "It is deafeningly loud, but that's the price you pay for such a buzzy atmosphere". Top Tip – "wonderful ice cream shop opposite which they also own". / W1D 7BB; www.boccadilupo.com; bocca_di_lupo; Mon-Sat 11 pm, Sun 9.30 pm.

BOCCONCINO RESTAURANT W1 £116

19 BERKELEY ST 020 7499 4510 3–*3C*

"You can't fail to impress with the food, vibes and service", according to fans of this Moscow-based chain, whose Mayfair offshoot is not short on glam. It provoked less feedback this year, though, in our annual diners' poll (too limited for a rating), but expansion is coming in the second half of 2023 with a new branch, below the Strand Palace Hotel. / W1J 8ED; www.bocconcinorestaurant.co.uk; bocconcino_london; Mon-Sat 12.30 am, Sun 10.30 pm.

BOISDALE OF BELGRAVIA SW1 £111 233

15 ECCLESTON STREET
020 7730 6922 2–*4B*

The Scottish roots of Ranald Macdonald (the eldest son of the 24th chief and captain of Clanranald) help explain the approach of this Belgravian stalwart, which – since 1986 – has majored in a menu of Scottish-sourced beef and burgers (plus lobster and a few other dishes); backed up by an 'old school' wine list informed by Ranald's original career in the wine trade; and topped off with a huge range of whiskies. "Live music helps make it fun" and there's also a cigar terrace. On the downside, although harsh critiques are absent, its overall rating suggests it is fully priced. (For traditional expense-accounters, though, it's tailor-made.) / SW1W 9LX; www.boisdale.co.uk; boisdale_uk; Mon, Sat, Tue-Fri 1 am, Sun 4 pm.

BOISDALE OF CANARY WHARF E14 £83 333

CABOT PLACE 020 7715 5818 12–*1C*

"If you are not planning a return to the office, the largest selection of whisky ever seen" helps round off a business lunch at this Canary Wharf branch of Ranald Macdonald's Caledonian group. "The restaurant prides itself on good Scottish ingredients… shellfish in season… excellent fillet steak" and "tables are sufficiently spaced for private conversation". Top Tip – "regular visitors may join a club which gives discounts on wines and they host musical events in the evenings". / E14 4QT; www.boisdale.co.uk; boisdale_restaurants; Tue, Wed 11 pm, Fri & Sat 2 am, Thu 1 am, Sun 4.30 pm.

BOMBAY BRASSERIE SW7 £94 333

COURTFIELD ROAD 020 7370 4040 6–*2B*

This grand Indian near Gloucester Road tube station was famous in the late 1980s, and nowadays has achieved a respectable semi-obscurity. Now owned by India's swish Taj Hotels group, all reports rate it well, and fans say it's been "year-in, year-out enjoyable" for four decades. / SW7 4QH; www.bombayb.co.uk; bombaybrasseriesw7; Tue-Thu, Sun 10 pm, Fri & Sat 10.30 pm.

BOMBAY BUSTLE W1 £79 534

29 MADDOX STREET 020 7290 4470 3–*2C*

"Imaginative dishes", which deploy "authentic and distinct spicing with just the right kick", "make for a cracking experience" at Samyukta Nair's "smartly decorated room on the edge of Mayfair, with memories of Old Bombay". It's "the casual little sister of Jamavar" and "almost as good as its more expensive sibling" – while probably more "fun". Top Menu Tip – "Jalebi cheesecake". / W1S 2PA; www.bombaybustle.com; bombaybustle; Mon-Sat 10.30 pm, Sun 9.30 pm.

BOMBAY PALACE W2 £69 442

50 CONNAUGHT ST 020 7723 8855 7–*1D*

"Don't be fooled by the 1990s looks – standards are right up to snuff!" This "old-fashioned, well-spaced, very comfortable" Indian near Edgware Road has – for decades – won surprisingly high scores for its "consistently good, traditional dishes of high quality served by knowledgeable waiters". It remains "highly recommended" but its ratings have been a bit more up-and-down since the pandemic; and the odd report says "a bit more consistency would be appreciated: the food can be excellent but can also be mediocre". / W2 2AA; www.bombay-palace.co.uk; bombaypalacelondon; Mon, Thu, Tue, Wed, Sun 10 pm, Fri & Sat 10.30 pm.

BONE DADDIES £46 322

NOVA, VICTORIA ST, SW1 NO TEL 2–*4B*
30-31 PETER ST, W1 020 7287 8581 4–*2D*
46-48 JAMES ST, W1 020 3019 7140 3–*1A*
1 PHILLIMORE GARDENS, W8
020 3668 5500 8–*1D*
24 OLD JAMAICA ROAD, SE16
020 7231 3211 10–*4D*
22 PUTNEY HIGH ST, SW15
020 8246 4170 11–*2B*
THE BOWER, 211 OLD STREET, EC1
020 3019 6300 13–*1A*

These funky (and noisy) 'rock 'n' roll ramen' bars shook up the capital's Japanese fast-food scene when the first outlet opened in Soho 11

Brooklands SW1

years ago, spawning a small group now reaching as far as Richmond. Their "super ramen" is served with 20-hour pork bone broth cooked these days at a kitchen on Bermondsey's 'beer mile'. But the business has not been immune to the industry's difficulties: a Putney spin-off only lasted a year before closing, and a long-touted outlet in the old Eurostar terminal at Waterloo has yet to eventuate. / www.bonedaddies.com; bonedaddies.

BONOO NW2 £63 333

675 FINCHLEY ROAD 020 7794 8899 1–1B

"A great local Indian, with tapas-style Indian dishes full of fresh, zingy flavours" – this family-run operation in Childs Hill is "definitely not your traditional curry house" and has proved a "really welcome addition to North London". / NW2 2JP; www.bonoo.co.uk; bonoo.indian.tapas; Mon-Sun 10.30 pm.

BOOKING OFFICE 1869, ST PANCRAS RENAISSANCE HOTEL NW1 £87 235

EUSTON ROAD 020 7841 3566 9–3C

"The scene is set for romance before you even step through the door" at this "very impressive and spectacular" yearling, with its location "next to Paul Day's sculpture of a couple kissing at St. Pancras International". Set inside the station's former ticket office (nowadays part of a glossy five-star hotel), "the majesty of the architecture is set off by elegant palm trees and it's a calm and wonderful oasis" (complete with a 22m bar). The only potential shortcoming is the all-day brasserie menu: even some fans concede it's "pricey" and there is the odd report of "really disappointing" dishes here. Top Menu Tip – "it's always been a stunning space and – now it's a restaurant – it's the perfect place to crash a hotel breakfast!"; "beautifully executed afternoon tea" too. / NW1 2AR; www.booking-office.co.uk; bookingoffice; Mon-Sun 10 pm.

THE BOOT & FLOGGER SE1 £69 334

10-20 REDCROSS WAY 020 7407 1184 10–4C

"Traditional, old favourites" characterise the British cooking at this "relaxed" and very atmospheric wine bar and dining room, just south of Southwark Street and the railway arches that ultimately run over nearby Borough Market. It has a "great atmosphere and good wine list" – like so much of the 15-strong Davy's wine bar chain, of which this was the original, opening in 1965. / SE1 1TA; www.davy.co.uk; davysoflondon; Tue-Sat 11 pm, Mon 10 pm, Sun 6 pm.

IL BORDELLO E1 £61 334

METROPOLITAN WHARF, 70 WAPPING WALL 020 7481 9950 12–1A

This neighbourhood Italian of almost 30 years' standing in a Wapping warehouse conversion "never disappoints" with its food and service, but "it's the lively atmosphere that really sells it", drawing a "great mix of local families and couples just getting together". / E1W 3SS; www.ilbordello.com; ilbordellorestaurant; Mon-Sat 11 pm, Sun 10.30 pm.

BOROUGH MARKET KITCHEN SE1 £66 422

JUBILEE PLACE 020 7407 5777 10–4C

"If you like street food and quick relaxed eating", seek out this three-year-old covered street-food area adjoining the famous market that's winning a consistent thumbs up; you can choose from about 15 different stands and there's a fair amount of communal seating. It used to be a car park! / SE1 9AG; www.applebeesfish.com; boroughmarket; Mon-Thu 10 pm, Fri & Sat 11 pm, Sun 9 pm.

IL BORRO W1 £132 233

15 BERKELEY STREET 020 3988 7717 3–3C

Owned by the Ferragamo fashion family and named after their Tuscan wine estate, this Mayfair two-year-old in the former premises of Nobu Berkeley (RIP) is certainly "a bit bling", but has won over a constituency of fans who say "it seems to be right for the occasion, whether business or pleasure". Plus points include "some fine dishes – including wonderful fish and vegetables" – and "a pleasant buzz". The big drawback, if you're footing the bill, is "the insane price point". / W1J 8DY; ilborrotuscanbistro.co.uk; tuscanbistrolondon; Sun-Thu midnight, Fri & Sat 1 am.

BOSSA W1

4 VERE STREET 020 3062 5844 3–1B

Opened in May 2023, just as our latest annual diners' poll was concluding, the debut of this Marylebone newcomer from Brazilian World's 50 best chef Alberto Landgraf has so far made remarkably few waves. It's clear from the pics that he's spent a packet on the svelte interior, but the menu – with mains for £30-£40 – has few distinguishing Latino inflections (e.g. a sample main – 'Pork Loin Chop, Apple Purée, Savoy Cabbage, Black Pudding'). Ignored in its initial months by the newspapers, including The Standard – reports please! / W1G 0DG; www.bossa.co.uk; bossa_uk; Tue-Sat 11 pm.

BOTTLE & RYE SW9 £62 342

GROUND FLOOR, 404-406 MARKET ROW NO TEL 11–2D

"Still dreaming about the anchovies on toast!" Robin and Sarah Gill's compact (28 covers) yearling aims to bring Parisian café culture to Brixton's Market Row. All feedback on the "daily changing menus of small and larger dishes" is upbeat: "a small place with a brilliant selection of options, good wine and drinks list. Staff are really on it, know the dishes inside out and steer you in the right direction for your order". / SW9 8LD; www.bottleandrye.com; bottleandrye; Tue-Sat 11 pm.

BOUCHON RACINE EC1 £88 553

66 COWCROSS STREET 020 7253 3368 10–1A

A "fabulous successor to the legendary Racine" (which closed in Knightsbridge in 2015) and "an amazing, blazing return to the stove for Henry Harris" – this "very lively room, up steep stairs" above Farringdon's Three Compasses pub is the opening of the year and, despite all the hype, it doesn't disappoint. "There's lots of passion and skill that goes into this quintessential cooking" – "French classics (basics even) taken to another level". Service, overseen by co-founder Dave Strauss, is "pitch perfect": "charming and from people who clearly love what they do". "One leaves uplifted and feeling that all is well with the world… that is, in the unlikely event that you can get a table!". Top Menu Tip – "a spot-on and delicious tête de veau sauce ravigote". / EC1M 6BP; www.bouchonracine.com; bouchonracine; Tue-Sat 10 pm.

BOUDICA SW11

BOUDICA HOUSE, 12 PALMER ROAD 020 8017 3400 11–1C

On the fringes of the new developments around Battersea Power Station, this modern all-day-brasserie opened in April 2023 – too late to generate any survey feedback. Instagram-worthy foliage is a feature, both inside and on the terrace. Let's hope chef Luigi Vairo (who provides an international menu) doesn't take too much inspiration from the restaurant's name… the legendary queen of the Iceni, who burnt London to the ground… / SW11 4FQ; www.boudicalondon.com; boudica_london; Mon-Sat midnight, Sun 10 pm.

BOULEVARD WC2 £62 233

40 WELLINGTON ST 020 7240 2992 5–3D

A "Covent Garden staple" for 33 years, this "bustling French bistro with packed tables but speedy service" serves "good-value, reliably cooked traditional Gallic fare" that belies its somewhat touristy looks. Top Tip – "a wide-ranging menu and the set menus and special deals add to its appeal; and it's a good choice for families with children". / WC2E 7BD; www.boulevardbrasserie.co.uk; boulevardbrasseriewc2; Mon-Wed 11 pm, Thu-Sat 11.30 pm, Sun 10 pm.

BRACKENBURY WINE ROOMS W6 £59 244

111-115 HAMMERSMITH GROVE 020 3696 8240 8–1C

This "cheerful" and "enjoyable" Hammersmith haunt carries a good selection of wines and its kitchen offers modern bistro food – but 'La Cave', its coffee house, generates the most feedback this year, for its "friendly staff", "superb coffee" and "the best chocolate brownies". / W6 0NQ; winerooms.london; wine_rooms; Mon-Sat 11 pm, Sun 4 pm.

BRADLEY'S NW3 £78 222

25 WINCHESTER RD 020 7722 3457 9–2A

Simon & Jolanta Bradley's "efficient" veteran of 30 years' standing near Swiss Cottage station "never lets you down" and it's a "great option if going to the Hampstead Theatre around the corner". But while fans say "the quality of the food is such that it shouldn't be only for pre-theatre", there's also a view that "it can feel rather soulless" as a destination in itself. / NW3 3NR; www.bradleysnw3.co.uk; bradleysrestaurant; Wed-Sat, Tue 9 pm, Sun 2.30 pm.

LA BRASSERIA £89 222

42 MARYLEBONE HIGH STREET, W1
020 7486 3753 2–1A
290 WESTBOURNE GROVE, W11
020 7052 3564 7–2B

For a "solid menu, with a wide variety" of "reliable Italian" options, this duo have a broad fanclub – both the Marylebone five-year-old and its year-old Notting Hill sibling. Their ratings are undercut, though, by a feeling that they are "expensive (but isn't everything nowadays…"), and can "lack atmosphere when they're not busy". Top Tip – for some folks, "the most important thing is that they welcome both families and doggies!" / www.labrasseria.com; brasseria_nottinghill.

BRASSERIE BLANC £62 222

119 CHANCERY LANE, WC2
020 7405 0290 2–2D
GOLDHURST HOUSE, PARR'S WAY, W6
020 8237 5566 8–2C
9 BELVEDERE RD, SE1
020 7202 8470 2–3D
60 THREADNEEDLE ST, EC2
020 7710 9440 10–2C

"For a reasonable pre-theatre/concert meal" on the South Bank, the SE1 branch of this Gallic brasserie chain is "a useful option behind the Royal Festival Hall"; its City and Legal-land outlets are serviceable for a working lunch; and its W6 branch has a "classy" position on the river. Over time, though, it has "declined from being one of the better multiples" and is nowadays "very, very average indeed" – with the possible exception of Hammersmith, you wouldn't make them a destination in their own right. BREAKING NEWS. In October 2023, a third branch was announced on the South Kensington site that – appropriately – traded for yonks in time gone by as La Brasserie (long RIP). / www.brasserieblanc.com. SRA – 3 stars

BRASSERIE OF LIGHT W1 £81 234

400 OXFORD STREET 020 3940 9600 3–1A

"Who would have believed you are eating in a department store!" – Richard Caring's "glitzy but useful" second-floor brasserie has "a real buzz". "With huge windows, the decor is fabulously glamorous and Damien Hirst's stunning 'Pegasus' dominates the scene". The "Ivy-style menu" is "appealingly eclectic, if with rather average execution", but by-and-large comes at "fair prices". / W1A 1AB; www.brasserie-of-light.co.uk; brasserieoflight; Mon-Sat midnight, Sun 11 pm.

BRASSERIE ZÉDEL W1 £60 124

20 SHERWOOD ST 020 7734 4888 4–3C

"Transport yourself to an imaginary 1930s world of Parisian glamour, as might be imagined by Fitzgerald or Hollywood", when you visit this Art Deco basement, "bang in the heart of town", just seconds from Piccadilly Circus. "The vast (Grade I listed) room is a crowded symphony of marble and gold leaf, with an immense buzz" and is "a faithful facsimile of a traditional French brasserie", complete with an excellent American Bar. Fans say "if you want to impress without spending a fortune then this is the place to go" and since its founding (in 2015) it's become a byword for "affordable luxury", with most folks tolerating its "dull and unmemorable" Gallic staples for the overall package. Since changes in the group, however, the equation is beginning to shift and fears are growing that "the package all-round is not quite good enough". "Service in particular has fallen notably in the post-Jeremy King era" and for more critical types "the whole experience is rather underwhelming" ("it was busy, but instead of making the atmosphere vibrant, there was a tired feel to the experience"). That's not yet the dominant verdict though: most diners still "never tire of visiting… it always feels like a wonderful and extravagant treat". / W1F 7ED; www.brasseriezedel.com; brasseriezedel; Mon-Sat 11 pm, Sun 10 pm.

BRAT E1 £87 543

FIRST FLOOR, 4 REDCHURCH STREET
NO TEL 13–1B

"Simple things are done very, very well on a smoking fire and every dish is a wow!" at Tomos Parry's Shoreditch superstar, which – now five years old – has proved "a superb addition to the London dining scene" ."It's casual in style, but the truly original cooking" and "enthusiastic and informed staff" generate "a real buzz about the place" and create a "cosy" atmosphere in what might otherwise might seem a "somewhat lacklustre" and tightly packed space (on the first floor, above Smoking Goat downstairs). As well as the signature turbot for which the restaurant is named, many dishes here are praised in reports ("spider crab toast to die for…"; "clever duck rice, like paella…"; "beautifully flavoursome and light Basque cheesecake"). / E1 6JJ; www.bratrestaurant.com; bratrestaurant; Mon-Sun 10 pm.

BRAT AT CLIMPSON'S ARCH E8 £101 432

CLIMPSON'S ARCH, 374 HELMSLEY PLACE
020 7254 7199 14–2B

"Such a treat on a summer's day" – ace chef Tomos Parry's railway arch pop-up-turned-permanent in London Fields "feels like a (rather smoky) house party", serving "great grilled meat and fish in a tent" – "the only issue is trying to limit the number of dishes one orders, and the quandary of whether to have THAT turbot or try something else!". / E8 3SB; bratrestaurant.com; bratrestaurant; Wed-Sat 10 pm, Sun 9 pm.

BRAVI RAGAZZI SW16 £51 422

2A SUNNYHILL ROAD
020 8769 4966 11–2D

"Excellent Neapolitan sourdough pizza" has carved a legendary reputation for Andrea Asciuti's cult Streatham pitstop, to which aficionados journey from far and wide. He also runs 081 Pizzeria – see also. / SW16 2UH; www.bravi-ragazzi.business.site; braviragazzipizzeria; Mon-Thu 10 pm, Fri 10.30 pm, Sat 11 pm, Sun 9.30 pm.

BRAWN E2 £78 554

49 COLUMBIA ROAD
020 7729 5692 14–2A

"Not missing a beat and at the very top of its game" – this culinarily renowned East End fixture, near Columbia Road flower market, scored highly all round in this year's annual diners' poll, putting any doubts about its staying power to one side. Its Med-influenced, superior bistro cuisine delivers "extraordinary flavours", service is very "charming" and all in all, it's "a delightful, unpretentious neighbourhood place" / E2 7RG; www.brawn.co; brawn49; Tue-Sat, Mon 10.30 pm.

BREAD STREET KITCHEN EC4 £78 223

10 BREAD STREET 020 3030 4050 10–2B

"Well-located in the power station", the new Battersea branch of Gordon Ramsay's upscale brasserie chain has inspired more interest than some others in this expanding group (which also now incorporates the Limehouse riverside pub GR has owned for ages, fka The Narrow). With their generously spaced, comfortable and quite stylish interiors they can be a versatile choice – especially on business – but their resolutely MOR standards mean they hardly set the pulse racing. / EC4M 9AJ; www.gordonramsayrestaurants.com; breadstreetkitchen; Mon-Wed 11 pm, Thu-Sat midnight, Sun 10 pm.

BREAKFAST CLUB £45 343

BRANCHES THROUGHOUT LONDON

"Plenty of yummy breakfast options" win praise for this "extremely well done" brunch specialist which launched 19 years ago in Soho and now has 13 self-described 'cafés', 10 of them around the capital, and another four bars and pubs. The fry-ups, pancakes and other comfort-food delights can be accompanied by cocktails if you fancy pushing the boat out early with a Breakfast Mai Tai. Any complaints? – "just the incredibly annoying queues". / www.thebreakfastclubcafes.com; thebrekkyclub.

BRICIOLE W1 £69 3 3 2

20 HOMER ST 020 7723 0040 7–1D

According to a fair few reports, this "charming neighbourhood Italian" near Edgware Road tube station offers "authentically tasty small plates and delicious classics", although "you do need to put up with the noise". Top Tip – "they are very good with children here". / W1H 4NA; www.briciole.co.uk; briciolerestaurant; Mon-Sun 10.45 pm.

BRICK LANE BEIGEL BAKE E1 £9 5 2 1

159 BRICK LN 020 7729 0616 13–1C

"The original and the best", agree fans of this legendary East End Jewish deli, which is "well worth a detour any time, day or night" (thanks to its 24/7 opening) for its "fantastic" beigels (stubbornly spelt in the traditional European manner), stuffed with classic fillings including salt beef, lox and pickled herring. "Amazing value" too – it feels like they've forgotten to change the prices for the last 20 years. / E1 6SB; www.beigelbake.co.uk; bricklanebeigelbake; Mon-Sun midnight.

BRIGADIERS, BLOOMBERG ARCADE EC2 £71 4 3 3

QUEEN VICTORIA STREET 020 3319 8140 10–3C

"Standards remain high" at JKS Restaurants' "Anglo-Indian sporting and military-themed eaterie" in the Bloomberg Arcade – "a go-to lunching spot (albeit that City lunching is significantly less prevalent than in days gone by)". The "amazing and different dishes" are "full of flavour and spices". Top Menu Tips – "the tandoori meats in particular are excellent" and "dum beef shin and bone marrow biryani is a must try!" / EC2R 8AR; brigadierslondon.com; brigadiersldn; Mon-Sat 10.30 pm.

THE BRIGHT COURTYARD W1 £90 3 2 2

43-45 BAKER ST 020 7486 6998 2–1A

A "big Chinese restaurant" – the London outpost of a Shanghai group – which serves Cantonese fare that's "really good and not too pricey". It occupies part of an office block near Portman Square in Marylebone – a setting that "can seem a bit sterile". / W1U 8EW; www.lifefashiongroup.com; brightcourtyard; Mon-Sat 10.30 pm, Sun 9.30 pm.

BRINKLEY'S SW10 £74 2 3 3

47 HOLLYWOOD RD 020 7351 1683 6–3B

For its Sloane Ranger crowd, wine merchant John Brinkley's long-established brasserie is a "still-buzzing Chelsea legend where you can drink well at almost-retail prices". But, while most fans feel the food is "decent" too, others say "you pay too much for what you get and folks are starting to vote with their feet". There are spin-offs in Wandsworth Bridge Road and beside Wandsworth Common (see Brinkley's Kitchen). / SW10 9HX; www.brinkleys.com; brinkleysrestaurant; Mon-Sun 11 pm.

BRINKLEY'S KITCHEN SW17 £76 2 2 3

35 BELLEVUE RD 020 8672 5888 11–2C

"Always busy local favourite" facing onto Wandsworth Common. It serves "competent modern British food" but what particularly helps keep its regulars coming back is a "keenly priced wine list" from owner John Brinkley, who has a string of wine-focused venues in southwest London. / SW17 7EF; www.brinkleys.com; brinkleyskitchen; Tue-Sat 11 pm, Sun 4 pm.

BROOKLANDS SW1

1 GROSVENOR PLACE 020 8138 6888 2–3A

When it opens in September 2023, this rooftop restaurant promises to be one of the capital's glossier debuts in recent times. It's on top of the Peninsular London – a branch of the landmark HK hotel, overlooking Hyde Park Corner (right next to The Lanesborough). The kitchen is under the culinary direction of Claude Bosi, the Lyon-born chef behind Bibendum in Chelsea, who will provide a contemporary European menu. Let's hope the cuisine really takes off… unlike the model of Concorde, which it is promised will soar above the heads of diners on the outside terrace. / SW1X 7HJ; www.peninsula.com; peninsulahotels; Mon-Sun.

BROOKMILL SE8 £56 3 3 3

65 CRANBROOK ROAD 020 8333 0899 1–4D

If you find yourself near Brookmill Park, between Deptford and Lewisham, this "lovely and friendly" corner pub (with garden) is worth knowing about for its "reliable" standard of cooking. / SE8 4EJ; www.thebrookmill.co.uk; brookmillse8; Sun & Mon 9 pm, Tue-Sat 10 pm.

THE BROWN DOG SW13 £63 3 3 4

28 CROSS STREET 020 8392 2200 11–1A

This "unspoilt, cosy and simply furnished" late-Victorian pub, "tucked away down a side street" in the cute 'Little Chelsea' enclave of Barnes, is "a joy to visit for its competently cooked food and excellent beer" – "not surprisingly it has loyal local support". Top Tip – sweet garden in summer. / SW13 0AP; www.thebrowndog.co.uk; browndogbarnes; Tue, Wed 11 pm, Thu-Sat 10 pm, Sun 6 pm.

BROWN'S HOTEL, THE DRAWING ROOM W1 £134 3 4 4

ALBEMARLE ST 020 7493 6020 3–3C

"Even better than The Ritz…", "on a par with Fortnum's…" – for many aficionados of London's top afternoon tea experiences, this wood-panelled drawing room within creaky old Brown's Hotel is the top dog. Built in 1837 (and with famous patrons including Queen Victoria and Agatha Christie) – it helps that it's "a lovely, traditional space": "delightful and just more intimate" than its main rivals. "Nothing is too much trouble (even to please a picky sub-teenager!)" and "the sandwiches and tea are just as good as elsewhere". / W1S 4BP; www.roccofortehotels.com; browns_hotel; Mon-Sun 9 pm.

BRUNSWICK HOUSE CAFÉ SW8 £64 3 2 5

30 WANDSWORTH RD 020 7720 2926 11–1D

"An architectural salvage display room" lit by chandeliers – in a Georgian mansion fronting the Vauxhall Cross gyratory system – provides a "lively, boho and very relaxed" backdrop for this unusual but successful venue. Amazingly, it "works so well", with "above average (if expensive) modern British fare" from highly regarded chef Jackson Boxer. ("Well worth the detour/ taking your life in your hands navigating the Vauxhall one way!"). / SW8 2LG; www.brunswickhouse.london; brunswick_house; Wed-Sat, Tue 9.45 pm, Sun 4.30 pm.

TRATTORIA BRUTTO EC1 £59 3 4 5

35-37 GREENHILL RENTS NO TEL 10–1A

Russell Norman's skillful love letter to Florentine trattorias is "hard to fault for a classic Italian" and, in particular, its "buzzy" ("if noisy" and "crowded") "glamourous" style is a brilliant escape from the grey streets of Clerkenwell (near Smithfield Market). The "Negronis are lethal" and the "heavy-hitting, rustic fodder" is "simply done, but top quality". An archetypal 'Bistecca alla Fiorentina' (T-bone steak) is a central menu feature, as are lesser-known treats such as "the moreish coccoli (or 'cuddles') of deep-fried dough that you stuff with soft cheese and prosciutto". For all its virtues, though, Russell is a darling of the foodie media, so the place receives regular "hype", and the only weaker reviews come from those expecting more culinary fireworks, given that "the food is good, but not great". / EC1M 6BN; msha.ke/brutto; bru.tto; Tue-Sat 11 pm.

BUBALA £41 4 4 3

15 POLAND STREET, W1 NO TEL 4–1C
65 COMMERCIAL STREET, E1 NO TEL 13–2C

"Every course hits harder than the next… and you don't even realise all are vegetarian!" – this former pop-up – now with outlets in Soho (on the site of the now-transferred Vasco & Piero's) and Shoreditch – serves "stunning" Middle Eastern-style dishes from founder Marc Summers (ex-Berber & Q) and head chef Helen Graham (ex-Palomar and Barbary). "If I could eat this food every day, I could easily become meat-free". Plan ahead – "it's hard to get a table!" / bubala_london.

THE BULL N6 £69 332

13 NORTH HILL 020 8341 0510 9–*1B*

This old Highgate pub with a big outside terrace makes a "good local" with "hearty gastropub fare", although its 2022 acquisition by the Metropolitan Pub Company may not have contributed to the atmosphere. / N6 4AB; thebullhighgate.co.uk; bull_highgate; Mon-Thu 11 pm, Fri & Sat midnight, Sun 10.30 pm.

BULL & LAST NW5 £79 433

168 HIGHGATE RD 020 7267 3641 9–*1B*

A "fabulous bistropub" – "now also a hotel with comfortable rooms" – in a "great location" near Parliament Hill and Hampstead Heath. "Giles Coren is not wrong" – the Times columnist is a local and a big fan. Any complaints? "If only they'd turn the music down...". / NW5 1QS; www.thebullandlast.co.uk; thebullandlast; Mon-Thu 11 pm, Fri & Sat midnight, Sun 10.30 pm.

BUND N2 £56 333

4-5 CHEAPSIDE, FORTIS GREEN
020 8365 2643 1–*1B*

"Good all round", say local fans of this Pan-Asian fixture, which offers East-meets-West presentation of dishes drawn from a variety of cuisines. It brings some light to the thinly provided boonies between Muswell Hill and East Finchley. / N2 9HP; bundrestaurant.co.uk; bundrestaurant; Tue-Sun 10 pm.

BURGER & BEYOND E1 £49 322

147 SHOREDITCH HIGH STREET
020 3848 8860 13–*1B*

This former food-truck and market-stall operation now has three bricks-and-mortar bars around the capital serving US-style burgers made from dry-aged Yorkshire-bred beef – and "wow, they're really good". You can enjoy them at home, too, thanks to a trio of delivery-only kitchens. Top Menu Tip – "the Bacon Butter Burger is great". / E1 6JE; burgerandbeyond.co.uk; burgerandbeyond; Mon-Thu 10 pm, Fri & Sat 11 pm, Sun 9 pm.

BURGER & LOBSTER £77 432

HARVEY NICHOLS, 109-125 KNIGHTSBRIDGE, SW1
020 7235 5000 6–*1D*
10 WARDOUR STREET, W1
020 3205 8963 5–*4A*
26 BINNEY STREET, W1
020 3637 5972 3–*2A*
29 CLARGES STREET, W1
020 7409 1699 3–*4B*
36 DEAN STREET, W1 020 7432 4800 5–*2A*
6 LITTLE PORTLAND STREET, W1
020 7907 7760 3–*1C*
18 HERTSMERE ROAD, E14
020 3637 6709 12–*1C*
52 THREADNEEDLE STREET, EC2
020 7256 9755 10–*2C*
BOW BELLS HS, 1 BREAD ST, EC4
020 7248 1789 10–*2B*

"The lobster roll is just lovely" at this surf'n'turf-meets-burger chain, where you'll find "plenty of very tasty grub". "I was expecting to be disappointed, but the food was excellent". A dozen years on from its launch, the group's nine London venues tend to be "full of people done up for a big night out, taking lots of selfies for their Insta". / www.burgerandlobster.com; burgerandlobster.

BUSABA £51 222

BRANCHES THROUGHOUT LONDON

After 25 years, this Thai-fusion group is generally regarded as "solid but far from spectacular". Creator Alan Yau (who also has Wagamama and Hakkasan among his credits) is no longer involved and out-of-town branches in Oxford and Cardiff have closed down, leaving 10 outlets in the London area. / www.busaba.com; busabaeathai.

BUTLER'S RESTAURANT, THE CHESTERFIELD MAYFAIR W1 £90 333

35 CHARLES ST 020 7958 7729 3–*3B*

Dover sole filleted at the table, "choosing from pick'n'mix from the sweet trolley" and "cocktails in a smoking glass" typify the retro flourishes favoured by the comfy dining room and bar of this traditional Mayfair venue. Feedback isn't super-plentiful, but all upbeat – "a lovely experience at a reasonable price". / W1J 5EB; www.chesterfieldmayfair.com; chesterfieldmayfair; Mon-Sun 10 pm.

BUTLERS WHARF CHOP HOUSE SE1 £85 223

36E SHAD THAMES 020 7403 3403 10–*4D*

"Handy for the location" by the Thames, with spectacular views of Tower Bridge from its terrace, this modern take on the British chop house was created by the late Sir Terence Conran as part of his 'Gastrodome' complex in the 1990s. Nowadays owned by D&D London, it is a useful spot for tourists and business diners. / SE1 2YE; www.chophouse-restaurant.co.uk; butlerswharfchophouse; Tue-Sat 9 pm, Mon 9.30 pm, Sun 6 pm. SRA – accredited

BYRON £47 223

BRANCHES THROUGHOUT LONDON

Now down to a dozen outlets nationally and just four in London from its 2018 peak of 67, this early 'better burger' chain has dropped ratings across the board this year. But, compared to other chains, feedback is far from rock-bottom – indeed complaints are notably absent – so perhaps there are still some legs in the brand? / www.byron.co.uk/about-us; ByronBurgersUK.

C&R CAFÉ W1 £36 422

3-4 RUPERT COURT 020 7434 1128 4–*3D*

"Please don't dress up to dine in this cheap little no-frills café" on the edge of Chinatown, but prepare to eat some "truly fantastic, highly spiced Malaysian food" – "the beef rendang is absolutely the best", and "the laksa lives up to expectations". / W1D 6DY; www.cnrcaferestaurant.com; c&r; Tue-Thu, Sun 10 pm, Fri & Sat 11 pm.

CABOTTE EC2 £86 343

48 GRESHAM ST 020 7600 1616 10–*2C*

"One of the best options for fine dining in the City" – "if you want a good French restaurant in the Square Mile, with a great wine list, look no further" than this "slick and intimate" venue which boasts "one of the best wine selections in London" – a particular "dream-list for lovers of Burgundy and Champagne". "Very good service is worth a shout out". / EC2V 7AY; www.cabotte.co.uk; cabotte_; Mon-Fri 10 pm.

THE CADOGAN ARMS SW3 £75 334

298 KING'S ROAD 020 3148 2630 6–*3C*

"When all that wealth and beauty on the King's Road become too much", this "tastefully restored" old pub (built in 1838) is something of an antidote. It wins praise all round for its "attentive" service and "traditional British fare" that's "on the button and carefully presented". If there's any reservation, it's that it doesn't dazzle quite as much as its restaurant royalty backing might lead you to hope (the owners of JKS Restaurants, with food overseen by Kitchen Table's James Knappett). Top Menu Tip – "prawn cocktail and skinny chips with a side order of hot sauce". / SW3 5UG; thecadoganarms.london; cadoganarmspublichouse; Mon-Thu 10 pm, Fri & Sat 10.30 pm, Sun 6 pm.

CAFE CECILIA E8 £65 444

CANAL PLACE, 32 ANDREWS ROAD
0203 478 6726 14–*2B*

"Cool places rarely fit the hype… but this one does!" Max Rocha's "low key and informal" Hackney two-year-old is going from strength to strength. "A light airy space by the canal, it's great for a relaxed meal", with service that – "though achingly hip – is very good". The "slightly unusual" food is all about small portions of intense flavours and "super-fresh seasonal ingredients", and results are "excellent". "Bonne chance getting a table!" Top Menu Tip – "the Guinness bread is very tasty". / E8 4RL; www.cafececilia.com; cafececilialondon; Thu-Sat 8.30 pm, Wed 3 pm, Sun 3.30 pm.

CAFÉ DECO WC1 £69 322

43 STORE STREET 020 8091 2108 2–*1C*

The "superb neighbourhood café we'd all love to have around the corner" – this upgraded greasy spoon "in a dead area of Bloomsbury" provides "particularly tasty, modern French fare" realised with a "delicious and light" touch by co-founder Anna Tobias, former head chef at Rochelle Canteen. / WC1E 7DB; www.cafe-deco.co.uk; cafe_deco_bloomsbury; Tue-Sat 9.30 pm.

CAFÉ DU MARCHÉ EC1 £62 345

2 CHARTERHOUSE SQ
20 7608 1609 10–*1B*

You actually feel as though you might be in a brasserie in France" at this City-fringe favourite", tucked away in an atmospheric former warehouse, near Smithfield Market (and long predating the trendification of the area). A great staple for both business and pleasure", "has a lovely atmosphere with a real, vibrant buzz which should surely impress" either a client or date. The "pleasing", solid Gallic fare offers "decent value", but "it is the overall experience that makes it stand out". / EC1M DX; www.cafedumarche.co.uk; cafedumarche; Tue-Fri 10 pm, Sat 9.30 pm.

CAFÉ IN THE CRYPT, ST MARTIN IN THE FIELDS WC2 £36 224

DUNCANNON ST 020 7766 1158 2–*2C*

A "long-established cafeteria" in the beautiful, brick-vaulted crypt of St Martin-in-the-Fields that's a useful venue for daytime and pre-theatre refuelling – "cheap and tasty and near the National Gallery". In summer, they open a 'Café in the Courtyard', too. / WC2N 4JJ; stmartin-in-the-fields.org; stmartininthefields; Mon, Wed, Fri-Sun 5 pm, Tue 7.30 pm.

CAFÉ JAPAN NW11 £41 332

626 FINCHLEY RD 020 8455 6854 1–*1B*

Some of the "best reasonably priced sashimi and sushi" in London has long been found at this basic but "friendly" café, near Golders Green Tube. In recent years, it's fallen under the ownership of top Japanese fish and seafood wholesaler T&S Enterprises, with outlets (usually under the Atariya brand) in Finchley, Kingston, Swiss Cottage and West Acton. / NW11 7RR; atariya.co.uk; cafejapanlondon; Wed-Sun 11 pm.

CAFÉ KITSUNÉ AT PANTECHNICON SW1 £47 334

19 MOTCOMB STREET
020 7034 5425 6–*1D*

'With the pâtisserie, the Japanese and Parisian influences are combined in such a wonderful way… and the coffee is sooo good", according to fans of this mezzanine and foyer café, within a beautiful Belgravia landmark. But, perhaps predictably considering the frou-frou nature of this luxe locale, it can also seem plain "overpriced". / SW1X 8LB; www.pantechnicon.com; _pantechnicon; Mon-Sun 6 pm.

CAFÉ LAPÉROUSE, THE OWO SW1

57 WHITEHALL PLACE AWAITING TEL
2–*3C*

Just the name of the Dior-affiliated designer (Cordeìlia de Castellane), evokes glamour at the courtyard eatery of this mega-development scheduled to open in late 2023. It's a spin-off from the 250-year-old Parisian venture of the same name – France's first restaurant with three Michelin stars back in the day (which it held, on and off, until 1968) – and looks set to be cut from the same (chic but extremely expensive) cloth as the original on the Place de la Concorde. / SW1A 2EU; Wed-Sat 10 pm, Sun 9.30 pm.

CAFE MURANO £74 342

33 ST JAMES'S ST, SW1
020 3371 5559 3–*3C*
36 TAVISTOCK ST, WC2
020 3371 5559 5–*3D*
PASTIFICIO, 34 TAVISTOCK STREET, WC2
020 3535 7884 5–*3D*
184 BERMONDSEY STREET, SE1
020 3985 1545 10–*4D*

"Reliably good Italian food at fair prices" and particularly "switched-on service" won revitalised support this year for Angela Hartnett's "very serviceable" mini-chain, which is generally a "very safe choice", and – at its best – "memorable" in the level of "very confident" cooking it can achieve. Even fans, though, concede the "atmosphere can be a bit low key", in particular at the "rather gloomy" WC2 branch (and the best reports are at St James's). / www.cafemurano.co.uk; cafemurano.

CAFÉ SPICE NAMASTE E16 £63 544

1-2 LOWER DOCK WALK, ROYAL DOCK
020 7488 9242 12–*1D*

"Cyrus and Pervin Todiwala have done it again, with the new incarnation of their bastion of Indian and Parsee food", on the Royal Docks "just moments from London Excel and City Airport". "After 26 years, they moved from the fringe of the City in E1 to Royal Albert Wharf E16" and "the food and the personal service remain of the highest nature". "It's just such original and delicious cuisine", "especially on nights when Cyrus cooks Parsee (but it's always good anyway)". Unless you happen to live out that way, though, the new spot could be mistaken for "the middle of nowhere": "we travel over two hours to dine here: the new menu is delicious, the themed evenings a joy… but I wish they were back in Prescott Street!". / E16 2GT; www.cafespice.co.uk; cafespicenamasteldn; Tue-Sat 10 pm.

CAFFÈ CALDESI W1 £86 332

118 MARYLEBONE LN
020 7487 0754 2–*1A*

"Very good Italian family food is served in a buzzy atmosphere" at chef Giancarlo Caldesi

Casa do Frango

and his wife Katie's Marylebone flagship – "all the classic dishes are available", accompanied by an "interesting wine list". The couple also have a country restaurant in Bray and a cookery school, while Tuscany-born Giancarlo has written a healthy cookbook following his diagnosis as a diabetic. / W1U 2QF; www.caldesi.com; caldesiinmarylebone; Mon-Sat 10 pm, Sun 4.30 pm.

CAH CHI KT3

79-81 KINGSTON ROAD
020 8949 8880 1–*4A*

A new location for an old restaurant: this latest incarnation of a family-run business opened in New Malden – serving the sizable local Korean expat community – in spring 2023. Grace Dent of The Guardian visited in May 2023 and was a fan of its "simple yet delicious" cooking – "Cah Chi isn't trying to change the world; it's just quietly representing skilful Korean cooking and creating a haven for hungry passers-by". / KT3 3PB; cahchi.co.uk; cahchibbq; Tue-Sat 10.30 pm, Sun 10 pm.

CAIA W10 £69 433

46 GOLBORNE ROAD 07927 328076 7–*1A*

"In a scruffy but lovely part of London, in the shadow of the Trellick Tower", this year-old, Portobello-fringe bar/restaurant is "top notch". It serves "small plates of interesting combinations charred on an open grill" and "bar seats offer great views of the actual cooking". Beyond the food, it's an "excellent night out" all round thanks to its "warm ambience", helped along by a brilliantly curated vinyl collection. / W10 5PR; caia.london; caia.london; Tue-Thu midnight, Fri & Sat 1 am.

CAKES AND BUBBLES, CAFÉ ROYAL W1 £89 343

70 REGENT STREET 020 7406 3310 4–*4C*

"Living up to the naturally high expectations"; this prime site within the Café Royal, off Piccadilly Circus, wins praise – albeit on limited feedback this year – for the "meticulous patisserie" you would hope for from Albert Adrià (who, back in the day, was pastry chef at his brother Ferran's world-famous destination restaurant: El Bulli, long RIP). / W1B 4DY; www.cakesandbubbles.co.uk; cakesandbubbleslondon; Mon-Sun 9 pm.

THE CAMBERWELL ARMS SE5 £67 444

65 CAMBERWELL CHURCH ST
020 7358 4364 1–*3C*

The "seasonal, generous and top-notch food" at this "great local" in Camberwell is delivered via "laid-back but professional service that exudes cool – much like the local clientele". Having established itself as one of the capital's best gastropubs over the past decade, there are no signs of easing off. Top Menu Tip – "get the pork fat and Scotch bonnet toast". / SE5 8TR; www.thecamberwellarms.co.uk; thecamberwellarms; Wed-Sat, Tue 11 pm, Sun 5 pm.

CAMBIO DE TERCIO SW5 £87 333

161-163 OLD BROMPTON RD
020 7244 8970 6–*2B*

"You leave feeling everything is good in the world" according to fans of Abel Lusa's accomplished stalwart (est. 1995) on the borders of South Ken and Earl's Court: one of London's original Spanish restaurants of quality and still at the cutting edge, with its "luxurious tapas", "excellent Iberian wines" and "wonderfully fun and atmospheric" style. A slip in ratings, though, accompanies one or two concerns that "it should offer better value"; or that "it risks slipping from a smart and exciting place to being lower-energy". But that didn't stop Wimbledon winner Carlos Alcaraz from eating here with his family five times during the Championships this year – and on the days he didn't go, he ordered deliveries to be sent to his accommodation. Apparently, his favourite dish is the crispy salmon nigiri (a Spanish version of sushi with sweet soy sauce, Spanish vinegar and chipotle mayonnaise). / SW5 0LJ; www.cambiodetercio.co.uk; cambiodetercio; Tue-Sat 11.30 pm, Sun & Mon 11 pm.

CAMINO £66 222

3 VARNISHERS YD, REGENT QUARTER, N1
020 7841 7330 9–*3C*
2 CURTAIN ROAD, EC2
020 3948 5003 13–*2B*
15 MINCING LN, EC3
020 7841 7335 10–*3D*

"Reliable tapas in handy locations" is the USP of this 16-year-old trio with a flagship near King's Cross station (by far the best known) and offshoots in Shoreditch and Monument. But while they're "decent enough", they offer "standard fayre" – it's "nothing exceptional". / www.camino.uk.com; caminolondon.

THE CAMPANER SW1

1 GARRISON CLOSE, CHELSEA BARRACKS
020 4580 1385 6–*3D*

Opened shortly before the 2023 Chelsea Flower Show, this svelte looking newcomer – with coffee and light bites during the day and food from the Josper oven available at lunch and dinner – aims to be an anchor attraction of the nearby Chelsea Barracks development, and is operated by José Parrado (who runs a number of high-profile Barcelona restaurants). A glance at the menu's panic-inducing prices suggests the cost-of-living crisis is in full swing, with a tomato juice at £9, a bowl of chips at £8.50, and most mains on the lunch or dinner menu around the £40 mark. Nor is our only early feedback encouraging: "there is a lot of marketing hype on this place… do not believe it". / SW1W 8BP; thecampaner.com; thecampanerchelsea; Tue-Thu 11.30 pm, Fri & Sat midnight, Sun 5 pm.

CANTO CORVINO E1 £83 233

21 ARTILLERY LANE
020 7655 0390 13–*2B*

This modern Italian bar/restaurant by Spitalfields is consistently well-rated in all feedback. There's a continued theme from last year, however, that even fans of its antipasti, pasta and grills from the Josper oven can find it plain "overpriced". / E1 7HA; www.cantocorvino.co.uk; cantocorvino; Mon-Sat 9 pm.

CANTON ARMS SW8 £62 334

177 SOUTH LAMBETH RD
020 7582 8710 11–*1D*

This "top-notch local boozer" in Stockwell offers arguably the "best pub food in South London" – "simple and hearty fare, but always served with verve and understanding" by on-the-ball service. Its slightly remoter address and a lack of theatres nearby means it is slightly less busy than its famous foodie stablemate, the Anchor & Hope in Waterloo. / SW8 1XP; www.cantonarms.com; Tue-Sat 9.45 pm, Sun 3.45 pm.

CAPEESH E14 £56 333

4 PAN PENINSULA SQUARE
020 7538 1111 12–*2C*

Dazzling views from the 48th-floor of a Canary Wharf tower help create a sense of occasion at this family-run, five-year-old Italian restaurant and 'Sky Bar'. Its long menu of pasta, pizza, grills and other fare doesn't inspire a huge volume of feedback, but the limited amount we have is all upbeat. / E14 9HN; www.capeesh.co.uk; capeeshlondon; Mon-Sun 10.30 pm.

CAPRI W4 £52 333

6 TURNHAM GREEN TERRACE
020 8994 3800 8–*2A*

"Lovely fresh seafood" and "excellent pasta dishes" – everything "brimming with flavour" – have won an enthusiastic welcome for this "new Italian run by a very experienced team" in Turnham Green. Founders Ben and Michael have worked together for more than 20 years, running an independent restaurant in Italy and in five-star hotels. / W4 1QP; caprirestaurant.uk; caprirestaurant.uk; Tue-Thu 10 pm, Fri & Sat 11 pm, Sun 9 pm.

CARACTÈRE W11 £139 333

209 WESTBOURNE PARK ROAD
020 8181 3850 7–*1B*

"Run by Michel Roux's daughter" Emily and her husband Diego Ferrari (former head chef of Le Gavroche), this Notting Hill five-year-old "gives us the best of two culinary worlds: French and Italian". The "precise, thoughtful and delicious dishes (celeriac, crab, turbot, veal)…" are "real high-end comfort food" and the "dining room is cool and buzzy without being overly formal". "Both wine list and cheeseboard are on the conservative side, but none the worse for that"; and "the Italian sommelier has an encyclopaedic knowledge of Italian wines and will always steer us to something new and unusual". Some reports note a "post-Covid blip amidst staff changes", and a slip in ratings generally backs up those who feel the experience is "not bad, and better than average, but not quite the quality it was previously". Top Tip – "lunch is particularly good value". / W11 1EA; www.caractererestaurant.com; caractererestaurant; Tue-Sat 9 pm.

CARAFFINI SW1 £73 243

61-63 LOWER SLOANE ST
020 7259 0235 6–*2D*

"Still as popular with its regular clientele as ever" – this "civilised old-favourite" near Sloane Square "doesn't change much", to the relief of its massive, silver-haired following ("you could do away with the menu, as all the customers know exactly what they will order before they arrive. It'll be the same as they've been ordering for the last 25 years!"). The traditional "comfort-Italian" food is "reliable", but it's the "extremely courteous service and wonderful greeting" that really carries the day. Top Menu Tip – "best calves' liver in London". / SW1W 8DH; www.caraffini.co.uk; caraffinirestaurant; Mon-Sat 10.30 pm.

CARAVAGGIO EC3 £66 232

107-112 LEADENHALL ST
020 7626 6206 10–*2D*

With its "classic menu" of "pricey but good-quality" food, this "friendly" Italian occupies a former banking hall in the heart of the City, where it entertains senior money men and women. Luciano Pavarotti, the late 'King of the High Cs', was a guest at its 1996 opening. / EC3A 4DP; www.caravaggiorestaurant.co.uk; caravaggio_ldn; Mon-Fri 10 pm.

CARAVAN £63 222

YALDING HOUSE, 152 GREAT PORTLAND STREET, W1 020 3963 8500 2–*1B*
30-35 DRURY LANE, WC2 AWAITING TEL 5–*1D*
1 GRANARY SQ, N1 020 7101 7661 9–*3C*
METAL BOX FACTORY, 30 GREAT GUILDFORD ST, SE1 020 7101 1190 10–*4B*
UNIT 2, REUTERS PLAZA, E14 020 3725 7600 12–*1C*
11-13 EXMOUTH MKT, EC1 020 7833 8115 10–*1A*
QUEEN VICTORIA STREET, EC4 020 3957 5555 10–*3C*

"The most original brunches" – with "a good selection of super-tasty, tapas-style dishes" fusing eclectic flavours from the Middle East to the Pacific – are the top feature of these "nicely vibey" haunts, which also boast "great coffee and pastries, plus interesting non-alcoholic drinks (like sodas and kombuchas)". And they serve "lots for vegans and veggies too". On the downside, they become "noisy"; staff can be "overstretched" and ratings are dragged down by those who find them "a convenient option, but, in truth, a slightly disappointing one". Expansion is still on the cards, though, with 2023 seeing a big new opening in Covent Garden, in a workspace on Drury Lane, complete with outside terrace. / www.caravanonexmouth.co.uk.

CARAVEL N1 £49 444

172 SHEPHERDESS WALK 020 7251 1155 14–*2A*

"So romantic!": "down a hidden waterway alley" near Angel, this debut venture from brothers Lorcan and Fin Spiteri – sons of John Spiteri (Quo Vadis, Sessions Arts Club) and Melanie Arnold (Rochelle Canteen) – is by all accounts "a little oasis of beauty". "Start the night with a cocktail on the jetty, then head down the stairs into a lovely converted barge with low-level lighting", where "very impressive Italian-leaning food is achieved in a tiny kitchen". / N1 7ED; thestudiokitchen.co.uk; caravel_restaurant; Thu-Sat, Wed 11 pm, Sun 4 pm.

CARLOTTA W1

77-78 MARYLEBONE HIGH STREET NO TEL 2–*1A*

"FUN FUN FUN!" – that's practically the only feedback we have so far on Big Mamma Group's fifth London opening, which threw open its doors in Marylebone in May 2023, just as our survey was concluding. Decked out in the maximalist style that characterises their approach – here it's a riff on a retro, Italian-glam theme with acres of ruched wall material, wood panelling, dark leather seating and loud carpeting. Cutting down on the calories? – don't go for the 10-tiered chocolate fudge cake… in fact, maybe avoid most of the Italian/American menu… / W1U 5JX; www.bigmammagroup.com; bigmamma.uk; Mon-Thu 9.30 pm, Fri & Sat 10, Sun 9 pm.

CARMEL NW6 £68 534

LONSDALE ROAD 020 3848 2090 1–*2B*

"Interesting Israeli/Middle Eastern dishes" served in a "fun, vibey setting" have created a big winner for the Berber & Q team at this Queen's Park two-year-old: a "great neighbourhood addition". "There are super veg options, but also fab meat and fish ones too". "The large shared table might not be for everyone" although there is also some more conventional seating (mostly for couples). Top Tip – the small terrace in summer is particularly "nice, as there are no cars outside". / NW6 6RR; www.carmelrestaurant.co.uk; carmelrestaurantldn; Tue-Sat 11 pm.

CAROUSEL W1 £72 442

19-23 CHARLOTTE STREET 020 7487 5564 2–*1C*

"Buy your ticket and wait and see… the chefs give their all and I've never had a disappointing evening!" – typical feedback on this Fitzrovia venue, whose "signature is a rotating selection of outstanding chefs cooking at the top of their game, for just a few weeks at a time" from the open kitchen. "It is a showroom (or perhaps a labour exchange!) for the rising stars of international dining… often the room is full of extra affection and praise as the chef's family or colleagues from past brigades offer enthusiastic support. The courses are skillful and generous, and stints reflect a wide range of global experience". "It's hard to compare the different chefs, but the standard generally is so high and service is very well done". / W1T 1RL; www.carousel-london.com; carousel_ldn; Tue-Sat midnight, Sun 6 pm.

THE CARPENTER'S ARMS W6 £62 333

91 BLACK LION LN 020 8741 8386 8–*2B*

A superior backstreet boozer in the cute enclave near Hammersmith's posh St Peter's Square – a "lovely spot" with a sweet garden serving a menu that's ambitious for pub cooking. / W6 9BG; www.carpentersarmsw6.co.uk; thecarpentersarmsw6; Mon-Sat 9 pm, Sun 6 pm.

CASA DO FRANGO £56 335

SIR SIMON MILTON SQUARE, SW1 NO TEL 2–*4B*
31-32 HEDDON STREET, W1 020 3535 5900 4–*3A*
32 SOUTHWARK STREET, SE1 020 3972 2323 10–*4C*
3 KING JOHN COURT, EC2 020 7654 3020 13–*1B*

"I would never have imagined chicken 'n' chips could be so delicious! It's like being on a mini holiday!" – the original, "über-busy" SE1 branch of this growing chain of "posh Nandos" is a smash hit. "The yummy food, the fabulous greenery, the buzzy atmosphere, the extensive vinho verde wine list. Who'd have thought such a gem would be found under a grubby railway arch in South London!" Expanding under owners MJMK (who also own Lisboeta and Kol), the group has a less-high-profile Shoreditch spin-off; and is also set to open in 2023 in Victoria, on the site last occupied by Hai Cenato (RIP). Top Tips – don't just stick to the peri-peri chicken – look out for the African rice, chorizo and other menu options. Also, at SE1 "there is a downstairs, but try to eat upstairs in the lovely loft-style space, with plenty of light and enough plants to require a full time gardener!" / www.casadofrango.co.uk; casadofrango_london.

CASA FOFÓ E8 £80 433

158 SANDRINGHAM ROAD 020 8062 2489 14–*1B*

"The depth of flavour which Adolfo brings out in his ever-changing menus means we visit at least once or sometimes twice a month: nowhere else would we ever dream of doing the same!" – Adolfo de Cecco's Hackney shop-conversion is "always a pleasure for its inventive dishes", which meld Asian influences with European ingredients into an intriguing and individual culinary mashup. At any one time, there is a single tasting option, and he "manages to maintain high standards with each iteration". "The front room is arguably more dull than the very light rear area, which is a sort of conservatory. And there are interesting choices of music at low levels". / E8 2HS; www.casafofolondon.co.uk; casafofolondon; Wed-Sun 9.30 pm.

CASA PASTÓR & PLAZA PASTÓR N1 £59 222

COAL DROPS YARD 020 7018 3335 9–*3C*

Within the arches of ever-so-hip Coal Drops Yard, this Hart Bros spin-off was one of the first tenants of the development. Surprisingly, given the trendy locale and regular queues, feedback in our annual diners' poll on its mix of tacos, tostadas and sharing plates is thin on the ground and rather lukewarm. / N1C 4AB; www.tacoselpastor.co.uk; tacos_el_pastor; Tue-Sat 11 pm, Sun 8 pm.

CASSE-CROUTE SE1 £69 434

109 BERMONDSEY ST 020 7407 2140 10–*4D*

"Visited with French friends. Their verdict: better than Paris! They loved it" – this "proper Gallic bistro" in Bermondsey is "very popular for good reasons", including "impeccable food" and a "delightful" atmosphere. It offers "a simple daily changing menu of three starters, three mains, and three desserts all done well, plus classic Gallic service". / SE1 3XB; www.cassecroute.co.uk; cassecroute109; Mon-Sat 10.30 pm, Sun 4.30 pm.

CAVITA W1 £85 323

55 WIGMORE STREET 020 3928 1000 3–*1B*

"Confidently spiced, really excellent Mexican dishes" washed down with "brilliant cocktails" have won high acclaim from aficionados of Latino cuisine for Adriana Cavita's lively itzrovia yearling, which – according to the T's Tim Hayward – "redefines the city's Iexican food scene". Not all our reporters re quite as sure though, a typical report eing: "pretty good, but it needed something nore to give it the wow factor". It doesn't elp that the menu can strike first-timers as incomprehensible"; and on some occasions aff can be "inarticulate" in explaining it. / V1U 1PU; www.cavitarestaurant.com; cavita. estaurante; Tue-Sun 10.15 pm.

:AY TRE £48 332

2-43 DEAN ST, W1 020 7317 9118 5–*2A*
01 OLD ST, EC1 020 7729 8662 13–*1B*

Thoughtful" Vietnamese food is served at fabulous prices for the generous portions" at nis duo in Soho and Hoxton from Hieu Trung ui, who has done much to popularise pho nd other southeast Asian dishes in London ver more than 20 years. That "plenty of sian people eat there too" speaks for its authentic" style. / www.caytrerestaurant.co.uk; aytrerestaurant.

:ECCONI'S £87 233

9-21 OLD COMPTON STREET, W1
20 7734 5656 5–*2A*
A BURLINGTON GDNS, W1
20 7434 1500 4–*4A*
8-60 REDCHURCH STREET, E2
20 3841 7755 13–*1C*
HE NED, 27 POULTRY, EC2
20 3828 2000 10–*2C*

it at the bar where there's "Prosecco on tap" nd hang with the Mayfair glam crowd at his "always buzzy" and "professional" Italian rasserie in Burlington Gardens, at the back f the Royal Academy: "a favourite for some ood people watching". Nowadays part of Soho Iouse, "there's something for everyone on the nenu" and it's a favoured lunch spot for local usiness types. On the downside, prices are igh, the food is "average" and service can be o-so. (Reports on its Soho 'Pizza Bar' spin-off nd City branches are few and far between). / ecconis.co.uk; cecconislondon.

:EDRIC GROLET AT THE 3ERKELEY SW1 £97 343

VILTON PLACE 020 7235 1200 6–*1D*

'arisian über-pâtissier Cedric Grolet's irst outpost outside Paris (which opened 1 early 2022) is to be found at this bright, hic bakery, within the swish Knightsbridge -star. Internationally he is renowned for his nsta-friendly, trompe l'oeil fruit and flowers - amongst London's fooderati he's famous for harging £135 per head for the chef-counter xperience. We have maintained its (fairly ood) rating on the basis of complimentary, f limited, feedback this year. But some other eviewers sound a warning note, including hat of Tanya Gold in the March 2023 Spectator who concluded: "It's too flimsy – too redulous, too fragile – to hate, and soon, like Dorothy [in The Wizard of Oz], it will blow way". / SW1X 8RL; www.the-berkeley.co.uk; edricgroletheberkeley; Mon-Sun 7 pm.

CENT ANNI SW19 £58 333

33 HIGH STREET 020 3971 9781 11–*2B*

"Standing out from the chain restaurants in the area, this vibrant Italian-inspired restaurant in the heart of Wimbledon Village" has a big fan club drawn from neighbouring postcodes. The more cautious view is that "it's nothing spectacular but the food standard is reliable with some good mid-week deals". / SW19 5BY; centanni.co.uk; centannirestaurant; Mon-Sat 11 pm, Sun 10.30 pm.

CEPAGES W2 £60 324

69 WESTBOURNE PARK ROAD
020 3602 8890 7–*1B*

"Great vibe", "wonderful cooking", "super wine list" and "so, so French!" – this "friendly and authentic" little wine bar/bistro in Westbourne Park celebrates its tenth anniversary this year. / W2 5QH; www.cepages.co.uk; cepages_london; Mon-Sat 11 pm, Sun 10 pm.

CERU £43 322

7-9 BUTE ST, SW7 020 3195 3001 6–*2C*
13 QUEENSWAY, W2 020 7221 2535 7–*2C*

"Ever-reliable, ultra-tasty sharing plates" and "brisk but jolly service" are the order of the day at "this buzzy South Ken local" (and its Queensway offshoot) from Barry & Patricia Hamilton. The "interesting" mix of Greek and Middle Eastern cuisines is backed up by a "very different wine list – Lebanese, Macedonian, Greek, Armenian". / www.cerurestaurants.com; ceruLondon.

CEVICHE SOHO W1 £60 323

17 FRITH ST 020 7292 2040 5–*2A*

This fresh Peruvian small-plates specialist is "still a lovely place for lunch in Soho", with "a range of interesting small plates to share". Some long-term fans feel it "doesn't quite reach the heady heights of yesteryear" (it opened in 2012) but that's maybe more to do with the capital's increasing familiarity with this style of cooking. / W1D 4RG; cevichelondon.com; cevicheuk; Mon-Sat 11.30 pm, Sun 10.30 pm.

CHAKRA W8 £59 333

33C HOLLAND STREET
020 7229 2115 6–*1A*

"Fragrant and tasty dishes" win approval at this cute Indian hidden away in a Kensington backstreet. Its siblings in Little Venice, Barnes and Kingston get very little notice from reporters. / W8 4LX; www.chakralondon.com; chakralondon; Tue-Thu 10 pm, Fri & Sat 10.30 pm, Sun 9 pm.

CHAMPOR-CHAMPOR SE1 £65 324

62 WESTON ST 020 7403 4600 10–*4C*

Unusual, eclectically decorated venue with an interesting Thai-Malay menu, in a sidestreet near Guy's Hospital and London Bridge station – it no longer attracts the attention it did a decade ago, but its ratings remain pretty solid. / SE1 3QJ; www.champor-champor.com; champorchamporldn; Mon-Sat 10 pm, Sun 9.30 pm.

CHARLIE'S AT BROWN'S, BROWN'S HOTEL W1 £118 455

ALBEMARLE STREET 020 7493 6020 3–*3C*

"The great Jesus Adorno and his team (aided by his no. 2 Paul Stabbins) have brought the charm and atmosphere of the hugely missed Le Caprice" to this "very smooth operation" within Rocco Forte's London flagship hotel, which fans say is "the new classiest place in town" (Adorno joined in 2021). It occupies a fine, panelled dining room that for traditionalists is "one of the loveliest in the capital", complete with "marvellous spacious tables". Since 2019, Adam Byatt (of Trinity, see also) has overseen the kitchen, which gives a modern spin to the preparation of top British ingredients: "wonderful" if not especially foodie. BREAKING NEWS: in early September 2023, it was announced that Jesus would be leaving Charlie's to re-join Jeremy King in founding a new restaurant back on the site of Le Caprice (but under a different name). These will be big shoes to fill here… / W1S 4BP; www.roccofortehotels.com; browns_hotel; Mon-Sun 10 pm.

CHATEAU W4 £52 342

213 CHISWICK HIGH ROAD
020 8742 2344 8–*2A*

"Cake shop by day, Lebanese by night" – this "very friendly and welcoming" spot on Chiswick High Road is an "excellent spot for lunch and a good dinner venue, too". "I've recently discovered their breakfasts – awesome!". / W4 2DW; chateau-chiswick.com; chateau_chiswick; Mon-Sun 10 pm.

THE CHEESE BARGE W2 £56 233

SHELDON SQUARE 07862 001418 7–*1C*

Mathew Carver's floating ode to the cheeses of Britain and Ireland is a 96 ft double-decker barge moored in Paddington Basin that delights turophiles with cheese-based meals accompanied by a "nice selection of wines at a reasonable price", with simpler cheese boards and toasties available in the afternoon. The group also operates a cheese conveyor belt in Seven Dials and a new cheese and natural wine bar, Funk, in Shoreditch. / W2 6HY; www.thecheesebar.com; thecheesebarldn; Tue-Sun 11 pm.

CHER THAI SW4 £47 343

22 NORTH STREET 020 3583 3702,ÄÄ 11–*1D*

The "warm welcome, good food and great prices all impress" at this "simple Thai restaurant" in Clapham, from a husband-and-wife team who are "trying to elevate it above the 'standard UK Thai' menu and doing

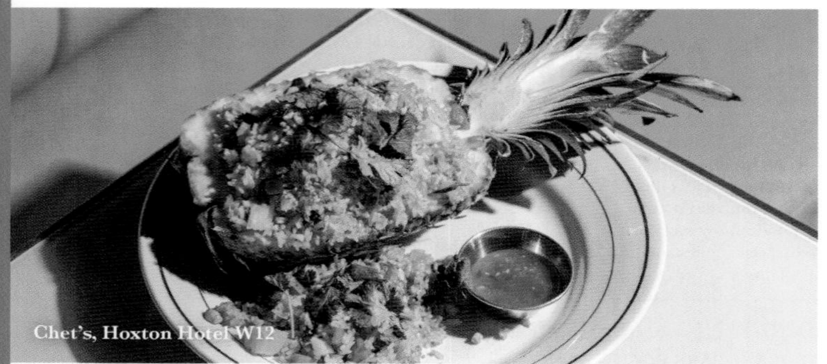
Chet's, Hoxton Hotel W12

a good job". The result: "a buzzing place with happy-looking customers". / SW4 0HB; www.cherthailondon.co.uk; cherthailondon; Tue, Thu, Wed 10.30 pm, Fri & Sat 11 pm, Sun 10 pm.

CHET'S, HOXTON HOTEL W12 £44 333

65 SHEPHERD'S BUSH GREEN
020 3540 3150 8–*1C*

"Part of the ongoing gentrification of Shepherd's Bush" – LA chef Kris Yenbamroong has found a permanent showcase for his US-style 'nu Thai' cuisine at the new Hoxton Hotel overlooking Shepherd's Bush Green. It's "surprisingly fun"… "lively, tasty, and fairly priced". The food is brash and impactful ("I had a delish bowl of fries, deep-fried chicken wings with hot sauce and tuna melt sandwich with a refreshing lychee lemonade"), while "large rounds of beer heading to most tables often contributes to the merriment". A few reporters do have quibbles – that the "sharing plate concept doesn't really work gastronomically"; or that the "LA influence is too horribly sweet, missing out on the salty and sour components of good Thai cooking". But even some critics feel it's "finding its feet: I've been back four times since December and the menu improves each visit". / W12 8QE; www.chetsrestaurant.co.uk; chets_ldn; Fri & Sat 1 am, Sun-Thu midnight.

CHEZ ANTOINETTE £47 332

THE CAXTON, 22 PALMER STREET, SW1
020 3990 5377 2–*4C*
UNIT 30 THE MARKET BUILDING, WC2
020 7240 9072 5–*3D*

This "bustling bistrot tucked down a side street near Victoria" feels "just like being in a small, rushed French café". Lyon-born founder Aurelia Noel-Delclos named the business after the grandmother who inspired her love of food. The 10-year-old original branch, in the tourist 'ground zero' of old Covent Garden market, is less reported-on, but said to be "decent" for "post-matinée early dinner".

CHEZ BRUCE SW17 £110 553

2 BELLEVUE RD 020 8672 0114 11–*2C*

"Long live Chez Bruce!". It has "a neighbourhood feel", but Bruce Poole's "jewel in south west London's crown" by Wandsworth Common is one of the capital's most revered restaurants and – for the 18th year running – is voted Londoner's No. 1 favourite in our annual diners' poll. Key to its appeal is the delivery of "top quality, but without the pretensions of some places". Chef Matt Christmas has worked with Bruce for over 10 years, and the kitchen produces modern British dishes that are "very memorable", but "without being fussy or fad-ish, nor horrendously overpriced". "Doing simple food this well is the ultimate in difficulty, there is just nowhere to hide!" "Professional and friendly service continues to excel", "seemingly effortlessly delivering a superb feeling of conviviality" and enlivening a space that's "classy and understated", but not intrinsically that special. "Bruce himself frequently still wanders around the dining room greeting and chatting informally to diners" and the whole operation practically "never puts a foot wrong". That all this can be enjoyed "without breaking the bank" seals the "absolute pleasure of eating there". / SW17 7EG; www.chezbruce.co.uk; chez.bruce; Tue-Thu 9.15 pm, Fri & Sat 9.30 pm, Sun 9 pm.

CHEZ ELLES E1 £61 333

45 BRICK LN 020 7247 9699 13–*2C*

"A simple menu with unexpectedly great food" is to be found at this 'bistroquet' on Brick Lane, which has flown the Tricolor in curry country for the past 11 years with a parade of Gallic classics including snails, frogs' legs and veal sweetbreads. / E1 6PU; www.chezellesbistroquet.co.uk; chezellesbistro; Tue-Sat 11.30 pm.

CHICAMA SW10 £91 333

383 KING'S ROAD 020 3874 2000 6–*3C*

"I keep coming back for all the ceviches" at this "excellent Peruvian seafood specialist" on the King's Road in Chelsea – an offshoot from Pachamama in Marylebone. The atmosphere is lively, too, although some reckon the music is just "too loud". / SW10 0LP; www.chicamalondon.com; Mon-Fri 11 pm, Sat & Sun 4 pm.

CHICK 'N' SOURS £43 43…

1 EARLHAM STREET, WC2
020 3198 4814 5–*2B*
390 KINGSLAND RD, E8
020 3620 8728 14–*2A*

"Full marks" say fans of the fried-chicken burgers, sarnies and other crispy poultry treats at these Haggerston and Covent Garden pit-stops. Order 48 hours in advance and you can enjoy the 'Whole Fry' – at £35 it's their 'iconic whole fried chicken' with two sides and the dressing of your choice… / www.chicknsours.co.uk; chicknsours.

THE CHILTERN FIREHOUSE W1 £113 22…

1 CHILTERN ST 020 7073 7676 2–*1A*

"It may not be quite as high on 'places to be seen' lists as it used to be", but – "having made a name for itself as a celebrity hotspot" – this beautiful-crowd haunt in Marylebone is provin[g] surprisingly enduring. "You're paying a pretty hefty premium for the trendy location": "the food/price ratio is off kilter, as the food really is not good and outrageously expensive". But does anyone care? For its many fans "you can't go wrong with the Firehouse – it always feels like a treat!" ("Our daughter was excited to spo[t] one of David Beckham's sons and his girlfriend so extra brownie points for me. LOL!") / W1U 7PA; www.chilternfirehouse.com; Mon-Sun 10 pm.

CHINA TANG, DORCHESTER HOTEL W1 £112 33…

53 PARK LN 020 7319 7088 3–*3A*

"Gorgeous" decor taking inspiration from 193[0s] Shanghai (particularly in the marvellous, small cocktail bar) has always won admiration for thi[s] deluxe basement (originally created by the late Sir David Tang). When it opened in 2005, it was a pioneer of serving dim sum at any time of day, but there's also a full menu offering blow-out dishes to share for £200-£300 including Peking duck with caviar, suckling pig, abalone and seafood hotpot. Complaints about pricing were absent this year, and praise for the cuisine and "romantic" atmosphere on the up. / W1K 1QA; www.chinatanglondon.co.uk; chinatanglondon; Mon-Sun 11 pm.

LA CHINGADA SE8 £16 33…

206 LOWER ROAD 020 7237 7448 12–*2B*

This "surprisingly good Mexican café in the back of nowhere" – well, deepest Surrey Quays – even imports soft drinks from Mexico for added authenticity. Top Menu Tip – "the prawn tacos are great – crispy, juicy and they come with a fiery salsa". / SE8 5DJ; lachingada.co.uk; lachingadalondon; Tue-Sat 10 pm, Sun 9pm

CHISHURU W1 £52

GREAT TITCHFIELD ST
7960 002150 3–1C

Adejoké 'Joké' Bakare moved in September 2023 to this new, 50-cover Fitzrovia location, having closed the SW9 site where she won the Brixton Kitchen competition in 2019 for her original supper club, offering the dishes of her Nigerian childhood but 'given a London sensibility'. Open-fire cooking will be a feature as well as an extended pastry selection. It has been very highly PR'd though, so let's hope it lives up to all the coverage – even in the former location there was the odd review along the lines of: "nice people, but disappointing after the hype". / W1W 8AX; www.chishuru.com; chishuru.

CHISOU £76 432

22-23 WOODSTOCK STREET, W1
020 7629 3931 4–1A
31 BEAUCHAMP PL, SW3
020 3155 0005 6–1D

The "absolute dogs for real Japanese dining" – this "authentic" duo in Mayfair (the original – "a welcome oasis from Oxford Street") and Knightsbridge (in posh Beauchamp Place) offer "exemplary sushi and cooked dishes" backed up by "a wide sake list". "As is always the case with this cuisine, it's never cheap, but great for a treat". / www.chisourestaurant.com; chisoulondon.

CHOOK CHOOK SW15 £46 434

137 LOWER RICHMOND ROAD
020 8789 3100 11–1B

This "great little local" in Putney "bills itself as an Indian railway kitchen and leans into the theme very nicely – the decor feels like an old-school carriage, and much of the menu is based on genuine street food, taken up a notch". It's certainly "not your standard curry house", and the "fresh, flavourful dishes are full of individual tastes". "It can be tricky to get a table if you don't book ahead, but once you're in, service is attentive". / SW15 1EZ; chookchook.uk; chookchooklondon_; Mon-Thu 10.30 pm, Fri & Sat 11 pm, Sun 10 pm.

CHOTTO MATTE £73 444

11-13 FRITH ST, W1 020 7042 7171 5–2A
26 PADDINGTON STREET, W1
020 7058 4444 2–1A

Kurt Zdesar's "loud and dark" haunts promise a culinary journey from Tokyo to Lima with some "brill cocktails" thrown in. It's "great fun" and the Nikkei food is an "interesting fusion" too, if also a pricey one. Since 2022, the London presence has doubled with the addition of a Marylebone branch to join the first Soho one. It also has six siblings in North America and a couple in the Middle East. / chotto-matte.com; chottomatteldn.

CHOURANGI W1 £66 443

3 OLD QUEBEC STREET
020 3582 2710 2–2A

"Craft cocktails and delicious upscale street food in a swank setting" is the proposition at this interesting Marble Arch two-year-old named after a historically important district of Calcutta (from chef-patron Anjan Chatterjee and airline entrepreneur Aditya Ghosh). "Finding good Bengali food from Calcutta has been a struggle, but not any more!" – this is "a taste of real Indian regional food crafted using exceptional ingredients which elevate the flavours of each dish". / W1H 7DL; chourangi.co.uk; chourangildn; Sun-Thu 10 pm, Fri & Sat 10.30 pm.

CHRISTOPHER'S WC2 £102 223

18 WELLINGTON ST 020 7240 4222 5–3D

This stunning Covent Garden mansion (once a high-class brothel) is named for the son of one of Thatcher's cabinet ministers, who launched it in its current guise as a grand American restaurant; and for about a decade it was the height of fashion. It retains a "great atmosphere" – and also, something of a following for business, brunch and its martini bar. But, given its location and dramatic interior, it attracts remarkably little feedback these days. / WC2E 7DD; www.christophersgrill.com; christopherswc2; Tue-Sat 10 pm, Sun 3.30 pm.

CHUCS £94 223

25 ECCLESTON STREET, SW1
020 3827 3000 2–4B
65 LOWER SLOANE STREET, SW1
020 3827 2999 6–2D
31 DOVER ST, W1 020 3763 2013 3–3C
97 OLD BROMPTON ROAD, SW7
020 8037 4525 6–2B

Inspired by La Dolce Vita lifestyle (indeed, there used to be an accompanying apparel resort-wear brand), this small Italian group strives to evoke the retro glamour of the 1960s 'jet set'. There's some enthusiasm for them amongst reporters, but a recognition that the food is "nice but not exceptional": "I had an excellent martini. But the dishes were either overly seasoned or (the salad) not dressed at all". / www.chucsrestaurants.com; chucsrestaurants.

CHUKU'S N15 £65 343

274 HIGH ROAD NO TEL 1–1D

"Billed as the first Nigerian tapas restaurant in London – this small but buzzy venue" in Seven Sisters "provides a modern spin on traditional Nigerian cuisine". The "friendly" siblings behind the project, Emeka and Ifeyinwa Frederick (motto 'chop, chat, chill'), attracted headlines in early 2023 when they were selected for an £8,000 grant by the BeyGood Foundation during the London leg of Beyoncé's world tour. / N15 5AJ; www.chukuslondon.co.uk; chukusldn; Tue-Sat 10.30 pm, Sun 8.30 pm.

CHUNGDAM W1

35-36 GREEK STREET
020 7287 0526 5–2A

On the Soho-fringe site of the much-lamented YMing (RIP), this April 2023 newcomer is a Korean BBQ bringing the pyeonbaek steam box to London – a three-tiered box made from hinoki wood, a type of cypress. It's named after Cheongdam-dong, an affluent – and foodie – district of Gangnam in Seoul. It opened too late to inspire survey feedback – reports please! / W1D 5DL; chungdam.co.uk; chungdam.london; Mon-Sat midnight.

CHURCH ROAD SW13 £74 342

94 CHURCH ROAD 020 8748 0393 11–1A

Fans of Rebecca Mascarenhas's Barnes fixture (which some may still recall as Sonny's, long RIP) say it "deserves higher recognition and praise", benefitting as it does from "the Phil Howard magic" (the co-owner, who lives nearby) in delivering "excellent" food (for example, "a perfect lobster and chips lunch") and a "thoughtfully compiled wine list". But what is a "sophisticated setting" for many supporters can also appear to "lack atmosphere". / SW13 0DQ; www.churchroadsw13.co.uk; churchroadsw13; Wed, Sat 10 pm, Thu & Fri 10.30 pm, Sun 3 pm.

CHURCHILL ARMS W8 £47 324

119 KENSINGTON CHURCH ST
020 7792 1246 7–2B

"Still a first choice for a fun, good-value Thai meal" – the "freshly cooked" scoff in the "bonkers" flower-filled dining conservatory of this quirky 1750 tavern, near Notting Hill Gate, still makes it a top destination for the budget conscious. Popularity comes at a price, though – "booking is essential after 6pm". Top Tip – the pub itself is worth a visit too – it was renamed in the statesman's honour, and his grandparents visited in the Victorian era. / W8 7LN; www.churchillarmskensington.co.uk; churchillarmsw8; Mon-Sat 9.30 pm, Sun 9 pm.

CHUTNEY MARY SW1 £91 444

73 ST JAMES'S STREET
020 7629 6688 3–4D

"Always a good experience" – this "upmarket Indian" in St James's is the original venture of Ranjit & Namita Mathrani, plus the latter's sister, Camellia Panjabi (who run other top Indians and the Masala Zone chain). One of London's first 'nouvelle Indians' (when it opened, on its former site, in SW10), its "complex and well-balanced" dishes are "done well enough to let them off the high prices" and served in a great space, whose "wonderful décor gives it character". Rishi's a regular apparently. / SW1A 1PH; www.chutneymary.com; chutneymary.london; Mon-Sat 10 pm, Sun 9.15 pm.

CHUTNEYS NW1 £25 332

124 DRUMMOND ST 020 7388 0604 9–4C

"A stalwart on London's cheap-eats itinerary for decades" – this canteen in the 'Little India' enclave behind Euston station "has moved a smidgen upmarket since the pandemic". Top Tip – the "lovely fixed-price vegetarian buffet" – a "longstanding favourite" – remains in place at lunchtime. / NW1 2PA; www.chutneyseuston.uk; chutneysnw1; Mon-Sat 11 pm, Sun 10 pm.

CIAO BELLA WC1 £54 345

86-90 LAMB'S CONDUIT ST
020 7242 4119 2–1D

"You could be in Italy" at this "authentic" old-school trattoria that has provided four decades of its "great atmosphere" in Bloomsbury – "it's like being at home but with no washing up". "Everyone looks like they are enjoying themselves" – as Boris Johnson did in his days as Mayor of London, when he shared chips and house red here with his squeeze-du-jour, Jennifer Arcuri. / WC1N 3LZ; www.ciaobellarestaurant.co.uk; ciaobella_london; Mon-Sat 10.45 pm, Sun 10.30 pm.

CIBO W14 £81 444

3 RUSSELL GDNS 020 7371 6271 8–1D

This tasteful backstreet 1980s Italian, with interesting art on the walls, sits in the no-man's-land between Kensington and Olympia; and has become less well-known since the death of Michael Winner ten years ago (who used to plug it remorselessly in The Sunday Times as his favourite restaurant). Its quiet virtues as a high quality and authentic venture have changed little over the years: "still love this venue, but best to go in the week when the kitchen isn't too busy". Top Menu Tip – go for fish and seafood here. / W14 8EZ; www.ciborestaurant.net; Mon-Sat 9.45 pm.

CIGALON WC2 £62 344

115 CHANCERY LANE
020 7242 8373 2–2D

A glass-ceilinged former auction house in Chancery Lane is home to this homage to Provençal cuisine from Pascal Aussignac's Club Gascon group – making it an "excellent place for a business lunch in an otherwise under-served area". Plus points include an interesting list of southern French and Corsican wines, and the downstairs cocktail bar Baranis. Top Tip – "ask for a booth to celebrate a special occasion". / WC2A 1PP; www.cigalon.co.uk; cigalon_london; Tue-Fri 9 pm.

CILANTRO PUTNEY SW15 £70 442

244 UPPER RICHMOND ROAD 02033439317 11–2B

'Fresh, Tasty, Healthy' is the mantra at this November 2022 newcomer on the site of Ma Goa (RIP), which aims for a "modern" variant of Indian cuisine. The first UK outpost of a family-owned group with restaurants in India itself – its "above average" standards make it a worthy successor to its long-established predecessor. / SW15 6TG; www.cilantro.london; cilantro_london; Tue-Sat 10.30 pm, Sun 9 pm.

CINDER £87 332

66 BELSIZE LANE, NW3
020 7435 8048 9–2A
5 ST JOHN'S WOOD HIGH STREET, NW8
0207 4358 048 9–3A

This "superb, cosy local" in Belsize Park now also has an offshoot that's proving "a great addition to St John's Wood". The focus is on "interesting food cooked with fire" from chef-owner Jake Finn (ex-LPM and The Ritz), who takes inspiration from Mediterranean, Peru and Japan: "a sharing concept from a menu that's not huge but with good variety and lots of veggie options". Both sites provide "wonderful combinations, simply done", with meat, fish and veggies that are "both charred and succulent". "It's not inexpensive, but great value given the quality of ingredients and cleverness of the cuisine". Top Menu Tip – "whole sea bream, fennel, radish and fresh herbs is a standout".

CINNAMON BAZAAR WC2 £64 543

28 MAIDEN LANE 020 7395 1400 5–4D

"From the pricing, you'd be forgiven for expecting a 'standard' Indian restaurant", but Vivek Singh's popular café is "surprisingly good" to those who've not yet discovered it and delivers outstanding value for somewhere in Covent Garden. "The menu is anything but run-of-the-mill, with interesting and creative twists on classics and some wholly new creations". The worst gripe this year? It can get "too noisy when it's packed". / WC2E 7NA; www.cinnamon-bazaar.com; thecinnamoncollection; Mon-Sat 11 pm, Sun 10 pm.

THE CINNAMON CLUB SW1 £82 445

OLD WESTMINSTER LIBRARY, GREAT SMITH ST 020 7222 2555 2–4C

"Fantastic food in a fabulous building – what more could you ask for?" So say fans of Vivek Singh's "impressive" HQ "in the beautiful setting of Westminster's former public library", which remains the most-mentioned non-European restaurant in our annual diners' poll. The "progressive" cuisine is "perfectly spiced and brings together the best of Indian and European cooking" with "exquisite" results. The "lovely light, spacious and glamorous" setting "lends real class to the occasion", but "it isn't stuffy, and staff are very welcoming". "It's just a shame so many politicians eat here too!" Top Tip – "the lunch menu offers exceptional value for money". / SW1P 3BU; www.cinnamonclub.com; thecinnamoncollection; Mon-Sat 11 pm. SRA – 2 stars

CINNAMON KITCHEN £60 433

4 ARCHES LANE, SW11
020 3955 5480 11–1C
9 DEVONSHIRE SQ, EC2
020 7626 5000 10–2D

"Attractive Indians with a good range of different dishes" – Vivek Singh's dynamic duo of affordable spin-offs from his celebrated Cinnamon Club inspire practically nothing but high praise. The long-established City outlet set inside a rather 1980s atrium development is "a solid option around Liverpool Street" (although at times "the cavernous interior can feel a bit odd and echoey"); the newer Battersea branch occupies a railway arch near the power station and feels "different" (in a good way). / www.cinnamon-kitchen.com; cinnamonrestaurants. SRA – 2 stars

CINQUECENTO £51 333

6 GREEK ST, W1 020 7287 7705 5–2A
1 CALE STREET, SW3 020 7351 9331 6–2C
115 NOTTING HILL GATE, W11
020 7792 8881 7–2B
233 PORTOBELLO ROAD, W11
020 3915 3797 7–1A
73 HAVERSTOCK HILL, NW3
020 7483 0113 9–2A

"Top pizza by the boys from Napoli!" – Carmelo Meli and Emanuele Tagliarina's "small" venues offer "great pizzas" (it's down to the San Marzano tomatoes and EVO oil apparently) and "a good atmosphere". The original in SW3 is the highest rated, and W11 also wins numerous favourable reports. Also now in Hampstead (since 2022) and – new in mid-2023 – Soho. / cinquecentopizzeria.com; cinquecentopizzeria.

CIRCOLO POPOLARE W1 £64 345

40-41 RATHBONE SQUARE NO TEL 5–1A

"Massive, Instagram-tastic and buzzy" – Paris-based Big Mamma Group's Sicilian trattoria in Fitzrovia is "great for a night out with the kids". "If only as much thought had been put into the food as the decor!" – although to be fair, the simple and generous Italian dishes are served at a quality and price that most find very acceptable. / W1T 1HX; www.bigmammagroup.com; bigmamma.uk; Mon-Sat 10.30 pm, Sun 10 pm.

CITRO N6 £62 442

15A SWAIN'S LANE 07840 917586 9–1B

This "authentic Italian" in Highgate "with an ever-changing seasonal menu" is "run by two brothers", Nunzio & Salvatore, who ensure that everything is "freshly made by hand" – ranging from pasta and pizza to "Dad's home-made cannolis" and "interesting small plates such as chickpea fritters with lemon mayonnaise or grilled lamb skewers with salsa Siciliana". The "attentive and welcoming service" makes it ideal for "casual lunch, family dinner or romantic meal". / N6 6QX; www.eatcitro.com; citro_restaurant; Tue-Sat 10 pm.

CITY BARGE W4 £61 2 2 3

27 STRAND-ON-THE-GREEN
020 8994 2148 1–3A

"I can forgive any failings for the riverside location", say fans of this pub at Strand-on-the-Green, "on the Thames near Chiswick" – a "great local" with "reliable food… nothing challenging". / W4 3PH; www.citybargechiswick.com; citybargew4; Mon-Fri 11 pm.

CITY SOCIAL EC2 £122 3 3 4

TOWER 42 25 OLD BROAD ST
020 7877 7703 10–2C

'Beautiful views from the old NatWest Tower" help seal the deal at Jason Atherton's City outpost. "It feels quite corporate but is a good place for business", and wins many recommendations from expense-accounters as their top venue for wining and dining. "The food is always very good with a good seasonal choice on the menu. Staff are well trained and happy to spend time chatting to guests even when they're busy. The setting is unique overlooking the Square Mile and the ambience is special". / EC2N 1HQ; www.citysociallondon.com; citysocial_t42; Tue-Sat 9.30 pm.

THE CLARENCE TAVERN N16 £66 3 3 3

102 STOKE NEWINGTON CHURCH STREET
020 8712 1188 1–1C

This Grade II listed Stokey boozer was taken under the wing of the gastropub magicians behind the Anchor & Hope and Canton Arms three years ago, and now boasts a "delicious seasonal menu" and "very good Sunday lunch". The move has been such a success that the Clarence team now has a West End outpost – at no less an address than Soho's historic Kettner's (see also). Top Menu Tip – "the pies for two: I'm still dreaming about the chicken and leek". / N16 0LA; www.clarencetavern.com; theclarencetavern; Tue-Sat 11 pm, Sun 6 pm.

CLARETTE W1 £100 2 3 3

44 BLANDFORD ST 020 3019 7750 3–1A

"The wine list is pricey, even by Marylebone High Street standards" at this Tudorbethan pub, with leaded windows and inset stained glass. That's to be expected, as it's backed by Alexandra Petit-Mentzelopoulos – part of the family who own the legendary Château Margaux – and you really have to be a lover of wine (some famous names are available by the glass using the Coravin system) to get the most out of the place, which has extensive listings – amongst other areas – of bottlings from Bordeaux and Burgundy: for example, there is a 'Château Margaux Experience': a 'degustation' of 50ml glass of 4 vintages for £95. Viewed purely as a place to get fed? "We liked it, the food is lovely, but there are options offering better value". / W1U 7HS; www.clarettelondon.com; clarettelondon; Tue-Sat 11 pm.

CLARIDGE'S FOYER & READING ROOM W1 £118 3 4 4

49 BROOK STREET 020 7107 8886 3–2B

"Endless sandwich and tea refills and no clock ticking in the background (unlike at some other London five-star establishments)" make this "comfortably opulent" foyer "a wonderful place to enjoy an immensely satisfying afternoon tea, which will obviate any need for dinner later". Fans also say there's "nowhere better for breakfast" either: "a marvellous tranquil setting with immaculate service" and "highly recommended". / W1K 4HW; www.claridges.co.uk; claridgeshotel; Mon-Sun 11 pm.

CLARIDGE'S RESTAURANT, CLARIDGE'S HOTEL W1

49 BROOK ST 020 7107 8886 3–2B

Plus ça change! After 20 years of mucking about with megastar chefs, like Gordon Ramsay, Simon Rogan and Daniel Humm – this landmark Mayfair hotel's glorious Art Deco dining room is finally going back to sailing under its 'own brand' flag: returning to an updated version of the format it abandoned two decades ago. Coalin Finn is to be at the stoves, and the food will be a bit fancier than when the space was something of an undiscovered traditional gem. Few five stars in the late '90s were serving barbequed radish skewers braised in homemade teriyaki, laced with horseradish; but grilled native lobster with crushed Jersey royals and sauce Américaine… that sounds more like it. / W1K 4HW.

CLARKE'S W8 £115 4 5 3

124 KENSINGTON CHURCH STREET
020 7221 9225 7–2B

"Terrific ingredients, cleverly but unfussily combined" has long been the hallmark of Sally Clarke's "impeccably run restaurant" in Notting Hill, which has been at the cutting edge of promoting seasonal, Californian-inspired cuisine since 1984. "It's on the pricey side, but quality remains superb"; the setting is "romantic"; and the service, from a loyal and seemingly well-looked-after contingent of staff is "excellent, all overseen by Sally herself". The "marvellous" wine list has an "unusual emphasis on North American wines" and some "reasonably priced alternatives to famous names". Top Tip – "the good-value daily lunch set menu is a fantastic way to try this restaurant out". / W8 4BH; www.sallyclarke.com; sallyclarkeltd and sallyclarkefood; Tue-Sat 10 pm.

CLIPSTONE W1 £86 3 3 2

5 CLIPSTONE STREET
020 7637 0871 2–1B

"An upmarket but wonderfully understated local without pretensions" that's "just 10 minutes' walk from Oxford Circus". Will Lander and Daniel Morgenthau's well-regarded – if "fairly cramped and noisy" – Fitzrovia corner site wins continues to win support with its "very competent, modern British cooking", "varied international wine list, with many options by the glass", and "staff who are friendly and passionate about what they serve". Is it the cost of living crisis though? – "rather small portions" is a repeat complaint this year. Top Tip – "great value lunch with an (always) interesting menu". / W1W 6BB; www.clipstonerestaurant.co.uk; clipstonerestaurant; Tue-Sat 9.45 pm, Sun 8.45.

CLOS MAGGIORE WC2 £98 3 4 5

33 KING ST 020 7379 9696 5–3C

"On more than one occasion we have observed someone 'popping the question' here!" – the "magical" setting "never fails to impress" at this Covent Garden oasis, yet again voted London's No.1 venue for romance in our annual diners' poll. "Sitting in the conservatory is a joy, especially in good weather when the retractable roof is open" and its "most beautiful interior courtyard is tailormade for a date". "The largely Provençal and Tuscan cuisine is good but the star of this show is the magnificent wine list, with choices from around the world and prices to suit all budgets. The only recommendation is to read the wine list at home in advance, otherwise you'll spend the first hour ignoring your date!". / WC2E 8JD; www.closmaggiore.com; clos_maggiore; Mon-Sat 10.30 pm, Sun 10 pm.

THE CLOVE CLUB EC1 £220 3 3 2

SHOREDITCH TOWN HALL, 380 OLD ST
020 7729 6496 13–1B

The UK's leading position on World's 50 best has helped underpin the longevity of this mould-breaking icon, which opened 10 years ago to phenomenal acclaim in the incongruous hipster surroundings of Shoreditch Town Hall. Fans "love the vibe of the room"; and say Isaac McHale's "awesome and imaginative" cuisine "just gets better and better". Even they, though, can concede that with the tasting menu now costing £195 per person it is "getting a little expensive now". And then there is a minority for whom it's not only "overpriced" but "vastly overrated and living off the PR" ("I adore fine dining and was fully prepared to spend on a fantastic meal. But the food, while technically fine, felt over-thought and overly fussy, with scant imagination or soul"). / EC1V 9LT; www.thecloveclub.com; thecloveclub; Tue-Sat 11 pm.

CLUB GASCON EC1 £167 4 3 3

57 WEST SMITHFIELD
020 7600 6144 10–2B

"Reliably inventive Michelin-quality tasting menus with quirky-but-good wine pairings" continue to inspire joy at Pascal Aussignac and Vincent Labeyrie's long-standing foodie temple to the cuisine of southwest France, which occupies a stately former Lyons Tea House near Smithfield Market. It partly achieved its renown originally by serving everything with foie gras, but nowadays a "superb vegetarian tasting menu" is also a feature. / EC1A 9DS; www.clubgascon.com; clubgascon; Tue-Sat 9.30 pm.

THE COACH EC1 £70 333

26-28 RAY STREET 020 3954 1595 10–*1A*

"Very decent" French-influenced food helps elevate this fine old Clerkenwell pub restaurant into being a "good all-rounder", as does its attractive, glazed dining area. That said, it doesn't attract the attention it did a few years ago when Henry Harris was at the stoves. / EC1R 3DJ; www.thecoachclerkenwell.co.uk; thecoachlondon; Mon-Sat 11 pm, Sun 4 pm.

COAL OFFICE N1 £78 444

2 BAGLEY WALK 020 3848 6085 9–*3C*

"Loud… buzzy… delicious" – this "original, exciting and cool" venue designed by the neighbouring Tom Dixon studio, by Granary Square, "is a full-on, in-your-face Tel Aviv sort of place". The "superb Israeli small plates, which you are invited to share" are overseen by executive chef, Assaf Granit: "very flavoursome food with some unusual combinations". "Tables are very close" inside, which is "noisy", with "drum and bass in the background" and lots of chatter; "so, it's best to go for lunch on a sunny day on the terrace and take in the views over the renovated King's Cross area". Top Menu Tips – "their signature polenta starter remains strong… a must. Octopus is amazing, tender and tasty. Desserts are also a high point… as is the powerful coffee!" / N1C 4PQ; coaloffice.com; coaloffice; Mon-Wed, Sat & Sun, Thu & Fri 11 pm.

COAL ROOMS SE15 £75 332

11A STATION WAY 020 7635 6699 1–*4D*

This "interesting" conversion of the Victorian booking hall and goods rooms at Peckham Rye station accommodates a café/restaurant whose modern menu is "thoughtful without being too crazy". The day-time brunch offering gets a thumbs-up, too, as "many steps ahead of the typical avo on toast". (A back-handed compliment from north of the river: "As an ex-north Londoner, I was amazed to find this in central Peckham. How things have changed!") / SE15 4RX; www.coalroomspeckham.com; coalrooms; Wed-Sat 11 pm, Sun 6 pm.

THE COAL SHED SE1 £84 322

ONE TOWER BRIDGE
020 3384 7272 10–*4D*

With its "straightforward" offering including "very good fish and lamb" and its "welcome service", this offshoot of a Brighton steakhouse is "a top option in the locality of The Bridge Theatre", near City Hall – "it just works". / SE1 2SE; www.coalshed-restaurant.co.uk; thecoalshed; Tue-Sat 11 pm, Sun 6 pm.

COCORO W1 £38 432

31 MARYLEBONE LANE
020 7935 2931 3–*1A*

They look modest, but "great value Japanese food" (for example, "delightful sushi" and "very fresh salmon and tuna") of "consistently high quality" is served by "lovely people" at this well-established Marylebone restaurant and its more deli-style offshoots in Highgate, Bloomsbury and Bayswater. / W1U 2NH; cocororestaurant.co.uk; cocorolondon; Mon-Sun 10.30 pm.

COCOTTE £58 332

271 NEW KING'S ROAD, SW6
020 7610 9544 11–*1B*
11 HARRINGTON ROAD, SW7
020 7589 1051 6–*2C*
95 WESTBOURNE GROVE, W2
020 3220 0076 7–*1B*
8 HOXTON SQUARE, N1
020 7033 4277 13–*1B*
79 SALUSBURY ROAD, NW6
020 7625 6606 1–*2B*

"Chicken with amazing sides" is the winning formula at Romain Bourrillon's rotisserie chain, which imports its chooks from France. "Nice brunch", too. / www.mycocotte.uk.

COLBERT SW1 £84 223

51 SLOANE SQ 020 7730 2804 6–*2D*

"Always a good place to meet people" – this Wolseley Group operation on a corner of Sloane Square feels like "a slice of Paris in London" and its supremely "convenient location" means it "can get very busy". Somehow standards have never quite gelled here as well as at the group's better-known sites: the "predictable, ersatz French brasserie fare" is merely "fine"; the service can be "quite patchy"; and the "buzzy atmosphere" can tip into bland anonymity. Harsh criticisms were absent this year, though, and seemingly there's "been no perceptible drop in quality since C&K's departure". / SW1W 8AX; colbertrestaurant.com; colbertchelsea; Mon-Sat 10.30 pm, Sun 10 pm.

THE COLLINS ROOM, THE BERKELEY HOTEL SW1 £131 334

WILTON PLACE 020 7107 8866 6–*1D*

Hermès, Loewe and Zimmermann help inspire the Spring/Summer 2023 Prêt-à-Portea collection on the 'cakewalk' of this Belgravia chamber, which takes annual inspiration for its wizard patisserie selection from the catwalk of the fashion industry. If you have money to burn, it's an impressively skillful and witty twist on the afternoon tea experience – tuck into "Hermès' tasselled bucket bag, crafted out of Victoria sponge sandwiched with apricot jam, wrapped in chocolate and finished with a chocolate feather plume!" / SW1X 7RL; www.the-berkeley.co.uk; the_berkeley; Mon-Sun 10.30 pm.

LE COLOMBIER SW3 £95 244

145 DOVEHOUSE STREET
020 7351 1155 6–*2C*

"My refuge when feeling homesick for France" – Didier Garnier's "long standing favourite" in a quiet Chelsea backstreet is "a typical French restaurant of the kind that you might find in the Dordogne". "It can get very crowded and there's not much privacy between the tables. But it has a very loyal following" particularly amongst a well-heeled, silver-haired crowd, for whom it's a "go-to" destination thanks to its "traditional, buzzy atmosphere", "dependable French-bistro cuisine" and a "wine list which has some great bargains" ("not your usual SW3 mark up – try the wines priced £30-£60, top value"). Didier himself presides over the "discreet and effortless service" and provides "excellent professional advice on the choice of vintage". The odd naysayer finds it all "shockingly old-fashioned"… but folks have been saying that for years. / SW3 6LB; www.lecolombier,restaurant; Tue-Sat 10.30 pm.

COLONEL SAAB WC1 £69 434

HOLBORN HALL, 193-197 HIGH HOLBORN
020 3004 0004 5–*1D*

"Great food, attentive service, and an overall lovely experience" are winning a small but very enthusiastic fan club for this quirky, late 2021 Indian two-year-old. Despite the interest of a historic building – Holborn's former Town Hall – it inhabits something of a restaurant graveyard site, which has seen off numerous previous occupants (Shanghai Blues, Gezellig, Burger & Lobster). And, shortly after opening, it too was written off as a 'Curry Catastrophe' by the Evening Standard's David Ellis. So kudos to owner Roop Partap Choudhary for persevering with his very personal vision for the enterprise. / WC1V 7BD; www.colonelsaab.co.uk; colonelsaab; Mon-Sat 10 pm.

COLONY GRILL ROOM, THE BEAUMONT W1 £101 334

8 BALDERTON STREET, BROWN HART GARDENS 020 7499 9499 3–*2A*

With its colourful murals, dark-wood features and plush leather seating, the "lovely" dining room of this Art Deco hotel near Selfridges faithfully recreates a rather Manhattan-esque style. The menu is likewise praised by some reporters for its "superb American fare" (although its mix of grills with caviar, oysters and more generic locally sourced dishes – such as Dover sole – equally fit the image of typical British clubland venues). No longer run by Corbin & King as once it was, it is "still consistent but now quite expensive". / W1K 6TF; www.colonygrillroom.com; thecolonygrillroom; Mon-Wed 9.30 pm, Thu-Sat 10 pm, Sun 3 pm.

:OMPTON EC1 £83 342

7-48 ST JOHNS SQUARE
20 4548 6939 10–*1A*

Somewhere to go that isn't fine dining but ; above the ordinary" – this Clerkenwell ıte became well-known under chef Anna Iansen as The Modern Pantry (RIP), and vas relaunched (under new ownership) as this ll-day restaurant and deli in 2022. It does do runch, but that's no longer the top feature : was in its former guise. The menu includes ome "retro" dishes such as prawn cocktail 'mains of Holstein chicken and mushroom agu were excellent") and has a something-for-verybody quality to it. What's more, "service ; a notch above the usual" helping to create a relaxed feel to the place". (In his November 2022 review, The Telegraph's William Sitwell noted the venue's "polite" qualities and thought t a place to "take my favourite aunt".) / EC1V JJ; www.compton.restaurant; compton.restaurant; Tue-Fri 11 pm, Mon 5 pm.

THE CONNAUGHT GRILL W1 £161

:ARLOS PLACE 020 7107 8852 3–*3B*

That there's too few reports in our annual diners' poll for a rating on this Mayfair chamber is remarkable given the lofty heritage of its famous name (for many decades applied to the room that's nowadays Hélène Darroze, upstairs). After a hiatus of many years, this new space opened in 2020 and has never inspired much press reviewer attention – perhaps due to its 'citizens of nowhere' contemporary styling and modern JG Vongerichten-curated menu. Still, such feedback as we do receive on results from the luxurious rotisserie and wood-burning grill is all good. / W1K 2AL; www.the-connaught.co.uk; theconnaught; Wed-Sat 10.15 pm, Sun 4.30 pm.

CONTIGO WC2

1-3 GRAND BUILDING, STRAND NO TEL 2–*3C*

Despite tons of money thrown at its numerous incarnations, the site of the former Strand Dining Rooms, just off Trafalgar Square, has never really cut through in recent years. Maybe this new Nikkei (Japanese/Peruvian) operation – a 'Coming Soon' as we go to press – will break the mould, which will feature a sushi counter and bar named Lima; a main open kitchen called Osaka; and an outdoor terrace. / WC2N 5HR; www.eatcontigo.co.uk; Tue-Sun 10 pm.

COPPA CLUB £64 224

29 BREWHOUSE LANE, SW15
020 3937 5354 11–*2B*
THREE QUAYS WALK, LOWER THAMES STREET, EC3 020 7993 3827 10–*3D*

"Sat in an outdoor pod with the family, drinking mimosas and with lovely views of the river" is a key feature of London's two outposts of these comfy venues (part of a national chain), both of which have riverside terraces featuring all-weather igloos for year-round fun. The Italian-ish food in the dining rooms is "unexceptional", but "their lounge areas are cosy and just the place for morning coffee or afternoon tea". / www.coppaclub.co.uk; coppaclub.

Cinnamon Bazaar WC2

COPPER & INK SE3 £74 333

5 LEE ROAD 020 3941 9337 1–*4D*

"A jewel in Blackheath's crown" – extravagantly moustachioed (and inked) chef Tony Rodd's "stunning monthly changing menu, using seasonal and mostly local ingredients, is worthy of a central London establishment". Partner Becky Cummings runs the FOH at this distinctive and distinguished neighbourhood spot. / SE3 9RQ; www.copperandink.com; copperandink; Wed-Sat 11.30 pm.

COPPER CHIMNEY W12 £54 333

SOUTHERN TERRACE, WESTFIELD LONDON, ARIEL WAY 020 8059 4439 1–*3B*

Near the main entrance to Westfield, this Indian venue will celebrate its fifth year in 2024, but is easily lost amongst the glossy anonymity of the surrounding units. It's the London outpost of a 45-year-old chain that's 15-strong in India itself. Although it doesn't inspire a huge volume of feedback, reports are consistently upbeat: "good value, freshly cooked dishes, lovely ambience". / W12 7GA; www.copperchimney.uk; copperchimney_uk; Sun-Thu 9.30 pm, Fri & Sat 10.30 pm.

COQ D'ARGENT EC2 £99 222

1 POULTRY 020 7395 5000 10–*2C*

"Signs of returning normality with a full Coq!". This "purring" D&D London operation sits on the top floor of No 1 Poultry – with leafy roof terraces in sight of the Bank of England – and is a well-established linchpin of the Square Mile lunching scene. For foodies, it can seem a disappointing experience, but for those packing corporate plastic it's valued as a "great location in the heart of the City for a pricey-but-decent business lunch serving upmarket staples with a French twist". Top Tip – "good for breakfast in the summer on the outside terrace". / EC2R 8EJ; www.coqdargent.co.uk; coqdargent; Mon-Sat midnight. SRA – accredited

COQFIGHTER W1 £37 322

75 BEAK STREET 020 7734 4001 4–*2C*

The "divine chicken" at these funky East-meets-West outlets – founded by three mates who missed the Korean fried chicken they ate in Melbourne's Chinatown – is "worth the pain of the uncomfortable seating and queue". The business has graduated from home cooking and pub pop-ups to five permanent sites with a Soho flagship and a thriving delivery arm. / W1F 9SS; www.coqfighter.com; coqfighteruk; Mon-Sun 11 pm.

CORA PEARL WC2 £86 344

30 HENRIETTA STREET
020 7324 7722 5–*3C*

With its "good short menu" of "delicious" (if sometimes "very rich") dishes; "very friendly service and great atmosphere", this is a "cosy, charming little restaurant in Covent Garden". It's a sibling to Kitty Fisher's in Shepherd Market, Mayfair – both named after historical local ladies of the night – and ideal for a "relaxed" occasion. / WC2E 8NA; www.corapearl.co.uk; corapearlcg; Mon-Sat 9.30 pm, Sun 3.30 pm.

CORD EC4 £89 434

85 FLEET STREET 020 3143 6365 10–*2A*

"Doing a grand job of showcasing the school" – "seemingly simple small dishes done with exemplary refinement" ("perfect pork belly and a delicate citrus tart slice") impress diners at this year-old restaurant, where you can sample the work of the august Le Cordon Bleu culinary institute (founded in Paris in 1895). Set in an "well-spaced, light-filled" dining room in Fleet Street's Grade II listed former Reuters building (designed by Lutyens), it also has a "clean lined and attractive" adjoining daytime café worth visiting for its "accurately toasted" sandwiches and cakes. / EC4Y 1AE; www.cordrestaurant.co.uk; cordrestaurant; Mon-Fri 10 pm.

CORE BY CLARE SMYTH W11 £231 554

92 KENSINGTON PARK RD
020 3937 5086 7–2B

"World-class cooking from the best female chef in the country" inspires nothing but reams of rapturous reports on Clare Smyth's "seemingly effortless and very special" Notting Hill HQ – again the No. 1 gastronomic choice in our annual diners' poll and "well deserving its three Michelin stars" (the same of which could not be said for most of London's other holders of these laurels). The "virtuoso" cuisine is "simply exquisite" yet "without seeming pretentious": it says something that one of this Northern Irish farmer's daughter's key signature dishes is made out of potato! "Everything from the welcome, the theatre of the kitchen, the execution of the cooking, the comprehensive wine list, the crisp, airy and bright dining room and the enthusiastic and delightful service" provides a "profoundly good experience with incredible attention to detail". "Clare is in the kitchen each time" and regularly greets guests personally, and "although the bill is high, it is not outlandish for the culinary performance that is delivered". "Always at the top of its game" – ratings here have held very steady in a year that has seen wobbles at many of its rivals. / W11 2PN; www.corebyclaresmyth.com; corebyclaresmyth; Thu-Sat, Tue, Wed 9.45 pm.

CORK & BOTTLE WC2 £69 234

44-46 CRANBOURN ST
020 7734 7807 5–3B

"A secret, below-ground escape from the mayhem of Leicester Square" for more than half a century – this "well-hidden", "old-school" wine bar has "only got better" over the years, first under founder Don Hewitson and latterly under Will Clayton. Top Menu Tip – "share the ham and cheese pie (it is absolutely enormous)", and has sold around a million portions since 1971. / WC2H 7AN; www.thecorkandbottle.co.uk; thecorkandbottle; Mon-Sun 10.30 pm.

CORNERSTONE E9 £97 554

3 PRINCE EDWARD ROAD
020 8986 3922 14–1C

"Tom Brown's single-minded passion for fish and seafood shines through" at his "mecca of fine dining" – a post-industrial space "tucked away not far from the canal" in "wondrously trendy Hackney Wick". "We love its informality and the friendliness of the staff" who give "detailed descriptions explaining the provenance of each dish" from "a stunning menu". "So, get your skinny jeans on, tousle that beard (man bun optional) and go!" Top Menu Tip – "fabulous crab bun with pear hoisin"; "shrimps in a sort of panna cotta, decorated with sprouting herbs and vegetables… inspired". / E9 5LX; cornerstonehackney.com; cornerstonehackney; Wed-Sat, Tue 9 pm.

CORRIGAN'S MAYFAIR W1 £139 344

28 UPPER GROSVENOR ST
020 7499 9943 3–3A

"Excellent traditional British cuisine with an Irish accent" helped win very consistent praise this year for Richard Corrigan's comfortable Mayfair bastion of 'all that is coastal, wild, furred and feathered'. It's a "classic dining experience" but service is "wonderfully welcoming" and is "pitch perfect" for business entertaining in particular. Top Tip – "the set lunch menu cushions the blow to the wallet". / W1K 7EH; www.corrigansmayfair.com; corrigans bar & restaurant; Tue-Sat midnight.

CÔTE £59 123

BRANCHES THROUGHOUT LONDON

"OK its a chain", but these faux French brasseries are one of the most talked-about brands in our annual diners' poll, due to their huge army of fans who see them as a "not-brilliant but consistent" standby for a "cheap 'n' cheerful meal disguised as something more upmarket" thanks to their "reasonable prices" and "very pleasant" ambience. For an easygoing breakfast, "family-friendly" meal or pre-theatre pit stop, they are particularly nominated. But while standards of service have held up relatively well here post-Covid, there was a strong feeling this year that the food is "on the wane" with lots of reports of "boring" or even "bad and unappealing" meals ("What has happened to Côte? It used to be so reliable, but we have had several experiences recently when we had to send dishes back because they'd been poorly cooked"). / www.cote.co.uk; coteuk.

COUNTER 71 N1

71 NILE ST NO TEL 13–1A

Opened in summer 2023, former Fenn head chef Joe Laker's debut project is a 16-seater chef's table with a focus on less familiar British produce, presented in a minimalist style. There's a touch of the TARDIS to it – on the outside, it looks like a bog-standard old corner pub; on the inside, it transforms into an open kitchen surrounded by a slick dining counter made from green marble. The venue has its own separate cocktail bar, Lowcountry, featuring whiskeys from the Georgia to North Carolina coast under Savannah-born mixologist Ryan Sheehan. Lowcountry also has a menu of southern US small plates such as shrimps and grits prawn toast. Top Menu Tip – "the custard tarts with fennel seeds are a real show-stopper". / N1 7RD; Mon-Sat 11 pm.

THE COW W2 £80 324

89 WESTBOURNE PARK RD
020 7221 0021 7–1B

One of London's original gastropubs, Tom Conran's Irish-themed "neighbourhood joint" in Bayswater still hits the spot after nearly 30 years. "Whoever is in the kitchen does a terrific job, as the food is delicious". It "can be noisy with bigger parties" and "the upstairs dining room is only small" – but you can always eat in the main bar. / W2 5QH; thecowlondon.com; thecowlondon; Mon-Sat 11 pm, Sun 10 pm.

COYA £116 22

118 PICCADILLY, W1 020 7042 7118 3–4
UNIT 1C ANGEL COURT, 31-33 THROGMORTON ST, EC2
020 7042 7118 10–2C

"Absolutely delicious" Peruvian food ("we took our foodie friends, who loved it too!") features in practically all reports on Arjun Waney's glossy haunts in Mayfair and near Bank (as well as Paris, Dubai, Mykonos…). There's a lot of feeling even amongst fans, though, that they're just "not worth the money any more" ("yes it's good, but at these prices it should be. Perhaps it's just their rents but spending just short of £200/head and being rushed off the table left me underwhelmed. I could rave about the wondrous dishes, but not sure it's worth it…") www.coyarestaurant.com; coyamayfair.

THE CRABTREE W6 £57 22

RAINVILLE ROAD 020 7385 3929 11–1A

Making the most of its "brilliant setting" – on the pedestrian path along the Fulham shore of the Thames, midway between Craven Cottage and The River Café, and with a big garden and small waterside terrace – this well-known and popular old tavern has a decent pub-grub offering, and gets rammed on summer weekends and Fulham match days. / W6 9HA; www.thecrabtreew6.co.uk; thecrabtreew6; Mon-Sat 11 pm, Sun 10.30 pm.

CRATE BREWERY AND PIZZERIA E9 £35 32

7, THE WHITE BUILDING, QUEENS YARD
020 8533 3331 14–1C

Hang with the hip crowd at this groovy Hackney Wick haunt – a canal-side warehouse ('The White Building') just across the water from the Olympic Park, with a big outside terrace. On the menu: affordable and yummy pizza, washed down with quality brews from the in-house microbrewery. Downside? At busy times it's a bit of a zoo. / E9 5EN; www.cratebrewery.com; cratebrewery; Sun-Thu 11 pm, Fri & Sat 1 am.

CRISP PIZZA, THE CHANCELLORS W6 £59 522

25 CRISP ROAD 020 8748 2600 8–2C

"Believe the hype… these pizzas are remarkable!" – there's nothing gastro in appearance when it comes to this mock Tudor pub: "a proper old man's boozer" behind Hammersmith's Riverside Studios. But self-taught pizzaiolo Carl McCluskey has set social media ablaze with folks travelling from far and wide and queuing round the block for his NYC-inspired creations. Even Harry Kane's a fan! It's a homespun and quirky set-up, which can struggle under weight of numbers. In particular

Dovetale by Tom Sellers, 1 Hotel Mayfair W1

"be sure to book your dough before you go!" – you can reserve your pizza (to ensure you don't go hungry and can take out if needs be), even if tables are reserved for walk-ins only. Is it the capital's best? Jimi Famurewa in his March 2023 Evening Standard review neatly captured the nigh-impossibility of living up to such legendary billing. "The fact that McCluskey's slices may not instantly supersede all the other half-remembered London pizzas you have eaten – and they didn't quite, for me – does not make them any less exceptional, rare or worth crossing town for". (Apparently, McCluskey is now on the hunt for a more conventional central London site). / W6 9RL; crisppizzaw6.

CROCKER'S FOLLY NW8 £58 333

23-24 ABERDEEN PLACE 020 7289 9898 9–*4A*

"Outstanding, really tasty Lebanese food" can be a surprise find at this "very ornate pub" – a beautifully restored, late-Victorian, Renaissance-style gin palace in St John's Wood, whose dazzling interior was originally supposed to act as that of a major railway hotel (due to the 'folly' of the owner, as the tracks ultimately ended up terminating in Marylebone). In its current guise, it's "one of the few Maroush group restaurants that survived post-Covid". / NW8 8JR; www.maroush.com; maroush; Mon-Sun midnight.

THE CRYSTAL MOON LOUNGE, CORINTHIA HOTEL LONDON SW1 £105 344

WHITEHALL PLACE 020 7321 3150 2–*3C*

The "gorgeous setting" of a lounge with a 1,001-crystal chandelier at this luxury hotel off Trafalgar Square is ideal for a "wonderful afternoon tea, especially after spending time in the spa". "The delightful little sweet creations will be topped up if required" to provide "a miracle! – tea for elderly mother's birthday done to her full satisfaction". / SW1A 2BD; www.corinthia.com; corinthialondon; Mon-Sun midnight.

THE CULPEPER E1 £61 333

40 COMMERCIAL STREET 020 7247 5371 13–*2C*

"Buzzing" old boozer on a Spitalfields corner site, which was very stylishly upgraded nine years ago and nowadays boasts an airy upstairs dining room with an "always interesting, always reliable" British bistro menu. "The roof terrace is a great bonus", too. / E1 6LP; www.theculpeper.com; theculpeper; Mon-Thu midnight, Fri & Sat 1 am, Sun 9 pm.

CUT, 45 PARK LANE W1 £188 232

45 PARK LN 020 7493 4545 3–*4A*

If it wasn't for the celebrity of chef Wolfgang Puck and its prime Park Lane location – across the door from the main entrance of The Dorchester – we would be tempted to skip an entry for this swanky Mayfair steakhouse. If you're not paying, you're likely to enjoy picking from its British-farmed steaks, USDA meat, Australian or Japanese wagyu. But it inspires very little feedback in our annual diners' poll, and even those who say it's "good all-round" feel it's "only for expense-accounters". / W1K 1PN; www.dorchestercollection.com; 45parklane; Mon-Sun 10 pm.

CYCENE E2 £218 544

9 CHANCE STREET 020 7033 6788 13–*1C*

"Akoko's chef and staff uprooted to here, this time without African-inflected cuisine… it's awesome!" – Theo Clench is now installed in the happening hipster venue in Shoreditch that was previously Mãos (part of the 'Blue Mountain School'). You start in the bar, in the lower portion of this two-floor space, which begins "an incredible evening from start to finish". Clench and his team serve a 10-course menu which promises to marry classic techniques with influences from Eastern Asia and Australasia. The result is "high-end dining, with amazing attention to detail but which feels very relaxed at the same time". The intimate and "stylish room" contributes to a "great experience all round". / E2 7JB; www.bluemountain.school; bluemountainschool.

CYPRUS MANGAL SW1 £48 332

45 WARWICK WAY 020 7828 5940 2–*4B*

"Delicious chops piled high, good gluggable house red – what's not to like?" at this long-running and "extremely good-value" Turkish-Cypriot grill near Victoria station in Pimlico. It's "not a place for a romantic tête-à-tête, but great fun – you'll leave very well fed and watered, and with a smile on your face". / SW1V 1QS; www.cyprusmangal.co.uk; cyprusmangal; Mon-Sun 11 pm.

DA MARIO SW7 £54 323

15 GLOUCESTER RD 020 7584 9078 6–*1B*

This "long-established" family-owned Italian in a Venetian Gothic building near the Albert Hall is "set up as a sort of homage to Princess Diana", who used to bring Princes Wills and Harry for pizza and pasta. / SW7 4PP; www.damario.co.uk; da-mario-kensington; Mon-Sun 11.30 pm.

DA MARIO WC2 £73 233

63 ENDELL STREET 020 7240 3632 5–*1C*

"Very friendly" and "authentic" – this "family-run traditional Italian trattoria" is a "dependable and good-value" option in Covent Garden, "with outside tables in decent weather". The food is "good but not exceptional". Top Menu Tip – "try the calves' liver and tiramisu". / WC2H 9AJ; www.da-mario.co.uk; da_mario_covent_garden; Tue-Sat 11 pm, Sun 9 pm.

DA TERRA, TOWN HALL HOTEL E2 £293 545

8 PATRIOT SQUARE 020 7062 2052 14–*2B*

Rafael Cagali provides "precise, innovative and fully-flavoured" Brazilian-influenced cuisine that's "some of the best food in London" at his acclaimed Bethnal Green venture – a site in the area's former town hall which has housed a number of the capital's most notable restaurants (The Typing Room, Viajante) over the last fifteen years. "The lovely setting is very good as it is intimate but still allows you to see the kitchen and how they prepare your food". / E2 9NF; www.daterra.co.uk; daterrarestaurant; Wed-Sat 8 pm.

DADDY BAO SW17 £34 433

113 MITCHAM ROAD 020 3601 3232 11–*2C*

"Our teen kids love this place and we do too!" – so say fans of Frank Leung's Tooting venue, which provides steamed Taiwanese buns, washed down with decent cocktails, in an atmospheric neighbourhood setting. See also 'Mr Bao' in Peckham. / SW17 9PE; www.daddybao.com; daddybao; Tue, Wed, Sun 9.45 pm, Sat, Fri 10.45 pm, Thu 9.45 pm.

DADDY DONKEY EC1 £18 432

50B LEATHER LANE 020 7404 4173 10–*2A*

"Reliable, generously proportioned burritos with a great range of extra fillings" keeps 'em coming to this fast-food café/takeaway, on a corner amidst Leather Lane Market. / EC1N 7TP; www.daddydonkey.co.uk; daddydonkeyburritos; Mon-Thu 7 pm, Fri 3 pm.

DAFFODIL MULLIGAN EC1 £72 443

70-74 CITY ROAD 020 7404 3000 13–*1A*

Richard Corrigan's "unassuming but amazing" bar/restaurant, just south of Silicon Roundabout, has – perhaps due to its pre-pandemic debut – never quite capitalised on his renown and its high quality. An "imaginative menu" of Irish-inflected dishes are "all matched by the superb, friendly, welcoming service" led by his son Richie. "Not cheap but equally not too expensive and certainly worth the visit". / EC1Y 2BJ; www.daffodilmulligan.com; daffodilmulligan; Wed-Fri 10 pm, Sun 8 pm.

LA DAME DE PIC LONDON EC3 £179 433

10 TRINITY SQUARE 020 7297 3799 10–*3D*

"A perfect marriage of traditional and modern culinary approaches" is to be found in the "impeccably-run" dining room of this impressive five-star hotel near the Tower of London. The Pic in question is Anne-Sophie, owner of Maison Pic near Lyon and Michelin's most decorated female chef. Fans say her team's contemporary French cuisine, led by head chef Evens López, is "on a different level from almost every other restaurant in the capital – presented like modern art and with each dish lovely surprise". In fact, given its consistent uality (as recognised by two of the tyre men's tars) it's surprising that – perhaps due to s Square Mile location – it still maintains relatively low profile in the capital's food cene. / EC3N 4AJ; ladamedepiclondon.co.uk; adamedepiclondon; Tue-Sat 9 pm.

DAPHNE'S SW3 £96 335

12 DRAYCOTT AVE 020 7589 4257 6–2C

'A terrific Italian with super service… that's more!", declare fans of this smart Chelsea aunt, founded in 1964 by Richard Burton's agent, Daphne Rye, and frequented in the 990s by Princess Di. Now part of Richard Caring's Caprice group, it seems to be lefying the ravages of time and remains a 'favourite, if expensive" rendezvous near Brompton Cross. Top Menu Tip – "the crab and chilli linguine is to die for". / SW3 3AE; www.daphnes-restaurant.co.uk; daphneslondon; Mon-Sat 10.45 pm, Sun 10.15 pm.

DAQUISE SW7 £67 234

20 THURLOE ST 020 7589 6117 6–2C

'A wonderful survivor", this old-world "gem" by South Ken tube has served "solid, Polish food" ("all the old hits: duck, goose, herring…") at "sensible prices" since 1947, and its devotees love its "real sense of authenticity" ("I feel happy when I walk in the door: the menu never changes and I hope it never will!"). It may be "a level down from Ognisko" culinary-wise, but "you're coming here for the charm, not the workmanlike fare". Top Tip – "it's well situated close to the South Kensington museums and a good alternative to the numerous expensive and unexciting chains!" / SW7 2LT; www.daquise.co.uk; daquise_london; Tue-Sun 11 pm.

DARBY'S SW11 £81 334

3 VIADUCT GARDENS ROAD, EMBASSY GARDENS 020 7537 3111 11–1D

In a style not dissimilar to an NYC steakhouse, Irish chef Robin Gill's "lovely" venue is an "excellent addition" to the new Nine Elms development – and should make staff at the US Embassy next door feel right at home with its "solid" menu of seafood and steaks and "nice cocktail bar vibe". "Oysters are good value in happy hour", accompanied by "spot-on martinis" or draught Guinness. Other highlights include breakfast, Sunday lunch with live music, and Southeast Asian BBQ treats from 'The Hatch' in the beer garden. / SW11 7AY; www.darbys-london.com; darbyslondon; Wed-Sat 10 pm.

DAROCO SOHO W1

MANETTE ST AWAITING TEL 5–2A

With siblings in the 2nd and 16th arrondissements of Paris, this October 2023 newcomer aims to import its brand of 'offbeat Parisian chic and sunny Italian generosity' to Soho (on an intriguing cut-through between Greek Street and Charing Cross Road). It's a large spot – with 100 covers and a 50-seater terrace – where the focus will be on pasta and pizza. / W1D 4AL; Mon-Sat 10.30 pm.

THE DARTMOUTH CASTLE W6 £58 323

26 GLENTHORNE RD 020 8748 3614 8–2C

"This unassuming pub tucked around the back of Hammersmith's one-way system serves good and hearty Mediterranean food", in particular some "lovely pasta dishes" – "don't miss the penne with Italian sausage ragu". It's also a "top sun trap for early-evening drinks on the patio". / W6 0LS; www.thedartmouthcastle.co.uk; thedartmouthcastle; Mon, Sat, Tue-Fri 9.30 pm, Sun 8.30 pm.

DARWIN BRASSERIE EC3 £88 224

1 SKY GARDEN WALK 033 3772 0020 10–3D

"The view from the gallery over the city is great" at this sky-high brasserie, on the 36th floor of the 'Walkie Talkie'. Reports this year were limited and rather uneven, so we've taken ratings down a peg. It won particular praise, though, as a glam breakfasting destination. / EC3M 8AF; skygarden.london; sg_darwin; Tue-Sun 10.30 pm, Mon 10 pm.

DASTAAN KT19 £49 543

447 KINGSTON RD 020 8786 8999 1–4A

"Well worth a detour by car, bus and/or train to eat in this small restaurant near Tolworth" – "looking just like your typical, noisy curry house on a dual carriageway… except that it is fully booked every night". "From pani puri to chicken Chettinad, the flavours are exquisite" with "a lasting intensity that can leave you punchdrunk". It's not utterly ridiculous to hail it as "the very best Indian food in the UK at any price point, and yet it's still very reasonably priced compared with the Indian palaces of Marylebone and Knightsbridge". Top Menu Tip – "the lamb chops are an absolute must". / KT19 0DB; dastaan.co.uk; dastaan447; Tue-Sun 10.30 pm.

DAYLESFORD ORGANIC £73 122

44B PIMLICO RD, SW1 020 7881 8060 6–2D
6-8 BLANDFORD ST, W1 020 3696 6500 2–1A
76-82 SLOANE AVENUE, SW3 020 3848 7100 6–2C
208-212 WESTBOURNE GROVE, W11 020 7313 8050 7–1B

Lady Bamford's quartet of London 'rus in urbe' cafés should have caught the zeitgeist, with their focus on home-produced organic ingredients from her estate. But the offering is variable, with food that's too often slated as "poor"; or incidents of "staff hanging around not knowing what to do". The Pimlico branch scores the best of the bunch, but it's worthy of note that visitors to the Daylesford farm mothership in the Cotswolds report an altogether different and "delightful" experience. / www.daylesfordorganic.com; daylesfordfarm. SRA - 3 stars.

DEAN STREET TOWNHOUSE W1 £78 244

69-71 DEAN ST 020 7434 1775 4–1D

"The warm and welcoming ambience is hard to beat" at this all-day brasserie, from the Soho House group – part of a hotel, which enjoys a "brilliant central location". The food? "Uncomplicated, nothing special, but very acceptable" (especially for brunch), if "expensive for what you get". But it's the "lovely" atmosphere that carries the day here. / W1D 3SE; www.deanstreettownhouse.com; deanstreettownhouse; Mon-Thu midnight, Fri & Sat 1 am, Sun 11 am.

DECIMO WC1 £97 324

THE STANDARD, 10 ARGYLE ST 020 3981 8888 9–3C

"A spectacular room with spectacular views (including from the loos!)" sets a high-octane scene at Peter Sanchez-Iglesias's dramatic Mexican venue: a high-ceilinged space on the top of King's Cross's über-hip Standard Hotel, with a breathtaking outlook over St Pancras station next door, and accessed via an exterior, red, glass-walled lift. "It seems less busy at lunch – it looks more like one for the cool kids after dark". Most reporters are "pleasantly surprised by the food" which majors in ribs, steaks and seafood from the grill "(I thought it was going to be yet another celebrity rip-off)". It's far from a cheap experience, though, and one or two dud meals were also reported. / WC1H 9JE; www.decimo.london; decimo.london; Tue, Wed midnight, Fri & Sat 2 am, Thu 1 am.

DEHESA W1 £60 222

25 GANTON STREET 020 7494 4170 4–2B

We're in two minds about the inclusion of this former star of London's tapas scene, which generates very little feedback nowadays despite a prime mid-Soho site. Fans do still laud its "well-crafted dishes and Spanish wines", but others say "the food has that 'here's one I made earlier' quality. OK, but not very exciting". / W1F 9BP; www.saltyardgroup.co.uk; dehesarestaurant; Mon-Sat 11 pm, Sun 9 pm.

DELAMINA £53 333

56-58 MARYLEBONE LANE, W1 020 3026 6810 3–1A
151 COMMERCIAL STREET, E1 020 7078 0770 13–2B

"Consistently very good food" results from the menu of small sharing plates at this modern Levantine duo in Marylebone and Shoreditch, created by Israeli-born cook Limor Chen and her husband Amir. There's a "buzzy atmosphere without being too noisy" and a playlist that channels the Tel Aviv vibe. / www.delaminaeast.co.uk; delaminakitchen.

Decimo WC1

THE DELAUNAY WC2 £72 244

55 ALDWYCH 020 7499 8558 2–2D

"Viennese in style" – this "elegantly understated" sibling to The Wolseley sits on the easterly fringe of the West End, and is "very much a power location": "the ambience is perfect for business meals – bustling but not too noisy – with well-spaced tables and comfortable seating"; and "obliging" service that's "efficient and warm". Its "Mittel European brasserie menu with schnitzel/goulash/wurst etc" is "nothing special, but it is consistent and very acceptable" and "with something amongst the selection of dishes that anyone and everyone can eat". "Despite the loss of founders Corbin and King, it is mercifully unaltered under its new ownership" with ratings practically identical to last year's. Top Tip – "fabulous for breakfast", whether you are dealmaking or not. / WC2B 4BB; www.thedelaunay.com; thedelaunay; Mon-Sat 10.30 pm, Sun 5 pm.

DELFINO W1 £80 332

121A MOUNT ST 020 7499 1256 3–3B

This family-owned Italian wins consistently good ratings for the straightforward menu of "authentic" pasta, pizza and more it has served – at a prominent corner site in Mayfair – for half a century now. Despite a recent refurb, prices remain exceptionally reasonable for this part of town. / W1K 3NW; www.delfinomayfair.com; delfinomayfair; Mon-Sat 10.30 pm.

DELHI GRILL N1 £40 423

21 CHAPEL MKT 020 7278 8100 9–3D

"Value for money! Truly punchy curries that sing on the tongue" continue to win fans for this street-food inspired cheap eat, on Islington's Chapel Market. / N1 9EZ; www.delhigrill.com; delhi_grill; Mon-Thu, Sat, Fri 10.30 pm, Sun 10 pm.

LES 2 GARCONS N8 £79 553

14 MIDDLE LANE 020 8347 9834 9–1C

"Jean-Christophe's Slowik's affability and lovely front-of-house wisdom and Robert Reid's fine cheffing remain delightful as ever" at this "happily old-school bistro in Crouch End, located firmly in the great late 80s dining scene"; and its February 2023 crowdfunded "move to (slightly) larger, nearby premises has made eating here a more comfortable experience". "If every neighbourhood had a restaurant as good as this", the world would be a better place. "Traditional, un-fancy French food is simply and lovingly prepared and served" – "… wish they had restaurants like this in France!". Top Menu Tip – "tarte Tatin is not to be missed; and if they are doing the pig's trotter Pierre Koffman, which chef Robert used to cook for MPW, then don't hesitate". / N8 8PL; www.les2garconsbistro.com; les2garconsbistro; Tue-Sat 9.30 pm.

THE DEVONSHIRE W1

17 DENMAN ST 020 7437 2445 4–3C

Fooderati favourite, Oisín Rogers – previously of The Guinea Grill – and Flat Iron founder Charlie Carroll created their dream pub in the heart of the West End at this refurbished boozer, just north of Piccadilly Circus (opposite Brasserie Zédel). Opened in Autumn 2023, it's no surprise given their joint heritage that prime steak – dry aged and butchered on the premises – is intrinsic to the formula. But so, too, is just dropping in for a pint. / W1D 7HW; Mon-Sat 11 pm.

DIBA £54 222

386 KING'S ROAD, SW3
020 7349 9499 6–3B
87 THE BROADWAY, SW19
020 8545 0207 11–2B

"Big portions of tasty Persian food" make this "friendly" duo in Chelsea and Wimbledon "great value for money". Top Menu Tip – "you must have the bread fresh out of the clay oven". / dibarestaurant.co.uk; diba_restaurant_.

DIM SUM DUCK WC1 £43 522

124 KING'S CROSS ROAD
020 7278 6018 9–3D

This tiny café whose menu is summed up in its name is one of the capital's champion cheap eats, with "stunning" Cantonese cuisine. "Just a shame it's not bigger as the queuing time and outdoor seating on the grimy King's Cross Road isn't ideal". The only solution is to go early or in the afternoon. / WC1X 9DS; dimsum-duck.business.site; dimsumandduck; Mon-Sun 10 pm.

DIN TAI FUNG £61 222

5-6 HENRIETTA STREET, WC2
020 3034 3888 5–3D
CENTRE POINT, TOTTENHAM COURT ROAD WC2 AWAITING TEL 5–1A

An international Taiwanese-based chain with a trio of UK outlets in Covent Garden, Selfridges and most recently Centre Point ("with a great view"). To well-travelled connoisseurs of the original, they are "more upmarket here and more expensive too" ("I lived in Asia for several years and ate at a DTF at least weekly, but here they've jacked the prices up to a level that is taking the p***"). But to the uninitiated, they can seem like "the best ever dumplings", and – Top Menu Tip – even their sternest critics say "don't ignore the Xian Long Bao" (soup dumplings). / www.dintaifung-uk.com; dintaifunguk.

THE DINING ROOM, THE GORING HOTEL SW1 £124 223

15 BEESTON PL 020 7396 9000 2–4B

Very often recommended as an "expensive but reliable" venue for a "perfect business lunch", this "decorous", family-run hotel near Buck House (where the Middletons stayed before Kate & Will's big day) has won renown as a "very classy", traditionally British affair, where "everything is done perfectly". Post-Covid, however, its dining room's performance seems to have been on the slide and the downward trend noted last year continued in this year's poll amidst gripes that it was "not as good as previously", serving "bland food" and with "too many high expectations dashed". Top Tip – "a quintessential English afternoon tea" in the lounges here is still a popular event. / SW1W 0JW; www.thegoring.com; thegoring; Mon-Sun 9.45 pm.

DININGS £101 532

22 HARCOURT ST, W1
020 7723 0666 9–4A
WALTON HOUSE, WALTON ST, SW3
020 7723 0666 6–2C

Such is their similarity, that we continue to write up this Japanese duo in a single entry, even though the chefs who own them split the business a few years ago and now run each independently. Both provide "dishes to wow the palate" – and "a feast for the eyes" too: "each beautiful, tiny dish tastes as good as it looks". If you're looking for differences, SW3 receives more attention nowadays, but fractionally lower ratings and can seem "crowded". / dinings.co.uk; dinings_sw3.

DINNER BY HESTON BLUMENTHAL, MANDARIN ORIENTAL SW1 £156 222

66 KNIGHTSBRIDGE 020 7201 3833 6–*1D*

"A menu of deep historical appreciation and stimulating intellectual connections adds up to a total experience that's much more than great fine dining", according to fans of Heston Blumenthal's Knightsbridge venue, whose "original takes on classic English cuisine" are, apparently, inspired by Heston's love of historic British gastronomy and research into cookbooks from the 14th century onwards. Supporters say "the signature meat fruit and tipsy cake are so good, you can just have them every time" and that his other more recent (re)creations can also be "magnificent". But that it's a case of "Emperor's new clothes" is another commonly held belief about this hotel dining room, which – in 1 in 3 reports – is said by diners to be their most "overpriced" meal of the year; and which, despite Hyde Park views from some tables, struggles to generate much in the way of atmosphere. "Seriously, a disappointment after The Fat Duck. Just not value for money!" / SW1X 7LA; www.dinnerbyheston.com; dinnerbyhb; Mon-Sun 9.30 pm.

DIPNA ANAND RESTAURANT & BAR WC2 £51

SOUTH WING, SOMERSET HOUSE, STRAND 020 7845 4646 2–*2D*

Within glorious Somerset House, Dipna Anand (part of the family who founded the famous Brilliant Restaurant in Southall) took over this stately, traditional chamber last year, and mostly earned recommendations for its Indian cuisine. Not all reports were 100% positive, though, and in summer 2023 it underwent a temporary closure (with re-opening slated for early September 2023). / WC2R 1LA; dipnasomersethouse.co.uk; dipnaatsomersethouse; Wed-Sat 10 pm, Sun 4 pm.

DISHOOM £52 345

22 KINGLY ST, W1 020 7420 9322 4–*2B*
12 UPPER ST MARTINS LN, WC2 020 7420 9320 5–*3B*
THE BARKERS BUILDING, DERRY STREET, W8 020 7420 9325 6–*1A*
STABLE ST, GRANARY SQ, N1 020 7420 9321 9–*3C*
WOOD WHARF, 15 WATER STREET, E14 020 7420 9326 12–*1C*
7 BOUNDARY ST, E2 020 7420 9324 13–*1B*

"You really can't go wrong with Dishoom". Shamil and Kavi Thakrar's phenomenal chain remains the most commented-on in our annual diners' poll and its "bustling and loud, throwback, Bombay-colonial-era atmosphere" and "distinctively superior" menu – such a "novel variation from what you get in a typical curry house" – have given UK diners a welcome jolt as to what can be expected from an Indian meal. This includes their "Asian-inspired alternative to the usual 'Full English' breakfast", which has revolutionised the start of the day for many folks. "Super-friendly staff do all they can to create a great experience", which – along with the "delectable cocktails" – helps to underpin the "good vibes" that makes their ambience so buoyant. Perhaps inevitably, ratings for its food have slipped a tad in recent times from being exceptional to merely good, but the overall verdict remains that the overall package is "relatively cheap and always really tasty". The ability to book is restricted at certain times and at certain branches, but "the queue is worth it!" Top Menu Tips – "stupendous black dahl"; "you could have their okra fries by the bucket"; "ruby murray is a must try"; "that bacon naan… with unlimited chai latte = heaven!". / www.dishoom.com; dishoom. SRA – 2 stars

DIWANA BHEL-POORI HOUSE NW1 £33 321

121-123 DRUMMOND ST 020 7387 5556 9–*4C*

"Terrific dosas" and other South Indian vegetarian fare have been on the menu for 60-odd years at this stalwart of the 'Little India' array of cheap 'n' cheerful canteens near Euston station. / NW1 2HL; www.diwanabph.com; diwanabhelpoorihouse; Mon-Sat 10.30 pm, Sun 9.30 pm.

DONOSTIA W1 £93 322

10 SEYMOUR PL 020 3620 1845 2–*2A*

"Delicious baby-brother alternative to Lurra" (the more formal restaurant across the road) – this "rather crowded" bar/restaurant provides a "superb Basque tapas" plus a "small but select wine list". "It's especially good sitting at the bar" – less so in the somewhat stranded rear tables. / W1H 7ND; www.donostia.co.uk; donostiaw1; Mon-Sat 10.30 pm, Sun 9 pm.

DOPPO W1

33 DEAN STREET 020 7183 2100 5–*2A*

On a Soho corner, this straightforward but stylish independent opened in early 2023. No survey feedback as yet, but The Standard's David Ellis was impressed on his February 2023 visit, hailing the "quiet elegance" of its interior and light, well-realised Tuscan-influenced cuisine to match, plus a strong wine list. / W1D 4PW; dopposoho; Wed & Thu, Tue 10 pm, Fri & Sat 11 pm.

DORIAN W11 £51 445

105-107 TALBOT ROAD 020 3089 9556 7–*1B*

With Chris D'Sylva's background (Notting Hill Fish Shop and Supermarket of Dreams) "the ingredient quality was always going to be superb" at this "constantly buzzing" new 'bistro for locals', which has instantly become something of a "modern classic" for the Notting Hillbilly in-crowd. Chef Max Coen "manages to make decadent dishes seem simple" ("steak is to die for"; or "feast on the most melting buttery liver pâté") and "counter seats are excellent for kitchen watching" – "you get the cooking show and a fantastic atmosphere with lots of interesting fellow diners". / W11 2AT; dorianrestaurant.com; thedoriansf; Tue-Sat 9.30 pm, Sun 4.15 pm.

DOROTHY & MARSHALL BR1 £59 233

BROMLEY OLD TOWN HALL, 4 COURT STREET 020 3989 9092 1–*4D*

"A super addition to Bromley" – the borough's old Town Hall has had £20m spent on a refit as a boutique hotel, complete with this new landmark dining room which launched in late 2022: an imposing chamber, with a soaring vaulted ceiling, wood-panelled walls and clerestory windows. It serves a menu of British classics, and is aiming to be a linchpin of the area. Our early feedback (and press reports) are up-and-down: one reporter liked the "very friendly staff and great building", but thought "the menu needs to be a little more adventurous". Another was "slightly disappointed all round, but went shortly after it opened and they were obviously still ironing out stuff". (Both comments have echoes of Grace Dent's review in The Guardian: "a gorgeous space…with a brief menu… service is delightful… prompt and friendly, but it's hard to regard the place as much more than a cafe"). / BR1 1AN; www.dorothyandmarshall.co.uk; dorothyandmarshall; Tue-Thu 10 pm, Fri & Sat 10.30 pm, Sun 7 pm.

DOUBLE STANDARD WC1 £68 355

THE STANDARD, 10 ARGYLE ST 020 3981 8888 9–*3C*

Conveniently sited bang opposite St Pancras, the authentically 1970s backdrop of the former Camden Town Hall Annexe provides the stylishly time-warped (and convenient) home for this hip haunt: the vibey ground-floor bar of Standard Hotels' London outpost. An ideal rendezvous – especially for creative types – the simple brasserie fare is reliable and staff are particularly professional and welcoming. Don't go if you don't like it loud though: expect the sounds of the seventies at 80-90dB with powerful bass. / WC1H 8EG; www.standardhotels.com; isla.london; Mon-Sun 11 pm.

THE DOVE W6 £50 345

19 UPPER MALL 020 8748 9474 8–*2B*

This "historic" venue on Hammersmith's Upper Mall (owned by local brewer Fuller's since 1798) is unquestionably "one of the nicest pubs in London": with its "delicious" pub grub, "cosy log fire in the winter, a terrace overlooking the river in the summer – what else would you want?". Top Menu Tip – yummy burgers. / W6 9TA; www.dovehammersmith.co.uk; the_dove_hammersmith; Mon-Sat 11 pm, Sun 10.30 pm.

DOVETALE BY TOM SELLERS, 1 HOTEL MAYFAIR W1

3 BERKELEY STREET 020 3137 4983 3–*3C*

Part of a swanky nine-story hotel that opened in summer 2023, primely located opposite The Ritz (on the junction of Piccadilly and Berkeley Street), this Mayfair newcomer is another recent initiative of Tom Sellers (who also opened Story Cellar in Covent Garden in April 2023). The launch is the UK's first from a luxury international chain whose styling includes lots of plant-filled spaces. According to the website, the dining room features an 'abundant raw bar' and is 'grounded in a deep respect for seasonal, organic, and locally sourced ingredients'. One heavily trailed feature: two dessert trolleys dispensing customisable, 'curated' knickerbocker glories, named 'Apollo One' and 'Apollo Two'. / W1J 8DJ; www.1hotels.com; dovetalelondon; Mon-Fri 2.30 pm.

DRAGON CASTLE SE17 £61 322

100 WALWORTH ROAD 020 7277 3388 1–3C

"You could be in Hong Kong" at this "barn-like" Chinese venue near Elephant & Castle, where you'll find "truly authentic", "super-fresh dim sum, alongside old-school Cantonese favourites". "So pleased it has found its mojo again" after a long post-pandemic closure. / SE17 1JL; www.dragoncastlelondon.com; dragoncastle100; Mon-Sat 11 pm, Sun 5 am.

THE DRAPERS ARMS N1 £67 333

44 BARNSBURY STREET 020 7619 0348 9–3D

This "very popular gastropub" in Islington has been transformed from an early Victorian boozer by Nick Gibson, and now "does so well you really need to book". The "consistently good food and great wine list" show a strong French influence, and it's "lovely outside at the back in summer". / N1 1ER; www.thedrapersarms.com; thedrapersarms; Mon-Sat 10.30 pm, Sun 8.30 pm.

THE DRAWING ROOM AT THE DUKES SW1 £70 344

35 SAINT JAMES'S PLACE 020 7318 6574 3–4C

"Ignore The Ritz around the corner, for afternoon tea this is the place to go" according to fans of this St James's bastion: "the scones are soft and freshly baked", "the sandwiches and cakes are divine", and the "famous Dukes 'James Bond' martini is an optional extra". / SW1A 1NY; www.dukeshotel.com; afternoonteauk; Mon-Sun 6 pm.

DROPSHOT COFFEE SW19 £23 344

281 WIMBLEDON PARK ROAD 07445 673405 11–2B

Don't be fooled by the tennis theme – this indie haunt a strong serve away from the All England Club is absolutely serious about its "delicious brews from different roast houses" and "tasty made-to-order toasties" – in fact, fans claim it's "without a doubt the BEST coffee shop in SW London", and "so friendly: only problem is it's too popular and the queues can be sooooo long". / SW19 6NW; dropshotcoffee.co.uk; dropshotcoffeeldn; Mon-Sun 5 pm.

THE DUCK & RICE W1 £76 323

90 BERWICK ST 020 3327 7888 4–2C

This "pub with an Oriental twist" on Soho's Berwick Street is a concept that "works well", with "lovely, tasty food"; even if – eight years after its launch by ace restaurateur Alan Yau – it has never matched the success of his hit concepts Wagamama, Hakkasan or Yauatcha. Top Menu Tip – "the pork scratchings are amazing". / W1F 0QB; www.theduckandrice.com; theduckandrice; Tue-Sat 11 pm, Sun 9 pm.

DUCK & WAFFLE EC2 £99 223

110 BISHOPSGATE, HERON TOWER 020 3640 7310 10–2D

Open 24/7 on top of the City's 40-storey Heron Tower, this elevated posh diner comes particularly recommended for a "great breakfast" or a chilled date ("when you get tired of looking into each other's eyes, the views over London are pretty impressive"). The food, including the signature duck, is mostly up to scratch, but "you just feel it could be better". / EC2N 4AY; www.duckandwaffle.com; duckandwaffle; Mon-Sun 11.30 pm.

THE DUCK TRUCK E1 £18 432

BISHOPS SQUARE 07919 160271 13–2B

"This truck at Spitalfields continues to be a favourite of everyone I take there" – parked just outside the market, it delivers generous filled buns of the eponymous roasted bird, or boxes with meat, chips and salad. / E1 6AN; www.theducktruck.com; theducktruck; Mon-Fri 4 pm.

DUCKSOUP W1 £79 443

41 DEAN ST 020 7287 4599 5–2A

This "cool spot" with a "tight menu that changes daily" is "a Soho go-to, even if you get turned away at the door because it's too damned successful!" Now in its second decade, it was way ahead of the curve with its modern Mediterranean/North African menu and biodynamic wine list ("tried orange and natural wines here before they became popular categories elsewhere"). / W1D 4PY; www.ducksoupsoho.co.uk; ducksoupsoho; Wed-Sat, Mon & Tue 10 pm, Sun 5 pm.

THE DUKE OF RICHMOND PUBLIC HOUSE & DINING ROOM E8 £60 333

316 QUEENSBRIDGE ROAD 020 7923 3990 14–1A

"Delicious food" and "attentive service" are the order of the day at this ambitious gastropub on the Dalston-Haggerston border, where the kitchen is headed by chef Tom Oldroyd, whose self-named restaurant in Islington closed down during the pandemic. / E8 3NH; www.thedukeofrichmond.com; thedukeofrichmond; Mon, Wed 9 pm, Fri & Sat, Thu 9.30 pm, Sun 8 pm.

THE DUKE OF SUSSEX W4 £67 223

75 SOUTH PDE 020 8742 8801 8–1A

"Avoiding a typical pub-forgettable menu" – this Victorian tavern on a prominent corner overlooking Acton Green Common "offers a tapas selection of real quality and a lovely interior to boot". That's it on a good day, though – it's not consistent and some "unexceptional" results dragged on the rating a little this year. You can eat anywhere in the pub, although the grand dining room at the rear is the most comfy location, and "the garden is very pleasant on a fine day". / W4 5LF; www.thedukeofsussex.co.uk; thedukew4; Mon-Wed 11 pm, Fri & Sat midnight, Thu 11 am, Sun 10 pm.

DUMPLINGS' LEGEND W1 £41 321

16 GERRARD ST 020 7494 1200 5–3A

"It's all about the dumplings" at this "efficient" and "good-value" Chinatown dim sum specialist – "and luckily they're worth it". "The best time to go is a Sunday just before the lunch rush". / W1D 6JE; www.dumplingslegend.com; dumplingslegend; Mon-Thu 11 pm, Fri & Sat 3 am, Sun 10 pm.

DURBAR W2 £43 332

24 HEREFORD RD 020 7727 1947 7–1B

This "brilliant local curry house" off Westbourne Grove has "been there forever (since 1956, in fact) for good reason" – "we've been going for over 40 years and it's always delicious and great value" and there's "always a friendly welcome". Top Tip – "it no longer has an alcohol licence and is now BYOB, so is even better value". / W2 4AA; www.durbartandoori.co.uk; durbarrestaurant; Mon-Sat 11.30 pm.

THE DUSTY KNUCKLE £39 523

429 GREEN LANES, N4 NO TEL 9–1D
ABBOT STREET, E8 020 3903 7598 14–1A

"Down a classic dodgy Dalston alleyway, this beautiful place awaits!" (there's also an offshoot in Green Lanes, Haringey). "I love the good old Dusty Knuckle", which inspires affection not just for its "absolutely top bread, pastries and sarnies" plus "excellent coffee"; but also for its social enterprise role supporting at-risk young East Londoners. / www.thedustyknuckle.com; thedustyknuckle.

THE DYSART PETERSHAM TW10 £94 544

135 PETERSHAM ROAD 020 8940 8005 1–4A

Kenneth Culhane's "superb cooking – inventive within the boundaries of modern British cuisine" – has generated a groundswell of interest in this "unique" venue: an Arts & Crafts home bordering leafy Richmond Park and near the Thames. "The building itself is absolutely stunning and, like the menu, feels both progressive and traditional"; the atmosphere of civilised luxury extends to monthly dinners featuring a classical recital on an antique rosewood Bechstein grand piano. / TW10 7AA; www.thedysartpetersham.co.uk; thedysartpetersham; Wed & Thu, Sun, Fri & Sat 8.30 pm.

E&O W11 £77 333

14 BLENHEIM CRESCENT
020 7229 5454 7–*1A*

Over more than 20 years, Will Ricker's Notting Hill stalwart – fuelled by cocktails, sushi, and other pan-Asian bites – has proved incredibly enduring. It still has a few big fans, particularly local ones, but one or two reporters feel it's now "lost its charm". / W11 1NN; www.eandolondon.com; eandonotthill; Mon-Sat midnight, Sun 10 pm.

THE EAGLE EC1 £45 334

159 FARRINGDON RD
020 7837 1353 10–*1A*

"Gastropub heaven!" – this basic boozer on the busy Farringdon Road is where the gastropub revolution started in 1991, and it's "still fabulous after all these years" – "no fuss, no pretence, just wholehearted focus, as ever, on simple yet perfect flavour combinations. Unbeatable!". Head chef Edward Mottershaw celebrates two decades as head chef this year, and still chalks up the daily changing menu of Mediterranean-influenced dishes a matter of minutes before service, ensuring "simplicity and perfection without scary prices". / EC1R 3AL; www.theeaglefarringdon.co.uk; eaglefarringdon; Mon-Sat 11 pm, Sun 5 pm.

EAT TOKYO £40 322

16 OLD COMPTON ST, W1
020 7439 9887 5–*2A*
50 RED LION ST, WC1
020 7242 3490 2–*1D*
27 CATHERINE ST, WC2
020 3489 1700 5–*3D*
17 NOTTING HILL GATE, W11
020 7792 9313 7–*2B*
169 KING ST, W6 020 8741 7916 8–*2B*
14 NORTH END RD, NW11
020 8209 0079 1–*1B*
628 FINCHLEY RD, NW11
020 3609 8886 1–*1B*

"Proper" Japanese food at a "very affordable price" ("the sushi is seemingly no more expensive than Yo! Sushi, but so much better quality") ensures that these Tokyo-inspired pitstops are "always busy" and there are "often queues". "The canteen atmosphere and sometimes inflexible service doesn't make you want to linger" but no-one cares given the "extensive menu – made with fresh ingredients and served up super quick – that's good overall value". Top Tip – "the bento boxes are tasty and authentic". / www.eattokyo.co.uk; eattokyoldn.

EATALY EC2 £58 223

135 BISHOPSGATE 07966 544965 10–*2D*

"A great place for anything Italian" – Oscar Farinetti's "huge" food mall concept has swept the world and its London outpost near Liverpool Street station (a relatively late arrival in 2021) boasts no fewer than 11 restaurants, bars and counters to feed you, alongside shops and stalls where you can pick up goodies to take home. Gastronomically, the sheer scale works against it, so even the flagship Terra elicits comparatively little praise, but the whole enterprise has a pleasant buzz; "staff work hard to please"; and simpler items in particular "benefit from the ready supply of super ingredients". / EC2M 3YD; www.eataly.co.uk; eatalylondon; Mon-Sat 11 pm, Sun 10 pm.

EDERA W11 £63 343

148 HOLLAND PARK AVE
020 7221 6090 7–*2A*

"Roberto, Francesco and Alberto are finally back" (after a prolonged closure during Covid) and "really go out of their way to make you feel welcome" at their "wonderful neighbourhood Italian" in posh Holland Park. Its large local fanclub sometimes acknowledge that "prices are too high", but don't mind because the food (including a number of Sardinian specialities) is "tasty and well presented" and the overall performance makes it "dependable for any occasion". / W11 4UE; www.edera.co.uk; Mon-Sun 11 pm.

EDIT E8

217 MARE STREET NO TEL 14–*1B*

Near London Fields, this 'hyper-seasonal' spot in Hackney (from Elly Ward and the team behind plant-based pioneer Super Nature) opened in spring 2023 and focuses on a low-waste philosophy. There's a short array of meat-free, modern British dishes, accompanied by a selection of low-intervention wines, beers and ciders. Or, in the evenings, you can go for an eight-course tasting menu with the option of a drinks pairing. No survey feedback as yet, but if you are avoiding meat, this is one of the more interesting-looking openings this year. / E8 3QE; www.edit.london; edit.restaurant; Mon & Tue, Sun 3 pm, Wed-Sat 9 pm.

THE EIGHT RESTAURANT W1 £38 322

68-70 SHAFTESBURY AVENUE
020 3332 2313 4–*3D*

"A top choice for a Hong-Kong-style café menu" – this "rushed" tearoom on the edge of Chinatown opened in 2022 and serves everything from light bites to full meals from its huge selection of dishes. The food is consistently well rated. / W1D 6LZ; www.theeightrestaurant.co.uk; theeightlondon; Mon-Sun 10.30 pm.

EKSTEDT AT THE YARD, GREAT SCOTLAND YARD HOTEL SW1 £118 343

GREAT SCOTLAND YARD
020 7925 4700 2–*3C*

"Niklas Ekstedt's trademark open-fire cuisine" has its first outpost (beyond Stockholm) in Westminster's Hyatt hotel, where the "relaxed and peaceful ambience, theatrical open kitchen and flames" and "unexpectedly delicate flavours" win over most reporters. Its ratings would be even higher, were it not for the occasional sceptic who feels the performance "relies on the drama of the grill rather than the quality of cooking". / SW1A 2HN; www.ekstedtattheyard.com; ekstedtldn; Tue-Sat 9 pm.

EKTE NORDIC KITCHEN EC4 £64 322

2-8 BLOOMBERG ARCADE
020 3814 8330 10–*3C*

Soren Jessen's "slick, Nordic cafe in the City of London" occupies part of the Bloomberg Arcade and contributes to the development's renown for offering "good food in the dry desert of the Square Mile". It majors in Danish smørrebrød (rye bread with toppings): "nice for a change", but "you can rack up a fair bill eating these delicate one-bite-and-they-are-gone appetisers" (though "there there are decent main courses such as fish, schnitzel and venison fillet"). On the downside, results can end up seeming "not as Scandi and varied as expected" – "I prefer IKEA meatballs, even if they are not as prettily presented!" / EC4N 8AR; www.ektelondon.co.uk; ektelondon; Mon-Sat 10 pm.

EL PASTOR £56 334

BREWER STREET, W1
020 3092 4553 4–*3C*
7A STONEY STREET, SE1 NO TEL 10–*4C*

"Properly authentic tortillas and tacos transport you to Mexico City" with their "spicy but very delicious" flavours, at this Mexican duo from the Hart Brothers, whose original venue in a "great location" on the edge of Borough Market is deservedly "very busy". The Soho branch has a late-night basement bar, 'Mezcaleria Colmillo', while 'big sister' Casa Pastor at Coal Drops Yard in King's Cross (see also) features live music. / www.tacoselpastor.co.uk; tacos_el_pastor.

EL TA'KOY WC2

3 HENRIETTA STREET 07377 220955 5–*3D*

Hawaiian street food marrying Latino and Asian cuisines is the promise at this small cellar and tiki bar, in a Covent Garden basement below three other restaurants. Open in 2021, it has yet to generate much in the way of survey feedback, but The Independent's Kate Ng describes a "fun, flirty little spot" with "generous plates" that are "middling to pretty damn good", plus "dangerously delicious" cocktails. / WC2E 8LU; el-takoy.com; el_takoy_london; Mon-Sun 11 pm.

ELA & DHANI SW13 £36 342

127 CHURCH ROAD 020 8741 9583 11–*1A*

"Surprisingly and deliciously different" Indian cooking can be found at this "smart little" two-year-old on the main drag in Barnes – a debut restaurant from three friends who grew up together in the Punjab, one of whom runs the upmarket Barnes Pantry just up the road. Local regulars say they "love this place and the staff". / SW13 9HR; www.eladhani.co.uk; ela_and_dhani; Tue-Thu 10 pm, Fri & Sat 10.30 pm, Sun 9 pm.

THE ELDER PRESS CAFÉ W6 £25 334

3 SOUTH BLACK LION LANE 020 3887 4258 8–*2B*

Very 'zen' for somewhere barely 100m from the A4 – this "delightful" Hammersmith café serves an "original and interesting" menu of light bites and luscious cakes and makes a handy stop-off from a riverside stroll. It was beautifully converted from a builders' merchants four years ago by chef Lindsay Elder; and its calm interior is a good match for the yoga and pilates sessions in the upstairs room. / W6 9TJ; www.theelderpress.co.uk; theelderpress; Mon-Sun 5 pm.

ELINE E2 £73 453

1C ROSEWOOD BUILDING, CREMER STREET 020 4547 2702 14–*2A*

"So special" and "clearly the product of two people who absolutely love what they do and want to share it with as many other people as possible" – Maria Viviani and chef Alex Reynolds' September 2022 newcomer "hasn't been open that long but has made such an impact" in Hoxton: It provides "really welcoming, accessible fine dining". "Alex showcases his exemplary skills in the kitchen" delivering "precise imaginative cooking" in the "cool dining room" (although "it can feel like a goldfish bowl on a quiet winter night"). "Meanwhile the lovely Maria is on hand to find you some of the most exciting and approachable low-intervention, natural wines around". Top Tip – "their bottle shop is an absolute bonus for those passing by and needing to pick up something spectacular for dinner at home!" / E2 8GX; www.restauranteline.co.uk; elinelondon; Wed-Sat 9.30 pm.

ELIS, TOWN HALL HOTEL E2 £69 442

PATRIOT SQUARE 020 7871 0460 14–*2B*

"I'm pleased they kept the hanging lights of the former Corner Room" – the previous occupant of this restaurant space within the monumental, erstwhile Bethnal Green Town Hall (nowadays a hotel). Chef Rafael Cagali runs the much-fêted Da Terra next door, and this October 2022 newcomer provides "a simplified version of the Michelin two-star cuisine" at its neighbour. Reports included plus points: "the quality combinations are full of flavour" and service is "decent", while on the debit side, ambience has sometimes proved elusive and sentiments seem a tad muted: there are no full-on raves at how marvellous and incredible it all is. Top Menu Tip – dulce de leite doughnuts. / E2 9NF; www.restaurantelis.co.uk; elis.ldn.

ELLIOT'S £79 332

12 STONEY ST, SE1 020 7403 7436 10–*4C*
121-123 MARE STREET, E8 020 3302 5252 14–*2B*

"Excellent modern cooking with Med influences" and a "good natural wine list" are the strengths of this Borough Market staple that has championed organic and biodynamic wine for more than a decade; and which was joined two years ago by a spin-off near London Fields. The cuisine is "down to earth, with some stonking small plates" and matched with "efficient service and a relaxed atmosphere" to provide a "very enjoyable meal". / www.elliots.london; elliotslondon.

ELYSTAN STREET SW3 £105 433

43 ELYSTAN STREET 020 7628 5005 6–*2C*

Former Square chef, "Philip Howard's magical touch" is evident in much of the "very well-realised, modern and light" 'flexitarian' cuisine at his grown-up HQ, in one of the posh side streets surrounding Brompton Cross. Ambience-wise, it's not a riot, but "unstuffy", "very civilised and not noisy". Incidents of "inept performance" post-Covid continue to drag on its rating for service, but most reporters are "very well looked after" and a typical report is of a "truly delightful" meal. / SW3 3NT; www.elystanstreet.com; elystanstreet; Mon-Thu 2145 pm, Fri & Sat 10.30 pm, Sun 4 pm.

EMILIA'S CRAFTED PASTA £56 333

12 GEORGE STREET, WOOD WHARF, E14 020 8176 1100 12–*1C*
77 ALIE STREET, E1 020 3358 0317 10–*2D*
UNIT C3 IVORY HOUSE, ST KATHARINE DOCKS, E1 020 7481 2004 10–*3D*

"Excellent pasta" is the straightforward proposition at this Italian trio, with a flagship in Canary Wharf, which takes its name and inspiration from Italy's Emilia-Romagna region. / www.emiliaspasta.com; emiliaspasta.

EMMANUELLE EC1

5A ROSEBERY AVENUE NO TEL 10–*1A*

Yuma Hashmi's latest venture is a seventies-styled wine bar (complete with a peacock rattan chair, famous from 1974's X-rated film Emmanuelle) directly opposite Tehran-Berlin (fka The Drunken Butler), his Persian restaurant in Clerkenwell. The wine list is modern, with natural and biodynamic options, and is backed up by French and Iranian snacks and small plates. / EC1R 4SP; emmanuellewinebar.com; Mon, Fri-Sun 10.30 pm.

EMPIRE EMPIRE W11

16 ALL SAINTS ROAD 020 3930 3658 7–*1B*

Aiming to 'epitomise India's groovy seventies scene', this disco-themed dive in Notting Hill features drinking, dancing and dining and is the brainchild of Harneet Baweja, the owner of Gunpowder. It launched too late for survey feedback, but early online buzz from fans of Gunpowder suggest it's worth a whirl. The menu – with dishes incorporating goat, duck and guinea fowl – reads well; while on the drinks list, 'sharing cider' is a feature, alongside a short wine selection and non-Indian beers. / W11 1HH; www.empire-empire.restaurant; empirempire_london; Mon-Sat 10 pm, Sun 4 pm.

THE EMPRESS E9 £58 334

130 LAURISTON RD 020 8533 5123 14–*2B*

Consistently one of London's better-performing gastroboozers, this substantial Victorian tavern near Victoria Park in Hackney was iconic in the area's gentrification over twenty years ago, and "just keeps delivering as a local pub and place to eat". It does a "perfect Sunday roast" while also catering well for non-meat-eaters. / E9 7LH; www.empresse9.co.uk; the_empress_e9; Mon-Sun 10 pm.

ENDO AT THE ROTUNDA, TV CENTRE W12 £280 545

101 WOOD LANE 020 3972 9000 1–*2B*

"A total one off" – Endo Kazutoshi's "zen-like" venue occupies a unique site, on the top of the old BBC Television Centre, and is "spectacular in all respects". "Chef Endo has ruined all other sushi restaurants for me… watching Endo and his team preparing individual pieces of sushi… the rice perfect and still slightly warm, the seafood surely all the best money can buy and prepared with utmost respect. It could be pretentious, but Chef Endo is such a warm and welcoming presence that it never feels like it". Despite the ruinous expense, all reports say it's "worth every penny": "The best meal ever… until you go back!" / W12 7FR; www.endoatrotunda.com; kazutoshi.endo; Tue-Sat 9 pm.

ENDO KAZUTOSHI, THE OWO SW1

57 WHITEHALL PLACE AWAITING TEL 2–*3C*

From the all-star team behind Endo at the Rotunda – another Japanese-influenced rooftop venture: this time a 60-seater on top of London's splashiest hotel opening in decades, complete with outside terrace. Kazutoshi is backed by Misha Zelman, the man who created the likes of Burger & Lobster and the Goodman steakhouse chain. / SW1A 2EU; Tue-Sat 10.30 pm.

ENOTECA TURI SW1 £ 343

87 PIMLICO ROAD 020 7730 3663 6–*2D*

"The personal touch is invaluable" at Giuseppe & Pamela Turi's "thriving" and "very confident" Italian stalwart, which "has gone from strength to strength since moving from Putney to Pimlico in 2015, and is always full" (often of long-term customers, who 'happily make the trek" into the centre of town). "If Italian wine is your thing, this is the place to go": Giuseppe's all-Italian list is a "masterpiece in its own right" and even if 'a ton of money is sometimes required, the vintages are not expensive for what they are". To match it: "refined cooking, with classics, specials, and seasonal variations, reflecting the team's heritage". It's a "grown-up" and "very confident experience, without bowing to fashion" – "the Turis be found at the restaurant every day, and there is always a smile to welcome you". BREAKING NEWS – In August 2023, the Turis announced their retirement, thus rendering the above entry otiose. A month later, just before we went to press, experienced restaurateur, Dominic Ford, and Liberty Wines owner, David Gleave, were announced as the new patrons. Much of the team remains in place, as does the cellar. But – as our read feedback clearly demonstrates – this whole enterprise has always been a supremely personal one and the Turis will be a hard act to follow. We've maintained its rating (but taking service down a notch, reflecting the very personal style of the founders). / SW1W 8PH; www.enotecaturi.com; enotecaturi; closed Sun.

THE ENTERPRISE SW3 £72 234

35 WALTON ST 020 7584 3148 6–*2C*

'Amusing locals and colourful regulars liven up the atmosphere" at this smart watering hole for the Chelsea set, where guests enjoy immaculate white tablecloths, "excellent, often entertaining service" and "perfectly fine gastropub food". / SW3 2HU; www.theenterprise.co.uk; theenterprise35; Mon-Sat 10.30 pm, Sun 10 pm.

EPICURUS NW1

UNIT 90, THE NORTH YARD, CAMDEN STABLES MARKET 07843 199560 9–*2B*

The latest venture from a pair of ex-Palomar chefs, in Camden Market's expansion into North Yard, marries North American diner food with Middle Eastern flair and flavours. Shiri Kraus and Amir Batito already run the Black Cow steakhouse nearby and the result here is an interesting twist on a seemingly familiar (fairly meaty) formula. It opened in late April 2023, too late to generate feedback in our annual diners' poll. / NW1 8AH; www.epicuruscamden.co.uk; epicuruscamden; Tue-Sun 11 pm.

L'ESCARGOT W1 £100 333

48 GREEK STREET 020 7439 7474 5–*2A*

This Gallic treasure (est. 1927, but ultimately dating back to 1896) is London's oldest French restaurant and – complete with its snail carpet – remains a Soho landmark. Its standards under owner Brian Clivaz have held up well over the years, and its ratings continued to be solid in this slightly turbulent year (which saw the establishment close from February to May 2023 to allow for a financial restructuring). The fairly classic menu is appealing and mixes affordable entry-level dishes (croque monsieur at £12) with more luxurious options (such as baked lobster with garlic butter, or fillet of beef 'Rossini', both at £54). Top Tip – superb-value prix fixe at lunch and early evening: two courses £19, three courses £24. / W1D 4EF; www.lescargot.co.uk; lescargotsoho.

ESCOCESA N16 £71 332

67 STOKE NEWINGTON CHURCH STREET 020 7812 9189 1–*1C*

An "excellent Stokey local", "deservedly very popular" for its Spanish tapas, in particular its "absolutely wonderful fish": its Glasgow-born founder, former record producer Stephen Lironi, has made it his mission to intercept some of the top-quality Scottish fish usually exported to Spain. One quibble this year: "surely it's time to upgrade the school chairs". Top Tip – "half-price oysters before 7pm". / N16 0AR; www.escocesa.co.uk; escocesa_n16; Mon-Thu 10 pm, Fri & Sat 11 pm, Sun 9.30 pm.

ESTIATORIO MILOS SW1 £140 224

1 REGENT STREET 020 7839 2080 4–*4D*

"One of the best fish restaurants anywhere" – Costas Spiladis's London outpost of his luxurious international chain channels the brilliance of the Mediterranean, with its bright, white walls and high ceiling. "The fish is displayed beautifully on ice at one end of the venue and hosed down every 20 mins or so" – "a fantastic selection that always delivers a fabulous meal". Sadly, though, you have to be a Greek shipping magnate to afford it nowadays ("just reading the menu is a shock"), and even those who think it's "worth the hype" can find it "so eye-wateringly expensive, I think it might be one visit per year from now on". Those less well disposed to it, say "if you like being served a smidgen of food and being charged a fortune, this restaurant is for you!" / SW1Y 4NR; www.estiatoriomilos.com; estiatoriomilos; Mon-Sat 11 pm, Sun 10 pm.

EVELYN'S TABLE AT THE BLUE POSTS W1 £161 543

28 RUPERT STREET 07921 336010 4–*3D*

"This intimate little counter-dining venue" in an ancient pub that nowadays finds itself part of Chinatown "shows levels of skill and technique to compete with much better-known places that leave you with a far higher bill". James Goodyear has taken over from Luke Selby (the latter departing to be head chef at Le Manoir), but all reports swoon over "a truly special experience" and a multi-course tasting menu that's "absolutely exceptional". "Love the counter-top layout of the restaurant and the chefs are very happy to talk, explaining in detail how things are made (important to me because I am a very keen cook!)". "It has a buzzy vibe and is a bit of a squeeze (in both space and time), making it a very different formula than nearby Aulis. Having said that, the cooking is consistently delightful, imaginative and bold. The menu feels well thought-through, building and balancing as it progresses". "File it under 'one to watch' as they plan to build out the ambition even further": from mid-2023 they are opening on Monday nights and also incorporating their wine bar, The Mulwray, and the pub, The Blue Posts, into the overall offering at Evelyn's Table. / W1D 6DJ; www.theblueposts.co.uk; evelynstable; Tue-Sat 11 pm.

EVEREST CURRY KING SE13 £32 332

24 LOAMPIT HILL 020 8691 2233 1–*4D*

"A staple fixture for the local Sri Lankan community, serving good portions of tasty grub for very reasonable prices", this Lewisham shopfront outfit (with a geographically misleading name) is "now slightly smartened-up, with a new glass frontage". Recent convert Jay Rayner of The Observer swooned at a beetroot curry of "all-engrossing, soothing power". / SE13 7SW; Mon-Sun 11 pm.

EVEREST INN SE3 £56 322

41 MONTPELIER VALE 020 8852 7872 1–*4D*

This Nepalese venue in Blackheath Village is popular with locals, who rate it "a cut above" standard curry-house fare. Ideal after a stroll on the common it overlooks. / SE3 0TJ; www.everestinn.co.uk; everestinn; Tue-Sat 11 pm, Sun 10 pm.

EVERNIGHT SW11 £64 333

3 RAVINE WAY 020 4547 6390 11–*1D*

Near the new American Embassy in Nine Elms, this modern izakaya opened in September 2022 and is the creation of Singapore-born Lynus Lim (ex-The Laughing Heart) and Chase Lovecky (formerly of The Clove Club). Foodwise, it's a bit of a mashup, aiming to 'highlight Japanese cookery techniques whilst engaging the micro-seasonality of produce from the British Isles'. Most reports say the result is "a super newcomer with really enjoyable food showing great balance of flavours and representing value for money". On the downside, there's the occasional view that "though good it's been very hyped up and some dishes work better than others (a bit overcomplicated)". / SW11 7BH; evernightlondon.co.uk; Tue-Sat 11 pm.

FADIGA W1 £38 453

71 BERWICK STREET 020 3609 5536 4–*1C*

"My own family comes from the Emilia Romagna and I can vouch for the authenticity of the delicious (and also generously proportioned!) dishes", says one fan of this "tiny, restaurant, run by a family from Bologna" in Soho. "Dad cooks, Mum is the sommelier, daughter serves tables. Excellent!" / W1F 8TB; www.fadiga.uk; fadiga_ristorantebolognese; Tue-Sat 11 pm.

FAIR SHOT CAFÉ W1

17 SOUTH MOLTON STREET
020 7499 9007 3–*2B*

Bianca Tavella's ground-breaking non-profit moved from Mayfair to splendid new Covent Garden premises in early 2023, bringing tasty treats, light lunches and a proper caffeine hit to guests, while its workforce of young people with learning difficulties get their first proper shot at a job. This social enterprise is a winner, too: 100% of its graduates move on to paid employment, against the UK's 95% unemployment rate among adults with learning difficulties. / W1K 5QT; fairshot.co.uk; fairshotcafe; Sun-Fri 6 pm, Sat 7 pm.

FALLOW ST JAMES'S SW1 £101 333

2 ST JAMES'S MARKET
07785 937900 4–*4D*

To instant acclaim two years ago, Jack Croft and Will Murray transplanted their renowned Heddon Street residency, known for its "interesting" small plates, to this large (150-cover) site, with open kitchen, chef's counter and bar, at the southern end of Haymarket. All accounts this year continue to vaunt its cooking and "fun" style, but ratings weakened across the board amidst a general feeling it risks becoming a victim of its own success: "it felt a bit rushed…"; "the food was good, but prices were crazy…" Top Tips – "smoked cod's head? Yes please!"; and breakfast is now available here both weekends and weekdays, and is highly recommended. / SW1Y 4RP; www.fallowrestaurant.com; fallowrestaurant; Mon-Sun 10.30 pm.

LA FAMIGLIA SW10 £85 234

7 LANGTON STREET 020 7351 0761 6–*3B*

Fans of this "old-fashioned" and datedly glam trattoria near World's End in Chelsea (est. 1966, and the haunt, in its heyday, of folks like Jack Nicholson) say it may "not be tops for food, but the atmosphere and ambience are addictive"(especially in its adorable garden in summer). Fears that it's becoming too long in the tooth have been around for years, with sceptics suggesting "they're just painting by numbers nowadays"; but true believers insist this view is "just snotty – the food is delicious and the service charming". Top Tip – for a blast from the past, "the dessert trolley is an attractive feature". / SW10 0JL; www.lafamiglia.co.uk; lafamiglia.sw10; Tue-Sat 9.45 pm, Sun 9.15 pm.

FARANG N5 £53 443

72 HIGHBURY PARK 020 7226 1609 9–*1D*

"Super spicy (in a good way) cooking", "really interesting dishes" and "roti to die for" keep aficionados of new-wave Thai cuisine coming back to Sebby Holmes's Highbury venue – originally a pop-up, but now firmly established after eight years on the scene. / N5 2XE; www.faranglondon.co.uk; farangldn; Wed-Sat 9 pm.

FARMACY W2 £76 434

74 WESTBOURNE GROVE
020 7221 0705 7–*1B*

Camilla Fayed's "wonderful" plant-based project in Bayswater, supplied by her biodynamic farm in Kent, offers "a wide range of options to keep you returning", with veggie versions of fashionable global dishes – ramen, tacos, pad thai and "juicy and delicious burgers, absolutely to die for". "You can certainly tell she's sunk millions into this place – it's really rather pretty, and the enormous central bar is impressive". / W2 5SH; www.farmacylondon.com; farmacy kitchen; Mon-Thu 9 pm, Fri & Sat 10 pm, Sun 8 pm.

THE FAT BADGER TW10 £69 322

15-17 HILL RISE 020 3743 0853 1–*4A*

Like its other five London ventures, the Gladwin family's Richmond bar/restaurant supplies modern (rather eclectic) British plates and wines sourced from its farm and vineyard in Sussex. Reports are relatively limited, mixing all-round good feedback with sentiment such as: "an average meal from a chain from which I would expect slightly more". / TW10 6UQ; www.thefatbadger-restaurant.com; thefatbadger_resto; Tue-Sat 10 pm, Sun 8 pm.

FATT PUNDIT £59 323

77 BERWICK STREET, W1
020 7287 7900 4–*1C*
6 MAIDEN LANE, WC2
020 7836 8883 5–*3D*

"Delicious small plates that are unusual, interesting and at times rather spicy" distinguish this Soho and Covent Garden duo presenting the Indo-Chinese cuisine developed by Kolkata's historic Hakka community. / www.facebook.com/fattpundit; fattpundit.

FATTO A MANO N1

3 PANCRAS SQ 020 3148 4900 9–*3C*

One minute's walk from Google HQ, amidst the clean-lined new canyons north of King's Cross, this is the year-old London outpost of Brighton & Hove's well-regarded chain (whose unit in Shoreditch's Boxpark is no longer in operation). Reports on the Brighton operations are all very upbeat, but this one has yet to spark much in the way of interest. / N1C 4AG; www.fattoamanopizza.com; fattoamanopizza; Sun-Thu 10 pm, Fri & Sat 10.30 pm.

FEELS LIKE JUNE E14

15 WATER STREET 02035307700 12–*1C*

LA came to Canary Wharf at this California-inspired venue, which opened in summer 2022, and whose all-day menu (also with brunch and dinner alternatives) aims to reflect the west coast's debt to the cuisines of Latin America and Italy. The sunny styling of the interior is a winner – regarding the grub we have limited (but upbeat) feedback. / E14 9SB; www.feelslikejune.com; feels_like_june; Mon-Sun 1 am.

FENCHURCH RESTAURANT, SKY GARDEN EC3 £110 334

20 FENCHURCH ST 033 3772 0020 10–*3D*

Limited feedback in this year's annual diners' poll on the 37th floor of the City's 'Walkie Talkie' – perhaps many Londoners regard it as touristy. Such accounts as we have, though, on the cooking under chef Kerth Gumbs is upbeat: you can have an eight-course tasting menu for £115 or eat à la carte (although the latter is not much less inexpensive with main dishes circa £50). Incredible views, of course. / EC3M 3BY; skygarden.london; sg_skygarden; Tue, Sun 9 pm, Wed & Thu 9.30 pm, Fri & Sat 8.30 pm.

FEZ MANGAL W11 £50 321

104 LADBROKE GROVE
020 7229 3010 7–*1A*

"Still one of the best Turkish grills in town" – this Ladbroke Grove fixture might be "a bit spartan", but "speedy service and BYO" make it a "cost-effective alternative to eating at home". Top Tip – there's "slightly less-packed seating in the extension next door". / W11 1PY; www.fezmangal.com; fezmangal; Mon-Sun 11.30 pm.

50 KALÒ DI CIRO SALVO WC2 £49 433

7 NORTHUMBERLAND AVENUE
020 7930 9955 2–*3C*

"Not quite as good as the original in Naples, but still a safe bet if you want a traditional Neapolitan pizza in the heart of the capital" – Ciro Salvo's offshoot of his award-winning chain (which is indeed headquartered in Napoli) serves "seriously great" pizza "as Naples intended" (using his special long fermentation dough); and its "busy and vibrant" quarters are "an excellent find so close to Trafalgar Square!". A few pizza anoraks say "it's fine, just not London's best". / WC2N 5BY; www.xn--50kal-yta.it; 50kalolondon; Mon-Sun 11 pm.

FIREBIRD W1 £80 333

29 POLAND STREET 020 3813 1430 3–*1D*

"They like grilling!" – in fact pretty well every dish at this "thoroughly enjoyable" Soho yearling, from St Petersburg restaurateurs Madina Kazhimova and Anna Dolgushina, has been 'touched by flames', resulting in some really "lovely food". It's served in a very contemporary interior, alongside a list of natural wines. / W1F 8QR; firebirdlondon.co.uk; firebird.london; Mon-Sat 11 pm.

FISCHER'S W1 £69 223

50 MARYLEBONE HIGH STREET
020 7466 5501 2–*1A*

"The Wolseley's popular little brother provides a setting somewhere between a Munich beer cellar and a Viennese Cafe" in fashionable Marylebone. You don't come here for the food – a "pretty underwhelming pastiche" of Austrian/German cuisine with schnitzel a

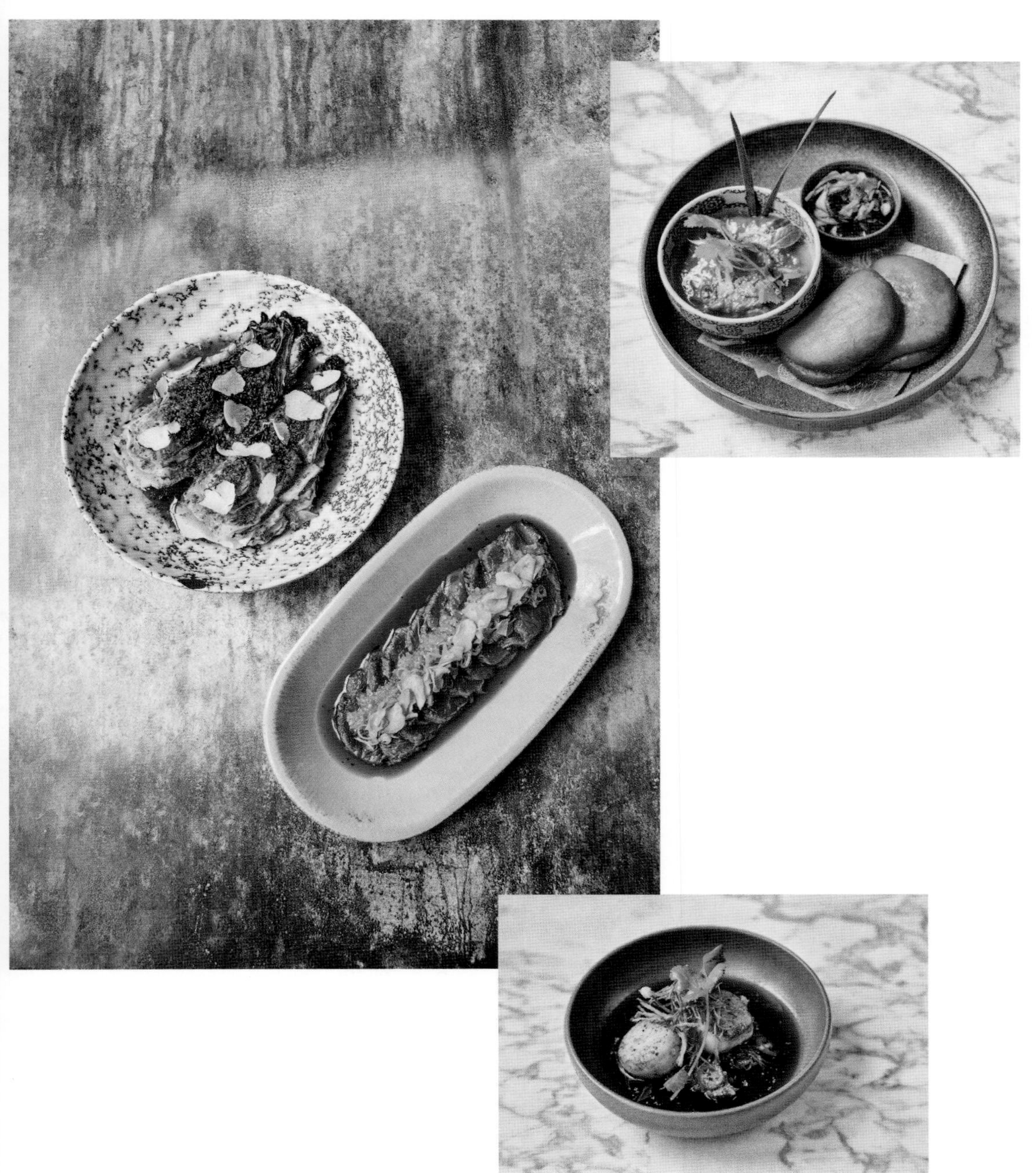

menu mainstay – and the feeling is widespread that "they should do better". But even the many who feel it's becoming ever-more "disappointing" given the "steep" prices often acknowledge that "it's a useful spot and usually busy". / W1U 5HN; www.fischers.co.uk; fischerslondon; Sun & Mon 9.30 pm, Tue-Sat 10 pm.

FISH CENTRAL EC1 £43 442

149-155 CENTRAL ST
020 7253 4970 13–1A

This "authentic chippy" in Clerkenwell – a Greek-Cypriot family-run veteran of more than 50 years' standing – scores well for its "excellent fish" and "warm, humorous service". / EC1V 8AP; www.fishcentral.co.uk; fishcentralrestaurant; Mon-Thu, Sat 10 pm, Fri 10.30 pm.

FISH! SE1 £78 323

CATHEDRAL ST 020 7407 3803 10–4C

This "great fish restaurant offering a range of seafood (and other) dishes" has been a fixture for more than 20 years, behind a glass frontage "in the middle of buzzing Borough Market". The fish is "the freshest" and there are "usually some unusual specials" – although many would argue that "the most appealing thing is its location". / SE1 9AL; www.fishkitchen.co.uk; fishboroughmarket; Sun-Wed 10 pm, Thu-Sat 11 pm.

FISHERS SW6 £46 332

19 FULHAM HIGH STREET 02073715555
11–1B

"The fish is consistently very good (whether battered, grilled or steamed)" at this "perennial favourite" chippy near Putney Bridge in Fulham, which offers "takeaway and a small dine-in area with a half-dozen tables". "The chips are not bad and the price is reasonable". / SW6 3JH; www.fishersfishandchips.co.uk; fisherslondon; Mon-Sun 10 pm.

FISHWORKS £82 332

7-9 SWALLOW ST, W1
020 7734 5813 4–2B
89 MARYLEBONE HIGH ST, W1
020 7935 9796 2–1A
2-4 CATHERINE STREET, WC2
020 7240 4999 5–3D

The "super-fresh fish" – "simply prepared" and "never overcooked" – "never disappoints" at this "good value" trio of West End seafood brasseries, in Covent Garden, Marylebone and Swallow Street, off Piccadilly. / www.fishworks.co.uk; FishworksUK.

FIUME SW8 £76 222

CIRCUS WEST VILLAGE, SOPWITH WAY
020 3904 9010 11–1C

This "elegantly decorated, modern Italian" with a terrace overlooking the river near the redeveloped Battersea Power Station is "useful in the neighbourhood" – a "safe bet", albeit "expensive for what it is". High-profile chef Francesco Mazzei parted company with the owners, D&D London, in early 2023, boosting the sentiment that this potentially spectacular venue has never fully realised its potential. / SW8 5BN; fiume-restaurant.co.uk; fiume.london; Mon-Sat 10 pm, Sun 8.30 pm. SRA – accredited

THE FIVE FIELDS SW3 £201 443

8-9 BLACKLANDS TER
020 7838 1082 6–2D

"For a very civilised meal", Taylor Bonnyman's "refined" and "romantic" venue – in a Chelsea townhouse, hidden way near Peter Jones – has become a huge hit: out of the PR limelight, but in the Top 40 most-mentioned restaurants in our annual diners' poll and "well worthy of its Michelin star" thanks to its "immaculate but unobtrusive" service and Marguerite Keogh's "superb and assured cooking": "wonderfully light, creative, beautiful and flavoursome food" from "their own kitchen garden in Sussex" (which the most ardent fans feel is "at a level above their tyre-company rating"). Its ratings slipped a little this year amidst cost of living concerns (and a number of reporters noting that "it's a pity that they only do a tasting menu"). As a result, its style can appear more "hushed" and "formal" and "very expensive" ("we find it just too costly to visit anymore, although we love this place as one of the most amazing providers of interesting and totally divine food"). That's still a minority view, though – for most diners it's just "just a brilliant experience". Top Tip – "stellar wine selection". / SW3 2SP; www.fivefieldsrestaurant.com; the5fields; Tue-Sat 10 pm.

500 N19 £58 342

782 HOLLOWAY RD 020 7272 3406 9–1C

Near Archway, this "great little local" (named after the diminutive Fiat Cinquecento) is both "reliable and good value". It may "feel a tad old school", but chef-patron Mario Magli and his team serve up "wonderful food with love and enthusiasm". ("I have had many meals here with friends and it has always been delightful and an example of how delicious Italian cooking can be".) / N19 3JH; www.500restaurant.co.uk; 500restaurant; Wed-Sat 10 pm, Sun 9 pm.

500 DEGREES SE24 £46 323

153A DULWICH ROAD
020 7274 8200 11–2D

"Great pizza that's very good value" is the USP of this Neapolitan-style shopfront outfit by Brockwell Park. It used to have three offshoots across South London, but now only the Herne Hill branch is ongoing. / SE24 0NG; www.500degrees.co; 500degreeshernehill; Mon-Sat 11 pm, Sun 10 pm.

FKABAM (BLACK AXE MANGAL) N1 £56 423

156 CANONBURY ROAD NO TEL 9–2D

"Nothing else quite like this in London!" – Lee Tiernan's renowned heavy-metal BBQ (renamed with a nod to Prince a couple of year ago) "may look closed from the outside, but inside, this tiny venue (30 seats) is jumping". It's known for its kick-ass flatbreads: "flavours pack a punch, the decor's wild and the music loud. We love it!" / N1 2UP; www.blackaxemangal.com; blackaxemangal; Wed-Sat 10.30 pm.

THE FLASK N6 £54 234

77 HIGHGATE WEST HILL
020 8348 7346 9–1B

Not to be confused with its namesake near Hampstead tube on the other side of the Heath – this classic, traditional pub (which boasts Dickens as a former patron) sits in a beautiful slice of period Highgate, and benefits from a large outside terrace, a characterful interior and dependable grub. / N6 6BU; www.theflaskhighgate.com; theflaskhighgate; Mon-Sat 10 pm, Sun 9 pm.

FLAT IRON £39 333

17 BEAK ST, W1 020 3019 2353 4–2B
42-44 JAMES STREET, W1 NO TEL 3–1A
17 HENRIETTA ST, WC2
020 3019 4212 5–3C
9 DENMARK ST, WC2 NO TEL 5–1A
9 YOUNG STREET, W8 NO TEL 6–1A
47-51 CALEDONIAN RD, N1 NO TEL 9–3D
112-116 TOOLEY STREET, SE1 NO TEL
10–4D
41-45 THE CUT, SE1 NO TEL 10–4A
SOHO WHARF, CLINK STREET, SE1
NO TEL 10–3C
88-90 COMMERCIAL STREET, E1 NO TEL
13–2C
77 CURTAIN ROAD, EC2 NO TEL 13–1B

"One of the best bangs for your buck in town" – this "well-priced" steak chain has a "sensible formula" and has "managed to keep standards up despite constant expansion" (its latest, 11th London site, opened in March 2023 in Kensington). "Surroundings are basic" and "their menu is very simplistic: you choose a cut of meat, sauce and sides – the cuts are cooked to perfection", "chips are hot, the service is punctual" and "free ice cream at the end ensures happy faces when people leave". / www.flatironsteak.co.uk; flatironsteak.

FLAT WHITE W1 £13 332

17 BERWICK ST 020 7734 0370 4–2D

This "small, often crowded" independent coffee shop by Soho's Berwick Street market is a pilgrimage site for caffeine junkies, as the source of Antipodean 'third wave' coffee culture in Britain since its 2005 opening. And yes, "the coffee's very good". / W1F 0PT; www.flatwhitesoho.co.uk; flat white; Mon-Fri 5 pm, Sat 6 pm, Sun 6.30pm.

FLESH AND BUNS £68 443

2 BERNERS STREET, W1
20 3019 3492 3–*1D*
BONE DADDIES, 41 EARLHAM STREET, WC2 020 7632 9500 5–*2C*

A taste-tingling sensation of Japanese and other Asian delights" – the "most amazing bao buns", plus "Korean wings, poke bowls and sushi that are all so good" – win a big thumbs up for this duo of "great Asian-fusion restaurants" (under the same ownership as Bone Daddies). If anything, their star has risen since they cut back to just two branches in Fitzrovia and Covent Garden. / www.fleshandbuns.com; fleshandbuns.

FLORA INDICA SW5 £60 333

42 OLD BROMPTON ROAD
20 7370 4450 6–*2A*

A quirky steampunk theme combined with an emphasis on cocktails and craft beers accompanies very sound modern Indian cooking" at this Earl's Court venture, whose name pays tribute to the 19th-century Scottish botanists who classified the subcontinent's plants. "After a few false starts on the site, this restaurant has found its forte under the same ownership as its predecessor Mr Wing (RIP)". / SW5 0DE; www.flora-indica.com; flora_indica; Tue-Sun 11 pm.

FLOUR & GRAPE SE1 £51 334

14 BERMONDSEY ST
20 7407 4682 10–*4D*

This new-wave Italian in Bermondsey is deservedly packed at all times" with fans of its very moreish" pasta-only dishes in "generous servings". "Not being able to book is a bit of a gamble", but you can queue in the downstairs cocktail bar, 'Two One Four'. / SE1 3TQ; www.flourandgrape.com; flourandgrape; Mon-Sun 10 pm.

FOLEY'S W1 £56 333

3 FOLEY STREET 020 3137 1302 2–*1B*

High ratings express continued satisfaction with this 70-seater in Fitzrovia, where an outside bar is something of a feature. The website promises 'Asian-inspired food, cocktails and sake' and steady feedback confirms that's what it consistently delivers. / W1W 6DU; www.foleysrestaurant.co.uk; foleysrestaurant; Mon-Thu 10 pm, Fri & Sat 10.30 pm, Sun 9 pm.

FORTNUM & MASON, THE DIAMOND JUBILEE TEA SALON W1 £90 334

181 PICCADILLY 020 7734 8040 3–*3D*

Delicious sarnies and pastries keep on coming" at this elegant chamber, just down the road from its rival The Ritz, to which it is a close second in votes as offering London's top afternoon tea. There is a huge selection of brews, plus "excellent homemade ice creams and sorbets" and "yummy savoury snacks as well". "Take a friend from overseas and pretend you come here all the time!" / W1A 1ER; www.fortnumandmason.com; fortnums; Mon-Sat 8 pm, Sun 6 pm.

45 JERMYN ST. SW1 £85 233

45 JERMYN STREET 020 7205 4545 3–*3D*

With its many booths, Fortnum & Mason's "comfortable" bar/restaurant (with its own, independent street entrance) provides a "discreet" and "decently located" venue that's ideal for a St James's light bite, meal, tea, coffee or cocktail; and is most often tipped as a handy option for a business get-together. Since its very promising launch in 2015, its ratings have waned, with its cooking increasingly judged "reliable but not spectacular". Top Menu Tip – "breakfast is always a pleasure; go for the Welsh rarebit". / SW1Y 6DN; www.45jermynst.com; 45jermynst; Mon-Sat 10.15 pm, Sun 4.45 pm.

40 MALTBY STREET SE1 £58 333

40 MALTBY ST 020 7237 9247 10–*4D*

Firmly established after more than a decade, highly rated chef Steve Williams's no-frills canteen is attached to a biodynamic wine warehouse in a railway arch behind London Bridge station. It's "always busy, but the trek is worth it for the food" – seasonal ingredients transformed in a basic-looking open kitchen and served "with a smile and a laugh". / SE1 3PA; www.40maltbystreet.com; 40maltbystreet; Wed-Sat 10 pm.

FORZA WIN SE5 333

29-33 CAMBERWELL CHURCH STREET
07454 898693 1–*3C*

"Inventive and delicious Italian cooking in a cheerful trattoria" is the straightforward but engaging offer at Bash Redford and Michael Lavery's Camberwell newcomer, relocated from its former well-known Peckham location in late 2022. Top Menu Tips – "the homemade focaccia is the best, either plain or with a dipping sauce such as nduja, wild garlic pesto or crab and lemon; the antipasti are so varied and good and – if you have room – the signature dessert, custardo, is terrific". / SE5 8TR; www.forzawin.com; forzawin; Mon-Sun 10.30 pm.

FORZA WINE SE15 £61 343

FLOOR 5, RYE LANE 020 7732 7500 1–*4D*

"Find of the year and worth the trek to Peckham" (although the foodie in-crowd have known about it and its sibling Forza Win, newly transferred to Camberwell, for several years now) – this rooftop wine bar with a "buzzing ambience, perched above Peckham Rye station", offers "a great selection of small plates" to nibble on while sipping "natural wine only, but a fair few easy-drinking bottles" (or cocktails if you prefer). In September 2023, they opened a large new offshoot on the terrace at the National Theatre: there are 100 covers inside with an open kitchen, and a sheltered outside area with seating for 70 drinkers and diners. / SE15 4ST; www.forzawine.com; forzawine; Sun-Thu 11.30 pm, Fri & Sat 12.30 am.

FOUR REGIONS TW9 £59 333

102-104 KEW RD 020 8940 9044 1–*4A*

This "stalwart neighbourhood Chinese restaurant" on the fringes of Richmond (as you head to Kew) is well known after more than 30 years for the "consistently good food" that means it's "usually busy". / TW9 2PQ; www.fourregions.co.uk; four regions; Mon-Sat 11 pm, Sun 10.30 pm.

FOUR SEASONS £68 411

11 GERRARD STREET, W1
020 7287 0900 5–*3A*
12 GERRARD ST, W1 020 7494 0870 5–*3A*
23 WARDOUR ST, W1 020 7287 9995 5–*3A*
84 QUEENSWAY, W2 020 7229 4320 7–*2C*

"It's worth the spartan interior and mixed service to eat the roast duck and/or char siu pork" at these Cantonese canteens, where "the best roast duck in the world is the claim" – from no less an authority than The FT – "and it must be up there" with "meat and crispy skin so well done (no pun intended)"; and don't forget "the crispy pork belly – an especial fat-lover's treat!". Launched in Queensway 34 years ago, the group now has three venues around Chinatown plus the new Chop Chop nearby in the Hippodrome Casino. Further afield there are outlets in Colindale's Bang Bang Oriental food hall, Oxford and Leicester. / www.fs-restaurants.co.uk; fourseasons_uk.

14 HILLS EC3 £96 224

120 FENCHURCH STREET
020 3981 5222 10–*3D*

"Great decor" in the shape of 2,500 living evergreen plants vie with the "stunning 14th-floor views" over the City for top billing at this D&D London venue in 120 Fenchurch Street. By comparison, the "expensive but good food" from an Anglo-French menu is somewhat in the shade. / EC3M 5BA; www.danddlondon.com; danddlondon; Mon-Sun 10.30 pm. SRA – accredited

FOX & GRAPES SW19 £63 343

9 CAMP RD 020 8619 1300 11–*2A*

"You feel miles away from London" at this Georgian gastroboozer on the edge of Wimbledon Common, which provides "a great atmosphere in very cosy surroundings". "There's a more relaxed vibe than when it originally emerged from its old 'boozer' days. The staff are lovely, attentive, fun but not over the top, and the food is perfect". / SW19 4UN; www.foxandgrapeswimbledon.co.uk; foxandgrapeswimbledon; Wed-Sat 9.15 pm, Sun 8 pm.

THE FOX & HOUNDS SW11 £70 343

66-68 LATCHMERE ROAD
020 7924 5483 11–*1C*

"Super-charming service" and a "great hidden garden" that feels "secluded and away from London life" are key ingredients behind the success of this "jolly pub-restaurant" on a prominent corner in Battersea; very "decent" Mediterranean-inspired food too. / SW11 2JU; www.thefoxandhoundspub.co.uk; thefoxbattersea; Mon-Sat 10 pm, Sun 9 pm.

THE FOX AND PHEASANT SW10 £61 334

1 BILLING ROAD 020 7352 2943 6–*3B*

A "charming 'country-pub-style' local, cutely hidden away in west Chelsea" in 'The Billings' close to Stamford Bridge; and which nowadays is "celeb-owned" (by singer James Blunt and his wife Sofia). "The food has always been of great quality and the fact that you can relax in the pub bit afterwards makes for a lovely lazy afternoon and evening". / SW10 9UJ; www.thefoxandpheasant.com; thefoxandpheasantpub; Mon-Sat 10 pm, Sun 9 pm.

FRANCO MANCA £39 222

BRANCHES THROUGHOUT LONDON

With its "delicious sourdough bases", and its "excellent choice of toppings with regularly changing specials" from "well-sourced ingredients", these "buzzing" cafés are still seen as "a refreshing angle on the pizza theme" and – if "nothing special" – "pretty decent and fairly priced". Those questioning "what the fuss is about" are growing in number though, as its ratings head south into PizzaExpress territory. (In April 2023, the Fulham Shore owners of the group were sold to Japanese investors, Toridoll Holdings, making its future direction hard to call.) / www.francomanca.co.uk; francomancapizza.

FRANCO'S SW1 £90 344

61 JERMYN ST 020 7499 2211 3–*3C*

"A great all-rounder in St James's", particularly popular amongst a well-heeled SW1 business clientele – this "reassuring" veteran provides the "careful service" of "no frills", "traditional" dishes and "has been going for years" – since 1945 in fact – "and long may it last". But even those for whom it's a favourite note that "you pay the price when the bill comes". / SW1Y 6LX; www.francoslondon.com; francoslondon; Mon-Sat 11 pm.

FRANK'S CANTEEN N5 £45 332

86 HIGHBURY PARK 020 7354 4830 9–*1D*

This "great local" on Highbury Corner has developed from a catering company and supper club into a fully fledged "neighbourhood restaurant, serving proper food at reasonable prices", with separate all-day brunch/lunch and evening menus featuring modern European dishes. / N5 2XE; www.frankscanteen.com; frankscanteen; Mon & Tue, Sun 4 pm, Thu-Sat, Wed 9.30 pm.

FRANKLINS SE22 £65 343

157 LORDSHIP LN 020 8299 9598 1–*4D*

"Lunching here is like a warm hug with a dear friend", say fans of Rod Franklin and Tim Sheehan's "perfect local restaurant" in East Dulwich – a "good balance of the classic and quirky" that celebrates its quarter century this year. Top Tip – "Sunday lunches are a particular local legend with extra Yorkshire puds on the side for the really hungry"; and "lots for vegans/veggies". / SE22 8HX; www.franklinsrestaurant.com; franklinsse22; Mon-Sat midnight, Sun 10.30 pm.

FRANTOIO SW10 £68 324

397 KING'S RD 020 7352 4146 6–*3B*

A meal is "always fun" at this long-running Chelsea trattoria near World's End, where host Bucci looks after his guests well. The service may "lack finesse", but the food is "fine" and comes in "massive portions". / SW10 0LR; frantoio.co.uk; frantonio_london; Mon-Sun 11 pm.

FREAK SCENE SW6 £44 443

28 PARSONS GREEN LANE
020 7610 9863 11–*1B*

Ace Aussie chef, Scott Hallsworth has revived his raved-about Freak Scene pan-Asian restaurant once again – this time off Parsons Green in Fulham in spring 2023. Based on a small number of initial ratings, his amped-up fusion fare (sushi plus wackier creations such as miso-yaki foie gras croissant with star anise jus) is in fine form. / SW6 4HS; www.freakscenerestaurants.com; freaksceneldn; Wed-Sat 10.30 pm, Sun 9.30 pm.

FREDERICK'S N1 £71 344

106 CAMDEN PASSAGE
020 7359 2888 9–*3D*

Set among the antiques shops of Camden Passage, this "comfortable" Islington institution has been superbly run by two generations of the Segal family for 55 years. The "simple but very good quality food is served in a bright and well-spaced conservatory dining room at the back", at tables that are "nicely spaced", with "just the right amount of buzz to have a conversation". Top Tip – huge garden area for summer dining / N1 8EG; www.fredericks.co.uk; fredericks_n1; Tue-Sat 10 pm.

THE FRENCH HOUSE W1 £72 445

49 DEAN STREET 020 7437 2477 5–*3A*

"The lovely Soho institution above this legendary pub" (where de Gaulle is said to have composed some of his speeches during WWII) is currently "in the very safe hands of Neil Borthwick" (Angela Hartnett's hubbie). There's "wizardry afoot" here but "no faff or fancy" – by "doing simple but really excellent things to top produce but not doing much to it" he creates "a tight menu of absolute bangers", with "big flavours singing out" ("a plate of greens can be as full of oomph as a tartare or a chop"). "Staff are tremendous" and for many reporters this is "a go-to destination in the West End". / W1D 5BG; www.frenchhousesoho.com; frenchhousesoho; Mon-Sat 11 pm, Sun 10.30 pm.

FRENCHIE WC2 £92 333

18 HENRIETTA STREET
020 7836 4422 5–*3C*

We have Jamie Oliver to thank for the name of this "quintessential modern French bistro" in Covent Garden, who gave the nickname to owner Gregory Merchand when he worked for him many years ago at Fifteen (long RIP). It's the spin-off to Marchand's (and wife Marie's) Parisian venue of the same name, "featuring the speed, simplicity, flavour and lightness, essential for a satisfying pre-theatre experience". "This is honest Gallic fare which does not disappoint": "dishes made with good ingredients, treated respectfully". "The counter is always a good area to sit if just two are dining. There's the

Gloria EC2

chance to engage with bar staff and have a good view of the comings and goings". / WC2E 8QH; www.frenchiecoventgarden.com; frenchiecoventgarden; Mon-Sat 10 pm, Sun 8 pm.

FROG BY ADAM HANDLING WC2 £241 4 4 3

35 SOUTHAMPTON STREET 020 7199 8370 5–*3D*

Many "magical and simply sublime" meals were reported this year at Adam Handling's "exceptional" Covent Garden HQ, whose open kitchen delivers "creative, passionate and sustainably resourced modern British cooking" ("intricate beyond belief in presentation; and a delightful explosion of taste and texture"). The "buzzing" setting is kept in "relaxed" mood by the "fun", "slightly irreverent" service. The catch? "You get an incredible meal, but it comes with an incredible price tag!" / WC2E 7HG; www.frogbyadamhandling.com; frogbyah; Wed-Sat, Mon & Tue 11 pm.

LA FROMAGERIE £56 3 3 3

2-6 MOXON ST, W1 020 7935 0341 3–*1A*
52 LAMB'S CONDUIT ST, WC1 020 7242 1044 2–*1D*
30 HIGHBURY PARK, N5 020 7359 7440 9–*2D*

'Simple food done well...and the cheese!!" – this small group has basic eateries attached to their stores as well as "an enormous selection of cheese to buy at retail". WC1 is by far the most popular outlet – "like wandering into a village restaurant in the heart of Bloomsbury". 'If you like cheese and wine, what's not to love about this place?" / www.lafromagerie.co.uk; lafromagerieuk.

FUMO WC2 £55 2 3 4

37 ST MARTIN'S LANE 020 3778 0430 5–*4C*

The "beautiful setting" and "elegant small sharing plates of tapas-like cicchetti" make this "great spot" from the San Carlo group "perfect for pre- or post-Coliseum dining" and it inspires uniformly positive feedback from a big and diverse fan base. / WC2N 4JS; sancarlofumo.co.uk; sancarlorestaurants; Sun-Fri 11 pm, Sat midnight.

GALLIPOLI AGAIN N1 £50 3 2 4

119 UPPER STREET 020 7226 8099 9–*3D*

This "cheap 'n' cheerful Turkish operation" has been an atmospheric fixture on Upper Street for more than 25 years, offering "well cooked and presented dishes in generous portions". "The smaller Gallipoli has gone, so all efforts have been put into this larger branch", which has "a relaxed style, with different areas to sit in depending on the occasion". / N1 1QP; gallipolicafe.co.uk; Sun-Thu 11 pm, Fri & Sat midnight.

GALVIN AT WINDOWS, PARK LANE LONDON HILTON HOTEL W1 £111 3 3 4

22 PARK LN 020 7208 4021 3–*4A*

"What a view you get over London" from the 28th floor of Hilton Hotel on Park Lane (when it opened in 1963, the capital's first skyscraper hotel). Run since 2006 by the Galvin Bros, there is the odd grumble that the fare is "pedestrian and overpriced", but most diners feel you get "wonderful service and food to match the vista", with head chef Marc Hardiman providing a variety of à la carte and tasting options. Top Tip – good-value set lunch. / W1K 1BE; www.galvinatwindows.com; galvinatwindows; Mon-Sun 9.30 pm.

GALVIN BISTROT & BAR E1 £68 3 4 2

35 BISHOPS SQUARE 020 7299 0404 13–*2B*

Occupying "an excellent spot in the City, overlooking a pedestrian square behind Bishopsgate" – this is, say fans, a "reliable" bistro, whose "great French food and friendly service" delivers "the Galvin experience, but at approachable prices", right next door to the brothers' high-end La Chapelle (see also). More critical reporters, though, diagnose price creep here, which they feel is starting to erode the level of value, especially given the relatively humble interior. Top Tip – "sit outside on the terrace". / E1 6DY; galvinrestaurants.com; galvinbistrot; Mon-Sat 9.30 pm.

GALVIN LA CHAPELLE E1 £121 4 4 5

35 SPITAL SQ 020 7299 0400 13–*2B*

"One of the best dining rooms in London", the Galvin Bros' "impressive" Spitalfields venue occupies a "spectacular" space that looks like a church, but which was actually part of a late-Victorian girls' school – a "real special occasion place" both for romantics or for an "unbeatable, proper business lunch in the City". It won improved ratings this year for its "fabulous", "classic" cuisine, its "professional" service and its "refined" wines from a "huge book of vintages". / E1 6DY; www.galvinlachapelle.com; galvinrestaurants; Mon & Tue 9.15 pm, Wed-Sat 9.15 pm, Sun 9 pm.

LA GAMBA SE1 £59 3 4 2

UNIT 3, ROYAL FESTIVAL HALL, 020 7183 0094 2–*3D*

Need a bite near the Southbank Centre? This new Galician-inspired tapas spot at the foot of the centre itself, complete with outside terrace, opened in February 2023. It is run by Jack, Harry and Matthew Applebee, who run the Applebee's at Borough Market (see also). Stylewise, the appeal is far from cutting edge, with almost-retro decor and with Spanish cuisine that's not designed to wow the fooderati. But amidst the anonymity of the area, our early reports say it creates good vibes: "very new...very good... family welcome absolutely perfect... tapas are fresh and plentiful... a great addition to the South Bank!" (And The Observer's Jay Rayner is a fan too. In a June 2023 review he blessed its "extremely solid and pleasing take on the Spanish repertoire" and he too notes its "personal" style: "You do not sense the dead hand of head office, as you might in the surrounding places"). / SE1 8XX; www.lagambalondon.com; lagamba.london; Mon-Sun 11 pm.

THE GAME BIRD SW1 £124 3 3 4

16-18 ST JAMES'S PLACE 020 7518 1234 3–*4C*

'Hoof, feather and field' is the billing given to the meaty options (which are the top choices) at this traditional dining room – a peaceful space, discreetly hidden away in St James's and overseen from afar by its 'food director', star-chef Lisa Goodwin-Allen of The Stafford's sister property, Northcote (in Lancs). Practically all reports applaud its all-round professional performance and also its "extensive" cellar. Top Tip – a shout out to the "sumptuous and plentiful" afternoon tea served on the "wonderful comfortable sofas" nearby complete with "free refills for the sandwiches!" / SW1A 1NJ; thestaffordlondon.com; thestaffordlondon; Mon-Fri 9 pm, Sun 9 pm, Sat 9 pm.

GANAPATI SE15 £45 4 4 3

38 HOLLY GROVE 020 7277 2928 1–*4D*

"A true neighbourhood go-to" – in her 20th anniversary year, Peckham food pioneer Clare Fisher is "still doing things with South Indian flavours that make the heart sing". Top Tip – "don't forget to buy a jar of homemade garlic or beetroot pickle to take home". / SE15 5DF; www.ganapatirestaurant.com; ganapati.peckham; Tue-Sat 10.30 pm, Sun 10 pm.

GANYMEDE SW1 £88 3 3 3

139 EBURY STREET 020 3971 0761 2–*4A*

"More gastro French than pub, but delicious" – the successor to much-missed Belgravia institution the Ebury Street Wine Bar (long RIP) has got off to a strong start, helped by a "very high standard of food and service" from "welcoming, friendly and courteous staff". / SW1W 9QU; ganymedelondon.co.uk; ganymedesw1; Mon-Sat 10 pm, Sun 6 pm.

THE GARDEN CAFE AT THE GARDEN MUSEUM SE1 £62 3 3 4

5 LAMBETH PALACE RD 020 7401 8865 2–*4D*

"Excellent food in a leafy setting, especially on a warm and bright day" makes the elevated café at Lambeth's Garden Museum "a complete go-to" for foodies in the know. George Ryle, the chef who co-founded it to great acclaim in 2017, left after five years to return to his native Yorkshire, but the kitchen has barely missed a beat under his successor Myles Donaldson (ex-Noble Rot and Anchor & Hope among others). / SE1 7LB; www.gardenmuseum.org.uk; gardenmuseum; Mon, Wed & Thu, Sat & Sun 3 pm, Tue, Fri 9 pm.

LE GARRICK WC2 £63 333

10-12 GARRICK STREET
020 7240 7649 5–*3C*

"Candlelit booths, rustic French food and wine, and discreet service" make this "little slice of France in Covent Garden" "perfect for a date or anniversary". If possible, "go downstairs and experience the brick arched cellar dining area, which is full of character and charm". The "classic bistro fare" is "adequately prepared and comes at very reasonable prices considering the location". / WC2E 9BH; www.legarrick.co.uk; le_garrick; Mon-Sat 11 pm.

THE GARRISON SE1 £84 333

99 BERMONDSEY STREET
020 7089 9355 10–*4D*

"Still a very good gastropub", this green-tiled ex-boozer was a leading light in Bermondsey's emergence as a foodie destination when it opened 21 years ago, and remains in the gastronomic high ground with its commitment to ethically sourced ingredients. / SE1 3XB; www.thegarrison.co.uk; thegarrisonse1; Mon-Thu 11 pm, Fri & Sat midnight, Sun 10.30 pm.

THE GATE £62 333

22-24 SEYMOUR PLACE, W1
020 7724 6656 2–*2A*
51 QUEEN CAROLINE ST, W6
020 8748 6932 8–*2C*
370 ST JOHN ST, EC1 020 7278 5483 9–*3D*

"A go-to favourite vegetarian… they have been going for 30 years" – this small group "still maintains high standards" with "very imaginative dishes that will even please your meat-eating friends". The W6 original – a characterful space, above a church behind Hammersmith's Eventim Apollo – is the most popular, but its spin-offs near Sadlers Wells and in Seymour Village are also well-regarded. / thegaterestaurants.com; gaterestaurant.

THE GATEHOUSE N6 £66 332

1 NORTH ROAD 020 8340 8054 9–*1B*

"A perfect rabbit stew" was one of the options given the thumbs up this year at this black-and-white gabled, 1930s pub in central Highgate, where many of the dishes have a Spanish spin. Notable features include a large garden area and even its own theatre upstairs. / N6 4BD; www.thegatehousen6.com; thegatehousen6; Mon-Wed 10 pm, Thu-Sat 10.30 pm, Sun 9 pm.

GAUCHO £87 222

BRANCHES THROUGHOUT LONDON

This Argentinian-inspired group celebrates its 30th anniversary this year, now with a dozen branches in London and another seven in provincial cities. In its heyday, it "used to be the best place for a steak", backed up by a "well-compiled list" of South American wines. But while fans still applaud it for "reliably good" meals (albeit acknowledging it "could do with a few more non-meat options"), critics – and its competition – have multiplied over the years, and there's a feeling "you can now find better elsewhere". / www.gauchorestaurants.co.uk; gauchogroup. SRA – 1 star.

GAUTHIER SOHO W1 £120 344

21 ROMILLY ST 020 7494 3111 5–*3A*

"Alexis is now 100% vegan and the result is outstanding", say disciples of his quirky Soho venture – a "beautiful townhouse with a series of intimate, romantic rooms", which he's run since 2010, and which went fully meat-free in 2021. Vegetarians of course worship it, but so do many meat-eaters too ("I am an avowed carnivore and my mind was blown by this restaurant – how anyone can create something so superb from the humble vegetable is beyond my comprehension"). But that's not to say it's all plain sailing as many diners are in two minds about the switch and "still not completely convinced that the vegan offering is as good as the old omnivorous one". One or two are just outright disappointed; but for most there's a feeling that "some menu items are trying too hard and miss the mark". A recurrent gripe is that "it seems odd that so much of his vegan menu imitates meat forms" ("I have no problems with a vegan establishment; my only annoyance is the tendency to imitate non-vegan dishes. I just wish they would stick to their guns and stop impersonating non-vegan cuisine because there is no question that Alexis and the team are very talented chefs"). The "slick service" and "fabulously atmospheric" space are the same as they ever were. / W1D 5AF; www.gauthiersoho.co.uk; gauthierinsoho; Tue-Sat 9.30 pm.

LE GAVROCHE W1 £160 334

43 UPPER BROOK ST 020 7408 0881 3–*2A*

"Perfect in so many ways" – Michel Albert Roux's Mayfair legend is part of the nation's gastronomic history. It was the first UK restaurant to win three Michelin stars in 1982 after his father Albert moved it to this basement near the former US embassy from its original Chelsea site. And it has been ably run by MasterChef judge Michel since 1992, when père moved over for fils (since which time it has held two stars). "The entrance leads to a small bar for pre-dinner drinks (arrive early), with a staircase down to the main restaurant": an old-fashioned space – all "soft furnishings and discreet dividers" – whose 1980s decor has a certain retro charm. Old traditions are maintained – for example, "some diners are surprised that only the person named in the reservation has prices shown on their menu". "Classic French cuisine is served with style and reverence: dishes are very much 'old-school'" and prepared with "flair and skill". "The wine list is to drool over", "if you have time to read it (it's so long!)". "Michel himself works the room, which adds to the experience", greeting guests in his whites, and with a longstanding team, including twins Sylvia & Ursula Perbersschlager managing the show. Post-Covid, the restaurant significantly cut its opening times, and – perhaps due to the pressures of soaring costs – concerns over value since the pandemic have taken ratings from being outstanding to merely good. Many guests still say "prices are reasonable given the excellent cooking and unique sense of occasion"; but there is a growing minority of regretful regulars for whom the experience is just "not as good as on previous visits", with some meals plain "disappointing". The lack of lunchtime service is a particular issue ("this was my favourite restaurant and lunch was a treat, but unfortunately it's no longer offered and we simply can't afford to eat there anytime. The prices are horrendous"). For the majority, though, it's still "worth it for a special blow out" and "there is a long waiting list so you need to book well in advance". Top Menu Tip – "the double cooked cheese souffle is incredible". BREAKING NEWS: in mid-August 2023, Michel announced that Le Gavroche will close in January 2024. Up till that point there will be a series of special dinners… but good luck getting a booking! In fact, given the fact that all available seats at the restaurant are pretty much now taken, we've listed it as closed. / W1K 7QR; www.le-gavroche.co.uk; le_gavroche_restauraunt; Tue-Sat 10 pm.

GAZETTE £65 223

79 SHERWOOD CT, CHATFIELD RD, SW11
020 7223 0999 11–*1C*
147 UPPER RICHMOND RD, SW15
020 8789 6996 11–*2B*
218 TRINITY ROAD, SW17
020 8767 5810 11–*2C*
17-18 TOOK'S COURT, EC4
020 7831 6664 10–*2A*

This popular small bistro group is "so very French", especially when eating at the original "buzzy" Battersea branch, which opened in 2007 "at an attractive location near the river". The other branches – in Putney, Wandsworth Common and the City (plus one inside the Institut Français in South Kensington) – are also applauded as "good value" options, but results can also seem a little "unadventurous". / www.gazettebrasserie.co.uk.

GBR (THE GREAT BRITISH RESTAURANT) AT THE DUKES HOTEL SW1 £90 323

35 ST JAMES'S PL 020 7491 4840 3–*4C*

Traditional, peaceful hotel brasserie, hidden away in a cute warren of St James's streets, which has successfully upped its profile in recent years. It provides a "very good standard of food and wine that's not expensive for the quality". The only recurrent gripe is service that can be a tad "erratic". Top Tip – "reasonably priced set menu". / SW1A 1NY; www.dukeshotel.com; dukeslondon; Sun & Mon 11 am, Tue-Sat 9.30 pm.

GEM N1 £48 333

265 UPPER STREET 020 7359 0405 9–*2D*

This "small and crowded" grill on Islington's main drag serves "reasonably priced Turkish,

Kurdish and Greek-style food" and is "clearly a local crowd-pleaser". The 'Hidden Gem' basement is available for private parties. / N1 2UQ; www.gemrestaurant.org.uk; gemrestaurantuk; Mon-Sat 11 pm.

GERMAN GYMNASIUM N1 £76 113

KING'S BOULEVARD
020 7287 8000 9–3C

"It occupies an amazing, high-ceilinged space" built in 1865 for the German Gymnastics Society – and venue for London's first indoor Olympic games), but "it's a shame other aspects of the offering are so weak" at this D&D London property, immediately behind King's Cross station. Fans do claim "all German food boxes are firmly ticked, with tasty and well-presented schnitzel and weißwurst", but even they admit "the building is the star of the show". And far too many reporters "expected much better than the very poor quality for the prices" – which are "on the high side" – "terrible service that doesn't seem to care" and cuisine that's somewhere between "pretty standard" and "below average". Top Menu Tip – breakfast with "pretzel to die for" is its most recommended feature. / N1C 4BU; www.germangymnasium.com; thegermangym; Mon-Sat 10 pm. SRA – accredited

GIACCO'S N5

176 BLACKSTOCK ROAD
020 3649 4601 9–1D

This micro Italian wine bar in Highbury's Blackstock Road (formerly the Light Eye Mind arts space) opened in March 2023 and operates as a bottle shop and café by day and a 20-cover wine bar by night, serving low-intervention Italian wines along with cheese and salumi from small producers and pasta. The cakes are from Forno in Hackney, and they produce their own small-batch gelato. Co-owner Leonardo Leoncini ran Highbury's Farewell Cafe, which closed in 2021. / N5 1HA; www.giaccos.bar; giaccos_ldn; Wed-Sat 11 pm, Sun 10 pm.

GIACOMO'S NW2 £52 332

428 FINCHLEY RD 020 7794 3603 1–1B

Home-made pasta and other Italian classics hit the spot at this "enjoyable local restaurant" in Child's Hill, a family-run business for more than four decades which moved to its present address 22 years ago. / NW2 2HY; www.giacomos.co.uk; Tue-Sun 10.30 pm.

GINGER & WHITE HAMPSTEAD NW3 £15 333

4A-5A PERRINS COURT
020 7431 9098 9–2A

Loyal locals endure the (sometimes lengthy) queue for this favourite Hampstead hang-out, thanks to its "very good coffee" and "top breakfast" (shakshuka something of a speciality). / NW3 1QS; www.gingerandwhite.com; gingerandwhitelondon; Mon-Fri 5.30 pm, Sat & Sun 6 pm.

GINZA SW1 £101 333

15 BURY ST 020 7839 1101 3–3D

With its counters for teppanyaki and sushi, this sizable St James's basement (with 70 covers) offers a high-quality, traditional Japanese dining experience. All reports on the food say it can be of an exceptional standard, but even ardent fans can also find it "overpriced". / SW1Y 6AL; www.ginza-stjames.com; ginzastjames; Mon-Sun 10.30 pm.

GIULIA W12 £61 432

77 ASKEW RD 020 8743 0572 8–1B

On the site that was for aeons the locally loved Adam's Café (RIP), this "relative newcomer" in 'Askew Village' "hits the right notes" as a replacement. It "still feels a bit like a café inside", but is warmed up by the personable service, who provide a "short but interesting menu of Italian dishes" including "delicious homemade pasta"; and other "well cooked, prettily presented food". / W12 9AH; www.giuliarestaurant.co.uk; giulia.restaurant; Tue-Sat 10.30 pm, Sun 4.30 pm.

GLORIA EC2 £66 235

54-56 GREAT EASTERN STREET NO TEL
13–1B

"Great for a fun dinner out with friends or family, thanks to the lovely cocktails and amazing decor!" – Big Mamma Group's happening Shoreditch Italian is a happy, overblown pastiche of retro Amalfi-coast style. Results are "inconsistent in quality, but some dishes are mind blowing" (if only in terms of their heart-attack-threatening creaminess). Top Menu Tip – yummo pizza. / EC2A 3QR; www.bigmammagroup.com; bigmamma.uk; Mon-Wed 10.45 pm, Thu-Sat 11 pm, Sun 10.30 pm.

GO-VIET SW7 £56 342

53 OLD BROMPTON RD
020 7589 6432 6–2C

South Kensington Vietnamese from former Hakkasan chef Jeff Tan, whose "incredibly consistent" food is "always prepared with the lightest of touches"; and where lunches are notably "good value". A warehouse-style older sibling, Viet Food, is often packed out in Chinatown. / SW7 3JS; vietnamfood.co.uk; govietnamese; Sun-Thu 10.30 pm, Fri & Sat 11 pm.

LA GOCCIA WC2 £64 333

FLORAL COURT, OFF FLORAL STREET
020 7305 7676 5–3C

"It's lovely to sit at the outside tables in the summer" in the "beautiful courtyard" of Covent Garden's Floral Court, dining on "interesting small plates" of Italian food – "albeit on the expensive side" – at the central London offshoot from the well-known Petersham Nurseries in Richmond. It's just "great for a girls' day lunch or dinner". / WC2E 9DJ; petershamnurseries.com; petershamnurseries; Mon-Wed 10 pm, Thu-Sat 11 pm, Sun 6 pm.

GODDARDS AT GREENWICH SE10 £27 343

22 KING WILLIAM WALK
020 8305 9612 1–3D

One of the vanishingly few traditional pie 'n' mash dynasties left in London, four generations of Goddards have run the family business since 1890. "Always friendly to regulars and tourists alike", they offer a "good choice of pies", from the standard beef mince to a vegan option. / SE10 9HU; www.goddardsatgreenwich.co.uk; Sun-Thu 7.30 pm, Fri & Sat 8 pm.

GOLD W11 £72 245

95-97 PORTOBELLO ROAD
020 3146 0747 7–2B

This "cool vibes" Portobello Road hang-out with a "let-your-hair-down ambience" was carved out of an old Notting Hill boozer by nightclub entrepreneur Nick House (Mahiki and Whisky Mist). The tapas-y food, by former River Café chef Theo Hill, divides opinion: it's either "exemplary" and "delicious", or "sloppy", "heavy-handed and over-priced". Top Tip – "if you don't like noise, ask for a table upstairs". / W11 2QB; goldnottinghill.com; goldnottinghill; Mon-Thu 12.30 am, Fri & Sat 1 am, Sun 11.30 pm.

GOLD MINE W2 £45 322

102 QUEENSWAY 020 7792 8331 7–2C

This classic Cantonese in Queensway specialises in "delicious dim sum" and roast meats; and though "there are better venues in the area" you may still face a long queue at busy times. It also has a Chinatown sibling at 45 Wardour Street, London W1D 6PZ. / W2 3RR; goldmine.bayswater; Sun-Thu 11 pm, Fri & Sat 11.15 pm.

GOLDEN DRAGON W1 £53 322

28-29 GERRARD ST 020 7734 1073 5–3A

This "very busy" Cantonese stalwart is "a cut above its rivals" on the Chinatown main drag. There's "nothing special about the environment, but it serves some of the best and best-value dim sum available in London". / W1 6JW; www.gdlondon.co.uk; goldendragon_uk; Mon-Sun 10 pm.

GOLDEN HIND W1 £52 332

73 MARYLEBONE LN 020 7486 3644 2–1A

"Going strong" since 1914, this Marylebone veteran is one of the oldest in central London, serving "reliable and authentic fish 'n' chips in a part of town where no-nonsense dining is not so easy to find". Unusually for a chippy there's "outdoor seating in warmer months", and when it's cold you can finish your meal with a traditional sponge pudding. / W1U 2PN; www.goldenhindrestaurant.com; Mon-Fri 10 pm.

GOOD EARTH £75 332

233 BROMPTON RD, SW3
020 7584 3658 6–*2C*
143-145 THE BROADWAY, NW7
020 8959 7011 1–*1B*
11 BELLEVUE RD, SW17
020 8682 9230 11–*2C*

This well-known family-owned quartet of "upmarket Chinese" operations – in Knightsbridge, Mill Hill, Wandsworth Common and Esher – are "longstanding favourites" for many reporters. "The menus may not excite any true aficionados of Asian cuisine, but its consistency excites us!" And even if it's "never cheap, it's always worth the price". / www.goodearthgroup.co.uk.

GOODMAN £89 343

24-26 MADDOX ST, W1
020 7499 3776 3–*2C*
3 SOUTH QUAY, E14 020 7531 0300 12–*1C*
11 OLD JEWRY, EC2 020 7600 8220 10–*2C*

"Steak, steak, and steak are all brilliant" at Misha Zelman's NYC-style grill-houses also praised for their "great wine pairings" and "knowledgeable staff". With branches in Mayfair, the City and Canary Wharf, they are a particular business favourite, and had the edge on their arch-rival Hawksmoor in survey results this year. Meat is sourced from Scotland, the US, Australia and Japan, dry-aged on site and cooked over charcoal. / www.goodmanrestaurants.com; goodman_london.

GORDON RAMSAY SW3 £231 222

68-69 ROYAL HOSPITAL RD
020 7352 4441 6–*3D*

The Hell's Kitchen chef's original Chelsea HQ is increasingly "trading on its reputation", attracting more criticism than it does praise nowadays. Even fans sometimes acknowledge this "rather beige" room has a "stilted" ambience, and opinions on the service vary widely: from "impeccable" to "overwhelming" or even "robotic". When it comes to the fairly classical cuisine, there's also a pick 'n' mix of views: from "unbeatable" to "overly fussy" or "safe". What both sides do often agree on is that the experience comes "at the most ridiculous second mortgage prices", with almost two in five of diners' voting it their most overpriced meal of the year. A fair middle view is that: "as you should expect from a three Michelin star restaurant, the food is lovely; but it's a struggle to work out in what way it is better than many other two-star or even one-star restaurants. It's good, but not that good". / SW3 4HP; www.gordonramsayrestaurants.com; restaurantgordonramsay; Tue-Sat 11 pm.

GOUQI SW1 £120 232

25-34 COCKSPUR STREET
020 3771 8886 2–*3C*

Fans hail an "excellent addition to the Asian fine dining scene" at this West End spring 2023 newcomer – the first solo restaurant from Tong Chee Hwee, the masterchef behind Hakkasan's rise to global fame over the past two decades, and focused on Chinese cuisine. Our few early reports unanimously applaud the high quality of its dishes, although one does gripe about it being too pricey or with a poor ambience. (Both of these negative sentiments are echoed by Times critic Giles Coren in his May 2023 review: while acknowledging the food "is in general fine", Giles really gives it both barrels for its "unforgivable" prices; what he considers a "horrid, horrid" location on the fringes of Trafalgar Square; and his suspicions that social media agencies have been used to paint it in an overly favourable light online). / SW1Y 5BN; Wed-Sat 10.30 pm, Sun 9.30 pm.

GOURMET BURGER KITCHEN £41 332

BRANCHES THROUGHOUT LONDON

"Still my favourite burger", proclaim loyalists of the brand that launched the contemporary vogue for upmarket burgers – although the original 2001 branch in Battersea's Nappy Valley is now gone, a victim of cost-cutting in recent years. Birmingham's 'chicken king' Ranjit Boparan bought the chain out of administration in 2020, with the closure of almost half its 60-odd outlets. Judging by the limited but positive feedback this year, he appears to have brought an upward trend to the surviving 35 branches plus eight delivery-only kitchens. / www.gbk.co.uk; gbkburgers.

GOYA SW1 £92 332

34 LUPUS ST 020 7976 5309 2–*4C*

This Pimlico veteran has served "tasty, reliable and good-value tapas" including "particularly enjoyable seafood" for more than 30 years – putting it well ahead of the more recent vogue for Hispanic cuisine. "The menu is always the same and always very good", which suits local regulars well. / SW1V 3EB; www.goyarestaurant.co.uk; Mon-Sat midnight.

GRANARY SQUARE BRASSERIE N1 £52 234

1 GRANARY SQUARE 020 3940 1000 9–*3C*

"Eating outside overlooking the square is extremely pleasant" at this "large brasserie", which is particularly well-located in the new developments north of King's Cross; and wins praise for its "great buzzy atmosphere". But it suffers from the Ivy Collection's habitual weakness of "disappointing and unimaginative food – all the classics not done that well". / N1C 4AB; www.granarysquarebrasserie.com; granarysquarebrasserie; Mon-Sun midnight.

GRANGER & CO £64 223

237-239 PAVILION RD, SW1
020 3848 1060 6–*2D*
105 MARYLEBONE HIGH STREET, W1
020 8079 7120 2–*1A*
175 WESTBOURNE GROVE, W11
020 7229 9111 7–*1B*
STANLEY BUILDING, ST PANCRAS SQ, N1
020 3058 2567 9–*3C*
THE BUCKLEY BUILDING, 50 SEKFORDE ST, EC1 020 7251 9032 10–*1A*

"Excellent breakfasts… you just need to be patient" – "after all these years, the queue outside is there for a reason" according to fans of this Aussie-inspired chain, owned by celeb chef Bill Granger. There are five nowadays, but it's still the OG Notting Hill branch – cited by fans as "the best brunch spot in West London!" – which receives the most attention. But whereas all feedback acknowledges the "nice buzz" they create, ratings are capped by reports of food that's merely "meh". / grangerandco.com; grangerandco.

GREAT NEPALESE NW1 £45 323

48 EVERSHOLT ST 020 7388 6737 9–*3C*

Fay Maschler's review from the 1980s is blown up for all to see as you enter this "old stalwart that's had a brush-up" in recent years: a low-key curry house (est. 1982) long known as one of the few bright culinary sparks near Euston station. Go for the smattering of Nepalese specials amidst the "simple and unchanging" selection of subcontinental dishes. Bills can end up higher, though, than its "basic" style might suggest. / NW1 1DA; www.great-nepalese.co.uk; Mon-Sat 10.30 pm.

GREEN COTTAGE NW3 £56 322

9 NEW COLLEGE PARADE
020 7722 5305 9–*2A*

This "typical local Chinese" amidst a parade of shops in Swiss Cottage has put in more than 50 years' service. Why? "The food is relatively good and prices reasonable". / NW3 5EP; www.greencottage22.com; Mon-Sun 10.30 pm.

GREENBERRY CAFÉ NW1 £63 233

101 REGENTS PARK ROAD
020 7483 3765 9–*2B*

This "fun and buzzy local restaurant" in Primrose Hill is especially a brunch favourite. The food menu is a bit "hit/miss", but it wins particular shout-outs for its "good coffee" and "hard to beat salads". / NW1 8UR; greenberrycafe.co.uk; greenberrycafe; Sun & Mon 3 pm, Tue-Sat 10 pm.

THE GRILL BY TOM BOOTON (FKA THE DORCHESTER GRILL) W1 £145

53 PARK LANE 020 7629 8888 3–*3A*

This illustrious chamber was closed during our annual diners' poll, awaiting a May 2023 relaunch under the brand of talented whippersnapper, Tom Booton (who has only just hit 30). It is the first time the grill has had a chef's name over the door in its 92-year history, and heralds a major change of gear for the space – no longer is it to be a hallowed foodie temple, but now more of a luxe brasserie with 'Tom's cheeky personality shining through' (at least that's what the press release says). In comes breakfast for the first time (with truffled egg

Harrods Dining Hall SW1

nd soldiers and omelette Arnold Benedict); unday lunch; a chef's counter; sharing dishes; nd a general culinary 'tie loosening' moment ith 'twists on British classics'. As part of this uddlier style we are also promised 'playlists and selected by Tom'; and 'playful cocktails nd artisan English beer'. / W1K 1QA; ww.dorchestercollection.com; thedorchester; Mon-at 10 pm, Sun 4 pm.

GRUMBLES SW1 £66 342

5 CHURTON ST 020 7834 0149 2–4B

ittle has changed at this "unstuffy" Pimlico istro since it opened 60 years ago (except hat, back then, a couple could eat here for nder £3!). The original wooden panelling nd furniture are still in place, the fish pie is ill topped with piped potato, and pricing is ill "cheap 'n' cheerful". It also does a "great unday lunch for the kids". / SW1V 2LT; ww.grumblesrestaurant.co.uk; grumblesrestaurant; Ion-Sun 10 pm.

THE GUILDFORD ARMS SE10 £60 333

5 GUILDFORD GROVE
20 8691 6293 1–3D

Co-owner Guy Awford's "brilliantly executed, lassically inspired" cooking is well above pub grub" standard, and has established this well-maintained, upmarket" Georgian tavern s a leading option in Greenwich. / SE10 8JY; ww.theguildfordarms.co.uk; guildfordarms_; Tue-at 11 pm, Sun 8 pm.

THE GUINEA GRILL W1 £111 213

0 BRUTON PL 020 7409 1728 3–3B

Yes, it is expensive (if not by Mayfair tandards) but it is a meat-lover's nirvana in a reat setting" – that's long been the accepted iew on this quirky, grill room (est. 1952) behind Young's pub, tucked away in a scenic central ews. "Old fashioned pies, mixed grills and xcellent steaks" are washed down with an impressive, if over-priced, wine list" and served n a quaint, period setting, whose "overcrowded ables are part of the experience". In the last ouple of years, though (even prior to the eparture last year of well-known manager Oisín Rogers), ratings have been on the ide. Some "shockingly bad" cooking has een reported, alongside service that's "so ndifferent"; and the current impression is that they are relying ever more heavily on their "captive market" of local business-lunchers. / W1J 6NL; www.theguinea.co.uk; guineagrill; Mon-Sun 10 pm.

THE GUN E14 £78 324

27 COLDHARBOUR 020 7515 5222 12–1C

A spectacular riverside setting, directly opposite The O2, sets the scene at this Grade II-listed Docklands tavern, ten minutes' walk from Canary Wharf. Run by Fuller's, its "enjoyable food and lovely cocktails" are best enjoyed from the large modern terrace in summer. / E14 9NS; www.thegundocklands.com; thegundocklands; Mon & Tue, Sun 10 pm, Wed-Sat midnight.

GUNPOWDER £63 433

20 GREEK STREET, W1
020 3813 7796 5–2A
ONE TOWER BRIDGE, 4 CROWN SQUARE, SE1 AWAITING TEL 10–4D
11 WHITES ROW, E1 020 7426 0542 13–2C

"Innovative small plates pack a flavour punch" ("the lamb chops are some of the most glorious things ever") at this "buzzy if rather cramped" Indian street-food trio, with operations near Tower Bridge, and in Spitalfields and Soho. Top Tip – "good, if limited, pre-theatre menu. Virtually no choice but, with tasty and large portions costing £22 for two courses or £25 for three, excellent value". / www.gunpowderlondon.com; gunpowder_london.

GURA GURA WC2 £52 344

19 SLINGSBY PLACE 07918 352879 5–3B

Festooned with foliage and feathers, this late 2022 newcomer is set in Covent Garden's 'The Yards' development. It's not made huge waves, but early reports on its cocktails and pan-Asian sushi and other fare are uniformly upbeat: "excellent and inexpensive pan-Asian tapas", "great choice" and "delicious dim sum". / WC2H 9DL; www.guragura.co.uk; guraguralondon; Mon-Thu 10 pm, Fri & Sat 11.30 pm, Sun 9.30 pm.

THE GURKHAS W1 £54 343

110 GREAT PORTLAND STREET
020 7637 4198 2–1B

From the Nepalese team behind Hot Stone in Islington, this upmarket new venue in Great Portland Street, Fitzrovia aims to showcase an 'elevated' take on classic Nepalese cuisine. Head chef Joe Allen has a Nepalese wife and Gurkha father-in-law, and has travelled extensively in Nepal to study some of its culinary secrets. An early visit backed up the initial positive feedback we have on the place, finding precisely prepared, slightly unusual dishes; and early days service that was at pains to get everything right. BREAKING NEWS. In October 2023, the restaurant announced its closure. / W1W 6PQ; www.thegurkhasrestaurant.com; thegurkhas_restaurant; Tue-Thu 9 pm, Fri & Sat 9.30 pm.

GUSTOSO RISTORANTE & ENOTECA SW1 £69 322

35 WILLOW PL 020 7834 5778 2–4B

This "good-value" Italian "with excellent-quality cooking" and "always-welcoming staff" near Westminster Cathedral in Pimlico "stands out in an area with not much else". / SW1P 1JH; www.ristorantegustoso.co.uk; gustoso_ristorante; Mon-Sat 9.30 pm.

GYMKHANA W1 £98 543

42 ALBEMARLE ST 020 3011 5900 3–3C

"Setting the benchmark for high-end Indian gastronomy in London" – "the capital may have a lot of hot new Indian destinations, but this Sethi family property in Mayfair is still at the top thanks to dazzling cuisine" – "interesting twists on the classics" with "exceptional spicing", all served by "thoroughly welcoming" staff in a "richly decorated and buzzy environment". / W1S 4JH; www.gymkhanalondon.com; gymkhanalondon; Mon-Sun 10.45 pm.

HACHÉ £61 332

95-97 HIGH HOLBORN, WC1
020 7242 4580 2–1D
329-331 FULHAM RD, SW10
020 7823 3515 6–3B
24 INVERNESS ST, NW1
020 7485 9100 9–3B
37 BEDFORD HILL, SW12
020 8772 9772 11–2C
153 CLAPHAM HIGH ST, SW4
020 7738 8760 11–2D
147-149 CURTAIN RD, EC2
020 7739 8396 13–1B

"Fab burgers with a posh turn" – including "awesome sweet potato fries" – still lead the charge at these Frenchified fast-food outfits, but they are transitioning into a brasserie group under the ownership of Hush Mayfair's Jamie Barber. The 20-year-old original – a "great, cosy little spot in Camden" – and its Balham offshoot are all that remain as pure burger bars, while Kingston, High Holborn and Chelsea are now branded as brasseries with an extended menu to match. / www.hacheburgers.com.

HAGEN CHELSEA SW3 £15 342

151 KINGS ROAD 07958 060036 6–3C

With nine branches scattered across the capital's wealthier neighbourhoods, this "popular" Copenhagen-inspired coffee-shop group offers the "best coffee" from hip

Danish roasters Prolog, plenty of "hygge" (if "limited seating" in some venues), and cinnamon buns commissioned from Blake's Kitchen in the Cotswolds. / SW3 5TX; www.thehagenproject.com; thehagenproject; Wed-Sat 9 pm, Sun 5.30 pm.

HAKKASAN £123 4 2 3

17 BRUTON ST, W1 020 7907 1888 3–2C
8 HANWAY PL, W1 020 7927 7000 5–1A

"Best Asian restaurant I've eaten in!" – these "beautiful" nightclubby haunts ("quite why they keep them so dark is beyond me") have maintained an impressive standard for over 20 years, and the Tottenham Court original has since been replicated not just in Mayfair but in numerous cities around the globe. Their ratings have fluctuated over many years, always around the same concerns – "success has got the better of them…"; "chaotic" and/or "attitude-y" service; punishing prices. The believers still carry the day, though, saying they are "always a special experience" with a "delectable" mix of dim sum, Peking duck (with or without caviar) and other classic Chinese dishes – "definitely take a big wallet, but I love it!" / www.hakkasan.com; hakkasanlondon.

HAM YARD RESTAURANT, HAM YARD HOTEL W1 £71 2 3 4

1 HAM YD 020 3642 1007 4–3D

"A quiet oasis on the fringe of messy Soho" – this hotel comes complete with a cute and rather unexpected courtyard and makes a "great setting" for a "comfortable and reasonably priced afternoon tea". The food at other times is "comforting but not exciting", although the set menu offers "good value for pre-theatre dining". / W1D 7DT; www.firmdalehotels.com; firmdale_hotels; Mon-Sun 10.30 pm.

THE HAMPSHIRE W6 £51 3 3 3

227 KING STREET 020 8748 3391 8–2B

A short step from Hammersmith Town Hall and its ongoing surrounding property developments – this "spacious" and stylish pub was taken over by an Indian restaurant during the pandemic (although you can still just drop in for a pint). The food is fair value and "very good" from "an extensive menu with some unusual dishes"; and the owners have invested heavily in the large and comfortable garden. / W6 9JT; www.the-hampshire.com; thehampshire; Tue-Sun midnight.

HANKIES W1 £47 3 3 2

67 SHAFTESBURY AVENUE
020 7871 6021 5–3A

In the heart of Theatreland, this Indian street-food operation is focused on dishes served with 'hankies' – hand-spun roti folded around the dish – and still receives good marks (if from a limited number of reports). There used to be offshoots in Marble Arch and Paddington, but both have closed over the last couple of years. / W1D 6LL; hankies.london; hankies_shaftesbury; Wed-Sat 8.30 pm.

HANNAH SE1 £138 3 3 2

SOUTHBANK RIVERSIDE, BELVEDERE ROAD 020 3802 0402 2–3D

This top-class Japanese dining room in the monolithic former County Hall near the London Eye is "a surprising delight in an area largely devoid of good eating options". Daisuke Shimoyama, previously head chef at Umu in Mayfair who began his career at 15 washing pots in Kanagawa, serves everything from "good-value lunch bentos to enticing main menus", including a 13-course omakase with the chef's sake pairing. / SE1 7PB; www.hannahrestaurant.london; hannah_japanese_restaurant; Wed-Sun 10 pm.

HANS' BAR & GRILL SW1 £87 3 3 3

164 PAVILION ROAD 020 7730 7000 6–2D

A very appealing looking spot, in one of Chelsea's more chichi little enclaves – this café bar is part of nearby boutique hotel, 100 Cadogan Gardens. It's not the cheapest venue, and service can lag, but for a breakfast or light shopping lunch it's praised (albeit in limited feedback) as "a good all-rounder". / SW1X 0AW; www.hansbarandgrill.com; hansbarandgrill; Mon-Sat 10 pm, Sun 7 pm.

HARE & TORTOISE £44 2 3 2

11-13 THE BRUNSWICK, WC1
020 7278 9799 2–1D
373 KENSINGTON HIGH ST, W14
020 7603 8887 8–1D
156 CHISWICK HIGH RD, W4
020 8747 5966 8–2A
38 HAVEN GRN, W5 020 8810 7066 1–2A
296-298 UPPER RICHMOND RD, SW15
020 8394 7666 11–2B
90 NEW BRIDGE ST, EC4
020 7651 0266 10–2A

"Where else can you get ramen and laksa in the same place?", ask fans of this "efficient and friendly" pan-Asian chain founded almost 30 years ago in Bloomsbury's Brunswick Centre and now with branches in Ealing, Putney, Kensington and Chiswick plus two delivery-only kitchens. / www.hareandtortoise.co.uk; hare_tortoise.

HARRODS DINING HALL SW1 £90

HARRODS, 87-135 BROMPTON ROAD 6–1D

From October 2023, this golden-hued space, with its stunning Edwardian tiling – originally built to house the Harrods Food Hall's meat and fishmongers counters, and converted into a dining hall four years ago – will be re-launched with four new outlets in addition to the existing Kerridge's Fish 'n' Chips (see also): Sushi by Masa (from NYC celeb chef Masayoshi ('Masa') Takayama); Kinoya Ramen Bar – an import from Dubai; Assembly Mezze & Skewers, from vaunted Lebanese chef Athanasios Kargatzidis ('Chef Tommy'); and an upgrade of the existin Pasta Evangelists outlet, in partnership with top Veronese chef Giancarlo Perbellini (which becomes 'Pasta Evangelists by Perbellini'). / SW1X 7XL; www.harrods.com/en-gb/restaurants https://www.instagram.com/harrods/.

HARVEST NW10

68 CHAMBERLAYNE ROAD
020 3848 8111 1–2B

In Kensal Green – just down the road from his well-established neighbourhood operation, Parlour – chef Jesse Dunwood Green launched this small, casual all-day haunt in June 2023, with green leather seating for about 40. It opened after our survey had concluded, but looks like a useful addition to the area, with service from breakfast onwards, and an array of cocktails. Steak is a feature and some main dishes – say, a whole sea bass or chicken – are available to share. / NW10 3JJ; www.harvestrestaurantuk.com; harvestrestaurantuk Mon-Sun 10 pm.

HARWOOD ARMS SW6 £89 4 3 3

WALHAM GROVE 020 7386 1847 6–3A

London's best pub (yet again No.1 in our annual diners' poll) "truly deserves its Michelin star and the old feel of creaky wood chairs and tables is what makes it a pub that still feels like a pub" (though space for drinkers is actually very limited). Lost deep in the backstreets near Fulham Broadway, it delivers "sublime British food at its best", in particular "good game, especially deer". Top Menu Tips – "amazing Sunday lunch" and "you must try the Scotch egg". / SW6 1QP; www.harwoodarms.com; theharwoodarms; Mon-Thu 9.15pm, Fri & Sat 9.15 pm, Sun 8.15 pm.

HATCHED SW11 £86 4 4 3

189 SAINT JOHN'S HILL
020 7738 0735 11–2C

Between Clapham Junction and Wandsworth Town, this grey-walled fixture (also with counte dining) puts the focus on the cooking from Shane Marshall's open kitchen. Choose from an à la carte menu of modern bistro fare, with a roast on Sunday – its small fan club from the SW postcodes rate it very highly. / SW11 1TH; www.hatchedsw11.com; hatchedsw11; Wed-Sat 11 pm, Sun 1.30 pm.

HAUGEN E20 £75

9 ENDEAVOUR SQUARE
020 4568 1444 14–1D

You can't miss this remarkable, oversized swiss-chalet-inspired structure run by D&D London, which sits on the fringes of the Olympic Park, a short walk from Westfield Stratford. Its roof terrace is a prime spot for drinks on a sunny day. When it comes to eating the Alpine-inspired fodder (fondue, rösti, schnitzel…) inspires remarkably little feedback: such as we have is positive, but insufficient to safely repudiate some of the brickbats thrown

at the place online. BREAKING NEWS. In September 2023, it was announced that Haugen will soon close, although a new occupant is being sought for this impressive site. / E20 1JN; www.haugen-restaurant.com; haugenldn; Mon-Thu 11 pm, Fri-Sun 11.30 pm. SRA – accredited

THE HAVELOCK TAVERN W14 £65 333

57 MASBRO RD 020 7603 5374 8–1C

This "lovely local pub with decent food" behind Olympia has been a significant presence on the West London gastropub scene for almost 30 years, with its distinctive blue-tiled facade and elevated menu. Long-time regulars feel "it's not like it was in the old days" (when folks flocked from miles around), but they still feel it's "good all round". / W14 0LS; www.havelocktavern.com; havelocktavern; Mon-Sat 11 pm, Sun 10 pm.

HAWKSMOOR £95 332

5A AIR ST, W1 020 7406 3980 4–4C
11 LANGLEY ST, WC2 020 7420 9390 5–2C
3 YEOMAN'S ROW, SW3
020 7590 9290 6–2C
16 WINCHESTER WALK, SE1
020 7234 9940 10–4C
WOOD WHARF, 1 WATER STREET, E14
020 3988 0510 12–1C
157 COMMERCIAL ST, E1
020 7426 4850 13–2B
10-12 BASINGHALL ST, EC2
020 7397 8120 10–2C

"Still one of the steak stalwarts of London…"; "still our go-to place for a relaxed night out…"; "still the place for a discreet business meeting in the City…". Few brands inspire as much long-term adulation as Huw Gott and Will Beckett's steakhouse chain, which has ridden the zeitgeist since its founding in 2006; and which is now (with the help of Graphite Capital, who own most of it nowadays) to be found in NYC and Dublin, as well as Manchester, Edinburgh and Liverpool. A "terrific" cocktail in the bar, precedes "awesome steaks with fantastic side dishes, all in a cool setting". At least, that's long been the accepted wisdom anyway, although there's a widespread feeling that quality "has dropped off a bit in recent years". In this year's annual diners' poll, ratings improved in some respects and declined in others, with historical concerns over stratospheric prices supplanted by niggles that maybe the formula is just "starting to look a tad tired" and that service – though often "excellent" – can also sometimes seem increasingly "impersonal" ("you are just a number!"). The majority verdict for the time being, though? Still "always hits the spot". / www.thehawksmoor.com; hawksmoorrestaurants; SRA – 3 stars.

HAWTHORN TW9 £65 353

14 STATION PARADE 020 8940 6777 1–3A

"A very worthy successor to the beloved Glasshouse (RIP)" – this new Kew favourite is co-owned by its predecessor's former manager, Patra Panas. Service is particularly "well-drilled and friendly"; and regulars are "delighted to find that little has changed" after a "seamless" changeover, with "many of the furnishings still in place" in the agreeable (a few feel, "slightly uninspiring") dining room. Diners dispute whether the "intelligent and carefully crafted" cuisine, from chef and co-owner Josh Hunter, is a step up or down from before, but practically all agree it's "very competent", and say "we shall definitely return and recommend it highly!" / TW9 3PZ; www.hawthornrestaurant.co.uk; hawthorn_kew; Tue-Sat 10 pm.

HAYA W11 £57 343

184A KENSINGTON PARK ROAD
0203 995 4777 7–1B

This appealing café/restaurant in Notting Hill is "just a gentle place to be", with a modern eastern Mediterranean menu inspired by founder Victoria Paltina's visits to Tel Aviv. / W11 2ES; haya.london; haya.ldn; Mon-Sun 11.30 pm.

HAZ £63 322

9 CUTLER ST, E1 020 7929 7923 10–2D
14 FINSBURY SQUARE, EC2
020 7920 9944 13–2A
34 FOSTER LN, EC2 020 7600 4172 10–2B
64 BISHOPSGATE, EC2
020 7628 4522 10–2D
6 MINCING LN, EC3 020 7929 3173 10–3D

"Good mezze and grilled meat" help tick the boxes for "delicious food that is not expensive" at this Turkish business with five branches in the City – making them suitable "for business or social occasions" (although they can be "noisy"). In summer 2023, the group made its West End debut with the opening of Olea Social in Covent Garden, with a more general Mediterranean focus. / www.hazrestaurant.co.uk; hazrestaurantofficia.

HÉLÈNE DARROZE, THE CONNAUGHT HOTEL W1 £175 332

CARLOS PL 020 3147 7200 3–3B

"Yes, the food is very, very good" – the tasting menu is "absolutely incredible (every dish a piece of art and served on stunning crockery)" – according to fans of this superstar French chef, who has presided over the main dining room of this most blue-blooded of Mayfair hotels since 2008. Her reign has always been a little controversial here – for example, no-one is wild about the uneventful recent makeover of this fine, period chamber. But since its elevation to three Michelin stars, prices have become "extortionate (and with numerous supplements on the menu!)" and those diners who feel "this all-round exceptional experience is worth every penny" vie with the 2 in 5 who feel "the wallet-destroying prices are beyond extravagant" – "if I have to sell a kidney to eat here, I expect the food to win my heart… I'm not sure it did!" / W1K 2AL; www.the-connaught.co.uk; theconnaught; Tue-Sat 9 pm.

HELIOT STEAK HOUSE WC2 £78 32

CRANBOURN STREET
020 7769 8844 5–3B

"A go-to place for top USDA steaks" – this unusual space, hewn out of the old circle of th former Hippodrome Theatre, is worth a trip, with food that's much better than you might expect. It's great value too (perhaps as a loss leader to get you into the casino?), making it ideal as a pre-theatre option; and on Monday you can BYO wine. NB. Under 25s must have ID. / WC2H 7AJ; www.hippodromecasino.com; hippodromecasino; Sun-Thu 10 pm, Fri & Sat 11 pm.

HELIX (SEARCY'S AT THE GHERKIN) EC3 £91 33

30 ST MARY AXE 0330 1070816 10–2D

Originally closed to the public when it opened 20 years ago, Norman Foster's 'Gherkin' – arguably the most iconic of the City's modern towers – now has a dining room run by catering company Searcy's on its 40th floor, which is "just so wonderful, with a glass-roofed bar and wall-to-wall windows in both bar and restaurant" – "it's my 'go-to' when I visit London for an excellent meal, first-class presentation, attentive staff, and all at a reasonable price. Win, win, win all round". / EC3A 8EP; searcysatthegherkin.co.uk; searcysgherkin.

HEREFORD ROAD W2 £60 44

3 HEREFORD RD 020 7727 1144 7–1B

"Interesting and reasonably priced seasonal British food, expertly cooked and full of flavour" has underpinned the winning formula for 15 years at this old butcher's shop in Bayswater from ex-St John chef Tom Pemberton. "This is farm-to-table, but done properly", "letting the ingredients speak for themselves with flawless cooking that you can watch in the open kitchen" – made to look "deceptively simple" and served in an appropriate "slightly spartan ambience". / W2 4AB; www.herefordroad.org; Fri & Sat, Tue-Thu 10 pm, Sun 3.30 pm.

HERITAGE SE21 £55 44

101 ROSENDALE ROAD
020 8761 4665 1–4D

"Just amazing food bursting with flavour… and in generous portions" inspires very enthusiastic reports for Dayashakar Sharmar's ambitious Dulwich Indian – "it's so good for a local!" – and its small-but-dedicated fan club travel from across south east London. / SE21 8EZ; www.heritagedulwich.co.uk; heritageindiandulwich; Tue-Sat 10.30 pm, Sun 9 pm.

HICCE N1 £73 22

COAL DROPS YARD 020 3869 8200 9–3C

It has a "good location and a buzzy atmosphere too", but this early linchpin of the Coal Drops ard development continues to produce mixed ports. Most feedback does acclaim Pip Lacey's nteresting menu" of "lovely sharing plates". ut "tiny portions at sky-high prices" remains mething of a theme ("I was shocked by the ll, especially as we'd eaten so little!)". Top ip – "a particularly nice spot on a summer's vening". BREAKING NEWS. In October)23, it was announced that the restaurant will ose in December. / N1C 4AB; www.hicce.co.uk; ccelondon; Wed & Thu, Tue 11 pm, Fri & Sat idnight, Sun 5 pm.

ICCE HART N1

3 PENTON STREET 020 3848 8168 9–3D

corner-pub (formerly the Day & Night), n Islington's Chapel Market, provides the te for high-profile chef Pip Lacey's late)22 newcomer. It's a spin-off from her first pening in Coal Drops Yard, with a focus on ooking over wood fire. No survey feedback yet, though social posts support the view that the alue provided here is similar to the good-but-ricey reports we receive on the original. / 1 9PZ; www.hiccehart.co.uk; hiccehart; Mon-Wed pm, Thu-Sat midnight, Sun 10 pm.

IDE W1 £177 323

5 PICCADILLY 020 3146 8666 3–4C

The views over the park make for a magical tting" at this luxurious venue near Green Park ation, where the kitchen is overseen by star hef Ollie Dabbous. Under the same ownership s famous merchants, Hedonism Wines, it hares their "spectacular list" ("by obsessives r obsessives"... and "with some surprising ockets of value nestling in its more obscure eaches" if you look hard enough). Hitherto, it aded as two distinct entities with 'Hide Below' place for a "high level breakfast" or informal uxe-brasserie meal any time of day; and Hide Above' reserved for Ollie's "innovative" sting menus – "terrific" but "don't mention e price... they're definitely not for everyday ining!" In mid-2023, though, they announced change of direction – the same combined ffering with the main features from both paces will now be available on either floor: so ou can now have breakfast with the same leafy istas previously reserved for diners in 'Above' r, tuck into the full, blow-out luxury menu hile seated 'Below'). / W1J 8JB; www.hide.co.uk; ide_restaurant; Tue-Sun 9.30 pm.

IGH ROAD BRASSERIE V4 £72 324

62-166 CHISWICK HIGH ROAD 20 8742 7474 8–2A

or the Chiswick fast-set (if there is such a hing?), this prominently sited outpost of the oho House empire (from the early days, efore it went global) is "THE best place for runch", and at weekends in summer it's all esigner sunnies and expensive casualwear ut on the deck. It doesn't generate a huge olume of feedback, but was well-rated his year. / W4 1PR; highroadbrasserie.co.uk; ighroadbrasserie; Sun-Thu 11 pm, Fri & Sat idnight.

HIGH TIMBER EC4 £70 332

8 HIGH TIMBER STREET 020 7248 1777 10–3B

"Hidden away on the north bank of the Thames" by the 'Wobbly Bridge', directly opposite Tate Modern, you'll find Neleen Strauss's "well-executed Western Cape restaurant", which is "big on steaks" but arguably most notable for its "very good and well structured" South African wine list. Top Tip – "I bring all my City contacts here". / EC4V 3PA; www.hightimber.com; hightimberrestaurant; Mon-Fri 10 pm.

HISPANIA EC3 £86 334

72-74 LOMBARD STREET 020 7621 0338 10–2C

Set over two spacious floors in the grand Victorian former HQ of Lloyds Bank, this "classy Spanish restaurant is a great place to eat and drink" – with food and atmosphere that are more than a match for most of its City rivals. / EC3V 9AY; www.hispanialondon.com; hispanialondon; Mon-Fri 10 pm.

HOLBORN DINING ROOM WC1 £89 213

252 HIGH HOLBORN 020 3747 8633 2–1D

For a "good solid business lunch" it remains recommendable, but otherwise reports are uneven regarding this grand hotel's 'British brasserie', where traditional pies are a big menu feature: the least enthusiastic diners feel it's "disappointing, since it is supposed to be a five star". / WC1V 7EN; www.holborndiningroom.com; holborndiningroom; Mon-Sat 10 pm, Sun 9.45 pm.

THE HOLLAND W8 £50 433

25 EARLS COURT ROAD 020 4599 1369 8–1D

"A fantastic new gastropub near Holland Park", in the no-man's-land location just south of Kensington High Street as you head down to Earl's Court. It was converted in September 2022 (from The Princess Victoria, RIP) with an upstairs dining room serving a modern British menu from chef Max de Nahlik, whose pop-up Oxalis was highly regarded. Initial high ratings and reports – "lovely Sunday roast...", "good and attentive service...", "deserves to be fuller than the night we went there..." – suggest it's worth discovering. / W8 6EB; www.thehollandkensington.co.uk; thehollandkensington; Wed-Sat 11 pm, Sun 6 pm.

HOLLY BUSH NW3 £79 323

22 HOLLY MOUNT 020 7435 2892 9–1A

This "hidden gem" – a picture-book Grade II-listed Georgian tavern down a Hampstead side street – is "a great place to take the day off work", particularly "now the food has been improved". / NW3 6SG; www.hollybushhampstead.co.uk; thehollybushpubhampstead; Mon-Thu, Sat 11 pm, Fri 10 pm, Sun 8 pm.

HOLY CARROT SW1 £59 444

URBAN RETREAT, 2-4 HANS CRESCENT 020 3897 0404 6–1D

"My find of the year... and I'm not vegetarian/vegan!" – former fashion model and producer Irina Linovich's two-year-old plant-based debut venture was scheduled to move into new Notting Hill premises in late 2023 from its original perch in a wellness salon near Harrods (and a vintage Airstream caravan by Battersea Power Station). There's a "really wide choice of imaginative food", with dishes such as 'Sexy Tofu' (eat your heart out, Richard Caring) that "certainly change your perception of vegan living". / SW1X 0LH; www.holycarrot.co.uk; holycarrotrestaurant; Mon-Sat 10 pm, Sun 5 pm.

HOLY COW SW11 £35 332

166 BATTERSEA PK RD 020 7498 2000 11–1C

"A cut above when it comes to delivered Indian food" – most reporters know this brand through its 'at home' business, with 15 sites delivering "a wide selection of always hot and very tasty dishes on time to your door". They do also have two restaurants though in Putney and – since January 2023 – in Canary Wharf. The few reports we have on them say they are "a bit better than your typical curry house". / SW11 4ND; www.holycowfineindianfood.com; Sat & Sun, Mon-Fri 9 pm.

HOMESLICE £63 323

50 JAMES STREET, W1 020 3034 0621 3–1A
13 NEAL'S YD, WC2 020 7836 4604 5–2C
2 TELEVISION CENTRE, 101 WOOD LANE WHITE CITY, W12 020 3034 0381 1–2B
374-378 OLD STREET, EC1 020 3151 1121 13–1B
69-71 QUEEN STREET, EC4 020 3034 0381 10–3C

This "hectic but enjoyable" trio of pizzerias from Alan & Mark Wogan (the late Sir Terry's sons) – in "lovely Neal's Yard", Marylebone and the City – specialises in large 20-inch pizzas (enough for 2 or 3), with "not the usual toppings" – air-dried wagyu beef with truffle creme fraiche, curried minced lamb with smoked burrata – "served alongside the usual ones". Top Tip – "you can have a half-and-half if you can't decide". / www.homeslicepizza.co.uk; homesliceldn.

HOMIES ON DONKEYS E11 £15 444

686 HIGH ROAD LEYTONSTONE 07729 368896 14–1D

"Delicious tacos in a lovely new location" are to be found at this hip-hop-blasting, graffiti-walled taqueria, which has taken over the old Spicebox site on Leytonstone High Road. Arriving with a strong reputation from a five-year stint in a smaller Walthamstow location, the selection mixes classic Mexican flavours with more local ingredients. In a June 2023 review, The Guardian's Grace Dent thought its "astonishingly good" food to be "one of the more exciting things to have happened to this distant area of east London for a while… This is not Claridge's – in fact, I've had a comfier seat at Costa Coffee – but they play Kool G Rap while you eat, you leave very full and the bill is utterly reasonable". / E11 3AA; www.homiesondonkeys.com; homiesondonkeys; Tue, Thu 10 pm, Fri & Sat 11 pm, Sun 2.30 pm.

HONEST BURGERS £51 3 2 2

BRANCHES THROUGHOUT LONDON

"Nearly but not quite the last man standing after the burger wars" – this "busy" chain offers "a limited menu" that's generally credited with being a "reliable" way to "hit the spot" when craving a "decent" burger with "fragrant rosemary fries". Ratings, though, do support those who say they are "not as good as they used to be" and risk becoming "nothing special" if the trend continues. / www.honestburgers.co.uk; honestburgers.

HONEY & CO WC1 £71 3 2 2

54 LAMB'S CONDUIT STREET
020 7388 6175 2–*1D*

"Warren Street's loss is Bloomsbury's gain as Honey & Co sets up in Lamb's Conduit St on the former site of Cigala (RIP)", bringing with it the "interesting" middle Eastern cuisine ("lots of choice for vegetarians") that has won TV appearances and recipe-book deals for husband and wife, Sarit Packer and Itamar Srulovich. But while this 2022 newcomer is "a good addition to WC1", it "is now a proper and comparatively large restaurant compared to its former location and has lost its 'special' ambience". And for a few regulars, this disappointment extends to the food too ("not a patch on the original… it was packed solid so others may disagree, but we felt they're now just cashing in on their previous good name"). / WC1N 3LW; www.honeyandco.co.uk; honeyandcobloomsbury; Mon-Sat 10.30 pm.

HONEY & SMOKE W1 £72 3 2 2

216 GREAT PORTLAND STREET
020 7388 6175 2–*1B*

"Different" and "interesting" Middle Eastern cooking wins praise for this grillhouse near Great Portland Street from influential husband-and-wife team Sarit Packer and Itamar Srulovich. It also attracts some criticism, though – the setting is "quite loud", service can be "amateurish" and some diners "were not blown away by the meal: it was good, but not amazing". / W1W 5QW; honeyandco.co.uk; honeyandsmokerestaurant; Tue-Sat 10.30 pm.

HOPPERS £49 3 3 3

49 FRITH ST, W1 NO TEL 5–*2A*
77 WIGMORE STREET, W1
020 3319 8110 3–*1A*
UNIT 3, BUILDING 4, PANCRAS SQUARE, NI
020 3319 8125 9–*3C*

"A fantastic menu of unusual Sri Lankan street food" with "lots of interesting ingredients (breadfruit, squid, dal, etc) in a mix-and-match format" has won a huge fan club for JKS Restaurants three-strong chain (with a fourth branch planned to open late in 2023 in Shoreditch). Ratings slipped across the board, though, this year – incidents of "hit 'n' miss service" and "packed and noisy" conditions can make them appear "a bit pricey". / www.hopperslondon.com; hopperslondon.

HOSHI SW20 £44 3 3 2

54 DURHAM ROAD 020 8944 1888 11–*2A*

This "relaxed local Japanese" in Raynes Park "opened recently on the site of (confusingly similarly named) Hashi". Reports suggest "the quality of the food is better", with "authentic, skillfully prepared dishes" including "good fresh sushi". / SW20 0TW; hoshirestaurant.co.uk; Tue-Sat 10.30 pm, Sun 10 pm.

HOT STONE N1 £91 2 2 2

9 CHAPEL MARKET 020 3302 8226 9–*3D*

Many diners do applaud "wonderful ingredients, impeccably presented" at this ambitious Japanese venue on Islington's Chapel Market, and say that the "signature sashimi, maki rolls and different types of wagyu that you cook on a hot stone are all spectacular". But a slew of critical reports – in particular regarding voucher promotions – has dented ratings; and such feedback is peppered with a variety of critiques and disappointments, including some "fairly average dishes" and some items charged at "outrageous prices". / N1 9EZ; www.hotstonelondon.com; hotstonelondon; Mon & Tue 9 pm, Wed & Thu, Sun 8.45 pm, Fri & Sat 9.30 pm.

HOUSE OF MING, ST JAMES'S COURT SW1

54 BUCKINGHAM GATE
020 7963 8330 2–*4C*

India's famous Taj group brought their take on the cuisines of Sichuan and Canton to their St James's Court hotel (near Buck House) in May 2021. It's stablemate to the establishment's Keralan superstar Quilon, and reflects the popularity of Chinese cuisine in India itself. As it launched after our annual diners' poll we have no direct user feedback, but early online reviews are upbeat. / SW1E 6AF; www.houseofming.co.uk; homlondon; Mon-Sun 11 pm.

HUMBLE CHICKEN W1 £38 4 3 4

54 FRITH STREET 020 7434 2782 5–*2A*

"One of the most exciting options in Soho nowadays": Angelo Sato's ambitious and

Imad's Syrian Kitchen W1

"really rather good multi-course omakase" – in the premises of the original Barrafina – features "really innovative dishes, executed to perfection in a casual, buzzing atmosphere". The Tokyo-born chef, who trained under Clare Smyth and headed the kitchen at Restaurant Story, originally opened the venue as a yakitori, specialising in chicken skewers, before upgrading in early 2023 to its present, rather less humble incarnation. Diners sit at the counter to enjoy the theatrical preparation. / W1D 4SJ; www.humblechickenuk.com; humblechicken_uk; Tue-Thu 10 pm, Fri & Sat 11 pm.

HUMBLE GRAPE £67 2 3 3

11-13 THEBERTON STREET, N1
020 3887 9287 9–*3D*
2 BATTERSEA RISE, SW11
020 3620 2202 11–*2C*
18-20 MACKENZIE WALK, E14
020 3985 1330 12–*1C*
8 DEVONSHIRE ROW, EC2
020 3887 9287 10–*2D*
1 SAINT BRIDE'S PASSAGE, EC4
020 7583 0688 10–*2A*

James Dawson's wine shops/clubs/bars are "great places to catch up with friends over a bottle you might never ordinarily have tried". "The staff are super-helpful, with lots of suggestions" of bottles from independent and sustainable producers. The food is "OK if a little uninspiring", but "who cares when there's one evening a week when you can drink wine at retail prices". / www.humblegrape.co.uk; humblegrape.

HUMO W1 £91 5 5 4

12 ST GEORGE STREET
020 3327 3690 3–*2C*

An "amazing newcomer" on the former Mayfair site of Wild Honey (RIP), where chef Miller Prada (who worked with Endo Kazutoshi at Endo at The Rotunda) infuses Japanese flavours into his dishes at a four-metre wood grill (using no electricity or gas in the cooking process). It's "a very cool setting" with "notably ood" service and the culinary invention of the chnique means "every dish has a wow factor". However, both Giles Coren of The Times nd William Sitwell of The Telegraph have ound the experience "great… but pretentious"; sublime… [but] somewhat self-satisfied"). / V1S 2FB; humolondon.com; humolondon; Tue-Sat).15 pm.

HUNAN SW1 £120 4 2 1

1 PIMLICO ROAD 020 7730 5712 6–*2D*

Course after course of utter deliciousness!" – omprised of "Chinese tapas that never ceases o impress" – has won renown for this Pimlico eteran, whose "very different 18-course asting menu is tailored in terms of spiciness nd dietary preferences" in discussion with e staff. It's a formula that's served the Peng amily well for over 40 years (although their ersonal service is not quite as intrinsic to a visit s once it was). "As other authentic Chinese uisine has become available across London", is perhaps no longer the leading destination once was, although all diners feel "the food eserves its excellent reputation". "The venue oes not create much in the way of ambience" owever and it is often noted in feedback hat a meal here has become "very expensive ow". Top Tip – "don't eat all day before you o". / SW1W 8NE; www.hunanlondon.com; unanlondon; Mon-Sat 11 pm.

HUO SW10 £72 3 3 3

PARK WALK 020 3696 9090 6–*3B*

This "always enjoyable" two-year-old on Chelsea Beach' entices a stylish local crowd with its fresh-tasting take on the cuisines of China and Southeast Asia, and bleached-pastel ontemporary decor. Regulars tip its "best urries". It's a sibling to Uli in Notting Hill and Marylebone, from restaurateur Michael Lim. SW10 0AJ; huo.london; huo.london; Mon-Sat nidnight, Sun 11 pm.

HUSH W1 £99 2 3 4

LANCASHIRE CT 020 7659 1500 3–*2B*

Perfectly located just away from the hubbub of Bond Street/Oxford Street/Regent Street but asy to get to", this slick Mayfair venue with a great outdoor courtyard" for summer dining makes "an excellent place to talk business over a meal and wine". The pleasure "comes at a price", though – "one the food struggles to ustify". Fun fact: the founding investors include Evgeny Lebedev, the son of a Soviet spy who now sits in the House of Lords. / W1S 1EY; www.hush.co.uk; hushmayfair; Mon-Sat 10 pm.

HUTONG, THE SHARD SE1 £125 3 4 4

31 ST THOMAS ST 020 3011 1257 10–*4C*

'You pay for the view… it stings the wallet…", but they seem to have pulled their socks up at this well-known Asian venue on the 33rd floor of the famous London landmark. True, 'large numbers of diners seem more interested in taking photos of themselves and their food rather than eating it… it's definitely an Insta trophy". But it avoided the usual harsh critiques this year and practically all reports acknowledged the "surprisingly good Chinese cooking AND nighttime vistas over London". / SE1 9RY; www.hutong.co.uk; hutongshard; Mon-Sun 10.30 pm.

IBÉRICA £67 2 2 2

ZIG ZAG BUILDING, 70 VICTORIA ST, SW1
020 7636 8650 2–*4B*
195 GREAT PORTLAND ST, W1
020 7636 8650 2–*1B*
12 CABOT SQ, E14 020 7636 8650 12–*1C*
89 TURNMILL ST, EC1
020 7636 8650 10–*1A*

This "buzzy but very noisy" Hispanic quartet (in Marylebone, Farringdon, Victoria and Canary Wharf) offers a "good range of tapas" and "interesting wines by the glass and the bottle". They still have plenty of admirers as a "reliable" option, even if they "no longer provide the novelty or the high standards they once did". / www.ibericarestaurants.com; ibericarestaurants.

ICCO PIZZA £19 3 3 2

46 GOODGE ST, W1 020 7580 9688 2–*1C*
21A CAMDEN HIGH STREET, NW1
020 7380 0020 9–*3B*

"Awesome, thin and crispy pizza" has built quite a following for this "fast, simple, really cheap and really cheerful" Goodge Street spot – where, "unless strip lighting, functional metal tables and chairs are your thing, the ambience is forgettable". Celebrating its quarter-centenary this year as 'The People's Pizzeria', it now has a branch in Camden and 'click & collect' kitchens in Wood Green, Colindale and Croydon. / www.icco.co.uk; icco_pizza.

IKEDA W1 £94 4 3 2

30 BROOK ST 020 7629 2730 3–*2B*

After half a century, this high-quality Mayfair veteran is "still one of the best Japanese restaurants in London", with particularly "good fish" – although it has a lower profile than many newer and more flashy rivals. "Having the kitchen open to the dining area adds some theatre to aid the digestion". / W1K 5DJ; www.ikedarestaurant.com; Tue-Fri 9 pm, Mon 9.15 pm.

IKOYI WC2 £345 2 3 2

180 THE STRAND 020 3583 4660 4–*4D*

Iré Hassan-Odukale and Jeremy Chan have won huge renown for their 'haute' interpretation of West African culinary themes, but this year saw very unsettled reports. Perhaps, in part, this owes to the disruption of a move to 180 The Strand, although the copper-hued, minimalist design there isn't wholly at odds with the look and feel of the former location in St James's Market. But to a large extent, this year's themes are a continuation of last year's; and complaints that seemed to set in after they jacked up their prices following all the Michelin and 'World's 50 Best' accolades. True, some reports do acknowledge an "outstanding gastronomic experience" from the blind tasting menu which sees jollof rice and plantain jostling with luxury ingredients, foams and emulsions. But too many are mixed: "we had a couple of stunners, but a dish that was so bitter it was unpleasant. So expensive and given the unpredictability it makes Core look like a bargain…"; "really did not enjoy this. Dull atmosphere, combinations of food which just did not work and service not firing on all cylinders. First time I've ever not enjoyed a two-star restaurant…"; "was expecting something so special: it wasn't!" / WC2C 1EA; www.ikoyilondon.com; ikoyi_london; Thu-Sat, Mon-Wed 8.45 pm.

IMAD'S SYRIAN KITCHEN W1 £28 3 4 4

KINGLY COURT, KINGLY STREET
07473 333631 4–*2B*

"The poignant history" of Syrian chef Imad Alarnab (who fled Damascus in 2015) helps inspire excellent reviews for his "convivial" venue: a "gem in Kingly Court". Our feedback – citing "delicious" Syrian cooking and "thoughtful service" – came just before his May 2023 move to a bigger unit in the same development (where breakfast is a new feature): "the fact that you have to book with plenty of notice says it all… I'm not surprised to hear they're expanding". / W1B 5PW; imadssyriankitchen.co.uk; imadssyriankitchen; Tue-Sat 10 pm, Mon 9 pm.

IMPERIAL CHINA WC2 £59 3 2 2

25A LISLE ST 020 7734 3388 5–*3A*

"Fresh and very tasty dim sum" ensures that this 30-year-old Cantonese over three storeys on the edge of Chinatown "soon fills up with regulars". "It may be a blessing that the ambience is not exactly chic – it keeps the tourists away". / WC2H 7BA; www.imperialchinalondon.com; imperialchinalondon; Mon-Thu 11 pm, Fri & Sat 11.30 pm, Sun 10.30 pm.

IMPERIAL TREASURE SW1 £147 4 3 2

9-10 WATERLOO PLACE
020 3011 1328 4–*4D*

"Expensive, but worth it for a treat!" is the positive view on this West End fixture – part of a Singapore-based group, whose London outpost occupies an expensively converted former banking hall in the West End, whose atmosphere has ended up somewhere between impressive and stilted. "Very good, classic Chinese cuisine is reverently served by a stream of waiters… but the prices!… £200 for Peking duck with caviar anyone?" Indeed, such is the size of the bill that there is a school of thought that the level of value doesn't stack up and that – irrespective of its many qualities – the overall experience is overpriced and/or disappointing. / SW1Y 4BE; www.imperialtreasure.com; imperialtreasureuk; Mon-Sun 11 pm.

INAMO £65 324

134-136 WARDOUR STREET, W1
020 7851 7051 4–1D
11-14 HANOVER PLACE, WC2
020 7484 0500 5–2D

"Launched in 2008 as the world's first interactive restaurant", these Soho and Covent Garden venues are "great for an alternative afternoon tea" and attract a "young, tech-savvy crowd". A meal here is "certainly an experience – you have to see it to believe it", and the pan-Asian "unlimited lunch" is "of a high standard". / www.inamo-restaurant.com; inamorestaurant.

INDIAN OCEAN SW17 £31 333

214 TRINITY RD 020 8672 7740 11–2C

This "fabulous, family-run" curry house near Wandsworth Common has built a loyal local following over the years for its "delicious food" and "always charming" welcome. / SW17 7HP; www.indianoceanrestaurant.com; Sun-Thu 11 pm, Fri & Sat 11.45 pm.

INDIAN ZING W6 £61 433

236 KING ST 020 8748 5959 8–2B

Reaching "classic" status after almost two decades of "outstanding food and great service", this Ravenscourt Park venue is a haven of "superb Indian cuisine", thanks to chef-patron Manoj Vasaikar's "well-spiced" cooking and "quality ingredients". The late Michael Winner was an early fan. / W6 0RS; www.indian-zing.co.uk; indianzinguk; Mon-Sun 10 pm.

INDIGO, ONE ALDWYCH WC2 £71 334

1 ALDWYCH 020 7300 0400 2–2D

This conveniently situated mezzanine venue in a luxury hotel near Covent Garden is a real treat thanks to its "lovely setting" and "high standard" of cooking. The kitchen is "particularly accommodating for those with dietary restrictions" – "the wheat and dairy-free afternoon tea is joyous, with wonderful flavours and ingenious combinations, plus a wide selection of unusual teas". / WC2B 4BZ; www.onealdwych.com; onealdwychhotel; Mon-Sat 9.30 pm, Sun 11.

INO W1 £58 344

4 NEWBURGH STREET
020 3701 6618 4–2B

One or two "outstanding" reports inspire interest in this modern Greek off Soho's Carnaby Street, whose name means 'wine' in ancient Greek (there's an all-Hellenic list), and where the menu focus is on plates from the charcoal grill. (It's from the team behind Opso, who also run the two-Michelin-star Funky Gourmet in Athens).Our rating errs on the conservative side, but we still don't get as many reports on the place as we would like. Top Tip – very good value set lunch. / W1F 7RF; www.inogastrobar.com; ino.restaurant; Mon-Sat 11 pm, Sun 10 pm.

ISHTAR W1 £71 332

10-12 CRAWFORD ST 020 7224 2446 2–1A

Celebrating its 20th anniversary this year, this smart Turkish operation in Marylebone wins consistently solid marks for the "excellent quality and taste" of its dishes – in particular the grilled meat and mezzes. / W1U 6AZ; www.ishtarrestaurant.com; ishtarlondon; Sun-Thu 11 pm, Fri & Sat midnight.

ISLA WC1 £66 354

THE STANDARD, 10 ARGYLE ST
020 3981 8888 9–3C

The gorgeous, glazed summer terrace adjoining the main lounges is a highpoint at this bar/restaurant opposite St Pancras. Its other features include the superb 1970s decor and shelves lined with books inherited from the hotel's former life as the Camden Council Library. Extra convenient if you need a meeting place near King's Cross – it serves a dependable all-day modern European menu and service is particularly friendly and efficient. / WC1H 8EG; www.islalondon.com; isla.london; Mon-Sun 11 pm.

ISSHO-NI E2 £43 442

185 BETHNAL GREEN ROAD
020 7366 0314 13–1D

"Top-end sushi for a fair price" is the deal at this Bethnal Green izakaya from Claire Su, who delights her guests with "the freshest sushi and some great hot dishes too". The weekday bento-box lunches are extremely good value, and the "unlimited brunch (starters, sashimi and maki rolls) on Saturdays is fantastic". Top Menu Tip – "don't get me started on the butter fish". / E2 6AB; issho-ni.com; isshoniuk; Tue-Thu 10.30 pm, Fri & Sat 11 pm.

ITALIAN GREYHOUND W1 £61 333

62 SEYMOUR STREET
020 3826 7940 7–1D

Attractive casual two-year-old not far from Marble Arch, whose mid-pandemic opening perhaps robbed it of PR it might otherwise have generated. Feedback remains limited, but the response is all very good when it comes to the stylish interior; 20-seat outside terrace; and Italian cuisine (from pizza and pasta to some more 'serious' dishes). / W1H 5BN; theitaliangreyhound.co.uk; greyhoundmarylebone; Mon-Sat 11 pm, Sun 10.30 pm.

THE IVY WC2 £97 223

1-5 WEST STREET 020 7836 4751 5–3B

The eclipse of this former icon of Theatreland by the nationwide chain it spawned (and its adjoining club) is continuing, and the volume of feedback it inspired sank significantly this year. A fair amount of glam still remains, but the A-listers are long gone, and standards are "hit and miss nowadays" to the extent that it too often delivers an experience that's "overpriced, formulaic and mediocre". / WC2H 9NQ; www.the-ivy.co.uk; theivyweststi; Mon-Sat 11 pm, Sun 10.30 pm.

THE IVY ASIA £84 324

8-10 NORTH AUDLEY STREET, W1
020 3751 4990 3–2A
201-203A KING'S ROAD, SW3
020 7486 6154 6–3C
20 NEW CHANGE PASSAGE, EC4
020 3971 2600 10–2B

"Wanted to hate this chain but it's actually really good" – Despite being totally un-PC in its level of cultural appropriation, it looks like Richard Caring's is going to make a go of this "extraordinary" new sub-branch of the Ivy brand (which has opened five further branches around the UK). True, "it's part of a big corporate machine with little intrinsic character"; the über-"kitsch" styling is "love-it-or-hate-it"; and some diners feel "these places are ghastly and overpriced". But even if "the jewelled floor is more interesting than the food" most folks feel that the "OTT decor" "justifies the trip in itself" and that the long, pan-Asian menu is "so much better than expected". / www.theivyasia.com; theivyasia.

THE IVY CAFÉ £88 112

96 MARYLEBONE LN, W1
020 3301 0400 2–1A
120 ST JOHN'S WOOD HIGH ST, NW8
020 3096 9444 9–3A
75 HIGH ST, SW19 020 3096 9333 11–2B
9 HILL STREET, TW9 020 3146 7733 1–4A

"Trading on a once-great name but disappointing in every category (except perhaps breakfasts)" – this brasserie brand themed around the Theatreland classic feels "very 'chain restaurant' now". Some reporters do suggest their "comfort food staples" and "buzzy interiors" make them useful destinations, but too many suggest they are "haphazard" and "not a place to return to". / ivycollection.com/our-restaurants.

THE IVY GRILLS & BRASSERIES £87 223

66 VICTORIA STREET, SW1
020 3971 2404 2–4B
26-28 BROADWICK ST, W1
020 3301 1166 4–1C
1 HENRIETTA ST, WC2
020 3301 0200 5–3D
197 KING'S RD, SW3 020 3301 0300 6–3C
96 KENSINGTON HIGH ST, W8
020 3301 0500 6–1A
ONE TOWER BRIDGE, 1 TOWER BRIDGE, SE1 020 3146 7722 10–4D
50 CANADA SQUARE, E14
020 3971 7111 12–1C
DASHWOOD HOUSE, 69 OLD BROAD ST, EC2 020 3146 7744 10–2D

With the "lovely decor" replicated from the Theatreland icon for which they are branded, Richard Caring's "always buzzy" spin-offs have found a gigantic audience nationally. But "these places live off the name for sure" and "it's the ambience that keeps them going" – while fans say the food is "reliable", more sceptical types ismiss it as "conveyor-belt cooking"; and say ervice is merely so-so. Some branches are etter than others: best in London is 'Chelsea arden', which has the same "distinctly verage" standards as the others, but reliably ffers an "uplifting" atmosphere and "great eople watching" (and "on a sunny afternoon iere is literally NO WHERE ELSE TO BE ut its large garden. HEAVEN!!"). Also worth ientioning is the outlet by The Thames in E1: "excellent views of Tower Bridge", "even etter if outside in summer and convenient for he Bridge Theatre". / theivymarketgrill.com.

ZAKAYA NIGHTS W11

UPERMARKET OF DREAMS, 126 HOLLAND ARK AVENUE 01904 610370 7–2A

fter shopping hours, the Supermarket of reams in Holland Park Avenue morphs into n upscale Japanese restaurant, with guests eated at a long central table. It started as a op-up, and announced it was to become a ermanent feature in March 2023. Dishes are reated by Juan Cardona (formerly of Endo at The Rotunda), and Jaime Finol (formerly of umi) and sushi is the mainstay of the menu as you'd hope, given the stellar renown of both hose places in that respect). Reports please! / V11 4UE; www.izakaya-york.co.uk; izakaya.york; Ved-Sat midnight.

ACUZZI W8 £72 124

4 KENSINGTON HIGH STREET NO TEL –1A

A fun place for the Insta crowd…" – "the etting is absolute bling (but enjoyable for hat)" at this mammoth Kensington newcomer rom the Big Mamma group (Gloria, Circolo Popolare, etc), complete with a Sicilian-styled nezzanine with retractable roof and glitter-ball disco toilet. But too often it's "all about he vibe and location" – the humongous portions of Italian fare can be tolerable, but strike unlucky and "OMG the food is bad"; and service "needs focus" not "annoying oud Italian-style showmanship". Top Menu Tip – "the pizza is pretty decent". / W8 4SH; www.bigmammagroup.com; bigmamma.uk; Mon-Sat 10.15 pm, Sun 9.45 pm.

JAM DELISH N1 £52 543

1 TOLPUDDLE STREET 07957 439777 9–3D

"Deserving all the plaudits and great value too" – siblings Jordan & Chyna Johnson graduated from residencies and pop-ups to this bricks-and-mortar perma-home in 2022: a hard-to-define, good-times restaurant and cocktail bar in Islington, with a "super soundtrack and slightly bonkers decor". What makes it particularly of interest is the "quirky-in-a-good-way" Caribbean cuisine that's not only hearty for meat-free cooking – and with "an unexpected range of flavours" – but also absolutely bangin'. Add in "lovely staff" and it's "a real find". / N1 0XT; www.jamdelish.co.uk; jam.delish; Tue-Sat 10.30 pm, Sun 7 pm.

JAMAVAR W1 £83 333

8 MOUNT STREET 020 7499 1800 3–3B

"A beautiful restaurant interior, plus warm, professional and attentive staff" have helped Samyutka Nair and family's "posh Indian" near Mayfair's Berkeley Square acquire a reputation as "one of the best subcontinental restaurants in London". Its ratings sank this year, though amidst a number of experiences of cooking that was "solid, but not as refined as expected" – "It was very nice… but is it so different to many others that have sprung up to justify the high price here?" Top Tip – "set lunch is a steal!" / W1K 3NF; www.jamavarrestaurants.com; jamavarlondon; Mon-Sat 10.30 pm, Sun 9.30 pm.

JASHAN N8 £42 332

19 TURNPIKE LN 020 8340 9880 1–1C

Nobody is entirely happy about the change of style at this "wonderful curry house" of more than three decades' standing in Turnpike Lane, following a recent "facelift", although "if that's what they had to do to survive the pandemic, then fair enough I suppose – but we really miss the old place". Some feel it's now "essentially a large takeaway counter with the restaurant area tucked behind under glaringly bright lights", while more positive types feel that overall it's "still recommended for a quick casual eating experience, but not for a relaxed evening out as in the past". / N8 0EP; www.jashan.co.uk; Mon-Sun 11 pm.

JEAN-GEORGES AT THE CONNAUGHT W1 £132 233

CARLOS PLACE 020 7107 8861 3–3B

Other than for a deeply cosseting afternoon tea, it's hard to be too thrilled by this blue-blooded hotel's luxurious conservatory dining room. Although it's branded with the name of the famous NYC chef, it's difficult to discern any trace of JGV's fingerprints in the design of the ubiquitous, international-luxe menu of caviar, fish, posh pizza, burgers, salads and so forth. Of course, if you find yourself in Mayfair, and are sanguine about spending £30+ for a bowl of mushroom bolognese or shrimp salad, it's a jolly pleasant experience. Viewed through a more demanding lens, though, it can seem "overpriced" for something with little in the way of distinctive culinary personality. / W1K 2AL; www.the-connaught.co.uk; theconnaught; Mon-Sun midnight.

JERU W1 £106 334

11 BERKELEY STREET 020 3988 0054 3–3C

"Two atmospheric dining rooms" make a "beautiful setting" for Aussie celeb chef Roy Ner to showcase his "pan-Middle Eastern" cuisine, featuring his signature chocolate-aged beef among other creations. But even some who feel the food is "perfectly acceptable" can quibble at the Mayfair prices. / W1J 8DS; jeru.co.uk; jerulondon; Mon-Thu 10.15 pm, Fri & Sat 11.15 pm.

JIJI N1 £70 333

6G ESTHER ANNE PLACE 020 7486 3929 9–3D

"An amazing variety of small, tasty and unusual combination dishes served in a very cool environment" continues to win a thumbs up – if from a tiny fan club – for this Israeli-Japanese one-year-old in the shiny new Islington Square development. / N1 1WL; jijirestaurants.com; jijirestaurant; Tue-Sun 11 pm.

JIKONI W1 £83 434

21 BLANDFORD STREET 020 7034 1988 2–1A

This "beautiful little restaurant with a neighbourhood feel" in Marylebone, from chef and food writer Ravinder Bhogal, offers a "wide-ranging and ever-changing selection of consistently good dishes" inspired by her 'no borders kitchen' philosophy. "It's a melange of Middle Eastern, African and Indian influences" that results in "very creative flavours – not just in the cooking but also outstanding cocktails such as a Negroni with pomegranate and rose". / W1U 3DJ; www.jikonilondon.com; jikonilondon; Tue, Sat 10 pm, Wed-Fri 11 pm, Sun 9 pm.

Kanishka W1

JIN KICHI NW3 £62 543

73 HEATH ST 020 7794 6158 9–1A

"Now happily doubled in size" – this favourite stalwart near Hampstead tube "hasn't been spoilt by its recent expansion" and remains "an atmospheric local gem", much to the relief of its large following. "You feel like you might be in Tokyo here", such is its unpretentious yet "elegantly bustling" nature; and "wonderful sushi and yakitori" (especially the latter) gives it a justifiable claim to offering "the best value Japanese food of its quality in London". / NW3 6UG; www.jinkichi.com; jinkichi_restaurant; Tue-Sun 10 pm.

JINJUU W1 £73 322

16 KINGLY ST 020 8181 8887 4–2B

The "small plates of big Korean taste bombs never disappoint" in this basement dining room (with a ground-level bar) off Carnaby Street, where traditional cuisine meets contemporary K-pop youth culture. Top Menu Tip – "prawn tacos and spicy cauliflower". / W1B 5PS; www.jinjuu.com; jinjuusoho; Mon & Tue 10 pm, Wed & Thu 11 pm, Fri & Sat midnight, Sun 9.30 pm.

JOE ALLEN WC2 £62 234

2 BURLEIGH ST 020 7836 0651 5–3D

The "Manhattan-esque atmosphere" is the perennial attraction of this Theatreland favourite (sibling to a famous NYC brasserie near Times Square), which retains the retro charm of a 1970s period piece, even though it was completely rebuilt on a new site just around the corner from the original one just four years ago. "Despite the luvvie buzz, the American food is decidedly second rate (though the off-menu burger is fine)". "Prices are not unreasonable for the location", however, and "the youthful staff do their best". / WC2E 7PX; www.joeallen.co.uk; joeallenlondon; Mon-Thu 9.45 pm, Fri & Sat 10.30 pm, Sun 4.30 pm.

JOIA SW11 £114 334

BATTERSEA POWER STATION, CIRCUS ROAD WEST 020 3833 8333 11–1C

"You feel like you're on the set of Blade Runner next to the floor-to-ceiling windows" of this striking newcomer on the 16th floor of the new Battersea art'otel, with gobsmacking sightlines over the top of the power station and of the London skyline. Fêted Portuguese chef, Henrique Sá Pessoa, provides a not-unaffordable selection of tapas, petiscos, tortilla, grills (from the Josper) and a few large plates. Our reporters were generally more enthusiastic than The Standard's Jimi Famurewa (whose food "lurched, haphazardly, from forgettably luxe to clumsily experimental"), referencing "classic Portuguese dishes, all executed with impeccable attention to detail". But one reporter did feel their meal was only "fine… like JimFam we were thinking of the much more interesting and better value menu at Lisboeta". Top Tip – dip your toe in the water by "heading to the rooftop bar next door which has stunning views: order some drinks and nibble on small plates". / SW11 8BJ; www.joiabattersea.co.uk; joiabattersea; Tue, Wed midnight, Thu-Sat 1 am.

JONES & SONS N16 £67 334

STAMFORD WORKS, 3 GILLETT STREET 020 7241 1211 14–1A

"Deservedly something of a local institution" – this industrial-style restaurant and grill "manages to provide a cut-above dining experience while retaining a low-key Hackney vibe" – making it the perfect location for the 2021 film Boiling Point, which was spun out into a BBC TV series in 2023. / N16 8JH; www.jonesandsonsdalston.com; jones.and.sons; Wed-Sat 10 pm, Sun 6 pm.

THE JONES FAMILY KITCHEN SW1 £85 334

7-8 ECCLESTON YARD 020 3929 6000 2–4B

"A great option near Victoria" – this indie venue in the stylish Eccleston Yards project provides a comfy spot for its Josper-grilled steaks, other grills from 'sea, land and field' and fish tartares. It's "relatively simple fare" but well-realised from a wide variety of menus, including Sunday roasts. And the venue "makes a virtue of its converted warehouse space" with "very friendly" service that helps it win votes both for business and as a good spot to spend "a lovely lazy afternoon". Top Tip – wonderful outside dining in summer. / SW1W 9AZ; www.jonesfamilykitchen.co.uk; jonesfamilyrestaurants; Mon-Sat 11.30 pm, Sun 9 pm.

JOSÉ SE1 £62 534

104 BERMONDSEY ST 020 7403 4902 10–4D

"For maybe a decade now, José has been London's most reliable and enjoyable restaurant", assert fans of the tiny tapas bar José Pizarro opened on Bermondsey Street in 2011, now the spiritual home of a growing culinary empire. "Whether it's a quick lunch or hours spent at the bar, it simply never misses". "Always incredibly fun, always worth the queue, always get the croquetas". / SE1 3UB; www.josepizarro.com; jose_pizarro; Mon-Sat 10.30 pm, Sun 10 pm.

JOSÉ PIZARRO EC2 £68 322

BROADGATE CIRCLE 020 7256 5333 13–2B

The Broadgate Circle tapas bar from the trailblazer of contemporary Hispanic cooking in London provides "excellent food in a modern environment" – even if aficionados of the more atmospheric original insist it "doesn't replicate the better José across the river" in Bermondsey. / EC2M 2QS; www.josepizarro.com; josepizarrorestaurants; Mon-Fri 10.30 pm, Sat 9.45 pm.

JOSÉ PIZARRO AT THE RA, ROYAL ACADEMHY W1 £60 334

BURLINGTON GARDENS, PICCADILLY 020 7300 5912 3–3D

"Talk about high ceilings and light" – this "really lovely addition to the RA" is "worth a trip just for the beautiful dining room". According to supporters, "it's a clear exception to the rule that restaurants in art galleries never live up to their surroundings, with imaginative tapas in good-sized portions and at very reasonable prices for the area". That said, its ratings have slipped since it first opened and there are one or two critics who say "we've always been fans of José, but the RA offering isn't as good as the other JPs". / W1J 0BD; josepizarro.com; jose_pizarro; Tue-Thu, Sat & Sun 6 pm, Fri 9 pm.

JUGEMU W1 £40 522

3 WINNETT ST 020 7734 0518 4–2D

Yuya Kikuchi's no-frills, very personal, small Soho six-year-old inspired little feedback this year, although we have received rave reviews in the past, particularly about the sushi. You can eat quite cheaply here, but aficionados of Japanese cuisine regularly go nuts for his £120, 18-course omakase. The FT's Tim Hayward was one such in February 2023, declaring it "the best Japanese food in London" where "the chef's attention to his ingredients is quite staggering… his craft skills second-to-none". We have never had any complaints, but read Tripadvisor reviews if you are at all sensitive to poor service… / W1D 6JY; jugemu.uk; Mon-Sat 10.30 pm.

THE JUGGED HARE EC1 £75 324

49 CHISWELL STREET 020 7614 0134 13–2A

The "excellent meat-driven menu" at this "busy bar opposite the Barbican" is led by British game in season, backed up by prime cuts of beef and such treats as Herefordshire snails. "It's not simple pub grub, and you do pay for it, but it's worth it", say fans. It's also "particularly useful pre- or post-events in the nearby arts centre". / EC1Y 4SA; www.thejuggedhare.com; thejuggedhare; Mon-Sun 11 pm.

JUNSEI W1 £74 342

132 SEYMOUR PLACE 020 7723 4058 7–1D

"Top-notch cooking that uses every bit of the chicken and won't cost a wing and a leg" draws an appreciative Marylebone crowd to this Japanese two-year-old which "specialises in yakitori skewers with some very interesting options (gizzard anyone?)". "Go sit at the counter to see the open kitchen at work" and "revel in the omakase menu". / W1H 1NS; junsei.co.uk; junsei_uk; Wed-Sat 10 pm, Sun 9 pm.

Kapara by Bala Baya W1

KAFFEINE £17 253

15 EASTCASTLE ST, W1
020 7580 6755 3–*1D*
66 GREAT TITCHFIELD ST, W1
020 7580 6755 3–*1C*

"One of the original Aussie coffee shops", founded in 2009 by Melburnian Peter Dore-Smith and now with two branches in Fitzrovia serving "fabulous artisanal brews". They make a "perfect escape from the chain experience of nearby Oxford Street" with their "great service and vibe", "fresh sandwiches" and "very good lunchtime salads". / kaffeine.co.uk; kaffeinelondon.

KAHANI SW1 £80 443

1 WILBRAHAM PLACE
020 7730 7634 6–*2D*

Peter Joseph (raised in Chennai) "has maintained high standards and always delivers value for money" at his culinarily "interesting" Indian venture near Sloane Square (behind Cadogan Hall), where he uses a robata grill and tandoor to "delicious" effect. "Initially, we thought it was an unpromising basement, but it was one of our best meals of the year". / SW1X 9AE; www.kahanilondon.com; kahani_london; Mon-Sat 10.30 pm, Sun 8 pm.

KAI MAYFAIR W1 £133 443

65 SOUTH AUDLEY ST
020 7493 8988 3–*3A*

"Chinese cuisine at its finest, with service to match" helps inspire high ratings this year for Bernard Yeoh's luxurious Mayfair fixture – now of two decades' standing – which describes its culinary focus as 'Liberated Nanyang Cooking'. Part of this freewheeling approach is the curation of a very comprehensive cellar: perhaps wash down your roasted Peking duck with a 1990 Château Pétrus at over £9,000 per bottle… / W1K 2QU; www.kaimayfair.co.uk; kaimayfair; Mon-Sun 11 pm.

KAIFENG NW4 £79 443

51 CHURCH ROAD 020 8203 7888 1–*1B*

One of North London's more consistent and interesting culinary success stories: Hendon's kosher Chinese restaurant "continues to operate at a very high standard", with "tasty and authentic cooking" and "a great ambience". It takes its name from a Chinese city with an ancient Jewish community. / NW4 4DU; www.kaifeng.co.uk; Sun-Thu, Sat 10.30 pm.

KAKI N1 £53 332

125 CALEDONIAN ROAD
020 7278 6848 9–*3D*

"Authentic, mostly fiery, Sichuan cooking" is showcased at this modern pub-conversion, "conveniently a few minutes' walk along the canal from King's Cross". The menu includes plenty of items that in Britain used to be hidden away behind untranslated Chinese characters – chicken feet, frog legs, pig intestines – and "given the large plates, you need a big group to do it justice". / N1 9RG; www.thekaki.co.uk; kaki_london; Sun-Thu 10 pm, Fri & Sat 11 pm.

KALIMERA N8 £53 433

43 TOPSFIELD ROAD 07446 981139 1–*1C*

It's "definitely worth a trip to Crouch End" to sample the "lovely Greek mezze, stews and fish dishes from a short and well-chosen menu" at Télémaque Argyriou's two-year-old venture, where the olives and oil are sourced directly from his family's farm in Laconia, close to Sparta. Now with spin-offs in Paris and Lille, it's pitched as a showcase for modern ("not tourist-oriented") Greek cuisine, with some "interesting Hellenic wines". / N8 8PT; kalimera.london; eatkalimera; Tue-Sat 11 pm.

KANADA-YA £42 422

3 PANTON ST, SW1 020 7930 3511 5–*4A*
28 FOUBERT'S PLACE, W1
020 3435 8155 4–*1B*
64 ST GILES HIGH ST, WC2
020 7240 0232 5–*1B*
3B FILMWORKS WALK, W5
020 3375 2340 1–*3A*
35 UPPER STREET, N1
020 7288 2787 9–*3D*

"The best ramen in London, IMO – the rich, porky broth is perfect", say fans of former pro-cyclist Kazuhiro Kanada's five noodle bars – in Angel, Piccadilly, Covent Garden, Carnaby and Ealing. "If you're going to do one thing, do it well, and they do" – so they "deserve the frequent queues". / www.kanada-ya.com; kanada_ya_ldn.

KANISHKA W1 £103 322

17-19 MADDOX STREET
020 3978 0978 4–*2A*

"Delicious and quite unusual dishes" help win praise for Atul Kocchar's Mayfair five-year-old, which is "handy to know about just off the West End's main shopping streets". Even fans, though, feel that the prices for some items are a bit "ridiculous". / W1S 2QH; kanishkarestaurant.co.uk; kanishkamayfair; Mon-Sat 10.30 pm, Sun 9.30 pm.

KAOSARN £42 343

110 ST JOHNS HILL, SW11
020 7223 7888 11–*2C*
181 TOOTING HIGH STREET, SW17
020 8672 8811 11–*2C*
BRIXTON VILLAGE, COLDHARBOUR LN, SW9 020 7095 8922 11–*2D*

This family-owned traditional Thai trio – in Brixton, Battersea and Tooting – is "always packed" – a tribute to the high levels of hospitality they have maintained over the years. The BYO policy means they are good value, too. / www.kaosarnlondon.co.uk; kaosarntooting.

KAPARA BY BALA BAYA W1

JAMES COURT, MANETTE STREET
020 8079 7467 5–*2A*

Inspired by Israeli home cooking as well as the Tel Aviv party scene (Kapara is Hebrew slang for 'darling'), this all-day-and-late-night, Soho-fringe newcomer is from Eran Tibi (the chef behind Bala Baya in Southwark). It opened shortly prior to our survey in Spring 2023, and didn't generate much in the way of reports. Early online buzz suggests that even if there's the odd wrinkle to iron out, it has potential. / W1D 4AL; www.kapara.co.uk; kapara; Mon-Sat 1 am, Sun 11.30 pm.

KAPPACASEIN SE1 £11 53

1 STONEY STREET NO TEL 10–*4C*

"Quite simply the best cheese and onion toastie ever" – and equally yummy raclette – is found at Bermondsey raw cheesemaker Bill Oglethorpe's Borough Market stall, named after one of the proteins in milk. / SE1 9AA; www.kappacasein.com; kappacasein; Thu-Sat 5 pm

KASA & KIN W1 £50 343

52-53 POLAND STREET
020 7287 5400 4–*1C*

"Worth a visit for the mural alone!" – this brightly decorated two-year-old, just off Regent Street, has "raised the bar for consistently good Filipino food in the West End". Admittedly that's not from a high base, but all reports on it BBQ-focused menu are enthusiastic: "you get little fuss, no hype, just great nosh and cocktails too". / W1F 7NQ; kasaandkin.co.uk; kasaandkin; Tue, Wed 9 pm, Thu-Sat 10 pm, Sun 6 pm.

KASHMIR SW15 £53 34

18-20 LACY ROAD 07477 533888 11–*2B*

"Very good food", "charming service" and what they claim is the 'only authentic Kashmiri cuisine in England' are the distinguishing features of this Putney venture from Rohit & Shweta Razdan, whose culinary journey took them to New Delhi and Singapore before settling here eight years ago. / SW15 1NL; www.kashmirrestaurants.co.uk; kashmirrestuk; Sun-Thu 10.30 pm, Fri & Sat 11 pm.

THE KATI ROLL COMPANY W1 £28 32

24 POLAND STREET 020 7287 4787 4–*1C*

A kati roll is made of skewer-roasted fillings wrapped in a paratha – tasty Indian street food that hits the spot for a small but enthusiastic fan club amongst our reporters. With branches in Soho and Bethnal Green, they are imports from a four-strong Manhattan-based chain. / W1F 8QL; www.thekatirollcompany.com; thekatirollcompany; Mon-Sun 11 pm.

KAZAN SW1 £64 33

93-94 WILTON RD 020 7233 7100 2–*4B*

"Honest Turkish food and very good value" continue to inspire enthusiasm for this Pimlico local of over two decades' standing: "meat is grilled to perfection" and there's "a high standard of service". / SW1V 1DW; www.kazan-restaurant.com; kazan_restaurant_london; Mon-Sat 10 pm, Sun 9.30 pm.

EBAB QUEEN
C2 £125 443

MERCER WALK 020 7439 9222 5–2C

know that I am not the first person to have en blown away by the imagination displayed this deconstruction of the kebab!" – this no-nger-secret 10-seater counter in the basement Kingly Court's Le Bab aims to rocket-propel e kebab taste-palate to new heights, with a ulti-course tasting menu served (smeared?) to a special heated countertop (you scoop ith your fingers). "Tasty… good patter from e chefs… engaging… quite the experience". August 2023, it relaunched with Pamir eydan as the new head chef (although he ad already been working here with departing Ianu Canales). The sort of dishes to expect? Dover sole kebab delivered on an ironed hispi abbage taco with roasted red pepper purée'. / C2H 9FA; www.eatlebab.com; eatlebab; Sun & Ion 9.30 pm, Wed-Sat 10.30 pm, Tue 10 pm.

EN LO'S MEMORIES
W1 £73 332

5-69 EBURY ST 020 7730 7734 2–4B

Iow in its fifth decade and almost 30 years fter Ken Lo's death, the Victoria venture he ounded to showcase his brand of Chinese uisine continues to feed a loyal (if now, erhaps somewhat ageing) band of regulars. ll rate it well, although it can seem "pricey ven for somewhere on the edge of Belgravia". SW1W 0NZ; www.memoriesofchina.co.uk; enlosmemoriesofchina; Wed-Sat, Tue, Sun 10.30 m.

KENNINGTON TANDOORI
E11 £57 343

13 KENNINGTON RD 020 7735 9247 1–3C

Kowsar Hoque's stylish Indian emporium" Kennington, opened by his father almost 40 ears ago, "continues to deliver excellent dishes which are reasonably priced for the high quality nd make you feel you're in the company f experts"… actually you are likely in the ompany of our less-than-expert ruling class, iven that the venue has long been a favourite f MPs from nearby Westminster, including David Cameron and BoJo. / SE11 4QE; www.kenningtontandoori.com; kennington andoori; Mon-Sun 10.30 pm.

KERRIDGE'S BAR & GRILL
WC2 £118 334

0 NORTHUMBERLAND AVENUE
20 7321 3244 2–3C

Within a "luxurious and pampering" five tar, the "unpretentious but stylish setting" of TV-star Tom Kerridge's high-ceilinged hamber provides a "wonderful" yet relaxed atmosphere to suit most types of occasion and he place is "always busy". However, the bill or the posh brasserie fare is "eye-watering" – o fans "pricey but terrific", but critics opine hat "some gastropubs do this better for half he cost… but then again you are in The Corinthia". Top Tip – unbelievably good-value set lunch, for £15 per person. / WC2N 5AE; www.kerridgesbarandgrill.co.uk; kerridgesbandg; Mon-Sat 10.30 pm, Sun 9 pm.

KERRIDGE'S FISH & CHIPS, HARRODS SW1 £105 234

87-135 BROMPTON ROAD
020 7225 6800 6–1D

Within the gorgeous tiled space of Harrods Dining Hall, TV Tom's seafood counter (as well as the National Dish, menu options include caviar, whole lobster, and seafood curry) is a favourite for the odd reporter, and no-one rates its food less than good. Even so it is sometimes rated as disappointing, due in large part to the Knightsbridge prices. / SW1X 7XL; www.harrods.com; harrods; Tue-Sat 10.30 pm, Mon 9 pm, Sun 6 pm.

KETTNERS W1

29 ROMILLY ST 020 7734 6112 5–2A

Dating from 1867, this fine Soho landmark should be famous, but has slipped off the restaurant map in recent years: initially due to its indifferent standards; and then due to Soho House's purchase of the building, and its closure to non-members since 2019. In July 2023, the club once again threw open its doors to the hoi polloi, with a food operation now run by the team behind the Stoke Newington pub The Clarence Tavern. Fingers crossed, this promising partnership helps it recoup some of its old mojo, rather than descending once again into the Theatreland tourist trap mode that's dogged it since PizzaExpress founder, the late Peter Boizot, sold it on in 2002. / W1D 5HP; www.kettners.com; kettnerssoho; Mon-Fri 1 am, Sat 2 am, Sun midnight.

KIBAKO W1

3 WINDMILL STREET 020 7419 0305 2–1C

From the team behind Islington's Hot Stone, this February 2023 newcomer is a re-imagining of their Fitzrovia site, which previously traded as Rai and with a not-completely-dissimilar format. The cuisine is 'contemporary Japanese' in style, with sushi, sashimi and Kagoshima wagyu beef, chosen omakase-style for each diner and served in a presentation box. / W1T 2HY; www.kibakolondon.com; kibakolondon; Tue-Thu, Sun 9 pm, Fri & Sat 9.30 pm.

KIBOU LONDON SW11 £62 223

175-177 NORTHCOTE ROAD
020 7223 8551 11–2C

Strikingly decorated with murals, this three-year-old modern Japanese from a Cheltenham-based group has proved a "great addition" to Battersea's 'Nappy Valley', and wins praise for "exceptional signature sushi rolls", "very good cocktails" and its lively style. Ratings are limited by those who find the success of the cooking to be a case of hit and miss. / SW11 6QF; kibou.co.uk; kiboucheltenham; Tue-Sat 11 pm, Sun 10 pm.

KIKU W1 £70 442

17 HALF MOON ST 020 7499 4208 3–4B

A short walk from the Japanese Embassy, this veteran family-run operation in a Mayfair backstreet offers "immaculately prepared food" and "superb service" in a "calm and grown-up atmosphere". It opened in 1978, well before Japanese cuisine became fashionable. / W1J 7BE; www.kikurestaurant.co.uk; kikumayfair; Mon-Sat 10.15 pm.

KILN W1 £54 544

58 BREWER STREET NO TEL 4–3C

"So cool, but with amazing food!" – Ben Chapman's "bustling" Thai BBQ in Soho continues to deliver exceptional value. With a "cramped but lovely vibe", "the best seats in the house are at the back where you can sit and watch the chefs cook over charcoal" (although "your clothes may be smelly afterwards due to the smoke from the open kitchen"). "Knowledgeable staff" provide a "menu full of things you never see at your average Thai restaurant, with stunning flavours" (and with "spice levels just on the right side of incendiary"). / W1F 9TL; www.kilnsoho.com; Mon-Sat 11 pm, Sun 9 pm.

KIMA W1

57 PADDINGTON STREET
07745 205136 2–1A

Opened in June 2023, from the team behind nearby Opso, this contemporary Greek seafood specialist in Marylebone follows a zeitgeisty, no-waste 'fin-to-gill' philosophy, with fish off-cuts, tails and bones either grilled or used to make stock. Expect some meat choices, and plenty of Hellenic wines. / W1U 4JA; www.kimarestaurant.com; kima.restaurant.london; Wed-Sun 11.30 pm.

KIN AND DEUM SE1 £49 323

2 CRUCIFIX LANE 020 7357 7995 10–4D

"Great, modern Thai food" is to be had at this stylish (although "rather cramped and noisy") pub conversion a short walk from the Shard by London Bridge station – "the kind of Thai you wish was just around the corner". It's run by siblings Roselyn, Shakris & Bank Inngern, the new generation of the family that operated Thai restaurant Suchard on nearby Tooley Street for more than 20 years, which has recently been re-opened as veggie specialist Plants of Roselyn. / SE1 3JW; www.kindeum.com; kindeum; Mon-Sun 10.30 pm.

KINDRED W6 £45 333

BRADMORE HOUSE, QUEEN CAROLINE STREET 020 3146 1370 8–2C

Need somewhere civilised to meet for an informal business lunch or catch-up with a pal in Hammersmith? Then it's well worth remembering this convivial haunt, improbably located in the cellars of a large Grade II mansion (Bradmore House – nowadays a

Kima W1

coworking space) marooned in the middle of trafficky Hammersmith Broadway, right by the tube. A short menu of simple fare is well-prepared and service is friendly. Top Tip – nice terrace on a sunny day too. / W6 9YE; www.wearekindred.com; londonkindred; Tue, Wed 11 pm, Thu-Sat midnight, Mon 6 pm.

KIPFERL N1 £55 433

20 CAMDEN PASSAGE
020 77041 555 9–*3D*

"Lovely Austrian spot in the middle of Islington" – a fixture of cute Camden Passage for more than a decade – that's perfect "when you fancy something a bit different": "think good coffee and amazing cakes by day and gorgeous goulash and schnitzel by night". "Interesting Austrian wine list, too". / N1 8ED; www.kipferl.co.uk; kipferl_london; Mon-Thu 10 pm, Fri & Sat 11 pm, Sun 7 pm.

KISS THE HIPPO £19 343

51 MARGARET STREET, W1
020 3887 2028 3–*1C*
50 GEORGE STREET, TW9
020 3887 2028 1–*4A*

"Great coffee and extremely moreish light snacks" is the simple-but-winning formula at this ethical and sustainable Scandi-style roastery that started life in Richmond six years ago and now has outlets scattered across some of central London's foodie enclaves. / kissthehippo.com; kissthehippo.

KITCHEN TABLE W1 £253 444

70 CHARLOTTE STREET
020 7637 7770 2–*1C*

James Knappett and Sandia Chang 18-seat, chef's-table experience is "an exceptional restaurant that never ceases to amaze and delight" and some would say it's "London's best Michelin two-star by far" ("I've had four visits in the last year, and this is the most imaginative cooking in the capital!"). Even fans, though, had come to see it as "ridiculously overpriced" – "I love Kitchen Table, I really do. I've dined there quite regularly since it first opened and the food is exquisite. However, the price per person of £300 is a step too far: it's a great establishment, but that feels extortionate". The penny has dropped however, and in late May 2023 – after our survey concluded – they slashed the price here by one third, to £200 per person for their 20-course experience. On that basis, we've rated it a little more optimistically than this year's feedback in our annual diners' poll would have suggested. / W1T 4QG; www.kitchentablelondon.co.uk; kitchentable1; Wed-Sat 11 pm.

KITCHEN W8 W8 £95 443

11-13 ABINGDON ROAD
020 7937 0120 6–*1A*

"I've had dinner here at least 20 times over the last 10 years and have never had a bad meal. I'm a fan!" – this smart and "very comfortable" ("slightly dull?") fixture sits in a side road off Kensington High Street and is very accomplished by the reckoning of neighbourhood venues (and is nowadays in the top-100 most mentioned London restaurants in our annual diners' poll). Star chef Phil Howard is a partner in its management, and standards are "very good all round", including the "really creative and delicious" modern European cuisine. / W8 6AH; www.kitchenw8.com; kitchenw8; Sun-Thu 9.30 pm, Fri & Sat 10 pm.

KITTY FISHER'S W1 £82 343

10 SHEPHERD'S MARKET
020 3302 1661 3–*4B*

"Consistent, tasty, dependable" food at a "price-point that's pretty competitive given its Mayfair location" is the deal at this Shepherd Market outfit named after an 18th-century courtesan. At almost 10 years old, the excitement it generated at launch has diminished, although fans reckon it "continues to excel" as both "a business destination with character" and "a romantic and atmospheric" spot. / W1J 7QF; www.kittyfishers.com; kittyfishers; Tue-Sat 9.30 pm.

KNIFE SW4 £79 443

160 CLAPHAM PARK ROAD
020 7627 6505 11–*2D*

This indie steakhouse on the Clapham-Brixton border "does that one thing very well, then adds a big helping of friendly service". A former Top Steakhouse winner in the Harden's London Restaurant Awards, it is a local favourite for Sunday roasts. / SW4 7DE; kniferestaurant.co.uk; kniferestaurant; Wed-Sat 9.30 pm, Sun 4.30 pm.

KOJI SW6 £86 44

58 NEW KING'S RD 020 7731 2520 11–*1B*

"You could be in the West End" at this "exceptional local restaurant" by Parsons Green, "serving contemporary Japanese cuisine" – "the ambience is glamorous and cool, the service friendly and efficient, and the food excellent, fresh and tasty". It also has an "elegant and classic cocktail bar". / SW6 4LS; www.koji.restaurant; kojirestaurant; Tue, Wed 10.3 pm, Thu-Sat 11 pm.

KOL W1 £124 44

9 SEYMOUR STREET 020 3829 6888 2–2

"A revelation: I don't think I really understood the beauty of chillies until I went to Kol, where they complement different ingredients in each dish… a gentle burn… never overpowering but genius!" – Santiago Lastra's smart and well-spaced dining room, just off Portman Square, is justifiably hailed by its fans as "one of the more interesting restaurants in the capital". "Top- quality, seasonal British produc is turned into amazing, refined Mexican food" and it "constantly surprises with its journey around Mexican spicing and cuisine, with man wonderful twists on traditional Latin flavours". To accompany the menu there is a list of mezcals (and indeed an adjoining 'mezcaleria' and cocktail bar) and "many unusual wines which explore the less well known parts of the globe". "Some of the cooking is clever, some beautifully presented, and it's all excellent". / W1H 7BA; kolrestaurant.com; kol.restaurant; Tue-Sat midnight, Sun 4.30 pm.

KOLAMBA W1 £39 43

21 KINGLY STREET 020 3815 4201 4–*2B*

"Interesting and original spicing" makes the "Sri Lanka-inspired small plates" and "amazin curries" at this "rather cramped" Soho four-year-old a "good choice if you like really spicy food". Top Menu Tip – "superb hot butter cuttlefish". / W1B 5QA; kolamba.co.uk; kolamba. ldn; Mon-Sat 10 pm, Sun 9 pm.

KOYA £46 44

50 FRITH ST, W1 020 7434 4463 5–*2A*
10-12 BROADWAY MARKET MEWS, E8
07342 236933 14–*2B*
QUEEN VICTORIA STREET, EC2 NO TEL
10–*3C*

"Love the original Koya, sitting at the long counter with a bowl of udon – even if you do have to queue", say fans of this Soho noodle bar. Top Tip – the "definitive zen breakfast" is well liked, too, both here and also at the Bloomberg Arcade and Hackney spin-offs. / www.koya.co.uk; koyalondon.

KOYN W1 £103 34

38 GROSVENOR STREET
020 3376 0000 3–*2B*

Samyukta Nair and family's 'contemporary izakaya' in Mayfair provides an evolved menu of sushi, tempura and robata dishes in a westernised style not dissimilar to that of obu or Roka, overseen by NZ-born chef hys Cattermoul. No-one has a bad word to y about the cooking, but there is the odd ipe about the size of the bill… / W1K 4QA; ww.koynrestaurants.com; koynlondon; Mon-Sat).45 pm, Sun 10.30 pm.

RICKET £56 544

2 DENMAN STREET, W1
20 7734 5612 4–3C
TELEVISION CENTRE, 101 WOOD LANE, 12 –2B
1-43 ATLANTIC ROAD, SW9 11–1D

Clever, subtly infused curries a wonderful ep up from your local Indian" ("the flavours every option are incredible with each dish piced to perfection") have catapulted this roject by university friends Will Bowlby and ik Campbell from a Brixton pop-up to three riving tapas-style restaurants, including a oho flagship with cocktail bar, in less than 10 ears. / closed Sun, SW9 Tue-Thu closed L.

UDU SE15 £60 443

19 QUEEN'S RD 020 3950 0226 1–4D

atrick Williams and Amy Corbin's original eckham opening (it now has siblings like Little udu, see also) has become a well-known pin n southeast London's restaurant map (owing nly partly to the celebrity of Amy's father, hris Corbin, among the capital's foodie ommentariat). Amidst the menu choices, ere is the occasional nod to Patrick's heritage outh African), but the inspiration for the asty, small plates" magpies from all over e globe. Brunch is a big occasion here for hich there's a dedicated menu; and "friendly" ervice is also a feature. Top Tip – eat in the ack garden on warmer days. / SE15 2EZ; ww.kuducollective.com; kudu_restaurant; Thu-un 10 pm.

UDU GRILL SE15 £53 443

7 NUNHEAD LANE 020 3172 2450 1–4D

High ratings all-round again this year for Amy orbin and Patrick Williams's spin-off venture an open-fire restaurant, which takes the outh African braai for part of its inspiration. occupies an attractively converted former ruman's pub in Nunhead. / SE15 3TR; ww.kuducollective.com; kudugrill; Wed-Sat 10 pm, un 2.30 pm.

URO EATERY W8 £73 443

HILLGATE STREET 020 7221 4854 7–2B

A super little spot in the 'hood" – Hillgate illage now boasts another reason to travel to is cute enclave, off Notting Hill Gate: an ffshoot of the coffee shop across the road. With its sparse, pale-wood interior, it has Nordic" looks, although the menu claims to e 'broadly Mediterranean inspired'. Whatever ou call it, there's "great innovation" from ndrianos Poulis's "interesting, exciting and asty" "fusion" cuisine. A downside? – "it's so oisy!" / W8 7SP; www.kuro-london.com; kuro__ ondon; Tue-Sat 11 pm, Sun 4 pm.

KUTIR SW3 £70 444

10 LINCOLN STREET 020 7581 1144 6–2D

"A surprise hidden treat just off the King's Road" – Rohit Ghai's Chelse townhouse is set in a series of "several small and intimate" chambers, and there's even a first-floor lounge bar with a "nice little roof terrace". His "deeply spiced", "non-generic" Indian cuisine is in the capital's premier league: "very original and authentic" and contributing to an overall experience that's "refined, without being splashily luxurious". Gripes? – "wish the menu was slightly longer". / SW3 2TS; kutir.co.uk; kutirchelsea; Tue-Sun 10 pm.

L'ANTICA PIZZERIA DA MICHELE £65 432

44 OLD COMPTON STREET, W1
020 7434 4563 5–2A
199 BAKER STREET, NW1
020 7935 6458 2–1A

"Outstanding pizzas" live up to the highest expectations at the London outposts of a Neapolitan original going back five generations and 150 years (even if these days they merrily break late founder Michele Condurro's commandment that only two types of pizza are allowed, the Marinara and the Margherita). The Naples flagship became a place of post-divorce pilgrimage following Elizabeth Gilbert's 2006 bestseller 'Eat Pray Love'. / www.anticapizzeriadamichele.co.uk; anticapizzeriadamicheleuk.

THE LADBROKE ARMS W11 £71 324

54 LADBROKE ROAD 020 7727 6648 7–2B

With its "perfect pub atmosphere", "pretty front garden" and "excellent, interesting food that never disappoints", this unusually gracious Ladbroke Grove local is "a real contender" as one the capital's better hostelries. On the debit side, service was often said to be "up and down" this year ("smiling and helpful, but run off their feet"). / W11 3NW; www.ladbrokearms.com; ladbrokearms; Mon-Sat 11 pm, Sun 10 pm.

LAHORE KEBAB HOUSE E1 £37 422

2-10 UMBERSTON ST
020 7481 9737 12–1A

"The original Pakistani joint" – this "perfect" East End pitstop of over half a century's standing is as "cheap and consistent as ever" (and as grotty…). For "legendary" lamb chops, "the best ever dry lamb curry" and "amazing chicken tikka", it can't be beat. / E1 1PY; www.lahore-kebabhouse.com; Tue-Sat 10 pm, Sun 9 pm.

LAHPET £60 432

21 SLINGSBY PLACE, WC2
020 3883 5629 5–3C
58 BETHNAL GREEN ROAD, E1
020 3883 5629 13–1C

"A revelation!" this "unpretentious" yet "awesome" outfit offers "a wonderful introduction to Burmese cuisine" – "intense, fragrant and refreshing", but "not as fierce as Thai" – at its new venue in Covent Garden's The Yards development. Founders Dan Anton and chef Zaw Mahesh started out in a Hackney warehouse, and still have a restaurant in Shoreditch. It's named after the "unique and superb tea leaf salad" on its menu. / lahpet.co.uk; lahpet.

LAKSAMANIA W1 £49 322

92 NEWMAN STREET 020 7637 9888 3–1D

"A great selection of different laksa and very tasty too!" – a key appeal of this street-food destination off Oxford Street, which is named for its Malaysian noodle soups (though other dishes are also served). / W1T 3EZ; www.laksamania.co.uk; laksamania; Mon, Wed & Thu 9 pm, Fri & Sat 9.30 pm, Sun 8 pm.

THE LANDMARK, WINTER GARDEN NW1 £85 335

222 MARYLEBONE RD
020 7631 8000 9–4A

"Wonderful afternoon tea in a huge glass-roof covered area with palm trees" is the big hit at "beautiful" Palm Court: a hotel atrium, eight storeys tall near Marylebone station (and one of London's more Instagrammed spaces). Not a bad spot for a business (or romantic) meal: the food – served from breakfast through to dinner – is uniformly well rated, and even those who feel it's "absurdly expensive" say "it was worth it to see the atrium!" / NW1 6JQ; www.landmarklondon.co.uk; the_landmark_london; Mon-Sun 10 pm.

THE LANESBOROUGH GRILL SW1 £93 224

HYDE PARK CORNER 020 7259 5599 2–3A

"The room is the star" at this swish hotel restaurant on Hyde Park Corner, with its gorgeous domed glass ceilings (providing natural light by day) and huge chandeliers. Formerly known as Celeste (RIP), it has now adopted a less fancy, more fashionably straightforward menu under chef Shay Cooper. The overall experience is much more consistently well-rated in this new guise, although there are still some quibbles over "so-so" results and "patchy" service. Most consistent is support for the "sublimely elegant", "reassuringly traditional, tasty and well-presented afternoon tea". / SW1X 7TA; www.oetkercollection.com; the_lanesborough; Mon-Sun 10 pm.

LANGAN'S BRASSERIE W1 £76 223

STRATTON STREET 020 7491 8822 3–3C

Were it not still considered "outrageously expensive" in over 40% of reports, it might be easier to recommend this "well-located", old-faithful brasserie (est. 1976). When it was relaunched under new ownership in late 2021, it was widely derided for its poor standards. But even though its cooking is still too often dismissed as "standard fodder", overall feedback on its food improved this year, with fans praising its "menu to suit all tastes, including many traditional and down-to-earth dishes". And anyway, cost-be-damned, it's "still the haunt of the business lunch crowd" thanks to its "long-established, buzzy ambience" and handy location near The Ritz. / W1J 8LB; www.langansrestaurants.co.uk; langansbrasserie; Mon-Sat 10.30 pm, Sun 9.30 pm.

PALM COURT, THE LANGHAM W1 £100 233

1C PORTLAND PLACE 020 7636 1000 2–1B

"Always a treat" – this luxurious lounge in a swanky five-star opposite the Beeb makes a "beautiful setting for a classic afternoon tea": indeed the hotel claims the ceremony started here! (The venue spent the latter half of 2023 hosting evening meals as 'The Good Front Room': south London chef Dom Taylor's celebration of his Caribbean heritage, with elevated versions of dishes including curry goat and rice and peas. The residency was his prize for winning Channel 4 show 'Five Star Kitchen', hosted by chef Michel Roux Jr, the Langham's culinary director.) / W1B 1JA; www.palm-court.co.uk; langham_london; Mon-Sun 11 pm.

LANGOSTERIA, THE OWO SW1

57 WHITEHALL PLACE AWAITING TEL 2–3C

With branches in Paris, near Portofino, St Moritz and – now here at this mega new five-star on Whitehall – Enrico Buonocore's Italian newcomer originates (like Paper Moon) from Milan. Seafood is the big deal here, and if it follows the template of the original no meat or veggie options will be served. / SW1A 2EU; Tue-Sat 10.30 pm.

LASDUN, NATIONAL THEATRE SE1

UPPER GROUND NO TEL 2–3D

Named for National Theatre architect Sir Denys Lasdun, the latest incarnation of this South Bank landmark's flagship eatery is an all-day brasserie, run by the team behind The Marksman. It opened in late May 2023 (after our annual diners' poll had closed) but the press immediately rushed in and drooled. It helps if you like the Brutalist design of the space: nearly all restaurant critics, it seems, get off on that kind of thing. One such is the FT's Tim Hayward, who in early June 2023 declared – "Go for the soul-nourishing architecture" and "pointedly British" fare that "operates in tune with the [surroundings]… austere but elegant… it honours its materials rather than obscuring them with decoration". The cynical would also say, go ASAP, before – like its predecessors – it is tempted to coast on the captive market its pre-theatre trade provides. / SE1 9PP; www.lasdunrestaurant.com; lasdunrestaurant; Mon-Sat 11 pm.

LAUNCESTON PLACE W8 £102 444

1A LAUNCESTON PLACE 020 7937 6912 6–1B

"Tucked away from the hustle and bustle", in the kind of ultra-picturesque Kensington backwater where one imagines Mary Poppins floating about on her umbrella – this "quirky" converted town-house provides a "special", "understated but comfortable setting" and "always impeccable personal service with attention to detail": it's "ideal for a romantic evening". "You might not expect much of the cooking as it's part of the D&D London Group – but you'd be wrong!" – Ben Murphy has been at the stoves since 2017 and his "refined and interesting" cuisine goes from strength to strength: "food that just makes you smile about how it looks and how it tastes". Top Tip – "good value at lunch". / W8 5RL; www.launcestonplace-restaurant.co.uk; launcestonplace; Wed-Sat 10 pm, Sun 9 pm. SRA – accredited

THE LAUNDRY SW9 £66 344

374 COLDHARBOUR LANE 020 8103 9384 11–2D

"A great place to have in the neighbourhood" – this "lovely" Antipodean-run fixture is set – with its own sizable outside terrace – in a large and characterful Victorian laundry; and "sitting next to Brixton Market means it always has a lively vibe with some added street theatre". "Lots of cocktails are enjoyed at the weekends here", when it's a favourite destination. But "it works for brunch, lunch or dinner" with an all-day menu incorporating a good selection of modern bistro dishes alongside more breakfast-ish staples. / SW9 8PL; thelaundrybrixton.com; brixtonlaundry; Mon-Thu 11 pm, Fri & Sat 11.30 pm, Sun 8 pm.

LAVO, THE BOTREE W1

30 MARYLEBONE LN 020 7309 9700 3–1B

An Italian September 2023 newcomer, from Tao Group Hospitality: the business which owns the (nowadays international) Hakkasan and Yauatcha chains. Within a swish new boutique hotel in Marylebone, the press release promises 'a vibrant space illuminated by a colour-changing light feature that expands across the ceiling', where you can enjoy pastas, pizzas, 'a showstopper Wagyu meatball topped with whipped ricotta' (wow!) and 'an indulgent 20-layer chocolate cake'. / W1U 2DR; Tue-Sat 10.30 pm.

LAXEIRO E2 £19 33

95 COLUMBIA ROAD 020 7729 1147 14–2

Well predating the gentrification of Columbia Road, this "small, local Spanish restaurant" (es 1982) is worth remembering when browsing fo blooms and designer flower pots. It probably won't re-frame your understanding of Hispani cuisine, but "prices are reasonable" and the "team are friendly and fun" (albeit sometimes under pressure at busy times). / E2 7RG; www.laxeiro.co.uk; laxeiro_restaurant; Tue-Sat 11 pm, Sun 4 pm.

LAYLA W10 £15 33

332 PORTOBELLO ROAD NO TEL 7–1A

"Go for the cinnamon buns, top-quality coffee and croissants and amazing sarnies too", say fans of this superb "artisanal bakery", towards the very northern end of the Portobello Road. / W10 5PQ; www.laylabakery.com; layla_w10; Mon-Sun 4 pm.

THE LEDBURY W11 £236 44

127 LEDBURY RD 020 7792 9090 7–1B

"Back with a bang!" – Brett Graham's "superlative" Notting Hill HQ 'pressed pause' during Covid, but re-opened in 2022 to near-universal acclaim. "Technically exquisite, with delicate preparation and flavour combinations" – "his cuisine was straight back in with two Michelin stars – zero surprise there!". (But ther are also widespread misgivings about prices tha risk becoming "just too expensive"). "Many of the old staff remain and balance efficiency and familiarity with aplomb" and "Brett is very visible to chat with". "To top it off, with the new interior it has such a relaxed vibe now". Top Menu Tip – "unbelievably brilliant mushrooms". / W11 2AQ; www.theledbury.com; Tue-Sat 9.15 pm.

LEGARE SE1 £52 44

CARDAMOM BUILDING, 31G SHAD THAMES 020 8063 7667 10–4D

"The tiny kitchen in this intimate restaurant" ir Shad Thames, near Tower Bridge, "produces the most imaginative and delicious Italian food". "It's run by a talented chef who will go places", Matt Beardmore, previously of Trullo, alongside founder Jay Patel, a former Barrafina manager. / SE1 2YB; legarelondon.com; legarelondon; Wed-Sat, Tue 10 pm.

LEMONIA NW1 £66 23

89 REGENT'S PARK RD 020 7586 7454 9–3B

"Everyone seems to be a regular" at this "old and long-established Greek restaurant" – a large Primrose Hill landmark which is still "buzzing from morning till night", as it has been for over three decades now. "The longstanding staff are very friendly" (but service is not too good at busy times"). "You an always find something to eat on this long enu, but – though filling – it is very basic". / W1 8UY; www.lemonia.co.uk; Mon-Thu 10 pm, i & Sat 10.30 pm, Sun 4 pm.

EO'S E5

9 CHATSWORTH ROAD
20 4559 8598 14–*1B*

x P Franco and Brawn chef Giuseppe elvedere (backed by the team behind Milk afé and Juliet's Quality Food) is inspired by is Sardinian heritage at this skillful revamp of e former Jim's Cafe on Clapton's Chatsworth oad. Serving café staples during the day, in the vening and at Sunday lunch he provides more mbitious Italian dishes cooked over a wood fire nd served alongside low-intervention Italian ines. It opened in May 2023 after our survey ad concluded, but in an early June write-up, he Standard's Jimi Famurewa lauded its vocative interior as an "Italian beauty". But, here the scoff was concerned, he was left with n "abiding feeling … of a short menu eliciting ots of intrigue but, also, a nagging urge for an ctual dinner". / E5 0LH; leos.london.

.EROY EC2 £96 443

8 PHIPP STREET 020 7739 4443 13–*1B*

On a quirky Shoreditch corner-site, this relaxed" haunt offers affordable and nteresting small plates, "good wine" and just e kind of "buzzy" ambience you'd hope or in these hipster environs. But for slaves to Le Guide Rouge' and their grading system here's a problem. "It's a really good restaurant. t's just not a Michelin star place – its star a distraction". ("If this was a Michelin bib gourmand' it would be spot-on, and it bsolutely deserves that sort of grade. But the tar creates an expectation of something more pecial than this place delivers. That's the only riticism. It is a cracking spot, but someone at he tyre place got a bit carried away".) / EC2A NP; www.leroyshoreditch.com; leroyshoreditch; Mon-Sat 9.30 pm.

.EVAN SE15 £63 322

-4 BLENHEIM GROVE
20 7732 2256 1–*4D*

An "interesting and very good menu" – "prefer he à la carte to the set" – with natural wines o match draws an appreciative crowd to his open-kitchen outfit, behind Peckham verground station. Inspired by the 'bistronomy' f Paris or Copenhagen, it no longer generates he volume of feedback or stellar ratings of a ouple of years ago. / SE15 4QL; levanlondon. o.uk; levanlondon; Tue-Sat 11.30 pm, Sun 3 pm.

THE LIGHT HOUSE SW19 £65 333

75-77 RIDGWAY 020 8944 6338 11–*2B*

"Almost part of Wimbledon's heritage nowadays!": after a quarter of a century's service, this local indie is a local contemporary classic, known for its "very good" Mediterranean-style food and "personable staff". Fans say it's "upped its game over the last year" too, although it "can struggle to cope when crowded". / SW19 4ST; www.lighthousewimbledon.com; lighthousewimbledon; Mon-Sat 10 pm, Sun 3 pm.

THE LIGHTERMAN N1 £59 222

3 GRANARY SQUARE 020 3846 3400 9–*3C*

Overlooking the canal at Granary Square behind King's Cross station, this striking modern gastropub certainly looks the part and packs in the crowds. It avoids harsh critiques, but feedback generally makes it clear that "the location is better than the dining experience". / N1C 4BH; www.thelighterman.co.uk; thelightermankx; Mon-Thu 11.30 pm, Fri & Sat midnight, Sun 10.30 pm.

LILIENBLUM EC1

80 CITY ROAD 020 8138 2847 13–*1A*

Israeli chef-restaurateur Eyal Shani has followed up pitta specialist Miznon, in Soho and Notting Hill, with this very different, more formal concept off the Old Street roundabout on the edge of the City. Opened (after our survey concluded) in late May 2023, it serves sharing plates from a menu divided by ingredients rather than courses. A very early June 2023 verdict from The Standard's Jimi Famurewa was mixed: "Shani's undeniable genius" is still present, "dishes were still cooked with unexpected flair, potency and restraint" but the "vast, echoing barn of a new-build space" does Lilienblum no favours, nor does the "menu construction" (split by ingredients with "wearying zaniness of… descriptions"). / EC1Y 2BJ; www.lilienblum.co.uk; lilienblumlondon; Tue, Wed 11.45 pm, Thu-Sat 11 pm.

LINA STORES £50 223

13 MARYLEBONE LANE, W1
020 3148 7503 3–*1A*
51 GREEK STREET, W1
020 3929 0068 5–*2A*
20 STABLE STREET, N1 AWAITING TEL
9–*3C*
22 THE PAVEMENT, SW4
020 3838 1343 11–*2D*
19 BLOOMBERG ARCADE, EC4
020 3002 6034 10–*3C*

"A nice pit-stop for pasta lovers" – this expanding chain is now up to its fifth restaurant spin-off from the original Soho deli (with the June 2023 opening of a new 80-seater, overlooking Clapham Common), and fans say it provides an "attractive", "buzzing" setting for "simple dishes, well cooked". A meal is "unlikely to live long in the memory though", and there's a growing fear that "as they have expanded the quality has dropped". Top Tip – at the W1 original (est. 1944 originally as a deli) "sitting upstairs or by the bar is lovely, the windowless basement is not particularly comfortable". / www.linastores.co.uk; linastores.

LISBOETA WC1 £78 432

30 CHARLOTTE STREET
020 3830 9888 2–*1C*

"Portuguese cooking at its addictive best" has delivered "yet another hit for Nuno Mendes" (in partnership with MJMK Restaurants) at this "really enjoyable" three-floor yearling in Fitzrovia, where "distinctive", "top-quality" dishes are "made from the best produce"; ("it already feels like a fixture on the dining scene – the sort of place you want to go to again and again, and to tell people about"). Fans also celebrate the "cool vibes" of its "buzzy (if slightly boomy)" café-style setting, although the interior can also seem "cramped" and not everyone's wild about the music ("I complained to Nuno, but he likes it loud!"). Success has also brought concern about "hype", or that "some prices risk becoming a joke" – "it tasted good, but the price stuck in the throat". Top Menu Tip – "love the pork fat dessert". / WC1B 4AF; lisboeta.co.uk; lisboeta.london; Mon-Sat 11 pm, Sun 5 pm.

LITTLE KUDU SE15

133 QUEEN'S ROAD 020 7252 8287 1–*4D*

Open in June 2023 from Peckham's Kudu Collective, Little Kudu replaces the Smokey Kudu cocktail bar in Queen's Road (which has shifted to the RIXO fashion emporium on Chelsea's King's Road). There's a strong focus on South African wine here, with simple, tapas-y/small plates food to soak it up (eg Braaibroodjie: a Saffa cheese toastie). / SE15 2ND; www.kuducollective.com; littlekudu; Wed-Sun 10 pm.

LITTLE PIZZA HICCE N1

99 CHAPEL MARKET 020 3062 5690 9–*3D*

Opposite their pub Hicce Hart in Islington's Chapel Market, chef Pip Lacey and business partner Gordy McIntyre have launched their first permanent pizzeria, with lots of stripped wood and a blackboard menu. Both are offshoots from Hicce, their fashionable flagship at Coal Drops Yard behind King's Cross station. / N1 9EY; www.littlepizzahicce.co.uk; littlepizzahicce; Tue-Sat 10 pm, Sun 9 pm.

LITTLE SOCIAL W1 £80 443

5 POLLEN STREET 020 7870 3730 3–*2C*

Jason Atherton's elegant, "professional" wine bar and bistro is decked out in an understated, classic style that's a little more retro than at his main gaff (Pollen Street), which is across the street. Here, chef Frankie van Loo offers less 'foodie' "bistro-style" dishes raised to a "superb" standard. The bar area is tiny, but "you can always have a pre-dinner drink at its big brother opposite, which has a great cocktail bar". Top Tip – visit in summer, when you can eat outside on the pedestrianised street. / W1S 1NE; www.littlesocial.co.uk; _littlesocial; Tue-Sat 9pm.

LITTLE TAPERIA SW17 £54 344

143 TOOTING HIGH ST
020 8682 3303 11–2C

"A local delight" near Tooting Broadway tube station – this "fantastic tapas restaurant brings together some wonderful Iberian tastes with brilliant service"; and "the lighting is great for an intimate meal out" (the "buzzy and upbeat atmosphere adds to the feeling that you're anywhere but on Tooting High Street!"). The founders, former food journalist Madeleine Lim and Hikmat Antippa, owner of nearby Meza, are two of the prime movers behind Tooting's growing food scene. / SW17 0SY; www.thelittletaperia.co.uk; littletaperiatooting; Sun-Thu 10 pm, Fri & Sat 11 pm.

LLAMA INN, THE HOXTON EC2

81 GREAT EASTERN ST
020 7550 1000 13–1B

Hot in NYC, this late summer 2023 newcomer is the latest incumbent on the rooftop of Shoreditch's 'The Hoxton' hotel, with its city-fringe vistas of The Barbican and the Square Mile. On offer – Americanised Peruvian fare – let's hope it's a better recipe for success than the previous occupant, Maya (RIP), which also had a US/Latino theme (then it was Baja-Mexican). / EC2A 3HU; Tue-Sun 11.30 pm.

LLEWELYN'S SE24 £75 333

293-295 RAILTON RD
020 7733 6676 11–2D

This "high-level local bistro" opposite Herne Hill station is "great for date night", and its kitchen team is "very accomplished at composing dishes that bring together familiar ingredients in unfamiliar combinations to good effect, rather than for curiosity value". The latest addition is a wine bar and shop next door, called Lulu's. / SE24 0JP; www.llewelyns-restaurant.co.uk; llewelynslondon; Tue-Thu 9 pm, Fri & Sat 9.30 pm, Sun 3.15 pm.

LA LLUNA N10 £59 332

462 MUSWELL HILL BROADWAY
020 8442 2662 1–1B

"A great find" on Muswell Hill Broadway, this "buzzy, lively restaurant with very efficient service and great Spanish food" ticks all the boxes for a "super local" – serving Iberian breakfasts, a good-value set lunch, plus a full menu of tapas and classic main dishes. / N10 1BS; www.lalluna.co.uk; lallunalondon; Sun-Thu 11 pm, Fri & Sat midnight.

LOCANDA LOCATELLI W1 £104 332

HYATT REGENCY, 8 SEYMOUR ST
020 7935 9088 2–2A

"Memorable food in a lively, buzzy but not hectic environment" maintains the appeal for fans of Giorgio Locatelli's "classic Italian", which he has run with wife Plaxy for over 20 years, in a "discreet" and stylish hotel dining room off Portman Square (and with its own entrance). There is a harsh view that "there's nothing special about it other than the outrageous prices". But that's a minority opinion, and for its majority of fans it remains an "exceptional all-rounder", as recommended for business as it is for being a "fantastic place to take the family". / W1H 7JZ; www.locandalocatelli.com; locandalocatelli; Wed-Sat, Tue 11 pm, Sun 10.30 pm.

LONDON SHELL CO. W2 £105 345

THE PRINCE REGENT, SHELDON SQUARE
07553 033636 7–1C

"Stunningly fresh fish, brilliant service and a jolly super wine list" ensure that a dining cruise along the Grand Union canal aboard the barge Prince Regent is "a fabulous part of the London restaurant scene" – while "tucking into a lobster roll with a beer on the Grand Duchess, permanently docked in Paddington basin, is just as good". The company's third venue – its first on dry land – is a combined fishmonger and seafood bar in Swains Lane, near Parliament Hill Fields in Highgate, where late-afternoon oyster-and-wine deals are a special draw. / W2 6EP; londonshellco.com; londonshellco; Wed-Sat 9.30 pm, Sun 3 pm.

LONDON STOCK SW18 £56 333

2 BUBBLING WELL SQUARE, RAM QUARTER 020 8075 3877 11–2B

In the centre of trafficky downtown Wandsworth, this "very plain room in the brewery development" is a somewhat unsung hero of the area. The young team is headed by Le Cordon Bleu alumni Assem Abdel Hady and Andres Bernal and brings genuine gastronomic ambition to the 'Ram Quarter' with an "eight-course tasting menu at a reasonable price" – "every course is tasty" and some nothing less than "superb". / SW18 1UQ; londonstockrestaurant.co.uk; ldnstockrestaurant; Wed-Sat 8 pm.

THE LORE OF THE LAND W1 £79 344

4 CONWAY STREET 020 3927 4480 2–1B

Perhaps our user-base isn't impressed by the c'leb ownership of Guy Ritchie's rustic Fitzrovia pub, where pal Becks has been seen pulling a pint, as we receive few reports. But such as we do get praise "fantastic food, attentive service and good value". / W1T 6BB; gritchiepubs.com; loreofthelandpub; Tue, Wed 11 pm, Thu-Sat 11.30 pm, Sun 9 pm.

LORNE SW1 £77 553

76 WILTON ROAD 020 3327 0210 2–4B

"Going from strength to strength... surviving a flood in its first year... then Covid… it shines triumphant!" – owner Katie Exton "has dedication in abundance" and her "superb and fairly priced" Pimlico favourite is the result. That the "lovely and intimate" room can also appear "a little understated" is the nearest any report gets to a criticism; and most are a full-o[n] hymn of praise to its "stunning, clean-flavoure[d] seasonal food" served with "enthusiasm and knowledge". La patronne is a top sommelier and "pound for pound her brilliant, eclectic an[d] accessible wine list is one of the best in Londo[n] punching well above its weight for a restaurant of its size and price-point". / SW1V 1DE; www.lornerestaurant.co.uk; lorne_restaurant.

LPM (FKA LA PETITE MAISON) W1 £127 33

54 BROOK'S MEWS 020 7495 4774 3–2B

A "gorgeous homage to the Côte d'Azur" – th[is] "exciting" operation, just around the corner from Claridges, serves beautiful, fresh-tasting Med-inspired sharing plates to an "urbane and international" crowd, who like its informal, somewhat "cramped" style. But while the prices here have always been eye-catching, its (previously stellar) ratings slumped this year amidst a feeling that you increasingly need "more money than sense" to pay them. ("Ther[e] is no doubting the cooking skill and the careful sourcing of produce. But the dishes are so simple that it feels eye-watering to pay so much for a lentil salad… that is literally just a lentil salad"). / W1K 4EG; www.lpmlondon.co.uk; lpmlondon; Mon-Sat 10.30 pm, Sun 9.30 pm.

LUCA EC1 £99 44

88 ST JOHN ST 020 3859 3000 10–1A

"An oasis of calm just outside the hustle of the City" (north of Smithfield Market): this "beautiful" bar and restaurant (linked – but you'd never know it – to The Clove Club) is increasingly recognised as "one of the top Italians in London", and a "special" overall experience ("everyone seems so happy just to b[e] there!"). Even fans acknowledge it as being "on the expensive side", but there are no quibbles about its "elegant and refined" cuisine which "never fails to hit the spot". And it's "also a good place for business". Top Tips – "the Parmesan fries are dreamy"; and "the bar has a great set lunch menu and wonderful booths". / EC1M 4EH; luca.restaurant; luca.restaurant; Wed-Sat, Tue 10 pm.

LUCE E LIMONI WC1 £64 33

91-93 GRAY'S INN RD
020 7242 3382 10–1A

"Family-run Italian" that helps add life to a du[ll] stretch of the Gray's Inn Road. It specialises in Sicilian cuisine presented by Fabrizio Zafarana an engagingly "well-informed and enthusiastic" host. / WC1X 8TX; www.luceelimoni.com; restaurant_luce_e_limoni; Mon-Thu 10 pm, Fri & Sat 11 pm.

Lavo, The BoTree W1

LUCIANO'S SE12 £60 3 4 3

131 BURNT ASH ROAD
020 8852 3186 1–*4D*

"So lucky to have this as our local in Lee" – this "perfect neighbourhood Italian" sparks joy with its home-made pasta and wood-fired pizzas. Owner Enzo Masiello named it after his father Luciano, who played football for Charlton Athletic. / SE12 8RA; lucianoslondon.co.uk; lucianoslondon; Tue-Thu 10.30 pm, Fri & Sat 11.30 pm, Mon 10 pm, Sun 9.15 pm.

LUCIO SW3 £98 3 2 2

257 FULHAM RD 020 7823 3007 6–*3B*

"Charming old-style service and delicious food" "still packs the locals in" at this "popular family-run Italian" in Chelsea from Lucio Altana and his sons Dario and Mirko, now in its twenty-first year. / SW3 6HY; www.luciorestaurant.com; luciorestaurant; Tue-Sat 10.30 pm, Sun 3 pm.

LUCKY & JOY E5 £48 4 3 3

95 LOWER CLAPTON ROAD
07488 965966 14–*1B*

This "fun local for Clapton hipsters" offers "exceptional" Chinese cooking from two well-travelled Western chefs, Ellen Parr (ex-Rochelle Canteen and Moro) and Peter Kelly (ex-Morito), who knock out "the freshest flavours at incredible value" – "what a great neighbourhood place!" But "expect to mime: the rendered walls and low ceiling amplify the bonhomie, so the volume is turned up to 11". / E5 0NP; luckyandjoy.co.uk; luckyandjoyldn; Tue-Sat 10.30 pm.

LUCKY CAT W1 £85 1 2 2

10-13 GROSVENOR SQUARE
020 7107 0000 3–*2A*

The "buzzing vibe", DJs and "showmanship of dishes being completed at the table" tends to "overshadow the food and service" at Gordon Ramsay's "Pan-Asian" joint on the former site of Maze in Mayfair. The "play-safe, please-all Asian menu" runs the gamut from sushi and bao to Korean-spiced black cod and Thai green curry stone bass – "but it lacks real flavour". "If it's trying to compete with the likes of Roka and Nobu, it doesn't… apart from on prices". / W1K 6JP; www.gordonramsayrestaurants.com; luckycatbygordonramsay; Mon-Wed midnight, Thu-Sat 2 am, Sun 11 pm.

LUME NW3 £88 3 2 2

38 PRIMROSE HILL ROAD
020 7449 9556 9–*2A*

"Owner/front-of-house Giuseppe is Sicilian, chef Antonio is Sardinian, and the cuisine is a mix of the two" at this cute Primrose Hill corner-site, praised for its "fabulous cooking and charming service". An impressive wine list explores biodynamic bottles from the two islands. / NW3 3AD; www.lume.london; lumelondon; Tue-Sun 10 pm.

LUPINS SE1 £55 4 4 4

66 UNION ST 020 3908 5888 10–*4B*

"It's amazing what they can achieve with simple ingredients", and there's "always cheerful and efficient service" at this "little sharing-plates restaurant" close to Tate Modern, which has won a solid reputation for its "very talented" founders Lucy Pedder and Natasha Cooke over the past six years. / SE1 1TD; www.lupinslondon.com; lupinslondon; Tue-Sat 9.30 pm.

LURE NW5 £52 3 2 3

56 CHETWYND RD 020 7267 0163 9–*1B*

This modern fish 'n' chip shop in Dartmouth Park is "a nice, healthy (and non-smelly) alternative" to the classic old-school chippy, with "good-quality" fresh fish. / NW5 1DJ; www.lurefishkitchen.co.uk; Wed-Sat 10 pm, Sun 9.30 pm.

LURRA W1 £73 4 3 3

9 SEYMOUR PLACE 020 7724 4545 2–*2A*

"Totally amazing in every way" – this Basque specialist in Seymour Village has a very short menu focusing on aged dairy beef ribs or whole turbot grilled over a wood fire, and is both "extraordinary, and eye-wateringly expensive" – "we spent well north of £1,000 for four, but it was worth it". "The morel and black garlic croquetas are sublime", too. Its sibling tapas bar Donostia is close by (see also). / W1H 5BA; www.lurra.co.uk; Mon-Sat 10.30 pm, Sun 3.30 pm.

LUSIN W1

16 HAY HILL 07768 447398 3–*3C*

Just around the corner from Berkeley Square, this 100-seater Mayfair newcomer opened in late 2022; and is part of a small international chain originating in Armenia and with outlets in Saudi Arabia. It offers a menu created by Armenian cookbook author Mme Anahid Doniguian and Monaco chef Marcel Ravin. We've not had a huge number of reports to-date for a rating: early feedback suggests it has potential but you suffer a typical Mayfair trade-off: "food not bad to very good… but expensive". / W1J 8NY; lusinrestaurant.com; lusinmayfair; Mon-Sun midnight.

LUSITANIA SW8 £61 3 3 3

353 WANDSWORTH ROAD
020 7787 0600 11–*1D*

"Great fun on a Friday night, when there's music and dancing" – this large Stockwell venue opened three years ago, near the new Thames-side developments surrounding Vauxhall and Battersea; and comes complete with an 'Olive Tree Garden' for the summer months. "The food is typically Portuguese – ample and fulfilling!" / SW8 2JH; www.restaurantelusitania.co.uk; lusitania_restaurant; Tue-Thu 10 pm, Fri & Sat 2 am, Sun 9 pm.

LUTYENS GRILL, THE NED EC2 £109 3 3 4

27 POULTRY 020 3828 2000 10–*2C*

"Is this what business lunching was like 50 year ago?" – this "elegant and wood-panelled" steakhouse, "hidden away in the vast opulence of the Ned" (itself the former Midland Bank HQ) "always impresses a client" with its "wonderful club-like atmosphere", "the smell of leather and the feeling of luxury" (it's where "old-school stockbroker dining meets Wolf of Wall Street"). "Power lunches abound within a serene ambience" – "the food leans heavily towards meat with beef Wellington a highlight". / EC2R 8AJ; www.thened.com; thenedlondon; Tue-Sat midnight.

LYLE'S E1 £105 5 3 2

THE TEA BUILDING, 56 SHOREDITCH HIGH STREET 020 3011 5911 13–*1B*

"Never wavering in its excellence" – James Lowe's acclaimed canteen sits at the foot of Shoreditch's 'Tea Building' and his seasonal modern British cooking is nowadays something of a benchmark (having achieved a listing for numerous years on the World's 50 Best). At lunch, small plates can be ordered tapas-style, whereas in the evenings there's just a single tasting option. "Individual dishes look simple: actually this belies a great deal of underlying complexity, and fantastic tastes". Service is informed and passionate too: "you do not think they are temps!" The post-industrial space it inhabits is "hard-surfaced, buzzy, and hence can be very noisy" (and there were a few more reservations this year that the overall effect can end up "slightly cold and soulless"). / E1 6JJ; www.lyleslondon.com; lyleslondon; Tue-Sat 9 pm.

LYON'S N8 £60 4 4 3

1 PARK ROAD 020 8350 8983 1–*1C*

This "brilliant, buzzy local seafood restaurant" is much-loved in Crouch End and beyond for its "exciting, high-quality dishes from a short menu" and "exceptionally friendly, knowledgeable and enthusiastic staff". It works equally well for a meal with a large group or a "snack at the bar". / N8 8TE; lyons-restaurant.com; lyonsseafood; Tue-Sat 10 pm.

M RESTAURANTS £99 2 2 2

NEWFOUNDLAND, E14
020 3327 7771 12–*1C*
2-3 THREADNEEDLE WALK, 60 THREADNEEDLE STREET, EC2
020 3327 7770 10–*2C*

Fans and foes alike agree on the essential value trade-off at Martin (the "M" in question) Williams's large 'Gastro Playgrounds' in the City, and Canary Wharf (Victoria and Twickenham branches having fallen by the wayside). To fans, they are "a bit expensive for what they are, but you can't fault the food or wine": to foes, they are "good but not worth the money". Japan and Provence provide the culinary inspiration for the steak-focused menu (Williams is also the CEO of the Gaucho group); and the menu is backed up by a very wide-ranging wine list, with a broad range of options (including some trophy vintages for over £7,000 per bottle). The least popular part of the formula is the atmosphere created by their ultra-glossy, London via Miami interiors: "chic but soulless". / www.mrestaurants.co.uk; mrestaurants. SRA – accredited

MA LA SICHUAN SW1 £50 432

37 MONCK STREET 020 7222 2218 2–4C

Though "well patronised by suited government types and Sky News executives", it's easy to overlook this "unassuming restaurant in an otherwise soulless building on a Westminster corner-site". "It's a pleasure to find" though, especially if you like "classic Sichuan cooking". Chef Zhang Xiaozhong provides "thoughtfully presented and delightful dishes, with punchy flavours and consistent quality" and "the menu indicates degrees of spice / heat for each item". "Always busy – it's best to reserve" and – though very "efficient" – service can also be seen as "brusque" or "rushed". Top Menu Tip – "some dishes you don't get in most Chinese restaurants, such as delicious preserved egg". / SW1P 2BL; malasichuan.co.uk; malasichuan; Mon-Sat 10.30 pm, Sun 10 pm.

MACELLAIO RC £73 223

39-45 SHAFTESBURY AVENUE, W1
020 3727 6161 5–3A
6 STORE STREET, WC1
020 3848 7230 2–1C
84 OLD BROMPTON RD, SW7
020 7589 5834 6–2B
ARCH 24, 229 UNION ST, SE1
07467 307682 10–4B
124 NORTHCOTE RD, SW11
020 3848 4800 11–2C
38-40 EXMOUTH MARKET, EC1
020 3696 8220 10–1A

Fans do still hail the "fabulous meat" at Roberto Costa's quirky Italian steakhouse group, but it has lost some of its red-blooded allure in recent years. "The restaurants look appealing and the menu looks promising", but lower ratings bolster those who feel "the quality has dropped with expansion", as it has grown to six venues across London (and a sister concept, Fish Game, opened in Canary Wharf in mid-2023); and at its worst, it can deliver "distinctly average steaks" at "steep prices". / www.macellaiorc.com.

MADDOX TAVERN W1 £79 223

47 MADDOX STREET 020 3376 9922 3–2C

"These very big premises were once a prestigious tailor's" – then more recently a branch of the Browns brasserie chain – and are now "a pub-like restaurant in the middle of Mayfair". Fans are impressed by "its competent realisation of a standard menu" of British classics. But service can be "somewhat patchy" and food can be "fairly average" as a result. / W1S 2PG; www.maddoxtavern.com; maddoxtavern; Tue-Sat midnight.

MADE IN ITALY £57 322

249 KING'S RD, SW3 020 7352 1880 6–3C
59 NORTHCOTE RD, SW11
020 7978 7711 11–2C

"The sourdough base is slow-fermented for 48 hours", and there's "a great selection of toppings (but you can't beat any with the burrata heart – so creamy, so addictive!") at these rustic venues in Chelsea and Battersea. / www.madeinitalygroup.co.uk; madeinitalylondon.

MAENE E1 £37 433

7-9 FASHION STREET
020 3011 1081 13–2C

"A new spin-off from Whitechapel Gallery's Townsend that's just opened": former Anglo chef Nick Gilkinson launched this hard-to-find all-day bistro, at the top of a four-storey Victorian warehouse in Spitalfields, in early April 2023. The choice of an Olde English name – meaning a sense of community, apparently – chimes with its short menu of determinedly seasonal British cuisine and we've optimistically rated it on initial reports describing "an awesome new opening, with fantastic, flavoursome food, locally sourced and provided by personable and knowledgeable staff". It is by all accounts a "lovely dining room too", with a roof terrace an expected addition. / E1 6PX; www.maenerestaurant.co.uk; maene_restaurant; Mon-Sat 9.30 pm, Sun 4.15 pm.

MAGENTA NW1 £83 343

23 EUSTON ROAD 0203 146 0222 9–3C

A trafficky location – right on Euston Road, opposite King's Cross station – doesn't augur well for this ambitious Italian bar/restaurant, within the recently revamped Megaro hotel. But, since it opened in November 2021, the limited feedback we receive suggests it can surprise with its quality and good value: "Four of us, all locals, dined here. We were delighted by everything and couldn't find anything to fault. A particular shout-out to the service!" / NW1 2SD; www.magentarestaurant.co.uk; magenta_kx; Tue-Sat 9.30 pm.

MAGGIE JONES'S W8 £69 344

6 OLD COURT PL 020 7937 6462 6–1A

This vintage Kensington haunt – named after the pseudonym used by the late Princess Margaret when wining and dining as a commoner – delights its guests with its gorgeous and romantic, rustic decor. Never a foodie fave rave: expect the kind of "delicious" 1970s brasserie-style comfort food which will not distract from a "lovely family meal", or more intimate tête-à-tête. / W8 4PL; www.maggie-jones.co.uk; maggiejonesrestaurant; Mon-Sun 9.30 pm.

Lasdun, National Theatre SE1

THE MAINE MAYFAIR W1 £106 223

6 MEDICI COURT, 20 HANOVER SQUARE
020 3432 2192 3–2C

"Taking you back to a different era", this glitzy American brasserie is spread over three floors of an extravagantly refurbed Georgian townhouse in Mayfair, where the entertainment runs to live jazz and burlesque shows. It's the creation of Montreal-born, Middle East-based 'tastemaker' Joey Ghazal. Naturally it does a "nice brunch", and the rather obvious menu – New England-style seafood plus some steaks and American-Italian favourites – is consistently well-rated. / W1S 1JY; www.themainemayfair.com; themainemayfair; Mon-Sun 11 pm.

MAISON BERTAUX W1 £16 335

28 GREEK ST 020 7437 6007 5–2A

"One of the few remaining eccentric Soho sites left" – this "long-established fixture" was founded in 1871 by an exile from Paris. "Individual, exceptional and entertaining", "the food still makes it a destination" – "including wonderful cakes better than any chain". It is, though, "very busy, clearly on the 'to-do' list of many tourists". / W1D 5DQ; www.maisonbertaux.com; maison_bertaux; Mon-Sun 6 pm.

MAISON FRANÇOIS SW1 £89 334

34 DUKE STREET ST JAMES'S
020 3988 5777 3–3D

This "smart bit of France in swanky St James's" is becoming an established favourite in the West End thanks in large part to its elegant and "buzzy" setting and the fact that it is "well organised". The classic menu of "French brasserie classics" has "lots of crowd-pleasers", but opinions divide on the results – to critics it is "a little expensive for what it is", but fans feel "the food is top-notch" and ratings tend to support those who say this is "a place for serious cooking, not just a big café". Top Tip – "the dessert trolley is an utter treat". / SW1Y 6DF; maisonfrancois.london; maisonfrancoislondon; Thu-Sat 1 am, Mon-Wed midnight, Sun 4 pm.

MALLOW SE1 £59 334

1 CATHEDRAL STREET
020 7846 8785 10–*4C*

"As non-vegans this was a revelation!" This "grown-up vegan restaurant" – a spin-off from the well-established Mildreds Group – has an excellent view of Borough Market and has won a strong reputation in its two years of operation. There's "no sense of a second-rate eating experience for lack of meat / fish etc" and its "inventive" cooking provides "really interesting flavours and combinations". On the downside, "the menu doesn't change that often"; and ratings weakened this year due to a few disappointed reporters who found it "overrated" due to lacklustre dishes and "intermittent" service. In June 2023, after our annual diners' poll had concluded, a new branch opened in Canary Wharf. / SE1 1TL; www.mallowlondon.com; mallowlondon; Mon-Sat 11 pm, Sun 10 pm.

MAMBOW SE15 £37 421

MARKET, 133A RYE LANE NO TEL 1–*4D*

"This Malaysian place at Market Peckham has wonderful food" – "the chicken satay is as good as I've had in the UK" and "the Hainanese chicken sando is delectable". It's "highly regarded, with fans including reviewers (Marina O'L)", but popularity has brought problems with "scaling up" – "they need more space, staff and flexible portions". BREAKING NEWS – in September 2023, they announced they have found their first 'forever home' at 78 Lower Clapton Road, Lower Clapton, London E5 0RN. The bigger space, with open kitchen, will have 40 covers, with 20 seats inside and 20 seats on a 'garden' terrace. / SE15 4BQ; www.wearemambow.com; mambow_ldn; Thu-Sat 11 pm, Wed 10 pm, Sun 5 pm.

MANDARIN KITCHEN W2 £71 442

14-16 QUEENSWAY 020 7727 9012 7–*2C*

"The lobster noodles are as legendary as ever" – "best in the world!" – chorus a legion of fans for this 45-year-old Queensway institution that's "tops for Chinese seafood in London". It's a "buzzy family restaurant" too, with "really lovely friendly staff", even if it's "a bit too brightly lit". / W2 3RX; www.mandarin.kitchen; mandarinkitchenlondon; Mon-Sat 11.15 pm, Sun 11 pm.

MANGAL 1 E8 £37 532

10 ARCOLA ST 020 7275 8981 14–*1A*

"One of the OGs and still one of the very best!" – this renowned Turkish dive in Dalston gets some diners' votes as "the best-value restaurant in London". "The smell of grilled meats entices you into the deservedly bustling interior", where it "delivers amazing food every time": "wonderful BBQ, lovely warm bread and generous salad". One of owner Ali Dirik's sons runs nearby Mangal 2, putting a more modern slant on grill cooking. / E8 2DJ; www.mangal1.com; mangal_ocakbasi; Sun-Thu midnight, Fri & Sat 1 am.

MANICOMIO £86 223

85 DUKE OF YORK SQUARE, SW3
020 7730 3366 6–*2D*
6 GUTTER LANE, EC2
020 7726 5010 10–*2B*

"Smart and buzzy", "reliable but expensive" – the underlying themes in reports over the years on this duo in Chelsea and the City, where "fresh Italian food is generally well done, if a little safe and uninspired". Top Tip – the Duke of York Square branch benefits from a heated terrace as well as conservatory and garden, making it a "happening place when the sun shines". / www.manicomio.co.uk; manicomiorestaurant.

MANTECA EC2 £52 544

49-51 CURTAIN ROAD
020 7033 6642 13–*1B*

"Packed fuller than a tube train, but the blinding food makes it all worth it!" – Chris Leach and David Carter's "bustling" two-year-old "in the heart of hipster Shoreditch" has "made huge waves and deservedly so" thanks to its "punchy, honest, original and surprisingly good-value" Italian cooking which includes some notable pasta dishes (e.g. "shout out for the duck fazzoletti – homemade, with a perfectly balanced sauce"); and whose meaty options "make full use of lesser cuts (the pig's head croquette is a special treat)". "Always a good night out"… "superb!" / EC2A 3PT; mantecarestaurant.co.uk; manteca_london; Mon-Thu, Sat & Sun, Fri 10.45pm.

MANTHAN W1 £64 332

49 MADDOX STREET 020 7491 9191 3–*2C*

Rohit Ghai's Mayfair two-year-old offers a "glam Indian street-food experience" – inspired by the home cooking of his childhood in Madhya Pradesh – from a "short but always very good menu". / W1S 2PQ; manthanmayfair.co.uk; manthanmayfair; Tue-Sun 10 pm.

MANUEL'S SE19 £65 444

129 GIPSY HILL 020 8670 1843 1–*4D*

"A high-quality Italian, with an ever-changing menu and wide range of specials depending on market availability" – this Gipsy Hill Sicilian is well worth discovering deep in the SE postcodes. In summer the terrace comes into its own, but fans say it's "always a pleasure to dine there". / SE19 1QS; www.manuelsrestaurantandbar.com; manuelsrestaurantgipsyhill; Tue-Sat 10.30 pm, Sun 9 pm.

MANUKA KITCHEN SW6 £61 333

510 FULHAM RD 020 7731 0864 6–*4A*

"Very popular at weekends with a good breakfast menu" – this NZ-inspired bistro near Parsons Green particularly comes into its own for brunches and light lunches. / SW6 5NJ; manukakitchen.co.uk; manukakitchen; Tue-Sat 11 pm, Mon 10 pm, Sun 4 pm.

MANZI'S W1

1 BATEMAN'S BUILDINGS
020 3540 4546 5–*2A*

Few openings are as long anticipated as this resurrection of a long-defunct, once-famous seafood destination. Conceived when its owning company was still run by Jeremy King and Christopher Corbin, the final debut is the first major test of the ability of its successor, The Wolseley Group, to launch a new site. The business that forms the inspiration for this debut was in Chinatown, just off Leicester Square, and shuttered in the early 1990s. This revivified version is in 'Bateman's Buildings', tucked between Soho's Greek and Frith Streets. Set over two floors, it's an all-day operation with a large outdoor terrace. Dishes encompass everything from moules marinière to a wide range of crustacea, a 'catch of the day' and a classic Dover sole. / W1D 3EN; www.manzis.co.uk; manzissoho; Mon-Sat 11 pm.

MAR I TERRA SE1 £56 333

14 GAMBIA ST 020 7928 7628 10–*4A*

Long-standing tapas bar in a tiny converted pub near Southwark tube that's "great fun and like being in Spain" – tucked away in a backstreet, it is handily close to the South Bank's arts venues, including Tate Modern, the Old Vic and the National Theatre. / SE1 0XH; www.mariterra.net; Tue, Thu, Wed, Fri & Sat midnight.

MARCELLA SE8 £48 343

165A DEPTFORD HIGH STREET
020 3903 6561 1–*3D*

Bright, white-walled local Italian on the high street in Deptford (sibling to Peckham's Artusi) named for food writer Marcella Hazan; according to locals the scran's "always reliable, delicious and great value". / SE8 3NU; www.marcella.london; marcelladeptford; Wed & Thu 9.30 pm, Fri & Sat, Tue 10 pm, Sun 4 pm.

MARCUS, THE BERKELEY SW1 £176 243

WILTON PL 020 7235 1200 6–*1D*

Opinions divided this year on Marcus Wareing's august Belgravia HQ, where the day-to-day is overseen by head chef, Craig Johnston. Most reports acclaim modern European cuisine that's "very, very, very good… amazing!" and applaud the flexibility of the kitchen to particular requests ("our food intolerances were brilliantly catered for and we felt our meal was just as special as other diners"). On he downside, though, ratings were capped by a growing number of disappointments citing hefty prices, and in one or two cases 'poor execution". BREAKING NEWS – in September 2023, Marcus announced it is to close on Boxing Day 2023 and Wareing is now a TV-chef without a restaurant attached. But he says he is not retiring yet, and that announcements will follow… / SW1X 7RL; www.marcusrestaurant.com; marcusbelgravia; Tue-Sat 10 pm.

MARE STREET MARKET E8 £57 324

117 MARE STREET 020 3745 2470 14–2B

This "cool hangar of a restaurant in Hackney" (part of the design-conscious Barworks group) sits in a repurposed and eclectically decorated 1960s office block and also incorporates a coffee shop, deli, barber and tattoo parlour. 'Recommended for large groups – the food is very good for the price" and includes a range of global favourites plus sourdough pizza, to be eaten in the spacious 'Open Kitchen' or the cosier 'Dining Room'. / E8 4RU; www.marestreetmarket.com; marestreetmarket; Mon-Sun 10 pm.

MAREMMA SW2 £65 333

36 BRIXTON WATER LANE
020 3186 4011 11–2D

This "cute little restaurant" near Brockwell Park in Brixton "really ticks all the boxes", with a "short selection of interesting Italian food" inspired by Tuscany's Maremma marshes – "you wouldn't expect an establishment of this quality to be hidden away here". Marks for food slipped a notch this year, although it's still "exciting and seasonal" at its best. / SW2 1PE; www.maremmarestaurant.com; maremma_restaurant; Wed-Sat 10 pm, Sun 3 pm.

MARESCO W1 £81 333

45 BERWICK STREET 020 7439 8483 4–1C

"Not a place for a quiet tête-à-tête: instead climb up to the bar and dig into a mixture of fine Scottish fish and seafood, prepared as Spanish-style tapas". That's the culinary mashup at Stephen Lironi's new "Soho seafood heaven" – a "lively, albeit slightly cramped" space with "lovely and engaging service and a fun atmosphere" ("as long as you are sitting upstairs" – downstairs is "a bit small and dingy"). On the downside, it can seem a bit "hyped" – "they need to smarten up if they are going to charge such high prices when you are perched on a bar stool". / W1F 8SF; www.maresco.co.uk; maresco_soho; Mon-Fri 11 pm, Sat & Sun 11.30 pm.

MARGAUX SW5 £76 343

152 OLD BROMPTON RD
020 7373 5753 6–2B

"Always reliable and first-class French cooking" is complemented by a serious wine list, including nine from Margaux, at this upmarket neighbourhood spot over two storeys at the Earl's Court end of South Kensington. / SW5 0BE; www.barmargaux.co.uk; barmargaux.

MARGOT WC2 £91 344

45 GREAT QUEEN STREET
020 3409 4777 5–2D

"A very sophisticated Italian restaurant" in Covent Garden that combines "gorgeous" cooking and "excellent wines" with "superb" service and an "elegant" interior. Just one catch, and you can probably guess what it is… it's no bargain ("the crab ravioli at £31 had only 6 ravioli on the plate…"). Top Top – "good value for the pre-theatre menu". / WC2B 5AA; www.margotrestaurant.com; margotldn_; Tue-Sat 9.30 pm.

MARIA G'S £59 333

20 CENTRAL AVENUE, SW6
020 3479 3867 11–1B
COE HOUSE, 1-4 WARWICK LANE, W14
020 3479 3772 8–2D

An "attractive riverside setting" (incorporating a 45-cover outdoor terrace, complete with retractable roof) is a major selling point at star chef Robin Gill's second opening under the 'Maria G' banner, on the ground floor of a shiny new residential development, in the deepest, darkest Fulham no-man's-land near Imperial Wharf (by the big Sainsburys). Despite its out-of-the-way situation, it's already attracting more feedback than the first Maria G, which opened two years ago. That's also hard to find, and also in a glossy new block – this time part of a retirement village on the Kensington/Olympia borders. At both outlets, the culinary theme is Italian although SW6 concentrates more on its raw bar and pasta, with reports praising "some innovative dishes" (The Telegraph's William Sitwell was also a fan, proclaiming it a "chic oasis" with "delicate and authentic Italian food"). Reports in our annual diners' poll on W8 were scant (but the Daily Mail's Tom Parker Bowles found it a "lush, lovely Italian oasis… [in] the sterile, anodyne surroundings of those deluxe flats").

MAROUSH £67 421

5 MCNICOL DRIVE, NW10
020 3941 3221 1–2A
II) 38 BEAUCHAMP PL, SW3
020 7581 5434 6–1C
VI) 68 EDGWARE RD, W2
020 7224 9339 7–1D

"Consistently delicious Lebanese food" remains a hallmark of Marouf and Houda Abouzaki's well-established restaurant group after more than 40 years. Even experienced Beirut hands report "very authentic" cooking, although service can be "inconsistent". The group shrank during the pandemic, but has bounced back with a large new restaurant/bar/emporium further west, in Park Royal. A sandwich wrap in the busy café on the ground floor of the Beauchamp Place branch is one of the top cheap eats in the Knightsbridge area. / www.maroush.com; maroush.

MARU W1 £266 543

18 SHEPHERD MARKET
020 3637 7677 3–4B

Taiji Maruyama – a third-generation sushi chef, who arrived in London via stints in Barcelona and Norway – delivers a 20-course omakase menu at this tiny Shepherd Market venue. All the fair number of reporters this year who made the £210 per person investment say it was money well spent. / W1J 7QH; www.marulondon.com; maru__london; Tue-Sat 11 pm.

MARUGAME UDON £18 332

ST CHRISTOPHER'S PLACE, W1 NO TEL 3–1B
UNIT 2.03 ENTERTAINMENT AVENUE, THE O2, SE10 NO TEL 12–1D
UPPER FLOOR, THE ATRIUM KITCHEN, CABOT PLACE, E14 NO TEL 12–1C
114 MIDDLESEX STREET, E1
020 3148 2780 13–2B

These "functional Japanese canteen-style restaurants" serve "lovely udon noodles at cheap prices" – "possibly the most reasonable in London" – along with tempura, rice bowls and "fabulous chicken katsu curry". The Kobe-based chain has more than 1,000 branches around the world, with a dozen across the capital since arriving in 2021. / marugame.co.uk; marugameuk.

MASALA ZONE £65 444

244 PICCADILLY, W1 020 7930 6622 4–4D
9 MARSHALL ST, W1 020 7287 9966 4–2B
48 FLORAL ST, WC2 020 7379 0101 5–2D
147 EARL'S COURT RD, SW5
020 7373 0220 6–2A

"There's a reason this chain has endured for so long" – its street food and curries are "so authentic", "imaginative" and "such good value for money": "you still have to go a long way to beat their thali deals". Owned by MW Eats (who own the posh Chutney Mary, Amaya, etc), they sold off their Camden Town and Bayswater sites in the last 12 months; and in mid 2023 launched a stunning new landmark branch on Piccadilly Circus, in one of London's most historic, but (in recent times) most-under-achieving restaurant sites: the magnificent, Neo-Byzantine, mosaicked chamber dating from 1873 that for many years was The Criterion (RIP). Innovations on the new site include breakfast, 'Indian High Tea' and late opening. / www.masalazone.com; masalazone.

MASTER WEI WC1 £34 422

13 COSMO PLACE 020 7209 6888 2–1D

"Hand-made and pulled noodles are the stars of the show" at this "authentic" canteen in a side-street near Russell Square, offering "fantastic Xi'an cooking" from chef-proprietor Wei Guirong. It attracts an "odd but pleasing mix of mainland Chinese businessmen & students, with tourists and the odd culinary adventurer" – and is much easier for most to visit than its sibling, Xi'an Impression near Arsenal's Emirates Stadium. / WC1N 3AP; master-wei.com; master.wei.3150; Mon-Thu 10 pm, Fri & Sat 10.30 pm, Sun 9 pm.

MAURO COLAGRECO, THE OWO SW1

57 WHITEHALL PLACE AWAITING TEL 2–*3C*

A past winner of the World's 50-best – chef Mauro Colagreco of Mirazur is to run three of the dining spaces at this new Raffles hotel in Whitehall's former Old War Office building. As well as his flagship dining room – which is to showcase 'hyper-local, hyper-seasonal ingredients for a culinary experience of discovery', there will be Mauro's Table (a private room with space for 10); and 'Saison', a brasserie in a fine high-ceilinged room. / SW1A 2EU; theowo.london; theowo.london; Wed-Sat 10 pm, Sun 9.30 pm.

MAYHA W1 £242 444

43 CHILTERN STREET
020 3161 9493 2–*1A*

"Not quite the best sushi omakase in the now very competitive London market but nevertheless very good" – this "beautiful and serene" Japanese venture arrived in Marylebone in early 2023 and early reporters are uniformly impressed. "Service is attentive but not overwhelming and the delicious food is prepared with a lot of care". It's an offshoot of a Beirut original from the Nothing But Love Group. (Lucy Thackray in The Independent was also a fan: "…confident and unshowy. This isn't theatrical "pan-Asian" dining made for Instagram… it's understated Japanese fine dining which takes its heritage seriously, but isn't afraid to add a twist here and there"). / W1U 6LS; www.mayhalondon.com; mayhalondon; Mon-Sat 7 pm.

MAZI W8 £78 443

12-14 HILLGATE ST 020 7229 3794 7–*2B*

"Very noisy" rustic-chic taverna tucked away near Notting Hill Gate station, which has won a sizable fan club thanks to its "delicious and inventive modern rendition" of the Greek classics. / W8 7SR; www.mazi.co.uk; mazilondon; Mon-Sun midnight.

THE MEAT & WINE CO MAYFAIR W1

17C CURZON STREET
0203 988 6888 3–*4B*

Limited but promising feedback so far on this August 2022, Mayfair newcomer – the first UK outpost of an Aussie-based chain – which aims to deliver 'what it says on the tin', with USDA steaks and Wagyu MB5 from Australian farms, as well as Prussian Black cuts from Finland. Early reports say "if steak is your thing then you will not do much better", and speak of "very friendly staff" and an "enjoyable" overall experience. / W1J 5HU; www.themeatandwineco.co.uk; themeatandwinecouk; Mon-Thu 9.30 pm, Fri & Sat 10.30 pm.

MEATLIQUOR £50 322

37-38 MARGARET STREET, W1
020 7224 4239 3–*1C*
15-17 BRUNSWICK CENTRE, WC1
020 3026 8168 2–*1D*
17 QUEENSWAY, W2 020 7229 0172 7–*2C*
133B UPPER ST, N1 020 3711 0104 9–*3D*
14-15 HOXTON MARKET, N1
020 7739 8212 13–*1B*
37 LORDSHIP LANE, SE22
020 3066 0008 1–*4D*
7 DARTMOUTH RD, SE23
020 3026 1331 1–*4D*
74 NORTHCOTE ROAD, SW11
020 7228 4777 11–*2C*

"The Dead Hippy burger is a dirty, dirty legend" – the best-named burger on British menus and "if not the easiest burger to eat definitely the tastiest" (especially when chased down by a boozy "hard shake") – at the "cool" chain founded 15 years ago by Scott Collins and Yianni Papoutsis. The expansion of recent years seems to have ground to a halt with the closure of branches in Boxpark Croydon and Clapham Old Town, with a new strategy based around boosting sales via a national network of delivery kitchens launched in 2023. Top Tip – "root beer is available if you want a bit of real Americana!" / meatliquor.com; meatgram.

MEDITERRANEO W11 £70 323

37 KENSINGTON PARK RD
020 7792 3131 7–*1A*

This "decent Notting Hill Italian" is "always mobbed (and the back area is particularly noisy), but the basic fare is great quality and the service is smiley". It has notched up a quarter of a century, and spawned two offshoots in the same street – Essenza and Osteria Basilico. / W11 2EU; www.mediterraneo-restaurant.co.uk; mediterraneo_nottinghill; Mon-Sun 10.30 pm.

MEDLAR SW10 £115 443

438 KING'S RD 020 7349 1900 6–*3B*

"It may not have the best location in an obscure end of the King's Road", but this "low-key" Chelsea operation (est. 2011) "continues to quietly excel" and is one of the most popular in our annual diners' poll. "Imaginative" modern British cuisine "with a good range of ingredients" is "expertly cooked by co-owner and chef Joe Mercer Nairne, and with excellent but unobtrusive service overseen by co-owner David O'Connor", including "well-targeted wine advice" on the "terrific list". Another "star of the show is the cheeseboard" ("I am still talking about it months later!"). "Much better than many one-starred Michelin restaurants in London", "it is incomprehensible that this restaurant has been passed over for regaining its star for so long". Top Tips – "the three-course lunch for £45 and lunchtime corkage of only £15 are some of the capital's great culinary bargains". "Old favourites on the menu include the Crab Raviolo." / SW10 0LJ; www.medlarrestaurant.co.uk; medlarchelsea; Mon-Sat 10.30 pm, Sun 9.30 pm.

MEET BROS W2

29-31 CRAVEN ROAD 020 7723 7101 7–*1C*

No less a figure than Queen Azizah of Malaysia (while she was over for Charles's coronation) cut the ribbon for the May 2023 opening of this first European venture from one of Malaysia's leading restaurant groups – a steakhouse in Craven Road, Paddington, that takes its name from the meeting of Eastern and Western food cultures. No alcohol is served and the meat is fully halal, with cuts flavoured by infusion in Asian marinades. Reports please! / W2 3BX; www.meetbros.co.uk; meetbros.uk; Mon-Sun 11 pm.

MEGAN'S £50 113

BRANCHES THROUGHOUT LONDON

"Fairy lights, greenery and charming decor create a warm and cosy atmosphere" at this still-expanding group, which is most popular as a "reliable and friendly brunch option". Its Med-inspired tapas is typically rated somewhere between "tasty" and "nothing special" and scores overall are dragged well down by those experiencing "chaotic service" and "food that doesn't live up to the pretty dining room". / megans.co.uk; megansrestaurants.

MEIWEI SW15 £17 332

315 PUTNEY BRIDGE ROAD
020 8789 3165 11–*2B*

This "surprisingly good Chinese" in Putney specialises in the cuisines of Shanghai and Sichuan, and the "flavours and produce" are by all accounts "excellent" (even better if you "ask for the Chinese menu"). Top Menu Tip – "particularly fine duck". / SW15 2PP; www.meiweilondon.co.uk; Mon-Sun 11 pm.

MELE E PERE W1 £54 333

46 BREWER STREET 020 7096 2096 4–*3C*

This "authentic Italian vermuteria" (they make their own vermouths) in the heart of Soho was founded 12 years ago by three brothers from northern Italy, and offers enjoyable cooking from their homeland, including "a great choice of pasta" and "the crispiest pizza ever – delicious!" / W1F 9TF; www.meleepere.co.uk; meleeperesoho; Mon & Tue, Sun 10 pm, Wed-Sat 11 pm.

THE MELUSINE E1 £71 444

UNIT K, IVORY HOUSE, ST KATHERINE DOCK 02077022976 10–*3D*

"Consistently delicious seafood" and a "lovely location" by St Katharine Dock have put this three-year-old securely on the map. The interesting wine list is strong on "Greek offerings" – thanks no doubt to co-founder Theodore Kyriakou, a veteran of Livebait and The Real Greek in the '90s. Top Tip – "go on Wednesdays for the half-price wine". / E1W 1AT; www.themelusine.co.uk; themelusine_skd; Mon-Sat 10.30 pm, Sun 9.30 pm.

Little
KUDU

Manzi's W1

and tasty" Lebanese cooking. / SW17 7RE; www.mezarestaurant.com; meza_res; Sun-Thu 11 pm, Fri & Sat 11.30 pm.

MICHAEL NADRA NW1 £78 332

42 GLOUCESTER AVE
020 7722 2800 9–3B

Michael Nadra's "reliable" cuisine from an eclectic modern menu has created a high-quality neighbourhood destination for the last 12 years in this corner of Primrose Hill: quirkily laid-out premises, with a cute courtyard, just off the Regent's Canal. His original restaurant in Chiswick closed down during the pandemic. / NW1 8JD; www.restaurant-michaelnadra.co.uk.

MERAKI W1 £85 434

80-82 GT TITCHFIELD ST
020 7305 7686 3–1C

London… Mykonos… er, Riyadh… – that's the lineup for this small international group of luxe Greek restaurants owned by Peter Waney (who, with brother Arjun, has created hits such as Zuma and Roka). It flies slightly under the radar compared with its more famous stablemates, but shares the same virtues: the vibe is buoyant and the food (a Greek-inflected mix of the raw seafood, fish, grills and pasta popular with globetrotting types) "is great… so fresh!" / W1W 7QT; www.meraki-restaurant.com; merakilondon; Tue, Wed 10.15 pm, Thu-Sat 10.45 pm, Sun 8.30 pm.

MERCATO METROPOLITANO SE1 £46 224

42 NEWINGTON CAUSEWAY
020 7403 0930 1–3C

Hosting a range of pop-up kitchens and bars, these "lively and fun" sustainable markets have sprung up across the capital since opening in an ex-paper factory near Elephant & Castle in 2016, a year after the concept was launched at Milan's World Expo. They make a flexible and affordable option that particularly comes into its own in summer – the Canary Wharf branch on Wood Wharf is "brilliant for sitting outside overlooking the dock"; and SE1 boasts London's biggest beer garden. / SE1 6DR; www.mercatometropolitano.com; mercatometropolitano; Mon-Wed 11 pm, Fri & Sat 1 am, Thu midnight, Sun 10 pm.

THE MERCER EC2 £82 332

34 THREADNEEDLE ST
020 7628 0001 10–2C

This solid English brasserie in a converted banking hall not far from the Bank of England continues to win a general thumbs-up as an "excellent business lunch venue" – although "it could do with tables further apart". / EC2R 8AY; www.themercer.co.uk; themercerrestaurant; Mon-Fri 9.30 pm.

LE MERCURY N1 £40 222

140A UPPER ST 020 7354 4088 9–2D

It's "not haute cuisine", but you'll find "reasonably well-cooked bistro fare that's very well-priced for the location" at this old-school haunt that has done sterling service for almost 40 years on the Islington main drag, opposite the Almeida Theatre. "The two-tier Parisian theatre boxes are a bit of a mad addition to the interior design", but they make "a great spot for a family meal before a show". / N1 1QY; www.lemercury.co.uk; lemercury; Mon-Sat midnight, Sun 11 pm.

MERE W1 £123 343

74 CHARLOTTE STREET
020 7268 6565 2–1B

TV star chef Monica Galetti often "hits the heights" at the Fitzrovia basement she runs with her husband David – an "unfailingly delightful" place, sometimes tipped for "romance", but mostly nominated by its large fanclub for its "exquisite cooking" ("superbly prepared fish" in particular) and "pampering" service. But ratings here are limited by a few more nuanced experiences: "I kept hoping some culinary magic would happen, but it never quite made it". / W1T 4QH; www.mere-restaurant.com; mererestaurant; Wed & Thu, Tue 9 pm, Fri & Sat 9.30 pm.

MESON DON FELIPE SE1 £52 224

53 THE CUT 020 7928 3237 10–4A

Many older Londoners tasted their first tapas at this "fun and reliable" Hispanic spot on a prominent corner of the Cut, near Waterloo – back in the days when you "had to queue (now you can book)" for a place in the "cramped interior". It's still "excellent before and after visiting the Old Vic" across the road. / SE1 8LF; www.mesondonfelipe.com; mesondonfelipe; Mon-Sat 11 pm.

MEZA TRINITY ROAD SW17 £45 333

34 TRINITY RD 07722 111299 11–2C

"A great neighbourhood place" – this Tooting café maintains its reputation with "reliably fresh

MIDLAND GRAND DINING ROOM NW1

EUSTON ROAD 020 7341 3000 9–3C

Set in the stunning Gothic Revival St Pancras Renaissance Hotel – and using the establishment's original name – this 'elevated brasserie' opened in May 2023 to replace The Gilbert Scott (RIP) just as our survey was concluding. Consequently even though we did have one (upbeat) initial report, there's too little feedback for a rating. But The Standard's Jimi Famurewa was also a fan, admiring the amazing "double-height main room… gilded cornice work… vast textured mirrors" (but also noting a "slight stiltedness of atmosphere"). Its modern interpretation of classic French cuisine is under ex-Chiltern Fire House chef Patrick Powell: JF notes "light kitsch… impeccable details… intricate presentation" but "a potentially ruinous bill" ("prices… can take you whistling past the £100 a head mark without even really trying"). / NW1 2AR; www.midlandgranddiningroom.com; midlandgrand; Tue-Sat 9.45 pm, Sun 4 pm.

MILDREDS £57 333

45 LEXINGTON ST, W1
020 7494 1634 4–2C
79 ST MARTIN'S LANE, WC2
020 8066 8393 5–3B
200 PENTONVILLE RD, N1
020 7278 9422 9–3D
9 JAMESTOWN RD, NW1
020 7482 4200 9–3B
1 DALSTON SQUARE, E8
020 8017 1815 14–1A

"So much better now it is fully vegan and more adventurous with its food" ("a wonderful range of plant-based dishes from around the world including Central America and the Middle East") – this long-established meat-free chain started with its "old favourite" Soho branch (est 1988) and has mushroomed in recent years to include five locations in all. "Tables are crammed in" and the sites can get "extremely busy", but its offering is reliably "tasty and interesting". / www.mildreds.co.uk; mildredsrestaurants.

MILK SW12 £25 323

0 BEDFORD HILL 020 8772 9085 11–2C

The fish sando of dreams" is one item that omes highly recommended at this "über rendy" Antipodean-inspired café in Balham, nown in particular as a key brunch venue. The menu items regularly contain ingredients ou've never heard of… doesn't matter, ll of them are delicious!" / SW12 9RG; ilklondonshop.uk; milkcoffeeldn; Mon-Fri 3.30 m, Sat & Sun 4 pm.

MILK BEACH SOHO V1 £48 343

ONA ROSE HOUSE, MANETTE STREET 20 4599 4271 5–2A

A fairly recent addition to Soho" – sibling an older venture in Queen's Park – this interestingly-styled", "Aussie-themed" yearling a handy option for "meeting up with friends". Über-cool", "very amiable" staff provide "a reat selection of unusual menu offerings to mpt the slightly adventurous or those jaded ith standard fare". A disgruntled minority ismiss "average food in a cavernous space", ut the main impression is of something genuinely different from most West End ptions". Top Tip – dedicated menus for reakfast and pre-theatre. / W1D 4AL; ww.milkbeach.com; milkbeachlondon; Tue, Wed 1 pm, Thu-Sat midnight, Sun 4 pm.

MIMI MEI FAIR W1 £97 344

5 CURZON STREET 020 3989 7777 3–3B

We went there a mite apprehensive that we ould be overwhelmed by pretension… but e dining rooms are beautiful!" – Samyukta air's Shanghai-inspired two-year-old ccupies a three-story Mayfair townhouse ecorated in an elegant, classic style based n a fictional 'Empress Mimi'. The chicness f the surroundings helps compensate for me "slightly overpriced" dishes, as does the enerally excellent level of service. Top Menu ip – "the fabled Peking duck is one of the est in town". / W1J 8PG; mimimeifair.com; imimeifair; Mon-Sat 10.30 pm, Sun 10 pm.

MIN JIANG, THE ROYAL GARDEN HOTEL W8 £105 445

24 KENSINGTON HIGH ST 20 7361 1988 6–1A

Fabulous Peking Duck and dim sum comes ith one of the best views of any restaurant in ondon" at this luxurious Chinese venue, which ntinues to break the normal rules applying anywhere with a decent outlook. On the p of a five-star hotel overlooking Kensington ardens and Palace, it's "very popular and eservedly so": service is "spot-on" and it's ust lovely". / W8 4PT; www.minjiang.co.uk; injianglondon; Mon-Sun 10.30 pm.

MIRCH MASALA SW17 £26 422

213 UPPER TOOTING RD
020 8767 8638 11–2D

"Always delicious", this well-known Pakistani canteen on Tooting's 'curry corridor' offers the "same fun and good-value food as it has for years". A favourite of local boy-made-mayor Sadiq Khan (so come on foot or by public transport), it has an offshoot in Coulsdon, on London's southern fringe. / SW17 7TG; mirchmasala-takeaway.co.uk; mirch masala; Mon-Sun 23.59 pm.

MIZNON £58 323

8-12 BROADWICK STREET, W1 NO TEL 4–1C
14 ELGIN CR, W11 NO TEL 7–1B

"Get a pitta the action!" say fans of these "fast, fun, loud and daft" outlets in Soho and now also Notting Hill – part of Eyal Shani's international chain, based out of Tel Aviv. Flatbreads filled with falafel, burgers, English breakfast – you name it – exemplify the "playful" Middle Eastern menu, which everyone agrees is a "great concept" ("different and certainly worth experiencing for its unique take on pitta fillings"). But dishes that are "well-priced, fresh and tasty" in most accounts can – to a few critics – seem "bland and sloppily served". Top Menu Tip – "outstanding roasted cauliflower".

LOS MOCHIS £56 333

2 FARMER ST, W8 020 7727 7528 7–2B
100 LIVERPOOL STREET, EC2 AWAITING TEL 10–2D

"Fun and interesting" (if sometimes "very noisy and exhausting"), is the verdict on this "buzzy" Notting Hill Gate hang out, complete with bold Mexican-inspired wall hangings (and soon to acquire a rooftop offshoot at 100 Liverpool Street in the City, scheduled to open in autumn 2023). "The menu is less fusion, more Mexican with a nod to Japan": "flavour-packed mouthfuls" dubbed 'Baja-Nihon cuisine' by founder Markus Thesleff.

MON PLAISIR RESTAURANT WC2 £71 234

19-21 MONMOUTH STREET
020 7836 7243 5–2B

"The charming warren of rooms helps make for a happy experience" at this "nostalgic", and "immensely charming" Gallic super-bistro, near Covent Garden, which opened just after WWII and which has rambled over the years into neighbouring buildings. "For many decades the menu has hardly changed and continues to reflect Parisian bistros with confit de canard, steak grillé and a fine chariot de fromages... warming in winter and equally welcoming the rest of the year". New owners, Fabio Lauro and Family took over in 2022 from Alain Lhermitte (who owned it since 1972) "leaving some people worried this place has gone off". But "the food was not what it was" before Alain retired, and ratings improved here somewhat this year – hopefully the start of a positive new chapter for this old veteran. / WC2H 9DD; www.monplaisir.co.uk; monplaisiragram; Mon-Sat 9.30 pm.

MONMOUTH COFFEE COMPANY £7 343

27 MONMOUTH ST, WC2
020 7232 3010 5–2B
SPA TERMINUS, UNIT 4 DISCOVERY ESTATE, SE16 020 7232 3010 12–2A
2 PARK ST, SE1 020 7232 3010 10–4C

"Decent croissants and the best brews", delivered by "unfailingly lovely service, however long the queues", still win legions of fans for London's original cool coffee shop group, even if it has real competition these days from more Antipodean-style challengers. "They've been my top choice for over 35 years, but I can no longer cope with the uncomfortable seating at the OG Covent Garden outlet, so SE1 it is", which is "perfect to combine with a Borough Market visit". There's also a third branch at Bermondsey's Spa Terminus. / www.monmouthcoffee.co.uk; monmouthcoffee.

MONMOUTH KITCHEN WC2 £69 343

20 MERCER ST 020 7845 8607 5–2B

"A good find for a pre-theatre meal" – this "efficient and friendly" Covent Garden dining room is quite stylish for somewhere inside a modern chain hotel, and serves an offbeat mix of Peruvian and Italian dishes: "a great selection", with "lots of small-plate choices and interesting combinations" – "just enough to choose easily and all delicious". / WC2H 9HD; monmouthkitchen.co.uk; monmouthkitchen; Mon & Tue 11.30 pm, Wed-Fri 10 pm, Sat 10.30 pm, Sun 7 pm.

MORITO £59 432

195 HACKNEY ROAD, E2
020 7613 0754 14–2A
32 EXMOUTH MKT, EC1
020 7278 7007 10–1A

The "lovely Moorish/Spanish sharing food" at the little sister of Sam & Sam Clark's Moro next door in Exmouth Market – and also its spin-off in Hackney Road – makes them "a go-to place when you don't know where to go": "an all-round crowd-pleaser, good for meat and non-meat- eaters alike". / www.morito.co.uk; moritotapas.

MORO EC1 £79 443

34-36 EXMOUTH MKT
020 7833 8336 10–1A

"Have loved it forever!" – "After all these years Sam and Sam Clark's vanguard player in the 1990s British restaurant revolution still punches well up to its weight" (and scored much more consistently again this year, with one or two diners noting a "marked improvement" after a soggy couple of years). "Still packed, still pushing out creative Spanish/Moorish food, still surprisingly good value, and still in a minimalist space that's fundamentally 1990s"; it's a "heartwarming delight" for its big and ultra-loyal fan club. Other plusses include "excellent Spanish wine list and relaxed-but-efficient service". The "only issue is the noise level, which can make it difficult to hear your companion, even on a small table". / EC1R 4QE; www.moro.co.uk; restaurantmoro; Mon-Sat 10.30 pm, Sun 3 pm.

MORSO NW8 £79 322

130 BOUNDARY ROAD
020 7624 7412 9–3A

A modern Italian on Abbey Road, whose menu is "not the biggest", majoring in pasta and light 'bites'. Feedback this year was a little up-and-down: "always enjoyable" to fans, but, to other regulars "less good and more pricey than it used to be". / NW8 0RH; www.morsolondon.co.uk; morsolondon.

MOTCOMBS SW1 £69 224

26 MOTCOMB ST 020 7235 6382 6–1D

Occupying a prime site with a large pavement terrace in an ever-plusher corner of Belgravia, this old-fashioned stalwart (est 1982) had its heyday in the era of 'The Sloane Ranger Handbook' (published in the same year). Even if some reports consider the experience "overpriced" and say "and service would be easy to improve" – our poll still rates its international assortment of dishes decently (although, there are some less favourable experiences reported elsewhere online). / SW1X 8JU; motcombsbelgravia.com; motcombsofbelgravia; Mon-Sun 1 am.

MOUNT STREET RESTAURANT, THE AUDLEY W1 £116 334

41-43 MOUNT STREET
020 3840 9860 3–3A

"Sitting next to a £1,000,000 painting does add a frisson" at this "gorgeous" autumn 2022 newcomer in the blue-blooded heart of Mayfair. An arm of international art promoters, Hauser & Wirth, it sits on the first floor of the newly refurbished Audley Pub and counted King Charles & Queen Camilla amongst its earlier customers. It's undoubtedly a "fabulous" space (hung with works by Matisse and Freud) that makes a very "interesting new addition to the Mayfair restaurant scene", but the menu is priced for plutocrats, and results are a little mixed. Most reporters do applaud "elegant surroundings with food to match". But there are also a number of doubters, who feel it lacks culinary finesse ("I was pleasantly surprised that it wasn't quite as extortionately priced as we'd anticipated. We shared the famous lobster pie (£96)… to be honest it was a bit disappointing. The remainder of the meal was competent if a bit unexciting"). / W1K 3AH; mountstrestaurant.com; mountstrestaurant; Mon-Sat 10 pm, Sun 4.45 pm.

MOUNTAIN W1

16-18 BEAK STREET 020 7437 6138 4–2B

Gwynedd meets Catalonia and beyond at Tomos (Brat) Parry's hotly anticipated summer 2023 newcomer: potentially one of Soho's brightest foodie sparks. A "wood grill and wine bar", Tomos channels the native cuisine of his upbringing on Anglesey (with nearby Snowdonia) through the lens of his travels across Spain. Supplied by farmers and fisherman in Wales and Cornwall, whole roast bream will be a feature as will lamb chops, and Anglesey lobster – all emerging, as at Brat, from an open kitchen and with a good deal of counter seating. / W1F 9RD; mountainbeakstreet.com; mountain.restaurant; Mon-Thu 11 pm, Fri & Sat 3 am, Sun 10 pm.

MR BAO SE15 £36 333

293 RYE LANE 020 7635 0325 1–4D

This "buzzy Taiwanese café" in Peckham is a "friendly neighbourhood joint" that does a good trade in "reliably tasty bao buns"; and has a "wonderful" brunch menu at weekends ("spicy beans with hash browns; kimchi pancake with onsen egg and smoked salmon and egg bao buns are all 'must-tries"). There's also a Daddy Bao in Tooting and a Master Bao in Westfield Shepherd's Bush. / SE15 4UA; www.mrbao.co.uk; mrbaouk; Sun-Thu 10 pm, Fri 11.30 pm, Sat 11 pm.

MR FALAFEL W12 £9 542

15 UXBRIDGE ROAD 07307 635548 8–1C

"The best falafel in town!" is a claim regularly made for this family-run gaff, to be found amongst the mêlée of Shepherd's Bush Market. Motto: 'We Speak Falafel Fluently' – you can order the dish in the style of Syria, Iran, Lebanon or the owners' native Palestine. / W12 8LH; www.mrfalafel.co.uk; mr_falafel_london; Mon-Thu, Sat 6 pm.

MR JI NW1 £39 333

63-65 PARKWAY 07857 592575 9–3B

With the closure of its Soho branch, this "creative and fun modern Chinese restaurant recently opened in Camden Town", in November 2022, complete with funky, hard-edged decor and serving an East-meets-West style of Asian cuisine, washed down with cocktails. "Not all the dishes are entirely successful but some are delicious. Service is sweet natured, helpful and knowledgeable". / NW1 7PP; mrji.co.uk; mrjirestaurant; Tue-Sat 10 pm, Sun 5 pm.

MRIYA SW5 £64 333

275 OLD BROMPTON ROAD
020 3089 4640 6–3A

Slava Ukraini! "Behind a scruffy streetscape" on the edge of Earls Court (near the Troubadour), this "enjoyable, if cramped and noisy" yearling was created by Ukrainian refugees, led by chef Yurii Kovryzhenko and his partner, Olga Tsybytovska. "It's a great project – a good cause, with charming service and distinctive cooking": "a modern and rather lighter interpretation of East European cuisine (e.g. courgette flowers used instead of cabbage leave for golubtsi: the Ukrainian take on the Polish golabki)". "Well worth a visit and supporting the Ukrainian refugees who work there". Top Menu Tip – "deep-flavoured bortsch". / SW5 9JA; mriya_neo_bistro; Tue, Wed, Sun 11 pm Fri 1 am, Sat midnight.

MU E8

432-434 KINGSLAND ROAD
020 7209 4187 14–1A

On a site that was Rotorino (RIP), this year-old music venue (named for a jazz album) is from the brothers behind Hackney's 'Brilliant Corners'. It has yet to generate much in the way of survey feedback, but London needs more jazz diners; and its Japanese-inspired robata cuisine received a big shout out from the Guardian's Grace Dent in November 2022 who found it be "far grander and ornately executed than it needs to be". / E8 4AA; mu-ldn.com; mu.ldn; Tue-Thu 11.30 pm, Fri & Sat 12.30 am, Sun 11 pm.

MURANO W1 £129 443

20-22 QUEEN ST 020 7495 1127 3–3B

"One of the best value top-end restaurants in London" – Angela Hartnett's London flagship (celebrating its fifteenth anniversary) scored consistently highly in this year's annual diners' poll and is the rare kind of fancy Mayfair destination where folks like spending their own money rather than needing corporate plastic. The Italian-inspired cuisine is "very accomplished", with "flavours seemingly so simply presented, you know the effort that must have gone into each elegant dish". Staff are "helpful but unobtrusive" and contribute to an overall experience that "never fails to hit the spot". In August 2023, the establishment announced a total refurb (complete with glass chandelier from Venice), and the appointment of George Ormond as Head Chef, who takes over from Emily Brightman. / W1J 5PP; www.muranolondon.com; muranolondon; Mon-Sa 10 pm.

MUSE SW1 £215 544

38 GROOM PLACE 020 3301 2903 6–1D

"Tom Aikens is back to his brilliant best!" at his "chic little Belgravia mews house", where he's created "an outstanding small restaurant with open kitchen". Set on two floors, "tables are a bit close", but the "intimate" style is a selling point for most diners (especially at the chef's counter), as is the fact that there's "plent of interaction with the chefs including patron Tom", all of whom "serve and explain with a remarkable personal touch". The menu – "exquisite food, delivered with passion and skill" – draws on Tom's upbringing – "love the story-telling… a truly special experience". / SW1X 7BA; www.musebytomaikens.co.uk; musebytomaikens; Tue-Sat 11 pm.

MYRTLE SW10 £84 543

A LANGTON STREET
20 7352 2411 6–*3B*

)ublin-born Anna Haugh "has created a abulous local restaurant which is nowadays destination" at her "warm and welcoming" Chelsea Townhouse. Her "imaginative" tasting nenu provides "fine, Irish-influenced modern European cuisine": "brilliantly executed food which doesn't take itself too seriously whilst eing superb" and "worth every penny in his challenging economic environment". Michelin continues to show they have no rain by failing to even list the place, never nind giving it the star it deserves! / SW10 0JL; ww.myrtlerestaurant.com; myrtlerestaurant; Tue-at 10 pm.

NAKANOJO W1

3-14 THAYER STREET
20 7993 4321 3–*1A*

This high-street Nikkei hangout's first Chelsea branch opened in 2021 and shut in nid 2023 in favour of a new Marylebone ocation. No feedback as yet on either site, which purveys a trendy fusion of sushi, tacos, eviche and robata bites, and of course pisco ours, sakes and cocktails aplenty. / W1U 3JR; ww.nakanojo.com; nakanojouk; Sun-Thu 10 pm, ri & Sat 11 pm.

NAMMOS SW7

3-17 MONTPELIER STREET NO TEL
–*1C*

Mykonos, it is promised, will come to Knightsridge in autumn 2023, with the opening f this self-consciously glam newcomer – a spin-ff from the celeb-filled Greek island original, which is jetting into the Harrods hinterland ia Cannes and Dubai to create 'a new ining concept with a relaxed neighbourhood tmosphere'. It's on a site that was for decades Montpeliano, and – with its reservations-only no walk-ins) policy – seems to be aiming to apture the same supercar-driving set as its redecessor did in its heyday. If the advance isuals are any guide, the bright interior will e rather gorgeous, in which to enjoy a sharing lates menu of Med-inspired surf 'n' turf. / W7 1HF; www.nammosneighbourhood.com.

NANDINE SE5 £36 333

5 CAMBERWELL CHURCH STREET
20 7703 3221 1–*3C*

The name means 'kitchen' in Kurdish – Pary Baban's Camberwell café reproduces the ishes of her homeland, to the satisfaction of eporters. Top Tips – brunch is a highlight; you an BYO at her simpler nearby outlet at 82 Vestry Street (but the branch at Peckham Levels s no more). / SE5 8TR; nandineuk; Mon-Sun 1 pm.

NAUGHTY PIGLETS SW2 £55 544

28 BRIXTON WATER LN
020 7274 7796 11–*2D*

"As brilliant as ever" – Joe Sharratt and Margaux Aubry's "unassuming space" in Brixton is "everything you'd want from a local and more" – making it stand out on the South London gastronomic scene. The "laid-back vibe belies a serious approach to food and wine", resulting in French-inspired "plates of pure pleasure" – "so much better than the fancy fly-by-night trendy places that are all queues, instagram and foam". Top Menu Tip – "they serve the BEST butter you will ever taste". / SW2 1PE; www.naughtypiglets.co.uk; naughtypiglets; Tue-Thu 9.15 pm, Fri & Sat 11 pm.

NAUTILUS NW6 £38 442

27-29 FORTUNE GREEN RD
020 7435 2532 1–*1B*

This "classic family-run chippy" in West Hampstead has served "top-notch fish 'n' chips or any grilled fish alternative at a more than fair price" for longer than anyone can remember. "George the owner is lovely" and "the staff welcome you like you're family – once you've been a couple of times they'll know your order off by heart". "The dining room, though, is very basic and has the atmosphere of a station waiting room, with its fluorescent lighting". Top Menu Tip – "the matzo meal batter is really light". / NW6 1DU; nautilusfishandchip; Mon-Sat 10 pm, Sun 9 pm.

NESSA W1 £70 334

1 WARWICK STREET 020 7337 7404 4–*3B*

"A beautiful setting in a new members' club" adds lustre to this autumn 2022 newcomer in Soho: a stylish co-working space complex that's a sibling to fashionable Mortimer House, and with ex-Duck & Waffle chef, Tom Cenci at the stoves. On its bistro menu "some quite traditional dishes are given modern makeovers" which err on the hearty side (Chicken Cordon Bleu, 'Nessabocker Glory') and fans say results, especially at brunch, are "fantastic". Ratings are limited, though, by the odd reporter who feels the cooking's little more than "food assemblage at top prices". (Many newspaper critics have rushed along, and the consensus is also somewhat mixed – Giles Coren of The Times – a member of Mortimer House – thought some of the cooking "epochal", while the Telegraph's William Sitwell found the whole enterprise a "public-facing cash cow" with a "total charisma bypass"). / W1B 5LR; www.nessasoho.com; nessasoho; Mon-Wed midnight, Thu-Sat 1 am, Sun 6 pm.

NEST EC1 £105 433

374-378 OLD STREET
020 8986 0065 13–*1B*

"One of the best neighbourhood restaurants in London", this "bold" and "inspirational" outfit "creates dishes out of a tiny kitchen that puts a lot of better-known places to shame – the menu, centred around using as much of one main ingredient as possible and changing every few weeks, is always creative and thought-provoking". BREAKING NEWS: we've maintained ratings from the original Hackney site, but in September 2023 they closed the "uncomfortable" digs of five years' standing, so gaining more space in a new double-fronted Victorian location by Shoreditch Town Hall. / EC1V 9LT; www.nestfood.co.uk; nest_food; Mon-Sat 11 pm.

NEWENS: THE ORIGINAL MAIDS OF HONOUR TW9 £43 343

288 KEW ROAD 020 8940 2752 1–*3A*

"Like taking tea in olden days" – this mock-Tudor tea room opposite Kew Gardens was built in the 1940s and is splendidly unmodernised. The Newens have been baking here since the Victorian era while their signature Maids of Honour tarts are said to have originated under the Tudors. Yes, it's "touristy – but very atmospheric, and the afternoon teas are good". / TW9 3DU; theoriginalmaidsofhonour.co.uk; theoriginalmaidsofhonour; Mon-Sun 6 pm.

1905 W1 £69 345

40 MORTIMER STREET
020 7436 8090 3–*1C*

This "interesting new Cretan" (named after Crete's 1905 revolution) in Fitzrovia claims to be the first Cretan restaurant anywhere outside Greece, and presents the island's distinctive version of eastern Mediterranean cuisine, along with natural wines from some of the world's oldest wine-producing regions. / W1W 7RQ; www.1905.london; 1905.london; Sun-Thu 11 pm, Fri & Sat 11.45 pm.

THE NINTH LONDON W1 £116 533

22 CHARLOTTE STREET
020 3019 0880 2–*1C*

"Exceptional food and an approach that's attentive and friendly but never overbearing or distant" wins nothing but high praise for Jun Tanaka's "consistently excellent and very enjoyable" HQ, on Fitzrovia's restaurant row. "It was closed from summer last year until mid March 2023 owing to a fire – post re-opening, the cuisine is of just the same standard as before". / W1T 2NB; www.theninthlondon.com; theninthlondon; Mon-Wed 9 pm, Thu-Sat 9.30 pm.

NO. FIFTY CHEYNE SW3 £116 335

50 CHEYNE WALK 020 7376 8787 6–*3C*

"An excellent venue for an intimate date…" – this beautiful and comfortable grill, just off Chelsea Embankment (with river views from its top-floor bar) is full of atmosphere. It's owned by Sally Green – who also owns Ronnie Scott's – who is celebrating her 10th year as proprietor in 2024. The menu focus is on grilled protein and Sunday roast is also a feature: results are very good, but some would still say it's "overpriced". / SW3 5LR; www.fiftycheyne.com; 50cheyne; Wed-Sat midnight, Sun 6 pm.

NOBLE ROT WC1 £78 345

51 LAMB'S CONDUIT STREET
020 7242 8963 2–1D

A "magnificent" operation – Mark Andrew and Dan Keeling's first venture has become one of the most popular destinations in London, hitting our Top 10 most-mentioned entries for the first time this year. Opened in 2015 – and named for the wine and food magazine they started in 2013 – it inhabits the "characterful" Bloomsbury premises that were for decades 'Vats', and its "dark, cosy spaces" are perfect for working through the "terrific wine list" they have assembled: very arguably "the best by-the-glass list in town", with many "rarities preserved by the Coravin system". The cooking is overseen by afar by executive chef, Stephen Harris of Seasalter fame: "slip soles in butter are almost as good as at The Sportsman, but the other dishes are a bit more standard" – the "food can be unexpectedly accomplished, but it's really all about the wine list which caters to all tastes and budgets". Service is "superb, passionate and friendly" ("but can be patchy during busy periods"). Fans say, of the three branches it's "the original and the best", but – though slightly less commented-on – its more recent spin-offs now actually outscore the mothership. / WC1N 3NB; www.noblerot.co.uk; noblerotbar; Mon-Sat 9.30 pm.

NOBLE ROT MAYFAIR W1 £61 454

5 TREBECK STREET 020 7101 6770 3–4B

"What a fabulous new bar and restaurant where Boudin Blanc (RIP) was" – this latest, April 2023 member of the well-known, wine-led group has been instantly hailed as a "wonderful addition" to picturesque Shepherd Market. "Thoroughly grown-up in style, it feels a bit more professional and slick than the lovely Holborn original". In particular, the superior bistro cooking is "more interesting than in WC1": "no culinary fireworks or cheffy tricks" but "worth it even for non-wine drinkers" and "reasonably priced considering the neighbourhood". As you might hope, there's an "exceptional" list of vintages "across a wide range of price points" with "random treasures at reasonable prices", delivered by "charming and engaged staff" who "can actually have a conversation about a given bottle". "Can't recommend it more highly!" / W1J 7LT; noblerot.co.uk; noblerotmayfair.

NOBLE ROT SOHO W1 £64 454

2 GREEK STREET 020 7183 8190 5–2A

"Replacement for the beloved Gay Hussar" – Dan Keeling and Mark Andrew's 2021 resurrection of this famous Soho site has pulled off the amazingly difficult task of being almost as popular as their Bloomsbury original. "Everything about this establishment is wonderful, but the wine list elevates it to the exceptional" – "the care that goes into it is astonishing" ("I could happily spend the rest of my life working through it!"). The hearty food is "always enjoyable" too and "expertly served" by particularly "knowledgeable" and "friendly staff" in "the delightful atmosphere of this gorgeous old restaurant, which has been brought back to life by the Noble Rot team". Top Top – "amazing value set lunch". / W1D 4NB; noblerot.co.uk; noblerotsoho; Mon-Sat 9.30 pm.

NOBU, METROPOLITAN HOTEL W1 £134 432

19 OLD PARK LANE 020 7447 4747 3–4A

"Still the best Nobu for food in my opinion" – many "superb" meals are still reported at Nobu Matsuhisa's first London outpost: the first floor of a boutique hotel on Park Lane (famous, in part, for Boris Becker once having fathered a child here in between courses in a cupboard off the main dining room). "The original black cod is definitely better than the many rip offs that abound" and its mix of sushi, tacos, steak, raw seafood and other luxurious Nikkei bites inspires uniformly high ratings. "The uninviting room undeniably needs a make-over"… but people have been saying that almost since it first opened. / W1K 1LB; www.noburestaurants.com; nobuoldparklane; Sun-Wed 10 pm, Thu-Sat 10.30 pm.

NOBU PORTMAN SQUARE W1 £114 433

22 PORTMAN SQUARE
020 3988 5888 2–1A

Nobu Matsuhisa's Marylebone three-year-old is higher-rated but less well-known than the original Nobu in Park Lane. Decor-wise, it's more modern in style. Food-wise, it purveys the same, wizard Japanese-fusion cuisine for which the brand is internationally famous: most notably mesmerising sushi plus sensational signature dishes such as Black Cod. Practically all reports acknowledge the essential trade-off here: "it really cannot be beaten for deliciousness… but boy do you pay for it!" / W1H 7BG; london-portman.nobuhotels.com; nobulondonportman; Sun-Thu 10 pm, Fri & Sat 10.30 pm.

NOBU SHOREDITCH EC2 £127

10-50 WILLOW ST 020 3818 3790 13–1B

Despite its famous brand, this chic Shoreditch-fringe boutique hotel has struggled to make waves since its 2017 launch (no survey feedback this year), and in summer 2023 relaunched (re-relaunched?) its basement restaurant with adjoining sunken garden as a 'destination bar', complete with 'world-renowned Nobu signature dishes, small plates and sushi' and a regular DJ. As well as the wizard Nikkei bits, options include the 'newly launched Monaka… a lightweight flat rice crispbread, branded with the Nobu logo and stuffed with fresh toppings'. / EC2A 4BH; london-shoreditch.nobuhotels.com; nobulondonshoreditch; Mon-Wed 10 pm, Thu-Sat 10.30 pm, Sun 11 am.

NOCI £45 323

4-6 ISLINGTON GREEN, N1
020 3937 5343 9–3D
CIRCUS ROAD WEST, SW11
020 3540 8252 11–1C
THE BOWER, 211 OLD STREET, EC1
020 3780 0750 13–1A

"The best vitello tonnato ever tasted" was one fan's recommendation at Louis Korovilas's Islington yearling, which serves a range of affordable pasta alongside Italian street-food dishes. Another supporter "raved about Noci last year, but found a recent lunch a little disappointing with cooking lacking the earlier refinement"; but even they still thought "this is a cut above the usual Italian fare and still something of a find". In any case, Korovilas must be doing something right, as in May 2023 (too late for our survey) he launched a new offshoot in Battersea Power Station; to be followed swiftly in August 2023 by one in Shoreditch.

NOIZÉ W1 £105 453

39 WHITFIELD ST 020 7323 1310 2–1C

"Hidden in a quiet street in Fitzrovia", Mathieu Germond "continues to oversee a brilliant operation", on the site that was once Dabbous, RIP. An "imaginative French-orientated menu" is well-realised ("but not exceptional or pointlessly innovative") and service is "truly exemplary". "But the real bonus is the interesting wine list expertly put together and presented by Mathieu himself", who is "not only completely charming but also hugely knowledgeable" and "it always includes something new and unusual to try". / W1T 2SF; www.noize-restaurant.co.uk; noize_restaurant; Wed-Fri, Tue, Sat 10 pm.

NOMAD LONDON WC2 £124 225

4 BOW STREET 020 3906 1600 5–2D

The 2021 opening of a London branch of New York's hip NoMad hotel brought a "wonderful transformation" of Covent Garden's Bow Street Magistrates' Court "into a bright, airy venue with lots of choice" for eating and drinking. Its "fab main dining room", 'The Atrium', is a three-storey-high glass-ceilinged space with an extra-glam atmosphere, although "sometimes the food doesn't match the setting", being merely "OK, but no more than that". The appointment of Lancashire-born chef Michael Yates, formerly of Northcote and Holland's famous Oud Sluis, may lift its game. / WC2E 7AH; www.thenomadhotel.com; thenomadhotel; Mon-Sat 10.30 pm, Sun 5 pm.

NOODLE & SNACK W1 £33 442

145 CLEVELAND STREET
020 3161 0735 2–1B

"Please whatever you do, don't dress up to dine here!" – "This is a tiny, cheap hole-in-the-wall" near Great Portland Street tube, serving "comfort noodles for Chinese students

Mayha W1

nd others": "magical broth that feels utterly uthentic and packed with flavour (we bsolutely wolfed ours down!)". "Everyone ets a warm welcome" too! (The Times's Giles oren is also a fan – "it drew tears of nostalgia or a 1970s Shenyang childhood that I never ad"). / W1T 6QH; Mon-Sun 9 pm.

OOR JAHAN £52 343

A BINA GARDENS, SW5
20 7373 6522 6–2B
6 SUSSEX PLACE, W2
20 7402 2332 7–1D

his family-run "stalwart" of the Earl's Court-outh Ken dining scene (and its 'Noor Jahan II' ayswater offshoot) has built a strong following or its "consistently good" Indian dishes over e past 60 years – and the smattering of celebs nd royals among its guests (Angelina Jolie, rince William…) has not gone to its head: after all this time it remains your typical curry ouse". / www.noorjahansw5.co.uk.

OPI W1 £97 322

1-22 WARWICK ST 020 7494 9584 4–3B

he Soho flagship of Israeli writer/chef Yotam ttolenghi is conceived as a step up from his eli-diners, and the food is generally considered wonderful". But a note of disappointment has ept in with complaints along the lines of "bad ervice" or "overpriced vegetables and wine" – I really don't know what all the fuss is about". W1B 5NE; ottolenghi.co.uk; nopi_restaurant; on-Sat 10.30 pm.

HE NORFOLK ARMS VC1 £53 332

3 LEIGH ST 020 7388 3937 9–4C

Looking like a typical London pub, but serving good range of tapas" makes this Victorian ozer in the backstreets between King's Cross nd Russell Square a little out of the ordinary. ut "while some dishes are very good, others an be a bit hit and miss". / WC1H 9EP; ww.norfolkarms.co.uk; Tue-Sat, Mon 11 pm, Sun).30 pm.

ORMA W1 £89 434

CHARLOTTE STREET
203 995 6224 2–1C

Feeling like a serious step up from your un-of-the-mill Italian, but not breaking the ank" – this unusual and stylish venture is spin-off from the Stafford Hotel. There's a Sicilian focus to the menu and the food is "absolutely delicious". "Booths make it a great spot for a business lunch – intimate enough to be quiet in a bustling restaurant", with very attentive service. Top Menu Tip – "dangerously delectable focaccia". / W1T 2LS; www.normalondon.com; norma_ldn; Mon-Sat 10.30 pm.

NORMAH'S W2 £29 332

23-25 QUEENSWAY MARKET
07771 630828 7–2C

"If you love Malaysian food, head for Normah's" – "a small and basic café serving street food at incredibly low prices". It's "a little difficult to find in a nondescript Bayswater market, but so worth the effort" as your host, Normah Abd Hamid, "is likely to both greet you and cook your meal" – taking "great care to produce delicious food". / W2 4QP; www.normahs.co.uk; normahs_place; Tue-Sat 9 pm.

NORMANS CAFE N19 £27 444

167 JUNCTION ROAD NO TEL 9–1C

"Proper caff food done right" in Tufnell Park by two highly skilled chefs "will whizz you back in time to your school days or nursery – except I don't remember it ever tasting this good!". Elliot Kaye and Richard Hayes quit their jobs at Leroy and Lyle's four years ago to "make the best fry-up in London" at this "utterly brilliant" re-creation of the traditional greasy spoon. Top Tip – "arrive early as there is no booking system, so the queue is often around the corner for this tiny cafe". / N19 5PZ; www.normanscafe.co.uk; normanscafelondon; Wed-Sun 3 pm.

EL NORTE W1 £108 333

19-20 DOVER STREET
020 3154 8182 3–3C

Madrid-born Arian and Alberto Zandi added this new Mayfair venture to their portfolio (alongside Zuaya and Como Garden) in November 2021. On the plus side, results from the Spanish menu can be excellent. On the downside, the bill here can mount and feedback is sufficiently up-and-down to preclude a fully wholehearted endorsement. / W1S 4LP; el-norte.co.uk; elnortelondon; Sun-Thu 12.30 am, Fri & Sat 1.30 am.

NORTH CHINA W3 £43 333

305 UXBRIDGE RD 020 8992 9183 8–1A

"The venerable kingpin of Chinese food in this part of west London is not giving up its crown easily" – opened by the Lou family in the outer reaches of Acton in 1976, it has served "exceptionally tasty Peking-style cuisine" with "considerate service and warm atmosphere" for almost 50 years. / W3 9QU; www.northchina.co.uk; northchinafood; Tue-Sun 10.30 pm.

NORTH SEA FISH WC1 £52 322

7-8 LEIGH ST 020 7387 5892 9–4C

"A hidden gem in the back streets of Bloomsbury" – this traditional chippie has been owned and run by the Beauchamp family for the best part of 50 years, and excels for its "exceptionally good grilled fish" and "super-generous portions" of "normal fish 'n' chips". / WC1H 9EW; www.northseafishrestaurant.co.uk; thenorthseafish; Mon-Sat 9.30 pm.

THE NORTHALL, CORINTHIA LONDON WC2 £143 333

10A NORTHUMBERLAND AVE
020 7321 3100 2–3C

"Incredible flower displays" add to the airy and gracious style of this comfortable dining room, within the plush five star near Embankment station. Partly because of the fame of Kerridge's next door, it has struggled over the years to raise its profile, but can be a handy option for a stately, high-quality West End setting. Top Top – in particular, "the set lunch is excellent value". / WC2N 5AE; www.corinthia.com; corinthialondon; Tue-Sat 9.30 pm, Sun 4 pm, Mon 10.30 am.

NOTTO W1 £62 433

198-200 PICCADILLY 020 3034 2190 3–3D

"It seems unlikely to find such good food at such a touristy location", but "the lovely homemade pasta" at Phil Howard and Louis Korovilas's bright and efficient new pasta spot is "a revelation" – "very tasty Italian small plates at astonishingly reasonable prices for Piccadilly", from a "focused menu of pastas and dessert". (It was originally to be known as Otto – after Howard's lockdown pasta business – but lost a legal battle with 'an unnamed existing venture with a similar name'). BREAKING NEWS. In October 2023, a second 90-cover branch was announced to open in November 2023 in Covent Garden's Henrietta Street. / W1J 9EZ; www.nottopastabar.com; nottopastabar; Tue-Sat 10 pm, Sun 8 pm.

NOVIKOV (ASIAN RESTAURANT) W1 £140 224

50A BERKELEY STREET
020 7399 4330 3–3C

Thin feedback this year on this glossy Eurotrash playground in Mayfair – London outpost of

Arkady Novikov's large restaurant empire (fun fact – according to Forbes in Nov 2022, this includes what used to be the Krispy Kreme Russian franchise, rebranded post-sanctions as 'Krunchy Dream'). Its sushi, seared seafood and other luxe Pan-Asian bites remain well-rated, if at prices designed for oligarchs. (There's also an imposing, ambitious dining room with an Italian menu to the rear that no-one mentions much). / W1J 8HA; www.novikovrestaurant.co.uk; novikovrestaurant; Mon-Sun midnight.

NUMA NW7 £42 342

8 THE BROADWAY 020 8912 1678 1–*1A*

This "Middle Eastern small plates sharing concept" is a "fantastic addition to Mill Hill Broadway", with "loads of veggie options" and "really tasty food" from brunch through to dinner. Founder Tomer Vanuna and head chef Michael Levi were school friends in Israel; Numa apparently means 'so what' in Hebrew. / NW7 3LL; www.numacafe.co.uk; numacafe; Tue-Sat 11 pm, Sun 10 pm.

NUMERO UNO SW11 £69 242

139 NORTHCOTE ROAD
020 7978 5837 11–*2C*

"Engaging service" is the strong suit at this "solid neighbourhood Italian" that has been a fixture on Clapham's Northcote Road for many years. The menu offers "no surprises", but the cooking is "more than adequate". / SW11 6PX; www.numerounorestaurant.co.uk; numerounoclapham; Mon-Sun 11 pm.

NUOVI SAPORI SW6 £57 333

295 NEW KING'S RD 020 7736 3363 11–*1B*

Small and family-owned, this "always reliable quality Italian" near Parsons Green wins consistently high ratings for its "friendly service" and "cheerful ambience". / SW6 4RE; www.nuovisaporilondon.co.uk; Mon-Sat 11 pm.

NUSR-ET STEAKHOUSE, THE PARK TOWER KNIGHTSBRIDGE SW1 £194 111

101 KNIGHTSBRIDGE 01821 687738 6–*1D*

With the closure of Nusret Gökçe's NYC branch, the vultures have started to gather around this Knightsbridge venture ('Is Salt Bae's empire beginning to crumble?' – Daily Mail, June 2023). The outlook is not super-positive. Our review last year suggested it was "suitable only for chavs and vulgarians" and our volume of reports this year was significantly reduced; while in summer 2023, the venue was close to being London's lowest-ranking restaurant on TripAdvisor (quite an achievement!). In a sign that suggests management also think change is needed, in July 2023 they cut prices with the introduction of a set lunch menu from £39 per person and burger and fries for 'just' £45. / SW1X 7RN; www.nusr-et.com.tr; nusr_et_steakhouse__; Mon-Sat 1.30 am, Sun 1 am.

O'VER £68 332

1 NORRIS STREET, ST JAMES'S MARKET, SW1 020 7930 9664 4–*4D*
44-46 SOUTHWARK STREET, SE1
020 7378 9933 10–*4B*

"Bouncy, chewy, doughy deliciousness – the crust is to die for" at this pizzeria that uses seawater to make its dough. "The lovely little restaurant in Borough doesn't look anything special during the day, but in the evening it's very romantic with candles and soft lighting". Some reckon "the food in St James's is nothing like as good as the original in Borough". / www.overuk.com; over_uk.

OAK £68 333

243 GOLDHAWK RD, W12
020 8741 7700 8–*1B*
137 WESTBOURNE PARK RD, W2
020 7221 3355 7–*1B*

"Great Roman-style crispy pizzas" along with a full selection of tapas, starters, "ever-changing Italian main courses" and a "fun Notting Hill vibe" ensure that this smart pub conversion is "a definite step up from the pizza chains" while "still reasonable value". Two offshoots further west – the Oak W12 near Ravenscourt Park and the Bird in Hand at Brook Green – repeat the trick. / www.theoaklondon.com; theoaklondon.

OAK & POPPY NW3 £67 343

48 ROSSLYN HILL 020 3479 4888 9–*1A*

"A useful, casual-dining addition to the area" – this old Hampstead village pub (formerly the Rosslyn Arms) was brought back to life in Autumn 2022, with a "stylish fit out" featuring a retractable glass ceiling. Fans say it's now the "perfect neighbourhood café/restaurant", with "the loveliest staff and reliably good food". / NW3 1NH; www.oakandpoppy.co.uk; oakandpoppyhampstead; Mon-Sat 11 pm, Sun 10.30 pm.

OBICÀ MOZZARELLA BAR, PIZZA E CUCINA £61 332

19-20 POLAND ST, W1
020 3327 7070 4–*1C*
1 WEST WINTERGARDEN, 35 BANK ST, E14
020 7719 1532 12–*1C*
UNIT 4 5-7 LIMEBURNERS LANE,, EC4
020 3327 0984 10–*2A*

These "upscalish Italians" – part of an international chain – serve pizza, pasta and other lighter dishes, featuring the trademark ingredient. It can be that the "quality of the food is a pleasant surprise"; they inspired nothing but positive feedback this year. / obica.com; obicamozzarellabar; E14 & EC4 Closed Sun.

OBLIX, THE SHARD SE1 £116 334

31 ST THOMAS ST 020 7268 6700 10–*4C*

"You book for the view, which is obviously incredible" at this 32nd-floor venue, run by Rainer Becker (of Zuma and many other top London restaurants). Like most places with a stunning outlook and "special occasion" suitability, it often takes flak for its sky-high pricing to match. This was absent in (admittedly thin) feedback this year, though, and the luxurious outputs from its open kitchen (with Josper oven, charcoal grill and rotisserie) were well-rated. (For cocktails or afternoon tea, head to Oblix East). / SE1 9RY; www.oblixrestaurant.com; oblixrestaurant; Mon-Sun 10.30 pm.

OCHRE, THE NATIONAL GALLERY WC2 £56 324

TRAFALGAR SQUARE
020 7747 2525 2–*2C*

It's "nice to find a good restaurant in a museum", and the National Gallery's latest, year-old incumbent within its atmospheric ground floor dining room has provided a step-up just in time to compete with the revamped culinary offerings at the NPG next door. The snazzily updated interior by architects Red Dee makes a great setting for a "beautiful afternoon tea", and there's an opulent bar for stronger drinks. / WC2N 5DN; www.nationalgallery.org.uk; nationalgallery; Sun-Wed 6 pm, Thu-Sat 11 pm.

ODETTE'S NW1 £83 332

130 REGENTS PARK ROAD
020 7586 8569 9–*3B*

Chef-patron Bryn Williams produces a "small and well-executed menu" showcasing north Wales at this high-quality local in lovely Primrose Hill, which he's owned for over 15 years now. But while it still attracts many favourable reviews, the magical atmosphere that was a hallmark of its original incarnation (it was founded nearly 50 years ago) has "faded" in more recent times. / NW1 8XL; www.odettesprimrosehill.com; odettesrestaurant; Thu-Sat, Wed 9 pm, Sun 8.30 pm.

OGNISKO RESTAURANT SW7 £63 345

55 PRINCE'S GATE, EXHIBITION ROAD
020 7589 0101 6–*1C*

This "opulent, high-ceilinged dining room" within a Polish émigré club in South Kensington ("a stone's throw from the Royal Albert Hall") provides a "truly elegant" backdrop for a meal. "Inviting and cosmopolitan in atmosphere", it is "unusually, equally good in summer and winter" thanks to its "delightful" covered rear outside terrace, which provides "a memorable location on a warm day". "Delicious" Polish fodder comes in "hearty" portions and "without any grand prices despite the grand setting"; there's a wide range of affordable central and eastern European wines; and "the cocktails and vodkas are well worth a shout out". / SW7 2PG; www.ogniskorestaurant.co.uk; ogniskorestaurant; Mon-Sat 9.45 pm, Sun 8.45 pm.

OKA £57 342

KINGLY COURT, 1 KINGLY COURT, W1
020 7734 3556 4–*2B*
19 NEW CAVENDISH STREET, W1
020 7486 4388 3–*1A*
251 KING'S ROAD, SW3
020 7349 8725 6–*3C*
71 REGENTS PARK RD, NW1
020 7483 2072 9–*3B*
88 CHURCH ROAD, SW13
020 8741 8577 11–*1A*

"A top tip for sushi and other interesting Japanese dishes" – this 11-year-old group from Israeli-born Ohad Kastro offers an "excellent quality and variety of options" that are "so much better than standard rivals" – and each branch "manages to feel like a comfy 'local', despite there being others around town". / www.okarestaurant.co.uk; okarestaurant.

THE OLD BULL & BUSH NW3 £59 224

NORTH END RD 020 8905 5456 9–*1A*

This renovated Victorian tavern makes a "great location" for refuelling "if you've been walking on Hampstead Heath". Its fame rests on Florrie Forde's music-hall song from the Edwardian era, when day-tripping Cockneys would visit, not on its cooking – the latter does have its fans, but there is also the view that it is "standard pub grub and rather indifferent" at that. Top Tip – "if you use the car park, make sure you check-in with the computer screen at the bar or risk a penalty charge". / NW3 7HE; www.thebullandbush.co.uk; oldbullandbush; Mon & Tue, Thu-Sat 11 pm, Wed 10 pm, Sun 10.30 pm.

OLIVETO SW1 £78 332

61 ELIZABETH ST 020 7730 0074 2–*4A*

Whether you choose pizza, pasta or a main dish, this all-rounder in Sardinian Mauro Sanna's smart Belgravia group "never disappoints". Following a fire, it has moved a few doors to the premises formerly occupied by stablemate Olivocarne (RIP). A major attraction is the "wine list to delight lovers of off-beat, small producer wines". / SW1W 9PP; www.olivorestaurants.com; olivorestaurants; Mon-Sun 10.30 pm.

OLIVO SW1 £87 332

21 ECCLESTON STREET
020 7730 2505 2–*4B*

In its day a pioneer of Italian 'peasant' cuisine in the capital, Mauro Sanna's original Belgravia Sardinian remains "steady and always reliable" in its 35th year – "this restaurant has never disappointed". If it's "quite pricey", that has never been an issue for the well-heeled locals who ensure it is perennially busy. / SW1W 9LX; www.olivorestaurants.com; olivorestaurants; Tue-Sun 10.30 pm.

OLIVOMARE SW1 £89 432

10 LOWER BELGRAVE STREET
020 7730 9022 2–*4B*

"Reliable Sardinian shellfish and pasta" win consistent high marks for this seafood specialist in Mauro Sanno's smart Belgravia group, which has been feeding well-heeled locals for 15 years. The pavement seating in the summer is a better bet than the sleek but stark modern interior. / SW1W 0LJ; www.olivorestaurants.com; olivorestaurants; Mon-Sun 10.30 pm.

OLLEY'S SE24 £39 342

65-69 NORWOOD RD
020 8671 8259 11–*2D*

"Love coming here", say fans of the "excellent fish 'n' chips" served for 36 years by Harry Niazi opposite Brockwell Park – where it's "great to eat a takeaway". It takes its name from Oliver Twist, in which Dickens refers to Londoners' favourite dish. / SE24 9AA; www.olleys.info; olleysfishexperience; Tue-Sun 9.30 pm.

OLYMPIC STUDIOS SW13 £59 223

117-123 CHURCH ROAD
020 8912 5170 11–*1A*

For "Barnes at brunch" – or as a "very useful and convenient place to eat before a film" – the "family-friendly" dining room in the "nice surroundings" of Barnes's iconic recording-studio- turned-indie-cinema "serves its purpose" (and the outdoor terrace further adds to its appeal as a social hub in decent weather). But the menu is "disappointingly limited and dull, even if pretty well executed". / SW13 9HL; www.olympiccinema.co.uk; olympicstudios; Mon-Thu 10 pm, Fri & Sat 10.30 pm, Sun 9 pm.

OLYMPUS FISH N3 £44 342

140-144 BALLARDS LN
020 8371 8666 1–*1B*

"Always fresh and good-value fish 'n' chips" – cooked "over charcoal as an alternative" and backed up by a selection of Turkish small plates – ensures this 25-year-old family-run operation remains "an attractive option" for eating in Finchley. / N3 2PA; www.olympusrestaurant.co.uk; Mon-Sun 9.30 pm.

OMBRA E2 £62

1 VYNER ST 020 8981 5150 14–*2B*

A superb location – on the Regent's Canal and complete with heated terrace – helps justify the continued inclusion of this Hackney Italian. Feedback is too thin and nuanced for a full rating this year – according to one fan it's "still good all round, but the ratio of hype to expectations is high". / E2 9DG; www.ombrabar.restaurant; ombrabar.restaurant; Mon, Thu-Sat 10 pm, Sun 3 pm.

108 BRASSERIE W1 £77 23

108 MARYLEBONE LANE
020 7969 3900 2–*1A*

This "well-run spot" with outdoor seating attached to a hotel on Marylebone Lane makes a "very useful venue for lunch when in the vicinity", with an offering that "seems to have something for everyone". "It's nothing exceptional in one sense, but a menu of properly prepared classics is the sort of thing that sounds easy but needs to be done well… and it is". / W1U 2QE; www.108brasserie.com; 108marylebonelane; Mon-Sat midnight, Sun 6 pm

104 RESTAURANT W2 £129 54

104 CHEPSTOW ROAD
020 3417 4744 7–*1B*

A focused menu of "high-quality ingredients with excellent provenance and preparation" together with "attentive and adaptive service" continue to win praise for Richard Wilkins's small (seating a maximum of 16) venue, which has an unobtrusive frontage on a corner-site in the Notting Hill/Bayswater borders. It has a comprehensive wine list, running to the likes of clarets and burgundies at over £1,000 per bottle. / W2 5QS; www.104restaurant.com; 104restaurant; Wed-Sun 9.30 pm.

101 THAI KITCHEN W6 £42 33

352 KING ST 020 8746 6888 8–*2B*

This "exciting local gem" near Stamford Brook serves "excellent Thai cuisine in a no-nonsense setting", attracting aficionados from far and wide who warm to an "authenticity" that makes it "almost an 'in-country' experience". The uninitiated may miss the point other than the good prices. Top Tip – "if they say something is hot, believe them!" / W6 0RX; www.101thaikitchen.uk; 101thaikitchen; Tue-Sun 10.30 pm.

1 LOMBARD STREET EC3 £94 22

1 LOMBARD ST 020 7929 6611 10–*3C*

"For a dependable City business breakfast or lunch venue", Soren Jessen's stalwart brasserie, in the beating heart of the Square Mile, is the epitome of a useful amenity for dealmakers, even if "the large, cavernous space remains a little tricky" ("the room is bright and airy, but depending on your table can feel cramped and noisy"). "Its modern European menu covers all the bases reliably. It does what it's meant to, but you are never coming away with a knockout meal. BTW, that's an observation not a criticism". / EC3V 9AA; www.1lombardstreet.com; 1lombardstreet; Mon-Fr 11 pm.

23V, FENWICK W1 £60 322

3 NEW BOND STREET
20 8132 9088 3–2B

The vegan sushi is a work of art" at this outlet the basement of Fenwick's department store Mayfair from Alexis Gauthier (the French ne-dining-chef-turned-evangelist for plant-ased eating). He has raided global cuisines r his concoctions – "the vegan burgers are orgeous" – but it's the Japanese specials which icit the most feedback, including "all-you-can-at sushi" (in two hours). / W1S 1RQ; 123vegan.).uk; 123vegan_w1; Mon-Wed 6 pm, Thu-Sat 30 pm, Sun 3.30 am.

NLY FOOD AND COURSES VC2 £72

LITTLE ESSEX STREET
7949 259067 2–2D

obbie Lorraine has upped sticks from rixton with his Del Boy-inspired pop-up – a itty, multi-course trip back in time to the uisine of the 80s and 90s (duck-liver paté, rawn cocktail…). This new home is part f a Grade II listed pub just off the Strand: ot to be confused with Ye Olde Cheshire heese on Fleet Street, which is about ten inutes' stroll away (although both claim ickens as a former patron). No survey edback as yet – reports please! / WC2R 3LD; ww.onlyfoodandcourses.com; onlyfoodandcourses; hu-Sat 10.30 pm.

ES 110 DE TAILLEVENT V1 £90 444

6 CAVENDISH SQUARE
20 3141 6016 3–1B

If you love wine… heaven!" – a "huge list lmost 2,000 bins)", "some with no mark-up om merchant prices" and including 110 vailable by the glass (hence the name), is the g attraction at this plush Cavendish Square enue from a famous Parisian operation. It inally seems to have found its footing as a al restaurant, not just somewhere that serves od as an afterthought to the wine list – there's me very good cooking here". / W1G 9DD; ww.les-110-taillevent-london.com; 110london; Ion-Sat 10.30 pm.

PERA TAVERN VC2 £60 322

3 CATHERINE STREET
20 7836 3680 5–3D

Handily located near the Royal Opera ouse", this converted pub serves Spanish and alian-style small plates of "food that's just a bit etter than its local competition" in the heart Covent Garden. It is "not the best of the alt Yard chain, but good for a quick pre-show eal". / WC2B 5JS; www.saltyardgroup.co.uk; peratavernldn; Mon-Sat 11 pm, Sun 8 pm.

OPSO W1 £101 333

10 PADDINGTON ST 020 7487 5088 2–1A

"Posh Greek food" – "very nice sharing plates" from a "well-designed menu" where "delicious moussaka" rubs shoulders with "caviar" and top steaks – wins praise for this Marylebone venture, as does its "great wine list". It's a sibling to INO (see also), and likewise run by an Athens-based team who hold a Michelin star for that city's 'Funky Gourmet'. / W1U 5QL; www.opso.co.uk; opso_london; Mon-Fri 11.30 pm, Sat 10.30 pm, Sun 10 pm.

ORANGE PEKOE SW13 £40 343

3 WHITE HART LN 020 8876 6070 11–1A

This pretty and professionally run tea shop close to the Thames in Barnes excels for its cakes and afternoon teas (for which booking is essential at busy times), although it no longer generates the copious feedback of earlier years. / SW13 0PX; www.orangepekoeteas.com; orangepekoeteas; Mon-Sun 5 pm.

THE ORANGE TREE N20 £63 223

7 TOTTERIDGE VILLAGE
020 8343 7031 1–1B

This smart 'country pub' overlooking the village pond in Totteridge, far North London, boasts a menu that ranges from steaks to sourdough pizza. But marks suffered this year on the basis of one or two reports saying recent standards have been "all a bit 'meh'". / N20 8NX; www.theorangetreetotteridge.co.uk; Mon-Sat 11 pm, Sun 10 pm.

THE ORANGERY BAR & KITCHEN EC2

5 SUN STREET 020 3988 7709 13–2A

A glass-roofed atrium dining room that's part of a new boutique hotel (created from six Georgian townhouses) on the City/Shoreditch fringes, that opened last year. No survey feedback as yet, but it looks well styled and potentially a useful option in the area either for a cocktail, or for a meal with a flexible all-day menu served: first a breakfast selection; later in the day of small and sharing dishes. (There's also a restaurant here serving South East Asian food called Quercus). / EC2A 2EP; www.sunstreethotel.com; sunstreetlondon; Mon-Fri 10 pm, Sat & Sun 2.45 pm.

ORASAY W11 £63 544

31 KENSINGTON PARK ROAD
020 7043 1400 7–1A

"Jackson Boxer's sublime Notting Hill outpost remains an out-and-out favourite, from the laid- back vibe to the small but perfectly formed menu" – that's the unanimous view on his "beautifully lit and cosy" four-year-old: a "consistent and fantastic neighbourhood restaurant" serving superb, "inventive" small plates all at a "very reasonable price". Top Menu Tip – "special kudos has to go to the caviar served simply with potato chips and sour cream just as it should be". / W11 2EU; orasay.london; orasay.london; Tue-Sat 10 pm.

OREN E8 £70 442

89 SHACKLEWELL LANE
020 7916 6114 14–1A

"Lovely and adventurous", Tel Aviv-style small plates "zinging with flavour" draw a busy crowd to Israeli chef Oden Oren's 30-seater in Dalston – an immediate hit from its opening in 2019. It's a "charming" place, but there's one catch: "it's hard to hear your companions over the din". A spin-off deli opened at Broadway Market in early 2023. / E8 2EB; www.orenlondon.com; Tue-Sat 11 pm.

ORIENT LONDON W1 £55 443

15 WARDOUR STREET
020 7989 8880 5–3A

With its "marvellous selection of dim sum" raised to a "fantastic" level; "amicable and chatty service"; and its "well-spaced tables", this low-key-looking venue "stands a cut above the usual Chinatown standard" in all respects. / W1D 6PH; www.orientlondon.com; orientlondon; Sun-Thu 11 pm, Fri & Sat 11.30 pm.

ORMER MAYFAIR BY SOFIAN, FLEMINGS MAYFAIR HOTEL W1 £149 443

7-12 HALF MOON STREET
020 7016 5601 3–4B

Although this luxurious Mayfair hotel dates from the 1850s, its swish basement dining room owes its looks to the 1930s. Under chef Sofian Msetfi, the "fabulous" cuisine (choose either a 6-course 'market' menu or 9-course 'tasting' option) continues to achieve high ratings and even the weakest report this year awarded "full marks for presentation and service". "A friend of mine who swears not to visit hotel dining rooms granted it high praise after our dinner there!" / W1J 7BH; www.flemings-mayfair.co.uk; flemingsmayfair; Tue-Sat 9 pm.

ORO DI NAPOLI W5 £41 442

6 THE QUADRANT, LITTLE EALING LANE
020 3632 5580 1–3A

"The pizza is phenomenal" – "always tasty, with fresh ingredients well cooked" – at this popular Ealing independent, whose offerings are named after Neapolitan heroes ranging from Maradona to Bud Spencer (the spaghetti western actor born Carlo Pedersoli in Naples). / W5 4EE; www.lorodinapoli-ealing.com; lorodinapoliealing; Tue, Sat, Wed-Fri 10 pm.

ORRERY W1 £100 224

55 MARYLEBONE HIGH ST
020 7616 8000 2–1A

A "gorgeous bright room, overlooking a churchyard" – "especially lovely on sunny days when you can get a terrace seat on the roof" –

this D&D London property above Marylebone's Conran shop provides a classy and intimate setting. It's no longer seen as a particularly gastro destination, as once it was, but the kitchen is currently putting in an "expensive but reliable" performance that avoids criticism and makes it a potentially useful choice, especially for a slightly "formal" or upscale occasion. / W1U 5RB; www.orrery-restaurant.co.uk; the_orrery; Mon-Sat 10 pm, Sun 9 pm. SRA – accredited

OSCAR WILDE LOUNGE AT CAFE ROYAL W1 £101 335

68 REGENT ST 020 7406 3333 4–4C

"Gorgeous finger sandwiches, very pretty patisserie" and "fantastic staff" are all par for the course at an upscale afternoon tea, but it's "the opulent surroundings that make it special" in this "beautiful room" – the architecturally dazzling, rococo former Grill Room from 1865, now named after its most famous denizen and a must-visit for gastronomic history buffs. / W1B 4DY; www.hotelcaferoyal.com; hotelcaferoyal; Wed-Sun 5.30 pm.

OSLO COURT NW8 £78 355

CHARLBERT STREET 020 7722 8795 9–3A

"For a birthday there's nowhere better to come, whether you're 80, 90… or older!" – this "fun trip down memory lane" at the foot of a Regent's Park apartment block just goes on and on. A perfectly preserved time capsule from the 1970s ("from the salmon tablecloths and napkins to the recently departed ruched curtains"), you "sit down to crudités with a garlic dip and Melba toast then move onto a three-course meal from an extensive Italian-biassed English menu": "it's the most comforting of comfort food" ("Steak Diane as a main… wonderful!"). Service-wise, it's "a well-oiled machine": "all ages are well looked after, especially the oldest and youngest" and it's a "go-to venue for family celebrations" for a large slice of north London. "Portions are huge" ("even the teenagers in the party struggle with the quantities"), but you must leave space for pud, delivered by Neil "the fabulous dessert waiter, who always 'saves his favourite just for you'!" / NW8 7EN; www.oslocourtrestaurant.co.uk; oslocourt; Mon-Sat 11 pm.

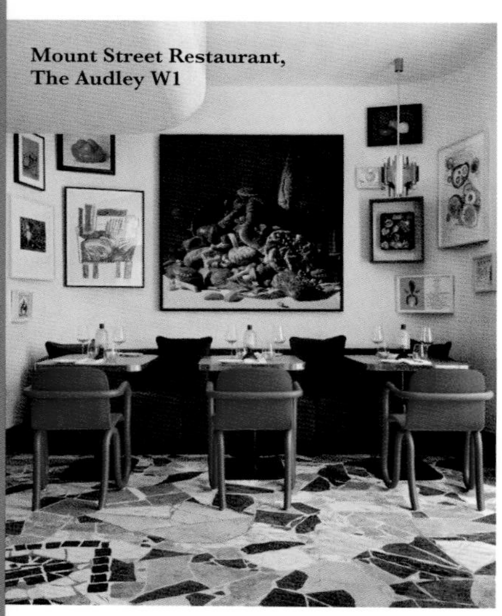

Mount Street Restaurant, The Audley W1

OSTERIA ANTICA BOLOGNA SW11 £67 332

23 NORTHCOTE RD 020 7978 4771 11–2C

This rustic Italian trattoria is a "reliable local favourite" which has fed generations of families in Clapham's 'Nappy Valley' over the past 30 years. The hearty cuisine "rarely disappoints", although the venue "can get extremely loud on a busy night (speaking volumes for its popularity!)". / SW11 1NG; www.osteria.co.uk; osteriaanticabologna; Tue-Fri 21.45 pm, Sat 10 pm, Sun 8.45 pm.

OSTERIA BASILICO W11 £78 333

29 KENSINGTON PARK RD 020 7727 9957 7–1A

A "local favourite" in Notting Hill for more than 30 years on account of its "always-consistent" cooking, this rustic Italian is the sort of place with something for "every member of the family". It has spawned two offspring in the same street, Essenza and Mediterraneo – an indication of how well it suits the neighbourhood. / W11 2EU; www.osteriabasilico.co.uk; osteriabasilico; Mon-Sun 10.30 pm.

OSTERIA TUFO N4 £66 343

67 FONTHILL RD 020 7272 2911 9–1D

"Crowded, buzzy and fun" – this "atypical Italian" ("one of the waiters even breaks into operatic arias") "round the back of Finsbury Park station is a real neighbourhood gem". "Owned and run by the incredibly friendly and attentive Paola", its "cuisine ranges across Neapolitan and southern Italian in general and is totally unpretentious – it could be described as a little rustic". "No dish disappoints but to nit-pick, the menu hardly changes". / N4 3HZ; www.osteriatufo.co.uk; osteriatufo; Mon-Fri 10.30 pm, Sat 22.30 pm, Sun 8.30 pm.

OTTO'S WC1 £103 554

182 GRAY'S INN ROAD 020 7713 0107 2–1D

"For extravagant excellence", look no further than this "quirky", "proper old-school French" establishment near Gray's Inn, where "splendidly off-the-wall" patron, Otto Tepasse, "is at times both chef, sommelier and confidant". "Old-fashioned silver service, rich dishes (including the signature 'canard à la presse'), a wine cellar that seems to have no limits, and waiters who prep the sauces in front of you" all make for "great theatre and superb food. It's slightly bonkers, but brilliant. Maybe wear elasticated trousers!" Top Menu Tip – "the scallops sealed in their shells, with the obligatory caviar, with puff pastry is a dish of the year". / WC1X 8EW; www.ottos-restaurant.com; ottos_restaurant; Wed-Fri, Tue, Sat 10 pm.

OTTOLENGHI £71 33

28 PAVILION ROAD, SW1 020 3824 2818 6–2D
63 MARYLEBONE LANE, W1 020 3148 1040 2–1A
63 LEDBURY RD, W11 020 7727 1121 7–1
287 UPPER ST, N1 020 7288 1454 9–2D
50 ARTILLERY PAS, E1 020 7247 1999 10–2D

"Stunning salads, amazing pastries" and a "lovely variety of interesting prepared dishes" have stood the test of time at Yotam Ottolenghi's "vibrant" deli-cafés – still hugely popular 22 years on from the launch of the first in Notting HIll. The Israeli-born chef and writer has had an enormous influence on the way people shop, eat and cook, helping to create a whole category of modern Middle Eastern cookery and "totally living up to his reputation as a leading expert in vegetarian cuisine" – even though his premises serve meat and fish. An occasional quibble – "the prices? Too high for a few stalks of broccoli even takin into account the undoubtedly skills of the Chef!" / www.ottolenghi.co.uk; ottolenghi.

THE OWO SW1

57 WHITEHALL PLACE AWAITING TEL 2–3C

A mega new hotel for London sees the Old War Office on Whitehall – in which Winston Churchill made many of the most important decisions of World War II – being taken over by Raffles, no less (their first venture in Europe and the Hinduja Group, to open in late 2023 a a new 125 bedroom property. It will have nine new restaurants, of which we list the five most notable individually: Café Lapérouse, Endo Kazutoshi, Langosteria, Mauro Colagreco and Paper Moon (see also). Other options include Mauro's Table and a fine high-ceilinge brasserie called 'Saison' – which fall under the Colagreco umbrella – as well as The Drawing Room (lounge and all-day dining) and Guards Bar. / SW1A 2EU; www.theowo.london; theowo.london.

OXO TOWER, RESTAURANT SE1 £113 11

BARGE HOUSE ST 020 7803 3888 10–3A

"The view is incredible, especially in the evening" from the posh section of this South Bank landmark – "anything with a view of St Paul's wins high marks in the romantic stakes". But too many of those acknowledging the "wonderful location" feel it "needs a revamp", or find the experience "very overpriced for the quality of food and service… One can't help but feel that OXO Tower trades off of its name and outlook rather than the actual virtues of its fering". / SE1 9PH; www.harveynichols.com; xo_tower; Mon-Sun 9.30 pm. SRA – 3 stars

XO TOWER, BRASSERIE E1 £92 113

ARGE HOUSE ST 020 7803 3888 10–3A

A table right by the windows here – verlooking the river – is frankly still one of the est restaurant views to be had in London"; nd some diners feel that the brasserie at is long-established Art Deco landmark rovides a good all-round experience. It ill gives rise to more than its fair share of sappointments, though, and the perennial omplaint that "you get a wonderful vista but very disappointing experience". / SE1 9PH; ww.oxotowerrestaurant.co.uk; oxo_tower; Mon-un 9.30 pm. SRA – 3 stars

HE OYSTERMEN EAFOOD KITCHEN & BAR VC2 £79 432

2 HENRIETTA ST 020 7240 4417 5–3D

Constantly updated on blackboards, you nd a selection of fresh oysters, crab, lobster, her seafood, and fish to choose from" at this brilliant little place" in Covent Garden, which despite its location in the central touristic area, oesn't feel expensive". "Tables and chairs e a bit basic" though – it's "pleasant and onvivial" enough, but "you do pretty much ave to accept being part of the next table's onversation". / WC2E 8NA; oystermen.co.uk; eoystermen; Tue-Sun, Mon 10 pm.

ZONE COFFEE OASTERS £45 333

MMA STREET, E2 020 7490 1039 14–2B
LEONARD STREET, EC2
20 7490 1039 13–1A

"spectacular breakfast" – "the options are ard to choose from, but none are a poor hoice" – is the top culinary feature at these iwi haunts, whose zeitgeisty vibe and in-house oasting (omg the smell in Shoreditch!) makes em a magnet for a "top notch coffee" at any me of day. / ozonecoffee.co.uk.

ACHAMAMA £76 333

8 THAYER STREET, W1
20 7935 9393 3–1A
3 GREAT EASTERN STREET, EC2
20 7846 9595 13–1B

A super choice to explore Peruvian cuisine with wide variety of dishes available on their tapas-yle menu" (ceviche, croquetas, churros…) these noisy and atmospheric, cocktail-fueled perations in Marylebone and Shoreditch ake for a fun night out: "a great evening was ad by all!" / www.pachamamalondon.com; achamamalondon/.

ADELLA £44 434

SOUTHWARK ST, SE1 NO TEL 10–4C

Love Padella! Both the one in Borough Market nd the one in Shoreditch". "It doesn't need any review as everyone seems to already know it" – a "go-to Italian" with "simple, perfect portions whose comforting flavours just sing" (freshly made every morning on the premises) all at "amazing value" prices. "It's so busy, you need to book way in advance (at least in EC2, unlike SE1 where you need to queue)". "All in all, the whole experience is devoid of pretence: nothing tries to be fancy, it is just damn good." "I take all my friends, all of whom have been impressed… and many have subsequently returned for themselves. Says it all!" / / padella_pasta.

PAHLI HILL BANDRA BHAI W1 £83 332

79-81 MORTIMER STREET
020 8130 0101 3–1C

"Authentic high-quality Indian food", including some "inventive and interesting dishes", are on the menu at the first London venture from New Delhi's Azure Hospitality, on the former site of veteran curry house Gaylord (RIP) near Selfridges. Named after a smart Mumbai district and with the 'Bandra Bhai' cocktail bar downstairs, it's definitely "worth remembering". A chef's counter – launched in summer 2023 – is a new addition. / W1W 7SJ; www.pahlihillbandrabhai.com; pahlihillbandrabhaiuk; Mon-Sat 10 pm.

PALADAR SE1 £66 444

4-5 LONDON ROAD 020 7186 5555 10–4A

"Amazing artworks on the walls" and "great, unobtrusive music" set the tone for an enjoyable and "easygoing" meal at this "fun" Latino in the "increasingly Bohemian neighbourhood" of St George's Circus (not far from Elephant & Castle), which offers "superb South American fusion food" and "lovely Argentinian wines". Founder Charles Tyler was also behind Malay-Asian restaurant Champor-Champor near London Bridge. / SE1 6JZ; www.paladarlondon.com; paladarlondon; Tue-Fri 9.45 pm, Mon 9 pm, Sat 10 pm, Sun 8 pm.

THE PALOMAR W1 £81 332

34 RUPERT STREET 020 7439 8777 4–3D

"Fabulous and unusual Middle East food" has carved a major reputation for Zoë and Layo Paskin's Tel Aviv-inspired grill, on the fringes of Chinatown (where the perches at the counter are the best seats in the house). Since its recent refurb, new menu and expansion, however, ratings have taken a knock: "service is still good and professional, but doesn't seem as cheerful as it used to be, and the new price tags on the dishes may blow your socks off!" / W1D 6DN; www.thepalomar.co.uk; palomarsoho; Mon-Sat 11 pm, Sun 9 pm.

PAPER MOON, THE OWO SW1

57 WHITEHALL PLACE AWAITING TEL
2–3C

One of the first restaurants to be announced at this major new five star in Whitehall, this Italian venue is part of a luxurious international chain that originated in Milan's fashion district in 1977. Nowadays with eight branches such as Doha, Istanbul and the Algarve, the promised offering here is a conventional chic Italian one. / SW1A 2EU; Tue-Sat 10.30 pm.

PAPI E8 £51 423

1F MENTMORE TERRACE
07961 911500 14–2B

"Any restaurant with five orange wines gets my vote!" – initial reports give a green light to this early 2023 newcomer in London Fields: the successor to 'Hot 4 U', a wacky former meal delivery service for hipsters that was born of the pandemic. "The small menu highlights some imaginative dishes" from chef Matthew Scott and there's an "extensive wine list" curated by Charlie Carr. / E8 3PN; papi.restaurant; Wed & Thu 10 pm, Fri & Sat 10.30 pm, Sun 4 pm.

PARADISE W1 £65 433

61 RUPERT STREET NO TEL 4–2D

The "fantastic Sri Lankan food" served at this brutalist-style Soho venue (formerly Spuntino, RIP) is part of the new wave of Asian restaurants, combining inspiration, spices and ancient-grain rice from Sri Lanka with high-quality British ingredients and natural wines from organic producers. Manager Sam Jones used to play rugby for Wasps. / W1D 7PW; www.paradisesoho.com; paradisesoho.

PARADISE HAMPSTEAD NW3 £36 343

49 SOUTH END RD 020 7794 6314 9–2A

"Consistently wonderful food and service" ensure that a loyal Hampstead crowd keeps coming back to this 55-year-old curry house, now run by the founder's son. It's "full of staff from the local hospital", who clearly know a good thing when they see it. / NW3 2QB; www.paradisehampstead.co.uk; Mon-Sun 11.30 pm.

THE PARAKEET NW5 £71 543

256 KENTISH TOWN ROAD
020 4599 6302 9–2C

"All the food is wood-grilled and tastes fantastic" at this exciting March 2023 newcomer – a converted boozer (a Victorian hostelry, previously called The Oxford Tavern) from former Brat chefs Ben Allen and Ed Jennings that's not just "a welcome addition to Kentish Town" but widely hailed from more distant postcodes as "the perfect gastropub". The "original" if quite limited menu is extremely highly rated in a slew of early reports (and just about every newspaper restaurant critic has waxed lyrical over it); there's also a "superb and well-priced wine list, plus great beers on tap". / NW5 2EN; theparakeetpub.com; the_parakeet; Mon-Sat midnight, Sun 10.30 pm.

THE PARK W2

123 BAYSWATER RD AWAITING TEL 7–*2C*

Jeremy King is back! (with a vengeance?) at this big, bold newcomer in a landmark new development opposite Kensington Gardens and on the corner of Queensway. Apparently it will be "very much within the 'Grand Cafés & Brasseries' mould that [he] love[s] so much but it is however very much of the early 21st Century rather than 20th". Perhaps that means less of the Edwardian (Ivy, Wolseley, Delaunay) or Victorian (Sheekeys) style that has characterised his earlier openings. BREAKING NEWS. In September 2023, King announced he is returning to the original site of Le Caprice, where he found fame. He sold the name long ago, but it's already being talked of as Le Caprice 2.0. / W2 3JH; Mon-Sat 11 pm.

PARK CHINOIS W1 £156 221

17 BERKELEY STREET
020 3327 8888 3–*3C*

An "extravagant setting" is central to the approach of this showy Chinese venue in Mayfair, whose website promises 'the ultimate Asian restaurant' and a 'world of hedonism' including 'devilishly curious entertainment' (such as burlesque). Its "excruciating prices" have always been an issue, but the view that the food (from a very wide-ranging menu, including dim sum, caviar, steak, noodles…) is "nothing special" gained ground this year, as did the concern that "I just didn't enjoy the experience" – "the shows are at least a distraction from what is a pretty lacklustre meal..." / W1S 4NF; parkchinois.com; parkchinois; Tue-Sat 2 am, Sun midnight.

PARK ROW W1 £114

77 BREWER STREET 02037 453 431 4–*3C*

Despite the larger-than-life Marvel theme (enter through a bookcase in a library) and big backing (including the involvement of DC Comics and Warner Bros), this sizable basement two-year-old near Piccadilly Circus doesn't make many waves – too few reports for a rating, although such feedback as we did receive was positive. That some aspects of its approach are surprisingly upmarket perhaps actually limits its appeal: instead of being a fun, cartoony schlockfest, the decor is in fact rather classy; and although there's now a cheap set menu option (including for 'Little Gothamites'), the à la carte or Monarch Theatre experience are priced beyond the reach of 'casual dining'. Still, with extensive AV in some areas, for a themed, business-related event it can be a natural. / W1F 9ZN; www.parkrowlondon.co.uk; parkrowlondon; Mon-Wed 1 am, Thu-Sat 1, Sun 9 pm.

PARLOUR KENSAL NW10 £67 334

5 REGENT ST 020 8969 2184 1–*2B*

Jesse Dunford Wood's quirky former pub in Kensal Rise "never disappoints". It's open for "lovely meals all day long" (from 10am), delivering a versatile set of dishes from "an ever-changing seasonal menu" made "with fresh ingredients and imaginative preparation". "Sunday lunch for both vegetarians and meat-lovers is a particular highlight". / NW10 5LG; www.parlourkensal.com; parlouruk; Mon-Sun 10 pm.

PARRILLAN £123 333

COAL DROPS YARD, N1
020 7018 3339 9–*3C*
BOROUGH YARDS, 4 DIRTY LANE, SE1
NO TEL 10–*4C*

"Taking the good bits from Parrillan Coal Drops Yard and improving on it X 2" – the attractive Borough Yards branch of the Hart Bros Hispanic duo has eclipsed its N1 sibling in terms of feedback. At both sites, the parrilla grill is a DIY job if you sit outside (you order para picar, and then chicken, seafood and meat for the BBQ); but at SE1 there's also a stylish, brick-lined interior section, complete with chefs and a more conventional menu-style service. The younger branch is not beyond criticism though: as in CDY it can seem "a good all-round experience, but overpriced" and the odd reporter finds it all too "hyped". / www.parrillan.co.uk; parrillanlondon.

PARSONS WC2 £71 432

39 ENDELL STREET 020 3422 0221 5–*2C*

"By no means a flashy restaurant and fairly cramped, but some of the very best fish that you will find in London" – this immensely popular Covent Garden fixture is a "premier choice" despite its humble looks thanks to a "daily changing menu dependent on the morning's catch" that's "accurately and sometimes interestingly, sometimes classically cooked" and delivered at a "really good-value" price. "The inside space is tiny, but they have managed to expand into an outside area which they heat on the pavement". / WC2H 9BA; www.parsonslondon.co.uk; parsons_london; Mon-Sat 10 pm.

PASCOR W8 £63 322

221 KENSINGTON HIGH STREET
020 7937 3003 8–*1D*

"Terrific posh Levantine food with a twist" is the story of this Kensington High Street three-year-old, whose kitchen is run by former Palomar head chef Tomar Amedi. The menu can seem "confusing" to first-timers ("what's a starter? a main? a side? did we order enough?") but the small plates are "interesting and all very tasty". / W8 6SG; www.pascor.co.uk; pascor_restaurant; Tue-Sun 11 pm.

PASTAIO W1 £57 323

19 GANTON STREET 020 3019 8680 4–*2B*

"Fantastic pasta" is the USP at high-profile chef Stevie Parle's Soho venue. In particular, it's "a top spot with kids, thanks to the fun and friendly staff and a notably good children's menu option". / W1F 7BU; www.pastaio.london; pastaiolondon; Mon-Thu 10.30 pm, Fri & Sat 11 pm, Sun 10 pm.

PATARA £74 33

15 GREEK ST, W1 020 7437 1071 5–*2A*
7 MADDOX ST, W1 020 7499 6008 4–*2A*
181 FULHAM RD, SW3
020 7351 5692 6–*2C*
9 BEAUCHAMP PL, SW3
020 7581 8820 6–*1C*
82 HAMPSTEAD HIGH ST, NW3
020 7431 5902 9–*2A*
18 HIGH ST, SW19 020 3931 6157 11–*2B*

"Generous portions" of "reliably excellent Thai food" have kept the six London branches of Khun Patara Sila-On's international group busy for more than 30 years. Although known for its value for money, there were one or two grumbles about "price increases" this year, but full agreement that you get "a consistently great bargain on their lunch deal". / www.pataralondon.com; pataralondon.

PATERNOSTER CHOP HOUSE EC4 £74 23

1 WARWICK COURT 020 7029 9400 10–2

Punters are often drawn to this D&D London operation because of its association with TV show 'First Dates', for which it was famously the location. Originally it was conceived by the group as a classic City steakhouse kind of place, but has never really made waves in that department. Still, the odd report says it's a "useful" option in the area (although, note, if you haven't visited for a little while, it's moved – it's no longer overlooking St Paul's from Paternoster Square and is now on Ludgate Hill / EC4M 7DX; www.paternosterchophouse.co.uk; paternosterchophouse; Mon-Fri 10 pm, Sat 10.30 pm, Sun 4.30 pm. SRA – accredited

PATRI £49 33

139 NORTHFIELD AVENUE, W13
020 3981 3388 1–*3A*
103 HAMMERSMITH GROVE, W6
020 8741 1088 8–*1C*

This West London pair of Indian street-food canteens, in Ealing and Hammersmith, elicits little in the way of commentary this year but wins its usual solid ratings for food and service.

PATTY AND BUN £44 32

18 OLD COMPTON ST, W1
020 7287 1818 5–*2A*
26 KINGLY STREET, W1
020 7287 9632 4–*2A*
54 JAMES ST, W1 020 7487 3188 3–*1A*
19 BOROUGH HIGH STREET, SE1
020 7407 7994 10–*4C*
12 NORTHCOTE ROAD, SW11
020 7223 0900 11–*2C*
15 PARK DRIVE, E14
020 3951 9715 12–*1C*
2 ARTHAUS BUILDING, 205 RICHMOND ROAD, E8 020 8525 8250 14–*1B*
22-23 LIVERPOOL ST, EC2
020 7621 1331 10–*2D*

"So tasty and messy – I love it", say fans of this 12-year-old London operation who insist it's the "best burger restaurant in town – others copy but this is consistently the best" "for when you ant a full-on dripping burger and to hell with e diet!". Expansion of the chain has proved fficult in the last year, with the Notting Hill anch shutting up shop just months after its mmer 2022 opening. / www.pattyandbun.co.uk; ttyandbun.

AVYLLON, THE FOUR EASONS HOTEL W1 £140

AMILTON PLACE 020 7319 5200 3–4A

arisian uber-chef Yannick Alléno – who holds total of 15 Michelin stars at 17 restaurants ross the globe – made his London debut this mmer at this July 2023 launch. Since the days Bruno Loubet in the early '90s, the quietly amorous Four Seasons has – for all its other rtues – lacked a high profile flagship eatery. et's hope that this newcomer inspires more cal excitement than its more established near ighbour on Park Lane, run by the holder of e world's most Michelin Stars (in that case): Alain Ducasse at the Dorchester. With ain dishes around £50, the à la carte pricing ere is a little vertigo-inspiring, but the offering a set two-course lunch option under £50 d a tasting menu under £100 suggest a desire tempt the locals to try it out. / W1J 7DR; ww.pavyllonlondon.com; pavyllon_london.

EARL LIANG W2 £54 322

SHELDON SQUARE 020 7289 7000 7–1C

uthentic and sensibly priced dim sum, a cut two above the quality of many traditional oho joints" (and with "some stand out shes") has carved a good reputation for is Cantonese basement, below the shiny ew towers of Paddington Basin. (Its ratings, ough, are not as high as once they were; and e or two reporters feel "it still hasn't fully covered its shine post pandemic"). / W2 6EZ; ww.pearlliang.co.uk; pearl_liang_restaurant; Mon-n 10.30 pm.

ECKHAM BAZAAR E15 £61 433

9 CONSORT RD 020 7732 2525 1–4D

he "great and original menu" at Albanian-orn John Gionleka's Peckham pub conversion inspired by the cuisine of the former ttoman Empire, stretching across the Balkans Greece and Anatolia, with an emphasis n cooking over a charcoal grill. Ingredients ange daily with seasonal availability. See so its sister restaurant, Dulwich Lyceum. SE15 3RU; www.peckhambazaar.com; eckhambazaar; Mon-Sat 11 pm, Sun 4 pm.

ECKHAM CELLARS E15 £60 343

25 QUEENS ROAD 020 7207 0124 1–4D

his "exceptional local wine room", one the prime movers and shakers in the eckham foodie scene, presents an "interesting st of wines" in a "fun and unpretentious mosphere". There's also a short but ell-received menu of modern European ibbles and larger plates. A long-heralded spin-off called 'Little Cellars' was due to open in Camberwell in 2023. / SE15 2ND; peckhamcellars.co.uk; peckhamcellars; Tue-Sat 11 pm.

THE PELICAN W11 £69 334

45 ALL SAINTS RD 020 4537 2880 7–1B

"A winner if only for people-watching" – "the great and the good-looking of Notting Hill gather in the beige but tasteful surroundings" of this year-old pub, whose popularity is such that it's regularly "heaving". "It's not that cheap", but all reviews applaud Owen Kenworthy's "top-end pub good", from an "interesting menu" of "reinvented pub classics". Top Menu Tips – mince on toast is a staple here; "bar snacks of crab and cheese on toast are a delicious counterpoint to the drinks". / W11 1HE; thepelicanw11.com; thepelican_w11; Mon-Sat midnight, Sun 10.30 pm.

E PELLICCI E2 £23 352

332 BETHNAL GREEN RD 020 7739 4873 13–1D

"Unbeatable for a classic full English breakfast" – but perhaps most popular for the accompanying bants – this Bethnal Green café, notable for its Grade II-listed Art Deco interior, has been run by four generations of the Pellicci family since 1900 – Maria, the current boss, has cooked here since 1966. / E2 0AG; epellicci.has.restaurant; pelliccicafe; Mon-Sat 4 pm.

THE PEM, CONRAD LONDON ST JAMES SW1 £101 443

22-28 BROADWAY 020 3301 8080 2–3C

Sally Abé's accomplished traditional British cuisine has rightfully succeeded in bringing media attention to this rather hotel-y chamber, in a comfortable but anonymous five-star a short walk from St James's Park tube. (Indeed, in his September 2022 review, the FT's Tim Hayward declared it "absolutely bloody cracking… some of the best food in town"). It still doesn't attract the volume of reports in our annual diners' poll we would like, but most (if not quite all) proclaim it "outstanding all round". BREAKING NEWS: in July 2023, the restaurant closed, for the installation of a new kitchen. We've left it with its former rating, but apparently on re-opening in autumn 2023 it will have an amended offering. Abé commented: 'We'll be back all guns blazing'! / SW1H 0BH; thepemrestaurant.com; thepemrestaurant; Tue, Sat, Wed-Fri 9.30 pm.

PENTOLINA W14 £67 454

71 BLYTHE ROAD 020 3010 0091 8–1C

A "perfect neighbourhood spot" near Brook Green – "Michele and Heidi's wonderful home from home" thrives on their "warm welcome", "honest" and "reasonably priced" Italian food and "lovely wine list". Most fans are local, but one or two cross London to visit. / W14 0HP; www.pentolinarestaurant.co.uk; pentolina_london; Tue-Sat 9.30 pm.

PERILLA N16 £82 333

1-3 GREEN LANES 020 7359 0779 1–1C

This "cosy yet elegant" neighbourhood restaurant overlooking Newington Green serves a "delicious and inventive menu" from highly rated young chef Ben Marks, who has The Square, Noma and Claridges on his impressive CV. Ratings have slipped slightly this year, but all reports here say it's a very good all-round experience. / N16 9BS; www.perilladining.co.uk; perilladining; Fri & Sat, Tue-Thu 11 pm, Sun 6 pm.

PERSIAN PALACE W13 £34 422

143-145 UXBRIDGE ROAD 020 8840 4233 1–3A

"Huge portions of very good Persian cuisine" are served at this Ealing local, where "very little has changed over the last ten years" – and it remains "excellent value". The menu encompasses kebabs, grills and traditional stews, while the decor adds to the authentic atmosphere. / W13 9AU; www.persianpalace.co.uk; persianppalace; Mon-Thu 10.30 pm, Fri-Sun 11 pm.

THE PETERSHAM WC2 £102 223

FLORAL COURT, OFF FLORAL ST 020 7305 7676 5–3C

"One of the prettiest restaurants in London – charmingly tucked away in Floral Court, Covent Garden" – this is the in-town offshoot of the famous Richmond plant nursery, and in fact houses two establishments – "La Goccia is the better of the two" (see also). There's "a lovely atmosphere in this light and bright room – it's the sort of place you might take your rich aunt to for lunch". The food, though, is "not especially memorable" and "weirdly expensive for average fare". / WC2E 9DJ; petershamnurseries.com; petershamnurseries; Mon-Sat 9.30 pm, Sun 4 am.

PETERSHAM NURSERIES CAFE TW10 £123 225

CHURCH LANE (SIGNPOSTED 'ST PETER'S CHURCH'), OFF PETERSHAM ROAD 020 8940 5230 1–4A

A series of converted greenhouses makes an "eccentric but wonderfully romantic setting" for a meal at this posh garden centre, near Ham Polo Club. A shabby-chic culinary hit when it opened under chef Skye Gyngell 20 years ago, it has often stood accused of "hype over substance" – but remains a "personal favourite" to many, especially for the "quite delicious reinvention of afternoon tea". / TW10 7AB; www.petershamnurseries.com; petersham nurseries; Tue-Thu, Sun 5 pm, Fri & Sat 11 pm.

THE PETERSHAM RESTAURANT TW10 £83 224

NIGHTINGALE LANE 020 8003 3602 1–4A

The "stunning dining room with spectacular views, high above the Thames" at this grand mid-Victorian hotel in Richmond "retains a fine atmosphere", and it serves "delicious cakes" at afternoon tea. "Many chefs have been through the kitchen here" and where more serious culinary occasions are concerned, verdicts are split: fans say it is "currently undergoing a renaissance", but others feel (as they have for years) that "the food is only average and the service likewise". / TW10 6UZ; petershamhotel.co.uk; thepetershamhotel; Mon-Sun 6 pm.

LE PETIT BEEFBAR SW3 £106

27 CALE STREET 020 4580 1219 6–2C

On the backstreet Chelsea site that was Tom's Kitchen (RIP) – this import from Monte Carlo via Dubai and Méribel (which may sum-up its patrons too) opened in late 2021. For a second year, its meaty offering still hasn't generated a huge volume of feedback in our annual diners' poll, even if such as we have is all positive. But they must be doing something right, as a spin-off sprang up in Edinburgh too in mid 2023. / SW3 3QP; lepetit.beefbar.com; beefbar_official; Sun-Thu 10.30 pm, Fri & Sat 11 pm.

LE PETIT CITRON W6 £58 333

98-100 SHEPHERDS BUSH ROAD 020 3019 1175 8–1C

This "dependable neighbourhood bistro", on a busy stretch linking Hammersmith and Shepherd's Bush, combines classic gingham tablecloths with a menu inspired by Provence – favoured holiday destination for proprietors Lawrence & Emily Hartley, who previously operated the site as Mustard. / W6 7PD; lepetitcitron.co.uk; lepetitcitronw6; Mon-Sat 10 pm, Sun 4 pm.

PETIT MA CUISINE TW9 £62 343

8 STATION APPROACH 020 8332 1923 1–3A

This "retro neighbourhood French bistro" in a parade of shops near Kew station is "massively popular with the locals due to its competitive prices" for "Gallic classics with a little twist" (and gets "very crowded at lunchtimes"). / TW9 3QB; www.macuisinebistrot.co.uk; Tue-Sun 10 pm.

LA PETITE AUBERGE N1 £56 332

283 UPPER ST 020 7359 1046 9–2D

"Calves' liver, perfect coq-au-vin, deeply flavourful venison stew" – this Gallic venue in Islington doesn't aim for foodie fireworks, but fans like its traditional approach, "warm" atmosphere and "willing" service. The less rosy view is that the cooking is "rather standard French food, if good enough for an evening with friends". Top Tip – the interior is split level in some areas and regulars say "the top section especially feels romantic". / N1 2TZ; www.petiteauberge.co.uk; lapetiteauberge_en4; Mon-Fri 10 pm, Sat 10.30 pm, Sun 9.30 pm.

PÉTRUS SW1 £167 233

1 KINNERTON ST 020 7592 1609 6–1D

"Interesting vintages, well introduced by the sommelier" helped win renewed praise this year for this slick, luxurious Belgravian (built around a central wine cage), which was also sometimes nominated for its "romantic" potential. However – as it approaches its 14th year – although its modern French cuisine was often favourably rated this year, there's little of the excitement in feedback that once distinguished it as one of the flagships of Gordon Ramsay's restaurant portfolio. / SW1X 8EA; www.gordonramsayrestaurants.com; petrusrestaurant; Wed-Sat 11 pm, Sun 6 pm.

PHAM SUSHI EC1 £53 232

159 WHITECROSS ST 020 7251 6336 13–2A

"There are so few dining choices near the Barbican, it's worth knowing that you can get decent sushi and other obvious Japanese options here at Pham", a short walk away; which particularly benefits from "fast and attentive" service. Some critics, though, feel that "evening visits without an expense account cannot justify the prices here". There's also a caution that "you should skip the house specials and stick to the simpler choices" as "several of the fancier options seem excessively performative". / EC1Y 8JL; www.phamsushi.com; phamsushi; Mon-Sat 9 pm.

PHAT PHUC, CHELSEA COURTYARD SW3 £41 333

151 SYDNEY STREET 020 7351 3843 6–3C

"Authentic street food at great prices" makes this Vietnamese noodle bar one of the better cheap grazing options in Chelsea. The name translates as 'happy Buddha' – which would not have sold many T-shirts. / SW3 6NT; www.phatphucnoodlebar.co.uk; phat_phuc_noodle_bar; Mon-Sun 6.30 pm.

PHOENIX PALACE NW1 £70 322

5-9 GLENTWORTH ST 020 7486 3515 2–1A

This "reliable old-school Chinese" near Baker Street tube is "great for big family lunches" – with its sheer scale, traditional décor and eight menus, "one could be in Hong Kong of old". It's also "pretty good value for money" for its address. / NW1 5PG; www.phoenixpalace.co.uk; thephoenixpalace; Mon-Sat 11.30 pm, Sun 10.30 pm.

PIAZZA ITALIANA EC2 £74 33

38 THREADNEEDLE STREET 020 7256 7223 10–2C

This "beautiful old banking hall" in Threadneedle Street makes for a "decent business venue" in the heart of the City, with "a well-executed if limited Italian menu, and wines priced for expense accounts". On a quie evening, though, it can "lack atmosphere". / EC2R 8AY; www.piazzaitaliana.co.uk; piazzaitalianauk; Mon-Wed 10 pm, Thu-Sat 11 p

PIDGIN E8 £87

52 WILTON WAY 020 7254 8311 14–1B

No journalistic round-up of East End restaurants is complete without mention of thi unassuming-looking Hackney eight-year-old (e 2015), which has been a darling of London's fooderati ever since winning (and quickly losin a Michelin star in the years after its opening. But feedback in our annual diners' poll – whil positive – was, surprisingly, too limited this year for a reliable rating on its experimental tasting menu of funky small plates. / E8 1BG; www.pidginlondon.com; pidginlondon; Wed-Sun 11 pm.

PIED À TERRE W1 £151 43

34 CHARLOTTE ST 020 7636 1178 2–1C

"Over 30 years on this is still a class act" – David Moore's Fitzrovia townhouse has prove one of London's enduring temples of top gastronomy – currently under chef Asimakis Chaniotis – and "this old favourite has also evolved over the years": "the introduction of a vegan alternative menu is pure genius (as an unreformed eater of meat and fish, I was well-and-truly wowed by the plant-based version)"; and "as always the wine list is a treasure trove". There are a few quibbles: that "commercial pressure seems to have limited choice" a little of late; the odd "unexceptional" meal is reported; and its "long and thin" premises can feel "a little crowded". But overall feedback is sunny, helped by "thoroughly welcoming and unobtrusive service" which also helps make it a strong "romantic" bet. / W1T 2NH; www.pied-a-terre.co.uk; piedaterrerestaurant; Thu Sat, Tue, Wed 10 pm.

PIERRE VICTOIRE W1 £56 32

5 DEAN ST 020 7287 4582 3–1D

"A teleport into France" is easily achieved at "this unfussy, efficiently run" operation off Soh Square, noted for its "good honest classics don well" at "very reasonable prices". "Service can suffer when busy, which it often is, but no matter". / W1D 3RQ; www.pierrevictoire.com; Sun-Wed 11 pm, Thu-Sat 11.30 pm.

The Silver Birch W4

IG & BUTCHER
1 £69 433

) LIVERPOOL ROAD 020 7226 8304 9–*3D*

his "great neighbourhood gastropub" in lington is "very strong all-round", and the -house butchery means it delivers a "stunning ast". It's still winning excellent ratings after dozen years, with just a single gripe this year "they only had one vaguely interesting beer 1 tap". / N1 0QD; www.thepigandbutcher.co.uk; gandbutcher; Mon-Sat 10 pm, Sun 9 pm.

HE PIG'S HEAD
W4 £78 344

7 RECTORY GROVE
20 4568 5830 11–*1D*

his two-year-old conversion of a "grand old arn of a tavern in Clapham" into a "beautiful ty-rustic gastropub with very good food" as been a real success for the team behind mokehouse and the Princess of Shoreditch. So happy to have a local worth staying near ome for", purr fans of its "meat-friendly enu that's packed with flavour". "Wide eggie options available", too. / SW4 0DR; ww.thepigshead.com; thepigshead; Mon-Fri 10 n, Sat 10.30 pm, Sun 9 pm.

IQUE NIQUE SE1 £79 233

2 TANNER STREET 020 7403 9549 10–*4D*

onverted from a building in Tanner Street ark, this Gallic fixture in Bermondsey is bling to nearby Casse-Croûte and known as a ulinary bright spark in the area. It can be a tad inconsistent" though ("three servings of the ame dish (saddle of lamb) produced one that as very good; one that was reasonable; and ne that had to be returned to the kitchen!") / E1 3LD; pique-nique.co.uk; piquenique32; Mon-at 11 pm, Sun 5 pm.

L PIRATA W1 £57 244

-6 DOWN ST 020 7491 3810 3–*4B*

"buzzy" atmosphere and "decent wine st" are strengths of this "reliable, traditional panish tapas bar"; and prices that represent great value for Mayfair" have helped sustain e jolly venue from its founding decades before e current vogue for Hispanic cuisine. Notable ns include Fred Sirieix and Caribbean pirate ohnny Depp. / W1J 7AQ; www.elpirata.co.uk; piratamayfair.

PIVOT BY MARK GREENAWAY WC2 £96 333

3 HENRIETTA STREET
020 3325 5275 5–*3D*

Scottish chef Mark Greenaway's two-year-old 'British bistro', set in the first-floor drawing room of an elegant Georgian townhouse overlooking Covent Garden piazza, flies somewhere under the radar given its grand address. (The name apparently refers to the way the menu 'pivots' with the changing seasons). Its pre-theatre options are useful for the area, while Sunday lunch is also favourably mentioned. / WC2E 8LU; 3henrietta.com; pivotbarandbistro; Mon-Sat 11 pm, Sun 9 pm.

PIZARRO SE1 £66 444

194 BERMONDSEY ST
020 7256 5333 10–*4D*

"Stunning and authentic" Spanish food in a "beautiful, always-convivial setting, and with a wine list to die for" is the attractive proposition at José Pizarro's massively popular Bermondsey restaurant. Its ratings are a shade below those of José, its older sister (by a few months) tapas bar across the road, due to a minority sentiment that it's "good rather than great". / SE1 3TQ; josepizarro.com; josepizarrorestaurants; Mon-Sat 10.45 pm, Sun 8.45 pm.

PIZZA EAST E1 £59 323

56 SHOREDITCH HIGH ST
020 7729 1888 13–*1B*

"Great pizzas in the heart of buzzing Shoreditch" made this "cool and buzzy", post-industrial pizza joint an early player in the area's rise as a gastronomic hub when it was opened by Soho House in 2009. The venue was taken over by Gordon Ramsay after closing briefly in early 2023 (a sister site in Portobello has closed permanently), so there may be changes afoot. It's in the 'Tea Building', whose "concrete interior makes the place pretty noisy, but isn't that why you go to Shoreditch?". / E1 6JJ; www.pizzaeast.com; Mon-Sat 10.45 pm, Sun 8.45 pm.

PIZZA METRO SW11 £60 322

64 BATTERSEA RISE
020 7228 3812 11–*2C*

Now 30 years old, this battered Battersea Neapolitan helped introduce the capital to the delights of pizza sold by the metre. Others, perhaps, have overtaken it over the decades, but for a good laugh and some very decent pizza, it still has a fan club. / SW11 1EQ; www.pizzametropizza.com; pizzametropizza; Tue-Thu 10 pm, Fri, Sun 11.30 pm, Sat midnight.

PIZZA PILGRIMS £41 332

BRANCHES THROUGHOUT LONDON

"The best whistle-stop pizza in London" for its army of fans – the Elliot brothers' successful chain continues to grow, with their latest opening in Queen's Park in June 2023. But even if "you can't knock the food" or the "realistic prices", the rest of the experience is somewhere between "pleasant" and "a bit underwhelming". / pizzapilgrims.co.uk; pizzapilgrims.

PIZZAEXPRESS £57 233

BRANCHES THROUGHOUT LONDON

Is this venerable high-street brand (est. 1965) finally getting back on track? Owned by its creditors since 2021, its volume of feedback and ratings rebounded significantly this year, with particular improvement in its "efficient and welcoming" service and the "pleasant ambience" for which the chain was previously known. And, although its food rating remains washed out, it does retain many fans (including Marcus Wareing apparently!) who feel a pizza here is "always enjoyable". Parents still love it – "they are very friendly and kind to kids" and "you know what you are going to get". / www.pizzaexpress.co.uk; pizzaexpress/.

PIZZERIA MOZZA, TREEHOUSE HOTEL W1 £48 433

14-15 LANGHAM PLACE
020 3988 4273 3–*1C*

"Miss it and miss out!" – the first UK venture from legendary LA baker-chef Nancy Silverton (founder of La Brea Bakery and a James Beard Award winner) is "this pizza joint, tucked away in a hotel opposite Broadcasting House". It's "just the best", with "fab sourdough crust and great toppings" – altogether "very special!" / W1B 2QS; www.treehousehotels.com; pizzeriamozzalondon; Mon-Sat 10 pm.

PLANQUE E8 £80 344

322 ACTON MEWS 020 7254 3414 14–*2A*

An "incredible wine list from a seriously passionate and knowledgeable team" is backed up by "lovely modern food" in this hip 'wine drinkers' clubhouse' set in a pair of Haggerston railway arches. "The restaurant has been designed beautifully and it feels like serious money has been spent on the project", even if wine is the primary focus. (Members enjoy priority booking and can store their reserves in the cellar.) / E8 4EA; www.planque.co.uk; _planque_; Wed & Thu 9 pm, Fri & Sat 9.30 pm, Sun 3 pm.

PLAQUEMINE LOCK N1 £46 434

139 GRAHAM ST 020 7688 1488 9–*3D*

"Amazing Creole food" including such delights as po'boys, gumbo and jambalaya liven up any meal at this Islington pub from Jacob Kenedy (of Bocca di Lupo) – a tribute to his Louisiana forebears. "If you're looking for something fun, lively and different without having to compromise on the cooking, Plaquemine Lock is an awesome night out". Top Tip – "great jazz at Sunday brunch". / N1 8LB; plaqlock.com; plaqueminelock; Sun & Mon 10 pm, Tue-Fri 11 pm, Sat midnight.

PLAZA KHAO GAENG, ARCADE FOOD HALL WC1 £36 432

103-105 OXFORD STREET NO TEL 5–*1A*

"Not a place to linger" – this "busy, basic and noisy" canteen from JKS Restaurants is a highlight of the Arcade Food Hall (see also) at Centrepoint. "Styled as street food" – it's "several notches above a typical Thai offering" and bangs out dishes that aficionados claim "are reminiscent of actually eating in the lesser-known corners of Thailand" (some of them "rip-your-face-off" spicy). Top Menu Tip – "sea bass in chilli and holy basil is just epic". / WC1A 1DB; plazakhaogaeng.com; plazakhaogaeng; Tue-Sat 10 pm, Sun 7.30 pm.

THE PLIMSOLL N4 £61 543

52 ST THOMAS'S ROAD NO TEL 9–*1D*

"Legendary Dexter cheeseburgers and well-flavoured small plates" of "delicious, unfussy grub" hit the jackpot at this "crowded Finsbury Park local" near the old Arsenal stadium, "if you want to eat down-to-earth cooking, served up with charm in a proper boozer". "With the exception of the burgers the menu changes constantly", and "attention is on the food not the decor" – although the 'Four Legs' duo, Jamie Allan & Ed McIlroy, did strip out the previous incarnation's Oirish-themed interior before launching here two years ago. / N4 2QW; theplimsoll.com; the.plimsoll; Mon-Fri 11 pm, Sat & Sun midnight.

THE PLOUGH SW14 £58 223

42 CHRIST CHURCH RD 020 8755 7444 11–*2A*

This attractive eighteenth-century inn is a short stroll from Sheen Gate and a good option following a walk in Richmond Park (especially in summer on the terrace). On the downside, "the cooking can be a bit hit and miss" – it's "under new management" since Fuller's fell out with the previous landlord a couple of years back, "so perhaps hasn't found its stride yet". / SW14 7AF; www.plougheastsheen.co.uk; ploughsheen; Mon-Fri 9 pm, Sat 10 pm, Sun 8 pm.

PLOUSSARD SW11 £34 433

97 SAINT JOHN'S ROAD 020 7738 1965 11–*2C*

"A more-than-welcome addition to Battersea Rise, with a Continental-style vibe" that opened in April 2023 (a revamp of the "small", 35-cover site that Tommy Kempson and chef Matt Harris used to run the as a branch of their Brixton-based 'Other Side Fried'). The eclectic menu is short but interesting, and accompanied by a selection of low-intervention vintages. "Grab a seat by the window to watch the world go by whilst enjoying delicious plates of food" – crumpet with lamb and anchovy is a prime example – plus a small-but-good wine list. / SW11 1QY; ploussardlondon.co.uk; ploussardlondon; Tue, Wed 10 pm, Fri & Sat 11 pm, Thu 10.30 pm, Sun 6 pm.

PLU NW8 £213 544

12 BLENHEIM TERRACE 020 7624 7663 9–*3A*

"If I won the lottery I would eat at PLU at least once a month!" – Elliot Moss has created something "so special" with this "cosy-yet-super-elegant" venue in St John's Wood: "a small luxurious room with impeccable attention from the single front-of-house person" (Helen, his wife). "The best part is the food": "dishes should score 10 out of 5 for their flavours, textures, aromas, presentation, anticipation, fun and excitement"; and "betray a lovely sense of humour too". "How on earth Michelin continually fails to recognise PLU is a travesty of justice!" / NW8 0EB; www.plurestaurant.co.uk; plurestaurant; Thu-Sat 10 pm.

PLUM VALLEY W1 £51 322

20 GERRARD ST 020 7494 4366 5–*3A*

"The dim sum is pretty good for this price range" ("all the stalwarts are available" as well as one or two "unusual/Hakkasan-like creations") at this Cantonese stalwart in Chinatown. / W1D 6JQ; plumvalley.co.uk; plumvalleyrestaurant; Mon-Sun 10 pm.

POLLEN STREET SOCIAL W1 £160 333

8-10 POLLEN ST 020 7290 7600 3–*2C*

"Jason Atherton's original solo venture in Mayfair remains a star" and it's "good to see him still at the helm and running the pass". His cuisine is "immaculately presented" with "many little delights in between courses" and "the wine list is special (not cheap but with some good bargains to be had if you look carefully"). The stylish interior can seem a fraction "soulless" for some tastes however; and there was the odd incident of "unhelpful" service this year. And even those acknowledging the "beautiful-looking and generally excellent cuisine" can go "Oh… the bill.....wow!!" Maybe that's why – as our survey was in progress – Jason slashed his prices, taking the tasting menu down from £185 to £145 per person; and the set lunch from £75 per person to £39.50 per person. The latter in particular is stunning value! / W1 1NQ; www.pollenstreetsocial.com; pollen_street_social; Tue-Sat 9.30 pm.

LE PONT DE LA TOUR SE1 £96 22

36D SHAD THAMES 020 7403 8403 10–*4*

"An outside table on the lovely riverside, complete with the spectacular and iconic view of Tower Bridge" is the best way to visit this D&D London venue (where the Blairs once entertained the Clintons, when both were in office). With its modern French cuisine and heavyweight wine list, there was a time when this was both the jewel in the crown of the late Sir Terence Conran's restaurant empire and the City of London's favourite entertaining spot. Times have moved on, though, and nowadays its middling performance gives it a dwindling reputation. For fans, it's still "worth it for a really special treat". Others, though, "won't be rushing back: the interior ambience is nothing to write home about and the food is pricey for what's served up". / SE1 2YE; www.lepontdelatour.co.uk; lepontdelatourldn; Mon Sat 10 pm, Sun 9 pm. SRA – accredited

POPOLO EC2 £61 33

26 RIVINGTON STREET 020 7729 4299 13–*1B*

"A find!" – "Sit at the ground-floor kitchen bar for a fun, close up experience" at this sophisticated Shoreditch joint, where Jon Lawson and his team provide accomplished sharing plates (often with Moorish touches) and deliver them in a "knowledgeable and friendly" manner. But ratings took a hit this year, with the odd review referring to cost-of-living concerns: "most of the food is excellent but the size of the portions for the price charged was ridiculously small and felt like a starter at the price of a main. For the premium cost, you might expect comfy seating too!" / EC2A 3DU; popoloshoreditch.com; popoloshoreditch; Mon-Wed 10.30 pm, Thu-Sat 11 pm.

POPPY'S £36 32

129-131 BRACKENBURY ROAD, W6 020 8741 4928 8–*1C*
30 GREYHOUND ROAD, W6 020 7385 9264 8–*2C*
78 GLENTHORNE ROAD, W6 020 8748 2351 8–*2C*

"Good home-cooked Thai food" at "bargain" prices keeps guests coming back to this trio of Hammersmith neighbourhood cafés, distinctively crammed full of retro bric-a-brac. They serve English breakfasts and afternoon teas by day.

PORTE NOIRE N1 £56 34

UNIT A GASHOLDER 10, 1 LEWIS CUBITT SQUARE 020 7930 6211 9–*3C*

Within the foot of one of King's Cross's histori gasholders – just behind Coal Drops Yard – thi handsome wine bar boasts a celeb investor

64 Goodge Street W1

(Idris Elba) as well as a large terrace with peaceful views over the canal and landscaped greenery. The business also makes Champagne and other vintages under the 'Porte Noire' brand and "an interesting wine list" is a key strongpoint, alongside its "buzzy" atmosphere and staff who are "well-balanced, friendly and knowledgeable". The food is relatively "basic", but some of the more ambitious dishes can really shine. / N1C 4BY; www.portenoire.co.uk; portenoirekx; Mon-Sat 11.30 pm, Sun 5.30 pm.

IL PORTICO W8 £74 233

277 KENSINGTON HIGH ST
020 7602 6262 8–*1D*

"Such traditional, family-run restaurants are quite a rarity in London these days"; and the Chiavarinis have maintained this "quintessential", "old-fashioned" trattoria, opposite the Design Museum, for over 50 years. Fans say the food is "terrific, albeit a bit pricey probably because of its posh postcode". But there is a less charitable school of thought, which says results are "uninspired, but it's always busy, possibly because the locals don't know how to cook…" / W8 6NA; www.ilportico.co.uk; ilportico.kensington; Mon-Sat 11 pm.

PORTLAND W1 £98 442

113 GREAT PORTLAND STREET
020 7436 3261 2–*1B*

Will Lander and Daniel Morgenthau have created an understated classic at this Fitzrovia fixture, with open kitchen on view. No-one minds that the "informal atmosphere is nothing particularly special" or that "tables are too close together" – they value the positive vibes generated by "low-key, friendly and unobtrusive staff who are helpful without hovering or being overly servile". Most importantly, "if the decor is slightly bland, the food is anything but": it can be "outstanding"; comes at "a very reasonable price given the location and quality"; and is backed up by "unusual and excellent wines". / W1W 6QQ; www.portlandrestaurant.co.uk; portlandrestaurant; Tue-Sat 9.45 pm.

PORTOBELLO RISTORANTE PIZZERIA W11 £75 334

7 LADBROKE ROAD 020 7221 1373 7–*2B*

"Make sure you sit in the front garden" or the "nice covered terrace" to get the most out of this "lovely local", not far from Notting Hill Gate. Despite the "fresh fish on display", lots of regulars "only ever have pizza, which is very good indeed with lots of very fresh-tasting toppings". "Nice gelato" too. And it's "excellent value for the quality and area". / W11 3PA; www.portobellolondon.co.uk; portobello_ristorante_pizzeria; Mon-Sun 11 pm.

THE PORTRAIT RESTAURANT BY RICHARD CORRIGAN, NATIONAL PORTRAIT GALLERY WC2

ST MARTIN'S PLACE 020 7306 0055 5–*4B*

Dazzling rooftop views accompany a trip to this landmark chamber overlooking the rooftops of Trafalgar Square towards Parliament. As part of the NPG's refurb it has been re-designed by design studio Brady Williams and re-opened in early July 2023 with acclaimed chef, Richard Corrigan at the helm. The bar operation has been beefed up and offerings will include a light afternoon tea and chef's dining counter (plus launch set lunch and pre-theatre menus from £29 per head). / WC2H 0HE; www.npg.org.uk; Mon & Tue, Sun 5.30 pm, Wed & Thu 9.30 pm, Fri & Sat 9.45 pm.

POSTBOX SW13 £43 343

201 CASTELNAU 07424 339379 11–*1A*

This yearling on the Barnes approach to Hammersmith Bridge is a "lovely little neighbourhood eatery" serving "amazing and homely fresh Indian dishes". Founder Leo Noronha, originally from Goa, presides over a "short menu of family recipes" – of the type jotted down on postcards to remind travellers of the food from home. / SW13 9ER; www.postboxrestaurantlondon.com; postbox_ldn; Tue-Thu 10 pm, Fri & Sat 10.30 pm, Sun 9.30 pm.

POTLI W6 £55 433

319-321 KING ST 020 8741 4328 8–*2B*

"An interesting street-food menu is very well executed" at this "real treat" of a Hammersmith café, with a comfortable, atmospheric interior and "friendly service". "It's not as flash as Indian Zing across the road, but dishes are full of flavour and good value!" / W6 9NH; www.potli.co.uk; potlirestaurant; Mon-Thu 10 pm, Fri & Sat 10.30 pm, Sun 9 pm.

LA POULE AU POT SW1 £76 345

231 EBURY ST 020 7730 7763 6–*2D*

Dark and candle-lit, this "unchanging French" old charmer in Pimlico has "lots of tiny tables squeezed into its intimate nooks"; and yet again comes highly recommended for a steamy date in our annual diners' poll. The very Gallic service "can be a bit hit 'n' miss (it helps if they know you)" but typically "makes you feel so cosseted and looked after". "There aren't so many restaurants left in Paris serving such traditional bistro fare" (Tarte à l'Oignon, Beef Bourguignon, Crème Brûlée…), all served in "very generous portions" and "with a sensibly priced wine list". Top Tip – "great terrace for al fresco dining" in summer. / SW1W 8UT; www.pouleaupot.co.uk; lapouleaupotrestaurant; Mon-Sun 11 pm.

PRAWN ON THE LAWN N1 £72 43

292-294 ST PAUL'S RD
020 3302 8668 9–*2D*

This 10-year-old fishmonger-turned-restaurant near Highbury Corner is a "great all-rounder" with "fresh fish" from Devon or Cornwall (it has another branch in Padstow) "often cooked originally". Even after a move to "slightly large premises on St Paul's Road" it's still "a simple space, so the ambience is not highly rated given the expense" – "shame it's so small that you can't always get a booking". / N1 2LH; prawnonthelawn.com; prawnonthelawn; Wed-Sat 10 pm, Sun 5 pm.

PRIMEUR N5 £65 33

116 PETHERTON RD 020 7226 5271 1–*1C*

A retro shopfront (left behind by a 1940s car showroom) adds to the street cred of this well-known East End foodie hotspot (linked to Westerns Laundry and Jolene). Its fashionable combination of small plates served with natura wines doesn't inspire as much feedback in our annual diners' poll as its fooderati renown might imply, but is all positive. / N5 2RT; www.primeurN5.co.uk; menuprimeur; Mon-Sat 11 pm, Sun 9 pm.

THE PRINCESS ROYAL W2 £84 33

7 HEREFORD ROAD 020 3096 6996 7–*1B*

"A very solid offering in a great space" – this restored late-Victorian tavern in Notting Hill provides "delicious food from Ben Tish", culinary director of the smart Cubitt House group. This extends from breakfast via a £15 'worker's lunch' to more sophisticated evening dining. / W2 5AH; www.cubitthouse.co.uk; princessroyalnottinghill; Mon-Sat 10 pm, Sun 9 pm

THE PRINCESS VICTORIA W12 £55 32

217 UXBRIDGE ROAD 020 8749 4466 8–*1*

This big, smartly restored 1829 gin palace in deepest Shepherd's Bush features a horseshoe bar stocking 100 different gins, and a modern gastropub menu appealing to all age groups – "kids love their pizzas and we love their Sunday roasts". / W12 9DH; www.princessvictoria.co.uk; threecheerspubs; Mon-Thu 11 pm, Fri & Sat midnight, Sun 10.30 pm.

PRIX FIXE W1 £49 33

39 DEAN ST 020 7734 5976 5–*2A*

For a "really good-value meal" (including a "pretty decent steak-frites") "in the heart of the West End" it's hard to beat this Soho brasserie. "The simplicity of the menu" and "wide variety of choices" mean "there's something for everyone", so it's "a real go-to", especially for its set-price lunch or pre-theatre deals. / W1D 4PU; www.prixfixe.net; prixfixesoho; Mon-Sun 11.30 pm.

HE PROMENADE AT HE DORCHESTER /1 £141 344

3 PARK LANE 020 7629 8888 3–3A

ollowing the refurb of the hotel's extremely ush lounge bar, fans hail it as "the most mazing new tea salon in London" thanks to its elegant and tasty" afternoon teas. Pastry chef Michael Kwan's creations take centre stage, and inge from 'Champagne' to 'vegan' options. W1K 1QA; www.dorchestercollection.com; edorchester; Mon-Sun 10.30 pm.

ROVENDER E11 £46 342

7 HIGH ST 020 8530 3050 1–1D

Typical French cuisine perfectly cooked" has on a solid reputation for this "great Wanstead cal" – a traditional-ish Gallic bistro, with rrace. Veteran restaurateur Max Renzland, ho founded it in 2011, stepped down in 2021, ith no evident change in its performance. E11 2AA; www.provenderlondon.co.uk; rovenderwanstead; Tue-Thu 10 pm, Fri & Sat 11 n, Sun 9 pm.

RUFROCK COFFEE C1 £15 333

3-25 LEATHER LN 020 7242 0467 10–2A

affeine aficionados beat a path to the eather Lane premises of "one of the early hampions of speciality coffee", where they nbibe information from the "friendly and nowledgeable staff" along with their brews. 's a "comfortable refurbished space", and here are "great pastries" and breakfast/ runch options to munch on. / EC1N 7TE; ww.prufrockcoffee.com; prufrockcoffee; Mon-Fri 30 pm, Sat & Sun 5 pm.

'UNJAB WC2 £49 343

0 NEAL ST 020 7836 9787 5–2C

It ain't Bibi or Tamarind, but it's less than alf the price and it's jolly good" – this ever-reliable" Covent Garden institution has arned devotion from generations of fans for s "authentic" Punjabi curries and "great staff" 'I've been coming here for excellent meals for ver 40 years"). Founded in 1946 – the year efore Indian independence – it claims to have een the UK's first north Indian restaurant nd is now run by the fourth generation of ie founding family. It's run with a conscience oo – "during lockdown they served over 45,000 neals to the needy and homeless". / WC2H PA; www.punjab.co.uk; punjabcoventgarden; Ion-Sat 11 pm, Sun 10 pm.

'URE INDIAN COOKING SW6 £56 443

7 FULHAM HIGH STREET 20 7736 2521 11–1B

'here's "always something new and original to empt you" at this understated and "very good alue" contemporary Indian on Fulham High treet near Putney Bridge. Chef-owner Shilpa Dandekar (who trained with both India's Taj Group and Raymond Blanc) "proves you can give a nod to tradition while being a little more modern, and not have to pay Mayfair prices to get it". Husband Faheem Vanoo ensures the front of house "always provides courteous service". Top Menu Tip – "the best black dhal". / SW6 3JJ; www.pureindiancooking.com; pureindiancooking; Mon-Wed, Sat, Thu & Fri 11 pm, Sun 10.30 pm.

QUAGLINO'S SW1 £93 234

16 BURY ST 020 7930 6767 3–3D

Thirty years ago, this vast basement – a 1929 ballroom which later fell on hard times to be rescued and relaunched with a tsunami of hype by the late Sir Terence Conran – was emblematic of the sweeping improvements in the capital's dining out scene. Nowadays run under the flag of D&D London, it's largely forgotten by the locals and most frequented for special occasions by out-of-towners and tourists, for whom its attractions include a large bar and regular live music. Reports on the food used to be awful, but have improved in recent years and although feedback on its posh-brasserie cuisine is limited it's much more upbeat than it once was. Top Menu Tip – good value prix-fixe options for brunch (£39 for two courses, with bottomless bubbles for £35); and dinner Mon-Thu till 7pm then after 8.30pm (£38 for three courses and a glass of fizz). / SW1Y 6AJ; www.quaglinos-restaurant.co.uk; quaglinos; Mon-Thu midnight, Fri & Sat 1 am, Sun 7 pm. SRA – accredited

THE QUALITY CHOP HOUSE EC1 £106 323

88-94 FARRINGDON RD 020 7278 1452 10–1A

"So what if the benches aren't that comfortable!" – the bum-numbing seating at Will Lander and Daniel Morgenthau's "characterful and closely packed" Clerkenwell institution is part of its proud history as a 'Progressive Working Class Caterer', built in 1869 to feed the masses. Nowadays, "as the name suggests", it mainlines on "butchery and quality of the meat" ("you can pop into their nextdoor butcher's shop to buy too"). Most reviewers feel it is "a great London venue and long may it continue", but it can also seem "a slightly odd mix of traditional English food with the tasting plate craze" and "some dishes can fall into the cracks between the price charged and their quality". / EC1R 3EA; thequalitychophouse.com; qualitychop; Tue-Sat 10 pm, Sun 3.15 pm.

LE QUERCE SE23 £58 342

66-68 BROCKLEY RISE 020 8690 3761 1–4D

Diminishing feedback in recent years makes it hard to recommend this "noisy and fun", family-run Sardinian on Brockley Rise quite as resoundingly as we used to. Fans, though, still say it's "a super, local Italian trattoria, with a great menu: especially the quirky ice cream and sorbet flavours". / SE23 1LN; www.lequerce.co.uk; le_querce; Wed-Sat 8.30 pm, Sun 5.30 am.

QUILON SW1 £92 432

41 BUCKINGHAM GATE 020 7821 1899 2–4B

"Delicate flavours" from dishes rooted in southwest Indian coastal cuisine establish this blandly luxurious hotel venue, near Buckingham Palace, as "the most interesting of London's Indians" for some of its fans. You wouldn't go there for riotous ambience though, particularly in the "gloomy back of the dining room". Top Tip – "the set lunch menu is great value considering its location" and there's also a "great weekend brunch". / SW1E 6AF; www.quilon.co.uk; thequilon; Tue-Thu, Sun 10 pm, Fri & Sat 10.30 pm.

QUO VADIS W1 £90 445

26-29 DEAN ST 020 7437 9585 4–1D

"One of the legends of the London food scene" – the Hart Bros' 'Grande Dame of Dean Street' is some reporters' "all-time favourite in the capital – especially now the dining room has been enlarged and transformed to feel much comfier". (At the end of 2022, the Harts reclaimed the space in this "beautiful, historic building" that had been given over to Barrafina for a few years, to return QV back to its former capacity). "Now with the refit, the environment has caught up with Jeremy Lee's dishes" – "fine British fare using seasonal ingredients" that's "top cuisine, without feeling too 'restauranty'" – all delivered in a "convivial atmosphere which takes us back to classic Soho days". "Superb all round" and "low-key in a good way, so ideal for business". Top Menu Tip – "that eel sandwich is still a winner". / W1D 3LL; www.quovadissoho.co.uk; quovadissoho; Mon-Sat 10 pm. SRA – 2 stars

RABBIT SW3 £71 222

172 KING'S RD 020 3750 0172 6–3C

The Gladwin family's faux-rustic, field-to-fork spot in quirky premises on the King's Road still scores more hits than misses, thanks to the "care taken sourcing the ingredients" and its "buzzy" atmosphere. It's perennially a "crowded" venue however, and a slip in ratings supports the odd reporter who feels that food-wise, its British small plates are "not quite punching up there like they used to". / SW3 4UP; www.rabbit-restaurant.com; rabbit_resto; Mon-Sat 10.30 pm, Sun 8 pm.

RAGAM W1 £36 421

57 CLEVELAND ST 020 7636 9098 2–1B

"The rather cramped interior isn't great but Keralan food is exceptional" at this "really good local independent Indian", near the Telecom Tower, which has delivered "very decent value for money" for four decades. ("More than a quarter of a century after my first visit, the dosas are still worth the trip. I think it's been redecorated as well!") / W1T 4JN; www.ragamindian.co.uk; Mon-Thu 11 pm, Fri & Sat 11.30 pm.

www.rasarestaurants.com; Mon-Sat 11 pm, Sun 9.30 pm.

RAMBUTAN SE1 £41 533

10 STONEY STREET NO TEL 10–*4C*

"A fantastic new Sri Lankan restaurant that really does things differently!": cookbook author Cythia Shanmugalingham opened her Borough Market newcomer in late 2022, and the dishes from its open kitchen – with much use of open grills – generated excellent ratings in our annual diners' poll. The press have utterly raved too: The Standard's Jimi Famurewa discovered a "buzzy, tropical playground" and had "an unforgettable, palate-rattling trip"; The Times's Giles Coren was "mesmerised by watching the chefs" and "such great use of different kinds of fire"; and the FT's Tim Hayward thought the food "so good it could heal wounds". / SE1 9AD; www.rambutanlondon.com; rambutan_ldn; Wed-Sat, Tue 10 pm.

RANDALL & AUBIN W1 £86 334

14-16 BREWER ST 020 7287 4447 4–*2D*

"A glorious spot for a boozy seafood bite, watching Soho stroll past" – this "always busy" and "buzzy" venue was converted over 25 years ago from an atmospheric old butcher's shop (est 1911) and oozes quirky Edwardian charm. Perch on a stool, and "exuberant staff" will serve you fizz and "expert fish dishes" ("simple, but cooked beautifully – fruits de mers, oysters, pints of prawns"). "It's not the most comfortable time, but worth it for the quality of the food and general ambience". "Long live R&A". / W1F OSG; www.randallandaubin.com; randallandaubin; Mon-Thu 11.30 pm, Fri & Sat midnight, Sun 10.30 pm.

RASA N16 £46 433

55 STOKE NEWINGTON CHURCH ST 020 7249 0344 1–*1C*

Still regarded as a "benchmark" for vegetarian cuisine – not just of the south Indian variety – Das Sreedharan's bright pink Stoke Newington fixture has for 30 years showcased the Keralan home cooking he grew up with. At one stage the flagship of a small group, these days the fleet is limited to here and its new 'Rasa Street' spin-off across the, er, street. / N16 0AR;

RASA SAYANG W1 £51 432

5 MACCLESFIELD STREET 020 7734 1382 5–*3A*

Ellen Chew's "always reliable" Chinatown outfit celebrates the Chinese-Malay street food she sold as a hawker in her Singapore youth, and is widely held to be "one of the better Malaysian restaurants" in town. Opened in 2008, it is now the flagship of her Chew On This group, with outlets across England. / W1D 6AY; www.rasasayangfood.com; rasasayang_london; Mon-Sat 10 pm, Sun 9 pm.

RASA STREET N16 £24 332

60-62 STOKE NEWINGTON CHURCH STREET 020 7254 8882 1–*1C*

"Well done Rasa!" – the revered veggie Keralan has "opened up a new restaurant in Stokey": opposite the original bright-pink Rasa, now in its 30th year, the latest venture from Das Sreedharan "stays true to the original, but also offers yummy fish dishes" with "a whole array of beautiful and tasty new options" – and "it's already a local hit". / N16 0NB; www.rasastreet.com; rasastreet; Tue-Sun 10 pm.

RAVI SHANKAR NW1 £35 322

133-135 DRUMMOND ST 020 7388 6458 9–*4C*

"Very well-priced vegetarian Indian thalis" have brought a steady ants' trail of diners to this fixture of the 'Little India' dining enclave behind Euston station for more than 40 years. "The buffets offer real value and choice". / NW1 2HL; www.ravishankarbhelpoori.com; Mon-Sun 11 pm.

THE RED LION & SUN N6 £63 333

25 NORTH ROAD 020 8340 1780 9–*1B*

"In an area where there's lots of options for dining out, it's not easy to get a reservation – that says it all" about this well-known Highgate gastropub – which serves "good seafood in addition to the usual pub favourites" and benefits from "an owner (Heath Ball) who knows his wine, with an excellent selection from his native NZ". It's also "rather grand" and "old established" – there's been a pub on the site for 500 years – and there are two gardens for eating al fresco. / N6 4BE; www.theredlionandsun.com; theredlionandsun; Mon-Sun 11 pm.

Story Cellar WC2

REGENCY CAFE SW1 £15 33

17-19 REGENCY STREET 020 7821 6596 2–*4C*

A definitive London caff – this Westminster institution has hardly changed since opening in 1946, and provides "the best fry-up you'll likely have had in years, with quality ingredients, well cooked and served in an iconic Art Deco setting". Breakfast here is "an experience every Londoner should try at least once in their life: consistent, quick and heavy" – and it's "as good as ever, even if there are lots of tourists now" ("you'll totally understand why people join the long queue"). / SW1P 4BY; regencycafe.co.uk; Mon-Fri 7.15 pm, Sat 12 pm.

LE RELAIS DE VENISE L'ENTRECÔTE £57 33

120 MARYLEBONE LN, W1 020 7486 0878 2–*1A*
5 THROGMORTON ST, EC2 020 7638 6325 10–*2C*

"So long as you don't mind queuing and the fact that there's just one item on the menu" – "entrecôte, salad, secret sauce and sublime frites" – this Gallic duo in Marylebone and the City can offer "a wonderful evening of no-frills dining", and it's an "obsession" to more ardent fans . "The only pressing question is 'house red or Bordeaux'" – while the "hugger-mugger seating and bustle is all part of the charm". The original Paris branch opened 60 years ago in a bankrupt Italian restaurant – hence the name. www.relaisdevenise.com; lerelaisdeveniseofficial.

REPUBLIC W4 £49 43

301-303 CHISWICK HIGH ROAD 020 8154 2712 8–*2A*

"Luscious, carefully spiced and original food" wins high ratings for this "very good upmarket Indian" in deepest Chiswick. Founders Kuldeep Mattegunta and Mustaq Tappewale (ex- Kricket, Amaya, Benares among others) took over the venue from the brilliant, much lamented Hedone (RIP), whose open kitchen makes it a "great place for chef watching". / W4 4HH; republicw4.com; republic_chiswick; Tue-Sat 10 pm.

ESTAURANT 1890 BY GORDON RAMSAY WC2 £211 344

TRAND 020 7499 0124 5–3D

Beautifully decorated", this small, gold-ecorated jewel box of a restaurant in the avoy opened in 2022 (a location that in days one by was a cheaper eatery called 'Upstairs', ng RIP). A major plus is its bird's-eye view f the comings and goings at the hotel's main ntrance, providing a superb talking-point r your date: the best use for the place as s few tables are mostly doubles and space tight. The main kitchens are elsewhere in e building, so the menu is "limited" but very good if you like what you receive". / /C2R 0EZ; www.gordonramsayrestaurants.com; staurant1890gordonramsay; Tue-Sat 11 pm.

HE RESTAURANT AT THE APITAL SW3 £98 332

2-24 BASIL STREET 020 7591 1202 6–1D

ack in the day, this small chamber – in a xury five-star near the back of Harrods was a much stiffer and foodie affair. In cent times the style has become laid-back bare tables and an all-day menu (much f it from a Josper grill). Feedback is a little p-and-down, but even a reporter who was a little disappointed" ultimately rated the xperience as "good all-round". / SW3 1AT; ww.therestaurantatthecapitallondon.com; ecapitalhotel; Mon-Sun 9.30 pm.

HE RESTAURANT AT THE WENTY TWO W1 £62 344

2 GROSVENOR SQUARE 20 3988 5022 3–2A

"stunning dining room" – stylishly decked ut in an elegant, traditional fashion – helps spire good vibes for this recently opened, understated-but-great" hotel (launched in pring 2022), just around the corner from e former American Embassy in Mayfair. hef Alan Christie aims for a 'Mediterranean ourish to modern British fare': the result is a cute menu that's expertly cooked". "Prices re steep but locally acceptable!" / W1K 6LF; ww.the22.london; the22.london; Mon-Sun idnight.

ESTAURANT ST. BARTS C1 £173 545

3 BARTHOLOMEW CLOSE 20 4547 7985 10–2B

ohnnie Crowe, Luke Wasserman and Toby Neill – "the team from Nest and Fenn – have rought their A-game" to this "beautiful" mithfield yearling, which opened in September 022. "No expense can have been spared in e design and fit-out of this wonderful space, tmospherically situated with a floodlit view of t-Bartholomew-the-Great through the massive windows". The "ambitious menu focuses on British ingredients" and each "adventurous" ourse is "cleverly delivered" and "with marvellous, personal service". "It's the finest of fine dining with some original and exceptional tastes from a fixed multi-course tasting menu". / EC1A 7BG; www.restaurant-stbarts.co.uk; restaurantstbarts; Wed & Thu, Tue 7.30 pm, Fri & Sat 8 pm.

REUBENS W1 £48 323

79 BAKER ST 020 7486 0035 2–1A

"Perennially popular and always great fun" – there's "nowhere better for excellent salt beef and chicken soup", say fans, than this classic Jewish deli in Baker Street – Britain's longest-running kosher restaurant, having opened (on a different site) in 1973. Restaurateur Lee Landau saved it from closure four years ago with plans for a revival of the basement fine-dining space, scheduled to open in late 2023. / W1U 6RG; www.reubensrestaurant.co.uk; reubens_restaurant; Sun-Thu 10 pm, Fri 2 pm.

RHYTHM & BREWS W4 £25 334

22 WALPOLE GARDENS 020 7998 3873 8–2A

"Brilliant vinyl in the background" – you can choose the records, and in the evenings listen to live music while sipping drinks from the licensed bar – sets the tone at this "wonderful and very relaxed neighbourhood café" not far from Turnham Green church. The coffee is notably good, staff are "lovely" and they "serve the best breakfast – complete with edible flowers!". / W4 4HA; rhythmandbrews.co.uk; rhythmandbrewscafe; Sun, Sat 5 pm, Mon-Fri 5pm.

THE RIB MAN E1 £11 44

BRICK LANE MARKET NO TEL 13–2C

"Messy but worthwhile!" – a trip to Mark Gevaux's acclaimed pitch on Sundays at Brick Lane, for his BBQ ribs and pork rolls from pigs reared outdoors in Norfolk and Suffolk. But the creator of 'Holy Fuck' hot sauce suffered an aneurism and underwent surgery in summer 2023 – wishing him all the best for a speedy recovery… not only is he a top bloke, but we all need him back at work… / E1 6HR; www.theribman.co.uk; theribman; Sun 2 pm.

RICCARDO'S SW3 £54 343

126 FULHAM RD 020 7370 6656 6–3B

This "fun" Tuscan tapas bar on a Chelsea corner is, say fans, "everything a local Italian should be", and celebrates its 30th anniversary next year. "It knows what it's good at and does it very, very well" – "though not exceptional, it's reasonably priced for SW3; and always relaxed and informal". / SW3 6HU; www.riccardos.it; riccardoslondon; Mon-Sun 11.30 pm.

RICHOUX W1 £56 333

172 PICCADILLY 020 3375 1000 3–3D

Decked out in cosy period style, this "slightly touristy"-looking Mayfair stalwart was rescued from administration in 2021 and is the surviving member of a now-defunct tearoom chain. Traditionally an afternoon tea place, there's more of an emphasis these days on its menu of "well-presented brasserie classics". At worst it's a "safe bet" for "a good pre-theatre supper", but some would argue that its "excellent offerings and well-spaced tables" means it can be more highly recommended. BREAKING NEWS. In September 2023, the restaurant closed as it was announced it will move to new premises in Soho, to open in late 2023. / W1Y 9DD; www.richoux.co.uk; richouxrestaurants; Tue-Sat 11 pm, Sun 5 pm.

RICK STEIN SW14 £90 222

TIDEWAY YARD, 125 MORTLAKE HIGH ST 020 8878 9462 11–1A

A "lovely location on the river" with "vistas over the Thames" is an uncontested attraction of the London outpost of the famous TV chef, near Barnes Bridge. It's not a huge advertisement for choosing a place according to the celebrity name over the door, as results are "hit and miss" to the extent that many diners view it as "consistently disappointing", "especially given the elevated prices". / SW14 8SN; www.rickstein.com; ricksteinrestaurants; Sun-Thu 9 pm, Fri & Sat 10 pm. SRA – accredited

RIDING HOUSE £64 223

43-51 GREAT TITCHFIELD ST, W1 020 7927 0840 3–1C
THE BRUNSWICK CENTRE, BERNARD STREET, WC1 020 3829 8333 2–1D

The "good-looking decor" and "varied menu with an enticing range of small plates, bowls and skewers" bring customers back to this well-established Fitzrovia haunt, now with a popular sibling in Bloomsbury's modernist Brunswick Centre ("nice place with lots of plants, like a conservatory"). They're a big hit for "a long lazy brekkie"; at other times the cooking can seem rather "uninspiring".

THE RISING SUN NW7 £70 343

137 MARSH LN 020 8959 1357 1–1B

"A true treasure in the leafy suburbs", this "small and quirky" 16th-century pub operates as a "restaurant spread over different rooms", "delivering a consistently high standard of high-quality British/Italian cooking". "Luca (Delnevo) and the team treat you as part of the extended family". / NW7 4EY; www.therisingsunmillhill.com; therisingsunmillhill; Tue-Sat 9.30 pm, Sun 8 pm.

RISTORANTE FRESCOBALDI W1 £89 233

15 NEW BURLINGTON PLACE 020 3693 3435 4–2A

This sumptuous Mayfair outpost from a Florentine banking dynasty offers a "great location"; "an atmosphere ideal for hedge fund types"; and wines "straight from the vineyards in Tuscany" (the family estates date back to 1308). There's also a "super outdoor space when the weather cooperates". Fans say the Italian cooking is "solid" – foes that it's "just not good enough – let alone for the price". / W1S 5HX; www.frescobaldi.london; frescobaldi_london; Mon-Sat 11 pm.

THE RITZ W1 £196 455

150 PICCADILLY 020 7300 2370 3–*4C*

"Like a holiday in heaven!" – this "simply wonderful" Louis XVI-style chamber is known for its "OTT but magnificent" decor, and creates an "unbeatable location" for a special celebration, particularly an important date. John Williams commands a brigade of 60 chefs in the kitchen to provide "absolutely wonderfully executed, classic dishes, some using gueridon service – so rare now – and always adding a sense of occasion". It's "some of the best cooking in London", and though "horrendously expensive" is justified by the "utterly sensational" all-round level of performance, which also includes "professional and kind" service and a wow of a wine list. "The Ritz is unusual in still having a jacket-and-tie dress code (about the only time I wear a tie these days!)". "A band provides music, for dancing, at dinner on weekends (although there is a significant supplement for this)". / W1J 9BR; www.theritzlondon.com; theritzlondon; Mon-Sun 9 pm.

THE RITZ, PALM COURT W1 £134 345

150 PICCADILLY 020 7493 8181 3–*4C*

"A truly iconic experience all round" – this "world famous", gilt chamber is "renowned for its elegant and sophisticated atmosphere" and provides "exactly what everybody expects from an Afternoon Tea", for which it remains London's No.1 choice: "a great treat for your mum on her birthday, with super sandwiches (loads of 'em – they don't scrimp here) and lots of tea options and other yummy bites"; "pricey and extravagant but worth it!". / W1J 9BR; www.theritzlondon.com; theritzlondon; Mon-Sun 7.30 pm.

RIVA SW13 £82 542

169 CHURCH RD 020 8748 0434 11–*1A*

"Really special cooking" – "simple, seasonal northern Italian dishes with excellent daily specials" – has won a star-studded following amongst food writers for Andreas Riva's Barnes fixture of over 30 years standing (Fay Maschler, Nigella Lawson and the late AA Gill have all cited it as a favourite). The uninitiated sometimes find its attractions pass them by and even fans admit that the "ambience, while OK, could do with a bit of a spruce up". "This is such an iconic restaurant" for its fan club though that all is easily forgiven – "I keep coming back year in year out and the quality of the food has not diminished and speaks for itself. Looking forward to our next meal already!" / SW13 9HR; Tue-Sat 10 pm, Sun 9 pm.

THE RIVER CAFÉ W6 £150 323

THAMES WHARF, RAINVILLE RD
020 7386 4200 8–*2C*

"Just keeping on delivering outstanding quality, year after year, with the highest-quality seasonal Italian food that's not over-elaborate" – Ruth Rogers' iconic Thames-side café in an obscure Hammersmith backstreet remains one of the most talked-about destinations in our annual diners' poll. Since its debut in 1987, it has helped drive culinary fashion. "They take the best fresh ingredients and the open-plan kitchen allows you to watch them work their magic" – an "exceptional" ingredient-led approach that's now practically ubiquitous in top kitchens. And it popularised the idea that top-notch food can be enjoyed in a "casual" setting, without flunkies and flummery: the bright, "noisy", "packed-in" space having originally been created as the canteen for her late husband's architectural practice (it helps that "it has a gorgeous riverside setting, especially outside on the terrace on a summer's day"). But, "while it's simply great, my God, do you pay for that simplicity". Yet again, it tops our list of 'most overpriced' restaurants as its "absurd prices seem to be multiplied by the number of years it has been open". As always our reporters have mixed feelings on this question of value. Some are unquestioning ("it's expensive, but you never feel ripped off"). For others, it's a struggle ("it never disappoints… so long as the heart attack when you get the bill doesn't end the evening prematurely"). And this year, those who "find it increasingly difficult to justify the expense" are gaining ground, particularly as the "beautiful" servers have seemed "very flakey" or "impersonal" on numerous occasions this year. "If you live near an airport, consider a day trip to Milan for lunch instead: it would work out cheaper…". Top Tip – "the winter weekday lunch is absolutely fantastic value and so delicious". / W6 9HA; www.rivercafe.co.uk; therivercafelondon; Mon-Sat 9 pm, Sun 3 pm.

RIVIERA SW1

23 ST JAMES'S STREET
020 7925 8988 3–*4D*

Aiming to bring Côte d'Azur style to stuffy old St James's – Arian & Alberto Zandi launched this bar and lounge in April 2023 on the interesting if offbeat 120-cover site (now with an open kitchen) that was formerly Sake no Hana (RIP). A 60-cover ground floor bar opened subsequently, together with a similarly sized terrace. Too few reports as yet for any rating – little in the MSM to-date either. / SW1A 1HA.

ROAST SE1 £80 224

STONEY ST 0845 034 7300 10–*4C*

The dramatic setting of a wrought-iron and glass portico – originally part of Covent Garden's Royal Opera House and now overlooking Borough Market – makes this "a great place for breakfasts or business lunches". More generally, though, its retro-British cuisine generates limited enthusiasm (the main problem is "it costs too much!"). / SE1 1TL; www.roast-restaurant.com; roast_restaurant; Tue-Fri, Mon, Sat 10 pm, Sun 6.30 pm.

ROCCA £51 22

73 OLD BROMPTON RD, SW7
020 7225 3413 6–*2B*
75-79 DULWICH VILLAGE, SE21
020 8299 6333 1–*4D*

With their "decent menu of Italian food at good prices" and terraces for al fresco dining, this low-key duo can be useful options – the South Ken branch is "perfect for a pre-museur or Sunday grazing trip", while its bigger Dulwich Village sibling is "filled with families and dogs". "You wouldn't make a special journey, but they're reliably pleasant". / www.roccarestaurants.com.

ROCHELLE CANTEEN E2 £70 23

16 PLAYGROUND GARDENS
020 7729 5677 13–*1C*

Melanie Arnold and Margot Henderson's (wife of St John's Fergus) not-so-secret venue near Spitalfields was converted in 2006 from the bik sheds of a former school. Aided by its hipster credentials, it has long been a regular inclusion on top-10 round-ups by food journalists. Feedback this year, however, invariably came with a catch: "good, but not quite as good as expected…", "food went downhill after the scrummy starters…", "overhyped and too cool for school…". / E2 7ES; www.arnoldandhenderson.com; rochelle canteen; Mon-Wed 2.45 pm, Thu-Sat 7.30 pm.

ROCK & ROSE £67 22

270-272 CHISWICK HIGH ROAD, W4
020 8948 8008 8–*2A*
106-108 KEW ROAD, TW9
020 8948 8008 1–*4A*

"Wonderful décor, a nice mix of cocktails and a lively buzz make this a very good local" that works equally "for a romantic meal or for celebrating a special event". The new branch in Chiswick generates most of the feedback this year, but Lorraine Angliss (also owner of Annie's and Little Bird) has run the Richmond original for 15 years.

ROCK & SOLE PLAICE WC2 £64 32

47 ENDELL ST 020 7836 3785 5–*1C*

A classic "cheap eats place" on the fringe of Covent Garden that's particularly handy for feeding groups on a budget, with "very good fish 'n' chips" that are "great for eating outside with the sun shining". There's been a chippie on the site since 1871 – although not under the current very 1970s name. / WC2H 9AJ; www.rockandsoleplaice.com; rockandsolelondon; Tue-Sat 11.30 pm.

ROJI W1 342

6B SOUTH MOLTON STREET NO TEL
-2B

One of London's top omakase-style experiences provided by husband and wife chef team, amas Naszi and Tomoko Hasegawa, at this nall 10-seater counter experience, in a yard ist off Mayfair's pedestrianised South Molton treet. Feedback in its first year of operation as been limited, so our rating is a conservative ne. / W1K 5SH; ro-ji.co.uk; ro_ji_ldn; Wed-Sat 30 pm.

ROKA £91 323

0 NORTH AUDLEY ST, W1
20 7305 5644 3–2A
7 CHARLOTTE ST, W1
20 7580 6464 2–1C
LDWYCH HOUSE, 71-91 ALDWYCH, WC2
20 7294 7636 2–2D
NIT 4, PARK PAVILION, 40 CANADA SQ,
14 020 7636 5228 12–1C

The pan-Asian food is yummy… the black cod exceptional" and the "buzzy" atmosphere "stunning", say fans of Arjun Waney and ainer Becker's svelte Japanese-inspired enues, where "you can either sit at the counter atching the kitchen (great if you're just two), r at a table"; and where "a typical meal is sushi r sashimi as a starter then a robata (charcoal rill) dish for a main". Its ratings slid this year, hough. Never cheap, prices are becoming "sky igh"; the cooking is "not as reliably good as it nce was"; and there was the odd incident of shocking" service. / www.rokarestaurant.com; okarestaurant.

ROKETSU W1 £294 543

2 NEW QUEBEC STREET
20 3149 1227 2–2A

This "completely original" two-year-old apanese restaurant in Marylebone offers "a reat and authentic kaiseki experience" with luxury ingredients and amazing presentation" rom chef-patron Daisuke Hayashi, who ained at Kyoto's famous Kikunoi. The nterior, complete with 10-seater counter, was ailor-made in the Sukiya style from 100-year-ld hinoki wood in Kyoto and shipped over, which means "being in the dining room is like eing transported to Japan". A la carte dining s also available in the Bo-sen 'wine and dining oom', where guests relax over a light meal n mid-century European armchairs, with a hoice of 500 wines and sakes. / W1H 7RW; ww.roketsu.co.uk; roketsulondon; Tue-Sat 10 pm.

ROMULO CAFÉ W8 £64 343

43 KENSINGTON HIGH STREET
20 3141 6390 8–1D

A pioneer in championing dishes from he Philippines" – this Kensington feature pened in 2016 and helped pave the way for what's nowadays a healthy level of interest n the cuisine in the Capital. It's named or a well-known Filipino diplomat whose randchildren own the venture; and who also run a number of similarly branded cafés back home in Asia. / W8 6NW; www.romulocafe.co.uk; romulocafelondon; Wed-Sun 9.30 pm.

ROOF GARDEN AT PANTECHNICON SW1 £90 225

19 MOTCOMB ST 020 7034 5426 6–1D

"Costa del Belgravia anyone? On a sunny day, you're entirely justified eating in your sunnies" in this "roof-top bar/restaurant" with a retractable glass ceiling on top of the landmark Pantechnicon building. But while all agree on the merits of the stunning location, views on the food range from "great" via "fairly standard" to frankly "awful": at the very least, it is inconsistent. / SW1X 8LB; www.pantechnicon.com; Tue, Wed 11 pm, Thu & Fri 00 , Sat 00 pm, Sun 10 pm.

THE ROSENDALE SE21 £56 333

65 ROSENDALE ROAD
020 8761 9008 1–4D

"Brilliant pub grub" wins a nod at this Victorian former coaching inn in West Dulwich, with plenty of outdoor space that is covered and heated in winter. It's family-friendly, so gets "a bit noisy" at times. / SE21 8EZ; www.therosendale.co.uk; therosendalepub; Mon-Thu 11 pm, Fri & Sat midnight, Sun 10.30 pm.

ROSMARINO SW17 £46 333

23 TRINITY ROAD 020 8244 0336 11–2C

"Tiny, buzzy and authentic Italian" in Tooting Bec – on the fringe of the area's burgeoning gastro zone – that's "a bit of a neighbourhood gem", with its smart modern styling and "some unusual menu offerings that lift it a cut above average". Owner-operators Daria & Giovanni set up on their own account five years ago after establishing themselves in the industry. / SW17 7SD; www.rosmarinorestaurant.co.uk; rosmarinorestaurant; Tue-Sat 10.30 pm, Sun 10 pm.

ROSSLYN COFFEE EC4 £8 343

78 QUEEN VICTORIA STREET NO TEL
10–3B

This five-year-old in the City (now with three outlets) has won international recognition for its "exceptional" coffee, sourced from some of the world's leading independent roasteries. The name? Founders James Hennebry and Mat Russell picked up the caffeine habit in Melbourne, location of Rosslyn Street. / EC4N 4SJ; Mon-Thu 10.30 pm, Fri-Sun 11 pm.

ROTI CHAI W1 £48 322

3 PORTMAN MEWS SOUTH
020 7408 0101 3–1A

"There's a wide range of options to explore" on the extensive menu of this "Indian street-food" café, in a side-alley near Selfridges: "great simple food at reasonable prices" and cooked to a "consistently high level". Upstairs makes a "perfect location for lunch". There's a more formal basement dining room, better suited to evening meals. / W1H 6AY; www.rotichai.com; rotichai; Mon-Sat 10 pm, Sun 9 pm.

ROTI KING £15 522

IAN HAMILTON HOUSE, 40 DORIC WAY, NW1
020 7387 2518 9–3C
CIRCUS WEST VILLAGE,
BATTERSEA POWER STATION, SW8
020 4580 1282 11–1C

"Huge queues are par for the course but worth it in spades", when visiting this "sensational" basement – "a great, basic pit stop" on "a dodgy street near Euston station" where you "pack in tight" for the "amazing, fresh and feather-light rotis", "excellent laksa" and other "stalwart Malaysian dishes". "For a satisfying, cheap meal" many would say this is "the best value in town". There's also now a larger spin-off in the Battersea Power Station development – "it's good, but the original is still the favourite". / rotikinguk.

ROTUNDA BAR & RESTAURANT, KINGS PLACE N1 £62 224

90 YORK WAY 020 7014 2840 9–3C

At the foot of the King's Place arts centre – a "lovely space overlooking water" with a glorious canal-side terrace – Green & Fortune's stylish venue offers a "good selection of small plates and excellent, if pricey, beef and lamb" from its own farm in Northumberland. "The pre-concert set menu is super value, but best of all is the Sunday roast lunch". / N1 9AG; www.rotundabarandrestaurant.co.uk; rotundalondon; Tue-Sat midnight, Mon 11 pm, Sun 9 pm.

ROVI W1 £89 333

59-65 WELLS STREET
020 3963 8270 3–1D

"I don't know how Ottolenghi comes up with those flavour combinations but the result is genius!", say fans of Yotam O's Fitzrovia flagship, which lives up to his renown for "exceptionally varied and delicious food with a focus on the Middle East (but also with some oriental influences)". "Served mostly as small plates so great for sharing", they're "particularly talented at vegetable dishes, but overall everything tastes good". There's also a "short but interesting wine list". It would score even higher but for the odd niggle: be it about "erratic, if charming" service; or toppish prices. Top Menu Tip – "in a high-quality field, the celeriac shawarma really stands out". / W1A 3AE; www.ottolenghi.co.uk; rovi_restaurant; Sun-Fri & Sat 10.30 pm.

ROWLEY'S SW1 £93 223

113 JERMYN ST 020 7930 2707 4–4D

"Steak, as many hot chips as you can handle, good claret... and that's about it really" – sums up the appeal of this "traditional" St James's steakhouse that occupies the site where Wall's became famous for their sausages. "Does exactly what it says on the tin", although it's seen as "rather overpriced" – "you're paying for the name and the location". / SW1Y 6HJ; www.rowleys.co.uk; rowleys_restaurant; Tue-Sat 11.30 pm.

ROYAL CHINA £67 322

24-26 BAKER ST, W1 020 7487 4688 2–*1A*
805 FULHAM RD, SW6
020 7731 0081 11–*1B*
30 WESTFERRY CIRCUS, E14
020 7719 0888 12–*1B*

"Sunday dim sum lunch is always full of happy families" at this popular Cantonese group with 1980s-nightclub decor – an occasion for which they "cannot be beaten" for many diners: so "arrive around 10:45 to join queue for 11am opening". With the closure of its Bayswater branch a few years ago, Baker Street and Canary Wharf are its preeminent spots (and SW6 can be "disappointing" by comparison). All feedback is about the lunchtime service – "the evening offering is a bit ordinary". / www.royalchinagroup.co.uk.

ROYAL CHINA CLUB W1 £76 432

38-42 BAKER STREET
020 7486 3898 2–*1A*

"Best dim sum I've had in a long time – everything was best-in-class": reporters are unanimous in their praise for the "always great" Cantonese cooking at the Marylebone flagship of the Royal China group. But there's some pushback against the prices: "eye-wateringly expensive, compared to the standard competition, if comparable to their Hakkasan/Yauatcha-peers". / W1U 7AJ; www.royalchinagroup.co.uk; Mon-Sun 9 pm.

RUDY'S W1 £34 343

80-82 WARDOUR ST 020 7734 0195 4–*2D*

From Naples via Manchester to Soho – this "really top-quality joint in a former Wahaca is definitely a positive addition to the London pizza scene". "The smiley, friendly service" and "big portions" – legacies perhaps of its Northern origins – "make the opposition look second rate". It's part of Manchester's expanding Mission Mars stable, which is planning more Rudy's and Albert's Schlosses in the capital and beyond. / W1F 0TG; www.rudyspizza.co.uk; wearerudyspizza; Sun-Thu 9 pm, Fri & Sat 10.30 pm.

RULES WC2 £83 335

35 MAIDEN LN 020 7836 5314 5–*3D*

"What's not to like about the oldest restaurant in London?" – in continuous operation on the same Covent Garden site since 1798. Of course, it's "popular with tourists", but its "quintessentially British" style makes it an "old favourite" for many Londoners too, and it provides "a beautiful, traditional experience". The atmosphere of the beautiful dining room is "exceptional" and the "old school cuisine, with an emphasis on meat and game", is very dependable; and backed up by an "extensive, if quite expensive wine list". Top Menu Tip – "lovely steak 'n' kidney pie". / WC2E 7LB; www.rules.co.uk; rules_restaurant; Mon-Sat 11.30 pm, Sun 10 pm.

SABOR W1 £68 555

35 HEDDON ST 020 3319 8130 4–*3A*

"Just wonderful: fresh… lively… exciting and always interesting!" – that's this year's worst (!) report of many lauding Nieves Barragan and José Etura's phenomenal slice of Spain, just off Regent Street. "A seat at the counter, if you can snag one (get there early, or be prepared to queue – it's well worth it) transports one to Andalucia or Castile, and the assured food is as good as it is there". Or "eat upstairs at the El Asador dining room" (which is bookable nowadays). "Seating can be a little cramped but it all adds to the atmosphere". Top Menu Tip – "crisp piglet never disappoints". / W1B 4BP; www.saborrestaurants.co.uk; sabor_ldn; Tue-Sat 10.30 pm.

LE SACRÉ-COEUR N1 £50 332

18 THEBERTON ST 020 7354 2618 9–*3D*

"French comfort food in a cosy setting in the heart of Islington" is just the ticket at this long-serving outfit, where "both cuisine and ambience resemble a bistro in France two or three decades ago". "Wines have a restrained mark-up", and there's a "super-value set lunch which is also available on Saturdays". Top Menu Tip – "boeuf bourguignon is particularly good". / N1 0QX; lesacrecoeurbistro.co.uk; lesacrecoeurfrenchbistro; Mon-Sun midnight.

SACRO CUORE £43 332

10 CROUCH END HILL, N8
020 8348 8487 1–*1C*
45 CHAMBERLAYNE RD, NW10
020 8960 8558 1–*2B*

"Top Neapolitan pizza", say fans of this Kensal Rise 11-year-old and its Crouch End offshoot, which offers a "limited and delicious menu (they stick to what they know) in cool surroundings". / www.sacrocuore.co.uk; sacrocuorepizza.

SAGAR £45 332

37 PANTON STREET, SW1
020 3093 8463 5–*4A*
17A PERCY ST, W1 020 7631 3319 3–*1D*
31 CATHERINE ST, WC2
020 7836 6377 5–*3D*
157 KING ST, W6 020 8741 8563 8–*2C*

The "absolutely delicious" South Indian vegan and vegetarian food at this quintet of low-key cafés – stretching from Harrow to Covent Garden – is "good enough to keep carnivores quiet": in particular "the dosas, which are just what you want from a dosa: crispy, tender, flavourful". The formula is "simple but it works, even if the menu is always the same"; and it helps that the experience comes at "very reasonable prices". / www.sagarrestaurant.co.uk.

SAINT JACQUES SW1 £87 43[illegible]

5 ST JAMES'S ST 020 7930 2030 3–*4D*

This "delightful" and "very trad (in a good way) French resto" in St James's thrives on its "unpretentious, classic cooking delivered by efficient and accommodating waiting staff" under an "entertaining boss who seems to know everyone". "There have been several very good restaurants on this site (Boulestin and L'Oranger inter alia) and Saint Jacques is up there with any of them". Top Menu Tip – "the theatre of crêpes Suzette cooked by the table is highly recommended". / SW1A 1EF; www.saintjacquesrestaurant.com; saintjacquesrestaurant; Mon-Fri 22, Sat 10 pm.

ST JOHN BREAD & WINE E1 £74 43[illegible]

94-96 COMMERCIAL ST
020 7251 0848 13–*2C*

"Wearing the 'nose-to-tail' mantle a little more lightly" than the Smithfield original, Trevor Gulliver and Fergus Henderson's Spitalfields canteen hits the nail on the head for many diners. Its robust British small plates are "seriously good – different, and utterly deliciou[s] with plenty of offal" – and "the wine list with lesser known bottles is also interesting". "The room may be clinical" but "its basic style is attractive… if you like that sort of thing". Top Menu Tip – "the best bacon butty in London!", plus "mega Eccles cakes with Lancashire cheese to fill you up". / E1 6LZ; www.stjohngroup.uk.com; st.john.restaurant; Mon-Sun 9.30 pm.

ST JOHN SMITHFIELD EC1 £82 44[illegible]

26 ST JOHN ST 020 7251 0848 10–*1B*

"Still love the place…" – Trevor Gulliver and Fergus Henderson's icon of British cuisine coined the concept of 'nose-to-tail dining' and hasn't missed a beat since it opened in 1994, in a "stark-but-chic" ex-smokehouse, near Smithfield Market. Known for its "sometimes challenging menu (not least for its selection of offal dishes)", it continues to deliver "totally brilliant", "straightforward" dishes ("the cuts may be humble, but the results are of the highest grade") from "good old-fashioned recipes" in its distinctive "white-walled, down-to-earth" setting, whose ultra-utilitarian style is livened up by "entertaining" service that's "very kind and personable". Top Menu Tip – "puddings are to die for (I don't have a sweet tooth but this is the only restaurant where I ALWAYS have a pudding)". / EC1M 4AY; stjohnrestaurant.com; st.john.restaurant; Mon-Sat 10.30 pm, Sun 4 pm.

ST JOHNS N19 £66 33[illegible]

91 JUNCTION RD 020 7272 1587 9–*1C*

Fans hail this Archway tavern as "the best for miles around" (it was George Michael's favourite back in the day) – "always welcoming", and with a "terrific menu of

ticks'n'Sushi

nainly British cuisine" served in the dining oom, which has "some charm as a former allroom". Top Menu Tip – the "great roast eef" is a treat for Sunday lunch. / N19 5QU; ww.stjohnstavern.com; stjohnstavern; Tue-Sat 10 m, Sun 6 pm.

T MORITZ W1 £66 333

61 WARDOUR STREET
20 7734 3324 4–*1C*

hat "you could almost be in the Alps" is the aison d'être of this chalet-style veteran in oho, celebrating its half-century this year. here is the odd long-term visitor who feels s performance is so-so nowadays, and that 's "time to call it a day on this long-time nstitution". But in general, reviews are positive or its "traditional Swiss menu which caters for ll lovers of the country's food". "It may be escribed as looking old-fashioned, but I have aten in many restaurants in Switzerland which ook exactly like this; absolute classics!" / W1F WJ; www.stmoritz-restaurant.co.uk; st.moritzsoho; Mon-Sat 11.30 pm, Sun 10.30 pm.

AKONIS £34 332

27-129 EALING RD, HA0
20 8903 9601 1–*1A*
30 UXBRIDGE ROAD, HA5
20 8903 9601 1–*1A*

n all-you-can-eat buffet – with options at reakfast, lunch and dinner – is a longstanding eature of this no-frills veggie veteran: a family usiness that started out as a market stall in 984. It also offers an à la carte menu, which ncludes a significant Indo-Chinese section. No alcohol, so knock yourself out on the array f milkshakes and lassis. (It also has offshoots n Hatch End and Kingsbury). / sakonis.co.uk; akonis_uk.

ALE E PEPE SW1 £83

-15 PAVILION ROAD 020 7235 0098 6–*1D*

Retired maître d' Tony and his team created n atmosphere that was "mad, crowded, noisy et still great fun" at this fifty-year-old Trattoria est. 1974), long known for providing relatively good value for somewhere not far from the ack door of Harrods. In February 2023, it was aken over by The Thesleff Group, whose press elease promises 'a revitalised energy and subtle hanges' to this old groover, which includes a trendified menu. No reports from the old egulars as yet on the new regime so we've left it un-rated for the time being. / SW1X 0HD; www.saleepepe.co.uk; saleepepelondon; Mon-Sat 10.30 pm, Sun 10 pm.

LE SALON PRIVÉ TW1 £73 333

43 CROWN RD 020 8892 0602 1–*4A*

For a quality meal out St Margaret's way, this conventional French restaurant – set in agreeably old-fashioned Victorian premises – provides a traditional and enjoyable experience that's consistently well-rated in our annual diners' poll. Top Tip – good-value 'menu du jour' available at lunch and at dinner early in the week. / TW1 3EJ; lesalonprive.net; lesalon_prive; Tue-Sat 21.30 pm, Sun 4 pm.

SALT YARD £61 322

54 GOODGE ST, W1 020 7637 0657 2–*1B*
THE SOUTHERN TERRACE, ARIEL WAY, W12 020 7749 3834 1–*3B*
NEW HIBERNIA HOUSE, WINCHESTER WALK, SE1 020 8161 0171 10–*4C*

"The original Salt Yard in W1 used to be one of London's best new tapas restaurants" – but it opened over 15 years ago and "the subsequent roll-out of the brand as multiple branches" under Urban Pubs & Bars "has seen quality drop quite a lot". As "a pleasant option for well-produced Med-inspired dishes", they maintain a fair number of fans, if without the pizzazz once conjured by the name. The year-old branch near the entrance to Westfield is the highest rated, and the newest near Borough Market is also seen as "a handy addition to the group". / www.saltyardgroup.co.uk; saltyardgroup.

SALTIE GIRL W1 £75 343

15 NORTH AUDLEY STREET
020 3893 3000 3–*2A*

"You will not believe how good canned fish can be!" – this late 2022 newcomer from a Boston chain maxes out on luxurious seafood treats ("delicious oysters, caviar, premium tinned seafood and of course lobster rolls!") and provides both "a nice change of pace" and also "a great addition to the Mayfair food scene". "The fresh fish is excellent. The dozens of tinned fish options are surprisingly varied and tasty – like having a North Sea picnic when you don't want a full meal". / W1K 6WZ; www.saltiegirl.com; saltiegirl.london; Mon-Sat 11 pm, Sun 4 pm.

SALUT N1 £79 444

412 ESSEX ROAD 020 3441 8808 9–*3D*

This "lovely neighbourhood restaurant" in Islington from brothers Martin & Christoph Lange thrives thanks to a "really good all-round menu" fusing Nordic, French and German influences, and a "New York-style ambience". / N1 3PJ; www.salut-london.co.uk; salut.restaurant; Mon-Thu 9.30 pm, Fri & Sat 10 pm, Sun 9 pm.

SAM'S CAFÉ NW1 £28 322

40 CHALCOT ROAD 020 7916 3736 9–*3B*

"This upmarket local café" with artistic leanings in Primrose Hill has a "great vibe, relaxed-yet-warm service and consistently good food". Founded by actor Sam Frears and novelist Andrew O'Hagan, who live nearby, it has an artist-in-residence programme and hosts readings, live music and community supper clubs. / NW1 8LS; www.samscafeprimrosehill.com; samscafeprimrosehill; Mon & Tue, Thu-Sun 10 pm, Wed 5 pm.

SAM'S KITCHEN W6

17 CRISP ROAD 020 8237 1020 8–*2C*

Just behind Sam's Riverside, on the site that was Café Plum (RIP) – Sam Harrison's vision of a 'perfect little local corner café' offers a full English breakfast and all-day bacon rolls alongside more contemporary dishes such as beetroot with halloumi and za'atar on sourdough with goat's cheese, crushed nuts, pickled red onion, roasted garlic confit and poached eggs. It opened in summer 2023, too late for feedback in our annual diners' poll. / W6 9RL; samsriverside.co.uk; samskitchenw6; Mon-Sun 4 pm.

SAM'S RIVERSIDE W6 £81 355

1 CRISP WALK 020 8237 1020 8–*2C*

"Sam himself is very much in evidence" at his "glamourous" brasserie, which has an "ideal location on the Thames" – "with a close-up view of Hammersmith Bridge" – and whose popularity is making it "a destination restaurant" for a huge fan club spread across west London. "You could describe it as the perfect local – but it's smarter than that", with a "lovely" (and expensively decorated) interior and "super vibe". "The menu is full of well-crafted crowd- pleasers" and – though not hugely 'gastro' – its "seafood orientation" (and "wonderful seafood platters") makes anything pescatarian a top choice. "Packed to the rafters", it's "a great night out". / W6 9DN; samsriverside.co.uk; samsriversidew6; Mon-Sat 10 pm, Sun 4 pm.

SAM'S WATERSIDE TW8

CATHERINE WHEEL ROAD AWAITING TEL 1–*3A*

Restaurateur Sam Harrison's smart neighbourhood restaurant and bar is designed to help anchor the new Brentford Project – an upscale, mixed-use development beside the

River Brent, open in summer 2023. It follows the success of Sam's Riverside at the re-opened Riverside Studios by Hammersmith Bridge, although it doesn't have the sweeping Thames -side vistas of the original. (There is also a Sam's Larder opposite). / TW8 8BD.

SAMBAL SHIOK N7 £47 322

171 HOLLOWAY ROAD
020 7619 9888 9–*2D*

"Fantastic laksa – available in vegetarian versions" – is a crowd-pleaser at Mandy Lim's hawker-style Malaysian spot on the Holloway Road. Her authentic version is in the 'campur' style found in Malacca – combining Kuala Lumpur's curry laksa with Penang's fiery assam. If you don't like noodles, rice bowls are also on offer. / N7 8LX; www.sambalshiok.co.uk; sambalshiok; Tue-Thu 9 pm, Fri & Sat 9.30 pm.

SAN CARLO SW1 £82 333

2 REGENT STREET SAINT JAMES'S
020 3778 0768 4–*4D*

"The warmth of the welcome and quality of the food can come as something of a surprise at such a central and well-known location" as this West End branch (just north of Pall Mall) of the national group, created by Sicilian-born Carlo Distefano and now with over 20 locations nationwide. Perhaps it's the "lovely atmosphere for either a business or social lunch or dinner" that's its key strength, but all reports suggest the "great and varied menu" is also "consistently good". / SW1Y 4AU; sancarlo.co.uk; sancarlorestaurants; Mon-Sun 11.30 pm.

SAN CARLO CICCHETTI £68 344

215 PICCADILLY, W1 020 7494 9435 4–*4C*
30 WELLINGTON ST, WC2
020 7240 6339 5–*3D*
6 HANS ROAD, SW3 020 7846 7145 6–*1D*

"Don't be put off by the tourist location or the gold frontage" if you visit the flagship branch of this successful Italian chain near Piccadilly Circus (which is due to double in size over 2023). For a national group, it and its siblings deliver a surprisingly high-quality formula that mixes "a great range of Venetian-style small plates" with "friendly and efficient" service and "bright and vibrant interiors" which create a "wonderful and buzzing atmosphere". Top Tip – "super for pre-theatre eating". / www.sancarlocicchetti.co.uk; sancarlorestaurants.

SAN PIETRO W8 £56 334

7 STRATFORD ROAD 020 7938 1805 6–*1A*

"A wonderful display of fresh fish on ice" ("including the biggest scallops with the coral attached") greets diners arriving at this "unique Italian" in a quiet corner of Kensington, whose "cooking is precise with a light touch". / W8 6RF; www.san-pietro.co.uk; sanpietro7; Mon-Sun 10 pm.

SANTA MARIA £47 423

160 NEW CAVENDISH ST, W1
020 7436 9963 2–*1B*
92-94 WATERFORD ROAD, SW6
020 7384 2844 6–*4A*
11 BOND STREET, W5
020 8579 1462 1–*3A*
189 UPPER STREET, N1
020 7288 7400 9–*2D*

"Glorious-tasting authentic Neapolitan pizza", "with interesting toppings that are quite unique", is the USP of this Ealing-based operation launched in 2010 by Naples-born duo Angelo and Pasquale, which has grown in recent years into a small group with outlets as far away as Islington and Fitzrovia. Their "aim is to transport you to Naples, and the pizzas live up to the ambition". / www.santamariapizzeria.com; santamariapizza.

SANTA MARIA DEL SUR SW8 £60 332

129 QUEENSTOWN ROAD
020 7622 2088 11–*1C*

"Friendly" Argentinian steakhouse that's clocked up 18 years in Battersea, with well-priced cuts of beef complemented by empanadas at lunchtime and a list of South American wines. Top Tip – on Sundays you can bring your own wine, with no corkage fee. / SW8 3RH; www.santamariadelsur.co.uk; stamariadelsur; Mon-Sun 10 pm.

SANTINI SW1 £116 233

29 EBURY ST 020 7730 4094 2–*4B*

Food writer Laura Santini nowadays oversees this datedly chic Belgravia Italian founded by her father Gino in 1984, and which had quite a celebrity following back in the day (Frank Sinatra was a fan). Ever since we started our guide in 1991, it's been priced for the rich residents of SW1 (a bowl of pasta is about £30), and most years don't see a huge volume of reports. Representative of feedback this year: "OK food on the whole (if unexciting)… and big wine list mark-ups". / SW1W 0NZ; www.santinirestaurant.com; santinirestaurant; Mon-Sat 11.30 pm.

SANTO MARE W1 £97 343

87-89 GEORGE STREET
020 7486 0377 2–*1A*

High-quality Italian seafood (some of it fresh from the tank) and elegant decor help win solid ratings for Andrea Reitano's Marylebone fixture, which is about to enter its fifth year. But there's the odd cavil from diners who say it has "excellent food and good service but is more expensive than it should be". / W1U 8AQ; www.santomare.com; santomare; Mon-Sun 11 pm.

SANTO REMEDIO £72 332

152 TOOLEY STREET, SE1
020 7403 3021 10–*4D*
55 GREAT EASTERN STREET, EC2
020 7403 3021 13–*1B*

"Proper home-made nachos" backed up by "awesome margaritas" top the "short but focused menu" at Edson & Natalie Diaz-Fuentes's authentic Mexican cantina in Bermondsey (with an offshoot in Shoreditch). Top Tip – "the reasonably priced pre-theatre menu is perfect before going to the Bridge Theatre".

SARAVANAA BHAVAN HA0 £53 422

531-533 HIGH RD 020 8900 8526 1–*1A*

"If feels like being transported to SB in Chennai", according to well-travelled fans of the Wembley branch of this global vegetarian chain offering "reasonably priced South Indian food", who say that "if you're hankering for a masala dosa, this is the place". There are actually seven branches around the capital (including Leicester Square and Tooting), but this is the most commented-on. (Historical footnote: P Rajagopal, who founded SB in 1981, died five years ago after being imprisoned for the murder of an employee whose wife he wanted to marry.) / HA0 2DJ; saravanabhavanlondon.co.uk; saravanaa bhavan london; Mon-Sun 10.30 pm.

SARTORIA W1 £94 333

20 SAVILE ROW 020 7534 7000 4–*3A*

This classic Italian set among the tailors of Savile Row (for which it is named and themed) serves "outstanding" dishes – most notably seafood – at admittedly "expensive" prices. Celebrity chef Francesco Mazzei departed in early 2023, leaving the D&D London venue lacking a high-profile figurehead, but thus far, this has seemingly had little effect on the quality of the cooking. / W1S 3PR; www.sartoria-restaurant.co.uk; sartoriarestaurant; Mon-Sat 10 pm. SRA – accredited

THE SAVOY HOTEL, SAVOY GRILL WC2 £154 224

STRAND 020 7592 1600 5–*3D*

A two-month closure facilitated a 'Gatsby makeover' this year at this elegant and famous grill room, which for the last 20 years has been part of Gordon Ramsay's culinary empire. (It now incorporates a chef's table, and a walnut wood-lined wine experience room for eight). With its Beef Wellington, Dover Sole and Lobster Thermidor – plus also a selection of steaks from now de rigueur charcoal grill – fans say it's "superb all round for celebrating that special occasion". Doubters, though, continue to focus on its "extortionate prices and very uninspired menu in this newly redecorated Art Deco space". / WC2R 0EU; www.gordonramsayrestaurants.com; savoygrillgordonramsay; Mon-Sat midnight, Sun 11.30 pm.

Sushi Kanesaka W1

THE SAVOY HOTEL, THAMES FOYER WC2 £115 2 4 5

91 THE STRAND 020 7420 2111 5–*3D*

"Is there a better way to spend the afternoon?", query fans of the "beautiful" foyer of this famous hotel – "a wonderful room with the piano playing and where the sandwiches just keep coming!" Supporters say "nothing can compare to the high level of cakes" and that service is "above par" too. Ratings are capped, though, by one or two more cautious reports, from those who "were expecting more of the tea" (too weak) and/or the victuals. When it comes to the music, there's also some debate – "I hated the Disney tunes being played on the piano, although admittedly I was tempted to stand and join in when it moved on to Les Mis!" / WC2R 0ER; www.thesavoylondon.com; thesavoylondon; Mon & Tue 4 pm, Wed-Sun 6 pm.

THE RIVER RESTAURANT, THE SAVOY WC2 £103 2 2 3

91 THE STRAND 020 7499 0122 5–*3D*

Gordon Ramsay's two-year-old tenure has yet to dazzle at this Thames-side dining room (which, two years ago – when Gordon took it over – returned to the name under which it was launched in 1890 and has traded under for much of the last century). From its days as Kaspar's (RIP), it continues a fish and seafood theme – now with a fashionable raw bar – and there are also a few meat grills on the menu. But few dishes catch the eye from the somewhat "unremarkable" selection and it can be "difficult to find something you fancy". And, when they arrive, too often results are "only moderately good" or plain "disappointing". / WC2R 0EU; www.gordonramsayrestaurants.com; riverrestaurantbygordonramsay; Mon-Sat midnight, Sun 11.30 pm.

SCALINI SW3 £95 3 4 3

1-3 WALTON ST 020 7225 2301 6–*2C*

This "really good old-school Italian" in Knightsbridge is a perfect fit for the Harrods shopping crowd it feeds, and "has hardly changed in 30 years". Expansion in recent years has seen spin-offs open in Cannes and the Middle East, which gives a clue to the prices charged. Top Menu Tip – "the bruschetta they give you as you sit down is great, but make sure you ask for cheese as well". / SW3 2JD; www.scalinilondon.co.uk; scaliniuk; Mon-Sat 10.45 pm, Sun 10 pm.

THE SCARSDALE W8 £67 2 3 5

23A EDWARDES SQ 020 7937 1811 8–*1D*

On one level it's like any other "friendly local", but few pubs have such a picturesque location as this popular tavern, on the kind of Regency square in Kensington that makes tourists swoon (and with its own cute outside terrace). "Great pub-like food" (without any gastro pretensions) is served in its "lively" dining room. Piers Morgan throws an annual Christmas party here, hosting celeb pals from TV and politics, with Gary Lineker in regular attendance… well, nowhere's perfect… / W8 6HE; www.scarsdaletavern.co.uk; scarsdalew8; Mon-Sat 11 pm, Sun 10.30 pm.

SCHNITZEL FOREVER N16 £51 3 3 2

119 STOKE NEWINGTON CHURCH STREET 020 7419 0022 1–*1C*

"Literally the size of a dinner plate", the schnitzels at this tiled Stoke Newington two-year-old are "freshly made", "tender & super-tasty", and come with "great sides – especially the pickled cucumber salad". The classics (veal, pork, chicken) take their cue from German-speaking central Europe, but the menu strays as far as Mexico and Japan to up the variety. A spin-off opened in Hoxton under the name Schnitzel Heaven in early 2023. / N16 0UD; www.schnitzelforever.co.uk; schnitzel_forever; Mon, Wed & Thu, Sat 10 pm, Fri 10.30 pm, Sun 9.30 pm.

SCOTT'S W1 £113 3 3 4

20 MOUNT ST 020 7495 7309 3–*3A*

"Always sparkling" – this "glamorous" Mayfair "classic" (007's favourite) is nowadays second only to its Theatreland stablemate Sheekeys in terms of the total number of nominations it receives in our annual diners' poll; and likewise in the rankings as a "go-to place for fish". More "sophisticated" (and expensive) than its rival, the crowd is better heeled and more A-lister here than in WC2 (and also, perhaps, with a greater share of "flash Harrys"). "Excellent Dover Sole", "the best crab" and "top-quality fruits de mer" are typical of the "superb seafood", "classily" delivered by "professional" staff, all of which make it popular for most occasions, including business entertaining. "It slipped down in the estimations" of one or two reporters this year due to general concerns that it risks becoming "overrated and overpriced". But for the vast majority, the feeling is still that although "it's obviously not cheap, it's a real treat and a totally reliable one at that". / W1K 2HE; www.scotts-restaurant.com; scottsmayfair; Mon-Sat 1 am, Sun 9.30 pm.

SCOTT'S RICHMOND TW9 £113 2 3 4

4 WHITTAKER AVENUE 020 3700 2660 1–*4A*

"They must have spent a fortune on the decor" of this "absolutely stunning" Richmond newcomer, with a "terrace overlooking the Thames": Richard Caring's first spin-off from Mayfair's legendary Scott's. But while everyone is sold on the "wonderful dining room with its riverside view", views on the cuisine diverge. Fans say its luxurious seafood menu "has transferred very well" delivering "top-quality" Fruits de Mer, Lobster Bisque and other fishy delights. But its ratings in our annual diners' poll are not nearly as strong as in W1. Firstly, there are numerous reservations about it being "totally overpriced". Secondly, it can seem like a poor substitute ("I was excited to visit the newly opened Scott's in Richmond, a great addition to the area, so I thought. But this version is nothing like the original, it is like an Ivy Café under another name"). / TW9 1EH; www.scotts-richmond.com; scottsrichmond; Mon-Sat 12.30 am, Sun midnight.

SCULLY SW1 £91 4 4 2

4 ST JAMES'S MARKET 020 3911 6840 4–*4D*

"Ramuel Scully gets flavour out of ingredients like no one else" at his ambitious St James's Market fixture, where he and his team serve a "wacky and interesting menu based on ferment and underused ingredients" from their open kitchen. Its ratings are not as stratospheric as when it first opened, due to the odd doubt that "the quality of foodstuffs can be lost in the plethora of flavourings". But the balance of feedback this year was highly enthusiastic: "it's my London go-to" with a "very different menu that changes enough to warrant a return". / SW1Y 4QU; www.scullyrestaurant.com; scully_chef; Tue-Sat 11 pm.

SEA CONTAINERS, MONDRIAN LONDON SE1 £83 2 2 3

20 UPPER GROUND 020 3747 1000 10–*3A*

This swish and "buzzy" hotel dining room on the South Bank walkway – designed by Tom Dixon with full-height windows and a terrace overlooking the river – makes a most "enjoyable place to meet friends" – "and there's a great bar" by Ryan Chetiyawardana, aka Mr Lyan. On the debit side, it's certainly "not cheap", and the food "could be so much better". / SE1 9PD; www.seacontainerslondon.com; seacontainersldn; Mon-Sun 9.30 pm.

THE SEA, THE SEA £175 5 4 4

174 PAVILION ROAD, SW3 020 7824 8090 6–*2D*
337 ACTON MEWS, E8 020 7824 8090 14–*2A*

"Incredible seafood in the most unique of settings" inspires outstanding feedback on chef Leandro Carreira and restaurateur Alex Hunter's "amazing and inventive" 14-seater chef's table experience under Haggerston railway arches, where the moodily-lit counter looks onto the gleaming open kitchen. A 12-course tasting menu involving every type of sustainable sea creature is presented at £150 per person. (Very good all-round ratings too for the original branch – a simpler and cheaper seafood bar in the bouji backstreets, off Sloane Street). / www.theseathesea.net; theseathesea_.

SEABIRD AT THE HOXTON, SOUTHWARK SE1 £90 4 3 5

40 BLACKFRIARS ROAD 020 7903 3000 10–*4A*

"Fresh fish and shellfish" – including "oysters to die for" from what is billed as 'London's longest oyster list' – make this glamorous modern venue in Southwark a genuine rarity: a swish ooftop restaurant worth visiting for its food. Set n the 14th floor of a hip hotel, it has "great anoramas over the capital, and the large errace is a top spot in good weather" – "loved ne atmosphere, views and food". / SE1 8NY; nehoxton.com; thehoxtonhotel; Sun-Thu midnight, ri & Sat 1 am.

'HE SEAFOOD BAR V1 £87 3 4 2

7 DEAN STREET 020 4525 0733 4–*1D*

'his "clean and spare-looking seafood estaurant" from Amsterdam's De Visscher amily is a "super addition to Soho", with platters both raw and roasted that are enerous, super-fresh, tasty and not exorbitantly ricey". It's also "a great place just to drop in or a martini and some oysters at the bar". / V1D 3SH; www.theseafoodbar.com; theseafoodbar; un-Thu 10 pm, Fri & Sat 10.30 pm.

SEAFRESH SW1 £60 3 2 2

0-81 WILTON RD 020 7828 0747 2–*4B*

This "absolutely reliable" chippie has done terling service in Pimlico for 59 years, with recent refurb enabling it to live up to its ame. "Dishes range from excellent fish 'n' hips to more complex and flavourful fare" - and it's "reasonably priced". / SW1V 1DL; eafreshrestaurant; Mon-Sun 10.30 pm.

SEARCYS ST PANCRAS GRAND NW1 £77 2 2 3

JPPER CONCOURSE 020 7870 9900 9–*3C*

Vith its gracious styling, this handsome brasserie (with a neighbouring Champagne bar overlooking the Eurostar tracks) is extremely omfortable and its location – and all-day ervice from early morning onwards – certainly means "it's a very convenient place for folk from around the country to meet up". But while it s tipped for business, breakfast and afternoon ea, it's hard to give it a ringing endorsement: o some diners, it feels like "everything is average, apart from the price…" / NW1 2QP; tpancrasbysearcys.co.uk; searcystpancras; Mon-Sat) pm, Sun 4 pm.

THE SEA SHELL NW1 £59 3 2 2

49-51 LISSON GROVE
020 7224 9000 9–*4A*

The very "essence of chip shop" – this century-old Lisson Grove institution serves 'lovely fresh fish" with a "great choice" of preparation ("plain grilled or deep-fried in batter or breadcrumbs") and "LOTS of chips – it's bottomless and they mean it!". "Staff can be a bit pressurised on a busy service, and not terribly engaged with customers". / NW1 6UH; www.seashellrestaurant.co.uk; seashellrestaurant; Tue-Sat 10 pm, Sun 7 pm.

SESSIONS ARTS CLUB EC1 £62 3 4 5

24 CLERKENWELL GREEN
020 3793 4025 10–*1A*

"A very special venue"; "hidden behind a nondescript door in Farringdon and accessed by an ancient brass lift, you pass beyond the heavy black curtain to a breathtaking dining room" at this "wonderfully atmospheric" two-year-old. "A historic setting" (mentioned in Dickens's 'Oliver Twist') – its "high ceilings, distressed walls and candle light" come highly recommended for "an illicit date". Fans of Florence Knight's "inventive" cuisine say it "holds its own in the space" – is "magical" even – but to others it is "unspectacular" in comparison to the backdrop. "Booking a table requires military advance planning but it's worth it". / EC1R 0NA; sessionsartsclub.com; sessionsartsclub; Tue-Sat 10 pm.

SEVEN PARK PLACE SW1 £170 3 2 2

7-8 PARK PL 020 7316 1621 3–*4C*

A "real favourite" of well-heeled foodies, this classy if relatively unsung Mayfair hotel dining room boasts in "William Drabble, the most underrated of chefs – and one of great longevity" after 15 years at the helm. There is an eight-course 'Menu Gourmand' (for £125), but also à la carte options (starting in the evening with a two-course meal for £82 – lunchtimes are cheaper). / SW1A 1LS; www.stjameshotelandclub.com; sevenparkplace; Thu-Sat, Tue, Wed 9 pm.

SEXY FISH W1 £104 1 1 2

1-4 BERKELEY SQUARE
020 3764 2000 3–*3B*

"Full of Eurotrashy tourists taking selfies" – if that's not you, a visit to Richard Caring's glitzy and "superficial" Mayfair seafood scene may be "an unhappy experience". True, fans do claim it can be a "very buzzy and atmospheric" place to try "for the people-watching and sushi" (plus other luxurious fishy treats). But 70% of reporters feel it's "overpriced"; and its "loud, echo-chamber" styling, "offhand service" and "food that – particularly given the cost – is terrible" can all grate. ("I'm surprised there isn't a tanning booth in the loos so the clientele can top up in between courses…"; "I get forced to go there on business: why anyone would go of their own free will is a mystery"). / W1J 6BR; www.sexyfish.com; sexyfishlondon; Sun-Wed 1 am, Thu-Sat 2 am.

SHAHI PAKWAAN N2 £36 3 2 2

25 AYLMER PARADE, AYLMER ROAD
020 8341 1111 1–*1B*

"You go for the food not the location" to this family-run Indian café, rated by locals as one of the best options for a curry in the purlieus of East Finchley. / N2 0PE; www.shahipakwaan.co.uk; shahi_pakwaan009; Mon-Sat 11 pm, Sun 10 pm.

THE SHED W8 £83 3 2 4

122 PALACE GARDENS TER
020 7229 4024 7–*2B*

This "noisy, fun" and "quirky little place" – just off Notting Hill Gate – was the first of the Sussex-based Gladwin brothers' 'farm-to-fork' restaurants to open in the capital, a dozen years ago, and is applauded for the "fresh ingredients" that one might hope for. One reporter feels that it's "not as good as it was", but ratings have held up decently over the years. / W8 4RT; www.theshed-restaurant.com; theshed_resto; Tue-Sat, Mon 11.30 pm.

J SHEEKEY WC2 £93 3 3 4

28-34 ST MARTIN'S CT
020 7240 2565 5–*3B*

Black & white pictures of actors past and present line the "iconic panelled dining rooms" of this "absolute classic" in Theatreland (est. 1896) – "still the benchmark for fish and seafood" in London; and still the capital's No.1 most-mentioned entry in our annual diners' poll; and still "always packed". Located in an unpromising back alley off St Martin's Lane, you navigate past the uniformed doorman and opaque windows to the "very classy" and "old school" interior, which is "divided into smaller rooms, lending a degree of privacy and keeping the noise down" (not always successfully). A superb variety of fresh dishes is "impeccably" (if "unadventurously") realised, with Dover Sole ("cooked on the bone then prepared by the waiter") and Fish Pie most often featuring in reports. This year, there's a feeling that "though very good, it's now relatively expensive for quality versus its peers": a particular gripe is the "rather overpriced" wine. / WC2N 4AL; www.j-sheekey.co.uk; jsheekeyldn; Mon-Sat 11 pm, Sun 10 pm.

J SHEEKEY ATLANTIC BAR WC2 £89 4 2 2

28-32 ST MARTIN'S CT
020 7240 2565 5–*3B*

"Pre or post-theatre, very much a favourite over many years" – this elegant seafood bar was added adjacent to the main restaurant fifteen years ago, and its more laid-back style means it's tailor-made for a luxurious bite and glass of fizz. That said, it's become "quite pricey" over time, and doesn't have quite the dazzling golden glow of yesteryear. / WC2N 4AL; www.j-sheekey.co.uk; jsheekeyldn; Mon-Sat 11 pm, Sun 10 pm.

SHEESH W1

1 DOVER STREET 020 8559 1155 3–*3C*

TOWIE comes to Mayfair at Dylan Hunt's March 2023 newcomer: a spin-off from his Chigwell original notorious for its crowd of Essex royalty from Harry Kane to Rod Stewart, and visitors including the Gypsy King himself, Tyson Fury. It also imports its luxurious comfort food menu ('let's begin', 'the main event', 'a bit on the side',…) to a prime spot on Piccadilly. Feedback is too limited for a rating but our

20 Berkeley W1

first report is not encouraging: "unbelievably over-priced… only the briefest nod to Turkish cuisine… all in all, very disappointing". There is also much outrage online at the restaurant's unusual practice of presenting prices ex VAT (so, be prepared for them to whack 20% on your bill…) / W1S 4LD; sheeshrestaurant.co.uk; sheesh_uk.

SHIKUMEN, DORSETT HOTEL W12 £73 4 2 2

58 SHEPHERD'S BUSH GREEN
020 8749 9978 8–*1C*

"Some of the best dim sum in London" and "outstanding, delicious Peking duck" is an unexpected find in this anonymous modern hotel dining room overlooking trafficky Shepherd's Bush Green. It's "good enough to impress visitors from the Far East" and has built a sufficiently strong reputation in its 10 years to be extremely busy at times. / W12 5AA; www.shikumen.co.uk; shikumen.w12; Mon-Sun 11 pm.

SHILPA W6 £37 4 2 2

206 KING ST 020 8741 3127 8–*2B*

Its "appearance is very basic", but this "slightly shabby" Hammersmith pit-stop is acclaimed by its local fans as "still some of the best Indian food in London, regardless of price". "The host in charge is very charming", too. / W6 0RA; shilpahammersmith.co.uk; Sun-Wed 11 pm, Thu-Sat midnight.

SHIP TAVERN WC2 £71 3 4 5

12 GATE STREET 020 7405 1992 2–*1D*

This historic Holborn tavern – dating from 1549, if rebuilt a century ago – deploys its wood-panelled Dickensian atmosphere to good effect, with appetising bites served in the bar and a more involved menu in the upstairs Oak Room, complete with dining booths and an open fireplace. / WC2A 3HP; www.theshiptavern.co.uk; theshiptavern; Mon-Sun 11 pm.

SHIRO EC2

100 LIVERPOOL STREET
020 3873 8252 13–*2B*

Neither its prime City location – overlooking Broadgate Circle – nor its experienced heritage (the Hong Kong-based Aqua group, with their Aqua-branded operations in the Shard and on Oxford Street) have helped garner huge attention for this glossy December 2022 newcomer: a minimalist Japanese, where chef Ken Miyake offers 'crystal sushi' (draping sushi rolls in coloured jelly slices with kimchi, ponzu or mint and sake favouring) plus robata-grilled meats and noodles. The exception is a January 2023 review from the Independent's Lucy Thackray, who said the "dizzying" selection of dishes "hit the mark, when it comes to the trifecta [of] presentation, flavour, quality". She also noted, though, that portions are "petite"; and that it's "easy to rack up quite a bill". / EC2M 7RH; www.shirosushi.co.uk; shirosushilondon; Mon-Sat 9.30 pm.

SHORYU RAMEN £59 3 2 2

9 REGENT ST, SW1 NO TEL 4–*4D*
3 DENMAN ST, W1 NO TEL 4–*3C*
5 KINGLY CT, W1 NO TEL 4–*2B*
35 GREAT QUEEN STREET, WC2 NO TEL 5–*1D*
190 KENSINGTON HIGH STREET, W8 NO TEL 8–*1D*
45 GREAT EASTERN STREET, EC2 NO TEL 13–*1B*
BROADGATE CIRCLE, EC2 NO TEL 13–*2B*

"The ramen is excellent" at this West End-based group from the Japan Centre's Tak Tokumine – although "the rest of the menu is not as good" and the venues tend to be "too cramped and/or noisy to be ideal". A drive to expand via franchise operations has apparently stalled since the summer 2022 opening of a branch in Kensington High Street – a possible sign that "we may have passed peak noodle". / www.shoryuramen.com; shoryu_ramen.

THE SICHUAN EC1 £50 3 2 2

14 CITY ROAD 020 7588 5489 13–*2A*

"Authentically fiery dishes" light up the menu at this City Road restaurant where head chef Zhang Xiao Zhong hails from Chengdu, the capital of Sichuan – a third-generation chef, his grandfather was personal chef to Deng Xiaoping, China's leader through the 1980s. / EC1Y 2AA; www.thesichuan.co.uk; Mon-Sun 11 pm.

SILK ROAD SE5 £28 4 3 2

49 CAMBERWELL CHURCH ST
020 7703 4832 1–*3C*

This "rapid-fire" canteen in Camberwell serves up "pungent and fiery spiced dishes" from Xinjiang in northwest China, homeland of the Muslim Uigurs. The food is "relatively cheap" and "a cut above" what you might expect – which makes a visit "well worth sharing a table and being hurried out afterwards". / SE5 8TR; silkroadlondon.has.restaurant; Mon-Sun 11 pm.

THE SILVER BIRCH W4 £86 4 3 2

142 CHISWICK HIGH ROAD
020 8159 7176 8–*2A*

"Great to have this restaurant on our doorstep" – Kimberley Hernandez's superior fixture is easily missed in the strip of pizza-stops and cafés on Chiswick's main drag; but it's well worth discovering for its "interesting, very well-prepared and presented" (and relatively healthy) cuisine. And in April 2023, they appointed Nathan Cornwell (recently of The Barn at Moor Hall) as head chef who has, if anything, further stepped up its performance. Not sure about the home-made elderflower wine though… / W4 1PU; silverbirchchiswick.co.uk; silverbirchchiswick; Tue-Sat 9 pm.

SIMPSON'S IN THE STRAND WC2 £100

100 STRAND 020 7420 2111 5–*3D*

This legendary temple to roast beef (opened in 1828) closed in March 2020 and has yet to re-open. In August 2023, the Savoy (of which it's a part) auctioned off many of the antiquities relating to the site, including fireplaces, furniture, crockery and its renowned carving trolleys. It has also posted on its website its 'intention to announce a re-opening date in 2024'. Clearly it will be a new non-heritage-based departure for this famous name, so, watch this space. / WC2R 0EW; www.simpsonsinthestrand.co.uk; simpsons1828.

SINGAPORE GARDEN NW6 £59 3 3 3

83A FAIRFAX RD 020 7624 8233 9–*2A*

"This place has not changed in 30 years, thank goodness!" – a Swiss Cottage "stalwart" that "packs 'em in every night" ("it gets very loud") with "slick service and consistently good cooking" from "an excellent range of Chinese and SE Asian specialities", all at very "reasonable prices". Top Menu Tip – "laksa is a favourite". / NW6 4DY; www.singaporegarden.co.uk; singapore_garden; Mon-Thu 10.30 pm, Fri & Sat 11 pm, Sun 10 pm.

SINGBURI ROYAL THAI CAFÉ E11 £28 422

93 LEYTONSTONE HIGH RD
020 8281 4801 1–1D

"Just go!" say fans of this "wildly popular" shopfront Thai BYO in Leytonstone, which "deserves a medal" for the "fabulous flavours" in its "authentic menu". Top Tip – "book in person for weeks ahead – no phone bookings". / E11 4PA; singburi_e11; Wed-Sat 10.30 pm, Sun 9.30 pm.

SIX BY NICO £70 333

33-41 CHARLOTTE STREET, W1
020 7580 8143 2–1C
1 CHANCELLOR PASSAGE, E14
020 3912 3334 12–1C

Glasgow chef Nico Simeone's distinctive concept has grown into a national chain with 11 restaurants (including Fitzrovia and Canary Wharf) in just six years, offering a quick-changing succession of themed six-course menus for under £50 a head. It's widely seen as "fantastic value" and has a sizeable fanbase amongst reporters ("every six weeks, the menu renews and for me, it is something to look forward to…"; "we simply love it and we've yet to miss a menu!" – "the Tokyo menu was so good we went back a second time"). Only a tiny few say, "you can feel you're on a conveyor belt with lots of upsells"; or that the whole thing is a dystopia of where restaurants will evolve". / www.sixbynico.co.uk; sixbynico.

SIX PORTLAND ROAD W11 £83 333

6 PORTLAND ROAD 020 7229 3130 7–2A

Nowadays owned by Jesse Dunford Wood, this "beauty of a local restaurant" is a "gem worth travelling to Holland Park for" – "with a warm welcome, efficient staff and a regularly changing menu". It's notably "small and cosy", which most reporters "love". / W11 4LA; www.sixportlandroad.com; sixportlandroad; Mon-Sun 10 pm.

64 GOODGE STREET W1

64 GOODGE STREET 020 3747 6364 2–1C

The team behind highly regarded central London trio Portland, Clipstone and the Quality Chop House is to open what promises to be a smart French bistro in Fitzrovia, in August 2023. Chef Stuart Andrews's knowledge of Gallic cuisine stems from his 18 months working in Paris, and he aims to offer 'French cooking from an outsider's perspective'. / W1T 4NF; 64goodgestreet.co.uk; Mon-Sat 11 pm.

SKAL NORDIC DINING N1 £38 343

149 UPPER STREET 07308 031151 9–2D

"Tasty and authentic" Scandinavian dishes including "excellent fish" are on the menu at this "surprisingly cosy and stylish" Nordic outfit in Islington, where "attentive service" ensures an enjoyable meal. Top Menu Tip – "the venison meatballs with lingonberry sauce deserve a special mention". / N1 1RA; www.skalnordicdining.co.uk; skalnordic; Fri & Sat, Tue-Thu 11 pm.

SKETCH, THE LECTURE ROOM AND LIBRARY W1 £245 445

9 CONDUIT ST 020 7659 4500 4–2A

This "simply stunning" fairytale chamber on the top floor of the well-known Mayfair palazzo won many 5/5 reviews this year, while avoiding the brickbats often thrown at it in former years. "In these curious post-Covid times, where even the most indifferent restaurants are charging hard, this one now seems good value", despite its notoriously vertiginous prices. Overseen by Gallic über-chef Pierre Gagnaire – Daniel Stucki provides a "divine" selection of intriguing modern French dishes, be it from the £190 tasting menu or £210 three-course à la carte. If this venue continues on its current "outstanding" form, we will have to finally agree that it is "deserving of its three Michelin stars". / W1S 2XG; sketch.london; lrl. sketchlondon; Fri & Sat, Wed & Thu 9 pm.

SKETCH, GALLERY W1 £101 234

9 CONDUIT ST 020 7659 4500 4–2A

A gorgeous, Grade II Palladian Mansion… glowing pink-hued walls, high ceilings, glam banquettes… incredible artworks from Yinka Shonibare… über-chef Pierre Gagnaire's menu… what's not to like about this famous Mayfair venue? The fact that it's seen as being mightily "overpriced" with forgettable food is the chief fault, which means that few other than fashionistas and first-timers are prepared to make the investment… even to go to the bog in a WC shaped like an egg! / W1S 2XG; sketch. london; sketchlondon; Sun-Thu 10 pm, Fri & Sat 11 pm.

SKEWD KITCHEN EN4 £70 433

12 COCKFOSTERS PARADE
020 8449 7771 1–1C

This "fantastic upscaled-local Turkish restaurant" in Cockfosters gives the traditional North London Anatolian grill a modern makeover – and fans say it's "wonderful to see it so deservedly busy" on account of its "excellent food and service". "They've just expanded", but it's "harder than ever to get a table on a Saturday night". / EN4 0BX; www.skewd.com; skewdkitchen; Mon-Sun midnight.

SKYLON, SOUTH BANK CENTRE SE1 £80 212

BELVEDERE ROAD 020 7654 7800 2–3D

"With spectacular views of London over the Thames, this is the place to bring out-of-towners", say fans of this huge, Brutalist chamber, built in the 1950s as the South Bank's original destination restaurant (when it was known as 'The People's Palace'). Supporters – particularly those on business – say the food is "perhaps a little formulaic, but reliably good too". This is not a universal experience, though, and too often this D&D group venue suffers from "complacent service" and "below-average cooking". (Some reports do also tip it as "a very nice spot to eat before a concert". But others have had a bad pre-show trip… "what we ordered never arrived in time"). / SE1 8XX; www.skylon-restaurant.co.uk; skylonrestaurant; Mon & Tue 9 pm, Wed-Sat 10 pm, Sun 5 pm. SRA – accredited

SKYLON GRILL SE1 £72 235

BELVEDERE RD 020 7654 7800 2–3D

"Still adore the room but the food should get a leg up at that price" – a verdict that has for many years dogged this landmark venue. Even though it's the cheaper section of the large operation run by D&D London, "you're most certainly paying for the location, when there are similarly priced restaurants along the South Bank which are much better". / SE1 8XX; www.skylon-restaurant.co.uk; skylonrestaurant; Mon-Sat 10.30 pm, Sun 4 pm. SRA – accredited

SMITH & WOLLENSKY WC2 £112 222

THE ADELPHI BUILDING, 1-11 JOHN ADAM ST 020 7321 6007 5–4D

Despite a fine NYC pedigree; a selection of top-quality imported USDA steaks; and a 'prestige' location, at the foot of the Adelphi (just off the Strand), this US steakhouse has never made waves in the capital. When it does, it's often for the wrong reasons, with too many complaints either that it's "overpriced" or "very disappointing". / WC2N 6HT; www.smithandwollensky.co.uk; sandwollensky; Mon-Thu 11.30 pm, Fri & Sat midnight, Sun 10 pm.

SMITH'S WAPPING E1 £82 434

22 WAPPING HIGH ST
020 7488 3456 12–1A

"A top selection of fish" – "simple and so fresh" – is served at this smart, white-tablecloth restaurant in a "fantastic setting, on the Thames at Wapping, with great views of Tower Bridge". "Service is slick and the atmosphere reflects the bright, buzzy feel of the whole place". The only drawback is that "it's always full and difficult to get into". The original Smith's was founded 66 years ago in Ongar, Essex. / E1W 1NJ; www.smithsrestaurants.com; smithsofwapping; Mon-Sat 10 pm, Sun 9 pm.

SMITHS OF SMITHFIELD, TOP FLOOR EC1 £88 333

67-77 CHARTERHOUSE ST
020 7251 7950 10–1A

"Amazing steak (though the rest of menu is good too)" and terrific views over the City and St Paul's share top billing at the flagship restaurant at the top of a handsome

Grade II-listed former Smithfield market warehouse. It can be "a bit noisy", but it makes for a "solid dining experience" that's "always good for business". / EC1M 6HJ; www.smithsofsmithfield.co.uk; thisissmiths; Mon-Fri 9.30 pm, Sat 9 pm.

SMOKE & SALT SW17 £53 543

115 TOOTING HIGH ST NO TEL 11–2C

Another year of stellar ratings confirms that Remi Williams and Aaron Webster's former pop-up in Tooting is no flash in the pan, offering "fine food in a bustling, vibrant atmosphere" and "set menus of delicious sharing plates" for which they make clever use of European salting, curing and smoking techniques. They made a name for themselves at Pop Brixton before moving to this permanent site in 2020. / SW17 0SY; www.smokeandsalt.com; smokeandsaltldn; Tue-Sat 10 pm.

SMOKESTAK E1 £56 433

35 SCLATER STREET 020 3873 1733 13–1C

"Boldly seasoned, flavourful – unashamedly meat-heavy" – dishes are the simple hallmark of BBQ obsessive David Carter's moodily dim-lit Brick Lane operation, inspired by the smokehouses of the American South. "Some interesting options on the menu" include salt-baked beetroot or charred greens with tahini and pomegranate. / E1 6LB; www.smokestak.co.uk; smokestakuk; Mon-Thu, Sat, Fri 11 pm, Sun 10 pm.

SMOKING GOAT E1 £62 533

64 SHOREDITCH HIGH STREET NO TEL 13–1B

"Thailand meets Shoreditch" at Ben Chapman's "still exciting" BBQ, with its "deliciously different", "confident and bold spicing" creating "amazingly flavoursome food". If there's a downside, it's "cramped" tables and that it becomes "understandably noisy", but regulars "love eating here whether solo or with friends". / E1 6JJ; www.smokinggoatbar.com; smokinggoatbar; Mon-Sat 11 pm, Sun 10 pm.

SMOKOLOKO E1 £18 433

OLD SPITALFIELDS MARKET, BETHNAL GREEN ROAD 07508 675363 13–2B

Meaty street-food dishes, smoked in an oven shaped like the boiler of an old steam engine, produce "fabulous food" in the "great setting" of Spitalfield Market. (In August 2023, they graduated to include a small unit with a few seats in the section of the market on Lamb Street.) / E1 6EW; smokoloko.uk; smokolokobbq; Mon-Fri 3 pm, Sat & Sun 5 pm.

SOCCA W1 £114 333

41 SOUTH AUDLEY STREET 020 3376 0000 3–3A

"Deliciously light and fluffy food" inspired by the sunshine cuisine of the south of France lights up the menu at this Mayfair yearling – a collaboration between Lyonnais-born chef Claude Bosi of Bibendum and restaurateur-du-moment Samyukta Nair (it's named after the chickpea flour flatbread made in Nice). Sadly, they have brought with them "plain ludicrous" Riviera-style pricing, which sours the tone of otherwise positive reports. (The Observer's March 2023 review from Jay Rayner was not-dissimilar: "I wanted that utter fabulousness to mitigate the price. But it was strange and uneven rather than the perfect it should be".) / W1K 2PS; soccabistro.com; soccabistro; Mon-Sun 10.30 pm.

SOCIAL EATING HOUSE W1 £97 322

58-59 POLAND STREET 020 7993 3251 4–1C

Having put in over ten years of services, the chilled Soho outpost of Jason Atherton's 'Social' brand no longer attracts a huge volume of feedback. But the food remains good, and the chef's table on the lower ground floor is particularly recommended as a "truly personal and excellent" (if "rather noisy") experience. / W1F 7NR; www.socialeatinghouse.com; socialeathouse; Tue-Sat 10 pm.

SOFFICE LONDON SW15 £47 332

236 UPPER RICHMOND ROAD 020 3859 4335 11–2B

"In Putney's fairly indifferent restaurant scene, this is a welcome addition" – a Sicilian 'gastro-bakery' with an interesting selection of pastries from that sweet-toothed island, plus pasta and pizza. / SW15 6TG; www.sofficelondon.com; soffice_london; Mon-Sat 11 pm, Sun 5 pm.

SOIF SW11 £66 322

27 BATTERSEA RISE 020 7223 1112 11–2C

With its charcuterie, gutsy small plates, cheese and wacky vintages, this venture from Les Caves de Pyrène (est 2011) helped inspire the current vogue for low intervention wine bars in the capital. Feedback is scarce nowadays, but still suggests it's worth a try if you're in the vicinity of Battersea Rise. / SW11 1HG; www.soif.co; soif_sw11; Wed-Sat, Tue 11 pm, Sun 5 pm, Mon 9 pm.

SOLA W1 £210 532

64 DEAN STREET 020 7734 8428 5–2A

"Slightly unorthodox" but "exceptional" Californian food "made with super, luxury ingredients" and backed up by "an interesting and mainly Californian wine list" mean Victor Garvey's acclaimed four-year-old is "the place to head for in Soho for an out-of-the-ordinary meal"; and some believe "it should have two stars from the tyre men". ("Highlights included flambéed langoustines with a dashi broth and foie gras; and that rare thing, a grapefruit dessert with jelly, sorbet, consommé and meringue"). If there's a reservation, it's about the "small and cramped-feeling" space, which critics feel "for a VERY expensive meal has really no sense of occasion at all" ("it is essentially an unremarkable café in Soho with staff who might have been officiating at some kind of sacred ceremony in a High Temple!"). W1D 4QQ; solasoho.com; solasoho; Wed-Fri, Tue 8.30 pm, Sat 9 pm.

SOLLIP SE1 £107 54[3]

8 MELIOR STREET 020 7378 1742 10–4C

"Perfect French cuisine with a Korean twist" has built an impressive reputation for Woongchul Park and Bomee Ki's ambitious and highly accomplished three-year-old – a patch of serenity in the gritty streets surrounding Guy's Hospital. The main event is an 8-9 course tasting menu, which is exciting in the freshness of its ideas and with "faultless" realisation. Top Tip – Bomee trained as a pastry chef so pace yourself for dessert. / SE1 3QQ; www.sollip.co.uk; sollip_restaurant; Tue-Sat 9 pm.

SOM SAA E1 £48 43[3]

43A COMMERCIAL STREET 020 7324 7790 13–2C

"Full of a young crowd who really want to enjoy the flavours of Thailand" – this "noisy" former factory near Spitalfields Market has won renown for offering "a unique flavour of 'real' Thai cuisine with a wonderful selection of zingy, spicy, aromatic and refreshing dishes". Top Menu Tip – "nothing can beat the whole deep-fried seabass with crunchy bones, and sitting at the counter they'll do half portions for a single diner. Excellent!" / E1 6BD; www.somsaa.com; somsaa_london; Mon-Wed 10 pm, Thu-Sat 10.30 pm, Sun 9 pm.

SÔNG QUÊ E2 £41 32[2]

134 KINGSLAND RD 020 7613 3222 14–2A

"Some of the best Vietnamese food on Kingsland Road" is to be found at this "no-frills dining room" in Shoreditch – everything is "fresh and fragrant": no wonder "they're always so busy". / E2 8DY; www.songque.co.uk; songquecafe; Mon-Sat 11 pm, Sun 10.30 pm.

SORELLA SW4 £69 32[2]

148 CLAPHAM MANOR STREET 020 7720 4662 11–1D

An "interesting range of modern, high-quality Italian dishes" means this "buzzy" Clapham Old Town venue – inspired by chef-patron Robin Gill's experience of working on the Amalfi coast – draws a more-than-local clientele. The Dairy, its influential older 'sister' around the corner, closed down in 2020. Top Menu Tips – "superb octopus arancini, fresh gnocchi and pappardelle ragu". / SW4 6BX; www.sorellarestaurant.co.uk; sorellaclapham; Tue-Sat 10 pm.

Sucre London W1

›OUTINE NW8 £67 224

) ST JOHN'S WOOD HIGH STREET
20 3926 8448 9–*3A*

Safe food and lovely decor" help maintain ›ns for this "beautifully decorated" and quintessentially French" brasserie – part of ›e Wolseley Group, and – according to such ıpporters – "everything you could want from neighbourhood restaurant". However, even ıose who say it's "one of the only decent ptions for a meal in St John's Wood", can ›el that "it's really gone downhill since the eparture of the Corbin & King founders"; nd a slip in ratings can be ascribed to nconsistent" standards here this year. Top Tip popular for breakfast. / NW8 7SH; soutine. ›.uk; soutinestjohn; Mon-Sat 10 pm, Sun 9 pm.

›OUVLAKI STREET SE22

8 NORTH CROSS ROAD NO TEL 1–*4D*

›fter nine years in various street markets ıcluding Pop Brixton (which came to an end ı late 2022), Greek street-food specialists Evi eroulaki and Conor Mills are moving into ermanent premises on North Cross Road in ast Dulwich. Expect Aegean classics using rime British ingredients such as rare-breed)ld Spot pork, plus Greek lager and cola. / E22 9EU; www.souvlakistreet.co.uk; souvlakistreet.

›PAGNOLETTI ›W1 £49 343

3 EUSTON ROAD 020 7843 2221 9–*3C*

A great little find right opposite King's Cross". The location is not the best" – immediately ff a busy pavement and bordering the trafficky ›uston Road – but, if you want a good-value efuel before you hop on a train (especially with ımily in tow), this bright pitstop at the foot f a boutique hotel is trying hard: "service is ood and they obviously care". Pasta (the main vent) is made in-house: if it lacks anything in erms of finesse, it compensates with ample ortions and "the food is very nice". In case ou've been wondering, the place is named fter the 19th-century Anglo-Italian inventor f the railway signalling system. / NW1 2SD; ww.spagnoletti.co.uk; spagnoletti_; Mon-Fri 9.30 m.

THE SPANIARD'S INN NW3 £59 235

SPANIARDS RD, HAMPSTEAD HEATH
020 8731 8406 9–*1A*

This "ancient characterful tavern" by Hampstead Heath has hosted an impeccable list of literary tipplers in its long history from 1585, from Byron and Dickens to Bram Stoker and local poet John Keats, who listened to a nightingale in the walled garden. These days it serves "good fish 'n' chips" and other pub staples, and an "excellent Sunday lunch". / NW3 7JJ; www.thespaniardshampstead.co.uk; thespaniardsinn; Mon-Sat 11 pm, Sun 10.30 pm.

SPARROW ITALIA W1 324

1-3 AVERY ROW 020 3089 9501 3–*2B*

"Request the elegant first-floor dining room" when you dine at this large Italian in Mayfair, imported from LA (there's also a ground-floor bar). It opened in late 2022 and reports are still not as numerous as we'd like; but early diners are wowed by the classily ritzy decor and high-quality cuisine. There's also a cigar lounge and terrace. / W1K 4AJ; www.sparrowitalia.com; sparrowitalia; Mon-Sat midnight.

SPEEDBOAT BAR W1 £54 444

30 RUPERT STREET NO TEL 4–*3D*

"They rock a vibrant, kitsch, Thai-sports-bar style beautifully" at JKS Restaurants's zany and "buzzy" Chinatown yearling, which is "very casual" and "great fun". "Full-flavoured dishes are authentically and unashamedly packed with the core Thai flavours of sweet, sour, fire and salt" – it's "fantastic, authentic, good-value" food, washed down with funky cocktails and a wide variety of other libations (you can just drink here). / W1D 6DL; speedboatbar.co.uk; speedboatbar; Fri & Sat 1 pm, Mon-Thu midnight.

SPRING RESTAURANT WC2 £123 444

NEW WING, LANCASTER PLACE
020 3011 0115 2–*2D*

"Simplicity and style are in abundance" at Skye Gyngell's dining room in Somerset House – not only "an absolutely beautiful space", but whose "seamless service" and "wonderful food" make it "a delightful experience from start to finish". Skye's cuisine has a deft delicacy of touch, but the most popular option is the 'Scratch' menu – "lovely reimagined 'leftovers' from earlier services, provided from a no-choice menu between 17.30 and 18.30 at £25 for three courses" ("designed to reduce food waste, it's a great idea and useful for a post-shopping pick-me-up before the train home or a pre-theatre supper"). Although this is the kind of venue that's "gorgeous for lunch with a visiting mother", it's actually most nominated as either a gastronomic highlight or for client-entertaining: "the slightly zen nature of the food and purist environment makes it a brilliant choice for a certain type of business"; and "clients are always impressed with Spring". / WC2R 1LA; www.springrestaurant.co.uk; spring_ldn; Tue-Sat 9.30 pm.

ST JOHN MARYLEBONE W1 £67 432

98 MARYLEBONE LANE
020 7251 0848 3–*1A*

Nose-to-tail dining returns to the West End, with Fergus Henderson and Trevor Gulliver's first opening in seven years (their Leicester Square project, St John's Hotel, closed in 2013). It's on a two-floor Marylebone site with a short menu of trademark punchy British dishes and baked items (for example: deep-fried rarebit, ox heart, Eccles cake and cheese). Ratings are high for the food, but also support the view that – as yet – it's "not as good as in Smithfield" or Spitalfields. More problematic is the interior, which echoes the stark utilitarian approach of its siblings: here it can seem merely "cold" or "dreary" ("like the 1960s!"). / W1U 2JE; stjohnrestaurant.com; st.john.restaurant; Mon-Sun 10 pm.

STANLEY'S SW3 £100 322

151 SYDNEY STREET 020 7352 7664 6–*3C*

This "pleasant spot off the King's Road" in Chelsea is at its "romantic best if you're sitting outside in the summer", in one of the courtyard booths. The seasonal British menu is well executed, if lacking real excitement. / SW3 6NT; www.stanleyschelsea.co.uk; stanleys_chelsea_; Mon-Sat 11.30 pm, Sun 7.30 pm.

STEVEN EDWARDS BINGHAM RIVERHOUSE TW10 £86 424

61-63 PETERSHAM ROAD
020 8940 0902 1–*4A*

"An incredible setting overlooking The Thames at Richmond" anchors the appeal of this "relaxing and enjoyable" dining room, with terrace: part of a small boutique hotel set in gardens right by the river. The "competent and consistent" realisation of high-quality dishes wins nothing but praise for cuisine created by chef Steven Edwards (winner of Masterchef: The Professionals a decade ago), which makes it one of this swanky borough's top culinary venues. / TW10 6UT; www.binghamriverhouse.com; binghamriverhouse; Wed-Sat 11 pm.

STICK & BOWL W8 £20 422

31 KENSINGTON HIGH STREET
020 7937 2778 6–1A

With its "delicious cheap 'n' cheerful Chinese food in an area of overpriced restaurants", this "brisk" family-run spot on Kensington High Street is "always popular and rightly so", including with "many Asian clients, which tells you everything you need to know". ("I've been coming for almost 30 years, and they recently updated the interior while remaining true to their unique concept of barstool dining tables"). / W8 5NP; stickandbowl.has.restaurant; stickandbowl; Mon-Fri 10.45 pm.

STICKS'N'SUSHI £72 322

3 SIR SIMON MILTON SQ, VICTORIA ST, SW1 020 3141 8810 2–4B
40 BEAK STREET, W1 020 3141 8191 4–2C
11 HENRIETTA ST, WC2
020 3141 8810 5–3D
113-115 KING'S ROAD, SW3
020 3141 8181 6–3C
1 NELSON ROAD, SE10
020 3141 8220 1–3D
58 WIMBLEDON HILL RD, SW19
020 3141 8800 11–2B
1 CROSSRAIL PLACE, E14
020 3141 8230 12–1C

"Expensive, but high-quality yakitori skewers and sushi" are a "delicious and original offering that suit all ages", and win little but praise for this "very consistent" chain, whose minimalist Scandi style reflects its origins in Copenhagen. Success continues to bring fast expansion, with recent openings in Westfield W12 (in December 2022) and Shoreditch (in March 2023) and more soon to follow in Richmond (October 2023) and Kingston (early 2024). Phew! Top Menu Tip – "truffle paste cauliflower side dish to die for (who knew?)". / www.sticksnsushi.com; sticksnsushi.

STICKY MANGO £61 322

33 COIN STREET, SE1
020 7928 4554 10–4A
36C SHAD THAMES, SE1
020 7928 4554 10–4D

"A well composed panoply of flavours from Southeast Asia" – curry puffs, crab dumplings, lobster, ox cheek Penang curry – have won a loyal following for Peter Lloyd's South Bank fixture, and over time fans "have become enamoured, and no longer mourn the loss of RSJ" (which preceded on the site for over 20 years). "Nothing is extraordinary, but it is our current first choice pre the National Theatre". He must be doing something right, as expansion is coming fast, with a sibling to open in July 2023 on the former site of Cantina del Ponte, RIP, with a large terrace overlooking Tower Bridge; and another in Islington later in the year.

STORY SE1 £272

199 TOOLEY ST 020 7183 2117 10–4D

"Quite an experience" – Tom Sellers has established his unique foodie temple near Tower Bridge as one of a kind. Each quixotic menu relates a culinary 'story' which unfolds over numerous courses and the "fabulous" results mean that quibbles regarding the mind-numbing prices – though often present – were a minor theme this year in diner feedback compared with satisfaction with the overall stellar performance. Just after our survey concluded in May 2023, the restaurant closed for the addition of a second floor, outside terrace, and the promise of new areas in which to dine. TS has also been busy with the openings of Dovetale and Story Cellar – hence for the time being we've left it unrated. / SE1 2UE; www.restaurantstory.co.uk; rest_story; Mon-Sun 11 pm.

STORY CELLAR WC2 £83 334

17 NEAL'S YARD 020 7183 0021 5–2C

A back-to-basics offshoot of Tom Seller's celebrated Restaurant Story, this new Covent Garden venue opened in April 2023, inspired by his love of Parisian brasseries. Dine on rotisserie chicken (the big deal here) or other brasserie fare including large cuts of meat from the grill to share. Most of the ground floor is counter seating, with more conventional tables in the cellar. It's an atmospheric winner on most accounts, and – when it came to the food – The Standard's Jimi Famurewa awarded it full marks, applauding "a careful Jenga tower of elements" that transforms "a deceptively basic concept" into "stylish, subtly affecting excellence". Not all our early reporters are quite as wowed though – it can also seem "perfectly good if expensive; and unclear what the Michelin background really adds to this type of cooking". / WC2H 9DP; storycellar.co.uk; story_cellar; Tue-Sat 10 pm.

STRAKER'S W10 £87 335

91 GOLBORNE ROAD 020 3540 8727 7–1A

"A hot new ticket north of the Portobello Road" – Insta fave-rave, Thomas Straker's "super-busy" new 40-seater opened in November 2022 and has a "brilliant atmosphere" driven by "passionate chefs creating unusual food in a sharing plates concept". At their best, results are electrifying, but the odd misfire is not unknown: "the famed butter-drenched flatbreads were over burnt, so the waiters trying to upsell us was annoying… the doughnuts and langoustines were heaven though!" / W10 5NL; www.strakers.london; strakers__; Tue-Sun 11 pm.

STREET BURGER £51 32

13-14 MAIDEN LANE, WC2
020 7592 1214 5–3D
24 CHARING CROSS ROAD, WC2
020 7592 1361 5–4B
222 KENSINGTON HIGH STREET, W8
020 7592 1612 8–1D
341 UPPER STREET, N1
020 7592 1355 9–3D
ENTERTAINMENT DISTRICT, THE O2, SE10
020 7352 2512 12–1D
26 COWCROSS STREET, EC1
020 7592 1376 10–1A
17 UPPER CHEAPSIDE PASSAGE, ONE NEW CHANGE, EC4 020 7592 1217 10–2B

The "fancy burgers" usually hit the spot this year at TV chef Gordon Ramsay's growing diffusion chain, with nine sites in the capital as of mid-2023 (and where the frozen chips are provided by another prominent chef now retired from front-line stove action: the venerable Pierre Koffmann). The odd "mixed experience" or "haphazard service" was still reported, but overall ratings were up. / www.gordonramsayrestaurants.com/street-burger; gordonramsaystreetburger.

STUDIO FRANTZÉN, HARRODS SW1 £160 34

87-135 BROMPTON ROAD
020 7225 6800 6–1D

"A beautiful space with a Michelin three-star chef overseeing the kitchen" – Harrods continues to reinvent itself as a gastronomic hub with this blockbusting 2022 debut from an acclaimed Nordic chef. It occupies a newly constructed site on the top floor of the world famous department store. "Surprisingly spacious with a very high ceiling": inside you can get a "nice view of the sparkling clean kitchen"; and outside there's a glam roof terrace overlooking the Knightsbridge rooftops. The cooking combines Asian and Scandi influences and most reports are rapturous. Top marks are only missed due to the odd more nuanced account – "I had palpable excitement to try this Swede's food, but was let down by ridiculous pricing and the mixture of some exquisite and some dud options". Top Menu Tip – "they are justifiably proud of their milk bread: a crisp crust similar to croissant and a fluffy centre like the Japanese variety, served with miso butter and borage honey" ("the best bread I have – dare I say – ever had!"). The 'Sweden vs Japan' menu option "allows you to compare meats prepared in the style of each cuisine. Both are good but there is a significant contrast in textures". / SW1X 7XL; www.harrods.com; Mon-Sat 11.30 pm, Sun 10.30 pm.

STUDIO GAUTHIER W1

21 STEPHEN STREET 020 8132 9088 5–1

Renowned vegan chef-patron, Alexis Gauthier has spun out his meat-free cuisine with the June 2023 opening of two new venues in the BFI Building in Stephen Street, north of Oxford Street. Studio Gauthier is a more relaxed showcase for the upmarket veggie cooking atured at his Soho flagship (Gauthier), while 23V Bakery offers lighter bites to eat in or ke away. / W1T 1LN; studiogauthier.co.uk; uthierinsoho; Mon-Fri 11 pm.

UCRE LONDON V1 £83 334

7B GREAT MARLBOROUGH STREET
20 3988 3329 4–*1B*

"great vibe" is the key selling point of this arge", "buzzing" chandeliered venue, where atino chef, Fernando Trocca aims to import e glam of Buenos Aires. Most reports also pplaud its "ace take on Argentinian cuisine, ith the asado fired up at the back of the om" delivering "a real variety of options, not st beef" in a "tasty tapas style". A minority f diners, though, are "a little disappointed" y the size of the bill: "not terrible, but at the rices I won't be rushing to return". Top Tip the basement bar is excellent. / W1F 7HS; ww.sucrerestaurant.com; sucre.london; Mon-Sat 1 n, Sun midnight.

UDU NW6 343

0 SALUSBURY ROAD
20 7624 3829 1–*2B*

Really succulent rendang" is a menu highlight this "great new Malaysian eatery": a opitiam' (café-style) venture which opened Queen's Park in late 2022. It's the creation siblings Fatizah and Irqam Shawal, whose arents opened London's most venerable Ialaysian – Satay House – in 1973. / W6 6NL; sudu.ldn; Mon-Sun 10.30 pm.

UKHO FINE THAI CUISINE W6 £55 442

55 FULHAM RD 020 7371 7600 11–*1B*

he "delicious and beautifully prepared Thai od" at this Fulham shop conversion makes it "great local restaurant" that attracts diners om across London. The surroundings are othing special, but everything is "served with harm". / SW6 5HJ; www.sukhogroups.com; ıkho_thairestaurant_fulhamsw6; Mon-Sat 10.30 m, Sun 9.30pm.

UMAK N8 £44 342

41 TOTTENHAM LANE
20 8341 6261 1–*1C*

One of the reasons we've yet to move house om Crouch End!" – local fans are sold on e virtues of this "stubbornly traditional urkish restaurant (with murals on every wall epicting famous Turkish and other global urist destinations... at least a step up from e glitzy establishments on Green Lane)". Despite recent price hikes, they are still very air considering the high standard of cooking, s well as the warm welcome". / N8 9BJ; ımakrestaurants.com; sumakrestaurant; Sun-Thu 1 pm, Fri & Sat 11.30 pm.

SUMI W11 £103 443

157 WESTBOURNE GROVE
020 4524 0880 7–*1B*

"Incredible sushi in an environment that is more relaxed and fun than many sushi joints of this quality" is a potent recipe for success at Endo Kazutoshi's "welcoming" venture ("all the more enjoyable as it affords the opportunity to people-watch in the rarefied atmosphere of Notting Hill"). "A simple menu is very well realised; service is good and friendly"; and since it expanded in late 2022 "the extra floor-space has made for a better atmosphere". / W11 2RS; www.sushisumi.com; sumilondon; Tue-Sat 10 pm, Sun 5 pm.

THE SUMMERHOUSE W9 £84 235

60 BLOMFIELD RD 020 7286 6752 9–*4A*

"Sitting by the canal is relaxing, and in cooler weather the heaters are turned on and the entire experience is warm and welcoming" at this "beautiful" spot by the Regent's Canal in Little Venice. Views diverge on the fish-centric cooking: to fans it produces "well-cooked staples", to the odd harsh critic the performance is verging on "unskilled". All agree, though, that "personal and un-rushed service" contributes to its appeal. / W9 2PA; www.thesummerhouse.co; the_summerhouse; Mon-Sat 11 pm, Sun 10.30 pm.

SUNDAY IN BROOKLYN W2 £73 224

98 WESTBOURNE GROVE
020 7630 1060 7–*1B*

If it didn't attract quite a few reports in our annual diners' poll, we might be tempted to overlook this NYC-import on a corner in Notting Hill, named for its fashionable elder sibling in Williamsburg. Mostly, feedback is from locals, who feel the place is "fun", but too often "very disappointing"; a natural choice for an authentic American brunch, but where "only the pancakes are above average". / W2 5RU; sundayinbk.co.uk; sundayinbrooklyn_ldn; Mon-Wed 4.30 pm, Thu-Sat 10 pm, Sun 8 pm.

SUPA YA RAMEN 332

191 RYE LANE, SE15 020 7358 0735 1–*4D*
499 KINGSLAND ROAD, E8
07440 066900 14–*1A*

Chef Luke Findlay brings his 'traditionally inauthentic' cult ramen (using ingredients such as Parmesan cheese or Cumberland sausages) to a duo of functionally kitted-out venues. First honed as a supper club, the Dalston original opened in March 2000, and a Peckham spin-off in late 2022. Not a huge volume of feedback, but all good for the big-flavoured bowls that had The Independent's Kate Ng hail "a perfectly imperfect take on fusion food" in January 2023.

SUPAWAN N1 £58 544

38 CALEDONIAN ROAD
020 7278 2888 9–*3D*

Some of the "most authentic Thai food you could ever experience in UK is prepared by a Thai chef and team" in the bizarre but "beautiful" surroundings of a florist's shop, near King's Cross station, where "the flowers are put aside in the evening to make room for extra tables". Chef Wichet Khongphoon delivers "incredible" and "powerful" flavours and the "attentive staff give helpful and useful guidance as to the potentially obscure treats" from the "interesting and deeply satisfying" menu. "You can get a green curry (a really good one!), but alongside more unusual starters, there are salads and slow-cooked meats, plus good vegan options with clear allergy pointers too". "Book well ahead: and you may have to wait for your table even so, as the place is very busy and popular". / N1 9DT; www.supawan.co.uk; supawan_thaifood; Tue-Sat 11 pm, Sun 10.30 pm.

SUPER TUSCAN E1 £70

8A ARTILLERY PASSAGE
020 7247 8717 13–*2B*

Post pandemic, the feedback on this small, quirky, City-fringe Italian (in the characterful tangle of streets near Spitalfields) has become more patchy. Fans still say its interesting wines and authentic cuisine are outstanding, but we don't have sufficient volume of reports for a reliable rating. / E1 7LJ; www.supertuscan.co.uk; enoteca_super_tuscan; Mon-Fri 9 pm.

THE SURPRISE SW3 £82 334

6 CHRISTCHURCH TERRACE
020 7351 6954 6–*3D*

"A gem of a place hidden away" in a quiet corner of SW3 close to Chelsea's 'Physic Garden', this "traditional" 1853 pub – a classic watering hole in the area – has been transformed by landlord Jack Greenall (scion of the Lancashire brewing dynasty), and now serves a high standard of "very reasonable value" British dishes, accompanied by "sensibly priced" Bibendum wines. "Service is spot-on, too". / SW3 4AJ; www.thesurprise-chelsea.co.uk; Tue-Sat 9.30 pm, Sun 8.30 pm.

SUSHI ATELIER W1 £70 433

114 GREAT PORTLAND STREET
020 7636 4455 2–*1B*

Sit on the ground floor at the counter and watch the chefs in action to get the most out of this clean-lined Japanese (part of the Chisou group) near Oxford Circus. The food here is consistently well-rated: choose from modern sushi options, ceviches, fish carpaccios and other Japanese-inspired bites like wagyu sliders. / W1W 6PH; www.sushiatelier.co.uk; sushiatelierlondon; Tue-Sat 11 pm.

SUSHI BAR MAKOTO W4 £44 431

57 TURNHAM GREEN TERRACE
020 8987 3180 8–2A

While you probably wouldn't cross town for it, this basic pit-stop near Turnham Green tube is worth remembering – the sushi is a cut-above what you'd expect from the nondescript exterior. / W4 1RP; sushi_makoto; Mon-Sat 10 pm, Sun 9 pm.

SUSHI KANESAKA W1

45 PARK LANE 020 7319 7466 3–4A

Aiming for 'a new benchmark for omakase dining in the city' – certainly when it comes to price… – this Dorchester Collection property (opposite the mothership itself across the road) opened in July 2023. It's a spin-off from Shinji Kanesaka's Tokyo Michelin two-star and will seat just 13 diners (9 at a counter, 4 in a separate room). Perhaps the UK's most expensive set menu: it offers a 20-course omakase experience for £420 per head, plus paired saké at £150 per head. Go easy on the Coco Mademoiselle though: 'we kindly request that you refrain from wearing perfume'. / W1K 1PN; www.dorchestercollection.com; 45parklane; Tue-Sun 11.30 pm.

SUSHI MASA NW2 £47 332

33B WALM LANE 020 8459 2971 1–1A

With its "surprisingly high-quality Japanese cooking for a nondescript suburban strip" in Willesden Green, this accomplished local spot offers a "delicious omakase experience in a calm environment" – making it an adequate replacement for its predecessor Sushi-Say (the epitome of a wonderful, family-owned Japanese, which inhabited this out-of-the-way site for over 30 years). / NW2 5SH; sushimasa_id; Tue-Sat 10 pm.

SUSHI MURASAKI W9 £58 442

12 LAUDERDALE ROAD
020 3417 8130 7–1C

"Tucked away in an unassuming suburban street, this Maida Vale Japanese is firmly established as a local favourite" for its "inventive and original" dishes that are "excellently executed" using "high-quality ingredients". "Standards are much higher than the dining room decor might suggest – it's somewhat functional!" / W9 1LU; sushi-murasaki.co.uk; sushimurasakiuk; Mon-Sat 11 pm, Sun 10.30 pm.

SUSHI REVOLUTION SW9 £39 442

240 FERNDALE ROAD
020 4537 4331 11–1D

This "really impressive" two-year-old from Aidan Bryan & Tom Blackshaw in Brixton's former Bon Marché department store is a "catch-all Japanese restaurant delivering high-quality, tasty dishes" that are "quirky, in a good way": "while not the most authentic sushi for the purists" – the clue is in the name – "it's definitely worth a visit". / SW9 8FR; www.sushirevolution.co.uk; sushirevolution; Mon-Sun 10 pm.

SUSHI TETSU EC1 £167 554

12 JERUSALEM PASSAGE
020 3217 0090 10–1A

"Still a top omakase experience in a very relaxed environment" – Toru Takahashi does not exactly need to go out of his way to attract customers to this tiny (7 seat) venue. You can only book online on Monday at 12:00pm onwards. There are no event bookings (max 4 in a party). There's no concession to vegans or vegetarians. No kids under 12. No Insta (yay!!) – photography and video are not permitted. No scent is to be worn by diners. The full shebang costs £167 per person and takes 3-4 hours, although he also does a shorter 2 hour version early on Saturday evenings for £117 (June 2023 prices). Everyone loves it… / EC1V 4JP; www.tetsusushibar.com; tetsusushibar_van; Tue-Sun 9.30 pm.

SUSHISAMBA £117 223

OPERA TERRACE, 35 THE MARKET, WC2
020 3053 0000 5–3D
HERON TOWER, 110 BISHOPSGATE, EC2
020 3640 7330 10–2D

Zooming up to the 38th floor of the Heron Tower in one of Europe's fastest lifts… looking out with a cocktail on an open terrace overlooking the scrapers of the City, it's easy to get swept up by the glamour of the original, "buzzy" branch of this US-based chain. And its popular WC2 spin-off is also "always a pleasure to visit": looking out onto the back of the Royal Opera House from the huge terrace on the top of Covent Garden Market. Fans say the luxe, Japanese/South American fusion cuisine in both locations – taquitos, sushi, steaks, samba rolls, black cod from the robata – is "delicious and remarkably inventive" too. But ratings for it have sunk post-Covid, and while pricing here has always been toppy, there is a growing gripe that "food which is average at best is accompanied by a bill that's distinctly not average!" / sushisamba.com; SUSHISAMBA.

SUSSEX W1 £81 223

63-64 FRITH STREET 020 3923 7770 5–2A

This Soho outpost from the Sussex-based Gladwin Brothers was launched in 2019 in the stylish quarters vacated by Arbutus (long RIP). As at the Gladwins' five other venues across London, feedback was somewhat limited and a little up-and-down this year. A particular plus is the "valiant focus on locally sourced produce" and a "friendly" approach. Negatives include meals that can be "pleasant but unmemorable" and the odd incident of "haphazard" service. / W1D 3JW; www.sussex-restaurant.com; sussex_resto; Tue-Fri, Mon, Sat 10.30 pm.

SUZI TROS W8 £88 44

18 HILLGATE STREET
020 7221 2223 7–2B

The "delicious and interesting modern Greek food" is enjoyed by all who visit this "fun" if "slightly cramped and noisy" Notting Hill four-year-old – the "less formal sister to Mazi" nearby. (Founders Christina Mouratoglou and Adrien Carre were inspired by the cuisine of northern Greece, and named it after a film character who has passed into contemporary Greek folklore.) / W8 7SR; suzitros.com; suzitros; Mon-Sun 11 pm.

THE SWAN W4 £67 344

1 EVERSHED WALK,119 ACTON LN
020 8994 8262 8–1A

A "top pub garden" is the trump card of this handsome, green-tiled tavern on the Chiswick-Acton border, and it's backed up by "super-attentive service, great food" and "a lively buzz". It's been "consistently good" in its current guise for more than 20 years. / W4 5HH; www.theswanchiswick.co.uk; theswanchiswick; Sun-Thu 10 pm, Fri 10.30 pm, Sat 11 pm.

THE SWAN AT THE GLOBE SE1 £70 224

21 NEW GLOBE WALK
020 7928 9444 10–3B

The "unforgettable setting" of this pub and restaurant adjoining Shakespeare's Globe theatre, "with a lovely view over the river" to St Paul's, provides much of the draw, although its food and service are (just about) up to scratch too. The wide range of menus makes it a "flexible option", providing afternoon teas, brunches, drinks and meals before and after performances. / SE1 9DT; www.swanlondon.co.uk; swanglobe; Mon-Sat 9 pm, Sun 6 am.

SWEET THURSDAY N1 £52 322

95 SOUTHGATE RD 020 7226 1727 14–1A

This lively bottle shop and local in De Beauvoir Town does a good trade in Neapolitan-style pizzas and a small selection of Italian starters and mains – not surprisingly, it attracts "loadsa families, so choose your time carefully". / N1 3JS; www.sweetthursday.co.uk; sweetthursdaypizza; Mon-Thu 10 pm, Fri & Sat 10.30 pm, Sun 9 pm.

SWEETINGS EC4 £92 324

39 QUEEN VICTORIA ST
020 7248 3062 10–3B

"It's as though time was paused 100 years ago" at this Square Mile legend, founded in the 1830s and on its current site since the 1920s. Arrive early if you want to beat the City pinstripes to a table or a spot at the counter, although "it's worth the wait for a seat while sipping a tankard of Black Velvet". "Traditional, hearty British fish is served in

a manner unchanged by time" – oysters, smoked eel, whitebait – and "the fish pie is still good and not too expensive". "Longstanding staff add to its stalwart appeal". / EC4N 4SA; sweetingsrestaurant.co.uk; sweetingslondon; Mon-Fri 3 pm.

SYCAMORE VINO CUCINA, MIDDLE EIGHT HOTEL WC2 £76 222

66 GREAT QUEEN STREET
020 7309 9300 5–1D

The timing of its debut, during Covid 19, couldn't have been harder for this Covent Garden three-year-old, and it has yet to attract a huge volume of feedback or a settled view from diners. One fan says "you get a twist on Italian cooking, and boy do they get it right" in a "superb, light and airy space that's ideal for a business meal". To a critic it's "bizarre eating in what feels like, and actually is, a hotel lobby, with some dishes very clumsily seasoned". / WC2B 5BX; www.middleeight.com; middle_eight_hotel; Mon-Sat 10 pm, Sun 5 pm.

TA KE SUSHI W5 £45 432

3-4 GROSVENOR PARADE
020 8075 8877 1–3A

"A favourite of local Japanese expats", this Ealing three-year-old offers a wide range of fresh-made dishes, including sushi, ramen, soba and udon. It's "not so cheap, but excellent value, and definitely cheerful". Top Tip – "the daily lunch special is a steal, with plenty of change from a tenner". / W5 3NN; take-sushi.co.uk; Mon-Sat 10.30 pm, Sun 10.30pm.

TAB X TAB W2 £38 343

WESTBOURNE HOUSE, 14-16 WESTBOURNE GROVE 020 7792 3445 7–1B

This "great meeting spot" in Bayswater is "ever-popular" for its "excellent coffee and snacks" served in immaculate minimalist surroundings, from founders Mathew and Charmaine Tabatabai. The menu stretches from breakfast/brunch dishes to afternoon cocktails. / W2 4UJ; tabxtab.com; tabxtablondon; Mon-Sun 4 pm.

TABLE DU MARCHE N2 £65 332

111 HIGH ROAD 020 8883 5750 1–1B

"This better-than-solid bistro" in East Finchley offers "excellent value and sound cooking – the very strong local following is justified". It's old-school in the best way – and "the staff are charming". / N2 8AG; tabledumarchelondon.co.uk; tabledumarche; Mon-Sat 11 pm, Sun 10.30 pm.

TAKA MARYLEBONE W1 £100 323

109 MARYLEBONE HIGH STREET
020 3637 4466 2–1A

An "upscale Japanese/fusion place" – "a modern take on Nipponese cuisine in a light and airy venue in the heart of Marylebone High Street". It scores higher this year: even those who consider it "overpriced" still say the culinary results are "very good". / W1U 4RX; takalondon.com; takarestaurants; Fri & Sat, Tue-Thu 10 pm.

TAKAHASHI SW19 £62 553

228 MERTON ROAD 020 8540 3041 11–2B

"The omakase experience borders on the sublime" – "it's food as art" – at this "hidden gem" of a Japanese restaurant, tucked away in an unpromising shopping parade near South Wimbledon tube for almost a decade now. Former Nobu chef Taka and his wife Yuko preside over a "very personalised food offering", with their "delightful and kind service". / SW19 1EQ; www.takahashi-restaurant.co.uk; takahashi_wimbledon; Wed-Sat 10.30 pm, Sun 7.30 pm.

TAKU W1 £378 533

36 ALBEMARLE STREET NO TEL 3–3C

Japanese chef Takuya Watanabe transfers his high-end skills from Paris (where he spent 10 years at restaurant Jin) to Mayfair, for this November 2022 debut. A visit is an investment – lunch is £130 per head, dinner £280 per head, or £380 for the 'prestige' offering. We have had limited but outstanding feedback to date in our annual diners' poll; Michelin rushed to award it an early star after less than six months in operation; and veteran blogger Andy Hayler – who knows his way around a chopstick – declared it "definitely some of the best sushi to be found in the capital" after an April 2023 visit. / W1S 4JE; www.takumayfair.com; takumayfair; Tue-Sat 11 pm.

TAMARIND W1 £87 433

20 QUEEN ST 020 7629 3561 3–3B

The world's first Indian restaurant to bag a Michelin star (in 2001) – this "sophisticated and glamorous" Mayfair linchpin has neither lost its way, nor remained pre-eminent: it just continues to plough its own distinctive path. The kitchen "always finds a neat twist to traditional favourites" and succeeds in delivering "stunning presentation and wonderful flavours". And "despite its top quality food and location, the bill isn't bad either". Top Tips – "the vegetarian fare is particularly delicious"; and "the lunchtime menu is great value". / W1J 5PR; www.tamarindrestaurant.com; tamarindofmayfair; Mon-Sat 10.15 pm, Sun 9.15 pm.

TAMARIND KITCHEN W1 £81 433

167-169 WARDOUR ST
020 7287 4243 4–1C

"A gem in Soho" – this large and stylish spin-off from the famous Mayfair mothership is "a very reasonable (and reasonably priced) option" that takes inspiration from regional cuisines across India. "The tasting menu is particularly good value by London standards". / W1F 8WR; tamarindkitchen.co.uk; tamarindkitchenlondon; Mon-Thu 10 pm, Fri & Sat 10.30 pm, Sun 9.30 pm.

THE TAMIL PRINCE N1 £48 43

115 HEMINGFORD ROAD
020 7062 7846 9–2D

"Truly brilliant" – this desi pub (formerly the Cuckoo) in Barnsbury is one of the most talked-about openings of 2022 thanks to "stellar" cooking that's "expertly spiced and oh-so-moreish", washed down with "great cocktails and beers on tap". On the downside, it is "squashed" and "oh-so-noisy" ("they won turn the music down!") but most folks like its "bustling" style. "You have to plan ahead" – "it's very difficult to get a reservation unless yo book four weeks in advance" – but "well wort the effort". / N1 1BZ; www.thetamilprince.com; the_tamil_prince; Tue-Sat, Mon 10 pm, Sun 9 pm

TAMP COFFEE W4 £29 34

1 DEVONSHIRE ROAD NO TEL 8–2A

Superb in-house roasted coffee and scrumptio pastries (speciality Portuguese Pastel de Nata) – made daily on the premises – make for a superior breakfast at this Chiswick café, just of the main drag. / W4 2EU; www.tampcoffee.co.u tampcoffee; Mon-Fri 3.30 pm, Sat & Sun 4 pm.

TANDOOR CHOP HOUSE WC2 £60 43

8 ADELAIDE STREET 020 3096 0359 5–4

"Tandoor as it is meant to be", with "bursts of authentic, deep and rich smoky flavours", earn an emphatic thumbs-up for this "energetic" operation just off Trafalgar Square. The "menu is limited but compelling, with bold an memorable spicing", "mouthwatering chicken and duck" and "well made naan", while "desserts are the weakest element". / WC2N 4HW; tandoorchophouse.com; tandoorchop; Mon Thu 11 pm, Fri & Sat 11.30 pm, Sun 10 pm.

TAPAS BRINDISA £68 22

46 BROADWICK ST, W1
020 7534 1690 4–2B
7-9 EXHIBITION RD, SW7
020 7590 0008 6–2C
18-20 SOUTHWARK ST, SE1
020 7357 8880 10–4C
UNIT 25 BATTERSEA POWER STATION, 25 CIRCUS ROAD WEST, SW11
020 8016 8888 11–1C
HOTHAM HOUSE, 1 HERON SQUARE, TW9
020 8103 8888 1–4A

"An excellent location overlooking the River Thames makes the Richmond branch very special if you are able to bag one of its outside tables on a balmy summer evening"; and it's a highpoint of this chain run by a firm of well-known Iberian food importers. On the plus-side, its branches are generally "buzzy", with "tasty" and "authentically flavoured" tapas. On the minus-side, for all the "high quality ingredients", dishes can end up "indifferent" and "pricey for the size of the portions"; and "service can be a little too uneven". / www.brindisakitchens.com; brindisaspanishfoods. SRA – accredited

AQUERIA £45 333

1-145 WESTBOURNE GROVE, W11
0 7229 4734 7–1B
10 EXMOUTH MARKET, EC1
0 3897 9609 10–1A

ℓeally tasty Mexican food in a fairly spartan tting" established this Notting Hill venue as e of London's original taco specialists, and 20 ars on it remains on some accounts "possibly e best". Now with an offshoot in Exmouth arket, it continues to serve "excellent ojitos" which makes it "a good choice for ıch… if one has nothing else planned for the ternoon". / taqueria.co.uk; taqueriauk.

ARO £39 332

CHURTON STREET, SW1
0 7802 9776 2–4B
BREWER STREET, W1
0 7734 5826 4–3C
6 REGENTS PARK ROAD, N3
0 4531 9124 1–1B
4 KENNINGTON ROAD, SE11
0 7735 7772 1–3C
3 BALHAM HIGH ROAD, SW12
0 8675 5187 11–2C
HIGH STREET, E17
0 8520 2855 1–1D

Vell produced, tasty morsels of delight" cluding "ace lunchtime bento boxes" e served at these "pared down" Japanese nteens, which provide "good value for money r what is generally an expensive cuisine". under Mr Taro is not one for fast food: he nceived the idea of opening an 'everyday ning room' on a visit to London in 1979 and unched it in Soho 20 years later. Two decades he is in expansion mode, and in February 23 opened a sixth branch in a former Manze e & Mash shop in Walthamstow, with a Grade listed interior now restored to its previous ory. / tarorestaurants.uk; tarorestaurants.

ATE MODERN, KITCHEN BAR, LEVEL 6 E1 £51 335

EVEL 6 BOILER HOUSE, BANKSIDE
20 7401 5108 10–3B

Vith its "great view over the river", the sixth-oor restaurant in this converted power station pposite St Paul's Cathedral is a "really rather lendid place for a decent set lunch". The od is "better than expected, perhaps better an it needed to be" – "appropriately arty", o, with dishes inspired by artists on display the gallery. (Over at Tate Britain, "the Rex histler dining room is sorely missed and real loss" – its closure brought about by a ombination of Covid and dilemmas about e depiction of slavery in its Whistler murals, owadays deemed 'unequivocally… offensive'.) SE1 9TG; www.tate.org.uk; tate; Mon-Sun 6 pm.

TATTU LONDON WC2 £120 233

THE NOW BUILDING ROOFTOP, DENMARK STREET 020 3778 1985 5–1A

Considering its prominent location in 'The Now Building' on Oxford Street, this glossy two-year-old from an Insta-friendly Manchester-based group inspires surprisingly little feedback. Most is positive, but it's not without the one or two disappointments, and some ongoing concern about high prices. / WC2H 8LH; tattu.co.uk; tattulondon; Tue-Sun 1 am, Mon midnight.

TAVERNAKI W11 £30 323

222 PORTOBELLO ROAD
07510 627752 7–1A

"An excellent Greek, with a brilliant, relaxed atmosphere. Being Mediterranean, the staff love children. Highly recommended!" – In the thick of Portobello, this cosy spot is only three years old, but fairly conventional in style, complete with 'traditional comfort cuisine' and live Greek music. / W11 1LJ; www.tavernakiportobello.co.uk; tavernaki.portobello; Mon-Sun 11 pm.

TAVOLINO SE1 £67 223

UNIT 1, 2 MORE LONDON PLACE
020 8194 1037 10–4D

"Fabulous views of the Thames" from this modern Italian in the new development next to City Hall make it "perfect for giving out-of-town guests the full London experience". "The food has sufficient interest, but the real draw is the panoramic view from HMS Belfast to Tower Bridge". / SE1 2JP; www.tavolino.co.uk; tavolinokitchen; Sun-Wed 10 pm, Thu-Sat 10.30 pm.

TAYYABS E1 £36 432

83 FIELDGATE ST 020 7247 6400 10–2D

"The grilled lamb chops are worth a visit in their own right" to this "affordable and ever-reliable Punjabi institution in Whitechapel" whose 500 seats are "guaranteed to be jam-packed on any particular evening". "BYOB means it is even better value for money". / E1 1JU; www.tayyabs.co.uk; 1tayyabs; Mon-Sun 11.30 pm.

TEHRAN BERLIN (FKA THE DRUNKEN BUTLER) EC1 £167 344

20 ROSEBERY AVENUE
020 7101 4020 10–1A

"What a find! Chef Yuma (Hashemi) produces the most amazing plates of delicious food which reflect his heritage and upbringing" at this quirky Clerkenwell operation, whose decor is akin to a retro Tehran living room. The menu plays out in 'four acts', with shifts of gear in the background music to enhance the experience. All this plus "great staff and a fabulous vibe". / EC1R 4SX; www.tehranberlin.com; tehran_berlin; Tue-Sat 11 pm.

THE TELEGRAPH SW15 £54 345

TELEGRAPH ROAD, PUTNEY HEATH
020 8194 2808 11–2A

Few London pubs enjoy as leafy a setting (complete with "lovely garden") as this "spacious" and "friendly" tavern on Putney Heath, which is "suitable for all ages" and makes a "good destination for Sunday lunch". Now capably run by Chester-based Brunning & Price, it takes its name from the visual shutter telegraph that linked the Admiralty in London with Portsmouth in the Napoleonic era. / SW15 3TU; www.brunningandprice.co.uk; telegraphputneyheath; Sun-Thu 11 pm, Fri & Sat midnight. SRA – 2 stars

TEMPER £58 212

25 BROADWICK STREET, W1
020 3879 3834 4–1C
5 MERCERS WALK, WC2
020 3004 6669 5–2C
78 GREAT EASTERN STREET, EC2
020 3758 6889 13–1B
ANGEL COURT, EC2 020 3004 6984 10–2C

An "open-plan kitchen" complete with fire pit is the theme unifying Neil Rankin's four-strong BBQ-group, which takes all its supplies of beef, pork, lamb and chicken from Yorkshire farmer Charles Ashbridge. Despite some favourable steak suppers being reported, ratings took a further dive in our latest poll, continuing last year's themes of "chaotic" service and a feeling that the overall experience can "promise more than it delivers". Lack of value, in particular, inspires repeated gripes ("plates were minuscule at ridiculous prices…"; "we joked that you needed a microscope to find the portions…") / temperrestaurant.com; temperlondon.

THE 10 CASES WC2 £82 343

16 ENDELL ST 020 7836 6801 5–2C

With its "unusual and interesting wines" (only 10 cases of each one are ordered, to ensure a steady turnover), "well complemented by delicious small bites to eat", this is "the wine bistro you want in your street". The fact that they can combine this with a "great, busy and bustling neighbourhood vibe in the middle of Covent Garden" is "simply astonishing", making it both "a pre-theatre restaurant and a destination in its own right". / WC2H 9BD; www.10cases.co.uk; 10cases; Mon-Sat midnight.

10 GREEK STREET W1 £70 443

10 GREEK ST 020 7734 4677 5–2A

A "reliable Soho favourite", where results from its blackboard menu are "always solidly good and can be excellent" – the same can be said of its handwritten 'little black book' of wines. "Small, relaxed and friendly", it "can become pretty noisy, but that's part of the fun". / W1D 4DH; www.10greekstreet.com; 10greekstreet; Tue-Sat 10.30 pm.

TENDIDO CERO SW5 £71 333

174 OLD BROMPTON ROAD
020 7370 3685 6–2B

"Every dish is good" at this long-running tapas bar in South Kensington. Regulars, though, reckon it's "not quite up to the experience" of its sibling opposite, Cambio de Tercio, with which it shares a list of "excellent" Spanish wines ("it's clearly tapas from a chef more familiar with fine dining, leaning towards the elegant rather than a solid punch of flavour"). / SW5 0BA; cambiodeterciogroup; Mon-Sun 11.30 pm.

TENDRIL W1 £58 433

5 PRINCES STREET 07842 797541 4–2C

The "interesting, unusual" and "occasionally really great" vegan cuisine at this "romantic and candle-lit restaurant close to Oxford Circus" has won enough fans to crowdfund its transformation from pop-up to permanent status at the same address. "The best test is that it continues to attract non-vegetarians because the food is so good". Former Fat Duck and Chiltern Firehouse chef Rishim Sachdeva was a committed meat-eater before challenging himself to create knock-out veggie dishes (with some cheese permitted). / W1B 2LQ; www.tendrilkitchen.co.uk; tendril_kitchen; Mon-Sat 10 pm, Sun 5 pm.

TERRA MODERNA NW3

2B ENGLANDS LANE 020 4568 8525 9–2A

Modern Italian cuisine with Antipodean influences – including an impressive list of Australian and New Zealand wines – is to be found at this new venture in the heart of Belsize Park from Aussie founder and coffee entrepreneur Jeffrey Young, who is also behind the England's Lane café next door. It opened in April 2023, too late to inspire survey feedback, but early online buzz suggests it's worth giving it a go. / NW3 4TH; www.terramodernalondon.com; terramodernaldn; Tue-Sat 11 pm.

TERRA ROSSA £67 444

139 UPPER STREET, N1
020 7226 2244 9–3D
62 CARTER LN, EC4 020 7248 6600 10–2A

"What a find!" – this Puglian specialist close to Islington's Almeida Theatre (it takes its name from the Salento peninsula's red earth) is "a cheap 'n' cheerful favourite", thanks to its "generous portions of absolutely delicious and comforting Italian food". It may "lack kerb appeal, but once inside you find an attractive dining room with quite a buzz" – making it a "classic and authentic neighbourhood restaurant". Since spring 2023, founder François Fracella also has now opened a second site near St Paul's.

THAI THO SW19 £22 333

20 HIGH ST 020 8946 1542 11–2B

"Wimbledon Village may have three Thai restaurants, but this independent family business is our favourite!" Nicky Santichatsak's "traditional" operation sits "in the centre of the village" and is a "preferred choice for celebs during the tennis". (There's also a long-established Soho sibling that inspires no feedback). / SW19 5DX; www.thaitho.co.uk; Tue-Sat 10.30 pm.

THALI SW5 £53 333

166 OLD BROMPTON RD
020 7373 2626 6–2B

With its "good North Indian cooking" from family recipes, this well-established venue with Bollywood posters lining the walls is these days a rival to veteran Noor Jahan for bragging rights on Earl's Court's "curry corner". / SW5 0BA; thali_london; Mon-Sat midnight.

Zahter W1

THEO RANDALL AT THE INTERCONTINENTAL LONDO[N] PARK LANE W1 £90 54[…]

1 HAMILTON PLACE 020 7318 8747 3–4[…]

"As good as anything you might experience in Verona or Florence" – Theo Randall's "divin[e] monthly regional tasting menus" produce "consistently great" results as well as adding interest to his Mayfair HQ, just off Hyde Par[k] Corner. "There's the option of wine matches" and "a good cocktail bar (especially the desig[n]-your-own-Negroni option!)". "Ok, the space isn't terrific" – windowless, and off the foyer o[f] a large 1970s hotel – but "it is one of the very few celebrity chef restaurants where the chef frequently to be seen". "Theo always seems to be there and comes out into the dining room most times you visit", helping create an overal[l] atmosphere that was surprisingly well-rated this year. Top Tip – "Sunday brunch at £65 including unlimited Prosecco, Negroni or Aperol Spritz is particularly good value". / W[…] 7QY; www.theorandall.com; theo.randall; Tue-Sa[t] 10 pm, Sun 6 pm.

THEO'S SE5 £41 33[…]

2 GROVE LANE 020 3026 4224 1–3C

The "doughy, chewy, charred base is a winner" at this "excellent quality" pizzeria duo in Camberwell and Elephant & Castle, whose "pared-back toppings deliver great tastes". They're backed up by a short but sharp selection of cocktails, craft beers and organic or skin-contact wines. / SE5 8SY; www.theospizzeria.com; theospizzeria; Tue-Thu 10.30 pm, Sun & Mon 10 pm, Fri & Sat 11 pm.

34 MAYFAIR W1 £133 23[…]

34 GROSVENOR SQ 020 3350 3434 3–3A

Richard Caring's American-style grill near the former US Embassy in Mayfair wins praise as "an all-rounder, with a menu to suit all tastes"; and as "a busy, vibrant place with attentive and knowledgeable staff". "The win[e] list (book really) is endless and if you want to be extravagant, very expensive"… in keeping with the general approach. / W1K 2HD; www.34-restaurant.co.uk; 34mayfair; Mon-Sat 11 pm, Sun 10 pm.

THE THOMAS CUBITT PUB BELGRAVIA SW1 £80 22[…]

44 ELIZABETH ST 020 7730 6060 2–4A

"Consistent over many years", this smart (and "not particularly cheap") Belgravia gastropub is named after the master-builder who developed the area in the Georgian era, and is the flagship of the ambitious Cubitt House group, which has hired chef-director B[e] Tish (ex-Salt Yard, The Stafford and Norma) and food journalist/hospitality expert Joe Warwick to bolster its standards. / SW1W 9PA www.thethomascubitt.co.uk; cubitt house london; Mon-Sat 10 pm, Sun 8.45 pm.

HREE FALCONS W8 £48 432

ORCHARDSON STREET
:0 7724 8928 7–1C

Jnder the radar of most who are not in the ow" – this large tavern and hotel off Edgware oad incorporates some "excellent Indian od" into a more conventional gastropub fering. "A number of TV screens to watch orts" are also a feature. / NW8 8NG; eefalcons.com; threefalcons.

HREE UNCLES £37 522

NIT 199 HAWLEY WHARF, 2ND FLOOR
ODHALL, NW1 07597 602281 9–2B
NIT 19&20, BRIXTON VILLAGE, SW9
0 3592 5374 11–2D
DEVONSHIRE ROW, EC2
:0 7375 3573 10–2D

antastic roast duck" and quite possibly "the st chicken rice in London" earn full marks this Cantonese roast meat specialist with tlets near Liverpool Street, in Hawley Wharf, amden, and Brixton Market. Founders Pui ng, Cheong Yew and Mo Kwok were inspired childhood memories of eating sui mei near an Chai market in Hong Kong. Their venues ay be "cramped and busy", but the cooking "consistently delicious, generously portioned d great value". / three.uncles.

LA SE8 £74 333

DEPTFORD BROADWAY
:0 8692 8803 1–3D

Iave been walking by literally for years… night we took the plunge for dinner... my odness… the food was superb! Every dish ed herbs to provide intense bursts of flavour. ioughtful, exciting cooking, both tasty and ll presented…" – Thumbs up for this brick-ed bar/restaurant between Deptford High reet and Deptford Bridge, which is heavily fluenced by the Eastern Med, with lots of eparation over fire. "The charred aubergine a must!" / SE8 4PA; www.tiladeptford.com; tila.ptford; Wed-Sat 10 pm, Sun 5 pm.

NG, THE SHARD E1 £95 335

ST THOMAS ST 020 7234 8108 10–4C

Vhat could be nicer than sitting on the th floor of the Shard with fantastic views London", while lingering over a "lovely rushed afternoon tea" or – later in the day ien the mood is "very romantic" – sampling "fresh Asian-inspired dishes". Not a huge lume of feedback, but ratings are better this ar as it escaped the customary complaints for erpricing. / SE1 9RY; www.ting-shangri-la.com; glondon; Mon-Sun 10.15 pm.

ISH NW3 £91 323

6 HAVERSTOCK HILL
:0 7431 3828 9–2A

ı "attractively presented dining room" is the tting for "excellent kosher food" at David Levin's modern brasserie in Belsize Park. "Usually the culinary experience is firmly in the back seat at kosher restaurants, but not here". / NW3 2AG; www.tish.london; tish_london; Sun-Thu midnight.

TOBA SW1

1 ST JAMES'S MARKET
020 3583 4660 4–4B

In slick-but-stilted St James's Market, this February 2023 newcomer inhabits the site that till recently housed Ikoyi (nowadays on The Strand). It's from Pino Edward Sinaga, and – like his successful Camden Market operation – serves Indonesian street food inspired by family recipes. For this posh SW1 locale, prices are very approachable. No survey feedback as yet, but in a March 2023 review, The Guardian's Grace Dent thought results were incentive enough to visit this "soulless" SW1 development. / SW1Y 4AH; tobalondon.co.uk; toba.london; Tue-Fri 11 pm, Sat 11.30 pm, Sun 4 pm.

TOFF'S N10 £54 342

38 MUSWELL HILL BROADWAY
020 8883 8656 1–1B

"Sensationally good grilled plaice" and the "freshest fish and prawns" help make this 55-year-old north London chippy a "favourite place to go to be cheered up" ("my partner and I think it's well worth catching the two buses needed to get there!"). "Snooker legend Ronnie O'Sullivan is known to frequent it when playing in the Masters Championships at nearby Ally Pally". Top Menu Tip – "always order the delicious Greek salad, with the family's own-recipe dressing". / N10 3RT; www.toffsfish.co.uk; toffsfish; Mon-Sat 10 pm.

TOFU VEGAN £23 432

105 UPPER STREET, N1
020 7916 3304 9–3D
28 NORTH END ROAD, NW11
020 8922 0739 1–1B
54 COMMERCIAL STREET, E1
020 7998 6640 13–2C

This "great vegan" with branches in Islington, Golders Green and Spitalfields Market "beats the hell out of anything left in Chinatown" with its "interesting Chinese options", full of "flavour and texture" and "leaning towards Sichuan peppercorns" (it's from the team behind non-vegan Xi'an Impression). "Go with half-a-dozen friends so you can try plenty of dishes" – "you won't miss the meat". / tofuveganlondon.

TOKIMEITE W1 £104

23 CONDUIT ST 020 3826 4411 3–2C

Since its founding in 2015, this ambitious Japanese – created with investment from Zen-Noh (Japan's agricultural cooperative) has struggled to make waves. Although Zen-Noh remains involved, ownership was taken over a couple of years ago by London food importers Atariya, whose sound restaurants elsewhere should underpin a decent level of performance here. Feedback in our annual diners' poll is still too thin for a proper rating, but we do receive the odd very favourable report. / W1S 2XS; www.tokimeite.com; tokimeitelondon; Tue-Sat 10.30 pm.

TOKLAS WC2 £84 333

1 SURREY STREET 020 3930 8592 2–2D

Who knew Arthur Andersen's previous HQ (also apparently a former car park) could look so chic! The founders of Frieze art fair are behind this "stylish and buzzing" yearling in a Modernist building, off the Strand – "an interesting mid-century space", which is "spacious" and "with a lovely secluded outside terrace". Chef Yohei Furuhashi delivers an "on-trend concept": "ingredients so fresh and of superior quality" are interfered with as little as possible: "this is how delicious food should taste, with flavours bursting in one's mouth, not dishes laced with salt lazily passed off as a meal in most restaurants" ("impeccable…. I'm still dreaming about the artichoke and pea salad"). "Prices seem to have jumped up in recent months" though, placing it in value terms as "pricey, but worth it". / WC2R 2ND; www.toklaslondon.com; toklas_london; Tue-Sat 11 pm.

TOMMI'S BURGER JOINT £36 332

30 THAYER ST, W1 020 7224 3828 3–1A
37 BERWICK STREET, W1
020 7494 9086 4–2D

"Well priced, tasty" burgers make this long-running Icelandic chain (with two outlets in London and one in Oxford; as well as Berlin and Copenhagen) a "cheap 'n' cheerful favourite" for some reporters. Veteran burger-slinger Tómas Tómasson founded the group 43 years ago, and in 2021 was elected to Iceland's parliament, the Althing, at the age of 72. / www.burgerjoint.co.uk; burgerjointuk.

TOMOE SW15 £43 442

292 UPPER RICHMOND ROAD
020 3730 7884 11–2B

This "outstanding family Japanese" in Putney has attracted a strong following across southwest London for its fresh and authentic cooking, presented in deceptively – but authentically Japanese – modest surroundings. / SW15 6TH; tomoe.london; Wed & Thu 9 pm, Fri & Sat 9.30 pm.

TONKOTSU £50 333

BRANCHES THROUGHOUT LONDON

"Tasty, good-value noodles" in a "relaxed environment" make this 12-year-old London chain (14 branches, plus Brighton and Brum) "worth a visit". The "ramen is deep and fabulous" if "limited in range (no fish-based dishes except prawn)", and is augmented by "quite acceptable katsu curry". Aficionados should head to the Haggerston branch to watch the noodles being made. / www.tonkotsu.co.uk; tonkotsulondon.

TOSA W6 £40 332

332 KING ST 020 8748 0002 8–2B

This "very decent" small café near Stamford Brook tube makes "a good change from the usual Japanese", with "yakitori grilled skewers the real draw". "The room is a little jaded but a seat at the grilling bar is an entertaining winner" ("the friendly chef chats all through the meal"). Top Menu Tip – "the grilled mackerel is truly holy". / W6 0RR; www.tosa.uk; tosa_authentic_japanese ??; Wed-Sun 11.30 pm.

TOULOUSE LAUTREC SE11 £69 333

140 NEWINGTON BUTTS
020 7582 6800 1–3C

This wood-panelled French brasserie with an "excellent fixed-price menu" of Gallic classics is particularly "useful in the location" – close to the Imperial War Museum in Kennington – and provides its own entertainment in the form of its upstairs jazz club. / SE11 4RN; www.toulouselautrec.co.uk; tlvenue; Mon-Sat midnight, Sun 10.30 pm.

TOWNSEND @ WHITECHAPEL GALLERY E1 £59 332

77-82 WHITECHAPEL HIGH STREET
020 7539 3303 10–2D

One of London's most appealing museum or art gallery dining rooms – this "cheerful operation with a small but delightful menu" presents chef Nick Gilkinson's "well sourced, flavoursome dishes", distinguished by the way the "clean, simple flavours of the ingredients come though". Named in celebration of the turn-of-the-century building's architect, Charles Harrison Townsend, "the room is lined with light wood and mirrors (which some may think a bit stark)". / E1 7QX; www.whitechapelgallery.org; whitechapelgallery; Tue, Sun 6 pm, Wed-Sat 11 pm.

TOZI £65 213

8 GILLINGHAM ST, SW1
020 7769 9771 2–4B
3A ELECTRIC BOULEVARD, SW11
020 38 338 200 11–1C

All-day Italian-style eating, inspired by the grand cafés of Europe and the culinary traditions of Venice, is the aim at this ground-floor venue in a hotel near Victoria station and its sibling in the Battersea Power Station development's new art'otel. Both can still be an "asset to the area", offering a "buzzing" setting, "amazing breakfasts" and "decent dining proposition", but there was also a high proportion of disappointments this year – in particular, poor service in both locations.

THE TRAFALGAR TAVERN SE10 £62 335

28 PARK ROW 020 8858 2909 1–3D

"On the river, next to the Royal Naval College buildings in the heart of Greenwich", this massive old tavern opened in the year of Queen Victoria's coronation, and its "period design, position and aspect give it a unique selling point". Perhaps because it doesn't have to try too hard, its culinary offering has fluctuated in quality over the years, but the view that "it's a mechanism to fleece tourists" took more of a back seat this year, with most reports being of "pub staples and British classics" that are "full of flavour". / SE10 9NW; www.trafalgartavern.co.uk; trafalgartaverngreenwich; Sun-Thu 11 pm, Fri & Sat midnight.

TRINCO SE22

20 LORDSHIP LANE 020 8638 7812 1–4D

In East Dulwich's restaurant row, Vibushan Thirukumar launched this 'community focused, sustainable restaurant' in April 2023 – too late for feedback in our annual diners' poll – inside the co-working and wellness hub Oru Space (which he co-founded with business partner Paul Nelmes in 2020). Named for his seaside home town back in Sri Lanka, its vegan and vegetarian cuisine is rooted in Tamil culture. / SE22 8HN; www.trinco.restaurant; Thu-Sat 11 pm.

TRINITY SW4 £103 332

4 THE POLYGON 020 7622 1199 11–2D

"A perfect mix of fine dining and neighbourhood restaurant" – Adam Byatt's celebrated flagship on Clapham Common has won renown as one of the most notable destinations south of the River, and a strong rival to Chez Bruce ten minutes away thanks to its "exquisite evolving menu" and "personal" service. But while still much-vaunted this year by very many reporters, its ratings slipped noticeably due to an unusual number of downbeat reports ("I can't understand why Trinity is so highly rated… I found the experience underwhelming"; "expensive and can lack atmosphere"; "until recently, this was a favourite, but it's now fallen out of my top ten"). In July 2023 – after our annual diners' poll had finished – a former member of the team, Harry Kirkpatrick, returned to the kitchen after stints at a number of top establishments having been appointed as a new head chef. Taking into account owner Adam Byatt's impressive track record here, our best bet is a swift return to form. And, still for the majority of diners in this year's poll, this is "a place we go to again and again for special occasions and it never disappoints us". / SW4 0JG; www.trinityrestaurant.co.uk; trinityclapham; Mon-Sun 8 pm.

TRINITY UPSTAIRS SW4 £70 44

4 THE POLYGON 020 3745 7227 11–2D

"Wonderful food", delivered in the format of "innovative and interesting sharing plates", is the draw at chef-patron Adam Byatt's casual option, upstairs from his Clapham flagship Trinity. The "high stool seating" doesn't please everyone, but that's more than made up for by the "good-value, high-class victuals" and "friendly and knowledgeable staff". / SW4 0JG; www.trinity-upstairs.co.uk; trinityclapham; Tue-Sat 8.30 pm, Sun 4 pm.

TRISHNA W1 £81 53

15-17 BLANDFORD ST
020 7935 5624 2–1A

"Wonderfully scented dishes" are "delicately and expertly prepared" at JKS Restaurants' exceptional Marylebone flagship, just off the high street, which fans claim "surpasses the Indian original" in Mumbai (which inspired it). But while its culinary performance impressively lives up to its reputation, perceptions of its "oddly shaped and slightly claustrophobic" premises are deteriorating. Top Menu Tip – "definitely get the Duck Keema Naan if it's on the menu". / W1U 3DG; www.trishnalondon.com; trishnalondon; Mon-Sat 10.15 pm, Sun 9.45 pm.

TRIVET SE1 £147 33

36 SNOWSFIELDS 020 3141 8670 10–4C

The Bermondsey location is "not the easiest to get to", but many reporters make the effort for this "very accomplished" four-year-old. Chef Jonny Lake provides "absolutely first-rate cooking" with "refined and exciting flavours" and sommelier Isa Bal curates a "fantastic and eclectic" wine list. But even numerous fans feel a tad daunted by the pricing – "I thought it was worth the trip and deserving of its reputation, but the bill here makes it a treat rather than just a meal out…"; "it was very good… luckily I wasn't paying!". / SE1 3SU; trivetrestaurant.co.uk; trivetrestaurant; Wed-Sat, Tue 11 pm.

LA TROMPETTE W4 £111 33

5-7 DEVONSHIRE RD 020 8747 1836 8–2

This "absolute gem of a neighbourhood restaurant" sits on a side street off Chiswick's bustling main drag, and – like its cousin Chez Bruce – has earned a London-wide reputation over the years thanks to its "fine modern British dining", "well-drilled service with a smile" and "comprehensive list of fine wines". There's been some "changing of the guard in the kitchen" in the last 12 months with Greg Wellman, formerly of The Glasshouse, Kew, taking over at the stoves. But whereas some fans say "it hasn't undermined what remains a very strong offering", others are less certain and ratings are not what they were: "I'm still the 'fan from E18' who schleps across town to go here, and remain a supporter, but it seems to have lost some of that elusive lustre that eviously made it so special". / W4 2EU; vw.latrompette.co.uk; latrompettechiswick; Wed & ıu 9 pm, Fri & Sat 10 pm, Sun 3 pm.

RULLO N1 £78 433

0-302 ST PAUL'S RD
0 7226 2733 9–2D

'he neighbourhood Italian everyone would ınt to have" – Tim Siadatan and Jordan ieda's "low-key and lovely" Islington fixture eels like a special meal every time", with mazing pasta" and other "delicious" dishes epared from "excellent ingredients". "Choose stairs in summer for lunch, and downstairs winter for a romantic dinner". "Just wish ey weren't so dog-friendly!". / N1 2LH; vw.trullorestaurant.com; Mon-Sat 10.30 pm, Sun 30 pm.

SIAKKOS & CHARCOAL 9 £74 343

MARYLANDS ROAD 020 7286 7896 7–1B

ıreat hosts and a wonderful bubbly venue" – t to mention affordable prices for its simple od, much of it from the charcoal grill – derpin the appeal of this cosy Greek-Cypriot fé, off the Harrow Road in Maida Vale. A uple of newspaper articles in 2022 have ought it to the attention of more people of e, but it's been there for yonks. / W9 2DU; akkos.co.uk; Tue-Sat 11 pm.

SUNAMI SW4 £57 323

7 VOLTAIRE RD 020 7978 1610 11–1D

his "modern Japanese" with a "clubby and uncy vibe" has been a hit on Clapham igh Street since three former Nobu chefs ened it 23 years ago, and it remains a "very pular" destination for cocktails and fusion tes. Always "a slightly idiosyncratic" place this issue was more to the fore this year with cidents of "erratic" or "uncoordinated" rvice, and one or two fears that the "huge" enu is being "dumbed down". / SW4 6DQ; vw.tsunamirestaurant.co.uk; tsunami_restaurants; ın-Thu 10.30 pm, Fri & Sat 11.30 pm.

URNIPS WITH OMAS LIDAKEVICIUS E1 £137 433

3 BOROUGH MARKET, OFF BEDALE TREET 020 7357 8356 10–4C

unique experience!" – "For a dinner with twist, sit 'outside' within Borough Market ıd enjoy a set menu with wine pairing" at omas Lidakevicius's offbeat venture, attached a greengrocer's stall. "You've no need to ıoose anything and everything is good": he lovely setting helps for sure, but the great od from a tasting menu with seasonal veg as centrepiece speaks for itself". "Loved it!". SE1 9AH; www.turnipsboroughmarket.com; rnipsborough; Tue-Sat 11.30 pm.

12:51 BY CHEF JAMES COCHRAN N1 £71 432

107 UPPER STREET 07934 202269 9–3D

"Fantastically fun and fabulous food" from accomplished chef, James Cochran, is the pay-off for a visit to his Islington venue. "It's definitely not a posh night out" – "the room is tiny" and it's "a tricky and very cramped space" – but "the vibe is very upbeat and the meal is great value and highly recommended". Top Menu Tip – "best fried chicken ever". / N1 1QN; www.1251.co.uk; 1251_twelve_fifty_one; Tue-Sat 10 pm, Sun 8 pm.

20 BERKELEY W1

20 BERKELEY STREET
020 3327 3691 3–3C

Misha Zelman's (Goodman, Burger & Lobster) Creative Restaurant Group (Endo at the Rotunda; Humo; Sumu) opened this luxurious May 2023 newcomer on a Mayfair site that's never been previously used as a restaurant. Online articles around its launch have recycled the PR claims to 'English Manor House' styling – but the reality seems to be nothing like a creaky old country home, other than in the names of rooms like 'pantry' and the addition of lots of posh finishes. Executive chef Ben Orpwood sources ingredients at the height of their short seasons to emphasise the cuisine's local British focus. No survey feedback or significant press reviews as yet. / W1J 8EE; www.20berkeley.com; 20berkeleylondon; Mon-Thu 9.30 pm, Fri & Sat 10 pm.

28 CHURCH ROW NW3 £61 444

28 CHURCH ROW 020 7993 2062 9–2A

Under a picturesque Georgian terrace, close to St John-in-Hampstead church, this basement tapas bar is a prime destination in the area thanks to its "consistently delicious food, attentive staff" and "lovely atmosphere". The menu adds Italian elements to its Spanish core, and there's a "very good wine selection". / NW3 6UP; www.28churchrow.com; 28churchrow; Mon-Sat 10.30 pm, Sun 9.30 pm.

28-50 £90 223

15-17 MARYLEBONE LANE, W1
020 7486 7922 3–1A
4 GREAT PORTLAND STREET, W1
020 7420 0630 3–1C
300 KING'S ROAD, SW3
020 7349 9818 6–3C
96 DRAYCOTT AVE, SW3
020 7581 5208 6–2C

A "fabulous wine list with so many wines available by the glass" is the key draw to this trio of wine-bar/kitchens from the West End to Chelsea (the Draycott Avenue branch closed this year). Dining can seem "quite pricey" for what it is, but most diners say they "love the food as well". / www.2850.co.uk; 2850marylebone.

24 THE OVAL SW9 £62 343

24 CLAPHAM ROAD 020 7735 6111 11–1D

In the thin area near Oval tube, this neighbourhood bistro is worth remembering. A sibling to Knife in Clapham, its "old-fashioned modern British cooking" puts a similar emphasis on steak and other grills, but there's a good selection of dishes and – albeit on limited feedback – it wins praise for "excellent all-round value". / SW9 0JG; www.24theoval.co.uk; 24theoval; Fri & Sat, Wed & Thu 9.30 pm, Sun 4.30 pm.

TWIST CONNUBIO W1 £69 332

42 CRAWFORD STREET
020 7723 3377 2–1A

"Tucked away in Marylebone, with a friendly vibe and tasty food", this creative outfit marries flavours from Spanish, Italian and Japanese cuisine. "Some of the tapas are very good indeed", and they are supported by a serious wine list focused on Spain and Italy. / W1H 1JW; www.twistconnubio.com; twistconnubio; Mon-Sat 10 pm.

TWO BROTHERS N3 £40 322

297-303 REGENT'S PARK RD
020 8346 0469 1–1B

"The fish is always fresh and the staff are friendly" at this "good local fish 'n' chip place" that has been a fixture in Finchley for three decades. "Best fish and chips in London?" – probably not, but just what you want in your neighbourhood. / N3 1DP; www.twobrothers.co.uk; Tue-Sun 10 pm.

222 VEGGIE VEGAN W14 £46 333

222 NORTH END ROAD
020 7381 2322 8–2D

Celebrating its 20th anniversary this year, chef Ben Asamani's "very good vegan" on Fulham's trafficky North End Road (near its crossroads with the Lillie Road) provides "a lovely dining experience" – "you certainly don't miss eating fish or meat". Top Menu Tip – the "veggie burgers" – made with asparagus and petits pois on gluten-free bread – "are the best!". / W14 9NU; www.222vegan.com; 222vegancuisine; Wed-Sun 9 pm.

2 VENETI W1 £59 232

10 WIGMORE STREET
020 7637 0789 3–1B

Handy as a "welcoming" spot near the Wigmore Hall – this straightforward Italian delivers "an enjoyable experience" at "surprisingly reasonable prices for a smart restaurant in a smart district". Some reports also applaud its "really good and authentically Venetian dishes", but a fair summary might be that the overall performance is "pleasant". / W1U 2RD; www.2veneti.com; 2veneti; Mon-Fri 9.45 pm, Sat 10 pm.

ULI £78 434

15 SEYMOUR PLACE, W1
020 3141 5877 2–2A
5 LADBROKE ROAD, W11
020 3141 5878 7–2B

"Relaxed and busy", Michael Lim's Notting Hill venue is "always a treat", with "great Singaporean and other Asian dishes". It has notched up 26 years, first in All Saints Road and more recently in smart new premises on Ladbroke Road. A second branch opened in Seymour Place, Marylebone, in June 2023. Top Tip – "fantastic in the summer with the roof open".

UMU W1 £166 344

14-16 BRUTON PL 020 7499 8881 3–2C

Opened 20 years ago as London's first exponent of Kyoto-style kaiseki dining (Japan's most refined cuisine), this low-key Mayfair fixture remains a key foodie destination under Ryo Kakatsu, who joined 10 years ago and was appointed executive chef in 2020. It also has one of the most extensive sake lists in Europe. While the occasional reporter flinches at the "incredibly expense and very small portions", nobody complains about the quality of the food. / W1J 6LX; www.umurestaurant.com; umurestaurant; Tue-Sat 10 pm.

UPSTAIRS AT THE GEORGE W1 £86 323

55 GREAT PORTLAND STREET
020 3946 3740 2–1B

This "grand but friendly" tavern, in "magnificent" 18th-century premises a short walk from Oxford Circus, offers Kitchen Table chef "James Knappett's take on traditional pub classics with inventive twists". In the main bar you'll find elevated snacks, while a "concise British menu" is served in the upstairs dining room, including "incredible roast dinners – huge slices of beef with what can only be described as a chimney-sized Yorkshire pudding!". / W1W 7LQ; thegeorge.london; thegeorgepublichouse; Tue-Sat 11 pm, Sun 7 pm.

LE VACHERIN W4 £77 344

76-77 SOUTH PARADE
020 8742 2121 8–1A

"The French bistro at its best", this "reliable" Gallic fixture by Acton Green is "a small bit of Paris in Chiswick", with "perfect food (including oysters) and an atmosphere for romance". Top Menu Tip – "delicious soufflés". / W4 5LF; www.levacherin.com; le_vacherin; Mon-Sat 10.30 pm, Sun 9 pm.

VARDO SW3 £75 223

9 DUKE OF YORK SQUARE
020 7101 1199 6–2D

Set in a striking purpose-built circular pavilion in Duke of York Square, this family-friendly venture is part of the Caravan group (it's named after the Romany travelling wagon). The menu of global favourites is "very good value for Chelsea" (but, in gastronomic terms, perhaps a bit "dull"). / SW3 4LY; vardorestaurant.co.uk; vardorestaurant; Tue-Thu, Sun 10 pm, Fri & Sat 10.30 pm, Mon 9.30 pm.

VASCO & PIERO'S PAVILION W1 £75 343

11 D'ARBLAY STREET
020 7437 8774 4–1C

"Still a special place even though it's moved site" – this veteran Soho Italian was evicted from its previous Poland Street home over Covid, and found these new digs last year. It still "exudes old world charm" and has retained many of the former "delightful" staff, who are really at the heart of this "unpretentious" experience as much as the "reliable Umbrian/Italian cooking". / W1F 8DT; www.vascosfood.com; Tue-Sat 10 pm.

VEERASWAMY W1 £101 434

VICTORY HOUSE, 99-101 REGENT STREET
020 7734 1401 4–4B

"First came here almost 60 years ago! And it's still one of my favourites" – London's oldest Indian restaurant "delivers fabulous food year after year". Opened in 1926, in a first-floor space at the Piccadilly end of Regent Street, it is nowadays part of the upmarket Amaya and Chutney Mary group who have ensured its offering has moved with the times. The decor is "lovely" but not old-fashioned, and the "imaginative food has lots of flavours". Top Menu Tip – "Rogan Josh on the bone". / W1B 4RS; www.veeraswamy.com; veeraswamy.london; Mon-Sat 10 pm, Sun 10.15 pm.

VIA EMILIA £48 343

10 CHARLOTTE PLACE, W1
020 8127 4277 2–1C 37A HOXTON SQUARE, N1 020 7613 0508 13–1B

"A relatively limited menu allows for a focus on quality" and authenticity at this duo showcasing the food of Emilia-Romagna: both the original "small and intimate" branch in Shoreditch; and the one "formerly known as 'In Parma by Food Roots' in Fitzrovia (since early 2023 now rebranded in line with its sister restaurant)". "Staff are very accommodating" and offer "Italian meats and cheeses and Bolognese/Emilian standbys, like Tagliatelle al Ragu (definitely not SpagBol!)". "Go back frequently as it's great value too".

IL VICOLO SW1 £72 232

3-4 CROWN PASSAGE
020 7839 3960 3–4D

Celebrating its 30th anniversary this year, this "family-owned Italian restaurant" has long seemed refreshingly down to earth for somewhere hidden in an alleyway in posh St James's: with its "simple Calabrian menu and good service", it's "especially good for lunch". As with many other central places, it has "appeared considerably more expensive" of late – perhaps they are saving up for a move to new premises: a relaunch a few doors down from its old site scheduled for September 202 / SW1Y 6PP; www.ilvicolorestaurant.co.uk; ilvic restaurant; Mon-Sat 10 pm.

THE VICTORIA SW14 £66 33

10 WEST TEMPLE SHEEN
020 8876 4238 11–2A

"Love this pub", hailed by fans (often parents for providing "one of the best Sunday lunche in this part of southwest London, just outside Richmond Park in East Sheen. Over the yea TV chef Paul Merrett has transformed the rambling Victorian tavern into a boutique ho with a large garden and spacious conservator for dining. / SW14 7RT; victoriasheen.co.uk; thevictoriasheen; Wed & Thu, Sat, Fri 9 pm, Sun 7 pm.

VIET FOOD W1 £43 32

34-36 WARDOUR STREET
020 7494 4555 5–3A

"Delicious morsels" of "good Asian food at l low prices" ensure that ex-Hakkasan chef Jeff Tan's warehouse-style Chinatown operation i often packed to the rafters – it's a "fun, busy place" if you don't mind squeezing in. / W1I 6QT; www.vietnamfood.co.uk; vietfoodlondon; Sun-Thu 10.30 pm, Fri & Sat 11 pm.

VIET GARDEN N1 £36 32

207 LIVERPOOL RD 020 7700 6040 9–3

"I couldn't love it more", say regulars of this Islington Vietnamese – "a family-run and family-oriented original, with reliable and delicious food". / N1 1LX; www.vietgarden.co. vietgardenuk; Sun-Thu 11 pm, Fri & Sat 11.30 p

VIJAY NW6 £41 34

49 WILLESDEN LN 020 7328 1087 1–1B

This "well-established" Kilburn curry house – purportedly the first to offer South Indian cuisine in the UK – celebrates its 60th anniversary this year. Little has changed since it opened, with its "plain good cooking", "authentic recipes" including dishes not found elsewhere and "lovely vegetarian meals" pleasing happy locals as well as a string of celeb visitors ranging from the late Michael Winner to Diana Ross, Harrison Ford and the Indian cricket team. / NW6 7RI www.vijayrestaurant.co.uk; vijayindiauk; Sun-Th 10.45 pm, Fri & Sat 11.45 pm.

VILLA BIANCA NW3 £75 33

1 PERRINS CT 020 7435 3131 9–2A

"There's an air of old-school sophistication as you enter" this "established Italian" with starched white linen "off an alleyway in Hampstead". It scored consistently well this year for its "charming and helpful" service an "fab food, without fab prices". Top Tip – "the wild boar ragu". / NW3 1QS; villabiancagroup com; villabiancanw3; Tue-Sat 11 pm, Sun 10 pm.

VILLA DI GEGGIANO W4 £93 344

66-68 CHISWICK HIGH ROAD
020 3384 9442 8–*2B*

This "beautiful courtyard" on the Chiswick High Road "feels like a little bit of (the expensive part) of Tuscany – but at least you've saved on the air fare", and the "delightful atmosphere, good fish and pasta" add to the impression. The Chianti estate it is named after has exported wine to London for 300 years. / W4 1SY; www.villadigeggiano.co.uk; villa_di_geggiano_london; Tue-Sat 10.30 pm, Sun 9 pm.

THE VINCENT ROOMS, WESTMINSTER KINGSWAY COLLEGE SW1 £46 334

76 VINCENT SQUARE 020 7802 8391 2–*4C*

One of "London's best kept foodie secrets", where you act as a guinea pig for the next generation of the UK hospitality trade within Westminster Kingsway College, on leafy Vincent Square. There are two restaurants: the relaxed 'Brasserie' and more formal 'Escoffier Room', where "the cooking by third-year students is often Michelin quality", while "the service by first years is lovely… if a bit rough at the edges". Not only is a meal here "terrific value (£35 for 5-course tasting menu, ditto wine pairings)", you also "support budding culinary careers". / SW1P 2PD; www.thevincentrooms.co.uk; thevincentrooms; Mon, Fri 3 pm, Tue-Thu 9 pm.

VINOTECA £62 222

18 DEVONSHIRE RD, W4
020 3701 8822 8–*2A*
ONE PANCRAS SQ, N1
020 3793 7210 9–*3C*
BOROUGH YARDS, STONEY STREET, SE1
020 3376 3000 10–*4C*
7 ST JOHN ST, EC1 020 7253 8786 10–*1B*
QUEEN VICTORIA STREET, EC4
AWAITING TEL 10–*3C*

"An exceptional list of wine with so many to choose by the glass that it's always possible to try something a bit different" is the key selling point of this popular modern wine bar chain. Its culinary attractions are less reliable – the food can be "surprisingly good" but is too often "essentially average"; service can be "accommodating" or "rushed"; and the ambience can be "better if you can sit outside". But its "excellent value" drinking and "lively" style carry the day. In particular, the "conveniently placed" King's Cross branch has a "great location, which makes it a winner". Top Tip – "creditable set lunch at a pretty restrained price". / www.vinoteca.co.uk; vinotecawinefood.

VIVAT BACCHUS £74 332

4 HAY'S LANE, SE1 020 7234 0891 10–*4C*
47 FARRINGDON STREET, EC4
020 7353 2648 10–*2A*

Now in its 21st year, this South African-owned duo in Farringdon and London Bridge thrive on their "good basics", including "delicious steaks" and a "lovely wine list" with a focus on South African vintages. Saffa-style dried meats and a dedicated cheese room complete the deal. / www.vivatbacchus.co.uk; vivatbacchus.

VOLTA DO MAR WC2 £66 332

13-15 TAVISTOCK STREET
020 3034 0028 5–*3D*

A move to Notting Hill in summer 2023 after four years in Covent Garden should have put new wind in the sails of this culinary celebration of Portugal and its historical maritime links with Asia, Africa and South America – a project from Salt Yard founder Simon Mullins and his Portuguese wife Isabel Almeida Da Silva. The "fancy versions of Portuguese classic dishes" are generally "very good" (if, according to the odd critic, "too well behaved"), and there's a "well-priced Portuguese wine list". / WC2E 7PS; voltadomar.co.uk; voltadomar_ldn; Thu-Sat, Tue, Wed 10.30 pm.

VORI W11 £88 333

120 HOLLAND PARK AVENUE
020 3308 4271 7–*2A*

Restaurateur Markos Tsimikalis closed his Shoreditch restaurant, Hungry Donkey, to open this brightly decorated Greek venue in Holland Park in late 2022. Our initial feedback is very upbeat all-round and – in April 2023 – The Independent's Kate Ng was likewise positive, including about the signature Cretan-style cheesecake made with sheep and goat's milk ("certainly up there with the greats"). / W11 4UA; vorigreekkitchen.co.uk; vorilondon; Tue-Sat 10.30 pm, Sun 9 pm.

VQ £64 223

ST GILES HOTEL, 111A GREAT RUSSELL STREET, WC1 020 7636 5888 5–*1A*
325 FULHAM RD, SW10
020 7376 7224 6–*3B*
9 ALDGATE HIGH STREET, EC3
020 3301 7224 10–*2D*

"Open 24 hours, with flexible options for breakfast" – these round-the-clock cafés are worth remembering if you're out on the town and need to refuel. Only the SW10 original generates much in the way of feedback – "the cuisine is not fine food, but it's a convenient option that's good value" and "reliable". (Aldgate also has a standalone bar with a 24-hour alcohol licence). / www.vqrestaurants.com; vqrestaurants.

WAGAMAMA £58 112

BRANCHES THROUGHOUT LONDON

As a "reliable standby", this Japanese-inspired ramen (noodle) chain still inspires many reports, and parents in particular see it as a "safe option". Even some fans, though, acknowledge that "it's not a gastronomic highlight" nowadays, and ratings are dragged significantly down by the few who feel it's "lost its way", with service that's "not the fastest" and "food that used to be nice, but which is now not so good". / www.wagamama.com; wagamama_uk. SRA – 1 star.

WAHACA £53 22

BRANCHES THROUGHOUT LONDON

These "lively, colourful" Mexican street-food joints are, say fans, "great for a quick bite" – "the food remains pretty good (if not where it was several years ago)" and "you can't compla at the prices". That's the majority view anywa although there is a small minority who feel it's "very average" now (and its ratings risk headi that way). Founded by MasterChef winner Thomasina Miers in 2007, the group hit the buffers during the pandemic and halved in size to 10 sites in London, with Dick Enthove of Nando's taking a controlling stake. / www.wahaca.com. wahaca; SRA – 3 stars.

THE WALLACE, THE WALLACE COLLECTION W1 £48 21

HERTFORD HOUSE, MANCHESTER SQUA
020 7563 9505 3–*1A*

This "beautiful space in a covered courtyard" the Wallace Collection museum and art galle makes an unusually "delightful" rendez-vous for lunch or afternoon tea near Oxford Street or it would if it were not for the "disappointin food and shambolic service". / W1U 3BN; www.peytonandbyrne.co.uk; peytonandbyrne; Mon-Sun 4 pm.

THE WATER HOUSE PROJEC E2 £197 45

1 CORBRIDGE CRESCENT
07841 804119 14–*2B*

"Wow! Terrifically innovative, technical cooki and a lovely supper club concept of common tables, complete with a welcome and farewell from the chef" inspires ongoing acclaim for Gabriel Waterhouse's excellent Bethnal Green venture (which relocated a couple of years ago to an airy new space). It's £155 for his 10-course menu with drinks pairings (and on Wednesday nights and Saturday lunchtimes a shorter selection is served for £100): "for this standard of cuisine, it's a great price when so much London serious 'fine' dining is nowadays just unaffordable". / E2 9DS; www.thewaterhouseproject.com; thewaterhouseproject; Wed-Sat 11 pm.

THE WATERMAN'S ARMS SW13

375 LONSDALE RD AWAITING TEL 11–*1*

Few pubs in London boast as fine a location as this riverside tavern, at the Thames-side end of Barnes High Street (and next to the also-picturesque Bull's Head). Abandoned to pizza and brasserie chains in recent decades, it's now to be relaunched as a passion project by Patty & Bun founder, Joe Grossmann; and with fron of house from Simon Walsh, who filled the same role at Hammersmith's excellent Anglese Arms. / SW13 9PY; Tue-Sat 10.30 pm.

HE WELLS TAVERN W3 £74 344

WELL WALK 020 7794 3785 9–1A

/ many accounts "by far the best gastropub the Hampstead area", this particularly velcoming and charming" Georgian tavern as been run for two decades by Beth Coventry ster of the doyenne of restaurant critics, Fay aschler). "Great outside seating… if you can ab it". / NW3 1BX; thewellshampstead.london; ewellshampstead; Mon-Sat 10 pm, Sun 9.30 pm.

ESTERNS LAUNDRY 5 £73 333

DRAYTON PARK 020 7700 3700 9–2D

Heavily embracing the post-industrial vibe" this "buzzy" hipster feature not far from the mirates and Drayton Park station ("did they out of their way to make it difficult to find?") akes elegant and appealing use of the high-ilinged space it occupies (originally, of course, laundry). Five years old now, it's something of classic of the contemporary East End genre "a small plates outlet of quality" combining nky tapas with low intervention wines. It oes attract the odd more downbeat critique ough: "the food, service and ambience are all ne but in no way justify the prices". / N5 1PB; ww.westernslaundry.com; westernslaundry; Tue-at 10.30 pm, Sun 9 pm.

HE WET FISH CAFÉ W6 £57 333

42 WEST END LANE 020 7443 9222 1–1B

A great local for brunch, quick lunchtime ite or impromptu dinner for two" – this small and always friendly neighbourhood avourite" occupies atmospheric premises in West Hampstead that started life as a 1930s shmonger (you can still buy fish retail here). The food is consistently good", "service speedy" and they do "excellent coffee" o. / NW6 1LG; www.thewetfishcafe.co.uk; hewetfishcafe; Mon-Sun 10.30 pm.

HE WIGMORE, THE ANGHAM W1 £65 344

5 LANGHAM PLACE, REGENT STREET 20 7965 0198 2–1B

Pub grub is elevated by Michel Albert Roux great effect at this "posh pub", "handily lose to the horrors of Oxford Circus" – a urprisingly "good place to meet for business" nd "worth going out of your way for". Top Menu Tip – "take friends and order the cheese oastie on the sly, then watch their faces light up when the magnificent beast of a sandwich is resented". / W1B 3DE; www.the-wigmore.co.uk; vigmorelondon; Mon-Sat 11 pm.

WILD HONEY ST JAMES SW1 £120 322

SOFITEL, 8 PALL MALL 020 7389 7820 2–3C

Anthony Demetre's "combination of balance, tastes and textures" inspires fans of this "grand hotel dining room" off Trafalgar Square ("a far cry from his original restaurant of this name" in Mayfair). It's most nominated for a "solid business lunch" although "the tasting menu is lovely" and also wins recommendations for it as a foodie destination in its own right. A setting that's "classy" to supporters, though, can – to critics – seem "a little soulless"; and service doesn't always live up to the occasion. Top Tip – "the set lunch and early evening menus offer excellent value". / SW1Y 5NG; www.wildhoneystjames.co.uk; wildhoneystjames; Wed-Sat 9.30 pm, Tue 2.30 pm.

WILD TAVERN SW3 £127 223

2 ELYSTAN STREET 020 8191 9885 6–2C

This Chelsea four-year-old (by Chelsea Green) with an Alpine-themed interior is from a duo involved in Beast and Burger & Lobster; and offers a raw bar along with prime cuts of steak and fish from the grill, sold per 100g – all of which attracts little commentary from reporters beyond the consistent complaint that it's "way over-priced". In September 2023, a new offshoot – Wild Notting Hill – will open on the site that was formerly 202 (RIP). / SW3 3NS; www.wildtavern.co.uk; wildtavern; Mon-Sat 10 pm, Sun 9.30 pm.

WILTONS SW1 £117 333

55 JERMYN ST 020 7629 9955 3–3C

"A last redoubt of traditional gastronomy" – London's oldest restaurant in St James's (est. 1742, but on this site since the 1980s) maintains its "quiet" and "calm" style, with "understated but excellent service" and "booths that make a superb place to do business". Classic fish dishes – for example "very good Dover sole off the bone" – are the speciality and "ever-reliable". A less welcome constant are its "eye-watering prices": "everything was as I hoped it would be… apart from the bill!" / SW1Y 6LX; www.wiltons.co.uk; wiltons1742; Mon-Sat 10.30 pm.

THE WINDMILL W1 £65 323

6-8 MILL ST 020 7491 8050 4–2A

The "focus on home-made British pies" makes this trad Mayfair pub a crowd-pleaser, "tucked away" off Regent Street close to Oxford Circus. From the same stable as the Guinea Grill, it now has a smarter restaurant upstairs, along with a rooftop terrace. Top Menu Tips – "the pastry pies are best for hungry young adult males, while the shepherd's pie is excellent if you want something lighter". / W1S 2AZ; www.windmillmayfair.co.uk; windmill_pub; Mon-Sat 9 pm, Sun 7 pm.

THE WINE LIBRARY EC3 £51 235

43 TRINITY SQ 020 7481 0415 10–3D

"Back to being busy, bubbly and bright" after the bleak pandemic years – this vaulted 19th-century cellar near Tower Hill offers a "great and interesting selection of wine", served at retail prices plus £9.50 corkage, with "informative staff" to help you choose. A "help-yourself" menu of cheeses, cold meats and other nibbles is on hand to provide ballast. / EC3N 4DJ; www.winelibrary.co.uk; thewinelibrary; Tue-Fri 8 pm, Mon 6 pm, Sat 5.30 pm.

THE WOLSELEY W1 £83 225

160 PICCADILLY 020 7499 6996 3–3C

"Reports of the death of The Wolseley are greatly exaggerated". After a well-publicised boardroom battle in 2022 ousted its original co-founders, even though its long-term fans are "annoyed at the ousting of Christopher Corbin & Jeremy King", there is "no evidence on the floor of any impact": "it's as good as it ever was (and just as full!"). This Continental-style Grand Café, near The Ritz (originally built as a car showroom, for which it is named) is celebrating its 20th year, and remains a hub of metropolitan living. The "impressive" and "always bustling" space is "one of the best dining rooms in London" and "if you want to wow a client or a foreigner, then bring them here": it remains London's No. 1 for business entertaining in our annual diners' poll. Its "great menu of classics" is executed to a "solid and reliable" if "lacklustre" standard, but you "go for the overall package and peerless people watching, not the food". The exception is "the most civilised breakfast anywhere on the planet" which is also our diners' poll's No. 1 choice in this category. The "varied menu, with something – and more – for everyone", helps "elevate the occasion to a special level"; and it is also "a power scene" amongst business-types. Top Tip – afternoon tea is also "always impressive with its elegance and high standards". / W1J 9EB; www.thewolseley.com; thewolseley; Mon-Sat 11 pm, Sun 10 pm.

THE WOLSELEY CITY EC4

68 KING WILLIAM STREET 020 7499 6996 10–3C

In Autumn 2023, the famous West End icon will start a new, ultimately global, roll-out. First stop is the City, with this conversion of the ground floor of the old House of Fraser building, near Monument tube and looking onto London Bridge. The site is considerably larger than that on Piccadilly and the website promise is of 'a younger sister to the original, not a replica'. / EC4N 7HR; thewolseleyhospitalitygroup.com; thewolseley; Mon-Sun 10 pm.

WONG KEI W1 £34 322

41-43 WARDOUR ST 020 7437 8408 5–3A

"No frills, no smiles but always fast and reliable" – this "Chinatown standby" has fed generations of West End revellers and theatre-goers with "great cheap Cantonese food", serving up to 500 people at a time over several floors. "Service is not what it was – the staff are no longer rude!" – but "the speed with which scoff arrives at the table remains utterly predictable". Top Menu Tip – "still love their Singapore noodles". / W1D 6PY; Mon-Sat 11.30 pm, Sun 10.30 pm.

WRIGHT BROTHERS £72 333

56 OLD BROMPTON RD, SW7
020 7581 0131 6–*2B*
11 STONEY ST, SE1 020 7403 9554 10–*4C*
26 CIRCUS ROAD WEST, SW8
020 7324 7734 11–*1C*

"Crowded… slightly crazy-busy… top oysters supported by a changing menu of fish and crustacea" – that's the package at this trio of "busy" bistros in Borough Market, Battersea Power Station and South Kensington. "You come here for the seafood, not to be fawned over. The decor's a little rough and ready but the food's so fresh and delicious". / thewrightbrothers.co.uk; WrightBrosLTD.

WULF & LAMB £57 323

243 PAVILION ROAD, SW1
020 3948 5999 6–*2D*
66 CHILTERN STREET, W1
020 8194 0000 2–*1A*

"The food pleases everyone, vegan or not" at this duo of "comfortable" and "enjoyable" meat-free cafés which occupy chichi enclaves in Chelsea and Marylebone. "Vegan eaters are bewildered at the choice on offer" ("great curries, veggie burgers etc") and "whether or not you eat meat, it represents good value for lunch or a light dinner in an otherwise pricey part of town". / www.wulfandlamb.com.

XI'AN IMPRESSION N7 £44 421

117 BENWELL RD 020 3441 0191 9–*2D*

"I could eat here every day and die happy", say fans of this Shanxi street-food canteen opposite Arsenal's Emirates stadium – "the homemade dumplings and noodles are consistently superlative and soooo moreish". "Service is matter-of-fact Chinese, seating is short and tight", "but you go just for the food and you're not disappointed!" / N7 7BW; www.xianimpression.co.uk; xianimpression; Mon-Sun 10 pm.

YAATRA SW1 £85 442

OLD WESTMINSTER FIRE STATION, 4 GREYCOAT PLACE 020 4549 1906 2–*4C*

This "no-expense-spared upmarket Indian restaurant" in Grade II listed Old Westminster Fire Station has impressed reporters with some "amazing and interesting dishes" in its first year. It was launched as "Atul Kochhar's Mathura, which didn't last long, but the new management has done some great marketing with customer deals" – "I'd certainly go again". / SW1P 1SB; www.yaatrarestaurant.com; yaatrawestminster; Tue-Sun 11 pm.

YAMA MOMO SE22 £65 323

72 LORDSHIP LN 020 8299 1007 1–*4D*

Buzzy Japanese in East Dulwich (younger sister of Clapham's long-established Tsunami), that's "always busy due to the reliably tasty (and never-changing) menu" of sushi and sashimi, plus more substantial fare, backed up by "excellent cocktails". / SE22 8HF; www.yamamomo.co.uk; yamamomo_eastdulwich; Mon-Thu 10 pm, Fri & Sat 10.30 pm, Sun 9.30 pm.

YARD SALE PIZZA £43 342

54 BLACKSTOCK ROAD, N4
020 7226 2651 9–*1D*
46 WESTOW HILL, SE19
020 8670 6386 1–*4D*
39 LORDSHIP LANE, SE22
020 8693 5215 1–*4D*
393 BROCKLEY ROAD, SE4
020 8692 8800 1–*4D*
63 BEDFORD HILL, SW12
020 8772 1100 11–*2C*
622 HIGH ROAD LEYTONSTONE, E11
020 8539 5333 1–*1D*
15 HOE STREET, E17 020 8509 0888 1–*1D*
184 HACKNEY ROAD, E2
020 7739 1095 14–*2A*
105 LOWER CLAPTON RD, E5
020 3602 9090 14–*1B*

"Delicious thin-crust pizzas" win consistently high ratings for this 10-strong chain across north, east and south London. They are a socially conscious bunch who contributed 8,000 meals to NHS staff during the pandemic. / yardsalepizza.com; yardsalepizza.

YASHIN £109 432

117-119 OLD BROMPTON RD, SW7
020 7373 3990 6–*2B*
1A ARGYLL RD, W8 020 7938 1536 6–*1A*

This offbeat, "really high-quality Japanese" outfit in a Kensington backstreet from Yasuhiro Minemo and Shinya Ikeda has carved out a niche for itself over the last 13 years with its "delicious sushi" and "extremely attentive staff". It's pricey, but "the lunch menu is great value". Its offshoot Ocean House is in the former Brompton Library, while the latest addition from 2022, Sushi Kamon in Arcade Food Hall on Oxford Street, offers a cut-price 45-minute omakase experience. / yashinsushi.com.

YAUATCHA £105 32

BROADWICK HOUSE, 15-17 BROADWICK STREET, W1 020 7494 8888 4–*1C*
BROADGATE CIRCLE, EC2
020 3817 9888 13–*2B*

"Cheung fun… just wow" – a highlight of the "brilliant" dim sum at this cool modern take on Cantonese cuisine, created by Alan Yau, the restaurant whizz behind Hakkasan and Wagamama. Now in its 20th anniversary year, there are two sites in the capital – a Soho basement (with ground-floor tea room) and a very much bigger and glossier venue in the City's Broadgate development (plus satellites in the Middle East and India). But even fans of the "delicious food" sometimes say, "I like it here, but the bill always surprises me… not in a good way!" / www.yauatcha.com.

THE YELLOW HOUSE SE16 £53 33

126 LOWER RD 020 7231 8777 12–*2A*

"Thank the stars they survived the pandemic!" – nearby residents cherish this "wonderful local" near Surrey Quays station. "Effectively, it has three menus – modern European, grill and pizza 'n' pasta – all are top-notch!" / SE16 2U; www.theyellowhouse.eu; theyellowhouserestaurant; Tue-Thu 9 pm, Fri & Sat 9.30 pm, Sun 5.30 pm.

ZAFFERANO SW1 £116 43

15 LOWNDES ST 020 7235 5800 6–*1D*

"Top-notch food and great service" continue to win praise for this chic Belgravia Italian. Compared with its 1990s heyday (when under Giorgio Locatelli it reigned supreme as London's best) it doesn't attract nearly the same level of attention, partly because it is "very, very expensive". But quality remains high and it's particularly popular amongst expense-accounters as a good way to "impress clients". / SW1X 9EY; zafferanorestaurant.com; zafferanorestaurant; Mon-Sun 10 pm.

The Waterman's Arms SW13

AIBATSU SE10 £40 432

TRAFALGAR RD 020 8858 9317 1–*3D*

;mall, rammed and pretty hectic, but that's part of the charm" at this Japanese café on e edge of Greenwich, serving "fantastic food at's insanely well priced" – "ribs in BBQ uce, mixed tempura, cod in tempura, sushi, odles... all amazing, fresh and such good lue". "A few things to note: it's cash only; YO for booze; it can be a tad cold in winter". SE10 9UW; www.zaibatsufusion.co.uk; Tue-Sat pm, Sun 9 pm.

AIKA OF KENSINGTON 8 £79 444

KENSINGTON HIGH STREET
0 7795 6533 6–*1A*

itunning food, service and ambience" make meal at this upscale Indian near Kensington ardens "a special experience". Set in a eautiful ex-bank building with great art roughout", fans feel it is "often overlooked ven the location (i.e. not Mayfair) but up ere with the best" ("I've tried several new dian places, but keep returning to this ie"). / W8 5NP; www.zaikaofkensington.com; ikaofkensington; Tue-Sat 10.15 pm, Sun 9.15 pm.

APOTE EC2 £40 444

LEONARD STREET
20 7613 5346 13–*1B*

Bringing an affordable higher-end Mexican perience to London, with inventive cuisine" chef Yahir Gonzalez and co-founder Tony eary have taken over the Shoreditch site that as St Leonards (RIP) to open this colourfully corated and attractive 60-seater. It has ceived some up-and-down reports in the edia (The Guardian's Grace Dent, a fan, ought it "a date-night kind of place, or for nner with a client you'd actually like to talk "; but it's "a modern Mexican muddle" cording to the FT's Tim Hayward; or with basic errors" in the view of online restaurant aven, Andy Hayler). But we've rated it ositively on our initial reports of "knockout atino food with imaginative and perfectly dged sharing plates", "interesting cocktails nd wines" and "warm and attentive service". EC2A 4QX; zapote.co.uk; Tue-Thu 10 pm, Fri & at 10.30 pm.

EPHYR W11 £80 444

00 PORTOBELLO ROAD
20 4599 1177 7–*2B*

'his "chic-casual" venture from the achamama group in Notting Hill focuses on modern Greek fusion food", and has picked p plenty of fans in its inaugural year thanks to s "sophisticated cooking" and "buzzy" vibe.)ne repeated gripe: "bringing dishes when the itchen fancies can lead to an odd sequence meals!" / W11 2QD; www.zephyr.london; phyrnottinghill; Mon-Sat 11 pm, Sun 10 pm.

081 PIZZERIA, PECKHAM LEVELS SE15 £37 522

95A RYE LANE 020 3795 8576 1–*4D*

"Best pizza for miles..." Andrea Asciuti's mega-popular pizza powerhouse has found its first permanent home in Peckham, opening in Feb' 2023 at this small, 20-cover unit. "Frantic service from Italians, but that doesn't matter because the pizza's so good!". (It also serves Napoli-inspired street food such as frittatina, arancina, crocche.... He also operates within pubs at the Smugglers Tavern in Fitzrovia and at Camden Town's Colonel Fawcett). / SE15 4ST; www.081pizzeria.com; 081pizzerialdn; Mon-Sun 11 pm.

ZHENG SW3 £80 332

4 SYDNEY ST 020 7352 9890 6–*2C*

Chelsea Malaysian whose menu mixes and matches Chinese dishes and other Asian inspirations. It's survived ten years on a site (off the King's Road) that was previously something of a restaurant graveyard, due to its straightforward if not earth-shattering virtues: "friendly service, good food, nice interior". / SW3 6PP; www.zhengchelsea.co.uk; Mon, Wed-Sun 11 pm.

ZIA LUCIA £53 332

61 BLYTHE ROAD, W14
020 7371 4096 8–*1C*
18 OLYMPIC WAY, HA9
020 3744 4427 1–*1A*
61 STOKE NEWINGTON HIGH STREET, N16
020 8616 8690 1–*1C*
157 HOLLOWAY ROAD, N7
020 7700 3708 9–*2D*
238 WEST END LANE, NW6
020 3737 9557 1–*1B*
65 BALHAM HIGH ROAD, SW12
020 3093 0946 11–*2C*
356 OLD YORK ROAD, SW18
020 3971 0829 11–*2B*
SOUTH QUAY PLAZA, 75 HAMPTON TOWER, E14 020 4503 8859 12–*1C*
12A PIAZZA WALK, E1
020 7702 2525 10–*2D*

"It's hard to be 'special' with pizza these days with so much competition, but the eye-catching options give an edge" to this popular nine-strong chain, whose calling card is a choice of four different 48-hour fermented pizza bases, including the distinctive black vegetable charcoal. Their latest opening is in Canary Wharf. / zialucia.com; zialuciapizza.

ZIANI'S SW3 £58 343

45 RADNOR WALK 020 7351 5297 6–*3C*

"Despite being off the beaten track" in Chelsea (albeit near the King's Road), this tiny trat' still packs 'em in. Founder Roberto Colussi died a few years back, but the front-of-house team has maintained his warm welcome and the very dependable cooking. / SW3 4BP; www.ziani.co.uk; Mon-Sun 10 pm.

ZOILO W1 £85 334

9 DUKE ST 020 7486 9699 3–*1A*

"Small, personal and romantic, with serious food for meat fans" – an Argentinian venue near the Wallace Collection in Marylebone, run by chef-patron Diego Jacquet, who trained in his native Buenos Aires under the legendary Francis Mallmann and worked at El Bulli in Spain and Aquavit in New York. Top Tip – "set lunch is a bargain". / W1U 3EG; www.zoilo.co.uk; zoilolondon; Tue-Sat midnight.

ZUMA SW7 £115 444

5 RAPHAEL ST 020 7584 1010 6–*1C*

"Buzzy and still heaving" – Rainer Becker and Arjun Waney's happening Eurotrash magnet, a short walk from Harrods, is "still a firm favourite after all these years" (and was the original site of what's now a 20-strong global luxury chain). As well as its moody cocktail bar, the draw is "top-notch Japanese food" – sushi, tempura, robata grills, black cod, lobster – "if with prices to match". "I feel like a cheat putting this as my top choice again... but it never fails to deliver!" / SW7 1DL; www.zumarestaurant.com; zumalondonofficial; Mon-Sat 11 pm, Sun 10.30 pm.

Llama Inn, The Hoxton EC2

The Parakeet NW5

Lilienblum EC1

LONDON AREA OVERVIEWS

Kima W1

CENTRAL

SOHO, COVENT GARDEN & BLOOMSBURY (PARTS OF W1, ALL WC2 AND WC1)

Price	Restaurant	Cuisine	Rating
£240+	Frog by Adam Handling	*British, Modern*	443
£230+	Aulis London	*British, Modern*	543
£210+	SOLA	*American*	532
	Alex Dilling	*British, Modern*	543
	Restaurant 1890	*French*	344
£160+	Evelyn's Table	*British, Modern*	543
£150+	The Savoy Hotel	*British, Traditional*	224
£140+	The Northall	*International*	333
£120+	Gauthier Soho	*Vegan*	344
	NoMad London	*American*	225
	Spring Restaurant	*British, Modern*	444
	Kebab Queen	*Turkish*	443
	Tattu London	*Chinese*	233
£110+	Kerridge's Bar & Grill	*British, Modern*	334
	Park Row	”	– – –
	Sushisamba	*Fusion*	223
	Smith & Wollensky	*Steaks & grills*	222
	The Savoy Hotel	*Afternoon tea*	245
£100+	Christopher's	*American*	223
	Simpson's in the Strand	*British, Traditional*	– – –
	The River Restaurant	*Fish & seafood*	223
	L'Escargot	*French*	333
	Otto's	”	554
	The Petersham	*Italian*	223
	Oscar Wilde Lounge	*Afternoon tea*	335
	Yauatcha	*Chinese*	322
£90+	Bob Bob Ricard	*British, Modern*	244
	Clos Maggiore	”	345
	The Ivy	”	223
	Pivot by Mark Greenaway	”	333
	Quo Vadis	”	445
	Social Eating House	”	322
	J Sheekey	*Fish & seafood*	334
	Frenchie	*French*	333
	Margot	*Italian*	344
	Nopi	*Mediterranean*	322
	Decimo	*Spanish*	324
	Hawksmoor	*Steaks & grills*	332
	Roka	*Japanese*	323
£80+	Balthazar	*British, Modern*	123
	Cora Pearl	”	344
	The Ivy Market Grill	”	223
	Sussex	”	223
	Holborn Dining Room	*British, Traditional*	213
	The Ivy Soho Brasserie	”	223
	Rules	”	335
	Firebird	*East & C. European*	333
	Fishworks	*Fish & seafood*	332
	Randall & Aubin	”	334
	The Seafood Bar	”	342
	J Sheekey Atlantic Bar	”	422
	Blanchette	*French*	332
	Story Cellar	”	334
	The 10 Cases	*International*	343
	Toklas	*Mediterranean*	333
	Cakes and Bubbles	*Spanish*	343
	Maresco	”	333
	Cecconi's Pizza Bar	*Pizza*	233
	Sucre London	*Argentinian*	334
	The Barbary	*North African*	544
	The Palomar	*Middle Eastern*	332
	Tamarind Kitchen	*Indian*	433
£70+	Big Easy	*American*	223
	Andrew Edmunds	*British, Modern*	345
	Dean Street Townhouse	”	244
	Ducksoup	”	443
	The French House	”	445
	Ham Yard Restaurant	”	234
	Heliot Steak House	”	322
	Indigo	”	334
	Nessa	”	334
	Noble Rot	”	345
	Only Food and Courses	”	– – –
	Ship Tavern	”	345
	10 Greek Street	”	443
	The Delaunay	*East & C. European*	244
	The Oystermen	*Fish & seafood*	432
	Parsons	”	432
	Mon Plaisir	*French*	234
	Café Murano	*Italian*	342
	Da Mario	”	233
	Sycamore Vino Cucina	”	222
	Vasco & Piero's Pavilion	”	343
	Lisboeta	*Portuguese*	432
	Barrafina	*Spanish*	544
	Il Teatro della Carne	*Steaks & grills*	223
	Burger & Lobster	*Burgers, etc*	432
	Barshu	*Chinese*	532
	The Duck & Rice	”	323
	Chotto Matte	*Japanese*	444
	Sticks'n'Sushi	”	322
	Jinjuu	*Korean*	322
	Patara Soho	*Thai*	332
£60+	Paradise	*Sri Lankan*	433
	Joe Allen	*American*	234
	Café Deco	*British, Modern*	322

Price	Restaurant	Cuisine	Ratings
	Caravan	”	222
	Double Standard	”	355
	Isla	”	354
	Noble Rot Soho	”	454
	Riding House	”	223
	VQ	”	223
	Cork & Bottle	British, Traditional	234
	Brasserie Blanc	French	222
	Brasserie Zédel	”	124
	Cigalon	”	344
	Le Garrick	”	333
	Boulevard	International	233
	Ave Mario	Italian	334
	Bocca di Lupo	”	443
	Dehesa	”	222
	La Goccia	”	333
	Luce e Limoni	”	332
	Obicà Mozzarella Bar	”	332
	San Carlo Cicchetti	”	344
	Volta do Mar	Portuguese	332
	Opera Tavern	Spanish	322
	Tapas Brindisa Soho	”	222
	St Moritz	Swiss	333
	Haché	Burgers, etc	332
	Rock & Sole Plaice	Fish & chips	322
	L'Antica Pizzeria	Pizza	432
	Homeslice	”	323
	Monmouth Kitchen	Sandwiches, cakes, etc	343
	Ceviche Soho	Peruvian	323
	Le Bab	Middle Eastern	432
	Berenjak	Persian	544
	Lahpet	Burmese	432
	Four Seasons	Chinese	411
	Din Tai Fung	Chinese, Dim sum	222
	Cinnamon Bazaar	Indian	543
	Colonel Saab	”	434
	Gunpowder Soho	”	433
	Masala Zone	”	444
	Tandoor Chop House	”	433
	Flesh and Buns	Japanese	443
	Inamo	Pan-Asian	324
£50+	El Pastor Soho	Mexican	334
	Tendril	Vegan	433
	The Black Book	British, Modern	344
	The Norfolk Arms	”	332
	Ochre	”	324
	Pierre Victoire	French	323
	INO	Greek	344
	La Fromagerie	International	333
	Bancone	Italian	233
	Ciao Bella	”	345
	Cinquecento	”	333
	Fumo	”	234
	Lina Stores	”	223
	Mele e Pere	”	333
	Pastaio	”	323
	Blacklock	Steaks & grills	344
	Block Soho	”	222
	Mildreds	Vegetarian	333
	MEATliquor	Burgers, etc	322
	Street Burger	”	322
	North Sea Fish	Fish & chips	322
	temper Covent Garden	Pizza	212
	temper Soho	BBQ	212
	Miznon London	Middle Eastern	323
	Fatt Pundit	Chinese	323
	Golden Dragon	”	322
	Imperial China	”	322
	Orient London	”	443
	Plum Valley	”	322
	Kasa & Kin	Filipino	343
	Dishoom	Indian	345
	Fatt Pundit	”	323
	Kricket	”	544
	Dipna Anand	Indian, Southern	– – –
	Oka	Japanese	342
	Shoryu Ramen	”	322
	Rasa Sayang	Malaysian	432
	Gura Gura	Pan-Asian	344
	Kiln	Thai	544
	Speedboat Bar	”	444
£40+	Hoppers	Sri Lankan	333
	Milk Beach Soho	Australian	343
	Chez Antoinette	French	332
	Prix Fixe	”	332
	Bar Italia	Italian	245
	Patty and Bun Soho	Burgers, etc	322
	50 Kalò di Ciro Salvo	Pizza	433
	Chick 'n' Sours	Chicken	433
	Barbary Next Door	North African	432
	Bubala Soho	Middle Eastern	443
	Dim Sum Duck	Chinese, Dim sum	522
	Dumplings' Legend	”	321
	Hankies	Indian	332
	Punjab	”	343
	Sagar	”	332
	Bone Daddies	Japanese	322
	Eat Tokyo	”	322
	Jugemu	”	522
	Kanada-Ya	”	422
	Koya-Bar	”	443
	Hare & Tortoise	Pan-Asian	232
	Cay Tre	Vietnamese	332
	Viet Food	”	323
	Bao Soho	Taiwanese	344
£35+	Kolamba	Sri Lankan	432
	Café in the Crypt	British, Traditional	224
	Arcade Food Hall	International	222
	Fadiga	Italian	453
	Flat Iron	Steaks & grills	333
	Tommi's Burger Joint	Burgers, etc	332
	Coqfighter	Chicken	322
	The eight Restaurant	Chinese	322
	Baozi Inn	Chinese, Dim sum	322
	Humble Chicken	Japanese	434

	Taro	”	332
	C&R Café	*Malaysian*	422
	Plaza Khao Gaeng	*Thai*	432
£30+	Rudy's	*Pizza*	343
	Master Wei	*Chinese*	422
	Wong Kei	”	322
£25+	Imad's Syrian Kitchen	*Syrian*	344
	The Kati Roll Company	*Indian*	322
£20+	Bageriet	*Sandwiches, cakes, etc*	422
£15+	Maison Bertaux	*Afternoon tea*	335
£10+	Flat White	*Sandwiches, cakes, etc*	332
£5+	Monmouth Coffee Company	*Sandwiches, cakes, etc*	343

MAYFAIR & ST JAMES'S (PARTS OF W1 AND SW1)

£390+	The Araki	*Japanese*	453
£370+	TAKU	*Japanese*	533
£340+	Ikoyi	*West African*	232
£270+	Alain Ducasse	*French*	332
£260+	Maru	*Japanese*	543
£240+	Sketch (Lecture Rm)	*French*	445
£180+	Bacchanalia	*British, Modern*	224
	Cut	*Steaks & grills*	232
£170+	Hide	*British, Modern*	323
	Hélène Darroze	*French*	332
	Seven Park Place	”	322
£160+	The Connaught Grill	*British, Modern*	– – –
	Pollen Street Social	”	333
	Le Gavroche	*French*	334
	Umu	*Japanese*	344
£150+	Park Chinois	*Chinese*	221
£140+	The Grill by Tom Booton	*British, Modern*	– – –
	Ormer Mayfair by Sofian	”	443
	Estiatorio Milos	*Fish & seafood*	224
	L'Atelier Robuchon	*French*	– – –
	Pavyllon	”	– – –
	Amazonico	*International*	234
	The Promenade, Dorchester	*Afternoon tea*	344
	Novikov (Asian restaurant)	*Pan-Asian*	224
£130+	Corrigan's Mayfair	*British, Modern*	344
	Il Borro	*Italian*	233
	34 Mayfair	*Steaks & grills*	232
	Brown's Hotel	*Afternoon tea*	344
	The Ritz	”	345
	Kai Mayfair	*Chinese*	443
	Nobu	*Japanese*	432
	Jean-Georges, Connaught	*Pan-Asian*	233
£120+	Wild Honey St James	*British, Modern*	322
	The Game Bird	*British, Traditional*	334
	Bar des Prés	*French*	243
	LPM	”	333
	Murano	*Italian*	443
	Gouqi	*Chinese*	232
	Hakkasan Mayfair	”	423
£110+	Charlie's at Brown's	*British, Modern*	455
	Mount Street Restaurant	”	334
	The Ritz	*British, Traditional*	455
	Wiltons	”	333
	Scott's	*Fish & seafood*	334
	Galvin at Windows	*French*	334
	Socca	”	333
	Bocconcino	*Italian*	– – –
	Aquavit	*Scandinavian*	– – –
	The Guinea Grill	*Steaks & grills*	213
	Claridges Foyer	*Afternoon tea*	344
	Coya	*Peruvian*	223
	China Tang	*Chinese*	334
£100+	Colony Grill Room	*American*	334
	Apricity	*British, Modern*	332
	The Maine Mayfair	”	223
	Bentley's	*Fish & seafood*	344
	Sexy Fish	”	112
	Sketch (Gallery)	*French*	234
	El Norte	*Spanish*	333
	Jeru	*Middle Eastern*	334
	Kanishka	*Indian*	322
	Veeraswamy	”	434
	Ginza	*Japanese*	333
	Koyn	”	344
	Tokimeite	”	– – –
£90+	The Barley Mow	*British, Modern*	333
	Hush	”	234
	Quaglino's	”	234
	Butler's Restaurant	*British, Traditional*	333
	GBR	”	323
	Scully	*International*	442
	Al Duca	*Italian*	323
	Chucs Dover Street	”	223
	Franco's	”	344
	Sartoria	”	333
	Theo Randall	”	543
	Hawksmoor	*Steaks & grills*	332
	Rowley's	”	223
	Fortnum & Mason	*Afternoon tea*	334

	MiMi Mei Fair	*Chinese*	344
	Benares	*Indian*	432
	Chutney Mary	"	444
	Gymkhana	"	543
	Humo	*Japanese*	554
	Ikeda	"	432
	Roka	"	323
£80+	The American Bar	*American*	334
	Bellamy's	*British, Modern*	344
	45 Jermyn St.	"	233
	Kitty Fisher's	"	343
	Little Social	"	443
	The Wolseley	"	225
	Fishworks	*Fish & seafood*	332
	Maison François	*French*	334
	Saint Jacques	"	434
	Cecconi's	*Italian*	233
	Ristorante Frescobaldi	"	233
	San Carlo	"	333
	Goodman	*Steaks & grills*	343
	Delfino	*Pizza*	332
	BiBi	*Indian*	554
	Jamavar	"	333
	Tamarind	"	433
	The Ivy Asia Mayfair	*Pan-Asian*	324
	Lucky Cat	"	122
£70+	Langan's Brasserie	*British, Modern*	223
	Maddox Tavern	"	223
	Saltie Girl	*Fish & seafood*	343
	Café Murano	*Italian*	342
	Il Vicolo	"	232
	Burger & Lobster	*Burgers, etc*	432
	Bombay Bustle	*Indian*	534
	Chisou	*Japanese*	432
	Kiku	"	442
	Patara Mayfair	*Thai*	332
£60+	123V	*Vegan*	322
	Noble Rot Mayfair	*British, Modern*	454
	Restaurant at The 22	"	344
	The Windmill	*British, Traditional*	323
	Notto	*Italian*	433
	José Pizarro at the RA	*Spanish*	334
	Sabor	"	555
	O'ver	*Pizza*	332
	Manthan	*Indian*	332
£50+	The Audley	*British, Modern*	324
	Casa do Frango	*Portuguese*	335
	El Pirata	*Spanish*	244
	Richoux	*Sandwiches, cakes, etc*	333
	Shoryu Ramen	*Japanese*	322

FITZROVIA & MARYLEBONE (PART OF W1)

£290+	Roketsu	*Japanese*	543
£250+	Kitchen Table	*British, Modern*	444
£240+	Mayha	*Japanese*	444
£160+	Akoko	*West African*	443
£150+	Pied à Terre	*French*	433
£120+	Kol	*Mexican*	444
	Mere	*East & C. European*	343
	Hakkasan	*Chinese*	423
£110+	The Chiltern Firehouse	*American*	224
	The Ninth London	*British, Modern*	533
	Nobu Portman Square	*Japanese*	433
£100+	The Berners Tavern	*British, Modern*	345
	Clarette	*French*	233
	Noizé	"	453
	Orrery	"	224
	Opso	*Greek*	333
	Locanda Locatelli	*Italian*	332
	Arros QD	*Spanish*	232
	Palm Court	*Afternoon tea*	233
	Dinings	*Japanese*	532
	Taka Marylebone	"	323
£90+	Portland	*British, Modern*	442
	28-50 Marylebone	"	223
	Santo Mare	*Fish & seafood*	343
	Les 110 de Taillevent	*French*	444
	Ampéli	*Greek*	332
	Donostia	*Spanish*	322
	The Bright Courtyard	*Chinese*	322
	Roka	*Japanese*	323
£80+	Cavita	*Mexican*	323
	Brasserie of Light	*British, Modern*	234
	Clipstone	"	332
	The Ivy Café	"	112
	Upstairs at The George	"	323
	Fishworks Marylebone	*Fish & seafood*	332
	Meraki	*Greek*	434
	La Brasseria Milanese	*Italian*	222
	Caffè Caldesi	"	332
	Norma	"	434
	ROVI	*Mediterranean*	333
	Zoilo	*Argentinian*	334
	Jikoni	*Indian*	434
	Pahli Hill Bandra Bhai	"	332
	Trishna	"	532
£70+	The Lore of the Land	*British, Modern*	344

	108 Brasserie	*”*	232
	Chotto Matte	*Fusion*	444
	Carousel	*International*	442
	Six by Nico	*”*	333
	Blandford Comptoir	*Mediterranean*	343
	Ottolenghi	*”*	333
	Lurra	*Spanish*	433
	Burger & Lobster	*Burgers, etc*	432
	Daylesford Organic	*Sandwiches, cakes, etc*	122
	Pachamama	*Peruvian*	333
	Honey & Co	*Middle Eastern*	322
	Honey & Smoke	*”*	322
	Ishtar	*Turkish*	332
	Royal China Club	*Chinese*	432
	Junsei	*Japanese*	342
	Sushi Atelier	*”*	433
	Uli Marylebone	*Pan-Asian*	434
£60+	Granger & Co	*Australian*	223
	Caravan	*British, Modern*	222
	St John Marylebone	*British, Traditional*	432
	The Wigmore	*”*	344
	Fischer's	*East & C. European*	223
	Twist Connubio	*Fusion*	332
	1905	*Greek*	345
	Briciole	*Italian*	332
	Circolo Popolare	*”*	345
	Italian Greyhound	*”*	333
	Riding House Café	*Mediterranean*	223
	Ibérica	*Spanish*	222
	Salt Yard	*”*	322
	The Gate	*Vegetarian*	333
	Homeslice	*Pizza*	323
	Royal China	*Chinese*	322
	Chourangi	*Indian*	443
	Flesh and Buns	*Japanese*	443
£50+	Wulf & Lamb	*Vegan*	323
	La Fromagerie Café	*International*	333
	Lina Stores	*Italian*	223
	2 Veneti	*”*	232
	Le Relais de Venise	*Steaks & grills*	333
	MEATLiquor	*Burgers, etc*	322
	Golden Hind	*Fish & chips*	332
	Chishuru	*West African*	– – –
	Delamina	*Middle Eastern*	333
	The Gurkhas	*Pan-Asian*	343
	Oka	*”*	342
	Foley's	*Thai*	333
£40+	Hoppers	*Sri Lankan*	333
	The Wallace	*French*	215
	Via Emilia	*Italian*	343
	Patty and Bun	*Burgers, etc*	322
	Pizzeria Mozza	*Pizza*	433
	Santa Maria	*”*	423
	Reubens	*Kosher*	323
	Roti Chai	*Indian*	322
	Sagar	*”*	332
	Bone Daddies	*Japanese*	322
	Laksamania	*Malaysian*	322
	Bao Marylebone	*Taiwanese*	344
£35+	Flat Iron Marylebone	*Steaks & grills*	333
	Tommi's Burger Joint	*Burgers, etc*	332
	Ragam	*Indian*	421
	CoCoRo	*Japanese*	432
£30+	Noodle & Snack	*Chinese*	442
£15+	Icco Pizza	*Italian*	332
	Kaffeine	*Sandwiches, cakes, etc*	253
	Kiss the Hippo	*”*	343
	Marugame Udon	*Japanese*	332

BELGRAVIA, PIMLICO, VICTORIA & WESTMINSTER (SW1, EXCEPT ST JAMES'S)

£250+	A Wong	*Chinese*	522
£210+	Muse	*British, Modern*	544
£190+	Nusr-Et Steakhouse	*Steaks & grills*	111
£170+	Marcus	*British, Modern*	243
£160+	Pétrus	*French*	233
	Studio Frantzén	*Scandinavian*	345
£150+	Dinner	*British, Traditional*	222
£140+	Imperial Treasure	*Chinese*	432
£130+	The Collins Room	*Afternoon tea*	334
£120+	The Dining Room	*British, Traditional*	223
	Hunan	*Chinese*	421
£110+	Santini	*Italian*	233
	Zafferano	*”*	433
	Ekstedt at The Yard	*Scandinavian*	343
	Boisdale of Belgravia	*Scottish*	233
£100+	Fallow St James's	*British, Modern*	333
	The Pem	*”*	443
	Kerridge's Fish & Chips	*Fish & seafood*	234
	The Crystal Moon Lounge	*Afternoon tea*	344
£90+	The Lanesborough Grill	*British, Modern*	224
	Roof Garden, Pantechnicon	*”*	225
	Harrods Dining Hall	*International*	– – –
	Chucs	*Italian*	223
	Goya	*Spanish*	332
	Cedric Grolet	*Sandwiches, cakes, etc*	343
	Amaya	*Indian*	444
	Quilon	*Indian, Southern*	432

Price	Restaurant	Cuisine	Ratings
£80+	Blue Boar Pub	British, Modern	222
	Ganymede	”	333
	Hans' Bar & Grill	”	333
	The Ivy Victoria	”	223
	The Jones Family Kitchen	”	334
	The Thomas Cubitt	”	223
	Olivomare	Fish & seafood	432
	Colbert	French	223
	Olivo	Italian	332
	Sale e Pepe	”	– – –
	The Cinnamon Club	Indian	445
	Kahani	”	443
	Yaatra	”	442
£70+	Daylesford Organic	British, Modern	122
	Lorne	”	553
	La Poule au Pot	French	345
	Caraffini	Italian	243
	Drawing Room, Dukes	Afternoon tea	344
	Burger & Lobster	Burgers, etc	432
	Oliveto	Pizza	332
	Ottolenghi	Middle Eastern	333
	Ken Lo's Memories	Chinese	332
	Sticks'n'Sushi	Japanese	322
£60+	Granger & Co	Australian	223
	Grumbles	International	342

Price	Restaurant	Cuisine	Ratings
	Motcombs	”	224
	Gustoso	Italian	322
	Tozi	”	213
	Ibérica	Spanish	222
	Seafresh	Fish & chips	322
	Kazan	Turkish	332
£50+	Holy Carrot	Vegan	444
	Casa do Frango	Portuguese	335
	Wulf & Lamb	Vegetarian	323
	Ma La Sichuan	Chinese	432
£40+	The Vincent Rooms	British, Modern	334
	Chez Antoinette	French	332
	Cyprus Mangal	Turkish	332
	Aloo Tama	Indian	432
	Sagar	”	332
	Bone Daddies	Japanese	322
	Café Kitsuné	”	334
	Kanada-Ya	”	422
£35+	Taro	Japanese	332
£25+	Bleecker Burger	Burgers, etc	422
£15+	Regency Cafe	British, Traditional	335

WEST

CHELSEA, SOUTH KENSINGTON, KENSINGTON, EARL'S COURT & FULHAM (SW3, SW5, SW6, SW7, SW10 & W8)

Price	Restaurant	Cuisine	Ratings
£230+	Gordon Ramsay	French	222
£220+	Bibendum	French	333
£200+	The Five Fields	British, Modern	443
£170+	The Sea, The Sea	Fish & seafood	544
£120+	Wild Tavern	Italian	223
£110+	Clarke's	British, Modern	453
	Medlar	”	443
	No. Fifty Cheyne	”	335
	Zuma	Japanese	444
£100+	Elystan Street	British, Modern	433
	Launceston Place	”	444
	Stanley's	”	322
	Le Petit Beefbar	Steaks & grills	– – –
	Min Jiang	Chinese	445
	Dinings	Japanese	532
	Yashin Ocean House	”	432

Price	Restaurant	Cuisine	Ratings
£90+	Bluebird	British, Modern	213
	Kitchen W8	”	443
	28-50 Chelsea	”	223
	The Restaurant at The Capital	British, Traditional	332
	Le Colombier	French	244
	Chucs	Italian	223
	Daphne's	”	335
	Lucio	”	322
	Scalini	”	343
	Hawksmoor	Steaks & grills	332
	Chicama	Peruvian	333
	Bombay Brasserie	Indian	333
£80+	Harwood Arms	British, Modern	433
	The Ivy Chelsea Garden	”	223
	The Shed	”	324
	The Surprise	British, Traditional	334
	Bibendum Oyster Bar	Fish & seafood	334
	Suzi Tros	Greek	443
	Myrtle	Irish	543
	La Famiglia	Italian	234
	Manicomio Chelsea	”	223
	Cambio de Tercio	Spanish	333
	Koji	Japanese	444
	Zheng	Malaysian	332
	The Ivy Asia Chelsea	Pan-Asian	324
£70+	Big Easy	American	223

	Brinkley's	*British, Modern*	233
	The Cadogan Arms	*"*	334
	Daylesford Organic	*"*	122
	The Enterprise	*"*	234
	Kuro Eatery	*"*	443
	Rabbit	*"*	222
	Wright Brothers	*Fish & seafood*	333
	Margaux	*French*	343
	Mazi	*Greek*	443
	Vardo	*International*	223
	Jacuzzi	*Italian*	124
	Il Portico	*"*	233
	Belvedere	*Mediterranean*	334
	Tendido Cero	*Spanish*	333
	Macellaio RC	*Steaks & grills*	223
	Alexandrie	*Egyptian*	333
	Akub	*Middle Eastern*	234
	Good Earth	*Chinese*	332
	Kutir	*Indian*	444
	Zaika of Kensington	*"*	444
	Akira at Japan House	*Japanese*	332
	Chisou	*"*	432
	Sticks'n'Sushi	*"*	322
	Huo	*Pan-Asian*	333
	Patara	*Thai*	332
£60+	The Abingdon	*British, Modern*	333
	The Fox and Pheasant	*"*	334
	Manuka Kitchen	*"*	333
	VQ	*"*	223
	Maggie Jones's	*British, Traditional*	344
	Mriya	*East & C. European*	333
	The Scarsdale	*International*	235
	Cicchetti Knightsbridge	*Italian*	344
	Frantoio	*"*	324
	Pascor	*Mediterranean*	322
	Daquise	*Polish*	234
	Ognisko Restaurant	*"*	345
	Tapas Brindisa	*Spanish*	222
	Haché	*Steaks & grills*	332
	Maroush	*Lebanese*	421
	Royal China	*Chinese*	322
	Romulo Café	*Filipino*	343
	Flora Indica	*Indian*	333
	Masala Zone	*"*	444
£50+	The Holland	*British, Modern*	433
	Los Mochis	*Fusion*	333
	Aglio e Olio	*Italian*	332
	Da Mario	*"*	323
	Made in Italy	*"*	322
	Maria G's	*"*	333
	Nuovi Sapori	*"*	333
	Riccardo's	*"*	343
	San Pietro	*"*	334
	Ziani's	*"*	343
	The Atlas	*Mediterranean*	344
	Street Burger	*Burgers, etc*	322
	Cinquecento	*Pizza*	333
	Rocca	*"*	223
	Cocotte	*Chicken*	332
	Diba	*Persian*	222
	Best Mangal	*Turkish*	442
	Chakra	*Indian*	333
	Dishoom	*"*	345
	Noor Jahan	*"*	343
	Pure Indian Cooking	*"*	443
	Thali	*"*	333
	Oka	*Japanese*	342
	Shoryu Ramen	*"*	322
	Sukho Fine Thai Cuisine	*Thai*	442
	Go-Viet	*Vietnamese*	342
£40+	Churchill Arms	*British, Traditional*	324
	Big Fernand	*Burgers, etc*	332
	Fishers	*Fish & chips*	332
	Santa Maria	*Pizza*	423
	Ceru	*Middle Eastern*	322
	Bone Daddies	*Japanese*	322
	Bibida	*Korean*	342
	Freak Scene	*Pan-Asian*	443
	Phat Phuc	*Vietnamese*	333
£35+	Flat Iron	*Steaks & grills*	333
£20+	Stick & Bowl	*Chinese*	422
£15+	Hagen Chelsea	*Sandwiches, cakes, etc*	342

NOTTING HILL, HOLLAND PARK, BAYSWATER, NORTH KENSINGTON & MAIDA VALE (W2, W9, W10, W11)

£230+	Core by Clare Smyth	*British, Modern*	554
	The Ledbury	*"*	444
£130+	Caractère	*Mediterranean*	333
£120+	104 Restaurant	*British, Modern*	544
£100+	London Shell Co.	*Fish & seafood*	345
	Sumi	*Japanese*	443
£90+	Assaggi	*Italian*	453
£80+	The Princess Royal	*British, Modern*	333
	Six Portland Road	*"*	333
	Straker's	*"*	335
	The Summerhouse	*Fish & seafood*	235
	Vori	*Greek*	333
	Zephyr	*"*	444
	The Cow	*Irish*	324
	La Brasseria	*Italian*	222
£70+	Sunday in Brooklyn	*American*	224
	Daylesford Organic	*British, Modern*	122
	Gold	*"*	245
	The Ladbroke Arms	*"*	324

	Tsiakkos & Charcoal	*Greek*	343
	Mediterraneo	*Italian*	323
	Osteria Basilico	*"*	333
	Portobello Ristorante	*"*	334
	Ottolenghi	*Mediterranean*	333
	Farmacy	*Vegetarian*	434
	Mandarin Kitchen	*Chinese*	442
	E&O	*Pan-Asian*	333
	Uli	*"*	434
£60+	Granger & Co	*Australian*	223
	Caia	*British, Modern*	433
	Orasay	*"*	544
	The Pelican	*"*	334
	Hereford Road	*British, Traditional*	443
	Cepages	*French*	324
	Edera	*Italian*	343
	The Oak W2	*"*	333
	Maroush	*Lebanese*	421
	Four Seasons	*Chinese*	411
	Bombay Palace	*Indian*	442
£50+	Dorian	*British, Modern*	445
	The Cheese Barge	*British, Traditional*	233
	Cinquecento	*Italian*	333
	Haya	*Mediterranean*	343
	MEATliquor	*Burgers, etc*	322
	Cinquecento	*Pizza*	333
	Cocotte	*Chicken*	332
	Miznon	*Middle Eastern*	323
	Fez Mangal	*Turkish*	321
	Pearl Liang	*Chinese*	322
	Noor Jahan	*Indian*	343
	Sushi Murasaki	*Japanese*	442
£40+	Taqueria	*Mexican*	333
	Ceru	*Middle Eastern*	322
	Gold Mine	*Chinese*	322
	Durbar	*Indian*	332
	Eat Tokyo	*Japanese*	322
£35+	Tab X Tab	*International*	343
£30+	Tavernaki	*Greek*	323
£25+	Normah's	*Malaysian*	332
£15+	Layla	*Sandwiches, cakes, etc*	333

HAMMERSMITH, SHEPHERD'S BUSH, OLYMPIA, CHISWICK, BRENTFORD & EALING (W4, W5, W6, W12, W13, W14, TW8)

£280+	Endo at The Rotunda	*Japanese*	545
£140+	The River Café	*Italian*	323
£110+	La Trompette	*British, Modern*	333
£90+	Villa Di Geggiano	*Italian*	344
£80+	Sam's Riverside	*British, Modern*	355
	The Silver Birch	*"*	432
	Cibo	*Italian*	444
£70+	High Road Brasserie	*British, Modern*	324
	Le Vacherin	*French*	344
	Shikumen	*Chinese*	422
	Sticks n Sushi	*Japanese*	322
£60+	The Anglesea Arms	*British, Modern*	435
	City Barge	*"*	223
	The Duke of Sussex	*"*	223
	The Havelock Tavern	*"*	333
	Rock & Rose	*"*	223
	Vinoteca	*"*	222
	Brasserie Blanc	*French*	222
	Annie's	*International*	234
	L'Amorosa	*Italian*	443
	Giulia	*"*	432
	The Oak W12	*"*	333
	Pentolina	*"*	454
	The Carpenter's Arms	*Mediterranean*	333
	The Swan	*"*	344
	Salt Yard	*Spanish*	322
	The Gate	*Vegetarian*	333
	Homeslice	*Pizza*	323
	Indian Zing	*Indian*	433
£50+	Brackenbury Wine Rooms	*British, Modern*	244
	The Crabtree	*"*	224
	The Dartmouth Castle	*"*	323
	The Dove	*"*	345
	The Princess Victoria	*"*	323
	Le Petit Citron	*French*	333
	The Andover Arms	*International*	344
	Capri	*Italian*	333
	Maria G's	*"*	333
	Avanti	*Mediterranean*	223
	The Bird in Hand	*Pizza*	333
	Crisp Pizza	*"*	522
	Zia Lucia	*"*	332
	Chateau	*Lebanese*	342
	Best Mangal	*Turkish*	442
	Copper Chimney	*Indian*	333
	The Hampshire	*"*	333
	Kricket	*"*	544
	Potli	*"*	433
£40+	222 Veggie Vegan	*Vegan*	333
	Kindred	*British, Modern*	333
	Oro Di Napoli	*Pizza*	442
	Santa Maria	*"*	423
	North China	*Chinese*	333
	Patri	*Indian*	332
	Republic	*"*	433

Price	Restaurant	Cuisine	Rating
	Sagar	”	332
	Eat Tokyo	Japanese	322
	Kanada-Ya	”	422
	Sushi Bar Makoto	”	431
	Ta Ke Sushi	”	432
	Tosa	”	332
	Hare & Tortoise	Pan-Asian	232
	Chet's	Thai	333
	101 Thai Kitchen	”	332
£35+	Base Face Pizza	Pizza	443
	Shilpa	Indian, Southern	422
	Poppy's Thai Eatery	Thai	323
£30+	Persian Palace	Persian	422
£25+	The Elder Press Café	British, Modern	334
	Bleecker Burger	Burgers, etc	422
	Rhythm & Brews	Sandwiches, cakes, etc	334
	Tamp Coffee	”	343
£5+	Mr Falafel	Middle Eastern	542

NORTH

HAMPSTEAD, WEST HAMPSTEAD, ST JOHN'S WOOD, REGENT'S PARK, KILBURN & CAMDEN TOWN (NW POSTCODES)

Price	Restaurant	Cuisine	Rating
£210+	PLU	French	544
£90+	Tish	Kosher	323
£80+	Booking Office 1869	British, Modern	235
	The Ivy Café	”	112
	The Landmark	”	335
	Odette's	”	332
	L'Aventure	French	454
	Lume	Italian	322
	Magenta	”	343
	Cinder	Mediterranean	332
	Cinder	BBQ	332
£70+	Bradley's	British, Modern	222
	The Parakeet	”	543
	Searcys St Pancras Grand	”	223
	The Wells Tavern	”	344
	Holly Bush	British, Traditional	323
	Michael Nadra	French	332
	Oslo Court	”	355
	Bull & Last	International	433
	Morso	Italian	322
	The Rising Sun	”	343
	Villa Bianca	”	334
	Skewd Kitchen	Turkish	433
	Good Earth	Chinese	332
	Kaifeng	”	443
	Phoenix Palace	”	322
	Patara	Thai	332
£60+	Greenberry Café	British, Modern	233
	Oak & Poppy	”	343
	Parlour Kensal	”	334
	Lemonia	Greek	233
	Soutine	International	224
	Carmel	Mediterranean	534
	28 Church Row	Spanish	444
	Haché	Steaks & grills	332
	L'Antica Pizzeria	Pizza	432
	Maroush Park Royal	Lebanese	421
	Bonoo	Indian	333
	Jin Kichi	Japanese	543
£50+	The Old Bull & Bush	British, Modern	224
	The Wet Fish Café	”	333
	Lure	Fish & seafood	323
	Authentique	French	333
	The Spaniard's Inn	International	235
	Anima e Cuore	Italian	432
	L'Artista	”	233
	Cinquecento	”	333
	Giacomo's	”	332
	Mildreds	Vegetarian	333
	The Sea Shell	Fish & chips	322
	Zia Lucia	Pizza	332
	Cocotte	Chicken	332
	Crocker's Folly	Lebanese	333
	Green Cottage	Chinese	322
	Saravanaa Bhavan	Indian	422
	Oka	Japanese	342
	Singapore Garden	Malaysian	333
£40+	Spagnoletti	Italian	343
	Berbere Pizza	Pizza	433
	Sacro Cuore	”	332
	Numa	Middle Eastern	342
	Great Nepalese	Indian	323
	Three Falcons	”	432
	Vijay	”	342
	Café Japan	Japanese	332
	Eat Tokyo	”	322
	Sushi Masa	”	332
	Bang Bang Oriental	Pan-Asian	322
£35+	Nautilus	Fish & chips	442
	Mr Ji	Chinese	333
	Three Uncles	”	522
	Paradise Hampstead	Indian	343
	Ravi Shankar	”	322

Price	Restaurant	Cuisine	Rating
	Anjanaas	Indian, Southern	342
£30+	Diwana Bhel-Poori House	Indian	321
	Sakonis	”	332
£25+	Sam's Café	British, Traditional	322
	Chutneys	Indian	332
£20+	Tofu Vegan	Chinese	432
£15+	Icco Pizza	Pizza	332
	Ginger & White	Sandwiches, cakes, etc	333
	Roti King	Malaysian	522

HOXTON, ISLINGTON, HIGHGATE, CROUCH END, STOKE NEWINGTON, FINSBURY PARK, MUSWELL HILL & FINCHLEY (N POSTCODES)

Price	Restaurant	Cuisine	Rating
£120+	Parrillan	Spanish	333
£90+	Hot Stone	Japanese	222
£80+	The Baring	British, Modern	433
	Perilla	”	333
£70+	Frederick's	British, Modern	344
	Hicce	”	223
	12:51	”	432
	Westerns Laundry	”	333
	Prawn on the Lawn	Fish & seafood	432
	Les 2 Garcons	French	553
	Jiji	Fusion	333
	German Gymnasium	German	113
	Salut	International	444
	Trullo	Italian	433
	Coal Office	Mediterranean	444
	Ottolenghi	”	333
	Barrafina	Spanish	544
	Escocesa	”	332
£60+	Granger & Co	Australian	223
	The Bull	British, Modern	332
	Caravan King's Cross	”	222
	The Clarence Tavern	”	333
	The Drapers Arms	”	333
	Humble Grape	”	233
	Pig & Butcher	”	433
	The Plimsoll	”	543
	The Red Lion & Sun	”	333
	Rotunda	”	224
	St Johns	British, Traditional	334
	Lyon's	Fish & seafood	443
	Table Du Marche	French	332
	The Orange Tree	International	223
	Primeur	”	334
	Citro	Italian	442
	Osteria Tufo	”	343
	Terra Rossa	”	444
	Vinoteca	Mediterranean	222
	Bar Esteban	Spanish	344
	Camino King's Cross	”	222
	The Gatehouse	”	332
	Chuku's	West African	343
	Arabica KX	Middle Eastern	333
£50+	Casa Pastór	Mexican	222
	Granary Square Brasserie	British, Modern	234
	The Lighterman	”	222
	Porte Noire	”	344
	Kipferl	East & C. European	433
	Schnitzel Forever	”	332
	Bellanger	French	– – –
	La Petite Auberge	”	332
	Le Sacré-Coeur	”	332
	Kalimera	Greek	433
	FKABAM	International	423
	The Flask	”	234
	La Fromagerie	”	333
	500	Italian	342
	Lina Stores	”	223
	La Lluna	Spanish	332
	Mildreds	Vegetarian	333
	MEATLiquor Islington	Burgers, etc	322
	Street Burger	”	322
	Toff's	Fish & chips	342
	Sweet Thursday	Pizza	322
	Zia Lucia	”	332
	Cocotte	Chicken	332
	Jam Delish	Caribbean	543
	Gallipoli Again	Turkish	324
	Kaki	Chinese	332
	Dishoom	Indian	345
	Bund	Pan-Asian	333
	Farang	Thai	443
	Supawan	”	544
£40+	Frank's Canteen	British, Modern	332
	Two Brothers	Fish & seafood	322
	Caravel	French	444
	Le Mercury	”	222
	Noci	Italian	323
	Via Emilia	”	343
	Olympus Fish	Fish & chips	342
	Sacro Cuore	Pizza	332
	Santa Maria	”	423
	Yard Sale Pizza	”	342
	Plaquemine Lock	Cajun/creole	434
	Gem	Turkish	333
	Sumak	”	342
	Xi'an Impression	Chinese	421
	Delhi Grill	Indian	423
	Hoppers	”	333
	Jashan	”	332
	Rasa	Indian, Southern	433
	Akari	Japanese	433
	Kanada-Ya	”	422
	Sambal Shiok	Malaysian	322
	The Tamil Prince	Pan-Asian	433

	Cafe Bao	*Taiwanese*	344
£35+	Skal Nordic Dining	*Scandinavian*	343
	Flat Iron	*Steaks & grills*	333
	The Dusty Knuckle	*Sandwiches, cakes, etc*	523
	Afghan Kitchen	*Afghani*	322
	Shahi Pakwaan	*Indian*	322
	Taro	*Japanese*	332

	Viet Garden	*Vietnamese*	322
£25+	Normans Cafe	*British, Modern*	444
	Bayleaf	*Indian*	433
£20+	Tofu Vegan	*Chinese*	432
	Rasa Street	*Indian*	332

SOUTH

SOUTH BANK (SE1)

£270+	Story	*British, Modern*	– – –
£140+	Trivet	*British, Modern*	333
£130+	Turnips	*British, Modern*	433
	Hannah	*Japanese*	332
£120+	Parrillan	*Spanish*	333
	Hutong	*Chinese*	344
£110+	Aqua Shard	*British, Modern*	224
	Oblix	"	334
	Oxo Tower (Rest')	"	111
£100+	Sollip	*French*	543
£90+	Oxo Tower (Brass')	*British, Modern*	113
	TING	"	335
	Seabird at The Hoxton	*Fish & seafood*	435
	Le Pont de la Tour	*French*	223
	La Barca	*Italian*	333
	Hawksmoor	*Steaks & grills*	332
£80+	The Garrison	*British, Modern*	333
	The Ivy Tower Bridge	"	223
	Sea Containers	"	223
	Skylon	"	212
	Butlers Wharf Chop Hs	*British, Traditional*	223
	Roast	"	224
	The Coal Shed	*Steaks & grills*	322
£70+	Santo Remedio	*Mexican*	332
	Elliot's	*British, Modern*	332
	Skylon Grill	"	235
	The Swan at the Globe	"	224
	Applebee's Fish	*Fish & seafood*	332
	fish!	"	323
	Wright Brothers	"	333
	Vivat Bacchus	*International*	332
	Cafe Murano	*Italian*	342
	Macellaio RC	"	223
	Barrafina	*Spanish*	544
	Pique Nique	*Chicken*	233
	Bala Baya	*Middle Eastern*	433
	Baluchi	*Indian*	334
£60+	The Anchor & Hope	*British, Modern*	433
	The Boot & Flogger	"	334
	Caravan Bankside	"	222
	Garden Café, Garden Mus'	"	334
	Vinoteca Borough	"	222
	Brasserie Blanc	*French*	222
	Casse-Croute	"	434
	Borough Market Kitchen	*International*	422
	Tavolino	*Italian*	223
	José	*Spanish*	534
	Pizarro	"	444
	Salt Yard Borough	"	322
	Tapas Brindisa	"	222
	O'ver	*Pizza*	332
	Paladar	*South American*	444
	Arabica	*Lebanese*	333
	Berenjak Borough	*Persian*	544
	Gunpowder	*Indian*	433
	Sticky Mango	*Pan-Asian*	322
	Champor-Champor	*Thai*	324
£50+	Mallow	*Vegan*	334
	El Pastór	*Mexican*	334
	40 Maltby Street	*British, Modern*	333
	Lupins	"	444
	Tate Modern	"	335
	Bancone	*Italian*	233
	Flour & Grape	"	334
	Legare	"	443
	Bar Douro	*Portuguese*	334
	Casa do Frango	"	335
	Andanza	*Spanish*	433
	La Gamba	"	342
	Mar I Terra	"	333
	Meson don Felipe	"	224
£40+	Rambutan	*Sri Lankan*	533
	Mercato Metropolitano	*Italian*	224
	Padella	"	434
	Patty and Bun	*Burgers, etc*	322
	Kin and Deum	*Thai*	323
	Bao Borough	*Taiwanese*	344
£35+	Flat Iron	*Steaks & grills*	333

Price	Restaurant	Cuisine	Ratings
	Baozi Inn	*Chinese*	3 2 2
£10+	Kappacasein	*Swiss*	5 3 2
£5+	Monmouth Coffee Company	*Sandwiches, cakes, etc*	3 4 3

GREENWICH, LEWISHAM, DULWICH & BLACKHEATH (ALL SE POSTCODES, EXCEPT SE1; ALSO BR1)

Price	Restaurant	Cuisine	Ratings
£70+	Coal Rooms	*British, Modern*	3 3 2
	Copper & Ink	"	3 3 3
	Llewelyn's	"	3 3 3
	Tila	"	3 3 3
	Sticks'n'Sushi	*Japanese*	3 2 2
£60+	The Alma	*British, Modern*	3 3 4
	The Camberwell Arms	"	4 4 4
	Franklins	"	3 4 3
	The Guildford Arms	"	3 3 3
	Levan	"	3 2 2
	Toulouse Lautrec	*French*	3 3 3
	Peckham Bazaar	*Greek*	4 3 3
	The Trafalgar Tavern	*International*	3 3 5
	Artusi	*Italian*	3 3 2
	Forza Wine	"	3 4 3
	Luciano's	"	3 4 3
	Manuel's	"	4 4 4
	Peckham Cellars	*Spanish*	3 4 3
	Kudu	*South African*	4 4 3
	Dragon Castle	*Chinese*	3 2 2
	Yama Momo	*Japanese*	3 2 3
£50+	Dorothy & Marshall	*British, Modern*	2 3 3
	The Rosendale	"	3 3 3
	Brookmill	*International*	3 3 3
	The Yellow House	"	3 3 3
	Le Querce	*Italian*	3 4 2
	The Dartmouth Arms	*Burgers, etc*	3 2 2
	Street Burger	"	3 2 2
	Rocca	*Pizza*	2 2 3
	Kudu Grill	*South African*	4 4 3
	Babur	*Indian*	4 4 3
	Everest Inn	"	3 2 2
	Heritage	"	4 4 3
	Kennington Tandoori	"	3 4 3
£40+	Marcella	*Italian*	3 4 3
	500 Degrees	*Pizza*	3 2 3
	Theo's	"	3 3 2
	Yard Sale Pizza	"	3 4 2
	Ganapati	*Indian*	4 4 3
	Bone Daddies	*Japanese*	3 2 2
	Zaibatsu	"	4 3 2
£35+	Olley's	*Fish & chips*	3 4 2
	081 Pizzeria	*Pizza*	5 2 2
	Nandine	*Middle Eastern*	3 3 3
	Taro	*Japanese*	3 3 2
	Mambow	*Pan-Asian*	4 2 1
	Mr Bao	*Taiwanese*	3 3 3
£30+	Everest Curry King	*Sri Lankan*	3 3 2
£25+	Goddards At Greenwich	*British, Traditional*	3 4 3
	Silk Road	*Chinese*	4 3 2
£15+	La Chingada	*Mexican*	3 3 2
	Marugame Udon	*Japanese*	3 3 2
£5+	Monmouth Coffee Company	*Sandwiches, cakes, etc*	3 4 3

BATTERSEA, BRIXTON, CLAPHAM, WANDSWORTH BARNES, PUTNEY & WIMBLEDON (ALL SW POSTCODES SOUTH OF THE RIVER)

Price	Restaurant	Cuisine	Ratings
£110+	Chez Bruce	*British, Modern*	5 5 3
	JOIA	*Portuguese*	3 3 4
£100+	Trinity	*British, Modern*	3 3 2
£90+	Rick Stein	*Fish & seafood*	2 2 2
£80+	Hatched	*British, Modern*	4 4 3
	The Ivy Café	"	1 1 2
	Darby's	*Irish*	3 3 4
	Riva	*Italian*	5 4 2
£70+	Church Road	*British, Modern*	3 4 2
	The Pig's Head	"	3 4 4
	Trinity Upstairs	"	4 4 3
	Wright Brothers	*Fish & seafood*	3 3 3
	Brinkley's Kitchen	*International*	2 2 3
	Archway	*Italian*	4 4 4
	Fiume	"	2 2 2
	The Fox & Hounds	*Mediterranean*	3 4 3
	Knife	*Steaks & grills*	4 4 3
	Macellaio RC	"	2 2 3
	Good Earth	*Chinese*	3 3 2
	Cilantro Putney	*Indian*	4 4 2
	Sticks'n'Sushi	*Japanese*	3 2 2
	Patara	*Thai*	3 3 2
£60+	The Laundry	*Australian*	3 4 4
	Bistro Union	*British, Modern*	3 3 2
	The Black Lamb	"	3 2 2
	Bottle & Rye	"	3 4 2
	The Brown Dog	"	3 3 4
	Brunswick House Café	"	3 2 5
	Coppa Club Putney	"	2 2 4
	Humble Grape	"	2 3 3
	24 The Oval	"	3 4 3
	The Victoria	"	3 3 3
	Canton Arms	*British, Traditional*	3 3 4
	Fox & Grapes	"	3 4 3
	Augustine Kitchen	*French*	3 2 3

	Gazette	”	223
	Soif	”	322
	The Light House	*International*	333
	Maremma	*Italian*	333
	Numero Uno	”	242
	Osteria Antica Bologna	”	332
	Pizza Metro	”	322
	Sorella	”	322
	Tozi Grand Cafe	”	213
	Lusitania	*Portuguese*	333
	Tapas Brindisa	*Spanish*	222
	Haché	*Burgers, etc*	332
	Santa Maria del Sur	*Argentinian*	332
	Le Bab	*Middle Eastern*	432
	Cinnamon Kitchen	*Indian*	433
	Evernight	*Japanese*	333
	Kibou London	”	223
	Takahashi	”	553
£50+	London Stock	*British, Modern*	333
	Olympic Studios	”	223
	The Telegraph	”	345
	The Plough	*British, Traditional*	223
	Smoke & Salt	”	543
	Cent Anni	*Italian*	333
	Lina Stores	”	223
	Made in Italy	”	322
	Little Taperia	*Spanish*	344
	Naughty Piglets	*Steaks & grills*	544
	MEATliquor	*Burgers, etc*	322
	Bravi Ragazzi	*Pizza*	422
	Zia Lucia	”	332
	Diba	*Persian*	222
	Kashmir	*Indian*	342
	Kricket	”	544
	Oka	*Japanese*	342
	Tsunami	”	323
£40+	Noci	*Italian*	323
	Rosmarino	”	333
	Soffice London	”	332
	Black Bear Burger	*Burgers, etc*	432
	Patty and Bun	”	322
	Yard Sale Pizza	*Pizza*	342
	Orange Pekoe	*Sandwiches, cakes, etc*	343
	Meza Trinity Road	*Lebanese*	333
	Black Salt	*Indian*	443
	Chook Chook	”	434
	Postbox	”	343
	Bone Daddies	*Japanese*	322
	Hoshi	”	332
	Tomoe	”	442
	Hare & Tortoise	*Pan-Asian*	232
	Cher Thai	*Thai*	343
	Kaosarn	”	343
	Bao Battersea	*Taiwanese*	344
£35+	Amrutha	*Vegan*	342
	Three Uncles	*Chinese*	522
	Balham Social	*Indian*	342
	Ela & Dhani	”	342
	Holy Cow	”	332
	Sushi Revolution	*Japanese*	442
	Taro	”	332
	Awesome Thai	*Thai*	332
£30+	Ploussard	*British, Modern*	433
	Indian Ocean	*Indian*	333
	Daddy Bao	*Taiwanese*	433
£25+	Milk	*Sandwiches, cakes, etc*	323
	Mirch Masala	*Pakistani*	422
£20+	Dropshot Coffee	*British, Modern*	344
	Thai Tho	*Thai*	333
£15+	Meiwei	*Chinese*	332
	Roti King	*Malaysian*	522

OUTER WESTERN SUBURBS KEW, RICHMOND, TWICKENHAM, TEDDINGTON

£120+	Petersham Nurseries Cafe	*British, Modern*	225
£110+	Scott's Richmond	*Fish & seafood*	234
£90+	The Dysart Petersham	*British, Modern*	544
£80+	The Ivy Café	*British, Modern*	112
	Steven Edwards Bingham Riverhouse	”	424
	The Petersham	”	224
£70+	Le Salon Privé	*French*	333
	A Cena	*Italian*	443
	Bacco	”	332
£60+	The Fat Badger	*British, Modern*	322
	Hawthorn	”	353
	Petit Ma Cuisine	*French*	343
	Tapas Brindisa	*Spanish*	222
	Rock & Rose	*Pan-Asian*	223
£50+	Black Dog Beer House	*British, Modern*	333
	Four Regions	*Chinese*	333
£40+	Newens	*Afternoon tea*	343
	Dastaan	*Indian*	543
£15+	Kiss the Hippo	*Sandwiches, cakes, etc*	343

EAST

SMITHFIELD & FARRINGDON (EC1)

Price	Restaurant	Cuisine	Rating
£220+	The Clove Club	*British, Modern*	332
£170+	Restaurant St. Barts	*British, Modern*	545
£160+	Club Gascon	*French*	433
	Tehran Berlin	*Persian*	344
	Sushi Tetsu	*Japanese*	554
£110+	Anglo	*British, Modern*	543
£100+	NEST	*British, Modern*	433
	The Quality Chop House	*British, Traditional*	323
£90+	Luca	*Italian*	444
£80+	Compton	*British, Modern*	342
	St John Smithfield	*British, Traditional*	443
	Bouchon Racine	*French*	553
	Smiths of Smithfield	*Steaks & grills*	333
£70+	The Coach	*British, Modern*	333
	The Jugged Hare	*"*	324
	Daffodil Mulligan	*Irish*	443
	Apulia	*Italian*	223
	Macellaio RC	*"*	223
	Moro	*Spanish*	443
£60+	Granger & Co	*Australian*	223
	Caravan	*British, Modern*	222
	Sessions Arts Club	*"*	345
	Vinoteca	*"*	222
	Bleeding Heart Bistro	*French*	334
	Café du Marché	*"*	345
	Ibérica	*Spanish*	222
	The Gate	*Vegetarian*	333
	Homeslice	*Pizza*	323
	Le Bab	*Middle Eastern*	432
	Berber & Q Shawarma Bar	*"*	543
£50+	Attica	*Greek*	233
	Trattoria Brutto	*Italian*	345
	Morito	*Spanish*	432
	Street Burger	*Burgers, etc*	322
	The Sichuan	*Chinese*	322
	Pham Sushi	*Japanese*	232
£40+	Taqueria	*Mexican*	333
	Fish Central	*Fish & seafood*	442
	Noci	*Italian*	323
	The Eagle	*Mediterranean*	334
	Black Bear Burger	*Burgers, etc*	432
	Bone Daddies	*Japanese*	322
	Cây Tre	*Vietnamese*	332
£15+	Daddy Donkey	*Mexican*	432
	Prufrock Coffee	*Sandwiches, cakes, etc*	333

THE CITY (EC2, EC3, EC4)

Price	Restaurant	Cuisine	Rating
£170+	La Dame de Pic	*French*	433
£120+	City Social	*British, Modern*	334
	Nobu Shoreditch	*Japanese*	– – –
£110+	Fenchurch Restaurant	*British, Modern*	334
	Angler	*Fish & seafood*	342
	Coya	*Peruvian*	223
	Sushisamba	*Japanese*	223
£100+	Lutyens Grill	*Steaks & grills*	334
	Yauatcha City	*Chinese*	322
£90+	Duck & Waffle	*British, Modern*	223
	14 Hills	*"*	224
	Helix	*"*	335
	Leroy	*"*	443
	1 Lombard Street	*"*	222
	Sweetings	*Fish & seafood*	324
	Bob Bob Ricard City	*French*	244
	Coq d'Argent	*"*	222
	Hawksmoor Guildhall	*Steaks & grills*	332
	M Restaurant	*"*	222
£80+	CORD	*British, Modern*	434
	Darwin Brasserie	*"*	224
	The Ivy City Garden	*"*	223
	The Mercer	*"*	332
	Cabotte	*French*	343
	Cecconi's	*International*	233
	Manicomio City	*Italian*	223
	Bibo by Dani García	*Spanish*	223
	Hispania	*"*	334
	Goodman City	*Steaks & grills*	343
	The Ivy Asia	*Pan-Asian*	324
£70+	Santo Remedio Café	*Mexican*	332
	Bread Street Kitchen	*British, Modern*	223
	High Timber	*"*	332
	Paternoster Chop House	*British, Traditional*	232
	Vivat Bacchus	*International*	332
	Piazza Italiana	*Italian*	332
	Burger & Lobster	*Burgers, etc*	432
	Pachamama East	*Peruvian*	333
	Brigadiers	*Indian*	433
£60+	Caravan	*British, Modern*	222
	Coppa Club	*"*	224
	Humble Grape	*"*	233
	Vinoteca City	*"*	222
	VQ	*"*	223

	Brasserie Blanc	*French*	222
	Gazette	”	223
	Caravaggio	*Italian*	232
	Gloria	”	235
	Obicà Mozzarella Bar	”	332
	Popolo	”	332
	Terra Rossa	”	444
	Ekte Nordic Kitchen	*Scandinavian*	322
	Camino Monument	*Spanish*	222
	José Pizarro	”	322
	Haché	*Burgers, etc*	332
	Homeslice	*Pizza*	323
	Haz	*Turkish*	322
	Cinnamon Kitchen	*Indian*	433
£50+	Los Mochis	*Fusion*	333
	The Wine Library	*International*	235
	Barbican Brasserie	*Italian*	333
	Eataly	”	223
	Lina Stores	”	223
	Manteca	”	544
	Casa do Frango	*Portuguese*	335
	Blacklock	*Steaks & grills*	344
	Le Relais de Venise	”	333
	temper Shoreditch	”	212
	Street Burger	*Burgers, etc*	322
	temper City	*BBQ*	212
	Shoryu Ramen	*Japanese*	322
£40+	Zapote	*Mexican*	444
	Padella Shoreditch	*Italian*	434
	Patty and Bun	*Burgers, etc*	322
	Ozone Coffee Roasters	*Sandwiches, cakes, etc*	333
	Koya	*Japanese*	443
	Hare & Tortoise	*Pan-Asian*	232
£35+	Flat Iron	*Steaks & grills*	333
	Three Uncles	*Chinese*	522
£25+	Bleecker Burger	*Burgers, etc*	422
£5+	Rosslyn Coffee	*Sandwiches, cakes, etc*	343

EAST END & DOCKLANDS (ALL E POSTCODES)

£290+	Da Terra	*Fusion*	545
£210+	Cycene	*Fusion*	544
£190+	The Water House Project	*British, Modern*	454
£170+	The Sea, The Sea	*Fish & seafood*	544
£140+	Behind	*Fish & seafood*	543
£120+	Galvin La Chapelle	*French*	445
£100+	Brat at Climpson's Arch	*British, Modern*	432
	Lyle's	”	532
£90+	Allegra	*British, Modern*	322
	Cornerstone	*Fish & seafood*	554
	Hawksmoor	*Steaks & grills*	332
	M Restaurant	”	222
	Roka	*Japanese*	323
£80+	Brat	*British, Modern*	543
	The Ivy in the Park	”	223
	Pidgin	”	– – –
	Smith's Wapping	”	434
	Planque	*French*	344
	Casa Fofó	*International*	433
	Canto Corvino	*Italian*	233
	Cecconi's Shoreditch	”	233
	Boisdale of Canary Wharf	*Scottish*	333
	Goodman	*Steaks & grills*	343
£70+	Big Easy	*American*	223
	Eline	*British, Modern*	453
	Elliot's	”	332
	The Gun	”	324
	Rochelle Canteen	”	233
	St John Bread & Wine	*British, Traditional*	433
	The Melusine	*Fish & seafood*	444
	Angelina	*Fusion*	534
	Six by Nico	*International*	333
	Super Tuscan	*Italian*	– – –
	Brawn	*Mediterranean*	554
	Oren	”	442
	Ottolenghi	”	333
	Haugen	*Swiss*	– – –
	Burger & Lobster	*Burgers, etc*	432
	Sticks'n'Sushi	*Japanese*	322
£60+	Barge East	*British, Modern*	435
	Cafe Cecilia	”	444
	Caravan	”	222
	The Culpeper	”	333
	The Duke of Richmond	”	333
	Humble Grape	”	233
	Jones & Sons	”	334
	Chez Elles	*French*	333
	Galvin Bistrot & Bar	”	342
	Il Bordello	*Italian*	334
	Obicà Mozzarella Bar	”	332
	Ombra	”	– – –
	Ibérica	*Spanish*	222
	Elis	*Brazilian*	442
	Le Bab	*Middle Eastern*	432
	Berber & Q	”	543
	Haz	*Turkish*	322
	Lahpet	*Burmese*	432
	Royal China	*Chinese*	322
	Café Spice Namaste	*Indian*	544
	Gunpowder	”	433
	Smoking Goat	*Thai*	533

Price	Restaurant	Cuisine	Ratings
£50+	The Empress	*British, Modern*	334
	Mare Street Market	"	324
	Papi	"	423
	Townsend	"	332
	Capeesh	*Italian*	333
	Emilia's Crafted Pasta	"	333
	Morito	*Spanish*	432
	Blacklock	*Steaks & grills*	344
	Mildreds	*Vegetarian*	333
	Ark Fish	*Fish & chips*	332
	Pizza East	*Pizza*	323
	Zia Lucia	"	332
	Acme Fire Cult	*BBQ*	213
	Smokestak	"	433
	Delamina East	*Middle Eastern*	333
	Dishoom	*Indian*	345
£40+	Provender	*French*	342
	Black Bear Burger	*Burgers, etc*	432
	Burger & Beyond	"	322
	Patty and Bun	"	322
	Yard Sale Pizza	*Pizza*	342
	Ozone Coffee Roasters	*Sandwiches, cakes, etc*	333
	Chick 'n' Sours	*Chicken*	433
	Bubala	*Middle Eastern*	443
	Lucky & Joy	*Chinese*	433
	Issho-Ni	*Japanese*	442
	Koya Ko	"	443
	Som Saa	*Thai*	433
	Sông Quê	*Vietnamese*	322
	Bao Noodle Shop	*Taiwanese*	344
£35+	Maene	*British, Modern*	433
	Flat Iron	*Steaks & grills*	333
	Crate	*Pizza*	323
	The Dusty Knuckle	*Sandwiches, cakes, etc*	523
	Mangal 1	*Turkish*	532
	Taro	*Japanese*	332
	Lahore Kebab House	*Pakistani*	422
	Tayyabs	"	432
£30+	Alter	*Vegan*	432
	Supa Ya Ramen	*Japanese*	332
£25+	Bleecker Burger	*Burgers, etc*	422
	Singburi Royal Thai Café	*Thai*	422
£20+	E Pellicci	*Italian*	352
	Tofu Vegan	*Chinese*	432
£15+	Homies on Donkeys	*Mexican*	444
	Laxeiro	*Spanish*	333
	The Duck Truck	*Burgers, etc*	432
	Smokoloko	*BBQ*	433
	Marugame Udon	*Japanese*	332
£10+	The Rib Man	*Burgers, etc*	44–
£5+	Brick Lane Beigel Bake	*Sandwiches, cakes, etc*	521

Lasdun, National Theatre SE1

Manzi's W1

Story Cellar WC2

Masala Zone W1

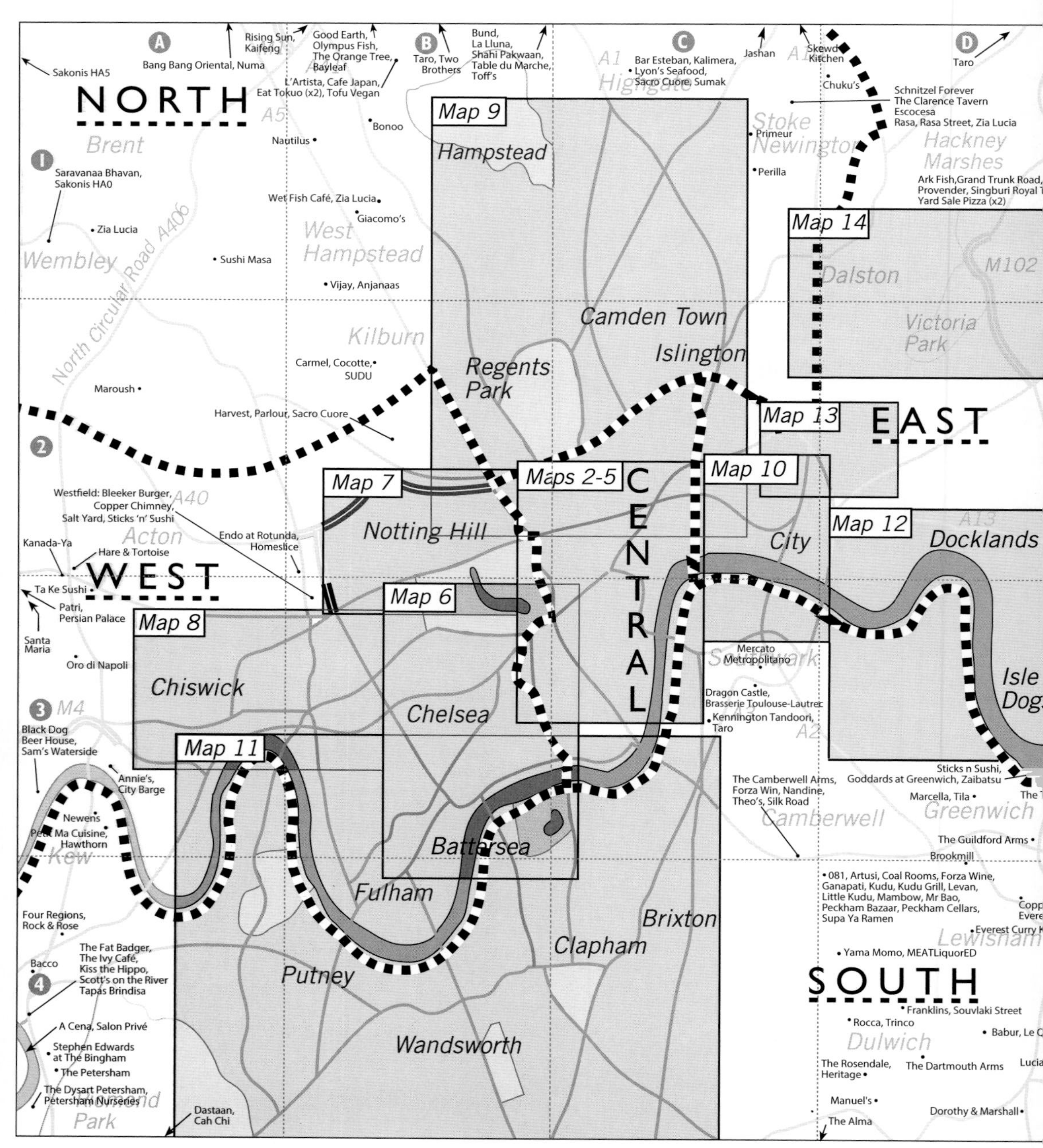
NORTH
WEST
CENTRAL
EAST
SOUTH
Map 9
Map 14
Map 13
Map 10
Map 12
Map 7
Maps 2-5
Map 6
Map 8
Map 11
Sakonis HA5
Bang Bang Oriental, Numa
Rising Sun, Kaifeng
Good Earth, Olympus Fish, The Orange Tree, Bayleaf
L'Artista, Cafe Japan, Eat Tokuo (x2), Tofu Vegan
Taro, Two Brothers
Bund, La Lluna, Shahi Pakwaan, Table du Marche, Toff's
Bar Esteban, Kalimera, Lyon's Seafood, Sacro Cuore, Sumak
Jashan
Skewd Kitchen
Chuku's
Taro
Schnitzel Forever
The Clarence Tavern
Escocesa
Rasa, Rasa Street, Zia Lucia
Bonoo
Nautilus
Primeur
Perilla
Saravanaa Bhavan, Sakonis HA0
Wet Fish Café, Zia Lucia
Giacomo's
Zia Lucia
Sushi Masa
Vijay, Anjanaas
Carmel, Cocotte, SUDU
Maroush
Harvest, Parlour, Sacro Cuore
Westfield: Bleeker Burger, Copper Chimney, Salt Yard, Sticks 'n' Sushi
Endo at Rotunda, Homeslice
Kanada-Ya
Hare & Tortoise
Ta Ke Sushi
Patri, Persian Palace
Santa Maria
Oro di Napoli
Black Dog Beer House, Sam's Waterside
Annie's, City Barge
Newens
Petit Ma Cuisine, Hawthorn
Four Regions, Rock & Rose
Bacco
The Fat Badger, The Ivy Café, Kiss the Hippo, Scott's on the River, Tapas Brindisa
A Cena, Salon Privé
Stephen Edwards at The Bingham
The Petersham
The Dysart Petersham, Petersham Nurseries
Dastaan, Cah Chi
Mercato Metropolitano
Dragon Castle, Brasserie Toulouse-Lautrec
Kennington Tandoori, Taro
The Camberwell Arms, Forza Win, Nandine, Theo's, Silk Road
Sticks n Sushi, Goddards at Greenwich, Zaibatsu
Marcella, Tila
The Guildford Arms
Brookmill
081, Artusi, Coal Rooms, Forza Wine, Ganapati, Kudu, Kudu Grill, Levan, Little Kudu, Mambow, Mr Bao, Peckham Bazaar, Peckham Cellars, Supa Ya Ramen
Yama Momo, MEATLiquorED
Franklins, Souvlaki Street
Rocca, Trinco
Babur, Le C
The Rosendale, Heritage
The Dartmouth Arms
Manuel's
The Alma
Dorothy & Marshall
Hampstead
West Hampstead
Kilburn
Camden Town
Islington
Regents Park
Notting Hill
Acton
City
Docklands
Chiswick
Chelsea
Battersea
Fulham
Putney
Brixton
Clapham
Wandsworth
Camberwell
Greenwich
Lewisham
Dulwich
Dalston
Victoria Park
Hackney Marshes
Stoke Newington
Highgate
Brent
Wembley
North Circular Road A406
Kew
Isle of Dogs
Southwark
A1
A5
A40
M4
A13
A2
M102

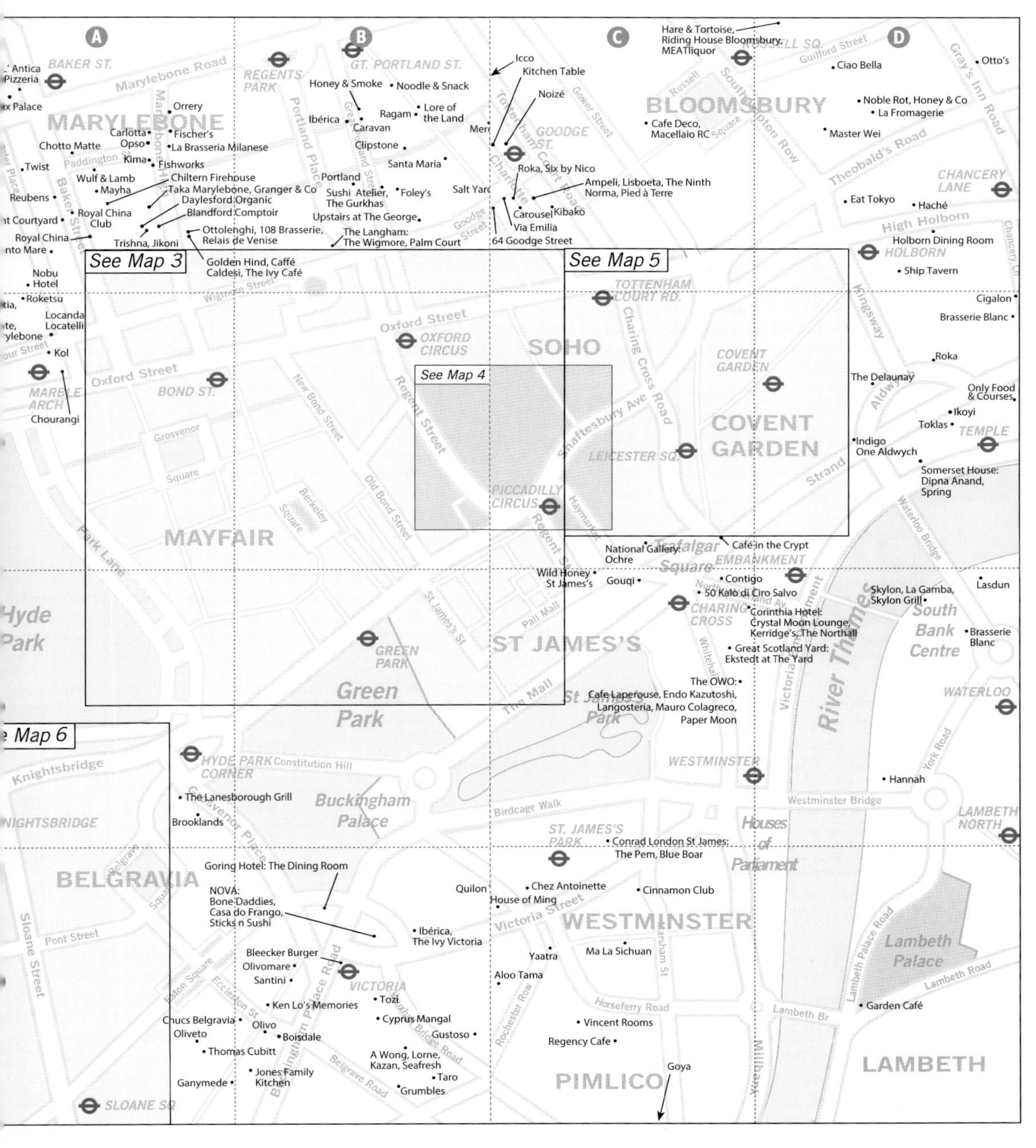

See Map 3
See Map 4
See Map 5
See Map 6
MARYLEBONE
BLOOMSBURY
SOHO
COVENT GARDEN
MAYFAIR
ST JAMES'S
BELGRAVIA
WESTMINSTER
PIMLICO
LAMBETH
Hyde Park
Green Park
Buckingham Palace
St James's Park
Houses of Parliament
Lambeth Palace
River Thames
South Bank Centre
Trafalgar Square
Orrery
Carlotta
Opso
Fischer's
La Brasseria Milanese
Kima
Fishworks
Chotto Matte
Twist
Wulf & Lamb
Mayha
Chiltern Firehouse
Taka Marylebone, Granger & Co
Daylesford Organic
Blandford Comptoir
Reubens
Royal China Club
Royal China
Trishna, Jikoni
Ottolenghi, 108 Brasserie, Relais de Venise
Golden Hind, Caffé Caldesi, The Ivy Café
Nobu Hotel
Roketsu
Locanda Locatelli
Kol
Chourangi
Honey & Smoke
Noodle & Snack
Ibérica
Caravan
Ragam
Lore of the Land
Clipstone
Santa Maria
Portland
Sushi Atelier, The Gurkhas
Foley's
Upstairs at The George
The Langham: The Wigmore, Palm Court
Salt Yard
Icco
Kitchen Table
Noizé
Roka, Six by Nico
Ampeli, Lisboeta, The Ninth Norma, Pied à Terre
Carousel
Kibako
Via Emilia
64 Goodge Street
Hare & Tortoise, Riding House Bloomsbury, MEATliquor
Cafe Deco, Macellaio RC
Ciao Bella
Otto's
Noble Rot, Honey & Co
La Fromagerie
Master Wei
Eat Tokyo
Haché
Holborn Dining Room
Ship Tavern
Cigalon
Brasserie Blanc
Roka
The Delaunay
Only Food & Courses
Ikoyi
Toklas
Indigo One Aldwych
Somerset House: Dipna Anand, Spring
Café in the Crypt
National Gallery: Ochre
Wild Honey St James's
Gouqi
Contigo
50 Kalò di Ciro Salvo
Corinthia Hotel: Crystal Moon Lounge, Kerridge's, The Northall
Great Scotland Yard: Ekstedt at The Yard
The OWO: Cafe Laperouse, Endo Kazutoshi, Langosteria, Mauro Colagreco, Paper Moon
Skylon, La Gamba, Skylon Grill
Lasdun
Brasserie Blanc
Hannah
The Lanesborough Grill
Brooklands
Goring Hotel: The Dining Room
NOVA: Bone Daddies, Casa do Frango, Sticks n Sushi
Ibérica, The Ivy Victoria
Quilon
House of Ming
Chez Antoinette
Conrad London St James: The Pem, Blue Boar
Cinnamon Club
Bleecker Burger
Olivomare
Santini
Ken Lo's Memories
Tozi
Cyprus Mangal
Gustoso
Chucs Belgravia
Olivo
Oliveto
Boisdale
Thomas Cubitt
A Wong, Lorne, Kazan, Seafresh
Jones Family Kitchen
Taro
Ganymede
Grumbles
Yaatra
Ma La Sichuan
Aloo Tama
Vincent Rooms
Regency Cafe
Goya
Garden Café

MAP 3 – MAYFAIR, ST. JAMES'S & WEST SOHO

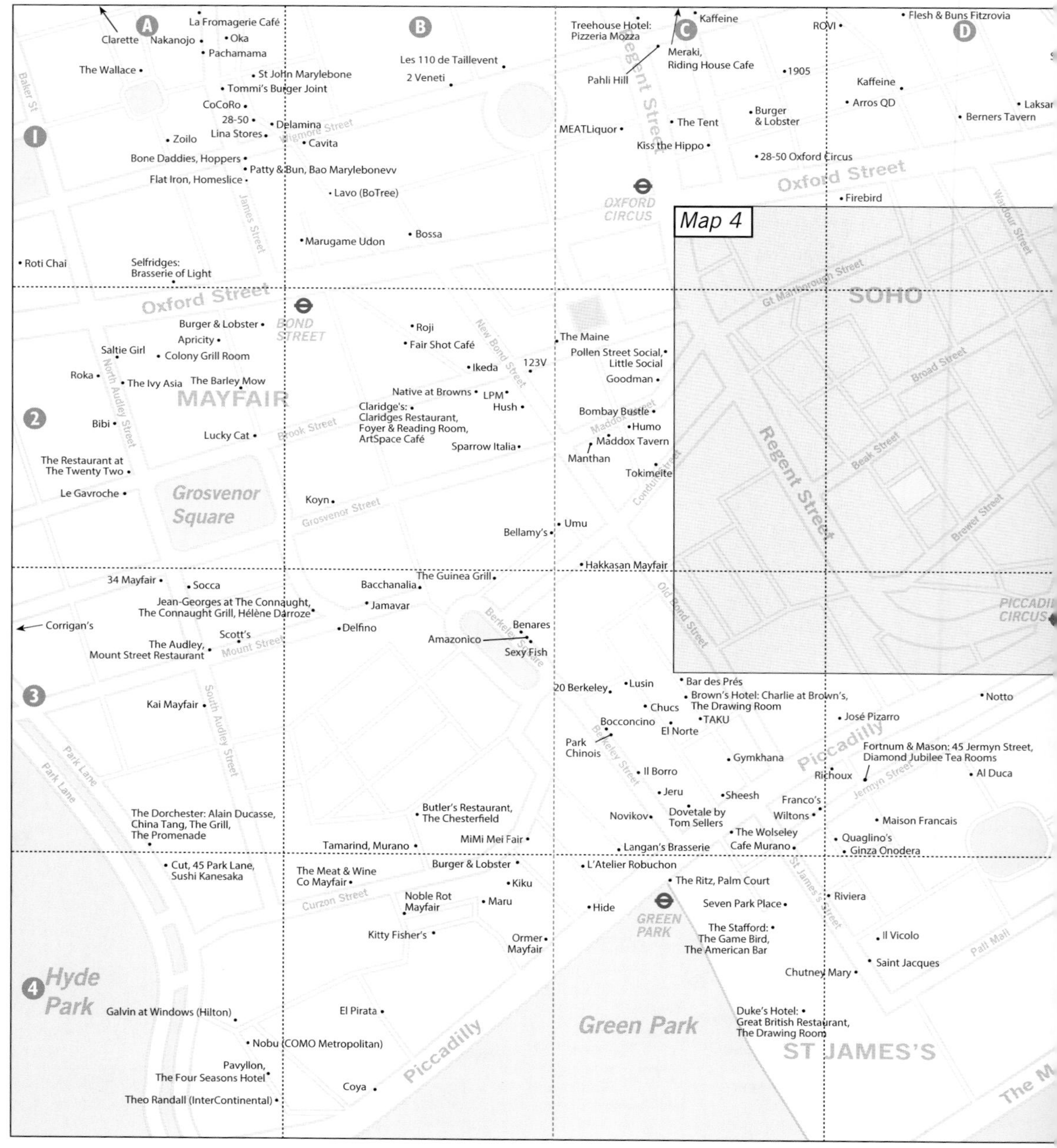
A
B
C
D
1
2
3
4
Clarette
La Fromagerie Café
Nakanojo
Oka
Pachamama
The Wallace
St John Marylebone
Tommi's Burger Joint
CoCoRo
28-50
Delamina
Lina Stores
Zoilo
Cavita
Bone Daddies, Hoppers
Patty & Bun, Bao Marylebonevv
Flat Iron, Homeslice
Lavo (BoTree)
Marugame Udon
Bossa
Roti Chai
Selfridges:
Brasserie of Light
Baker St
Wigmore Street
James Street
Les 110 de Taillevent
2 Veneti
Treehouse Hotel:
Pizzeria Mozza
Kaffeine
ROVI
Flesh & Buns Fitzrovia
Meraki,
Riding House Cafe
Pahli Hill
1905
Kaffeine
Arros QD
Laksa
Berners Tavern
Burger
& Lobster
MEATLiquor
The Tent
Kiss the Hippo
28-50 Oxford Circus
Regent Street
Oxford Street
OXFORD
CIRCUS
Firebird
Map 4
Wardour Street
Gt Marlborough Street
SOHO
Broad Street
Beak Street
Brewer Street
Regent Street
PICCADILLY
CIRCUS
Oxford Street
BOND
STREET
Burger & Lobster
Apricity
Saltie Girl
Colony Grill Room
Roka
The Ivy Asia
The Barley Mow
MAYFAIR
North Audley Street
Bibi
Lucky Cat
Brook Street
The Restaurant at
The Twenty Two
Le Gavroche
Grosvenor
Square
Roji
Fair Shot Café
New Bond Street
Ikeda
123V
Native at Browns
LPM
Hush
Claridge's:
Claridges Restaurant,
Foyer & Reading Room,
ArtSpace Café
Sparrow Italia
Koyn
Grosvenor Street
Bellamy's
Umu
The Maine
Pollen Street Social,
Little Social
Goodman
Bombay Bustle
Maddox Street
Humo
Maddox Tavern
Manthan
Tokimeite
Conduit Street
Hakkasan Mayfair
34 Mayfair
Socca
Jean-Georges at The Connaught,
The Connaught Grill, Hélène Darroze
Corrigan's
Scott's
The Audley,
Mount Street Restaurant
Mount Street
Bacchanalia
The Guinea Grill
Jamavar
Delfino
Benares
Amazonico
Sexy Fish
Berkeley Square
Old Bond Street
Kai Mayfair
South Audley Street
Park Lane
Park Lane
The Dorchester: Alain Ducasse,
China Tang, The Grill,
The Promenade
Butler's Restaurant,
The Chesterfield
MiMi Mei Fair
Tamarind, Murano
20 Berkeley
Lusin
Bar des Prés
Brown's Hotel: Charlie at Brown's,
The Drawing Room
Chucs
TAKU
Bocconcino
El Norte
Park
Chinois
Berkeley Street
Il Borro
Jeru
Gymkhana
Sheesh
Novikov
Dovetale by
Tom Sellers
The Wolseley
Cafe Murano
Langan's Brasserie
Notto
José Pizarro
Piccadilly
Fortnum & Mason: 45 Jermyn Street,
Diamond Jubilee Tea Rooms
Richoux
Jermyn Street
Al Duca
Franco's
Wiltons
Maison Francais
Quaglino's
Ginza Onodera
Cut, 45 Park Lane,
Sushi Kanesaka
The Meat & Wine
Co Mayfair
Burger & Lobster
Kiku
Curzon Street
Noble Rot
Mayfair
Maru
Kitty Fisher's
Ormer
Mayfair
L'Atelier Robuchon
The Ritz, Palm Court
Hide
GREEN
PARK
Seven Park Place
St James's Street
Riviera
The Stafford:
The Game Bird,
The American Bar
Il Vicolo
Pall Mall
Saint Jacques
Chutney Mary
Hyde
Park
Galvin at Windows (Hilton)
El Pirata
Nobu (COMO Metropolitan)
Piccadilly
Green Park
Duke's Hotel:
Great British Restaurant,
The Drawing Room
ST JAMES'S
Pavyllon,
The Four Seasons Hotel
Coya
Theo Randall (InterContinental)
The M

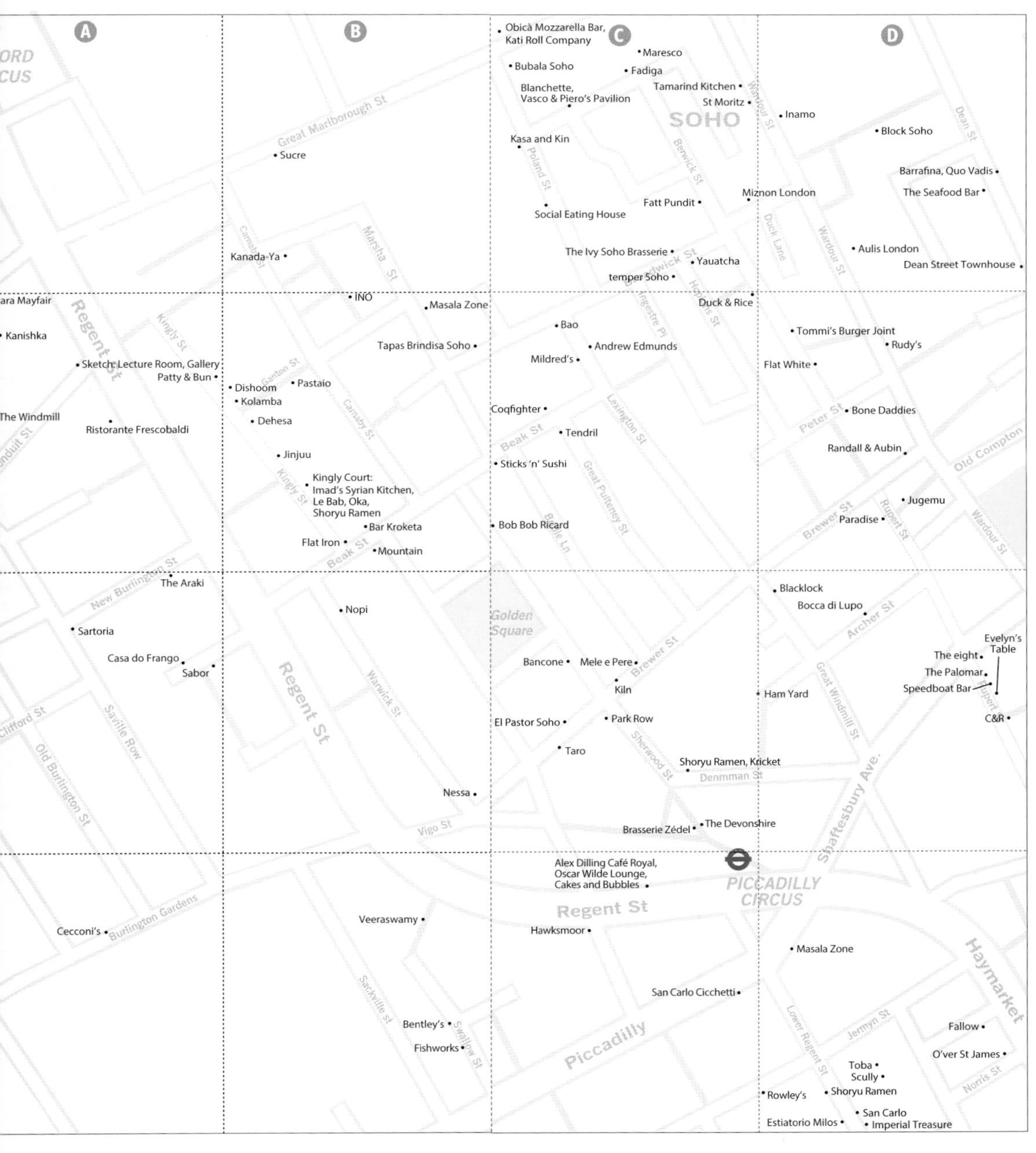

A
B
C
D
SOHO
GOLDEN Square
PICCADILLY CIRCUS
Regent St
Great Marlborough St
Carnaby St
Marshall St
Kingly St
Ganton St
Beak St
Poland St
Berwick St
Wardour St
Dean St
Duck Lane
Lexington St
Great Pulteney St
Bridle Ln
Brewer St
Peter St
Rupert St
Old Compton
Archer St
Great Windmill St
Sherwood St
Denmman St
Shaftesbury Ave.
Warwick St
Vigo St
New Burlington St
Clifford St
Saville Row
Old Burlington St
Burlington Gardens
Sackville St
Swallow St
Piccadilly
Jermyn St
Lower Regent St
Norris St
Haymarket
Obicà Mozzarella Bar, Kati Roll Company
Maresco
Bubala Soho
Fadiga
Blanchette, Vasco & Piero's Pavilion
Tamarind Kitchen
St Moritz
Inamo
Block Soho
Sucre
Kasa and Kin
Barrafina, Quo Vadis
The Seafood Bar
Miznon London
Fatt Pundit
Social Eating House
The Ivy Soho Brasserie
Yauatcha
Aulis London
Dean Street Townhouse
Kanada-Ya
temper Soho
ara Mayfair
INO
Masala Zone
Duck & Rice
Kanishka
Bao
Tommi's Burger Joint
Rudy's
Tapas Brindisa Soho
Andrew Edmunds
Sketch: Lecture Room, Gallery
Mildred's
Flat White
Patty & Bun
Dishoom
Pastaio
Kolamba
Coqfighter
Bone Daddies
The Windmill
Dehesa
Ristorante Frescobaldi
Tendril
Randall & Aubin
Jinjuu
Sticks 'n' Sushi
Kingly Court: Imad's Syrian Kitchen, Le Bab, Oka, Shoryu Ramen
Jugemu
Paradise
Bar Kroketa
Bob Bob Ricard
Flat Iron
Mountain
The Araki
Blacklock
Nopi
Bocca di Lupo
Sartoria
Evelyn's Table
The eight
Casa do Frango
Bancone
Mele e Pere
The Palomar
Sabor
Kiln
Speedboat Bar
Ham Yard
El Pastor Soho
Park Row
C&R
Taro
Shoryu Ramen, Kricket
Nessa
Brasserie Zédel
The Devonshire
Alex Dilling Café Royal, Oscar Wilde Lounge, Cakes and Bubbles
Veeraswamy
Cecconi's
Hawksmoor
Masala Zone
San Carlo Cicchetti
Bentley's
Fallow
Fishworks
O'ver St James
Toba
Scully
Rowley's
Shoryu Ramen
San Carlo
Estiatorio Milos
Imperial Treasure

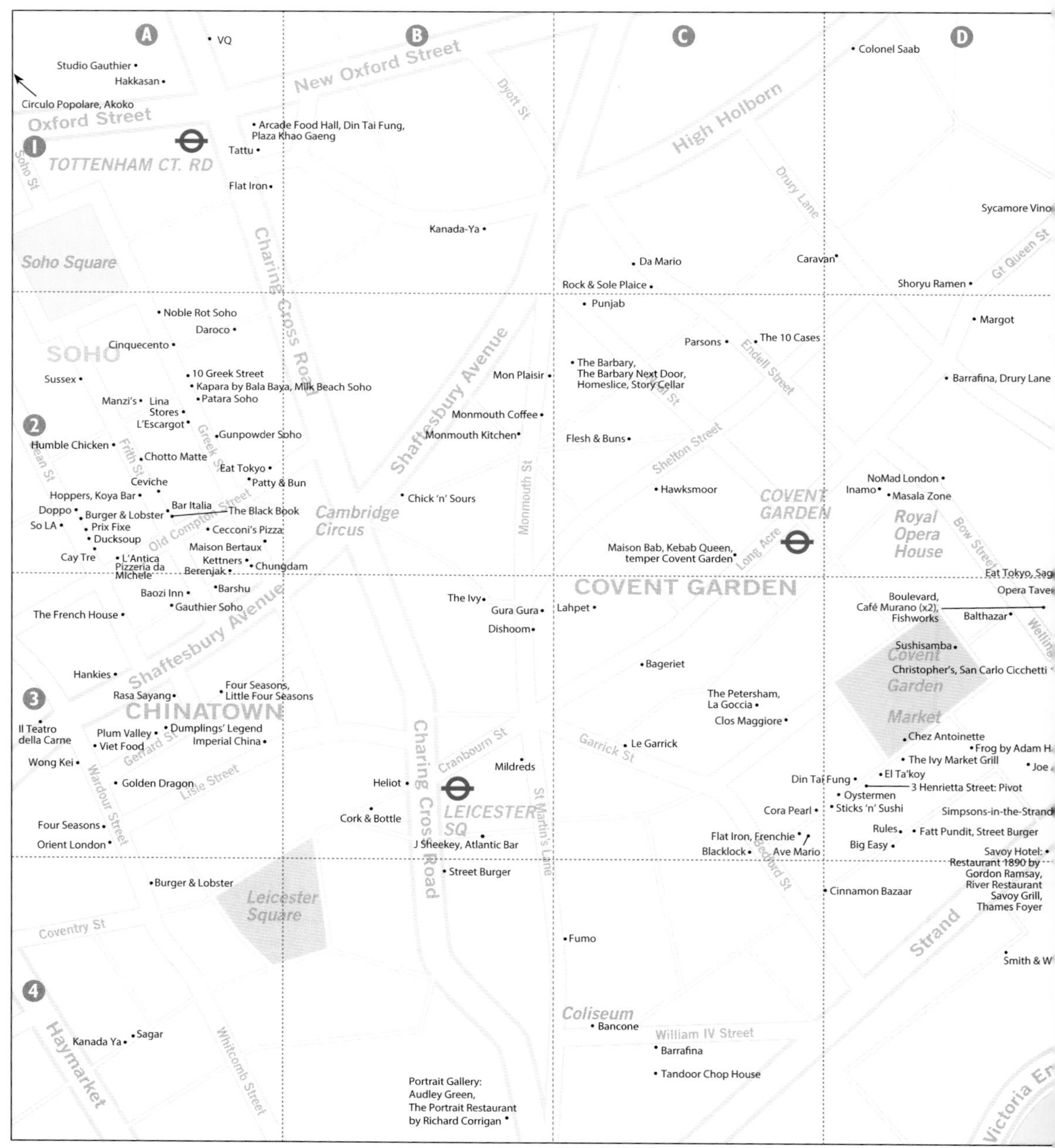
A
B
C
D
1
2
3
4
VQ
Studio Gauthier
Hakkasan
Circulo Popolare, Akoko
Oxford Street
New Oxford Street
Dyott St
High Holborn
Colonel Saab
Arcade Food Hall, Din Tai Fung, Plaza Khao Gaeng
Tattu
TOTTENHAM CT. RD
Soho St
Flat Iron
Drury Lane
Sycamore Vino
Kanada-Ya
Soho Square
Charing Cross Road
Da Mario
Caravan
Gt Queen St
Rock & Sole Plaice
Shoryu Ramen
Punjab
Noble Rot Soho
Daroco
Margot
SOHO
Cinquecento
Parsons
The 10 Cases
Endell Street
Shaftesbury Avenue
The Barbary, The Barbary Next Door, Homeslice, Story Cellar
Sussex
10 Greek Street
Kapara by Bala Baya, Milk Beach Soho
Mon Plaisir
Barrafina, Drury Lane
Manzi's
Lina Stores
Patara Soho
L'Escargot
Monmouth Coffee
Gunpowder Soho
Monmouth Kitchen
Flesh & Buns
Greek St
Humble Chicken
Chotto Matte
Shelton Street
Dean St
Frith St
Eat Tokyo
Monmouth St
NoMad London
Ceviche
Patty & Bun
Hawksmoor
Inamo
Masala Zone
Hoppers, Koya Bar
Chick 'n' Sours
COVENT GARDEN
Bar Italia
The Black Book
Doppo
Burger & Lobster
Cambridge Circus
Royal Opera House
So LA
Prix Fixe
Cecconi's Pizza
Bow Street
Ducksoup
Old Compton Street
Maison Bertaux
Maison Bab, Kebab Queen, temper Covent Garden
Long Acre
Cay Tre
L'Antica Pizzeria da Michele
Kettners
Chungdam
Berenjak
Eat Tokyo, Sag
Barshu
COVENT GARDEN
Opera Tave
Baozi Inn
The Ivy
Gauthier Soho
Gura Gura
Lahpet
Boulevard, Café Murano (x2), Fishworks
Balthazar
The French House
Dishoom
Sushisamba
Hankies
Bageriet
Covent Garden Market
Christopher's, San Carlo Cicchetti
Rasa Sayang
Four Seasons, Little Four Seasons
The Petersham, La Goccia
CHINATOWN
Clos Maggiore
Il Teatro della Carne
Plum Valley
Dumplings' Legend
Chez Antoinette
Viet Food
Gerrard St
Imperial China
Garrick St
Le Garrick
Frog by Adam H
Cranbourn St
Wong Kei
Mildreds
The Ivy Market Grill
Joe
El Ta'koy
Wardour Street
Golden Dragon
Lisle Street
Heliot
Din Tai Fung
3 Henrietta Street: Pivot
Oystermen
Sticks 'n' Sushi
Cora Pearl
Simpsons-in-the-Strand
Cork & Bottle
LEICESTER SQ
Four Seasons
Rules
Fatt Pundit, Street Burger
Flat Iron, Frenchie
Orient London
J Sheekey, Atlantic Bar
Big Easy
Blacklock
Ave Mario
Savoy Hotel: Restaurant 1890 by Gordon Ramsay, River Restaurant Savoy Grill, Thames Foyer
Bedford St
Street Burger
St Martin's Lane
Burger & Lobster
Cinnamon Bazaar
Leicester Square
Coventry St
Strand
Fumo
Smith & W
Coliseum
Bancone
William IV Street
Barrafina
Haymarket
Kanada Ya
Sagar
Whitcomb Street
Tandoor Chop House
Portrait Gallery: Audley Green, The Portrait Restaurant by Richard Corrigan
Victoria Em

MAP 6 – KNIGHTSBRIDGE, CHELSEA & SOUTH KENSINGTON

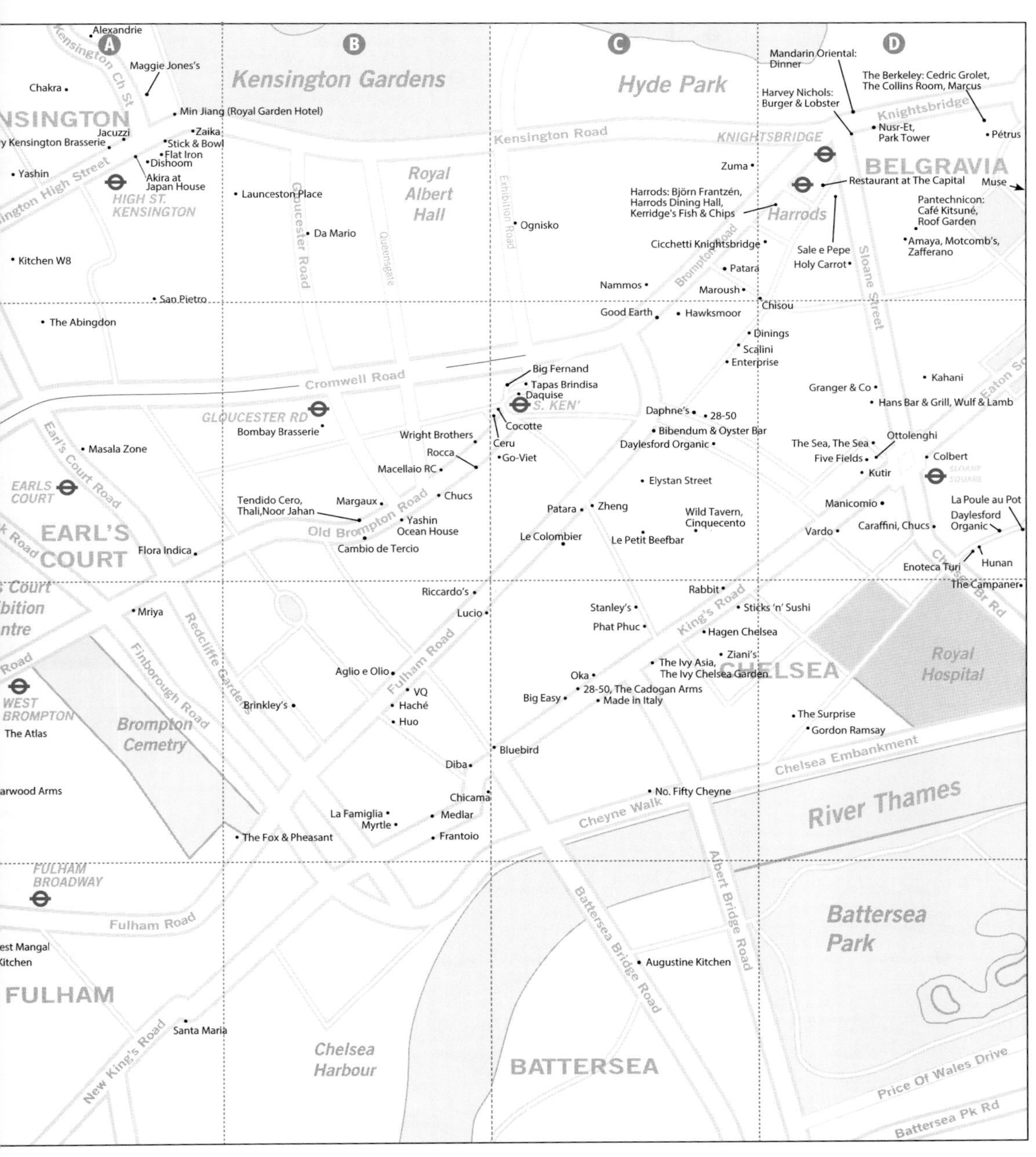
A
B
C
D
Alexandrie
Kensington Ch St
Maggie Jones's
Chakra
Kensington Gardens
Hyde Park
Min Jiang (Royal Garden Hotel)
Jacuzzi
Zaika
y Kensington Brasserie
Stick & Bowl
Flat Iron
Dishoom
Yashin
Akira at
Japan House
HIGH ST.
KENSINGTON
Launceston Place
Royal
Albert
Hall
Da Mario
Gloucester Road
Queensgate
Exhibition Road
Ognisko
Kitchen W8
San Pietro
The Abingdon
Kensington Road
Mandarin Oriental:
Dinner
Harvey Nichols:
Burger & Lobster
The Berkeley: Cedric Grolet,
The Collins Room, Marcus
Knightsbridge
KNIGHTSBRIDGE
Nusr-Et,
Park Tower
Pétrus
Zuma
BELGRAVIA
Restaurant at The Capital
Muse
Harrods: Björn Frantzén,
Harrods Dining Hall,
Kerridge's Fish & Chips
Harrods
Pantechnicon:
Café Kitsuné,
Roof Garden
Amaya, Motcomb's,
Zafferano
Cicchetti Knightsbridge
Sale e Pepe
Holy Carrot
Brompton Road
Sloane Street
Patara
Nammos
Maroush
Chisou
Good Earth
Hawksmoor
Dinings
Scalini
Enterprise
Big Fernand
Tapas Brindisa
Daquise
Cromwell Road
S. KEN'
GLOUCESTER RD
Bombay Brasserie
Cocotte
Ceru
Go-Viet
Wright Brothers
Rocca
Macellaio RC
Daphne's
28-50
Bibendum & Oyster Bar
Daylesford Organic
Granger & Co
Kahani
Hans Bar & Grill, Wulf & Lamb
Eaton Sq
The Sea, The Sea
Five Fields
Ottolenghi
Colbert
Kutir
SLOANE SQUARE
Masala Zone
Earl's Court Road
EARLS COURT
EARL'S COURT
Elystan Street
Tendido Cero,
Thali,Noor Jahan
Margaux
Chucs
Old Brompton Road
Yashin
Ocean House
Cambio de Tercio
Flora Indica
Patara
Zheng
Le Colombier
Le Petit Beefbar
Wild Tavern,
Cinquecento
Manicomio
Vardo
Caraffini, Chucs
La Poule au Pot
Daylesford
Organic
Enoteca Turi
Hunan
The Campaner
Chelsea Br Rd
Riccardo's
Lucio
Mriya
Redcliffe Gardens
Finborough Road
Rabbit
Stanley's
Sticks 'n' Sushi
Phat Phuc
King's Road
Hagen Chelsea
Ziani's
The Ivy Asia,
The Ivy Chelsea Garden
CHELSEA
Royal
Hospital
Aglio e Olio
Fulham Road
VQ
Haché
Huo
Oka
28-50, The Cadogan Arms
Made in Italy
Big Easy
Brinkley's
WEST
BROMPTON
The Atlas
Brompton
Cemetry
The Surprise
Gordon Ramsay
Bluebird
Diba
Chelsea Embankment
River Thames
arwood Arms
No. Fifty Cheyne
Cheyne Walk
Chicama
La Famiglia
Myrtle
Medlar
Frantoio
The Fox & Pheasant
FULHAM
BROADWAY
Battersea Bridge Road
Albert Bridge Road
Battersea
Park
Fulham Road
est Mangal
Kitchen
Augustine Kitchen
FULHAM
Santa Maria
New King's Road
Chelsea
Harbour
BATTERSEA
Price Of Wales Drive
Battersea Pk Rd

MAP 7 – NOTTING HILL & BAYSWATER

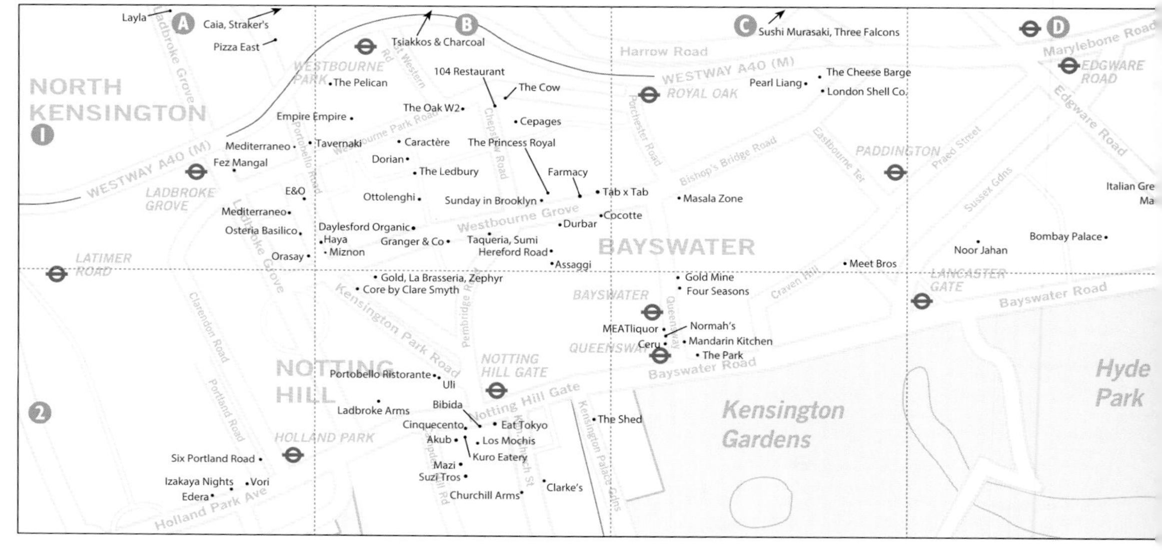

MAP 8 – HAMMERSMITH & CHISWICK

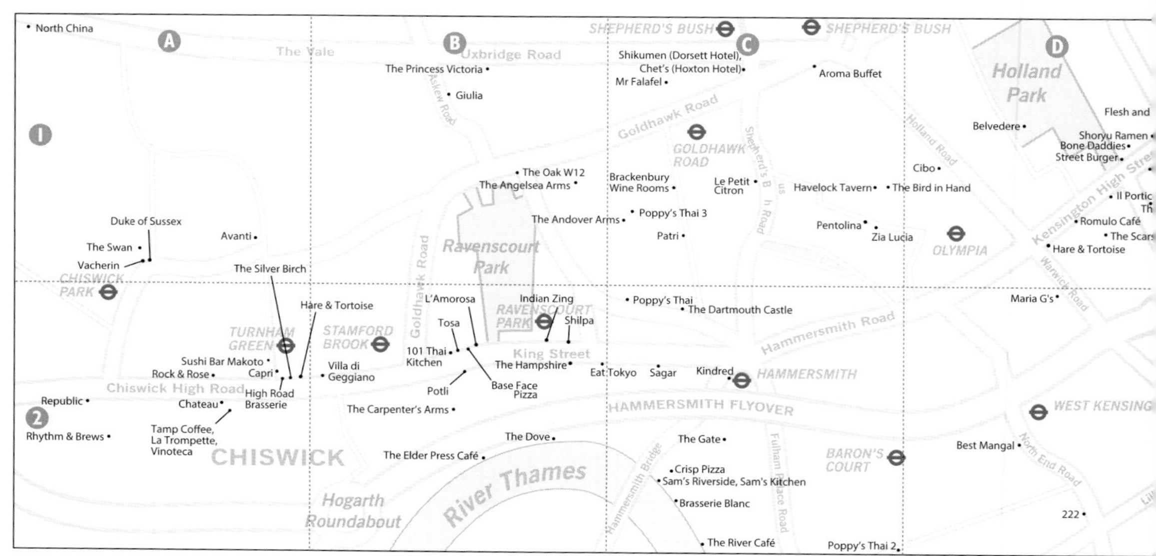

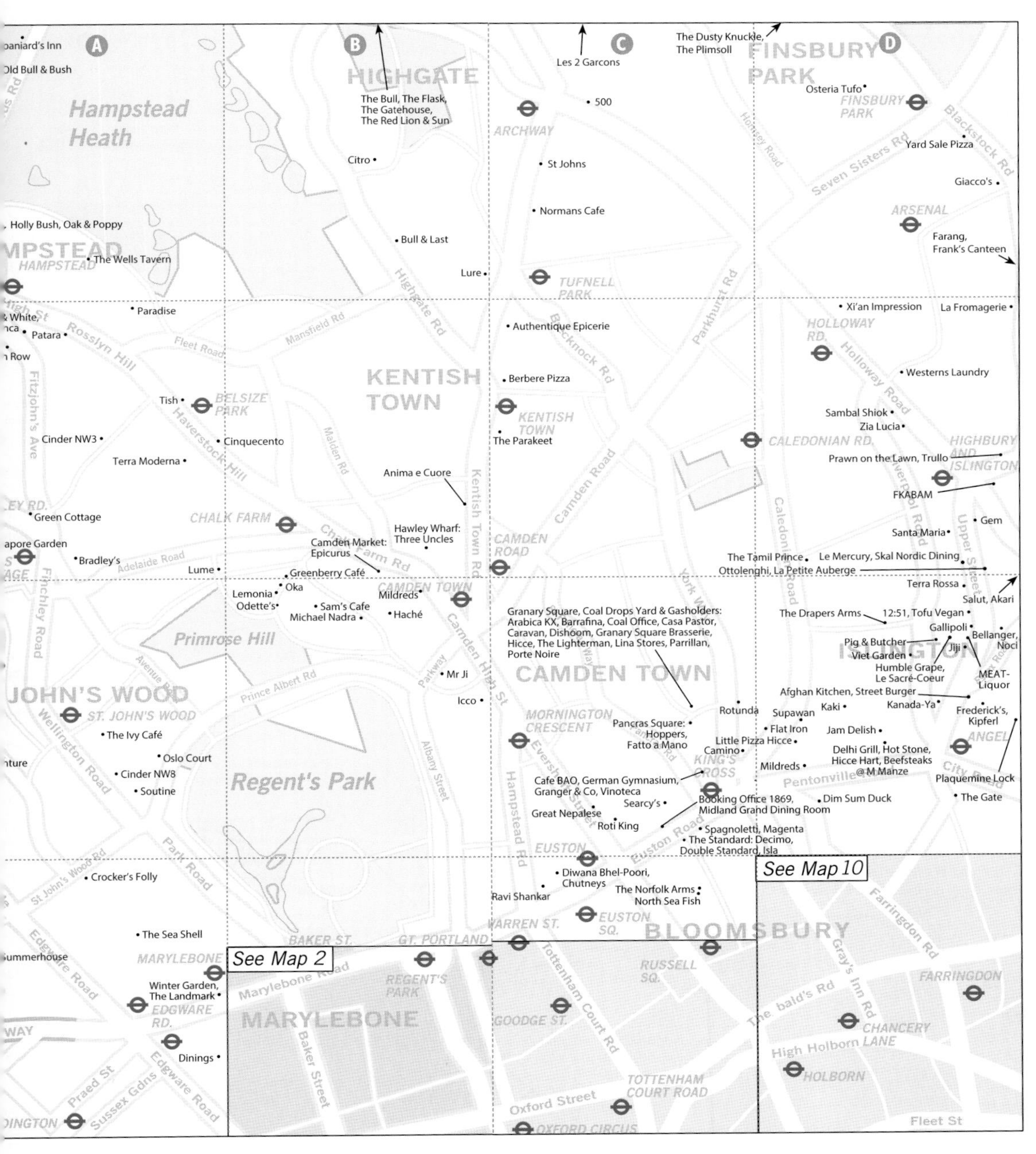
Hampstead Heath
HIGHGATE
KENTISH TOWN
FINSBURY PARK
HOLLOWAY RD.
CAMDEN TOWN
Primrose Hill
Regent's Park
ISLINGTON
BLOOMSBURY
MARYLEBONE
See Map 2
See Map 10
The Bull, The Flask, The Gatehouse, The Red Lion & Sun
Les 2 Garcons
The Dusty Knuckle, The Plimsoll
Osteria Tufo
500
Citro
St Johns
Yard Sale Pizza
Giacco's
Normans Cafe
Holly Bush, Oak & Poppy
Bull & Last
Farang, Frank's Canteen
The Wells Tavern
Lure
Paradise
Xi'an Impression
La Fromagerie
Patara
Authentique Epicerie
Berbere Pizza
Westerns Laundry
Tish
Sambal Shiok
Zia Lucia
Cinder NW3
Cinquecento
The Parakeet
Prawn on the Lawn, Trullo
Terra Moderna
Anima e Cuore
FKABAM
Green Cottage
Hawley Wharf: Three Uncles
Gem
Camden Market: Epicurus
Santa Maria
Bradley's
The Tamil Prince
Le Mercury, Skal Nordic Dining
Lume
Greenberry Café
Ottolenghi, La Petite Auberge
Oka
Terra Rossa
Lemonia
Mildreds
Salut, Akari
Odette's
Sam's Cafe
The Drapers Arms
12:51, Tofu Vegan
Michael Nadra
Haché
Granary Square, Coal Drops Yard & Gasholders: Arabica KX, Barrafina, Coal Office, Casa Pastor, Caravan, Dishoom, Granary Square Brasserie, Hicce, The Lighterman, Lina Stores, Parrillan, Porte Noire
Gallipoli
Bellanger, Noci
Pig & Butcher
Jiji
Viet Garden
Humble Grape, Le Sacré-Coeur
MEAT-Liquor
Mr Ji
Afghan Kitchen, Street Burger
Icco
Kaki
Kanada-Ya
Rotunda
Frederick's, Kipferl
Supawan
The Ivy Café
Pancras Square: Hoppers, Fatto a Mano
Flat Iron
Jam Delish
Little Pizza Hicce
Camino
Delhi Grill, Hot Stone, Hicce Hart, Beefsteaks @M Manze
Oslo Court
Mildreds
Cinder NW8
Plaquemine Lock
Cafe BAO, German Gymnasium, Granger & Co, Vinoteca
Soutine
Booking Office 1869, Midland Grand Dining Room
Dim Sum Duck
The Gate
Searcy's
Great Nepalese
Roti King
Spagnoletti, Magenta
The Standard: Decimo, Double Standard, Isla
Crocker's Folly
Diwana Bhel-Poori, Chutneys
The Norfolk Arms
North Sea Fish
Ravi Shankar
The Sea Shell
Winter Garden, The Landmark
Dinings

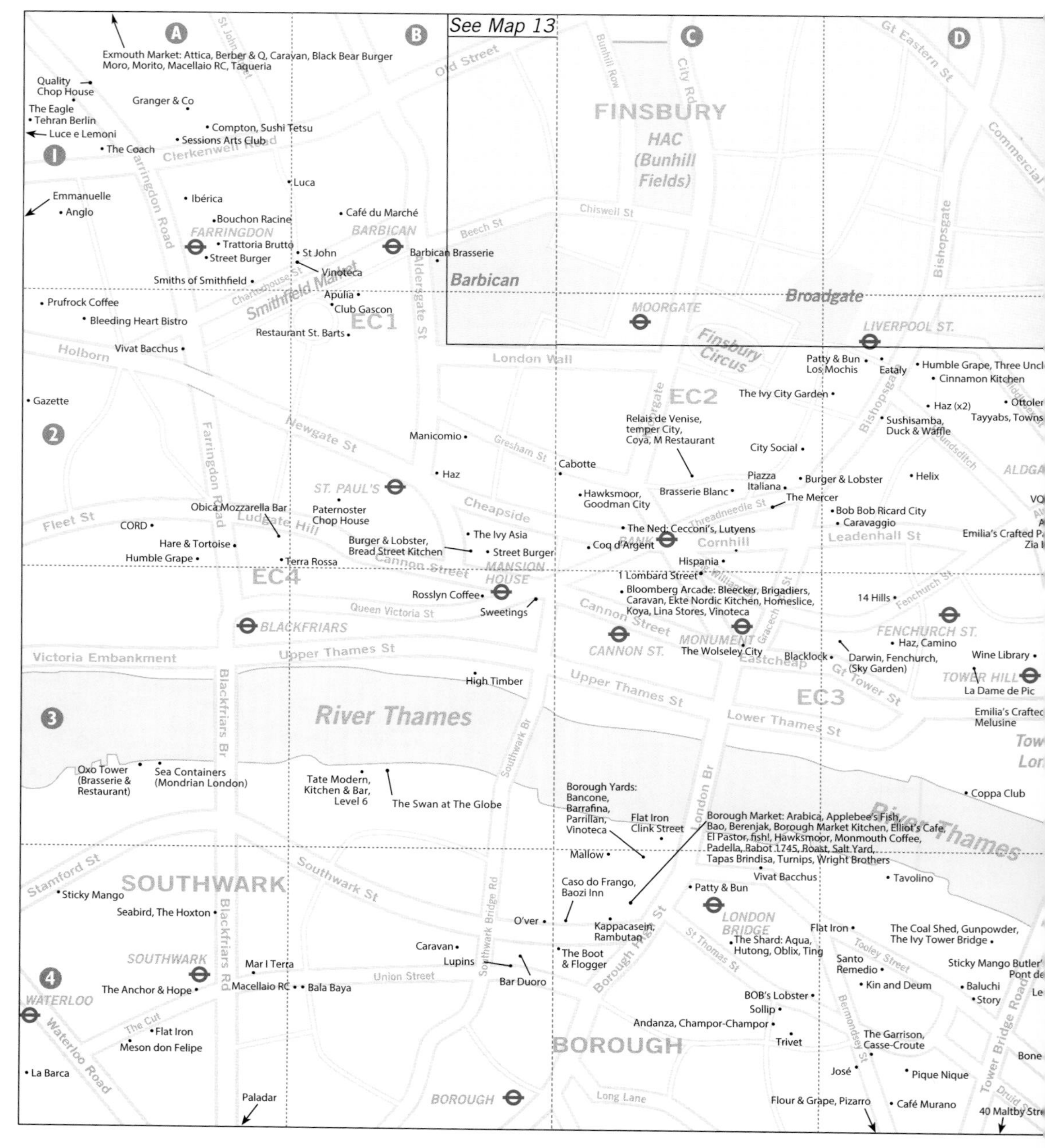

See Map 13
A
B
C
D
1
2
3
4
Exmouth Market: Attica, Berber & Q, Caravan, Black Bear Burger
Moro, Morito, Macellaio RC, Taqueria
Quality Chop House
Granger & Co
The Eagle
Tehran Berlin
Luce e Lemoni
Compton, Sushi Tetsu
Sessions Arts Club
The Coach
Clerkenwell Road
Old Street
Gt Eastern St
Commercial
FINSBURY
HAC (Bunhill Fields)
Bunhill Row
City Rd
Luca
Emmanuelle
Anglo
Ibérica
Bouchon Racine
Café du Marché
Farringdon Road
FARRINGDON
BARBICAN
Trattoria Brutto
Street Burger
St John
Vinoteca
Barbican Brasserie
Smiths of Smithfield
Smithfield Market
Chiswell St
Beech St
Bishopsgate
Barbican
Broadgate
MOORGATE
LIVERPOOL ST.
Apulia
Club Gascon
EC1
Aldersgate St
Prufrock Coffee
Bleeding Heart Bistro
Restaurant St. Barts
Holborn
Vivat Bacchus
London Wall
Finsbury Circus
Patty & Bun
Los Mochis
Eataly
Humble Grape, Three Uncl
Cinnamon Kitchen
The Ivy City Garden
EC2
Gazette
Haz (x2)
Ottolen
Tayyabs, Towns
Sushisamba, Duck & Waffle
Relais de Venise, temper City, Coya, M Restaurant
City Social
Newgate St
Manicomio
Gresham St
Cabotte
Haz
ALDGA
Helix
Piazza Italiana
Burger & Lobster
ST. PAUL'S
Hawksmoor, Goodman City
Brasserie Blanc
The Mercer
Obica Mozzarella Bar
Paternoster Chop House
Cheapside
Bob Bob Ricard City
Caravaggio
Fleet St
CORD
Ludgate Hill
Threadneedle St
Leadenhall St
Emilia's Crafted P
Zia L
The Ned: Cecconi's, Lutyens
Cornhill
The Ivy Asia
Hare & Tortoise
Burger & Lobster, Bread Street Kitchen
Street Burger
Coq d'Argent
Humble Grape
Terra Rossa
Hispania
Cannon Street
MANSION HOUSE
EC4
1 Lombard Street
Bloomberg Arcade: Bleecker, Brigadiers, Caravan, Ekte Nordic Kitchen, Homeslice, Koya, Lina Stores, Vinoteca
14 Hills
Fenchurch St
Rosslyn Coffee
Sweetings
Queen Victoria St
Cannon Street
BLACKFRIARS
MONUMENT
FENCHURCH ST.
Haz, Camino
CANNON ST.
The Wolseley City
Victoria Embankment
Upper Thames St
Blacklock
Darwin, Fenchurch, (Sky Garden)
Wine Library
Eastcheap
TOWER HILL
La Dame de Pic
High Timber
Upper Thames St
EC3
Gt Tower St
River Thames
Lower Thames St
Emilia's Crafted
Melusine
Blackfriars Br
Southwark Br
Oxo Tower (Brasserie & Restaurant)
Sea Containers (Mondrian London)
Tate Modern, Kitchen & Bar, Level 6
The Swan at The Globe
Borough Yards: Bancone, Barrafina, Parrillan, Vinoteca
Flat Iron Clink Street
London Br
Borough Market: Arabica, Applebee's Fish, Bao, Berenjak, Borough Market Kitchen, Elliot's Cafe, El Pastor, fish!, Hawksmoor, Monmouth Coffee, Padella, Rabot 1745, Roast, Salt Yard, Tapas Brindisa, Turnips, Wright Brothers
River Thames
Coppa Club
Mallow
Stamford St
SOUTHWARK
Southwark St
Vivat Bacchus
Tavolino
Sticky Mango
Caso do Frango, Baozi Inn
Patty & Bun
Seabird, The Hoxton
O'ver
Kappacasein, Rambutan
LONDON BRIDGE
Flat Iron
The Coal Shed, Gunpowder, The Ivy Tower Bridge
The Shard: Aqua, Hutong, Oblix, Ting
Caravan
The Boot & Flogger
Southwark Bridge Rd
Borough High St
St Thomas St
Tooley Street
Lupins
Santo Remedio
Sticky Mango Butler'
Pont de
SOUTHWARK
Mar I Terra
Bar Duoro
Union Street
Kin and Deum
Baluchi
Story
The Anchor & Hope
Macellaio RC
Bala Baya
Blackfriars Rd
BOB's Lobster
WATERLOO
Sollip
Waterloo Road
The Cut
Flat Iron
Meson don Felipe
Andanza, Champor-Champor
Trivet
BOROUGH
Bermondsey St
The Garrison, Casse-Croute
Tower Bridge Road
José
Pique Nique
La Barca
Paladar
BOROUGH
Long Lane
Flour & Grape, Pizarro
Café Murano
40 Maltby Stre
Druid St

MAP 11 – SOUTH LONDON (& FULHAM)

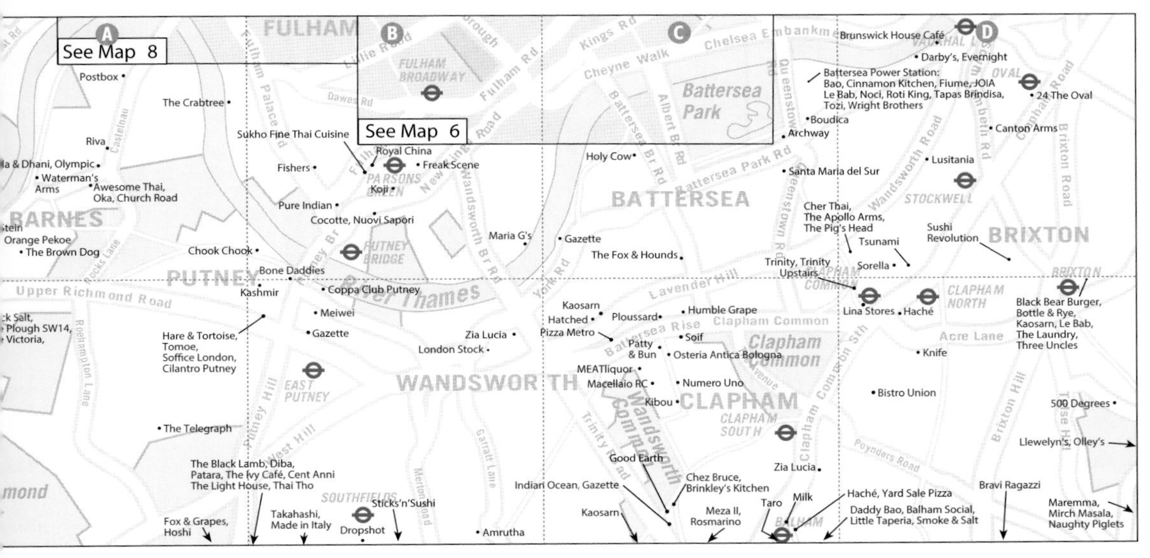

MAP 12 – EAST END & DOCKLANDS

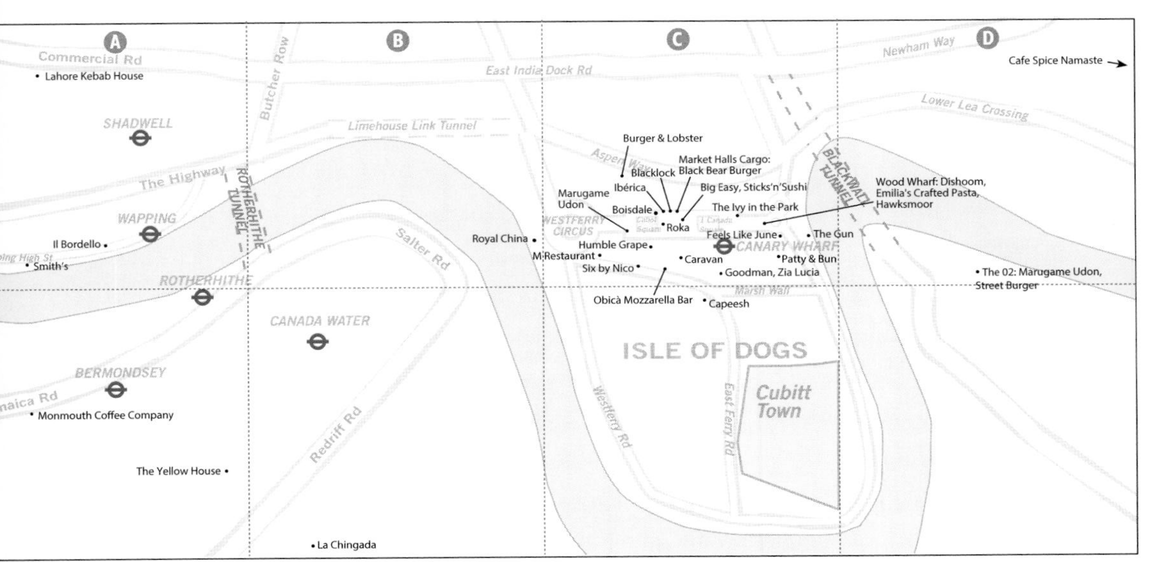

MAP 13 – SHOREDITCH & BETHNAL GREEN

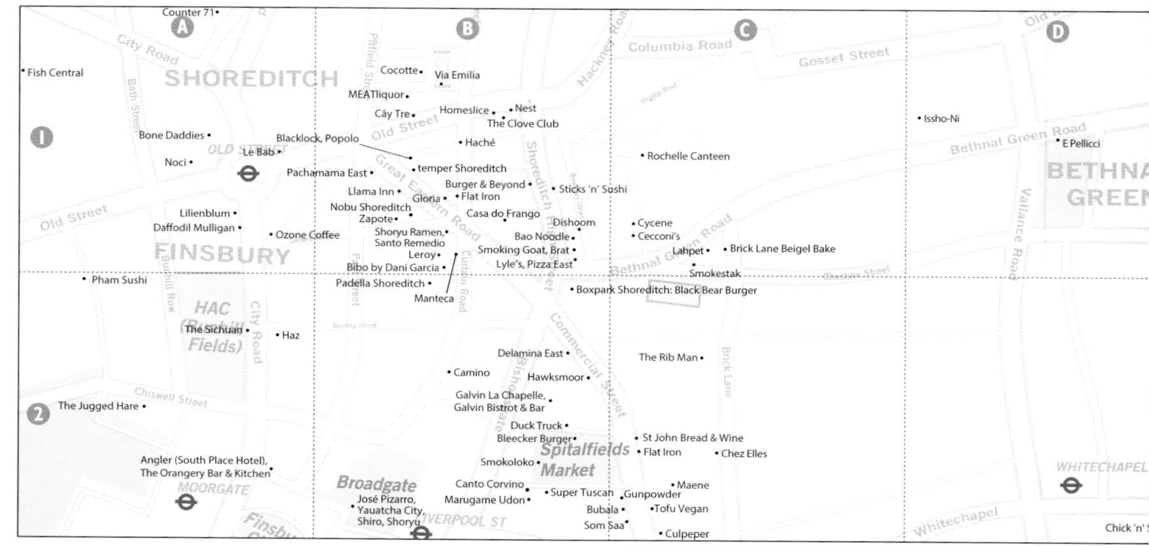

MAP 14 – EAST LONDON

UK SURVEY RESULTS AND TOP SCORERS

Restaurant Twenty Two, Cambridge

Lympstone Manor, Exmouth

Woven, Coworth Park, Ascot

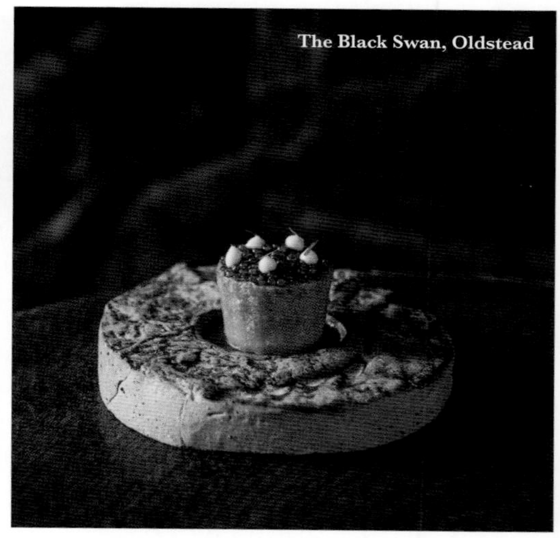
The Black Swan, Oldstead

TOP SCORERS

All restaurants whose food ratings is 5; plus restaurants whose formula price is £60+ with a food rating of 4.

Price	Restaurant	Ratings
£430	Ynyshir Restaurant and Rooms *(Eglwys Fach)*	433
£320	Midsummer House *(Cambridge)*	433
£300	L'Enclume *(Cartmel)*	545
	Aulis at L'Enclume *(Cartmel)*	554
	Raby Hunt *(Summerhouse)*	432
£270	Moor Hall *(Aughton)*	544
£250	Waterside Inn *(Bray)*	445
£230	The Glenturret Lalique Restaurant *(Crieff)*	444
£220	Solstice *(Newcastle upon Tyne)*	544
£210	Outlaw's New Road *(Port Isaac)*	544
	The Black Swan *(Oldstead)*	433
	Sosban & The Old Butcher's *(Menai Bridge)*	432
£200	Lympstone Manor *(Exmouth)*	544
	Mana *(Manchester)*	544
	Restaurant Sat Bains *(Nottingham)*	443
£190	Gidleigh Park *(Chagford)*	445
£180	House of Tides *(Newcastle upon Tyne)*	544
	Latymer, Pennyhill Park Hotel *(Bagshot)*	544
	Paul Ainsworth at No6 *(Padstow)*	544
	Shaun Rankin at Grantley Hall *(Grantley)*	544
	Condita *(Edinburgh)*	543
	Woven by Adam Smith at Coworth Park *(Ascot)*	444
£170	Pine *(East Wallhouses)*	544
	ChefsTable at TRUEfoods *(Melmerby)*	553
	Number One, Balmoral Hotel *(Edinburgh)*	444
	The Forest Side *(Grasmere)*	444
	Morston Hall *(Morston)*	434
	Roots *(York)*	434
	Home at Penarth *(Penarth)*	443
£160	Hjem *(Wall)*	544
	The Cellar *(Anstruther)*	544
	Cail Bruich *(Glasgow)*	553
	Meadowsweet *(Holt)*	543
	Sorrel *(Dorking)*	533
	Gravetye Manor *(East Grinstead)*	445
	The Bow Room Restaurant *(York)*	444
	The Whitebrook, Restaurant with Rooms *(Whitebrook)*	433
	The Olive Tree, Queensberry Hotel *(Bath)*	432
£150	Andrew Fairlie, Gleneagles Hotel *(Auchterarder)*	554
	The Kitchin *(Edinburgh)*	534
	Restaurant Martin Wishart *(Edinburgh)*	553
	Loch Bay Restaurant *(Stein)*	543
	Hambleton Hall *(Hambleton)*	445
	Àclèaf at Boringdon Hall *(Plympton)*	434
	Annwn *(Lawrenny)*	453
	Restaurant Hywel Jones by Lucknam Park *(Colerne)*	433
£140	Adam Reid at The French *(Manchester)*	444
	Grace & Savour *(Hampton-in-Arden)*	444
	Allium at Askham Hall *(Penrith)*	434
	Ugly Butterfly *(St Ives)*	434
	The Nut Tree Inn *(Murcott)*	433
£130	Northcote *(Langho)*	544
	The Three Chimneys *(Dunvegan)*	544
	The Wilderness *(Birmingham)*	544
	SY23 *(Aberystwyth)*	543
	Pensons at Netherwood Estate *(Stoke Bliss)*	434
	Aizle *(Edinburgh)*	443
	Alchemilla *(Nottingham)*	443
	Lake Road Kitchen *(Ambleside)*	433
£120	Paris House *(Woburn)*	545
	Adam's *(Birmingham)*	553
	Etch *(Brighton)*	543
	Etive *(Oban)*	543
	Roski *(Liverpool)*	543
	The Hare Inn Restaurant *(Scawton)*	543
	Salt *(Stratford upon Avon)*	533
	Restaurant Roots *(Southbourne)*	542
	Artichoke *(Amersham)*	444
	Tyddyn Llan *(Llandrillo)*	444
	Where The Light Gets In *(Stockport)*	444
	Cleaver & Wake *(Nottingham)*	434
	Timberyard *(Edinburgh)*	434
	Furna *(Withdean)*	443
	The Fernery, Grove of Narberth *(Dyfed)*	443
	The Little Fish Market *(Brighton)*	443
	Toffs *(Solihull)*	443
	Haar *(St Andrews)*	433
	Harborne Kitchen *(Birmingham)*	433
	Rafters *(Sheffield)*	433
	Unalome by Graeme Cheevers *(Glasgow)*	433
£110	The Muddlers Club *(Belfast)*	544
	Fhior *(Edinburgh)*	543
	Old Stamp House *(Ambleside)*	543
	Outlaw's Fish Kitchen *(Port Isaac)*	543
	Restaurant Twenty Two *(Cambridge)*	543
	The Peat Inn *(Cupar)*	543
	The Shore *(Penzance)*	543
	Vanderlyle *(Cambridge)*	543

Price	Restaurant	Rating
	64 Degrees *(Brighton)*	542
	Le Champignon Sauvage *(Cheltenham)*	542
	The Seafood Ristorante *(St Andrews)*	435
	The Art School *(Liverpool)*	454
	Heron *(Edinburgh)*	444
	Longueville Manor *(Jersey)*	444
	Purnells *(Birmingham)*	444
	Simpsons *(Birmingham)*	444
	The Box Tree *(Ilkley)*	444
	Kintsu *(Colchester)*	453
	L'Ortolan *(Shinfield)*	443
	The Royal Oak *(Whatcote)*	443

Price	Restaurant	Rating
£100	The Small Holding *(Goudhurst)*	544
	The Sportsman *(Seasalter)*	544
	Beach House *(Oxwich)*	534
	Lumière *(Cheltenham)*	553
	Hide & Fox *(Saltwood)*	543
	Joro *(Sheffield)*	543
	Osip *(Bruton)*	543
	So-lo *(Aughton)*	543
	The Dining Room, Beaverbrook *(Leatherhead)*	543
	The Fordwich Arms *(Fordwich)*	543
	The Neptune *(Old Hunstanton)*	543
	White Swan at Fence *(Fence)*	543
	Bulrush *(Bristol)*	533
	Bohemia *(Jersey)*	454
	Coombeshead Farm *(Lewannick)*	444
	Coast *(Saundersfoot)*	434
	Elderflower *(Lymington)*	443
	Fishmore Hall *(Ludlow)*	443
	Harry's Place *(Great Gonerby)*	443
	Henrock *(Windermere)*	443
	Home *(Leeds)*	443
	The Angel *(Hetton)*	443
	The Feathered Nest Inn *(Nether Westcote)*	443
	Seafood Restaurant *(Padstow)*	433

Price	Restaurant	Rating
£90	Stark *(Broadstairs)*	544
	Upstairs by Tom Shepherd *(Lichfield)*	544
	John's House *(Mountsorrel)*	543
	Wheelers Oyster Bar *(Whitstable)*	543
	The Poet *(Matfield)*	542
	Ninth Wave *(Fionnphort)*	454
	Freemasons at Wiswell *(Wiswell)*	444
	Melton's *(York)*	444
	Read's *(Faversham)*	444
	Rocpool *(Inverness)*	444
	The Greyhound *(Beaconsfield)*	444
	The Ingham Swan *(Ingham)*	444
	The Loch & The Tyne *(Old Windsor)*	444
	The Sir Charles Napier *(Chinnor)*	444
	Vero Gusto *(Sheffield)*	444
	La Table d'Alix at The Plough *(Great Haseley)*	434
	MUSU *(Manchester)*	434
	The Angel Inn *(Stoke-by-Nayland)*	434
	21 *(Newcastle upon Tyne)*	443
	HRiSHi, Gilpin Lodge *(Windermere)*	443
	La Chouette *(Dinton)*	443
	La Popote *(Marton)*	443
	Orwells *(Shiplake)*	443
	Pentonbridge Inn *(Penton)*	443
	The Beehive *(White Waltham)*	443
	The Old Bank *(Westerham)*	443
	Catch at The Old Fish Market *(Weymouth)*	433
	Heaney's *(Cardiff)*	433
	Inver Restaurant *(Strachur)*	433
	Oxheart *(Long Compton)*	433
	The Newport *(Newport On Tay)*	433
	The Old Bank Bistro *(Snettisham)*	433
	One Fish Street *(Saint Ives)*	432

Price	Restaurant	Rating
£80	The French Table *(Surbiton)*	543
	Vaasu by Atul Kochhar *(Marlow)*	543
	Verveine Fishmarket Restaurant *(Milford-on-Sea)*	543
	Wilson's *(Bristol)*	543
	Arras *(York)*	533
	The Bridge Arms *(Bridge)*	533
	Prithvi *(Cheltenham)*	542
	Portmeirion Hotel *(Portmeirion)*	435
	Old Downton Lodge *(Ludlow)*	444
	Roux at Skindles *(Taplow)*	444
	The Little Chartroom *(Edinburgh)*	444
	The Pig & Pastry *(York)*	444
	The Pipe & Glass *(Beverley)*	444
	Wild Flor *(Brighton)*	444
	Rafters at Riverside House *(Ashford-in-the-Water)*	434
	The Barn at Moor Hall *(Aughton)*	434
	Jew's House Restaurant *(Lincoln)*	453
	33 The Homend *(Ledbury)*	443
	Black & Green *(Barnt Green)*	443
	Crab Shed *(Salcombe)*	443
	Dining Room *(Rock)*	443
	Gem 42 *(Newport)*	443
	Peace & Loaf *(Newcastle upon Tyne)*	443
	Purslane *(Edinburgh)*	443
	Rogan & Co *(Cartmel)*	443
	Roger Hickman's *(Norwich)*	443
	Sindhu *(Marlow)*	443
	The Bailiwick *(Englefield Green)*	443
	The Clockspire *(Milborne Port)*	443
	The Seahorse *(Dartmouth)*	443
	The Westwood Restaurant *(Beverley)*	443
	Thomas by Tom Simmons *(Cardiff)*	443
	Benedicts *(Norwich)*	433
	Celentano's *(Glasgow)*	433
	Folium *(Birmingham)*	433
	Henry's Restaurant *(Bath)*	433
	Red Lion Freehouse *(East Chisenbury)*	433
	The Coach *(Marlow)*	433
	The Olive Branch *(Clipsham)*	433
	Gingerman *(Brighton)*	442
	5 North Street *(Winchcombe)*	432
	The Unruly Pig *(Bromeswell)*	422

Price	Restaurant	Rating
£70	Maison Bleue *(Bury St Edmunds)*	544
	Opheem *(Birmingham)*	544
	Forage Kitchen *(Rougham)*	543

	Restaurant	Score
	Tallow *(Southborough)*	543
	Thompson's *(Newport)*	543
	Pierhouse Hotel *(Port Appin)*	445
	Pea Porridge *(Bury St Edmunds)*	454
	Stones *(Matlock)*	444
	The Parsons Table *(Arundel)*	444
	World Service *(Nottingham)*	444
	Shell Bay *(Studland)*	434
	The Horse Guards Inn *(Tillington)*	434
	The Lake Isle *(Uppingham)*	434
	Whitstable Oyster Fishery Co. *(Whitstable)*	434
	Odos *(Barnet)*	453
	1921 Angel Hill *(Bury St Edmunds)*	443
	Catch *(Plymouth)*	443
	Eileen's *(Ampthill)*	443
	Hawkyns by Atul Kochhar *(Amersham)*	443
	Hitchen's Barn *(Oakham)*	443
	Kentish Hare *(Bidborough)*	443
	Kysty *(Ambleside)*	443
	Spiny Lobster *(Bristol)*	443
	The Vanilla Pod *(Marlow)*	443
	Tolcarne Inn *(Penzance)*	443
	Upstairs at Landrace *(Bath)*	443
	Wedgwood *(Edinburgh)*	443
	Yalbury Cottage *(Lower Bockhampton)*	443
	Chapter One *(Locksbottom)*	433
	Duke Street Market *(Liverpool)*	433
	Fig Tree *(Plymouth)*	433
	Glebe House *(Southleigh)*	433
	Kota *(Porthleven)*	433
	Scran & Scallie *(Edinburgh)*	433
	Smith's Brasserie *(Ongar)*	433
	Star Inn *(Sparsholt)*	433
	The Alice Hawthorn *(Nun Monkton)*	433
	The Dog & Gun *(Skelton)*	433
	The Dog at Wingham *(Wingham)*	433
	The Pack Horse *(Hayfield)*	433
	The Seaview Restaurant *(Saltburn)*	433
	The Suffolk (fka L'Escargot sur Mer) *(Aldeburgh)*	433
	Arthur *(Belper)*	442
	Butley Orford Oysterage *(Orford)*	432
	Terre à Terre *(Brighton)*	432
	The Anchor *(Ripley)*	432
£60	Edinbane Lodge *(Edinbane)*	544
	The Parkers Arms *(Newton-in-Bowland)*	544
	Crab House Café *(Weymouth)*	543
	Prévost at Haycock *(Wansford)*	543
	Leaping Hare Vineyard *(Stanton)*	435
	Shibden Mill Inn *(Halifax)*	454
	Chapters *(Hay-on-Wye)*	444
	Noble *(Holywood)*	444
	Ondine *(Edinburgh)*	444
	Paco Tapas *(Bristol)*	444
	Riddle & Finns *(Brighton)*	444
	Riddle & Finns On The Beach *(Brighton)*	444
	The Cartford Inn *(Little Eccleston)*	444
	The Fox & Goose *(Fressingfield)*	444
	The Rocket Store *(Boscastle)*	444
	The Swine That Dines *(Leeds)*	444
	Crabshakk Botanics *(Glasgow)*	434
	Kendells Bistro *(Leeds)*	434
	Lyzzick Hall Country House Hotel *(Keswick)*	434
	Nick's at Port of Menteith *(Port of Menteith)*	434
	Silver Darling *(Aberdeen)*	434
	The Three Fishes *(Whalley)*	434
	Fat Olives *(Emsworth)*	453
	Bilash *(Wolverhampton)*	443
	Indian Essence *(Petts Wood)*	443
	Jon & Fernanda's *(Auchterarder)*	443
	Kala *(Manchester)*	443
	La Boheme *(Lymm)*	443
	Noto *(Edinburgh)*	443
	Prawn on the Lawn *(Padstow)*	443
	Pythouse Kitchen Garden *(West Hatch)*	443
	Restormel Kitchen *(Lostwithiel)*	443
	Rick Stein *(Winchester)*	443
	Root *(Bristol)*	443
	Skosh *(York)*	443
	The Alan *(Manchester)*	443
	The Black Bull Inn *(Sedbergh)*	443
	The Inn at Welland *(Welland)*	443
	The Jolly Cricketers *(Seer Green)*	443
	The Wild Mushroom *(Westfield)*	443
	Tytherleigh Arms *(Tytherleigh)*	443
	Watson & Walpole *(Framlingham)*	443
	YU *(Copster Green)*	443
	Zhang Ji *(Oxford)*	443
	Beckford Canteen *(Bath)*	433
	Clay's Hyderabadi Kitchen *(Reading)*	433
	Clos du Marquis *(Stockbridge)*	433
	Coarse *(Durham)*	433
	Crabshakk *(Glasgow)*	433
	Fish and Forest *(York)*	433
	Muse Brasserie *(Cheltenham)*	433
	No 7 Fish Bistro & Wine Bar *(Torquay)*	433
	Pasture *(Cardiff)*	433
	The Black Bear Inn *(Usk)*	433
	The Easy Fish Company *(Stockport)*	433
	The Felin Fach Griffin *(Brecon)*	433
	The Gaff *(Abergavenny)*	433
	The Moorings *(Blakeney)*	433
	The Scallop Shell *(Bath)*	433
	The Walrus *(Shrewsbury)*	433
	Trakol *(Gateshead)*	433
	The Shed at Porthgain *(Porthgain)*	423
	Augustus *(Taunton)*	442
	The Perfect Match *(Sale)*	442
	COR *(Bristol)*	432
	Fishmarket *(Edinburgh)*	432
	Goodfellows *(Wells)*	432
	Lasan *(Birmingham)*	432
	Marmo *(Bristol)*	432
	Provenance Brix + Mortar *(Whittlesford)*	432
	Samphire *(Whitstable)*	432
	Ee-Usk (Seafood Restaurant) *(Oban)*	422
	The Mount by Glynn Purnell *(Henley-in-Arden)*	422

£50	Crocadon *(Saltash)*	544
	Engine Social Dining *(Sowerby Bridge)*	544
	Angela's *(Margate)*	543
	Socius *(Burnham Market)*	543
	Kushi-ya *(Nottingham)*	533
£40	Manifest *(Liverpool)*	543
	Ebi Sushi *(Derby)*	542
	The Cod's Scallops *(Wollaton)*	542
£30	Riley's Fish Shack *(Tynemouth)*	545
	Paesano Pizza *(Glasgow)*	543
	Beefy Boys *(Hereford)*	533
	Dungeness Snack Shack *(Dungeness)*	532
	Anstruther Fish Bar *(Anstruther)*	522

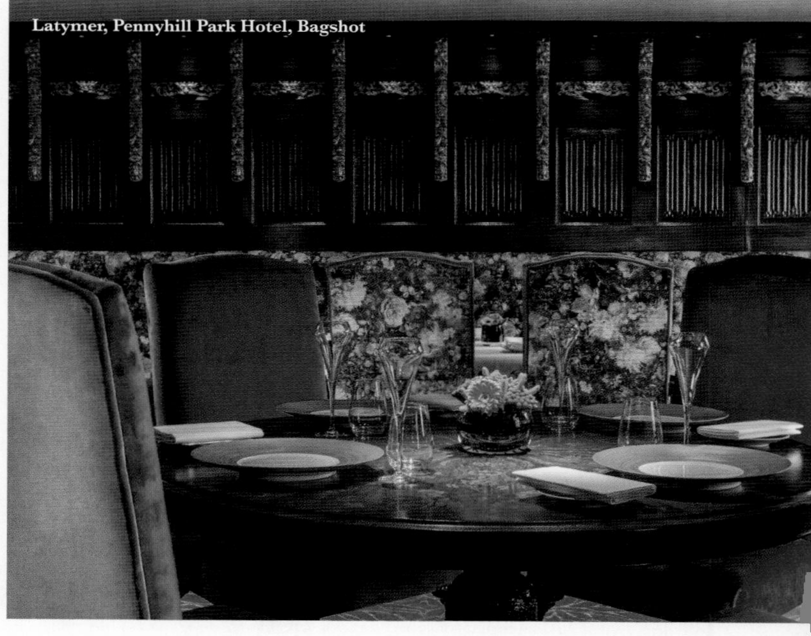
Latymer, Pennyhill Park Hotel, Bagshot

UK DIRECTORY

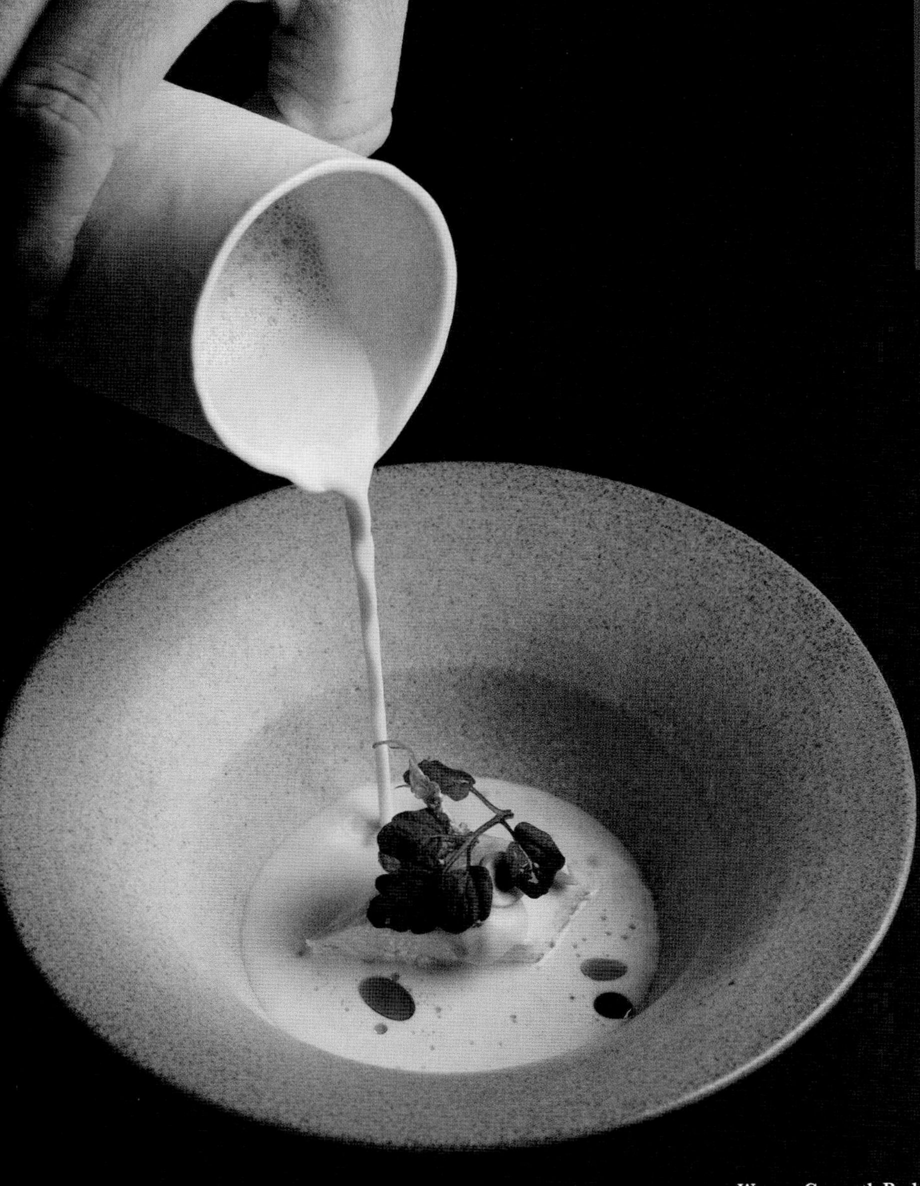

Woven, Coworth Park, Ascot

UK DIRECTORY

ABERAERON, CEREDIGION 4-3C

HARBOURMASTER £58 343

2 QUAY PDE SA46 0BT 01545 570755

"Situated at the end of the quay in Aberaeron, this well commented-on converted harbourmaster's house is now solely dedicated to hotel and restaurant service, dispensing with the bar area which drew many people to it" before its takeover by the Cardigan-based FlatRock hospitality group. While that might seem like a worrying development (one which has "somewhat reduced the atmosphere"), for "excellent-quality fresh fish and seafood it is still worth the visit". / harbour-master.com; hmaberaeron; Mon-Sun 9 pm.

ABERDEEN, ABERDEENSHIRE 9-2D

MOONFISH CAFE 333

9 CORRECTION WYND
AB10 1HP 01224 644166

This "cosy restaurant with welcoming staff", next to the 12th-century kirk of St Nicholas, has done sterling service for two decades "serving great food with the emphasis on fish". Chef Brian McLeish, a MasterChef finalist in 2014, presides over a well-thought-out menu that runs from two to four courses. / moonfishcafe.co.uk; moonfishcafeaberdeen; Tue-Sat 11.30 pm.

SILVER DARLING £62 434

NORTH PIER HOUSE, POCRA QUAY
AB11 5DQ 01224 576229

"One of the best views you will get, watching the comings and goings of boats in Aberdeen harbour," combines with "excellent fish", "beautifully cooked and presented" at this venue set on top of the old Customs House by the water. The vistas are "especially amazing at night", so "try for a window table" to make the best of your meal here. / thesilverdarling.co.uk; thesilverdarlingrestaurant; Mon-Fri 8.30 pm, Sat 9 pm, Sun 8 pm.

ABERGAVENNY, MONMOUTHSHIRE 2-1A

THE ANGEL HOTEL £82 333

15 CROSS ST NP7 5EN 01873 857121

This classy coaching inn not far from the English border is a real all-rounder: whether you want "great cocktails" in the bar, an "amazing" afternoon tea, or a prix-fixe meal, the "interesting and ever-changing menu" is "always cooked with skill". There are two local siblings: the mostly vegetarian The Chapel, a five-minute walk away, and acclaimed restaurant The Walnut Tree, ten minutes away by car. / angelabergavenny.com; the_angel_abergavenny; Sun-Thu 11 pm, Fri & Sat 11.30 pm.

BEAN & BREAD £15 334

36 LION STREET NP7 5PE 01873 778575

This "stylish café" – directly inspired by the coffee culture experienced by founder Jess Fletcher in New Zealand – is a "lovely spot for brunch and always the best coffee". There's a short menu of plant-based goodies, and on Friday and Saturday evenings wine and cocktails are served. / beanandbread.co.uk; beanandbread_; Mon-Sun 5 pm.

THE CHAPEL £15 333

MARKET STREET
NP7 5SD 01873 736430

"Locally sourced fresh produce is teased into interesting dishes" at this indie arts-centre café, with a menu of inexpensive bistro fare, alongside coffee and bakes. / artshopandchapel.co.uk; theartshopandchapel; Tue-Sat 4 pm.

THE GAFF £65 433

4 THE COURTYARD, LION STREET
NP7 5PE 01873 739310

The success of its younger Bath sibling is helping to bring more attention to this bright, high-roofed space converted from three sheds and sitting in a courtyard in the town centre. Owners Danielle Phillips and Dan Saunders were previously front of house and head chef at The Walnut Tree and their "tapas-style" small plates are "unfailingly brilliant – food that smacks you in the face and service that makes you feel like you're royalty". / thegaffrestaurant.co.uk; thegaffinbath; Wed-Sat 8.30 pm, Sun 2 pm.

ABERYSTWYTH, CEREDIGION 4-3C

SY23 £135 543

2 PIER STREET SY23 2LJ 01970 615935

"Remote but worth the journey" (at least "if you are lucky enough to get a table") – Nathan Davies's industrially styled venue has a "great many similarities to Ynyshir, where he used to work" and is "going from strength to strength". The lively, moodily lit dining room delivers an "excellent tasting menu" strong on foraging, fermenting and charcoal grills, but there's also an "outside area serving barbecued lighter snacks". / sy23restaurant.com; sy23restaurant; Wed-Sat 11 pm.

ULTRACOMIDA £56 33

31 PIER ST SY23 2LN 01970 630686

"Genuine Spanish food" and a "long list of great Spanish wines" are available at this restaurant/bar that developed out of a deli founded in 2001 by Paul Grimwood & Shumana Palit, moved into wholesaling, and during the pandemic found a new focus on wine. They have a second branch in Narberth and two tapas bars in Cardiff (Curado and Vermut). / ultracomida.com; ultracomida; Mon-Wed 3 pm, Thu-Sat 8.30 pm.

ACHILTIBUIE, ROSS-SHIRE 9-1B

SUMMER ISLES HOTEL 43

IV26 2YG 01854 622282

"Unbeatable fresh fish and lobster" – much of it fresh from the waters you see from the dining room windows – are "cooked to perfection either in the restaurant or adjacent bar" of this remote Highlands hotel, named after the island it looks at across the sound. The bar has been used by the region's crofters for more than 150 years. / summerisleshotel.com; Mon-Sun 9 pm.

ALBOURNE, WEST SUSSEX 3-4B

THE GINGER FOX £69 33

MUDDLESWOOD ROAD
BN6 9EA 01273 857 888

With its "beautiful setting nestling under the South Downs" and "inventive, superbly presented dishes," this "lovely thatched country pub" from Brighton's Gingerman group is "well worth the trip inland from the coast". The wine list is strong on local Sussex wines. / thegingerfox.com; gingerfoxbrighton; Tue-Sun 8.30 pm.

ALDEBURGH, SUFFOLK 3-1D

ALDEBURGH FISH AND CHIPS £15 32

226 HIGH ST IP15 5DB 01728 454685

There's "always a long queue" at this well-known and much-commented-on fixture – "but it's worth the wait" for "great fish 'n' chips to eat on the beach" while trying to "avoid the seagulls" poised to pounce on your meal. Owner Peter Cooney was 11 when his parents bought the business in 1967, and he's still frying. Top Tip – "grab a pint of excellent Adnams from next door while you wait". / aldeburghfishandchips.co.uk; aldefishnchips; Tue, Wed, Fri 8.30 pm, Thu, Sat 8 pm, Sun 2 pm.

'HE LIGHTHOUSE £59 354

7 HIGH STREET
P15 5AU 01728 453377

Always reliable"; "always a cheery welcome"; always fun"; "always something new to try"… and moreover, they charge reasonable prices!" These are some of the prime virtues of Sam & Maxine Hayes's local stalwart which remains he most commented-on venue in this seaside own even after almost three decades in service, hanks to its "dependable" delivery of "simple, onest fare". "The fisherman was carrying is catch through the restaurant and my wife potted skate… 15 minutes later it was served to er!" / lighthouserestaurant.co.uk; aldelighthouse; Mon-Sun 9.30 pm.

REGATTA £39 332

71 HIGH STREET
P15 5AN 01728 452011

My favourite restaurant in Aldeburgh" this long-running operation from twins Alex (FOH) and Oliver (chef) Burnside, lso behind local haunts The Plough & Sail nd The Golden Key, "specialises in fish nd seafood, but the meat dishes are also mpressive". / regattaaldeburgh.com; Mon-Sun 0 pm.

'HE SUFFOLK (FKA L'ESCARGOT SUR MER) £73 433

52 HIGH STREET
P15 5AQ 07557 333453

With its "great fish dishes – we had a whole rill for two served at the table with chips and ollandaise sauce, which was… 'bril' (geddit?)" this yearling from George Pell, formerly of L'Escargot in Soho, "has ambitions to be the ew east coast superstar. Another year will ell whether they have made it". Locally born ead chef Tom Payne, 25, certainly made good start, mightily impressing Observer ritic Jay Rayner a week after his promotion o run the kitchen, with a 'menu that is certain of its mission'. It's certainly "a welcome ddition locally – a treat", and the "nice new edrooms" and "well-made cocktails are a plus". (It's one of the few good legacies from Covid, as the team from L'Escargot shifted ere during the pandemic). / the-suffolk.co.uk; hesuffolkaldeburgh; Wed-Sun 2.30 am.

ALDERLEY EDGE, GREATER MANCHESTER 5–2B

SAN CARLO ALDERLEY EDGE

LONDON ROAD SK9 7QD 01625 599995

The WAGs of Cheshire's Golden Triangle may t last have a restaurant HQ worthy of them s the San Carlo group has come into town, with a view to importing the success of their ong-standing Manchester city-centre venue o these plush, Bentley-filled 'burbs. On the ite of Gino D'Acampo's Luciano's (RIP), its lassic Italian cooking is served in a suitably plashy setting, where the dining terrace complete with retractable roof) is centre stage, complete with open-flame fireplace and palm trees. / sancarlo.co.uk.

ALDFORD, CHESHIRE 5–3A

THE GROSVENOR ARMS £55 334

CHESTER RD CH3 6HJ 01244 620228

This unusually grand and "busy gastropub" near the gates of the Duke of Westminster's Cheshire estate is "probably the best Brunning & Price". "We've eaten here many times over the years, and while the food has had its ups and downs, recently it's been of top quality" – "it's best to avoid weekends though, as it can get very busy: the price of success!" Top Tip – lovely garden in summer. / brunningandprice.co.uk; grosvenor.arms; Mon-Sun 11 pm. SRA – 3 stars

ALFRISTON, EAST SUSSEX 3–4B

THE TASTING ROOM, RATHFINNY WINE ESTATE 333

RATHFINNY WINE ESTATE
BN26 5TU 01323 870 022

Panoramic views of the vineyards and South Downs accompany a trip to this seasonal dining room (which is closed in October during the wine harvest). Some reports are of outstanding cuisine from chef Chris Bailey, although there is the odd concern about some "huge mark-ups" on certain items. You can always opt for the "really relaxed" Flint Barn dining room also on the estate ("keenly priced, lovely posh grub with a large choice of wines to wash it all down"). There is also The Hut at Rathfinny – a wine bar with week-round opening. / rathfinnyestate.com; rathfinnyestate; Wed & Thu, Sun 3 pm, Fri & Sat 8.30 pm.

THE STAR £80 334

HIGH STREET BN26 5TA 01323 870495

In a medieval village at the foot of the South Downs, a "fifteenth-century inn transformed into a delightful boutique hotel and restaurant" by hospitality guru Olga Polizzi, who acquired it in 2021 for her now three-strong chain. Most (if not all) reporters laud River Café alumnus Tim Kensett's "delicious" locally sourced food, though "what makes this place is the service and setting" (the "very sophisticated" decor includes Bloomsbury Set artworks, and, in the dining room, a striking monochrome Elizabethan-style floor). / thepolizzicollection.com; thestar; Mon-Sun 9 pm.

ALTRINCHAM, GREATER MANCHESTER 5–2B

ALTRINCHAM MARKET £44 323

GREENWOOD STREET WA14 1SA NO TEL

Nick Johnson's "fun food hall" in a covered Victorian market is "still delivering on all fronts", with "an excellent choice of stallholders" ensuring a "casual and vibrant lunch or dinner". "To their credit they're maintaining high standards" – although things can get fraught at busy times, with "pushy" fellow diners the main problem. / altymarket; Tue-Sat 10 pm, Sun 6 pm.

SUD (WAS SUGO) £55 443

22 SHAW'S ROAD
WA14 1QU 0161 929 7706

"Forget flying to southern Italy – go to Sud for wonderful pasta and other Italian dishes", say fans of the "fresh, vibrant, authentic food" served at this "fun" Altrincham outfit with "slick and friendly service" – the original of a group now with outposts in Ancoats, Sale and Manchester city centre, and which changed its name from Sugo to avoid a clash with a Glasgow operation of that name. "Lots of eye-rolling, and funny noises came out of my mouth, and my wife and I literally didn't speak for 15 minutes during the main course – I'll never eat pasta with a knife and fork again!". / sudpasta.co.uk; sudpasta; Tue-Sat 10 pm, Sun 8.30 pm.

AMBERLEY, WEST SUSSEX 3–4A

AMBERLEY CASTLE £133 224

BN18 9LT 01798 831992

This luxury hotel restaurant in a semi-ruined medieval castle (complete with portcullis) is part of the Andrew Brownsword group, and certainly makes for a "wonderfully romantic" destination. "The dining room is situated upstairs in the castle" – replete with a rare barrel-vaulted ceiling – so may not be good for the mobility-impaired, "but the staff are obliging" and the food "good" (if not exceptional). / amberleycastle.co.uk; brownswordhotels; Wed-Sun 9 pm.

AMBLE, NORTHUMBERLAND 8–1B

FISH SHACK £40 433

29 HARBOUR ROAD
NE65 0AP 01665 661301

"Fish doesn't come any fresher", say fans of Martin & Ruth Charlton's "casual and characterful" spot, purpose-built beside Amble harbour from an old boat, where the "astonishing seafood platter – whole lobster, whole bream, hot and cold smoked salmon, mackerel, beer-battered cod, prawns, langoustines, mussels, oysters, crusty bread and triple-cooked chips – feeds four for £88. Crikey!" / boathousefoodgroup.co.uk; Mon-Sun 8 pm.

THE OLD BOAT HOUSE AMBLE £51 333

LEAZES STREET
NE65 0AA 01665 711 232

"A good range of locally caught fish and shellfish" can be enjoyed at this "recently refurbished building" in a "fantastic setting right on the quayside in Amble, with views up to Warkworth along the Coquet and out towards the sea". It's "our go-to place when we want to give foreign visitors a taste of traditional fish 'n' chips" – with the bonus that you can "watch the boats arriving" with tomorrow's fish. The owners also run the Fish Shack close by. / boathousefoodgroup.co.uk; oldboathousefoodgroup; Mon-Sun 9 pm.

AMBLESIDE, CUMBRIA 7–3D

DRUNKEN DUCK £84 3 2 3

BARNGATES LA22 0NG 01539 436347

Also home to the Barngates Brewery – whose brews are on tap – this rural pub is a popular destination on the Lakeland tourist trail. It didn't generate much attention in our annual diners' poll this year, but such as we received was 'all good' (although some feedback suggested "mains aren't as good as the starters and puds"). / drunkenduckinn.co.uk; Mon-Sat 8 pm, Sun 3 pm.

KYSTY £75 4 4 3

3-4 CHEAPSIDE LA22 0AB 015394 33647

"Delicious food, beautifully presented in a relaxed environment", has won plenty of admirers for this spin-off from the nearby Old Stamp House, where head chef Dan Hopkins's "modern, accurate cooking" makes excellent use of prime Lakeland ingredients, including Herdwick lamb. It's "good value", too – especially for the "brilliant set lunch". 'Kysty' apparently means fussy in the Cumbrian dialect. / kysty.co.uk; kystyamble; Thu-Sat, Wed 9.30 pm.

LAKE ROAD KITCHEN £138 4 3 3

3 SUSSEX HOUSE, LAKE ROAD LA22 0AD 015394 22012

Chef James Cross returned to the Lake District after doing time at acclaimed eateries Noma, Per Se and Simpsons to set up this new Nordic restaurant with suitably Scandi styling (wooden plank walls, sheepskin throws on the chairs). The dinner-only dining room turns out eight- or twelve-course tasting menus, and wins raves for the "absolutely faultless cooking, amazing service and atmosphere". / lakeroadkitchen.co.uk; lakeroadkitchen; Wed-Sun 9 pm.

OLD STAMP HOUSE £118 5 4 3

CHURCH ST LA22 0BU 01539432775

Ryan Blackburn and general manager brother Craig's decade-old venture – the poet Wordsworth's office when he was the local stamp distributor – is a truly "first-class" affair; the "cellar-type interior gives a cosy atmosphere", while the "unique" tasting menu of locally sourced food (acclaimed by the tyre men since 2019) is abetted by staff who take "evident pleasure" in their work. Is it cheap? Well, "a full-blown evening tasting menu at £95 per person seems really quite reasonable" to one reporter… "anyway, it raised the bar for cooking in Cumbria for me". / oldstamphouse.com; oldstamphouseambleside; Wed-Sat 9 pm.

ROTHAY MANOR 3 3 4

ROTHAY BRIDGE LA22 0EH 01539 433605

This "beautiful country house hotel restaurant" has long held a reputation for "wonderful food in a really wonderful Lakeland setting". It "continues to offer high-class, interesting cuisine in the chef Daniel McGeorge era", with "innovative and delicious cooking" – "so seasonal, the entire meal evoked autumn on a plate". / rothaymanor.co.uk; rothaymanor; Mon-Sun 8.30 pm.

ZEFFIRELLI'S £52 2 3 3

COMPSTON RD LA22 9AD 01539 433845

"Such a pleasant place to eat with lots of customers who don't even realise they're in a vegetarian restaurant" – this Lakeland fixture of four decades' standing is part of a town-centre complex incorporating a cinema and jazz bar. Pizza and pasta are staples of the vegetarian Italian menu, and for £28.95 you can book a complete evening out including a two-course dinner and reserved cinema seat. / zeffirellis.com; zeffsfellinis; Mon & Tue, Thu-Sat 10 pm, Wed 11 pm, Sun 9 pm.

AMERSHAM, BUCKINGHAMSHIRE 3–2A

ARTICHOKE £123 4 4 4

9 MARKET SQ HP7 0DF 01494 726611

"Brilliant, Brilliant, Brilliant.....and tucked away in sleepy Amersham"; Laurie Gear's "classy" venue is celebrating over 20 years in its sixteenth-century grade II listed site in Old Amersham (although it took Michelin until 2019 to cotton on and give it a star). It is one of the most commented-on venues in our annual diners' poll on the fringes of the capital "Stunning", relatively traditional cuisine is "served by people who actually understand the job of hospitality", in a Scandi-influenced interior. / artichokerestaurant.co.uk; artichokeche Fri & Sat, Wed & Thu 11 pm.

GILBEY'S £71 2 3 3

1 MARKET SQ HP7 0DF 01494 727242

"Tasty bistro food" is enjoyed in the "lovely setting" of a seventeenth-century former school in Old Amersham, a "cosy" local spot opened by the Gilbey's gin dynasty 35 years ago. Founder Michael Gilbey passed away in summer 2022, and his widow, Lin, has put the site up for sale. (She also runs its sister restaurant in Eton.) / gilbeygroup.com; gilbeysoldamersham; Mon, Thu-Sat 9.30 pm, Sun 3 pm.

THE GROCER AT 15 £27 3 3 3

15 THE BROADWAY HP7 0DT 01494 722925

This "great local" has had an up-and-down time of it of late, with the Gerrards Cross branch under new management, and The Grocer at 91, which had pivoted to being a food shop in the pandemic, now closed. On the plus side, this "very busy" outpost is still going strong with its "reliable" (if pricey) sandwiches, salads and toasties, and they also recently opened a new Amersham venue, The Grocer a 2 (Whielden St), spanning a grocery store and café. / thegrocershops.co.uk; thegrocershops; Wed Sat 4.30 pm, Sun 4 pm.

HAWKYNS BY ATUL KOCHHAR, THE CROWN INN £74 4 4 3

16 HIGH STREET HP7 0DH 01494 721541

A surprise find in an ancient sixteenth-century pub on the high street – Atul Kochhar's "super upmarket Indian" is a "delight", where the set menus are "outstanding value" ("would happily have paid more", says a fan) and service "very attentive from the outset". The ambience is sometimes rated no better than "OK" – for some tastes it's not as immensely characterful as one might think given the venue's cameo in 'Four Weddings', as the backdrop to Hugh and Andie's romance. / hawkynsrestaurant.co.uk; hawkynsamersham; Wed-Sat 9.30 pm, Sun 7 pm.

Andrew Fairlie, Gleneagles, Auchterarder

·LUMA £86 322

8 HIGH STREET HP7 0DJ 01494 728383

Refined" and "interesting" tapas ("the Iberico ork is the best thing on the menu") married ith creative cocktails and sherries are the allmark of this high street three-year-old, from duo with Heston B pedigree. Amongst a high olume of reports in our annual diners' poll, attracted the odd critic this year ("the menu ould do with changing"), but even they "simply ved the fact that there is a buzzing, good panish restaurant in the locale – a rare treat in his neck of the woods (which is why it is always ıll!)". / plumarestaurants.com; pluma_amersham; ue-Sat 9 pm.

'OM YUM £38 332

01 SYCAMORE ROAD
P6 5EJ 01494 728806

Super Thai food" makes this "rather ramped" but otherwise "lovely" local fixture really worth a visit" according to fans (albeit ne that's also popular for takeaway) and it's reat value for money too; from Tuesday to aturday they do a lunchtime noodle bar. / omyum.net; Tue-Thu 9 pm, Fri & Sat 10 pm.

AMPTHILL, BEDFORDSHIRE 3–2A

:ILEEN'S £72 443

6A DUNSTABLE STREET
1K45 2JP 01525 839889

Bedfordshire-born Steven Barringer opened his popular restaurant alongside wife Amy seven years after starring on the 2011 eason of MasterChef: The Professionals. The "great taster menu" (coming in five- or even-course versions that change monthly) nd "knowledgeable staff" have contributed o its local success – so do think to book in dvance. / eileensampthill.co.uk; eileensampthill; Ved-Sat 11 pm.

ANGMERING, WEST SUSSEX 3–4A

'HE LAMB AT ANGMERING £56 333

'HE SQUARE BN16 4EQ 01903 774300

Next to the South Downs, this Georgian pub (with rooms) has been owned by the Newbon family since 2011. The menu mixes classics' (burger, fish 'n' chips, steak) with more brasserie-style items. It was highlighted this year for its "good-value set lunch and pleasant service". / thelamb-angmering.com; thelambatangmering; Mon-Sat 8.30 pm, Sun 3 pm.

ANSTRUTHER, FIFE 9–4D

ANSTRUTHER FISH BAR £39 522

2-44 SHORE ST
KY10 3AQ 01333 310518

'Not many people visit Anstruther, or Ainster as the locals call it, without visiting this famous institution" – a veteran chippie est. 2003) run by the Smiths, who were born into the local fishing industry and also run the Argofish processing business. "Be prepared to wait during high season, but it will be worth it, as their fish renderings are second to none (no wonder they win lots of awards)". / anstrutherfishbar.co.uk; anstrutherfishbar; Mon-Fri 8.30 pm, Sat & Sun 9 pm.

THE CELLAR £160 544

24 EAST GREEN
KY10 3AA 01333 310378

"Hidden away in Anstruther", Billy Boyter's renowned fixture in a "beautiful" former smokehouse is celebrating the tenth year of his tenure in style, having recently won both the AA's and TripAdvisor's 2023 crown for being the best restaurant in Scotland. Our feedback also repeats the raves of recent years, for this "quiet and intimate venue" with "exceptional, imaginative and excellently presented food and superb matching wines". / thecellaranstruther.co.uk; THE_CELLAR_ANSTRUTHER; Wed-Sat 8.30 pm.

APPLECROSS, HIGHLAND 9–2B

APPLECROSS INN £48 433

SHORE ST IV54 8LR 01520 744262

"Wow, this is indeed a find if you can stomach the drive over the highest road in the British Isles" – a sentiment felt for more than a century for this far-flung destination, which was recommended as the 'Temperance Hotel' in the 1911 Michelin Guide. Owned and run by the redoutable Judith Fish for more than 30 years, it's noted these days for excellent local seafood and drinks including beer from the Applecross Brewery. Top Menu Tip – "the scallops are to die for". / applecrossinn.co.uk; Wed, Mon, Thu-Sun 10 pm.

ARMSCOTE, WARWICKSHIRE 2–1C

THE FUZZY DUCK £62 333

ILMINGTON ROAD
CV37 8DD 01608 682635

Within striking distance of Stratford upon Avon (about seven miles away), this boutique inn has been spruced up by Adrian and Tania Slater – the owners of Baylis & Harding – in 'Contemporary Cotswolds' style and offers pub classics (steak, chicken pie, fish 'n' chips) alongside more brasserie-style items (e.g. tortellini, duck breast). / fuzzyduckarmscote.com; fuzzyduckarmscote; Tue-Sat 10 pm, Sun 4 pm.

ARUNDEL, WEST SUSSEX 3–4A

CAMPANIA £32 332

51 HIGH ST BN18 9AJ 01903 884500

A beamed high street boozer has made way for this "buzzing" and "wonderful Italian", a short walk from the castle in this "lovely town"; as per the name, it focuses on SW Italian food – pizza, spaghetti, cannelloni, etc. – with a dedicated fish night on Wednesdays, and steak night on Thursday. / lacampania.co.uk; lacampania_arundel_; Mon-Sat 10 pm, Sun 9 pm.

THE PARSONS TABLE £76 444

2 & 8 CASTLE MEWS, TARRANT STREET
BN18 9DG 01903 883477

Launched in 2015 after a stellar career (Claridge's, Le Manoir aux Quat' Saisons, many a high-end Canadian hotel), Lee (& FOH wife Liz) Parsons' small indie is a real local "favourite" that inspires many comments in our annual diners' poll (booking is thus essential) focussing on "exquisite fresh ingredients whose combinations tantalise the tastebuds". The "great-value set lunch" merits investigation, and "fish is the outstanding choice" as always. / theparsonstable.co.uk; tpt_restaurant; Tue-Sat 9 pm.

THE PIG IN THE SOUTH DOWNS £88 324

MADEHURST BN18 0NL 01243 974500

"What a lovely setting" – on a hilltop in the South Downs National Park – for a "very typical 'Pig'": Robin Hutson's well-known litter of shabby-chic hotels (now sold to private equity). At almost two acres, the kitchen garden enables "a good exhibition of farm-to-fork", although the most critical diners feel "the cooking is not particularly interesting or exciting (possibly because it has been replicated by so many)". There's a "great list of Sussex and Kent wines", soon to be joined by bottles from the estate's own vines – a 'Pig' first – and a herd of South Downs sheep. / thepighotel.com; thepig_hotel; Mon-Sun 9.30 pm.

ASCOT, BERKSHIRE 3–3A

WOVEN BY ADAM SMITH AT COWORTH PARK, COWORTH PARK £181 444

BLACKNEST RD SL5 7SE 01344 876 600

"An amazing new dining room! The experience from start to finish is personal, thought provoking and the cooking is inspired. a true destination!" – so say fans of the revamp of the "well appointed" flagship dining room at this Dorchester Collection property, where a new contemporary look has brought the decor much more into line with the quality of chef Adam Smith's cuisine. Reports acclaim both its "exceptional food and dining experience on a consistent basis". You choose from a five-course menu for £145 per person. / dorchestercollection.com; coworthpark; Wed-Sat 9 pm, Sun 2 pm.

ASENBY, NORTH YORKSHIRE 8–4C

CRAB & LOBSTER £76 223

DISHFORTH RD YO7 3QL 01845 577286

This quirky fish specialist, with exotically styled bedrooms in the 18th century Crab Manor, certainly has an "original ambience" ("if Victoria Wood's Acorn Antiques ran a restaurant", it might look like this, replete with assorted "sea-fishing paraphernalia"); there was the odd blip on the service front this year, but also continued praise for some of the "best seafood around". / crabandlobster.co.uk; crabandlobster; Mon-Sun 11.30 pm.

ASHBOURNE, DERBYSHIRE 5-3C

THE COW DALBURY £80 343

THE GREEN, DALBURY LEES DE6 5BE 01332 824297

"It's nowhere near the sea, but they have great suppliers" and this handsome 19th-century Peak District village pub (fka The Black Cow) six miles from Derby is now a boutique inn (with six bedrooms) where Cornish-born chef, Nathan Senior, specialises in fresh seafood delivered daily from his home county. "They also do a fantastic steak. All round a perfect pub for a meal and stopover". / cowdalbury.com; thecowdalbury; Mon-Sat 9 pm, Sun 7 pm.

THE HORSESHOES LONG LANE £70 323

LONG LANE DE6 5BJ 01332 824625

"A lovely (if small) bar and outside space" add to the appeal of this "nice old pub in the middle of nowhere but set in a pleasant Derbyshire Dales setting". Run by chef Gareth Ward (a namesake of the chef-patron at Ynyshir in Wales), it offers "a good modern menu" with beer-battered haddock about the only dish on the menu that might qualify as 'pub grub'. / horseshoeslonglane.co.uk; thehorseshoeslonglane; Wed-Sat 9 pm, Sun 6 pm.

ASHBURTON, DEVON 1-3D

EMILIA £70 333

2 EAST STREET TQ13 7AA 01364 653998

"This really was a very pleasant surprise" – a "small but very lively" osteria, set in a former Lloyds bank, that draws its name and inspiration from the Emilia-Romagna region; the "interesting, daily changing menu" is chalked up on the old vault door, and revolves around a "selection of delicious small plates" (including a particularly "stunning" 'offal of the day' option). / emiliaashburton.co.uk; emilia.ashburton; Wed-Sat 9 pm.

ASHFORD-IN-THE-WATER, DERBYSHIRE 5-2C

RAFTERS AT RIVERSIDE HOUSE £89 434

RIVERSIDE HOUSE HOTEL, FENNEL STREET DE45 1QF 01629 814275

"A lovely place, with excellent food, high levels of service, great wine list and a perfect location" – this prettily located Peak District restaurant with rooms occupies a solid, ivy-clad period mansion (complete with walled garden) and is owned by John and Alex Hill, but with a dining room run by Alistair Myers and Tom Lawson who run Rafters in Sheffield (see also). / riversidehousehotel.co.uk; raftersrh; Wed & Thu, Sun 8 pm, Fri & Sat 8.30 pm, Mon 9 am.

AUCHTERARDER, PERTH AND KINROSS 9-3C

ANDREW FAIRLIE, GLENEAGLES HOTEL £156 554

PH3 1NF 01764 694267

"A brilliant annual treat!" that's "worth the enormous drive to get there!" – this stunning venue regularly tops our annual diners' survey as the UK's best venue, and was once again applauded unanimously in reports this year for its "exceptional cuisine". The flagship for the world-renowned golf resort, it's a cosseting, dark-walled space whose elegant decor helps offset its windowless position within the heart of the hotel. "Unique flavours are beautifully presented" by chef Stephen McLaughlin who worked with Andrew Fairlie for 26 years before the latter passed away in 2019; and GM Dale Dewsbury presides over an "amazing" front of house team. As well as the 'Degustation' menu "it offers a three-course à la carte for £125 per person, which is a nice find in these days of taster-only options". Top Menu Tip – "the signature home smoked lobster is a great dish". / andrewfairlie.co.uk; restaurant_andrew_fairlie; Mon-Sun 10 pm.

JON & FERNANDA'S £69 443

34 HIGH STREET PH3 1DB 01764 662442

"Beautifully prepared, super tasting food from local producers" is on the menu at this "small restaurant on Auchterarder's high street", which makes a "great choice for dinner out one night" for guests holidaying at the nearby Gleneagles hotel (J&F are "former employees"). "I just wish this was on our local high street – we'd be there every week!". / jonandfernandas.co.uk; Wed-Sat 9 pm.

STRATHEARN RESTAURANT, GLENEAGLES HOTEL £111 343

PH3 1NF 0800 731 9219

"Food, service and ambience are all excellent", as one might expect of this grand resort hotel's traditional dining venue, which focuses on spectacular Scottish seafood and roast meat, leaving more adventurous interpretations to Restaurant Andrew Fairlie (its neighbour along the corridor). Even some diehard fans, though, complain that "the price has gone up and up over the years". / gleneagles.com; thegleneagleshotel; Mon-Sun 9 pm.

AUGHTON, LANCASHIRE 5-2A

THE BARN AT MOOR HALL £82 434

PRESCOT RD L39 6RT 01695 572511

The more casual 'second' restaurant at Mark Birchall's all-conquering project still offers a "sumptuous dining experience", with the "incredible attention to detail" expected from such a venue. Some reporters even "like its chilled style more than its more prestigious neighbour. Service is genuinely more friendly, and there's less genuflecting at the stuff on the plate – I've come to eat, not worship!". As for the clientele, it's "a bit less footballer WAGish" than next door – and there's "an excellent valu lunch menu, considering the elevated nature of the cooking". / moorhall.com; thebarnmh; Wed-Sat 9 pm, Sun 6.30 pm.

MOOR HALL £273 54

PRESCOT RD L39 6RT 01695 572511

"There is nothing not to love about the experience – from the tour of the kitchen on the way to your table through the ballet of service to the final bites of deliciousness, all done with great charm and humour" – Mark Birchall's converted manor house a short drive north of Liverpool has captured the imagination of the UK food scene since it first launched in 2014 and – "a candidate for a thir Michelin star" – it still regularly tops media To 100s of UK restaurants. At the heart of the offering is the "outstanding tasting dinner-time menu of 17 small but exceptional courses" for £225 per person, but the gorgeously refurbished medieval setting, cheese room, kitchen garden, and landscaped five acres with long drive and lake all add to its mystique. Just one issue presents itself – the jaw-dropping bills. For most reporters the verdict remains that it's "worth every penny", but its high cost means its top rating from our annual diners' poll is becoming borderline. "It's wonderful, and I know prices are rising everywhere, but it feels expensive now… even compared to The Ritz!" / moorhall.com; restaurantmoorhall; Thu-Sun, Wed 8.30 pm.

SO-LO £104 54

17 TOWN GREEN LANE L39 6SE 01695 302170

"Superb food every time", say early converts to high-flying chef Tim Allen (ex-Launceston Place, Wild Rabbit, Flitch of Bacon)'s first venture as chef-patron, a "former Seafood Pub Company outpost" that he opened in late 2021 down the road from superstar Moor Hall. "The cuisine is terrific with a few interesting surprises thrown in" – and "with just Tim Aller and one other in the open kitchen – a model of calmness – it's all the more remarkable how good and refined the cooking is. There's a very light touch and freshness to it all that's just delightful". "The pricing at Moor Hall (while never not worth it) has always put it into a rare treat category… the arrival of this place is approaching an epiphany of more affordable fine dining!" / restaurantsolo.co.uk.

AUSTWICK, LANCASHIRE 8-4A

THE TRADDOCK HOTEL £65 33

LA2 8BY 01524 251224

Run by the Reynolds family for over two decades, this "lovely hotel" in the Yorkshire Dales National Park is imminently "suitable as a touring base" for the gorgeous countryside in these parts. Despite its considerable ambitions ı the cooking stakes (a ten-course tasting ıenu is amongst the offer, which has received a oveted 3 'AA' Rosettes), it remains a "friendly nd relaxed" sort of place. / thetraddock.co.uk; ıe_traddock; Mon-Sun 8.30 pm.

AYLESBURY, BUCKINGHAMSHIRE 3–2A

·IARTWELL ·IOUSE £118 234

·XFORD ROAD HP17 8NR 01296 747444

Splendid surroundings for a plentiful and ısty afternoon tea" are again noted as a ighpoint at this Jacobean/Georgian stately ome spa hotel, with grounds laid out originally y Capability Brown and nowadays owned y the National Trust. Top Tip – "they are appy to give you a box for anything you can't nish!" / hartwell-house.com; hartwellhouse; Aon-Sun 9 pm.

BAGSHOT, SURREY 3–3A

.ATYMER, PENNYHILL PARK ·IOTEL £184 544

.ONDON ROAD GU19 5EU 01276 486150

Steve Smith hits all the right notes" in this pulent dining room: "a real treat that's xpensive but worth it". "While the hotel may eel a bit big and corporate, The Latymer just eels special. From the moment you walk in, to he time you leave. Each course is craft-fully ıapped out with little cards explaining what is and where it originated from". On all ccounts this year, its six-course menu – for vhich you should allow three hours – delivers n "outstanding" experience for £175 per erson. / latymerrestaurant.co.uk; latymer_ estaurant; Wed-Sun 8.30 pm.

BAKEWELL, DERBYSHIRE 5–2C

·IEDANIELS £62 333

·ATH ST DE45 1BX 01629 812687

Great-value French cuisine" has drawn uests for more than 25 years to this amily-run venture from Eric & Christiana ·iedaniel – both career chefs. It makes a lovely quiet environment for lunch" just 0 minutes' drive from historic Chatsworth Iouse. / piedaniels-restaurant.com; Wed-Sat 1 pm.

·ESTAURANT LOVAGE BY .EE SMITH £61 343

·ATH STREET DE45 1DS 01629 815 613

This is the restaurant the Peak District has een waiting for" – a "chilled and unfussy" our-year-old, in a former stable block, which .ee Smith (ex-of the acclaimed Samphire n Jersey) opened after a crowdfunding lrive. The staff's "enthusiasm for the place nakes for a happy experience, but most of ll it's the modern English cooking done ery well in a lovely room… I'm lucky it's ny local". Some reporters feel we rate it too onservatively, but to go further: more reports lease! / restaurantlovage.co.uk; lovagerestaurant; Thu-Sat, Wed 9 pm.

BALA, GWYNEDD 4–2D

PALE HALL HOTEL RESTAURANT £100

PALE ESTATE, LLANDDERFEL LL23 7PS 01678 530 285

On the edge of Snowdonia National Park, this Relais & Châteaux property occupies a former hunting lodge once owned by the Duke of Westminster, and was relaunched in 2016 as a luxury hotel. Its culinary ambitions have always run high, and were underpinned in May 2023 with the recruitment of Sam Griffths (Welsh Chef of the Year 2021) as their new head chef; Gareth Stevenson who had run the kitchen here since opening is stepping back. Griffiths was formerly the executive sous chef in The Chester Grosvenor's restaurant Arkle. / palehall.co.uk; palehallhotel; Mon-Sun 9 pm.

BALLATER, ANGUS 9–3C

THE FISH SHOP £66

3 NETHERLEY PLACE AB35 5QE 01339 720250

"Newly opened but with great potential" – this April 2023 newcomer threw open its doors just before our annual diners' poll concluded and elicited just this single comment. But it had already been visited by HM The King and Queen thanks to its sustainability credentials (it supports the Ocean Recovery Project). On the former site of the Rothesay Rooms, it's now part of ArtFarm's expanding portfolio – "an impressive and immersive place that you won't forget in a hurry, and the same goes for the food", according to The Scotsman's Rosalind Erskine in her May 2023 review, where she enjoyed "fresh seafood in stylish surroundings" (which becomes more understandable when you find out that "at the helm of this new venture is Jasmine and Marcus Sherry, who worked at the Fife Arms in Braemar" up the road). Rosalind's choices were "light, fresh, local and unfussy". / fishshopballater.co.uk; fishshopballater; Wed-Sun 11 pm.

BAMBURGH, NORTHUMBERLAND 8–1B

THE POTTED LOBSTER £76 333

3 LUCKER ROAD NE69 7BS 01668 214088

"Seafood so fresh it's practically still swimming" – including Lindisfarne oysters and locally caught lobsters – is the trump card at Alnick-born chef Richard Sim's "gem" of a restaurant – "a real must if you ever venture near Bamburgh". There's a sibling venture on the far side of the country, at Abersoch on the Llyn Peninsula in Wales. / thepottedlobster.co.uk; thepottedlobster; Mon-Sun 9 pm.

BAMPTON, CUMBRIA 7–3D

MARK GREENAWAY AT THE HAWESWATER HOTEL £96

LAKESIDE ROAD CA10 2RP 01931 713673

"Amazing stay and experience, the dishes were out of this world" – early praise for this January 2023 Lake District newcomer from the high-profile Edinburgh chef. It occupies an Art Deco hotel on the banks of Haweswater Reservoir, now transformed into a self-named fine-dining outfit focusing on local seasonal produce serving some of his signature dishes (shiitake mushrooms on toast; 11-hour slow-roast pork belly; sticky toffee soufflé). There's also the more informal Brasserie 37, named after the year the hotel was opened. More reports please! / markgreenaway.com; chefmarkgreenaway; Mon-Sun 9.30 pm.

BARLASTON, STAFFORDSHIRE 5–3B

LUNAR £132 332

WEDGWOOD DRIVE ST12 9ER 07494 073091

"You are served in a large dining room under a giant moon" in this striking eatery – a centrepiece of the World of Wedgwood – which was added to this factory-visit and museum experience in late 2021. Named for a seventeenth-century dining club filled with luminaries of the Midlands Enlightenment, and overseen by local lad Niall Keating (who left behind two Michelin stars to take up the opportunity), it brings a pleasing level of ambition to underserved Staffs and The Potteries. There's a relatively affordable à la carte menu, or an eight-course tasting menu for £120 per person. Given that its mere presence is a minor miracle in the area, it's not hard to be bowled over and it delivers "frequently excellent dishes – often containing luxury ingredients, formally but attentively and helpfully served, if in a space that is perhaps a little large to feel completely at home in". On the flip-side, even those who think it "very good" can still find it "overpriced". / lunarwedgwood.com; lunarwedgwood; Thu-Sat midnight, Sun 7 pm.

BARNET, HERTFORDSHIRE 3–2B

ODOS £73 453

238-240 HIGH STREET EN5 5TD 020 8440 6222

This "hidden gem in Barnet" has a "fabulous Greek/Mediterranean menu, made 'posh' with additions such as ceviche and miso aubergine". The "food is fresh, tasty and always delicious", and "they're so welcoming". Founder Louis Loizu promoted former apprentice chef Gerry Sands to co-ownership last summer, at the tender age of 21. / odosrestaurant.co.uk; odosrestaurant; Tue-Sat 10 pm, Sun 9 pm.

BARNT GREEN, WEST MIDLANDS 5–4C

BLACK & GREEN £88 4 4 3

49 HEWELL ROAD
B45 8NL 0121 655 5550

"A very small restaurant in the small, attractive, well-heeled north Worcestershire village of Barnt Green with tables and a counter at which some diners are sat in very close proximity of the culinary action". With just 18 seats, it's owned by chef Andrew Sheridan, and although he recently left Brum for his native Liverpool, he continues to show an interest locally with the August 2023 acquisition of nearby coffee and brunch venue, The Garrity. At Black & Green, his team "delivers a well-balanced six-course tasting menu, often with original ingredients. Many of the dishes are brought to table by the chefs themselves". / aboutblackandgreen.co.uk; Wed-Sat 11.30 pm.

BARTLOW, CAMBRIDGESHIRE 3–1B

THE THREE HILLS, BARTLOW £70 3 3 3

DEAN ROAD CB21 4PW 01223 890500

In a village about 30 minutes' drive south of Cambridge, this "excellent village pub with rooms" is praised as a "fab restaurant with very friendly staff". You can choose between the orangery dining room, bar and large outside terrace; early morning breakfast (including a Champagne option) is also a feature. / thethreehills.co.uk; thethreehillsbartlow; Wed-Sat 9 pm, Sun 4 pm.

BARTON-ON-SEA, HAMPSHIRE 2–4C

PEBBLE BEACH £72 3 3 3

MARINE DRIVE BH25 7DZ 01425 627777

This "excellent beachside restaurant" from experienced chef Andy Waters – one of the few in Britain to have worked under the late, great Paul Bocuse in Lyons – has a fitting focus on "good fish", alongside classic pasta dishes and steaks. The terrace has lovely views across the Solent to the Isle of Wight. / pebblebeach-uk.com; pebblebeachuk; Wed-Sun 9 pm.

BASLOW, DERBYSHIRE 5–2C

FISCHER'S AT BASLOW HALL £125

CALVER RD DE45 1RR 01246 583259

This well-known Peak District property has been run by Max & Susan Fischer since 1988 and is currently managed by their son Neil, who is credited in reports with keeping standards at least as high under his parents. In mid-2023, though, the house went up for sale so – although it continues to operate as normal for the time being – change may be afoot (and we've left it un-rated for the time being). / fischers-baslowhall.co.uk; FischersBaslow; Thu-Sun 8 pm.

THE GALLERY RESTAURANT AT THE CAVENDISH HOTEL £85

CHURCH LANE DE45 1SP 01246 582311

This swish country house hotel, in one of the Peak District's most picturesque villages, is transforming before visitors' eyes as part of an ongoing, £1.1 million makeover. As we went to press, the more casual 'Garden Room' had already been reborn, with chef Adam Harper (ex-of the acclaimed nearby Fischer's) overseeing a new menu with impeccable local sourcing such as Chatsworth beef; this, the more formal fine diner, will follow suit, but meanwhile won praise this year – well "on its way to a Michelin star" by some accounts. All reports acclaim the "brilliant food and ambience in all areas" and it's also tipped for afternoon tea. / cavendishbaslow.co.uk; cavendishhotelbaslow; Mon-Sun 9 pm.

BATCOMBE, SOMERSET 2–3B

THE THREE HORSESHOES

BA4 6HE 01749 850359

"Tom Parker Bowles was dining near us and William Sitwell apparently was in earlier in the week so we will be reading about it the the press!" – and indeed we have, regarding this bucolically located inn (with five bedrooms), which has been lovingly and stylishly restored. It has proved one of the most hotly anticipated openings of the year, due to owner Max Wigram's long-trailed invitation to the stoves to star chef Margot Henderson OBE (of East London's Rochelle Canteen) who he has known since her teens. It opened in the middle of our survey and generated too little feedback for a firm rating, although what we do have mentions of "admirable" service and some "very good lemon sole with exotic homemade tartare sauce and excellent tossed chicken". Meanwhile the aforementioned press critics have fallen over themselves to swoon… although given Margot's impeccable in-crowd credentials this was always likely. / thethreehorseshoesbatcombe.co.uk; thethreehorseshoesbatcombe; Mon-Sun 11 pm.

BATH, SOMERSET 2–2B

THE BECKFORD BOTTLE SHOP £63 3 4 4

5-8 SAVILLE ROW
BA1 2QP 01225 809302

This "interesting restaurant set in a bottle shop" (est. 2015) is part of the Beckford group, which runs four SW England inns, and – as of December 2022 – Bath's Beckford Canteen, set in a Georgian greenhouse. The "tapas-style food" is "very moreish" and there's unsurprisingly a "good, reasonably priced wine list" to go with it, making it "very popular" and "deservedly so". / beckfordbottleshop.com; beckfordbottles; Tue-Sat 11 pm.

BECKFORD CANTEEN £65 4 3 3

11-12 BARTLETT STREET
BA1 2QZ 01225 338470

This widely fêted newcomer is a "welcome restaurant version" of the nearby Beckford Bottle Shop (see also), set "in a lovely old greenhouse" with "very nicely done décor". "The food is very good indeed" under highly rated ex-Kitty Fisher's/Cora Pearl chef George Barson, and has wowed critics including Grace Dent of The Guardian ("a delicious paean to modern British classics and comfort foods") and Giles Coren of The Times ("staggering beef tongue crumpet"). Top Menu Tip – "the fried pommes Anna are to die for". / beckfordcanteen.com; beckfordcanteen; Wed-Sat 11 pm, Sun 6 pm.

CHEZ DOMINIQUE £69 3 2 2

15 ARGYLE STREET
BA2 4BQ 01225 463482

"Very enjoyable French food in a convivial atmosphere" ensures the continued high success of Chris Tabbitt (ex-of London haunt Bibendum) and Sarah Olivier's modern European, est. 2016 and named after their first child. It's a "comfortable and not showy" sort of place with "casual" service, where no one doubts the "very proficient" cooking ("not cheap, but definitely felt good value for the overall meal"). / chezdominique.co.uk; chezdominique; Sun-Thu 9 pm, Fri & Sat 9.30 pm.

THE CIRCUS £57 3 4 2

34 BROCK ST BA1 2LN 01225 466020

"Pleased to say standards remain high in this popular and much commented-on bistro serving modern European food", in a useful central location. it's "one of the best choices in a city served mainly by the chains". / thecircusrestaurant.co.uk; thecircusrestaurant; Mon-Sat midnight.

CLAYTON'S KITCHEN £92 3 3 3

15A GEORGE ST
BA1 2EN 01225 585 100

"Buzzy" and "very popular city centre spot" that excels for its "great food, friendly ambience and good value". Chef-patron Rob Clayton opened it 12 years ago, after seven years as head chef at the Bath Priory Hotel. He has worked in top kitchens for 35 years, including a stint at Chez Nico in London. / claytonskitchen.com; claytons_kitchen; Wed & Thu 9.30 pm, Fri & Sat 10 pm, Sun 9 pm.

COLONNA & SMALLS £14 3 4 4

6 CHAPEL ROW BA1 1HN 07766 808067

"If you like coffee, this is the place to go" – founder Maxwell Colonna-Dashwood, three-times UK barista champion, has "unbeatable coffee knowledge" and his "friendly, engaged" staff also "really know their stuff", which includes some "unusual" eans! / colonnacoffee.com; colonnacoffee; Mon-at 5.30 pm, Sun 4 pm.

CORKAGE (CHAPEL ROW) £75

CHAPEL ROW BA1 1HN 01225 423417

imited but positive feedback this year on is well-established wine bar and bottle op, whose distinguishing feature is a large, arn-like extension and terrace that really omes into its own during the warmer onths. / corkagebath.com; corkagebath; Mon-at midnight.

THE ELDER AT THE INDIGO HOTEL 3 3 3

SOUTH PARADE A2 4AB 01225 530616

Great for game if you are in Bath" – a pleasant" and clubby hotel-restaurant that's e brainchild of Mike Robinson, of London's cclaimed Harwood Arms, and accordingly rong on venison et. al. The venue occupies everal adjoining Georgian townhouses, and the ictuals are "gusty" and "immensely satisfying", s The Telegraph's William Sitwell put it in Nov 2022 review (also proclaiming that he ould "rave about this joint well into the New ear"). / theelder.co.uk; theelderrestaurant; Wed-at 11 pm, Sun 9 pm.

THE GAFF BATH £38 4 4 4

9 MILSOM PLACE A1 1BZ 01225 984834

A brilliant new addition to the city" – this late 022 newcomer is a sibling to the Abergavenny mall plates restaurant from Daniel Saunders nd Danielle Phillips and is tucked away n the centre, off Broad Street. Feedback "outstanding" but more limited than we ould like, but in an August 2023 review, The elegraph's William Sitwell also raved over its bang-on-trend" formula, dubbing it "top notch nd stunning value". / thegaffrestaurant.co.uk; egaffinbath; Wed-Sat 9 pm, Sun 3 pm.

GREEN PARK BRASSERIE £43 2 3 3

GREEN PARK STATION A1 1JB 01225 338565

A good, no-nonsense place to eat, with outside eaters" – this local landmark is housed in an ld 1870s station on the fringe of the city centre next to the old Ironbridge railway line) and is elebrating over 30 years in business. Billing self as a steakhouse and jazz bar – and they lso do a good line in pizza – it doesn't aim for oodie fireworks, but is well-rated across the oard. / greenparkbrasserie.com; GreenParkBraz; un-Thu 10 pm, Fri & Sat 11.30 pm.

HARE & HOUNDS £71 3 3 4

ANSDOWN ROAD A1 5TJ 01225 482682

Outstanding views from the dining rea" and "lovely garden" over the urrounding countryside (top walking territory) characterise this well-liked stone gastroboozer; there are plaudits too for its "small menu of good classics" (plus latterly small plates). / hareandhoundsbath.com; harehoundsbath; Mon-Sun 9 pm.

HENRY'S RESTAURANT £89 4 3 3

4 SAVILLE ROW BA1 2QP 01225 780055

Chef-patron Henry Scott offers "two inventive set menus" at his 'zero waste' Georgian townhouse (five and seven courses, each also available as vegetarian, plus a simpler lunchtime option) – both of which are by all accounts "delicious". "The five-course vegetarian 'Earth' menu was perfection – every course delightful and each one managed to complement the next". / henrysrestaurantbath.com; henrysrestaurantbath; Wed-Sat, Tue 8.30 pm.

THE IVY BATH BRASSERIE £84 2 2 3

39 MILSOM ST BA1 1DS 01225 307 100

The "gorgeous room" is the highlight of a visit to this popular outpost of the "ever-expanding chain", whose interior design based on the famous London original in Theatreland trumps the "unremarkable" cuisine. Flexibility is much of the appeal – there's a "good varied all day menu, plus options for brunch or afternoon tea". / theivybathbrasserie.com; the_ivy_collection; Mon-Thu 10 pm, Fri & Sat 10.30 pm, Sun 9.30 pm.

MARLBOROUGH TAVERN £61 3 2 2

35 MARLBOROUGH BUILDINGS BA1 2LY 01225 423731

This gastropub with a garden, in an attractive setting near Victoria Park, is handy for the city centre and won solid support all-round this year in our annual diners' poll. / marlborough-tavern.com; marlboroughtavern; Mon-Sat 9 pm, Sun 8 pm.

NOYA'S KITCHEN £56 4 4 3

7 SAINT JAMES'S PARADE BA1 1UL 01225 684439

"Brilliant Vietnamese venue, owned by chef Noya who was taught to cook by her mum". "Honest and fresh-flavoured dishes" are "prepared with flair" in this "vibrant", "reasonably priced" townhouse restaurant, where the "consistently friendly and enthusiastic service contributes to a lovely experience" – "every time I go here, I come out with a smile!" / noyaskitchen.co.uk; noyaskitchen; Tue-Sat 3.30 pm.

OAK £51 4 3 3

2 NORTH PARADE PASSAGE BA1 1NX 01225 446059

"Creative and mesmerising cooking" – including "magical vegan sauces with astonishing creaminess" – draws an appreciative crowd to this vegetarian spot "in the heart of Bath". The modern small-plates menu with a five-course tasting option is backed up by a list of natural wines, and many of the ingredients are grown in its own chemical-free market garden a few miles away. Fans say it's "one of my favourite places on Earth – and such friendly service!" / oakrestaurant.co.uk; oakrestaurantbath; Mon-Sun 9.30 pm.

OLE TAPAS £49 3 4 3

1 JOHN STREET BA1 2JL 01225 424274

This "tiny upstairs tapas bar" turns out plates (tortillas, patatas bravas, calamari) so "authentic" that "if you don't look out the one window, you could be in Barcelona" (instead of round the corner from the city's Jane Austen Centre); fans "just wish it was bigger". / oletapas.co.uk; oletapasuk; Wed-Fri, Sun 10 pm, Sat 11 pm.

THE OLIVE TREE, QUEENSBERRY HOTEL £163 4 3 2

RUSSELL ST BA1 2QF 01225447928

"An incredible, unpretentious dining experience" with "varied and sumptuous tastes and service that's attentive but not fussy" is hailed in all reports on Chris Cleghorn's long-established venue. "The nine-course tasting menu is imaginative, beautifully presented and very tasty with some unusual flavours" (it's £160 per person, with a six-course option available for £130, and other cheaper menus available at lunchtime and earlier in the week). It's located in the cellar of a 'proudly independent' boutique hotel and is currently the city's only establishment to hold a Michelin star. / olivetreebath.co.uk; olivetreebath; Tue-Sun 9 pm.

PLATE £60 3 3 3

18-19 PULTENEY ROAD BA2 4EZ 01225 580438

This "quirky, bright dining room" offers "excellent service and pretty decent food for a hotel restaurant". "They also have a very good stab at breakfast for residents in the morning". / thebirdbath.co.uk; Mon-Sat 9.30 pm.

ROBUN £60

4 PRINCES BUILDING, GEORGE STREET BA1 2ED 01225 614 424

Too limited feedback for a rating, but that which we received is promising on this central Japanese two-year-old, which – as well as offering sushi – specialises in Yakiniku, which is cooking over charcoal (it's named for the Japanese food writer who introduced western-style BBQ into Japan in the 1870s). / robun.co.uk; robunrestaurant; Mon-Sun 11 pm.

THE SCALLOP SHELL £67 4 3 3

22 MONMOUTH PLACE BA1 2AY 01225 420928

This "exceptional" and rather posh chippy is reputedly MPW's favourite restaurant in the region, and all of the many reporters who commented on it this year praised its "truly excellent" food ("whether you opt for fish 'n' chips or grilled skate wing, it'll impress!"). In recent years, they've added a roof terrace – plus a sibling, The Oyster Shell, near the Theatre Royal, which offers fishy treats and fritters to go. / thescallopshell.co.uk; thescallopshell; Mon-Sat 9.30 pm, Sun 3 pm.

UPSTAIRS AT LANDRACE £77 443

61 WALCOT STREET
BA1 5BN 01225 424722

"A favourite in Bath" – this "intimate and relaxed small space" upstairs from the popular Landrace bakery "produces beautiful, well-cooked plates of local, in season, produce". "The couple that run it" (ex-Quality Chop House and Brawn chef Rob Sachdev and ex-Big Jo manager Jude Copperman, who re-thought their London lives during lockdown) "are passionate about their business, and the menu changes weekly with typically small-plate starters of salads, cold cuts and amazing cheese fritters. Mains usually consist of a meat, fish or vegetarian option, typically a pasta dish which is silky and delicious". / landracebakery.com; landraceupstairs; Tue-Sat 9.45 pm.

BAUGHURST, HAMPSHIRE 2–3D

THE WELLINGTON ARMS £76 333

BAUGHURST RD
RG26 5LP 0118 982 0110

"Every village should have one" – a "really pretty pub (with rooms) and a beautiful garden" in the "lovely" setting of the Wellington Estate. Chef Jason King does not trade on its location, as his elevated pub-style classics (featuring produce plucked from the garden) are "imaginative" and "cooked to perfection" too. Top Tip – they sell their own bread and gin over the bar. / thewellingtonarms.com; thewellingtonarms; Tue-Sat 8.30 pm.

BEACONSFIELD, BUCKINGHAMSHIRE 3–3A

THE CAPE GRAND CAFE & RESTAURANT £62

6A, BURKES PARADE
HP9 1NN 01494 681137

This "great independent cafe recently changed hands when the owner sold it on to the longstanding manager" and, having initially been open just during the day ("very good salads and quiches" plus other South African-slanted breakfasts and brunch dishes and "excellent coffee"), it's now also back to offering more complex meals at weekend dinners. Insufficient reports for a rating at this time of change. / thecapeonline.com; thecapebeaconsfield; Mon-Sat 4 pm, Sun 3 pm.

THE GREYHOUND £95 444

33 WINDSOR END
HP9 2JN 01494 671315

Four years down the line, Daniel Crump and Margriet Vandezande-Crump's "gorgeous" converted seventeenth-century coaching inn is simply "perfection" to the very many diners who comment on it: "not only do you experience fine dining" (an "innovative menu" whose "consistency is something to behold"), "but you get the choice of great beers too, because it's a pub!" On the food front, "excellent" tasting menus (including dedicated vegetarian and vegan options) are ably abetted by a "brilliant-value set lunch". Add in "incredible" service and "what more could you want?" / greyhoundbeaconsfield.co.uk; greyhoundbeaconsfield; Tue-Sat 8.30 pm.

RIWAZ BY ATUL KOCHHAR £78 323

41 AYLESBURY END
HP9 1LU 01494 728126

Slightly mixed feedback this year on this Indian two-year-old run by well-known chef, Atul Kochhar. Some reports acclaim it as "outstanding" in all respects. A medium view is that it's "not fine dining and still finding its level", while the least positive report says, "it attracts the 'look at me, me, me' brigade and is overpriced". Still, local popularity is such that in late 2023 they've now added takeaway to its offering. / riwazrestaurants.co.uk; riwazbucks; Wed-Sat 10 pm, Sun 9.30 pm.

THE ROYAL STANDARD OF ENGLAND £63 234

FORTY GREEN HP9 1XT 01494 673 382

This "fantastic" brick-and-timber boozer is a properly historic venue which, at 900 years old, may even be England's oldest free house; its warren-like rooms have featured on many a TV show (not least 'Midsomer Murders', which is namechecked by their chicken pie), and its menu of pleasing classics (burgers, fish pies) plays an admirable supporting role. / theoldestpub.com; theoldestpub; Mon-Sat 10 pm, Sun 9 pm.

BEAMINSTER, DORSET 2–4B

THE OLLEROD £77 333

3 PROUT HILL DT8 3AY 01308 862200

Former The Pig alumnus Silvana Bandini (FOH) and ex-Bath Priory/Mandarin Oriental chef Chris Staines are behind this "hidden gem" – a "comfortable" hotel-restaurant, set in a characterful fourteenth-century building, and with an "attractive outside space". The "delicious, sophisticated" small-plates menu is strong on SW produce and offers solid (fans would say "exceptional") value. / theollerod.co.uk; theollerod; Mon & Tue, Thu-Sat 9 pm, Sun 6 pm, Wed 10 am.

BEAULIEU, HAMPSHIRE 2–4D

THE TERRACE, MONTAGU ARMS HOTEL £118 333

SO42 7ZL 01590 612324

In the heart of Beaulieu, this Arts & Crafts building set in lovely gardens is one of the New Forest's best known luxury hotels. You can eat pub grub in 'Monty's Inn', but the main event is The Terrace: a comfortably plush dining room, which achieves good all-round (if limited feedback for its traditional – but not super-expensive – fare, backed up by an impressive 300-bin wine list. / montaguarmshotel.co.uk; montaguarms; Sat & Sun, Wed-Fri 9 pm.

BECKENHAM, GREATER LONDON 3–3B

CHAI NAASTO £52 433

2 - 4 FAIRFIELD ROAD
BR3 3LD 020 3750 0888

This suburban subcontinental offers an unusual take on Indian street food, having been set up by three brothers keen to pay homage to their grandmother's cooking, inflected by her travels in Africa and Saudi Arabia; its "authentic" recipes attract nothing but positive reports. / chai-naasto.co.uk; chai_naasto; Wed-Sat 9.45 pm, Sun 8 pm.

BEDFORD, BEDFORDSHIRE 3–1A

CHAAT HAUS £25 333

32 THE BROADWAY
MK40 2TH 01234 351870

"Fab! – small, well-run, and serving freshly cooked Asian street food"; given the above, plus the stylish setting and "great selection of curries, more unusual than most curry houses", it's certainly one of the city's most enticing options. / chaathaus.co.uk; chaathausbedford; Mon, Wed-Sun 10.30 pm.

BELFAST, COUNTY ANTRIM 10–1D

DEANES EIPIC £121 343

28-40 HOWARD STREET
BT1 6PF 028 9033 1134

"I was able to eat Alex Greene's GBM-winning Incredible Edible Book and it was just as delicious as it looked, topping off a great meal!" – Michael Deane's flagship destination in the city-centre won nothing but praise for its ambitious and much-accoladed cuisine, with chef Alex offering an à la carte selection or menu surprise at quieter times, but with the main event being the £100 per head tasting menu. Eipic itself is on the top floor of a three-floor operation run by Deane, and you enter via the other spaces. / deaneseipic.com; DEANES_EIPIC; Thu-Sat 9 pm.

EDO £49 433

3 CAPITAL HOUSE, UNIT 2 UPPER QUEEN STREET BT1 6FB 028 9031 3054

Jonny Elliott's "buzzing restaurant a short walk from Belfast City Hall" is set around "an open kitchen where you can sit and watch the busy chefs prepare your food" – "Spanish (and

Wilson's, Bristol

more)-style plates with fresh local produce (the scallops were fabulous), a good wine list and friendly, attentive staff" make it an attractive option. Linguistic note: 'edo' is Latin for 'I eat'. / edorestaurant.co.uk; edobelfast; Tue-Sat 9.30 pm.

MOURNE SEAFOOD BAR £55 443

34 - 36 BANK STREET BT1 1HL 028 9024 8544

"Very atmospheric, rustic and friendly, and with exceptional seafood" – this cosy venue is one of the best-known in the city (and also has a sister establishment in Dundrum) – "have eaten here several times and would certainly recommend it". Last year we commented on its excellent newly extended beer garden with gazebos, which in July 2023 was the victim of an arson attack – here's hoping it's soon restored to its former glory. / mourneseafood.com; Mourne Seafood Bar; Tue-Thu 9.30 pm, Fri & Sat 10 pm, Sun 6 pm.

THE MUDDLERS CLUB £113 544

1 WAREHOUSE LANE BT1 2DX 028 9031 3199

"Adding to Belfast's improving food scene" – Gareth McCaughey's "buzzy" fixture opened in 2015 "in the thriving Cathedral Quarter of the city" and has emerged as one of the top destinations in Northern Ireland. The contemporary style of its glazed frontage and industrial design is carried into its seven-course menu for £90 per person: "a series of fabulous delights, with friendly attentive service and a great wine list or wine matching recommendations from their sommelier and an open kitchen to see all the activity of the chefs". / themuddlersclubbelfast.com; themuddlersclubbelfast; Wed-Sat 9.30 pm.

BELPER, DERBYSHIRE 5–3C

ARTHUR £77 442

1C CAMPBELL STREET DE56 1AP 07709 209260

BYOB fine dining? That's the unlikely formula at this relaxed 24-cover restaurant in the backstreets, run by local couple Leo Hill and Amelia Hawkins, and lauded by the Observer Food Monthly amongst others. On the basis of positive but thin feedback: expect "tasting menus only" (five- and ten-course versions that change monthly and are marked by a nostalgia for childhood classics) wherein "every mouthful is amazing". Unusual gripe: there's just "too much of the fabulous food!" / arthursbelper.co.uk; arthursbelper; Wed-Sat 8.30 pm.

BEMBRIDGE, ISLE OF WIGHT 2–4D

BEST DRESSED CRAB £35 444

FISHERMAN'S WHARF, EMBANKMENT ROAD, PO35 5N5 01983 874 758

This "great seafood restaurant, on a pontoon on the harbour" at Bembridge, serves only fresh local lobster, crab and prawns in season, with some mussels and clams. Now in its third decade, it is run by Graham Henley, a second-generation fisherman and former lifeboat crewman. With only five tables, booking is essential – but you can buy crustacea to take home. / thebestdressedcrabintown.co.uk; Mon-Sun 3 pm.

THE CRAB AND LOBSTER INN £64 333

32 FORELANDS FIELD RD PO35 5TR 01983 872244

"Situated on the seafront at Bembridge", on the eastern side of the isle, this early nineteenth century gastropub-with-rooms provides "a nice range of delicious seafood dishes", including the trademark crab and lobster. / characterinns.co.uk; Mon-Sun midnight.

BEVERLEY, EAST YORKSHIRE 6–2A

THE PIPE & GLASS £86 444

WEST END HU17 7PN 01430 810246

"Always-excellent food in beautiful, quaint surroundings" has made James & Kate Mackenzie's former coaching inn a real East Yorkshire destination for almost 20 years – "and everyone is so friendly". There's "no tasting menu, but with such good options amongst the selection of dishes, that makes a refreshing change". Top Tip – with seven boutique bedrooms, it's "a great place to stay because the breakfast is amazing: five or so choices of fish for breakfast, most places you'd be lucky to get one!". / pipeandglass.co.uk; pipeandglass; Tue-Sat 11 pm, Sun 4 pm.

THE WESTWOOD RESTAURANT £84 443

NEW WALK HU17 7AE 01482 881999

A Grade II-listed Georgian courthouse is the setting for siblings Michele (FOH) and Matt (chef) Barker's long-running restaurant (est. 2007), whose "fantastic" locally sourced British cooking and appealing atmosphere make it "great for business, romance or lunch" (not least the "really good" set lunch in the case of the latter). / thewestwood.co.uk; the_westwood_restaurant; Tue-Sat 9.30 pm.

BIDBOROUGH, KENT 3–3B

KENTISH HARE £76 443

95 BIDBOROUGH RIDGE TN3 0XB 01892 525709

In a "pretty village setting" ("what's not to like about sitting under a pergola in the Kent countryside?"), seasoned restaurateurs the Tanner brothers run this much-garlanded gastroboozer. The food choices are "simply cooked" but "not mundane like you could do yourself" (indeed, "to call this pub food would be truly a disservice"). / thekentishhare.com; thekentishharepub; Wed-Sat 9.30 pm, Sun 3.30 pm

BIDDENDEN, KENT 3–4C

THE THREE CHIMNEYS £54 33

HAREPLAIN RD TN27 8LW 01580 29147

This "delightful country pub" has a characterful fifteenth-century setting and five modern bedrooms in a converted nuttery above the gardens; it won praise this year for its "interesting and well-executed" locally sourced cuisine – served across five different dining areas – and even one reporter who had an off-visit rated it "very good". / thethreechimneys.co.uk; Mon-Sat 11 pm, Sun 10.30 pm.

THE WEST HOUSE RESTAURANT WITH ROOMS £100 33

28 HIGH ST TN27 8AH 01580 291341

Former rock drummer Graham Garrett's quirky 16th century restaurant-with-rooms in a "lovely village" in the Kent Weald has been beating off the competition since back in 2002. The set menus showcase some "very good cooking" based on "top-quality ingredients" – and while "just a few tables can mean there is a certain formality to it all", it's "none the worse for that". / thewesthouserestaurant.co.uk; thewesthouserestaurant; Thu-Sat 9.30 pm, Sun 2.30 pm.

BIGBURY-ON-SEA, DEVON 1–4D

THE OYSTER SHACK £69 33

MILLBURN ORCHARD FARM, STAKES HILLS TQ7 4BE 01548 810876

"Shack is the right word for this ultra-casual restaurant specialising in delicious oysters but also serving freshly caught fish" – one reporter summarises the limitations (but mostly charms) of this former oyster farm, where you can now dine inside by the fire or on the outdoor terrace. / oystershack.co.uk; theoystershack; Mon-Sun 7.30 pm.

BILTON IN AINSTY, NORTH YORKSHIRE 5–1D

TICKLED TROUT £31 33

CHURCH STREET YO26 7NN 01423 359006

On the main road to York, and handy for the Wetherby Racecourse, this "lovely old pub" with rooms has had a new lease of life since its 2019 takeover by the Mainey family, who reopened its fireplaces and restored its beams and flagstone floors. The "food is of a good gastropub level, and the outside areas (two big tents and a covered and heated area) are very pleasant" too. / tickledtrout.co.uk; the_tickled_trout_inn; Mon-Sat 9.30 pm, Sun 7 pm.

BINFIELD HEATH, BERKSHIRE 2–2D

HE BOTTLE & GLASS NN £64 343

ONES LANE RG9 4JT 01491 412 625

Everything you want in a country pub" ccording to fans of this thatched free ouse on the Phillimore Estate, a short rive outside Henley-on-Thames and on e edge of the Chilterns. Run by David olliday and with chef Alex Sargeant – both -Harwood Arms in Fulham – it has a lelightful dining room with food that's at e top end of gastropub grub" and for less nbitious fare, head to the adjoining 'burger arn'. / bottleandglassinn.co.uk; bottleandglassinn; 'ed-Sat 11 pm, Sun 6 pm.

BIRMINGHAM, WEST MIDLANDS 5–4C

DAM'S, NEW OXFORD OUSE £127 553

6 WATERLOO ST B2 5UG 0121 643 3745

Smart, chic, highly professional" – Adam & atasha Stokes's "commendably consistent" peration is "outstanding in every respect" nd "one of the leading lights in Brum's gh-quality restaurant scene": in fact the No. in the city in our annual diners' poll this ear where European cuisine is concerned. Not cheap but worth every penny", its entral location and "unfailingly impressive ombination of brilliant cooking and resentation with excellent service" makes it ust the setting for a business meal" (the top ption is to be "royally looked after at the ef's table"). Top Tip – "the set menu at lunch brilliant value". / adamsrestaurant.co.uk; estaurantAdams; Tue-Sat 9 pm.

SHA'S INDIAN BAR AND ESTAURANT £60 333

2-22 NEWHALL STREET 3 3AS 0121 200 2767

rooftop fire in July 2023 briefly shuttered is hugely popular hangout of stars, and fering northwest Indian food that's packed ith taste; it's now back in business and while not cheap", you can expect "a stand-out eal every time with a proper cocktail bar nd Bollywood ambience" befitting its owner nonagenarian singer Asha Bhosle, who was amechecked in Cornershop's hit 'Brimful of sha'. / ashasbirmingham.co.uk; ashasuk.

ARTERS OF OSELEY £165

C WAKE GREEN RD 13 9EZ 0121 449 8885

July 2023, after our annual diners' poll ad concluded, Brad Carter and his team pped sticks from the rather moody premises ey previously inhabited in Birmingham's Ioseley to move to one of the glasshouses Westlands UK, providers of the produce at they used daily in the city, in a pop- p supported by boutique English winery, usbourne, to showcase Westlands' produce. riginally due to run till September 2023, its future is unknown as we go to press so this is something of a holding entry. All feedback, though, acknowledges Brad's cuisine as "often exceptional with many excellent, often original dishes" and his team "really know how to run a restaurant" with service that's "friendly but respectful, usually knowledgeable and always helpful". (Westlands UK, Station Road, Offenham, Worcestershire, WR11 8LW – booking is online.) / cartersofmoseley.co.uk; cartersofmoseley; Fri & Sat, Wed & Thu midnight.

CHAKANA £54 333

140 ALCESTER ROAD B13 8HS 0121 448 9880

Chef Robert Ortiz has introduced his "delicious and extraordinarily colourful Peruvian cuisine" to the West Midlands at the converted bank in Moseley he opened five years ago – a "relaxing place for a meal, with a spacious dining area and good service". Only authentic ingredients are used, and the bar stocks an impressive range of pisco, the national spirit. / chakana-restaurant.co.uk; chakana. restaurant; Wed & Thu 10 pm, Fri & Sat 11 pm, Sun 6 pm.

DISHOOM £41 445

1 CHAMBERLAIN SQUARE B3 3AX 0121 809 5986

"Excellent Indian food that's amongst the very best in an area where such restaurants are plentiful" – this outpost of London's smash-hit chain wins strong ratings, despite the local tradition of brilliant subcontinental cuisine, for its innovative – often "exceptional" – dishes and winning retro style (influenced by the Parsi cafés of 1940s Mumbai). It's in a big, 330-cover site, overlooking Birmingham Town Hall from the city's Paradise development. / dishoom.com; dishoom; Sun-Thu 11 pm, Fri & Sat midnight. SRA – 2 stars

FOLIUM £86 433

8 CAROLINE STREET B3 1TR 0121 638 0100

Noma alumnus Ben Tesh and partner Lucy Hanlon run this "lovely smallish restaurant" in the Jewellery Quarter, whose "fantastic tasting menus" (comprising "classic dishes with a twist") come in 'short' or 'long' versions – the latter going 14 rounds. The "brilliant" venture, which was launched in 2017, elicited real raves again this year: for one fan, this is "perhaps the finest, truest expression of modern British cuisine in the West Midlands". / restaurantfolium.com; restaurantfolium; Wed & Thu 8 pm, Fri & Sat 9 pm, Sun 1.30 pm.

HARBORNE KITCHEN £121 433

175-179 HIGH ST B17 9QE 01214399150

This "absolute jewel of a place" in Harborne, two miles from Birmingham city centre, is hailed by fans for its "outstanding food and divine tasting menus", while "the unusual wine pairings work really well" – "how it doesn't have a Michelin star is beyond us all!". Midlands-born chef-patron Jamie Desogus (formerly of Gordon Ramsay's Pétrus) opened the venue in 2016, and has not faltered since. Top Tip – the reduced five-course weeknight menu offers "exceptionally good value". / harbornekitchen.com; harbornekitchen; Wed & Thu 7.45 pm, Fri 8 pm, Sat 9 pm.

LASAN £68 432

3-4 DAKOTA BUILDINGS, JAMES STREET B3 1SD 0121 212 3664

This "glitzy post-modern Indian" in the Jewellery Quarter serves "solid accomplished food" in a "stunning dining room". Now 21 years old, it was an early pioneer of ambitious modern British-Indian cuisine but these days faces "lots of competition" in this field – not least from founding chef Aktar Islam, who left to open Opheem (see also). / lasan.co.uk; lasan_restaurant; Tue-Fri 10 pm, Sat 11 pm, Sun 9 pm.

OPHEEM £73 544

65 SUMMER ROW B3 1JJ 0121 201 3377

"Just wow!" – Aktar Islam's city-centre HQ reliably "lives up to expectations… and more!"; and remains Brum's most commented on and highest-rated destination in our annual diners' poll. "His unique twist on his family's ancestral dishes with superb matching wine flight provided by sommelier Stefan" (Liperowski) "magnificently takes Indian food to the highest possible level" – "flavours are off the scale" – and "the range and variety of each distinctly different meal is glorious". / opheem.com; opheemrestaurant; Wed-Sat 9.30 pm.

ORELLE 335

103 COLMORE ROW B3 3AG 0121 716 8186

A "stunning location" (and suitability for business dining) are undisputed attractions of this year-old newcomer from D&D London, whose huge windows offer a bird's eye view of Brum from the 24th floor of the city's tallest office building. All reports are fundamentally positive regarding the modern brasserie cuisine (top slot on the menu is côte de boeuf or châteaubriand to share) if with the caveat that the odd dish is "rather ordinary". / orellerestaurant; Mon-Sat 10 pm, Sun 4.30 pm.

THE OYSTER CLUB £92 333

43 TEMPLE STREET B2 5DP 0121 643 6070

Adam Stokes' more casual – but still very posh, down to the marble-topped tables – offshoot to his acclaimed Adam's, on nearby Bennett's Hill; it "not surprisingly specialises in fish and seafood dishes", reflecting the name, and while ratings tend to be rather up and down, there are early reports of some "lovely" cooking since the 2023 arrival of new chef Stuart Langdell, whose CV includes Simpson's in Birmingham, and MPW's Pear Tree Inn in Whitley, Wiltshire. / the-oyster-club.co.uk; the_oysterclub; Wed & Thu 11 pm, Fri & Sat 00 am, Sun 10 pm.

PLATES BY PURNELL'S £35 333

121 EDMUND STREET B3 2HJ 0121 461 9254

"Glynn Purnell's most recent addition to his Birmingham portfolio specialises in Spanish tapas" and opened, just around the corner from his main gaff, in spring 2023. It's rated on the basis of a couple of early-days reports, which say that "dishes are mostly very tasty and reasonably portioned" and that the space is "nicely decorated (if narrow and L-shaped"). / platesbypurnells.com; platesbypurnells; Wed-Sat 10 pm.

PURNELLS £115 444

55 CORNWALL ST B3 2DH 0121 212 9799

An "enjoyable if slightly flash" Birmingham "icon" that "continues to deliver fine cuisine with wit" – TV chef (and 'Yummy Brummie') Glynn Purnell's "guvnor of West Midlands cuisine" continues to win high praise with "on-the-ball service" and "clever" cuisine that's "thoughtful, robust, balanced… everything you'd hope for". One or two diners this year noted that "there can be a tendency to place too many old favourites on the menu, albeit often with a new twist", but even they feel that quality is "still consistent". Top Tip – "an extremely fine long lunch" wins tips for this it as "the best place to do business in Birmingham". / purnellsrestaurant.com; purnellsrestaurant; Tue-Sat midnight.

SABAI SABAI £47 333

25 WOODBRIDGE ROAD B13 8EH 0121 449 4498

Torquil and Juree Chidwick's Moseley Village fixture is celebrating its twentieth year (est. 2003) and continues to inspire solid feedback for its 'true taste of Thailand'. Over the last twelve months, they expanded further with a new Solihull outpost, complete with outside seating. / sabaisabai-restaurant.co.uk; sabaisabai_restaurant; Mon-Sun 11 pm.

TROPEA £39 433

27 LORDSWOOD RD B17 9RP 0121 427 9777

Inspired by the Calabrian town of the same name, this "tiny" Harborne two-year-old from Kasia Piatkowska and Ben Robinson-Young (who met while studying to be chefs at the University College of Birmingham) is making waves with its "delicious small plates for sharing". It's "very good value indeed" – "the courgette flowers stuffed with ricotta drizzled with local honey was a standout dish and their aubergine parmigiana is the best ever!" / tropea.uk; tropea_harborne; Tue-Sat midnight.

THE WILDERNESS £131 544

27 WARSTONE LANE B18 6JQ 0121 233 9425

"Unmissable!". "Chef-patron Alex Claridge with head chef Marius Gedminas are at the cutting edge of modern British cuisine" at this Jewellery Quarter venue, which is "very much of 2023" with its moodily decorated black-painted brick walls, dark wood, dark leather and open kitchen. "It produces superbly original, highly inventive, exciting and ultimately delicious tasting menus with a passion which one could only wish that all British chefs brought with them, with some exceptional items that could only be described as works of art". / wearethewilderness.co.uk; thewildernessrestaurant; Tue-Sat 8.30 pm.

BLAIRGOWRIE, PERTH AND KINROSS 9–3C

KINLOCH HOUSE £93 333

PH10 6SG 01250 884 732

"Always a pleasure, combining excellence all round" – this luxurious, family Relais & Châteaux property (built in 1840) has long been a mainstay of the surrounding area, with its "assured cooking of quality ingredients, particularly excellent meat". / kinlochhouse.com; kinlochhouse; Mon-Sun 8.30 pm.

BLAKENEY, NORFOLK 6–3C

THE MOORINGS £67 433

HIGH STREET NR25 7NA 01263 740 054

A "great-value" menu featuring plenty of fresh fish, along with local meat and game, has attracted a loyal following for this "very friendly" family-run North Norfolk venue over more than 20 years. Co-chef/founder Angela Long has ensured that standards remain high since the loss of her husband, Richard, two years ago. / blakeney-moorings.co.uk; themooringsblakeney; Tue-Sat 9 pm.

BOGNOR REGIS, WEST SUSSEX 3–4A

CHEZ MOI £54 342

49 ALDWICK ROAD PO21 2NJ 01243 825445

"Fantastic food from an ex-Gavroche husband and wife team" – Nathalie and Michael Newton-Young, who met working for the Roux brothers 30 years ago – "who would have thought Bognor could do this? (sorry, Bognor)". This is "classic French cooking by a very experienced chef who trained alongside Gordon Ramsay and spent his early career working at the highest level before settling with his family"; decor-wise "piles of acquired trinkets on the walls lend an olde-worlde type feel". / chezmoialdwick.com; chezmoi_aldwick; Thu-Sat 8.30 pm, Sun 7.30 pm.

BOLNHURST, BEDFORDSHIRE 3–1A

THE PLOUGH AT BOLNHURST £83 343

MK44 2EX 01234 376274

This "lovely 'olde worlde' village pub" (dating from the Tudor era) puts in a "consistently assured performance" under Martyn & Jayne Lee, owners since 2005, with "terrific food and excellent service" – "nothing much changes (which is not a criticism!)". / bolnhurst.com; ploughatbolnhurst; Wed-Fri 10.30 pm, Sat 11 pm, Sun 4 pm.

BOLTON ABBEY, NORTH YORKSHIRE 5–1C

THE BRASSERIE AT THE DEVONSHIRE ARMS HOTEL AND SPA, THE DEVONSHIRE ARMS £70 23

BD23 6AJ 01756 718100

The more casual (and vividly hued) dining option at this hotel owned by the Duke and Duchess of Devonshire turns out "good food" of a brasserie bent, featuring plenty of produce grown on the estate and in the hotel's kitchen garden. A "great open-plan wine cellar" and terrace add to its charms. / devonshirehotels.co.uk; devarmsboltonabbey; Mon-Sun 9 pm.

BOLTON BY BOWLAND, LANCASHIRE 5–1E

COACH AND HORSES £43 34

MAIN STREET BB7 4NW 01200 447 331

In a "lovely setting in an archetypically unspoilt Ribble Valley village, complete with stocks on the village green", Susan Lord and Dutch husband Ko Labeij's slick village inn is a "wonderful find" by all accounts; "the menu reads well: simple and manageable" pub classics (or more adventurous tasting menus on Fri & Sat nights), and it's a proper boozer too – "now with its own microbrewery" tapping the local well water in its 4 Mice ales. / coachandhorsesribblevalley.co.uk; coachandhorsesrv; Wed-Sat 9 pm, Sun 5.30 pm.

BOREHAMWOOD, HERTFORDSHIRE 3–2A

KIYOTO £30 33

31 SHENLEY ROAD WD6 1AE 0203 489 6800

The original in a small family-owned group specialising in sushi that is "always quick and super-fresh, with great presentation and delicious". Brothers Jason & Adam Balsam launched the business in 2015, hiring Japanese chefs in their mission to bring high-quality sush at reasonable prices to the north London 'burb Branches have followed in West Hampstead, Mill Hill, Cockfosters and most recently Hatch End. / kiyotosushi.co.uk; kiyotosushi; Mon-Sun 9.30 pm.

BOSCASTLE, CORNWALL 1–3B

THE ROCKET STORE £61 44

BOSCASTLE HARBOUR PL35 0HD 01840 250310

This diminutive seafood bar/restaurant in Boscastle Harbour is "excellent in every way", from the "lovely atmosphere" to the "ever-changing seasonal menu", which is chalked up on the blackboard, and features "divine", "really fresh" fishy fare from their boat, plus meat from eir nearby farm. / therocketstore.co.uk; erocketstoreboscastle; Tue-Sat 10 pm.

BOURNEMOUTH, DORSET 2–4C

RBOR RESTAURANT, HE GREEN HOUSE OTEL £59 333

GROVE RD BH1 3AX 01202 498900

central wood installation of a tree helps add lidity to the name of this seaside hotel dining om. Chef Andy Hilton produces a relatively market brasserie menu framed around 'bay, rn and butcher' and results are consistently ell-rated. / arbor-restaurant.co.uk; Mon-Sun 30 pm.

HEZ FRED £36 343

SEAMOOR RD H4 9AN 01202 761023

his "fantastic family-run" chippy, now in 35th year under three generations of the apel family, serves "some of the best fish " chips to be found anywhere" – and is "a odel of consistency". Top Tip – head for e "value meals: 'Fred's finest' or 'Fred's ast' are very well priced", with "endless ips". / chezfred.co.uk; chezfreduk; Tue-Sat 30 pm.

OLAS £52 333

COMMERCIAL ROAD H2 5RT 07588 065360

"cracking find in the centre of ournemouth", this "tiny little restaurant up off e main shopping street" is "worth the climb" r "tasty" and sometimes "superb" tapas and efreshing sangria". Top Menu Tip – "our rmally carnivorous children demand the ubergine with honey". / lolasrestaurant.co.uk; ashomemadetapas; Mon-Thu 11 pm, Fri & Sat idnight, Sun 9 pm.

BOWDON, GREATER MANCHESTER 5–2B

ORAGE £59 443

VALE VIEW, VICARAGE LANE A14 3BD 0161 929 4775

n excellent local restaurant with talent in e kitchen (Miarisuz Dobies) and professional ont of house" (his wife); regulars are never disappointed" by the French- and entral European-inflected food (including ve- or seven-course tasting menus), with every detail wonderful and made in- ouse". / boragebowdon.co.uk; boragerestaurant; hu-Sat 9 pm, Sun 5 pm.

BRACKLESHAM, WEST SUSSEX 3–4A

ILLYS ON THE EACH £55 333

RACKLESHAM LANE O20 8JH 01243 670373

verything is "just deliciously fresh" at this busy and popular beach-side café" serving hearty breakfasts" followed later in the day "fish and seafood" along with burgers and other simple dishes. "Views of the Isle of Wight are a bonus." / billysonthebeach.co.uk; billysonthebeach; Mon-Wed 5 pm, Thu-Sat 9 pm, Sun 3.30 pm.

BRADFORD, WEST YORKSHIRE 5–1C

AKBAR'S £39 322

1276 LEEDS RD BD3 8LF 01274 773311

"Just like going back to the 1970's… but on a larger scale!" – this city-centre veteran has grown over the years as well as spawning a national chain. The "old school Indian food is very tasty with large portions and the biggest naans anywhere". The menu features 'Chef's Challenges' for the Big Man (quantity) and for the Brav (heat). / akbars.co.uk; akbars.restaurants; Mon-Thu 11.30 pm, Fri & Sat midnight, Sun 11 pm.

MUMTAZ £38 343

386-410 GREAT HORTON RD BD7 3HS 01274 571861

One of the biggest restaurants in our guide, seating 500 guests – this Bradford institution started out 45 years ago as a tiny Kashmiri shop close to its present "very comfortable" premises. Well-known for its "high-quality food", fans include retired footballer Steven Gerrard and politico George Galloway, and there's now a spin-off in Leeds and a national brand of ready meals. / mumtaz.com; mumtazbradford; Tue-Thu, Sun midnight, Fri & Sat 1 am.

BRAEMAR, ABERDEENSHIRE 9–3C

THE CLUNIE DINING ROOM, THE FIFE ARMS £96 333

MAR ROAD AB35 5YN 01339 720200

Limited feedback this year on this grand hotel near Balmoral (opened by HRH Charles III back in 2019) – one of the first properties in Hauser + Wirth's ArtFarm portfolio. Such reports as we have say it can be "outstanding", and The Scotsman's Rosalind Erskine branded it "bonkers but beautiful" in an August 2023 review. It's by no means a cheap experience, though, with the simple, if high-quality main dishes typically in the £35-£40 price range… and that's before the chips (only £5, but mash or veg are closer to a tenner). / thefifearms.com; thefifearms; Mon-Sun 9.30 pm.

BRANCASTER STAITHE, NORFOLK 6–3B

THE WHITE HORSE £63 344

MAIN RD PE31 8BY 01485 210262

"A fabulous seaside pub and restaurant serving local produce, including smoked goods from their own smokehouse" – this "high-quality" and much commented-on north Norfolk venue fits the bill at all times of the year, whether "enjoying the warmth of the open fires in December" or "dining on the open deck in the summer, looking out over the salt marshes". Top Tip – "Brancaster mussels are excellent". / whitehorsebrancaster.co.uk; whitehorsebranc; Mon-Sat 9 pm, Sun 8 pm.

BRANSCOMBE, DEVON 2–4A

MASONS ARMS £53 343

MAIN ST EX12 3DJ 01297 680300

A "pretty setting" in a fourteenth-century thatched inn adds to the charms of this restaurant-with-rooms, which is run by the St Austell Brewery, and an easy walk from Branscombe beach. The pub classics and more ambitious dishes achieve "very high standards" ("the lunch menu is particularly good value") and the "quirky" spot offers a warm welcome too (also to dogs). / masonsarms.co.uk; Mon-Sun 8 pm.

BRAY, BERKSHIRE 3–3A

CALDESI IN CAMPAGNA £90 343

OLD MILL LN SL6 2BG 01628 788500

Giancarlo & Katie Caldesi's country venue – a counterpart to their Marylebone flagship – offers classic Italian cuisine in "a lovely atmosphere with fabulous service". It's "good-value", too – at least certainly compared to the nearby Fat Duck and Waterside Inn… / caldesi.com; caldesi_in_campagna; Wed-Sat 9.30 pm, Sun 2.30 pm.

THE FAT DUCK £399 332

HIGH ST SL6 2AQ 01628 580333

"Not only did it live up to the hype and our expectations… it exceeded them!" "The theatre of a meal at the Fat Duck is like nowhere else" and for many reporters the "absolute culinary sorcery" and showmanship at Heston Blumenthal's converted pub in bijoux Bray make for a "once-in-a-lifetime culinary blow out", with a dazzling array of dishes that are "either divine or merely mind boggling". All that conjuring can fall flat though ("the science lab style, and focus on sounds and lighting actually detracted from what was probably exquisite food"); or equally it may not stand up to a repeat visit ("maybe I have been too often but the experience is becoming repetitive – we need some renewal!"). And then there's the fact that for about one in three of our reporters, more prosaic matters of value for money intrude on their consciousness, and their main takeaway is: "how expensive was that!?" "Some courses were fantastic, others not so good, but to be honest I've had better food at other restaurants that didn't charge us £1,200 for two people". / thefatduck.co.uk; thefatduck; Tue-Sat 8.30 pm.

THE HIND'S HEAD £98 334

HIGH STREET SL6 2AB 01628 626151

There's no doubting that Heston Blumenthal's fifteenth-century tavern, a short walk from his Fat Duck flagship, is a "good gastropub", and the majority of reporters are thrilled by its upscale pub food. But the celeb chef's exalted reputation (reflected in the prices) means that expectations are sky-high – and though a majority of diners are well satisfied, visits "can be disappointing" ("our battered fish was hard and dry on the inside. Not acceptable at these prices!)" / hindsheadbray.com; thehindsheadbray; Wed-Sat 8.45 pm, Sun 3 pm.

WATERSIDE INN £250 445

FERRY RD SL6 2AT 01628 620691

"Traditional but still at the peak of its appeal" – Alain Roux's Thames-side "stalwart of French haute cuisine" is "still the most glorious of gastronomic treats". Founded by his late father, Michel, in 1972 – with the closure of Le Gavroche in early 2024, it now becomes the surviving flagship of the famous Roux dynasty. "Service is incredible", with "the friendly staff offering the warmest of welcomes"; and the "magical setting" by the river "is very hard to beat" and means a summer meal here can start with a glass of fizz either on the waterside terrace, or actually on the river in their electric launch. The "sublime" cuisine is resolutely of the old school (a signature dish is 'Lobster Medallions with Vegetable Julienne and White Port sauce); and backed up by an "exciting wine list" in a similar vein. "Obviously it's also incredibly expensive" – to an extent a few regard as "clearly overpriced" – and some would argue "surpassed by quite a few other restaurants, despite its three stars". But, "if you can afford it, this is THE place to go for romance and if you really want to splash out, the rooms overlooking the Thames are a perfect location for a night away (because one night is all you will be able to afford…)" / waterside-inn.co.uk; rouxwatersideinnbray; Wed-Sat 11.30 pm, Sun 2.30 pm.

BRECON, POWYS 2–1A

THE FELIN FACH GRIFFIN £63 433

FELIN FACH LD3 0UB 01874 620111

This "top-of-the-range gastropub" on the edge of the Brecon Beacons National Park has long been one of the most famous in Wales for good reason and is "always busy" as a result. "If only there were a lot more rural pubs working so hard on all aspects of the dining experience" – from "impeccable and considerate service" that creates "a lovely, welcoming, characterful ambience" to "flawless meals with an excellent selection of brilliant-value wines". The menu changes daily with seven starters and seven mains showcasing meat from the lowland hills, vegetables from nearby Penpont and fish delivered fresh from Cornwall. / eatdrinksleep.ltd.uk; thefelinfachgriffin; Mon-Sun 11 pm.

BRENTWOOD, ESSEX 3–2B

ALEC'S £90 344

NAVESTOCK SIDE
CM14 5SD 01277 375 696

"In the heart of Essex, this fabulous fish restaurant" (est. 2010, and revolving around the "plush conversion of an old pub") "offers amazing dishes and attentive service in a truly beautiful setting". "It can be fun watching the TOWIE types amongst fellow diners", but if that loses its appeal, divert your eyes to the "pleasant views from the terrace on a sunny day". / alecsrestaurant.co.uk; alecsrestaurant; Tue-Sat midnight, Sun 7 pm.

BRIDGE OF ALLAN, STIRLINGSHIRE 9–4C

NAIRNS BRIDGE OF ALLAN

HENDERSON STREET
FK9 4HR 01786 831616

Opened in July 2023 (after our annual diners' poll had concluded), veteran Scottish TV chef Nick Nairn and his wife Julia re-launched this Stirlingshire restaurant on the site of their previous venue, which was destroyed in a fire two years ago. The business is a modern, family brasserie that's not particularly foodie in approach and this is reflected in early reviews. For Murray Chalmers in The Courier it is "…great. Not life-changing, not genre-defining and not likely to win awards for innovation, but it all worked so well". The Herald's Ron Mackenna found it "strangely inconsistent… but is Nick's worth a try? Yeah. Definitely". / www.nairns.co.uk; chefnicknairn; Wed-Sat 10 pm, Sun 6 pm.

BRIDGE, KENT 3–3D

THE BRIDGE ARMS £85 533

53 HIGH STREET CT4 5LA 07818 567671

This old drovers' inn just outside Canterbury is "very atmospheric and comfortable, but the food is truly the star" – "really well executed but not overly fussy" and "a real dining treat". Former Clove Club chef Daniel Smith and his wife Tasha, herself a pastry chef, have settled in the village and created a "chilled pub with food that surprises" with its excellence. They also run the nearby Fordwich Arms. Top Menu Tip – "best lobster and chips ever". / bridgearms.co.uk; thebridgearms; Wed-Sat 9 pm, Sun 5 pm.

THE PIG AT BRIDGE PLACE £84 334

BREWERY LANE CT4 5LF 0345 225 9494

Four miles from Canterbury, this much-commented-on manor house is part of the now ten-strong Pig litter (the latest porcine offering, in Stratford-upon-Avon, is due in 2024) and "does not disappoint". The "buzzy" dining room – "like a large potting shed, its walls lined with preserved vegetables and pulses" – backdrops "lovely" gastrofare, and "in summer you can eat casually and drink in the garden" at their new 'Garden Oven', focusing on wood-fired snacks. On the downside, as at others in the chain, a minority of reports characterise its cooking as "pleasant, but nothing special". / thepighotel.com; thepig_hotel; Mon-Sun 6.30 pm.

BRIGHOUSE, WEST YORKSHIRE 5–1C

BROOK'S £43 433

6 BRADFORD RD
HD6 1RW 01484 715284

"An airy space with unusual dishes and great cooking" – this comfortable independent opposite the civic hall scored highly in this year's annual diners' poll. The focus is on small plates, some of them very original: who's for 'honey, soy and gochujang roast carrots, toasted sesame, with tahini satay'? / brooks-restaurant.co.uk; brooksrestaura[nt]; Wed & Thu 9 pm, Fri & Sat 9.30 pm, Sun 5 pm.

BRIGHTON, EAST SUSSEX 3–4[B]

BINCHO YAKITORI £40 44[3]

63 PRESTON STREET
BN1 2HE 01273 779021

"This real hidden gem" serving "Japanese yakitori skewers with sensational flavours" is "the favourite restaurant of many people in and around Brighton" – "the only problem is it's so popular it's hard to get a table". "We love sitting at the counter watching the chefs", led by founder David Miney, who picked up the authentic techniques while working in Japan before opening here nine years ago. / binchoyakitori.com; binchoyakitori; Tue-S[at] 10 pm.

BURNT ORANGE £36 23[3]

59 MIDDLE STREET
BN1 1AL 01273 929923

Brighton success story the Black Rock group's "packed" two-year-old is a "fun, open, casual restaurant" that doubles as a DJ-fuelled late-night hangout. The Middle Eastern small plates, "centred around wood-fired cooking", can be "too much on the same theme", but the majority verdict is that it's still amongst "the best culinary experiences" in town. Italian fan? The empire (inc. The Salt Room, and The Coal Shed, now with a London spin-off) also spawned Italian haunt Tutto, in a former Brighton banking hall, in autumn 2022. / burnt-orange.co.uk; burntorangeuk; Mon-Wed midnight, Thu-Sat 1 am, Sun 11 pm.

THE CHILLI PICKLE £49 33[3]

17 JUBILEE ST BN1 1GE 01273 900 38[3]

"Still one of Brighton's top Indians" – this Arts Quarter operation (est. 2008) offers "very good authentic cuisine, with dishes you usually never see here in the UK" – barbecue surf and turf, say, or interesting regional curries – and benefits from a "great atmosphere" too. / thechillipickle.com; thechillipickle; Wed-Sun 9.30 pm.

CHINA GARDEN £42 34[3]

88-91 PRESTON ST
BN1 2HG 01273 325124

Over four decades since its launch, this "longstanding Brighton Chinese" with sea view is still "one of the most authentic Cantonese around", and accordingly something of a local institution; the vast enterprise is especially rated for its dim sum, and is often filled to capacity with Chinese families, making booking essential. / chinagarden.name; Mon-Sun 10 pm.

N CIN HOVE £63 3 3 3

WESTERN ROAD
3 1JD 01273 726 047

` you want proper Italian in Hove (or now zrovia), this is the place to go" – Italian-stralian David Toscano's relaxed outfit ering seasonal small plates and handmade stas, with counter seating to watch the efs at work. Top Tip – look out for their gional banquet nights spotlighting particular lian regions. / cincin.co.uk; cincinuk; Tue-Sat 30 pm.

HE COAL SHED £69 3 4 2

BOYCES ST BN1 1AN 01273 322998

proper meat restaurant!" – Razak Helalat's pular destination (which has a London sibling ar Tower Bridge) is known for its "perfectly ne steaks" (although "if you don't like your ak and red meat, you may feel a bit stuck"); d also wins praise for its "great and attentive vice" too. Even those who feel it's "very od", though, can also feel it's "expensive what it is". / coalshed-restaurant.co.uk; coalshed; Mon-Sat 11 pm, Sun 9 pm.

URRY LEAF CAFE £53 3 2 2

SHIP ST BN1 1AE 01273 207070

at well in Brighton" at this South Indian eet food café – a firm fixture of the buzzing nes that was launched in 2014 (and for some ars also operated from a kiosk inside the al train station); the rather "bohemian" (or that "garish"?) artwork isn't to all tastes "but food is truly homemade and spectacular d authentic to its roots" – and, as befits any ho joint, there's a great line in craft beers to with it. / curryleafcafe.com; curry_leaf_cafe; on-Thu 9.30 pm, Fri & Sat 10 pm, Sun 9 pm.

UE SOUTH 3 3 3

9 KINGS ROAD ARCHES
N1 2FN 01273 721667

ob Shenton's recent switch-up of his local ini-empire – moving Champagne and oyster nt Riddle & Finns On the Beach, which ng sat here on the front, to a new site, and turning to the former branding of this outfit – d cause a few waves, but marks and comments re relatively solid this year. There's a "lovely w if you can get a table by the window" d the food, which favours the nose-to-tail hos and cooking over wood, is "delicious". duesouthrestaurant.co.uk; duesouthrestaurant; on-Sat 10 pm, Sun 6 pm.

NGLISH'S £72 3 3 4

-31 EAST ST BN1 1HL 01273 327980

Traditional seafood in pleasant surroundings" s proved an enduring formula for this seafood teran in the Lanes – one of the UK's few storic provincial restaurants, dating as it does om the 1890s and run by the Leigh-Jones mily since 1945. More critical reports say e "food quality can be a little hit or miss"; alternatively that it's "very good, but more icey than it needs to be". But "sat outside enjoying the sun, with great service and full-on Brighton atmosphere, you can have a great meal". / englishs.co.uk; englishsofbrighton; Sun-Thu 9 pm, Fri & Sat 9.30 pm.

ETCH £122 5 4 3

216 CHURCH RD BN3 2DJ 01273 227485

"Exceptional food, wonderful service and great ambience" combine to provide an "amazing special-event evening" at MasterChef: The Professionals winner Steven Edwards's conversion of a former Hove bank, now with a basement 'speakeasy' bar. There's a selection of tasting menus: from five courses for £70 per person to nine courses for £120. "If Etch was in London, it would cost three times as much", agree local fans of its "always interesting menus". "A very good selection of English wines is a bonus". / etchfood.co.uk; etchfood; Wed-Sat 8 pm.

FATTO A MANO £38 3 2 2

25 GLOUCESTER ROAD
BN1 4AY 01273 693221

This popular Neapolitan-style pizza pie joint (born in 2015) now has three outlets in Brighton and Hove – plus a newer one in King's Cross; solid ratings, if little in the way of feedback this year, but what there was reported the pizzas "excellent" (they do pizzas of the month, and also run a pizzaiolo competition). / fattoamanopizza.com; fattoamanopizza; Mon-Thu 10 pm, Fri & Sat 10.30 pm, Sun 9.30 pm.

FLINT HOUSE £57 4 4 3

13 HANNINGTON'S LANE
BN1 1GS 01273 916333

"Every dish is packed with flavour" at this "crowd-pleasing", modern British small plates venue from Pamela & Ben McKellar's Gingerman group, with a "bright and friendly dining room above the bucolic Lanes of Brighton": there's a "really something for everyone", backed up with "super-friendly service". / flinthousebrighton.com; theflinthouse; Mon-Sun 10 pm.

FOOD FOR FRIENDS £55 3 3 2

17-18 PRINCE ALBERT ST
BN1 1HF 01273 202310

"Highly recommended by locals", this Lanes veteran of more than 40 years serves up "gorgeous, colourful veggie food" in a "glam and romantic" environment. Juggling "exotic flavours" from various Mediterranean and Asian cuisines, the kitchen sends out dishes that are "great, even for carnivores". Its younger sibling, Botanique, offers similar options in nearby Hove. / foodforfriends.com; foodforfriendsrestaurant; Mon-Sun 10 pm.

FOURTH AND CHURCH £42 3 4 3

84 CHURCH ROAD
BN3 2EB 01273 724709

Eat "surrounded by bottles in this friendly and informal bistro", which also doubles as a wine bar and shop. Reporters love the "inventive small-plates food and excellent wine list" – especially the set menu, which is "full of more adventurous things you might not normally order à la carte". / fourthandchurch.co.uk; fourthandchurch; Wed-Sat 6 pm.

THE GINGER PIG £68 3 4 3

3 HOVE ST BN3 2TR 01273 736123

"A favourite restaurant" (and one of GQ magazine's Top 10 UK pubs) – this outpost of a much-liked and four-strong local chain, near the Hove seafront, is an "always-dependable" choice for its "brilliant food and service" (the latter consisting of gastroboozer fare plus fancier options like vegetarian tasting plates). / thegingerpigpub.com; gingerpighove; Mon-Sun midnight.

GINGERMAN £84 4 4 2

21A NORFOLK SQ
BN1 2PD 01273 326688

This "little gem of a side-street restaurant, just up from the sea front" delivers "tastes that go Wow!". The first in chef Ben McKellar & his wife Pamela's successful local group, it has maintained "the same standards as ever" for more than 25 years now. Top Menu Tip – "there's always a delicious soufflé for pudding!". / gingermanrestaurant.com; thegingermanrestaurant; Tue-Thu 8.30 pm, Fri & Sat 9 pm, Sun 3 pm.

IVY BRASSERIE £53 2 2 3

51A SHIP STREET
BN1 1AF 020 3971 2404

This five-year-old offshoot of the London It-hangout has transformed what was previously the city's central post office; as per its siblings, it turns out an all-day menu of "Asian-style tapas and small plates" that invariably play second fiddle to the glamorous décor (and are "not cheap either"). / ivycollection.com; the_ivy_collection; Mon-Sun 12 pm.

THE LITTLE FISH MARKET £126 4 4 3

10 UPPER MARKET ST
BN3 1AS 01273 722213

"What a spot!" – working solo, chef Duncan Ray "turns out five-star dishes, each one meticulously thought out, beautiful and tasty", to just 20 guests at a sitting in this "hidden away" seafood specialist in Hove. With a big reputation after 10 years in business, it's now "hard to actually get a table in such a small venue" – but "well worth trying" for the "sublime experience". / thelittlefishmarket.co.uk; littlefishhove; Tue-Sat 10.30 pm.

MANJUS £23 4|4|3

6 TRAFALGAR ST
BN1 4EQ 07400 620567

This "lovely little vegetarian Indian venture in North Laine" serves "authentic" Gujarati dishes that are "full of flavour". The titular Manjula Patel is one of Britain's most remarkable restaurateurs: exiled from Uganda with her family by Idi Amin in 1968, she worked as a machine operator in a London factory until retiring at 65. On her 80th birthday, seven years ago, her sons Naimesh & Jaymin bought her the restaurant she had always dreamt of running – and the family now operate it together. / manjus.co.uk; Thu & Fri 10 pm.

MURMUR £57 3|3|3

91-96 KINGS ROAD ARCHES
BN1 1NB 01273 711 900

Former Great British Menu winner Michael Bremner's "fish specialist" – a "not too expensive" all-day diner that's more casual than his Lanes flagship 64 Degrees; it sits in a magical location under The Arches overlooking the West Pier (and is thus "best on a summer evening" when you can dine outside). / murmur-restaurant.co.uk; murmur_restaurant; Mon-Thu 9 pm, Fri & Sat 11 pm, Sun 6 pm.

PALMITO £43 4|4|3

16 WESTERN ROAD
BN3 1AE 01273 777588

This "spectacular little place" (just 20 seats) occupies a former takeaway near the Brighton-Hove border; its "excellent menu, changed weekly", offers an unusual "mash-up of South American and Indian cooking" courtesy of chef-owners Kanthi Thamma, who is Indian, and Diego Ricaurte, an Ecuadorian. The spice-driven venture began as a series of pop-ups, and its new bricks-and-mortar incarnation is a "a real find" by all accounts. / palmito.co.uk; palmito.restaurant; Tue-Sat 11 pm.

PETIT POIS £43 3|4|3

70 SHIP STREET BN1 1AE 01273 911211

With a "uniquely buzzing atmosphere" befitting its Lanes location, this little bistro has a winning line in "classic French cooking that's beautifully executed" and "good quality for the price" as well; the "simple steak frites and fish soup are a must", and fans are "always interested to see what cheeses are chalked up on the board". / petitpoisbrighton.co.uk; petitpoisbrighton; Mon, Thu-Sun 10 pm.

THE REGENCY RESTAURANT £54 3|3|2

131 KINGS RD BN1 2HH 01273 325014

This "great traditional seafood restaurant on the seafront" has been "very popular for decades" (some nine decades in fact) owing to its "always good" victuals, which range from "basic fish 'n' chips to lobster" plus Champagne-fuelled platters. / theregencyrestaurant.co.uk; theregencyrestaurant; Mon-Sun 10 pm.

RIDDLE & FINNS £69 4|4|4

12B MEETING HOUSE LN
BN1 1HB 01273 721667

This "cracking hidden gem, tucked away in the Lanes" is "a bit of a Brighton institution now, and rightly so" – an "intimate and romantic" place where "the seafood is fresh, the dishes filling yet light and the service unobtrusive but friendly". "It provides a great selection of crustacea and everything from mackerel to Dover sole". There is now also a beachside offshoot in the Rotunda on Brighton's Promenade. / riddleandfinns.co.uk; riddlesandfinnsBN1; Sun-Fri 10 pm, Sat 11 pm.

RIDDLE & FINNS ON THE BEACH £68 4|4|4

65 KINGS ROAD BN1 1NA 01273 721667

This "very professional brasserie-style" operation has moved to a "stand-out location surveying Brighton Beach" – the restored late-Victorian Rotunda on the Promenade – and serves a "large and delicious choice" of "classic seafood dishes". It's a successful spin-off from the long-established Lanes oyster bar of the same name. Top Tip – "smoked haddock and tempura tiger prawns hit all the right notes". / riddleandfinns.co.uk; riddleandfinnsbrighton; Sun-Fri 10 pm, Sat 11 pm.

THE SALT ROOM £75 3|3|3

106 KINGS ROAD
BN1 2FA 01273 929 488

This "buzzy seafood restaurant on the seafront" with views over the skeletal West Pier features some "innovative cooking" and "fantastic sauces", with whole fish cooked over fire a speciality. Some reporters consider it "a little pricey", but "the lunchtime menu offers good value". / saltroom-restaurant.co.uk; thesaltroombrighton; Mon-Sat 11 pm, Sun 9 pm.

THE SET, UNIQUE HOTEL £116

50 PRESTON ROAD
BN1 4QF 01273 933795

In June 2021, Dan Kenny found a new home for his project in Café Rust, not far from Preston park and underneath the viaduct. It's a small place, with a two-person team in the kitchen aiming for big, umami flavours from a fixed 14-20 course tasting menu over two-and-a-half hours, and though it inspires somewhat limited feedback, fans say results are "just flawless". / thesetrestaurant.com; theset_restaurant; Wed-Fri 11 pm.

64 DEGREES £116 5|4|2

53 MEETING HOUSE LANE
BN1 1HB 01273 770 115

GBM winner Michael Bremner's open-kitchen Lanes joint has been one of Brighton's most interesting culinary venues for years, and remains "sensational" thanks to tasting menus that are "full of surprises" (as much the veggie option as the carnivorous one). Add in "attentive service and a buzzing atmosphere" ("sitting at the pass is a fantastic experience") and it's "highly recommended" by its very many fans. (It's priced for the evening taster menu, but you can also make a meal of individual small plates here for a much more modest cost). / 64degrees.co.uk; chef64degrees; Mon, Fri-Sun, Thu 9 pm.

TERRE À TERRE £71 4|3|

71 EAST ST BN1 1HQ 01273 729051

"So many dimensions of flavour on each plate each excellently balanced" and service with "just the right balance of the professional and the friendly" mean this veteran of The Lanes remains, for most reporters, "a revelation of how pleasing a vegetarian restaurant can be (and I am an omnivore!)" thanks to its "complex" dishes and "truly original flavour combinations". Indeed, this "lively" venue is the most commented-on destination in town in our annual diners' poll and the UK's most prominent meat-free venue. Ratings, though, were dragged down a little this year by a few more cautious reporters who feel "it used to be a trail blazer but hasn't moved on" and is "not as pleasing as it was". On most accounts, though, it remains "worth the trip to the south coast": "you don't feel like you're missing out on meat or fish". / terreaterre.co.uk; terreaterrebrighton; Wed & Thu, Tue 9 pm, Fri-S 10 pm.

URCHIN £57 4|4|

15-17 BELFAST ST
BN3 3YS 01273 241881

"A shellfish gastropub? Yes, exactly" – the winning formula at this much commented-on corner boozer with a "quirky dining area". By all accounts the grub is "fabulous" ("simply and expertly cooked") and "the homebrewed beer adds an additional dimension which makes it really good to visit". / urchinpub.co.uk urchinpub; Tue-Sat 9.30 pm, Sun 5.30 pm.

WILD FLOR £80 4|4|

42 CHURCH ROAD
BN3 2FN 01273 329111

Well established as "a real favourite" since launching in 2019, "what it does – modern British cooking in a relaxed bistro setting – it does brilliantly", while "the wine list brings it a cut above many other locals. Rob (Maynard, co-founder with James & Faye Thomson) seem to find amazing different things to drink". Top Menu Tip – "don't miss out on side orders: blue cheese and leek gratin and pommes Anna are both amazing". / wildflor.com; wildflorhove; Tue-Sat 9.15 pm.

BRISTOL, CITY OF BRISTOL 2-2

ADELINA YARD £97

QUEEN QUAY, WELSH BACK
BS1 4SL 0117 925 6682

Olivia Barry and Jamie Randall opened this straightforward-looking but ambitious venue in Queen's Quay in 2015, building on their experience in top London restaurants such as Odette's and Murano. A nine-course tasting

:nu is £70 per person (with matching wine
ȝht for £60). Too limited feedback this year
· a rating, but such as we have applauds "a
:at treat with welcoming service, lovely food
d some interesting wines". / adelinayard.com;
elinayard; Wed-Sat 11 pm.

ANK £65

7 WELLS ROAD
ƽ4 2BS 0117 452 7536

nited but positive feedback, including from ondon-based reporter, on this revamped ·mer branch of Lloyds in Totterdown, which ened in 2021 and relaunched in spring 23 with a menu based around open-fire oking. / bankbristol.com; bankbristol; Wed-Sat pm, Sun 5 pm.

OSCO PIZZERIA £48 334

WHITELADIES RD
ƽ8 2QX 01179 737 978

Iigh standards have been maintained" at this tremely popular and well commented-on hiteladies Road pizza joint – firmly back in siness despite undergoing the (double) blow a fire breaking out amidst the pandemic and where the wood-fired Neapolitan-style zzas (plus other classic Italian dishes) are reat" by all accounts. It now has spin-offs in eltenham and Bath, and the Clifton Village ling was also due to reopen for delivery the time of writing. / boscopizzeria.co.uk; scopizzeria; Mon-Sun 10 pm.

OX-E £52 443

IIT 10, CARGO 1, WAPPING WHARF
ƽ1 6WP NO TEL

mall restaurant – great food"; that's still : deal at Elliott Lidstone's 14-seaters in two pping containers at Bristol harbour's Cargo velopment. There's an à la carte menu of ordable modern bistro cooking, or you can the whole hog and opt for their seven-course written tasting menu, which costs £55 per rson (with optional wine flight at £40 a ad). / boxebristol.com; boxebristol; Wed-Sat pm.

ULRUSH £107 533

COTHAM ROAD SOUTH
ƽ6 5TZ 0117 329 0990

John alumnus George Livesey's "lovely ighbourhood restaurant" might look modest, t it's a star of the Bristol dining scene with Michelin star to match – "unreservedly mmended" for the staff ("clearly proud of : food"), to the "no-nonsense atmosphere" d the "brilliant tasting menu at a fair price": ne courses for £90 per person at dinner, the glo-French cooking combining with Scandi luences and some dishes that are "very clearly panese-influenced". / bulrushrestaurant.co.uk; rushrestaurant; Fri & Sat, Wed & Thu 7.30 pm, n 1.30 pm.

L'Enclume, Cartmel

CAPER & CURE £38 432

THE OLD CHEMIST, 108A STOKES CROFT
BS1 3RU 0117 923 2858

"Outstanding food" – "both interesting and tasty" – is on the menu at this small independent in Stokes Croft from founders who cut their teeth at the late, lamented Wallfish Bistro, Craig Summers & part-time actor Giles Coram. "Don't like crab in general but months later I've not forgotten the race to extract as much tasty buttery goodness as possible before the plate was taken away!" / caperandcure.co.uk; caperandcure; Wed-Sat 11 pm, Sun 5 pm.

CASA £33

THE GENERAL, LOWER GUINEA STREET
BS1 6FU 0117 959 2884

The Sanchez-Iglesias have considerably reformatted their Michelin-starred Casamia (RIP), which closed in summer 2022. In the place of that boundary-pushing (and extremely expensive) flagship, comes this more conventional, modern Italian replacement, whose open kitchen delivers a menu inspired by the family's original trattoria in Wesbury-on-Trym, with a selection of antipasti, pastas and reworkings of classic dishes such as chicken Milanese. / casabristol.co.uk; casa.restaurant.bristol; Wed-Sat 11 pm.

CLIFTON SAUSAGE £50 333

7 PORTLAND ST BS8 4JA 0117 9731192

"Working well as a straightforward venue with good fare" – the clue is in the name at Simon & Joy Quarrie's stalwart fixture, which is now over twenty years old. / cliftonsausage.co.uk; cliftonsausage; Mon-Sun midnight.

COR £65 432

81 NORTH STREET
BS3 1ES 0117 911 2986

This brightly painted Bedminster corner site opened in late 2022 and delivers a selection of diverse European small plates of French, Italian and Spanish inspiration. Quickly awarded one of the tyre men's 'bib gourmand's, we've rated it on limited feedback to-date, which is all complimentary. More reports please! / correstaurant.com; correstaurant; Tue-Sat 11 pm.

GAMBAS £47 334

UNIT 15 CARGO 2, WAPPING WHARF
BS1 6WD 0117 329 6887

This "lively place on Wapping Wharf does what it does very well" – namely tasty tapas (as per its sister Bravas), with a focus on seafood, especially the headline prawns. There's no denying the "cool location" – an "intimate shipping container on the harbour with a nice terrace" – though for one hipster-averse reporter "less focus on the 'cool' and more on the food would be welcome". / gambasbristol.co.uk; gambastapasbar; Mon-Sat 10 pm, Sun 4.30 pm.

HARBOUR HOUSE £32

THE GROVE, HARBOURSIDE
BS1 4RB 0117 925 1212

"Really a little gem in Bristol": the former Severnshed has morphed, post-pandemic, into an "amazing place that has bags of character and history", being set in a boatshed designed by Clifton Suspension Bridge engineer Isambard Kingdom Brunel (and also hosting a well-known eatery with a River Café chef in the '90s, and an exhibition by Banksy in 2000). Too limited feedback for a rating, but reports say Ross Gibbens now turns out "really competent food using SW ingredients priced sensibly" (and with a particular nod to St Mawes seafood); minor quibble: "the interior is a bit of a barn so wait for good weather and get a table on the terrace". Need more convincing? Jay Rayner called it "a delightful place to be" in a 2022 review. / hhbristol.com; _harbourhouse_; Tue-Sat 11 pm, Sun 10 pm.

THE IVY CLIFTON BRASSERIE £77 233

42-44 CALEDONIA PLACE
BS8 4DN 0117 203 4555

Thoroughly at home in Bristol's smartest village, the first branch outside London of Richard Caring's national chain is "a very good place to go for a relaxed business lunch" or similar occasion on smart, neutral ground – the food doesn't inspire much in the way of feedback either good or bad. / theivycliftonbrasserie.com;

the_ivy_collection; Mon-Thu 10 pm, Fri & Sat 10.30 pm, Sun 9.30 pm.

THE KENSINGTON ARMS £57 343

35-37 STANLEY RD
BS6 6NP 0117 944 6444

"Standards remain consistently high" at this Redland boozer – "part of the Pony and Trap Group" and offering "a step above pub food" (though not straying from the classics and laying on proper Sunday roasts). Top Tip – "there are two rooms upstairs you can have for exclusive use of groups". / thekensingtonarms.co.uk; thekensingtonarms; Wed-Sat 9 pm, Sun 6 pm.

LIDO £66 333

OAKFIELD PLACE
BS8 2BJ 0117 933 9533

It's "slightly surreal watching swimmers while eating a selection of Mediterranean/Middle Eastern tapas" at this restored Grade II-listed mid-Victorian swimming pool in Clifton, which offers a "warm welcome and some very accommodating touches". "Great breakfasts and small plates" are available poolside and fuller meals served upstairs, with windows overlooking the pool. "Overall it's pleasant but not perhaps memorable". / lidobristol.com; lidobristol; Mon-Sat 9.30 pm, Sun 4 pm.

LITTLE FRENCH £65 342

2B NORTH VIEW, WESTBURY PARK
BS6 7QB 01179 706276

It's "hard to get a table in this tiny French bistro" in Westbury Park (one of the most commented-on destinations in Bristol this year), where locally born "chef Freddie Bird's classics with a twist" make an "outstanding addition to the Bristol scene", with "proper gutsy French cooking, and delicious to boot". Top Menu Tip – "the pommes aligot alone is worth the trip, absolutely delicious and indulgent". / littlefrench.co.uk; littlefrench_bristol; Mon-Sat 9.30 pm, Sun 4 pm.

LONA GRILL HOUSE £31 344

281 GLOUCESTER ROAD
BS7 8NY 0117 942 6100

This ultra-vivid Gloucester Road hangout "done out like an exotic tent" is "fun for the family" or on birthdays "with all the staff clapping and serving a fantastic cake"; the "wonderful Lebanese food" (chargrilled meats and mezze) is "fresh and very tasty", with "great juices" to wash it down. Expect a "constant stream of people" at what's "clearly a local favourite" ("I went eight times the month of my first visit!"). / lonagrillhouse.com; Mon-Thu, Sat 10.30 pm, Sun 10 pm.

MARMO £63 432

31 BALDWIN STREET
BS1 1RG 0117 316 4987

St John and Brawn alum Cosmo Sterck and FOH wife Lily "serve up exceptional wine" at their stylish debut solo venture (est. 2019), in the city-centre – "an interesting, predominantly French wine list featuring some very unusual options". It's accompanied by a "short" and "delicious" seasonal menu that's consistently highly rated in a good number of reports (including a well-priced weekday lunch). / marmo.restaurant; marmo.restaurant; Mon-Sat 9.45 pm.

THE METROPOLITAN £39

72 WHITELADIES ROAD
BS8 2QA 0117 985 6769

This Clifton late-2022 newcomer serves brunch all day and Asian dishes in the evenings. No feedback as yet, but if Bristol Live are to be believed it's a promising new option on this well-known restaurant strip that's something of a "hotspot" at weekends. / metropolitanbristol.com; themetbristol; Tue, Thu-Sun 4 pm, Wed 10.30 pm.

THE MINT ROOM £60 443

12-16 CLIFTON RD
BS8 1AF 01173 291 300

It's "rare to eat Indian cuisine made to such high standards and with an imaginative touch to the food", but one place you can is this sophisticated Clifton operation (with Bath spin-off); "the decor is stylish and nothing like the traditional look", while the "fragrant" food is more than a match for it (not least "superb" pies "with all sorts of curried delights under the lid"). / themintroom.co.uk; themintroom; Mon-Sat 11 pm.

PACO TAPAS, THE GENERAL £63 444

LOWER GUINEA ST
BS1 6SY 0117 925 7021

"Yes, it comes at a cost, but it's worth it…" – The Sanchez Group's harbourside HQ (next to relaunched Casa) is a highlight of the city, combining "impeccable" Hispanic dishes and tapas with a thoughtful list of Spanish wines and sherries and "has an air of self-confidence (just the right side of arrogance) that sets it apart in Bristol". The "really helpful front of house team" also wins consistent praise. That it's "not cheap" features in practically all reports, but the value stacks up, although it is "a bit noisy". / pacotapas.co.uk; pacotapas_; Tue-Thu 10 pm, Fri & Sat 10.30 pm.

ROOT £61 443

WAPPING WHARF
BS1 6WP 0117 930 0260

"A container with a terrace" on the docks which, despite not being strictly veggie, "elevates even the humblest of veg to mouth-watering delights". In December 2022, chef Rob Howell and partner Megan Oakley (ex-of the Pony & Trap) launched a sister restaurant, Root Wells, in Wells, Somerset, following the same 'more veg, less meat' ethos. / rootbristol.co.uk; rootbristol; Mon-Sat 11 pm.

SAN CARLO £73 33

44 CORN STREET
BS1 1HQ 0117 922 6586

"Surprisingly good food" that is "a significant cut above that of a typical Italian chain" – an which is "in the current climate reasonable value for money" – ensures that this long-established venue in Carlo Distefano's nationa chain is "always busy". Some even rate it the "best Italian in Bristol", and it has "excellent fish, too". / sancarlo.co.uk; sancarlorestaurants; Mon-Sun 11 pm.

SERGIO'S £57 33

1-3 FROGMORE STREET
BS1 5NA 0117 929 1413

Near the Hippodrome, this "amazing place" has "been a favourite of thousands for over 30 years" (and is also a "big celeb hangout… anyone who is anyone has been there"); add in "super tasty", "very large portions" of "old-school" Italian cooking and "OTT servic (reminded me of the 1990s!)" and it makes for a "fantastic night out". / sergios.co.uk; sergiosbristol; Mon-Sat 11 pm.

SONNY STORES £51 44

47 RALEIGH ROAD
BS3 1QS 01179 028 326

This "delightful genuine neighbourhood restaurant" on a quiet street corner in Southville is "almost perfect – unpretentious, effortless and with sublime food and drinks". Launched after lockdown, it serves a "deliciou Italian-inspired menu" from chef-owner Pegs Quinn, who spent four years at the famous River Café, while his wife Mary Glynn ensure a "friendly and welcoming service, so it's like being a guest in someone's home". "The roon is nothing to speak of but that doesn't matter as it's about the conviviality and the awesome cooking". / sonnystores.com; sonnystores; Tue-S 10 pm.

SPINY LOBSTER £72 44

128-130 WHITELADIES ROAD BS8 2RS
0117 9737384

"Small, friendly, super fish" – the MO of Mit Tonks's longtime Bristol outpost, the former Rockfish Grill, which is "slightly old-fashioned (a "proper restaurant with proper tablecloths" but whose "beautifully fresh" catch, shipped in daily from Cornwall, makes it "so good" by absolutely all accounts. / thespinylobster.co.uk; thespinylobster; Tue-Sat 10 pm.

WILSON'S £87 54

24 CHANDOS RD
BS6 6PF 0117 973 4157

"A combination of casual style and fine dining – Jan Ostle & Mary Wilson's modern bistro in Redland is "well worth seeking out" for the "always excellent, ethically unquestionable" cooking (much of it using home-grown produ that they're "always pushing to improve". "Tl food is most definitely refined but the venue, a small Victorian shop in a shabby-chic part of istol, is relaxed and the vibe is more cafe than staurant". "At lunchtime, you can opt for a t-down tasting menu which is great value at s level". / wilsonsbristol.co.uk; wilsonsbristol.

RIXHAM, DEVON 1–3D

HOALS £52 3 2 4

SOUTH WEST COAST PATH
Q5 9AF 01803 854874

'he menu has become a little more phisticated with the new chef, and prices have creased" accordingly, say fans of this much-ved joint above the lido. Given that "this y restaurant is best at simply prepared fish sh from that morning's auction at Brixham" here owners the Perkes are wholesalers), the anges are not always supported, but even the d critic "would still return for the freshest h and that view to die for across the bay" to rquay. In 2022, that view got even better, th a new rooftop terrace area where they ll the catch outdoors and bring it directly table. / shoalsbrixham.co.uk; shoals_brixham; on-Sun 11 pm.

ROADSTAIRS, KENT 3–3D

EBBELLS £61 3 4 3

VICTORIA PARADE
T10 1QS 01843 319002

'rimarily a fish restaurant, but one with cellent vegetarian and vegan options, and ekend brunches, all with a Mediterranean be, from Michelin-trained chef Craig ather": one reporter neatly summarises e virtues of this "reasonably priced" and idback" bistro, of recent vintage; sit on the nny terrace for "al fresco dining with views ross Viking Bay". / kebbells.com; kebbells_ oadstairs; Tue-Sun 9 pm.

TARK £94 5 4 4

OSCAR ROAD
T10 1QJ 01843 579786

n & Sophie Crittenden's tiny 12-seater "is unique example of how a small, focused am can delight the diner", with "superb oking" and "terrific" six-course tasting enus that "never disappoint". The couple ened the restaurant eight years ago so they uld spend more family time with their three ildren; they closed their nearby tapas bar os at Christmas 2022 in the face of escalating sts. / starkfood.co.uk; starkbroadstairs; Wed-Sat pm.

ROADWAY, WORCESTERSHIRE 2–1C

RILL BY JAMES ARTIN £87

IE LYGON ARMS, HIGH STREET
R12 7DU 01386 852255

mes Martin is the latest in the line of c'leb efs to have his name over the door of the rrel-vaulted dining room of this historic dor coaching inn (which accommodated th Charles I and Oliver Cromwell at fferent times during the Civil War). Iconic xury Hotels Group (who run Cliveden and Chewton Glen) have managed the property for some time, and pre-rebrand the feedback continued the downbeat tenor – "such a disappointment…", "trading on its name and reputation" – of recent decades. Here's hoping James can bring some of the magic here that's created in Chewton Glen and that this fine space finally starts to live up to its potential. / lygonarmshotel.co.uk; lygoncotswolds; Mon-Sun 9.30 pm.

RUSSELL'S OF BROADWAY £73 3 4 2

20 HIGH STREET
WR12 7DT 01386 853555

This "lovely, chic restaurant in a pretty and historic Worcestershire Cotswold town" offers "a great dining experience" with "some excellent dishes, beautifully served and delightfully prepared". A new owner, Birmingham-based Roger Dudley, has taken over from Andrew & Gaynor Riley, who ran the property for 18 years, but chef George Santos and his kitchen team have carried on much as before. / russellsofbroadway.co.uk; russellsofbroadway; Wed-Sat 9 pm, Sun 6.15 pm.

BROCKENHURST, HAMPSHIRE 2–4D

THE PIG £85 3 2 4

BEAULIEU ROAD
SO42 7QL 01590 622354

"The setting is off the charts" at the New Forest original of Robin Hutson's shabby-chic country house hotel group (which was sold to private equity in late 2022) – "a beautiful manor house with incredible gardens and a fascinating, walled kitchen garden". "Finally made it here for my wife's birthday this year: we'll definitely be returning!". The food (better rated this year) is generally considered "fine" or better, albeit "with the continuous expansion of the chain, the meals become a little more hotel-like – though we certainly enjoyed our visit". / thepighotel.com; the_pig_hotels; Mon-Sun 9.30 pm.

BROCKHAM, SURREY 3–3A

THE GRUMPY MOLE £49 3 3 3

BROCKHAM GREEN
RH3 7JS 01737 845 101

This "great family pub" – "aka The Inn on the Green, part of the small Grumpy Mole chain" – attracts a fair number of reports and "is a delightful spot overlooking the Surrey countryside", with a "relaxed atmosphere" and a "tempting menu" that ticks most boxes. "The only issue is that you have to book a long time in advance for Sunday lunch". / thegrumpymole.co.uk; the_grumpy_mole; Mon-Sat 9.30 pm, Sun 8.30 pm.

BROMESWELL, SUFFOLK 3–1D

THE UNRULY PIG £87 4 2 2

ORFORD RD IP12 2PU 01394 460 310

"Difficult to find better", say the many fans of this "stylish" gastropub (est. 2015), whose 'Britalian' food "nails the authenticity" of its influences, be it arancini; "leftfield but delicious lavender and honey custard tart"; or "simply great seafood" (not to mention the beloved 'Be Unruly' tasting menu, yours for a discounted £49 per person on Thursdays). Admittedly, it's "well-hyped" these days – having garnered 'best gastropub' awards from many a national authority – and where there's hype, there are inevitably skeptics, for whom it's generally "far from cheap" and in a rather "unspectacular" roadside location too (albeit one handy for the A12, though). Top Tip – good for a business lunch. / theunrulypig.co.uk; unrulypig; Mon-Thu 9 pm, Fri & Sat 9.15 pm, Sun 8 pm.

BROOK, HAMPSHIRE 2–4C

BELL INN £48 3 3 3

NEW FOREST SO43 7HE 023 8081 2214

"The locals of Alresford are fortunate to have this place on their doorstep" – an "attractive" red-brick inn with flagstone floors and oak-paneled walls that has been in the same family since 1782, and is situated in the desirable locale of the New Forest National Park. On the dining front, the bistro offers "varied, good and well-priced" gastropub fare, from Sunday roasts to prix fixe menus and afternoon teas. / bellinn-newforest.co.uk; Mon-Sun 9 pm.

BRUNTINGTHORPE, LEICESTERSHIRE 5–4D

THE JOINERS £58 3 3 3

CHURCH WALK
LE17 5QH 0116 247 8258

With its oak beams and flagstone floors, this family-run rural gastropub between Leicester and Lutterworth continues to win a solid thumbs up from Midlands-based reporters in our annual diners' poll. The fairly traditional, bistro-style cooking (e.g. chicken liver parfait, steak or seabass, panna cotta) is in a more ambitious mould than typical pub grub. / thejoinersarms.co.uk; thejoinersarmsinbruntingthorpe; Tue-Sat 9 pm, Sun 3 pm.

BRUTON, SOMERSET 2–3B

AT THE CHAPEL £63 3 3 2

28 HIGH ST BA10 0AE 01749 814070

This stunning converted chapel (with rooms, artisan bakery and wine shop) was long in the hands of Catherine Butler, but in summer 2022 slotted into the Stay Original Company's roster of SW boutique hotels and pubs. "For a small town Bruton has plenty of places to enjoy good food" – and, albeit "less fancy than the others", this remains a safe choice for "straightforward, well-cooked fare" (including "a lovely lunch after a walk round the wonderful Newt" country estate). / atthechapel.co.uk; atthechapel; Mon-Sun 9 pm.

THE BOTANICAL ROOMS AT THE NEWT £104 334

THE NEWT IN SOMERSET
BA7 7NG 01963 577777

"A treat after viewing the interesting gardens" – this 'Country House Reimagined' is a handsome, limestone Georgian pile in lovely Somerset countryside and is the brainchild of billionaire Koos Bekker and his wife Karen Roos's (ex-editor of Elle Decoration). Where eating is concerned, the main event is a "gorgeous" panelled traditional chamber (for more inexpensive meals, head for The Garden Café – "a beautifully designed glass box" overlooking the kitchen garden and orchards –). "Good local produce, much from the grounds just outside" is presented alongside meat from heritage breeds on a three-course menu for £85 per person. One or two reports suggest "it's good but doesn't quite hit the heights it's aiming for" but on most accounts it's merely a "fantastic" experience – "love the range of Newt ciders" too. / thenewtinsomerset.com; thenewtinsomerset; Mon-Sun 9 pm.

GARDEN CAFE, THE NEWT £33 334

BA7 7NG 01963 577777

"The more casual restaurant at the Newt" – a simply spectacular country resort opened in 2019 by South African power duo Koos Bekker and his former 'Elle Decoration' editor wife Karen Roos, and housing everything from a reconstructed Romano-British villa, to a bottling plant, gardening museum, apiary and (attracting the most attention) an ultra-plush hotel. The Garden Café overlooks the kitchen gardens, from which much of its "interesting, different and fresh" vegetable-led menu is sourced (and there's also "the option to add a small meat plate as a side"). / thenewtinsomerset.com; Mon-Sun 6 pm.

OSIP £101 543

1 HIGH STREET
BA10 0AB 01749 813322

"Worth the trip to the pretty, hip rural Somerset village of Bruton for an occasion" – Merlin Labron-Johnson's "incredible" venue enjoys a massive following out of all proportions to its tiny size; and is one of the most commented-on destinations outside London in our annual diners' poll this year. There's no menu at this "very farm-to-table oriented place" – for £120 per person (with a cheaper, cut-down lunch alternative) you put yourself in his hands and the "expertly prepared" results are "exquisite… bursting with flavour". "Service is light but gracious and the atmosphere, in the small but beautifully decorated room, is lovely if lacking a bit of life…" but all that's about to change since, in autumn 2023 he successfully completed an oversubscribed £125,000 kickstarter campaign to create 'Osip 2.0' in a new space. Details to follow. / osiprestaurant.com; osiprestaurant; Thu-Sun, Tue, Wed 9.30 pm.

ROTH BAR & GRILL £74 323

DURSLADE FARM, DROPPING LN
BA10 0NL 01749 814060

This "excellent part of the Hauser & Wirth Somerset gallery, garden and cultural centre" was founded 10 years ago, as the opening gambit in the Swiss art dealership's Artfarm hospitality wing, which now has venues from Scotland to Los Angeles, including The Groucho Club in London. Named after Dieter Roth, one of their stable of artists, it's a "very attractive location", with "efficient service, a generally laid-back, happy ambience and good, generous cooking", using home-produced Durslade Farm ingredients. / rothbarandgrill.co.uk; rothbarandgrill; Tue, Wed, Sun 4 pm, Thu-Sat 10 pm.

BUCKFASTLEIGH, DEVON 1–3D

RIVERFORD FIELD KITCHEN £57 334

WASH BARN TQ11 0JU 01803 762074

The "really imaginative, fresh and creative food served by engaged and enthusiastic staff" in the canteen at this organic veg box company's HQ is "top, top grub – enough to turn the staunchest of meat-eaters into a temporary veggie!" – although some meat is served, albeit in a supporting role. Long-term admirers, though, regret that "the buffet of puds is no more, so you have to choose just one pud off the menu. I understand why COVID had this impact, but I do hope it isn't permanent". / fieldkitchen.riverford.co.uk; riverford; Wed-Sat 10 pm, Sun 7 pm.

BUNBURY, CHESHIRE 5–3B

THE DYSART ARMS 334

BOWES GATE ROAD
CW6 9PH 01829 260 183

This "lovely, cosy pub" in "a nice location in rural Cheshire" wins admirers for its "exceptionally friendly and helpful staff", who are "a credit to Brunning & Price", the Chester-based national chain. "We tried it on spec, and have been back several times since". / dysartarms-bunbury.co.uk. SRA – 3 stars

BURNHAM MARKET, NORFOLK 6–3C

SOCIUS £52 543

11 FOUNDRY PLACE
PE31 8LG 01328 738307

"You think it's a strange building in a car park! Then you go in and have just the best food…" – Self-taught chef Dan Lawrence and partner Natalie's purpose-built five-year-old is well "worth seeking out for some of the best food in this part of north Norfolk" (or even beyond, if you trust the AA's 2022 'Restaurant of the Year' accolade). It has a "small plates ethos" with "dishes designed for sharing" and "results are outstanding". / sociusnorfolk.co.uk; sociusnorfolk; Wed-Sat 9 pm, Sun 2.30 pm.

BURROUGH ON THE HILL, LEICESTERSHIRE 5–4

STAG & HOUNDS £67 33

4 MAIN STREET LE14 2JQ 01664 4542

This "fascinating old pub in a quiet village in rural Leicestershire" is now in its fifth year under "top-notch chef Dom Clarke (ex-Moor Hall) doing his own thing in a small kitchen, which produces unusual combinations of high-quality ingredients, mostly locally grown and supplied". The "menu is very limited" (3 starters and 3 mains), but that's "easy to overlook when the dishes are expertly constructed and presented, and rarely disappoint". "Add to this friendly service and a great atmosphere". / stagnhoundspub.co.uk; stag_n_hounds; Tue-Sat 9 pm, Sun 4.30 pm.

BURTON BRADSTOCK, DORSET 2–4

HIVE BEACH CAFE £63 32

BEACH ROAD DT6 4RF 01308 897 070

"Excellent fish, super-efficient service and a wonderful outlook on the beach" – three reasons to love this Jurassic Coast staple (est. 1991), and with siblings in West Bay and West Bexington; yes, the "seating is basic, but comfortable enough and with those views and the quality of the food, who cares?!" Top Tip – "look out for 'Lobster Wednesday'! It's the best deal on the coast!". / hivebeachcafe.co.uk; hivebeachcafe; Mon-Sun 7 pm.

THE PARLOUR 33

BREDY FARM, BREDY LANE
DT6 4ND 01308 897899

"A bit of Italy in Dorset" – this quirky, "friendly" and "busy" eatery is part of the freewheeling 300-acre Bredy Farm complex, host to summer music festivals, camping, a microbrewery (their range of ciders includes the racily titled 'Monika Lewinsky'), and live music venue 'The RattleShack' – essentially a beach barn with sand on the floor. "Top pizza" is the pick of the menu, though Italian fare makes way for roasts on Sundays. / theparlour-bredyfarm.com; theparlourbredyfarm; Mon-Thu, Sat, Fri 10 pm, Sun 3 pm.

THE SEASIDE BOARDING HOUSE HOTEL £82 23

CLIFF ROAD DT6 4RB 01308 897 205

A "stunning setting" is a highpoint at this contemporary dining room with outside terrace, overlooking the beach and sea on the Jurassic Coast on Lyme Bay. It continues to enjoy good ratings all-round although there is the odd gripe that it's "a bit too pricey". / theseasideboardinghouse.com; theseasideboardinghouse; Tue-Sun 9 pm.

The Three Chimneys, Dunvegan

BURY ST EDMUNDS, SUFFOLK 3–1C

LARK £31 444

6A ANGEL HILL IP33 1UZ 01284 652244

This "new, fresh and creative" venue – a former bus shelter with room for 23 diners – from "a young chef with a great pedigree", James Carn (ex-Pea Porridge) and his wife Sophia, is already making waves with "really personal cooking and personal service". Two reporters had their best meal of the year here this year, while The Observer's Jay Rayner in his July 2023 review was also bowled over on an early visit, describing it as "ambitious, clever, relaxed and hugely enjoyable; in one word, it's special". It's named after the river which flows through the town. / larkrestaurant.co.uk; lark.restaurant; Wed-Sat 9.30 pm.

MAISON BLEUE £70 544

30-31 CHURCHGATE ST IP33 1RG 01284 760 623

"Always delivers (if you can get in)" – "Karine, front of house, and Pascal (Canavet) in the kitchen are a fab combination" at this "gem" of a converted townhouse, invariably a much commented-on feature on our national diners' poll. The French fine-dining fare is "very creatively plated" and word is that new spin-off Léa, offering artisan ready meals à la française, reaches the same impressive heights; "they also supply suppers for the local theatre" if you're craving dinner and a show. / maisonbleue.co.uk; maisonbleuesuffolk; Tue 8.30 pm.

1921 ANGEL HILL £78 443

19-21 ANGEL HILL IP33 1UZ 01284 704870

"Interesting food of great quality and at a good price" from chef Zack Deakins is the attraction at this Grade II-listed townhouse on Angel Hill: one of the city's better established culinary destinations. It "has seemed really busy and vibrant this year, which is great to see and really builds a good ambience". / nineteen-twentyone.co.uk; 1921_angel_hill; Tue, Thu-Sat 9.15 pm.

THE ONE BULL £58 343

25 ANGEL HILL IP33 1UZ 01284 848220

"Great beer (including from their own craft brewery), an award-winning wine list and refined pub food": three excuses to visit this gastroboozer from the Gusto Pronto group (even if there were slight quibbles with the rotating cast of chefs this year). In 2022, they opened a wine shop, Vino Gusto, on Hatter Street, offering self-serve wine tasting via an Enomatic machine. / theonebull.co.uk; theonebullbury; Tue-Thu 11 pm, Fri & Sat midnight, Sun 10 pm.

PEA PORRIDGE £72 454

28-29 CANNON ST IP33 1JR 01284 700200

"Mediterranean (meets Middle Eastern) fine-dining without the Michelin faffing or prices" awaits at this "quirky" restaurant (est. 2009) from Justin Sharp and FOH wife Jurga. It's "in a most unlikely location" (a residential square), but there's no quibbling with Justin's "unusual" food, and "in a world of commoditised wine lists", Jurga's "perfectly curated list is a joy", with "plenty of interesting wines from small producers, including organic options, natural wines, etc.". / peaporridge.co.uk; peaporridgerestaurant; Thu, Wed 8.30 pm, Fri & Sat 9.30 pm.

BUSHEY, HERTFORDSHIRE 3–2A

ST JAMES £65 322

30 HIGH ST WD23 3HL 020 8950 2480

"A stalwart in a desert for decent cooking" that's still recommended after 25 years "under Alfonso La Cava's friendly eye" and where there's some "delicious food" to be had (be it light lunches, à la carte dinners or a newer set menu); afternoon tea is served in the recent (by the venue's standards) Betsy's Tearoom, which launched in 2018. / stjamesrestaurant.co.uk; stjamesbushey; Tue-Sat 9 pm, Sun 2 pm.

BUXTON, DERBYSHIRE 5–2C

SANTIAGO £32 333

GEORGE STREET SK17 6AY 01298 384577

"A good bet in Buxton", this "genuine Spanish tapas" joint ("plus on-site shop – brilliant!") was set up in 2021 by a family who had enjoyed holidaying to Spain's San Pedro Del Pinatar region for over two decades. "Most of the usual options are on the menu, with some interesting salad variants" and larger plates or 'raciones' (including "some that you rarely see elsewhere such as fabada asturiana", a rich bean stew). / santiagorestaurants.co.uk; santiago_restruk; Tue-Thu 10 pm, Fri & Sat 10.30 pm, Sun 7 pm.

CAISTOR ST EDMUND, NORFOLK 6–4C

MARK POYNTON AT CAISTOR HALL £75

STOKE ROAD NR14 8QN 01508 502205

Ex-Alimentum chef Mark Poynton opened an eponymous restaurant at this country house hotel ten minutes' drive from Norwich in March 2023, with Byron Franklin as his head chef. The debut allowed little time for feedback in our annual diners' poll on their offering which features a five-course menu for £75 per person; or a nine-course menu for £100 per person. / caistorhall.com; caistor_hall's profile picture caistor_hall; Thu-Sat, Wed midnight.

CAMBER, EAST SUSSEX 3–4C

THE GALLIVANT £81 343

NEW LYDD RD TN31 7RB 01797 225 057

"You wonder what's in store when you driving up to The Gallivant" – built in the 1960s as a beachfront motel by Camber Sands – but "you enter an oasis of calm, with a light and airy restaurant" serving "outstanding and interesting food" from MasterChef contestant Nico Fitzgerald. The venue operates as a wellness retreat, whose "friendly and knowledgeable team" provide a "truly relaxed environment". / thegallivant.co.uk; thegallivant; Mon-Sun 9 pm.

CAMBRIDGE, CAMBRIDGESHIRE 3–1

THE CAMBRIDGE CHOP HOUSE £57 32

1 KINGS PARADE CB2 1SJ 01223 359506

This "always reliable" outfit in a prime tourist location pleases carnivores with its selection of classic British cuts of meat – while the "midweek early evening short menu is very reasonable". "The ambience is much better if you can get a ground-level table" with views of King's College Chapel – ("but usually you can't!"). / cambridgechophouse.co.uk; cambscuisine; Mon-Thu 9.30 pm, Fri-Sun 10 pm.

FANCETT'S £57 44

96A MILL ROAD CB1 2BD 01223 35409

Holly & Dan Fancett's "fantastic, French-influenced bistro" is "going from strength to strength" after two years in business (the pair previously ran the North Street Bistro on the North Norfolk coast). The "small, intimate" venue is particularly of note for its "excellent set-price lunch menu" (dinner is also a two- or three-course prix fixe) and service is just as "excellent" too. / fancetts.com; fancettsbistro; Wed-Sat 11 pm.

FIN BOYS £51 44

2 MILL ROAD CB1 2AD 01223 354045

"The superlatives are fully justified" at this yearling from well-travelled chefs Jay Scrimsha and Richard Stokes, serving "grown-up seafoc dishes in a charming setting". It's a "simple and informal place but still quite serious", with "knowledgeable and passionate staff" and "every dish outstanding, in decent-sized portions and at very fair prices". / fin-boys.com thefinboys; Tue-Sat midnight.

HOT NUMBERS £27 33

4 TRUMPINGTON STREET CB2 1QA 01223 612207

This "buzzy" trio (with live jazz at its Gwydir Street branch) has grown over a dozen years since founder Simon Fraser returned to his hometown from Melbourne, bringing a taste for Antipodean coffee culture. "All three branches including their roastery in Shepreth offer excellent coffee and light food, but their bread is the main event – it's world standard!" / hotnumberscoffee.co.uk; hotnumberscoffee; Mon-Sun 5 pm.

THE IVY CAMBRIDGE BRASSERIE £85 22

16 TRINITY STREET CB2 1TB 01223 344044

Like the other links in Richard Caring's ubiquitous national chain, this "bustling" brasserie is a "very slick operation, with eat decor", and it's useful for "breakfast at will set you up for the day" or "lunch a shopping trip to Cambridge". But hough it's consistently decently rated and ought to be "a nice clone", it "has lost y magic associated with the Theatreland iginal". / theivycambridgebrasserie.com; eivycambridge; Mon-Thu 10 pm, Fri-Sun .30 pm.

ARKET HOUSE £83 334

/12A MARKET HILL
B2 3NJ 01223 455560

very well-balanced wine list" is an traction at this autumn 2022 newcomer, hich combines both a restaurant and wine r (the latter evenings-only in a crypt- e space). Early feedback is quite limited, it says the modern British cuisine can be xcellent" (and The Telegraph's William twell was also a fan, hailing – in a very early ors visit – "wholesome, generous cooking", beit with a few "experimentally disastrous" shes). / markethouse.co.uk; markethouse_ mbridge; Wed-Sat 10.30 pm, Sun 5 pm.

IDSUMMER OUSE £321 433

IDSUMMER COMMON
B4 1HA 01223 369299

Still at the very top level, with some nforgettable dishes" – Daniel Clifford's rilliantly situated Victorian villa is one of the ountry's better-established and most renowned ulinary destinations. It helps that it has a harming location – next to the River Cam pposite the varsity's many boathouses and the middle of the greenery of Midsummer ommon – and its overall approach "has an r of formality without being formal!" There's n eight-course evening tasting menu for £250 er person (or a four-course lunch for £150 per erson), which on practically all accounts is a dreamy" gastronomic voyage created by head hef Mark Abbott; and backed up by a "hugely teresting" wine list (introduced by a "brilliant mmelier"). As always, there is the odd gripe bout the level of expense here, absent which atings might be even higher. But the most ommon sentiment this year? – "everything was erfect!" / midsummerhouse.co.uk; midsummer_ ouse; Tue-Sat 8.30 pm.

AK BISTRO £64 234

LENSFIELD ROAD
B2 1EG 01223 323 361

Invaluable in the centre of Cambridge", nis smart independent bistro (est. 2009) naintains a "consistently high standard" with s Anglo-European cooking, and the "covered ourtyard area makes a lovely place for dinner" n more clement months. / theoakbistro.co.uk; neoakbistrocambridge; Tue-Sat, Mon 9.30 pm.

OLD BICYCLE SHOP £69 233

104 REGENT STREET
CB2 1DP 01223 859 909

This industrially-styled spot once housed not just any old bicycle shop, but the oldest one in the country, where Charles Darwin is rumoured to have bought a bike. It was reborn seven years ago as Cambridge Brew House's sibling and has won a local army of fans for its "good range of brunch dishes" (and more) and "lovely vibe". Top Menu Tip – "don't miss the lamb kebab". / oldbicycleshop.com; oldbicycleshop; Mon-Fri 9 pm, Sat 9.30 pm, Sun 8 pm.

PARKER'S TAVERN £67 224

1 PARK TERRACE
CB1 1JH 01223 606266

Starry local chef Tristan Welch (whose CV includes stints with Rhodes, Ramsay, Roux Jr. et. al.) is behind this "wonderful brasserie" in a "lovely setting" at the recently revamped University Arms hotel, overlooking Parker's Piece green. East Anglian produce informs the cooking, which is "good" (if not spectacular) by all accounts, and makes it never less than "a reliable choice" when in this varsity town. / parkerstavern.com; parkers_tavern; Mon-Thu, Sat & Sun, Fri 10 pm.

PINT SHOP £56 224

10 PEAS HILL CB2 3PN 01223 352 293

"A fantastic selection of beers (and gins)" makes the popular former home of E. M. Forster "a very useful and welcome gastro-choice in central Cambridge, where other options are not great". The food is "reliable" and "decently done but nothing earth-shattering". Top Tip – "stay downstairs: the upstairs dining room can have a chilly ambience". / pintshop.co.uk; pint_shop; Sun-Thu 9 pm, Fri & Sat 9.45 pm.

RESTAURANT TWENTY TWO £111 543

22 CHESTERTON ROAD
CB4 3AX 01223 351880

"Wow, the food is the real winner here. So many flavours leave you begging for more" – Sam Carter and Alexandra Oliver's "very intimate Victorian terrace house" sits a short walk outside the city centre. "Electrified by young and clever passion", "it has been on excellent form for years and seems to get better on each visit", was "the deserved recipient of a Michelin star in the latest 2023 guide" and has a "warm, friendly unpretentious feel" to it that is in contrast to many foodie temples. "One relaxes into a small array of sensational snacks on arrival": "sophisticated and bursting with flavour". "This is followed by a sublime, unforgettable malty light bread that signals you are in for a great taste sensation of an evening" – a "seriously complex", but "well thought out" set menu with "superb and exciting flavour combinations". Service is "highly professional and knowledgeable" and "you're allowed to eat at your own pace with no interruption". "Pity it's really difficult to get a table!" Top Menu Tip – the "flight of soft drinks is a riot of whacky creativity". / restaurant22.co.uk; restaurant22_ cambridge; Wed-Sat 8 pm.

SCOTT'S ALL DAY £43 333

MILL ROAD CB1 2AZ 01223 311105

"Good, well-made pizzas" are served by "cheerful and helpful staff" at Scott Holden's modern all-day operation, carved out of a pair of 200-year-old shop fronts on a Mill Lane corner. By day the menu leans toward American-style brunch dishes, turning towards Italy with pasta dishes in the evening. / scottsallday.com; scottsallday; Tue-Sat 9.30 pm, Sun 4 pm.

TIFFIN TRUCK £22 333

22 REGENT STREET
CB2 1DB 01223 366111

"Lovely tasty Indian street-food dishes" – "not the usual curries" – are served at this casual offshoot from the more formal Indian restaurant Navadhanya, nearby. The menu of "dosas with fillings and good rice dishes" can also be taken away in the classic stainless-steel tiffin boxes famous in Indian cities. / thetiffintruck.co.uk; Mon-Sun 11 pm.

TRINITY £76 332

15 TRINITY STREET
CB2 1TB 01223 322130

"Delicious" and "imaginative cooking" from an "inventive menu" ensures this "lovely, comfortable" venue with a "lively atmosphere" is "still very popular" – although one or two skeptics suggest this is "possibly down to its central Cambridge location" – bang opposite the Great Gate of the college it's named after. / trinitycambridge.co.uk; restauranttrinity; Thu & Fri 10 pm, Sat 10.30 pm, Sun 9.30 pm, Wed 9 pm.

VANDERLYLE £110 543

38 MILL ROAD CB1 2AD NO TEL

Former MasterChef finalist Alex Rushmer's follow-up (est. 2019) to the nearby Hole in the Wall in Little Wilbraham "goes from strength to strength", offering what's clearly a "top gastronomic experience" (and, for one reporter, "a favourite restaurant of all time"); the rather "eye-opening" plant-based menu uses only local, ethical and regeneratively grown produce, but this is "such clever food you barely notice that there is no meat". / vanderlyle-restaurant.com; vanderlylerestaurant; Tue-Fri 11 pm.

CANTERBURY, KENT 3–3D

CAFÉ DES AMIS £55 334

95 ST DUNSTAN'S ST
CT2 8AA 01227 464390

Ignore the Gallic name – this "busy, bustling and friendly" outfit in Westgate in fact deals in "excellent" Mexican fare and is "just such a happy place" where "the atmosphere sizzles" as much as the fajitas; the "long-established" venture ("it's been going since 1987 and hasn't lost its spark…in fact it just gets better and better") has a namesake sibling in Paia, Hawaii, and is also related to Canterbury's Café du Soleil. / cafedez.com; Sun-Thu 9.30 pm, Fri & Sat 10 pm.

THE COOK'S TALE (FKA THE AMBRETTE CANTERBURY) £59 443

14 - 15 BEER CART LANE CT1 2NY 01227 200 777

"Back to its very best since chef-owner Dev Biswas closed his other venues in Rye and Margate" (and "changed the name of this venue from Ambrette to The Cook's Tale", in homage to Chaucer). The "busy" and well commented-on fine diner offers an "alternative take on Indian cuisine" (albeit now also featuring that popular staple, curry, for the first time) and the results are "exceptional" and "good value", whether you opt for the tasting menu or "adventurous" sets, both of which boast hyper-local sourcing and "Kentish touches". / thecookstale.co.uk; thecookstalerestaurant; Fri & Sat 11 pm, Sun-Thu 10.30 pm.

COUNTY RESTAURANT, ABODE CANTERBURY £80 343

HIGH ST CT1 2RX 01227 766266

A "real bright light in an otherwise scrappy pedestrian high street", this polished and "very well-run" hotel dining room takes the original name of the hotel that stood here back in 1892 and brings a rare fine dining option to the centre of Canterbury; add in "wonderful" cocktails, and it's "a treat" for its many local fans. / abodecanterbury.co.uk; abodehotelsuk; Wed-Sun, Mon & Tue 9.30 pm.

THE GOODS SHED £60 444

STATION ROAD WEST CT2 8AN 01227 459153

"Above the farmers' market, cheese shop, and wine merchants in a converted goods shed", a "lovely" destination where "the menu is determined by what local produce is available just a few feet away"; it's "very romantic in the evening", when they do formal candlelit dinners. / thegoodsshed.co.uk; thegoodsshed_; Tue, Wed, Sun 3 pm, Thu-Sat 9 pm.

CARBOST, ISLE OF SKYE 9-2A

OYSTER SHED £35 323

IV47 8SE 01478 503141

"What an experience! Lobster and chips from a cardboard plate, sitting on a wall in the open air" – overlooking the Talisker distillery, Paul McGlynn's shed was an extension of his oyster-farming business, opening as a full 'seafood kitchen' nine years ago. It's "takeaway only, though they provide barrels for you to stand around and enjoy the fish". "We had a couple of oysters each, four large scallops each with chips and shared a whole lobster, with change from £50". Top Tip – BYOB. / theoysterman.co.uk; the_oyster_shed_skye; Mon-Sat 5 am.

CARDIFF, CARDIFF 2-2A

HEANEY'S £91 433

6-10 ROMILLY CRESCENT CF11 9NR 029 2034 1264?

"Tommy (Heaney) is a great chef and a great character", say fans of the chef's swanky five-year old, in the Cardiff 'burbs, which he launched after working at Bridgend's Great House hotel (an appearance on Great British Menu boosting his profile). Sample tasting menus or à la carte, or hit up his next door oyster and wine bar, Uisce (pronounced 'ish-ka', meaning 'water' in Gaelic). / heaneyscardiff.co.uk; heaneyscardiff; Wed-Sat midnight, Sun 6 pm.

KINDLE £57 444

SOPHIA GARDENS CF11 9SZ 029 228 01448

"A great place for warm summer evenings" – Phill and Deb Lewis's sustainably focused outdoors venue (sibling to Nook) is built around Sophia Gardens' old Warden's House and offers a menu of well-prepared dishes cooked over fire, complete with natural wines and blankets to keep the cold at bay. It's rated on limited but highly enthusiastic feedback. / kindlecardiff.co.uk; kindle_cardiff; Wed-Sat 11.30 pm, Sun 2.30 pm.

MATSUDAI RAMEN AT THE BANK £45 443

185 CLARE ROAD CF11 6QD 029 2022 6510

"Really impressed by my visit!" – 'cult ramen from Wales' is the promise of this "relaxing" Japanese-inspired yearling in Grangetown, from James Chant (whose start-up became a lockdown meal-kit phenomenon). In a February 2023 review, The Observer's Jay Rayner also gave it the thumbs up: "a broad, brightly lit space" with some "impeccable" and "revelatory" dishes, including a "thrillingly vegan take on crispy squid". / matsudai.co.uk; matsudairamen; Tue-Sat 10 pm.

PASTURE £69 433

8-10 HIGH STREET CF10 1AW 07511 217422

"Amazing food" cooked over fire – including "the best steak ever" – "and really good value for money" earn this contemporary steakhouse from Sam Elliott strong ratings across the board. The sibling to the original in Bristol, it now has a bar next door called Parallel, serving small plates. / pasturerestaurant.com; pasture_cardiff; Mon-Sat 9.30 pm, Sun 5 pm.

PURPLE POPPADOM £57 443

185A, COWBRIDGE ROAD EAST CF11 9AJ 029 2022 0026

The "stunning quality of the food" served at Keralan-born chef Anand George's flagship over the past dozen years has made it one of Wales's best known Asian restaurants. The subtly spiced cuisine is matched by "very efficient and professional service, so a meal here is like going to the theatre". Top Menu Tip – "the sea bass in mango (aka 'Tiffin sea bass', chef Anand's signature dish) is delicious". / purplepoppadom.com; purple_poppadom; Tue-Sat 11 pm, Sun 9 pm.

Lumière, Cheltenham

SILURES £81

55 WELLFIELD ROAD CF24 3PA 029 2280 6369

Two former Gordon Ramsay and Galvin Bros staffers have joined forces to launch this ambitious restaurant and cocktail bar in the suburb of Roath. Its May 2023 debut occurred just as our annual diners' poll was concluding – too late for feedback – but it aims to provide 'something for everyone, whether you're visiting post-dog-walk for a cocktail on our terrace or celebrating your 25th wedding anniversary'. The name? – as you probably know, the Silures were a powerful tribe of ancient Britain, occupying what is now south east Wales. / silures-amh.com; silurescardiff; Wed & Thu 11.30 pm, Fri & Sat midnight, Sun 6 pm.

THOMAS BY TOM SIMMONS £85 443

3-5 PONTCANNA STREET CF11 9HQ 029 2116 7800

"Excellent in all aspects!" – so say fans of Tom Simmons's ambitious Pontcanna HQ, who moved back from three years running his eponymous restaurant in London to open here in early 2020. In addition to the à la carte selection – he provides a seven-course tasting menu for £75 per person. His cuisine is traditionally grounded (e.g. chicken liver parfait with sourdough, braised pork cheek, turbot with caviar) rather than striving for flash odie fireworks. / thomas-pontcanna.co.uk; omasbytomsimmons; Wed-Sat midnight.

ISCE £31

ROMILLY CRESCENT
F11 9NR 029 2037 3009

ext door to the more formal Heaney's, is two year old spin-off (whose name eans water in Gaelic) is a no-booking fair, serving small plates. Oysters are the eciality. / heaneyscardiff.co.uk; uiscebyheaneys; ed-Sat midnight.

CARDIGAN, PEMBROKESHIRE 4–4B

IZZATIPI £38 323

AMBRIAN QUAY
A43 1EZ 01239 612259

nis "fun and buzzing" operation was started four brothers and their friends, and benefits om an atmospheric location in a riverside urtyard; despite the "open fires", it "can t chilly as you sit in a rustic tipi (hence the me) or equally rustic booths", but the "good zzas" it specialises in are worth the mild scomfort. / pizzatipi.co.uk; pizzatipi; Thu-Sat om, Sun 3 pm.

CARLISLE, CUMBRIA 7–2D

LEXANDROS GREEK ESTAURANT AND ELI £50 343

WARWICK ROAD
A1 1DR 01228 592227

here's "no case of resting on their laurels" this vibrant, family-run operation with adjoining deli – all ably overseen by triarch Aris, who is "passionate about the ality of his food and his ingredients"; the Greek classics are just as good as ever, and ere's always something new to try on the ecials". / thegreek.co.uk; alexandros-greek-staurant-deli; Tue-Sat 9 pm.

CARTMEL, CUMBRIA 7–4D

ULIS AT 'ENCLUME £300 554

AVENDISH ST LA11 6QA 015395 36362

As we booked for 3 people, we ended up with e place to ourselves. This was our second sit to Aulis and this was every bit as good as e first and in some ways better as we had e full private dining experience!" – Simon ogan's 'development kitchen in the Lakes' sits ext door to L'Enclume and its six seats aim provide guests with a 'behind the scenes' linary adventure, with insight into the perimental, creative process and partnership ith 'Our Farm' behind this Lakeland enomenon. All feedback acclaims it as a antastic dining experience". / lenclume.co.uk; nclume; Wed-Sat, Tue 9 pm.

L'ENCLUME £302 545

CAVENDISH STREET
LA11 6QA 01539 536362

"Wonderful! Have been coming here since 2005 and this was the best food I've had, fully deserving its third star!" – Simon Rogan's converted blacksmith's workshop was, in 2022, the first restaurant in the North to achieve a third Michelin gong, and it's impressive that – despite its remote Lakeland location – it is nowadays the second most commented-on destination in our annual diners' poll outside of London. Head chef Paul Burgalieres marshalls the finest local produce – much of it from Simon's 'Our Farm' on the surrounding hillsides – to provide "a symphony of beautifully orchestrated food" in a 17-course meal offering "a completely faultless experience that's luxurious in its ingredients, cooking, time and space". Another positive is the "smooth and welcoming service" with "immensely impressive teamwork from the staff from start to finish". Of course, the cost is "exorbitant", but for most diners it delivers "everything that was hoped for": "was it worth the journey? Absolutely!" – "100% we would go back". ("Second visit in less than twelve months… was able to really enjoy the food without being overawed which you do get on the first visit as everything is so exquisite. Cannot fault. If I could afford the outlay I'd be going more often!") / lenclume.co.uk; lenclume; Tue-Sun midnight.

ROGAN & CO £81 443

DEVONSHIRE SQUARE
LA11 6QD 01539 535917

"Very slick and professional, and more relaxed than L'Enclume" – this spin-off from Simon Rogan's mothership around the corner affords a more buzzy and approachable (and bookable!) alternative to his main operation (and there is also the option to stay the night). "Super tasty and joyful" dishes are "impeccably served" from a three-course menu for £79 per person. "Stayed with them too and the breakfast was spectacular!" / roganandcompany.co.uk; rogan_and_co; Wed-Sun, Tue 9 pm.

CASTLE DOUGLAS, DUMFRIES AND GALLOWAY 7–2B

MR POOK'S KITCHEN £58 343

THE OLD BANK, 38 KING STREET
DG7 1AD 01556 504000

"An excellent meal with a very interesting menu!" – praise for this modern venue with an open kitchen which occupies a grand former banking hall in the centre of this regional market town. The Guardian's Grace Dent is also a fan – in her April 2023 review she applauded "a special-treat place… and one that the community clearly loves": "fancy, hearty and possibly a little more pricey than everywhere else around these parts" – a "menu of fine-quality local meat, fish and veg, served in painstakingly concocted ways". / mrpooks.co.uk; mrpookskitchen; Wed-Sat 11.30 pm.

CASTOR, PETERBOROUGH 6–4A

THE CHUBBY CASTOR £98 343

34 PETERBOROUGH ROAD PE5 7AX
01733380801

Adebola Adeshina (ex-Gordon Ramsay) left London to set up this restaurant in a Grade II-listed thatched pub. Fans say that this fine diner is "very romantic" and "superb all round" – while, for the odd critic, "dishes are picture perfect but tastes lack follow-through". PS – Adeshina has now developed the open space behind the pub into a casual summer lunch spot, The Yard. / thechubbycastor.com; chubbycastor; Wed-Sat 10.30 pm, Sun 3 pm.

CHAGFORD, DEVON 1–3D

GIDLEIGH PARK £193 445

TQ13 8HH 01647 432367

"Wow, what a treat… old world style and service… food all locally supplied, including from the hotel's own kitchen garden… thoroughly deserving their new Michelin star!" – chef Chris Eden has delivered the goods at Andrew Brownsword's stalwart destination, which lost its long-held accolade from the tyre men in 2019 and finally won it back in spring 2023. There's nowhere else quite like this large, comfortable property, whose "lovely country house vibe" isn't completely of a piece with its Tudorbethan styling, which would not be out of place in Surrey – yet here it is down a winding lane, beautifully situated in gardens on the fringes of Dartmoor. It became famous over 40 years ago under the Hendersons who were pioneers of the boutique hotel format, and has been owned by Brownsword since 2005. / gidleigh.co.uk; brownswordhotels; Tue-Sat 8.30 pm.

CHALFONT ST PETER, BUCKINGHAMSHIRE 3–3A

THE JOLLY FARMER £98 333

GOLD HILL WEST
SL9 9HH 01753 887 596

This "good local gastropub" offers food that is a step up from most rivals (think soufflés at both ends of the meal), thanks to being "part of the Raymond Blanc outfit" – the former White Brasserie Group, renamed as Heartwood Inns in summer 2023. / jollyfarmerchalfont.com; jollyfarmer.chalfont; Mon-Thu 9.15 pm, Fri & Sat 10 pm, Sun 9 pm.

CHANDLER'S CROSS, HERTFORDSHIRE 3–2A

PRIME STEAK & GRILL, THE CLARENDON £84 343

REDHALL LANE
WD3 4LU 01923 264 580

"Prime manages to feel special and cosy all at once" – a family-friendly steak specialist where the main event is dry-aged on the bone and "not cheap but well worth it" for a "special occasion choice". This branch recently added a new canopied gin garden with heating in winter, and you can also check out a trio of siblings in St Albans, Beaconsfield and Berkhamsted. / primesteakandgrill.com; primesteak; Mon-Sat 11 pm, Sun 10 pm.

CHARD, SOMERSET 2–4A

THE CANDLELIGHT INN £56 433

BISHOPSWOOD TA20 3RS 01460 234476

As the name suggests, "a great, intimate atmosphere" is found at this seventeenth-century village inn, which is "a cut above the usual for style and service". Charlotte Vincent was crowned 'pub chef of the year' in the 2023 Great British Pub Awards – she sends out "a varied range of dishes, nearly all locally sourced and precisely cooked", such as a bar snack of roasted marrow bone and Porlock Bay oyster with garlic butter and sourdough bread. / candlelight-inn.co.uk; candlelightinnsomerset; Wed-Sat 11 pm.

THE COTLEY INN £59 333

WAMBROOK TA20 3EN 01460 62348

"Seemingly off the beaten track down increasingly narrow country lanes in the beautiful Blackdown Hills but with easy access from the A358 if you are en route to Devon and Cornwall" – this rural inn wins praise as a "great local" ("very dog friendly!") "producing lovely food in a picturesque setting". Meat is smoked onsite and "game seems to be a speciality (as we were leaving, the beaters and dogs were arriving back at the pub with several brace of pheasants!)" / cotleyinnwambrook.co.uk; thecotleyinn; Sun & Mon 10 pm, Wed-Sat 11 pm.

CHATHAM, KENT 3–3C

PUMPROOM RESTAURANT AT COPPER RIVET DISTILLERY £54 334

ME4 4LP 01634 931121

You couldn't ask for a much better location than this characterful Victorian pump house attached to Chatham dockyard, whose outside terrace enjoys fine views of the Medway. Converted into a distillery seven years ago by the Russell family, it has relatively recently added a restaurant and cocktail lounge serving "interesting" cooking. / crdpumproom.com; copperrivetdistillery; Thu-Sat 8.30 pm, Wed 2.30 pm, Sun 3.45 pm.

CHELMSFORD, ESSEX 3–2C

FETE GRAYS YARD £43 333

10-13 GRAYS BREWERY YARD CM2 6QR NO TEL

A "fun addition to the lacklustre Chelmsford food scene", "this small city-centre independent" started out as a socially distanced coffee van under lockdown, and is now a permanent coffee shop with a "really interesting evening menu of Middle Eastern tapas": "try it – it's great!" / fetegraysyard.co.uk; fete_graysyard; Tue, Wed, Sun 5 pm, Thu-Sat midnight.

MOTO PIZZA £36 332

24 BADDOW ROAD CM2 0DG 01245 257819

Press the green light for service, and then "eat until you can eat no more" – the "simple but effective" formula at this bottomless Neapolitan pizza joint, also with a Colchester spin-off; the "deliciously thin" pies support "fantastic food combinations" (but perhaps best to "go for lunch so that you have the rest of the day to digest all of the offerings!"). / motopizza.co.uk; Tue-Sat 10 pm, Sun 8 pm.

PIG & WHISTLE RESTAURANT 333

CHIGNAL ROAD, CHIGNAL SMEALY CM1 4SZ 01245 443 186

In a village a short drive outside Chelmsford, this converted sixteenth-century pub has fine countryside views and provides a traditionally comfortable destination, complete with linen tablecloths, candles and cut glass. It wins good all-round feedback (if not a huge volume of reviews) and its modern brasserie fare (with steak, beef Wellington and cote de boeuf to share a highlight) helps it regularly feature in Essex food awards. (Owners Brendan Curran & Justin Mullender are also known for the quality of their put-downs on Tripadvisor!) / pigandwhistlechelmsford.uk; PigWhistleChelmsford; Wed-Sat 10 pm, Sun 6 pm.

CHELTENHAM, GLOUCESTERSHIRE 2–1C

L'ARTISAN £64 333

30 CLARENCE ST GL50 3NX 01242 571257

The Ogrodzki's "traditional neighbourhood bistro" is a real local magnet for its accomplished Gallic cooking, with Jay Rayner's 2021 review in The Observer also praising its beautiful homage to the '80s. In June 2022, after almost a decade in business, the fine diner pivoted to a more casual bistro/'Café du Midi', offering breakfast and set lunch menus from 10am-4pm. Whether or not less is more, it was praised this year for its "changing seasonal menus, authentic dishes, pleasantly cluttered" decor and "delightful service that's so verrrrry French". / lartisan-restaurant.com; lartisanchelt; Wed-Sat 4 pm, Tue 9 pm.

BHOOMI £55 343

52 SUFFOLK RD GL50 2AQ 01242 222 010

"Stylish decor, food bursting with flavour and charming staff" win consistently high ratings across the board for local restaurateur Michael Raphel's venue, inspired by the flavours his chef-grandfather brought to the UK from South India. Fans feel "it's less ambitious than Prithvi (same ownership) but in some ways nicer". Top Tip – "lunchtime thali is a delightful bargain, with great tastes for a snip". / bhoomikitchen.co.uk; bhoomikitchen_; Tue-Sun 9.30 pm.

LE CHAMPIGNON SAUVAGE £114 54

24-28 SUFFOLK RD GL50 2AQ 01242 573449

"The yardstick against which we compare everything and few, if any, can compete with the quality and value" – an oft-repeated compliment for David & Helen Everitt-Matthias's long-established temple of foodie pilgrimage ("it is lucky we live 2.5 hours away as if it was closer I doubt we would go anywhere else"). David's cuisine is "always original, seasonal and well judged and – though carefully presented – avoids the irritating Instagrammability sometimes found elsewhere". "Helen presides over the room and also the wine with grace" in a manner that's both "friendly and professional" and the "very good list" is an attraction in itself with "the ample selection of half bottles being a bonus"; and "the cheese basket is a tour de force". Even devotees concede that "some might find the atmosphere sedate" – a more critical view is that "excellent food and wine is let down by an overly formal approach and lack of ambience" ("the reverential tone is not where we are in 2023!"). Overall, though, the verdict is of a stalwart that's "serene, calm, well-spaced and good humoured… if there's a better place to enjoy terrific cooking whilst having a good conversation, I'd like to know about it!" / lechampignonsauvage.co.uk; Lechampsauvage; Wed-Sat 8.30 pm.

THE IVY MONTPELLIER BRASSERIE £77 22

ROTUNDA TERRACE, MONTPELLIER STREET GL50 1SH 01242 894 200

"The rotunda is wonderful", and "can make a visit stand out" at this branch of the ubiquitou chain, which otherwise conforms to type with "food and service that are professional, reliabl and entirely anonymous" – "one could eat the same dish every day and find it unvarying, while being treated politely but distantly by the staff". / theivycheltenhambrasserie.com; ivycheltenham; Mon-Sun 11 pm.

LUMIÈRE £101 55

CLARENCE PARADE GL50 3PA 01242 222200

"At last! A well-deserved Michelin star" for John and (FOH) Helen Howe's "small, intimate and sophisticated modern British venture" and its considerable fan club is "absolutely delighted" that it is "finally getting the recognition it deserves" (although, to be fair, the question is what took them so long, as we've been raving about this place for many years). "Every element is perfectly crafted" to deliver "sublime cooking and stunning presentation" (with much of the produce sourced from a relative's farm) all "delightfully served", combining to make Lumière "as good as it gets" – "just what a perfect restaurant should be". / lumiererestaurant.co.uk lumiererestaurantcheltenham; Fri & Sat, Wed & Thu 8.30 pm.

USE BRASSERIE £67 4|3|3

ST GEORGE'S PLACE
.50 3PN 01242 239447

"fabulous selection of French/Indian cuisine, l of flavour and beautifully presented", is anks to an unusual collaboration between o chefs from very different traditions – enchman Franck Grillet, a graduate of e Parisian 'bistronomie' movement, and dian Pramod Tirunagari. The success of e combination has led to the opening of a cond branch in Bristol. / musebrasserie.com; isebrasserie; Mon-Thu 10 pm, Fri & Sat 11 pm.

RITHVI £87 5|4|2

BATH ROAD GL53 7HG 01242 226229

)utstanding and imaginative cooking th an Indian twist" is key to the success this "elegant and evolved restaurant" er the past dozen years. Locally born under Jay Rahman worked at top-ranked rmingham venues Lasan and Purnell's fore taking over and transforming his cle's traditional curry house, fka Hassan's. line with its evolution, "the sommelier ggests some interesting and well-thought- t wine pairings". / prithvirestaurant.com; ithvirestaurant; Tue-Sat 9.30 pm.

URSLANE £73 3|3|3

RODNEY RD GL50 1JJ 01242 321639

hef-patron Gareth Fulford's small indie is "friendly" location in which to dine upon stainable seafood and Cotswolds produce either from the "great set-price lunch", iich changes weekly, or the bi-monthly- anging à la carte. It doesn't inspire a huge lume of feedback, but fans say it's an nderrated" restaurant that outperforms the cal competition. / purslane-restaurant.co.uk; rslane_restaurant; Thu-Sat 12.30 am.

CHESHUNT, HERTFORDSHIRE 3–2B

HE ZEBRA RIDING CLUB, IRCH £54 3|4|4

IRCH, LIEUTENANT ELLIS WAY
N7 5HW 01992 645522

ırt hotel, part members' club, part co- orking space – this three-year-old eatery in e high-ceilinged and modernified stable- ocks of the 140-room property (set in over) acres) is overseen from afar by star chef obin Gill. It's a brasserie selection of dishes, any from the wood-fired oven, and feedback, still relatively limited, is uniformly upbeat. Whether or not the fancier tasting menu for 58 is a good investment is more of a moot oint). / birchcommunity.com; birchcommunity; 'ed-Sat 10 pm, Sun 8 pm.

CHESSINGTON, SURREY 3–3B

AFFRON SUMMER £58 3|4|2

ACE PARADE KT9 1DR 020 8391 4477

his haute Indian, in the Surrey 'burbs ıere's also a Reigate sibling) was set up by -Oberoi/Cinnamon Club chef-patron Awanish Roy; it offers "a different Indian meal experience", with the "lovely" food sampling Goan seafood specialities, or game from the Karnataka region, alongside more trad Punjabi dishes. / saffronsummer.co.uk; saffronsummersurrey; Tue-Thu, Sun, Fri & Sat 10.30 pm.

CHESTER, CHESHIRE 5–2A

ARCHITECT £53 2|3|4

54 NICHOLAS STREET
CH1 2NX 01244 353070

This Georgian pub near the city's picturesque racecourse, from the Brunning & Price stable, is popular for its "wonderful location and comforting decor". Reports on the food are more muted, although "if you like fish 'n' chips you'll love it – they offer more combinations of batter/fish/sides than most places". It was built by prominent Chester architect Thomas Harrison as his own home – hence the unusual name. / brunningandprice.co.uk; architectchester; Mon-Thu 11 pm, Fri & Sat 11.30 pm, Sun 10.30 pm. SRA – 3 stars

ARKLE, THE CHESTER GROSVENOR £120 3|3|3

56-58 EASTGATE STREET
CH1 1LT 01244 324 024

Chef Elliot Hill has big shoes to fill at this well-known dining room, which is one of the North West's most consistent culinary icons, having held a Michelin star under Simon Radley from 1998-2021 (at a time when such recognition was thin on the ground in this and neighbouring counties). Lacking natural light, this stately chamber sits deep within this unusually grand provincial hotel, which is owned by the Duke of Westminster, and is right next to the city's emblematic Eastgate Clock on its medieval walls. While acknowledging that it's "pricey", all reports are very positive on the start he's made with a "scrumptious five-course tasting menu"; staff who "make you feel valued and well looked after"; and the "elegant, comfortable and quiet (but not too quiet!)" interior. "An incredible, if expensive, experience" that's "well set to regain his predecessor's accolades". / chestergrosvenor.com; arkle.chester; Wed-Sat 9 pm.

LA BRASSERIE, CHESTER GROSVENOR, CHESTER GROSVENOR £78 3|3|5

EASTGATE CH1 1LT 01244 324024

In the shadow of the Eastgate Clock, this glam pavement-side brasserie (the second restaurant in a fine old hotel in the city centre) makes a luxurious spot to break from retail therapy in this shopping-mad city. There's a "varied menu", and although results have been "up and down" over time, locals say that "of late it's much improved". Top Menu Tip – "always oysters" (served with a selection of Champagnes). / chestergrosvenor.com; chestergrosvenor; Mon-Sat 9 pm, Sun 8.30 pm.

CHESTER NEW MARKET 3|3|4

NORTHGATE ST CH1 2AR NO TEL

This food hall is a "new concept for Chester" although the award-winning new purpose-built marketplace it inhabits (which opened in November 2022) traces its origins back to the city's first market charter in 1159. Fans say it's "well worth a visit" – "lively and busy all the time", "it caters for all" with dishes ordered from a wide range of traders to be consumed in a central dining area – "and it has a bar". (Few tears are being shed for the demise of the unlovely former Chester Market in the Forum Shopping Centre which was created in the 1960s to replace a demolished Victorian building). / newchester.market; Mon-Thu 10 pm, Fri & Sat 11 pm.

THE FORGE 3|3|2

HOTEL INDIGO, GROSVENOR PARK ROAD
CH1 1QQ 01244 735765

Feedback is more limited than we would like, but is enthusiastic over this grey-hued boutique hotel dining room, run from afar by game expert Mike Robinson. Chef Dan Regan oversees the preparation of a menu that majors in 40-60 day, dry-aged beef steaks from a selection of sirloin or ribeye cuts. / theforgechester.co.uk; the_forge_restaurant_chester; Mon-Thu 9.30 pm, Fri & Sat 9.45 pm, Sun 8.30 pm.

HAMAYUU £21 3|3|2

59 WATERGATE STREET
CH1 2LB 01244 350005

For "genuine Japanese food in the city-centre, this Japanese-owned and -run restaurant", near the cathedral, is just the ticket; the sushi and sashimi are especially "excellent", but there are other "authentic" dishes from gyoza to katsu curry on offer too. / hamayuu.co.uk; hamayuuchester; Mon, Wed-Sun 10 pm.

PORTA £73 3|3|3

140 NORTHGATE STREET
CH1 2HT 01244 344295

"You feel like you're in Madrid or Barcelona in these really authentic tapas bars" from Joe & Ben Wright – "the vegetable dishes are especially strong". The three branches – in Chester, Altrincham and Salford– have proved so popular that the brothers closed down their original Chester bistro, Joseph Benjamin, three years ago to turn it into a larger Porta. / portatapas.co.uk; porta_chester; Tue-Sat 10.30 pm, Sun 9 pm.

STICKY WALNUT £66 3|4|4

11 CHARLES ST CH2 3AZ 01244 400400

"We had heard the hype and were very pleasantly surprised that it lived up to it!" – Gary Usher's original venture in his nowadays-famous Elite Bistros group occupies the gentrified suburb of Hoole outside the city centre. "A small menu of reliably tasty food is provided by engaging and knowledgeable staff",

"It's only small, so it could get a bit awkward if it was quiet, but it always seems to be bustling. I really like it here!" / stickywalnut.net; Sticky_Walnut; Mon-Thu 9 pm, Fri & Sat 10 pm, Sun 5 pm.

STILE NAPOLITANO £35 442

49 WATERGATE STREET CH1 2LB 01244 320543

"What a find!" – a "fabulous authentic pizzeria" in a "buzzing city-centre location" right under half-timbered shopping hub The Rows. The "family favourite sort of place" is the second venture from Ischia-born chef Giacomo Guido, a former winner of the London Pizza Festival, who launched this homage to Neapolitan pies a year later, in 2018. Mains are "solely pizza", but that's a joy given their "perfect thin base – slightly charred with just the right amount of topping". / stilenapoletanopizzeria.co.uk; stilenapoletanochester; Mon, Wed & Thu 10 pm, Fri & Sat 10.30 pm, Sun 9 pm.

CHETTISCOMBE, DEVON 1–3D

THE LOST KITCHEN 322

THE LONG BARN EX16 7PT 01884 242427

This informal, wood-fired restaurant set in a 'feasting barn' with a terrace garden and beautiful views of the rolling hills of mid-Devon was started by a couple who used to run events across Somerset and Devon. "It can get very busy, but it's worth the journey down the lanes" from Tiverton for its sourdough pizzas and what Telegraph critic William Sitwell, in an admiring March 2023 review, called its "enveloping, welcome-to-our-cave spirit" and "exotic menu" ("more Shoreditch than Devon"). / lostkitchen.co.uk; thelostkitchendevon; Wed & Thu, Sat & Sun 6 pm, Fri 10 pm.

CHEW MAGNA, CITY OF BRISTOL 2–2B

LAZY LOBSTER £44 332

5D S PARADE BS40 8SH 01275 333996

It's "worth a trip out of town to this old village" east of Bristol to visit this "slightly quirky" (plus "small and lively") establishment, launched in 2018 by local couple Don and Donna; the former hairdressing shop turns out "rustic but good" tapas-style seafood from Brixham and beyond, and there are tempting gins from their son's on-site distillery to go with it. / lazylobsterltd.com; lazylobsterchewmagna; Tue-Sat 11 pm, Sun 6 pm.

CHICHESTER, WEST SUSSEX 3–4A

BRASSERIE £57 332

1-2 RICHMOND HOUSE CHURCH SQUARE PO19 7BG 01243 534200

A "perfect location for the theatre" as a matter of course, this venue also shines for its "well-cooked food", "enthusiastic and professional service from a young team" and "good value". / brasserieblanc.com; Mon-Fri 10 pm, Sat 10.30 pm, Sun 9 pm.

CASSONS RESTAURANT & BAR £63 332

ARUNDEL ROAD, TANGMERE PO18 0DU 01243 773294

It's "a little old-fashioned", but that does little to dent the appeal of Viv Casson's "lovely" restaurant, a short drive from the Goodwood Estate; the venue celebrated its twentieth anniversary in 2023, and whether you go for the Sunday lunch or regular themed dinners, it "delivers on efficiency and solidly good food". / cassonsrestaurant.co.uk; Thu-Sat 11 pm, Sun 3 pm.

THE HORSE & GROOM £65 333

PO18 9AX 01243 575339

Four miles from Chichester, and bordering the South Downs National Park, this 200-year-old pub-with-rooms is part proper boozer (upfront) and part tastefully arty restaurant offering ambitious gastrofare. Reporters this year praised the "warm ambience" and a "treat" of a menu that features some "standout courses" such as scallops and venison. / thehorseandgroom.pub; horseandgroompubeastashling; Mon-Sat 9 pm, Sun 4 pm.

PALLANT RESTAURANT AND CAFE £57 223

EAST PALLANT PO19 1TJ 01243 770827

A "lively, bright restaurant-cum-café looking out on a lovely courtyard" at this art gallery; following a recent trend, there were reports of some "average food" and service this year, but the majority deemed it "very pleasant", and the "delightful" location makes it a "good place for a coffee and a snack". / pallantcafe.co.uk; Tue-Sun 5 pm.

PURCHASES RESTAURANT 332

31 NORTH STREET PO19 1LX 01243 771444

"In the heart of Chichester", Nick Sutherland's "consistently good" and "reasonably priced" restaurant "with conservatory and garden rooms" is "perfect for pre-theatre dining". It has a "slightly old-fashioned ambience", as the bow-fronted Georgian premises it occupies previously housed a well-known wine merchant of the same name. / purchasesrestaurant.co.uk; Tue-Sat 11 pm, Sun 5 pm.

THYME & CHILLIES INDIAN KITCHEN £51 333

149 SAINT PANCRAS PO19 7SH 01243 778881

Mayank Gupta (orthopaedic surgeon) and wife Nita (dentist) set up this red-brick venture as a bastion against the dodgy provenance of some UK curry houses – and the "very good" curries (marked by "delicious spicing" and reasonable pricing) have made it a hit. Mayank also runs importer Wines In India, so why not skip the Kingfisher for something more adventurous to wash the food down? / thymeandchillies.co.uk; thymechilli; Sun-Thu 10.30 pm, Fri & Sat 11 pm.

CHINNOR, OXFORDSHIRE 2–2

THE SIR CHARLES NAPIER £97 44

SPRIGGS ALLEY OX39 4BX 01494 483011

"Delightfully out of the way" with a "tremendous location" in the leafy Chilterns: Julie Griffiths' hidden-away restaurant (too posh really to be called a pub as it originally was) is "worth the trip out of London" or makes a "perfect lunch stop off the M40". Its impressive standards over the years make it one of the top 100 most commented-on destinations outside of the capital in our annu diners' poll and it provides "flavoursome" (if not especially foodie) traditional fare backed u by a "serious wine list". "Julie always maintair the highest standard" (as she has done for ove 50 years at the helm now) and it is particularly "a perfect location on a fine summer day". / sircharlesnapier.co.uk; sircharlesnapier; Tue-Sat 9 pm, Sun 3.30 pm.

CHIPSTEAD, KENT 3–3

THE GEORGE & DRAGON 33

39 HIGH ST TN13 2RW 01732 779 019

This sixteenth-century pub, complete with beams, log fires and an updated interior, has a "great small menu which changes constantly". A "lovely spot" for a meal, "whether inside in the winter or in the garden in the summer". / georgeanddragonchipstead.com; georgechipstead; Mon-Sat 8.45 pm, Sun 5.45 pm.

CHISLEHURST, KENT 3–3

CINNAMON CULTURE £60 32

97 HIGH ST BR7 5AG 020 8289 0322

This contemporary curry house wins solid ratings for its food, with unusual chef's signatu dishes including a mixed grill of achari ostrich filet, chicken tikka and lamb chop. Family-run it transferred to Chislehurst after a decade in Plaistow Lane, Bromley. / cinnamonculture.com cinnamonculture; Tue-Sat 11 pm, Sun 10 pm.

CHRISTCHURCH, DORSET 2–4

THE JETTY, CHRISTCHURCH HARBOUR HOTEL & SPA £85 33

95 MUDEFORD BH23 3NT 01202 40095

This "top spot" – a modern, glass-walled venue with a terrace for outdoor dining at a "lovely location on Christchurch Harbour" (in the grounds of the Harbour Hotel and with superb views) – is an ideal showcase for chef Alex Aitken's "consistently high-quality, locally sourced seafood". / thejetty.co.uk; jettymudeford Mon-Sat 09.30 pm, Sun 8 pm.

Sorrel, Dorking

HE KINGS ARMS OTEL 344

CASTLE STREET
H23 1DT 01202 588933

good position in the town centre and on the ver Avon only adds to the appeal of this bstantial Georgian property – nowadays a xurious four-star hotel. The restaurant is erseen by Alex Aitken of the nearby Jetty d provides some surprisingly affordable tions, including "a daily changing £17.50 o-course market menu with ingredients urced within 15 miles". (Some change ay be afoot, though, as in June 2023 the vners since 2005 put the property on e market.) / thekings-christchurch.co.uk; ngsarmschristchurch; Mon-Sat 2 pm, Sun 9 pm.

CHURCHILL, OXFORDSHIRE 2–1C

HE CHEQUERS £60 344

HURCH LANE OX7 6NJ 01608 659393

nartly renovated with a 'no foam' menu elevated pub grub to match, this honey-loured boozer in an idyllic Cotswold village is "benefited from the 'Country Creatures' eatment" (now known as Lionhearth) under e co-ownership of locally based billionaire operty developer Sir Tony Gallagher, nchpin of the Chipping Norton set. hese days, "the main problem is getting a ble". / countrycreatures.com; lionhearthgroup; on-Sun 11 pm.

CHURTON, CHESTER 5–3A

HE WHITE HORSE £57 343

HESTER ROAD CH3 6LA 01829 272200

Bistro meets pub to create a really enjoyable xperience" at Gary Usher's year-old gastropub, hich opened in early 2023. It's off to a smooth art ("we ate on the fourth day of opening, nd expected some minor teething troubles, but ere were none!") and seems to succeed in his iginal aim, which was 'to serve great drinks, elicious unpretentious food by a team that ve what they do' (even despite a minor furore the national press over the pricing of a £20 urger). / elitebistros.com; whitehorsechurton; on-Thu 8 pm, Fri & Sat 9 pm, Sun 7 pm.

CLANFIELD, OXFORDSHIRE 2–2C

THE DOUBLE RED DUKE 213

BOURTON ROAD
OX18 2RB 03339 398875

"Everything a quaint and cosy country pub should be" – this ambitious venue was converted from a seventeenth-century coaching inn three years ago, and all reports agree it looks the part. "Amateur service" took the gloss off a number of experiences though – it can seem "just too busy and big" – even in reports that acknowledge a "delicious Sunday lunch". / countrycreatures.com; doubleredduke; Sun-Thu 9 pm, Fri & Sat 9.30 pm.

CLAUGHTON, LANCASHIRE 5–1B

THE FENWICK ARMS £68 322

LANCASTER RD LA2 9LA 01524 221250

This 250-year-old Lune Valley gastroboozer-with-rooms has the claim to fame of having appeared on Ramsay's 'Kitchen Nightmares' back in 2006. Fast-forward 17 years and several owners, and it's in the hands of The Oakman Group, and now, say fans, "always worth a visit" – being "probably the best place to go for fish in the Lancaster area" (quite the turnaround, then!). / fenwickarms.co.uk; fenwickarms; Sun-Fri 11 pm, Sat midnight.

CLIFTON, CUMBRIA 8–3A

GEORGE & DRAGON £65

CA10 2ER 01768 865381

Just a couple of miles from its stablemate, Askham Hall, which provides much of the produce for its kitchens – Charles Lowther's charming Cumbrian pub (with 10 bedrooms) near the M6 reopened in mid-2023 following a year's closure after a fire in June 2022. Previously one of the more commented-on destinations in this neck of the woods, fans have been "awaiting its return". / georgeanddragonclifton.co.uk; georgeanddragonclifton; Mon-Sun .

CLIMPING, WEST SUSSEX 3–4A

BAILIFFSCOURT HOTEL £92 334

CLIMPING ST BN17 5RW 01903 723511

This "charmingly higgledy-piggledy venue" may look like it springs from medieval times, but was in fact created in 1927, when a member of the Guinness brewing family commissioned it from an antiquarian and architect. Nowadays it sprawls over thirty acres leading to the coastline, replete with numerous houses and cottages offering accommodation, a hotel and spa, and a dining room with tapestry-hung walls, where diners can enjoy a solid menu based on Sussex produce. / hshotels.co.uk; hshotels; Mon-Sun 10 pm.

CLIPSHAM, RUTLAND 6–4A

THE OLIVE BRANCH £81 433

MAIN ST LE15 7SH 01780 410355

This "lovely and buzzy" and incredibly popular gastropub is situated near the A1 "on the edge of England's smallest county" and – "with its cosy open fires" – represents "the modern English pub at its best": "drink excellent local ales on draft at the bar" (or "there's an intriguing wine list as long as your arm"); "sit and eat delicious, upmarket food which is both straightforward and sophisticated… or do both!" (and you can also "stay in one of the beautifully appointed rooms in a neighbouring property for the perfect away break"). "Not only are most of the ingredients sourced locally, many of them are actually grown on the land surrounding the pub". / theolivebranchpub.com; olivebranchclipsham; Wed-Sat 9.30 pm, Sun 9 pm.

CLITHEROE, LANCASHIRE 5–1B

THE INN AT WHITEWELL £71 345

FOREST OF BOWLAND
BB7 3AT 01200 448222

"A great escape" – this famous country inn (dating from the sixteenth century) provides a "delightful setting" thanks both to its picturesque situation, by the River Hodder in the Forest of Bowland, and also its cosy and traditional interior and rooms: "idyllic for a romantic break". Chef Jamie Cadman has been at the stoves for the last 20 years and maintains a very high quality of traditional-with-a-twist cuisine, backed up by the impressive wine list one would expect of an establishment with its own onsite retail wine merchants ('Bowland Forest Vintners', which has operated for over 40 years). "Dining outside in summer on the terrace is a particular pleasure". / innatwhitewell.com; inn_at_whitewell; Fri-Sun, Mon-Thu 9 pm.

COBHAM, SURREY 3–3A

COPPA CLUB COBHAM £65 223

13-15 BETWEEN STREETS KT11 1AA 01932 500608

From a growing popular chain of 'no membership' clubs, this comfortable venue has a bar, lounge, orangery and terrace, along with "fun" all-weather igloos on the roof, in which to graze on a pretty standard all-day menu of Italian-inspired dishes, including pizza and pasta. Not a culinary fave rave, but handy for many occasions. / coppaclub.co.uk; coppaclub; Mon-Thu 11 pm, Fri & Sat 11.30 pm, Sun 10 pm.

THE CRICKETERS £61 343

DOWNSIDE COMMON KT11 3NX 01932 862 105

Given its attractive setting on Downside Common, this "lovely country pub" (part of Raymond Blanc's White Brasserie chain) in the heart of plush stockbroker belt would likely be a local destination come what may. But it also goes the extra mile and – though it's not particularly 'gastro' – wins consistently high acclaim for its "cheerful welcoming staff" and high quality of cooking. "It was done up over the winter; and although there is no longer a set menu, the prices are reasonable in the current climate". Top Menu Tip – "well-prepared steak and very good tartiflette starter". / cricketerscobham.com; The Cricketers; Mon-Thu 9.15 pm, Fri & Sat 10 pm, Sun 9 pm.

THE IVY COBHAM BRASSERIE £77 233

48 HIGH ST KT11 3EF 01932 901777

A "buzzy, colourful atmosphere" reigns supreme at this Surrey offshoot of The Ivy's flashy brasserie chain, with a beautiful orangerie the best of the seating options. As for the food, "it is perfectly acceptable" but "this place lives off the name for sure" and is "very expensive for what it is" (not that this necessarily deters repeat visitors, who "return for its lovely ambience"). / theivycobhambrasserie.com; the_ivy_collection; Mon-Thu 10.30 pm, Fri & Sat 11 pm, Sun 9.30 pm.

THE PLOUGH INN £82 332

PLOUGH LANE KT11 3LT 01932 589790

The Rarebreed Dining Group's boozer is far from your regular beast: the in-house butchery and smokery turns out "excellent" meaty cuts including chateaubriand, t-bone or sous-vide sirloin; in August they also run an outdoor cinema if you'd like some celluloid after your steak. / theploughinncobham.co.uk; theploughinncobham; Tue-Thu 9 pm, Fri & Sat 10 pm, Sun 8 pm.

COCKERMOUTH, CUMBRIA 7–3C

KIRKSTILE INN £42 333

LOWESWATER CA13 0RU 01900 85219

The "traditional pub food in generous portions" is just the ticket "for hungry walkers after a day on the fells" at this 400-year-old Lake District inn with "amazing views over Melbreak". "We love the choice between the bar or more formal dining room", and the beer brewed by its own Cumbrian Ales brewery also goes down well – especially the prizewinning Loweswater Gold. / kirkstile.com; thekirkstileinn; Mon-Sat 11 pm, Sun 10.30 pm.

COLCHESTER, ESSEX 3–2C

KINTSU £111 453

11A NORTH HILL CO1 1DZ 01206 570005

This "lovely local restaurant" with a "cool London vibe in a hard-to-find location off the High Street" showcases chef-patron Paul Wendholt's "just fantastic" modern British cooking. It's a "tiny place", so "sitting at the bar overlooking the open kitchen is really interactive". The venue changed its name and direction two years ago – "I loved when it was Grain, and I'm so glad the new name and menu live up to expectations". / kintsu.co.uk; kintsu_colchester; Wed-Sat midnight.

COLERNE, WILTSHIRE 2–2B

RESTAURANT HYWEL JONES BY LUCKNAM PARK, LUCKHAM PARK HOTEL £158 433

SN14 8AZ 01225 742777

"'Old school' dining… perhaps a bit stuffy, but the food's good" – the dining room of this well-known luxury spa hotel has had, since 2006, chef Hywel Jones at the stoves. You can eat à la carte for £110 per person for three courses, or there's an eight-course tasting menu for £140 per person, and the deft cuisine won nothing but praise this year. "The wild and woody setting of The Estate and the slightly faded grandeur of The House just make it a rather special place to stay" and it's also praised for a "delicious afternoon tea in beautiful, elegant surroundings". / lucknampark.co.uk; lucknam_park; Thu-Sun 9 pm.

COLWELL BAY, ISLE OF WIGHT 2–4D

THE HUT £79 334

COLWELL CHINE ROAD PO40 9NP 01983 898 637

The "fabulous seaside location", "lively, super-buzzy atmosphere" and resident DJ lend a Balearic Islands vibe to Matt & George Adams's 10-year-old venue – helped by a roof that closes when the British weather disobliges. Getting there can be an adventure in itself, either by charter boat from Lymington on the mainland opposite, or via ex-army one-tonne truck shuttle from Yarmouth Harbour. "Food (mostly seafood) is fine", but "can be a bit hit-and-miss". / thehutcolwell.co.uk; thehutcolwell; Mon-Sun midnight.

COLWYN BAY, CONWY 4–1

BRYN WILLIAMS AT PORTH EIRIAS £61 33

THE PROMENADE, LL29 8HH 01492 577 525

"With a window seat, smart service and very reliable cooking, this is one of the better place to eat in North Wales", is a generally agreed take on this outlet from high-profile Welsh chef Bryn WIlliams, in a modern beachside development owned by the local council. Although there's a view that it's "not a patch" on his more gastronomic Odette's in London, it's "clearly popular" and "even if the menu could be more exciting, it's good at what it does". / portheirias.com; Sun-Thu 4 pm, Fri & S 8.30 pm.

CONWY, CONWY 4–1

THE JACKDAW

HIGH STREET LL32 8DB 01492 596922

Llandudno-born chef/patron Nick Rudge cut his culinary teeth at The Fat Duck; his small two-year-old venue occupies part of a gothic building that was formerly a cinema and bingo hall. It has won some renown for his ambitious, locally rooted cuisine, and our feedback this year was also enthusiastic (if still too limited for a rating): "lucky to get last table for two at short notice: great menu and wine flight with links to Wales for both food and wine, with strong results across all courses and very attentive and professional service… would recommend". / thejackdawconwy.co.uk; thejackdawconwy; Tue-Sat 11 pm.

COPSTER GREEN, LANCASHIRE 5–1

YU £65 44

500 LONGSIGHT RD BB1 9EU 01254 240665

Victor Yu's "exceptional" Ribble Valley landmark celebrates its 20th anniversary this year, serving delicious Cantonese meals with a real sense of occasion. "Love this place, servic is brilliant and Victor is an absolute star", say fans – "the tasting menu offers something for everyone; it's expensive, but worth it". / yucopstergreen.co.uk; yu_copstergreen; Tue Thu, Sun 10 pm, Fri & Sat midnight.

CORBRIDGE, NORTHUMBERLAND 8–2

THE VALLEY £52 44

OLD STATION HS NE45 5AY 01434 633434

"Consistently excellent" local curry house which has spawned a couple of spin-offs in Newcastle and Hexham (badged Cilantro). From Newcastle, you can follow in Michael Portillo's footsteps (on his 'Great Coastal Railway Journeys' TV Series), and book their well-known 'Passage to India' train service from Newcastle (which includes your meal, plu travel by train). / valleyrestaurants.co.uk; Mon-S 10 pm.

:ORTON DENHAM, SOMERSET 2–3B

HE QUEEN'S RMS £55 333

'9 4LR 01963 220317

ɪis "newly refurbished family-owned pub th rooms" – originally a mid-Victorian cider ›use – in a "lovely village" near Sherborne, akes for a "perfect stop-over en route to :von or Cornwall", with "agreeable service" d "reliable food including interesting h dishes". Co-owner Doune Mackenzie-ancis has a foodie background as a former arketing manager for Leith's School of Food WIne. / thequeensarms.com; queensarmspub; on-Sat 9.30 pm, Sun 9 pm.

:OTTENHAM, CAMBRIDGESHIRE 3–1B

URRY PALACE £24 332

5 HIGH STREET
324 8QP 01954 250257

"brilliant Asian venue" in this village outside ambridge where the "really fresh and tasty od" in generous portions are matched by "amazing, very diverse menu selection" o. / currypalacecottenham.com.

:OVENTRY, WARWICKSHIRE 5–4C

URNELL'S CAFÉ BISTRO AT HARTERHOUSE £75 334

HARTERHOUSE PRIORY OF ST ANNE,)NDON ROAD CV1 2JR 0121 212 9799

nly recently opened, in early 2023, 'Yummy ummie' Glynn Purnell (operating in artnership with Historic Coventry Trust), unched this cafe and pizzeria in the cloisters a Grade I-listed 14th Century former arthusian monastery. "It's similar to Purnell's ates in Birmingham serving delicious and ry good-value small dishes, tapas style" and he setting is beautiful – a spacious, modern d comfortable conservatory in this historic ilding in a lovely park on the outskirts Coventry". / historiccoventrytrust.org.uk; storiccoventrytrust; Thu-Sat 8.30 pm, Sun 5 pm.

:RASTER, NORTHUMBERLAND 8–1B

OLLY FISHERMAN £55 334

AVEN HILL NE66 3TR 01665 576461

Great seafood platters" and "wonderful noked fish from the smokehouse next door" e the standout menu items at this "cosy place) metres from the sea" – a proper pub with good ales too", that has welcomed guests since arly Victorian times. The beer garden at the ont has views along the Northumberland ast that take in Dunstanburgh astle. / thejollyfishermancraster.co.uk; ejollyfisherman; Mon-Thu 8.30 pm, Fri & Sat pm, Sun 6 pm.

CRASWALL, HEREFORDSHIRE 2–1A

THE BULL'S HEAD £55 333

HR2 0PN 01981 510616

"What a pub dining experience should be like" – this "lovely old drovers' pub at the foot of Black Hill" may be remote (the Welsh border isn't far off) but "if you can find it, you will not be disappointed"; after long lying idle, it was reinvented by John Stead of Longtown's Wild By Nature group, and its ingredient-led gastropub menu is winning highly positive reports. Watch out for rooms coming soon. / wildbynaturellp.com; wildbynaturellp; Thu-Sat 11 pm, Sun 6 pm.

CRAWLEY, HAMPSHIRE 3–4B

THE FOX £69 333

PEACH HILL LANE
SO21 2PR 01962 461302

"Your standard pub this is definitely not" – in fact it's "quite likely one of the best places to eat in the Winchester area" – a "quintessential Victorian village pub" updated six years ago with a "large, modern dining area" offering a "monthly, small and very well considered menu" along with "excellent service". / the-fox.pub; the_fox_crawley; Wed-Sat 11 pm.

CREDITON, DEVON 1–3D

THE RING OF BELLS £50 343

THE HAYES, CHERITON FITAPAINE
EX17 4JG 01363 860111

"Such a good spot, always developing and always aware of customers' needs and likes", say fans of this thatched country pub, which landlady Binka Caven has restored in stages since bringing it back to life 10 years ago. The building was originally five Tudor-era cottages, knocked together into a pub during the 1800s. / theringofbells.com; the_ring_of_bells; Wed-Sat 9 pm, Sun 7 pm.

CRIEFF, PERTH AND KINROSS 9–3C

THE GLENTURRET LALIQUE RESTAURANT £235 444

THE GLENTURRET DISTILLERY, THE HOSH PH7 4HA 01764 656565

"An interesting venue in beautiful countryside" – this Lalique-branded two-year-old is sited within Scotland's oldest working distillery, and has quickly won recognition for its extremely ambitious tasting menu (at £195 per person). For those in striking distance of Crieff, it can be "a perfect and special place for a business lunch – there's good spacing between the tables; discreet but efficient service" plus of course "great whisky and wines" to complement the cuisine. / theglenturretrestaurant.com; TheGlenturretLalique; Wed-Sat 8 pm.

CROMER, NORFOLK 6–3C

NO. 1 £53 333

1 NEW ST NR27 9HP 01263 515983

This "excellent fish venue with locally sourced produce" is owned by Galton Blackiston, chef-patron of Norfolk's grand Morston Hall, and operates both as a seaside chippie for eat-in or takeaway and as a bookable restaurant upstairs, with views of the pier and fancier dishes such as king prawn Goan curry with roti and coconut rice. Sauces and ice creams are all produced in-house. / no1cromer.com; no1cromer; Mon-Sun 8.30 pm.

CROSTHWAITE, CUMBRIA 7–4D

THE PUNCH BOWL INN £67 333

LA8 8HR 01539 568237

This "consistently enjoyable" and much commented-on gastropub – originally a village blacksmiths from 1829 – wins plaudits for its "helpful and friendly staff" under owner Richard Rose, and for its signature "cheese soufflé that always hits the spot – which is why they keep it on the menu"; other dishes also go down well, not least a "raspberry soufflé to die for". / the-punchbowl.co.uk; punchbowlinncr; Mon-Sun 9 pm.

CROYDON, GREATER LONDON 3–3B

ELODIE, BIRCH SELSDON £76

126 ADDINGTON ROAD
CR2 8YA 020 3953 3000

A sibling to Birch in Cheshunt, set in a very large, 18th-century mansion in 200 acres which follows a similar formula combining hotel, club and co-working space. The top culinary attraction is this dining room in the heart of the old property offering foraged fine dining from ex-Typing Room chef, Lee Westcott. It opened in August 2023 (after our annual diners' poll had concluded) and offers a five-course tasting menu for £69 per person (with a wine pairing at £49 per person). There is also Vervain: an all-day brasserie (plus three bars, a spa, and Lido). / birchcommunity.com; birchcommunity; Wed-Sat 10 pm.

MCDERMOTTS FISH & CHIPS £38 442

5-7 THE FORESTDALE SHOPPING CENTRE FEATHERBED LN
CR0 9AS 020 8651 1440

Tony McDermott's "great fish 'n' chip shop" has earned an enviable reputation for its "fantastic fish and really good service" over almost 40 years – making a less-than-glamorous corner of Croydon "well worth a visit". / mcdermottsfishandchips.co.uk; Tue-Thu, Sat 8 pm, Fri 9 pm.

CRUDWELL, WILTSHIRE 2–2C

THE POTTING SHED £60 333

THE ST SN16 9EW 01666 577833

This cute whitewashed and beamed village pub "just outside Malmesbury" has its own two-acre organic kitchen garden and wins support for its "well prepared dishes from a nice menu" and "friendly staff". / thepottingshedpub.com; thepottingshedpub; Mon-Sun 9 pm.

RECTORY £56 334

WILTSHIRE SN16 9EP 01666 577194

"Promise… creativity… I would gladly go back" – the worst review this year on this "comfy and welcoming" country house boutique hotel, whose culinary credentials were boosted by the recent arrival of Rob Weston, a veteran head chef in top London kitchens including Le Gavroche, The Square, and most recently La Trompette. The hotel, an 18th-century former rectory built in Cotswold stone, has been transformed in recent years by Alex Payne, a locally born music industry executive in his first hospitality project. The pub opposite, the Potting Shed, is part of the package. / therectoryhotel.com; therectoryhotel.

CUCKFIELD, WEST SUSSEX 3–4B

OCKENDEN MANOR £103 332

OCKENDEN LN RH17 5LD 01444 416111

Chef Steve Crane's "excellent food" has been a feature of this "delightful" Elizabethan country-house spa-hotel for 23 years. Some reporters see it as very much an "old school, ladies who lunch, white tablecloths" venue – "no fireworks, just a decent meal in a quiet, refined setting". / hshotels.co.uk; hshotels; Mon-Sun 8.30 pm.

CUPAR, FIFE 9–3D

THE PEAT INN £114 543

KY15 5LH 01334 840206

In prime golfing territory a short drive from St Andrews, Geoffrey and Katherine Smeddle's well-known and highly acclaimed restaurant-with-rooms "never disappoints". It again won praise this year for its "quiet excellence" – both its service and its modern Scottish cooking which can be accompanied by a vintage from their very extensive (and in places expensive!) cellar. "Good news, lunch is back on Fridays and Saturdays". / thepeatinn.co.uk; thepeatinn; Tue-Sat 7 pm.

DARLINGTON, COUNTY DURHAM 8–3B

CAFE SPICE £28 433

19 CLARKS YARD DL3 7QH 01325 468783

"An institution" in Darlington after 15 years, Brian Miah's Bengali venue is a "consistently wonderful place to eat curry" – "the yummy food and high-quality service are never less than perfection", so you "won't be disappointed". / cafespicedarlington.co.uk; cafespicerestaurant; Mon-Thu 10 pm, Fri-Sun 11 pm.

THE ORANGERY, ROCKLIFFE HALL £106 333

DL2 2DU 01325 729999

"A lovely location for a special event" – this five-star property sits in over 365 acres on the North Yorks border, and its more formal dining option (you can also eat in the clubhouse overlooking the golf course) lives up to its name – a tall, striking pillared space with glass roof. Chef Paul Nicholson offers a four-course à la carte menu for £70 per person, or there's a six-course tasting option for £95 per person, backed up by an impressive 400-bin wine list. / rockliffehall.com; rockliffe_hall; Tue-Sun 9 pm.

DARSHAM, SUFFOLK 3–1D

TWO MAGPIES £24 343

LONDON ROAD IP17 3QR 01986 784370

This "must be the ultimate transport caff for foodies", say fans of this artisan bakery on the A12 – part of founder Rebecca Bishop's nine-strong East Anglian group – which draws more than just passing trade with its "lovely bread and lovely baked stuff". / twomagpiesbakery.co.uk; 2magpiesbakery; Sun-Fri 5 pm, Sat 8 pm.

DARTMOUTH, DEVON 1–4D

ROCKFISH £56 332

8 SOUTH EMBANKMENT TQ6 9BH 01803 832800

The original and "still the best of the Rockfish chain", founded by Mitch Tonks in 2010 and now with 10 satellite venues around the southwest coast, as well as its own boat and supply chain in Brixham. It's an "upmarket fish 'n' chip restaurant" with prices to match – and the "daily choice is always worth having". / therockfish.co.uk; therockfishuk; Tue-Thu 8.45 pm, Fri & Sat 9 pm, Sun 4 pm.

THE SEAHORSE £83 443

5 SOUTH EMBANKMENT TQ6 9BH 01803 835147

The harbourside flagship of Mitch Tonks's West Country group is a "great all-rounder", majoring in "superb fish and seafood". The Italian-influenced cooking is "delicious and unfussy", the wine list "interesting at all price points" – "and to cap it all, diners are made to feel really welcome. It's hard to find this level of hospitality nowadays". Top Menu Tip – "the focaccia and anchoiade is legendary". / seahorserestaurant.co.uk; seahorse.restaurant; Tue-Thu 4 pm, Fri & Sat 8 pm.

DAYLESFORD, GLOUCESTERSHIRE 2–1

DAYLESFORD ORGANIC FARM, TROUGH CAFÉ £61 23

DAYLESFORD NEAR KINGHAM GL56 0YG 01608 731700

Lady Bamford's two-decade-old farm shop an café may be "home to the Chipping Norton set" but it's "delightful" nonetheless, especially "when the weather is pleasant enough to sit ou under the brollies in the courtyard and people watch while having something tasty for lunch". Popularity doesn't come cheap, but one report found it "very reasonably priced" this year, bucking the usual critiques. / daylesford.com; Mon-Sat 10 pm, Sun 16.30 pm.

DEAL, KENT 3–3

DEAL PIER KITCHEN £75 33

DEAL PIER, BEACH STREET CT14 6HY 01304 368228

"You deserve a break after the pier walk" to reach this four-year-old establishment which, though technically not afloat, "makes you feel like you're on a boat"; watch out for their "surf 'n' turf weekend evenings", and "healthy" bottomless brunch (if your idea of healthy is unlimited prosecco, Bellinis and Bloody Marys!). / dealpierkitchen.com; www.facebook.com; Sun-Thu 4 pm, Fri & Sat 5 pı

THE ROSE £73 33

91 HIGH STREET CT14 6ED 01304 389127

This "lovely little pub" on the high street has had quite the history: it was long under John Matthews, owner of Thompson & Son brewery; in 2016, his great-grandson Christopher Hicks took over, and has transformed it into a very stylish hotel replete with Emin artworks and a tandem bicycle for guests. The "really good, mostly local produce is "beautifully done" and features an "excellen value lunch" as well as popular Scandi-style breakfasts. / therosedeal.com; therosedeal; Wed-Sat 10.30 pm, Sun 4 pm.

UPDOWN £75 33

UPDOWN ROAD CT14 0EF 07842 244192

Oli Brown (ex-of Rowley Leigh's Le Café Anglais) and FOH Ruth (Leigh's daughter) are behind this "brilliant place, both food and hotel", set in a "gorgeous location": a seventeenth-century farmhouse on seven acres, where guests eat in an open conservatory. The "truly delightful menu" is short and hyper-seasonal, with everything cooked over wood in the open kitchen and, while service can be "a bit on the slow side", the "ambience means that it goes relatively unnoticed". In 2022, Grace Dent called it "one of those places that shows how life could be" – high praise indeed! NB – open Thu-Sat dinner and Fri-Sat lunch, with a bargain £40 per person summer set

Pine, East Wallhouses

menu on Thu night. / updownfarmhouse.com; updownfarmhouse_; Wed-Sat 10 pm, Sun 4 pm.

DEDHAM, ESSEX 3–2C

MILSOMS £52 223

STRATFORD RD CO7 6HW 01206 322795

This attractive hotel in Constable Country is "a very pleasant place to eat", owing to its terraced gardens and "good basic bistro food" ("plus it's always open", which doesn't hurt). Service is not always a highpoint though, and can be "slow". / milsomhotels.com; milsomsdedham; Mon-Sun 11 pm.

THE SUN INN £58 433

HIGH ST CO7 6DF 01206 564325

"An excellent" stopping-off point in the heart of Constable Country, this centuries-old coaching inn has all the beams and wood panelling you'd hope for – as well as "very tasty meals with nice accompaniments". There are "lots of tourists", of course, but it's a "fun" and "reliable" operation under the same independent ownership for 21 years. / thesuninndedham.com; suninndedham; Mon-Sat 9.30 pm, Sun 4 pm.

LE TALBOOTH £98 235

GUN HILL CO7 6HP 01206 323150

"The delightful setting in Constable Country" makes this famous landmark – opened in 1925 – ideal for "special occasions and memorable meals", and the beamed interiors are almost a match for the dreamy Dedham Vale location. But the pricey food has too often been judged "average" over many years – critics feel it "doesn't live up to its reputation or ideal surroundings". / milsomhotels.com; milsomhotels; Mon-Sat 9 pm, Sun 4 pm.

DEGANWY, CONWY 4–1D

PAYSANNE £45 332

147 STATION ROAD
LL31 9EJ 01492 582079

"Probably unchanged in years, but a very good traditional French venue" – this "excellent, popular and consistent" bistro has been in operation since 1988, and is nowadays run by the son (Cai) of the original founders (Bob & Barbara Ross). Chef David Hughes produces pleasingly traditional Gallic fare, accompanied by wine sent home by the Ross's (who have now retired to the Languedoc). / paysannedeganwy.co.uk; paysannedeganwy; Wed-Sat 9 pm, Sun 2 pm.

DELL QUAY, WEST SUSSEX 3–4A

CROWN & ANCHOR £81 322

DELL QUAY RD PO20 7EE 01243 781712

For "enjoyable gastro-fare in a funky gastro-atmosphere", there's plenty to recommend this very attractive and popular pub, whose "interesting" menu focuses on fish and shellfish; the "lovely creek-side setting" is best enjoyed on the terrace, but you can also enjoy the views of Dell Quay Marina from inside. / crownandanchorchichester.com; crowndellquay; Mon-Sat 11 pm, Sun 10 pm.

DERBY, DERBYSHIRE 5–3C

ANOKI £44 333

OLD PICTURE HALL, 129 LONDON ROAD
DE1 2QN 01332 292 888

"Great food served by very helpful staff" has attracted a busy crowd for more than 20 years to Naveed Khaliq's flagship, a stylishly converted former picture palace with a gilded vaulted ceiling. A well-known name for good-quality Indian cuisine in the north Midlands, it now has offshoots in Nottingham and Burton. / anoki.co.uk; anokirestaurant; Mon-Sat 10.30 pm.

EBI SUSHI £49 542

59 ABBEY ST DE22 3SJ 01332 265656

"Continuing to provide high-quality Japanese food, if a bit limited in range, for very reasonable prices in something resembling a Tokyo cafe but in the middle of the north Midlands ... Why? It's just down the road from the Toyota factory!" / ebi_sushi_derby; Tue, Wed, Fri & Sat 10 pm.

DINTON, BUCKINGHAMSHIRE 2–3C

LA CHOUETTE £97 443

WESTLINGTON GRN
HP17 8UW 01296 747422

Frederic Desmette's cosy old sixteenth century cottage on the village green is a "real family-run restaurant" that's "not influenced by current fashion", but instead turns out a "fairly static" but "excellent quality" Belgian menu all "served up by Freddie with great aplomb!" / lachouette.co.uk; Wed-Sat 9 pm.

DOLLAR, CLACKMANNANSHIRE 9–4C

THE FORAGER £57

19-23 BRIDGE STREET
FK14 7DE 01259 742200

No reports as yet on this spring 2023 newcomer – the latest opening in the expanding empire of MasterChef: The Professionals 2018 finalist Dean Banks. But The Scotsman's Gaby Soutar is a fan – in her February 2023 review she noted that the "foraging theme only seems to extend as far as the branding" with a menu that only "features the prerequisite pub classics, like fish 'n' chips, Sunday roast, pies" along with some "fancier bits". But she concluded that "Scotland has another excellent country pub". / foragerpub.com; theforagerpub; Mon-Sat 9 pm, Sun 8 pm.

DORCHESTER, DORSET 2–4B

THE CLUB HOUSE £61 344

BEACH ROAD DT2 9DG 01308 898302

A "great location, with outside seating" overlooking Chesil Beach; an Art Deco atmosphere, thanks to its original 1930s styling, and a "tasty" seafood-based menu combine to good effect at this pleasing seaside venue. / theclubhousewestbexington.co.uk; theclubhouse2017; Wed & Thu 4 pm, Fri & Sat 10.30 pm, Sun 7 pm.

DORKING, SURREY 3–3A

SORREL £169 553

77 SOUTH STREET
RH4 2JU 01306 889 414

"Steve Drake is at the top of his game" and "continues to turn out beautifully prepared dishes, visit after visit" according to practically all reports on this much commented-on fixture: a "smart destination suited to a special occasion" in the centre of "lucky Dorking". There's "a very high level of professionalism in both kitchen and front-of-house" and the result is "a brilliantly devised, modulated and presented menu" full of "inventive and original flavours"; together with "an excellent choice of wines". One caveat, though – "check your bank balance before booking!" / sorrelrestaurant.co.uk; sorrel_restaurant_dorking; Wed-Sat 8.30 pm.

DOUGLAS, ISLE OF MAN 7–4B

ENZO'S £24 343

52 BUCKS ROAD IM1 3AD 01624 62265

This "small, intimate, nicely decorated" Italian is noted for its "superb, old-fashioned service" and "excellent food" – and hailed by admirers as one of the best serious restaurants on the Isle of Man. Founder Enzo Ciapelli has spent more than 40 years on the island, having moved from another – Sicily. / Mon-Sat 9.30 pm.

1 QUAY RESTAURANT £82 332

QUAY WEST BRIDGE ROAD
IM1 5AG 01624 617755

In the prestigious Quay West development in Douglas, this well-appointed Mediterranean restaurant is run by local restaurateur Mario Ciappelli, whose brother manages the city's Mailbox eatery. The cooking is "excellent", albeit not cheap, and there's "ample space for confidential conversation" whether you're there for business or romance. (It changed its name in mid-2023 from Portofino, but as near as we can tell from the website the team is unchanged hence we've maintained this listing). / 1quaywest.im; portofinoiom.

WINE DOWN £57 333

24 DUKE STREET IM1 2AY 01624 62477

In 2018, restaurant Macfarlane's morphed into this winning wine bar/shop near the promenade, where the "excellent selection of wines" (over 100) comes "at a fair mark-up" (with "only a limited corkage for choosing off the shelf"); the "much locally sourced" sharing plates hold their own, and while the "menu does not change often, there are great daily specials" to compensate. / winedown.im; winedowniom; Mon & Tue 8.30 pm, Wed & Thu 9 pm, Fri & Sat 9.30 pm.

DUNGENESS, KENT 3–4C

UNGENESS SNACK HACK £32 532

UNGENESS ROAD
N29 9NB 07549 377527

It's a shack on a working fisherman's beach ut the fresh fish and seafood is excellent" (be it obster and crab rolls, or smoked cod chowder) t this humble outfit, set next to their own shmonger. Want to impress clients? Between the food, the view and the mad giant train set ou travel on" (that'll be the Romney, Hythe nd Dymchurch Railway), you'll "clinch the nega deal for less than a tenner on food". Still eed convincing? "You have to go, basically… ut don't, please, because you doing so makes it nore likely they'll sell out before we get there". dungenesssnackshack.net; dungenessfishhut; Ion-Sun 3.30 pm.

DUNMOW, ESSEX 3–2C

IG & TRUFFLE £102 342

HE ST CM6 3HT 01371 821 660

Iaving changed its name from the Flitch of acon last year to signal the switch to a more ccessible à la carte approach, this smart enue remains "superior to anything else" in ne area – and to its most ardent fans "not ıst the best food in Essex but also the best-alue food". Under the same ownership as Cambridge heavyweight Midsummer House, s reputation rose under former chef Tim llen, whose successor Paul Croasdale is now naking his own name here on the basis of s "high quality". Top Tip – "the amazing alue lunch". / www.pigandtruffle.co.uk; igandtrufflelittledunmow; Wed-Sat 9.30 pm, Sun pm.

DUNVEGAN, HIGHLAND 9–2A

HE THREE CHIMNEYS £133 544

COLBOST IV55 8ZT 01470 511258

'Some of the freshest and best seafood in he UK" ("the double-dived local scallops vere divine; but everything was excellent!") s provided by chef Scott Davies at this elebrated former crofter's cottage, which vas established over 40 years ago by Shirley & Eddie Spear, then sold to the Wee Hotel Company run by Gordon Campbell Grey n 2019. As an overall experience it's 'simply spot on" – "a delightful table, with amazing views and passionate matching of astes and textures". / threechimneys.co.uk; hethreechimneysskye; Mon-Sun 9.30 pm.

DURHAM, COUNTY DURHAM 8–3B

COARSE £65 433

REFORM PLACE, NORTH ROAD
DH1 4RZ 0191 374 1123

Chef Ruari MacKay (former head chef of the city's now defunct Bistro 21) – with collaborators Gemma Robinson and Craig Lappin-Smith – raised £100,000 from crowd-funding to launch this simply decorated newcomer, which launched in late 2022, in a courtyard just over the river from the ancient city centre. The only option is a six-course tasting menu: feedback is still limited but says that "overall for the price it's excellent, and served by friendly staff". / coarse.restaurant; coarsedurham; Wed-Sat 11 pm.

FARU

26 SILVER STREET
DH1 3RD 0191 380 5451

Jake & Laura Siddle – long-term senior staff at Newcastle's House of Tides – quit their jobs to launch their own ambitious restaurant in the centre of Durham, with the blessing of their mentor, House of Tides founder Kenny Atkinson. Heaven knows, it's a town that could use a venue of some ambition. It opened in April 2023 (late in the day to inspire feedback in our annual diners' poll) and offers a 10-course menu for £98 (lunch is shorter and simpler for £60). Faru means journey in Old English. / faru.co.uk; restaurantfaru; Wed-Sat 8.30 pm.

DYFED, PEMBROKESHIRE 4–4B

THE FERNERY, GROVE OF NARBERTH £127 443

MOLLESTON SA67 8BX 01834 860915

"In a wonderful setting in Pembrokeshire", Neil & Zoe Kedward's modern luxury property (part of their Seren hotels collection) is a "lovely and quiet operation" decorated in a fresh, contemporary style. Chef Douglas Balish is in charge of its destination dining room (there's also the simpler, brasserie-style 'Artisan') which all reports acclaim as "a delight in every way" (if a rather "pricey" one). "Inventive cooking with locally sourced ingredients" is matched with a "very interesting wine list"; "the environment is warm and cosy" and "staff are obliging – nothing is too much trouble". / thegrove-narberth.co.uk; groveofnarberth; Wed-Sat 9 pm.

EAST CHISENBURY, WILTSHIRE 2–3C

RED LION FREEHOUSE £83 433

SN9 6AQ 01980 671124

North of Stonehenge, this thatched pub "continues its high standards" and is a "firm favourite" for a widespread fan club who travel to visit it. "It's a lovely team for whom the food is the star of the show": "we've never had a bad meal and just wish we lived nearer!". "It looks like a pub, but it's more like fine dining". / redlionfreehouse.com; redlionfreehouse; Thu, Wed 8.30 pm, Fri & Sat 9 pm.

EAST GRINSTEAD, WEST SUSSEX 3–4B

GRAVETYE MANOR £164 445

VOWELS LANE RH19 4LJ 01342 810567

"Truly beautiful and with superb food" – "the gracious room with stunning gardens beyond (including a unique walled kitchen garden) help make for a very special experience" at this "fabulous location" – an Elizabethan country house deep in the Sussex countryside (whose grounds were laid out in the 1880s by its then-owner, a famous landscape gardener). A hotel since 1958, it was relaunched in 2018 with a new "brilliantly architecturally conceived modern dining room" – a "light and airy space" whose "gorgeous views" mean "you actually feel it's part of the outside". And – having largely sunk from view in terms of gastronomy – nowadays its "quietly impressive" performance under chef George Blogg is establishing itself as one of the top 10 most commented-on destinations outside the capital in our annual diners' poll. He "has significantly upped the kitchen's game, with a three-course menu, perfectly prepared and exquisitely presented, incorporating wonderfully fresh herbs and vegetables" backed up by a heavyweight wine list. Top Tip – stay the night and "breakfast is every bit as good as dinner!" / gravetyemanor.co.uk; gravetyemanor; Mon-Sun 9.30 pm.

EAST LAVANT, WEST SUSSEX 3–4A

THE ROYAL OAK £66 333

POOK LN PO18 0AX 01243 527 434

This 200-year-old local pub at the foot of the South Downs is "well run and popular", with a "well-executed and great-value menu" of superior gastropub fare. / royaloakeastlavant.co.uk; Royaloaklavant; Mon-Sat 11 pm, Sun 9 pm.

EAST MOLESEY, SURREY 3–3A

MEZZET £52 332

43 BRIDGE RD KT8 9ER 020 89794088

"The best Middle Eastern for miles" – a smart operation, handy for Hampton Court Palace, that offers "bold flavours a world away from many Lebanese places"; there is "lots on offer to explore – if anything perhaps too much", and also a newer offshoot, Mezzet Dar, a couple of doors down, that turns out Spanish and Lebanese-inspired tapas. / mezzet.co.uk; Mon-Sun 9.45 pm.

LE PETIT NANTAIS 443

41 BRIDGE ROAD
KT8 9JE 020 8979 2309

Still on top form after 27 years, scrum-half-turned-chef JP (Jean-Philippe) Gravier and his FOH English wife Kim won particularly strong feedback this year for the "fresh and creative dishes in a charming environment" at their classic Gallic bistro across the river from Hampton Court Palace. It's "family-run from top to bottom", with daughter Victoria working in the kitchen these days – so "what's not to love"? / lepetitnantais.co.uk; lepetitnantais; Wed-Sat 9 pm, Sun 3 pm.

Restaurant Martin Wishart, Edinburgh

EAST WALLHOUSES, NORTHUMBERLAND 8–2B

PINE £173 544

VALLUM FARM, MILITARY ROAD
NE18 0LL 01434 671202

In the multi-tasking (shop, eat, stay) Vallum Farm complex near Hadrian's Wall, and occupying an old cow barn, there's "lots to love" about this "absolutely amazing" venture, which was set up by Cal Byerley and partner Siân Buchan several years back. Together the duo delivers a "fantastic experience", from Cal's "ever-developing and sophisticated", Nordic-inspired tasting menus, fuelled by produce from the kitchen garden and Northumberland countryside, to Vanessa's "incredible" matching wines. / restaurantpine.co.uk; restaurantpine; Wed-Sat midnight.

EAST WITTON, NORTH YORKSHIRE 8–4B

THE BLUE LION £79 333

DL8 4SN 01969 624273

Part of the Marquess of Downshire's Clifton Castle and Jervaulx estates, this well-known eighteenth-century Wensleydale inn is, apparently, a favourite watering hole of King Charles III. "Well worth a drive" for its high-quality cooking – the kitchen team come into their own during the game season when "they demonstrate their mastery of cooking grouse, in the traditional and best way" – and it's "dog friendly too". / thebluelion.co.uk; bluelioneastwitton; Mon-Sun 9 pm.

EASTBOURNE, EAST SUSSEX 3–4B

THE MIRABELLE, THE GRAND HOTEL £85 344

KING EDWARDS PARADE
BN21 4EQ 01323 412345

"The only true fine dining restaurant in Eastbourne" – Hrvoje Loncarevic "continues to gradually restore the reputation of the fine dining room of the elegant Grand Hotel": a large, 150-bedroom grande dame of a property on the seafront and "an excellent venue for business or celebrations". "Beautifully laid out courses" are provided by "service of the high level you'd expect from a five-star hotel, and the wine list has a very broad range of fine vintages". "We had a table in the window overlooking the garden on a lovely summer's evening, all the while being accompanied by an excellent pianist playing a mixture of standards and modern jazz". / grandeastbourne.com; grandhoteleastbourne; Tue-Sat 9 pm.

EASTON GREY, WILTSHIRE 2–2C

THE DINING ROOM, WHATLEY MANOR £218 324

SN16 0RB 01666 822888

Chef "Ricki (Weston) and the team do amazing work" at this Cotswolds country house hotel – "a lovely place to unwind", which has been a gastronomic highlight of the area for two decades now. Those who visited during the previous tenure of chef Niall Keating report that the "food was amazing then, but Ricki has taken it further", his "truly exceptional" tasting menu featuring some nicely performative touches too ("the whole experience of eating the first bites in the kitchen before being led into the Dining Room means the link between the chefs and the diners is well integrated"). / whatleymanor.com; Thu-Sun 9.15 pm.

EDGBASTON, WEST MIDLANDS 5–4C

SIMPSONS £116 444

20 HIGHFIELD ROAD
B15 3DU 0121 454 3434

Some would say "the doyen of Birmingham fine-dining restaurants" – fans feel that "owner Andreas Antona and chef Luke Tipping still deliver the best fine-dining experience in Birmingham, even after so many years" at this gracious-looking Edwardian villa "in leafy Edgbaston". And even those who feel it's "not the market leader it once was" say it's "very good all-round": "service is very good and delivers the high-quality dishes the Birmingham diner expects in a setting that's excellent and very relaxing". / simpsonsrestaurant.co.uk; simpsons_restaurant; Wed & Thu 9 pm, Fri & Sat 9.30 pm, Sun 2 pm.

EDINBANE, HIGHLAND 9–2A

EDINBANE LODGE £66 544

OLD DUNVEGAN ROAD
IV51 9PW 01470 582217

"The tasting menu is a real journey around Skye, sampling the best of local produce" at Calum Montgomery's converted hunting lodge (built in 1543, revamped in 2018) – the ten-course meal is £125 per person. The result is "some of the most exciting cooking you will find, with THE freshest and most local Scottish produce". But while all reports here say results are "unbeatable", they still haven't been blessed with a star by the tyre manufacturers based in Clermont-Ferrand… just a matter of time surely? / edinbanelodge.com; edinbanelodge; Wed-Sun 9 pm.

EDINBURGH, CITY OF EDINBURGH 9–4C

AIZLE £139 443

THE GARDEN ROOM IN THE KIMPTON HOTEL, 38 CHARLOTTE SQUARE
EH2 4HQ 0131 662 9349

Stuart Ralston relocated this ambitious venue from a previous location in 2020, and it continues to go from strength to strength in this modern, glass-roofed 'Garden Room' of a hotel. The "excellent tasting menu is very creative and not too expensive by the yardstick of comparable ventures", with "skillful" preparation of an "impressively eclectic array of ingredients". / aizle.co.uk; aizle_edinburgh; Wed-Sun 8.30 pm.

CAFÉ MARLAYNE £45 443

1 THISTLE STREET
EH2 1EN 0131 226 2230

Run by Marcelline Levicky, this lovely "small bistro" in the New Town is a real longtime favourite owing to its "well-presented" Gallic dishes that don't make too much of a dent in the wallet (its two-course lunches and dinners ringing in at £17/£27 per person respectively). / cafemarlayne.com; cafemarlayne; Tue-Sat 10 pm.

THE CAFÉ ROYAL BAR £76 334

19 WEST REGISTER STREET
EH2 2AA 0131 556 1884

With its imposing facade, stained glass, corniced ceilings, polished wood and brass, we maintain a listing for this busy Victorian institution (est. 1863 and nowadays run by the Metropolitan Pub Company) as much as a cultural experience as it is a culinary one. Seafood dishes and platters are the best choices here. / caferoyaledinburgh.com; caferoyaledn; Sun-Wed 11 pm, Fri & Sat 1 am, Thu midnight.

CAFÉ ST-HONORÉ £67 344

34 NW THISTLE STREET LN
EH2 1EA 0131 226 2211

"Step back in time to an old-school Parisian bistro in the heart of Edinburgh New Town" at this "cosy and unpretentious establishment down a side street off Princes Street" that "serves food as Elizabeth David might have ordered and admired" – "long may it continue". / cafesthonore.com; cafesthonore; Mon-Thu 9.30 pm.

:ONDITA £180 543

5 SALISBURY PLACE
H9 1SL 0131 667 5777

:onor Toomey's "outstanding food continues › surprise and delight" all who experience his :xcellent" three-hour no-choice tasting menus t £150 per person), while there is "good ıteractive service" and the "wine pairings are ıe best ever". The only criticism is directed at ıe dining room, which is "a little sparse" – with iners saying that cuisine of this monumental ıality "deserves a better setting than a glorified ıop". / condita.co.uk; condita_restaurant; Tue-at 10.30 pm.

›AVID BANN £46 443

6-58 ST MARYS ST
H1 1SX 0131 556 5888

ıst off the Royal Mile, this aubergine-hued alwart café (est. 2002) is one of Scotland's est known veggie/vegan haunts, owing to its imaginative dishes" that deftly incorporate ıfluences from the Mediterranean to ıe Pacific and subcontinent; "pleasant :rvice" adds to its appeal. / davidbann.com; avidbannrestaurant; Mon-Sun 10 pm.

)EAN BANKS AT THE ›OMPADOUR, THE :ALEDONIAN £109 234

/ALDORF ASTORIA EDINBURGH - HE CALEDONIAN, PRINCES STREET
H1 2AB 07770 451668

Vere our reporters just unlucky this year at ıis famous dining room in one of the city's ıost imposing hotels? Named for King ,ouis XV of France's favourite mistress, its ıuralled ceiling and opulent decor are in ontrast to the cutting-edge style of star chef)ean Banks's eight-course tasting menu for ;105 per person. But whereas there's a host f enthusiastic reviews of the experience to e found online, our feedback this year was mited and downbeat: "was expecting great ıings from DB at the Pompadour but ended ıp really disappointed". / deanbanks.co.uk; eanbankspompadour; Wed-Sun midnight.

)ISHOOM :DINBURGH £38 443

A ST ANDREW SQUARE
:H2 2BD 01312 026 406

The fun and lively Indian street food is lways reliable" according to all reports on this orthern outpost of the phenomenal chain – ıspired by the Parsi cafés of Mumbai – which ccupies a large three-floor site dating from the 920s. But while popular, it hasn't perhaps been he sell-out sensation it's proved in London, lthough there is one constant… "that bacon ıaan, with unlimited chai latte = breakfast ıeaven!" / dishoom.com; dishoom; Sun-Wed 1 pm, Thu-Sat midnight.

DULSE £82 333

17 QUEENSFERRY STREET
EH2 4QW 0131 573 7575

This "bustling and lively upstairs venue" in the New Town is the latest from chef Dean Banks (also of the nearby Pompadour and Haar in St Andrews), who "certainly knows how to cook fish – the octopus in the starter was tender and tasty, and the sole main course was well cooked". The Scotsman's Gaby Soutar was also impressed, in particular by the "sybaritic and rich" lobster crumpet. / dulse.co.uk; dulseseafood; Sun & Mon 11 pm, Tue-Sat 2 am.

DUSIT £54 333

49A THISTLE ST
EH2 1DY 0131 220 6846

"This very stylish and well-run restaurant" in the New Town serves "excellent appetising food" that is "not your standard Thai" – and all the better for it. In operation for 22 years, it has built a considerable following – which means it "can be noisy at times". / dusit.co.uk; Mon-Sun 10 pm.

ELEANORE £33 443

30-31 ALBERT PLACE
EH7 5HN 0131 600 0990

The younger sibling of the Little Chartroom (and occupying its old premises) certainly holds its own against its forebear; the cosy wine bar and restaurant with high stools and wooden tables turns out "lovely inventive cooking" (often fish-centric) "with exemplary service" to boot; bonus points for the "great music!". / eleanore.uk; eleanore_leithwalk; Fri & Sat-Mon 11 pm.

FHIOR £111 543

36 BROUGHTON STREET
EH1 3SB 0131 477 5000

Scott Smith's "intricate and exquisite cooking" and "amazing use of ingredients" produces "some pitch-perfect seafood, fish and vegetarian courses" from, in the evening, a seven-course menu for £85 per person (or a nine-course option for £105 per person) – delivered via his wife Laura's "absolutely brilliant, knowledgeable, professional, relaxed and fun service" at their ultra-seasonal venue: a follow-up to their equally vaunted Norn in Leith. Scott grew up in rural Aberdeenshire, and grows much of the produce in his own kitchen garden. / fhior.com; fhiorrestaurant; Thu-Sun midnight.

FISHERS IN THE CITY £69 343

58 THISTLE ST EH2 1EN 0131 225 5109

In a converted city-centre warehouse, this "popular and well-run fish venue" is a "dependable" and "excellent value" spot that has been going strong for a decade (and earned a special shout-out this year for its "delicious lobster"). You'll find the original Fishers near the Leith shore, right by their Shore Bar and Restaurant, offering classic British food with a Euro spin. / fishersrestaurants.co.uk; fishersinthecity; Mon-Sun midnight.

FISHERS LEITH £63 333

1 THE SHORE EH6 6QW 0131 554 5666

This "lovely restaurant by the Water of Leith" is "just the perfect place for a business lunch", with "lovely staff, simple fish dishes and rock-solid wines". Set in a seventeenth-century watchtower, it has been running for more than 20 years and is the flagship of a small group with a branch in the city as well as The Shore next door. / fishersrestaurants.co.uk; fishersleith; Mon-Sun midnight.

FISHMARKET £64 432

23A PIER PLACE
EH6 4LP 0131 552 8262

"Great fish 'n' chips" are one of the joys of this Victorian-style harbourside venture, a classy collab between Welch Fishmongers and top seafood restaurant Ondine, that also offers fancier and always "fresh" catch (oysters, grilled langoustines, smoked salmon). Just a "shame it's not bigger – wish they'd move into one of the vacant units around and expand!" / thefishmarketnewhaven.co.uk; thefishmarketnewhaven; Mon-Sun 10 pm.

LA GARRIGUE £72 333

31 JEFFREY ST EH1 1DH 0131 557 3032

Jean-Michel Gauffre is the mastermind behind this "pleasing, modest French establishment", in the Old Town; a firm fixture since its launch in 2001, it turns out hearty Gallic cooking with a particular focus on the Languedoc, alongside an excellent value lunchtime 'Menu du Jour'. / lagarrigue.co.uk; la_garrigue; Mon-Sat 9 pm.

HAWKSMOOR £95

23 WEST REGISTER STREET
EH2 2AA 0131 526 4790

The grand hall of the former Bank of Scotland HQ provides a dramatic setting for this northern outpost of the famous London-based steakhouse chain. As with last year, feedback on its menu of native-bred beef and Scottish seafood remains surprisingly limited, hence we've removed a rating for the time being. / thehawksmoor.com; hawksmoorrestaurants; Mon-Sat 10 pm, Sun 9 pm.

HENDERSONS £48 323

7-13 BARCLAY PLACE
EH10 4HW 0131 202 1635

Barrie Henderson's Bruntsfield two-year-old has revived a near-sexagenarian institution: Britain's oldest veggie, which was run by his grandmother Jan on Hanover Street before being scuppered by the pesky pandemic. The gorgeous-looking spot, with woven pendant lights and a grass installation on the ceiling, turns out impressive salads, pastas and tagines – which, despite receiving very solid marks, elicited little in the way of feedback. / hendersonsrestaurant.com; hendersonseatbetter; Mon-Sun 10 pm.

HERON £115 444

87-91 HENDERSON STREET EH6 6ED 0131 554 1242

Born during lockdown, and helmed by twenty-something chef-owners Tomas Gormley and Sam Yorke, this "lovely neighbourhood restaurant" with views of Leith Waters is – according to its biggest supporters – "so new and yet so 5/5". Expect "brilliant" modern Scottish dining (tasting menu or à la carte) paired with "amazing local cocktails". "More!" / heron.scot; heron.scot; Mon, Wed-Sun 9 pm.

THE IVY ON THE SQUARE £74 123

6 ST ANDREW SQUARE EH2 2BD 0131 526 4777

As per its siblings, this offshoot of Richard Caring's brasserie format woos diners with its "lovely surroundings" and location in a "handy spot" overlooking St Andrew's Square; also as per its siblings, there are critics of the "disappointing food, service and ambience", for whom this endlessly expanding empire is "a chain taken too far". / theivyedinburgh.com; the_ivy_collection; Sun-Thu 10 pm, Fri & Sat 10.30 pm.

JUNK £41 433

58 S CLERK ST EH8 9PS 0131 563 9085

This "new, super-fun" spot on Edinburgh's Southside offers small plates of 'a sophisticated take on junk food' from Cam & Jude Laidlaw, whose lockdown recipe blog led to a food vendor stall which won a triple crown of Scottish, British & European street food championships in 2022. The bricks-and-mortar site opened last year, and their "Asian fusion" dishes (for example, hand-dived Orkney scallop with confit oxtail) converts guests into "big fans". / wearejunk.co.uk; we.are.junk; Mon-Sun 2.30 pm.

KA PAO £38 332

UNIT 420, ST JAMES QUARTER EH1 3AE 0131 385 1040

"Once you get over the shopping mall outside" – namely the upmarket new St James Quarter development – this is "a great place": the sibling (est. 2022) to an Glasgow-based South-East Asian restaurant, and offering "fun fusion cooking" ("try the corn dogs and red curry"); "watch out" though – "it's rammed each evening". / ka-pao.com; kapaofeeds; Mon-Sun midnight.

THE KITCHIN £158 534

78 COMMERCIAL STREET EH6 6LX 0131 555 1755

"One of the stalwarts of the Edinburgh scene" – Tom & Michaela's flagship venue opened in this converted warehouse in Leith in 2006 and was yet again the city's most commented-on destination in our annual diners' poll. "A real treat", it's "simply superb at every level" with "wonderful" cooking that "changes with the seasons", "a beautiful setting" and "professional service". "Even though it's a 250-mile trip for us with a stop over it's well worth it: our favourite eating experience in the UK by far!" / thekitchin.com; Tue-Sat 10 pm.

KORA 344

14-17 BRUNTSFIELD PLACE EH10 4HN 0131 342 3333

Tom Kitchin's "fantastic" follow-up to his short-lived bistro Southside Scran, which shut in 2020 post-flood and pandemic; this "informal" yearling turns out relaxed Scottish dining, combining "great food and great service from a well-managed team". Kitchin's empire currently includes The Bonnie Badger in Gullane, East Lothian; Stockbridge pub The Scran & Scallie; and his acclaimed Edinburgh flagship, The Kitchin. / korabytk.com; korabytk; Sun-Thu 8.45 pm, Fri & Sat 9 pm.

LEFTFIELD £57 334

12 BARCLAY TERRACE EH10 4HP 0131 229 1394

This "marvellous" seafood bistro beside Edinburgh's Meadows from chef Phil White and FoH Rachel Chisholm pleases guests with "carefully prepared food" – "and if you get a seat at the window you see a mile of green space with a volcano in the distance (inert), in the middle of a capital city". Top Menu Tips – "lovely hake, and the octopus was cooked to perfection". / leftfieldedinburgh.co.uk; leftfieldedinburgh; Tue-Sun 9 pm.

THE LITTLE CHARTROOM £84 444

14 BONNINGTON ROAD EH6 5JD 0131 556 6600

"The food is good… really good" at Roberta Hall-McCarron's popular operation, where "the queue to get in has dropped from a five-month wait to a couple of weeks" following a move to larger premises a couple of years back (the original is now open as Eleanore, see also). It offers "very friendly service and a great location" – and "happily it's a place you can go for a three-course meal, not a ten-course tasting menu" (although there is also a five-course option available). / thelittlechartroom.com; thelittlechartroom; Wed-Sun 8.15 pm.

THE LOOKOUT BY GARDENER'S COTTAGE £134 335

CALTON HILL EH7 5AA 0131 322 1246

"Really enjoyable experience (apart from the walk in the dark on icy paths to reach the place from the Royal Terrace!") – few restaurants can match the location of this dramatically cantilevered structure, whose floor-to-ceiling windows ensure superb views over the city from Calton Hill. On limited feedback this year, some "outstanding" results were reported from a no-choice, four-course menu for £85 (shorter and cheaper at lunch). On the downside, in March 2023, Chitra Ramaswamy in The Times had an up-and-down trip: it "ha[d] everything going for it: fabulous taste, music, service and ingredients in a world-class setting" but was "simply too expensive for what you get". / thelookoutedinburgh.co; thelookoutbygc; Thu-Sat 11 pm, Wed 4 pm.

LUCKY YU £32 43[illegible]

53-55 BROUGHTON STREET EH1 3RJ 0131 259 7719

Handmade speciality dumplings, bao buns, small plates and chicken wings comprise the menu at this pan-Asian small plates restaurant (with cocktails), which relocated in 2023 from Leven Street in Bruntsfield. On limited feedback in our annual diners' poll, our early reporters are enthusiastic all-round as was The Scotsman's Gaby Soutar in her May 2023 review, who applauded "big fun flavours, lovely staff and the sort of space you want to linger in" – plus tatties "I haven't enjoyed this much in ages". / luckyyu.co.uk; luckyyuedinburgh; Thu-Sun 11 pm.

MOTHER INDIA'S CAFE £42 43[illegible]

3-5 INFIRMARY ST EH1 1LT 0131 524 9801

This spin-off from the famous Glasgow original "never fails to hit the spot" with its "terrific" Indian cooking, served in tapas-sized portions to taste and share. It's "great for lunch after a visit to the Dovecot Studios", a contemporary tapestry gallery next door in Edinburgh's Old Town. / motherindia.co.uk; officialmotherindia; Sun-Thu 9.30 pm, Fri & Sat 10 pm.

NEW CHAPTER £71 33[illegible]

18 EYRE PL. EH3 5EP 0131 556 0006

"The food is of the highest standard" at chef Maciej Szymik's modern European spot, tucked away in the New Town – "we were lucky to stumble on it". There's "only a handful of tables in each room, which gives the feel of quasi-private dining". "My only real criticism is the portion sizes are too large – it just wasn't possible to leave room for dessert". / newchapterrestaurant.co.uk; newchapterrestaurant; Wed-Sat 8.30 pm, Sun 4 pm

NOK'S KITCHEN £40 44[illegible]

8 GLOUCESTER STREET EH3 6EG 0131 225 4804

"If you've ever been in Thailand, you'll know how authentic the food is" at this "very popular Stockbridge restaurant" (which also has an offshoot near the castle). It's "small, intimate and always busy, but the efficient staff try their best to provide you with a good dining experience". Top Tip – "the chili crab signature dish". / nokskitchen.co.uk; nokskitchenuk; Mon-Sun 11 pm.

OTO £63 443

'A THISTLE STREET
H2 1DY 0131 241 8518

uart Ralston's New Town follow-up to izle combines a "cool, NY-style vibe with sian-inspired plates" (and is named after a rmer NY roomate of his); by all accounts s a "fun place to be" (if "a little dark as a ace"), particularly for those who "love small ates" that are "absolutely delicious" too you could feel the care and passion from the :chen"). / notoedinburgh.co.uk; notoedinburgh; .on-Sun 9 pm.

UMBER ONE, BALMORAL OTEL £170 444

PRINCES STREET
H2 2EQ 0131 557 6727

\ must visit when in town" – chef Matthew herry delivers a "high-class tasting menu ith ingredients to match" (seven courses for '115 per person) at this famous dining room a "beautiful" and "club-like" space in the asement of one of Scotland's most famous otels. It's an all-round experience too that's very comfortable" (and business-friendly) with professional and friendly service". "The wine st is not cheap but some good bins are to be ound". / roccofortehotels.com; numberoneedin; Ion, Thu-Sun 9.30 pm.

NDINE £69 444

GEORGE IV BRIDGE EH1 1AD
131 2261888

he "superb choice and quality" of the fish nd seafood at chef Roy Brett's "lovely" 5-year-old venue in the Old Town make it an Edinburgh favourite". "The food (which iese days includes some meat dishes) is always ooked to perfection". / ondinerestaurant.co.uk; ndine_edinburgh; Tue-Sat 10 pm.

X £33 333

9-51 LONDON STREET
H3 6LX 0131 556 9808

n "understandably very popular" Bonnington astroboozer set at the foot of foodie-riendly Broughton Street; its name reflects ie no-nonsense ethos, resulting in a "great ienu" of satisfying pub grub. The highlight the "terrific Sunday lunch" – amongst the JK's finest, according to a 2022 Guardian eature – featuring "giant Yorkshire puddings, oast beef and plentiful horseradish… erfect to take student offspring out for a ieal". / theoxedinburgh.com; the_ox_edinburgh; un-Thu 9 pm, Fri & Sat 9.30 pm.

A P'TITE FOLIE 333

1 FREDERICK ST
H2 1LH 0131 225 7983

\ "quirky French restaurant with great food nd service", set in a Tudor house in the West End, that has been wooing diners since 2003 and also has an adjoining wine bar, 'Le Di-Vin'). / laptitefolie.co.uk; Tue-Sat 10 pm.

THE PALMERSTON £55 434

1 PALMERSTON PLACE
EH12 5AL 0131 220 1794

This "absolutely flawless" two-year-old has been a "wonderful surprise in Edinburgh", both for Aussie chef Lloyd Morse's "brilliant" food and ex-Harwood Arms GM James Snowdon's "warmth and hospitality". Alex Sage (formerly of East London bakery Jolene) contributes "heavenly bread baked on site", while the "good-value prix-fixe lunch", made with offcuts from whole animals butchered on site, is highly recommended. / thepalmerstonedinburgh.co.uk; the_palmerston; Tue-Sat 9.30 pm, Sun 3.30 pm.

PURSLANE £83 443

33A ST STEPHEN STREET
EH3 5AH 01312 263500

Paul Gunning's casual Stockbridge fine-diner, set in a "small" but classy basement, combines "friendly staff" and "wonderful food": either a five- or seven-course tasting menu by night, or the "excellent value" two- or three-course set lunch. (We've continued its ratings this year, albeit on relatively limited feedback). / purslanerestaurant.co.uk; purslane1; Wed-Sat 7.30 pm, Sun 1.30 pm.

RESTAURANT MARTIN WISHART £152 553

54 THE SHORE EH6 6RA 0131 553 3557

"In the historic port of Leith, overlooking the Water of Leith from its converted warehouse setting" Martin Wishart's well established HQ has proved one of our annual diners' poll's most consistent over-achievers for the last two decades. It's not a place for ego and gimmicks: just "exceptional food" ("the unusual combinations of flavours, especially of the amuse-bouches, are a delight") that's "well deserving of its accolades". Service is notably "charming" too ("although we don't visit frequently, as we live in London, we are always recognised and warmly welcomed"). / restaurantmartinwishart.co.uk; Wed-Fri 9 pm, Sat 9.30 pm.

RHUBARB, PRESTONFIELD HOTEL £82 334

PRIESTFIELD RD
EH16 5UT 0131 225 1333

Set in 20 acres near Arthur's Seat, this opulent boutique hotel is part of James Thomson's portfolio (he also owns the Witchery) and "continues to deliver excellent ambience". The food is dependable too – it's not especially foodie, but did in September 2023, for example, win Boutique Hotelier's Restaurant of the Year awards. The venue also wins nominations for a fine afternoon tea. / prestonfield.com; prestonfieldhouseedinburg; Mon-Sun 10 pm.

SCRAN & SCALLIE £78 433

1 COMELY BANK RD
EH4 1DT 0131 332 6281

Now in its 11th year, Tom & Michaela Kitchin's "friendly" and "sometimes hectic" Scottish gastropub wins consistently high ratings for its "clever (if rich)" and "yummy" food. "Of course we had the famous steak pie, but the rest was pretty good as well". / scranandscallie.com; scranandscallie; Mon-Sun 9 pm.

THE SPENCE AT GLENEAGLES TOWNHOUSE 345

39 ST ANDREW SQUARE
EH2 1AF 0800 917 4655

"A stunning setting in a former banking hall" – the former HQ of the Bank of Scotland, complete with eye-catching cupola – provides a hard-to-beat setting for this year-old spin-off from the world-famous sporting estate: the first-ever extension of the brand (a property with 33 bedrooms). The focus of the (less reviewed) à la carte is on posh brasserie fare – the dedicated brunch menu is the most commented-on feature here ("amazing crab omelette"). Prices could be much worse given the level of grandeur. It's also tipped for a "good business venue". / gleneagles.com; gleneaglestownhouse; Mon-Sun 10 pm.

SUSHISAMBA

W HOTEL EDINBURGH, ST JAMES'S QUARTER EH1 3JD AWAITING TEL

Promising 'dynamic interiors' plus an 'outdoor terrace with sweeping views of Edinburgh's skyline' from the 10th floor of W Edinburgh in the St James Quarter – this heavily trailed third branch of the super-glossy US chain at long last is set to open in November 2023. The London Sushisambas blazed a trail on opening, and the heady blend of Japanese, Brazilian and Peruvian cuisine has the potential to be a major addition to the Scottish capital (if, likely, not an especially affordable one). / sushisamba.com; sushisamba; Mon-Sun 1 am.

TIMBERYARD £124 434

10 LADY LAWSON ST
EH3 9DS 01312 211222

Credited with introducing the principles of 'new Nordic' cuisine to Scottish ingredients, the Radford family's converted Victorian warehouse (originally built as a props & costume store) impresses all who visit with its foraged or pickled produce and low-intervention wines. Last year it celebrated its tenth anniversary and opened a spin-off wine bar/restaurant, Montrose House, in the Abbeyhill area. The entry-level option for dining here is a five-course tasting menu for £95 per person. / timberyard.co; timberyard10; Thu, Sun 8.30 pm, Fri & Sat 9 pm.

TIPO £53 343

110 HANOVER STREET
EH2 1DR 0131 226 4545

High marks in early feedback suggest a positive start for this small plates newcomer from Noto and Aizle's Jade Johnston and Stuart Ralston, on the site of The Perch (RIP). It's a view supported by The Scotsman's Gaby Soutar who, in her May 2023 review, hailed "a very appealing venue" (named for the grade of flour used to make the dishes) with excellent pasta and small plates that she termed "compulsive eating", and an "elevated combination of dreams": apparently, it has instantly become "part of [her] fantasy perfect day in the Capital". / tipoedinburgh.co.uk; tipoedinburgh; Mon-Sun 9 pm.

VALVONA & CROLLA £61 333

19 ELM ROW EH7 4AA 0131 556 6066

"The best choice of wine anywhere" is the main reason to visit the Caffè Bar at the rear of this famous deli and wine merchants (est. 1934) where any of the "extensive range of bottles from the shop" is available to accompany a meal for super-modest (£6) corkage. By comparison, the food is very straightforward, but provides dependable sustenance from breakfast onwards. / valvonacrolla.com; valvonacrolla; Mon-Sat 6 pm.

WEDGWOOD £75 443

267 CANONGATE EH8 8BQ 0131 558 8737

Paul and Lisa Wedgwood's basement on the Royal Mile again wins consistent praise this year for its "very good" cuisine, which provides a good trade off between its level of ambition and its relative affordability. There's a seasonally changing à la carte menu, or you can opt for the 'Wee Tour of Scotland' tasting menu at £80 per person. / wedgwoodtherestaurant.co.uk; wedgwoodtherestaurant; Sun-Thu 9 pm, Fri & Sat 10 pm.

THE WITCHERY BY THE CASTLE £109 224

CASTLEHILL, THE ROYAL MILE EH1 2NF 0131 225 5613

With its incredible wood-paneled interior (candle-lit, with antique furnishings and tapestries) and an alternative 'Secret Garden' space, James Thomson's restored old house near the castle (dating from 1595) provides a supremely romantic destination (there are also rooms), and has been one of the city's landmark destinations for decades. It has long been accused of "resting on its reputation" foodwise and this year those fears were to the fore, with concerns about the "pretty uninspiring food and eye-watering prices for such unexciting choices". Still, there's always compensation in the vast wine list. And its most upbeat fans have different concerns: "It's always nice to eat here, but it can be too dark to read the menu and you have to use the torch on your mobile phone to see it properly!" / thewitchery.com; the.witchery; Mon-Sun 10.30 pm.

EGHAM, SURREY 3-3A

THE TUDOR ROOM, GREAT FOSTERS HOTEL £95 344

STROUDE RD TW20 9UR 01784 433822

The intimate, seven-table dining room at this grand manor-house hotel features a tapestried wall and spectacular Tudor fireplace, making it an ideal showcase for ambitious and refined classical meals from chef Alex Payne, who grew up a mile away in Egham and trained under Heston Blumenthal and Gordon Ramsay. The hotel also serves smart afternoon teas in the Anne Boleyn drawing room and relaxed meals in the Estate Grill, with an impressive vaulted ceiling. / alexanderhotels.co.uk; greatfosters; Wed-Sat 9 pm.

EGLWYS FACH, POWYS 4-3D

YNYSHIR RESTAURANT AND ROOMS, YNYSHIR HALL £436 433

SY20 8TA 01654 781 209

"Was it expensive, yes. Was it challenging, yes. Was it worth it, YES!" Gareth Ward's famous matt-black painted mansion in the mists of mid-Wales isn't one of the nation's most expensive culinary pilgrimages for nothing, and fans of its maximalist style – complete with loud music and no end of restaurant 'theatre' – say that even if its 20-30 course menus are "a bit too protein-centric" (to be fair, the website does say they claim to be 'protein-obsessed') that "you can't fault the cooking or the passion" that drives "an incredible all-round experience" hailed by some as "the best in the UK". It still gets the thumbs up from a majority of reporters, but – as its prices have ballooned over its 10 years in operation – doubts have crept in and there's a significant minority for whom it risks becoming "pretentious and overpriced". ("It used to be exceptional, but IMHO has now jumped the shark with loud music, arrogant service, and stratospheric prices detracting greatly from its outstanding and interesting cooking…"; "It used to be a favourite of ours but is now more like a boot camp. Arrive when told, dine when told, leave when told… and all at a cost far greater than many Michelin star restaurants in Mayfair!") / ynyshir.co.uk; ynyshirrestaurant; Tue-Fri 11 pm.

ELLASTONE, DERBYSHIRE 5-3C

THE DUNCOMBE ARMS £45 433

MAIN RD DE6 2GZ 01335 324 275

An "absolute gem just north of Uttoxeter" – this rather glamorous peak District venture is "the local we all wish we had", to quote The Daily Mail's Tom Parker Bowles; "the tarte Tatin alone is worth the visit" but the modern British menu (more casual in the bar) also features "excellent dishes such as omelette Arnold Bennett and crispy belly pork" and their rooms are "brilliant" if you stay overnight. / duncombearms.co.uk; duncombe_arms; Mon-Sat 8.30 pm, Sun 8 pm.

ELY, CAMBRIDGESHIRE 3-1B

OLD FIRE ENGINE HOUSE £56 342

25 ST MARY'S ST CB7 4ER 01353 662582

"A place very much in keeping with its proprietor", Ann Jarman, who founded the restaurant and art gallery in 1968, in Georgian premises near the cathedral. Its personal approach and "old-school ambience" is very much part of its charm, and, combined with the "good" home cooking, wins it a "very loya[l] following" indeed. / theoldfireenginehouse.co.u[k]; theoldfireenginehouse; Tue-Sat 8.30 pm, Sun 5.15 pm.

EMSWORTH, HAMPSHIRE 2-4[D]

FAT OLIVES £65 45[.]

30 SOUTH ST PO10 7EH 01243 377914

"Satisfyingly simple and unpretentious" – the verdict on Lawrence & Julia Murphy's long-running (est. 2000) and "rustic" venture in a cute, seventeenth-century fisherman's cottage, on the road down to the quay; the "varied menu" features "plenty of fresh fish, beautifully prepared and served" and coming "at a reasonable price" to boot. / fatolives.co.u[k]; fatolives1; Wed-Sat 10.30 pm.

36 ON THE QUAY £87 34[.]

47 SOUTH ST PO10 7EG 01243 375592

In 2019, locally born chef Gary Pearce and hi[s] wife Martyna took over this well-established restaurant-with-rooms right on Emsworth harbour from Ramon & Karen Farthing, who had developed it into one of the South Coast's better-known dining options over two decades. Gary's "complex and innovative cooking" – honed in top kitchens including Le Champignon Sauvage in Cheltenham and Belgium's De Wulf – scored consistently well this year, if on somewhat limited feedback. / 36onthequay.com; 36onthequay; Tue-Sat 11.30 pm.

ENFIELD, HERTFORDSHIRE 3-2[B]

MARCUS KITCHEN AND BAR £50 44[.]

16 BURLEIGH WAY EN2 6AE 020 8367 3339

"It's located down a small mews which doesn't look particularly prepossessing, but what a trea[t] awaits any diner who ventures to this small, family run restaurant": a Neopolitan/Southern Italian specialist where the eponymous Marcus turns out the "most delicious seafood" and other dishes that "don't depend upon lots of fancy trimmings". "I'm loath to recommend this place because it is so special but Marcus deserves the plaudits and I am happy to give them in platefuls". / marcuskitchenandbar.com; Tue-Sat 11 pm, Sun 5 am.

ENGLEFIELD GREEN, SURREY 3-3A

THE BAILIWICK £88 44[.]

WICK ROAD TW20 0HN 01784 682888

Ex-Core chef Steven Ellis & pastry-chef wife Ami's "temple-of-gastronomy-wolf in a comfy-pub-sheep's clothing" launched two years back and it has a particular focus on local game. Th[e] "highly distinctive and skilfully crafted cuisine" (with "venison to the fore") plus "attentive and courteous service" place it "at the top gastropu[b] level". NB – while "parking is potentially tricky, one could enjoy a delightful walk in indsor Great Park before or after a meal ·re". / thebailiwick.co.uk; thebailiwickfreehouse; ed-Sat 9.30 pm, Sun 4 pm.

RBISTOCK, WREXHAM 5–3A

HE BOAT AT RBISTOCK 333

.13 0DL 01978 280 205

"great location and very good pub food" are e twin attractions of this seventeenth century ıb, a short drive from Wrexham, which has a autiful location next to the Dee. The menu ntains an eclectic international selection of shes (moussaka, red Thai curry, osso bucco…) d in warmer weather they fire up their wood-ed pizza oven. / theboataterbistock.co.uk; eboataterbistock; Sun-Thu 10 pm, Fri & Sat pm.

ESHER, SURREY 3–3A

OOD EARTH £72 332

- 18 HIGH STREET
T10 9RT 01372 462489

ne "only upmarket Chinese in the area" – and rt of an eight-strong, otherwise London-sed, chain; admittedly the "menu hasn't anged in decades" (this location opened 1980) and they don't tend to treat diners specials, but reporters "love it" all the me – and "the outstanding team match the ality of the food". / goodearthgroup.co.uk; odearthgroup; Tue-Sat 10.30 pm, Sun 10.45 pm.

OSÉ PIZARRO AT THE SWAN IN ESHER £64 332

HARE LANE KT10 9BS 01372 462 582

od TV staple José Pizarro's first outfit outside e capital – and first gastroboozer (with rooms) s set in "a not-completely-obvious location" the Surrey 'burbs. Reviews were slightly ıted this year: while most praised the "great odern Spanish food" (including "fabulous pas"), others noted a lack of atmosphere wouldn't be hard to make it feel a bit more timate"). / josepizarro.com; Jose? Pizarro's staurants; Tue-Thu, Sat & Sun 6 pm, Mon , Fri om.

ETON, BERKSHIRE 3–3A

ILBEY'S £72 223

- 83 HIGH STREET
.4 6AF 01753 854921

nis "stylish restaurant" near the bridge to indsor has been run for almost 50 years by -founder Lin Gilbey, who is responsible for interior design. Her husband and business rtner Bill (scion of the Gilbey's Gin dynasty) dly passed away in 2022, but Lin has essed ahead with improvements, acquiring e premises next door to offer corporate tertainment and private dining facilities. odern British cooking is generally felt to be olid". / gilbeygroup.com; gilbeys_eton; Mon-u 9.30 pm, Fri & Sat 10 pm, Sun 3.30 pm.

Lympstone Manor, Exmouth

EVERSHOT, DORSET 2–4B

SUMMER LODGE, SUMMER LODGE COUNTRY HOUSE £125 333

DT2 0JR 01935 482000

The Red Carnation group's "very comfortable and traditional country house hotel is set in a time warp", in prime Hardy Country (Evershot having been fictionalised as Evershead by the novelist, who also designed part of the hotel when he was an architect). The "very accomplished food" ("but at a high price!") has some "nice touches", with "desserts especially good". / summerlodgehotel.co.uk; summer_lodge; Mon-Sun 9 pm.

EXETER, DEVON 1–3D

GOTO £47 342

38 NEW BRIDGE STREET
EX4 3AH 01392 437734

"When it opened, it was pretty straightforward snagging a table – good luck right now!". Dan & Katie Goto moved their Plymouth business to Exeter a couple of years ago after their lease expired, and its "really good" sushi, sashimi and other traditional Japanese dishes have won it quick popularity locally: "it could thrive in bigger premises". / Mon-Sat 9 pm.

RENDEZVOUS WINE BAR £65 334

38-40 SOUTHERNHAY EAST
EX1 1PE 01392 270 222

A "lovely" Southernhay restaurant plus basement wine bar that's handy for Cathedral Yard. The "excellent wine list and menu showcase local producers", contributing to what is an invariably "reliable" spot. / rendezvouswinebar.co.uk; rendezvouswinebar; Mon-Sat 9 pm.

EXMOUTH, DEVON 1–3D

LYMPSTONE MANOR £201 544

COURTLANDS LANE
EX8 3NZ 01395 202040

"Michael Caines continues to deliver an exquisite dining experience, wherein locally sourced produce is transformed into joy on a plate in a gloriously beautiful location", according to practically all feedback on this Georgian mansion, set amidst its own vineyards and overlooking the Exe estuary. "The dining space is split across three rooms" (Berry Head has the best views) and the cuisine is "outstanding: in particular the Estuary Tasting menu is a triumph of fish cooking". "Also his own wines are very good". Minority concerns include the odd incident of "disengaged service" or a "slightly sterile" atmosphere. More common though is applause for the "stunning setting and views", "efficient" approach and "exceptional" overall standards. "Why only 1 star? It's right up there with the big guns!" / lympstonemanor.co.uk; lympstone_manor; Wed & Thu 9 pm, Fri-Sun 9.30 pm.

THE POOL HOUSE, LYMPSTONE MANOR £90 344

COURTLANDS LANE
EX8 3NZ 01395 202040

"An impressive new building (albeit noisy when full due to hard surfaces)" and "incredibly professional service" help win praise for this newish addition to Michael Caines's luxurious HQ, overlooking the hotel's recently added outdoor heated pool. The culinary aims here are more straightforward than in the main building with burgers and pasta dishes alongside more substantial brasserie fare, but even so dishes are not priced individually: you need to choose either a two-course (£48 per person) or three-course (£60 per person) meal. / lympstonemanor.co.uk; lympstone_manor; Mon-Thu 9 pm, Fri-Sun 9.30 pm.

FAIRLIGHT, KENT 3–4C

THE COVE £41 333

53 WAITES LANE
TN35 4AX 01424 814772

Opened on April Fool's Day 2022, but set on a site which has seen many incarnations (it was converted into a hotel from a cowshed back in the 1920s), this "wonderful" new arrival from husband-and-wife team Olivia and Henry is already a local hit. Chef Nick Hales oversees the "unfussy and well-executed" menu – "defo more restaurant than pub" in quality – with the "catch of the day supplied by a local fishmonger" and greens grown 400 yards away. Bonus points for the staff ("nothing was too much trouble"). / thecovefairlight.co.uk; thecovefairlightpub; Mon & Tue, Sun 9 pm, Wed-Sat 11 pm.

FAIRSTEAD, ESSEX 3–2C

THE SQUARE AND COMPASSES £54 333

FULLER STREET
CM3 2BB 01245 361477

You feel like you're in the middle of nowhere at this country pub north of Chelmsford (and dating from 1652) – "a perfect venue for those that enjoy a country walk followed by a decent lunch". "It really delivers on food" (generously portioned pub grub). "Great beers too!" / thesquareandcompasses.co.uk; squareandcompasses; Wed-Sat 8.30 pm, Sun 4 pm.

FAKENHAM, NORFOLK 6–4C

SCULTHORPE MILL £59 343

LYNN ROAD NR21 9QG 01328 633001

This "gorgeous pub/restaurant in a bucolic setting right next to a ford" was built as a watermill in the eighteenth century, became a pub in the nineteenth, and was taken over and spruced up in 2021 by Siobhan and Caitriona Peyton (sisters of well-known caterer Oliver). "More gastro than traditional pub", it's a "great destination" that's "unique in Norfolk" – "especially in the summer when you can sit in the sensational garden" and dine on "great seasonal cooking and very good pies". / sculthorpemill.uk; sculthorpemillnorfolk; Mon-Sat 8.30 pm, Sun 5 pm.

FALMOUTH, CORNWALL 1–4B

CULTURE £97

CUSTOM HOUSE QUAY, 38B ARWENACK STREET TR11 3JF 01326 313001

Hylton Espey and his wife Petronella are already winning awards for their hyper-seasonal approach with many foraged ingredients at their ambitious yearling, on Custom House Quay: a 30-seat venue presenting a seven-course menu for £75 per person. As yet, we've had too limited feedback for a definitive rating, but all reports to-date are ecstatic. / culturerestaurant.co.uk; culture.restaurant; Wed-Sat 10 pm.

HOOKED ON THE ROCKS £75 234

SWANPOOL ROAD, SWANPOOL COURT
TR11 5BG 01326 311886

A "buzzy atmosphere and great views" over Swanpool beach and nature reserve add to the charms of this cliffside venture; the "best scallops" are a feature of the menu, which has a strong focus on sustainability. Ratings for the food are a little middling overall, but the worst anyone has to say is that its popularity means some dishes soon run out – and that "starter portions were more like mains" (first-world problems, eh?). / hookedontherocksfalmouth.com; Tue-Sat 9 pm.

THE MULBERRY 333

29 HIGH STREET
TR11 2AD 01326 761055

Tucked away near the high street, this "small plates" venue is the debut restaurant from Cornish-based chefs Harry Cartwright and Nathan Outlaw-trained Jay Brady, with a focus on seasonal local ingredients, and delivers "very good, Cornish-style tapas" in a modern ("acoustically reverberant") setting. There's also a six-course tasting menu. / themulberryfalmouth.co.uk; the_mulberry_falmouth; Tue-Sat 11 pm.

RESTAURANT MINE £44 444

4 THE OLD BREWERY YARD
TR11 2BY 01326 211073

"What a find" – a "very small" outfit run by Angus Bell, previously of The Star Inn at Harome, and Michel Roux Jr's Le Gavroche. "You sit within ten feet of the 'kitchen' and can watch everything" as well as "chat to the chefs after service". Modern British cooking is "very, very good" ("something more interesting than most") and "good value too". It is rated positively on a relatively small number of reports. / restaurantmine.co.uk; restaurantmine; Mon-Sat 9.30 pm.

THE VERDANT SEAFOOD BAR £38 333

QUAY STREET TR11 3HH NO TEL

"A must if you're in Falmouth" – this "hipsterish bar" from Penryn's Verdant craft brewery "serves very hoppy cloudy beers and some seriously good seafood, in all its forms from raw to frittered". "Knowledgeable staff" are on hand to help you pair tapas-size plates with the brews on offer. "The cheese fritters are also stunning, light but flavoursome and perfect with that edgy beer!" / verdantbrewing.co; verdantbrew; Tue-Sat 11 pm.

FARINGDON, OXFORDSHIRE 2–2C

THE LAMB TAVERN BUCKLAND £55

POUNDCORNER SN7 8QN 01367 709196

No reports as yet on this modern retread of an ancient village boozer in the Oxfordshire countryside. It's a new showcase for the 'elevated gastro-pub cooking' of chef Nathan Richardson, who took over the property from former tenants of 15 years' standing and who previously worked at Mayfair's acclaimed Guinea Grill. You can eat in the bar (80 covers) or the restaurant (40 covers). / lambtavernbuckland.com; thelambtavern; Tue-Sat 11 pm, Sun 5 pm.

FAVERSHAM, KENT 3–3

QUAY £50 33

CONDUIT ST ME13 7DF 01795 530388

"A great restaurant-with-rooms a little away from the centre of Faversham but near the creek", and on the former site of the Swan and Harlequin pub (amongst other incarnations). The "young, keen chef" – Nick Martin, who previously ran the Carriage Restaurant, in the town's Railway Hotel, again with partner Tania Bourne – "provides a short but good selection of dishes" and "friendly staff" contribute to the "above average ambience". / thequayfaversham.co.uk; thequayfaversham; Wed-Sat 9 pm, Sun 4 pm.

READ'S £99 44

MACKNADE MANOR, CANTERBURY RD
ME13 8XE 01795 535344

Fans are "sad to hear that the Pitchfords are selling up" when it comes to this village restaurant with rooms – run by David and Ro Pitchford since 1977 and "a go-to for special family events" for many in this part of Kent. "The menu is conservative but the food alway of a very high standard", with items such as 'A Prawn Cocktail the way we used to do it back in when we opened'. It went on the market for £3m in April 2023, but we've left its rating untouched in the hope that any purchaser maintains its "traditional excellence" – "alway a treat especially the soufflés". / reads.com; reads_restaurant; Tue-Sat 9 pm.

FENCE, LANCASHIRE 5–1

WHITE SWAN AT FENCE £106 54

300 WHEATLEY LANE RD
BB12 9QA 01282 611773

This "proper local pub but with Michelin star food" is many reporters' "restaurant of the year" – with service that's both "fun and professional, not at all stuffy" and "stunningly good food" from chef Tom Parker, who trained at nearby Lancashire powerhouse Northcote. Top Menu Tip – "the beetroot ice cream is sublime". / whiteswanatfence.co.uk; whiteswanatfence; Tue-Thu 8.20 pm, Fri & Sat .

FERRENSBY, NORTH YORKSHIRE 8–4

GENERAL TARLETON £66 33

BOROUGHBRIDGE RD
HG5 0PZ 01423 340284

"A warm welcome, prompt service and tasty cooking" make it worth remembering this comfortable, modernified pub, not far from e A1, where chef Varun Khanna produces bistro-style selection of dishes. / the-gt.co.uk; neraltarleton; Mon-Sat 9 pm, Sun 8.30 pm.

FIONNPHORT, ARGYLL & BUTE 9–3A

INTH WAVE £90 454

RUACH MHOR PA66 6BL 01681 700757

ny meal at this Isle of Mull moorland croft is "wonderful occasion", with "delicious food" nd "great hosts" – gardener/fisherman John nd chef Carla Lamont, whose Canadian ritage brings Northwest Pacific Rim fluences to bear on "top-notch ingredients" mostly local, many grown, foraged, smoked cured on site. (Note they close for the winter ason from October-May; the only option this time is a luxury four-course lunch, for oup bookings). / ninthwaverestaurant.co.uk; rlaglamont; Wed-Sun .

FLAUNDEN, HERTFORDSHIRE 3–2A

HE BRICKLAYERS RMS £68 344

OGPITS BOTTOM
P3 0PH 01442 833322

"very pleasant country pub" helmed by lly & Alvin Michaels for two decades, and nose "good food" of Anglo-French bent ncluding home-smoked fish and meat, and cal game) "attracts diners from well beyond area"; indeed, one reporter who took far-ng American visitors found that they "loved e location and quaintness" of this attractive eorgian locale – also handy for the Harry otter experience at Warner Bros Studio earby. / bricklayersarms.com; Mon-Fri 8.30 pm, t 9 pm, Sun 7 pm.

FLETCHING, EAST SUSSEX 3–4B

HE GRIFFIN INN £79 332

N22 3SS 01825 722890

Family friendly and lively" Sussex pub-th-rooms that was taken over by the ational Young's chain in 2022, after over ur decades under the Pullan family. There the odd grumble about the switch, but ost reports remain positive and its "lovely rrace" in particular continues to win pproval. / thegriffininn.co.uk; thegriffininn; Mon-t 9.30 pm, Sun 8.30 pm.

FOLKESTONE, KENT 3–4D

OCKSALT £66 224

5 FISHMARKET
T19 6AA 01303 212 070

his stunning curved modern restaurant was pened in 2011 by Saga billionaire Sir Roger e Haan and his son Josh, and won widespread claim for its seafood under founding chef Mark Sargeant. But since Mark's departure in te 2021, ratings have softened a little – "the od is a bit up and down and on the pricey de to cater for the London crowd, but it has n ideal position overlooking the water and e harbour arm". / rocksaltfolkestone.co.uk; rocksaltfolkestone; Mon-Thu 10 pm, Fri & Sat 10.30 pm, Sun 5 pm.

STEEP STREET COFFEE HOUSE £21 333

18-24 THE OLD HIGH STREET
CT20 1RL 01303 247819

"Great coffee and a small and interesting lunch menu" keep customers coming back to this "super coffee shop complete with library in Old Folkestone High Street", a key component of the town's 'Creative Quarter'. Owners Alice Larkin and Stephen Brothwell were inspired by the literary cafés of Paris, and host writers' events. / steepstreet.co.uk; steep_street; Mon-Sat 6 pm, Sun 5 pm.

FONTHILL GIFFORD, WILTSHIRE 2–3C

BECKFORD ARMS £61 334

SP3 6PX 01747 870 385

This "superb country pub with fabulous food" on the Fonthill Estate dates from 1740 and boasts a "country-house ambience and upper-crust service" that make it "popular with the local gentry" (and very well commented-on in our annual diners' poll by the standards of venues in the area). An ivy-clad facade and "roaring log fires" are complemented by a smartly modernised interior, while "seasonal menus mix traditional country fayre and touches of the more exotic" – so there's "truly something for everyone". / beckfordarms.com; thebeckfordarms; Mon-Sun 11 pm.

FORDWICH, KENT 3–3D

THE FORDWICH ARMS £103 543

KING STREET CT2 0DB 01227 710444

"Each time we come we are impressed by the attention to detail and outstanding quality of the food at this well-regarded gastropub" – Daniel & Natasha Smith purchased this "beautiful old pub on the River Stour" in 2017 and has become one of the most commented-on venues outside the capital in our annual diners' poll. "The style of cuisine is that of fine dining with locally sourced produce and the flavours bring out the best in the ingredients". "Tables are well-spaced and the staff certainly know their stuff" – "incredible value". Top Tip – "Lovely wisteria-covered terrace by the river on a sunny day". / fordwicharms.co.uk; thefordwicharms; Wed-Sat 9.30 pm, Sun 5 pm.

FOWEY, CORNWALL 1–4D

APPLETONS £58 443

19 FORE STREET
PL23 1AH 01872 228738

"This is a great find in the centre of Fowey" – a "new favourite" that was first set up back in 2016 in a vineyard en route to Padstow, and relocated to the centre of this seaside town three years ago. Andy Appleton (former head chef at Jamie Oliver's Fifteen Cornwall) oversees the "wonderfully fresh Italian-inspired dishes", and wife Lyndsey the "very welcoming" and "knowledgeable" staff. / appletonsrestaurant.com; _appletons; Mon-Sat 10 pm.

THE RESTAURANT AT OLD QUAY HOUSE £62 334

28 FORE STREET
PL23 1AQ 01726 833302

"Continuing to be a reliable place for a quality meal in a lovely riverside setting" – the dining room and outside deck of this Victorian hotel provide wonderful estuary-side vantage-points for a meal. There are two-course and three-course menu options for about £40, and all-in-all it makes "an affordable special treat". / theoldquayhouse.com; oldquayhouse; Mon-Sun 8.30 pm.

FRAMLINGHAM, SUFFOLK 3–1D

WATSON & WALPOLE £68 443

3 CHURCH STREET
IP13 9BQ 01728 666556

"Really exceptional and genuinely Italian food, beautifully prepared, cooked and presented with brio", makes this three-year-old from Ruth Watson, TV's 'Hotel Inspector', her husband Dave and Rob Walpole "a very special place". With its "airy, light interior" and "exemplary service", it's "everything a neighbourhood restaurant should be" – and "not what you expect to find in a Suffolk town". / watsonandwalpole.com; watsonandwalpole; Tue-Sat 9.30 pm.

FRAMPTON MANSELL, GLOUCESTERSHIRE 2–2B

JOLLY NICE FARM SHOP £17 343

THE OLD WHITE HORSE FILLING STATION, CIRENCESTER ROAD
GL6 8HZ 01285 760868

"Just keeps getting better… it's gone from derelict petrol station to Airstream caravan selling ice cream to a shop and drive-thru where you can buy very local produce in the shop, and eat excellent rare-breed burgers" – this converted fuel stop was quoted in a 2023 Times article as being the type of local farm store that boosts rural property prices! "Outdoor seating in the meadow is on hand for fine days; there's a yurt with log burner on cooler days together with a covered area with a fire pit". "The quality is always excellent and the staff unfailingly friendly, knowledgeable and enthusiastic about what they sell". "Great coffee and pastries for early mornings… bigger breakfasts are also available". Top Menu Tip – "The Kentucky Fried Pheasant always goes down well". / jollynicefarmshop.com; jollynicefarmshop; Mon-Sun 7 pm.

FRESSINGFIELD, SUFFOLK 3–1D

THE FOX & GOOSE £61 444

CHURCH RD IP21 5PB 01379 586247

"Well worth a detour from the coast" for "delicious food and an interesting menu": Paul & Sarah Yaxley's "exceptional" venue – a beamed former guildhall – is "an oasis in the middle of East Anglia". "I've been coming here since I was a teenager 45 years ago, and despite many changes over that time it still never disappoints". / foxandgoose.net; Tue-Sat 11 pm, Sun 3.30 pm.

FRILSHAM, BERKSHIRE 2–2D

THE POT KILN £78 234

YATTENDON ESTATE
RG18 0XX 01635 201366

Kate Middleton's favourite pub, apparently (Raymond Blanc is a fan too) is this rural inn deep in the Berkshire countryside, where noise from the nearby M4 doesn't impinge on its tranquility. Much-expanded in recent years with the addition of a cookery school, it's nowadays run by Kate Robinson and her partner, musician Rocky Rockliff (Kate's ex-husband, game expert Mike Robinson, is no longer involved). Though still popular with our reporters too, there's a feeling that "the menu has been scaled back in recent times" with meals that are increasingly "good but not special". / potkiln.org; Mon-Thu 10 pm, Fri & Sat 11 pm, Sun 6 pm.

FRITHSDEN, HERTFORDSHIRE 3–2A

THE ALFORD ARMS £60 344

HP1 3DD 01442 864480

This "great country pub" in a Chilterns village makes a handy "all year round" escape from the big city, and has a cleverly constructed menu that changes every week and majors on local produce. / alfordarms.co.uk; alfordarms.

GATESHEAD, TYNE AND WEAR 8–2B

TRAKOL £69 433

HILLGATE QUAYS
NE8 2BH 0191 737 1120

An unabashedly carnivorous outfit in a "fantastic location on the quayside" – part of the container-bound By The River Brew Co. – housing brewery, street-food market, and bike shop. The "brilliant food is cooked over flame", with a "lovely use of different cuts" doled out in "hearty servings" ("the pig's head crackling is so plentiful you have to share it with other tables!"). / bytheriverbrew.co; bytheriverbrewco; Wed-Sat 10 pm, Sun 6 pm.

GATTONSIDE, SCOTTISH BORDERS 9–4D

THE HOEBRIDGE £73 332

HOEBRIDGE ROAD EAST
TD6 9LZ 01896 823082

This "very bright white" (in a cool way) indie, in the Borders, was opened in 2015 by New Yorker Kyle Tidd and his chef-husband Hamish Carruthers; the monthly changing seasonal small plates are "highly regarded in Scottish media" (not least The Scotsman, who gave it a rave 2022 review), and all reports this year rate results as good or very good. / thehoebridge.com; thehoebridge; Wed-Sat 8.30 pm.

GERRARDS CROSS, BUCKINGHAMSHIRE 3–3A

MALIKS £53 443

14 OAK END WAY
SL9 8BR 01753 889634

Malik Ahmed's traditional but "exceptional" curry house has achieved consistently high ratings for more than 20 years. Part of a trio with siblings in Cookham and Marlow, it's run hands-on by a family with 150 years in the business – the restaurant Malik's great-great-grandfather founded in what is now Bangladesh is still going strong! / maliks.co.uk; maliksgroup; Mon-Sat 11 pm, Sun 10.30 pm.

THREE OAKS £65 333

AUSTENWOOD LN
SL9 8NL 01753 899 016

Katherine (daughter of the late Terry Wogan) and Henry Cripps have long stewarded this top-class, good-value gastroboozer, in a "nice location" near the local golf club; the "seriously good food" makes it "much more than a pub" and "friendly staff" ensure a good welcome. / thethreeoaksgx.co.uk; thethreeoaksgx; Wed-Sat 11 pm, Sun 6 pm.

GISBURN, LANCASHIRE 5–1B

LA LOCANDA £60 443

MAIN STREET BB7 4HH 01200 445303

"The closest you will get to a true Italian Restaurant, without leaving the UK" – Maurizio and Cinzia Bocchi's "discreet and intimate" "landmark of authentic Italian cooking" occupies a converted weaver's cottage on the A59 in the Ribble Valley, and is "rare (if not unique) in the north" in terms of its genuine style and high level of accomplishment. Don't expect pizza – the repertoire is faithfully north Italian and there's a wide selection of Italian wines, beers and aperitivi. (Although the restaurant runs events supporting Italian produce – for example for olive oil importers – Maurizio is also Marketing Lancashire's 'Taste Lancashire Ambassador' and over 80% of the restaurant's produce is locally sourced). / lalocanda.co.uk; lalocandagisburn; Tue-Thu 9.30 pm, Fri 10 pm, Sat 10.30 pm, Sun 8 pm.

GLASGOW, CITY OF GLASGOW 9–4C

BANCA DI ROMA £55

31 ROYAL EXCHANGE SQUARE
G1 3AJ 0141 648 7662

"A brash, grand and ambitious new Italian" from owner Guiseppe Marini, which opened to much fanfare in spring 2023 in the expensively revamped city centre premises that were previously a branch of Zizzi. It immediately inspired upbeat reviews in our annual diners' poll ("just what Glasgow city centre needs"; "excellent pastas and promising-looking meat and fish options"; "really committed to its Italian wine list and to weaning its crowd off premium Champagne"). But in August 2023, the three Cozzolini brothers who used to work for Francesco Mazzei at Sartoria in London's Mayfair parted ways with the projec[t]. Consequently, we've left it un-rated for the time being while its culinary direction become[s] clearer. / bancadiroma.co.uk; bancadiromauk; Mon-Sun midnight.

BATTLEFIELD REST £42 33[…]

55 BATTLEFIELD ROAD
G42 9JL 0141 636 6955

Occupying an interesting looking Edwardian landmark (built in 1914 as a tram stop), this "classic Italian" wins praise for its "well-cooke[d] Italian food" (pizza, pasta, plus classic Italian staple dishes). "It can be crowded, but is very friendly". It generated national headlines in 2023 (including in the fun-filled Sun), when owner Marco Giannasi 'secretly' sold the business to waiter Alex Matheson and his wife Jen Doherty (although Giannasi and his wife still own the freehold). Top Tip – "good value lunchtime offers". / battlefieldrest.co.uk; restbattlefield; Mon-Sat 8.45 pm.

BEAT 6 £31

149 MILNGAVIE ROAD
G61 3DY 0141 486 8666

This April 2023 opening is the brainchild of Nico Simeone (of Six by Nico fame) whose wi[fe] Valentina recovered from Hodgkin lymphoma some years ago and was supported at Beatson Cancer Charity. 100% of profits from this relocated 48-seat venture (which previously operated in Whitehill Street) go to supporting the same charity. No feedback as yet in our annual diners' poll, but The Scotsman's Rosalind Erskine was impressed: the "chefs in charge… have come from Unalome by Graem[e] Cheevers… so the expectation is high, and the[y] do not disappoint". / beat-6.co.uk; beat6_uk; Wed-Sat 10.30 pm, Sun 9.30 pm.

CAFÉ GANDOLFI £57 33[…]

64 ALBION ST G1 1NY 0141 552 6813

"Just a home from home" for its many long-term fans – this Merchant City institution (est 1979) provides a cosy setting, characterised by its paneled walls and custom-made furniture ([b]y Tim Stead). The fare is straightforward rather than of any huge aspiration, but it makes for an affordable destination. / cafegandolfi.com; cafegandolfi; Sun & Mon 5 pm, Tue-Sat 10.30 pm.

CAIL BRUICH £168 55[…]

725 GREAT WESTERN RD
G12 8QX 01413 346265

"Worth the effort to get a table in this excellent star of Glasgow's culinary scene" – this nowadays renowned fixture in the city's dining line-up opened in 2008 in the West End, but emerged as a foodie hotspot in 2019 with the appointment of chef Lorna McGee; and it is acclaimed in our survey as "clearly the best fine dining in town", with a tasting menu that's "imaginative, seasonal and based on Scottish ingredients where possible"; all backed up by staff who are "enthusiastic and knowledgeable". On the downside, "this has taken to being

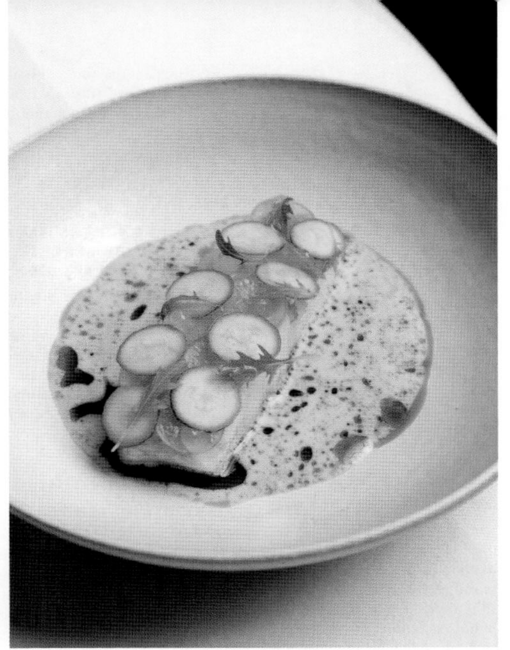

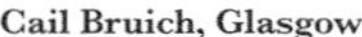

Cail Bruich, Glasgow

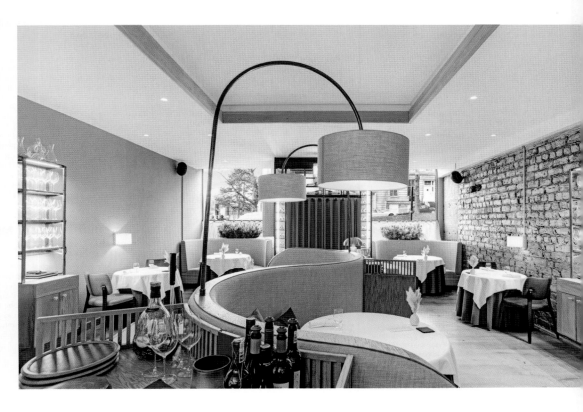

rather pricey for the city, but to complain over-much would be churlish as quality is brilliant and the welcome too". Top Menu Tip – "we particularly enjoyed a scallop starter with hazelnut and caviar". / cailbruich.co.uk; cailbruich; Tue-Sat midnight.

CELENTANO'S £80 433

28–32 CATHEDRAL SQUARE G4 0XA 0141 552 3519

This "buzzy" and "friendly" two-year-old, in a city-centre Scottish baronial landmark Cathedral House, is a "nice addition to Glasgow" by all accounts. It was launched by Anna Parker and chef-husband Dan (ex-of London venues Darby's and The Dairy), who fell in love with Italian cooking on their honeymoon and have brought "a different kind of Italian" to Anna's hometown. Expect much "sourcing locally from small suppliers", as well as a focus on fermenting, preserving and curing. / celentanosglasgow.com; celentanos_glasgow; Wed-Sat 10.30 pm, Sun 6 pm.

COIAS £62 322

473-477 DUKE STREET G31 1RD 0141 554 3822

"A great place to stop in for a coffee, a pastry or an ice cream" (or heartier "all-day classics done well") – this "authentic Italian" has "been family-run for as long as anyone can remember", having opened back in 1928, and been taken over by the third generation in the 1980s. These days the expanded premises includes a dedicated deli section. / coiascafe.co.uk; coiasglasgow; Sun-Thu 8.45 pm, Fri & Sat 9.45 pm.

CRABSHAKK £65 433

1114 ARGYLE ST, FINNIESTON G3 8TD 0141 334 6127

John Macleod's original venue – this quirkily laid out Finnieston fixture is one of the best-known destinations on this foodie strip and you can eat either at the counter or in the small warren of seating areas. Reports this year still included some "outstanding" fish and seafood cookery but there was also the odd "disappointment" – perhaps the strain of managing two places at once? / crabshakk.com; crabshakkfinnieston; Mon, Thu-Sun midnight.

CRABSHAKK BOTANICS £67 434

18 VINICOMBE STREET G12 8BE 0141 530 4407

The "truly exceptional food" at John Macleod's year-old follow-up to his long-established hit seafood venue Crabshakk shows he can repeat the successful formula, with "the same excellent fish but in more refined surroundings than Finnieston". The new site by the Botanic Gardens in the West End is a beautifully restored Art Deco garage from 1912, shared with Ka Pao (see also). / crabshakk.co.uk; crabshakkbotanics; Tue-Sun midnight.

DAKHIN £36 332

89 CANDLERIGGS G1 1NP 0141 553 2585

Nothing but good feedback again this year for this Merchant City venture, which – celebrating its twentieth anniversary this year – claims to be the 'first authentic South Indian restaurant in Scotland'. / dakhin.com; dakhinglasgow; Mon-Sun 10.30 pm.

THE DHABBA £46 342

44 CANDLERIGGS G1 1LE 0141 553 1249

"Slick and friendly service" adds to the appeal of this modern-looking north Indian restaurant, which has been a feature of the Merchant City for over twenty years now. / thedhabba.com; thedhabba; Mon-Sun 10.30 pm.

EUSEBI DELI £60 433

152 PARK ROAD G4 9HB 0141 648 9999

"The best Italian deli-restaurant in Glasgow and one of the best in the UK!" – this operation near Kelvinbridge subway station has been going strong for over four decades, and serves "just the most likable, interesting, superb" food (including "cannoli and other pasticceria delights you will happily remember long after a visit"). The "fantastically warm and smart service" and "amazing value" are further reasons why it's so "hard to get into" (and why you "must book at weekends"). / eusebideli.com; eusebi_deli; Mon-Sun midnight.

GA GA £36 322

566 DUMBARTON ROAD G11 6RH 0141 334 9407

"Not to be missed" – "having closed down her majorly successful Southside restaurant Kopitiam, chef Julie Lin (a former MasterChef quarter-finalist) has moved to the West End, in partnership with the local Thornwood Bar" and is now "raising the standard of cooking with her wonderful homely dishes" tapping her own half-Malaysian heritage. / gagaglasgow.com; Tue-Thu, Sun 11 pm, Fri & Sat midnight.

GAMBA £80 342

225A WEST GEORGE ST G2 2ND 0141 572 0899

This "treat of a seafood restaurant" in a centrally located basement is thriving after 25 years on the strength of chef-patron Derek Marshall's "tasty and generally faultless" cooking – no wonder "there has been little attempt to change the basic formula and experiment with new techniques and flavours". Top Menu Tip – the famous "fish soup is superb". / gamba.co.uk; gambaglasgow; Wed-Fri 9 pm, Sat 10 pm.

THE GANNET £57 343

1155 ARGYLE ST G3 8TB 0141 2042081

"The Gannet is towards the top end of Glasgow's gastronomy scene" – a chilled Scotch fine dining venture, in Finnieston, whose "superb food, both vegetarian and non-vegetarian" has won it a firm reputation over the past decade – although "it comes at a price of course" (tasting menu £90 per person and multi-course lunch nudging £40 per person). / thegannetgla.com; thegannetgla; Wed, Fri & Sat, Thu 10.30 pm.

KA PAO £52 33

BOTANIC GARDENS GARAGE, 26 VINICOMBE STREET G12 8BE 0141 483 6990

This fun venue by the Botanical Gardens "continues to be inventive with its pan-Asian fusion", using mainly Scottish produce. "Fish dishes are made to order and brought to your table fresh from the kitchen". Success has led to a second in Edinburgh's St James's Quarter. / ka-pao.com; kapaofeeds; Mon-Sun midnight.

MOTHER INDIA £47 43

28 WESTMINSTER TER G3 8AD 0141 339 9145

Home-style Punjabi dishes arrive in "astonishing quantities and variety" at Monir & Smeena Mohammed's West End curry institution, which has provided "thoroughly decent and tasty meals" for nearly 35 years. / motherindia.co.uk; officialmotherindia; Sun-Thu 9.45 pm, Fri & Sat 10 pm.

111 BY MODOU £59 34

111 CLEVEDEN ROAD G12 0JU 0141 334 0111

"Modou Diagne never ceases to amaze us" – "the strength of his cooking is unsurpassed" and the 'Total Trust' no-choice menu at £25 a head (served on Sunday and Monday nights) is an absolute bargain – even those who found the occasional dish "disappointing" reckon "the concept is good... We'll be back to give it another try". The story behind the chef's rise brings tears to the eyes of hardened reviewers: Modou was a penniless and homele[ss] refugee from Senegal, and worked his way up from kitchen porter under Glasgow chef Nico Simeone (of Six by Nico) to a level where Nico gave him his own restaurant to run. / 111bymodou.co.uk; 111bymodou; Mon, Thu 11 pm, Fri-Sun 11.30 pm.

OX AND FINCH £56 34

920 SAUCHIEHALL ST G3 7TF 0141 339 8627

"Tasty tapas-style food" to share at "very reasonable prices", plus "laid-back and friendl[y] service" draw a "great crowd" to Jonathan MacDonald's "vibrant and funky venue" in Kelvingrove. Top Tip – "try ordering 2 or 3 dishes at a time, as they are brought out as soon as they are ready and arrive in a random order". / oxandfinch.com; oxandfinch; Tue-Sun 1 am, Mon midnight.

AESANO PIZZA £37 5 4 3

MILLER STREET
1DT 0141 258 5565

here's a "wonderful buzz" around Sugo owner ul Stevenson's city-centre pizza joint – also th a West End spin-off; cooked in artisan-ilt, wood-fired ovens imported from Naples, e pizzas are "exceptional", while a "limited enu ensures quality" – and is rounded out, any case, by "always amazing specials" (e.g. ncetta, roasted violet potatoes and fior di te). / paesanopizza.co.uk; paesanopizzaglasgow; n-Thu 10.30 pm, Fri & Sat 11 pm.

HUCKS £59 4 4 3

8 HYNDLAND ROAD
2 9HZ 0141 473 0080

ecommended for seafood, this fish-focused arling from the team behind Cail Bruich ened in the West End of the city in ring 2022 to high acclaim and it receives gh ratings all-round in this year's annual ners' poll (if not yet with a huge volume of edback). "Waiting staff are well informed and tremely hard working" and "the 'Taste of e Sea' tasting menu is excellent value: very voursome and extremely well cooked"; you ed the whole table to order it, but there is à la carte alternative with meat options. p Menu Tip – "kingfish carpaccio was a ghlight". / shucksglasgow.com; shucks_glasgow; on-Sat midnight, Sun 10 pm.

TRAVAIGIN £62 3 3 4

GIBSON ST G12 8NX 0141 334 2665

Continuing its outstanding reputation in the est End, Stravaigin has been given a recent celift, which adds greatly to the ambience" this thirty-year-old landmark of the West nd was sold to new owners the Metropolitan ub Company in 2022 and their investment is eathing new life into this Glaswegian foodie on. Both The Scotsman and The Times viewed it after the change and according to osalind Erskine of the former, "the food and ink… is a lot like the new look, it's a refresh it still recognisable for what it always was, hich will be a comfort to regulars and new sitors alike". / stravaigin.co.uk; stravaigin_g12; on-Sun midnight.

WO FAT LADIES AT THE UTTERY £70 3 3 5

52 ARGYLE ST G3 8UF 0141 221 8188

A clear recommendation when visiting lasgow" – Ryan James' comfortable, d-school fixture occupies an extremely aracterful Victorian building (the site is ought to be Glasgow's oldest culinary tablishment) filled with "awesome antiques". he "very good" and "not overpriced" dishes aw on the rich Scottish larder (and there's "separate vegetarian menu, so worth a visit you've got veggies in your group!"). RIP its est End sibling Two Fat Ladies in the City, hich was still listed on the website as we went press, but has been put up for leasehold since 2022. / twofatladiesrestaurant.com; Mon-Fri 10 pm, Sat 10.30 pm, Sun 9 pm.

UBIQUITOUS CHIP £137 3 3 4

12 ASHTON LN G12 8SJ 0141 334 5007

This large, rambling West End institution was an early-days pioneer of 'Modern Scottish' cuisine and "still represents great Scottish food and character", making it a "fantastic setting for a special occasion at any age". Owned since summer 2022 by Greene King, the UK's largest pub group, it was founded in 1971 by Ronnie Clydesdale, who taught himself to cook while on all-night sentry duty during national service. It quickly became "the first Glasgow restaurant at a standard which you would accept in London", and after Ronnie's death in 2010 was run for a dozen years by his son Colin. / ubiquitouschip.co.uk; ubiquitouschip; Wed-Sun midnight.

UNALOME BY GRAEME CHEEVERS £127 4 3 3

36 KELVINGROVE STREET
G3 7RZ 0141 564 1157

This two-year-old Finnieston venture is the debut as patron from Graeme Cheevers, winning instant acclaim for his "excellent cooking" – he's a "fantastic chef, I've followed him from his days at Martin Wishart's Cameron House" (he also ran the kitchen at the Isle of Eriska Hotel). "The fish courses are particularly good" and there's a "generous and well chosen accompanying wine flight". / unalomebygc.com; unalomebygc; Wed-Sun 10.30 pm.

GLINTON, RUTLAND 6-4A

THE BLUE BELL £57 3 3 3

10 HIGH STREET PE6 7LS 01733 252285

"An ever-dependable gastropub in a delightful village north of Peterborough" – Will and Kelly Frankgate have run this attractively extended property for over 10 years now. It serves a menu of high-quality fare, supplemented by some "mostly Italian" dishes. / thebluebellglinton.co.uk; Wed & Thu 10 pm, Fri & Sat 11 pm, Sun 8 pm.

GOATHLAND, NORTH YORKSHIRE 8-4C

THE HOMESTEAD KITCHEN £51 4 3 3

PRUDOM HOUSE
YO22 5AN 01947 896191

Peter Neville made his name in these parts with venues including The Pheasant in Harome, which he co-owns; in 2021, he and partner Cecily Fearnley upped sticks to her home village to open this converted farmhouse restaurant (plus on-site holiday cottage), and by all accounts it's a "lovely spot" amidst the moors, whose "beautifully presented" local/seasonal cooking wins consistently high ratings. / thehomesteadgoathland.com; homestead_goathland; Wed-Sat 8.30 pm, Sun 3.30 pm.

GOLDSBOROUGH, NORTH YORKSHIRE 8-4B

GOLDSBOROUGH HALL £110 3 3 4

CHURCH ST HG5 8NR 01423 867321

"High-quality dining in the elegant, opulent surroundings of this former home of Princess Mary" – a sixteenth-century country house hotel with "beautiful" landscaped gardens. By day or night, "there is only a tasting menu" ("extremely good value", "tasting as good as it looks") in the dining room, but they've recently added a more casual 'Tapas on the Terrace' option, too. / goldsboroughhall.com; Wed-Sat 8.30 pm, Sun 2 pm.

GOUDHURST, KENT 3-4C

THE SMALL HOLDING £104 5 4 4

RANTERS LANE, KILNDOWN
TN17 2SG 01892 890105

A visit to this "lovely restaurant way out in the country" is "like a trip to the theatre only better – with amazing cooking" on "a top-value tasting menu". "Dishes are often surprising – I love that much of the produce is from the garden or nearby", in line with Kent-born chef-patron Will Devlin's ultra-local and sustainable ethos. He also runs Birchwood, a daytime venue in the nearby Flimwell Park sustainable woodland development, but was forced to close The Curlew in Bodiam due to rising costs in late 2022. / thesmallholding.restaurant; the_small_holding_; Wed-Sun 8.30 pm.

GRANDTULLY, PERTH AND KINROSS 9-3C

THE GRANDTULLY HOTEL BY BALLINTAGGART £46 3 3 3

PH9 0PX 01887 447000

You'll pay "London prices but it's worth it" as "quality shines through" at this "just lovely" restaurant in a newly relaunched 1866 railway hotel, now run by nearby Ballintaggart Farm cookery school. "There's some imaginative cooking here and good use of local and foraged ingredients", along with "very knowledgeable and friendly staff" – although "the bar has more atmosphere and better acoustics than the dining room". / ballintaggart.com; ballintaggart; Mon-Sun 8.30 pm.

GRANTCHESTER, CAMBRIDGESHIRE 3-1B

THE RUPERT BROOKE £60 2 3 4

2 BROADWAY CB3 9NQ 01223 841875

In scenic Grantchester just outside Cambridge, this "modern and not overcrowded" inn makes an attractive run out of town and generates consistent reports of its "decent" cooking. And 'is there honey still for tea?' – as Rupert Brooke famously asked in his 1912 poem set in Grantchester. The answer is a resounding No: the owners seem to have missed a trick with

Shaun Rankin at Grantley Hall, Grantley

their afternoon tea menu. / therupertbrooke.com; therupertbrookeuk; Wed-Sat 9 pm, Sun 5 pm.

GRANTLEY, NORTH YORKSHIRE 8–4B

FLETCHERS AT GRANTLEY HALL £105 344

HG4 3ET 01765 620070

This ultra-opulent seventeenth-century country house was reborn as a hotel in 2019 replete with pool, snow room and altitude training chamber. Its many eateries include a haute operation by former Ormer chef Shaun Rankin – and this tartan-clad, baronial-style brasserie, praised this year for its "amazing welcome and lovely food" (especially patisserie, if you put your trust in Jay Rayner's otherwise slightly mixed 2022 review). / grantleyhall.co.uk; grantleyhall_; Mon-Fri 7 pm, Sat & Sun 5.30 pm.

SHAUN RANKIN AT GRANTLEY HALL £186 544

HG4 3ES 01765 620070

This "handsome old house" makes a "brilliant" showcase for Yorkshire-born chef Shaun Rankin's talents, honed by decades in Jersey and London. Valeria Sykes spent £70 million converting the country pile into a hotel, and given its almost "intimidating" level of luxury naturally "you may need a second mortgage before booking" ("from the iron gates policed by a uniformed guard, along a coiffed drive, we found a forecourt occupied by four Rolls-Royces, a Lamborghini and assorted top-model Range Rovers!"). On all accounts, though, it's "quite outstanding in all respects", not least results from the ten-course 'Taste at Home' menu for £145 per person. / grantleyhall.co.uk; shaunrankinrestaurant; Wed-Sat 8.30 pm, Sun 8 pm.

GRASMERE, CUMBRIA 7–3D

THE FOREST SIDE £171 444

KESWICK ROAD
LA22 9RN 01539 435 250

"Simply outstanding in all areas" – Andrew Wildsmith's "luscious" Lakeland hotel occupies a stone-clad Victorian mansion and it's, say fans, "well worth the hype and prices" thanks to its "wonderful and romantic setting", "exemplary service" and "faultless cuisine" from chef Paul Leonard and his team, all combining to create a "top gastronomic experience" – "we've been going here for several years since it opened, and it gets better and better: worth the journey!" That said, the pricing is a sticking point for some reporters, who feel "it's good but not outstanding judged against the strong local competition, and heartier appetites than mine may not be satisfied". For those of more modest tastes, though, it may be a blessing that you are not constrained to a tasting menu format (although an eight-course menu is available for £140 per person): the entry-level option is a four-course meal for £85 per person. / theforestside.com; the_forest_side; Wed-Sun 9 pm.

THE JUMBLE ROOM £70 334

LANGDALE ROAD
LA22 9SU 01539 435 188

Chrissy & Andy Hill's vibrant Lake District veteran has been turning out "fantastic food" of a relaxed but appealing bent in a "lovely atmosphere" for over two decades now. / thejumbleroom.co.uk; thejumbleroom; Thu-Sat 11 pm.

GREAT GONERBY, LINCOLNSHIRE 5–3D

HARRY'S PLACE £107 443

17 HIGH STREET
NG31 8JS 01476 561780

"Outstanding!" – Harry & Caroline Hallam accommodate a maximum of 10 guests at a time in the "so cosy" front room of their Georgian house: a "long-running and great restaurant". It has been in operation for over 30 years (long before the term 'pop-up' was invented) and most folks have nowadays forgotten that for many years they held a Michelin star (until about 2010). Caroline is front of house, Harry in the kitchen and the menu depends on what Harry has decided to buy that day (you must book ahead). The experience is somewhat dependent on the quantity and personality of fellow diners but – even if the level and tenor of feedback has perhaps become slightly more muted in recent years – no reports this year suggested that the experience remains anything but very good or excellent. / Tue-Sat 9.30 pm.

GREAT HASELEY, OXFORDSHIRE 2–2

LA TABLE D'ALIX AT THE PLOUGH £95 43

RECTORY ROAD
OX44 7JQ 01844 279283

This "very nice old village pub" has been transformed into an "authentic French restaurant" by "fabulous hosts" Antoine & Camille Chretien, who named it after their son. It's a "lovely venue" that "stands out in the area" for its "superb cuisine" – no mean achievement when the next door village is hos to Raymond Blanc's famous Le Manoir aux Quat'Saisons. / latabledalix.co.uk; latabledalix; Thu-Sat 11 pm, Sun 4 pm.

GREAT MILTON, OXFORDSHIRE 2–2

LE MANOIR AUX QUAT' SAISONS, BELMOND £293 35

CHURCH ROAD OX44 7PD 01844 2788

"Romantic, extravagant, memorable… and expensive" – Raymond Blanc's "magical" fifteenth-century manor in a quiet village sout of Oxford remains the most commented-on destination in our annual diners' poll outside London. For some lucky diners, it's "an annua pilgrimage" for "a perfect weekend away" – "lunch can take all afternoon with a wander around the glorious garden" and an overnight stay in one of its cosseting suites contributes to the "best experience ever". Even though it's actually owned by LVMH nowadays, M Blanc himself is still often on-hand and contributes t a hands on approach that's "so professional". And aficionados say that: "yes, you pay a lot o money; yes, some may find it a little less trend in its decor and outlook; and yes, the cooking is in a specific style; but, this is an experience in wellbeing and one of life's treats". All that said, concerns over "gigabucks" pricing were more in evidence in a year that saw some discontinuities in the kitchen as chef Luke Sel took over from Gary Jones. While most report still drooled over "outstanding cuisine that's hard to better", there were more who – while acknowledging "first-world problems" – found the food "underwhelming, having dreamt abo going for years" ("was expecting to be wowed and enchanted like at other top rivals, but I rather found it all rather oversimplistic and non-memorable"). Still, for the majority the verdict remains "an absolute delight from star to finish" – "an indulgent place to dine and stay". / manoir.com; belmondlemanoir; Thu-Sur Mon-Wed 9 pm.

GREAT OXENDON, NORTHUMBERLAND 5–4

THE GEORGE £56 33

HARBOROUGH ROAD
LE16 8NA 01858 465205

Stephen and Tracy Fitzpatrick, who also run The Joiners Arms at Bruntingthorpe, are the winning duo behind this sixteenth-century village inn with four rooms, three miles south of Market Harborough; the wide-ranging menu tips its hat to fish 'n' ips on Friday, and takes in thrice-weekly ıberge Suppers', and there are "lovely rdens to go with the excellent food". Tip p – it's "worth staying for the superb veggie eakfast". / thegeorgegreatoxendon.co.uk; georgegreatoxendon; Mon-Fri 8.30 pm, Sat om, Sun 3 pm.

REAT WALTHAM, ESSEX 3–2C

ALVIN GREEN AN £65 333

OWE ST CM3 1BG 01245 408 820

'he Galvins' rural outpost" – on home turf the Essex-born-and-bred chef brothers – much commented-on: a "great gastropub ep in the countryside", where it's "an sis in an area with very little in the way good eating". The "smartly decorated" ırteenth-century venue is "well worth the p" for its "consistently excellent food", pecial atmosphere" and "lovely views over extensive garden". / galvingreenman.com; vingreenman; Thu, Wed 8 pm, Fri & Sat 10 pm, n 5 pm.

REETHAM, RUTLAND 5–3D

HE WHEATSHEAF £59 342

RETTON RD LE15 7NP 01572 812325

ıis "classy neighbourhood pub/restaurant" a "perennial favourite for quality food, lcome, service and all-round atmosphere ong may it flourish", chorus the many mirers of chef Carol & husband Scott addock's Grade II-listed stone pub, ıere "you dine on the freshest of fish and afood, their own herbs, wild garlic and od-quality locally raised meat". Top Tip 'full marks for the home-baked breads d fancy butters (wild or black garlic are vourites)". / wheatsheaf-greetham.co.uk; eatsheafgreetham; Wed-Sat 11 pm, Sun 7 pm.

RESFORD, WREXHAM 5–3A

ANT-YR-OCHAIN £53 234

D WREXHAM ROAD
12 8TY 01978 853525

xteenth-century inn 'the Pant' (as owners unning & Price fondly call it) occupies a bstantial, "very comfortable" Victorian operty a short drive outside Wrexham; and conversion has created "a great pub: warm d bustling in the winter, loads of outside ace in the summer" and offering a "reliably od beer selection" too. Given its high ındards, the odd reporter this year did quibble th the food, but overall this "very busy" stination remains a "favourite year after ar". / brunningandprice.co.uk; pantyrochain; on-Sat 11 pm, Sun 10.30 pm. SRA – 3 stars

GUILDFORD, SURREY 3–3A

THE IVY ASIA GUILDFORD £103 334

UNIT 23 TUNSGATE QUARTER
GU1 3QT 01483 958880

In the chic Tunsgate Quarter, this "vibey" pan-Asian has set local tongues wagging since its spring 2022 opening; it's a "fun place to visit" – the Ivy Asias being even more flamboyant than Richard Caring's other (brasserie) spin-off chain – and the eclectic mix of Japanese and Chinese inspired dishes is ably abetted by "super serving staff who greet you like their favourite customers". / theivyasiaguildford.com; theivyasia; Mon-Fri midnight, Sun 11 pm.

THE IVY CASTLE VIEW £78 333

TUNSGATE SQUARE, 98-100 HIGH STREET
GU1 3HE 01483 920100

"The view is unbeatable" (and what it overlooks is incorporated into the name) of this highly rated link in Richard Caring's national chain; as for the rest, you can expect the usual "pretty" decor and a "decent menu selection" ("including healthy choices that don't feel like a sacrifice"); "it isn't cheap though, so save it for an occasion". / theivyguildford.com; theivyguildford; Mon-Sun midnight.

RUMWONG £41 333

18-20 LONDON RD
GU1 2AF 01483 536092

This "reliable and busy Thai" has been a highlight of the local dining scene for over 45 years. The comfortable 'Khan Tok' dining room has been revamped, its cushions replaced by lounge seating – and is very popular. / rumwong.co.uk; Tue-Sun 10.30 pm.

GULLANE, EAST LOTHIAN 9–4D

THE BONNIE BADGER £81 333

MAIN STREET EH31 2AA 01626 21111

"What a cracking spot after a round of golf!" say fans of Tom & Michaela Kitchin's East Lothian outpost, which is handy for nearby Muirfield. It serves "excellent food, and an amazing breakfast if you stay overnight". / bonniebadger.com; bonniebadgergullane; Sun-Thu 11 pm, Fri & Sat 12 pm.

GULVAL, CORNWALL 1–4B

TREMENHEERE KITCHEN £60 333

TREMENHEERE SCULPTURE GARDENS
TR20 8YL 01736 448089

Set within a "beautiful sculpture park" outside Penzance hosting works by art-world stars James Turrell and Richard Long amongst others, this pleasant eight-year-old restaurant offers an "excellent selection of vegetarian dishes" (but not just) and classic cream teas. Stop in for the "lovely brunch and then walk it off" in the grounds – or else grab a takeaway from their hut, and picnic on the hill with views of St Michael's Mount. / tremenheerekitchen.com; Mon-Thu 3 pm, Fri & Sat 8.30 pm, Sun 4 pm.

GULWORTHY, DEVON 1–3C

THE HORN OF PLENTY, COUNTRY HOUSE HOTEL & RESTAURANT £88 333

COUNTRY HOUSE HOTEL & RESTAURANT
PL19 8JD 01822 832528

Expanded over its 50 years in operation – now to 16 rooms – this converted mansion on the Devon/Cornwall border enjoys good views of the Tamar Valley from its dining room. Dinner is a three-course table d'hôte or you can opt for the (only somewhat more expensive) six-course tasting menu for £85 per person. It was well-rated all round this year. / thehornofplenty.co.uk; the_hornofplenty; Mon-Sun 10 pm.

HAIGHTON GREEN, LANCASHIRE 5–1B

HAIGHTON MANOR £36 323

HAIGHTON GREEN LANE
PR2 5SQ 01772 706350

This crowd-pleasing pub once served as a hospital, but since its takeover and refurb' by the Brunning & Price group some years back, it's now a proper country gastroboozer (also with a handful of rooms); on the menu – high-quality British dishes abetted by some more exotic influences from around the world. / brunningandprice.co.uk; haightonmanor; Mon-Sun 11 pm. SRA – 3 stars

HALE, GREATER MANCHESTER 5–

CIBO £66

6-10 VICTORIA RD
WA15 9AF 0161 503 5022

"Book ahead" if you want to visit this "favourite in Hale" (a standby of Sir Alex Ferguson, Cristiano Ronaldo and myriad influencers hoping to bump into them). While the glam factor is certainly paramount – not least on the leafy rooftop terrace – its solid Italian cooking certainly doesn't hurt. The owners also run Disley's Sasso restaurant, and a sibling in Wilmslow, where they're shortly to launch a grand café. Too few reports for a reliable rating, but all positive. / ciborestaurants.co.uk; Mon-Sat 11 pm, Sun 10 pm.

SIGIRIYA £61 332

173 ASHLEY ROAD
WA15 9SD 0161 941 3025

Don Buddhika's accomplished operation in this fancy Manchester suburb delivers "delicious Sri Lankan food that's perfectly cooked", whether you opt for the small plates, curries or grills – many being notably healthy to boot; it's named for the imposing Sri Lankan Buddhist settlement Sigiriya rock. / sigiriya.co.uk; Tue, Sun 10 pm, Wed & Thu 10.30 pm, Fri & Sat 11 pm.

HALIFAX, WEST YORKSHIRE 5–1C

SHIBDEN MILL INN £66 454

SHIBDEN MILL FOLD
HX3 7UL 01422 365840

"A real must-try with a lovely convivial atmosphere", this historic former mill combines a "dining room and bar in heavy, dark wood that feels like it hasn't changed much since the eighteenth century and the days of the BBC's Gentleman Jack" (which was filmed here) with "food that's much more modern (though retaining a Yorkshire heartiness)" from "very talented and inventive chef Will Webster". There's also a "fabulous wine list, with many offered by the glass". / shibdenmillinn.com; shibdenmillinn; Mon-Fri 11 pm, Sat 11.30 pm, Sun 10.30 pm.

HALL GREEN, WEST MIDLANDS 5–4C

RAJA MONKEY £26 333

1355 STRATFORD ROAD
B28 9HW 0121 777 9090

This modern Indian street food restaurant (run by the Lasan Group) inspires only a limited amount of feedback, but such as we have suggests it's a very good bet in this leafy burb. It must be doing something right, as in 2023 they announced the opening of a spin-off in Harborne. / rajamonkey.co.uk; rajamonkey; Tue-Thu 10 pm, Fri & Sat 11 pm, Sun 9 pm.

HAMBLETON, RUTLAND 5–4D

FINCH'S ARMS £51 223

OAKHAM RD LE15 8TL 01572 756575

"A lovely old pub in the bar and more ancient parts (the newer additions are slightly less appealing – tip: avoid the dining room and stay in the original section if you can!)" – this characterful inn with its great Rutland Water setting put in a "less checkered" performance this year. That said, standards can still be "more ordinary than in the past – pleasant enough" and "readers are advised to be cautious in their expectations!". "Beautiful walks for after a meal though!" / finchsarms.co.uk; thefinchsarms; Mon-Sat 9 pm, Sun 6 pm.

HAMBLETON HALL £156 445

LE15 8TH 01572 756991

The "quintessential country house" – Tim & Steffa Hart's fine property was owned by the Hoare banking family prior to its conversion into a hotel; and long predates the 1970s reservoir over which it nowadays provides "stunning views". That it's "pleasantly old-fashioned" (or, if you prefer, rather old-school) is intrinsic to its charm. The "hushed tones in the dining room might not suit everybody", but can provide "a perfect setting in which to enjoy a significant occasion, with magnificent service and a glorious setting". Chef Aaron Paterson has overseen the kitchen for over thirty years now: and his classical cuisine remains "superb" (if "very expensive"). And it's matched with a "varied and well-chosen wine list, backed up by the excellent Dominique Baduel (Sommelier) who is always happy to recommend and advise". Stay the night and there are "excellent English breakfasts cooked to order". Top Menu Tip – "highlights this year included marinated scallops with a fennel and cucumber essence; gazpacho with celery granita; and slow-cooked octopus with squid ink pasta, chorizo, lemongrass and ginger". / hambletonhall.com; hambleton_hall; Mon-Sun 8.45 pm.

HAMPTON-IN-ARDEN, WEST MIDLANDS 5–4C

GRACE & SAVOUR £149 444

HAMPTON MANOR, SHADOWBROOK LANE
B92 0EN 01675 446080

"A unique setting in a building in the garden area of Hampton Manor, and a dining area that's spacious and modern and crisp" both help inspire a wave of superlatives for this hip yearling, built into the walled Victorian garden of Hampton Manor (and, according to The FT in April 2023, an 'epicurean delight' that's already 'a byword for chic sustainability'). It didn't win top ratings in our annual diners' poll due to the odd accusation that "it may have grace, but definitely lacked flavour! (the surroundings were stunning but the food was not worth the trip"). That's very much a minority view of chef David Taylor's cuisine, though – more commonly it's acclaimed as "an exceptional dining experience with a 15-course tasting menu for £155 per person made up of finely judged, precisely prepared, often original dishes" ("modern British cooking at its best – the mushroom broth was my favourite dish of the year"). / hamptonmanor.com; hamptonmanor; Thu-Sat midnight.

SMOKE AT HAMPTON MANOR 334

SHADOWBROOK LANE
B92 0EN 01675 446080

This "atmospheric restaurant" serves "excellent, very tasty and well-presented dishes" cooked over fire – appropriately in an old Victorian furnace house in the walled garden of Hampton Manor ("close to Grace & Savour and a short distance from the Manor itself"). Head chef Stuart Deeley won MasterChef: The Professionals in 2019. / hamptonmanor.com; hamptonmanor; Wed-Sat 10.30 pm, Sun 4 pm.

HARLYN, CORNWALL 1–3B

THE PIG AT HARLYN BAY £83 334

PL28 8SQ 01841 550240

The "stunning location" of a 15th-century manor house near Padstow ensures this Cornwall venue is among the most popular in Robin Hutson's shabby-chic Pig hotel group, helped by its "wood-paneled dining room oozing history, with friendly and helpful staff and great food" – including vegetables grown in the 200-year-old kitchen garden along with fish and seafood sourced nearby. There's also the 'Lobster Hut', a "slick indoor/outdoor restaurant", serving "reliable food" under canvas. / thepighotel.com; the_pig_hotels; Mon-Sun 9.30 pm.

HAROME, NORTH YORKSHIRE 8–4

THE PHEASANT HOTEL £88 34

YO62 5JG 01439 771241

"If you want a hotel with a really good restaurant, this is the place for you" – Jacquie Pern's "slightly formal" but reliably "quality" venture, occupies a "lovely setting" in a North Yorks village. "With the terrible fire at The Star Inn (next door, and run by Pern's ex-husband), the Pheasant was taking the lead in looking after dining for the two operations" – but thankfully the Star reopened in Nov 2022, a year after it was laid low by an arson attack. / thepheasanthotel.com; thepheasant_ho Mon-Sun 9 pm.

THE STAR INN £101 34

HAROME YO62 5JE 01439 770397

"Back after the terrible fire which is great news!" – Andrew Pern's famous pub in rural Yorkshire is, say fans, "back at the top of its game" and – having "recently refurbished" out of necessity is "everything a top restaurant should be". One of the top 100 most commented-on destinations outside London in our annual diners' poll: "it's not really a pub" anymore and the interior is "as beautiful as the food": "delicious cooking, using mainly local produce". It would have scored even higher ratings this year, were it not for a couple of reporters who felt the offering didn't live up to its high billing, but even they still rated it decently well. And most regulars are just plain delighted to have it bac "I make the pilgrimage there from London twice a year and have done so since 2004. It is just a fantastic all-round experience that never disappoints!" / thestaratharome.co.uk; thestarinnatharome; Tue-Sat 11 pm, Sun 7 pm.

HARPENDEN, HERTFORDSHIRE 3–2

LUSSMANNS £55 23

20A LEYTON ROAD
AL5 2HU 01582 965393

"One of a small chain of reasonably priced eateries in Hertfordshire specialising in sustainability and quality ingredients", born off the Portobello Road in 2002; even if it's not hitting its original heights, by all accounts "you're on safe ground" at the eighteenth-century converted coach house (fish is particularly rated) and fans just "love the outside courtyard space" too. / lussmanns.com lussmanns; Tue-Thu 9 pm, Fri & Sat 10 pm, Sun 8.30 pm.

THE SILVER CUP £96 34

5 ST ALBANS ROAD
AL5 2JF 01582 713095

"The best food in the culinary desert that is Harpenden" (including "a really delightful tasting menu" rounded out by "pub dishes – pricey, but beautifully presented and well ought-out"), awaits at local lads Matthew ader (chef) and Michael Singleton's imagined pub", on the edge of the mmon. Both the "creative menu and friendly vice from the young team belong in a more market situation than what is essentially a ozer" (also with four rooms) – impressive a venue in these 'burbs. / thesilvercup.co.uk; silvercup; Tue-Sat 11 pm, Sun 9 pm.

ARROGATE, NORTH YORKSHIRE 5–1C

ETTYS £43 345

PARLIAMENT STREET
G1 2QU 01423 814070

Yorkshire "legend" – "the epitome of an l-fashioned afternoon tea room, and with great pianist too". "You might have a long it in the queue to get in, but it's worth for the "delicious pastries and well-filled ndwiches" served at this flagship of a mily-owned business founded in 1919, w with five venues across North Yorkshire. laces that are described as an 'institution' e often a stuffy, stilted let-down – Betty's is ne of the above": "even the fish 'n' chips are lish". / bettys.co.uk; bettys; Mon-Sun 5 pm.

ETTYS GARDEN CAFÉ, HS GARDENS HARLOW ARR £42 434

RAG LANE, BECKWITHSHAW
G3 1QB 01423 505604

is outpost of the celebrated Yorkshire arooms has "more space than the branch in e centre of Harrogate" and a fine location verlooking a wonderful garden" (the RHS rdens at Harlow Carr); add in "good food" nging from pastries and cakes to more hearty pasts and it makes "a good place to meet siness colleagues and friends". / bettys.co.uk; on-Sun 5 pm.

LOCKTOWER RESTAURANT, UDDING PARK HOTEL 233

JDDING PK, FOLLIFOOT
G3 1JH 01423 871350

tached to a luxurious spa hotel, this modern asserie is open all day (with other options in e hotel being the more ambitious Horto, or ernoon tea in the Conservatory). One fan tes it as a good place for a relaxed business eal, but there is also the odd concern that its ood ambience can be let down by average sults at excessive prices". / ruddingpark.co.uk; ddingparkhotel; Tue-Sun 9 pm, Mon 10 pm.

RUM & MONKEY £59 443

MONTPELLIER GDNS
G1 2TF 01423 502650

is "amazingly busy" Montpellier Quarter teran (est. 1971) is "just as good as it's always en" – credit to Ray & June Carter, who've erseen it for a decade (and have also run e Sportsman's Arms, Wath-in-Nidderdale, r three). The "very interesting and delicious enu" spotlights "fish cooked absolutely ght" – "try the queenies (aka queen scallops) followed by fish pie". / drumandmonkey.co.uk; drumandmonkeyhgte; Mon-Fri 9 pm, Sat 9.30 pm.

JINNAHS £37 233

34 CHELTENHAM PARADE
HG1 1DB 01423 563333

Named after the founder of Pakistan, the Harrogate branch of this five-strong Yorkshire chain has been offering "interesting Kashmiri" fare in the setting of a converted school for 25 years; there's a "wide choice" of dishes on the menu – so large, in fact, that one reporter this year "took an eternity to select dishes". / jinnahharrogate.co.uk; jinnahharrogate; Sun-Thu 10.30 pm, Fri & Sat 11 pm.

ORCHID £56 332

28 SWAN ROAD HG1 2SE 01423 560 425

Ignore the "dated surroundings", this well-known local institution under the Studley Hotel "continues to deliver a first-class experience" after more than two decades, and "never lets you down" with its "amazing pan-Asian cooking", "matched by high-quality service and a good wine selection". "Whenever we visit Harrogate we make a bee-line for this restaurant". / orchidrestaurant.co.uk; studleyandorchid; Sun-Thu 8.30 pm, Fri & Sat 9.30 pm.

ROYAL BATHS £44 334

CENTRAL HALL, CRESCENT RD
HG1 2WJ 01423 536888

"Fantastic surroundings" – the owners spent an eye-watering £1.5 million transforming the Royal Baths into this upscale restaurant – and a "really nice feel and vibe at all times" set this two-year-old apart from the competition; the contemporary and trad Cantonese food is also worthwhile. "We still prefer Orchid, but this place has great decor!" / royalbathschineserestaurant.co.uk; Mon-Sun 9 pm.

SASSO £57 344

8-10 PRINCES SQUARE
HG1 1LX 01423 508 838

This "excellent Italian restaurant" is "a real treat to visit", with a menu of "well presented food" from Emilia Romagna. Its founding chef-patron Stefano Lancellotti, a well-known figure in Harrogate, died suddenly last summer, soon after celebrating the venue's 25th anniversary; his son Nico subsequently joined the team with a view to carrying on the family tradition. / sassorestaurant.co.uk; Mon-Thu 9 pm, Sat, Fri 10 pm.

SPICE CULTURE £34 332

31 CHELTENHAM CRESCENT
HG1 1DH 01423 500021

This "small" Indian of recent vintage is the first venture from a team with extensive restaurant experience in India, Dubai and the U.K. Reporters "love" the tapas-style formula, extending to well-known favourites plus more unusual northern Indian items (and all "a cut above the usual"). / spiceculture.co.uk; spicecultureuk; Mon-Sat 11 pm.

STARLING £23 333

47 OXFORD STREET
HG1 1PW 01423 531310

"Increased in size" – this "dog friendly" bar/café/kitchen is "still best in class locally despite the new look and expansion" and makes "the perfect location for working, socialising and relaxing". Expect "Darkwoods coffee, great value breakfasts and brunches, and the friendliest service" plus a selection of beers (10 craft keg taps and 6 cask hand pulls on the bar), pizzas and poutine (Quebec comfort food mixing chips, gravy and cheese) but with a Yorkshire twist. / murmurationbars.co.uk; starlinghgte; Mon-Sun 9 pm.

STUZZI £53 333

46B KINGS ROAD
HG1 5JW 01423 705852

"Well worth a visit", an Italian small plates spot (also with a Leeds spin-off), whose "regularly changing menu goes a little off-piste" at times but is "usually great"; it's "buzzy and great fun for an informal night out" (an especially fun night if you try the "exceptional" Negronis). / stuzzi.co.uk; Wed-Sat 9 pm, Sun 6 pm.

SUKHOTHAI 333

17-19 CHELTENHAM PDE
HG1 1DD 01423 500 869

Leeds entrepreneur, Ban Kaewkraikhot's local outpost is a large, modern and fairly glam venue that wins praise as a "busy restaurant with very consistent cooking". "Don't publicise the fact that it's your birthday!" if you don't want a fair amount of fuss… / sukhothai.co.uk; sukhothai_; Sun-Thu 10 pm, Fri & Sat 11 pm.

THE TANNIN LEVEL £64 333

5 RAGLAN ST HG1 1LE 01423 560595

In business for nearly four decades now (est. 1985), this stalwart operation occupies a cosy cellar space in the lower ground of a solid Victorian mansion in the city centre (with a small outside seating area for warmer days). The well-rated, traditional-ish cuisine has something of a meat and steak bias; despite the name, the wine list is not huge, but offers quality vintages from a range of countries up to a little over £100 per bottle. / tanninlevel.co.uk; tanninlevel; Mon-Fri 9 pm, Sat 9.30 pm, Sun 4 pm.

HARROW, GREATER LONDON 3–3A

MUMBAI LOCAL £44 333

207 STATION ROAD
HA1 2TP 020 8427 7960

"All the classic Indian veggie favourites" (chaat, dosas, thalis) are on the menu at this meat-free sibling of a Wembley original, and the "delicious, zingy food" is "great value" too. / mumbailocal.co.uk; mumbailocaluk; Mon-Sun 10 pm.

HARWICH, ESSEX 3–2D

THE PIER AT HARWICH £62 233

THE QUAY CO12 3HH 01255 241212

"Another from the Milsoms' stable" (whose flagship is The Talbooth at Dedham), this delightful small hotel dating from 1860 has a dining room that is "fish-focused to reflect the setting", on the historic Harwich waterfront. / milsomhotels.com; pieratharwich; Mon-Sun 11 pm.

HASTINGS, EAST SUSSEX 3–4C

THE CROWN HASTINGS £47 334

64 - 66 ALL SAINTS STREET TN34 3BN 01424 465100

"A tasty range of dishes" made from "simple ingredients treated with respect and creativity" is the recipe for happy dining at this "busy" and well commented-on pub in Hastings Old Town. Tess & Andrew Swan celebrate 10 years as owners this year, having created "a very pleasant environment" – they're "really trying to push things, and succeeding". / thecrownhastings.co.uk; thecrownhastings; Mon-Sat 11 pm, Sun 10.30 pm.

MAGGIE'S £30 442

ROCK-A-NORE ROAD TN34 3DW 01424 430205

This family-run chippy in a wooden shack right on the town's fishermen's beach is now in its third decade, and wins plaudits for its "excellent fresh seafood", straight off the boat. "Friendly staff" and "generous portions" make it a "great location for a family seaside lunch" – although it's at its "best when not too busy". "Booking is highly recommended – you may have to wait for a dull midweek in the 'off' season to get a walk-in table!" / maggiesfishandchips.co.uk; maggiesfishandchipshastings; Tue-Sat 8 pm, Sun & Mon 4 pm.

ROCK A NORE KITCHEN £44 443

23A ROCK-A-NORE RD TN34 3DW 01424 433764

This "tiny converted fisherman's hut by the harbour" serves "amazing fish, straight off the beach-launched day boats, so it couldn't be fresher". "Exceptional cooking" is backed up by a "delightful owner", "brilliant service" and a "very good wine list". Not surprisingly, it's "essential to book". / rockanorekitchen.com; Fri & Sat 10 pm, Sun 3.30 pm.

WEBBE'S ROCK-A-NORE £54 333

1 ROCK-A-NORE ROAD TN34 3DW 01424 721650

East Sussex luminary (and foraging pioneer) Paul Webbe's Old Town venture (est. 2009) offers "a good selection of mainly seafood to reflect its position on the seafront (but also meat and veggie dishes for those who need them)". "Friendly service and a reasonable atmosphere" contribute to its continuing success. / webbesrestaurants.co.uk; RockaNoreWebbes; Tue-Thu 9 pm, Fri & Sat 9.30 pm, Sun 8.30 pm.

HATFIELD PEVEREL, ESSEX 3–2C

THE BLUE STRAWBERRY £61 334

THE STREET CM3 2DW 01245 381333

You "can't go wrong" at this stalwart off the A12, where a rendered timbered façade gives way to a conservatory and covered patio. For over two decades it has been turning out traditional and consistent cuisine and, as ever, "the Beef Wellington is the pick of the menu". / bluestrawberrybistro.co.uk; bluestrawberrybistrot; Mon-Sat midnight, Sun 5 pm.

HAY-ON-WYE, HEREFORDSHIRE 2–1A

CHAPTERS £67 444

LION STREET HR3 5AA 07855 783799

"Highly recommend if you are around Hay on Wye" – a "small but perfectly formed restaurant" which puts its emphasis on "very locally sourced dishes that are well prepared" from a "carefully-put-together tasting menu" (five courses for £60 per person) "with unexpected but lovely flavour combinations". / chaptershayonwye.co.uk; chapters_hayonwye; Wed-Sat 9 pm.

HAYFIELD, DERBYSHIRE 5–2C

THE PACK HORSE £71 433

3-5 MARKET STREET SK22 2EP 01663 749126

It's "well worth a trip out" to the Peak District National Park to find this "exceptional" small village gastroboozer; chef Luke Payne's "upmarket food with a northern twist" has won the seal of approval from many a national restaurant critic, and there are excellent walks from the door. / thepackhorsehayfield.uk; thepackhorsehayfield; Wed-Sat 9 pm, Sun 7 pm.

HEBDEN BRIDGE, WEST YORKSHIRE 5–1C

COIN HEBDEN 333

ALBERT STREET HX7 8AH 01422 847707

A "great fit-out" of a former bank has resulted in this very cool destination, run by two alumni of the Moorcock Inn at Sowerby Bridge. It's "a lovely place to while away a couple of hours" (in the company of your canine if you like), where the concise menu revolves around punchy and "great small plates, including charcuterie and cheese" and there's "a dependable wine list too". / coinhebden.co.uk; coinhebden; Wed & Thu 10 pm, Fri & Sat 11 pm, Sun 6 pm.

HECKFIELD, HAMPSHIRE 2–3

MARLE, HECKFIELD PLACE £118 33

HECKFIELD PLACE RG27 0LD 0118 932 6868

Aussie chef Skye Gyngell's "ambitious establishment" – a Georgian country house dining room in a "beautiful location" overlooking a lake and parkland. They are "very conscious of their environmental responsibility", with "almost all ingredients locally grown or reared" and served in pared-back style. But while it received strong ratings all-round for its luxury hotel setting, a couple of reports did note "a feeling one has to be on one's best behaviour!" / heckfieldplace.com heckfield_place; Mon-Sun 10 pm.

HELFORD PASSAGE, CORNWALL 1–4

THE FERRYBOAT INN £54 33

TR11 5LB 01326 250625

"People come for the glorious view" over the Helford estuary at this "lovely pub", in a three-century-old building – accessible either by car, in which case you risk battling for a space, or "on the foot ferry from the other side of the Helford river"; despite the "beautiful setting", it's no one-trick pony, and the "above-average pub food" includes "great local fresh fish but also a superb and original take on chicken schnitzel and vegetarian choices full of originality and flavour". / ferryboatcornwall.co.uk; Mon-Sat 10 pm, Sun 6 pm.

HELMSLEY, NORTH YORKSHIRE 8–4

BANTAM £36

8 BRIDGE ST. YO62 5BG 01439 77047

This relaxed market town bistro turns out son "very tasty" Mediterranean-inspired plates w pleasingly little primping; it's run by Yorkshire boy Sam Varley, whose very wide-ranging CV spans Soho's Duck Soup and the celebrated Kinneuchar Inn in Fife. Unusually, there's als a "hatch for good burgers to eat al fresco". Too few reports for a rating, but all rate it well. / bantamrestaurant.co.uk; Wed-Sat 3 pm, Tue 9 pm.

HENLEY-IN-ARDEN, WARWICKSHIRE 5–4

THE MOUNT BY GLYNN PURNELL £66 42

97 HIGH STREET B95 5AT 01564 79213

This year-old operation in a 200-year-old Hig Street building from the 'Yummy Brummie' chef serves "typically delicious Glynn Purnell food" – "well-cooked, high-quality versions of (often) familiar pub dishes" – and is already tipped as "the place to go to in Henley". Seve reporters point out that "the garden (weather permitting) and pub areas are preferable to the main dining room", which "can be noisy". / themountpub.co.uk; themountpubhenl Wed-Fri 8.30 pm, Sat 9 pm, Sun 4 pm.

ENLEY-ON-THAMES, OXFORDSHIRE 3–3A

ISTRO AT THE BOATHOUSE, HE BOATHOUSE £78 334

E BOATHOUSE
9 1AZ 01491 577937

erhaps the best located restaurant on the hames" in these parts provides a "great er view and a good buzz". Run by Shuan cken, it provides an all-day menu that offers easygoing selection of straightforward shes, especially a "top breakfast". It used offer fancier fare, though, and the odd porter feels the ambition is a little "basic" wadays. / bistroattheboathouse.co.uk; stroattheboathouse; Wed-Sat 8.30 pm, Sun 30 pm, Mon 2.30 pm.

HE GREYHOUND £67 333

ALLOWSTREE RD, PEPPARD COMMON
9 5HT 0118 972 2227

short drive from Henley, Antony & Jay orrall Thompson's attractive gastropub rves a globally inspired menu with rgers and steaks a highlight of the lection. Fans – including those on a trip t of 'the smoke' – rate it as a "reliable" stination. / awtgreyhound.com; awtawtawt; ed-Sat midnight, Sun 5 pm.

HE LITTLE ANGEL 335

EMENHAM LN RG9 2LS 01491 411 008

his "very old pub in a great location next Henley Bridge" has been a scenic boozer r yonks, but now comes in a "fabulous new carnation", having been taken over by asoned restaurateurs Matt Dockray and Phil enner, who relaunched in late 2022. The gely stylish interior (not least in the vaulted ning room, strewn with trinkets) makes it "great place for a first date", and there are sitive early reports on the elevated pub assics by head chefs Joshua Wilde and George 'Leary – both previously senior sous-chefs at om Kerridge's Marlow joints The Coach, and he Hand and Flowers. / thelittleangel.co.uk; elittleangelhenley; Mon-Sat 9 pm, Sun 5 pm.

ILLA MARINA £65 333

THAMESIDE RG9 1BH 01491 575262

t on the water by the town bridge over e Thames, a "typically old-school" outfit at's "family-run", "long-established" and xcellent value for money" for what is uthentic Italian food"; you dine in a smart, ed room with a "nice buzz" and "well-paced rvice". / villamarina-henley.com; villamarina_ nley; Tue-Sat 10 pm, Sun 9 pm.

HEREFORD, HEREFORDSHIRE 2–1B

EEFY BOYS £33 533

LD MARKET HR4 9HU 01432 359209

defy anyone to find a more yummy, juicy urger" than those produced at this high-hieving Hereford independent, launched a quartet of local burger fanatics in 2015, and now with venues in Shrewsbury and Cheltenham. Early success in competitions, including second place at the 2015 world championship in Las Vegas, was no flash in the grill: their 'The Old Boy' won burger of the year at the 2023 UK National Burger Awards, while Beefy Boy Anthony Murphy was declared chef of the year. / thebeefyboys.com; thebeefyboys; Mon-Sat 9.30 pm, Sun 8.30 pm.

CASTLE HOUSE RESTAURANT, CASTLE HOUSE HOTEL £73 323

CASTLE ST HR1 2NW 01432 356321

"A lovely setting – tucked away in a quiet-but-central location" beside the remains of Hereford's castle moat adds to the joys of the Watkins family's Grade II-listed Georgian hotel. Reports are limited, but all approve the cooking from Hungarian-born chef Gabor Katona (with much produce from the owners' farm at Ballingham Hall, nearby). / castlehse.co.uk; castlehousehotel; Wed-Sat 4 pm, Sun 3 pm.

HESWALL, MERSEYSIDE 5–2A

BURNT TRUFFLE £61 343

104-106 TELEGRAPH ROAD
CH60 0AQ 0151 342 1111

"A top Sunday roast" is but one attraction of Gary Usher's Wirral fixture – the original follow-up to Chester's Sticky Walnut, which opened in 2015 in this Grade-II sandstone building; and which follows the format of its predecessor. Most reports rate its appealing modern bistro cuisine between "very good" and "outstanding", but ratings slipped a tad this year on the odd report of an "off night". / burnttruffle.net; burnt_truffle; Wed & Thu 9 pm, Fri & Sat 10 pm, Sun 5 pm.

HETTON, NORTH YORKSHIRE 5–1B

THE ANGEL £104 443

BD23 6LT 01756 730263

"The original gastropub" – this North Yorks inn has been famous for decades for cuisine that's unusually accomplished for a pub (featuring, for example, in The Trip, in 2010) and was purchased in 2018 by current owner Michael Wignall, who swept aside its former old-fashioned looks in favour of a stylish, if perhaps "clinical" new interior ("I've lost an old friend, but found a bright, young thing!"). All reports agree that he has successfully re-established the place on the UK's foodie map: the "really interesting and unusual cooking features some unusual pairings and over three hours engaging staff popped up everywhere and are willing to discuss the food, its preparation and its great presentation, all at a very reasonable price". At dinner, choose from a three-course menu for £110 per person, or there's a nine-course tasting option for £165 per person. / angelhetton.co.uk; angelathetton; Mon, Fri-Sun, Thu 8 pm.

HEXHAM, NORTHUMBERLAND 8–2A

THE BEAUMONT £49 343

BEAUMONT STREET
NE46 3LT 01434 602331

"Fun restaurant serving excellent food" from an open kitchen in a classic Victorian hotel in the town centre that has been cleverly modernised in recent years. "It's a super place to stay, too (and the breakfast is good)". / thebeaumonthexham.co.uk; thebeaumonthexham.

BOUCHON BISTROT £57 344

4-6 GILESGATE NE46 3NJ 01434 609943

Loire Valley native Greg Bureau's "reliable, welcoming and brilliant value" neighbourhood staple, where the "authentic" bistro-style cooking means it "really is like being in France". As per France, you're "not expected to rush a meal" and a recent refurb' has added more joy in the form of a flashy glass balcony. / bouchonbistrot.co.uk; Bouchonbistrot; Tue-Sat 9.15 pm.

THE RAT INN £67 334

ANICK NE46 4LN 014 3460 2814

This "delightful old inn" with a conservatory is "good for lunch with a view" over the Tyne Valley; a "short blackboard announces half a dozen starters and mains" – "all tasty" and "not your normal pub grub" (no surprise given that chef Phil Mason and wife Karen, who took over the venue in 2007, used to run the Michelin-starred Green Room nearby). / theratinn.com; theratinn; Tue-Sat 8 pm, Sun 3 pm.

HINTLESHAM, SUFFOLK 3–1D

HINTLESHAM HALL £91 334

HINTLESHAM IP8 3NS 01473 652334

This "impressive" Grade I listed country house in Suffolk dates from the reign of Henry IV and is a "glorious hotel to stay in". It is sometimes said to be "uninspiring given the pricing", but the majority of accounts this year were upbeat, hailing cuisine "worthy of its late owner, Robert Carrier" – who was a famous TV chef in the 1970s – "but up-to-date and interesting". Dip your toe in the water one afternoon, for the "large tea, with excellent scones, served in a lovely old hall". / hintleshamhall.co.uk; hintleshamhall; Mon-Sun 9 pm.

HITCHIN, HERTFORDSHIRE 3–2A

THE FARMHOUSE AT REDCOATS £55 223

REDCOATS GREEN
SG4 7JR 01438 729500

The "beautiful, charming setting" and "smart atmosphere" of this farmhouse hotel less than half an hour from London win general applause, and "in an area which is something of a desert in respect of 'fine dining', it provides cooking that's a notch above the usual gastropub fare". "On a warm summer's day, a table in the garden is ideal for a long, relaxed lunch". / farmhouseatredcoats.co.uk; farmhouse redcoats; Mon-Sat 9 pm, Sun 4 pm.

KAZOKU 332

36 BANCROFT SG5 1LA 07438 853471

This "crowded" and "noisy" outfit, featuring hanging lanterns and a water window, turns out "very tasty Japanese food", with "excellent value for money" bento boxes their calling card, though the sushi and sashimi are also "delightfully fresh". Top Tip – "this restaurant is tiny so you will need to book ahead". / kazoku.hitchin; Wed-Sat 9.30 pm, Sun 9 pm.

HODNET, SHROPSHIRE 5–3B

THE BEAR INN £58 433

DRAYTON ROAD TF9 3NH 01630 685214

Mel & Martin Board, who reinvented the Haughmond Inn at Upton Magna, have worked wonders since taking on this village pub-with-rooms, opposite a Norman church, two years back. The "beautifully refurbished" (to the tune of £2 million) venue's food "has also gone up a considerable notch", offering "inventive" and "excellent value" locally sourced British grub with greens from the 200-year-old walled garden of Hodnet Hall. While it "still caters for a local clientele", perhaps not for long, after critic William Sitwell's glowing review (headline "civilisation has hope"). / thebearinnhodnet.com; thebearinnhodnet; Wed-Sat, Tue 8.30 pm.

HOLKHAM, NORFOLK 6–3C

THE VICTORIA AT HOLKHAM, HOLKHAM HALL £69 224

. NR23 1RG 01328 711008

The attractive dining room of this ivy-clad independent hotel on the Holkham Estate, not far from the beach, has a focus on locally sourced food that mirrors the estate's ambitions in the sustainability stakes. In keeping with the tenor of reports over the years, the food continues to be "a little hit-and-miss, but it's a terrific setting and the service is usually reliable" at least. / holkham.co.uk; holkhamestate; Mon-Sun 10.30 pm.

HOLT, NORFOLK 6–3C

MEADOWSWEET £163 543

37 NORWICH ROAD
NR25 6SA 01263 586954

"Holt in Norfolk is a jewel of a market town, and Meadowsweet is a little jewel of a restaurant with rooms" that's won acclaim as "a superb addition to the county" since its 2021 launch by Greg Anderson and Rebecca Williams. "Service is personal and spot on" and "the house and dining room feel warm and friendly without trying to be bleeding edge". When it comes to the "ambitious" ten-course menu for £130 per person – "every dish is thoughtful and delicious" with "chefs all working out of a tiny space and involved in introducing the courses". "Prices seem to have risen sharply since they got their Michelin star, but we think it's worth it!" – "worth the journey… bravo!" / meadowsweetholt.com; meadowsweetholt; Wed-Sat 8 pm.

HOLYMOORSIDE, DERBYSHIRE 5–2C

THE BULLS HEAD £88 323

NEW ROAD S42 7EW 01246 569999

Mark Aisthorpe again wins consistent feedback (if not a huge volume of it) for his Peak District pub (the accommodation has five AA stars), where he presides over a kitchen providing a high standard of cooking at very reasonable prices: the five-course lunchtime and early evening menu is £35 and the eight-course option is £80. (There are also à la carte and Sunday lunch options). / bullsheadholymoorside.co.uk; bullsheadholymoorside; Fri & Sat 9 pm, Wed 10 pm, Thu 8.30 pm, Sun 5 pm.

HOLYWOOD, COUNTY DOWN 10–1D

NOBLE £63 444

27A CHURCH RD
BT18 9BU 028 9042 5655

Pearson Morris and Saul McConnell's modern first-floor venue with daily specials up on the blackboard has become one of Northern Ireland's best-known destinations and continues to win strong support in feedback (and in the foodie press): "we love this stylish bistrot – quintessential French food is served with a smile and charm. Looking forward to seeing the new downstairs addition!" (a bar with wine and small plates). / nobleholywood.com; nobleholywood; Thu-Sat 9.30 pm, Sun 6.30 pm.

HONITON, DEVON 2–4A

THE PIG AT COMBE £82 224

COMBE HOUSE, GITTISHAM
EX14 3AD 01404 540400

A "great location" – an "interesting renovation" of an Elizabethan mansion – contributes to the atmosphere of this Otter Valley outpost of the trendy Pig empire. Increased reports this year of rather "average" cooking ("unmemorable apart from the price", ouch), though fans insist that, albeit "slightly hit-and-miss", it's "generally hit". / thepighotel.com; the_pig_hotels; Mon-Sun 9.30 pm.

HOPE VALLEY, SOUTH YORKSHIRE 5–2C

LOSEHILL HOUSE HOTEL & SPA £80 343

LOSEHILL LANE, EDALE ROAD
S33 6AF 01433 621 219

Down a lane near the lovely Hope Valley, Paul and Kathryn Roden's Peak District property has a marvellous setting and wins consistent praise from a loyal fan club for its "beautifully presented" food, and "pleasant" staff. The choice is primarily à la carte, with the evening selection offering three courses for £60 per person. / losehillhouse.co.uk; losehillhouse; Mon-Sun 8.30 pm.

HORNINGSHAM, WILTSHIRE 2

THE BATH ARMS £51 32

THE LONGLEAT ESTATE
BA12 7LY 01985 844308

In a picturesque location on the Longleat Estate, this old rural pub with rooms is consistently well-rated. Wine is sourced by a sister business – The Beckford Bottle Shop in nearby Bath (about 30 minutes' drive) – while meat and game from the estate help supply the kitchen. In April 2023, The Telegraph's William Sitwell pronounced himself a fan, an enjoyed "a faultless lunch of amped-up pub classics". / batharmsinn.com; thebatharmsinn; Mon-Sun 11 pm.

HORSTEAD, NORFOLK 6–4

RECRUITING SERGEANT £61 33

NORWICH ROAD
NR12 7EE 01603 737077

A "favourite go-to place" – this "very friendly, busy and reliable" gastroboozer-with-rooms h "something available for all tastes" (not least t "absolutely amazing" steak and kidney puddi which features on the "decent" pub menu), and is also a "fine place to stay". It's part of local pub group Colchester Inns, whose latest opening is Salhouse Lodge, which reportedly sold a week's worth of pints on its summer 20 opening day. / recruitingsergeant.co.uk; recruitin sergeant; Mon-Sat 8.30 pm, Sun 8 pm.

HOVINGHAM, NORTH YORKSHIRE 8–4

MYSE £160

MAIN STREET YO62 4LF NO TEL

Chef Josh Overington and his wife Victoria opened this new restaurant with three rooms i North Yorkshire at the end of June 2023 (well after our annual diners' poll had concluded) in a converted old pub, formerly called the Malt Shovel (but still replete with beams, flagged floors and characterful details). Myse (which rhymes with cheese) is a follow-up to their Le Cochon Aveugle in York (which enjoyed stellar ratings in our survey) and provides a tasting-only formula, with fifteen courses for £125 and wine pairings from £65. Early vibes – for example from arch northern foodie Thom Hetherington – are ve upbeat. / restaurantmyse.co.uk; restaurantmyse; Wed & Thu 1.30 pm, Fri & Sat 8.30 pm.

HUDDERSFIELD, WEST YORKSHIRE 5–1

ERIC'S £72 33

73-75 LIDGET ST HD3 3JP 01484 6464

Chef-patron Eric Paxman trained under Marc Pierre White in London and Bill Granger in Australia, and has cooked for luminaries including Arnold Schwarzenegger, who vowed 'I'll be back' – a sentiment shared by numerous guests at the venture he opened in his hometown 14 years ago. "Lunch and early-bird evening specials are an exceptional rgain". / ericsrestaurant.co.uk; erics_restaurant; e-Sat 10 pm, Sun 6 pm.

HUNGERFORD, BERKSHIRE 2–2D

UNGHI CLUB £33 453

HIGH STREET
G17 0DN 07826 808407

Wow! A most delicious meal in café-like rroundings" from Laurent Lebeau, former ecutive head chef at the Chez Gérard group d the Wimbledon tennis championships, no these days runs this "small traiteur in ungerford high street, with tables", where rilliant staff" serve "fantastic French dishes" at can be consumed on the spot or taken me. / thefunghiclub.com; thefunghiclub; Tue-u 4 pm, Fri & Sat 9 pm.

HUNSDON, HERTFORDSHIRE 3–2B

HE FOX AND HOUNDS ESTAURANT & AR £61 343

HIGH STREET
G12 8NH 01279 843 999

hef James & Bianca Rix celebrate 20 years at eir smart pub/restaurant this year, recording gh levels of feedback and satisfaction for eir "much better than usual pub operation" – ood and service are great and it's reasonably iced". Top Menu Tip – "the clams and fish e always good". / foxandhounds-hunsdon.co.uk; efoxandhoundshunsdon; Wed-Sat 10 pm, Sun pm.

HUNTINGDON, CAMBRIDGESHIRE 3–1B

LD BRIDGE OTEL £65 233

HIGH ST PE29 3TQ 01480 424300

his ivy-clad Georgian coaching inn is the "a p destination for wine in Cambridgeshire" and "also a good all-rounder" – thanks to s long ownership by Master of Wine, John oskins. "Sadly" for their many admirers, hn and his wife Julia sold up after 29 ears in summer 2023, although the new wners, East Anglia's Chestnut Group, ave promised a 'seamless transition' with inimal changes. / oldbridgehuntingdon.co.uk; dbridgehuntingdon; Mon-Sun 9 pm.

HURLEY, BERKSHIRE 3–3A

EW DROP INN £37 433

ONEY LANE SL6 6RB 01628 829293

What a return" – chef Simon Bonwick is ack on home turf at this diminutive and lovely" sixteenth-century village pub, not far om The Crown at Burchetts Green, where e established a stellar reputation for classic rench cooking over the previous decade. His ood is "fabulous" – "precisely cooked with all e flavour you expect and more" (not least the renowned" pies), and front of house (including ife Deborah) are "delightful, warm and elcoming with a smile". PS – the chef himself reated the artwork lining the quirky venue's walls. / dewdropinnhurley.com; Wed-Sat 10 pm, Sun 3 pm.

HURWORTH, COUNTY DURHAM 8–3B

THE BAY HORSE £76 333

45 THE GRN DL2 2AA 01325 720 663

Marcus Bennett's fifteenth-century village gastroboozer – a regular on 'best' UK gastropubs lists, and a consistent scorer in our annual diners' poll – is a "very dependable" sort of spot, offering "beautifully presented food, especially game in season"; there was the odd quibble this year ("are prices higher" now?) but it still makes for "a good all-round treat now and again". / thebayhorsehurworth.com; bayhorsehurworth; Mon-Sat 11 pm, Sun 10.30 pm.

ICKHAM, KENT 3–3D

THE DUKE WILLIAM £63 333

THE ST CT3 1QP 01227 721308

This "lovely gastropub in a pretty Kent village" wins praise for its "good menu selection, including unusual dishes like homity pie" alongside the more standard burgers, steak and fish 'n' chips. It is part of Saga heir Josh De Haan's Pickled Egg pub group. / thedukewilliamickham.com; dukewilliamickham; Mon-Thu 9 pm, Fri & Sat 9.30 pm, Sun 5 pm.

ILKLEY, WEST YORKSHIRE 5–1C

THE BOX TREE £116 444

35-37 CHURCH ST
LS29 9DR 01943 608484

Without huge fanfare, Simon Gueller and wife Rena have moved on as owners of this 'Gavroche of the north' – set in one of the town's oldest buildings; a restaurant since 1962; and famously a springboard for the career of the young Marco Pierre White. Since September 2022 it's moved into the hands of local businessman, Adam Frontal (who ran Cookridge Hall Golf Club for nearly 20 years) and – although reports this year were not super-numerous – feedback is encouraging: "Under new ownership this great old timer is getting back its mojo, with great food and service in a traditional, if quirky, setting… not fully back to their old selves yet but they are getting there". In October 2023, chef Kieran Smith moved on, perhaps as a result of his recent brush with a serious heart condition – no news as yet as to who will be replacing him, but his Insta suggests a smooth transition is in place, so we have maintained ratings. Top Menu Tip – "a very classy Sunday lunch". / theboxtree.co.uk; boxtreerestaurant; Wed-Sat 8 pm, Sun 2.30 pm.

ILMINGTON, WARWICKSHIRE 2–1C

THE HOWARD ARMS £74 333

LOWER GREEN CV36 4LT 01608 682226

This "excellent inn" on the northern edge of the Cotswolds (West Midlands Tourism's Best Pub of the Year 2023) is "exactly what a large village local should be, but so rarely is". The menu is a bit posh to be described as pub grub and there are alternative options, both for vegans, and for special evenings (for example, game suppers in season). / howardarms.com; thehowardarms; Mon-Sat 9 pm, Sun 8 pm.

ILMINSTER, SOMERSET 2–3A

THE BARRINGTON BOAR £55 443

MAIN STREET TA19 0JB 01460 259 281

"We're so lucky to have this on our doorstep", agree locals who enjoy the "top-class pub grub" served in this smart 18th-century inn run by locally born chef Alasdair Clifford (ex-Chez Bruce & Glasshouse) and his wife Victoria Collins – who make "a brilliant team, well regarded by the village and their other customers". Now in their sixth year here, the couple recently bought the farm next door to provide extra accommodation, a bakery, orchard and kitchen garden. / thebarringtonboar.co.uk; the_barrington_boar; Thu-Sat, Wed 11 pm, Sun 6 pm.

INGHAM, NORFOLK 6–4D

THE INGHAM SWAN £97 444

SEA PALLING ROAD
NR12 9AB 01692 581099

Locally born chef-patron Daniel Smith's smartly thatched country restaurant-with-rooms "never disappoints and has the best food for some miles around". Relying mainly on local produce, it's "a great place to eat either the set lunch menu or the tasting menu" – and is also "very pleasant to stay in". / theinghamswan.co.uk; theinghamswan; Mon-Sun 9 pm.

INVERNESS, HIGHLAND 9–2C

ROCPOOL £95 444

1 NESS WALK IV3 5NE 01463 717274

This cool modern European brasserie has an attractive corner location on the banks of the River Ness – but "the use of local Scottish produce and very imaginative menu is the reason this restaurant buzzes" (as is the fact that "it stands out in an area that lacks good restaurants"). / rocpoolrestaurant.com; rocpool; Tue-Sat 9.45 pm.

IPSWICH, SUFFOLK 3–1D

TRONGS £35 443

23 ST NICHOLAS ST
IP1 1TW 01473 256833

Foo Trong and his family "always meet expectations" at the "traditional high street Chinese" – always one of the more commented-on restaurants in these parts. They have established the place as a local institution over 26 years, serving "delicious, generous and thoughtfully spiced food" using "high quality of ingredients" in a "warm and relaxing ambience". / trongschineserestaurant.com; Mon-Sat 10 pm.

JERSEY, CHANNEL ISLANDS –

BOHEMIA, THE CLUB HOTEL & SPA £101 454

GREEN ST, ST HELIER JE2 4UH 01534 876500

Callum Graham's "sublime tasting menus are a real treat for the senses" at this much-accoladed dining room within a 38-bedroom boutique hotel – the best-known gastronomic destination on the island – and "the pescatarian version justifies the trip to Jersey with the knowledge that the fish was landed that morning!". If you don't want to go the whole hog, there is also a four-course menu for £89 per person, but in either case you have the benefit of a "fantastic wine list with a good heavy presence of French classics also but with some interesting New World vintages". / bohemiajersey.com; bohemiajersey; Mon-Sun 10 pm.

LONGUEVILLE MANOR £113 444

LONGUEVILLE RD, ST SAVIOUR JE2 7WF 01534 725501

A "wonderful home-from-home" – Jersey's poshest, Relais & Châteaux-affiliated hotel (offering yacht charters, a pool, and other mod cons) has long been in the hands of the Lewis family; Andrew Baird oversees the fifteenth-century, wood-paneled dining room, his "classic" fine dining plates drawing on the hotel's Victorian kitchen garden. Further plaudits for the "amazing sommelier and great wine list" (a reflection of the serious 600-bin cellar on-site). / longuevillemanor.com; longuevillemanor; Mon-Sun 9 pm.

MARK JORDAN AT THE BEACH £64 333

LA PLAGE, LA ROUTE DE LA HAULE, ST PETER JE3 7YD 01534 780180

A sibling to the Ocean Restaurant at The Atlantic Hotel, where chef Mark Jordan (who runs this airy venue with wife Magda) held down a star for eleven years. The "casual fine dining" menu focuses on fish, and is deemed "great value for money". / markjordanatthebeach.com; mark_jordan_at_the_beach; Tue-Sun 9.30 pm.

KENILWORTH, WARWICKSHIRE 5-4C

THE CROSS AT KENILWORTH £108 332

16 NEW ST CV8 2EZ 01926 853840

"In the Premier League of food pubs", this "beautiful old building with a pleasant garden and an intimate atmosphere" offers highly ambitious "fine dining" food that's both "delicious and prettily presented" from Adam Bennett, formerly head chef at the grand Simpson's in Birmingham (a sister venue also owned by Andreas Antona). The cooking is "very well executed, while service combines the professional with the friendly". "Prices are inevitably rising, but it's always good value" and "still the local top restaurant" – "there's nowhere else we prefer to go… after 125 visits and counting!!". / thecrosskenilworth.co.uk; thecrossatkenilworth; Wed-Sat 9 pm, Sun 3 pm.

KESWICK, CUMBRIA 7-3D

THE COTTAGE IN THE WOOD £109 344

WHINLATTER FOREST CA12 5TW 01768 778409

"Capitalising on the stunning views down from Whinlatter Pass", this converted coaching inn above Keswick (in the Whinlatter Forest) is the epitome of a beautifully located Lakeland property; and fans say it's "a great place to stay and go walking, then come back for amazing meals". Chef Sam Miller has lots of top Scandi names on his CV (including Noma and Faviken) and his eight-course tasting menu for £110 per person achieves some high ratings in our annual diners' poll. Not everyone is wowed – a couple of reporters found it "disappointing given its reputation", or with dishes that had "too much pickling and cooking techniques that were not to my taste". But for the majority, it's 'mission accomplished' – "we had high expectations and the food was excellent and service efficient and friendly". / thecottageinthewood.co.uk; thecottageinthewoodkeswick; Tue-Fri 4 pm.

FELLPACK £56 343

34 LAKE ROAD CA12 5DQ 01768 771177

Food and fell-running trips combine at the multi-tasking adventure brand's bistro, whose eclectic dishes race all over the place and are "better than pub fare" (though the venue does enjoy a "quality pub ambience") plus "good value" to boot. Their growing local empire includes Airstream-set burrito joint the Fellshack, cocktail and burger bar The Round, set on hallowed fell-running territory in Keswick's Market Square, and (most recently) small hotel The Hazeldene, located on The Heads, a few minutes' walk from the bistro. / fellpack.co.uk; Fellpack_kitchen; Mon-Sat 9 pm.

LYZZICK HALL COUNTRY HOUSE HOTEL £63 434

UNDERSKIDDAW CA12 4PY 017687 72277

On the lower slopes of Skiddaw, England's third highest mountain, a luxury mid-Victorian Lakes hotel that "never fails to impress". The restaurant has been relocated over the years to amplify the "wonderful views", and it continues to please with its "good variety of dishes" (from Sunday lunch to salads and Cumbrian rarebit) that are also "exceptional value for money". / lyzzickhall.co.uk; lyzzickhall; Mon-Sat 1 pm.

KETTLESHULME, CHESHIRE 5-2B

THE SWAN INN £48 333

MACCLESFIELD RD SK23 7QU 01663 732943

"A pub that can serve ultra-fresh, skillfully cooked seafood is a rare treat" – "this country inn in the hills above Macclesfield" has a "light and comfortable small dining room adjacent t[o] the old bar". It enjoys "strong support from th[e] village", which clubbed together 20 years ago [to] buy the freehold when the pub was threatene[d] with closure. / swaninnkettleshulme.com; Sun & Mon 8 pm, Tue-Sat 11 pm.

KEYSTON, CAMBRIDGESHIRE 3-1A

THE PHEASANT AT KEYSTON £62

LOOP RD PE28 0RE 01832 710241

Open again from October 2023 (shortly after our guide goes to press) – this "lovely thatched pub just off the westbound A14 trun[k] road" is 'under exciting new management' (at least that's what the website says…). It received consistent praise as a "go-to place for many years", with good-value cuisine and a high-quality wine list – here's hoping that continues. / thepheasantatkeyston.co.uk; thepheasantatkeyston; Wed-Sat 9 pm, Sun 4 pm.

KILCHOAN, ARGYLL AND BUTE 9-3A

MINGARY CASTLE 34[5]

PH36 4LH 01972 614380

On the Ardnamurchan Peninsula, this "stunning, remote restaurant with rooms is set in a 13th century castle overlooking the Atlantic" (complete with battlements); restored to its former glory in 2016, it reopened in 2021. You could be forgiven for anticipating anticlimactic results in the dining room, but (on admittedly thin feedback) there is nothing but praise for the "warm service and great food". / mingarycastle.co.uk; Wed-Sat midnight.

KILLINGHALL, NORTH YORKSHIRE 5-1C

PARADISE CAFÉ AT DALESIDE NURSERIES £39 43[4]

RIPON ROAD HG3 2AY 01423 755196

"The new venture from the old Yorke Arms team is absolutely perfect in every way" – "to see Frances Atkins preparing your lunch in the open kitchen is a wonderful experience". Following the sad ending of her long tenure at the famous moorland inn, the first woman to earn a Michelin star in the UK is now wowing guests at a garden centre near Harrogate, alongside her trusted lieutenants chef Roger Oliver and manager John Tullett. There's "a high-quality menu available throughout the da[y] while dinner is only on Fridays" (twice a month) – and it's all "Michelin-quality food without th[e] pretensions of a star". / paradisewithfrj.co.uk; paradise_foods_; Tue-Sat 5 pm.

KINETON, GLOUCESTERSHIRE 2-1C

THE HALFWAY AT KINETON £45 333

GL54 5UG 07425 970507

"Newly refurbished Cotswolds inn now serving high-end pub food" from Nathan Eades and Liam Goff, formerly of The Wild Rabbit in Kingham. "Definitely one to watch", its cookin[g] is "delicious, well executed and hearty" and

Grace & Savour, Hampton-in-Arden

"service charming". / thehalfwayatkineton.com; halfway.kineton; Wed-Sat 9 pm, Tue 11 pm, Sun 3 pm.

KINGHAM, OXFORDSHIRE 2–1C

THE KINGHAM PLOUGH £71 333

THE GREEN OX7 6YD 01608 658327

This high-profile Cotswold gastroboozer near Chipping Norton is "always worth a visit" for its "relaxed ambience" and "consistent and tasty" food, from an "interesting menu which uses great local produce". Matt & Katie Beamish, who have worked for luminaries including Raymond Blanc and Fergus Henderson, took over a few years ago from Emily Watkins, who put the pub on the map – and have created a local group by snapping up The Hare at Milton under Wychwood and The Crown at Church Enstone, too. / thekinghamplough.co.uk; kinghamplough; Mon-Sat 9 pm, Sun 8 pm.

THE WILD RABBIT £88 333

CHURCH ST OX7 6YA 01608 658 389

This fancy Cotswold gastropub is popular with the Chipping Norton set, being owned by Lady Bamford, the driving force of Daylesford Organic (who supply much of the produce). Chef Sam Bowser's food elicited very solid marks this year, despite the occasional critic who feels it's "overpriced, even for those of us used to London mark-ups". Best way to do it? "Go for a country walk before or after and grab a room for the night". / thewildrabbit.co.uk; thewildrabbitkingham; Wed-Sun 9 pm.

KINGSTON UPON THAMES, SURREY 3–3A

ROZ ANA £48 432

4-8 KINGSTON HILL KT2 7NH 020 8546 6388

Set in a parade of shops, Deepinder Sondhi's subcontinental (with smarter dining room upstairs) is a fixture in these parts for its high-quality cooking, including some more adventurous dishes (think chocolate samosas, or chicken tikka with Laphroaig masala). If you wish, you can kick things off in style in the cocktail bar. / roz-ana.com; therozana; Sun-Thu 10 pm, Fri & Sat 10.30 pm.

KNOWLE, WARWICKSHIRE 5–4C

CHEAL'S £76 333

1630 HIGH STREET B93 0JU 01564 393333

Stop Press – in February 2023, ex-Simpson's head chef Matt Cheal closed down his popular Henley-in-Arden venture, which was too small for his planned expansion, and upped sticks eight miles down the road to Knowle High Street, where he now co-runs things with the manager of the Jacques fine dining restaurant which previously stood in the new location. According to early reports, "the exceptional quality of Cheal's food, not up till now as appreciated as it ought to be, has not deteriorated in its relocation", while the new space – a former bank with a posh cocktail bar – is "comfortable" (if "a little too glitzy" for some tastes). / chealsofhenley.co.uk; chealsofknowle; Wed & Thu 9 pm, Fri & Sat 9.30 pm, Sun 3 pm.

KNOWSTONE, DEVON 1–2D

THE MASON'S ARMS £74 334

SOUTH MOLTON EX36 4RY 01398 341231

"Located in a charming chocolate box north Devon village", this "quintessential country pub" in a thirteenth-century cottage is "well worth the outing" by all accounts. Chef Mark Dodson, formerly of the famed Waterside Inn, is in charge of the seasonal food, which a couple of reports note is still "worthy of its Michelin star". "If the cuisine isn't wow wow in its originality, the whole package is what you want from a place like this": an "all-round special experience" that spans everything from the "warm welcome" to the "fabric of the building itself" to "a great selection of dishes, all lovely". / masonsarmsdevon.co.uk; Tue-Sat 9 pm.

KNUTSFORD, CHESHIRE 5–2B

APRIL'S KITCHEN £54 343

37 REGENT STREET WA16 6GR 01565 651111

"Fabulous breakfasts to start the day with excellent omelettes; flavour-packed soups; and great coffee" ("with that rare accompaniment, a glass of iced water") are all highlights of the "imaginative creations from the open kitchen" at this funkily decorated, brick-walled bar/diner, which is "open all day" – a model of "simplicity with highly efficient service". / aprils-kitchen.co.uk; aprilskitchenknutsford; Mon-Sun 5 pm.

KYLESKU, HIGHLAND 9–1B

KYLESKU HOTEL £62 334

IV27 4HW 01971 502231

"A fantastic and remote setting with views outside over the waters" of Loch Glendhu are the special attractions of this distant hotel, just off NC500 (a 516-mile scenic route around the north coast of Scotland, starting and ending at Inverness Castle). It caught the national press this year on charges of being overpriced, and our reports do include the accusation that it has become a "rip off". For the majority, though, it's still "a destination spot whose food and service do not let the location down: lobster mac'n'cheese, catch of the day, monkfish curry all worthy of praise in a place that's nicely balanced between pub and a hotel". / kyleskuhotel.co.uk; kylesku_hotel; Mon-Sun 9 pm.

LANGAR, NOTTINGHAMSHIRE 5–3

LANGAR HALL £103 33

CHURCH LN NG13 9HG 01949 860559

This famous country-house "continues to be a great location for special occasions" – more than 40 years after the late Imogen Skirving converted it from her family home. Long-serving exec chef Gary Booth pursued the seasonal and local route – including game from the nearby Belvoir estate – long before it became a bandwagon and continues to win solidly good ratings for his cuisine. The venue still has the personality of a family-run estate, with Imogen's granddaughter Lila Arora nowadays at the helm. / langarhall.com; langarhall; Thu-Sat 8.30 pm, Sun 7.30 pm.

LANGFORD, OXFORDSHIRE 2–2

THE BELL INN £50 33

GL7 3LF 01367 860249

A "beautiful village pub (with rooms) in the Cotswolds" that's often "packed to the rafters" local boys Peter Creed and Tom Noest took it over in 2017 – with the latter turning out "all the modern pub classics delivered with panach along with some more unusual offerings" ("venison scrumpets", anyone?); add in "smilin service", and a beer garden overlooking the open countryside, and it's an "outstanding" proposition all-round. / thebelllangford.com; thebelllangford; Sun-Fri 9.30 pm, Sat 10 pm.

LANGHO, LANCASHIRE 5–1

NORTHCOTE £133 54

NORTHCOTE RD BB6 8BE 01254 24055

"Going from strength to strength under the stewardship of Lisa Goodwin-Allen" – this much-extended manor house in the Ribble Valley (just off the A59) built its renown under chef Nigel Haworth and his former-protégée Lisa's "exceptional and innovative" cuisine maintains its reputation in fine style, thanks to the "really excellent layers of flavour and texture running through all her dishes". Although its nowadays in the same group as that of The Stafford in London's St James's, long term MD Craig Bancroft remains at the helm and "the fact that he is so closely involved and so passionate about wine just shines through in the wine list (of course there are well-known vintages from France etc, but many other interesting options)". The odd regular fears that "a corporate approach is taking over the uniqueness that is Northcote", but most accounts applaud the "lovely" setting A highpoint of the year here is the annual Obsession food festival, which runs annually for two weeks in January and February with a series of guest meals from famous chefs – it has established itself now as a key event in the UK's annual foodie calendar. / northcote.com; northcoteuk; Mon-Sun 8.30 pm.

AWRENNY, PEMBROKESHIRE 4–4B

NNWN £153 4 5 3

MARKET SQUARE
A67 7AU 07308 313107

mazing dishes, with unusual foraged gredients" are winning some renown for att Powell's ten-seat yearling – a converted tting shed near the Cleddau Estuary. verything is prepared in front of you, then scribed by the chef before you eat in a ry intimate experience". It's a ten-course eal taking 3-4 hours, with the current base st of £130 per person – if you want to ake a day of it sign up to go foraging with att before you eat the ingredients you've scovered that evening. / annwnrestaurant.co.uk; nwnrestaurant; Thu-Sun 11.30 pm.

EATHERHEAD, SURREY 3–3A

HE DINING ROOM, EAVERBROOK £104 5 4 3

IGATE ROAD KT22 8QX 01372 571300

he very, very best of Japanese cuisine" is und in the unlikely setting of a luxurious rrey Hills mansion once owned by press ron Lord Beaverbrook, where Wojciech pow, founder of the Polish Association Sushi Chefs, presides over a "wonderful panese tasting menu" that delivers "an forgettable feast". Through the summer ests can dine in the heated basket of a tionary hot-air balloon in the formal Italian rden, on prized cuts of o-toro tuna and Kobe d wagyu beef cooked on their own yakiniku ill – a "great and expensive experience" 245 per person). / beaverbrook.co.uk; averbrook; Mon-Sun 9 pm.

EDBURY, HEREFORDSHIRE 2–1B

3 THE HOMEND £81 4 4 3

THE HOMEND HR8 1BP 01531 634451

Vonderful every visit" – a candlelit micro-staurant "with much ambience" in a Grade -listed building, and run by husband-and-fe team the Winters; "Elizabeth is a great stess" offering service "with panache", and er chef husband James must be a magician" turn out such "interesting" seasonal menus, owcasing rare-breed meats and Cornish tch. NB – this really is micro, seating just 14 ners between two rooms, so you will want book ahead. / 33thehomendledbury.co.uk; thehomendledbury; Thu-Sat 9 pm.

LEEDS, WEST YORKSHIRE 5–1C

AAGRAH £47 3 3 3

T PETER'S SQ LS9 8AH 0113 2455667

They always go the extra mile" according to ns of this city-centre outpost of Yorkshire's ne-strong chain of well-regarded curry ouses – a family-run business established in 977. / aagrah.com; aagrah; Mon-Sat 11 pm, Sun).30 pm.

BUNDOBUST £33 4 4 3

6 MILL HILL LS1 5DQ 0113 243 1248

"A craft beer pub with fabulous Indian vegetarian street food. What's not to like?" agree fans of the Manchester-based operation whose formula is equally popular in Leeds. It's "great to be able to take meat-lovers to a veggie restaurant and know they'll enjoy it!". / bundobust.com; bundobust; Mon-Thu 9.30 pm, Fri & Sat 10 pm, Sun 8 pm.

CHEF JONO AT V&V £105 3 3 3

68 NEW BRIGGATE
LS1 6NU 0113 345 0202

Yorkshire-born chef, Jonathan 'Jono' Hawthorne (a MasterChef: The Professionals 2020 finalist) presides over this city-centre hotspot, presenting a nine-course menu for £79 per person (as well as a five-course alternative, and various other vegan, vegetarian and Sunday lunch options). Many of the city's fooderati feel he is unfairly overlooked by the tyre men, but it inspired limited and slightly mixed feedback this year in our annual diners' poll: from "Wow!... what an experience... lovely lovely food" to the odd let down. / chefjonoatvandv.co.uk; vandvleeds; Wed-Sat 9.30 pm, Sun 3 pm.

DASTAAN LEEDS £48 4 4 2

473 OTLEY ROAD
LS16 7NR 0113 230 0600

Nand Kishor and Sanjay Gour's July 2022 launch follows on from the phenomenal success of their first Dastaan, in the outer London 'burbs. This northerly sibling is a tad more upmarket than in Ewell, but many dishes are shared between the restaurant's two menus. Local popularity has quickly propelled it to No. 1 in the Leeds Tripadvisor rankings, but our local reporters seem harder to impress – they say its "small but well-executed menu is very good", but have so far stopped short of awarding it an outstanding average rating. / dastaan.co.uk; dastaan447; Mon-Sun 10.30 pm.

HOME £105 4 4 3

3 BREWERY PLACE
LS10 1NE 0113 430 0161

"If you are looking for a truly haute cuisine experience this is the place to be" – Elizabeth Cottam's strikingly black venture (black floor, black décor, black uniforms), which has been given a new lease of life since relocating to Brewery Wharf two years ago. "From the moment you arrive you are made to feel welcome" and "the attention to detail and quality of ingredients" showcased in the five- or eight-course tasting menus (sometimes served by the chefs themselves) make for "an absolutely wonderful experience from start to finish". / homeleeds.co.uk; home_leeds; Wed, Fri & Sat 8.30 pm, Sun 3.30 pm.

THE IVY ASIA £80 3 3 5

55-57 VICAR LANE
LS1 6BA 0113 531 7990

Above its sister Ivy and one of three Ivys in the county, Richard Caring's showy pan-Asian beamed down in late 2022, complete with trademark green onyx flooring, mirrored ceilings, interior foliage and expensive culinary pick 'n' mix from a huge menu of of diverse inspiration, leaning heavily on Japan (sushi, sashimi, black cod), but also taking in China ('black pepper and szechuan [sic] glazed chicken', aromatic half duck); and with time to spare for Afternoon Tea. No quibbles about cultural appropriation in feedback, though – all feedback rates it solidly well (certainly better than its more traditional namesakes). / theivyasia.com; theivyasia; Sun-Wed 10.45 pm, Thu-Sat 1 am.

KENDELLS BISTRO £62 4 3 4

ST PETERS SQUARE LS9 8AH
0113 2436553

An "unpretentious, candlelit French bistro" that offers the "perfect romantic experience", replete with "authentic" cuisine and "lovely old-fashioned" vibes. Well-established locally, it remains of particular note for its attractive early-bird deals – handy before a trip to the nearby Leeds Playhouse. / kendellsbistro.co.uk; kendellsbistro; Tue-Thu 9 pm, Fri & Sat 10 pm.

KINO

34 NEW BRIGGATE
LS1 6NU 0113 223 3700

Attached to the Grand Theatre of Opera North, this brasserie makes for a "very handy new addition to the Leeds dining scene, especially if you're going to a show at the Grand". While it was initially dedicated to extended residencies from small food businesses they appear to have changed tack, with former MasterChef: The Professionals semi-finalist Josh Whitehead appointed head chef in May 2023. Here's hoping that it doesn't lose its initial momentum. / kinoleeds.co.uk; kino_leeds; Tue-Sat 10 pm.

THE MAN BEHIND THE CURTAIN £208 3 3 2

LOWER GROUND FLOOR FLANNELS
LS1 7JH 0113 2432376

The "culinary theatre" of Michael O'Hare's moody basement (to which it relocated a few years ago) has made it one of the UK's better known gastronomic temples, and it's become something of a standard-bearer for the city's foodie credentials. But it put in a very mixed performance in this year's annual diners' poll. Even those who "love it and feel its place in the Michelin is well deserved" – and there are still many of them – can find it "witheringly expensive". Meanwhile, skeptics worry that it's becoming "all show and no go": "I liked the first iteration, when it was located on the top floor of Flannels, but two subsequent visits to the current basement location have led me to conclude it's just soulless, with food that's

OK but which has not moved on" ("putting a prawn on top of a telephone doesn't make it taste better!") and "an entry-level price for wine that's ridiculous". The message may be getting through, as – with much fanfare – in May 2023 Michael launched a 'Menu Rapide' in response to the cost of living crisis, providing four courses for £40 or six courses for £60 per person. BREAKING NEWS. Actually, it looks like the penny has completely dropped, as – in late October 2023 – Michael announced that the restaurant is to close at the end of 2023 and relaunch under a new name; and with a 'more accessible' (we think that means less expensive) format in February 2024. Don't worry though: the style will still be 'out there' – it's to be themed around a seafood surf shack, and called 'Psycho Sandbar'. / themanbehindthecurtain.co.uk; ohare.michael; Wed-Sat 8 pm.

THE OWL £92 333

LOCKSIDE. MUSTARD APPROACH, MUSTARD WHARF LS1 4EY 0113 5316621

This "wonderful canalside restaurant, flooded with light" was originally at Kirkgate Market, moving to the Mustard Wharf development two years ago, where it is "a great addition to Leeds" – "the food is delicious but the relaxed atmosphere is also a key to its success". Liz Cottam, a MasterChef semifinalist, and Mark Owens (ex-head chef at the Box Tree) also run Home at Brewery Wharf. / theowlleeds.co.uk; theowlleeds; Wed-Sat 11 pm, Sun 5 pm.

OX CLUB £73 332

19A THE HEADROW LS1 6PU 07470 359961

This modern outfit in a glazed-brick former textile mill focuses on locally sourced ingredients including Yorkshire beef and the famous rhubarb that turns up in its signature take on Basque cheesecake as well as the house Negroni. Fans include Tim Hayward of the FT, who rated it "very close to the ideal of a restaurant". / oxclub.co.uk; oxclubleeds; Wed-Sat 10 pm, Sun 5 pm.

Bohemia, The Club Hotel & Spa, Jersey

PRASHAD £52 433

137 WHITEHALL RD BD11 1AT 0113 285 2037

The Hairy Bikers and Gordon Ramsay number amongst the fans of Bobby and Minal Patel's West Yorkshire legend (est 1992 in Bradford before the move here in 2012) and "it continues to maintain a high standard" of "delicious vegetarian cuisine". / prashad.co.uk; prashad_veggie; Tue-Thu 10.30 pm, Fri & Sat 11 pm, Sun 10 pm.

SALVO'S £62 322

115 & 107 OTLEY ROAD LS6 3PX 0113 275 2752

This "reliable Leeds stalwart" has served up "good Italian cooking" for 46 years under two generations of the Dammone family. Founder Salvatore's sons John & Gip retired in summer 2023, but the new owners have promised to carry on their traditions, with the same staff in place. / salvos.co.uk; salvosleeds; Sun-Thu 9 pm, Fri 9.30 pm, Sat 10 pm.

SOUS LE NEZ EN VILLE £68 333

QUEBEC HS, QUEBEC ST LS1 2HA 0113 244 0108

This "vibrant and busy" basement venue with an "interesting French menu" is a "longstanding favourite", whose "very good lunch" makes it an "ideal and consistent business brasserie". Opened in 1991 and still run by founders restaurateur Robert Chamberlain and exec chef Andrew Carter, its many fans are happy that it has "not changed in 20 years". / souslenez.com; sous_le_nez_chez_vous; Tue-Sat 9.45 pm.

SUKHOTHAI £44 334

15 SOUTH PARADE LS1 5QS 0113 242 2795

Ban Kaewkraikhot's small group of Thai restaurants started in Chapel Allerton and is now over 20 years old. She has invested in the lavish styling of this city-centre spin-off. A popular venue locally for celebrating an occasion, it wins upbeat (if limited) feedback for results from its very large (200+ dishes) menu. / sukhothai.co.uk; sukhothai_; Mon-Thu 10 pm, Fri & Sat 11 pm, Sun 9 pm.

THE SWINE THAT DINES £69 444

58 NORTH STREET LS2 7BF 0113 244 0387

The "personal service" at Stuart & Jo Myers' "fantastic small restaurant" in Mabgate – which they opened twelve years ago as a café called the 'Greedy Pig Kitchen' – is "the very definition of hospitality". "The unconventional cooking is great", too (including winning cakes). "It's a 140-mile round trip for us but sooo worth it!" / swinethatdines.co.uk; Thu-Sat 10.30 pm, Sun 5 pm.

TATTU £77 23

29 EAST PARADE, MINERVA HOUSE LS1 5PS 0113 245 1080

"Amazing decor, complete with cherry blossor sets a glossy scene at this outpost of the nation chain, where the pan-Asian selection adds Thai dishes and sushi to a menu backbone of Chinese dishes. Feedback was relatively limited this year, but all upbeat. / tattu.co.uk; tatturestaurant; Mon-Sun midnight.

THARAVADU £48 43

7- 8 MILL HILL LS1 5DQ 0113 244 050C

"Don't be put off by the outside!" – this "very popular" Keralan (a favourite, it is claimed, of India cricket ace Virat Kohli) wins a hymn of praise for its "authentic" cuisine and is "a must for fish and seafood fans": "the meen koottan (fish curry) was a standout dish, bursting with flavour and expertly prepared. The mango lassi is also delicious. Highly recommended!" / tharavadurestaurants.com; tharavadu; Mon-Sat 9.30 pm.

ZAAP £39 33

16 GRAND ARCADE LS1 6PG 0113 243 2586

A "great Thai street food" venture (est. 2015) with a "fun atmosphere" that replicates Bangkok markets, down to the tuk tuks in whic you can enjoy a menu featuring an impressive 80 dishes; the colourful mini-chain now has fiv northern spin-offs. / zaapthai.co.uk; Mon-Sun 10 pm.

ZUCCO £46 34

603 MEANWOOD ROAD LS6 4AY 01132 249679

This "authentic local Italian with a difference" benefits from an "excellent variety of imaginative small plates" and "enthusiastic service led by the family owners". One of "the most enjoyable dining experiences in Leeds", it's "worth the trip out of town" to Meanwood. / zucco.co.uk; Tue-Thu 9.30 pm, Fr & Sat 10.30 pm, Sun 8.30 pm.

LEICESTER, LEICESTERSHIRE 5–4D

BOBBY'S £28 32

154-156 BELGRAVE RD LE4 5AT 0116 266 0106

"Incredible Indian street food" has been enjoyed at this Gujarati vegetarian fixture on Leicester's 'Golden Mile' since 1976, when it was opened by the late Bhagwanjibhai and Manglaben Lakhani. Now run by their son Dharmesh, it has been refurbished taking inspiration from the classic Bollywood film 'Bobby', the source of its name. / eatatbobbys.com; eatatbobbys; Mon, Wed-Sun 10 pm.

AYAL £45 332

3 GRANBY ST LE1 6FE 0116 255 4667

ıis "excellent South Indian" near Leicester gers' Welford Road stadium is "the real deal", d "never disappoints" with its "superb food ved by a wonderful team". Top Menu Tips 'the fish curry is a delight, as is the masala sa". / kayalrestaurant.com; kayal_restaurants; on-Sat 11 pm, Sun 10 pm.

EWANNICK, CORNWALL 1–3C

OOMBESHEAD ARM £109 444

OOMBESHEAD FARM
.15 7QQ 01566 782 009

Gorgeous and remote", this "inviting farm-to-k restaurant" from well-known big-city chefs pril Bloomfield (New York's Spotted Pig) and m Adams (London's Pitt Cue) goes "super-cal and super-rustic with their menu – and u can't help loving the wonderful converted one barn dining room and attentive service". me find it "a marmite experience": "the shes are so few and so stripped-back that a gging voice kept asking 'is this it?', even while e quality of cooking was superb". But a large ajority reckon it's "well worth the journey", as u "come away having fallen in love with the ace". Its influence stretches far: Coombeshead ead crops up regularly on smart menus London. / coombesheadfarm.co.uk; oombesheadfarm; Thu-Sun 11 pm.

EWES, EAST SUSSEX 3–4B

ORK £68 333

STATION STREET
N7 2DA 01273 809445

his "tiny restaurant with big-flavoured food" as opened without much pizzazz in 2021 by rmer Ledbury and Dairy chef Richard Falk, d has attracted positive reviews from the uardian's Grace Dent and the Telegraph's 'illiam Sitwell. It has yet to generate much edback, but what there is, is uniformly ositive. / fork-lewes.co.uk; forklewes; Wed-Sat 30 pm, Sun 4.30 pm.

QUISITO £51 453

EST STREET BN7 2NZ 01273 958890

his yearling from four friends serves a antastic set menu at an accessible price" – ight courses for £40 per person, unbelievably ood value!" – of what they describe as nauthentic Italian' cuisine, including ome-cured meats and fresh-made pasta. Top enu Tip – "the best tiramisu ever (order conds!)". / squisito.co.uk; squisitolewes; Thu-Sat) pm, Sun-Wed 5 pm.

LEYBURN, NORTH YORKSHIRE 8–4B

HE SANDPIPER NN £64 333

ARKET PLACE DL8 5AT 01969 622206

nathan & Janine Harrison's eighteenth-entury inn in a Wensleydale market town continues to attract solid ratings all-round for its well-priced, modern bistro fare. / sandpiperinn.co.uk; thesandpiperinn; Wed-Sat 8.30 pm.

LICHFIELD, STAFFORDSHIRE 5–4C

UPSTAIRS BY TOM SHEPHERD £99 544

25 BORE STREET
WS13 6NA 01543 268877

"Getting a booking is no mean feat" at Tom Shepherd's "absolutely brilliant" operation – a "bright and crisp" 28-cover space "above his father's jewellery shop" which in two short years has established itself as one of the Midlands' most celebrated culinary destinations. "If you do, you will be rewarded with exciting and original cooking" with dishes that are "thoughtful in their concept, prepared meticulously and served beautifully". BREAKING NEWS – In September 2023, Tom announced a second, more informal venture in the city ('we're going to open up with the mindset of small plates, drinks orientated, and the small plates will develop so you can almost have your own tasting menu'). / upstairs. restaurant; rest_upstairs; Wed-Sat 8.30 pm.

LILLESHALL, SHROPSHIRE 5–3B

RED HOUSE £58 343

WELLINGTON RD
TF10 9EW 01952 739048

"Though part of a small chain of pubs" – the Paragon Group, who utterly transformed it with a £950k makeover prior to relaunching it in 2019 – this gastroboozer "has a very individual feel to it", with attractive décor and an outdoor 'secret garden'. The menu is "always interesting" and the food "consistent", with a focus on the pizzas emerging from the impressively large oven. / theredhouselilleshall.co.uk; red_house_lilleshall; Tue-Sat 11 pm.

LINCOLN, LINCOLNSHIRE 6–3A

JEW'S HOUSE RESTAURANT £85 453

15 THE STRAIT LN2 1JD 01522 524851

"Very good food – probably the best in Lincoln" is "matched by a lovely location in a historic building on Steep Hill", dating from 1170. Chef-patron Gavin Aitkenhead, who worked under legendary Germain Schwab at Winteringham Fields before setting up here on his own account in 2006, is behind a "thoughtful, interesting and imaginative tasting menu", which is "spiced up with fun conversation from the staff", headed by FOH Samantha Tomkins. / jewshouserestaurant.co.uk; thejewshouserestaurant; Wed-Sat 9 pm.

LINDFIELD, EAST SUSSEX 3–4B

LIMES THAI KITCHEN 332

67 HIGH STREET
RH16 2HN 01444 487858

"Really impressive and tasty food that's a cut above usual Thai fare" and "attentive service" win praise for this local Thai, on the high street of a super-cute village. Top Tip – "top delivery" too: "speedy delivery and delicious food; and a good range for vegans too". / limesoflindfield.co.uk; limeslindfield; Mon-Sat 10.30 pm.

LISS, HAMPSHIRE 2–3D

NATHAN MARSHALL CLARKE HOUSE £79 342

FARNHAM ROAD
GU33 6JQ 01730 779360

A "great little spot" in what was once a courthouse – though it's not necessarily evident from the façade or the rustic interior either; the "husband-and-wife team (Nathan and Evi Marshall) work well together", and the modern European food "continues to improve", making it "a welcome addition to an area surprisingly thin on exceptional restaurants". / nathanmarshallsrestaurant.co.uk; n.marshall_chef; Thu-Sat 11 pm.

LITTLE ECCLESTON, LANCASHIRE 5–1A

THE CARTFORD INN £67 444

CARTFORD LANE
PR3 0YP 01995 670 166

"A beacon of hospitality and gastronomy in the desert of the Fylde" – "the Beaume family's quirkily decorated riverside inn" is "a great example of what can be done in a pub with rooms to make it interesting" (and incorporates a deli, art gallery, farm shop, plus greenhouses for all-year dining). Amidst the selection of hearty yet enticing dishes, "there's lots of good stuff". Top Tips – "the French Onion Soup is still the best I've had, and oxtail suet pudding is always impressive. And if you can get one of the tables with a river view, you may get to see the striking sight of the river changing direction when the tide starts coming in. If you are very, very lucky, you may even see the tail end of the Wyre Bore". / thecartfordinn.co.uk; cartfordinn; Mon & Tue 8.30 pm, Wed-Sat 9 pm, Sun 6 pm.

LITTLE HUCKLOW, DERBYSHIRE 5–2C

THE BLIND BULL £47 444

SK17 8RT 01298 211949

Visit England's pub of the year in 2023, this renovated, twelfth-century Peak District inn's other claim to fame is being the fifth oldest pub in the country. Feedback on its conservatory dining room was more limited than we'd like this year, but acclaims its "excellent food, lovely view and proficient service". There's an eclectic selection of modern pub grub, or you can choose to dine from the focused (four choices for each course) dinner menu at £39.50 for two courses. / theblindbull.co.uk; theblind_bull; Thu-Sat, Wed 9 pm, Sun 5 pm.

LITTLE PETHERICK, CORNWALL 1–3B

THE OLD MILL BISTRO 332

THE OLD MILL HOUSE PL27 7QT 01841 540388

"Well prepared food (excellent Cornish fish) and friendly service" win enthusiastic (if limited) feedback in our annual diners' poll for this prettily located small (24 covers) bistro, in a converted sixteenth-century mill. It helps that it's very reasonably priced. / oldmillbistro.co.uk; the_old_mill_house; Tue-Sat 10 pm.

LIVERPOOL, MERSEYSIDE 5–2A

THE ART SCHOOL £111 454

SUGNALL ST L7 7DX 0151 230 8600

"Best in Liverpool" is a credible claim made by fans of Paul Askew's "classy" venue: a bright, contemporary dining room, next to 'The Phil' (built in 1888 as a 'Home for Destitute Children'), which provides "a 'proper' fine-dining experience that's exceptional in every way"; not least "perfect service" and "top-notch" cuisine that makes "excellent use of local produce from the Wirral and Lancashire". Top Tip – "the prix fixe menu lunchtime and early evening is brilliant value". / theartschoolrestaurant.co.uk; theartschoolrestaurant; Tue-Sat 9.15 pm.

BARNACLE £64 334

MEZZANINE, DUKE STREET MARKET, 46 DUKE STREET L1 5AQ 0151 245 5113

This "lively place" on the mezzanine of the city centre's Duke Street food market serves "nicely presented dishes", and benefits from the involvement of Merseyside food heroes Paul Askew (of The Art School) and Harry Marquart (Bone & Block). Aiming to provide an 'intimate Scouse brasserie', it launched in late 2021. / barnacleliverpool.co.uk; barnacleliverpool; Wed-Sat 8.30 pm, Sun 4 pm.

BELZAN £56 343

371 SMITHDOWN ROAD L15 3JJ 0151 733 8595

This "lovely modern British neighbourhood restaurant" has made a name for itself with "very good cooking and some standout dishes" from chef Sam Grainger. Co-owners Chris Edwards & Owain WIlliams ensure that "staff are very friendly and attentive and know their stuff" – "it's great to have a local bistro that's going places". / belzan.co.uk; belzan_lpl; Wed-Sat 11 pm, Sun 6 pm.

BUYERS CLUB £48 333

24 HARDMAN ST L1 9AX 0151 7092400

A very hip neighbourhood restaurant from the team behind local food icon Bold Street Coffee; the menu is "mostly pizza and pasta, all of a good quality" and there are "great natural wines" to go with it. Given the "big outdoor area", it's particularly "popular in the summer", though the bar is rather "cosy" too. / buyers-club.co.uk; buyersclubliverpool; Mon-Thu midnight, Fri & Sat 12.30 am, Sun 11 pm.

DUKE STREET MARKET £76 433

46 DUKE STREET L1 5AS NO TEL

"Fun" city-centre food hall offering a "great choice of stalls in half a dozen food styles" – the cuisines range from Italian and Japanese to Mexican and Cuban – with meals eaten "in a buzzy courtyard on shared canteen-style long tables". Upstairs on the mezzanine is a more standard restaurant, Barnacle (see also), from a team of top Merseyside kitchen stars. / dukestreetmarket.com; dukestreetmarket; Mon-Sun 2 am.

HAWKSMOOR £95 343

INDIA BUILDINGS, 31 WATER STREET L2 0RD 0151 294 6710

Occupying the Grade II-listed India Buildings, this Scouse outpost of the famous steakhouse chain "is an amazing venue, and the Hawksmoor team have kept the interior design true to the original decor, with a period Liverpool/New York vibe". Launched in November 2022, its sustainable steaks and seafood have not wowed quite as much as its older Manchester sibling did on launch: "the staff are lovely and it's a smooth operation, with good cocktails too; but the main meal didn't quite match the hype. Even so, it's early days for the ever growing Hawksmoor empire!" / hawksmoorliverpool; Mon-Thu 9.30 pm, Fri & Sat 10 pm, Sun 8 pm.

THE ITALIAN CLUB FISH £64 332

128 BOLD ST L1 4JA 0151 707 2110

A "long-standing, mainly fishy" sibling to The Italian Club, a stone's throw away down shopping hub Bold Street, and blending the backgrounds of Puglia-born chef Maurizio Pellegrini and his Scottish partner Rosaria Crolla; the "busy" outfit "never ceases to produce tasty dishes" – be it seafood platters, battered oysters or their "super fish 'n' chips". / theitalianclubfish.com; theitalianclubfish; Mon-Sat 10 pm, Sun 9 pm.

THE LONDON CARRIAGE WORKS, HOPE STREET HOTEL £64 333

40 HOPE STREET L1 9DA 0151 705 2222

"Superb food… comfortable surroundings, friendly but not obsequious staff, a very decent wine list, reasonable prices…" – this boutique hotel dining room (named after the original 1860 business that occupied the premises) was part of the early wave of culinary reinvention to hit 'The Pool' and opened in 2003. It's often overlooked nowadays, but reports this year suggest unfairly so. / thelondoncarriageworks.co.uk; Ldncarriageworks; Mon-Sat 10 pm, Sun 9 pm.

LUNYA £70 33

55 HANOVER STREET L1 3DN 0151 706 9770

Peter & Elaine Kinsella's "fun" tapas bar has introduced a generation of Scouse foodies to the delights of Catalan cuisine over the past 15 years. "Sadly the Manchester branch was a victim of lockdown, but the original is still going strong", along with its deli and Lunyalit offshoot in the Albert Dock. / lunya.co.uk; lunyadeli; Mon-Sat 10 pm, Sun 8.30 pm.

LUNYALITA £63 34

UNIT 5, BRITANNIA PAVILION, ROYAL ALBERT DOCK L3 4AD 0151 317 7199

A sunny days outside terrace and an attractive location by the waterside of the famous Alber Dock adds to the appeal of Lunya's little sister. It serves a range of tapas and sharing platters – this year it won particular praise for its "brilliant and friendly service with great attention given". / lunya.co.uk; lunyadeli; Mon Tue 8.30 pm, Wed & Thu 9 pm, Fri 9.30 pm, Sat 10 pm, Sun 8 pm.

MANIFEST £40 54

4A WATKINSON STREET L1 0AG 07729 129873

Chef Paul Durand's Baltic Triangle follow-up to the now shuttered city brasserie/micro bakery The Little Shoe has built up quite the momentum since opening in 2022. Set on the ground floor of a converted warehouse, and dominated by counter seats overlooking the open kitchen, it turns out "amazing small and large plates" from a menu that rotates by four or five dishes every couple of weeks. Wine is very much a focus, with a "good selection" of bottles by the glass "and not silly prices" too. / manifestrestaurant.com; manifestliverpool; Wed-Sat 9 pm.

MARAY £45 33

91 BOLD STREET L1 4HF 0151 709 5820

This "cosy bistro" in Albert Dock has built a strong reputation over the past decade with its "tasty food with bright, sunny flavours" inspired by Middle Eastern dishes encountere in the Marais, Paris. An "interesting short wine list covering some unusual locations" adds to the fun. Branches in Bold Street and Manchester have followed, although the branc in Allerton closed down after six years in 2022. / maray.co.uk; marayrestaurants; Sun-Thu 10 pm, Fri & Sat 11 pm.

MOWGLI £43 34

69 BOLD ST L1 4EZ 0151 708 9356

Ex-barrister Nisha Katona is nowadays one of the UK's foremost restaurateurs on the success of her national chain, of which this "welcoming" and still mega-popular street-food café in a converted former bank was the original (and celebrates its tenth year in 2024). "Always a good choice for all the family: even the young ones will try the food here" – "a very different take on Indian food, including me Indo-Chinese dishes that don't normally t much of an airing". Top Menu Tips – avourite items include Gunpowder Chicken, aa's Lamb Chops, Butter Chicken and House amb Curry… the cocktails are definitely orth trying too". / mowglistreetfood.com; owglistreetfood; Sun-Thu 9.30 pm, Fri & Sat .30 pm.

ORD £81

E PLAZA, 100 OLD HALL STREET 9QJ 0151 559 0654

strong new opening with great food!" – in Sixties-tastic building that used to be the Q for Littlewoods (once home to the football ools), Liverpudlian chef Daniel Heffy (ex-cret Diners Club & Buyers Club) returned om Stockholm to helm this ambitious wcomer. It opened in April 2023 – rather late the day to generate feedback in our annual ners' poll – hence we've left it unrated, despite e very upbeat early-days report (and the verpool Echo and the Confidentials have both axed lyrical about it). / nordrestaurant.co.uk; tdrinknord; Tue-Sat 10 pm.

ANORAMIC 34, WEST OWER £69 335

ROOK STREET L3 9PJ 0151 236 5534

ust watch the sunset over Liverpool from is 34th-floor restaurant", say fans of this ectacular venue in the West Tower, the y's tallest. Run by Cathy Frost, whose veloper husband Hugh built the tower, e operation's modern British cuisine has nsistently impressed reporters, and new ad chef Nathan Booth has settled in well llowing the departure of Elliot Hill to e Chester Grosvenor. / panoramic34.com; noramic34liverpool; Tue-Sat 9.30 pm, Sun 8 pm.

EN FACTORY £41 343

HOPE ST L1 9BQ 0151 709 7887

iverpool legend" Paddy Byrne "keeps flying e flag for everyday, good-value eating in a brant atmosphere" at his follow-on act to his ng-term stint at the Everyman Bistro (from hich he moved to found here in 2015). It presents "good casual dining with a mix of gh quality, small modern dishes and main eals, plus good wine options all available the glass" and a "fine choice of real ale". t gets very busy and noisy on Fridays and aturdays" but on a warm summer's evening, ash through the interior to discover its outside ourtyard seating. / pen-factory.co.uk; the_pen_ ctory; Tue, Wed 11 pm, Thu-Sat midnight.

UEENS WINE BAR £60 334

QUEEN AVENUE L2 4TX 0151 345 6646

fantastic find!" – "neatly tucked way" down a smart city alleyway, this nderstated wine bar/bistro "feels like a cret discovery" that is "perfect for a cozy journ". / queensliverpool.co.uk; queens_ verpool; Mon-Thu 9 pm, Fri & Sat 9.30 pm.

RESTAURANT 8 BY ANDREW SHERIDAN £92

16 COOK STREET L2 9RF 0151 5590 397

Native Liverpudlian Andrew Sheridan upped sticks from Brum to relocate '8' to a Victorian building in the city centre (next to the original Cavern Club) in April 2023. Seating is at one of two counters for, appropriately, eight diners; the lighting is low; much of the décor is black or slate-grey; and the level of ambition in the cooking is high, with the aim of delivering 'an immersive sensory experience'. The eight courses (for £110 per head) are of very diverse inspiration and there's also a wine pairing option (for £80 per head). / about8.co.uk; Wed-Sat 11.30 pm.

ROSKI £122 543

16 RODNEY STREET L1 2TE 0151 708 8698

This "exquisite" venue from MasterChef: The Professionals winner Anton Piotrowski is "a must-visit if you're in Liverpool" – and "worth a special visit to the city" if you're not. In the evening, for £115 per person, they serve a seven-course course tasting menu only. One mightily impressed recent visitor, Daily Telegraph reviewer William Sitwell, reported that 'the Lancashire haggis toastie was the most scrumptious thing I've eaten in ages'. / roskirestaurant.com; roskirestaurant; Thu-Sat, Wed 9.30 pm.

SALT HOUSE £64 333

1 HANOVER STREET L1 3DW 0151 706 0092

"Still serving great tapas with some influences from different countries" – this bright modern café opposite John Lewis is a well-known standby in the city, with the main drawback being that "the noise-level can be difficult at busy times". Opened in 2010, it was the first peg in a local chain that nowadays incorporates Hanover Street Social, Bacaro and Bouchon. / salthousetapas.co.uk; salthousetapas; Mon-Thu 10 pm, Fri & Sat 10.30 pm, Sun 9 pm.

SANSKRUTI 322

BIXTETH STREET L3 9LP 0151 236 8886

The "lovely veggie food" at this duo in Liverpool and Manchester takes inspiration from the regional vegetarian traditions found across India ('sanskruti' means tradition or culture). Their popularity means they "sometimes get a bit noisy with groups". / sanskrutirestaurant.co.uk; sanskrutirestaurant; Tue-Sat 10.30 pm, Sun 9.30 pm.

SPIRE £54 443

1 CHURCH ROAD L15 9EA 0151 734 5040

This "gem of a neighbourhood restaurant" near Penny Lane from brothers Matt & Adam Locke is "still one of the best in Liverpool" – it's "top-class in every respect", and the modern European cooking is of a "quality that never varies or disappoints". / spirerestaurant.co.uk; spirerestaurant; Wed-Fri 9 pm, Sat 9.30 pm, Sun 5.30 pm.

WRECKFISH £58 343

60 SEEL STREET L1 4BE 0151 707 1960

"Very good bistro cooking" and "amazing service" are turning Gary Usher's six-year-old fixture into a "Liverpool institution"; and it's become one of the best and best-known outlets in his Elite Bistros chain. But apparently he's toying with the idea of changing the name of this 90-cover venue, because too many people think it just serves fish! / wreckfish.co; wreckfish_ bistro; Mon-Sat 10 pm, Sun 5 pm.

LLANDAFF, CARDIFF 2–2A

HEATHCOCK £61 333

58 - 60 BRIDGE STREET CF5 2EN 029 2115 2290

A sister pub to Aberthin's Hare & Hounds, this gastropub on the fringes of Cardiff wins praise for its "always cheerful/funny" staff and dependable cooking, not to mention its "sublime" beers. It's not a twee, traditional place – the aesthetic is stark and modern, with bare wooden floors and tables and white walls. / heathcockcardiff.com; heathcock_cardiff; Mon & Tue, Sun 11 pm, Wed & Thu 11.30 pm, Fri & Sat 12.30 am.

LLANDEWI SKIRRID, MONMOUTHSHIRE 2–1A

THE WALNUT TREE £107 333

LLANDDEWI SKIRRID NP7 8AW 01873 852797

"We've been coming for twenty years, and it remains fantastic!" This famous rural gastropub won fame in the 1970s (founded by Ann & Franco Taruschio) and celebrated chef Shaun Hill has been in charge of the kitchen for the last 15 years now. "The cuisine is not super-innovative": "classic cooking of a high standard" that's "just very dependable and hugely enjoyable" – "excellent local ingredients prepared with flair" and served alongside "a modestly marked-up wine list carefully chosen by someone who cares". "Service can be a bit random" and one or two long-term fans feel it's "living somewhat on a strong regular clientele who value it dearly". But it remains in the top 100 most commented on restaurants in our annual diners' poll outside London – an impressive feat for a chef who's hit his 76th year. "Please don't let him retire!" / thewalnuttreeinn.com; lovethewalnuttree; Wed-Sat 9.30 pm.

LLANDRILLO, DENBIGHSHIRE 4–2D

TYDDYN LLAN £129 444

LL21 0ST 01490 440264

"The very best quality ingredients, the very best cooking and excellent service" have long singled out Bryan & Susan Webb's upscale converted shooting lodge, in the rolling Dee Valley; while it no longer has the tyre men's acclaim, the "cooking is still of a very high standard" indeed, and "this combined with the spacious dining room and lounge makes for a memorable evening". Top Tip – "just visit quick before they sell": after 20 years, the duo put the property on the market recently and are looking to retire. / tyddynllan.co.uk; Thu-Sun 9 pm.

LLANDUDNO, CONWY 4–1D

THE SEAHORSE £51 333

7 CHURCH WALKS
LL30 2HD 01492 875315

"The only recognised fish restaurant in the area" – this Grade II listed building has housed Don & Gill Hadwin's split-level venture for two decades, with an informal bistro downstairs and a Victorian-style dining room on the upper level. / the-seahorse.co.uk; seahorse_llandudno; Mon, Thu, Sun 10.30 pm, Fri & Sat 11 pm.

LLANGOLLEN, DENBIGHSHIRE 5–3A

THE CORN MILL £51 224

DEE LN LL20 8PN 01978 869555

It would be "difficult to find a more perfect setting" for a pub than this former watermill "nestling on the side of the River Dee, with decking overhanging the water and stunning views in all directions" – "in the evening there are candlelit tables with views looking out from the mill building, some situated directly above the original water wheel". "Part of the Brunning & Price chain, it offers well prepared and varied food on a daily changing menu" and "a large selection of wines to suit all pockets". / brunningandprice.co.uk; cornmillpub; Mon-Sat 11.30 pm, Sun 11 pm. SRA – 3 stars

LOCKSBOTTOM, KENT 3–3B

CHAPTER ONE £78 433

FARNBOROUGH COMMON
BR6 8NF 01689 854848

"A jeweled oasis" in the southeastern London 'burbs – this "exceptional venue continues to maintain the highest standards of hospitality" in an area a short drive from Bromley where there's "not much competition". Chef/Patron Andy McLeish trained under Nico Ladenis and has been at the stoves here since 2000 (with head chef Dean Ferguson joining shortly thereafter). "Reliably high-quality food" is provided in a "well-appointed" setting. Top Menu Tip – "jugged hare was a particular treat, not often seen on menus nowadays!" / chaptersrestaurants.com; chapteronekent; Wed & Thu 9 pm, Fri & Sat 9.30 pm, Sun 3 pm.

LONG COMPTON, WARWICKSHIRE 2–1D

OXHEART £94 433

50 MAIN STREET
CV36 5JJ 01608 684505

Mark Ramshaw's 'micro-restaurant' serves a "seriously inventive menu at a great price" to no more than 11 guests a night on just Fridays and Saturdays. "We sat at the kitchen counter and enjoyed a brilliant modern British menu, strong on local produce and full of lovely bitter-fermented-charred-umami flavour combinations. Pork, peas and pickled strawberry was a yummy main course". It opened in June 2021, with Marina O'Loughlin of the Sunday Times an early enthusiast. / oxheart.co.uk; restaurant.oxheart; Fri & Sat 10 pm.

LONG MELFORD, SUFFOLK 3–1C

BLACK LION £57 333

THE GRN CO10 9DN 01787 312356

A fifteenth century inn overlooking the local green that's ably helmed by the Chestnut Group, who run a series of characterful boozers across East Anglia; it's praised for a "well-balanced menu" (steaks, fish, veggie options like risotto) and its handy location for visiting local stately homes, with NT property Melford Hall just a five-minute walk away. / blacklionhotel.net; Mon-Sat 9 pm, Sun 7 pm.

LOOE, CORNWALL 1–4C

THE SARDINE FACTORY £41 323

QUAY ROAD WEST
PL13 2BX 01503 770262

"Excellent fresh fish" landed from day boats on the quay opposite is the mainstay of the menu at the restaurant chef-patron Benjamin Palmer opened in his hometown six years ago. "The Sunday lunch is perfect, too – so tasty". / thesardinefactorylooe.com; thesardinefactorylooe; Wed-Sun 9 pm.

LOSTWITHIEL, CORNWALL 1–3B

RESTORMEL KITCHEN £65 443

3 FORE STREET
PL22 0BP 07841 649261

"Jordan Cook and his partner Kerris have made a great success of Restormel Kitchen" – a "truly unique" venue with just 4 tables in a 400-year-old townhouse that's "almost like dining in someone's front room". Cook used to work as head chef in its former incarnation as the Trewithen Restaurant; having "taken the brave to step to start this business during Covid" (Kerris is FOH) his "amazing" rendition of the "small menu" makes it "a real go-to in the area". It's just pipped to an outstanding mark this year by one critical report ("full marks for enterprise, but some inconsistency in my meals there"). / restormelkitchen.wixsite.com; Tue-Sat 9 pm.

LOUGHBOROUGH, LEICESTERSHIRE 5–3D

THE HAMMER & PINCERS £75 343

5 EAST RD LE12 6ST 01509 880735

Now a restaurant with rooms, thanks to two bedrooms added during the covid-enforced closure, this former village forge has offered "consistently good, high-quality" cuisine for more than 20 years under the ownership of former Savoy chef Danny Jimminson and his wife Sandra. It's a "relaxed, really enjoyable" venue, with a range of menus from two to seven courses. / hammerandpincers.co.uk; thehammerandpincers; Tue-Sat 9.30 pm, Sun 4 pm.

LOWER BEEDING, WEST SUSSEX 3–4

THE PASS RESTAURANT, SOUTH LODGE HOTEL £190

BRIGHTON ROAD
RH13 6PS 01403 891711

This pioneer of the open kitchen concept (launched in 2008) is nowadays in the hands of chef Ben Wilkinson. Despite its renown in foodie circles, it achieved relatively little feedback in our annual diners' poll, hence we've left it unrated. But such reports as we did receive were ecstatic, and the AA have awarded the place an un-scruffy three stars. / exclusive.co.uk; southlodge_spa; Thu-Sun Wed 8.30 pm.

LOWER BOCKHAMPTON, DORSET 2–4

YALBURY COTTAGE £78 44

DT2 8PZ 01305 262382

"The food is always reliably delicious" at this 300-year-old thatched cottage across the road from Thomas Hardy's old school (the author was born in the neighbouring village) – which "must be one of the best restaurants in Dorset Former Four Seasons exec chef Jamie Jones assembles a "relatively short menu that caters for all tastes and appetites" – "you know as so as you taste the canapes that the food is going to be excellent". / yalburycottage.com; yalbury_ Tue-Sat 8.30 pm, Sun 2 pm.

LOWER CHICKSGROVE, WILTSHIRE 2–3

THE COMPASSES INN £58 33

SP3 6NB 01722 714318

This "lovely old pub" with rooms – a thatched survivor from the 14th century – wins solid ratings for its "friendly service", "great atmosphere and interesting food", which ranges from standard pub burgers to Turkish eggs and Goan pork vindaloo. Owner Ben Maschler, son of restaurant critic Fay, ran Soh House's food operations before heading to rur Dorset. / thecompassesinn.com; thecompasses; Mon-Sat 8.30 pm, Sun 7.30 pm.

LOWER ODDINGTON, GLOUCESTERSHIRE 2–1C

THE FOX AT ODDINGTON £46 33

HIGH STREET GL56 0UR 01608 692872

"The Fox has had a major makeover since the old days when it had the ambience of a venerable Cotswold pub" – as you'd expect since the July 2022 takeover by Lady Bamford and her Daylesford empire. Some old timers feel "the money lavished on its gentrification has not resulted in improvement", although ıey concede the result is "very comfortable" ınd deliver a thumbs-up to its selection of posh ub grub (pizza, steak, burgers and Cornish fish ır the most part). In early 2023, Giles Coren eclared himself a fan too, even if there was owhere close to park that wasn't already taken y "gleaming Land Rovers and Porsches, piled ıree deep in the narrow lanes and stacked n pavements". / thefoxatoddington.com; ıefoxatoddington; Mon & Tue 9 pm, Wed & Thu, un 8 pm, Fri & Sat 9.30 pm.

LOWER SLAUGHTER, GLOUCESTERSHIRE 2–1C

'HE SLAUGHTERS MANOR IOUSE £133 333

OPSEHILL RD GL54 2HP 01451 820456

'his archetypal Cotswolds manor house, just utside Bourton on the Water, occupies a eventeenth century property that's nowadays art of Andrew Brownsword's hotel group. 'he cuisine – under chef Nik Chappell – wins consistent thumbs-up ("we do enjoy going ere... results can be a bit hit and miss, but are ıostly good! while service is very good and ıe dining room attractive"). As well as a fairly ricey à la carte (three courses for £80) there's a elatively affordable all-day menu served in the ar and lounges (with dishes such as omelette ırnold Bennett, steak, posh sarnies, and so n). / slaughtersmanor.co.uk; brownswordhotels; ue-Thu 9 pm, Fri & Sat 9.30 pm.

LUDLOW, SHROPSHIRE 5–4A

'HE CHARLTON ARMS, :HARLTON ARMS IOTEL £63 344

UDFORD BRIDGE
Y8 1PJ 01584 872813

The view from the dining room over the iver is one of the best in the county" at :edric (brother of Claude) Bosi and wife ımy's well-established inn, on the Ludford ridge (and also with outside seating), vhere the food – relatively traditional and osher than pub grub – "continues to be f high quality". / thecharltonarms.co.uk; harltonarmsludlow; Mon-Sun 8.15 pm.

'HE CLIVE RESTAURANT VITH ROOMS £57 323

ROMFIELD SY8 2JR 01584 856565

.imited but positive feedback on the eating ossibilities afforded by this 17-room B&B n a Georgian House a short drive from .udlow. It offers a straightforward menu ıajoring in steaks, burgers and cuts of enison. / theclive.co.uk; theclivearms; Mon & Tue .30 pm, Wed-Sat 10.30 pm, Sun 5 pm.

:SONS AT THE GREEN :AFE £52 344

INHAM MILLENNIUM GREEN
Y8 1EG 01584 879872

Interesting and well-prepared local food" – now with a Middle Eastern influence" – is ın the menu at this idyllic spot from the four Crouch brothers, aka the CSONS. "The pleasure of dining here is derived not just from the good food but also the location at Dirham Weir, beside the River Teme, with wildlife to watch and even the chance of spotting an otter". / thegreencafe.co.uk; csons_food; Mon-Thu, Sat & Sun 4 pm, Fri 10 pm.

FISHMORE HALL £100 443

FISHMORE RD SY8 3DP 01584 875148

A "lovely restaurant with a view of distant Clee Hill, and situated in a pretty conservatory on one side of the gorgeously restored Fishmore Hall hotel" (replete with fancy spa since 2016). Chef Phil Kerry worked his way up from sous chef, and turns out "superb" tasting menus and à la carte dishes that are "really innovative". The venue also hosts a more casual bistro. / fishmorehall.co.uk; fishmorehall; Tue-Sat 9 pm.

THE FRENCH PANTRY 333

15 TOWER ST SY8 1RL 01584 879133

This "great little French brasserie serves all the classics in an unpretentious, enjoyable and charming way", close to the centre of this historic market town. In summer 2023, proprietors Olivier & Lynette Bossut took over the shop next door, launching it as a café and deli called Marmalade, with their son Ryan in charge. / frenchpantry.co.uk; thefrenchpantryludlow; Wed-Sat 10 pm.

GOLDEN MOMENTS £40 433

50 BROAD STREET
SY8 1NH 01584 878 488

"Still serving some of the best Indian food you can find!", this family-run curry house has earned a solid local reputation for its "great cooking… although you may have to wait as it's all freshly cooked". After more than 20 years, it may be living on borrowed time, with the landlord planning to return the site to domestic use. / goldenmomentsofludlow.co.uk; Mon, Wed-Sun 10 pm.

MORTIMERS £101 333

17 CORVE ST SY8 1DA 01584 872 325

"This lovely Ludlow restaurant" makes a suitable setting for "old-fashioned high-end dining" that showcases "top-notch" cooking from well-travelled chef Wayne Smith, who has worked for luminaries including Pierre Koffmann, Richard Corrigan, Tom Aikens and Claude Busi – the latter having put this address on the gastronomic map as Hibiscus. The venue "has been a little inconsistent over the years", going bust as La Bécasse, but Wayne has brought stability since 2015, and "recent meals eaten there have been excellent, each course finely prepared and very tasty". / mortimersludlow.co.uk; mortimersludlow; Thu-Sat, Wed 8 pm.

OLD DOWNTON LODGE £86 444

DOWNTON ON THE ROCK
SY8 2HU 01568 771826

Ideal for a "hideaway date night in the shires", with a "combination of discrete modern features melded into an ancient, beautiful and comfortable building" (whose stone dining room was built at the time of the Norman Conquest) – Pippa & Willem Vlok's country-house guarantees a "really great experience". "Truly remarkable staff" include head chef Nick Bennett, whose "highly skilled cooking" produces meals to savour. / olddowntonlodge.com; olddowntonlodge; Mon-Sun 8.30 pm.

LYME REGIS, DORSET 2–4A

HIX OYSTER & FISH HOUSE £72 334

COBB RD DT7 3JP 01297 446910

Set in a "perfect location overlooking Lyme Bay" from Lister Gardens, chef Mark Hix's "terrific fish restaurant" is "a real oasis in Dorset". It inspires a high volume of feedback and ratings would be even higher were it not for a minority opinion that "the culinary ideas remain sound, but the execution is wildly variable". Last year, the celeb chef was forced to remove a wooden decking area installed during the pandemic, after losing a long battle with the local council. / theoysterandfishhouse.co.uk; theoysterandfishhouse; Mon-Sat 9.15 pm, Sun 3 pm.

LILAC £62 333

CELLAR 57-58 BROAD STREET
DT7 3QD 07308 079427

"What an unexpectedly good find!" – a 400-year-old cellar housing a "wine bar doing small plates of very good", "fresh and locally sourced food", alongside "enjoyable cocktails, mocktails", "and a decent wine list described as 'low intervention'". "Service is efficient and unobtrusive", "staff charming", and "everyone is obviously enjoying themselves". Owner Harriet Mansell also operated her stellar restaurant Robin Wylde near here until September 2023, at which time it closed as its lease expired. Harriet is currently looking for a new site, but may offer special evenings here in the meantime. / lilacwine.co.uk; lilacfoodandwine; Sun, Wed-Fri 8 pm, Sat 8.30 pm.

ROBIN WYLDE £80

63 SILVER STREET
DT7 3QE 07717 227094

"Without a doubt the best meal and experience for many years"… but Harriet Mansell had to call time on her "intimate" venture in September 2023 as the lease ran out. We received "outstanding" reports on her tasting menus and "excellent drinks pairs, both alcoholic and nonalcoholic" here, so have maintained a holding entry, as she is looking for a new site nearby and continuing to operate out of her Lilac wine cellar. / robinwylde.com; robinwyldedining; Thu-Sat 10 pm.

TOM'S LYME REGIS £87 333

MARINE PARADE
DT7 3JQ 01297 816018

Try to nab a window seat – or in fine weather a place on the terrace – if you visit this brilliantly well-situated venue. All reports rate its "good fresh fish" from "rather a short menu" (which also features local beef as an alternative to the seafood). One supporter also muses that it's "quite expensive – is it trading on its excellent position"? / tomslymeregis.com; toms_lymeregis; Wed-Sat, Mon & Tue 8.30 pm, Sun 3.30 pm.

LYMINGTON, HAMPSHIRE 2–4C

ELDERFLOWER £103 443

QUAY ST SO41 3AS 01590 676908

"A set selection with superb balance of flavours and textures" (with options "you might not ordinarily choose") makes for "very interestingly presented and great-tasting food" ("we even ate a tulip!") according to fans of the "amazing tasting menus" at Andrew & Marjolaine du Bourg's "professional" fine-dining venue in a pretty cobbled street, near the harbour. "Too many elements on a plate" can leave some diners feeling "confused", though ("lovely people, who are trying very hard but we thought the food was unnecessarily complicated"). / elderflowerrestaurant.co.uk; theelderflowerrestaurant; Wed-Sat 9 pm, Sun 2 pm.

HIGHSTREET KITCHEN £39 443

68 HIGH STREET
SO41 9AL 01590 673000

A relaxed venture in a Grade II-listed building – this "new local has become a firm favourite for its sensible set menus and great cooking" of seasonal ingredients. The restaurant has been a longtime dream for Gavin Barnes, formerly of Hotel TerraVina (which metamorphosed into Spot in the Woods under his tenure), and of MasterChef: The Professionals, where he made it to the final ten. / thehighstreetkitchen.co.uk; thehighstreetkitchen; Tue-Sat 10.30 pm, Sun 2 pm.

RIVAAZ £43 443

7 SAINT THOMAS STREET
SO41 9NA 01590 679999

"An absolute gem of an Indian" that's "always busy with a great atmosphere" and "well worth a visit" for its "fantastic food" and "superb staff who really know their menu" (no wonder it has snaffled the Asian Curry Awards' 'Best Asian Restaurant on the South Coast of England' title for five years running). / rivaazdining.com; rivaazlymington; Tue-Sun 11.30 pm.

SAMPHIRE AT STANWELL HOUSE £60 343

14-15 HIGH STREET
SO41 9AA 01590 677123

"The new kid on the block", this ambitious new restaurant opened in November 2022 in a "boutique hotel on Lymington's High Street" that had been closed for a year-long renovation. It has quickly established a solid reputation for its "simply prepared and beautifully presented fish, straight from the local boats". / stanwellhouse.com; stanwellhousehotel.

LYMM, CHESHIRE 5–2B

LA BOHEME £67 443

3 MILL LANE WA13 9SD 01925 753657

"Truly fine dining without being stuffy" isn't an easy act to pull off, but Olivier Troalen's "traditional Gallic" venture (he first worked in England at the French Embassy in London) in the Cheshire suburbs does it with aplomb; by all accounts it "never fails to satisfy", its "healthy northern portions" pairing with "meticulous presentation and high-quality ingredients" ("you can invite anyone, assured they won't be disappointed"). / laboheme.co.uk; oliviertroalen_laboheme; Wed & Thu, Sat, Fri 8.30 pm, Sun 7 pm.

LYNDHURST, HAMPSHIRE 2–4C

HARTNETT HOLDER & CO, LIME WOOD HOTEL £114 323

BEAULIEU RD SO43 7FZ 02380 287177

"The Italian-style food is a treat to behold" at this out-of-town retreat from Anglo-Italian chef Angela Hartnett (of Murano in Mayfair) with chef Luke Holder, in a New Forest hotel that's "a place to be seen in, for a special occasion". "Full of character and brimming with fine furnishings", it's "a beautiful venue for a (pricey) treat", although lapses drag the ratings down: more critical diners feel "it's a very good restaurant, but it never seems to get everything completely right at the same time!" and service in particular can be "surprisingly varied". Top Tip – "ask for a table in the more attractive main room when booking". / limewoodhotel.co.uk; limewoodhotel; Mon-Sun 9 pm.

MACHYNLLETH, GWYNEDD 4–3D

GWEN £130

21 HEOL MAENGWYN
SY20 8EB 01654 701100

Fully open in May 2023, as our annual diners' poll concluded, Ynyshir chef Gareth Ward has opened this wine bar / restaurant, named after his mother, to offer a more affordable taste of nearby Ynyshir in this un-touristy Welsh market town. Head chef Corrin Harrison cooks 10-course meals for just eight diners at £100 per head. The wine-bar (also selling craft beers) is walk-in only and drinks-led for the time being, but there are also plans to open a pizzeria, using a pizza oven bought from fellow-chef Peter Sanchez-Iglesias following the closure of his Pi Shop in Bristol. / gwenrestaurant.co.uk; gwenrestaurant; Wed-Sat 11 pm.

MAIDEN BRADLEY, SOMERSET 2–3B

THE BRADLEY HARE £56 323

CHURCH STREET
BA12 7HW 01985 801018

This Victorian boozer on the Duke of Somerset's estate reopened in 2021 (with rooms) after a posh refit by Andrew Kelly and James Thurstan Waterworth (the ex-European design director at Soho House). Despite the rather rapid exit of initial chef Nye Smith – to Rochelle Canteen boss Margot Henderson's new venture, 'The Three Horseshoes', in Batcombe – its local/seasonal menu gained solid marks this year. / thebradleyhare.co.uk; thebradleyhare; Tue-Sat 9 pm, Sun 4.30 pm.

MANCHESTER, GREATER MANCHESTER 5–2B

ADAM REID AT THE FRENCH, MIDLAND HOTEL £143 444

PETER ST M60 2DS 01612354780

"Such a wonderful experience" – this famous Grade II listed chamber has been at the heart of the City's dining culture for over a century (Charles Rolls first met Henry Royce here in 1904 before going on to found Rolls Royce). Under chef Adam Reid's ten-year stint, it has yet to recapture the Michelin star (the city's firs that it lost in 1975, but his twelve-course tasting menu (for £130 per person, £145 per person on Saturday night) is consistently rated as "good" to "outstanding" in our annual diners' poll. Top Menu Tip – "wonderful afternoon tea with a glass of bubbly; a massive choice of tea and coffee (bottomless) and really good selection of savory and sweet treats" served in the nearby 'Tea Room', overlooking St Peter's Square. / themidlandhotel.co.uk; thefrenchmcr; Wed-Sat 8.30 pm.

THE ALAN £66 443

18 PRINCESS STREET
M1 4LG 0161 236 8999

"A brilliant addition to the Manchester scene" – this boutique hotel yearling is already "a place to see and be seen" thanks in no small part to "excellent cooking of the sort that's not often found in hotel restaurants": "locally sourced and very high quality, with dishes that are well cooked and well presented". But while "the space may be stunning, it can be difficult to please all of the guests all of the time in such a varied space (I went to dine, not to discover the playlist played at ear-splitting volume!)" / thealanhotel.com; Mon-Sun 9.45 pm.

ALBERT'S SCHLOSS £53 234

27 PETER STREET
M2 5QR 0161 833 4040

"Always busy and buzzing," not least when it lays on dedicated Oktoberfest antics, this

ıucous Bavarian-style beer hall serves up
great food" of a heavy Alpine bent, from
:hnitzel, spätzle and fondue to other rib-
ɔating fare. Manchester-based Mission Mars,
hich owns the joint, is clearly in an expansive
ɪood: following siblings in Birmingham and (as
f December 2022) Liverpool, another Schloss
due to take over the former Rainforest Café
te on London's Leicester Square, in Spring
024. / albertsschloss.co.uk; albertsschloss; Mon-
at 10 pm, Sun 9 pm.

AR SAN JUAN £47 344

6 BEECH RD M21 9EG 0161 860 0498

'his tiny spot is "the real deal for Spanish
ood", its "authentic and delicious tapas"
ırning a Chorlton backstreet into "Las
amblas of Manchester". So well-known after
3 years that it "fills its tables from opening
me to closing time", it "now takes bookings,
ith the outside barrel table reserved for walk-
ıs". / barsanjuan.com; barsanjuan; Tue-Sun
).30 pm.

'HE BLACK FRIAR £68 333

3 KING STREET M3 6BD 0161 667 9555

This old Salford pub has risen from the dead"
ollowing its long-time closure after a fire; "the
ne Victorian building now has a brilliantly
esigned dining area incorporating much glass,
ıd opening onto a garden with tables", but it's
lso a proper boozer too. Chef Ben Chaplin's
ɔod ranges from "excellent pub grub" to more
mbitious fare and "service and ambience are
oth wonderful". / theblackfriarsalford.co.uk;
ıeblackfriarsalford; Sun-Thu 10 pm, Fri & Sat
1 pm.

UNDOBUST £35 324

1 PICCADILLY M1 2AQ 0161 359 6757

:elebrating its 10th anniversary, this northern-
ased operation "still delivers very high-quality
ıdian street food with super craft beers at
xcellent value – keep it up!". Now with two
ranches in Manchester, one each in Leeds
nd Liverpool and a new venture as far south
s Birmingham, it's "very good for a quick
urry fix" – and nobody seems to notice that
ıe Gujarati food is vegan. / bundobust.com;
undobust; Mon-Thu 9.30 pm, Fri & Sat 10 pm,
un 8 pm.

:ANTO £34 333

:UTTING ROOM SQUARE, BLOSSOM TREET M4 5DH 0161 870 5904

'his "really good tapas" spot in Ancoats is
hugely popular", so "booking is a must" –
the only drawback is that tables are reserved
or 1.5-hour slots, so it's difficult to make a
ight of it no matter how much you spend
n wine!". Billed as a Portuguese follow-up to
imon Shaw's El Gato Negro when it opened
ve years ago under head chef Carlos Gomes,
he venue now describes its food puzzlingly
s 'Mediterranean tapas' – which would
xclude the many Portuguese dishes on the
ɪenu… / cantorestaurant.com; cantomcr; Mon-
un midnight.

CLIMAT £60 434

8TH FLOOR BLACKFRIARS HOUSE, ST MARYS PARSONAGE M3 2JA 0161 710 2885

"A promising addition to the Manchester scene" which "burst onto the stage with a hell of a bang" a year ago from the team behind Chester's Corvino, with The Observer's Jay Rayner an early enthusiast. It's "a fabulous rooftop spot" on the eighth floor of a city-centre building, with "excellent and innovative modern British small plates" backed up by "a really interesting wine list" (top Burgundies, but also vintages from Greece and other less famous wine growing regions). Top Menu Tips – "don't miss the ever-changing vol-au-vent which smacks of nostalgic 1970s happiness, or the hash browns with perfectly judged taramasalata". / restaurantclimat.co.uk; restaurantclimat; Mon-Thu 11 pm, Fri & Sat 11.30 pm, Sun 8 pm.

CROMA £47 333

500 WILBRAHAM RD M21 9AP 0161 881 1117

"Pizza with an inventive streak" – plus all the standards "for those who are less adventurous" – is the offer at this surviving branch of an independent Manchester group founded in 2000. The flagship in the city centre and the Didsbury branch have closed down in recent times, to the dismay of their many fans, leaving just Chorlton and Prestwick standing. / cromapizza.co.uk; cromapizza; Mon-Thu 9 pm, Fri & Sat 9.30 pm, Sun 8.30 pm.

DISHOOM £49 445

32 BRIDGE STREET M3 3BT 0161 537 3737

"Impossible to fault and always totally reliable" – this charismatic Indian group has stormed Manchester as it stormed London before it. "The building is fabulous and beautifully fitted out and the waft of incense as you walk into the restaurant sets the scene for what's to follow" – "extremely authentic cuisine that tastes as good as it looks, with staff who are very informative and helpful when choosing dishes you have not come across before": "perfect chicken tikka, ruby murray and house black dhal are must-tries" not to mention "THE best okra fries". Early morning here is an attraction too, but they are "busy! Get there early for the best breakfast naans ever!" / dishoom.com; dishoommcr; Sun-Thu 11 pm, Fri & Sat midnight. SRA – 2 stars

THE EDINBURGH CASTLE £53 343

BLOSSOM STREET M4 5AN 0161 414 0004

This splendid 1811 pub with upstairs restaurant has been rescued as part of the ongoing redevelopment of Ancoats, winning praise for its "brilliant pub food", plus "good beer and wines" and an "awesome Sunday lunch!" / ec-ancoats.com; ec_ancoats; Wed-Sat 9 pm, Sun 6 pm.

ELNECOT £36 433

41 BLOSSOM STREETCUTTING ROOM SQUARE M4 6AJ 07412 574324

This industrial-chic small plates joint is "one of the best, most interesting, most notable, places to eat in an area that has received plenty of press attention over the last few years" – namely Ancoats, to which chef-patron Michael Clay was "committed long before it became the fashionable foodie destination it is today". Now "virtually an old-stager", his "passion comes across in his original dishes and locally sourced ingredients", with "almost everything somewhere between vg and excellent". Clay also runs Dokes Pizzeria, which sits in Central Manchester's Society food hall, and spawned a standalone restaurant, in Prestwich, in June 2022. / elnecot.com; elnecot; Mon-Fri 9 pm, Sat 9.30 pm, Sun 8.30 pm.

ERST £27 444

9 MURRAY STREET M4 6HS 0161 826 3008

"Definitely one of the stars of the buzzing Ancoats scene… in fact, the Manchester scene overall" – "a minimalistic interior sets the scene for simple but brilliantly executed dishes designed for sharing" at this low-key zeitgeisty hit: the most commented-on destination in the city in our annual diners' poll this year. "The highly professional kitchen team are at the top of their game providing fare which is as clever as it is straightforward" (e.g. "the best bread and potato dishes I've ever had!"). Aided by its "very helpful" approach to service: "it's the kind of place you wish was in your neighbourhood. Small plates and a natural (but not too funky) list of wines make it as good a place as any you will find to spend a couple of hours when in Manchester". / erst-mcr.co.uk; erst_mcr; Tue-Sat 10.30 pm.

EVUNA £56 333

277 - 279 DEANSGATE M3 4EW 0161 819 2752

For 22 years, this pioneer of Hispanic food and wine in Manchester has provided "great tapas, with interesting choices", while "showcasing the very best in world-class, award-winning Spanish wines from family-run bodegas". It remains one of the most commented-on spots in town, and now has four branches (in Deansgate, the Northern Quarter, Knutsford and Altrincham). Some would say that "it doesn't feel like it's kept up with how Spanish food and flavours have evolved in the City" or note the food is "good but no better than that". But "it's big, it's comfortable" and "even it has been overtaken as the top destination for tapas in Manchester, you can still spend many pleasant afternoons and evenings here". / evuna.com; evunarestaurants; Mon-Sat 11 pm, Sun 9 pm.

FLAWD £58 433

9 KEEPERS QUAY M4 6GL 07900 588801

"Meg and the gang are now driving it forward to the next level" at this no-bookings natural wine bar and bottle shop, which took over this "perfect canalside location" in the New Islington neighbourhood in 2022. "Very much of its time", the minimal-chic venue serves "small plates, almost all plant-based" (and invariably "competent") and is "very casual but in a good way". / flawdwine.co; flawdwine; Wed & Thu 11 pm, Fri & Sat midnight, Sun 10 pm.

EL GATO NEGRO £69 334

52 KING STREET M2 4LY 0161 694 8585

Simon Shaw's well-known "Spanish restaurant goes from strength to strength" – "there's always a good atmosphere when you walk in, the place is buzzing, the staff are very welcoming" and "the food is really high quality". "Service can be a bit chaotic", but it's "hard to criticise – everything is done really well". / elgatonegrotapas.com; elgatonegromanc; Mon-Sun 10 pm.

GREENS £52 433

43 LAPWING LN M20 2NT 0161 434 4259

Foodie TV regular Simon Rimmer's Didsbury veteran was doing the plant-based thing way before it was trendy and the "longstanding favourite" is "still great after all these years" (and now boasts a sibling in Sale); the ultimate compliment – "meat-eaters tend to enjoy it too". / greensdidsbury.co.uk; greensdidsbury; Mon-Thu 8.30 pm, Fri & Sat 9 pm, Sun 7.30 pm.

HABESHA £23 431

29-31 SACKVILLE STREET M1 3LZ 0161 228 7396

The "very basic setting" shouldn't put you off a visit to this cheap 'n' cheerful Ethiopian pitstop, above a kebab shop on Canal Street. As is typical for the cuisine, many dishes are served on an injera (a large circular bread) – "there are excellent veggie options on the short menu with reasonably priced beer". / habesharestaurant.co.uk; Mon-Sun 11 pm.

HAWKSMOOR £71 344

184-186 DEANSGATE M3 3WB 0161 836 6980

"A first-class experience we look forward to with each visit" – this Deansgate outpost of what's nowadays an international chain provides a stylish destination, owing to its location in a late- Victorian courthouse, with plenty of interesting reclaimed décor (including glazed bricks from a Liverpool public lav). "Tender and delicious" meat is, of course, the calling card, but you'll also find some "very tasty" non-carnivorous options too (an expanding range of fish; and "even as a vegetarian I love Hawksmoor"). But while all reports rate it well, it didn't inspire any full-on rave reviews this year. / thehawksmoor.com; hawksmoorrestaurants; Mon-Thu 9.30 pm, Fri & Sat 10 pm, Sun 9 pm.

HIGHER GROUND £75 343

FAULKNER HOUSE, NEW YORK STREET M1 4DY 0161 236 2931

With its "small plates, mainly plant-based, and natural wines", this "very promising Manchester newcomer" generates a good amount of feedback: "very much of its time" and "one to keep an eye on". Long delayed by the pandemic, it is from the trio behind Cinderwood Market Garden in Cheshire and Flawd wine bar in Ancoats, who have worked at high-profile restaurants in Copenhagen and New York. / highergroundmcr.co.uk; highergroundmcr; Wed-Sat 9.30 pm.

HISPI BISTRO £69 343

1C SCHOOL LANE M20 6RD 0161 445 3996

A former bank in Didsbury doing things in the "best bistro style" – and part of Cheshire-based chef Gary Usher's crowdfunded Elite Bistros group. Less commented-on than many in the group this year, but reporters applaud its "pitch-perfect service", "buzzy environment" and "tasty, distinctively flavoured dishes" (including "great Sunday lunches" and early three-course set dinners for a modest £28 per person). / hispi.net; hispi_bistro; Mon-Thu 9 pm, Fri & Sat 10 pm, Sun 5 pm.

INDIQUE £47 433

110-112 BURTON ROAD M20 1LP 0161 438 0241

"Simply the best Indian cuisine ever!" – fans don't stint in their praise of this posh West Didsbury curry house that's both 'Indian' and 'Unique'… It lives up to its name with a menu incorporating a few dishes not seen elsewhere. / indiquerestaurant.co.uk; indique_manchester; Sun-Thu 10.30 pm, Fri & Sat 11 pm.

THE IVY ASIA £78 234

THE PAVILION, BYROM STREET M3 3HG 0161 5033222

"It's noisy and chaotic" at this glossy Asian-themed operation, upstairs from the Spinningfields Ivy – "but if you want to give your teens or twenty-somethings a good lunch/night out, you won't go far wrong". For all the glam styling of the interior – even the floor shimmers with semi-precious stones – some diners complain that the pan-Asian food can "taste a little processed". / theivymanchester.com; Mon-Thu 1, Fri & Sat 2 , Sun 1 am.

JAJOO STREET FOOD DIDSBURY 332

846 WILMSLOW ROAD M20 2SG 0161 434 5151

"Absolutely superb" regional Indian street food is the MO of this well-performing joint, also with a sibling in Hale; "usually everything they do is very good to excellent" (be it biryanis, dumplings or cocktails) and while "prices have crept up" a tad of late, "no surprise there and it could be much worse". / jajoostreetfood.co.uk; jajooindianstreetfood; Tue-Sat 10 pm.

JAMES MARTIN £62 34[illegible]

2 WATSON ST M3 4LP 0161 820 9908

TV chef James Martin's over-18s-only, industrial-chic flagship shares a home in the historic Great Northern Warehouse with Manchester235 Casino; the location is "slightly odd", to be fair, "but once you're seated in the restaurant you forget about it" – and can focus on the "absolutely delicious food" (be it an "excellent tasting menu" or slap-up afternoon tea). / jamesmartinmanchester.co.uk; jamesmartinmcr; Wed-Sat 10 pm, Sun 4 pm.

KALA £63 44[illegible]

KING STREET M2 7AT 0800 160 1811

Gary Usher's "slick, very smart" operation was the best performing member of his well-known Elite Bistros chain this year in our annual diners' poll. "Fundamentally a traditional bistro (whatever that might be these days?), but here it's kind of different, with locally sourced ingredients assembled with care and consistency. Presentation of dishes is without pretension, as is the service, which is efficient and attentive. Kala has a lot going for it!" Top Tip – "good value lunch". / kalabistro.co.uk; kala_bistro_manchester; Mon-Thu 8.30 pm, Fri & Sat 9.30 pm, Sun 5 pm.

THE LIME TREE £54 44[illegible]

8 LAPWING LN M20 2WS 0161 445 1217

"Fantastic food" has been a consistent refrain of guests at Patrick Hannity's West Didsbury brasserie for more than 35 years – many of whom return again and again – "we only go on my birthday (due to distance) but it's the meal I most look forward to each year". The modern British cooking with European touches is always up-to-date on seasonality, and in 2008 Patrick became one of the first restaurateurs to invest in his own smallholding to provide ingredients for the kitchen. "The fixed-price menu (weekday lunch and early evening) is fairly short on options but reliably high on quality" – and at £16 per person for two courses or £20 for three represents tremendous value. / thelimetreerestaurant.co.uk; thelimetreeres; Tue-Sat 9.30 pm, Sun 4 pm.

LITTLE YANG SING £58 322

17 GEORGE ST M1 4HE 0161 228 7722

Warren Yeung (cousin to Harry of the big Yang Sing) runs this long-serving staple (on the site of the original Yang Sing) which is still a treasured linchpin of Chinatown for some Mancunians and is still consistently well-rated for its Cantonese cuisine and dim sum. This year's worst comment? "service is patchy at busy times". / facebook.com; littleyangsing; Mon-Sat 11 pm, Sun 10.30 pm.

LUCKY CAT MANCHESTER £89

100 KING STREET M2 4WU 0161 424 915[illegible]

Will Gordon Ramsay succeed 'up north', where he's failed to make waves 'darn sarf'? In terms of grandeur alone, this May 2023

Mana, Manchester

opening (too late for feedback in our annual diners' poll) eclipses the London original as it occupies the former banking hall of a gobsmackingly grand building – a Portland-stone-clad monolith designed by Lutyens for the Midland Bank in the 1930s – also home in its time to Jamie's Italian. On the menu, the same rather pricey pan-Asian small plates. / gordonramsayrestaurants.com; luckycatbygordonramsay; Tue, Wed midnight, Thu-Sat 2 am.

MACKIE MAYOR £44 334

1 EAGLE STREET M4 5JY NO TEL

A "lovely conversion" of the old Smithfield market, by the Altrincham Market team, has given rise to this "fabulous food hall"; it's a "noisy, busy and fun" sort of place ("outside feels like the Meatpacking District of old") but "if you can nab a table, watch the world go by and enjoy the great selection of food and drinks". The latter includes nine outfits, with one reporter singling out New Wave Ramen as having "really hit their stride" ("worth going to MM for this alone"). / mackie.mayor.co.uk; mackiemayor; Tue-Sat 10 pm, Sun 6 pm.

MANA £203 544

SAWMILL COURT M4 6AF 01613927294

"Simply the best" – Simon Martin's Ancoats superstar continues to maintain the "outstanding all-round" form that secured its place in the history books in 2019 when it carried back to Manchester the city's first Michelin star since 1977. "Sublime dishes are cooked with invention and precision" by the squadron of chefs put on display by the open kitchen (you can walk between workstations as the chefs are plating up). They deliver a £195 per person tasting menu, although you can fight the cost-of-living crisis with a cut-down version at £95 per person. Combinations are clever and each dish is intricately crafted. The contemporary space it occupies – at the foot of a modern block – is also full of drama, with a very high ceiling and huge windows. / manarestaurant.co.uk; restaurant.mana; Wed-Sat midnight.

MARAY £45 332

14 BRAZENNOSE STREET M2 6LW 0151 347 0214

Inspired by bold Middle Eastern flavours via Le Marais district in Paris, this yearling is "a great place to visit" thanks to its intriguing menu selection and "relaxed and friendly service". Founders James Bates, Tom White and Dom Jones launched the concept in Liverpool before heading across to Manchester. / maray.co.uk; marayrestaurants; Mon-Sat 10 pm, Sun 6 pm.

MUSU £95 434

64 BRIDGE STREET M3 3BN 0161 883 7753

"A real feast for the senses and already very popular"; "a quite incredible fit-out for this newish opening" is just one of the attractions at this October 2022 debut, on the site that was previously Randall & Aubin (RIP), but which has been subject to a £3.5m refit. The name means 'infinite possibilities': here, that translates into seven-course or eleven-course Japanese omakase menus for up to £150 per person – "expensive to visit but quite fabulous ingredients prepared by Michael Shaw and his team" (he was previously at a traditional pub in Lydgate, near Oldham so this is quite the change, but his pedigree includes stints at Le Manoir, Ramsay's Aubergine and Richard Neat). In a March 2023 review, The Guardian's Grace Dent declared it "gigantically ambitious and pointedly bonkers", resembling "nothing so much as the Starship Enterprise, albeit one with geishas on the walls" and with "outstanding… Japanese food served in the manner of Le Manoir… Every bowl is a minuscule portion of exquisite pleasure". / musumcr.com; musumcr; Wed-Sat midnight.

THE OYSTERCATCHER £63 343

123 MANCHESTER ROAD M21 9PG 0161 637 5890

A "great, popular local fish restaurant" where the "brilliant" and "affordable" catch often comes chargrilled, or with influences from other seafood-loving nations ("favourites include the Thai curry prawn dish"); the "recent addition of outside covered tables" is an added boon. After six years in the game, a much-touted sibling in Sale's foodie-oriented Stanley Square development was due to launch in summer 2023. / theoystercatcher.org; theoystercatcherchorlton; Mon-Thu 9 pm, Fri & Sat 10 pm, Sun 8 pm.

RUDY'S £42 443

9 COTTON STREET, ANCOATS M4 5BF 0161 660 8040

"The high-quality, authentic pizzas" are "just the best" – "especially the plain old Neapolitan" – at the "really buzzing" Ancoats original of what has become a fast-growing chain. Founded by Jim Morgan & Kati Wilson nine years ago, it is now has 18 branches around the country as part of the Mission Mars/Albert's Schloss operation – but is "still very good" by all accounts, and if it "does get a bit noisy in there, that only adds to the atmosphere". / rudyspizza.co.uk; wearerudyspizza; Mon-Sat 10 pm, Sun 9 pm.

SAKURA £36

8 SALISBURY HOUSE, ST STEPHEN STREET M3 6AX 0161 834 9988

Opened in August 2022 in a former Chinese takeaway/chip shop, this 'authentic Hong Kong' (their words) venue shot to local fame on the back of an April 2023 review from The Observer's Jay Rayner, who enjoyed its "profoundly comforting" dishes, with the "textural joys" of both traditionally Asian "slippery foods" and plenty of deep-fried, crunchy ones (including "very good chicken wings"). Reports please! / sakura-japanese-restaurant.co.uk; sakurainstagram; Mon & Tue, Thu-Sat 9 pm.

SAM'S CHOP HOUSE £54 33

BACK POOL FOLD OFF CROSS STREET M2 1HN 0161 834 3210

A true "gem" – this "recently reopened Manchester institution" dates back to 1868, when it was founded by Sam Studd (whose brother Tom had opened nearby Tom's Chop House a year before), and later became L.S. Lowry's favourite watering hole. It serves a menu of "traditional British staples that are actually quite hard to find done well, as they are here". Top Menu Tip – "the corned beef hash is a must-try-before-you-die dish". / samschophouse.com; samschophouse_; Mon-Thu 11 pm, Fri & Sat midnight, Sun 10 pm.

SAN CARLO £73 33

40 KING STREET WEST M3 2WY 0161 834 6226

This "buzzy Italian in central Manchester" (opened in 2004) is one of the better-known locations both in the city and in the national chain of which it is part; and at lunch it "buzzes with business people" (evenings are overwhelmingly social). "Good traditional food is well cooked with delicious pasta and fish" and the old-school service is "friendly, efficient and well organised". / sancarlo.co.uk; sancarlorestaurants; Mon-Sat 11 pm, Sun 10 pm.

SEXY FISH

UNIT 1 & 2 SPINNINGFIELDS SQUARE M3 3AE 020 3764 2000

Open from mid-October 2023 (after we go to press), this new 200-cover outpost of Richard Caring's showy and luxurious fish and seafood brand has been a long time in the making. At the gateway to Spinningfields where the Armani Emporium used to be, it is set to feature fish tanks; a bar made of glowing pink onyx and glass; and a water-feature (or 'cascading waterfall' as the press release prefers to call it). Will Finchley-born Caring find a new spiritual home amidst Manc's bevvy of star footie players and WAGs ? / sexyfish.com; sexyfishlondon; Sun-Wed 1 am, Thu-Sat 2 am.

STREET URCHIN £51 44

72 GREAT ANCOATS STREET M4 5BG 07470 804979

"This excellent small restaurant is not to be missed" – "a gem hidden in plain sight on Great Ancoats Street". "The menu changes frequently and is driven by seasonal locally sourced produce and the passions of Kevin and Rachel Choudhary". "It's a relaxing space, an oasis full of potted plants and herbs, where conversation is easy, portions are generous, and dishes combine traditional ideas and concepts with innovative contemporary additions". / street-urchin.co.uk; st_urchin; Wed-Sun 11 pm.

UD (WAS SUGO) £58 443

BLOSSOM STREET
4 6BF 0161 236 5264

Seriously the best pasta (and great starters too)" can be found at this "consistently excellent" operation from brothers Mike & Alex de Martiis, who changed its name from Sugo Pasta Kitchen to Sud in early 2023 following a legal wrangle with a similarly named Glasgow outfit. "You can't fault the food at any of the branches – the new one in Sale is our current favourite"; it follows the Altrincham original, which opened in 2015, and the follow-up in Ancoats. The brothers opened a fourth branch in August 2023 in the city centre's Exhibition building (on the site of the 1817 Peterloo Massacre), which it shares with Basque live-fire restaurant Baratxuri and Scandi small-plates specialist OSMA. / sudpasta.co.uk; sudpasta; Tue-Sat 10 pm, Sun 8.30 pm.

ATTU £79 234

HARDMAN SQ, GARTSIDE ST
3 3EB 0161 819 2060

ces of expensive, moodily dark wood paneling and other luxurious surfaces contribute to the sta-friendly scene at this original outpost of what's now become a national chain of glam an-Asian destinations. Feedback was relatively limited this year, but raised no complaints regarding its mix of Chinese dishes with sushi and Thai favourites. / tattu.co.uk; tatturestaurant; un-Thu midnight, Fri & Sat 1 am.

0 TIB LANE £45

0 TIB LANE M2 4JB 0161 833 1034

With its thoughtful cocktail and drinks menu and interesting modern European menu, this two-year-old bar/restaurant in the city centre isn't trying too hard but is worthy of attention. It has yet to inspire much in the way of feedback in our annual diners' poll, but ay Rayner found "a lot to be stimulated by" in his March 2023 review: "somewhere along the way Manchester was culinarily twinned with Hackney… modern trends have been attended to… but there's also a wonderful old-school sensibility at work" and even "a couple of flourishes" like "a version of Fergus Henderson's hot, wobbly roasted bone marrow with salty, vinegary parsley salad". Reports please! / 10tiblane.com; 10tiblane; Wed-Sat 1 am, Sun 10 pm.

'HIS & THAT £24 422

SOAP ST M4 1EW 0161 832 4971

Still the best-value food in Manchester city centre – perfect for a good cheap daytime filler" (not least their famous 'rice and three curries deal', inching up in price but only at snail's pace); "apart from a minor refit a few years back", this Northern Quarter curry house "has been doing the same thing since forever – and when it remains this good, why change?" / thisandthatcafe.co.uk; Sun-Thu 8 pm, Fri & Sat 9 pm.

TNQ RESTAURANT & BAR £74 343

108 HIGH ST M4 1HQ 0161 832 7115

"An exemplar of city-centre neighbourhood bistros" – this "popular Northern Quarter restaurant" (that's the NQ in the name) has "settled down into a pleasing rhythm of knowing exactly who they are and what they need to do (kind-of like your favourite comfy pair of high-quality shoes… in the best possible way!)"; and "consistently delivers excellent food that doesn't cost the earth". / tnq.co.uk; tnqrestaurant; Mon-Sat 10 pm, Sun 7 pm.

20 STORIES £97 234

NO 1 SPINNINGFIELDS, 1 HARDMAN SQUARE M3 3JE 0161 204 3333

"Spectacular views over the Manchester city skyline and beyond" can make this "slick" D&D London operation "a breathtaking venue (but don't look down – the clue is in the name)". Fans also hail its "well-prepared" modern brasserie dishes, but for such a landmark venue, reports remain surprisingly limited, so we've maintained last year's conservative food rating. / 20stories.co.uk; 20storiesmcr; Sun-Thu 11 pm, Fri & Sat 1 am.

YANG SING £54

34 PRINCESS STREET
M1 4JY 0161 236 2200

We maintain a holding entry for this Manchester icon, founded in 1977 and a mainstay of the city's dining scene ever since. Closed since early 2022, co-owner Bonnie Yeung told the Manchester Evening News in late 2022 of hoping to reopen in 2023 or 2024, dependent on renegotiating the lease to reduce the operation's footprint ("we won't be across all four floors, but we really want to knuckle down and focus on the restaurant"). "We're hoping for next year, but we're happy to hang on and make sure it's the right time"… "so I look forward to us being more versatile and moving more seasonally". / yang-sing.com; yangsingmcr; Mon-Sun 9.30 pm.

YUZU £37 332

39 FAULKNER STREET
M1 4EE 0161 236 4159

This "excellent Japanese restaurant" – now 10 years old – offers "unpretentious homely Japanese cooking and a great sake menu". All the favourites are here, from noodles and tempura to kara-age chicken and gyoza, with the exception of sushi – but you can replicate its flavours by ordering assorted sashimi over the bowl of sushi-seasoned rice. / yuzumanchester.co.uk; yuzumanchester; Tue-Sat 10 pm.

MARGATE, KENT 3–3D

ANGELA'S £56 543

21 THE PARADE CT9 1EX 01843 319978

"Stunning seafood within walking distance of the Turner Contemporary gallery and Margate seafront" has won fame for Lee Coad's "tiny" sibling venue to Dory, that he opened in 2017 with his wife Charlotte Forsdike and chef Rob Cooper. "Gorgeous fresh fish is served in a very relaxed dining space": "a café-like setting that's enjoyable if not special". "Service is fabulous too", helping to account for why this is nowadays the most commented-on venue in town in our annual diners' poll and "booking is essential" ("having finally landed a table, the memory of the roasted turbot skin will remain with me for a very long time!") / angelasofmargate.com; angelas_of_margate; Tue-Sat 10 pm.

BOTTEGA CARUSO £58 343

BROAD STREET CT9 1EW 01843 297142

Herald of the new, cool, foodie-friendly Margate scene, this Old Town venue (Grace Dent is a fan) showcases the produce of Foglianise, where co-owner Simona Di Dio's family runs a farm; the food (meatballs, caponata, gnocchi, etc.) is "delicious as are the wines" – and if you want to learn to pimp your pasta, they also run the next-door Margate Cookery School. / bottegacaruso.com; bottegacaruso; Wed & Thu 3 pm, Fri & Sat 9 pm.

BUOY & OYSTER £66 332

44 HIGH STREET CT9 1DS 01843 446631

This "lovely seafood restaurant" is a "good find in Margate", with an "extensive and varied menu" that features fresh oysters and "delicious seafood platters" but also "includes local meat and vegetarian options". "Staff couldn't be friendlier" and "the whole experience is very enjoyable". / buoyandoyster.com; buoyandoyster; Mon-Sun 9 pm.

DORY'S £43 443

24 HIGH STREET
CT9 1DS 01843 520 391

The "little sister to Angela's", a seafood restaurant-with-rooms round the corner, "never fails to satisfy" with its menu of "creative, unique fishy small plates" that are raw, pickled, cured or smoked. The owners run a co-op producing their own fruit and veg, and this site also has a wine shop stocking bottles from England and beyond. / dorysofmargate.com; dorys_of_margate; Mon, Thu-Sun 9.30 pm.

FORT ROAD HOTEL 344

18 FORT ROAD CT9 1HF 01843 661313

"Lovely food and attentive service" are the standout features of this newly opened boutique hotel in a "prime position in Margate" – once a Regency boarding house, rescued from dereliction by Frieze art fair founder Matthew Slotover. Works by Tracey Emin and other Margate-related artists hang in the bar. Top Menu Tip – "delicious breakfast: black pudding and the most orange eggs I've ever seen". / fortroadhotel.com; fortroadhotel.

SARGASSO £60 434

MARGATE HARBOUR ARM, STONE PIER CT9 1AP 01843 229270

In a "great location on the harbour wall", Ed Wilson & Josie Stead's "perfect" and "amazing" follow-up to beloved E London venue Brawn is "a fantastic addition to Margate" by all accounts; the self-styled 'wine bar with food' may affect a casual air ("great soundtrack" included), but the seafood and vegetable-centric food is "interesting and at times very good" indeed. / sargasso.bar; sargasso.bar; Fri & Sat 9.30 pm, Sun 3 pm, Thu 8.30 pm.

MARKET HARBOROUGH, LEICESTERSHIRE 5–4D

ASCOUGH'S BISTRO £50 323

24 ST MARY'S ROAD LE16 7DU 01858 466 966

This "great local restaurant" from Chris & Abby Ascough has built a solid reputation over 19 years for its "beautifully cooked and presented food" at "exceptionally good value" – including a £20 set lunch and a six-course tasting menu for £48 per person with matching wines for £20 per person. / ascoughsbistro.co.uk; Tue-Sat 9.15 pm.

MARLBOROUGH, WILTSHIRE 2–2C

DAN'S AT THE CROWN £56 343

6-7 THE PARADE SN8 1NE 01672 512112

Australian Dan Bond's unpretentious restaurant, which gained an outdoor marquee in covid times, is a real local hit; "you know everyone will like the food, you know it will be fair value" and "you know they'll work their socks off to give you a good time"…."plus, Dan's just a good bloke", so "how could it not be everyone's favourite?" Top Tip – "their occasional wine dinners are great fun too". / dansrestaurant.co.uk; dans_restaurant; Tue-Sat 9 pm, Sun 3 pm.

RICK STEIN £68 233

LLORAN HOUSE, 42A HIGH STREET SN8 1HQ 01672 233333

"One of Rick Stein's smarter outposts" – this centrally located outpost of the celeb chef family's empire occupies a period building on the high street, and is a useful option in this surprisingly thinly provided area, including for "a business chat with friends". Limited but positive feedback this year on its cooking, although the indication is that it's "very decent". / rickstein.com; ricksteinrestaurants; Mon-Wed 9 pm, Thu-Sun 10 pm. SRA – accredited

MARLOW, BUCKINGHAMSHIRE 3–3A

THE BUTCHER'S TAP £31 433

15 SPITTAL STREET SL7 3HJ 01628 401535

"After a minor revamp where the butchery emphasis was toned down and the pub feel improved", this highly rated boozer ("a noisy part of the Kerridge empire") "now has a great atmosphere". "The meat is exceptional" too, whether you select your cut from the counter and watch as the chefs grill it, or just pop in for the "superb burgers" (including the in-demand special burger of the month). / thebutcherstapandgrill.co.uk; thebutcherstapandgrill; Mon-Sun 9 pm.

THE COACH £83 433

3 WEST STREET SL7 2LS 01628 483013

"The best of Tom Kerridge's places" – his no-bookings local in the centre of the town may look "pleasant, if nothing exceptional", but it is the one the locals head to in preference to any other. "Normally it is difficult to get excited about a soup and a fishcake" but here the "simple but excellent food makes it worth a special journey" and "service is very welcoming and professional". / thecoachmarlow.co.uk; thecoachmarlow; Wed-Sun 8.45 pm.

THE HAND & FLOWERS £131 222

126 WEST STREET SL7 2BP 01628 482277

What to make of TV-star Tom Kerridge's Thames Valley pub, which helped catapult him to stardom in 2012 when Michelin awarded the place two stars. The choice of this ordinary-feeling inn on the edge of town was always "a little quirky", but for many years satisfaction levels here held up even if the "ambience varies depending on where you are sat, as it can be nice and atmospheric, or you can feel very much shunted to one side". But for the most part, folks historically didn't quibble: they just focused on the down-to-earth style and "very high-quality British cooking". The latter is still sometimes applauded, even if dishes can seem "more traditional and less interesting/ exciting than expected". But the overall tide of sentiment has turned in recent years, with a growing view that "it's such a pity that what was a fantastic restaurant has now become overpriced and overrated". Even those who still hail it as "quite possibly the best gastropub in Britain" can still view it as "seriously overpriced and certainly not worthy of two Michelin stars". And that's still the upbeat verdict. More representative of feedback are those who say it's "horrendously overpriced for what is only reasonable pub food" ("two stars? I'm sorry, but that really is a case of the 'Emperor's New Clothes'"). Despite this being one of Michelin's worst ongoing conclusions, with their history of kowtowing to TV celebrities we're not betting on a re-rating any time soon. / thehandandflowers.co.uk; handfmarlow; Mon-Sat 9.15 pm, Sun 5 pm.

THE IVY MARLOW GARDEN £77 22[illegible]

66-68 HIGH ST SL7 1AH 01628 902777

There's no doubting the "wonderful location, especially in summer" at this outpost of Richard Caring's brasserie empire, where the "lovely décor" inside is matched by a pretty garden. While caveats remain over the service and food (Caring's venues are "never knowing under-priced"), for the majority the overall package is "solidly pleasing" ("even for a non-chain- lover"). / theivymarlowgarden.com; the_ivy_collection; Mon-Fri 10 pm, Sat 10.30 pm, Sun 9 pm.

THE OARSMAN £67 33[illegible]

46 SPITTAL STREET SL7 1DB 01628 617755

This ever-gentrifying 'bistropub and wine bar' (their designation) was launched by Nigel Sutcliffe and James McLean, co-founders of restaurant consultancy Truffle Hunting, in 2021, and picked up a 'Newcomer of the Year' award from the folks at Estrella Damm. Chef Scott Smith (ex-of acclaimed haunts Arbutus and Wild Honey) oversees the carnivorous British bistro dishes and, while there's the odd skeptical review submitted, even they acknowledge "most people seem positive as it slowly builds a reputation in the town". / theoarsman.co.uk; theoarsmanmarlow; Mon-Sat 9.45 pm, Sun 5.30 pm.

SINDHU, MACDONALD COMPLEAT ANGLER HOTEL £86 44[illegible]

THE COMPLEAT ANGLER SL7 1RG 01628 405 405

"Atul Kochhar's Marlow outpost is in the charming Compleat Angler hotel by the side of the Thames" – a marriage of traditional British setting and Indian cuisine that's proving enduringly popular. At night the room is less characterful, "whereas in daylight, there is the fabulous view of the River Thames's Marlow Weir". "Service is top notch and very welcoming" and the cuisine "is an inventive fine-dining take on Indian cuisine, beautifully presented" – "every element is spiced marvellously and cooked perfectly". There are "interesting wine pairings too (I'd never previously heard of mango wine. I certainly wouldn't have ordered it had it not been selected for us… it worked well!") / sindhurestaurant.co.uk; sindhumarlow; Sun-Thu 9.30 pm, Fri & Sat 10 pm.

VAASU BY ATUL KOCHHAR £84 54[illegible]

2 CHAPEL STREET SL7 1DD 01628 362274

"The best Anglo-Indian food tasted this year!" is a typical view of this three-year-old venture from high-profile chef Atul Kochhar, which just might be the best of his half-dozen restaurants (which include Sindhu at the Compleat Angler, also in Marlow). Inspired by the cuisines of the Punjab and Rajasthan, it has a "lovely tasting

enu" as well as shorter set and à la carte
›tions, and serves some "interesting and very
:asant Indian wines". / vaasurestaurant.co.uk;
asumarlow; Wed-Sun 9.30 pm.

HE VANILLA POD £76 443

WEST ST SL7 2LS 01628 898101

Dut-performing many more feted restaurants" Michael Mcdonald "runs a fantastic family-n restaurant that never fails to hit the spot" at is "quiet and discreet" fixture, which occupies rt of a house that was once home to TS iot. The dining room itself is "small, but well d out" and buoyed along by its "very good, endly and professional service". "The menu limited, but every dish is enticing" and all-·all it provides "a proper dining experience" at's "consistently great value" (and one of the 0 most-commented-on outside London in r annual diners' poll). / thevanillapod.co.uk; ·vanillapodmarlow; Tue-Sat 9 pm.

IARTON, CHESHIRE 5–2B

A POPOTE £92 443

IURCH FARM, MANCHESTER ROAD
:11 9HF 01260 224785

'errific French cooking" by Cheshire-born ef-patron Joseph Rawlins combines with maculate presentation from his FOH rtner, Parisienne Gaëlle Radigon, in a art, "contemporary setting" ("love having a olecloth: so many restaurants don't") at this nverted farmhouse in a village famous for its nber-framed church and ancient 'Marston k' (Britain's largest tree). Top Tip – "the set :al is exceptional value". / la-popote.co.uk; opoteuk; Thu-Sat 11 pm, Sun 6 pm.

IASHAM, NORTH YORKSHIRE 8–4B

AMUEL'S, SWINTON PARK OTEL & SPA £97 334

VINTON PARK HG4 4JH 01765 680900

'he formal dining room at Swinton Estate" – country house hotel in a beautiful setting that oplies much of its food from local sources" d its own 20,000 acres of grounds. Ruth nsom has been in charge of the kitchens ring 2023 – a year that saw solid all-round ings for its ambitious cuisine – in advance of nding over to former Roux Scholar Nicole nham-Corlette following a £500,000 refurb complete in early 2024: part of the property's tate-to-plate' philosophy which aims to luce its carbon footprint to being neutral by 30. / swintonestate.com; swintonestate; Mon-n 9 pm.

IATFIELD, KENT 3–3C

HE POET £91 542

AIDSTONE RD TN12 7JH 01892 722416

'he service and food are simply sublime" at s "lovely pub" – named in honour of the 'st World War poet Siegfried Sassoon, who ed nearby – which has served "the most omplished food" for some years. South rican-born chef-patron Petrus Madutlela, o has masterminded the venue's gastronomic rise since 2015, departed in early 2023 and is replaced by Lee Adams, who worked for the late Gary Rhodes and returns to his native Kent after a decade running kitchens in Dubai and Hong Kong. Early reports suggest standards remain very high under the new regime, although consistency may be an issue. / thepoetatmatfield.co.uk; poetatmatfield; Tue-Sat 9 pm, Sun 6 pm.

MATLOCK, DERBYSHIRE 5–3C

STONES £70 444

1C DALE RD DE4 3LT 01629 56061

Kevin Stone (the chef), wife Jade and sister Katie Temple provide "very good cooking and service" at this converted pub, whose glazed dining room, opening onto an outside terrace, makes the most of its "lovely setting" overlooking the River Derwent. Despite the heritage of the building, the menu – with a tasting option – is restaurant-style fare, not pub grub. / stones-restaurant.co.uk; stonesmatlock; Tue-Sat 8.30 pm.

MAYFORD, SURREY 3–3A

THE DRUMMING SNIPE £60 332

GUILDFORD ROAD
GU22 9QT 07849 088460

The second link in the growing Brucan Pubs group, set up by James Lyon Shaw and Jamie Dobbin, who met during their days at the famous Ivy. By all accounts the three-year-old venture is "surprisingly good for a somewhat unprepossessing area", and with "good-value set menus" to boot. Top Menu Tip – "in my experience the best dishes are the slow-cooked ones". / thedrummingsnipe.co.uk; thedrummingsnipe; Mon-Sat 9.30 pm, Sun 9 pm.

MELMERBY, NORTH YORKSHIRE 8–3A

CHEFSTABLE AT TRUEFOODS £172 553

9 HALLIKELD CLOSE
HG4 5GZ 01765 640927

"A true gem" – chef-patron Mitch Mitchell's utterly unlikely venture, located within a factory unit on an industrial estate that manufactures sauces and stocks. The 14-course tasting menu (Fri/Sat night only) caused Giles Coren to invoke Noma no less, and reporters this year all concurred that it is "an experience not to be missed". The "only tiny issue is who you sit next to, as your neighbour could be totally loud and full of self-importance – but this place deserves a star at least!" / truefoodsltd.com; truefoodsltd; Mon-Fri 5 pm.

MENAI BRIDGE, GWYNEDD 4–1C

DYLAN'S RESTAURANT £60 223

ST GEORGE'S ROAD
LL59 5EY 01248 716 714

There's no dissent about the "great setting" of this "busy, buzzy" modern waterfront establishment, overlooking the Menai Straits; the food, however, tends not to live up to it, being "competent rather than interesting" (though "vegetarian dishes perform better than fish"). Despite recurrent grumbles, the business opened its fourth North Wales link in September 2023: a baked goods and general store, on Conwy's High Street, and with a restaurant offering epic views to the castle. / dylansrestaurant.co.uk; dylansrestaurants; Mon-Sun 10 pm.

SOSBAN & THE OLD BUTCHER'S £212 432

1 HIGH ST, MENAI BRIDGE
LL59 5EE 01248 208 131

Stephen Stevens continues to impress those who visit this converted butcher's shop just over the Menai Bridge, which has won renown as one of Wales's top culinary destinations. You are encouraged to 'Forget the menu and savour the experience', which is only available three nights per week and remains at £175 per person. / sosbanandtheoldbutchers.com; Thu-Sat 11 pm.

MILBORNE PORT, DORSET 2–3B

THE CLOCKSPIRE £87 443

GAINSBOROUGH
DT9 5BA 01963 251458

A "beautifully renovated building" – originally an 1860s school, with impressive vaulted ceilings and now a mezzanine bar – plays host to this exceptional outfit on the Dorset/Somerset border. Chef Luke Sutton (ex-the acclaimed L'Ortolan, in Berkshire) oversees the "varied" and "very interesting" British menu, which remains of note for its particularly "good-value" set menu. / theclockspire.com; Wed-Sat 9.30 pm, Sun 4.30 pm.

MILFORD-ON-SEA, HAMPSHIRE 2–4C

LAZY LION £47 333

32 HIGH STREET
SO41 0QD 01590 641111

This "great local pub" with rooms on the High St, and handy for the beach, was taken over by new owners four years back, when it also adopted its current name – echoed inside by various lion artworks. With its "great Sunday roast" and "delicious rest of menu" (including a specials board and vegan menu) it's "always busy" and they're particularly "famous for their pies!" / thelazylion.co.uk; Mon-Sun 10 pm.

VERVEINE FISHMARKET RESTAURANT £81 543

98 HIGH ST SO41 0QE 01590 642 176

"Constantly innovative, super-fresh fish dishes" from chef-patron David Wykes have established this "small, warm space" with an in-house fishmonger as a true "destination restaurant", invariably hailed as a "great discovery" by first-time visitors. The "outstanding tasting menus" are presented in an unusual format, with guests nominating the number of courses but not their content. They arrive with "imaginative accompaniments" and "charming, attentive service". / verveine.co.uk; 98verveine; Tue-Sat 9.15 pm.

MILTON UNDER WYCHWOOD, OXFORDSHIRE 2–1C

HARE £54 333

3 HIGH STREET OX7 6LA 01993 835 763

Taken over and transformed some years back by Sue Hawkins of Bar Humbug fame, a "great little pub" where chef Matt Date turns out "competent" British food from a "varied menu", including a seafood specials board and a "nice Sunday lunch". Bonus points for the "always delightful service" ("you're not rushed at all and made to feel welcome"). / themiltonhare.co.uk; thehare_miltonunderwychwood; Mon-Sat 11 pm, Sun 10.30 pm.

MISTLEY, ESSEX 3–2D

THE MISTLEY THORN RESTAURANT & ROOMS £55 343

HIGH ST CO11 1HE 01206 392 821

Californian Sherri Singleton's "marvelous neighbourhood restaurant" occupies a 1723 coaching inn, with great views of the River Stour, and bedrooms set above the pub or on top of kitchen shop and cookery school. The "consistent" and "sophisticated seafood menu" (but not just) ensures that it's "always popular", and there was praise this year for the "good-value set menu" (two courses £24.95 or three courses £27.95 per person). / mistleythorn.co.uk; TheMistleyThorn; Mon-Sun 9 pm.

MOBBERLEY, CHESHIRE 5–2B

BULLS HEAD £46 333

MILL LANE WA16 7HX 01565 873395

This quintessential village pub delivers "very good food" (they're especially proud of their Steak and 'Wobbly Ale' Pie, but also do "great desserts"), and is part of the also "very good Cheshire Cat Pubs and Bars co.", a seven-strong group of characterful venues. Impressively, the Bull's Head has not one but two of its own car clubs: the '3P', for Porsche owners, and fierce rival the 'Good Fellows', dedicated to owners of any car that isn't a Porsche! / thebullsheadpub.co.uk; bullsheadmobberley; Mon-Thu 9.15 pm, Fri & Sat 9.45 pm, Sun 8.45 pm.

THE CHURCH INN £63 333

CHURCH LANE WA16 7RD 01565 873178

Opposite a twelfth-century church, this "really good" village outfit is "exactly what you'd want from a good-quality pub": a "relaxed, friendly and chatty" spot turning out some "perfectly judged" food (not least fish 'n' chips, though the desserts are also "technical and brilliantly flavoured"). / churchinnmobberley.co.uk; Mon-Fri 5 pm, Sat & Sun 10 pm.

MORECAMBE, LANCASHIRE 5–1A

MIDLAND HOTEL £72 334

MARINE ROAD WEST LA4 4BU 01524 424000

The "best afternoon tea ever" – arguably the main event at this "Art Deco masterpiece" of a hotel, in a "stunning location" overlooking Morecambe Bay. The food in the dining room – the 'Sun Terrace' – is "always enjoyable", too; although the odd cynic says "you're paying for the views". / inncollectiongroup.com; theinncollectiongroup; Mon-Sun 9 pm.

MORSTON, NORFOLK 6–3C

MORSTON HALL £176 434

MAIN COAST RD NR25 7AA 01263 741041

"A favourite place in Norfolk" – "Galton Blackiston and team continue to be at the top of their game" at this highly commented-on destination (amongst the top 50 outside the capital in terms of the volume of feedback in our annual diners' poll) near the north Norfolk coast, where the "conservatory-style dining room overlooking the gardens is a lovely setting". A favourite choice for a gastronomic break, "the wide repertoire of outstanding tasting menus changes every day" (seven courses for £135 per person): "reliably wonderful food" from "locally sourced produce" with "exceptional presentation" and "portions that are just right". But while all the many reports it attracts rate it well this year, a number also note that "sadly prices have risen, and it seems really expensive now". / morstonhall.com; morstonhallhotel; Mon-Sun 6 pm.

MOULSFORD, OXFORDSHIRE 2–2D

THE BEETLE & WEDGE BOATHOUSE £57 234

FERRY LN OX10 9JF 01491 651381

"It's in such an amazing spot" – a "romantic setting by the Thames" on a stretch of riverbank immortalised in the 'Wind in the Willows': this riverside inn (which housed a ferry until 1967) has had its looks updated in recent years, and is nowadays more pub-like that it once was. Some old-timers say it's "not as good as before", but for others it's "very good" and everyone agrees that on a sunny day few places are nicer than its outside terrace. / beetleandwedge.co.uk; thebeetleandwedgeboathouse; Mon-Sun 11 pm.

MOULTON, CAMBRIDGESHIRE 3–1C

THE PACKHORSE INN £68 333

BRIDGE ST CB8 8SP 01638 751818

"Consistently solid gastropub food" earns ratings to match at this well-presented inn from the East Anglian Chestnut Collection of pubs. / thepackhorseinn.com; thepackhorseinn; Wed-Sat 8.30 pm, Sun 7.45 pm.

MOUNTSORREL, LEICESTERSHIRE 5-4

JOHN'S HOUSE £95 54

139-141 LOUGHBOROUGH ROAD LE12 7AR 01509 415569

"The on-site farm is great for a wander" before or after a meal at John Duffin's family-owned venue, which uses produce from the surrounding property where he grew up (and you can also stay in one of his family's converted cottages). A renowned culinary spark in part of the Midlands with a dearth of decent eateries, all reports applaud it as a "ger with superb food" and "such friendly staff" too. / johnshouse.co.uk; johnshouserest; Wed-Sat 7.30 pm.

MOUSEHOLE, CORNWALL 1–4

THE OLD COASTGUARD £69 22

THE PARADE TR19 6PR 01736 731222

An "impressive location" commanding sea views to St Clement's Isle makes this seaside hotel a "great place for fish and seafood" landed just two miles away at Newlyn. It's a lesser-known (and less highly rated) sibling to the Gurnard's Head and the Felin Fach Griffin in Wales. / oldcoastguardhotel.co.uk; theoldcoastguard; Mon-Sun 11 pm.

2 FORE STREET RESTAURANT £59 43

2 FORE ST TR19 6PF 01736 731164

This "busy" bistro a short walk from the harbour serves "fabulous fish-based food with wonderful accompaniments" from chef-patron Joe Wardell, who trained in the classics under Raymond Blanc. "We're regulars in Cornwall and celebrate anniversaries here – tl fresh seafood and blackboard specials never disappoint". / 2forestreet.co.uk; 2Forestreet; Mo Sun 9.30 pm.

MUDEFORD, CORNWALL 2–4

NOISY LOBSTER £75 33

AVON BEACH BH23 4AN 01425 272162

This beachfront diner is a "post-covid success story – bigger and better since reopening" and doing a roaring trade in ultra-local lobster and other seafood. It also offers real "value for money in Sandbanks – now there's a thing…" / avon-beach.noisylobster.co.uk; thenoisylobster; Mon-Sun 11 pm.

MURCOTT, OXFORDSHIRE 2–1

THE NUT TREE INN £145 43

MAIN STREET OX5 2RE 01865 331253

Mike (chef) & FOH Imogen North's "stunning historic venture is "always a treat"; "it's a proper pub", yes, but also doubles as an acclaimed restaurant, where Mike's "simply sublime" food (seven-course tasting menus or à la carte at lunch, and tasting menus only by night) "cannot be recommended highly

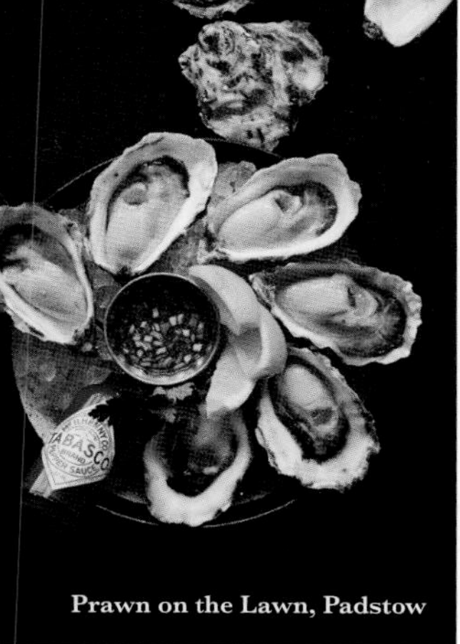

Prawn on the Lawn, Padstow

ough". / nuttreeinn.co.uk; Nuttreeinn; Wed-Sat 30 pm.

NAILSWORTH, GLOUCESTERSHIRE 2–2B

ILLIAM'S £63 333

FOUNTAIN STREET
L6 0BL 01453 832240

ow in its 49th year and ten years on from e retirement of founder William Beetson, appily, William's continues to thrive" as an nusual fishmonger/deli/restaurant, "far away om the sea". The refurbishment under new wners Ed & Helen Playne "has worked well", guests can enjoy "really good fish, always well ooked and nicely presented, but now served a better space". / williamsfoodhall.co.uk; lliamsfoodhall; Tue-Thu 4 pm, Fri & Sat 11 pm.

NANTGAREDIG, CARMARTHENSHIRE 4–4C

POLYN £72 343

APEL DEWI SA32 7LH 01267 290000

Still barely missing a beat on food, wine and rvice", Mark & Sue Manson's unpretentious stro is "a welcome oasis in West Wales" that's rticularly "ideal for visits to the National otanic Garden of Wales", two miles off. he "seasonal menu with local ingredients" akes the most of the local Welsh larder d is "professionally presented and always licious". / ypolyn.co.uk; polyncarmarthen; Tue-t 9 pm, Sun 2.30 pm.

NARBERTH, PEMBROKESHIRE 4–4B

LTRACOMIDA £56 333

HIGH ST SA67 7AR 01834 861491

nce 2005, Paul & Shumana Grimwood's spin-f from their original business in Aberystwyth s been one of Wales's brighter culinary arks. Adjoining a deli selling Spanish produce d wines, the café/bar is a daytime-only eration: "a tapas menu at lunch served shared tables (with no booking which is a in); then there's coffee or drinks till about ". / ultracomida.co.uk; ultracomida; Mon-Sat pm.

NETHER BURROW, CUMBRIA 7–4D

THE HIGHWAYMAN £55 333

BURROW LA6 2RJ 01524 273338

This much commented-on Brunning & Price stalwart in a Lune Valley hamlet is a "justifiably popular" place at any time of the day thanks to its menu of "consistently good" food (the "crispy beef salad is an all-time favourite"), its "nice atmosphere" and service that is "very relaxing and unhurried" too. / brunningandprice.co.uk; highwaymanpub; Sun-Thu 10 pm, Fri & Sat 11 pm. SRA – 3 stars

NETHER WESTCOTE, OXFORDSHIRE 2–1C

THE FEATHERED NEST INN £105 443

OX7 6SD 01993 833 030

"Sample Michelin-chef food" (that chef being Matt Weedon, who won the honour at Glenapp Castle and Lords of the Manor) at this ex-malthouse-turned-country-bolthole in a chocolate-box Cotswolds village. Not only is the setting "wonderful" – ideally placed between Burford and Stow-on-the-Wold, and with "great views" over the Evenlode Valley from the garden – Weedon's locally sourced cooking (not least the six-course tasting menu) is "wonderful" too. / thefeatherednestinn.co.uk; thefeatherednestinn; Mon, Thu-Sun 11 pm.

NETTLEBED, BERKSHIRE 2–2D

THE CHEESE SHED 323

HIGH STREET RG9 5DA 01491 642127

"Great cheese toasties" – dripping with home-produced cheese and consumed "before or after a walk" – are the attraction at this ultra-casual spot on a family-run dairy farm which believes in "keeping things simple": it is literally a modern agricultural shed to keep off the rain with bales of straw to sit on. / nettlebedcreamery.com; nettlebedcheese; Mon-Sun 3 pm.

NEW MILTON, HAMPSHIRE 2–4C

CHEWTON GLEN £111 343

CHEWTON GLEN RD
BH23 5QL 01425 282212

"Five-star service and food on the South Coast", say fans of this "special" venue – a famous Relais & Châteaux property, set in gorgeous grounds on the edge of the New Forest and 30 minutes' drive from Bournemouth: the "perfect hotel to be spoilt in with its lovely summery restaurant and first-class staff". Perennial gripes about high prices here were absent this year, and Luke Matthews's cuisine won nothing but praise. Top Tip – "The lunch menu is very good value"; and "the quality and quantity of afternoon tea here is so very impressive – we didn't need dinner!!" / chewtonglen.com; chewtonglen; Mon-Sun 8.30 pm.

THE KITCHEN AT CHEWTON GLEN £94 344

CHEWTON FARM ROAD
BH23 5QL 01425 275341

"Showing that the food doesn't have to be fancy to be good" – fans applaud the "great menu of varied choices" in the relaxed alternative eatery of this famous country-house hotel, whose menu line-up includes posh burger and pizza options. The addition was completed a few years ago and is an attractive modern space with pitched roof, whose features include views over the kitchen gardens, an outdoor terrace and a cookery school overseen by James Martin. An "ideal venue for a special occasion – expensive, but worth it". / chewtonglen.com; chewtonglen; Mon-Sun midnight.

NEWARK, NOTTINGHAMSHIRE 5–3D

KOINONIA £43 443

19 ST MARKS LN
NG24 1XS 01636 706230

"A firm favourite for over 12 years, this Keralan restaurant tucked away in Newark is always a delight and very well worth seeking out" for its "true" South Indian flavours and "friendly service" ("the 'railway mutton curry' is a particular hit, as are the delicious dosas"). / koinoniarestaurant.com; Mon-Thu 10 pm, Fri & Sat 11 pm, Sun 7.30 pm.

NEWBURY, BERKSHIRE 2–2D

THE WOODSPEEN £95 334

LAMBOURN RD
RG20 8BN 01635 265 070

"I was expecting rather standard Home Counties fare, but instead I found delicious cooking and charming service all in an attractive barn-style setting": this successful ten-year-old – a restored 'run-down pub' in West Berkshire countryside – boasts a "very lovely", high-ceilinged contemporary dining extension and has become one of the most commented-on restaurants in our annual diners' poll. Run by Alastair Storey (a top catering CEO), reporters are "delighted and frankly a bit surprised by the excellence of the experience" and – unusually for a rural venue – its "ambience and level of quiet formality make it a place in which you'd be happy to do business". Its scores slipped a fraction this year though, on the back of some incidents of "mechanical" service ("in the old-style, fancy-restaurant way)" or the odd "ordinary" meal ("we have had better here"). / thewoodspeen.com; thewoodspeen; Tue, Wed 9 pm, Thu-Sat 9.30 pm, Sun 5 pm.

NEWCASTLE UPON TYNE, TYNE AND WEAR 8–2B

BLACKFRIARS RESTAURANT £63 334

FRIARS ST NE1 4XN 0191 261 5945

A "very historic dining room" – set in a thirteenth-century former refectory that may be the oldest of its kind in the UK – adds a sense of occasion to a visit to this "atmospheric" outfit, but it's arguably even better in summer "when you can eat outside in the courtyard garden". The brasserie menu is "quality" (think "good seasonal produce such as game") and "you can hear yourself talk, so it's good for taking your parents too if they like traditional with a slight twist". / blackfriarsrestaurant.co.uk; BlackfriarsRestaurant; Mon-Sat 9.30 pm, Sun 4 pm.

THE BROAD CHARE £68 333

25 BROAD CHARE
NE1 3DQ 019 1211 2144

"This lively pub close to Newcastle's waterfront" has an "excellent bar downstairs where local brewery offerings can be tried with proper pork scratchings, scotch eggs or a pint of prawns. Upstairs offers more choice and a good wine list" – "I'm looking for an excuse to visit Newcastle again so I can return" to this "great venue". Through a unique arrangement, a proportion of its profits helps fund the Live Theatre next door, a haven for new dramatic writing. / thebroadchare.co.uk; _thebroadchare; Mon-Fri 9.15 pm, Sun 5 pm, Sat 10 pm.

COOK HOUSE £71 343

FOUNDRY LANE NE6 1LH 0191 276 1093

This Ouseburn outfit is "worth seeking out, even though it is off the beaten track", for its "quirky but delicious food and really good service". Founder Anna Hedworth worked at Quo Vadis and Rochelle Canteen in London before setting up in a shipping container in Newcastle, and moved on to the current open-kitchen venue six years ago. / cookhouse.org; cookhouse_anna; Wed-Sat, Tue 11 pm, Sun 4 pm.

DABBAWAL £41 323

69-75 HIGH BRIDGE
NE1 6BX 0191 232 5133

Near the Theatre Royal, this early pioneer of Indian street food (which opened in 2008) continues to generate upbeat (if limited) feedback on its "delicious curries". / dabbawal.com; dabbawal; Sun-Thu 10.30 pm, Fri & Sat 11 pm.

DOBSON AND PARNELL £56 333

21 QUEEN ST NE1 3UG 0191 221 0904

Troy Terrington's casual fine-dining venue (sibling to Blackfriars and Hinnies in Whitley Bay) occupies the well-known Quayside address which became famous as '21 Queen Street' (long RIP) in days gone by. There was the odd "disappointing" experience this year, but for the most part feedback praises its "excellent" cuisine, including the optional five-course and seven-course tasting menus (£40/£65 per person lunches and Thursday, £60/£75 per person at weekend dinners) praised for "some exceptional dishes". / dobsonandparnell.co.uk; dobsonandparnell; Thu-Sat, Wed 9.30 pm, Sun 4 pm.

FRANCESCA'S £39 334

134 MANOR HOUSE RD
NE2 2NE 0191 281 6586

For a "cheap 'n' cheerful" occasion, this Jesmond institution of decades standing is just the job. It bills itself as a pizzeria, but there are lots of other choices on its long menu. / francescasjesmond.co.uk; Mon-Sat 9.30 pm.

HOUSE OF TIDES £180 544

28-30 THE CLOSE NE1 3RN
0191 2303720

"A historic building with some lovely original features" – Kenny & Abbie Atkinson's Grade I-listed sixteenth-century merchant's house on the Quayside remains one of the city's 'crown jewel' eateries. It inspired less feedback than its sibling this year, but all rated it as "outstanding": "the cuisine was delicious and presented very precisely; the sommelier was very knowledgeable and engaging. I would certainly recommend". / houseoftides.co.uk; houseoftides; Wed-Sat 9 pm.

JESMOND DENE HOUSE £82 323

JESMOND DENE RD
NE2 2EY 0191 212 6066

This "lovely hotel" in a "beautiful" Grade II-listed Arts and Crafts house remains a satisfying getaway, being particularly "perfect for afternoon tea". There are several dining spaces, ranging from a bar offering light snacks to the dedicated Fern Dining Room for heartier meals. / jesmonddenehouse.co.uk; jesmonddenehouse; Wed-Sat 9.30 pm.

KHAI KHAI £50 443

29 QUEEN STREET
NE1 3UG 0191 261 4277

"Some of the best and most authentic Indian food you can get" in these parts awaits at this "really good addition to the varied Quayside scene", founded in 2020; while superficially there's a "similar menu and ambience to Dishoom", the point of pride here is the Josper grill, which lends its smoky magic to the menu of retro regional classics. / khaikhai.co.uk; khaikhaincl; Mon-Thu 10.30 pm, Fri & Sat 11 pm, Sun 9.30 pm.

PANI'S £46 344

61-65 HIGH BRIDGE
NE1 6BX 0191 232 4366

With its "buzzy atmosphere, friendly staff" and "good Sardinian specialities", Roberto & Walter Pani's deceptively "cheap 'n' cheerful" spot is quite possibly "the best, most consistent and interesting Italian in town". Just short of 30 years after opening, it remains for many "the go-to place when I return to Newcastle". / paniscafe.co.uk; Pani's Italian; Mon-Thu 9 pm, Fri & Sat 10 pm.

PEACE & LOAF £81 44

217 JESMOND ROAD
NE2 1LA 0191 281 5222

Le Gavroche-trained chef Dave Coulson came home to open this "firm favourite" in Jesmond with a winningly puntastic name; the "very good" seasonal tasting menus "mostly favour grown-up tastes" – and if you want to try them for less, there's a "great-value lunch deal called '2,1,2,1,2'". / peaceandloaf.co.uk; peaceandloafj Wed-Sat 9 pm.

SACHINS £46 33

FORTH BANKS NE1 3SG 0191 261 903

"Always a favourite" – this smart Punjabi curry house is "still one of the best Indian restaurants in town", even approaching its fourth decade; the "traditional food" is "very dependable", having been overseen by chef-owner Bob Arora (a former regular) since the millennium. / sachins.co.uk; sachins_newcastle_bob; Mon-Sat 9.30 pm.

SIMLA £40 44

39 SIDE NE1 3JE 07917391319

"Fabulous food and great customer service" are the hallmarks of a meal at this Quayside fixture founded in 1981 as a 'fast and furious' curry house by the late Ashraf Ali and re-launched as an upmarket destination eight years ago by his daughter, Shelly Muktadir. / simlarestaurant.ne Tue-Thu, Sun 11 pm, Fri & Sat 11.30 pm.

SOLSTICE £220 54

5 - 7 SIDE NE1 3JE 0191 222 1722

Kenny Atkinson's "fantastic inventive food", delivered across a "truly exceptional menu of 17 bitesize courses" (for £175 per person) in this "intimate" yearling, next-door to his flagship House of Tides, is "an absolute must-do if you are in Newcastle". "It might be expensive, it might be exclusive and it might b incongruous in the current economic climate, but it's also exceptional and well worth the treat if you can afford it" – and is many of our diners' choice as "the best cooking eaten in the last 12 months". / solsticencl.com; solstice_ncl; Wed-Sat 8 pm.

21 £98 44

TRINITY GARDENS, QUAYSIDE
NE1 2HH 0191 222 0755

The venue where it all began for local restaurant hero and 21 Hospitality Group owner Terry Laybourne; even well into its third decade, the Quayside icon (though not as commented-on as it once was) is still a "very dependable destination" ("good for celebration meals" especially), and turning out "well prepared and beautifully presented" food that owes a debt to French classics. / 21newcastle.com; 21newcastle_; Tue-F 9 pm, Sat 10 pm, Sun 5 pm.

NEWLYN, CORNWALL 1–4A

RGOE £33 433

R18 5HW 01736 362455

ou'll find the "best sardines outside of ortugal" and "delightful grilled lobster" this "tiny little restaurant right on the arbourside" that was opened in 2021 by cal fishmonger Rich Adams and ex-Rochelle anteen head chef Ben Coombs to celebrate ewlyn's connection with the sea. In decent eather, eat on the terrace "looking out over e boats which landed most of the items on e menu". / argoenewlyn.co.uk; argoenewlyn; e-Sat 10.30 pm.

ACKEREL SKY £40 433

EW ROAD TR18 5PZ 01736 448982

ina & Jamie MacLean's "very busy" no-ookings seafood bar is "an astonishing find" at elicited strong all-round feedback this ar. The "superb" small plates menu "is a umph" and, unusually, "half the fun of ting at this tiny roadside brasserie is queuing get in" ("it's great chatting with prospective low diners"). Such is its success that, in 2023, ey launched an extension, 'The Shack', two oors down, which offers the same menu and also walk-in only. / mackerelskycafe.co.uk; ackerelskyseafoodbar; Mon-Sun 10 pm.

NEWPORT ON TAY, FIFE 9–3D

HE NEWPORT £92 433

HIGH STREET DD6 8AA 01382 541 449

asterChef: The Professionals winner "Jamie ott is one of the UK's finest unsung chefs" etting aside that 2014 honour), say fans of the staurant-with-rooms he launched with wife elly in 2016; "the wonderful food together ith the young, local but knowledgeable serving am" make for a winning combination and window seat looking over the Tay estuary is bonus" (indeed, the room has "some of the est-ever views"). / thenewportrestaurant.co.uk; enewportrestaurant; Thu-Sat 9 pm, Sun 8.30 pm.

NEWPORT, ISLE OF WIGHT 2–2A

HOMPSON'S £79 543

TOWN LANE PO30 1JU 01983 526118

op Press – as of January 2023, much-arlanded chef Robert Thompson is "back his own establishment after a brief venture Cowes' North House" (now rebranded as oresters Hall), a fancy boutique hotel that as reportedly not fancy enough to make good match for his high-end cooking. ans couldn't be more delighted that his mazing" venue is back in business, and vhile the food is centre stage", the "service d theatre of it all are a great support act" articularly if you sit downstairs – home to e open kitchen). / robertthompson.co.uk; efrobertthompson; Fri & Sat 10 pm, Sun 30 pm.

NEWPORT, MONMOUTHSHIRE 2–2A

GEM 42 £85 443

42 BRIDGE STREET
NP20 4NY 01633 287591

"How this business survives in Newport is unbelievable! It's far too good!" – twin brothers Sergio and Pasquale Cinotti (the latter the pastry chef) established this brave destination in 2018, and – some would say against all odds – continue to go from strength to strength (in 2022 they were the AA's Welsh Restaurant of the Year). For the full blow-out, you can opt for a ten-course 'Essenza' menu which changes daily at £180 per head; but there are much more affordable 'entry-level' options, ranging from £65 per head. / gem42.co.uk; gem42newport; Mon-Sat 10.30 pm.

NEWQUAY, CORNWALL 1–3B

RENMOR £83

THE HEADLAND, FISTRAL BEACH,
HEADLAND RD, TR7 1EW 01637 872211

Costing £3 million and aiming to provide a 'world class experience', the new flagship destination at this landmark five-star hotel – a gigantic Victorian pile overlooking Fistral beach – opened in May 2023, too late for any feedback in our annual diners' poll. The Headland offers tremendous sea views, and the new menu aims to showcase the best of Cornish fish and farm produce (RenMor means 'restaurant by the sea' in Cornish). Maybe scope it out with a visit to one of the adjoining lounges for sarnies and cakes first – "afternoon tea looking out to sea couldn't be more perfect". / renmor.co.uk; Mon-Sun 9.30 pm.

NEWTON IN CARTMEL, CUMBRIA 7–4D

HEFT £145 333

LA11 6JH NO TEL

This "old pub is now a high-class restaurant with a lot of character", opened in summer 2021 by locally born couple Kevin & Nicola Tickle – Kevin spent 10 years in the kitchen of the exalted L'Enclume and was also head chef at Forest Side in Grasmere. There are "lots of options for eating, from the full gastronomic evening tasting menu to tasty snacks and pies in the dog-friendly bar" along with a "good wine list and great draft beers from Lakes Brew in Kendal". One or two reporters feel the performance here is no better than good all-round, but most would go further and feel it's "a great experience that anyone would happily repeat". / hefthighnewton.co.uk; heft_high_newton; Thu-Sat 7 pm, Sun 6 pm.

NEWTON-IN-BOWLAND, LANCASHIRE 5–1B

THE PARKERS ARMS £67 544

HALL GATE HILL
BB7 3DY 01200 446236

"The pies are world-beating and the staff are the friendliest people ever!" at this ever more famous pub in the Forest of Bowland – nowadays one of the top 100 most commented-on destinations outside London in our annual diners' poll, and fans still say "impossible to fault" thanks to its "brilliant and varied cuisine at great-value prices". "Chef Stosie Madi's star is burning bright, and rightly so, with daily- or twice-daily-changing menus using produce that's as local and as seasonal as possible (which often means foraged by Madi on the days they're not open)". "The food continues to be exceptional, and the most reliable for miles, combining an unerring flair for simple deliciousness with a remarkable mastery of a whole range of techniques". All this said, popularity is starting to weigh somewhat on feedback. "Prices are still not punishing, but they are much-increased, and the menu is now restricted to a three-course format, with appearances on the Hairy Bikers and the Top 50 Gastropubs keeping them full". And disappointments – though still largely drowned out by fanboying feedback – are no longer completely unknown ("it's just a pie when all's said and done, but the cost!") / parkersarms.co.uk; theparkersarms; Thu-Sat 8.30 pm, Sun 4 pm.

NOMANSLAND, WILTSHIRE 2–3C

LES MIRABELLES £59 443

FOREST EDGE RD
SP5 2BN 01794 390205

"Fab French food in the middle of nowhere" – on the edge of the New Forest – has won a devoted fan club for Claude Laage's establishment, now 30 years old and an "all-time favourite restaurant" to many for its "wonderful Gallic experience" and "superb wine list". You can also eat inexpensively here, from its 'Le Frog bistro' menu – same space and servers but much less fancy Gallic fare. / lesmirabelles.co.uk; Wed-Sat 9.30 pm.

NORTH BERWICK, EAST LOTHIAN 9–4D

LOBSTER SHACK £43 432

45 VICTORIA ROAD
EH39 4JL 07910 620480

"It's just a shack on the port but the lobster or fish 'n' chips are spectacular" at this venue perched on North Berwick Harbour, which is open seasonally from April to October. Their suppliers are accredited by Marine Scotland, and if you fancy a change from the national dish opt for crab tacos or chowder. / lobstershack.co.uk; lobstershacknb; Wed & Thu, Sun 5 pm, Fri & Sat 6 pm.

OSTERIA £60 343

71 HIGH STREET
EH39 4HQ 01620 890589

This "great local Italian" has been a popular success over the past 17 years, and owner "Angelo Cocchia is brilliant as front of house, supported by his team". "Shortage of staff means some services have now stopped, and two sittings for dinner has been normal in recent times". / osteria-no1.co.uk; osterianb; Tue-Sat 10 pm.

NORTHALLERTON, NORTH YORKSHIRE 8–4B

BETTYS £47 234

189A HIGH ST DL7 8LF 01609 775154

An offshoot of the time-capsule tearoom chain offering (once you get past the queues) genteel service, plus afternoon tea, sandwiches and other things more substantial. Fans claim that it's "great for brunch with very professional staff", although it's perhaps not the pick of the Bettys bunch, and there was the odd caveat this year over rising prices and shrinking portions. / bettys.co.uk; bettys; Sun-Fri 4.30 pm, Sat 5 pm.

ORIGIN SOCIAL £50 333

2 FRIARAGE STREET DL6 1DP 01609 775900

"If you happen to find yourself in Northallerton, a sure place to go!" – this two-year-old small plates venture focuses on live-fire cooking, and is a good bet in this thinly provided town. / originsocial.co.uk; originssocial_; Tue-Thu 11 pm, Fri & Sat midnight.

NORWICH, NORFOLK 6–4C

BENEDICTS £83 433

9 ST BENEDICTS ST NR2 4PE 01603 926 080

Chef-patron Richard Bainbridge's "brilliant, fresh and exciting food" wows reporters at the restaurant he opened with his partner Katja almost 10 years ago. With "great staff and a wonderful ambience", it is yet again plugged by many diners as "the best in Norwich", but its local rival Hickman's just had the edge in our annual diners' poll this year, due to a small minority of critics who found the food "hyped and average" ("but we might have hit them on a bad day"). / restaurantbenedicts.com; restbenedicts; Tue-Sat 10 pm.

BENOLI £62 332

5 ORFORD STREET NR1 3LE 01603 633056

"Lovely" daily-made pasta wins star billing at this "really good Italian" from former Roux at the Landau head chef Oliver Boon and his brother Ben (Ben & Oli). The "short but varied menu" is "creative, tasty yet somehow still traditional in feeling – in the Italian way rather than a British take on Italian". / benolirestaurant.com; benoli_restaurant_norwich; Mon-Sat 10 pm, Sun 9 pm.

FARMYARD RESTAURANT £55 344

23 SAINT BENEDICTS STREET NR2 4PF 01603 733 188

Chef Andrew Jones returned to his Norfolk origins seven years ago after working for Richard Corrigan and Claude Bosi, to open this modern venue that "never fails" with its locally sourced meals – "we love going there for lunch". He and his partner, Hannah, also ran The Dial House restaurant-with-rooms in Reepham for five years, before selling up in autumn 2023. / farmyard.restaurant; farmyard_frozen; Tue-Fri 9 pm, Sat 9.30 pm.

THE GUNTON ARMS £68 335

CROMER RD NR11 8TZ 01263 832010

"Set in the deer-filled grounds of a stately home" and owned by Chelsea art dealer Ivor Braka, this much commented-on pub-with-rooms "shows more contemporary art on its walls than the average West End gallery" (Tracey Emin, Lucian Freud, Damien Hirst, Anthony Caro and co.). Mark Hix alumni Stuart & Simone Tattersall oversee the victuals: mostly "meat and game from local estates" ("some cooked on the open fire"), but the "broad and inventive" menu isn't just for carnivores. "Top Menu Tip – the whole shared-chicken Sunday Roast is beautifully done and excellent value". / theguntonarms.co.uk; guntonarms; Mon-Sat 9.30 pm, Sun 9 pm.

L'HEXAGONE 334

22 LOWER GOAT LANE NR2 1EL 01603 926886

"A lovely, authentic French bistro run by friendly couple with lots of favourites on the menu that's been a great addition to Norwich" – husband and wife team Thomas Aubrit and Gemma Aubrit-Layfield are celebrating their third year in the Norwich Lanes, having launched just as covid struck at the start of 2020. / hexagonebistrofrancais.com; lhexa_gone; Tue-Thu 2.30 pm.

ROGER HICKMAN'S £86 443

79 UPPER ST. GILES ST NR2 1AB 01603 633522

"The best restaurant in Norwich (which is not intended to damn with faint praise!)", according to fans of Roger Hickman's "classy" and long-established dining destination in the city centre (which narrowly edged ahead of nearby Benedicts this year in our annual diners' poll). All reports applaud the "very assured cooking" – "deeply flavoured with deft presentation and lovely combinations, without a single gimmick or fad". Service is "willing" ("polite, charming, considerate, good-humoured!") and "the room itself is elegant, and the napery satisfying". One gripe – "it would be better to have their more extensive à la carte menu back in the evenings, but I guess the focus on a tasting format is a sign of the times". / rogerhickmansrestaurant.com; rogerhickmans; Tue-Sat 10 pm.

XO TAVERN £50 433

13-15 SAINT GEORGES STREET NR3 1AB 01603 660825

"A fresh and vibrant menu with a fusion of local foods and inspired cooking" inspires enthusiastic (if limited) feedback on Jimmy Preston's funky two-year-old, which started as a pop-up and went permanent in late 2021. In early 2023, The Observer's Jay Rayner also raved over its "face-slapping flavours" and "cheeky, magpie-like romp across Asia" (including XO seasoning which includes Frazzles, Scampi Fries and Monster Munch). / xo__kitchen.

NOTTINGHAM, NOTTINGHAMSHIRE 5–3

ALCHEMILLA £131 44

192 DERBY ROAD NG7 1NF 0115 941 3515

"There is a real buzz to this serious foodie venue near central Nottingham" where an "energetic team of chefs deliver a top gastronomic experience" with a "high, Michelin-starred standard of innovation and flavour". Occupying a converted former Victorian coach house on the Park Estate with brick-vaulted rooms: "once inside, it has a cellar-like vibe that certainly distinguishes it from other culinary destinations in the area". Sat Bains alumnus Alex Bond focuses on a tasting menu format with five courses for £95 per person and seven courses for £120 per person: "the selection is long on interesting ingredients, and the wine pairings very diverse and excellent". / alchemillarestaurant.uk; alchemillarestaurant; Wed-Fri 7.30 pm, Sat 8 pm.

ANNIE'S BURGER SHACK £29 32

5 BROADWAY NG1 1PR 01156849920

This 15-year-old Lace Market venue offers "a bewildering number and variety" of "very satisfying burgers to choose between", inspired by founder Anmarie Spaziano's childhood home in Rhode Island, where US diner culture began. She acquired a taste for the craft beer served alongside them here in the Midlands. There's now a second branch in Derby. / anniesburgershack.com; anniesburgershacknotts; Mon-Thu 10 pm, Fri & S 11 pm, Sun 10.30 pm.

BAR GIGI

15 FLYING HORSE WALK NG1 2HN 0115 9799997

On the first floor at the 14th-century Flying Horse Walk building, complete with beams and stained-glass windows, this offbeat venue was inspired by Milan's Fashion Week, and imports Italian tapas into a space above Gigi Bottega boutique. It's entering its third year of operation: too limited feedback for a full review but such as we have on its small plates and low intervention wines is promising. / bargigibotteg Tue-Thu 9 pm, Fri & Sat 10 pm.

CAFE ROYA £53 44

130 WOLLATON RD NG9 2PE 0115 922 1902

"Amazingly creative vegan and vegetarian food" continues to win raves for this fixture by chef Roya Bishop, who did time at Hansa's restaurant in Leeds, before finessing her style alongside Michelin-starred chef Sat Bains; the food is so "deeply satisfying" that even non-veggies "never fail to be stunned" by a visit. / caferoya.com; caferoya130; Tue-Sat 10 pm

LEAVER & WAKE £120 434

THE GREAT NORTHERN CLOSE
G2 3JL 0115 660 1151

very welcome addition to Nottingham's ›die scene" that is attached to the upcoming and Quarter regeneration project, and thus "somewhat stranded on a ring road", but th "great views of the canal" and a superb aterside setting in compensation. 'MasterChef: e Professionals' winner Laurence Henry asterminds the "very accomplished and tasty od" (two- or three-course lunch £37/£47 per rson, dinner £75 per person), while there's o praise for the impressive interior – "upscale thout being too grand". / cleaverandwake.com; averandwake; Tue, Wed, Sat 9 pm, Thu & Fri om, Sun 4 pm.

HE CUMIN £41 442

-64 MAID MARIAN WAY
G1 6BQ 0115 941 9941

is "stalwart of the Nottingham Indian staurant scene" is now in its seventeenth year, d "continues to serve very tasty and well- iced food". It's very much a family affair, with nny Anand and his wife Monika running e service with his cousin Shelley Anand king charge of the kitchen. / thecumin.co.uk; _cumin_indian_restauraunt; Mon-Thu 11 pm, & Sat 11.30 pm.

VERYDAY EOPLE £45 343

BYARD LANE
G1 2GJ 0115 958 2445

e "best fusion ramen" is the focus of is new noodle specialist from the crew cluding MasterChef finalist Pete Hewitt) hind food truck Homeboys; the "very od value" spot also adds charcoal grills, sian small plates and a hip hop soundtrack the mix. / theeverydaypeople.co.uk; erydaypeoplenottingham; Thu-Sat 10 pm, Wed pm, Sun 6 pm.

RENCH LIVING £53 333

KING ST NG1 2AY 0115 958 5885

Nottingham lunch place of choice" – orsican Stéphane Luiggi and local wife ouise's relaxed city-centre Gallic fixture is a al local treasure; they "also do good dinners d speciality evenings" where you can explore specific region of France through more aborate six-course dinners with matching ines. / frenchliving.co.uk; frenchlivinguk; Tue-Sat idnight.

ART'S KITCHEN £71 243

TANDARD HILL, PARK ROW
G1 6GN 0115 988 1900

hen the original venue of this name opened 1997 in a different location, it became a odern British icon (Times critic Jonathan eades was a major fan) and there's a pool goodwill towards Tim Hart's (of Rutland's ambleton Hall) hotel brasserie, which located to his nearby boutique hotel in 2019. Fans say "it is heartening to see the place getting busier with each passing year since the downsizing, as service is impeccable and the kitchen can produce some lovely food". Even they, though, can find the menu too "mainstream" or "frustratingly samey" nowadays or results "run of the mill". But they say "nonetheless, this is a cherished neighbourhood option". / hartsnottingham.co.uk; hartsnotts; Mon-Sun 9.30 pm.

IBERICO £69 343

THE SHIRE HALL, HIGH PAVEMENT
NG1 1HN 01159 410410

This "fabulous Spanish cellar-bar" is a long-term attraction in the Lace Market with "quality cooking", "vaulted ceilings and perfect service" which makes it "just right for special occasions". A spinoff tapas bar in Hockley is not so highly regarded. / ibericotapas.com; iberico_tapas; Tue-Fri 11 pm, Sat midnight.

KUSHI-YA £57 533

1A CANNON COURT, LONG ROW WEST
NG1 6JE 0115 9411369

"Everything is exquisitely conceived and executed… not to mention supremely tasty!" at this "unique and creative" Japanese-inspired destination (which received a boost in October 2022 when Jay Rayner of The Observer declared it his 'restaurant of the year'). "Hidden down a backstreet", "the compact (hard to get a booking) cool dining room is a surprise discovery after the unprepossessing external building" but "while it may be small it produces the best food": "delicious tapas-style Japanese dishes, each one tastier than the last" ("we get everything on the menu because it's too hard to choose!"). It was the most commented-on venue in the city this year in our annual diners' poll. / kushi-ya.co.uk; kushi_ya; Wed-Sat 10 pm.

MEMSAAB £47 343

12-14 MAID MARIAN WAY
NG1 6HS 0115 957 0009

"A large restaurant near several other rival establishments" – Amita Sawhney's 200-seater in the city centre has become one of the better-known venues in the city since it opened over 20 years ago, thanks to its "consistently good" standard of cooking. / mem-saab.co.uk; memsaabnottingham; Mon-Thu 10.30 pm, Fri & Sat 11 pm, Sun 10 pm.

NO.TWELVE £53 443

2 - 3 ELDON CHAMBERS
NG1 2NS 0115 958 8446

This highly rated plant-based restaurant produces what many consider the "best vegan tasting menu" they have tried, with "some really inventive flavours" – "the vegan camembert is a revelation: it tastes identical to the real thing". Menus are available in both gluten-free and nut-free versions, and there are "great cocktails too". / no12nottingham.co.uk; no12nottingham; Wed-Sat 10 pm.

PELICAN CLUB £62

55 ST. MARY'S PLACE NG1 1PH_
01159 242 932

A "fantastic little Italian in what would have been a smoky jazz joint" (if smoking had not been banned) in the Lace Market; the chefs serve "authentic and very tasty Umbrian food", and the "moodily lit" space is "perfect for a romantic meal" that won't be disrupted by terrible music (the guest artists being "carefully chosen" for the purpose). Too limited feedback for a rating, but what we have is promising. / thepelicanclub.co.uk; instagram.com; Tue-Thu 11 pm, Fri & Sat 1 am.

PIZZAMISU £51 334

9 HIGH PAVEMENT
NG1 1HF 01159 586682

Certified "authentic" pizza (it's Nottingham's only venue to gain the hard-won favours of the True Neapolitan Pizza Association) ensures many fans for this "buzzing" venue, which was born during lockdown, and set up shop in the Lace Market area in 2021. The "quality ingredients" play into "very tasty" sourdough pizzas that are "great value" to boot. / pizzamisu.co.uk; pizzamisunottingham; Tue, Wed, Sun 9 pm, Fri & Sat 10 pm, Thu 9.30 pm.

RESTAURANT SAT BAINS £200 443

LENTON LANE NG7 2SA 0115 986 6566

"Still at the top of its game" and "very much worth the trip" – Sat & Amanda Bains's converted motel remains Nottingham's flagship destination, even if its location leaves a little to be desired (just off a large dual carriageway, next to an industrial estate, beside a National Grid pylon and the concrete banks of the River Trent). Once inside, the stylish interior lives up to the high ambitions of the extensive tasting menus: either ten courses for £195 per person; or blow out with the 15-course option at £275 per person. In either case, reports say "the flavours are so well-crafted that you want to give each mouthful plenty of time, and before you know it you are well into your third hour". One or two reporters find it hard to get over the "extortionate price tag", but even they describe the cooking as "outstanding". (Aside from the main dining room, which seats 28, other options for a meal include the Tasting Room for 4-6 diners, and the kitchen Tasting Bench for 4 people). / restaurantsatbains.com; restaurant_sat_bains; Wed & Thu 7 pm, Sat 7.45, Fri 7.30 pm.

SHANGHAI SHANGHAI £49 332

15 GOOSE GATE
NG1 1FE 0115 958 4688

"Very authentic and reliable Sichuan cooking" gives this Chinese venture near the Lace Market an added string to its bow, that complements its large menu of more standard Cantonese fare. "The ma po bean curd is very moreish". / shanghai-shanghai.co.uk; Sun-Thu 10 pm, Fri & Sat 11 pm.

WORLD SERVICE £79 444

NEWDIGATE HOUSE, CASTLEGATE
NG1 6AF 0115 847 5587

"Always a real treat to visit" – this well-established local institution is to be found near the castle in the atmospheric surrounds of the seventeenth century Newdigate House (also home to networking haunt the Nottingham Club), and – especially in summer when its terrace comes into its own – provides "a calm escape from the city streets". Its rather ambitious food has proved "consistently good" over many years (and even "fabulous" on a good night) and reports this year suggest that it has attained a more consistent standard of late. / worldservicerestaurant.com; worldservice_restaurant; Wed & Thu 9 pm, Fri & Sat 9.30 pm, Sun 3.30 pm.

ZAAP £37 343

UNIT B, BROMLEY PLACE
NG1 6JG 0115 947 0204

"Fine food and a great atmosphere make you feel you're in Bangkok" at this funky street-food operation from Thai chef Ban Kaewkraikhot, who launched her UK business with Sukhothai in Leeds 22 years ago. She now has six Zaap sites across the north. / zaapthai.co.uk; zaap_thai_streetfood; Sun-Thu 10 pm, Fri & Sat 11 pm.

NUN MONKTON, NORTH YORKSHIRE 5–1D

THE ALICE HAWTHORN £73 433

THE GREEN YO26 8EW 01423 330 303

An "excellent gastropub-with-rooms in a delightful village" – and right on the village green, which has the rare honour of hosting the country's tallest maypole. Yorkshire hospitality royalty John & Claire Topham, who put the General Tarleton at Ferrensby on the map, are behind its recent national hype, and added award-winning rooms to the picture in 2022. Hearty dishes make the most of local produce and "very professional" staff don't bat an eyelid if you choose to linger a few hours. PS – they now do pizzas in the garden in summer on Fri/Sat nights. / thealicehawthorn.com; thealicehawthorn.

OAKHAM, RUTLAND 5–4D

FIKA 343

10D MILL STREET
LE15 6EA 01572 352935

"A great Rutland secret" from a brother-sister duo: a "tiny café serving delicious brunches and lunches" that come "Swedish-style" (hence the reference to 'fika', the Scandi institution of coffee and cake breaks) and feature much local produce. The hep spot also has spin-offs on Stamford High Street and at nearby members' club Woolfox, for that post-gym cinnamon roll. / fikacafe.co.uk; Mon-Sat 4.30 pm, Sun 4 pm.

HITCHEN'S BARN £74 443

12 BURLEY ROAD
LE15 6DH 01572 722255

"There's a great atmosphere in this country town restaurant, run by husband and wife team Neil & Louise Hitchen" – "Neil turns out superb dishes from the barn-conversion kitchen while Louise is in charge of front of house. Many of the ingredients are sourced locally in Rutland and the well-briefed team can answer any questions instantly". Set in a "venerable old building in the heart of lovely Oakham", with "mismatched furniture and crockery adding to the charm", it's "a mainstay of the town" and about "as good as a proper neighbourhood restaurant can get". "Better still, a huge effort has been made to construct dishes which achieve this whilst being affordable, so a dinner for two with some very good, interesting, wines is still possible for south of £100. No small achievement these days" – and it means "you leave smiling and probably happier than when you arrived. Even nearby Hambleton Hall (where the Hitchens met working in the 90s) can't better that!" Top Menu Tip – "scotch eggs are a speciality and well worth trying". / hitchensbarn.co.uk; hitchensbarnoakham; Tue-Sat 11 pm.

OARE, KENT 3–3C

THE THREE MARINERS £66 333

2 CHURCH RD ME13 0QA 01795 533633

This Grade II listed Georgian pub near Oare Marshes Nature Reserve is "a lovely spot on a warm day to sit and enjoy lovely grub on the outdoor terraces" – "while it does not outshine its near neighbour The Sportsman, it's cosy, well run, with excellent food and great service – all without having to book weeks in advance and much easier on the wallet". It has seen "a resurgence in the standard of cooking under new management" – experienced ex-Londoners Tom Gravett & Renny Peret. / thethreemarinersoare.co.uk; thethreemarinersoare; Tue-Sat 9 pm, Sun 5 pm.

OBAN, ARGYLL AND BUTE 9–3B

EE-USK (SEAFOOD RESTAURANT) £65 422

NORTH PIER PA34 5QD 01631 565666

"An incredible find" for seafood lovers – a modern, glass-fronted pierside outfit with views across the waters from which the menu is sourced. Run by the MacLeod family for more than 25 years, it is "exceptionally good and very busy" – the sort of place you "have to keep on going back to". / eeusk.com; eeusk; Mon-Sun 9 pm.

ETIVE £127 543

43 STEVENSON STREET
PA34 5NA 01631 564899

John McNutty & David Lapsley's understated venture is named after the loch where it started life – and its cuisine, celebrating the Scottish lochs and land, "never disappoints" by absolutely all accounts. The "wonderful" tasting menu (the only option) and presentatio "worthy of pictures" elicit real raves – indeed, for one reporter, it was "the best meal I have ever had!" Top Tip – "if you book on the whisky and wine pairing evenings, you are in f a treat". / etiverestaurant.co.uk; etiverestaurant; Wed-Sun 9 pm.

OBAN SEAFOOD HUT £18 42

CALMAC PIER PA34 4DB 07881 41856

This celebrated green shack sits on Oban pier, and was established in 1990 by fisherman John Ogden, who wanted to marry top catch with affordable prices. That's still very much the MO: get quality lobster, scallops and crabs either to go, or make a beeline for the outside seating. / seafoodloversrestaurantguide.co.uk; Mon-Sun 6 pm.

OLD HUNSTANTON, NORFOLK 6–3

THE NEPTUNE £103 54

85 OLD HUNSTANTON RD
PE36 6HZ 01485 532122

This "Norfolk gem", a former coaching inn on the north coast, is well-known for chef-patron Kevin Margeolles's "fantastic, precise and experimental cooking", "produced with absolute dedication", while his wife "Jackie is tireless at front of house". It's undoubtedly "expensive but worth it", with "comfortable, very well equipped rooms for an overnight stay" as well. / theneptune.co.uk; theneptuneoldhunstanton; Wed-Sat 8.30 pm.

OLD LANGHO, LANCASHIRE 5–1

BLACK BULL £65 33

OLD LANGHO ROAD
BB6 8AW 01254 248801

This "fab pub with cracking food and beer garden" has a small but very enthusiastic fan club – with more reports ratings might be higher. Landlord Michael Jowett's parents launched the business more than 50 years ago, and made its name with signature platters of seafood (to be ordered three days in advance at £160 for 2 or £200 for 3 people). / theblackbulloldlangho.co.uk; blackbull_oldlangho.

OLD WINDSOR, BERKSHIRE 3–3

THE LOCH & THE TYNE £91 44

10 CRIMP HILL SL4 2QY 07722 293359

"A stunning tasting menu where every course offers a unique experience" wins nothing but praise this year for Adam Handling's out-of-town operation, in a "charming converted pub in Old Windsor", acclaimed for the "same high-quality, creative cuisine as his other 'Frog' restaurants" ("my favourite was brill with hispi cabbage and lobster bisque emulsion!"). There are a number of menus including an à la carte selection and one dedicated to Sunday lunch; and "at £65 per head for six courses it's tasting menu is great value" too. In September 2023,

Cleaver & Wake, Nottingham

it was crowned 'Dining Pub of the Year' in the Great British Pub Awards. / lochandtyne.com; lochandtyne; Thu-Sat, Wed 11 pm, Sun 7 pm.

OLDSTEAD, NORTH YORKSHIRE 5–1D

THE BLACK SWAN £213 4 3 3

YO61 4BL 01347 868 387

"It's very difficult to find fault" at Tommy Banks and his family's famous pub out in the boonies of North Yorks – head chef Callum Leslie's ten-course tasting menu is £175 per person, and even if "you may be heading for bankruptcy at this level of pricing, the cooking is astonishing": "we even thought it good value! with some of the most interesting and tasty desserts encountered in any starred restaurant"; "it lived up to all expectations despite (well-founded) cynicism about these things!" / blackswanoldstead.co.uk; blackswan_oldstead; Tue-Sat 8 pm.

ONGAR, ESSEX 3–2B

SMITH'S BRASSERIE £74 4 3 3

FYFIELD RD CM5 0AL 01277 365578

Established in 1958, this Essex institution is well known for its "excellently cooked fish with some imaginative and well-executed dishes", served in "generous portions" by "well-trained and extremely welcoming staff who provide great customer service". It's "always buzzing with a great atmosphere" – "and if you're lucky you might spot Rod Stewart… a regular". / smithsrestaurants.com; smithsofongar; Tue, Wed 11.30 pm, Fri & Sat 12.30 am, Thu midnight, Sun 8 pm.

ORFORD, SUFFOLK 3–1D

BUTLEY ORFORD OYSTERAGE £70 4 3 2

MARKET HILL IP12 2LH 01394 450277

The Pinney family's fishy institution "hasn't changed for 40 years, apart from the odd tweak to the menu – and why not, when it's as perfect as this?" A "simple setting" doesn't detract from its charms – including the fact that "it was doing local before it became a trendy buzzword, with fish (both fresh and smoked) and oysters from down the road"; "after you've eaten, you can wander through this impossibly picturesque village to their shop to take more home". / butleyorfordoysterage.co.uk; Mon-Sun 9 pm.

THE CROWN & CASTLE £64 3 3 3

MARKET HILL IP12 2LJ 01394 450205

This red-brick hotel with rooms was formerly owned by TV 'Hotel Inspector' Ruth Watson, but is nowadays under local group The Hotel Folk; "the menu is seasonal and consistent" and features "lots of lovely fish" landed in Orford, as well as locally reared meats, with "professional" service thrown into the mix. / crownandcastle.co.uk; crownandcastleorford; Mon-Sat 8.15 pm, Sun 2.30 pm.

ORPINGTON, KENT 3–3B

XIAN £55 3 3 2

324 HIGH ST BR6 0NG 01689 871881

"Still hitting the mark" – this family-run Cantonese flies more under the radar than once it did, but inspires nothing but positive reports from its loyal fan club ("consistently good… never had a bad meal here"). / Tue-Sun 10 pm.

OTLEY, WEST YORKSHIRE 5–1C

BUON APPS £60 3 2 4

HARTLEY HOUSE, 50 MILL WAY LS21 1FE 01943 468 458

A "fantastic setting beside the River Wharfe" provides the perfect backdrop for "good Italian food and friendly service" from Alessandro & Sofia Elena Tocca, who have established a strong local following over more than 20 years. Their Italian take on the classic Sunday roast is a highlight of the menu. / buonappsotley.co.uk; buonapps; Wed & Thu, Sun 8.30 pm, Fri & Sat 9.30 pm.

OUNDLE, RUTLAND 6–4A

TAP & KITCHEN £57 3 3 2

STATION ROAD PE8 4DE 01832 275069

Celebrating its 10th year, this "very lively option with good cooking on Oundle Wharf" is "now a stalwart of the local dining scene", with an "interesting menu that showcases local produce" – and "the beers are not too bad either, being brewed next door" at the Nene Valley brewery. / tapandkitchen.com; tapandkitchen; Mon-Sat 11 pm, Sun 9 pm.

OXFORD, OXFORDSHIRE 2–2D

ARBEQUINA £55 3 4 3

74 COWLEY RD OX4 1JB 01865 792777

A chemist's shop has made way for this highly rated and hip tapas spot, established in 2016 by the crew behind oversubscribed local Oli's Thai. Grab a spot at the long zinc bar, or enjoy cocktails and a "very Spanish wine list" at the dedicated bar, which now sits alongside the premises at no. 72. / arbequina.co.uk; arbequinaoxford; Thu-Sat 10 pm.

ASHMOLEAN DINING ROOM £57 2 2 4

BEAUMONT ST OX1 2PH 01865 553 823

"Light and spacious, with friendly service", "everything is excellent" at this dining room, cleverly positioned in a modern glass box on the roof of this famous museum – "except the food, which is just OK: unimaginative and overpriced, which is such a pity". / ashmolean.org; ashmoleanmuseum; Mon-Sun 4 pm.

BRANCA £56 2 3

111 WALTON ST OX2 6AJ 01865 55611

Even after two decades, they're "constantly looking for ways to improve the menu" at this "good-value" staple – an attractive Continenta brasserie in Jericho. The "eclectic" cooking tips its hat to the Mediterranean and "never disappoints" ("bring anyone and they will enjoy the meal"). Further joys include a "great deli" and expanded outdoor seating; as we went to press, they were finally due to open five long-awaited bedrooms, rounding out the package. / branca.co.uk; branca_oxford; Wed-Sa 9 pm, Sun 7 pm.

BRASSERIE BLANC £60 2 3

71-72 WALTON ST OX2 6AG 01865 510999

"I've been going for 25 years and it's always reliable" – Raymond Blanc's original branch of his spin-off chain still inspires loyalty from long-time fans who claim this Jericho brasserie is "sadly underrated". It certainly elicits few complaints and can be depended on for a solid meal and – it might not happen often, but ever now and then 'le patron mange ici' – when he's on a break from his nearby flagship, Le Manoir aux Quat' Saisons. / brasserieblanc.com brasserieblanc; Mon-Thu 9.15 pm, Fri & Sat 10 pm, Sun 9 pm. SRA – 3 stars

CHERWELL BOATHOUSE £59 2 3

BARDWELL ROAD OX2 6ST 01865 552746

"A table by the river on a summer day is idyllic at this magical Oxford institution, where "lovely food is served in a romantic setting alongside the River Cherwell in a location where punts are still built and operated". Run by two generations of the Verdin family for the past 55 years, it invariably has "great staff and a nice ambience" – although "food is not the main objective, but it's still very good – we tend to visit for the wine-tasting nights" (the lis is very good here). / cherwellboathouse.co.uk; cherwellboathouse; Mon, Wed & Thu 9 pm, Fri & Sat 9.15 pm, Sun 8.45 pm.

CHIANG MAI £51 3 3

KEMP HALL PASSAGE, 130A HIGH STREET OX1 4DH 01865 202233

Now of three decades' standing, this much commented-on "family favourite" is still the spot for "reliably good authentic Thai food in a lovely environment" ("an Elizabethan house tucked down an alley off the High"). Even if it is "not the force it once was", the food is "neve below very good" ("the green chicken curry remains the benchmark"), and even for those who have patronised the place for nearly as lor as it exists, "over-familiarity still does not dull the pleasure" of a visit. / chiangmaikitchen.co.u chiangmaikitchenoxford; Mon-Sat 10 pm, Sun 9 pm.

HE COCONUT REE £49 332

SAINT CLEMENT'S STREET
X4 1AH 01865 421865

om a now nine-strong "cheap 'n' cheerful" i Lankan chain that wants to create a laxed island vibe – candles in coconut ells, upbeat music – and has found a real idience for its "very tasty" and "excellent-lue" small plates (including many vegan-endly options) plus potent cocktails ka 'cocotails'). / thecoconut-tree.com; ecoconuttreeuk; Sun & Mon 11 pm, Tue-Thu .30 pm, Fri & Sat 1 am.

UTTLEFISH 333

ST CLEMENT'S STREET
X4 1AB 01865 243003

"wonderful selection of delicious fish" – cluding "the best fritto misto ever" – and with nteresting daily specials" is the draw at this pular and "good-value" spot with "helpful d friendly service, close to Magdalen Bridge". u can also opt for a burger if you don't l like seafood, and there's a decent range veggie dishes, too. / cuttlefishoxford.co.uk; ttlefishoxford; Mon-Sat 10.30 pm, Sun 9.30 pm.

DAMAME £35 433

HOLYWELL ST
X1 3SA 01865 246916

n Oxford institution in its 26th year, Meiko Peter Galpin's "tiny restaurant", "close to e historic Holywell Music Room", serves op-quality authentic Japanese home cooking", cluding "large bowls of tasty ramen soup d daily specials", with "one sushi evening a eek" (much in demand, on Thursdays). Top p – "it's cramped", very popular, and there's o advance booking" – so it pays to arrive very rly. / edamame.co.uk; Thu-Sat 8.30 pm, Wed 30 pm, Sun 3.30 pm.

EE'S £58 234

BANBURY RD OX2 6PE 01865 553540

his "lovely greenhouse" – originally a late-ctorian florist's – has been a landmark dining stination in north Oxford for almost 40 years, d benefited from a £1.5 million revamp a uple of years ago that boosted capacity to 0. It's a delightful spot for a meal, although e Italian-leaning cooking is generally felt be "hit and miss"; the appointment of w head chef Lee Parsons should improve atters. / gees-restaurant.co.uk; geesrestaurant; on-Sun 10.30 pm.

HE IVY OXFORD RASSERIE £96 324

0 - 121 HIGH STREET
X1 4DF 01865 416333

ith its "lovely decorations and plants", this rmer neo-Gothic bank in the High Street transformed by a £5 million makeover e years ago – elicits reports similar to stablemates across the country, with its eautiful interior" being its most important selling feature. That said, its brasserie fare is better rated than at many of its siblings. / theivyoxford.com; the_ivy_collection; Mon-Thu 10.30 pm, Fri & Sat 11 am, Sun 10 pm.

THE MAGDALEN ARMS £61 333

243 IFFLEY ROAD
OX4 1SJ 01865 243159

Now in its 15th year, this gastropub's "reputation has perhaps fallen from its earliest days, when it was the best restaurant in Oxford, but it seems to have returned to form with tasty and reasonably priced dishes". It's a sibling to London's stellar Anchor & Hope and Canton Arms. / magdalenarms.co.uk; magdalenarms; Wed & Thu, Tue 9 pm, Fri & Sat 10 pm, Sun 8 pm.

NO.1 SHIP STREET £68 333

1 SHIP STREET OX1 3DA 01865 806637

"A real find in central Oxford" – this "small backstreet restaurant" not far from the Ashmolean wins nothing but praise from its very large local fan club. "Good-quality food (well cooked rather than inspired)" is central to its appeal, but it's an all-rounder with service that's "fully engaged without being familiar", a "relaxing" setting, and a "thoughtful choice of wines at reasonable mark-ups". Top Tip – "the fixed-price lunch is the best deal in Oxford". / no1shipstreet.com; no1shipstreet; Mon-Sat 10 pm.

PARSONAGE GRILL £80 334

OLD PARSONAGE HOTEL, 1 BANBURY ROAD OX2 6NN 01865 292305

With its "log fire and paintings on the walls" and "pleasant terrace outside for better weather", this small hotel in a 17th-century "former rectory in central Oxford" makes for an atmospheric bolthole in the 'City of Dreaming Spires' – and the perfect setting for a "generous set tea" or relaxing lunch. / parsonagegrill.co.uk; parsonagegrill; Mon-Sun 10.30 pm.

THE PERCH £59 334

BINSEY LN OX2 0NG 01865 728891

"In an idyllic setting in the village of Binsey, very close to Oxford but along a rural lane, and with a lovely setting by the Thames" surrounded by Port Meadow, this cosy and popular pub "offers indoor dining by the fire in the winter, plus a spacious and airy conservatory with views of the garden; and tables on the terrace outside, or pub benches on the grass, with an outdoor bar". It serves "a good variety of dishes at reasonable prices, plus daily specials". / the-perch.co.uk; theperchoxford; Mon-Sun 9 pm.

PIERRE VICTOIRE £52 433

LITTLE CLARENDON ST
OX1 2HP 01865 316616

This "reliable bistro" in a useful central location "can't be beaten on price for lunch or pre-theatre, and the food is as near to authentic French as anywhere below comic prices". It "seems to have been here forever", having split off from a national chain of the same name that collapsed in 1998. / pierrevictoire.co.uk; pierrevictoireoxford; Mon-Sat 11 pm, Sun 10 pm.

POMPETTE £73 333

7 SOUTH PARADE
OX2 7JL 01865 311166

This "relaxed French bistro offering contemporary cuisine and good service" from chef-patron Pascal Wiedermann (ex-Terroirs) and his wife Laura has established a strong niche in Summertown, north of the city centre. A meal here is "always an enjoyable experience" – on a relatively "limited" menu, top billing goes to the steak frites. / pompetterestaurant.co.uk; pompetterestaurant; Tue-Sat 11 pm, Sun 3 pm, Mon .

QUOD, OLD BANK HOTEL £66 234

92-94 HIGH ST OX1 4BJ 01865 202505

A "perfect" location right in the centre of town is one of the draws to this "spacious" and "buzzy" fixture, set in the Old Bank Hotel, and also profiting from a "lovely" rear terrace. It's one of the more commented-on spots in town, although the "well thought-out" brasserie fare is arguably "solid"… "nothing wrong with it". Still, it's "worth booking to avoid disappointment" (not least come graduation, when it tends to "get packed"). / quod.co.uk; quodrestaurant; Mon-Sun 11 pm.

SICHUAN GRAND £58 322

THE OLD SCHOOL, GLOUCESTER GRN
OX1 2DA 01865 236 899

"Good Sichuanese cooking and a good variety of dishes" (albeit "not as extensive as the 'My Sichuan' restaurant it replaced") make this venture "in the lovely Gloucester Green Old School building" more than "enough to tickle the tastebuds at very affordable prices". The Westfield Stratford sibling has now been joined by a second Big Smoke offshoot, in Holborn. / sichuangrand.com; sichuan_grand; Mon-Sun 10.30 pm.

THE VAULTS AND GARDEN CAFE £32 334

UNIVERSITY CHURCH OF ST MARY THE VIRGIN, RADCLIFFE SQ
OX1 4AH 01865 279112

"A great choice for lunch in atmospheric church vaults close to the famous Radcliffe Camera and Bodleian Library" – guests sit "on long trestles" or in the garden feasting on "good freshly cooked food, with vegetarians and vegans particularly well catered for". After 20 years, the café's future is in the balance, its church landlord wanting to replace it with a social enterprise. / thevaultsandgarden.com; vaultsandgardencafe; Mon-Sun 4.30 pm.

VICTORS 332

307 THE WESTGATE QUEEN STREET OX1 1PG 01865 689064

This faux-wisteria-hung rooftop venue above the Westgate Centre offers "surprisingly well cooked dishes for an ambitious range from all over the world". Victors has branches in Newcastle, Alderley Edge and Hale in Manchester, and takes inspiration from American-Asian cuisine. / victors.co.uk; victors_restaurants; Tue-Thu 4 pm, Fri & Sat 9 pm.

WILDING £60 344

11 LITTLE CLARENDON STREET OX1 2HP 01865 985630

Wine expert Kent Barker's two-year-old wine bar/restaurant has a sharp focus on ethical sourcing and sustainability, with more than 400 mainly biodynamic wines available – "a wide range by the glass" and in "brilliant small taster measures", with "very knowledgeable staff to guide you through". The cooking was already rated "very reliable", but should have gone up a notch since our survey with the installation of a new kitchen and chef's table last autumn, accompanied by the appointment of Michael Carr and Ben Wood as co-head chefs. / wilding.wine; wilding_ox; Mon-Sun 11 pm.

ZHANG JI £68 443

170 COWLEY ROAD OX4 1UE 01865 248158

An "absolute find", this standard-looking Chinese on the Cowley Road showcases "delicious Sichuan cooking at its most authentic", along with relatively unknown specialities from northeast China. / zhangji.co.uk; Mon-Thu 10.30 pm, Fri & Sat 11 pm, Sun 10 pm.

OXSHOTT, SURREY 3–3A

THE VICTORIA OXSHOTT £93 332

HIGH STREET KT22 0JR 01372 841900

"A great addition to the local Oxshott/Cobham area" – this smartly converted pub in the heart of the plush commuter belt from chef Matt Larcombe and front-of-house Simon King is universally applauded for standards that are a cut above in all respects. But even fans note that "while superb, it's definitely on the pricey side", to the extent some consider it "expensive for what it is". Top Menu Tip – "good and varied wine list", with one or two trophy vintages (at well over £1,000 per bottle). / thevictoriaoxshott.com; thevictoriaoxshott; Mon & Tue 10 pm, Wed-Sat 11.30 pm, Sun 9 pm.

OXTED, SURREY 3–3B

KINJO £28 443

46 STATION ROAD EAST RH8 0PG 01883 771601

"Amazing Japanese food that you don't have to travel up to London for" was a cause for celebration at the late 2022 opening of this "great Japanese restaurant" in a former shop close to Oxted station. / kinjo.co.uk; kinjo_oxted; Tue-Fri 10 pm, Sat 10.30 pm, Sun 9 pm.

OXWICH, SWANSEA 1–1C

BEACH HOUSE £102 534

OXWICH BEACH SA3 1LS 01792 390965

The "amazing cooking", including "fabulous seafood", at chef Hywell Griffith's former coalhouse in a "fantastic beach setting" is "worth the trek to the Gower Peninsula whatever the weather". "Sitting looking out over a wide expanse of beach", "sipping an unusual cocktail", "you could be in the Med". You can push the boat out for six-course or eight-course tasting menus here, but the entry level is a three-course menu for £89 per person. / beachhouseoxwich.co.uk; beachouseoxwich; Wed-Sat 9 pm.

PADSTOW, CORNWALL 1–3B

CAFFÈ ROJANO £59 332

9 MILL SQUARE PL28 8AE 01841 532093

Paul Ainsworth's casual spot is a "surprising crowd-pleaser", turning out "perfect arancini", "brilliant salty house fries" and "excellent pizza with blistered crust" ("other dishes are available, but I've never got past the pizza"). While the odd skeptic who hasn't visited since its 2020 bistro relaunch rues the disappearance of the "formerly excellent pasta dishes", the vast majority love the "amazing" small-plates menu and, for dessert, "the brown butter soft-serve ice cream with your own toppings to add is SO Paul Ainsworth – fun!". / paul-ainsworth.co.uk; themarinersbeachclub; Mon-Sun 9.30 pm.

MUSSEL BOX £34 333

11 BROAD ST PL28 8BS 01841 532846

This "good-value-for-money seafood restaurant in Padstow" was FKA The Basement, but changed its name in 2020; as per the new name, local mussels from the Padstow estuary (served with bread or skinny fries) are the star of the menu – which you can enjoy in the slick interior or take away and munch on the nearby harbour wall. / musselbox.co.uk; musselbox; Mon-Sun 9 pm.

PAUL AINSWORTH AT NO6 £182 544

6 MIDDLE ST PL28 8AP 01841 532093

"Out of this world!!" – "Paul Ainsworth's flagship restaurant goes from strength to strength" and few restaurants in the UK achieve such a high level of esteem in our annual diners' poll. "A culinary haven in the middle of, and yet a world apart from, the tourist crowds of Padstow": it certainly eclipses its local rivals nowadays, with Nathan Outlaw a few miles down the coast its most serious nearby culinary competition. Set in a bijou Georgian townhouse, "the open kitchen shows off the enthusiastic team and it's a case of selfies all round with the chefs after the meal". "No, it isn't cheap, but we found ourselves wondering how the team managed to set such high standards for the money". "Special mention go to the dessert… and we don't usually like desserts!" "All around an amazing gastronom experience"! / number6inpadstow.co.uk; no6padstow; Tue-Sat 10 pm.

PRAWN ON THE LAWN £65 44

11 DUKE STREET PL28 8AB 01841 532223

Rich & Katie Toogood's Cornish offshoot – a tiny spot near the harbour – generates much less feedback than their Highbury Corner original in London, but the ratings for its smal plates of local seafood remain high. They also run a seasonal pop-up called Barnaby's on similar lines, at Trevibban Mill Vineyard a sho drive from Padstow. / prawnonthelawn.com; prawnonthelawn; Tue-Sun 10 pm.

RICK STEIN'S CAFÉ £59 33

10 MIDDLE STREET PL28 8AP 01841 532700

This casual venue – one of five outlets the TV chef and his family run in their adopted home town – is "not your typical café": "prices are reasonable and the dishes spot-on". The all-da menu runs from breakfast staples through to a lively mix of bistro and Asian dishes alongside seafood and steak sarnies. / rickstein.com; ricksteinrestaurants; Mon-Sun 9 pm. SRA – accredited

ST PETROC'S HOTEL & BISTRO £85 33

4 NEW STREET PL28 8EA 01841 53270

One of the lesser-known venues in the local Stein empire, set in an old stone building in the heart of Padstow, this low key bistro serves "excellent" and "reliable meals that never disappoint" – "we usually enjoy fish". Importantly for some visitors, there's "a small indoor dog-friendly space". / rickstein.com; ricksteinrestaurants; Mon-Sun 9.30 pm. SRA – accredited

SEAFOOD RESTAURANT £105 43

RIVERSIDE PL28 8BY 01841 532700

"Continues to impress after 25 years or more since our first visit" – the Stein family's harbourside HQ continues to deliver the good for the very many people who report on it in our annual diners' poll. Opened in 1975, it is nowadays run primarily by Rick's ex-wife Jill and her sons, and achieves the hard task of living up to the world fame of TV chef Rick (who nowadays spends a good chunk of his year living down under in Aus'). If you were to quibble, you would say the food is "lovely but not brilliant" or that it's "not cheap by any means", but to an impressive extent serious disappointments are completely absent in feedback this year: "you get the excellent seafood that you would expect with a good mix mix of interesting dishes alongside more inly cooked options that allow you to fully preciate the quality of the fish". "Well worth trip to Cornwall: the freshest seafood ved with care and love!" / rickstein.com; steinrestaurants; Mon-Sun 9.30 pm. SRA – redited

ATCHETTS GREEN, ERTFORDSHIRE 3–2A

HE THREE OMPASSES £60 333

GMIRE LANE
)25 8DR 01923 857655

ourmet cooking at reasonable prices in a lightful village pub" encapsulates the appeal this five-year-old venture from well-travelled ef James Harkin, whose parents ran the oine Restaurant in nearby Bushey for 48 urs, and his partner Magda. The menu xes pub classics with more refined Italian hes. / thethreecompassesaldenham.co.uk; eecompasses; Tue-Thu 9 pm, Fri & Sat 9.30 pm, n 8.30 pm.

EASMARSH, KENT 3–4C

LLINGHAM £68 334

W FARM, DEW LANE
31 6XD 01797 208226

n a 70-acre estate with views to Rye and Romney salt marshes, Gusbourne CEO n Walgate's farmhouse winery-with-rooms d tents in the grounds if preferred) enjoys "superb setting" and "the space itself is oulous". New chef Brendan Eades worked zero-waste pioneer Silo, so a field-to- k ethos prevails (already winning them a een Michelin star); despite limited opening urs (lunch Fri-Sun, a 6-course tasting enu by night) it garners a large volume positive reports – as does the "perfectly od" sourdough pizzeria in the barn posite. / tillingham.com; tillinghamwines; Wed Thu, Sun 8 pm, Fri 9 pm, Sat 9.30 pm.

ENARTH, CARDIFF 1–1D

OME AT ENARTH £175 443

ROYAL BUILDINGS, STANWELL ROAD
64 2AB 029 2071 0686

n exceptional experience, with excellent food, tstanding wines and professional service, but done in a friendly way" – James Sommerin d family continue to inspire high praise for is small and highly personal venue (at which quickly reclaimed his Michelin star after e forced closure of a former starred venue the Penarth seafront in 2020) and where cooks with his daughter Georgia in an en kitchen, with wife Louise and daughters gharad and Cath also working in the siness. "James has always produced top-class od and this is certainly true of this latest nture". / homeatpenarth.co.uk; home.penarth; ed-Sat 9 pm.

PENMAENPOOL, GWYNEDD 4–2D

PENMAENUCHAF HALL

LL40 1YB 01341 422129

Promising feedback on the dining room (with conservatory) of this very attractive, Snowdonian Victorian hotel, which was purchased by the Seren Collection in mid-2022. Not enough reports for a rating as yet, but praise for "a lovely Sunday lunch and excellent value too, with generous portions and beautiful preparation". / penhall.co.uk; Mon-Sat midnight, Sun 10.30 pm.

PENRITH, CUMBRIA 7–3D

ALLIUM AT ASKHAM HALL £147 434

ASKHAM CA10 2PF 01931 712350

"The most incredible wine list – in the league of the best three-star restaurants, with the added advantage of being relatively reasonably priced" is "coupled with a five-star level of food" from chef Richard Swale (who has held a Michelin star since 2019) at this dazzlingly good operation. It occupies a Grade I listed mansion dating from the 1200s, which has been inhabited by the family of the current owners since 1724. Converted to a restaurant with rooms in 2013, it offers an "amazing all-round experience": "we had a stunning 1952 Pomorol, and then sat in front of the lounge fire with a gentle Cognac!" / askhamhall.co.uk; Askham_hall; Tue-Sat 9.30 pm.

FOUR & TWENTY £50 443

42 KING ST CA11 7AY 01768 210231

"Behind a rather nondescript exterior of the local red sandstone", this converted old bank near the town's market square "was once the sister restaurant of the remarkable Mrs Millers at Culgaith, which disappeared with the closure of the garden centre which housed it" a few years ago. "It continues where Mrs Millers left off, with an attractive and attractively priced short menu": "very comforting, hearty dishes, but also delicious" and "beautifully presented". "We live in Darlington but regularly drive over to Four and Twenty. The food is amazing value! The staff go above and beyond to make us feel welcome and comfortable" ("jugs of iced tap water come unbidden to the table!"). / fourandtwentypenrith.co.uk; four_and_twenty_; Tue-Thu 10.30 pm, Fri & Sat 11 pm.

PENTON, SCOTTISH BORDERS 7–2D

PENTONBRIDGE INN £99 443

B6318 CA6 5QB 01228 792 732

"I remember it from fifty years ago as a dirty, swirly-carpeted local drinking hole. So much nicer now! Well worth the detour". Gerald and Margo Smith transformed this Cumbrian inn in 2017 and it has been much accoladed ever since thanks to chef Chris Archer's "very well-balanced" five- or eight-course tasting menus. The Guardian's Grace Dent is also a fan: "in recent times especially, it has felt wrong to glorify expensive, unabashedly poncy food, but cooking at this level is something Britain should be proud of". And before or after your meal, there are "beautiful walks just down the road". / pentonbridgeinn.co.uk; pentonbridgeinn; Wed-Sat 8.30 pm.

PENZANCE, CORNWALL 1–4A

THE SHORE £119 543

13-14 ALVERTON STREET
TR18 2QP 01736 362444

"Exquisite cooking, with fish straight from the Atlantic" again wins very high ratings for Bruce Rennie's very personal 14-seater, where service is by the man himself. Seafood is the speciality here and there are lots of Japanese accents used in the preparation of the six-course tasting menu. No walk-ins, as the fish is purchased in the morning for the number of reservations. / theshorerestaurant.uk; shore_pz; Tue-Sat 10.30 pm.

TOLCARNE INN £74 443

TOLCARNE PL TR18 5PR 01736 363074

Ben Tunnicliffe's centuries-old pub with a "lovely" terrace serves a "menu that's almost exclusively fish and can change twice a day" depending on the catch – "unsurprising given its location next to Newlyn harbour". "Nothing beats a great plate of fish that was landed only a few hundred yards away… if you close your eyes and picture a fisherman's inn in an old Cornish port, the Tolcarne is what you're seeing". / tolcarneinn.co.uk; tolcarneinn; Tue-Sat 8.45 pm.

PERTH, PERTH AND KINROSS 9–3C

CARDO £42 344

38 SOUTH ST PH2 8PG 01738 248784

This "spot-on neighbourhood place" serves "brilliant bistro-style food", including "great specials and pizzas". Now in its 18th year, it has established a strong reputation for "excellent value and friendly, professional service". / cardo.restaurant; cardorestaurant; Tue-Thu 9 pm, Fri & Sat 9.30 pm.

THE NORTH PORT £59 433

8 NORTH PORT PH1 5LU 01738 580867

This wood-paneled "gem" occupying a seventeenth-century building, from the husband-and-wife team of chef Andrew Moss & FOH Karen Milne, celebrates its 10th anniversary this year – the "exceptional cooking and wine list are a joy". We've rated it on relatively thin feedback – more reports please. / thenorthport.co.uk; northportperth; Tue-Sat 10 pm.

PETTISTREE, SUFFOLK 3–1D

GREYHOUND £71 343

THE STREET IP13 0HP 01473 932168

"A lovely old pub that has now been taken on by a young team who have tidied it up and not overdone it – the welcome is lovely and the menu is great", featuring "really tasty, down-to-earth pub food with a creativity missing from

The Angel, Hetton

so many places". "Ex-River Café chef Harry McKenzie really knows how to delight", while the front-of-house (Suffolk-born Will Orrock and his wife Cassidy Hughes) "is like your new best friend". / greyhoundpettistree.co.uk; Wed-Sat 10.30 pm, Sun 6 pm.

PETTS WOOD, KENT 3–3B

INDIAN ESSENCE £69 443

176-178 PETTS WOOD RD
BR5 1LG 01689 838 700

TV chef Atul Kochhar's smart subcontinental, in the SE London 'burbs, is "still a joy" – the "delicious and succulent" cooking being "a far cry from the average Indian cuisine". The two- or three-course weekend lunch attracted particular acclaim this year for its "excellent value" ("it was packed and I can see why!"). / indianessence.co.uk; indianessenceak; Mon-Fri 10 pm, Sat 10.30 pm, Sun 9.30 pm.

PETWORTH, WEST SUSSEX 3–4A

E STREET BAR & GRILL £81 334

NEW STREET GU28 0AS 01798 345111

"Looks can deceive at this understated venue" – a stylish haunt with numerous characterful spaces, whose rather metropolitan style is somewhat at odds with this antique-dealer-infested town. The upscale brasserie menu majors in seafood selections and steaks – fans tip the "well-priced three-course set lunch and affordable wine list". / estreetbarandgrill; Thu-Sat 11 pm, Sun 6 pm.

PITTENWEEM, FIFE 9–4D

DORY £67 332

15 EAST SHORE
KY10 2NH 01333 311222

"Simply a joy" – a "lovely local seafood restaurant on the harbour" (est. 2018) which also doubles as an art gallery, with maritime-themed works on its walls. "They also have a boat!" Some of the catch comes "straight out of the sea", and the rest from not much further off, so that "within a couple of hours of them swimming in the North Sea, you can eat the freshest mussels, crabs, lobsters and beautiful fish" here. / thedory.co.uk; bistrodory; Wed-Sun 8.30 pm.

PLYMOUTH, DEVON 1–4C

CATCH £71 443

47 SOUTHSIDE ST
PL1 2LD 01752 371461

"A welcome tiny addition to Plymouth's limited food scene", this "great new neighbourhood seafood joint" is also a fishmonger and cookery school, turning out some "simple" but "exceptional" food that ranges from the day's catch to fishy tapas. "It's extremely small, only 14 covers, so when a table leaves it suddenly feels very quiet, but we will deffo be back". / thecatchplymouth.co.uk; thecatchplymouth; Mon-Sun 10 pm.

FIG TREE £71 433

36 ADMIRALTY STREET
PL1 3RU 01752 253247

Being "tucked away in a quiet residential street", this "lovely small" family-owned restaurant (est. 2017) "has to excel, and does"; the locally sourced bistro cooking includes a "very good value set menu with plenty of fresh fish" and their "'Trust the Chef' evenings on Wednesdays and Thursdays are justly popular" (you specify meat, fish or veggie, and leave the rest to chef-patron Ryan). / figtree36.co.uk; thefigtreeat36; Wed-Sat , Sun 3 pm.

HONKYTONK WINE LIBRARY £53 234

2 NORTH EAST QUAY, SUTTON HARBOUR
PL4 0BN 01752 257968

"On a summer's day, there isn't a better place to sip vino!" than this wine shop/deli, which has an excellent setting with views over Sutton Harbour. There's a selection of generous (not inexpensive) sharing platters, cheeses, and nibbles. The best bets are the Honkytonk Creole Dishes (say spatchcock chicken with fries and slaw for £25). / honkytonkwinelibrary.com; honkytonkwinelibrary; Wed & Thu 10 pm, Fri & Sat 10.30 pm, Sun 5 pm.

PLYMPTON, DEVON 1–4C

ÀCLÈAF AT BORINGDON HALL £156 434

BORINGDON HALL
PL7 4DP 01752 344455

In early 2023, Scott Paton and his team added a Michelin star to their list of accolades at this impressive-looking five star near Plymouth, which is now in its fourth year of operation. The dining area occupies a raised gallery inside the great hall which it overlooks via a wooden balustrade, and is the venue for a fou course meal for £120 per person. Although there are modern flourishes, the cuisine is traditionally rooted and includes numerous luxury ingredients (lobster, truffle, caviar, crab wagyu…). / acleaf.co.uk; acleafrestaurant; Mon-Sun 11 pm.

POOLEY BRIDGE, CUMBRIA 7–3

1863 RESTAURANT WITH ROOMS £99 33

ELM HOUSE, HIGH STREET CA10 2NH
017684 86334

"Fair prices for food that's consistently pleasar to excellent" wins ongoing praise for this converted blacksmith's – nowadays a restaura with rooms in the centre of this scenic Lakela village on Ullswater. Cumbrian born chef Phi Corrie offers a choice of three-course à la car menu and seven-course tasting menu (the latte for £105 per person). / 1863ullswater.co.uk; 1863_restaurant; Mon, Thu-Sun 8.30 pm.

PORT APPIN, ARGYLL AND BUTE 9–3

OLD INN £36 33

PORTNACROISH
PA38 4BH 01631 730186

"If you like steak (especially "cooked over flame on the real fire") then this is the daddy of dinners in Argyll" – a "very busy" and atmospheric gastroboozer that was resurrecte in 2014, and whose roots go back to Jacobean times, making it among the Highlands' oldest inns. While the steaks are the main event, the are "other excellent pub-style meals" on offer, "vast range of malt whiskies" and epic views c Stalker Castle opposite, too. / Mon-Thu 10 pm Fri & Sat 11 pm.

PIERHOUSE HOTEL £76 44

PA38 4DE 01631 730302

"The best view in the world" – over Loch Linnhe and the island of Lismore – elevate a visit to this "lovely" hotel-restaurant in the "fantastic setting" of an ex-piermaster's house. "Seafood is king here", with "generous platters of local produce" amongst the "simple and brilliant" offering (none of which will dent your wallet as much as a trip to its famed Skye sibling, the Three Chimneys). / pierhousehotel.co.uk; thepierhousehotel; Mon-Sun 8.45 pm.

PORT ISAAC, CORNWALL 1–3

OUTLAW'S FISH KITCHEN £111 54

1 MIDDLE ST PL29 3RH 01208 881138

"So small… how do they produce such great food from that tiny kitchen? Incredible!" – Nathan Outlaw's "tiny, so quite cosy" No 2. venue sits on the quayside of this picturesque fishing village and is "just the best place" on account of food that's "beautifully prepared d full of flavour": "a wonderful combination tapas-style eating and Michelin-starred oking". / nathan-outlaw.com; outlawsgrubclub; on-Sat 9 pm.

UTLAW'S NEW OAD £218 544

NEW RD PL29 3SB 01208 880896

gainst a backdrop of wild sea views we joyed small plate after small plate of stunning afood, each one different" – Nathan Outlaw's rbourside HQ inspired a dazzling level of isfaction this year, with all of the numerous ports we received on it acclaiming it as an utstanding" performer and very arguably he best seafood and fish restaurant in the K". "You know everything is fresh and urced locally and this shines through with erything they serve" in dish after "fabulously eative" dish, "beautifully presented on agnificent ceramics". Its "impeccable but per-friendly Cornish service tops off" the xceptional" standards. / outlaws.co.uk; tlawsnewroad; Tue-Sat 9 pm.

ORT OF MENTEITH, STIRLING 9–4C

ICK'S AT PORT OF ENTEITH £68 434

K8 3RA 01877 389900

mited but very enthusiastic feedback on this o-year-old outpost of the Nairns' empire, hose most notable feature is a vast outdoor ace, but whose attractions also include a me shop run by the celebrity chef's wife. aul's Pizza' is a mainstay of a menu of fairly aightforward brasserie-style fare (burger, icken Milanese, venison meatballs, steak…). he Scotsman's Gaby Soutar is also a fan in her February 2023 review she dubbed "a beautiful space" that's "well worth a tour" and "hard to leave". / nicknairn.com; cksatportofmenteith; Thu-Sat, Wed 10 pm, Sun pm.

ORTHGAIN, PEMBROKESHIRE 4–4B

HE SHED AT ORTHGAIN £61 423

A62 5BN 01348 831518

Great fish 'n' chips" and other straightforward shes is the MO of this relaxed-but-mfortable, old-school seafood bistro – a long-tablished fixture on the Pembrokeshire coastal ath not a million miles from St David's, and cordingly popular with walkers. The "menu aters to all ages and appetites", featuring "ten fferent types of fish to go with your chips" nd now a range of specials too). "Eat out n the harbour wall" to take in the slightly ark drama of this small harbour (with much ncient quarry machinery on display), or kick ack in the appealing dining room under the aves. / theshedporthgain.co.uk; theshedporthgain; Mon-Sun 8.30 pm.

PORTHLEVEN, CORNWALL 1–4A

KOTA £79 433

HARBOUR HEAD
TR13 9JA 01326 562407

"Jude Kereama's blend of Asian, New Zealand and West Country cuisines never fails to delight" (with "exciting" tasting menus a highlight) at this harbourside restaurant-with-rooms – and, "despite the increasing competition for quality cooking in Porthleven, it remains ahead of the pack". The chef (also behind Kota Kai) was due to add a third string to his bow in Carnon Downs holiday apartment complex the Valley, but the long-awaited arrival was apparently nixed by Covid. / kotarestaurant.co.uk; Tue-Sat 9 pm.

KOTA KAI £53 443

CELTIC HOUSE, HARBOUR HEAD
TR13 9JY 01326 574411

"Amazing ramen" is just one highlight of the "lovely menu" at chef Jude Kereama's second venue, sister to nearby Kota. There's plenty of seafood, along with dishes inspired by Jude's New Zealand and Asian heritage. "Fab views over the harbour just across the road" are another reason to visit. / kotakai.co.uk; kota_kai; Tue-Sat 9 pm.

PORTISHEAD, SOMERSET 2–2B

SEAROCK £37 322

313 NEWFOUNDLAND WAY
BS20 7QH 01275 390022

This four-year-old in the Marina "looks like a fish 'n' chip shop – and it is. But it's also a fantastic fish restaurant, with the freshest of fresh fish, cooked quickly and served immediately". "The chef cooks as if he were in a backstreet bar in Marseilles – wonderful!" Top Menu Tip – "the best fritto misto". / searockrestaurant.co.uk; searockportishead; Tue-Thu 8.30 pm, Fri & Sat 9 pm, Sun 6 pm.

PORTMEIRION, GWYNEDD 4–2C

PORTMEIRION HOTEL £83 435

LL48 6ET 01766 772440

"The setting in the hotel within Portmeirion village is completely unique" – "wonderfully situated overlooking the water" of the Dwyryd estuary and at the heart of the incredible 'Mediterranean' village constructed between 1925 and 1975 by the late Clough Williams-Ellis. "They are happy for you to dress to impress or just feel comfortable" and "the quality of the food is of the highest standard". (You can even stay in Patrick McGoohan's room if you are old enough to remember cult 1960s TV series 'The Prisoner'.) / portmeirion.wales; visit_portmeirion; Mon-Sun 6.30 pm.

PORTPATRICK, DUMFRIES AND GALLOWAY 7–2A

KNOCKINAAM LODGE £106 345

DG9 9AD 01776 810471

"A wonderful country-house hotel in a beautiful setting" whose place in the history books is anchored by Churchill and Eisenhower's D-Day planning here and its inclusion in John Buchan's 'The 39 Steps'. Its place in this guide continues to be secured by its "superb food with regional produce" and "fortunately the chef has resisted the move to ever-increasing numbers of (ever-smaller) courses" while maintaining "an emphasis on excellent local ingredients". "Some of the décor is very 'Edwardian shooting lodge' but the dining room is light and bright, particularly on a summer's evening". / knockinaamlodge.com; knockinaamlodgehotel; Mon-Sun 10 pm.

PORTSMOUTH, HAMPSHIRE 2–4D

ABARBISTRO £65 323

58 WHITE HART RD
PO1 2JA 02392 811585

This "pleasant" and "airy" bistro on the seafront has shaken up its offering thanks to new head chef Adam Maker, who has introduced small plates and ambitious locally sourced cuisine alongside ongoing fixtures such as the "excellent fish 'n' chips" and pizzas. Oenophiles are also well served as "in partnership with Camber Wines, there's plenty of choice for all tastes and budgets" when it comes to the tipples. / abarbistro.co.uk; abarbistro_; Mon-Sun 11 pm.

PORTSTEWART, COUNTY LONDONDERRY 10–1D

HARRY'S SHACK £64 343

118 STRAND ROAD
BT55 7PG 028 7083 1783

"Less a shack than a real wooden beach restaurant", "owned by the National Trust on the amazing beach at Portstewart" – this unusual spot is "all about fish, as you would expect", with "smashing fish 'n' chips, and huge and delicious turbot. More surprising was the excellent desserts". It's run by Donal Doherty (son of the late Harry), who "keeps an eye on the proceedings". Top Tip – "it's right on the beach so you can walk off your meal after lunch". / harrys_shack; Mon & Tue, Sun 10 pm, Wed-Sat 11 pm.

PRESTON, LANCASHIRE 5–1A

ROASTA PRESTON £20

43 PLUNGINGTON ROAD
PR1 7EP 01772 827958

"Went here after reading Jay Rayner's Nov 2022 review. Superb!" – this no-frills café near the Central Lancashire University campus (from Hong Kong natives Fai Tsang and her husband, Wai) is "very much a café rather than a restaurant but you can (need to) book", thanks to brilliant Cantonese cooking that's worth rolling up your sleeves for. Top Menu Tip – "The roast duck and siu yuk are delicious with the crisp skin contrasting the tender meat. Soy chicken is very flavourful and the brisket tender, tasty and well spiced". / roasta-preston.co.uk; roastapreston; Mon & Tue, Fri-Sun 9 pm.

READING, BERKSHIRE 2–2D

CLAY'S HYDERABADI KITCHEN £61 433

22-24 PROSPECT STREET RG1 4PS 0118 959 6888

Nandana & Sharat Syamala's part-crowdfunded venue is "not your standard Indian restaurant" – "more like home cooking" inspired by the regional cuisines of Hyderabad and Andhra Pradesh, with "some interesting specials always available". "The venue was previously a Wetherspoons, so it's a large space which is a challenge to make entirely comfortable but it's got a good ambience and is well worth a visit". / clayskitchen.co.uk; clayskitchenbar; Tue-Thu 10.30 pm, Fri & Sat 11 pm, Sun 5 pm.

THAMES LIDO £66 234

NAPIER ROAD RG1 8FR 0118 207 0640

Located in the "quirky but fun setting" of a refurbished Grade II listed Edwardian swimming pool, this venue is an "oasis of decent food in the wasteland of Reading", serving "very good Mediterranean-style food across all three courses". With views over the pool through plate-glass windows, it's "great to eat while watching others exercise!". / thameslido.com; thameslido; Mon-Sun 9.15 pm.

REIGATE, SURREY 3–3B

LEBNANI £42 433

11 CHURCH STREET RH2 0AA 07495 528919

"A very nice selection of Lebanese fare" helps win an early thumbs-up for this three-year-old venue, which occupies a simple, modern café space in the town centre. In his September 2022 review, The Observer's Jay Rayner was also a fan: "a small but perfectly judged, perfectly run restaurant with… open kitchen pumping out the smells of good things grilling over charcoal" cooker "with an especially light, fresh touch". / lebnani.co.uk; lebnaniuk; Tue-Thu 9.30 pm, Fri & Sat 10.30 pm.

MONTE FORTE £46 333

12 WEST STREET RH2 9BS 07584 833810

"Top-notch pizza" of the wood-fired Neapolitan variety "and beer from the local brewery opposite" combine to form a winning formula at brothers Paolo and Luca's crowd-pleasing venture, which began life as a market food truck in 2017. In addition to a bigger Horsham branch, you can also get their pizzas (limited hours only) at The Hatch pub in Redhill. / monteforte.co.uk; montefortepizza; Tue-Thu 9 pm, Fri & Sat 9.30 pm, Sun 8 pm.

REYNOLDSTON, SWANSEA 1–1C

KING ARTHUR £45 234

HIGHER GREEN SA3 1AD 01792 390775

This Victorian inn on the Gower peninsula is a "longstanding staple for good reliable pub food" – "I was so pleased not to have been disappointed after a long absence". / kingarthurhotel.co.uk; Mon-Sun 9 pm.

RHAYADER, POWYS 4–4D

LOST ARC £22 332

THE OLD DRILL HALL, BRIDGE STREET LD6 5AG 01597 811226

This crowd-pleasing arts centre café is a bit of a secret amongst vegans, but its wide-ranging menu includes lots of "excellent" and "good-value" options, from quiches to salads and falafel wraps. It won praise this year for its particularly good Sunday lunch and the wood-fired pizza night on Fridays. / thelostarc.co.uk; thelostarccafe; Mon, Thu, Sat & Sun 4 am, Fri 9 pm.

RHOSNEIGR, ISLE OF ANGLESEY 4–1C

OYSTER CATCHER £53 333

MAELOG LAKE LL64 5JP 01407 812829

This unusual beachside destination – a contemporary glass-walled and environmentally friendly Huf Haus – is a "lively and colourful place, full of character", serving "quick and efficient" meals that tick all boxes for "families and surfers". With its "great views", it might well be "the best of what's available on Anglesey". / oystercatcheranglesey.co.uk; oystercatcherandwillsbar; Mon-Sun 8.30 pm.

RIDGE, HERTFORDSHIRE 3–1A

OLD GUINEA £33 333

CROSSOAKS LANE EN6 3LH 01707 660 894

"A lovely country pub" in a "nice village" between Shenley and Potters Bar, where the "really attractive outside area" offers fine views of the Herts countryside. "Superb pizzas and pastas" (the latter also coming 'al forno') hog most of the limelight, though there are also more exotic dishes such as calzone and koftas on the menu. / theoldguinea.co.uk; theoldguinea; Mon-Sun 11 pm.

RIPLEY, SURREY 3–3A

THE ANCHOR £70 432

HIGH STREET GU23 6AE 01483 211866

"The food is always fantastic" – "especially for the price" – at this dining pub owned and run for five years now by chefs Mike Wall-Palmer and Dave Adams, who met working at top chef Steve Drake's former venue in the village. / ripleyanchor.co.uk; ripleyanchor; Wed-Sat 9 pm.

THE CLOCK HOUSE £154 34

THE CLOCK HOUSE, HIGH STREET GU23 6AQ 01483 224777

"One of the very few top-class restaurants in Surrey" celebrates its 20th anniversary this ye under owner Serina Drake (who rebranded it few years back following her split from former husband, chef Steve Drake). Head chef Luke Spier (ex-Gordon Ramsay Group and Simon Rogan's Roganic) has brought his Nordic-influenced modern British cuisine to the kitch in the past year. / theclockhouserestaurant.co.uk theclockhouse_restaurant; Wed-Sat 9 pm.

ROCK, CORNWALL 1–3

DINING ROOM £89 44

PAVILION BUILDINGS, ROCK RD PL27 6JS 01208 862622

Limited but still all-round enthusiastic feedback this year for Fred & Donna Beedles's low-key operation, in a parade of shops away from the harbour. The menu is a two-course or three-course à la carte, whose seeming straightforwardness belies the skill of the cuisine. / thediningroomrock.co.uk; Thediningroomrock; Tue-Sat 8.30 pm.

KARREK, ST ENODOC HOTEL £127

ROCK ROAD PL27 6LA 01208 863394

The dining room at this smart century-old hotel has long been one of Cornwall's prime culinary destinations, but the volume and tenor of feedback was more muted this year, so we've left it un-rated for the time being. There's a choice of tasting menus in six or nine courses, and less of a focus on seafood than in the Nathan Outlaw era of a few years back. Karrek is apparently Cornish for Rock. / enodoc-hotel.co.uk; Karrekrock.

THE MARINERS £60 43

PL27 6LD 01841 532796

"Paul Ainsworth's pub in Rock" – "a pleasant ride across on the ferry from Padstow and then a short stroll" – "goes from strength to strength". One of the more commented-on venues locally, it achieves "that perfect combination of offering classic British pub grub, without the huge portions or the stodge" It has an enticing terrace, and "the views over the Camel estuary are glorious on a fine day". It's part of a seven-strong 'family' of local venues from the chef, who settled in the area almost 20 years ago. / paul-ainsworth.co.uk; themarinersbeachclub; Mon-Sat 9.30 pm, Sun 9 pm.

ROSEVINE, CORNWALL 1–4B

DRIFTWOOD HOTEL £97 23

TR2 5EW 01872 580644

"Wonderful views of the cliffs, beach and sea" help inspire fans to this boutique hotel dining

›m, which occupies a clifftop Georgian ›ilding on the Roseland Peninsula. Opinions the operation were a little up-and-down s year, citing "slightly erratic service" or ›d that's "OK but variable"; but on the plus e, serious concerns were absent and ratings nain healthy all-round. / driftwoodhotel.co.uk; ftwood_hotel; Thu-Sun, Mon-Wed 9 pm.

ROUGHAM, SUFFOLK 3–1C

›ORAGE KITCHEN £75 5 4 3

ACKTHORPE FARM HOUSE
30 9JG 01359 720350

›uite exceptional and such a pleasure to visit", s "wonderful concept is very different from ›st restaurants" – "an intimate open kitchen ›-20 covers only)" serving "superb local ›redients, many of which are foraged by the ›efs" on the surrounding 3,000-acre Rougham ›ate. "All courses are delivered to your table the chefs and carefully explained" – it's ›mazing value for money too", at between ›0 per person and £75 per person for as ›any as ten courses. "Almost don't want to ›ite a review in case too many people find out out it!" / Tue-Thu 4 pm, Fri & Sat 9 pm.

ROWSLEY, DERBYSHIRE 5–3C

›HE PEACOCK AT ›OWSLEY £117 3 3 3

›AKEWELL RD DE4 2EB 01629 733518

›is "old manor house" handy for ›atsworth (and "not to be confused with ›e Peacock Inn in nearby Bakewell"), may ›el old-fashioned", but its "great food and ›eresting menu" (from tasting menus to ›ore "relaxed" options, both taken in the ›ne dining room") make it "a pleasure" by all counts. Local ingredients (beef and lamb, ›y) are sourced from the Haddon Estate › which it sits. / thepeacockatrowsley.com; ›epeacockatrowsley; Mon-Sun 9 pm.

RYE, EAST SUSSEX 3–4C

›ANDGATE BISTRO £61 3 3 2

- 6 LANDGATE
›N31 7LH 01797 222829

›his "really lovely small restaurant", housed in ›terlinked Georgian shops, has "been excellent ›r years" owing to its "short, interesting menu" ›locally sourced British food (some foraged) ›d its "charming and efficient service" ›o. / landgatebistro.co.uk; landgatebistro; Wed-Sat ›pm.

›ERMAID 2 3 5

›ERMAID ST TN31 7EY 01797 223065

›he "historic location" (a 600-year-old ›ilding with mullioned windows and many a ›am) certainly adds to the charms of this old ›ugglers' inn – "a little old-school, but that's ›l part of the experience". It's been under the ›me owners for three decades, and while it's ›t the main draw, the "lovely food" also has its ›ns. / mermaidinn.com; Mon-Sun 11 pm.

STANDARD INN 3 3 3

33 THE MINT TN31 7EN 01797 225 231

A "lovely old pub" with rooms in the Citadel, whose fifteenth-century charms (beams, etc.) have been restored to their full glory; the "buzzy" atmosphere and "good-value" local food (e.g. Romney Marsh lamb) create, for one reporter, "the best gastropub I've been to this year (and I've been to many!)" – an opinion backed by CAMRA, who have voted it the 'Best Pub in SE England' for two consecutive years. NB: "the lack of booking is both annoying and an advantage" ("be there by 17.45… or wait 'til about 19.30!"). / thestandardinnrye.co.uk; Mon-Sat 11 pm, Sun 10.30 pm.

WEBBE'S AT THE FISH CAFE £61 3 2 2

17 TOWER STREET
TN31 7AT 01797 222 226

"If you like fish, come here" – chorus the many fans of Paul Webbe's "reliable" spot, which serves some of "the freshest seafood ever" at "good VFM" prices – such as a "stonking portion of sprats with super-light batter for under a fiver" and "scallops which melt in the mouth". "Acoustic panels have been fitted to the ceiling to absorb noise" but the setting can still appear a little bare. / webbesrestaurants.co.uk; webbesrye; Sun-Thu 9 pm, Fri & Sat 9.30 pm.

SALCOMBE, DEVON 1–4C

CRAB SHED £81 4 4 3

GOULD ROAD TQ8 8DU 01548 844 280

This local business started processing crab in 2008 and opened this simple café in 2014. "Outside is challenging in the autumn and winter, but even then, they have wonderful blankets that you can use to savour the great seafood they serve. Absolutely love it". / crabshed.com; crabshedsalcombe; Mon-Sun 8.30 pm.

SALE, GREATER MANCHESTER 5–2B

THE PERFECT MATCH £68 4 4 2

103 CROSS STREET
M33 7JN 0161 204 3665

"What a wonderful find" in Sale – this "outstanding neighbourhood restaurant" combines "awesome food and a unique wine-matching option which never fails to impress". Manchester-born chef Jacinda (Jazz) met sommelier Andrea – from a prosecco-producing family near Venice – working at Gordon Ramsay's Savoy Grill, and they decided their talents were a 'perfect match'. Each dish on the menu is accompanied by a wine suggestion from Andrea. / theperfectmatchsale.co.uk; Fri & Sat 10.30 pm, Wed 9.30 pm, Thu 10 pm, Sun 6 pm.

SALISBURY, WILTSHIRE 2–3C

ANOKAA £54 3 3 2

60 FISHERTON ST
SP2 7RB 01722 414142

"Brilliant, delicately spiced food – in decent portions and well priced" – has established Farsi Solman's "really good Indian" as one of Salisbury's prime dining destinations over more than 20 years. "No wonder you must book". / anokaa.com; Mon-Sun 10 pm.

NOLE ON THE SQUARE £15 3 3 3

4 BUTCHER ROW
SP1 1EP 01722 445447

This intimate venue – spilling out onto the marketplace in warmer months – was opened in 2021, and has offshoots at The Pembroke Arms in Wilton, The Grosvenor Arms in Hindon and The Dog and Gun in Netheravon. It delivers "wonderful sourdough pizza with interesting, locally sourced toppings and combinations (Westcombe ricotta and local truffle is a favourite, as is local pepperoni with honey)". / nolepizza.co.uk; nolepizza; Mon, Wed-Sun 9 pm.

SALTASH, DEVON 1–3C

CROCADON £50 5 4 4

ST MELLION PL12 6RL NO TEL

"Without a doubt this was well and away my best meal of the year!" – "Dan Cox's delightful, new regenerative farm-to-fork project" opened in February 2023 and is destined for great things, inspiring rapturous early reports. "You can instantly tell that he owes a lot to his long tenure under Simon Rogan at L'Enclume and then Fera". He took over this former sawmill and organic farm on the Devon/Cornwall border in 2018 and spent five years planning and planting and raising rare-breed livestock in order to open this 25-cover ultra-sustainable restaurant with an open kitchen which occupies an old barn on the farm. The result is a "a wonderfully sparse, yet cosy and warm place" whose cuisine inspires a full-on rave: "we had the 13-course tasting menu, which was innovative and totally delicious, with everything sourced from the farm or like-minded local producers with the menu dependent on availability. The matching wines were also excellent. Well worth a journey!" – "The Lion's Mane steak was powerful and full of umami notes, so much so that even our diehard carnivore of a daughter enjoyed it. The pork belly and leg dish was exquisite. Hit all the right notes in this unstuffy dining experience where the chef serves your food. After only three months open it thoroughly deserves its Michelin Green Star and is destined to go far". (In his August 2023 review, The Telegraph's William Sitwell also pronounced himself a fan: "I can honestly say this was a collection of magnificent, original and quite breathtaking food".) / crocadon.farm; chefdancox; Thu-Sat 10 pm, Sun 4 pm.

SALTBURN, NORTH YORKSHIRE 8–3C

THE SEAVIEW RESTAURANT £70 433

THE FORESHORE BUILDING, LOWER PROMENADE TS12 1HQ 01287 236015

"Great fish and chips, but also a good number of other locally caught seafood options" are served "all with a lovely view over Saltburn beach and pier" at this well-named local feature. "The crab sandwich that featured in a Nadiya Hussein BBC TV show is good but pricey!" / theseaviewrestaurant.co.uk; seaviewrestaurant; Mon-Sun 10.30 pm.

SALTHOUSE, NORFOLK 6–3C

DUN COW £53 333

PURDY ST NR25 7XA 01263 740467

This "thoroughly reliable pub" is "just a short stroll from the coast" with views across the salt marshes. "Everything works well despite the casual, almost laid-back approach", while "the imaginative menu is definitely a notch above the pub norm". / salthouseduncow.com; theduncowsalthouse; Mon-Sun 10 pm.

SALTWOOD, KENT 3–4D

HIDE & FOX £102 543

THE GREEN CT21 4BT 01303 260915

"A real treat of a place" – this stylish restaurant was opened five years ago by a talented pair, Kent-born chef Allister Barsby (head chef at Gidleigh Park on Dartmoor at 24) and Italian Alice Bussi (food & beverage manager of the year in the 2018 Catey awards). The praise is unanimous: "we go when there's something to celebrate. We've been three times over the last few years and it has never failed to be a joy – the food is fabulous and the service and front of house exceptional". "One of the most amazing dinners I have had, in a very serene environment with exceptional service". / hideandfox.co.uk; hideandfox; Wed-Sat 8.30 pm, Tue 8 pm.

SANDBANKS, DORSET 2–4C

RICK STEIN £77

10-14 BANKS RD BH13 7QB 01202 283 000

You can hang with the local mansion-owners and beachgoers at this Poole Harbour outpost of the Stein empire, which has a brilliant location overlooking the water. It inspired less feedback this year than its stablemates, hence we've left it unrated. / rickstein.com; ricksteinrestaurants; Mon-Thu 9 pm, Fri-Sun 10 pm.

SANDSEND, NORTH YORKSHIRE 8–3D

THE FISH COTTAGE £73 333

FISH COTTAGE YO21 3SU 01947 899342

This modern 'posh chippy' (est. 2020) just 20 yards from the sea has a "first-class fish menu to suit all tastes", from fish 'n' chips to consume on the beach to a menu of more elevated international seafood dishes to eat in the dining room. There's a second branch in York's Shambles Market. / fishcottage.co.uk; thefishcottage; Mon, Thu-Sun 8 pm.

SAUNDERSFOOT, PEMBROKESHIRE 4–4B

COAST £101 434

COPPET HALL BEACH SA69 9AJ 01834 810800

"Overlooking the sea and beach in a wonderful location" – a striking wood-and-glass structure backdrops Fred Clapperton's "outstanding" food ("especially fish"). The local sourcing is impeccable (including bivalves from Atlantic Edge Oysters, who use regenerative farming methods), as is the "wow-factor attention to detail" – e.g. charcoal-rich cocktail 'The 1829', which nods to the year an act was passed to create the railway line on which the building sits. NB – watch out for the new summer terrace, offering tipples and fancy sharing plates. / coastsaundersfoot.co.uk; coastsaundersfoot; Wed-Sat 8.45 pm.

SCARBOROUGH, NORTH YORKSHIRE 8–4D

LANTERNA £74 332

33 QUEEN STREET YO11 1HQ 01723 363616

"We go regularly and are always sated and often delighted", say fans of the authentic Italian cooking at this stalwart on the Yorkshire coast, owned since 1997 by chef-patron Giorgio Alessio – a champion of the cuisine of his native Piedmont and the white truffles that are its crown jewels. He first talked of retiring five years ago, so don't postpone your visit too long. / lanterna-ristorante.co.uk; Thu-Sat 9.30 pm.

SCAWTON, NORTH YORKSHIRE 8–4C

THE HARE INN RESTAURANT £125 543

YO7 2HG 01845 597769

"What an amazing experience: loved it!" – "husband and wife team" Paul & Liz Jackson "deliver quality in every department" at the 12th-century inn on the North York Moors they've run since 2012. Paul's cooking is anything but traditional, featuring "Asian-inspired flavours in a tasting menu that doesn't overwhelm", alongside "interesting drinks pairings – not all of them are wines", while the "small number of tables" means "service is attentive and friendly". There are also "very pleasant rooms to stay overnight". / thehare-inn.com; Thu-Sat 9 pm.

SEASALTER, KENT 3–3C

THE SPORTSMAN £106 544

FAVERSHAM ROAD CT5 4BP 01227 273370

"Pretty much my idea of gastronomic heaven": Stephen Harris's "tricky-to-get-to old-looking pub" represents "a friendly and pleasurable approximation of perfection" for its enormou fan club and – as one of the top-5 most commented-on destinations in our annual diners' poll – is viewed by many as "simply th best pub-orientated restaurant in the UK". Set out on the salt marshes by the Thames just outside Whitstable, "don't be fooled by the external décor" (which makes it look like any old seaside pub). Inside, it "still retains its original charm" and its unforced style makes i "a place to return to on a regular basis". "Th local produce mirrors its estuary-side position' with each "simple but magnificent" componen of the five-course menu "representing the best of the locality at that time of year". "The cooking itself is a revelation" with "prodigious attention to flavour" and the most often-cited offerings including excellent fish, oysters and lamb (including, of course, the signature slip soles). "The wine list reflects the tastes of the Patron who only lists wines that he would choose to drink himself". "Many pilgrims make the journey but you have to book months in advance". "A joy to visit before or, preferably, after a bracing walk on the beach" (and with it being "just a short step to their delightful self-catering cabins, what could be more romantic?)" / thesportsmanseasalter.co.uk; sportsmankent; Tue-Sat 8.30 pm, Sun 2.30 pm.

SEDBERGH, CUMBRIA 7–4

THE BLACK BULL INN £62 44

44 MAIN STREET LA10 5BL 015396 20264

"A charming old pub with a lot of atmosphere – James Ratcliff and Nina Matsunaga's "well-run operation" is to be found in a "lovely town" between the Yorkshire Dales and the Lake District. The "really good" cuisine makes an unusual find in these parts, reflecting as it does chef Nina's Japanese heritage with some interesting Asian inflections to the traditional Yorkshire fare. / theblackbullsedbergh.co.uk; theblackbullsedbergh; Wed-Sat 8 pm.

SEER GREEN, BUCKINGHAMSHIRE 3–3

THE JOLLY CRICKETERS £62 44

24 CHALFONT RD HP9 2YG 01494 676308

"Worth the drive out" – Chris & Amanda Lillitou's "quintessential English country pub" has a super-cute village location in the lush Chilterns countryside surrounding Beaconsfield. The cuisine is down-to-earth, but it comes with the spin one might expect from Amanda's Tante-Claire training: the sou might be Jerusalem artichoke; the fish 'n' chips may incorporate Newlyn hake and battered cod's cheek; and a typical pie would feature game with a suet crust. / thejollycricketers.co.uk thejollycricketers; Mon-Sat 9 pm, Sun 6 pm.

Allium at Askham Hall, Penrith

SEVENOAKS, KENT 3–3B

NUMBER EIGHT £61 332

8 LONDON ROAD TN13 1AJ 01732 448088

"A welcome indie" launched by Stuart Gillies (whose starry CV includes stints at Le Caprice and NYC's Restaurant DANIEL) and wife Cecilia in 2022; the "informal" venue specialises in "delicious small plates", and while the "bill can add up", it's "the best option in Sevenoaks" by most accounts. / no8sevenoaks.com; no8sevenoaks; Tue-Thu 10 pm, Fri & Sat 11 pm, Sun 6 pm.

SHEFFIELD, SOUTH YORKSHIRE 5–2C

DOMO £57 334

34-36 COTTON MILL WALK S3 8DH 0114 322 1020

An "outstanding experience" awaits at this family-run Sardinian restaurant, bar and deli, on the ground floor of the Eagle Works building in the happening Kelham Island district. "The owner Raffa has a very clear vision of what he is trying to create": an "authentic yet modern" joint where "semi-casual fine-dining is lifted to a level of unexpected excellence" ("well above typical Italian pizza fare") and where "passion and humour are very much in evidence" amongst the staff. A sibling cocktail bar and snack spot, Kelu, has also now launched at the entrance to Kelham Island. / domorestaurant.co.uk; domo.restaurant; Mon-Thu 9 pm, Fri & Sat 9.30 pm, Sun 6.30 pm.

JORO £100 543

294 SHALESMOOR S3 8US 0114 299 1539

"Blessed to have this in Sheffield… it is bold and surprising!" – Luke & Stacey Sherwood "go from strength to strength" at this linchpin of the city's dining scene "set in a shipping container" and which opened in 2016. "When it comes to consistent, flavourful, creative food that's technically clever without being pretentious, it's hard to beat" and a number of reporters feel "it's a mystery as to why it hasn't got a Michelin star". "A new, larger venue might help with the slight feeling of overcrowding" ("hopefully the restaurant will move to a larger location where the timings do not have to be so rigid"). Top Menu Tip – "their soft drinks pairings are the work of alchemy: matching dishes with unique skill". / jororestaurant.co.uk; restaurant_joro; Thu-Sat, Wed 11.30 pm.

KONJÖ £25 443

CUTLERY WORKS, 73–101 NEEPSEND LANE S3 8AT NO TEL

"A must-visit for anyone in Sheffield who wants great food in an informal setting", this spin-off of the hit Kelham Island venue Joro is situated in indie food hall The Cutlery Works; the 'robotayaki' kitchen features Scandi/Japanese fusion plates cooked over a BBQ grill, and happily "the food quality is as good as Joro, but the prices more accessible". / konjo.business.site; konjokitchen; Fri & Sat 10 pm, Tue-Thu, Sun 9 pm.

RAFTERS £129 433

220 OAKBROOK RD, NETHERGREEN S11 7ED 0114 230 4819

"Tucked away in a leafy suburb in the posh west of the city", this comfortably appointed 26-seat venue from Tom Lawson & Alastair Myers has a dedicated local fan club. It's "now entirely focused on set menus, from 4 courses for £65 to the 'Kitchen Bench' for £120 – highly priced for round here" but scoring decent ratings or better in all reports. / raftersrestaurant.co.uk; raftersrestaurant; Wed-Sat 11.30 pm.

TONCO £48 343

2 DYSON PLACE S11 8XX 0114 349 3996

Flo Hiller and Joe Shrewsbury's "great, informal" small-plates restaurant, in what is a happening dining 'hood, has wowed the likes of Marina O'Loughlin since opening in 2019; you "can see the influence of Moro", the famously creative Clerkenwell icon, on its "exciting menu", and bonus points for its soft drink pairings, "many homemade". In 2023, they opened a bakery/café/essentials shop, 100m away on Sharrow Vale Road, with plans to create a laid- back extension to the main restaurant. / tonco.co.uk; toncosheffield; Wed-Sat 9.30 pm.

V OR V £44 332

WHARNCLIFFE WORKS, CORNISH STREET S6 3FB 01142 724370

"Great fine-dining vegetarian food" (and vegan, the other 'V' of the title) has won a big following for this Kelham Island outfit, whose attractive interior mines the same industrial-hip vibe as the quarter at large. The plant-based sharing plates are often cooked over an open fire, and come accompanied by vegan wines and beers. In early 2023, they launched fast-food spin-off V or V Grill House, offering Middle Eastern kebabs and more, at Sheffield Plate food hall in the city centre. / vorvsheffield.co.uk; vorvrestaurant; Wed-Sat 11 pm, Sun 6 pm.

VERO GUSTO £99 444

12 NORFOLK ROW S1 2PA 0114 276 0004

Opened in 2006 in an elegant townhouse on a cobbled street in the city centre, this well-known family-run venue "will not disappoint", with Naples-born Ester's "real Italian food" and her partner Saverio's "excellent Italian wine list" (with some truly notable vintages) winning high praise. / verogusto.com; verogusto; Wed-Sat 10.30 pm.

SHENLEY, HERTFORDSHIRE 3–2B

ITALIANA £53 333

142 LONDON ROAD WD7 9BT 01923 852584

This "lovely family-run Italian" has been a "reliable" local standby for 17 years, with its "extensive menu of old standards as well as interesting new dishes" and "the best pizza". "Service is friendly and helpful", too. / litaliana.co.uk; Sun-Fri 10 pm, Sat 10.30 p

SHERBORNE, DORSET 2–

THE GREEN £65 33

3 THE GREEN DT9 3HY 01935 813821

"Great modern European food using locally sourced ingredients at very reasonable prices" again wins praise for this local fixture. Chef-patron Sasha Matkevich grew up in south Russia but has lived in England for 30 years. / greenrestaurant.co.uk; thegreenrestaurar Tue-Sat 9.30 pm.

THE NEWELL £45 33

GREENHILL DT9 4EP 01935 710386

A "small restaurant in Sherborne, owned by an Australian couple", and where the "good" and "unusual" food pays testament to chef Paul Merrony's Gallic training with the likes of Albert Roux at Le Gavroche; there's an "interesting list of well-chosen wines at reasonable prices to match the excellent food" / newell.restaurant; Wed-Sat 9 pm, Sun 3 pm.

SHERE, SURREY 3–3

KINGHAMS £60 34

GOMSHALL LN GU5 9HE 01483 20216

"Set in a delightful village" in the Surrey Hills this 17th-century red-brick cottage now house a "delightful restaurant" where the "mild Moroccan influence on modern British food makes for a superb dining experience" ("I live in London and go specially"). "The staff cann do enough to make your meal enjoyable – and that includes the charming owner", Jack Forre Foster. / kinghams-restaurant.co.uk; kinghams_restaurant's profile picture kinghams_restaurant; Tue-Sat 9 pm, Sun 2.15 pm.

SHINFIELD, BERKSHIRE 2–2

L'ORTOLAN £112 44

CHURCH LN RG2 9BY 0118 988 8500

This "superb" restaurant in "a beautiful country house in a small village" on the edge c Reading celebrates its 40th anniversary under its current name this year – and has gathered a large number of fans who say "we've been visiting for years and it's brilliant". The loss of its long-held Michelin star in 2022 has not dampened enthusiasm, with reporters in our annual survey praising the "well executed" meals sent out by young head chef James Greatorex – "it's not cutting edge but very pleasant modern French-influenced cuisine". "As with so many fine-dining restaurants, lunch is much more affordable than dinner: the 5-course lunch at £49 was excellent value". / lortolan.com; lortolan; Wed-Sat 8 pm, Tue 1 pm.

SHIPLAKE, OXFORDSHIRE 2–2D

RWELLS £92 443

HIPLAKE ROW RG9 4DP 0118 940 3673

ıst a thoroughly super place to eat innovative od, beautifully presented, enjoy good mpany and feel thoroughly pampered!" Ryan & Liam Simpson-Trotman's rural ır has firmly established itself since 2010 a major highlight near Henley. Set in a nverted pub, service is charming, but the ot of its appeal is the "outstanding" modern uropean cuisine, which is available à la rte during quieter services but is usually esented as either a six-course tasting menu r £100 per person or ten courses at £150 per rson. / orwellsrestaurant.co.uk; orwells_rest; ed-Sat 9.30 pm, Sun 3.30 pm.

SHOREHAM, KENT 3–3B

OUNT VINEYARD £41 243

HURCH STREETSHOREHAM
N14 7SD 01959 524008

a "beautiful location" in the Darent alley – as close as country Kent gets to ondon – this vineyard was planted 20 years go and is now an attraction complete with staurant serving "predominantly cheese nd charcuterie boards as well as stone-baked zza". "The staff are fabulous – attentive ut not OTT) and great at recommending ine". It's a relaxed and "dog-friendly" ace for an outing. / themountvineyard.co.uk; emountvineyardkent; Wed-Sat 11 pm, Sun 6 pm.

SHREWSBURY, SHROPSHIRE 5–4A

SONS £52 323

MILK STREET SY1 1SZ 01743 272709

Owned & run hands-on by four brothers with passion for quality food" – Reuben, Adam, en and Josh Crouch (hence CSONS), who so run Ludlow's Green Café – this mainly aytime venue majors in "locally sourced asonal ingredients served in interesting ays", with "a Middle Eastern influence that akes for aromatic dishes". It's "not strictly egetarian/vegan, but many options are vailable". / csons-shrewsbury.co.uk; csons_food; un-Thu 4 pm, Fri & Sat 11 pm.

IOUSE OF YUM £13 334

ARKET HALL, CLAREMONT STREET
Y1 1QG 07526 673195

Cheap but good Thai food" (noodles, soups, shy specials) is the basis for "an excellent reet-food experience within Shrewsbury Iarket Hall", at this local hot ticket; "don't e put off by the Market Hall's rather nabby Sixties exterior, the interior is fine nd the food venues all worth a visit". / ouseofyumshrewsbury; Mon-Sat 4 pm.

NUMBER FOUR £40 333

4 BUTCHER ROW
SY1 1UW 01743 366691

This appealing indie café/restaurant, in a quiet side street, has a modish industrial-style interior, while the open kitchen turns out seasonal eats spanning small plates, steaks and lots of snackable 'things on toast'. / number-four.com; numberfourbutcherrow; Mon-Thu 4 pm, Fri midnight, Sat 5 pm.

THE WALRUS £65 433

2 LOWER CLAREMONT BANK
SY1 1RT 01743 240005

Local lad Ben Hall worked at the acclaimed Gidleigh Park, among others, before teaming up with partner Carla Cook to launch this ambitious five-year-old; in November 2022, they upped sticks from their former premises in Roushill to a larger, ex-warehouse setting on Claremont Bank in the city centre. The "really excellent food" (tasting menu only on Fri/Sat nights) remains intact at what is, for fans, "the best restaurant in Shrewsbury". / the-walrus.co.uk; thewalrusrestaurant; Wed-Sat 10 pm.

SKELTON, CUMBRIA 7–3D

THE DOG & GUN £70 433

CA11 9SE 01768 484301

"Another ex-boozer I remember from adolescence, with patterned carpets and glowering locals now replaced by worshippers of the Michelin divinity" – and by all accounts Ben Queen-Fryer's gentrified rural gastroboozer (est. 2017) "merits the star" it has held since 2022. "The food never disappoints with quality, quantity and interest" – all the more impressive given that this is a one-man band. / dogandgunskelton.co.uk; dog_and_gun_skelton; Tue-Sat 11 pm.

SKIPTON, NORTH YORKSHIRE 5–1C

THE BURLINGTON AT THE DEVONSHIRE ARMS HOTEL AND SPA £107 344

BOLTON ABBEY
BD23 6AJ 01756 718100

This "beautiful hotel at Bolton Abbey", the Duke of Devonshire's classic country estate, is a well-known getaway, and its very posh and "very good" dining room has also proved a testing ground for exciting chefs (Michael Wignall, Peter Howarth). Chris O'Callaghan, who arrived in 2021, now oversees the British cuisine (afternoon teas and fancier fare), while the open-plan wine cellar feeds into the "superb and very extensive wine list". / devonshirehotels.co.uk; devarmsboltonabbey; Mon-Sun 9 pm.

THE DEVONSHIRE FELL HOTEL, DEVONSHIRE HOTELS & RESTAURANTS £71 333

BURNSALL VILLAGE
BD23 6BT 01756 729000

Leafy views over glorious Dales countryside and the river Wharfe add to the occasion at this attractive hotel, convenient for Bolton Abbey. The cooking – Hardwick lamb, market fish, steaks – is not particularly 'gastro' in style but contributes to a comfortable and affordable experience, and one that comes at a reasonable price. / devonshirefell.co.uk; devonshirefell; Mon-Sun 9 pm.

SLAUGHAM, WEST SUSSEX 3–4B

HERITAGE £140 334

THE CHEQUERS INN
RH17 6AQ 01444 401102

In the "dream location" of this sleepy but charming West Sussex hamlet, Matt Gillan's "romantic" restaurant-with-rooms "continues to be a strong all-rounder" offering a "very convivial and relaxing experience" (especially if you opt for the "brilliant tasting menus"). Add in "superbly decorated bedrooms" and "breakfast – the icing on the cake". / heritage.restaurant; heritage_mattgillan; Thu-Sat 8 pm, Sun 1.45 pm.

SLEAT, HIGHLAND 9–2B

KINLOCH LODGE £129 344

SLEAT IV43 8QY 01471 833333

A meal at the former clan Macdonald hunting lodge is full of "delicious temptations, with a wine list full of delights and spirits to follow" from a bar which stocks 122 different whiskies. The setting is magical, on the shore of Loch na Dal with views of the Cuillin mountains, and the lodge – a hotel since 1972 and still owned and run by the family – has all the comforts and fireplaces you might need – and "their Sunday lunch is the best ever!". / kinloch-lodge.co.uk; kinloch_lodge; Mon-Sun 9 pm.

SNAPE, SUFFOLK 3–1D

THE PLOUGH AND SAIL £57 332

SNAPE BRIDGE IP17 1SR 01728 688413

This "busy pub on the Snape Maltings site offering rather more than good pub grub" is "perfect for pre-concert" but is "winning lots of local regulars, not just the concert crowd", with its "interesting menu and good service". Run for 12 years by twins Alex & Oliver Burnside, who "also manage Regatta in Aldeburgh and the Golden Key around the corner", the pub "has really improved over recent years". / theploughandsailsnape.com; ploughandsailsnape; Mon-Sun 2 am.

SNETTISHAM, NORFOLK 6–4B

THE OLD BANK BISTRO £95 433

10 LYNN ROAD PE31 7LP 01485 544080

Norfolk chef Lewis King and wife Aga have "struck a winning balance" at this small ex-coffee shop, whose honours include the GFG's accolade for Best Local Restaurant in Britain – and where "the atmosphere and décor is nothing outstanding in the best possible way – a simple yet tasteful interior that feels very calm, cosy and welcoming". In the kitchen, Lewis turns out "extremely high-quality and creative food" (much locally sourced) from short and long set menus, while "passionate yet knowledgeable" Aga ensures a "fantastic" welcome and wines. / theoldbankbistro.co.uk; theoldbankbistro; Wed-Sat 11.30 pm.

SOLIHULL, WEST MIDLANDS 5–4C

TOFFS £120 443

16 DRURY LANE B91 3BG 0121 824 4166

"This must be the most 'undiscovered' fine-dining restaurant in the West Midlands", say fans of this yearling from locally born and trained Rob Palmer, formerly head chef at Hampton Manor, whose debut as patron is a 26-seat open-kitchen venue in a former computer game shop. "Food and service are first-class", and if it's "a little pricey, it's worth it". In the evening, the five-course menu is £85 per person; or there's a seven-course option for £99 per person. / toffsbyrobpalmer.com; toffsbyrobpalmer; Wed-Sat 9 pm.

SONNING-ON-THAMES, BERKSHIRE 2–2D

THE BULL INN £53 224

HIGH ST RG4 6UP 0118 969 3901

"Cracking Sunday lunches with football-sized Yorkshires" are the culinary highlight of this "pretty village inn" in a glorious spot just by the Thames (which gets a mention in Jerome K Jerome's classic 'Three Men in a Boat'). It's a notably "stylish" and "buzzy venue" with a "lovely outdoor area" but has never been a particularly foodie destination. Local heart-throb George Clooney was rumoured to want to buy the pub when he moved into the area with his wife Amal – he told Graham Norton "it's fantastic and we drink all kinds of pints and things". / bullinnsonning.co.uk; BullInnSonning; Mon-Sat 11 pm, Sun 10 pm.

THE FRENCH HORN £126 345

RG4 6TN 0118 969 2204

"Three generations of the same family have been pleasing visitors" to this Thames Valley bastion of traditional haute cuisine, owned by the Emmanuel family since 1972 and with a first-class position overlooking the water at Sonning Eye. The famous signature "roast duck on the spit is the best", while "the fab wine list is worth taking home to salivate over". While a minority of reporters caution that it is "very good but too expensive", most feel the high quality justifies the investment. / thefrenchhorn.co.uk; frenchhornsonning; Wed-Sat 9.30 pm, Sun 4.30 pm.

SOUTH FERRIBY, LINCOLNSHIRE 6–2A

THE HOPE & ANCHOR £74 334

SLUICE ROAD DN18 6JQ 01652 635334

This capacious boozer-with-rooms near the Humber Bridge has a "great atmosphere" and estuary views. On the food front, their original British cooking embraces the zero-waste approach, with greens foraged in Broughton Woods, and meats (even fancy Wagyu) aged in a glass-front drying cabinet, before finishing in the trendy Josper oven. / thehopeandanchorpub.co.uk; thehopeandanchorpub; Tue-Sat 8.30 pm, Sun 5 pm.

SOUTH PETHERTON, SOMERSET 2–3B

HOLM 334

28 ST JAMES STREET TA13 5BT 01460 712470

"A great addition to the food scene in Somerset" – this two-year-old operation from chef-patron Nicholas Balfe (previously of the team behind Peckham's Levan, now flying solo) occupies a converted bank, with a dining room in the original vault, open kitchen and diners' counter. Foodwise, the focus is on reasonably priced modern bistro fare not a million miles from its original stablemate's 'bistronomy'. Other features include an outside terrace (for coffee or snacks) and rooms for a stay. Top Tip – "good value lunch menu". / holmsomerset.co.uk; holmsomerset; Wed-Sat midnight, Sun 6 pm.

SOUTH SHIELDS, TYNE AND WEAR 8–2B

COLMANS £37 443

182-186 OCEAN RD NE33 2JQ 0191 456 1202

Not all chippies can boast 100 years of operation (the business started as a hut on the foreshore in 1905) – this traditional operation is one of the few that can, but has moved with the times and only uses wild fish from sustainable fishing grounds, fried in additive-free vegetable oil. Nowadays its 'Temple' spin-off generates more interest in our poll, but the original remains highly rated for what it does. / colmansfishandchips.co.uk; Mon-Sun 6 pm.

COLMANS SEAFOOD TEMPLE £56 433

SEA ROAD NE33 2LD 0191 511 1349

"Ask for a table overlooking sea" when you visit this beachfront landmark (known locally as Gandhi's Temple and dating from 1921), which was relaunched in 2017 as the flagship of local institution Colmans (see also): "excellent fish is served in a dining room with wonderful views". / colmansseafoodtemple.co.uk; colmansseafoodtemple; Mon-Thu 7.30 pm, Fri & Sat 8.30 pm, Sun 5 pm.

SOUTHAMPTON, HAMPSHIRE 2–3

BLUE JASMINE £59 33

UNIT 3-4 ALEXANDRA WHARF, MARITIME WALK, OCEAN WAY SO14 3QS 023 8063 6387

An "excellent culinary experience" is again reported – if on quite limited feedback – at this very contemporary four-year-old venue in Southampton's Ocean Village Marina. Chef Daren Liew – whose CV includes Hakkasan – aims to create 'Asian gastronomy that's been elevated to fine-dining standards'. / bluejasmine.co.uk; bluejasmine_uk; Tue-Sun 11 pm.

JETTY £33 33

5 MARITIME WALK SO14 3QT 023 8110 3777

"Great seafood" combining "consistent quality and excellent value" is on the menu at "the flagship hotel and restaurant of the Harbour Hotels group". Self-taught chef Alex Aitken started his working life as a trawlerman and was for many years patron of Le Poussin in Brockenhurst. Top Menu Tip – "tempura soft shell crab is fantastic". / harbourhotels.co.uk; southamptonharbourhotel; Mon-Thu 9 pm, Fri & Sat 9.45 pm, Sun 8.30 pm.

LAKAZ MAMAN £43 32

22 BEDFORD PLACE SO15 2DB 023 8063 9217

"It's the only place to eat in Southampton!" according to fans of this Mauritian street kitchen run by Shelina Permalloo. Don't expect huge comfort, but the curries, soups, fry-ups and funky burgers are "interesting, beautifully cooked and presented and full of flavour". / lakazmaman.com; lakazmaman; Mon-Sat 10 pm, Sun 9 pm.

SOUTHBOROUGH, KENT 3–4B

TALLOW £70 543

15A CHURCH ROAD TN4 0RX NO TEL

It's been a good year for Rob & Donna Taylor, who moved to this "charming, cramped little room in a fun stripped-out townhouse in Southborough – a near-neighbour of Tunbridge Wells" – and who topped the Good Food Guide's list of Top 100 local restaurants in July 2023 just two years after their opening (having moved here in 2021 from The Compasses Inn in Crundale). For a second year it is one of the more commented-on venues outside the capital in our annual diners' poll: the "highly skillful" food is "out of this world" and available à la carte (yay!) as well as in an alternative tasting format. Dishes include "plenty of well-judged strong touches" and "the presentation, balance and clarity of flavours are standout" ("meat cookery is a highlight, but the pastry section runs it a close second"). "Staff are super-sweet too and know their stuff!". "The overall feeling is of a place that's fairly priced (if not cheap) and a special place for a special occasion". / tallowrestaurant.co.uk; tallow_restaurant; Tue-Sat 9.30 pm.

SOUTHBOURNE, DORSET 2–4C

ESTAURANT OOTS £127 542

41 BELLE VUE ROAD H6 3EN 01202 430005

Still blown away with Jan & Stacey's ability deliver top-quality food and service" is a pical report on the Bretschneiders' very cused small restaurant, now in its ninth ear. Berlin-born Jan's "very personal" tasting enu (eight courses for £95 per person, or velve courses for £150 per person), which is so available in a "wonderful veggie version", omes "with notes about his childhood that d to the thought process behind the dish". he couple have also opened the more casual out still ambitious) Cork & Lobster next oor. / restaurantroots.co.uk; restaurant_roots; Ved-Sat midnight.

SOUTHEND-ON-SEA, ESSEX 3–3C

HE PIPE OF PORT £60 343

4 HIGH ST SS1 1JN 01702 614606

awdust floors and shelves of wine for sale add the atmosphere of this 'Wine Merchant & Dining Rooms' – a Dickensian-style space that's een a linchpin of the town's eateries since 976. It continues to win consistent support for s traditional fare, and is well-suited to business unches. / pipeofport.co.uk; thepipeofport; Mon-at 11 pm.

SOUTHLEIGH, DEVON 2–4A

GLEBE HOUSE £79 433

X24 6SD 01404 871368

Hugo Guest (ex-of London haunts Sorella and Marksman) grew up in this hilltop Georgian icarage, when his parents ran it as a B&B; fast-orward to 2020, and he and wife Olive set out o create an English-style 'agriturismo' on this 5-acre smallholding in a "delightful location" verlooking the Coly Valley. The victuals are plit between casual kitchen suppers (for guests nly) and more formal four-course fixed dinners or all), and both showcase a "high standard of ooking"; stay on for the night to profit from the excellent" breakfast. / glebehousedevon.co.uk; lebehousedevon.

SOUTHPORT, MERSEYSIDE 5–1A

BISTROT VÉRITÉ £53 444

' LIVERPOOL ROAD PR8 4AR 01704 564 199

This "great French bistro" is a true family affair rom the Vérité family, with owners Marc & Michaela nowadays joined by their two sons; 'there is always a great choice of imaginative easonal dishes, expertly cooked and well-presented", and the "recently acquired adjacent premises" (Petite Verité, a bar/overspill area for the restaurant) is also a "welcome addition". / bistrotverite.co.uk; bistrotverite; Wed-Sat 9 pm, Tue 10 pm.

THE VINCENT HOTEL V-CAFE £70 333

98 LORD STREET PR8 1JR 01704 883 800

This "buzzy and consistent" brasserie at a stylish modern hotel and wedding venue offers "excellent service and good food", with an eclectic menu that stretches from "delicious steaks and fish 'n' chips" to sushi and other Asian delights, then back to comforting domestic desserts including chocolate mousse and fruit crumble. / thevincenthotel.com; thevincent.southport; Mon-Sun 11 pm.

SOUTHROP, GLOUCESTERSHIRE 2–2C

OX BARN AT THYME £81 334

SOUTHROP MANOR ESTATE GL7 3NX 01367 850174

Opened in 2020 after a lavish conversion, the Hibbert family's "stunning" former barn is "one of the most stylish and delicious places to eat in the Cotswolds", serving "interesting and top-quality ingredients, beautifully presented" by Ballymaloe-trained chef Charlie, whose mother Caryn led the 18-year-long development project which also includes a cookery school, pub and beauty business. / thyme.co.uk; thyme.england; Mon-Sun 9 pm.

SOUTHWOLD, SUFFOLK 3–1D

THE CROWN, ADNAMS HOTEL £79 223

90 HIGH ST IP18 6DP 01502 722275

Back in the day, this characterful, Adnams-owned Georgian tavern in the heart of the town was an easy entry in London-based journos' round-ups of day-escapes from the capital. For many years now, however, it's been a less commented-on and less reliable attraction: for the majority, "still a favourite in Southwold after forty-something years" and some would say "back on form"; but there is still the odd disastrous trip reported here. / thecrownsouthwold.co.uk; crownsouthwold; Mon-Sat 9 pm, Sun 8 pm.

SOLE BAY FISH COMPANY £58 332

22E BLACKSHORE IP18 6ND 01502 724241

A fire in May 2023 engulfed this beloved clapboard-shack-style venue with town-centre spin-off, as well as its quayside neighbours, but they were already up and running as a takeaway the following month, with plans to re-open the restaurant (for now there's limited outdoor seating). Despite the setback, it continues to win raves for "fish 'n' chips as good as it gets", featuring "crispy batter" and "crunchy/soft" chips, "all cooked in umami-packed beef dripping"; add in "a dollop or two of mushy peas as contrasting texture…and who could ask for more?" / solebayfishco.co.uk; solebayfishcompany; Mon-Sun 3 pm.

SUTHERLAND HOUSE £63 334

56 HIGH ST IP18 6DN 01502 724544

"Excellent fish" is the highlight of the "imaginative" menu at this "delightful restaurant", which is "probably the best place for dinner in Southwold". The ancient building dates from 1455 and has been run for 15 years (10 as owners) by Kinga & Andy Rudd – the latter "a fun host who really cares about making sure everything goes very well". Al-fresco dining is available in semi-private outdoor timber 'pods'. / sutherlandhouse.co.uk; Tue-Sat 9 pm.

THE SWAN £57 223

THE MARKET PL IP18 6EG 01502 722186

On the market place, the Adnams brewery's grand seventeenth century hotel attracted some positive reviews this year for its "good food" and "warm, buzzy atmosphere", but also critics in equal measure, for whom the food is "OK, nothing special" – contributing to a lingering sense that "it was far better before the botched refurbishment" back in 2017, which added fancier design cred and fancier prices to go with it. Top Tip – for a cheaper meal, head to the Tap Room, not the main dining room. / theswansouthwold.co.uk; swansouthwold; Mon-Sun 8 pm.

SOWERBY BRIDGE, WEST YORKSHIRE 5–1C

ENGINE SOCIAL DINING £51 544

72 WHARF STREET HX6 2AF 01422 740123

"Blimey, these guys can cook" – the tenor of most reports on chef Mark Kemp's converted pub (est. 2018); "the menu (all in the tapas/small plates mode) ranges far and wide" ("something like gyozas stuffed with sobrasada and basil, served with a makhani sauce"), but despite such adventurous combinations, there "isn't a single duff note" on the menu – which is also "tremendous value" and "utterly, indulgently delicious". Top Tip – "it now opens Wednesday to Saturday and getting a table at the last minute is nigh on impossible. Book in advance and enjoy… just don't take my seat!" / enginesocial.co.uk; enginesocialsb; Wed-Sat 9 pm.

MUSTARD £39 333

5 WHARF STREET HX6 2EG 01422 553700

This "new addition to Sowerby Bridge" sees David Duttine, ex-chef at the former Design House in Halifax, cooking solo and turning out "incredibly reasonable" tasting menus ("£40 per person for seven courses and £60 per person for ten courses"), with some "outstanding and complex dishes". "There's a lot of work going on in that tiny kitchen but my word, the chef is firing out dish after dish that hits the spot" – "this is a local gem and deserves to be supported". / mustard_restaurant; Wed-Sat 9 pm, Sun 7 pm.

SPARSHOLT, OXFORDSHIRE 2–2D

STAR INN £75 433

WATERY LANE OX12 9PL 01235 751 873

Dating from 1720, this "pub in a lovely village near Wantage" ("highly rural in the Lambourn valley") offers a "warm welcome and superb food, backed up by a beefy wine list and high-quality service". With a strong gastro history, it was taken over and renovated two years ago by the team behind Newbury's highly rated Woodspeen and fans say "it has great potential". / thestarsparsholt.co.uk; thestarsparsholt; Wed-Sat 11 pm, Sun 4.45 pm.

SPEEN, BERKSHIRE 3–2A

HARE AND HOUNDS £47 333

BATH ROAD RG14 1QY 01635 521152

"What was once an average kind of roadhouse place is now a pleasant surprise" – a "beautiful, airy" Georgian venue taken over back in 2020 by eleven-strong chain Grosvenor Pubs Limited, and fancily refurbished to include bedrooms named after the equestrian world or historical luminaries. The all-day farm-to-table menu offers "large portions" of "upper average cooking". / hareandhoundsnewbury.co.uk; Mon-Sat 9.30 pm, Sun 8 pm.

ST ALBANS, HERTFORDSHIRE 3–2A

DYLANS KINGS ARMS £57 343

7 GEORGE STREET AL3 4ER 01727530332

"One of the best in the area" – this fifteenth-century hostelry in the cathedral quarter (named for the landlord's dog) only has "a small dining area at the back of the pub", but provides "a very good menu – it's limited to a few dishes which is encouraging as they are all very good!" / dylanskingsarms.com; dylanskingsarms.

LUSSMANNS £52 233

WAXHOUSE GATE, HIGH ST AL3 4EW 01727 851941

"Long established in St Albans", and part of a five-strong, sustainability-oriented chain, this glass-roofed outfit by the cathedral continues to please with its "jolly good" bistro cooking (the latter recommended for its "consistent quality" and equally "good value"). / lussmanns.com; Tue-Thu 9 pm, Fri & Sat 10 pm, Sun 8.30 pm.

THOMPSON £116 334

2 HATFIELD RD AL1 3RP 01727 730 777

Phil Thompson has owned this city-centre casual fine-dining spot (offering à la carte or seven-course tasting menus) for over a decade, and oversaw what was another solid performance this year; the dining area "consists of a number of small rooms, which gives a feeling of intimacy" (there's also a charming Victorian-style courtyard), and Thompson's classical training alongside the Galvin bros and MPW means "there's always a good spin on traditional ideas". / thompsonstalbans.co.uk; thompsondining; Tue-Sat midnight.

ST ANDREWS, FIFE 9–3D

HAAR £120 433

1 GOLF PLACE KY16 9JA 01334 473387

"Tucked away near the golf courses in St Andrews" (by the 18th hole of the Old course) – Dean Banks moved this ambitious venue here (to the former 'Golf Inn') from another location in town two years ago. Ratings slipped a tad this year as views were split on its virtues: to a majority of reporters his multi-course tasting menu provides "fantastically flavoured fish and seafood with innovative textures and at sensible price too"; and "a wonderful experience at the chef's table". Others, though, found it "overpriced" for food that was "just OK", not helped by a couple of incidents of "poor" or "unwelcoming" service. / haarrestaurant.com; Mon-Sun .

THE SEAFOOD RISTORANTE £113 435

THE SCORES, BRUCE EMBANKMENT KY16 9AB 01334 479475

The "magnificent setting" in a glass box perched on the shore, just along from the A&R clubhouse, is the USP of this "excellent fish restaurant" with an Italian accent, run by Stefano Pieraccini of the family-owned Rocca group. "Book a window seat for the sea view" – although, in fact, the 360-degree views are pretty spectacular from every table. / theseafoodrestaurant.com; theseafoodsta; Tue-Sat 21.30 am.

ST BRIDES MAJOR, CARDIFF 1–1D

FOX £62 343

EWENNY ROAD CF32 0SA 01656 881048

"Wow what a find!" – former Welsh rugby golden boy Gavin Henson is "making a real success" of this "delightful" gastropub that he bought after retiring five years ago. "The recently appointed chef" is sending out "delicious" meals that are "a real treat", as well as being "very reasonably priced". / thefox-stbridesmajor.co.uk; the_fox_stbridesmajor; Wed-Sat 9 pm, Sun 4 pm.

ST DAVIDS, PEMBROKESHIRE 4–4A

BLAS RESTAURANT, TWR Y FELIN HOTEL, TWR Y FELIN HOTEL £52 432

SA62 6QT 01437 725 555

This modern boutique hotel dining room which opened in the heart of Britain's smallest city in 2015 achieved a mixed bag of feedback – albeit mostly positive – in our annual diners' poll. On the downside, many reports included an element of criticism, and the least well-rated part of the experience is the "very dark dining room" whose artwork is not to all tastes. But on the larger, positive side of the scorecard, no-one rates the food anything less than "good" and most reports say it's "very good". / twryfelinhotel.com; twryfelinhotel_stdavids; Mon-Sun 9 pm.

ST IVES, CORNWALL 1–4

ONE FISH STREET £97 43

1 FISH STREET TR26 1LT NO TEL

"Innovative fish dishes", a "fab location" and "good value" are the strong points at this "accomplished" small restaurant. It has moved to an unusual dual format, switching between an eight-course fish-based tasting menu and a more casual 'grill house' option (with a range of meat as well as fish choices) on three nights a week. / onefishstreet.net; onefishstreet_stives; Tue-Sat 11 pm.

PORTHGWIDDEN BEACH CAFÉ 22

PORTHGWIDDEN BEACH TR26 1PL 01736 796791

There's no quibbling with the "view to die for" at this beachside café, and they also turn out some "delicious food" including "great fish 'n' chips"; while it's not quite what it was, having unsuccessfully essayed various formats in recent times, and is "now closed for breakfast (they do takeaway) which is the best time of day to visit", "its location continues to be perfect". / porthgwiddencafe.co.uk; porthgwiddenbeach; Mon-Sun 6 pm.

PORTHMINSTER CAFÉ £72 34

PORTHMINSTER BEACH TR26 2EB 01736 795352

The "brilliant setting" with "unbeatable views over Porthminster Beach and across St Ives Bay" makes this long-running venue a "great restaurant" to visit. Ratings have held firm, although a number of reporters are questioning the pricing – "the PBC has been our favourite and we're regulars on our trips to Cornwall, but the last meal we had was not up to their usual standard and prices have increased hugely". / porthminstercafe.co.uk; Wed-Sat 9 pm, Mon & Tue, Sun 3 pm.

PORTHMINSTER KITCHEN £56 33

WHARF RD TR26 1LG 01736 799874

"St Ives has so many places to eat, but this is a favourite" – "right in the middle of the seafront, and because it's on the first floor you have a great view of the harbour and beach". "The menu has plenty of fish options, but the meat-eater is also catered for", while "the food quality is good, even if the options are not that innovative". / porthminster.kitchen; porthminster_kitchen; Mon-Sun .

SOURCE KITCHEN £75 342

6 THE DIGEY TR26 1HR 01736 799487

"A real find" – this "outstanding small eats" spot has an open kitchen which sources its fish, seafood, beef, charcuterie, salad leaves, potatoes pinot noir, rosé, beer, cider, gin, vodka, rum,

ft drinks and more from Cornwall – "keep
› the good work", say fans, who apparently
clude Rick Stein! / sourcekitchen.co.uk;
urcekitchenstives; Mon-Sun 8 pm.

GLY BUTTERFLY £149 434

ARBIS BAY ESTATE
R26 2NP 01736 805800

seriously interesting tasting menu and a
ew to die for!" are helping to win ever-greater
claim for Adam Handling's (of London's
rog' fame) "beautiful venue overlooking
arbis Bay" from a new luxury beachside
tate on the fringes of St Ives. Menus start
ith a five-course selection for £110 per
ad, with the option to add oysters, caviar,
uffles and wine matching. "It doesn't come
eap", but most reporters felt this year that
t's worth every penny": "from the brilliant
cktails to the 'snacks' you feed on faultless
novative courses (crab, turbot, asparagus,
mb, desserts) and some dishes are mind-
owing (e.g. sourdough muffin with brown
abmeat butter and a reveal of an exquisite
ab tart)". "Incredible to have this high-class
staurant in Cornwall". / uglybutterfly.co.uk;
glybutterflybyah; Wed-Sat, Tue 10 pm.

ST KEW, CORNWALL 1–3B

T KEW INN £61 333

L30 3HB 01208 841259

This beautifully situated Cornish pub" off the
adstow tourist trail has a pleasant location
a fifteenth-century stone building replete
ith a garden overlooking the local church;
lid marks if little feedback this year for its
pen-fire cooking, and especially "good-value
t lunches". / stkewinn.co.uk; STKEWINN;
on-Sat 11 pm, Sun 6 pm.

ST LEONARDS-ON-SEA, EAST SUSSEX 3–4C

ALF MAN HALF URGER £36 332

MARINE COURT
N38 0DX 01424 552332

Really satisfying" burgers using 100% Sussex
eef are accompanied by "cool drinks"
raft beers, etc.) at this winning joint (est.
015) in the posh setting of an Art Deco
afront complex; in 2021, the owners, who
et on the Brighton music scene and do
Glastonbury pop-up every year, added a
bling: 'The Yard', set in a converted stable
ock in Hastings. / halfmanhalfburger.com;
alfmanhalfburger; Mon-Sun 9 pm.

HE ROYAL £58 244

SAINT JOHNS ROAD
N37 6HP 01424 547797

his "beautifully presented pub" – a run-down
360s hotel until a renovation five years ago –
fers "great service" and a "hearty menu with
enerous portions". "The choice of dishes at
nch seems more limited in recent months" –
sign of the times?" / theroyalstleonards.co.uk;

Hide & Fox, Saltwood

the_royal_st_leonards; Tue-Sat 10 pm, Sun 5.30 pm.

ST CLEMENT'S £47 433

3 MERCATORIA TN38 0EB 01424 200355

"On top form" since the pandemic, this low-key spot in a townhouse away from the seafront, founded by former Le Caprice chef Nick Hales almost 20 years ago, does not generate a huge volume of feedback in our annual survey, but what we do receive is uniformly positive. The menu favours locally caught fish and seafood. / stclementsrestaurant.co.uk; Wed-Fri 9 pm, Sat 9.30 pm, Sun 3 pm.

ST MAWES, CORNWALL 1–4B

HOTEL TRESANTON £97 323

27 LOWER CASTLE ROAD
TR2 5DR 01326 270055

Olga Polizzi's "wonderful hotel" – a whitewashed former yacht club – is the stuff of interior mag dreams, with its ultra-chic rooms and unbeatable seafront location on the edge of picturesque St. Mawes; it's not all about show, though, with credit again this year for the "delicious food" (even if, according to one regular, "service is not what it once was"). Visitors can eat in the main dining room, with views of St Anthony's Lighthouse, or more informal Dog's Head bar. / tresanton.com; hoteltresanton; Mon-Sun 9.30 pm.

THE IDLE ROCKS £126 334

HARBOURSIDE TR2 5AN 01326 270270

"A new chef since our last visit but still excellent" – this Relais & Châteaux property is perched right over the sea and won nothing but praise in this year's annual diners' poll (as well as a hard-to-win three stars from the AA). In July 2023, Dorian Janmaat left as executive head chef, but we've maintained a rating for the time being. / idlerocks.co.uk; idlerocks; Mon-Sat 8.30 pm, Sun 2 pm.

ST MERRYN, CORNWALL 1–3B

THE CORNISH ARMS £62 333

CHURCHTOWN PL28 8ND 01841 520288

Rick Stein's large, much extended village pub has had its ups and downs in the past, but continues its recent upward curve; the worst that anyone had to say about the British pub grub on offer is that it was "OK" (and one fan praised the vegetable tart as a "little pie of dreams"). If the "barn-like dining area" doesn't appeal, opt for the garden in summer – or make a night of it in one of the six new 'shepherds' huts' on the property (far less rustic than they sound). / rickstein.com; ricksteinrestaurants; Mon-Sun 9 pm.

STALBRIDGE, DORSET 2–3B

THYME AFTER TIME £15 332

SPIRE HILL FARM
DT10 2SG 01963 362202

Despite the "basic surroundings" and "limited opening hours/menu", this "café but also caterer" is "well worth stopping off for" thanks to its "excellent ample food" (hearty breakfasts, brunches and lunches, alongside afternoon teas). / thymeaftertimecafe.com; Mon-Sun 2 pm.

STAMFORD, LINCOLNSHIRE 6–4A

THE GEORGE HOTEL £114 244

71 ST MARTINS PE9 2LB 01780 750750

This enormous, plush, ivy-clad coaching inn has played host to luminaries including Charles I and Sir Walter Scott and sits on the Great Northern Road as it enters this stunning Georgian town. "Afternoon tea is a speciality – truly an English tradition that should not just be for tourists, but for everyone!", while the august oak-panelled dining room offers old-fashioned traditional delights such as rib of beef carved from the trolley, backed by a selection from their biblical wine list. It is noted that "prices have continued to creep up", but this venue has long been a 'hang the expense' kind of treat. / georgehotelofstamford.com; Mon-Sun 10.30 pm.

PIZZA DA MARIO £39 333

1 SHEEP MARKET
PE9 2QZ 01780 917029

This "new addition to the town", set near the bus station, and featuring an outdoor dining space, is a "cheerful" and "cosy" spot where the Italian pizza oven turns out Neapolitan-style pies with "lovely dough" and "a good selection of toppings"; just be sure to "book early". / pizzadamario.co.uk; pizzadamario.

STANHOE, NORFOLK 6–3B

THE DUCK INN £63 333

BURNHAM RD PE31 8QD 01485 518 330

"Eating is simply a delight" at this "lovely old pub with quirky little dining rooms" and a menu that "focuses on top-quality local ingredients". Chef Jeremy Parke and his wife Rachael, formerly of Relish in Newton Flotman and Number 29 in Burnham Market, took over after our annual diners' poll in summer 2023 from Ben & Sarah Handley, who left after 10 years at the helm; we are leaving the ratings untouched, with Rachael saying the approach would remain largely the same, with the addition of small plates to the food menu and cocktails to the bar. / duckinn.co.uk; duckinnstanhoe; Wed-Sat 9 pm, Sun 6 pm.

STANTON, SUFFOLK 3–1C

LEAPING HARE VINEYARD £65 435

WYKEN VINEYARDS
IP31 2DW 01359 250287

"A beautiful high-ceilinged 400-year-old old barn in the middle of a vineyard" makes an "amazing setting" for the "great food" served at this restaurant, now in its third decade. "Wines made on site and in the local area" are a special feature, and you can "walk through woodland to view the vines" before or after eating. Post-lockdown there's also the outdoor Moonshine pizza café. / wykenvineyards.co.uk; wykenvineyards; Wed & Thu, Sun 5.30 pm, Sat, Fri 11 pm.

STAUNTON IN THE VALE, NOTTINGHAMSHIRE 5–3D

STAUNTON ARMS £61 233

NG13 9PE 01400 281218

"Another good country pub with rooms" – and former CAMRA Pub of the Year – that's set in a 200-year-old listed building, and has two East Midlands sister pubs. "The Sunday roast is a firm favourite with families", though their good-value (if not especially foodie) grub can be "equally satisfying" for a midweek lunch, with a "tempting" variety of dishes. / stauntonarms.co.uk; thestauntonarms; Mon-Fri 10 pm, Sat & Sun midnight.

STEIN, HIGHLAND 9–2A

LOCH BAY RESTAURANT £154 543

1 MACLEODS TERRACE
IV55 8GA 01470 592235

"A tiny converted front room in a row of waterside cottages" hosts Michael & Laurence Smith's "wonderful" destination – a nowadays much-accoladed 18-seater in an old fishing village at the north end of the Isle of Skye. Seafood is the speciality and there's only one option for a meal here – the 'Skye Fruits de Mer' menu at £140 per person. / lochbay-restaurant.co.uk; lochbayskye; Tue-Sat 10.30 pm.

STIRCHLEY, WEST MIDLANDS 5–4C

YIKOUCHI AT CHANCER'S CAFÉ £20 332

1418 PERSHORE ROAD B30 2PH NO TEL

"This is a real oddity" – "a micro-restaurant in trendy hipster Stirchley run by a charming couple" in a "tiny cafe converted into a Chinese part of the time" (Thursday & Friday) by chef James Kirk-Gould and his partner Cassie, inspired by their time in Beijing. There's a "lovely squashy buzz" and some "delicious, excellent food with fresh ingredients and good spicing" (if from a menu that "offers very little choice"). Top Menu Tip – "the crispy fried chilli chicken is a treat". / chancers_cafe; Thu & Fri 9 pm, Sat 2 pm, Sun 1 pm.

STIRLING, FALKIRK 9–4C

BREA £41 322

5 BAKER STREET
FK8 1BJ 01786 446277

Handy for Stirling Castle and the train station, this well-established venture has won an embarrassment of accolades over the years, including 'Restaurant of the Year – Scotland' at the country's 2022 Food Awards. Reporters love its "retro menu of good old-fashioned cooking" (haggis with mash, chicken supreme), "though the layout and ambience make it feel a little more like a café than a really good eatery, which is what it is". / brea-stirling.co.uk; breastirling; Sun-Thu 9 pm, Fri & Sat 10 pm.

STOCK, ESSEX 3–2B

THE HOOP £42 322

HIGH STREET CM4 9BD 01277841137

This "lovely old Essex pub" with a white wooden facade serves food that is "well above average for pub grub" – and its popularity means it "gets overcrowded and noisy" at times. Originally three weavers' cottages from 1460, the building was converted two centuries later using beams salvaged from naval vessels docked at Tilbury. Top Menu Tip – "the skate wing is delicious". / thehoop.co.uk; thehoop; Tue-Sat 8.30 pm, Sun 4 am.

STOCKBRIDGE, HAMPSHIRE 2–3

CLOS DU MARQUIS £68 43

NOMADS HOUSE, HIGH STREET
SO20 6HE 01264 810738

"Garth (maître d') and his wife (Maranda, the chef) run a truly delightful restaurant", say fans of this long-running French venture, which the duo took over a decade ago from Paris-born chef German Marquis, and recent shepherded from its former setting on the A30 to a handier high street location. By all accounts, Maranda's cooking is "superb" (prompting "possibly the best meal" one reporter had this year) and service is "excellen too. / closdumarquis.co.uk; Tue, Wed 2 pm, Thu Sat 9 pm.

GREYHOUND £64 34

31 HIGH STREET
SO20 6EY 01264 810833

In a "beautiful setting on the Test" in prime fly-fishing territory, Lucy Townsend's decade-old hotel inspires strong feedback as both a romantic destination and a top dining pub. The "British-style food with nods to the Orient" is uniformly well-rated and abetted by "confident and skilled" service (they're equally "welcoming to dogs, with generous treats included"). "I very rarely, if ever, say this but I couldn't fault it!" Top Tip – the courtyard is "absolutely perfect for quality outdoor eating". / thegreyhoundonthetest.co.uk; ghstockbridge; Mon-Sat 9.30 pm, Sun 7 pm.

STOCKCROSS, BERKSHIRE 2–2

THE VINEYARD AT STOCKCROSS £103 34

RG20 8JU 01635 528770

To say it has "an exceptional wine list" doesn't quite do justice to the cellar of more than 30,000 bottles at winemarker Sir Peter Michael's Berkshire passion project – the 49-room five-star property that he opened in 1998 and which celebrates its 25th year of operation this year. All rooms (both bedrooms and public spaces) are named after famous vintages and reference his family's vineyards in Sonoma County and the Napa Valley. Chef Tom Scade's cuisine has its work cut out to compete but is consistently well-rated in all reports. New this year: the addition of a summer pavilion dedicated to seafood – Catch. / the-vineyard.co.uk; thevineyardhotel; Mon-Sun 9 pm.

STOCKPORT, GREATER MANCHESTER 5–2E

THE EASY FISH COMPANY £65 43

117 HEATON MOOR ROAD
SK4 4HY 0161 442 0823

"The fish couldn't be any fresher if it was straight off the boats", at this "fish restaurant a the rear of a fishmonger's shop" – a family-rur business now in its fourth generation. "Portion are generous and the traditional fish 'n' chips ke some beating". They have another shop/ staurant in Wilmslow. / theeasyfishco.com; eeasyfishco; Wed-Sat 11.30 pm.

HERE THE LIGHT ETS IN £123 444

ROSTRON ROW
K1 1JY 016 1477 5744

very different but great experience" – Sam ickley's hipster hotspot has won fame at ese atmospheric brick-walled premises in a rmer coffee warehouse with huge windows, hich opened in 2016. It's "a super space for romantic dinner", especially if your date is a foodie disposition; the "gorgeous food" om a tasting menu at £110 per person its a major emphasis on sustainability id local sourcing and there are "delicious ine pairings, introducing you to novel ines", all served by "lovely staff". / wtlgi.co; estaurantwherethelightgetsin; Wed-Sat 10 pm.

STOKE BLISS, WORCESTERSHIRE 2–1B

ENSONS AT NETHERWOOD STATE £135 434

ETHERWOOD ESTATE, PENSONS YARD
R15 8RT 01885 410333

Brilliant flavours in a sublime setting" have elped win renown for this "lovely" converted arn on owner Peta Darnley's 1,200 acre mily estate, where head chef Chris Simpson elped it carry off Visit England's 'Taste of ngland' award as best restaurant in 2023. n the downside, its ratings took a slight iock this year, with a few diners being "a bit nderwhelmed given the hype": they query, as it all gone to their heads?" and discern "a ght preciousness" in the overall approach. ost accounts, though, continue to applaud its xceptional" overall standards. / pensons.co.uk; nsonsrestaurant; Wed-Sat 11.30 pm, Sun 5 pm. RA – 2 stars

STOKE D'ABERNON, SURREY 3–3A

RILL AT THE OLD LOUGH £51 343

STATION ROAD
T11 3BN 01932 862244

t's difficult to get a table" at this top-class astropub around the corner from Chelsea C's training ground – it "really earns its opularity", so regulars "learn to book ead". "We're so lucky to have our local ib serve great food – and there's a super irden too". / oldploughcobham.co.uk; dploughcobham; Mon-Thu 9 pm, Fri & Sat 30 pm, Sun 8 pm.

STOKE HOLY CROSS, NORFOLK 6–4C

TOKE MILL £73

ILL ROAD NR14 8PA 01508 493 337

n the River Tas, this 700-year-old mill as once home to the business that became olman's Mustard and has been run by Ludo id Andy Rudd since 2013. We had good, if ghtly guarded reviews about its longstanding staurant, but none of its new, more exciting offshoot – Store – which opened in 2021 and where Hazel Yuill and Liam Nichols won a Michelin star in early 2023 for their seven-course tasting menu at £110 per person (hence we've left it unrated). / stokemill.co.uk; stokemill; Wed & Thu 9.30 pm, Fri & Sat 10 pm, Sun 2.30 pm.

THE WILDEBEEST ARMS £90 334

82-86 NORWICH RD
NR14 8QJ 01508 492497

Locally born chef Daniel Smith's "modern British" cuisine at his village pub-restaurant on the edge of Norwich is "always a winner" for its "imaginative flavours" and "excellent service". "We eat here regularly and it's first-rate both for the food and the pleasant atmosphere", while "the set lunch and the tasting menu are both brilliant". The venue's name is left over from a previous African-themed incarnation. / thewildebeest.co.uk; thewildebeestnorfolk; Mon-Sun 9 pm.

STOKE ROW, OXFORDSHIRE 2–2D

THE CROOKED BILLET £79 344

NEWLANDS LN RG9 5PU 01491 681048

"Great food, great live music and great attention to detail" add up to "a perfect venue" at this country pub, run for 35 years by former rock musician and self-taught chef Paul Clerehugh (ex-Sweet). It's a "lovely building with great décor and a nice atmosphere", and if the "portions are way too big" – most guests are very happy with that. / thecrookedbillet.co.uk; crookedbillet_stokerow; Mon-Sun midnight.

STOKE-BY-NAYLAND, SUFFOLK 3–2C

THE ANGEL INN £90 434

POLSTEAD ST CO6 4SA 01206 263245

"At last Suffolk has somewhere very special again" – this "relatively new, upmarket" outfit is set in a five-hundred-year-old country inn that has long had a culinary reputation. Fans say it's "the best-looking restaurant for miles around", and is "trying hard" – they're "obviously chasing a star" in the kitchen, which is praised for its "great tasting menu" (the only option by night). / angelinnsuffolk.co.uk; angelinnsuffolk; Thu-Sat 9 pm, Sun 8 pm.

STONE, STAFFORDSHIRE 5–3B

LITTLE SEEDS £55 343

16 - 18 RADFORD STREET ST15 8DA
01785818925

The "lovely garden" at Sophie Hardman and Jake Lowndes's 'bar and kitchen' received a major boost this year as it was expanded and improved; and it has a "snug" interior too. There's the odd quibble that results are "pricey for Stone!" but all feedback says the modern British cuisine is "good" or "very good". / littleseedsstone.co.uk; littleseedsstone; Thu-Sat 9 pm, Sun 4 pm.

STOW ON THE WOLD, GLOUCESTERSHIRE 2–1C

THE OLD BUTCHERS £78 333

PARK ST GL54 1AQ 01451 831700

"Simple food, well executed" and service to match are the watchwords at this seafood specialist with a mismatched name from former Bibendum head chef Pete Robinson and his wife Louise. The couple launched the venue in 2005, and their two children are increasingly members of the team. / theoldbutchers.squarespace.com; the_old_butchers; Tue-Sat 9 pm.

STRACHUR, ARGYLL AND BUTE 9–4B

INVER RESTAURANT £98 433

STRACTHLACHLAN
PA27 8BU 01369 860 537

Pam Brunton and Rob Latimer, who honed their craft at the legendary Noma, took over this fisherman's croft (with rooms) on Loch Fyne back in 2015. The "excellent food" privileges local wild ingredients and forgotten Scottish dishes to straightforward but often stunning effect. This is also a romantic spot if you wish to overnight, with a "ruined castle beside the Loch to explore". / inverrestaurant.co.uk; inverrestaurant; Fri-Sun, Thu 8.30 pm.

STRATFORD UPON AVON, WARWICKSHIRE 2–1C

LAMBS £57 334

12 SHEEP STREET
CV37 6EF 01789 292554

"Situated in a fine historic timbered house (one of the city's oldest), Lambs of Sheep Street has been satisfying its customers for about a quarter of a century", with "more of a feel of authenticity to it" than the many eateries in this tourist-trap town. The reasonably priced fare may be "a little predictable" but is reliably "pleasing" – and you won't need to chase the "attentive" staff to make curtain-up at the nearby RSC. / lambsrestaurant.co.uk; lambsrestaurant; Mon-Sat 9 pm, Sun 8.30 pm.

LOXLEYS £61 333

3 SHEEP ST CV37 6EF 01789 292128

"More of a bistro/wine bar, but with a reasonably varied and interesting menu" – this two-floor operation has "modern décor" contrasting with its historic location near the RSC, and wins consistent praise, "particularly the set menu which is very good value". "Kind staff" help make it "a real local favourite". / loxleysrestaurant.co.uk; loxleysrestaurantandwinebar; Mon-Sat 11 pm, Sun 10.30 pm.

THE OPPOSITION £43 332

13 SHEEP STREET
CV37 6EF 01789 269980

"A great and very consistent local restaurant that always looks after you well" – this "cheap 'n' cheerful" bistro near the RSC is well worth remembering if you are looking for a decent meal in this touristy town: "the food is excellent and pricing keen". / theoppo.co.uk; theoppostratford; Mon-Sat 9 pm.

ROOFTOP RESTAURANT, ROYAL SHAKESPEARE THEATRE £56 234

WATERSIDE CV37 6BB 01789 403449

"The location is great, the staff are helpful and a good ambience is generated by the pre-theatre buzz" at the RSC's in-house top-floor venue. Food-wise, "there are better places in Stratford for a pre-theatre meal", although some reporters reckon "the standard of cooking has improved" and it's now "worth a visit even if you're not going to the theatre". Top Tip – "book early enough & you're more likely to get a coveted window table overlooking the river and swans". / rsc.org.uk; thersc; Mon-Sat 6 pm, Sun 3.30 pm.

SABAI SABAI £52 333

19-20 WOOD STREET
CV37 6JF 01789 508 220

Limited but good all-round feedback for this modern Thai restaurant – part of Torquil and Juree Chidwick's Midlands-based small group (this is the only one outside Birmingham). Menu options include a pre-theatre deal, as well as a bottomless lunch option at weekends. / sabaisabai.com; sabaisabai_restaurant; Mon-Sat 11 pm, Sun 10.30 pm.

SALT £125 533

8 CHURCH ST CV37 6HB 01789 263566

"Just sit back and enjoy the spectacular cooking that comes from a passionate chef's imagination… and Paul Foster's imagination is worth the journey for an evening's adventure in wonderland!" – This "rather quirky restaurant" in a timbered building is "more comfortable" after a recent renovation, and "the location close to a number of historical Stratford sites also adds to the pleasure of dining there". "Dinner is tasting-menu only, but at an amazingly good-value price"; and "it's a testament to the standard of cuisine that despite opening only a few years before Covid it survived and has now expanded to provide a chef's table and cookery school". / salt-restaurant.co.uk; salt_dining; Wed-Sat 8.30 pm.

THE VINTNER 233

4-5 SHEEP ST CV37 6EF 01789 297259

This half-timbered town-centre fixture is useful for a "consistent offering" that includes "good-value lunch and pre-theatre menus". "First ate here in the mid-80s with a Sixth Form school trip – it was good then and still is". / the-vintner.co.uk; the_vintner; Mon-Sat 9 pm, Sun 4 pm.

THE WOODSMAN, HOTEL INDIGO £84 334

CHAPEL STREET
CV37 6HA 01789 331535

Game guru Mike Robinson's "lovely, spacious" Shakespearean-era beamed dining room in the "very smartly renovated Indigo hotel"; "head chef Greg Newman has revitalised the venue since arriving in 2022" and the food ("very generous, almost excessively so, portions of locally sourced food, with a particular emphasis on game and wood-fired cooking") comes with "lots of flavour". / thewoodsmanrestaurant.com; thewoodsmanrestaurant; Mon-Sat 9.30 pm, Sun 8.30 pm.

STUDLAND, DORSET 2-4C

PIG ON THE BEACH £66 244

MANOR HOUSE, MANOR ROAD
BH19 3AU 01929 450 288

"Wonderful location and friendly staff" are the big draws at this branch of the shabby-chic hotel group, with views over Studland Bay and a range of accommodation including shepherds' huts and converted dovecotes. The kitchen serves up "classic Pig fare – simple, tasty food, much from the garden right outside". / thepighotel.com; the_pig_hotels; Mon-Sun 9.30 pm.

SHELL BAY £74 434

FERRY ROAD BH19 3BA 01929 450363

"Super-fresh fish in simple surroundings with wonderful views" over Poole Harbour and Brownsea Island makes a winning deck of cards for this waterside spot on the Isle of Purbeck, on the beach by the chain-link ferry. "Delicious puddings", a "respectable wine list" and "friendly staff" complete the deal. / shellbay.net; shellbayrestaurant; Mon-Sat 9 pm, Sun 8.30 pm.

SUDBURY, SUFFOLK 3-2C

THE SECRET GARDEN CAFÉ & RESTAURANT £56 343

BUZZARDS HALL, 17 FRIARS STREET,
CO10 2AA 01787 372030

"An unexpected delight in Sudbury" – a "lovely old house" with beams plays host to Stéphane Chapotot and Alain Jacq's "excellent French eatery", long a local light (and veggie-friendly too); post-pandemic, it has fused with the formerly separate café, and now serves "very well-sourced and presented" breakfasts and lunches, plus more gastronomic dinners on Fri/Sat. / tsg.uk.net; thesecretgardensudbury; Tue-Thu 4.30 pm, Fri & Sat 9.30 pm.

SUFFIELD, NORFOLK 6-4

SUFFIELD ARMS £50 33

STATION ROAD, THORPE MARKET
NR11 8UE 01263 586858

Relaunched in 2021, this "genuine gastropub" opposite Gunton station is the second local boozer to be reimagined by London art dealer Ivor Braka, after its sister the Gunton Arms, a mile up the road. It "specialises in tapas" (of "excellent variety and quality") and do "try the upstairs saloon which serves amazing cocktails in a setting that resembles a madame's boudoir!" (The rest of the building isn't far behind, with a whole page of the website dedicated to the hip artists on its walls, not least Michael Landy and Diane Arbus, who are both situated in the bogs, so to speak.) / suffieldarms.com; suffieldarms; Mon-Sat 9 pm, Sun 8 pm.

SUMMERHOUSE, COUNTY DURHAM 8-3

RABY HUNT £304 43

DL2 3UD 01325 374 237

Since its debut in 2009, James Close has put this Grade-II-listed former pub firmly on the UK's foodie map, despite its out-of-the-way location in the County Durham countryside, not far from Darlington. Once a real ale booze in its converted state it has maintained two Michelin stars since 2016 and is one of the culinary flag-bearers for the Northeast with its extensive tasting menu – £195 per person for over 10 courses (or you can eat at the chef's table for £300 per person). Compared with some other places of gastronomic pilgrimage, it didn't attract a huge volume of feedback in our annual diners' poll this year. But there were none of last year's critiques, and all acclaimed "an excellent dining experience" that's "outstanding all-round", so we've maintained its ratings. / rabyhuntrestaurant.co.uk; rabyhunt; Fri & Sat, Wed & Thu 8 pm.

SUNBURY ON THAMES, SURREY 3-3A

INDIAN ZEST £60 44

21 THAMES STREET
TW16 5QF 01932 765 000

"Contemporary Indian cooking with flair and finesse" makes for an attractive dining option in the outer 'burbs at this colonial-style villa – a sister venue to Manor Vasaikar's highly regarded Indian Zing, near Hammersmith. "The taste-stimulating amuse bouche to kick-off is definitely a harbinger of things to come" – (and "the loo decor must be seen…"). / indianzest.co.uk; indianzest; Mon-Sun 10.30 pm.

SUNNINGDALE, BERKSHIRE 3-3A

BARN AT COWORTH PARK £120 34

BLACKNEST RD SL5 7SE 01344 876 60

The more casual brasserie restaurant (muddy boots welcome) at the Dorchester Collection's ultra-ritzy countryside hotel, which also includes acclaimed fine-diner 'Woven by Adam

Haar, St Andrews

Smith'; its "tasty, wholesome and interesting" comfort food includes "quality fish 'n' chips and burgers but also more inspired dishes" too. / dorchestercollection.com; Mon-Sun 9 pm.

SURBITON, SURREY 3–3A

THE FRENCH TABLE £83 5 4 3

85 MAPLE RD KT6 4AW 020 8399 2365

"A local treasure" – Eric & Sarah Guignard's long-established "little gem" in "a tree-lined road 10 minutes walk from Surbiton station" ("handy if you wish to enjoy their brilliant wine list") remains a shining and much commented-on beacon in the 'burbs. "Eric and his team consistently create high-class modern French cuisine while Sarah and her front-of-house team provide very professional, very genuine service – dining here is first-class". Even those who note "the somewhat unpromising shape of the room" say it "continues to provide an excellent experience year after year" and one that's "very good value". Top Tip – "they also have a great little pastry counter next door". / thefrenchtable.co.uk; the_french_table_surrey; Tue-Sat 9 pm.

NO 97 £59 3 4 3

97 MAPLE ROAD KT6 4AW 020 3411 9797

Sam & Alex Berry are cooking up excitement in the 'burbs at their "lovely local" – a rather posh venture whose "food is way above its prices" and accompanied by "friendly service" to boot. If you want more of the Berry magic, they also run gin bar/school/micro-distillery Bone Idyll, pizzeria Cento Uno in Surbiton, and Teddington restaurant One One Four. / no-97.co.uk; numberninetyseven; Tue-Thu midnight, Fri & Sat 12.30 am, Sun 4 pm.

SWANAGE, DORSET 2–4C

1859 PIER CAFE & BISTRO £52 3 3 3

MARINE VILLAS HIGH STREET BH19 2AP 01929 425806

It's "well worth the extra hundred yards around the corner from the centre past the chip shops" to get to this café at the start of the town's Victorian pier. On the menu: "delicious" shellfish and other "rustic and freshly produced fare" that's "served with village enthusiasm" amidst "lovely views across Swanage Bay". / swanagepiertrust.com; swanagepier; Sun-Thu 4.45 pm, Fri & Sat 9 pm.

SWANSEA, SWANSEA 1–1D

BISTRO PIERRE £39 2 3 3

MUMBLES ROAD, 3 OYSTER WHARF SA3 4DN 01792 824117

Critics may find it slightly "formulaic" – it's part of a now 19-strong chain that was born a quarter of a century ago – but this "buzzy bistro" is still a solid choice for its "perfectly serviceable food" and (arguably even more so) its stellar views of Swansea Bay. / bistrotpierre.co.uk; Mon-Fri 11 pm, Sat & Sun midnight.

SWERFORD, OXFORDSHIRE 2–1D

THE BOXING HARE £69 2 3 3

BANBURY ROAD OX7 4AP 01608 683212

This Cotswold local for the Chipping Norton set is a "very busy pub on a Sunday, with great beef choices" and meat – sourced from a farm just six miles away – and is a mainstay on weekdays too: "even if it's expensive, it's well worth while ordering the very best of the menu". Owner Antony Griffith Harris and chef Nick Anderson first worked together more than 35 years ago before teaming up here in 2017. / theboxinghare.co.uk; hare_2017; Wed-Sat 9 pm, Sun 3.30 pm.

SWINTON, SCOTTISH BORDERS 8–1A

THE WHEATSHEAF AT SWINTON £60 3 3 3

MAIN ST TD11 3JJ 01890860257

Above-average sustenance in the Borders is to be found at this solid-looking inn, with a light-filled dining room overlooking the village green. It serves bistro/brasserie-style fare (Haggis bon-bons, venison or sirloin steak, pork stuffed with apricot…) as well as simpler lunchtime pub-grub options. / eatdrinkstaywheatsheaf.com; thewheatsheafswinton; Mon-Sun 9 pm.

TANKERTON, KENT 3–3C

LAND AND SEA £53 4 4 3

139D TANKERTON ROAD CT5 2AW 01227 668098

This "small independent" restaurant/deli was set up by a "young chef with a talent for flavours and originality" (Ben Stead) and offers a "short" but "amazing" menu "with a focus on local produce". It's "a firm favourite with the locals", so "whether it be breakfast, lunch or dinner (for which it is open on select nights only) you are lucky to find a seat!" We've introduced it into the guide and rated it this year on relatively limited feedback. / landandseatankerton.com; landandseatankerton; Mon-Sun 11.30 pm.

TAPLOW, BERKSHIRE 3–3A

THE ASTOR GRILL 2 3 4

CLIVEDON ROAD SL6 0JF 01628 607 107

Former stables have been converted into a "wonderful dining room" for the cheaper eating option in the "amazing setting" of Cliveden, the Astor family's country pile forever famous for hosting the scandalous 1961 pool party at which war minister John Profumo met showgirl Christine Keeler. "Service is friendly and fun" but the food can seem rather "ordinary" – which is "disappointing given the excellent location" ("the menu has the usual staples such as fish 'n' chips or burger" plus an array of more ambitious brasserie items, but is "not much better than you would get in a pub"). / clivedenhouse.co.uk; clivedenhouse; Mon-Sun 10 pm.

THE DINING ROOM AT CLIVEDEN, CLIVEDEN HOUSE £116 2 3

CLIVEDEN RD SL6 0JF 01628 668561

The "lovely location overlooking the Thames" – a spectacular Grade I listed country house dating from 1666, now owned by the National Trust and operated as a Relais & Châteaux hotel – is enough in itself to make any meal a "wonderful experience" here; especially if accompanied by "an interesting walk around the parkland" where historical figures from Queen Victoria to Christine Keeler came for R&R. The dining room occupies a prime site within the property with stunning views, where you can enjoy cuisine that's "good but not inspirational" considering the "eye-watering" prices. / clivedenhouse.co.uk; clivedenhouse; Mon-Sun 10 pm.

ROUX AT SKINDLES £83 4 4

TAPLOW RIVERSIDE, MILL LANE SL6 0AF 01628 951100

This former coaching inn has "everything you expect from a Roux Brothers brasserie" – plus a fascinating history as one of the world's top nightclubs in the '70s, when John and Yoko dropped in; it was reborn again when Alain Roux and his late father Michel Roux senior took over in 2017, and the "superb atmosphere by the river" currently abets "top-quality" French cooking at "reasonable prices" too (a snip compared to their Waterside Inn, a couple of miles away). / rouxatskindles.co.uk; rouxatskindles; Tue-Sat 9 pm, Sun 3 pm.

TAUNTON, SOMERSET 2–3A

AUGUSTUS £65 4 4

3 THE COURTYARD, ST JAMES ST TA1 1JR 01823 324 354

A "small but perfectly formed bistro-style" venue which was set up by Richard Guest and FOH Cedric Chirrosel in 2011, and has since firmly made its mark on the local dining scene with its impeccable local sourcing and "nice French-style cooking" (also inflected by British and Asian touches). Fans say that the "idiosyncratic" venture is "as good as it gets locally" ("when it is open we never go anywhere else"). / augustustaunton.co.uk; Tue-Sat 9 pm.

TAVISTOCK, DEVON 1–3C

CORNISH ARMS £72 3 3 3

15 WEST STREET PL19 8AN 01822 612145

John Hooker and wife Emma's "lovely pub" en route to Cornwall was praised this year for some "really clever cooking without being fussy or complicated" (including "good venison from local stalkers"). Despite the "exciting things happening in the kitchen" of late, it has reassuringly "not lost its 'pubbiness'". / thecornisharmstavistock.co.uk;

e_cornish_arms_tavistock; Mon-Thu 11 pm, Fri Sat midnight, Sun 10.30 pm.

EDDINGTON, MIDDLESEX 1-4A

UBA £41 333

2 HIGH STREET
W11 8JB 020 8977 7700

Really delicious Lebanese food" awaits at this ractive and "great-value" High Street venue st. 2018), whose owner hails from Lebanon d worked alongside his aunt and uncle in eir London restaurant for a decade. On e menu: an authentic selection of hot and ld mezze (including "very good" fattoush d moutabal) and "charming service by the vner and his wife". / rubarestaurant.co.uk; barestaurant; Mon-Thu 10 pm, Fri & Sat .30 pm, Sun 9.30 pm.

HE WHARF £55 332

MANOR RD TW11 8BG 020 8977 6333

Great views of the river" near Teddington ock undoubtedly elevate a visit to this velcoming" brasserie and jazz bar; the od also seems to be on an even keel of late, th reports of "well-cooked and enjoyable" shes (including a "fantastic afternoon tea") at can seem "surprisingly good given the ghtly rickety/plasticky interior". Best in mmer, when you can make the most of e riverside terrace. / wharfteddington.com; ewharfteddington; Mon, Wed-Sat 9.45 pm, Sun pm.

EIGNMOUTH, DEVON 1-3D

RAB SHACK £72

QUEEN ST TQ14 9HN 01626 777956

Simple and small, sited right on back beach" is popular shack is "heaven for seafood vers!" according to its fans. Too limited edback for a rating this year, but there ere none of last year's gripes about rising rices: "all you need is a whole crab, truffle ies, some hardware, glass of something ld and an hour, then you forget about e cost!" / crabshackonthebeach.co.uk; ecrabshackteignmouth; Mon, Wed-Sun 9 pm.

TEWKESBURY, GLOUCESTERSHIRE 2-1B

AFFE E VINO £43 334

CHURCH STREET
L20 5RX 01684 491078

A family-run traditional Italian café" born 2014, and still "busy with regulars" nearly decade on owing to its "authentic offerings, ith a large selection of antipasti and daily ecial pasta dishes", plus "superb" desserts nd "excellent coffee". The "warm enjoyable mosphere" and "reasonable prices" round out s assets. / caffeevino.uk; Tue-Sat 10 pm.

THORNBURY, GLOUCESTERSHIRE 2-2B

THORNBURY CASTLE £120 344

CASTLE ST BS35 1HH 01454 281182

"We first went 50 years ago… it was wonderful then and absolutely amazing now!" – this luxurious property (built in the 1520s and part of Henry VIII and Anne Boleyn's honeymoon itinerary) is "so quintessentially English in its historic ambience" ("it was fun watching overseas tourists being overawed with their surroundings!"). "A recent refurbishment of the Hotel, elevation to Relais & Chateaux membership and appointment of Carl Cleghorn as Executive Chef, have put Thornbury Castle firmly back on the culinary map. The menu and standard of cooking, particularly in the desserts, coupled with friendly and welcoming staff are now a match for the quite stunning rooms and grounds of the Castle itself". / thornburycastle.co.uk; thornburycastle; Sun, Mon-Sat 9 pm.

THORNHAM, NORFOLK 6-3B

ERIC'S FISH & CHIPS £35 432

DROVE ORCHARD, THORNHAM RD
PE36 6LS 01485 472 025

Titchwell Manor chef Eric Snaith's mini-chain (also with branches in Holt and St Ives) is set on an apple orchard with a popular farm shop; "lovely large pieces of fresh fish" feature in their standard chippie and more non-trad fare "and they can do the batter gluten-free!" NB – "There's not always much atmosphere here, so maybe best to take them home" (or picnic in the orchard if you can't wait that long). / ericsfishandchips.com; ericsfandc; Mon-Sun 8 pm.

THORNTON HOUGH, MERSEYSIDE 5-2A

THE RED FOX £55 333

LIVERPOOL ROAD
CH64 7TL 0151 353 2920

This handsome gastropub from Brunning & Price, set in a spacious Victorian property with extensive gardens, is "popular with locals" and "always busy – but the large restaurant easily accommodates a large number of diners without feeling cramped". / brunningandprice.co.uk; redfoxwirral; Mon-Sat 11 pm, Sun 10.30 pm. SRA – 3 stars

THORPE LANGTON, LEICESTERSHIRE 5-4D

BAKERS ARMS £47 333

MAIN ST LE16 7TS 01858 545201

This "beautiful old country pub" – thatched and beamed, with a "lovely cosy atmosphere, open fire and low lighting" – serves "top-quality food" from chef Emilie Bull, backed up with an "impressive wine list" overseen by proprietor Tim Hubbard, here for 22 years with his wife Kate. "Kate and Tim know what they're doing and they do it very well indeed" – "they're always so friendly and happy to see you again". / thebakersarms.co.uk; Wed-Sat 9 pm, Sun 2.30 pm.

THORPENESS, SUFFOLK 3-1D

THE DOLPHIN INN £36 333

PEACE PLACE IP16 4NA 01728 454994

This "very good pub" (with rooms and a "lovely garden") attracts a good amount of feedback and is "actually more of a restaurant now as the entire place is used for dining", but that's all to the good given its "cooking of a calibre expected in this upscale resort". The owners also run a sister pub, The Parrot in Aldringham. / thorpenessdolphin.com; the_dolphin_thorpeness; Mon-Sat 10 pm, Sun 9 pm.

TILLINGTON, WEST SUSSEX 3-4A

THE HORSE GUARDS INN £78 434

UPPERTON RD GU28 9AF 01798 342 332

"If only more pubs were like this" – a "perfect local", on the edge of the Petworth estates, where "the food is largely locally sourced and much better than standard pub grub" (indeed, the "innovative daily changing menu" comes "from a chef who obviously cares"). Bonus points for the appealing garden, and there's a "good atmosphere inside too, unless you're in the overflow room". / thehorseguardsinn.co.uk; horseguardsinn; Wed-Sat 9 pm, Sun 4 pm.

TITLEY, HEREFORDSHIRE 2-1A

STAGG INN £63 333

HR5 3RL 01544 230221

This well-known border-country inn is "still one of the best places to eat in the area", with "well prepared and flavoursome food". Long-time regulars miss Steve & Nicola Reynolds, who retired a couple of years ago, but the new management team of chef Tom Tudor and his partner Vittoria Turolla, FOH, have settled in well and the place is now "performing better again". / thestagg.co.uk; Wed-Sat 9 pm, Sun 4 pm.

TIXOVER, LINCOLNSHIRE 6-4A

THE SLANTED DOOR £60 323

43 SAINT MARY'S STREET
PE9 2DS 01780 757773

"Quirky in a good way" – a modern bar/restaurant in sixteenth-century premises owned by brothers Oliver & Joseph Regis, who decided Stamford needed something a little different back in 2020. Chef Dameon Clarke (ex-of Rywell's Wicked Witch) is at the pass of the "very snug restaurant" where the "ever-changing" menu includes "small plates which are a little eclectic but excellent value". / theslanteddoor.co.uk; theslanteddoorstamford; Tue-Sat 9 pm, Sun 3.30 pm.

TOOT BALDON, OXFORDSHIRE 2–2D

THE MOLE INN £65 323

OX44 9NG 01865 340001

This characterful pub has a "very pleasant location" in a village five miles from Oxford, and is best enjoyed in summer in the "lovely garden"; with meat from the local Sandy Lane Farm in Tiddington, and game from Oxfordshire estates, the food is "good" by all accounts, and the service "acceptable". / themoleinn.com; moleinn; Mon-Thu 8.45 pm, Fri & Sat 9.15 pm, Sun 4.30 pm.

TOPSHAM, DEVON 1–3D

THE GALLEY £53 344

41 FORE ST, TOPSHAM
EX3 0HU 01392 876078

"Fresh fish is the attraction at this small bistro in Topsham village", situated near the historic quay; the "first-class" cooking from chef James Checkley, one of four finalists in 2022's 'BBC MasterChef: The Professionals', is well "deserving of its recent Bib Gourmand", with particular praise directed at the "good-value" midweek lunch. / galleyrestaurant.co.uk; galleytopsham; Tue-Sat 9 pm.

THE SALUTATION INN £80 333

68 FORE STREET
EX3 0HL 01392 873060

"Beautifully presented, interesting modern cuisine" is on the menu at this "Georgian coaching inn, centrally located in a lovely unspoilt historic port in the Exe estuary", with "a conservatory-style dining room created by an intriguing glass roof over the former carriage yard". "Seafood and fish is a speciality", and post-pandemic they also operate a fishmonger's. / salutationtopsham.co.uk; salutationinn; Mon-Fri 9 pm, Sat 21 pm, Sun 17 pm.

TORQUAY, DEVON 1–3D

ELEPHANT RESTAURANT & BRASSERIE £81 333

3-4 BEACON TER, HARBOURSIDE
TQ1 2BH 01803 200044

Decorated TV chef Simon Hulstone's longstanding home base on the harbour was the first restaurant in Torquay to gain a Michelin star – an honour it has retained ever since; produce is largely sourced from Hulstone's 100-acre Brixham farm, feeding into a brilliant value set-lunch (it's thus tipped as a "superb lunchtime meeting place") and more elaborate tasting menu. / elephantrestaurant.co.uk; hulstone; Wed-Sat 9 pm.

NO 7 FISH BISTRO & WINE BAR £61 433

7 BEACON TERRACE
TQ1 2BH 01803 295055

"Divine fish and seafood" from Brixham is the mainstay of the blackboard menu at the Stacey family's "small, intimate" and "good-value" spot, now in its fourth decade. "Have been going for years and the fantastic fresh fish never disappoints – have taken American friends who vow it's the best they have ever had!". There's also a wine bar upstairs. / no7-fish.com; No7fishbistro.

TOTNES, DEVON 1–3D

THE BULL INN £60 323

ROTHERFOLD SQUARE, LITTLE TOTNES
TQ9 5SQ 01803 640040

This "amazing organic pub-with-rooms, serving great food with a conscience and really lovely wine list" is "different from the usual". It's owned and run by Geetie Singh-Watson, a self-proclaimed feminist and ethical publican who moved to Devon after meeting her husband, Riverford founder Guy Watson, on Soil Association business. She sold her London flat to finance the rescue of the run-down pub, which is "becoming an established favourite for Totnes residents and visitors, so it's wise to book". / bullinntotnes.co.uk; bullinn_totnes; Mon-Sun 9 pm. SRA – 3 stars

TREEN, CORNWALL 1–4A

THE GURNARD'S HEAD £65 334

TR26 3DE 01736 796928

This famous dining pub-with-rooms on the wild and woolly coast between St. Ives and St. Just is part of a three-strong empire spanning The Old Coastguard hotel in Mousehole and the further-flung Felin Fach Griffin, in the Brecon Beacons. Feedback this year was generally sound, and even if it has scored higher for food in some previous years, "the surrounding coast and countryside" (not to mention "the mustard-yellow exterior", which "pops in the landscape") both still "make it a destination" place. / gurnardshead.co.uk; gurnardshead; Mon-Sun 11 pm.

TRING, HERTFORDSHIRE 3–2A

CROCKER'S TABLE £155 333

74 HIGH STREET
HP23 4AF 01442 828971

It's "a fun experience to celebrate a special occasion" at Scott Barnard's chef's table-oriented venture seating just 16 people – particularly if you sit upstairs, where chefs plate up the "excellent" eight-course tasting menus before your eyes (ranging from £95 per person for weekday dinner to £120 per person at weekends); downstairs offers a more relaxed sample of the same menu without the drama, and there's also a glamorous cellar bar if you want to get a head start on the fun. / tring.crockersuk.com; crockers_tring; Tue-Sat 11 pm.

TROTTISCLIFFE, KENT 3–3C

BOWLEY'S AT THE PLOUGH £48 33

6 TAYLORS LANE
ME19 5DR 01732 822233

This cute weatherboard-fronted pub in a North Downs village is "well worth finding" for its "beautifully presented food" that "goes beyond local gastropub standards" – "great flavours and marvellous balance provide a real gastronomic experience". Owned as a community asset by villagers who raised money to save it from developers, the venue is operated by the Yates family: David, an ex-Balls Brothers wine merchant, and his son Alex, a "chef very engaged in his craft who loves to get feedback on his superb dishes". He and his young kitchen team have high aims for the 26-cover restaurant – whose regulars would "love it to go from strength to strength". / theploughkent.com; Tue-Sat 10.30 pm, Sun 6 pm.

TRURO, CORNWALL 1–4B

HUBBOX £38 32

116 KENWYN STREET
TR1 3DJ 01872 240700

Richard Boon's "slowly expanding West Country chain" – which emerged from his original venue, the Hub in St Ives, which opened 21 years ago – owes its success to doing simple things properly: namely "good burgers" from grass-fed Cornish beef. "Cheerful staff" and "fabulously crunchy onion rings" add to the appeal and it inspired a good degree of feedback in this year's annual diners' poll. / hubbox.co.uk; hubbox_; Sun-Thu 10 pm, Fri & Sat 11 pm.

TRUSHAM, DEVON 1–3D

CRIDFORD INN £29 33

NEWTON ABBOT
TQ13 0NR 01626 853694

"A typical English country pub doing not-so-typical English country pub food" based on "a wide selection of locally sourced and seasonal ingredients"; it's so "unusual to find this level of creativity in what is basically a Devon village boozer" – but then again the thatched Teign Valley spot isn't so run-of-the-mill after all, laying claim to being the oldest inn in Devon – if not England (the building was cited in the 1086 Domesday Book, but dates back even further). / thecridfordinn.co.uk; thecridford; Mon-Sat 9 pm, Sun 8 pm.

TUDDENHAM, SUFFOLK 3–1C

TUDDENHAM MILL, TUDDENHAM MILL HOTEL £87 32

HIGH ST IP28 6SQ 01638 713 552

A gloriously situated old watermill set on twelve acres strewn with weeping willows plays host to this venture, juggling a more formal upstairs dining room and casual outdoor hangout Tipi on the Stream, for cocktails and seafood. Chef-owner Lee Bye's seasonal field-to-fork

od is "done to perfection" (with one reporter
eferring the à la carte to the tasting menu)
id if you want to overnight, the rooms
e "fantastic" too. / tuddenhammill.co.uk;
ddenhammill; Mon-Sun 6.30 pm.

TUNBRIDGE WELLS, KENT 3–4B

HE BEACON ITCHEN £90 334

EA GARDEN LANE
N3 9JH 01892 524252

his "smart and trendy location" from the ll Be Mother' group, set in an Arts & Crafts ouse with "lovely views" over Happy Valley, fers "high-quality food, attentive service id great surroundings". There's also "a nice rrace for meals, if the weather permits". Not rprisingly, it's "popular and often hard to ook". / the-beacon.co.uk; thebeacon_tw; Sun-ed 10.30 pm, Thu-Sat 2.30 pm.

ANTUCCIO £28 343

CAMDEN ROAD
N1 2QD 01892 542047

ncredible pizza with the best ingredients – alian mozzarella, Cobble Lane cured meats id sourdough fermented for 72 hours" – is the ghlight of the "simple menu" at this corner staurant, offering a "pared-down but cheerful tting" ('cantuccio' meaning a small, cosy rner in Italian). / cantuccio.co.uk; cantuccio_zza; Tue-Sun 9 pm.

OCO RETRO £51 343

VALE RD TN1 1BS 01892 522773

ear the train station, a "lovely, intimate ighbourhood restaurant" (est. 2017) split tween ground-floor bistro with daily specials ard, and more romantic top-floor dining om with open kitchen (given its Gallic fluence, naturally there's also a wine cellar). ccording to one reporter who has patronised since its debut, it "felt back on top form this ar". / cocoretro.co.uk; Mon-Sat 10 pm.

ANKEY'S THE OLD ISHMARKET £94 323

THE UPPER PANTILES TN2 5TN
892511422

n "excellent choice of oysters" from Essex, orthumberland and Jersey – served raw, essed or cooked – are the centrepiece the seafood-focused menu at this smart ster bar in the historic Pantiles. There is a ter 'seafood kitchen' across town at Mount ohraim; and they also run a fishmongers in e town. / sankeys.co.uk; sankeysrtw; Tue-Sat idnight.

HACKERAY'S £100 334

LONDON RD TN1 1EA 01892 511921

erhaps the most luxurious restaurant in inbridge Wells" – this "very smart Regency la where [W.M.] Thackeray lived" provides "very attractive" location for a meal; and also praised for its "lovely, finely pitched service". But while Patrick Hill's well-regarded cuisine continues to win praise, there was also the odd reporter this year who felt it was "technically fine but with some over-fussy dishes that didn't let the good-quality ingredients fully shine". / thackerays-restaurant.co.uk; thackeraysrestaurant; Wed-Sat 10.30 pm, Sun 3 pm.

TWICKENHAM, SURREY 3–3A

MASANIELLO £45 332

22 CHURCH STREET
TW1 3NJ 020 8891 5777

"A very friendly and reliable local" named after a Neapolitan revolutionary, and doing a swift trade since its 2009 opening (hence the Surbiton spin-off). The "excellent pizzas" ("giving Napoli a run for its money") are by all accounts the highlight of the Campanian menu: "the dough is so light yet flavoursome that even my kids fight over the crusts". / masaniello.org; Wed-Sat 10 pm, Sun 8 pm.

ONE ONE FOUR £59 333

114-116 HIGH STREET
TW11 9BB 020 3745 8114

"Definitely on my list of places to eat" – with its "changing menu and great food", Sam and Alex Berry's "noisy" operation is a real favourite with locals, including the business set; the ambitious couple's mini-empire also includes Surbiton restaurants Cento Uno, No. 97 and The Hideaway, plus gin bar/distillery The Good Life, and (most recently) crowdfunded newbie Bone Idyll Gin School, which launched on Kingston's riverside in September 2022. / oneonefour.co.uk; numberoneonefour; Tue-Sat midnight, Sun 4 pm.

SHIULI £51 333

128-130 HEATH ROAD
TW1 4BN 020 8703 8201

"A cut-above Indian in Twickenham" from owner Alfred Prasad, who was the youngest Indian to receive a Michelin star during his days at London luminary Tamarind, and which was born during the pandemic. The venue, which is a short walk to the Stoop and Twickenham Stadium, is rated for its "above average set menu on match days" (particularly "for the price point"), and its "tasty and well-constructed" dishes include a vegetarian menu for non-carnivores. / shiulirestaurant.com; restaurantshiuli; Mon, Wed-Sat 10.30 pm, Sun 9 pm.

TSARETTA SPICE £40 433

55 CHURCH STREET
TW1 3NR 020 8892 1096

Former Tamarind and Dishoom chef Yousuf Mohammed has "a different take on traditional Indian cuisine, with tapas-style dishes and cocktails making it a great dining experience". Fans acclaim it as "my type of Indian", with a focus on "quality not quantity". Look out for pre- and post-match specials when England or Harlequins are in action at nearby Twickenham or the Stoop. / tsarettaspice.com; tsarettaspice; Tue-Sat 11 pm, Sun 9 pm.

UMI £47 442

30 YORK STREET
TW1 3LJ 020 8892 2976

This "well-established Twickenham no-frills Japanese restaurant" has an "unchanging menu that never fails to deliver" – "it's so difficult to get a table and you know why when you eat there: high-quality food at sensible prices". "Bobby on front of house is great – he knows his locals and welcomes everyone like an old friend". "The food is fantastic too – we always leave feeling we have had a feast". / umiedinburgh.com; umiedinburgh; Wed, Sun 10 pm, Thu-Sat 10.30 pm.

TYNEMOUTH, TYNE AND WEAR 8–2B

LONGSANDS FISH KITCHEN £45 332

27 FRONT STREET
NE30 4DZ 0191 272 8552

"Beautifully cooked fish and really good chips" (and a good approach to dietary requirements, like "good gluten-free options served without any fuss") help make this well-located fixture "the best in the local area". / longsandsfishkitchen.com; longsandsfish; Mon, Wed & Thu, Sun 7.30 pm, Fri & Sat 8.15 pm.

RILEY'S FISH SHACK £34 545

KING EDWARD'S BAY
NE30 4BY 0191 257 1371

"If you are lucky with the weather it's the best place to eat on earth", according to fans of this funky converted shipping container on Tynemouth Beach. "Surroundings are basic", but "the view is superb and the food is top notch": "fabulous fresh fish" brought in from North Shields round the corner. "Dinner overlooking the sea… log fires… amazing food and service… what could be better?" / rileysfishshack.com; rileysfishshack; Mon, Thu-Sun 9.30 pm.

TYTHERLEIGH, DEVON 2–4A

TYTHERLEIGH ARMS £65 443

EX13 7BE 01460 220214

A "great and reliable gastropub in an area that's not blessed with super eating venues", this sixteenth-century coaching inn, on the Devon/Dorset border, was a hit with all reporters this year; "prices are a bit high", but given that the "lovely food" (modern British with a Euro slant) "keeps getting better", no one seems to care too much. / tytherleigharms.com; tytherleigharms; Wed & Thu 9 pm, Fri & Sat 9.30 pm, Sun 2.30 pm.

UMBERLEIGH, DEVON 1–2D

NORTHCOTE MANOR £81 344

BURRINGTON EX37 9LZ 01769 560501

Sitting in 20 acres of Devon countryside with very pleasant views, this old manor house boasts a muralled Georgian dining room praised for its "consistently good cooking". A particular attraction is the "extensive, albeit pricey selection of wines, featuring some obscure names". / northcotemanor.co.uk; northcotemanor; Mon-Thu 9.30 pm, Fri & Sat 10 pm, Sun 9 pm.

UPPINGHAM, RUTLAND 5-4D

THE LAKE ISLE £76 434

16 HIGH STREET EAST
LE15 9PZ 01572 822951

"In an attractive village near Rutland Water", this seventeenth-century hotel-restaurant near the cute market place "has much to commend it" – not least its "really good food at a very nice price"; its many longtime fans ("as good today as it was for our wedding breakfast 28 years ago"), some of whom visit specifically to eat here, claim that it "never disappoints, whether it be for a celebratory dinner, a set lunch or fishcakes for breakfast". "The rooms are excellent too" if you want to overnight. / lakeisle.co.uk; thelakeisle; Tue-Sun 2 pm.

UPTON MAGNA, SHROPSHIRE 5-4A

THE HAUGHMOND £54 443

SY4 4TZ 01743 709918

"In the centre of the gorgeous village of Upton Magna", Martin Board & wife Mel's "lovely country pub-with-rooms" won nothing but praise this year; despite the seventeenth-century setting, the "food is far from traditional and leans towards modern British – all absolutely delicious and expertly served" (with "particularly good fish dishes" a highlight); add in "sensible prices", and it's a "standout restaurant in Shropshire". / thehaughmond.co.uk; thehaughmond; Tue-Sat 8 pm.

USK, MONMOUTHSHIRE 2-2A

THE BLACK BEAR INN £65 433

BETTWS NEWYDD
NP15 1JN 01873 880701

Josh & Hannah Byrne's "remote country pub" punches way above its weight with a "small, exceptional menu that changes every day" of "innovative cuisine", featuring "bold, delicious flavours" and "locally sourced ingredients, perfectly cooked". Top Menu Tip – "the deep-fried oysters are a gem"... "even if you're ambivalent about oysters!" / theblackbearinn.co.uk; theblackbearusk; Wed-Sat 10 pm, Sun 4 pm.

VENTNOR, ISLE OF WIGHT 2-4D

GERANIUM RESTAURANT AT THE ROYAL £85

BELGRAVE RD PO38 1JJ 01983 852186

"Sit in chandeliered grandeur in the dining room, or enjoy your food whilst looking out of the conservatory over the garden" when you dine at this grande old dame of a hotel. Too limited feedback for a rating in our annual diners' poll on the à la carte fare, which is more posh brasserie (fresh fish, rump steak, risotto) than it is particularly 'haute'. / royalhoteliow.co.uk; theroyaliow; Mon-Sun 8.30 pm.

WADDINGTON, LANCASHIRE 5-1B

THE HIGHER BUCK £52 333

THE SQUARE BB7 3HZ 01200 423226

Chef-patron Michael Heathcote has established a solid following for this Ribble Valley establishment, where he celebrates a decade this year. The "top-value Sunday lunch" is a big attraction – along with "exceptional fish soup". / higherbuck.com; thehigherbuck; Mon-Sat 8.30 pm, Sun 7 pm.

WADEBRIDGE, CORNWALL 1-3B

STEPPING STONE 333

POLMORLA RD PL27 7ND 01208 816377

This "exceptionally good-quality small restaurant, tucked away in Wadebridge", offers a "changing menu with a delightful range of food" – chef-patron Ryan Tomkins was born and bred nearby, and returned home to open his first venture as boss. It's often "packed out with locals and tourists alike (always a good sign)", so "booking is essential". / thesteppingstonewadebridge.co.uk; thesteppingstone.id; Tue-Sat midnight, Sun 3 pm.

WADHURST, KENT 3-4B

WHITE HART £55

HIGH STREET TN5 6AP 01892 351230

In a cute market town in prime English wine country on the Kent-Sussex border, this wine-focused pub from Sam Maynard (ex-Hotel du Vin) opened three boutique bedrooms in 2023. The 30-cover restaurant offers local seasonal dishes from chef Adam Sear alongside a list of 80 English wines (and there's also a more conventional bar menu). Too little feedback for a rating as yet, but such as we have is 'all good'. / thewhitehartwadhurst.com; whitehartwadhurst; Mon-Sat 11 pm, Sun 8 pm.

WALL, NORTHUMBERLAND 8-2A

HJEM £165 544

THE HADRIAN HOTEL
NE46 4EE 01434 681232

"We are so lucky to have this very special restaurant in Northumberland" – Swedish chef Alex Nietosvuori and his Northumberland-born partner Ally Thompson inspire nothing but superlatives for their acclaimed destination: a bright, contemporary 24-seater with open kitchen at a pub-with-rooms next to Hadrian's Wall. "It is evident that they seek out the best ingredients and are not afraid to change suppliers if they find something more in keeping with their ethos, with lots of local produce used". The result is "high class, inventive" Scandi-inflected cuisine served as a mixture of small bites and larger dishes comprising a £150 per person tasting menu. "Wonderful... even on a second visit – not every eatery can do that!" / restauranthjem.co.uk; restauranthjem; Wed-Sat 11 pm.

WALLINGFORD, OXFORDSHIRE 2-2

FIVE LITTLE PIGS £47 33

26 ST MARY'S STREET
OX10 0ET 01491 833999

"Long may it thrive" – an "engaging" neighbourhood joint with links to the local gin and craft-beer outfit, The Keep. "The menu changes regularly, and there's always somethin to love". Top Menu Tip – "save room for desserts...they're very good" ("the doughnuts are a guilty pleasure"). / fivelittlepigs.co.uk; fivelittlepigs_wallingford; Tue-Fri 11.30 pm, Sat midnight, Sun 6 pm.

HOME SWEET HOME INN £52 34

ROKE OX10 6JD 01491 838249

"Excellent pub food in Chilterns countryside" is to be had at this cosy seventeenth-century country pub in the hamlet of Roke, near Wallingford. The straightforward menu specialises in grills, and if you still have room for cheese afterwards there's a notably good selection. / hshroke.pub; hshroke; Tue-Sat 9 pm, Sun 4 pm.

WANSFORD, CAMBRIDGESHIRE 6-4

PRÉVOST AT HAYCOCK, HAYCOCK HOTEL £66 54

HAYCOCK MANOR
PE8 6JA 01780 782223

"Exquisite food with fabulous presentation, every time" is again hailed at Lee Clarke's relocated venue, which moved in 2021 into the revamped Grade II-listed Haycock Manor Hotel, in a lovely village near Peterborough. "My wife and I had eaten three times at Prevo when it was in town – standards have remaine high as Lee's imagination and the technique of his chefs is perhaps even more precise here, with a multi-course menu that's a delightful taste journey". / haycock.co.uk; haycock_manor wansford; Mon-Sun 8.30 pm.

WARWICK, WARWICKSHIRE 5-4C

LA MESA 33

5B OLD SQUARE
CV34 4RA 07528 080151

"Creative and interesting chef" Gerald Magui is behind this idiosyncratic townhouse indie, whose website baldly announces that its "aim i to improve your life, not f*** it up" via surpris Spanish food; there's "no menu, you just eat th six courses he puts in front of you and relax ar enjoy with a glass of one of his recommended wines... bliss". / lamesawarwick.co.uk; Mesa.la; Wed-Sat 11 pm.

WASHINGTON, WEST SUSSEX 3–4A

HALK ESTAURANT £73 3 3 4

ORTH FARM RH20 4BB 01903 877845

n a beautiful high-ceilinged barn-style ilding on the Wiston wine estate" – between orsham and Worthing in West Sussex – this nue was relaunched in 2022, with a "wine st not confined to Wiston wines, although ese feature heavily in the sparkling section". odwise, it offers produce from the estate epared by Tom Kemble, who made waves London at the Bonham's auction house in e years before Covid. "The menu provides ree-four choices on each course – on a od day it can be very pleasant". (You can so visit for breakfast, from 8.30 am on eekends). / wistonestate.com; wistonestate; Tue-hu, Sun 3 pm, Fri & Sat 9 pm.

WASS, NORTH YORKSHIRE 5–1D

HE STAPYLTON RMS £56 3 4 3

O61 4BE 01347 868280

Great pub food and proper Yorkshire ospitality" are the defining features of ob & Gill Thompson's whitewashed inn, a xture in the village for almost four centuries. Everything is a big cut above the average – ghly recommended". / stapyltonarms.co.uk; apylton_arms_wass; Tue-Sat 9 pm.

WATERGATE BAY, CORNWALL 1–3B

MILY SCOTT AT WATERGATE AY £65 3 3 3

R8 4AA 01637 860543

ne of a handful of restaurants in this famous otel, this ultra-romantic outpost was born as beachside pop-up, and is ably overseen by cott, a fast-rising Cornish chef and cookbook thor; whether opting for the lobster lunches six-course seafood menus, you're in for some antastic food" (although one or two regulars el it comes at a cost). / emilyscottfood.com; nilyscottfood; Tue-Sat 9.30 pm.

WELLAND, WORCESTERSHIRE 2–1B

HE INN AT VELLAND £63 4 4 3

OOK BANK, DRAKE STREET R13 6LN 01684 592317

"a wonderful spot between Upton and Ialvern", overlooking the rolling countryside specially if you dine al-fresco under the ass canopy), this "reassuringly consistent" astropub "consistently ticks all the boxes". The quite adventurous" food makes it a staple in ir annual diners' poll, and if anything "they ave upped their game of late"… add in "lovely ecorations" and "friendly, fun staff" and "what ore could you want"? / theinnatwelland.co.uk; einnatwelland; Wed-Sat 8.30 pm, Sun 3 pm.

WELLS NEXT THE SEA, NORFOLK 6–3C

WELLS CRAB HOUSE £61 3 4 3

38 FREEMAN ST
NR23 1BA 013 2871 0456

"The best we found in this popular holiday resort" – a "lovely, relaxed" local staple from Kelly (FOH) and Scott (chef) Dougal which has "excelled for many years" thanks to its "consummate" service and "original ways with fish"… "plus they have their own gin!". "Reasonable prices" contribute to the fact that "it's always busy", but if you can't get a spot "they offer 'take home and cook' too". / wellscrabhouse.co.uk; wellscrab; Tue-Sun 8.30 pm.

WELLS, SOMERSET 2–3B

GOODFELLOWS £63 4 3 2

7B ST THOMAS STREET
BA5 2UU 01749 676774

"This small family-run restaurant never fails to please" – Adam & Martine Fellows celebrate the 20th anniversary of their fish-focused, French-inspired bistro this year, having moved to a new townhouse address in 2022. Their dishes are always "beautifully cooked and presented" and there's a "variety of menus to suit different budgets". Top Menu Tip – "excellent scallops in a champagne sauce with samphire and asparagus". / 7bwells.co.uk; Thu-Sat 11 pm.

WELWYN, HERTFORDSHIRE 3–2B

AUBERGE DU LAC, BROCKET HALL £96 2 2 3

AL8 7XG 01707 368888

"Not yet back to its old self" seems to be the frustrating verdict on this former hunting lodge, scenically located with a large terrace by the lake of the luxurious Brocket Hall estate. In the early 2000s it was a national name under chef Jean-Christophe Novelli, but has since had its ups and downs. After a hiatus, "its re-opening has been long awaited and eagerly anticipated locally with the pop-ups fully booked". Early feedback suggests "it still seems to be a work in progress. Menu, food and cooking have been very good, suitably refined and up to the standard expected. However, service can be poor, with staff unable to cope and long waits to order. The general decor is also very dated and doesn't appear to have changed much during the past three years of closure. Hopefully, it will find its feet but it is taking longer than expected!" / brocket-hall.co.uk; brockethall; Thu-Sat 9 pm, Sun 3 pm.

THE WAGGONERS £63 3 3 2

BRICKWALL CLOSE, AYOT GRN
AL6 9AA 01707 324241

"The food in this small and atmospheric pub is unabashedly French – tasty, interesting and reasonably priced" with "just the right amount of an English touch". "Splendid service from host Laurent (Brydniak) and his team, who pay a lot of attention to getting the details right", adds to the appeal of a venue that is "often busy by midday as a walkers' reward" after strolling around the neighbouring Brocket Hall estate. / thewaggoners.co.uk; thewaggonersayot; Mon-Sat 11 pm, Sun 6 pm.

WEMBLEY PARK, GREATER LONDON 3–3A

STUDIO FIVE £58 4 4 4

128 WEMBLEY PARK DR HA9 0EW
NO TEL

"A bit of a gem a few minutes' walk from the stadium" and "set within a venue that offers a fascinating history of popular culture in the UK" – the site having variously hosted the fine- dining restaurant for the British Empire Exhibition of 1924, a Fox films studio, the UK's largest purpose-built sound stage (Freddie Mercury did his last music video here) and now a theatre. The "surprisingly good food" fuses Goan chef Ronald's roots and director Rob's experience of Michelin restaurants in London and Paris (think chili chutney fish and masala fries). "It's rare to get a truly unique dining experience these days, but that's what I got at Studio Five". / studiofive.restaurant; studiofiverestaurant; Wed-Sat 9 pm, Sun 6 pm.

WEST CLANDON, SURREY 3–3A

THE ONSLOW ARMS £63 2 2 3

THE STREET GU4 7TE 01483 222447

This smart gastroboozer is "a jolly nice place to go, whether à deux, or as a large group"; its "outstanding" British menu sets the local "benchmark for fish 'n' chips" and "the fact that it is always busy says it all (even we, as regulars, who always book way in advance, sometimes cannot get our first-choice table!"). / onslowarmsclandon.co.uk; onslowarmsclandon; Mon-Sat 11 pm, Sun 10.30 pm.

WEST HATCH, WILTSHIRE 2–3C

PYTHOUSE KITCHEN GARDEN £62 4 4 3

SP3 6PA 01747 870444

"In a beautiful setting in the Wiltshire countryside", Darren Brown's "most wonderful" venture occupies an eighteenth-century walled garden and "makes full use of the produce grown" there in its "wholesome, creative fare". "The fire pit conjures smoke, fire and primal appetites" which are ably slaked by the "superb" meats and "imaginatively done" vegetables – limited mostly to lunch, plus the odd Equinox-themed dinner. In summer they also run the 'Slow Food Kitchen' from Thursday to Sunday, while you can overnight year-round in their Shepherd's Hut. / pythousekitchengarden.co.uk; kitchengardenco; Wed-Sun 4.30 pm.

WEST HOATHLY, WEST SUSSEX 3–4B

THE CAT INN £67 334

NORTH LANE RH19 4PP 01342 810369

This "great country pub" – a free house dating from the sixteenth century – benefits from inglenook fireplaces and beams inside and an inviting garden in the summer, and offers some "delicious" grub. It makes an "excellent stop when touring the local gardens". / catinn.co.uk; Wed & Thu, Sat, Fri 8.30 pm, Sun 3.30 pm.

WEST MALLING, KENT 3–3C

THE SWAN £56 333

35 SWAN ST ME19 6JU 01732 521910

This modernised village inn "never fails to please" with an attractive brasserie-style menu that's "great for a casual lunch". A covered garden adds to the package. / theswanwestmalling.co.uk; Mon-Sat 10 pm, Sun 5.45 pm.

WEST MERSEA, ESSEX 3–2C

THE COMPANY SHED £43 423

**129 COAST ROAD
CO5 8PA 01206 382700**

"No frills" it may be (you must "BYO wine and bread"), but the "great seafood" – including the "freshest platters around", plus hot options – at this very "quirky establishment" (basically a clapboard shack) mean that a visit is "always great fun". / the-company-shed.com; the_company_shed; Wed-Sun 5 pm.

WEST RUNTON, NORFOLK 6–3C

ROCKY BOTTOMS £24 443

**CROMER ROAD
NR27 9QA 07848 045607**

"You can't get fresher than the beautiful seafood" at this clifftop perch "in a wonderful setting overlooking the sea", run by local lobster and crab fisherman Richard Matthews and his wife Ali. "The freshly caught crab is delicious", and last year they added a range of vegan options to the menu. / rockybottoms.net; rockybottoms.uk; Sun-Thu 5 pm, Fri & Sat 8 pm.

WEST WITTON, NORTH YORKSHIRE 8–4B

THE WENSLEYDALE HEIFER £87 343

MAIN ST DL8 4LS 01969 622322

In a "superb setting in the Dales", father-and-son team Lewis & David Moss are behind this quintessential gastropub-with-rooms (including one room with a James Bond theme). "The team is superb, and the food (including seafood) speaks for itself as getting a table at short notice is extremely difficult". NB – canines will love it ("the most dog-friendly pub I've ever visited!"), down to getting their very own sausages for brekko. / wensleydaleheifer.co.uk; wensleyheifer; Mon-Sun 9.15 pm.

WESTERHAM, KENT 3–3B

THE OLD BANK £98 443

**8 MARKET SQUARE
TN16 1AW 01233 659890**

Adam & Emma Turley's converted bank in this Kent town just beyond the M25 wins high ratings all-round: "a cool place", with "wonderful food and very good wine", plus "a lovely engaging front of house crew": "highly recommended". There's a five-course tasting menu for £75 per person, or go the whole hog and have the eight-course version for £105 per person. / oldbank-westerham.co.uk; theoldbankkent; Wed-Sat 9 pm.

SQUERREYS £60 234

**SQUERRYES WINERY
TN16 1QP 01959 562345**

This "restaurant attached to a winery" is ideal for "a very pleasant lunch – you can just eat or try a tasting, or both!". The North Downs estate has been home to eight generations of the Warde family since 1722, but they planted their vines as recently as 2006, winning early acclaim for their sparkling whites. / squerryes.co.uk; squerryes; Wed & Thu 5 pm, Fri & Sat 11 pm.

WESTFIELD, EAST SUSSEX 3–4C

THE WILD MUSHROOM £65 443

**WOODGATE HOUSE, WESTFIELD LANE
TN35 4SB 01424 751137**

This "pleasantly traditional and old-fashioned restaurant" "has been a favourite for years" – and is these days "serving a more modern style of food" without losing any of its attractions. It was chef-patron Paul Webbe's first opening more than 25 years ago, and has been followed by his fish specialist venues in Hastings and Rye. / webbesrestaurants.co.uk; webbesrestaurants; Wed-Fri 9 pm, Sun 2.30 pm, Sat 9.30 pm.

WESTGATE-ON-SEA, KENT 3–3D

QUINCE £57 443

**39 STATION ROAD
CT8 8QY 01843 833864**

A "great new local" set up by Ben Hughes and Rafael Lopez, both grads of Canterbury's The Goods Shed, and which has gained "rapid Michelin recognition" (having made it into the 2023 guide since launching in May 2022). The owners' British and Spanish backgrounds inform the "brilliant" modern bistro cooking, enriched by high-quality ingredients and "attentive service". / quincewestgate.co.uk; quince_westgate.

WESTON TURVILLE, BUCKINGHAMSHIRE 3–2A

THE CHEQUERS INN 333

**35 CHURCH LANE HP22 5SJ
01296613298**

Chef-owner Dritan and maître d' Ranka (husband and wife) took over this country pub in the Bucks countryside in 2010. It inspired limited feedback this year, but all upbeat regarding its fairly traditional fare whose high level of aspiration makes this more a 'restaurant in a pub' than a gastropub. / thechequerswt.co.uk; thechequersinnwt; Wed-Sat 11 pm, Sun 5 pm.

WEYMOUTH, DORSET 2–4

CATCH AT THE OLD FISH MARKET £91 43

**THE OLD FISH MARKET, CUSTOM HOUS
QUAY DT4 8BE 01305 590555**

In the exciting setting of the 1855 fish market this two-year-old sustainable seafood specialist delivers "an earnest love letter to seafood and the fishermen who provide it" (as The Independent's Kate Ng put it), with dishes changing to accommodate the catch even between customers – an "extraordinary way t run a restaurant" but one that "really works". "It's only a no-choice tasting menu" these day which may not be to all tastes, but the results are "inventive" and "very reasonably priced for the quality". / catchattheoldfishmarket.com; catchattheoldfishmarket; Thu-Sat, Tue, Wed 9.30 pm.

CRAB HOUSE CAFÉ £69 54

**FERRYMANS WAY, PORTLAND ROAD
DT4 9YU 01305 788 867**

"A hot sunny evening. A table outside with a view over Chesil Beach. A glass of local English white. Two whole crabs, one plain, on spicy Chinese. A sticky, messy heaven worth planning a voyage to Weymouth around!" – this "quirky", "rustic venue in a shack" sitting "just yards from the sea" is one of the hundred most commented-on restaurants in the UK in our annual diners' poll on account of its "awesome" fish, oysters, crab and other seafood. The main complaint? "wish I lived nearer!" / crabhousecafe.co.uk; Wed & Thu 9 pm Fri & Sat 9.30 pm, Sun 3 pm.

WHALLEY, LANCASHIRE 5–1E

KING STREET KITCHEN 33

**73 KING STREET
BB7 9SW 01254 822462**

"Quiet" and "small" it may be, but this new British bistro (with the odd Gallic-inspired dish on Whalley's main thoroughfare turns out som "exceptional" food ("especially Sunday lunch" and its low-key ambience makes it "perfect for business" too. / kingstreetbistro.co.uk; kingstreetbistro; Wed-Sat 10 pm, Sun 5 pm.

THE THREE FISHES £65 43

MITTON RD BB7 9PQ 01254 826888

"It's well worth the drive out to Mitton" to sample "fantastic food prepared by an exceptional chef" – "Nigel Howarth, back where he belongs cooking up a storm in Lancashire". Formerly the culinary force behind nearby regional powerhouse Northcote

Ugly Butterfly, St Ives

he "has revived this lovely restaurant" (a pub he was originally involved with 20 years ago, when it was part of the Ribble Valley Inns chain) "and made it is own" with "food that represents his character and seasonal dishes that keep the menu changing, so there's always something different to try". "The service is really good and the ambience is very friendly and relaxed". / thethreefishes.co.uk; thethreefishesmitton; Wed-Sat 8.30 pm, Sun 9 pm.

WHATCOTE, WARWICKSHIRE 2–1D

THE ROYAL OAK £115 443

2 UPPER FARM BARN CV36 5EF 01295 688 100

Richard & Solanche Craven's "exceptional" venue in a converted village pub on the northern fringe of the Cotswolds is "well worth the detour" for its "well-judged menu" of "beautifully cooked" dishes (many with foraged ingredients) and "democratically inclined wine list" in a "very attractive space". You don't have to endure a massive number of courses either, with evening options starting with a four-course menu for £80 per person. / theroyaloakwhatcote.co.uk; the_royal_oak_whatcote; Thu-Sat 11 pm, Sun 10 pm.

WHITBY, NORTH YORKSHIRE 8–3D

THE MAGPIE CAFÉ £51 443

14 PIER RD YO21 3PU 01947 602058

"Always the best fish 'n' chips in the UK" – this "unfailing" café on the harbour is "a must-visit when in Whitby" and remains the most commented-on chippie nationally in our annual diners' poll. "Yes, it does all the usual seaside dishes" and yet some fans "have never had the fish 'n' chips here because the daily specials board of other seafood dishes is so good" – an "expansive choice of fish, shellfish and molluscs all ideally prepared" as "the kitchen is imaginative and the combinations, which sometimes sound unusual, can always be relied on". "If you can bag a window seat (not easy in peak times… which is just about always) the view over the harbour is very atmospheric". / magpiecafe.co.uk; magpiecafewhitby; Mon-Sun 9 pm.

TRENCHERS £53 442

NEW QUAY RD YO21 1DH 01947 603212

"Watch out Magpie!" is a perennial cry of loyal fans of this Whitby fixture. But even if its more famous rival undoubtedly has won the popular vote, fans say this nearby chippie is "excellent of its kind". / trenchersrestaurant.co.uk; trencherswhitby; Mon-Sun 8.30 pm.

WHITCHURCH, SHROPSHIRE 5–3A

ETZIO £41 424

58 - 60 HIGH STREET SY13 1BB 01948 662248

"The trat' every neighbourhood needs" – "amazing value and consistently good food" (pizza, pasta, seafood, meat) make this relaxed "cheap 'n' cheerful" Italian on the high street "a firm favourite that is booked out two months ahead at weekends"; further plaudits for the "great atmosphere", too. / etzio.co.uk; Tue-Sat midnight, Sun 3 pm.

WHITE WALTHAM, BERKSHIRE 3–3A

THE BEEHIVE £92 443

WALTHAM RD SL6 3SH 01628822877

The "elevated food" served at Dominic Chapman's smart village-green venue is "certainly worthy of its top cooking grade", and "takes Home Counties pub fare up a level – the amuse-bouches and petits-fours make a pub lunch here a real occasion". "We hope to return when there's cricket on the adjacent field". / thebeehivewhitewaltham.com; thebeehivetweet; Tue-Thu 9.30 pm, Fri & Sat 10 pm, Sun 4 pm.

WHITEBROOK, MONMOUTHSHIRE 2–2B

THE WHITEBROOK, RESTAURANT WITH ROOMS £166 433

NP25 4TX 01600 860254

"Hidden in the Wye valley", Chris and Kirsty Harrod's "charming" restaurant with rooms is often hailed as "the Welsh version of Noma" – "lots of foraging and sustainability is in evidence and Chris will spend time talking you through ingredients and cooking methods". Most diners "really love the ethos of using local seasonal produce to produce such delicious food" and "the absence of silly combinations to deliver a seriously well put-together menu, with reasonable wine pairings". Its ratings slipped a fraction this year, as it struck the wrong note on the odd occasion. The tenor of most reports though? – "unique and certainly worth seeking out". Top Tip – lovely terrace for a summer's day. / thewhitebrook.co.uk; thewhitebrook; Fri-Sun, Thu 8.30 pm.

WHITLEY BAY, TYNE AND WEAR 8–2B

HINNIES £46 343

10 EAST PARADE NE26 1AP 0191 447 0500

With its "well-presented and substantial local food" – including classic comfort dishes with a Geordie twist – this café on the seafront is a "very welcoming place on a cold day" and "excellent for lunch after a walk by the sea", whatever the weather. / hinnies.co.uk; hinniesrestaurant; Tue-Fri 9 pm, Sat 9.30 pm, Sun 4 pm.

WHITSTABLE, KENT 3–3C

CASTELLUM £48 332

27A OXFORD ST CT5 1DB 01227 941352

A short walk from the beach, there's a "fantastic new Italian in town"; Salerno-born Carmine Cioffi is behind the three-year-old, which is doing a swift trade in Neapolitan pizzas ("definitely the best" in these parts) and elevated pasta and seafood dishes. Add in "very friendly" service and a "lovely garden" and it's "definitely one for a return visit". / castellumpizzeria.com; castellumpizzeria; Tue-Sat 9.30 pm, Sun 9 pm.

JOJO'S £54 44

2 HERNE BAY RD CT5 2LQ 01227 274591

You get "the Mediterranean diet writ large" a this "relaxed, informal, spacious and friendly" outfit opened in 2000 by cook Nikki Billingtor and her partner Paul Watson, originally in their own home. It's "the perfect place for a leisurely lunch, with delicious and mostly healthy cooking" including "the freshest tapas fish dishes", along with "professional and charming service" that ensures "every visit fee memorable and special". / jojosrestaurant.co.u jojostankerton; Thu-Sat 10.30 pm, Sun 5 pm.

THE LOBSTER SHACK RESTAURANT £28 32

EAST QUAY CT5 1AB 01227 771923

Operated by the Whitstable Oyster Company, this shack tucked away at the end of the harbour serves oysters from the beds visible at low tide from its terrace, as well as lobsters and fish from the nearby waters. "We're lucky to have such a place for fresh quality fish on our doorstep". / thelobstershack.co.uk; thelobstershackwhitstable; Mon-Sun 9 pm.

SAMPHIRE £67 43

4 HIGH STREET CT5 1BQ 01227 77007

This "always busy and buzzing brasserie on Whitstable High Street", from Australian-trained chef Sam, has built an impressive reputation in these parts for its use of "local ingredients lovingly prepared" (and its "interesting combination of choices" too); "really nice staff" are an added joy. / samphirewhitstable.co.uk; samphire_whitstable; Sun-Thu 9.30 pm, Fri & Sat 10 pm.

WHEELERS OYSTER BAR £94 54

8 HIGH STREET CT5 1BQ 01227 27331

"Tiny but perfectly formed!" – The very first Wheelers (est. 1856, and the original and last branch of an increasingly forgotten chain that ceased trading in 2014) is a "quaint but charming" venue whose "magical qualities make it a memorable and special place". "There is a counter at which you can order items to take away (to the nearby beach) or sit in the very bijoux parlour" – a "really lovely, family-run space where the attention to detail and freshness of the seafood is second to none". "Exceptional oysters" are the headline attraction on a "wow of a tasting menu" that "is of course centred on fish". "It's made even more affordable by their BYO policy" – "just pop to the offy over the road for a great bottle of wine" ("there's a small charge for corkage"). Top Tip – "book well in advance". / wheelersoysterbar.com; wheelersoysterbar; Mon & Tue, Thu, Sun 5 pm, F & Sat 8 pm.

HITSTABLE OYSTER SHERY CO. £70 434

·YAL NATIVE OYSTER STORES, ·RSEBRIDGE CT5 1BU 01227 276856

ı unrivalled seashore location" right "on the ach at Whitstable" and "with plain wooden bles" sets the scene at this "very popular" stination. "It's not fancy cooking, but the ality of the fish is very good" and "simply d ably prepared, although prices are not eap". "Best to go when there is an 'r' in month, when natives are available as they fantastic". / whitstableoystercompany.com; itstableoystercompany; Mon-Sat 9 pm, Sun 0 pm.

HITTLESFORD, AMBRIDGESHIRE 3–1B

ROVENANCE BRIX + ORTAR £68 432

LL FARM RD CB22 4AN 01223 839993

oads of appetising and well-cooked od" (locally sourced meat and fish, plus ggie options) comes out of the wood- ed hearth at this 'fast slow food' venture, ich started life in an Airstream but oved to this 'brix' and mortar location 2019. The "slightly odd" location (on oad outside town) and simple decor twithstanding, "this is a gem – consistently od and value for money" (particularly the near desert of the Cambridge stro scene"). / provenancekitchen.com; ovenancekitchen; Wed & Thu 4 pm, Fri & Sat pm, Sun 5 pm.

VINCHCOMBE, LOUCESTERSHIRE 2–1C

NORTH STREET £83 432

NORTH ST GL54 5LH 01242 604566

onstant high quality both in taste and entiveness" has been a hallmark of chef- tron Gus Ashenford's cooking at the "always lightful" small restaurant, a converted tswold tea room, he has run with his wife ate for two decades. His modern British hes, underpinned by the French classical hniques he learned under his mentor, the late ichel Roux Senior, invariably "look beautiful the plate". / 5northstreetrestaurant.co.uk; d-Sat, Tue 9 pm, Sun 1.30 pm.

VINCHESTER, HAMPSHIRE 2–3D

ANGKOK BISTRO 334

JEWRY ST SO23 8RY 01962 841811

th its "superb range of dishes" plumbing ser-known regions of Thailand, and also ombined with swift service", this three-year- l operation strikes reporters as quite the d – and if you're a vegan, they work miracles placing the fishy sauces Thai classics are so en based around. / bangkok-bistro.co.uk; ngkokbistrowinchester; Mon-Sun 9.45 pm.

THE CHESIL RECTORY £74 344

1 CHESIL ST SO23 0HU 01962 851555

This "quietly excellent" destination inhabits a 600-year-old building five minutes' from the city centre, and has operated as a restaurant for over 75 years (the current owners took over in 2008). It is second only to Rick Stein locally in terms of the amount of feedback it generates thanks to offering a "very high standard in everything": "the setting is classical yet relaxed; service is discreet and effective; and the cuisine elegant and well-prepared". "I am delighted that such restaurants still exist – there are so few like this". Top Menu Tip – "the lunch and early evening menu is exceptional value". / chesilrectory.co.uk; chesil_rectory; Mon-Thu 9 pm, Fri & Sat 9.30 pm, Sun 8.30 pm.

GANDHI RESTAURANT £48 343

163-164 HIGH ST SO23 9BA 01962863940

This 36-year veteran "continues to provide the best Indian food in Winchester", with an "interesting and wide-ranging menu of well-cooked dishes". There's an "obliging staff", although "the ambience is occasionally let down by noisy groups". / gandhirestaurant.com; Wed & Thu, Sun, Tue 10.30 pm, Fri & Sat 11 pm.

THE IVY WINCHESTER BRASSERIE £77 234

103-104 HIGH STREET SO23 9AH 01962 790700

The national brand's handy High Street perch is "THE place to have breakfast or brunch" locally, attracting uniformly positive reports this year. "The food is on the pricey side, but you get what you pay for" and despite being "always busy", it's "still somehow always able to deliver", with "excellent service" from the "polite and efficient" staff. / theivywinchester.com; theivywinchester; Mon-Fri midnight, Sat 12.30 am, Sun 11.30 pm.

KYOTO KITCHEN £51 444

70 PARCHMENT STREET SO23 8AT 01962 890895

Miff Kayum's top-performing and "authentic" Japanese offers "an amazing experience every time" (so much so that some fans "visit Winchester solely to visit"). The sushi and sashimi are invariably "excellent", with the famed 'Winchester Roll' a world's first, being wrapped in wasabi leaf rather than the usual seaweed. They now do an omakase (chef's choice) menu on Thu-Sat evenings if you feel like pushing the boat out. / kyotokitchen.co.uk; kyotokitchen; Mon-Sun 9.45 pm.

RICK STEIN £69 443

7 HIGH STREET SO23 9JX 01962 353535

This "very busy" venture is both the most commented-on restaurant in the city and also the most popular spin-off from the Stein family's original Padstow operation. Aside from the fact that it's "a little expensive", no-one has a bad word to say about the place: it has a "fantastic location" and "maintains a high quality of skillful fish cooking" with "frequent changes to the menu"; all delivered by "calm and attentive staff". "Some say it's overhyped – it's actually brilliant!" / rickstein.com; ricksteinrestaurants; Mon-Sun 9 pm. SRA – accredited

SHOAL £37 333

GUILDHALL, THE BROADWAY, SO23 9GH 01962 861919

This "thoroughly modern take on fish 'n' chips" in the ground floor of Winchester's Guildhall is "a real local favourite" with a "great atmosphere"; and it's much commented-on in our annual diners' poll. The fish is "outstanding", served with "homemade sauces and gelato to follow". Chef-patron Lenny Carr-Roberts learned his trade at Le Gavroche and Claridges, as well as Chez Fred in Bournemouth. Top Menu Tip – "the lemon meringue pie ice cream is to die for". / shoal.uk.net; shoalwinchester; Mon-Sat 8.30 pm.

WYKEHAM ARMS £58 335

75 KINGSGATE ST SO23 9PE 01962 853834

"Part of the Fuller's group but a cut above the city's other pubs", this famous boozer with rooms (betwixt Cathedral and college) is a "wonderfully atmospheric" spot that's "the spiritual heir to Orwell's 'Moon Under Water', or ideal public house". For non-literary types that means "a varied clientele, with some eccentrics", "a series of cosy and pleasantly cluttered rooms… convivial rather than noisy; no music or TV; and staff who are amiable and helpful". The food, helmed by 2022 Roux Scholarship semi-finalist Luke Emmess, was consistently well-rated this year. / wykehamarmswinchester.co.uk; thewykeham; Mon-Sat 11 pm, Sun 10 pm.

WINDERMERE, CUMBRIA 7–3D

GILPIN SPICE, GILPIN LODGE £68 343

CROOK ROAD LA23 3NE 01539 488818

This modern Lakeland dining room – an Asian dining alternative in this luxuriously updated small hotel – is nowadays presided over by Aakash Ohol, who – prior to the departure of Hrishkesh Desai in December 2022 – was sous chef of Hrishi (since relaunched as Source, see also). Notwithstanding the odd disappointment registered this year, feedback suggests its diverse dishes (inspired by countries along the Spice Route) can be a useful relief to the native fare generally prevalent in this neck of the woods; even if "sometimes it's difficult to choose and the dishes come as and when they're ready". / thegilpin.co.uk; gilpinhotel; Mon-Thu, Sat & Sun 9.30 pm, Fri 9 pm.

HENROCK £109 4|4|3

LINTHWAITE HOUSE, CROOK ROAD LA23 3JA 015394 88600

The "outstanding" if "lesser-known and more relaxed cousin of the Lake District's most famous culinary destination" – L'Enclume in nearby Cartmell – "Henrock is a fabulous option for those struggling to save up for (or not quick enough to book)" at the former. You still get real "Simon Rogan excellence", "overlooking Lake Windermere" in the "lovely Linthwaite Hotel", complete with "brilliant artwork, great views, delicious and innovative food, and delightful staff and service". / henrock.co.uk; henrocksimonrogan.

HRISHI, GILPIN LODGE £94 4|4|3

CROOK RD LA23 3NE 01539 488818

"Never failing with the quality of food and service" – ex-Fat Duck chef Ollie Bridgwater did well to hang onto the Michelin star at the Cunliffe family's Lakeland hotel, where he succeeded Hrishikesh Desai (who previously ran the dining room as Hrishi) just a matter of weeks before it was due to be re-rated. Despite the constant updating of the property, it is a relatively traditional space. There's a three-course à la carte for £90, or a six-course tasting option for £120 (£200 if you go for the accompanying wine-tasting accompaniment). There is also a less informal option of the Knipe Grill at Gilpin Lake House, which is a waterside building elsewhere on the estate. And see also Gilpin Spice. / thegilpin.co.uk; gilpinhotel; Mon-Sun 9 pm.

LANGDALE CHASE £65

AMBLESIDE ROAD LA23 1LW 015394 32201

Positioned on the edge of Lake Windermere, the restaurant at Langdale Chase is closed at the time of writing while it undergoes a multi-million pound refit, with re-opening planned for late 2023. In July 2023, owner Daniel Thwaites announced the appointment of chef Michael Cole to steer the kitchen for the main dining room, whose floor-to-ceiling windows overlook the lake and the Coniston Fells. / langdale.co.uk; Mon-Sat 9.30 pm, Sun 2 am.

WINDSOR, BERKSHIRE 3-3A

AL FASSIA £50 3|4|3

27 ST LEONARDS RD SL4 3BP 01753 855370

"Very welcoming hosts have time to chat even during a busy service" at the Chab family's popular Moroccan stalwart, which has been a fixture for over 25 years thanks to food that's "fresh, flavoursome and delicious". It's run by the children of the founder, Mustapha, who passed away in 2020. / alfassiarestaurant.com; alfassiarestaurant; Mon-Thu 10 pm, Sat, Fri 10.30 pm, Sun 9 pm.

THE GREENE OAK £50 3|3|3

DEADWORTH RD, OAKLEY GRN SL4 5UW 01753 864294

This smart boozer is a "great all-rounder with reliable gastropub fare and a fine garden with covered seating". It's the flagship of Brucan Pubs, a small group of ambition founded by a pair with strong credentials, ex-Savoy, Ivy and Groucho club chef Jamie Dobbin and James Lyon-Shaw , formerly operations manager at the ETM group. / thegreeneoak.co.uk; Mon-Fri 11 pm, Sat 9.30 pm, Sun 9 pm.

WINGHAM, KENT 3-3D

THE DOG AT WINGHAM £77 4|3|3

CANTERBURY ROAD CT3 1BB 01227 720339

"A warm, lovely and welcoming pub (complete with log fire for cold days) set in a village not far from Canterbury". Service is "attentive" but it's the food that "carries the experience: a good choice with some gorgeous flavours". / thedog.co.uk; dogwingham; Mon-Sat 9 pm, Sun 6 pm.

WINTERINGHAM, LINCOLNSHIRE 5-1D

WINTERINGHAM FIELDS £219 3|3|3

1 SILVER ST DN15 9ND 01724 733096

"If food is love, there is no better place to feel totally wined and dined!" according to fans of this converted sixteenth-century manor house, near the southern banks of the Humber. As the holder of the only Michelin star in North Lincs, it has long been a culinary beacon in this thinly provided neck of the woods and won particular praise this year for "a tasting menu that's second to none… and the fact that you can stay over too for the perfect date!". "Really interesting wines from some unusual locations" is another feature that attracts praise. Overall, the establishment's ratings were dragged down a little this year by a couple of "average" or "overpriced" meals. But, in April 2023 – late in the day for feedback in our annual diners' poll – the restaurant relaunched with 'a new immersive experience' that promises to be 'like nothing you've experienced before' ('by knocking through walls and incorporating our kitchen into the restaurant itself, you can [apparently] taste, smell and fully immerse yourself in an unrivaled restaurant experience'). We've maintained the former ratings but they are less certain than usual at this time of change. / winteringhamfields.co.uk; winteringham_fields; Wed-Sat 7.30 pm.

WISLEY, SURREY 3-3A

THE TERRACE 2|3|4

RHS GARDEN WISLEY, WISLEY LANE GU23 6QB 01483 668015

"How nice to have a decent restaurant to round off your visit to the RHS gardens", with a "short menu of good-quality food" in "attractive surroundings". Wisley can get enormously busy, though, and service can struggle to cope with the sheer numbers. / rhs.org.uk; The_RHS; Mon-Sun 5.30 pm.

WISWELL, LANCASHIRE 5-1

FREEMASONS AT WISWELL £99 4|4

8 VICARAGE FOLD CLITHEROE BB7 9DF 01254 822218

"Set in a tiny hamlet in Lancashire's Ribble Valley", Steve Smith's "fine-dining destination disguised as a pub with rooms" is one of the top 50 most commented-on destinations outside London in our annual diners' poll. "The food superb, and the wine list well chosen" and it's served "in an easygoing atmosphere… you can even take the dog!" Even amongst fans, though opinions divide sharply over the level of value it provides: what is "very fair" to some is – to others – becoming more borderline ("I know everything is more expensive now, but sadly the is now in the sphere of me not being able to justify the expense"). / freemasonsatwiswell.com; Wed & Thu 8 pm, Fri & Sat 8.30 pm, Sun 5 pm.

WITHDEAN, EAST SUSSEX 3-4

FURNA £125 4|4

6 NEW ROAD BN1 1UF 01273 031594

"My new favourite restaurant!" – well-known to diners at Brighton's Coal Shed, Gingerman and Salt Room, chef David Mothersill makes his debut as patron with this highly ambitious, tasting-menu-focused newcomer near the Pavilion, which is hailed by early guests for some "incredible food and wine" (in the evenings, from a six-course menu) and an "all-round great experience" – "hope they get the recognition they deserve". (Initial feedback this year was relatively thin on the ground, and we've rated it relatively conservatively – you could argue for full marks here!) / furnarestaurant.co.uk; furnarestaurant; Wed-Sat 11 pm.

WIVETON, NORFOLK 6-3

WIVETON BELL £66 2|3

BLAKENEY RD NR25 7TL 01263 740 1

Overlooking the green, this village pub-with-rooms was acquired by East Anglia's Chestnut Group in 2022. Some reports this year suggest that "things have started to slip" under the new regime, and that what "used to be a favourite" is "no longer quite as special as it once was", but "at its best, the food is excellent" still (and, despite the critiques, its locally sourced pub classics have so far retained their Bib Gourmand). / wivetonbell.co.uk; wivetonbell; Mon, Thu-Sat 9 pm, Sun 7.30 pm.

WOBURN, BUCKINGHAMSHIRE 3-2

BIRCH 3|3

20 NEWPORT RD MK17 9HX 01525 290295

"All food pubs should be like this!" – according to fans of this "perfect pit stop" on the outskirts of town. "You can't fault

Paris House, Woburn

e intent or enthusiasm of the service
d the food, if unadventurous, is very
cent". / birchwoburn.com; Sun-Thu 10 pm, Fri
Sat 10.30 pm.

ARIS HOUSE £125 545

OBURN PARK
K17 9QP 01525 290692

)f course it has a wonderful location… but
e food more than surpassed this". "In a
onderful parkland setting" (22 acres of the
uke of Bedford's Woburn Estate), this striking
ock-Tudor timber building (originally built in
ance in 1878) is nowadays the stage for chef/
tron Phil Fanning's highly ambitious cuisine.
he main event is a "memorable six-course
sting menu" for £99 per person, which on
actically all accounts delivers a "thoroughly
ofessional and delightful" experience: "each
urse is exceptional, with complex assemblies
often more than 10 components, but all
mplementing each other". "It is fortunate
u can have a two-hour walk amongst the
er after your meal!" / parishouse.co.uk;
rishousechef; Thu-Sat 8.30 pm, Sun 2 pm.

VOLLATON, NOTTINGHAMSHIRE 5–3D

HE COD'S CALLOPS £41 542

'0 BRAMCOTE LN
G8 2QP 0115 985 4107

bout as good as fish 'n' chips gets" – some
varieties of catch come 'baked, battered
naked' at John Molnar's award-winning
staurant and takeaway, now with five outposts
ross Nottingham and Birmingham; nor is the
nue, launched in 2011, just a mere chippie
her: alongside sashimi-grade tuna, the menu
fers the vegetarian 'Momma Bains' menu
samosas and curries, conceived by local
ichelin hero Sat Bains plus his ma (hence its
me). / codsscallops.com; Mon-Thu 9 pm, Fri &
t 9.30 pm.

VOLVERHAMPTON, WEST MIDLANDS 5–4B

ILASH £64 443

CHEAPSIDE WV1 1TU 01902 427762

Can't beat it" – there are "lots of Indian
staurants to choose from" in these parts "but
ake sure you book this one": Bangladesh-born
ef Sitab Khan's veteran destination (est. 1982), where "unusual dishes are all prepared to a great standard" and "your tastebuds will not be disappointed". / thebilash.co.uk; the.bilash; Wed-Sat 9 pm.

WOODHOUSE, WEST YORKSHIRE 5–1C

MANJIT'S KITCHEN £40 432

333 KIRKSTALL ROAD
LS4 2HD 07941 183132

"You don't miss the meat as the flavours are delicious" in Manjit Kaur's veggie cooking, available at her restaurant on Kirkstall Road and her stall at Kirkgate Market – which is "still a favourite for street food in Leeds". Manjit started out making food in her kitchen at home for delivery in 2010, slowly developing the business with her husband Michael Jameson over the next 10 years. / manjitskitchen.com; manjitskitchenuk; Wed-Sat 11 pm.

WOOFFERTON, SHROPSHIRE 5–4A

SALWAY ARMS £44 332

SY8 4AL 01584 711510

"A real find", with a "brilliant menu and smiley staff" – this seventeenth-century former coaching inn a short drive from Ludlow "takes you by surprise with the quality of its food". But there was also the odd 'off' report this year, and owner Sue Moss is looking to sell up so she can enjoy a well-earned retirement in her mid-70s. / thesalweyarms.co.uk; Mon-Sun 10 pm.

WOOTTON, OXFORDSHIRE 2–1D

THE KILLINGWORTH CASTLE 333

GLYMPTON ROAD
OX20 1EJ 01993 811 401

In 2021, after selling The Ebrington Arms near Chipping Campden, which they'd run for 15 years, Jim & Claire Alexander were able to fully focus their attentions on this seventeenth-century inn, handy for Blenheim Palace; chef Adam Brown (a Ramsay alum) oversees the locally sourced food, which inspired solid marks this year, if little in the way of commentary (other than to say that it's "good again at last" – perhaps a result of the Alexanders' renewed focus). / thekillingworthcastle.com; thekillingworthcastle; Tue-Sat 8.30 pm, Sun 4 pm.

WORTHING, WEST SUSSEX 3–4A

ANDALUCIA £46 323

60 FERRING STREET
BN12 5JP 01903 502605

"Good-value tapas" are served in a "lovely" setting at Luis and Miguel Quirosa's longstanding venue, opened by their parents 38 years ago and modernised when the brothers took over. Top Menu Tip – "don't miss the pork ribs!" / andaluciasussex.co.uk; andaluciasussex; Tue-Sat 11 pm, Sun 5 pm.

CRABSHACK £53 344

2 MARINE PARADE
BN11 3PN 01903 215070

"If you love fish you'll love CrabShack", say fans of this "rustic" family-owned spot "right on the seafront", with a "short and consistent menu". It's "a bit crowded, a bit noisy, but if you don't mind that, just relax and enjoy fish tacos, crab cakes, crispy squid and more – it's all gorgeous". / crabshackworthing.co.uk; crabshack_worthing; Tue, Wed, Sun 6 pm, Thu-Sat 10 pm.

WYKE REGIS, DORSET 2–4B

BILLY WINTERS BAR & DINER, CRAB HOUSE LTD £34 333

FERRY BRIDGE BOATYARD, PORTLAND ROAD DT4 9JZ 01305 774954

"Quirky diner, right on the beach" – "a simple, relaxed waterside venue, incorporating a plastic marquee overlooking Weymouth Bay". It "serves a wide range of delicious food: their amazing fish/shellfish tacos are a favourite" as are "fresh oysters from their own farm" (and there's also pizza and burgers). / billywinters.co.uk; billywintersweymouth; Wed-Sun 7 pm.

YORK, NORTH YORKSHIRE 5–1D

AMBIENTE £42 322

31 FOSSGATE YO1 9TA 01904 638 252

This "lively" and well commented-on venue with a "good choice of tapas" celebrates its 10th anniversary this year, now with two more branches in York as well as outposts in Leeds and Hull. A meal here is a "good opportunity to explore sherries, with various flights available". / ambiente-tapas.co.uk; ambientetapas; Mon-Sun 10 pm.

ARRAS £82 533

THE OLD COACH HOUSE, PEASHOLME GREEN YO1 7PW 01904 633 737

"Fabulous food at a reasonable price" is endorsed by every report on Adam & Lovaine Humphrey's stylish city-centre venue – and the "surprise extras" including "high-quality canapés, amuse bouches and the English cheese takes on worldwide alternatives" all go down a treat. Adam is originally from Yorkshire, but the couple ran restaurants in Australia for almost 20 years – more conservative diners may feel "the startling white decor would fit better in trendy Sydney" but most reports give it a strong thumbs up. / arrasrestaurant.co.uk; arras_york; Wed-Sat 9.30 pm.

BETTYS £43 3 4 5

6-8 ST HELEN'S SQUARE YO1 8QP 01904 659142

"An institution in York, and a 'must' on any visit to the city" – this central branch of Bettys dates from 1936, with an interior inspired by the ocean liner Queen Mary, and its Belmont Room – named after Frederick Belmont, the Swiss confectioner who founded the Harrogate original in 1919 – is "a real treat". "There's no place like Bettys if you want to enjoy a classic afternoon tea with as many of the trimmings as you want" – "the quality of the food offering is never in doubt but what is exceptional is the professionalism and efficiency of the staff". / bettys.co.uk; bettys; Sun-Thu 5.30 pm, Fri 6 pm, Sat 7 pm.

THE BLUE BARBAKAN £57 3 3 2

34 FOSSGATE YO1 9TA 01904 672 474

An "excellent" Polish restaurant (also drawing on wider European influences) that is "doing well in its enlarged setting" in Fossgate – having swapped its former Walmgate home for the old premises of the Blue Bicycle in 2020 (and having added blue to its name in tribute). Top Tip – "go hungry as the portions (of pierogi, stews, etc.) are huge, hearty and tasty", and you may then be "too full to try the excellent-looking selection of cakes". / bluebarbakan.co.uk; bluebarbakanyork; Sun & Mon 9 pm, Wed-Sat 10 pm.

THE BOW ROOM RESTAURANT, GRAYS COURT £160 4 4 4

GRAYS COURT HOTEL, CHAPTER HOUSE STREET YO1 7JH 01904 612613

In summer 2023, Ian Doyle (an alum' of the legendary Noma, who gained a star at previous haunt the Cliff House Hotel, in Waterford, Ireland) stepped in to fill the shoes of Adam Jackson, who has now moved to the Rattle Owl in Micklegate. Early reports suggest that his tasting menu is "just fabulous" ("exceeded our expectations") and "what a wonderful setting" the restaurant has in this "amazing ancient property" – York's oldest inhabited house – situated near York Minster. Top Tips – "make sure to have a stroll around the garden before enjoying the top-notch cuisine" and "also book a room so you don't have to rush home". / thebowroomyork.com; TheBowRoomYork; Tue-Thu 10.30 pm, Fri & Sat 11.30 pm.

CHOPPING BLOCK 3 3 2

25 WALMGATE YO1 9TX 01904 629222

"In a charming and historic building" dating from the 17th century, the Hjort family's "really pleasant and relaxing" venue was reborn some years ago in this guise, which reprises the ethos of their original York venue, Melton's. The "regularly changing menu" offers top Gallic fare, with fishy options recommended this year as an "excellent choice" on a visit. / walmgateale.co.uk; choppingblockyork; Wed-Sun 11 pm.

CRESCI £16 3 4 3

20 PICCADILLY YO1 9NU 01904 639395

"Top pizzas" make Armando Imparato and Berardo Caggiano's relaxed three-year-old, near Shambles Market, "worth traveling for" by all accounts; impressively, just five months after opening, it received the much-coveted approval of the Association Verace Pizza Napoletana, becoming just the eighth UK pizzeria to achieve the feat. "Great service too". / crescipizzeria.com; crescipizzeria; Mon-Sun 10 pm.

FISH AND FOREST £67 4 3 3

110 MICKLEGATE YO1 6JX 01904 220587

"The menu is determined daily by catch", and the result is "a wide and varied choice" of "fresh and excellent fish" at this popular bistro, near the city walls. Game and foraged food also feature in their menu repertoire, but inspire less feedback in our annual diners' poll. / fishandforestrestaurant.com; fishandforest_york; Wed-Sat 9 pm.

MANNION & CO £49 3 2 2

1 BLAKE ST YO1 8QJ 01904 631030

This deli-café in a former grocer's shop is "worth the queue" for a coffee and a treat, while the "surf 'n' turf lunch is also very good". Success has led to spinoffs in Helmsley and, last year, in Easingwold (where it's called OPC after the old police cells on the premises). / mannionandco.co.uk; mannionsofyork; Mon-Sat 5 pm, Sun 4.30 pm.

MELTON'S £93 4 4 4

7 SCARCROFT RD YO23 1ND 01904 634 341

"A high-end restaurant without all the flummery and fuss that is often associated with good restaurants" has cemented the longstanding appeal of this modern British bistro (est. 1990) from the Roux-trained Michael Hjort (director of York Food Festival) and FOH wife Lucy. "Melton's has long been a mainstay of the York food scene and long may it continue"! / meltonsrestaurant.co.uk; meltons_restaurant; Wed-Sat, Tue 9.30 pm.

LOS MOROS £61 3 3 3

15-17 GRAPE LANE YO1 7HU 01904 636834

Born as a Shambles Market stall in 2015 (the stall is still going strong), Tarik Abdeladim's venture branched out into this bricks-and-mortar incarnation three years later. It wins praise for "very enjoyable North African food" with "plenty of interesting sharing options" and Brew York's branded Los Moros pale ale and lager to wash it down. Top Tip – "sit downstairs if you can". / losmorosyork.co.uk; losmorosyork; Fri & Sat 9.30 pm, Tue-Thu 9 pm.

THE PIG & PASTRY £86 4 4

35 BISHOPTHORPE ROAD YO23 1NA 01904 675115

"A great place for a very reasonably priced brunch or lunch with Interesting home bakes that you have to get there early to get your hands on!" – this top neighbourhood café (est. 2008) is again well recommended thanks to its simple but high-quality fare, which includes yummy sarnies and breakfast dishes. / thepigandpastry.com; thepigandpastry_2.0; Tue-Sat 3 am.

ROOTS £179 4 3

68 MARYGATE YO30 7BH NO TEL

"Combining skill and originality in equal measure – with a menu that's is unexpected and exciting"; Tommy Banks's converted pub in the city centre is applauded in all reports as a "fabulous" destination: "knowledgeable service coupled with the beautiful presentation and amazingly flavoured food makes for a truly unforgettable meal". However, even those who acknowledge that it's "excellent" still often feel that "bills are simply excessive" ("we love Tommy Banks, but won't be returning"). The overall verdict? "Excellent… but at a price". / rootsyork.com; rootsyork; Wed-Sat 8 pm

SKOSH £63 4 4

98 MICKLEGATE YO1 6JX 01904 63484

"Clever small plate dishes with exciting flavour combinations" have established Neil Bentinck's city-centre destination as one of York's most popular in recent years. "Some seats are up at a counter watching the chefs at work, whilst the remainder still have the atmosphere of being in a busy kitchen restaurant". "Getting a table can sometimes feel like trying to get tickets for Glastonbury, but it is really worth it for amazing British-Japanese fusion food that's so inventive but not too expensive, with new dishes being created all the time". "Relaxing, with a buzz of warmth and efficiency": "It leaves you with a deeper love of humanity and a sense of what a great local can give!". "Looking forward to the knock through to next door" – planning permission was finally granted in early 2023 and work is due to be complete by the end of the year. / skoshyork.co.uk; skoshyork; Wed-Sat 10 pm.

STAR INN THE CITY £71 2 2

LENDAL ENGINE HOUSE, MUSEUM STREET YO1 7DR 01904 619208

In a "great location" by the River Ouse, this characterful gastropub was opened 11 years ago by chef Andrew Pern as a city counterpart to his acclaimed Star Inn at Harome in North Yorkshire. "The cuisine still fails to meet expectations", though – a recurrent theme, with reporters describing it as "good but not spectacular" or at best "better than expected given the poor reviews". / starinnthecity.co.uk;

estarinnthecityyork; Mon-Thu 11 pm, Fri & Sat idnight, Sun 10 pm.

ABANCO BY .MBIENTE £77 342

)-63 WALMGATE O1 9TY 01904 809565

his superior Walmgate venture draws its ame from Southern Spanish tabanco bars, here diners eat hot and cold tapas washed own with sherry or vermouth in an informal mosphere. There are several appealing spots which to dine, with the brick-lined patio perfect suntrap. / tabancobyambiente.co.uk; bancobyambiente; Mon-Sun 9.30 pm.

HE WHIPPET INN £77 333

5 NORTH ST YO1 6JD 01904 500660

Hidden away on one of York's least-hotogenic streets" (their words), and spread cross "several cosy rooms", this decade-'d establishment revolves around "very sty steaks" featuring flavoursome and hical beef from ex-dairy cows sourced in ngland, Galicia and France. The owners so run The Stone Trough Inn in Kirkham bbey. / thewhippetinn.co.uk; thewhippetinn; Ion-Thu 11 pm, Fri & Sat midnight, Sun 10 pm.

'HE YORK MINISTER EFECTORY ESTAURANT 334

EANGATE YO1 7JA 01904 307399

Unbeatable views of the Minster from the rrace" set the scene at this new April 2023 ndmark, which has a "fabulous location next York Minster" and which was opened with reat fanfare shortly before his coronation by ing Charles III and Queen Camilla. Despite s relatively recent opening, it instantly inspired ery encouraging feedback in our annual iners' poll – "an amazing new restaurant by cal restaurateur Andrew Pern with a simple enu on the 150-seat terrace and fuller menu side". There's "a very characterful interior in n old school" (the original use for this space, uilt in 1833) and – by the standards of touristy cations – promising reports of "excellent od": "raw dishes and delicate starters followed p by interesting taste combinations", with a eavy emphasis on local sourcing. / Wed-Sat 1 pm, Sun 6 pm.

The Terrace, Montagu Arms Hotel, Beaulieu

Aizle, Edinburgh

Holm, South Petherton

The Kitchin, Edinburgh

Pale Hall Hotel Restaurant, Bala

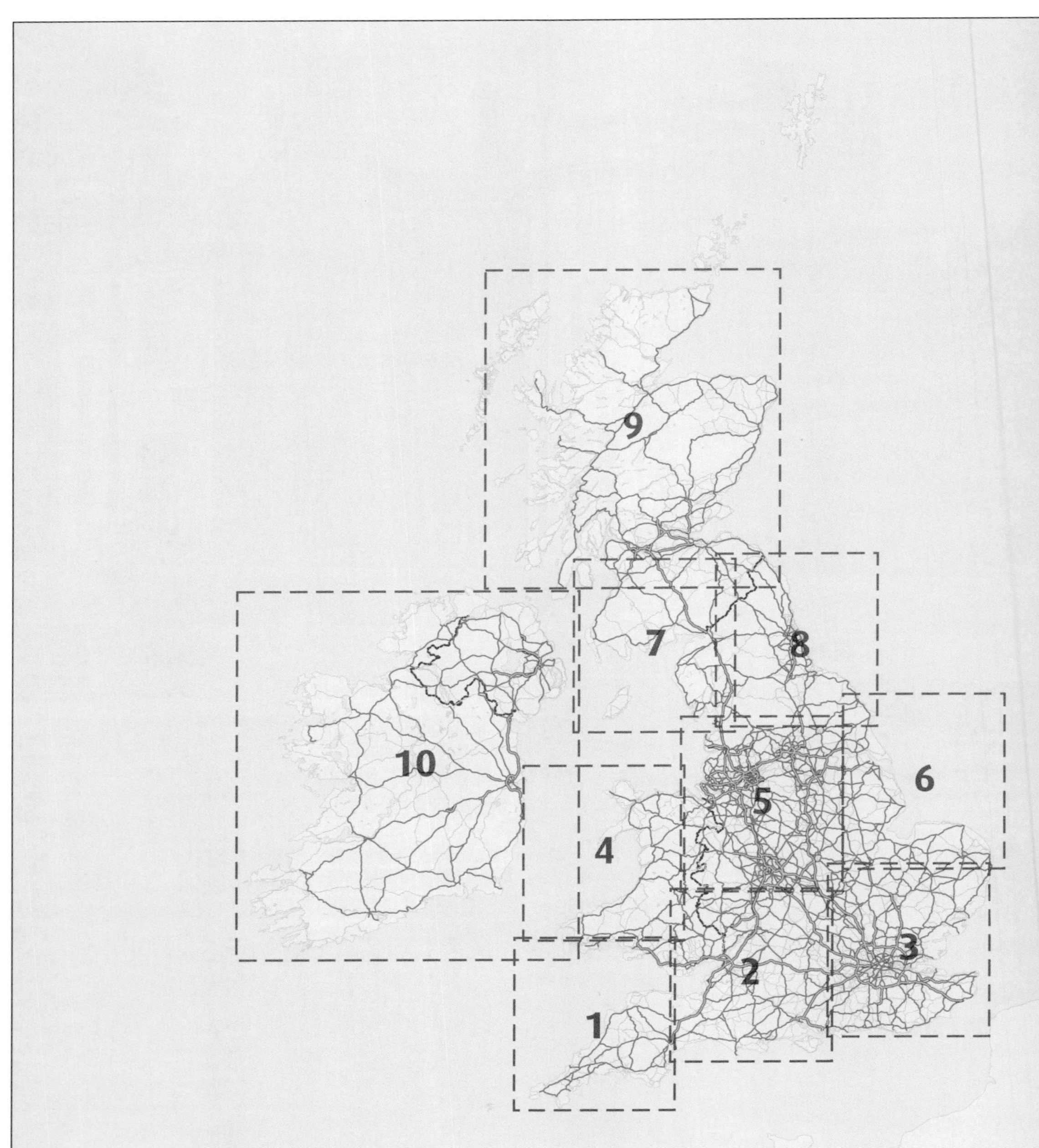
9
10
7
8
6
5
4
3
2
1

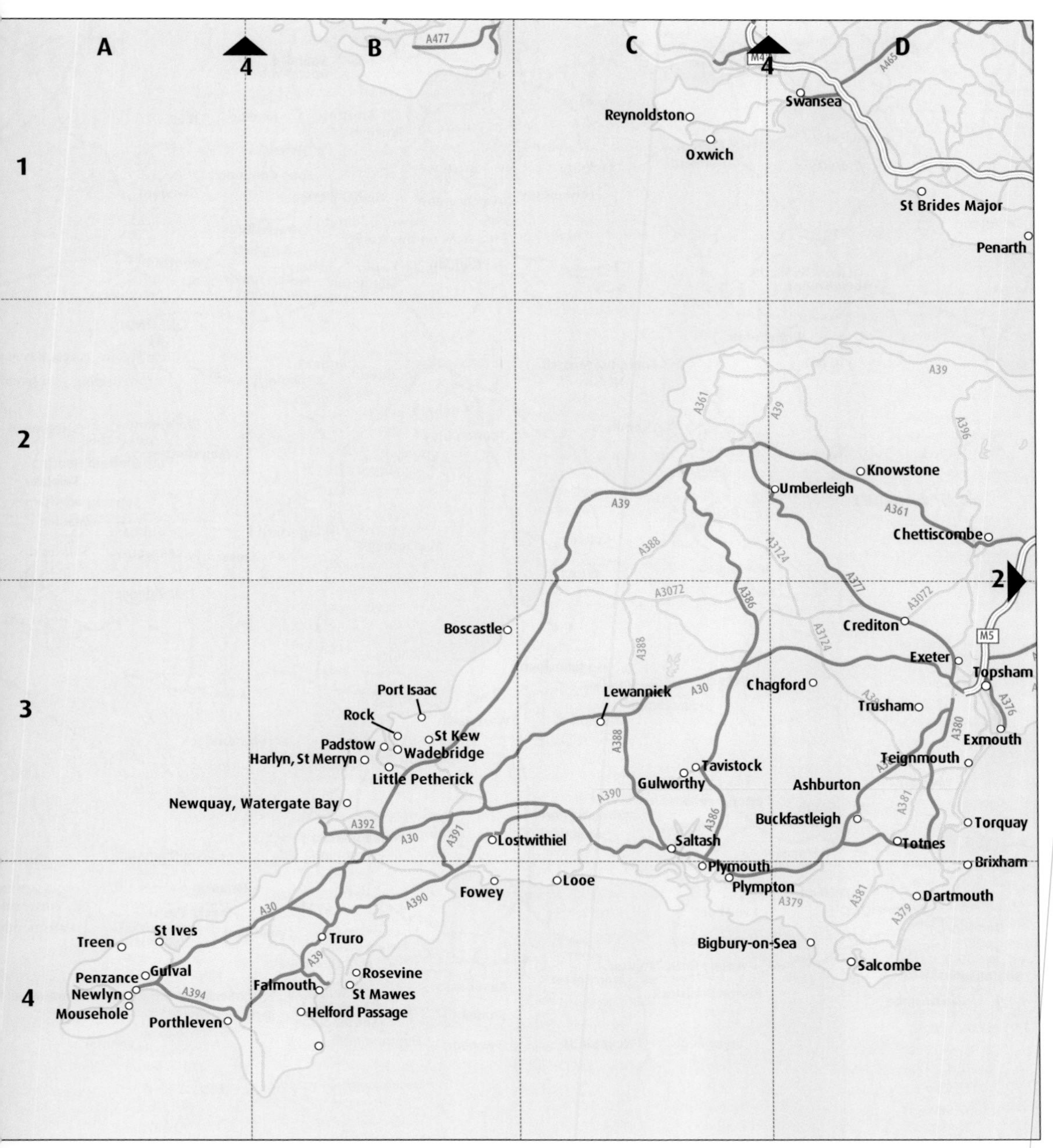

A
B
C
D
1
2
3
4
A477
M4
A465
Swansea
Reynoldston
Oxwich
St Brides Major
Penarth
A39
A361
A396
Knowstone
Umberleigh
Chettiscombe
A388
A3124
A377
A3072
A386
Boscastle
Crediton
M5
Exeter
Topsham
Chagford
Lewannick
A30
Trusham
A376
A380
Exmouth
Port Isaac
Rock
St Kew
Padstow
Wadebridge
Harlyn, St Merryn
Little Petherick
Tavistock
Gulworthy
Teignmouth
Ashburton
A381
A390
Newquay, Watergate Bay
A392
A391
Lostwithiel
Saltash
Buckfastleigh
Torquay
Totnes
Plymouth
Brixham
Fowey
Looe
Plympton
A379
Dartmouth
Treen
St Ives
Truro
Bigbury-on-Sea
Salcombe
Penzance
Gulval
Rosevine
Newlyn
A394
Falmouth
St Mawes
Mousehole
Porthleven
Helford Passage

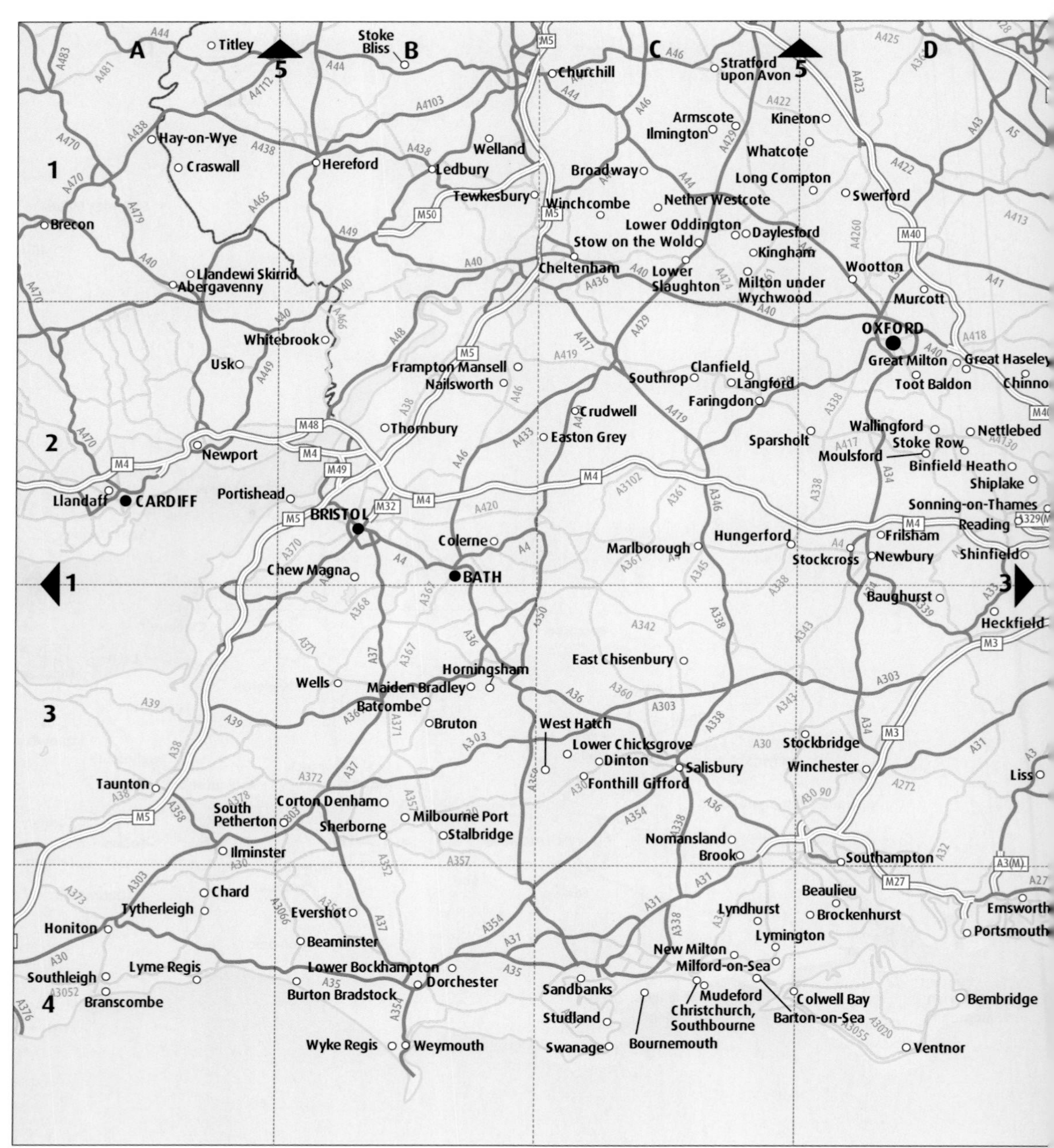
A
B
C
D
1
2
3
4
5
Titley
Stoke Bliss
Churchill
Stratford upon Avon
Armscote
Ilmington
Kineton
Whatcote
Hay-on-Wye
Craswall
Hereford
Welland
Ledbury
Tewkesbury
Broadway
Long Compton
Swerford
Winchcombe
Nether Westcote
Lower Oddington
Daylesford
Brecon
Stow on the Wold
Kingham
Llandewi Skirrid
Abergavenny
Cheltenham
Lower Slaughton
Milton under Wychwood
Wootton
Murcott
OXFORD
Whitebrook
Usk
Frampton Mansell
Nailsworth
Clanfield
Southrop
Langford
Faringdon
Great Milton
Great Haseley
Toot Baldon
Chinnor
Crudwell
Thornbury
Easton Grey
Wallingford
Nettlebed
Sparsholt
Stoke Row
Moulsford
Binfield Heath
Shiplake
Newport
Portishead
Llandaff
CARDIFF
BRISTOL
Sonning-on-Thames
Reading
Hungerford
Frilsham
Colerne
Marlborough
Stockcross
Newbury
Shinfield
Chew Magna
BATH
Baughurst
Heckfield
East Chisenbury
Horningsham
Wells
Maiden Bradley
Batcombe
Bruton
West Hatch
Lower Chicksgrove
Dinton
Stockbridge
Salisbury
Winchester
Taunton
Fonthill Gifford
Liss
South Petherton
Corton Denham
Milbourne Port
Sherborne
Stalbridge
Nomansland
Ilminster
Brook
Southampton
Chard
Beaulieu
Tytherleigh
Evershot
Lyndhurst
Brockenhurst
Emsworth
Honiton
Portsmouth
Beaminster
Lymington
New Milton
Milford-on-Sea
Lyme Regis
Lower Bockhampton
Southleigh
Dorchester
Sandbanks
Mudeford
Colwell Bay
Bembridge
Branscombe
Burton Bradstock
Christchurch, Southbourne
Barton-on-Sea
Studland
Bournemouth
Wyke Regis
Weymouth
Swanage
Ventnor

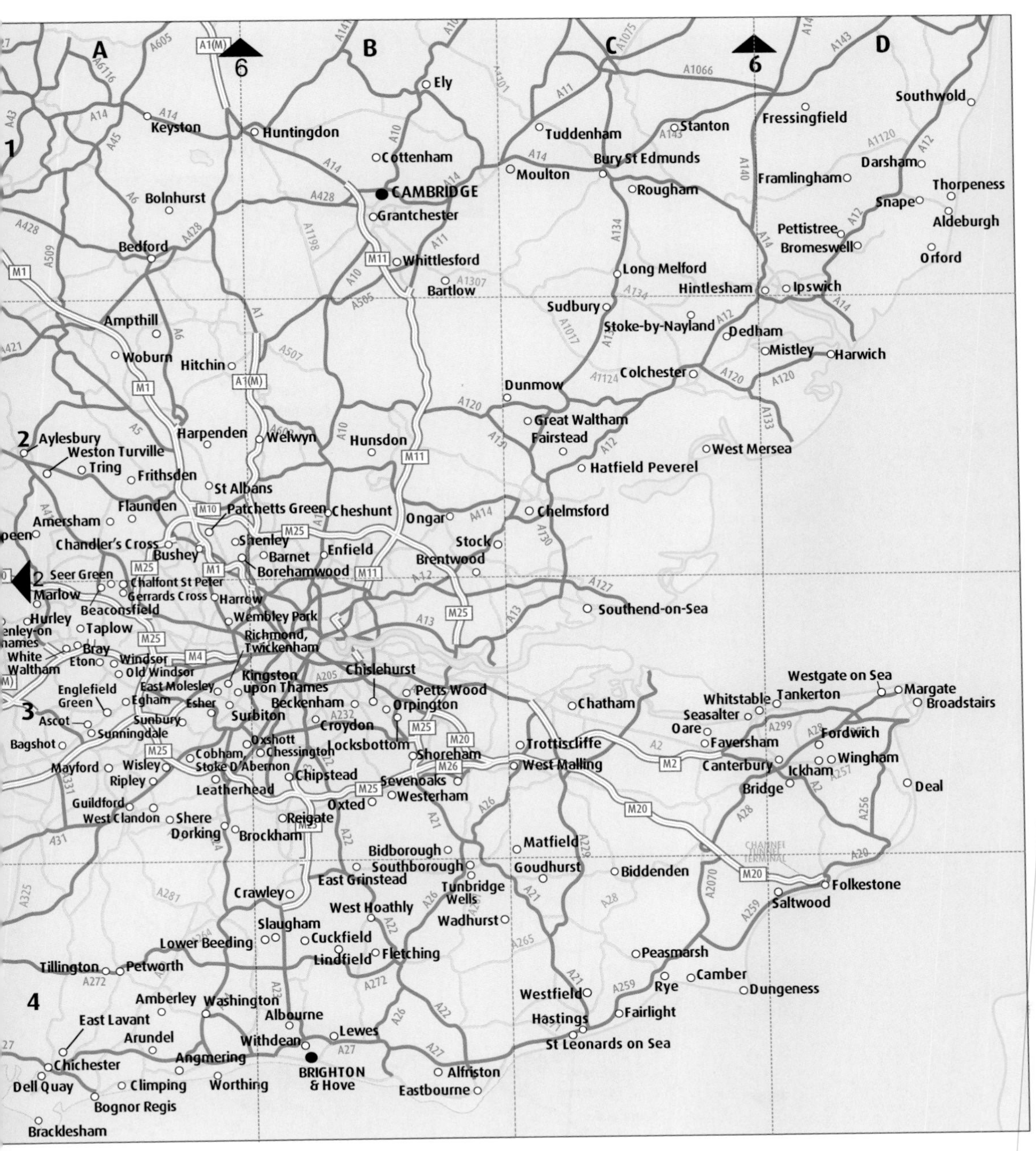
A
B
C
D
1
2
3
4
6
Ely
Southwold
Keyston
Huntingdon
Tuddenham
Stanton
Fressingfield
Cottenham
Moulton
Bury St Edmunds
Framlingham
Darsham
CAMBRIDGE
Rougham
Thorpeness
Snape
Bolnhurst
Grantchester
Pettistree
Aldeburgh
Bedford
Bromeswell
Whittlesford
Orford
Bartlow
Long Melford
Hintlesham
Ipswich
Ampthill
Sudbury
Stoke-by-Nayland
Dedham
Woburn
Hitchin
Mistley
Harwich
Colchester
Dunmow
Great Waltham
Harpenden
Fairstead
Aylesbury
Welwyn
Hunsdon
West Mersea
Weston Turville
Tring
Hatfield Peverel
Frithsden
St Albans
Flaunden
Patchetts Green
Cheshunt
Chelmsford
Amersham
Ongar
Chandler's Cross
Shenley
Stock
Bushey
Barnet
Enfield
Brentwood
Seer Green
Borehamwood
Chalfont St Peter
Marlow
Gerrards Cross
Harrow
Southend-on-Sea
Beaconsfield
Hurley
Wembley Park
Taplow
Richmond, Twickenham
Bray
White Waltham
Windsor
Eton
Old Windsor
Kingston upon Thames
Chislehurst
Westgate on Sea
Englefield Green
East Molesley
Petts Wood
Margate
Egham
Esher
Beckenham
Tankerton
Whitstable
Broadstairs
Orpington
Chatham
Seasalter
Ascot
Sunbury
Surbiton
Sunningdale
Croydon
Oare
Fordwich
Bagshot
Oxshott
Faversham
Chessington
Locksbottom
Trottiscliffe
Cobham, Stoke D'Abernon
Shoreham
Wingham
Mayford
Wisley
West Malling
Canterbury
Ripley
Chipstead
Sevenoaks
Ickham
Leatherhead
Deal
Westerham
Bridge
Guildford
Oxted
West Clandon
Shere
Reigate
Dorking
Brockham
Matfield
Bidborough
Goudhurst
Southborough
Biddenden
East Grinstead
Tunbridge Wells
Folkestone
Crawley
Saltwood
West Hoathly
Wadhurst
Slaugham
Lower Beeding
Cuckfield
Peasmarsh
Lindfield
Fletching
Tillington
Petworth
Camber
Rye
Dungeness
Westfield
Amberley
Washington
Fairlight
East Lavant
Albourne
Hastings
Arundel
Lewes
Withdean
St Leonards on Sea
Angmering
Chichester
BRIGHTON & Hove
Alfriston
Dell Quay
Climping
Worthing
Eastbourne
Bognor Regis
Bracklesham
CHANNEL TUNNEL TERMINAL
A1(M)
M1
M10
M11
M25
M4
M2
M20
M26
M23
A14
A428
A1066
A12
A120
A13
A127
A21
A22
A26
A27
A28
A259
A272
A281
A325
A331
A31
A24
A23
A2070
A256
A257
A20
A2
A299
A229
A228
A264
A265
A232
A205
A414
A130
A131
A133
A1124
A1017
A134
A143
A140
A1120
A1307
A505
A10
A11
A1198
A507
A602
A5
A6
A509
A41
A45
A43
A6116
A605
A1101
A1075
A1
A421
A4

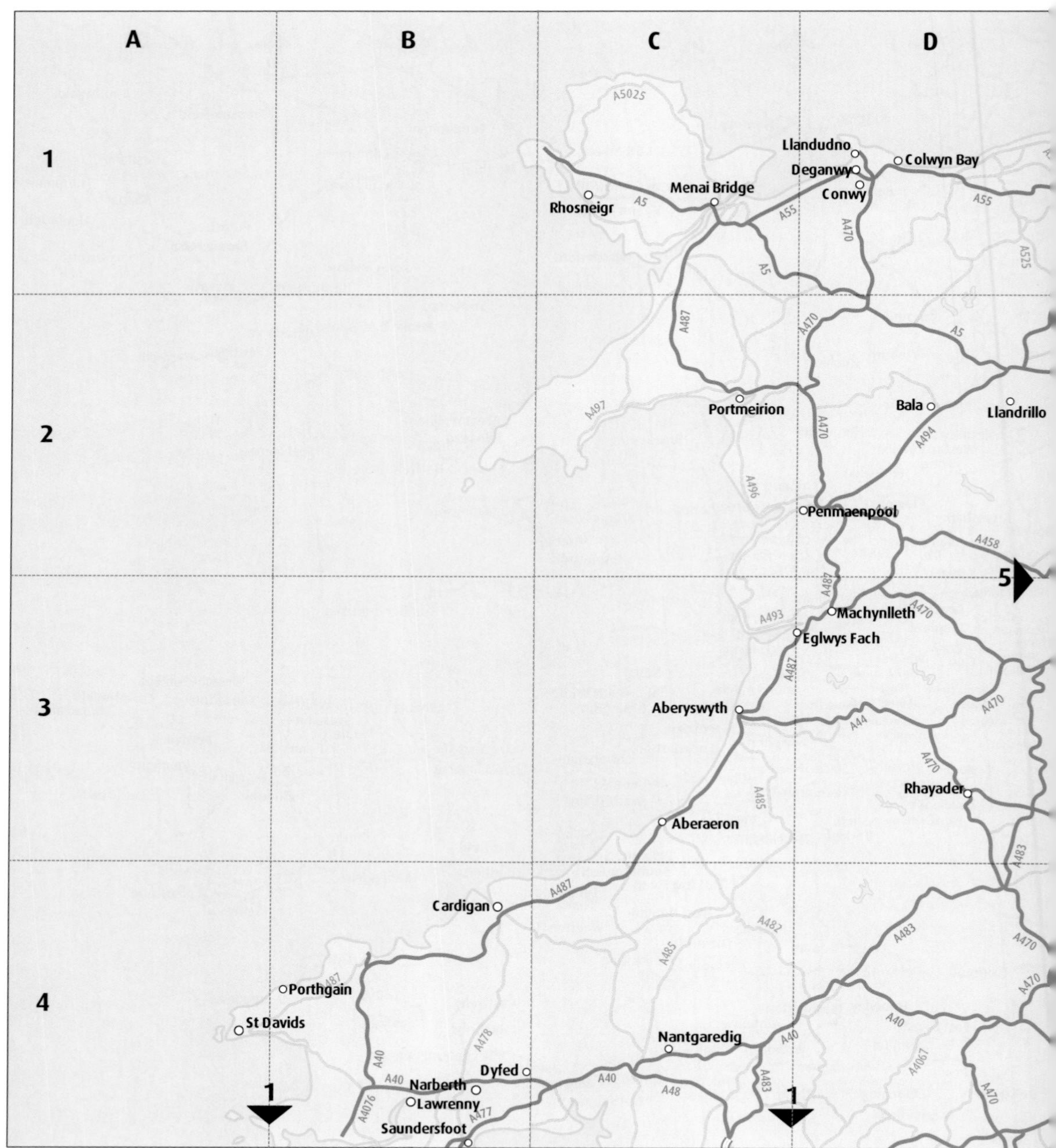
A
B
C
D
1
2
3
4
Llandudno
Colwyn Bay
Deganwy
Conwy
Menai Bridge
Rhosneigr
Portmeirion
Bala
Llandrillo
Penmaenpool
Machynlleth
Eglwys Fach
Aberystwyth
Rhayader
Aberaeron
Cardigan
Porthgain
St Davids
Nantgaredig
Dyfed
Narberth
Lawrenny
Saundersfoot
5
1
1
A5025
A5
A55
A470
A525
A487
A497
A496
A494
A458
A493
A44
A485
A483
A482
A40
A4067
A478
A4076
A477
A48

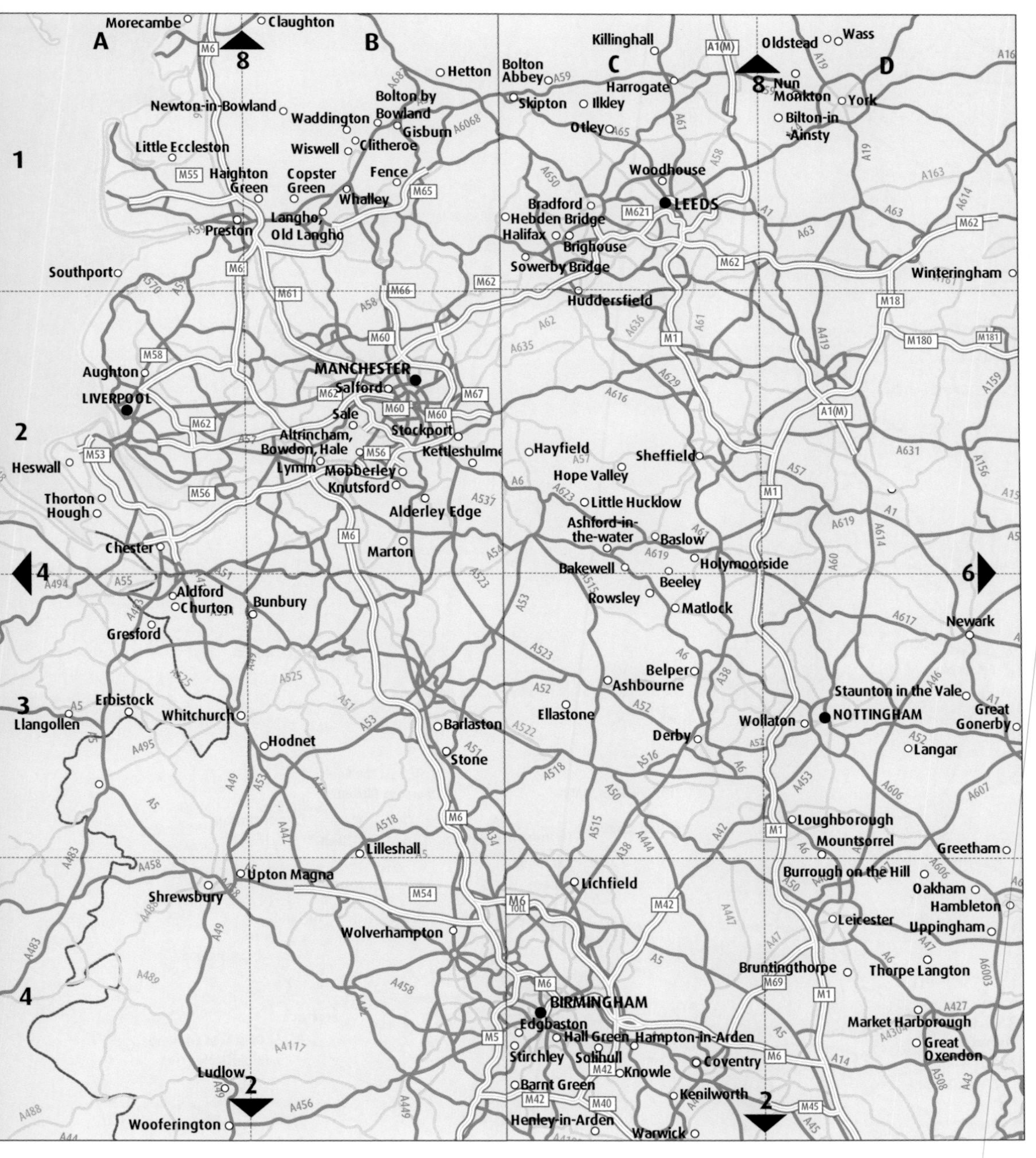
Morecambe
Claughton
A
8
B
Hetton
Bolton Abbey
Killinghall
C
Oldstead
Wass
D
Harrogate
Nun Monkton
York
Newton-in-Bowland
Waddington
Bolton by Bowland
Gisburn
Skipton
Ilkley
Bilton-in-Ainsty
Little Eccleston
Wiswell
Clitheroe
Otley
1
Haighton Green
Copster Green
Fence
Whalley
Woodhouse
Bradford
LEEDS
Hebden Bridge
Halifax
Brighouse
Preston
Langho, Old Langho
Sowerby Bridge
Southport
Winteringham
Huddersfield
Aughton
MANCHESTER
Salford
LIVERPOOL
Sale
Stockport
2
Altrincham, Bowdon, Hale
Kettleshulme
Hayfield
Sheffield
Heswall
Lymm
Mobberley
Knutsford
Hope Valley
Thorton Hough
Little Hucklow
Alderley Edge
Ashford-in-the-water
Baslow
Chester
Marton
Holymoorside
4
Bakewell
Beeley
6
Aldford
Churton
Bunbury
Rowsley
Matlock
Gresford
Newark
Belper
Ashbourne
Staunton in the Vale
3
Erbistock
Ellastone
Great Gonerby
Llangollen
Whitchurch
Barlaston
Wollaton
NOTTINGHAM
Hodnet
Derby
Langar
Stone
Loughborough
Mountsorrel
Greetham
Lilleshall
Burrough on the Hill
Upton Magna
Lichfield
Oakham
Shrewsbury
Hambleton
Leicester
Uppingham
Wolverhampton
Bruntingthorpe
Thorpe Langton
4
BIRMINGHAM
Market Harborough
Edgbaston
Hall Green
Hampton-in-Arden
Great Oxendon
Stirchley
Solihull
Knowle
Coventry
Ludlow
Barnt Green
Kenilworth
Wooferington
Henley-in-Arden
Warwick

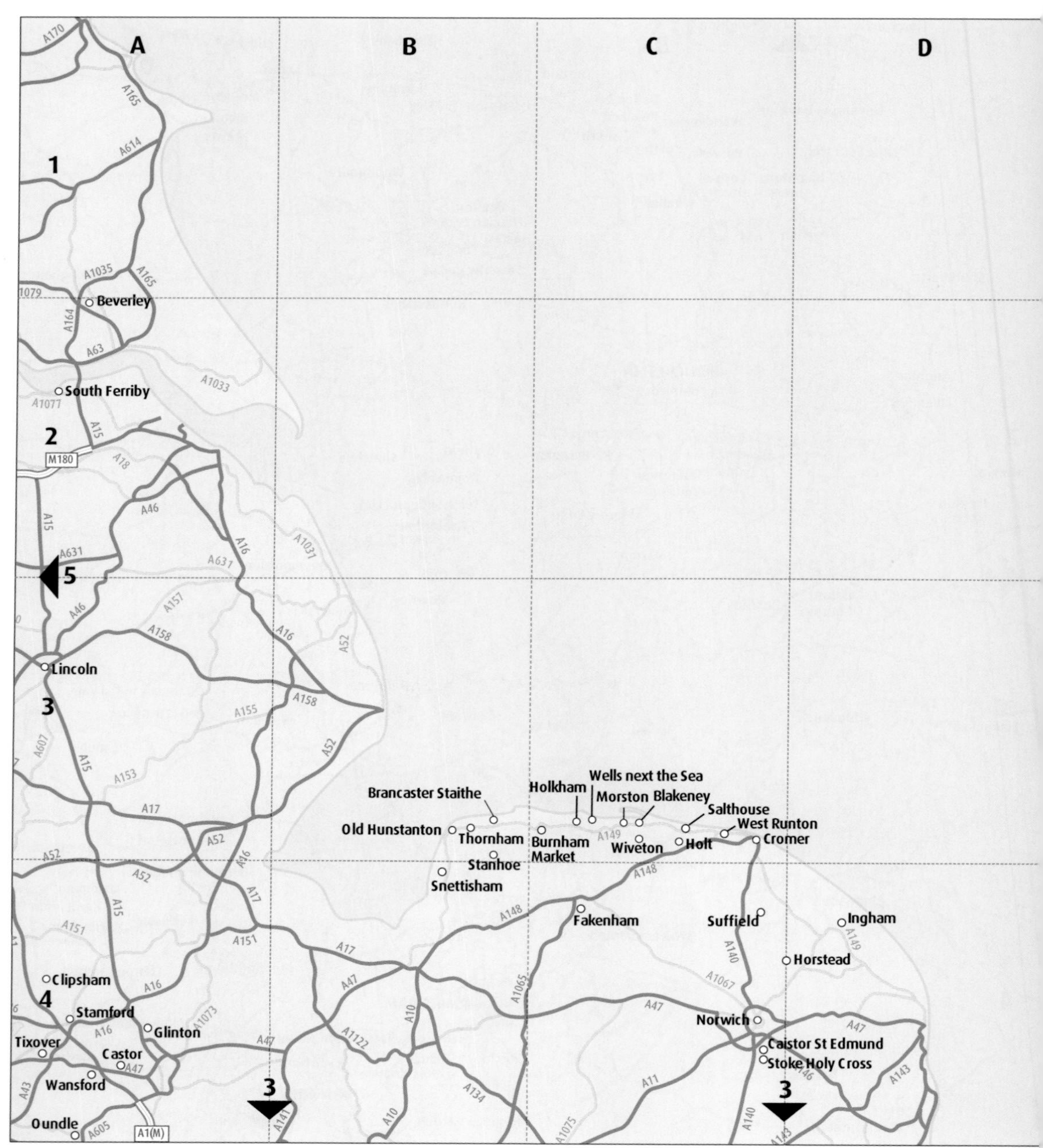
A
B
C
D
1
2
3
4
5
3
3
Beverley
South Ferriby
Lincoln
Clipsham
Stamford
Glinton
Tixover
Castor
Wansford
Oundle
Brancaster Staithe
Holkham
Wells next the Sea
Morston
Blakeney
Salthouse
West Runton
Cromer
Old Hunstanton
Thornham
Burnham Market
Wiveton
Holt
Stanhoe
Snettisham
Fakenham
Suffield
Ingham
Horstead
Norwich
Caistor St Edmund
Stoke Holy Cross
A170
A165
A614
A1035
A165
A164
A63
A1033
A1077
A15
M180
A18
A46
A15
A631
A16
A1031
A631
A46
A157
A158
A16
A52
A158
A155
A607
A15
A52
A153
A17
A52
A52
A52
A16
A17
A15
A151
A151
A17
A16
A47
A1073
A16
A47
A43
A605
A1(M)
A141
A1122
A10
A10
A134
A1065
A148
A148
A149
A47
A11
A1075
A140
A1067
A140
A149
A47
A143
A143

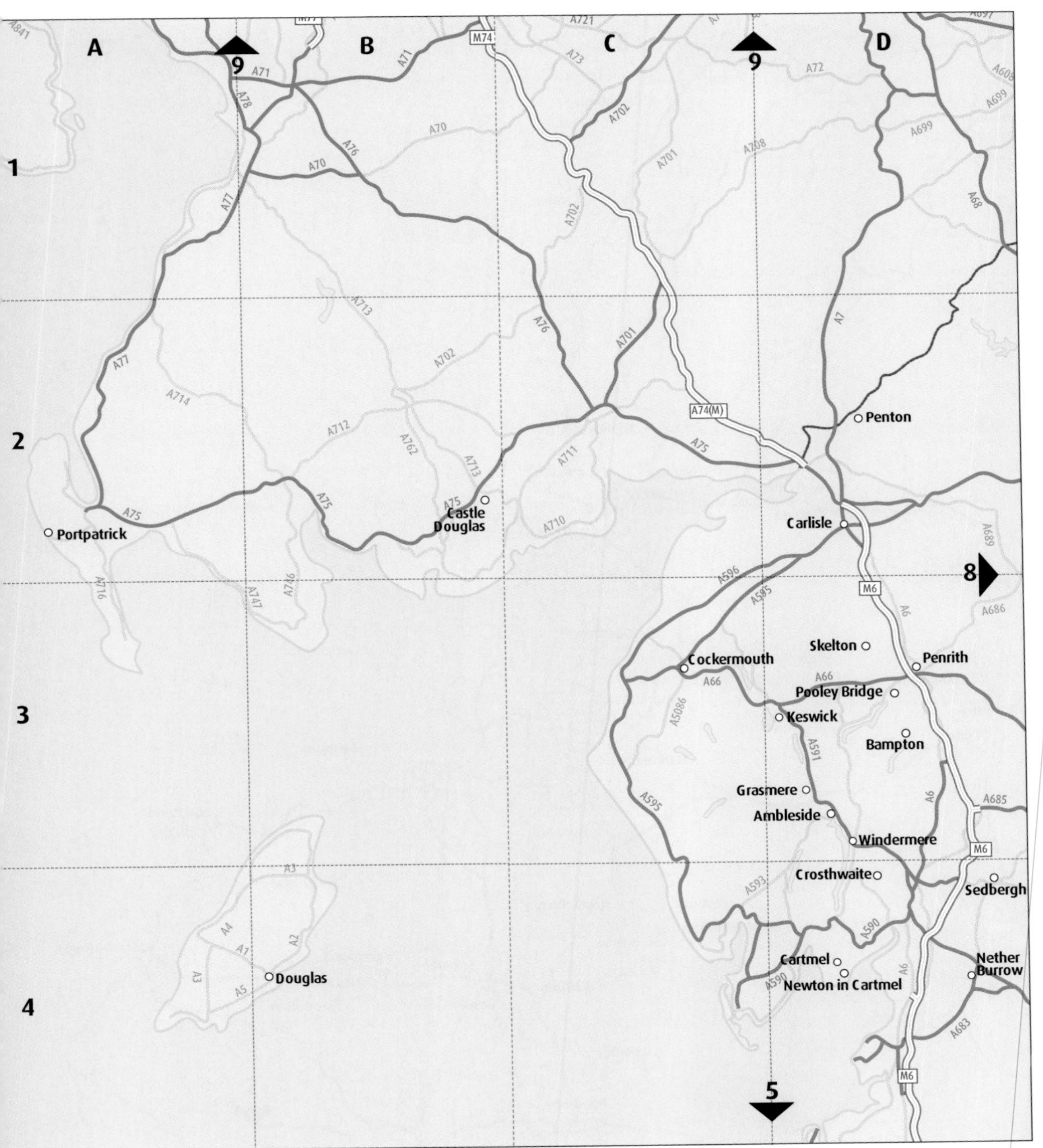
A
B
C
D
1
2
3
4
9
9
8
5
Penton
Carlisle
Portpatrick
Castle Douglas
Skelton
Penrith
Cockermouth
Pooley Bridge
Keswick
Bampton
Grasmere
Ambleside
Windermere
Crosthwaite
Sedbergh
Cartmel
Newton in Cartmel
Nether Burrow
Douglas
M74
A74(M)
M6

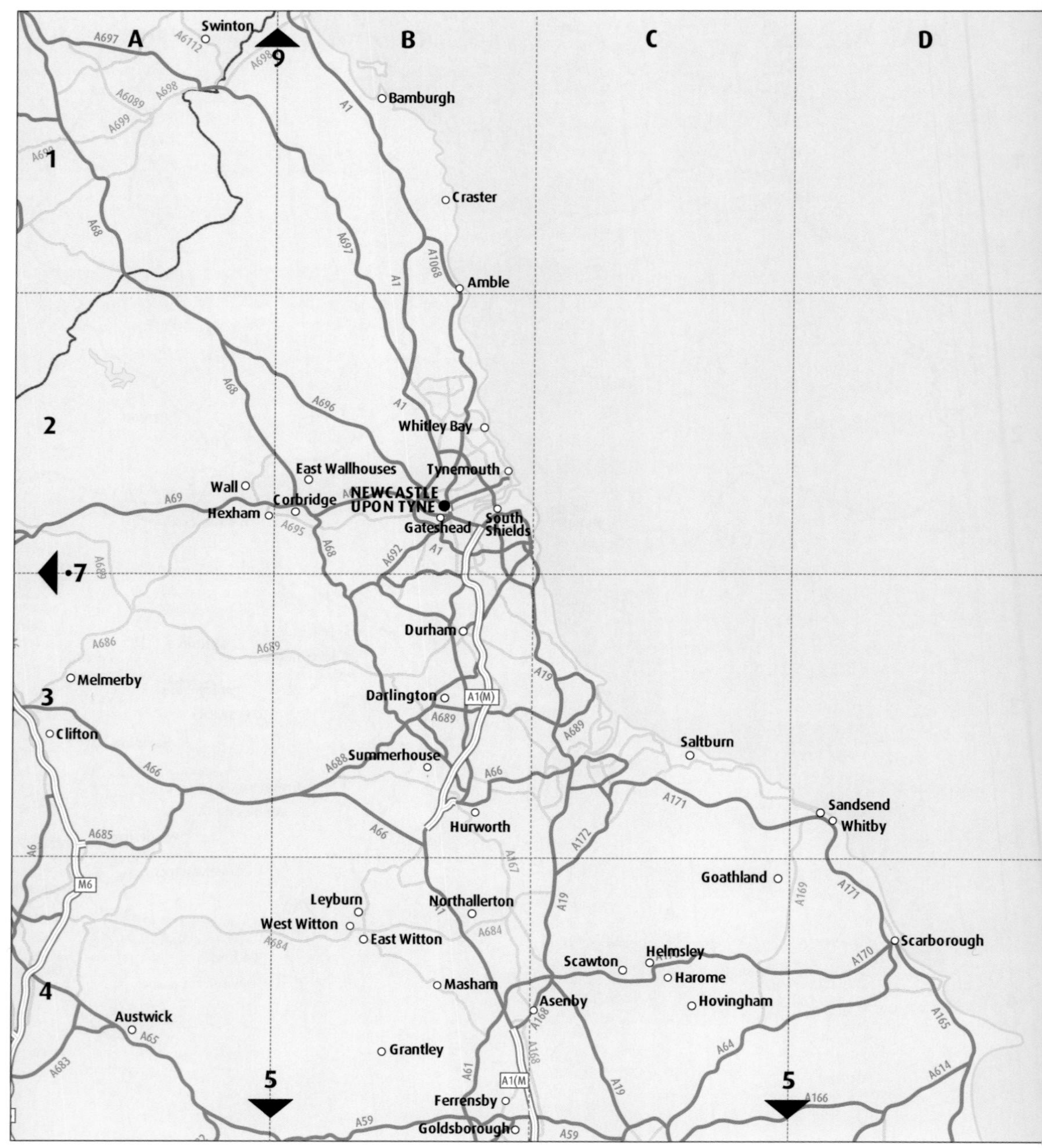
A
B
C
D
1
2
3
4
9
7
5
5
Swinton
Bamburgh
Craster
Amble
Whitley Bay
East Wallhouses
Tynemouth
Wall
NEWCASTLE UPON TYNE
Corbridge
Hexham
Gateshead
South Shields
Durham
Melmerby
Darlington
Clifton
Saltburn
Summerhouse
Hurworth
Sandsend
Whitby
Goathland
Leyburn
Northallerton
West Witton
East Witton
Scarborough
Scawton
Helmsley
Harome
Masham
Asenby
Hovingham
Austwick
Grantley
Ferrensby
Goldsborough
A697
A6112
A698
A6089
A699
A68
A1
A697
A1068
A696
A69
A695
A692
A689
A686
A19
A1(M)
A688
A66
A685
M6
A171
A172
A167
A169
A684
A170
A165
A64
A614
A61
A168
A683
A65
A59
A166

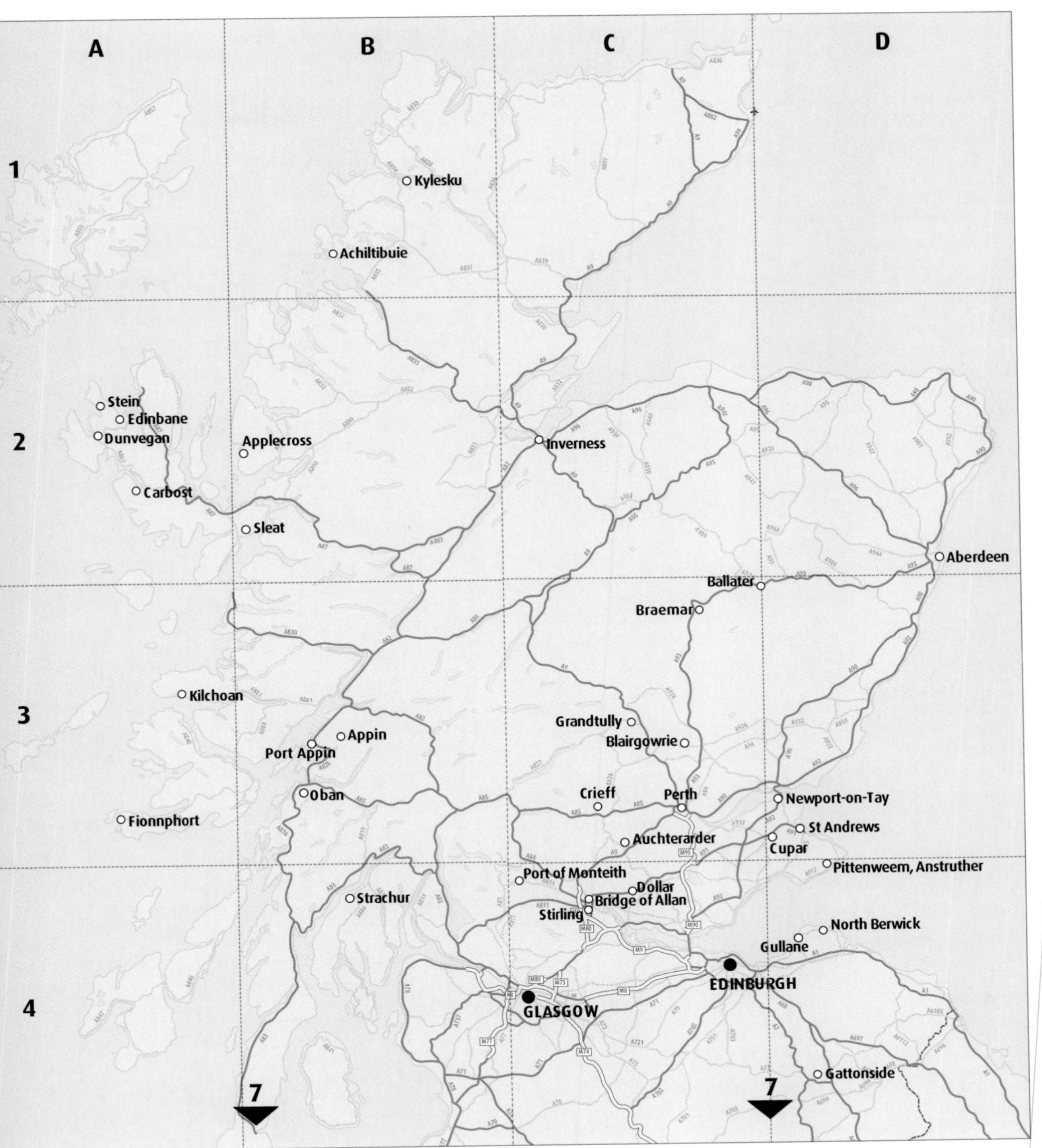
A
B
C
D
1
2
3
4
Kylesku
Achiltibuie
Stein
Edinbane
Dunvegan
Applecross
Carbost
Sleat
Inverness
Aberdeen
Ballater
Braemar
Kilchoan
Appin
Port Appin
Oban
Fionnphort
Grandtully
Blairgowrie
Crieff
Perth
Newport-on-Tay
St Andrews
Cupar
Auchterarder
Pittenweem, Anstruther
Port of Monteith
Dollar
Bridge of Allan
Stirling
Strachur
North Berwick
Gullane
EDINBURGH
GLASGOW
Gattonside
7
7

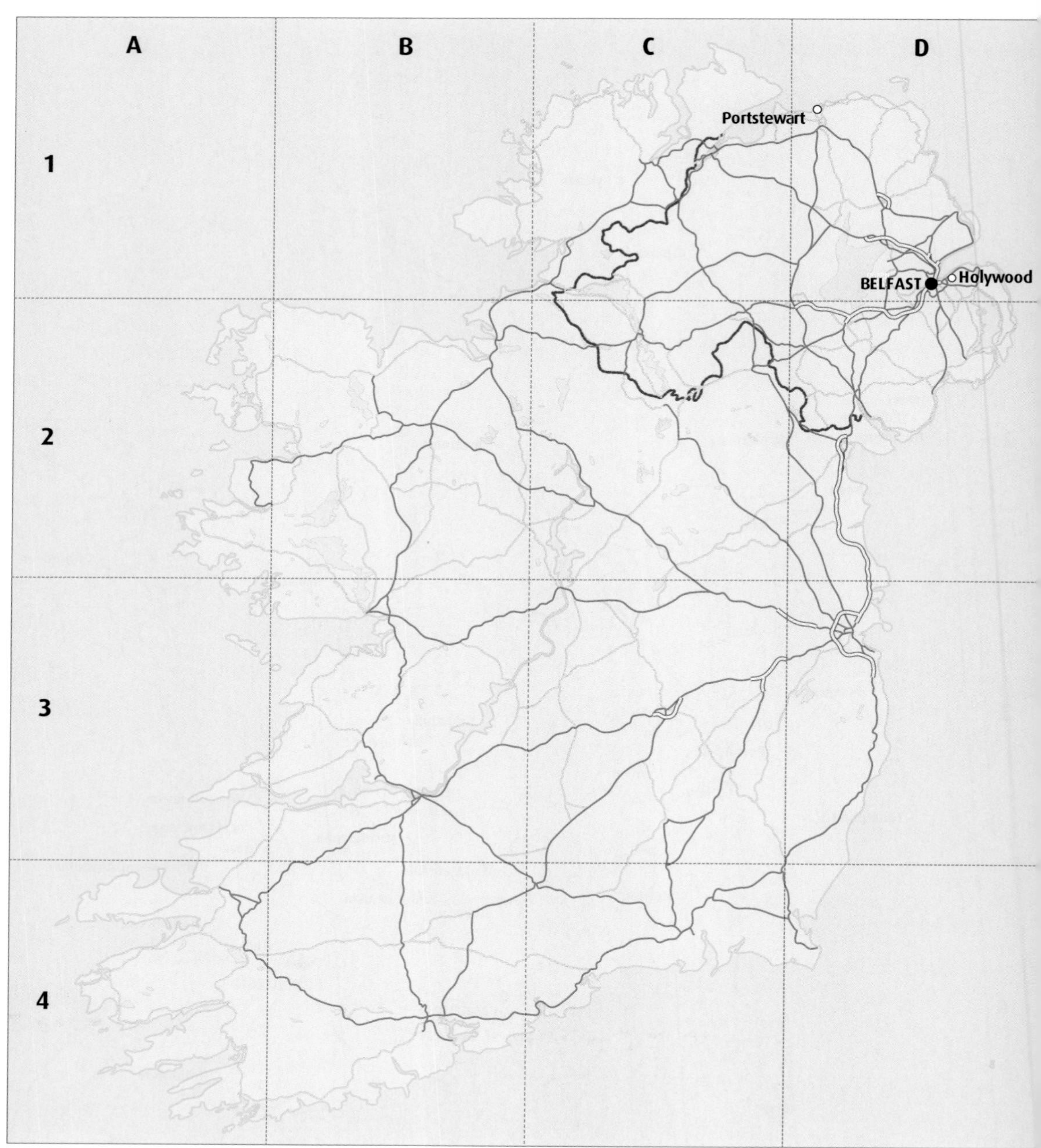
A
B
C
D
1
2
3
4
Portstewart
BELFAST
Holywood

ALPHABETICAL INDEX

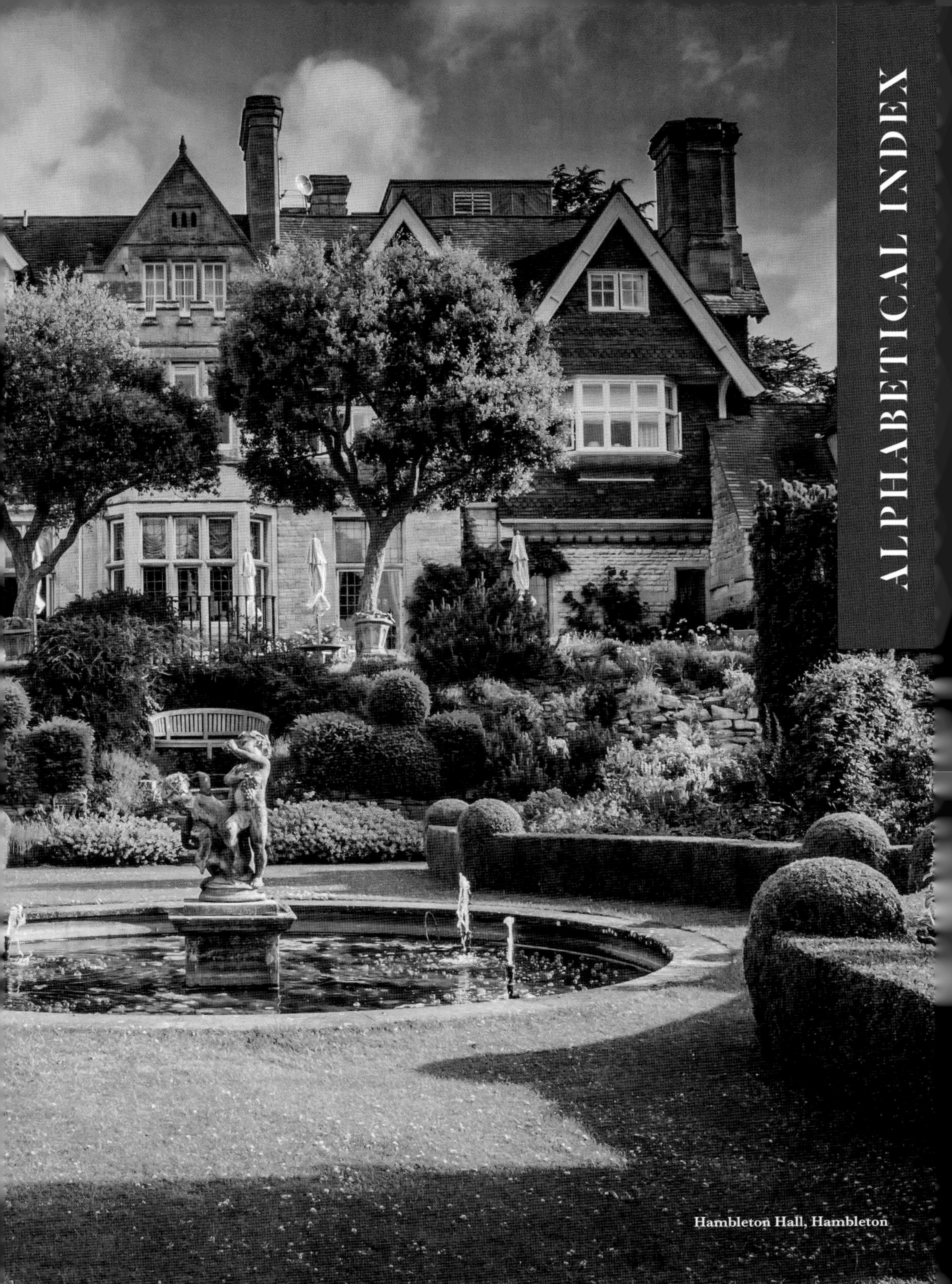

Hambleton Hall, Hambleton

ALPHABETICAL INDEX

Pale Hall Hotel Restaurant, Bala